1001 BEERS
YOU MUST TASTE BEFORE YOU DIE

1001 BEERS
YOU MUST TASTE BEFORE YOU DIE

GENERAL EDITOR ADRIAN TIERNEY-JONES

PREFACE BY NEIL MORRISSEY

UNIVERSE

A Quint**essence** Book

First published in the United States of America in 2010 by
UNIVERSE PUBLISHING
A Division of Rizzoli International Publications, Inc.
300 Park Avenue South
New York, NY 10010
www.rizzoliusa.com

Sixth printing, 2013
2013 2014 2015 / 10 9 8 7 6

ISBN: 978-0-7893-2025-4
QSS.BDD

Library of Congress Control Number: 2009936360

This book was designed and produced by
Quint**essence**
226 City Road
London EC1V 2TT
www.1001beforeyoudie.com

Project Editors	Philip Contos, Chrissy Williams
Editors	Rob Dimery, Becky Gee, Fiona Plowman
Editorial Assistant	Simon Ward
Designer	Nicole Kuderer
Design Assistant	Joel Foster
Research Assistant	Helena Baser
Production Manager	Anna Pauletti
Editorial Director	Jane Laing
Publisher	Tristan de Lancey

Color reproduction by Chroma Graphics Pte Ltd., Singapore.
Printed in China by Midas Printing International Ltd.

CONTENTS

PREFACE
By Neil Morrissey

It seems to me that the binge drinker has replaced the lager lout and provided yet more negative imagery for the beleaguered alcoholic drinks trade. Whatever next—Prohibition? However, there is hope. A sea change of thinking is in the air—and it's all about the most unlikely candidate to stage a cultural and taste-based revival for alcohol: beer. This beautiful book features 1001 beers in all their glory—from craft beers to traditional real ales, from gastronomic specialties to brews for serious hopheads—and all are world-class. Beer is making its way upmarket: ex-Gordon Ramsay workplace The Aubergine now boasts a beer list, and, back in the spiritual home of French cuisine chez Le Gavroche, I have actually attended a beer-tasting dinner!

In the face of such overwhelming top-end endorsement, one could be forgiven for thinking that beer is the new wine. But that's silly—beer was being enjoyed as a beverage of culinary importance when wine was just a twinkle in the great vine's eye. The oldest known recipe—carved into a stone tablet from ancient Mesopotamia and dating back to a few thousand years B.C.E.—is, of course, a recipe for beer.

From the pharaoh kings and Sumerian warriors to modern-day beer buffs, such as beer writers Adrian Tierney-Jones and Pete Brown (and not forgetting vintage brewers and consumers like Foxy and me), beer as a beverage of quality has been enjoyed for thousands of years. The ancient Egyptians revered it as a royal drink and were buried with pitchers and barley grains to sustain them in the afterlife—bring it on! A few years later, King Wenceslas—living up to his good name—imposed the death penalty for anyone caught exporting his prized Saaz hops. Back in medieval England, it was allegedly a floggable offense to serve poor-quality beer.

Of course, several thousand years is a long time to perfect a recipe, but it's only now that we're beginning to appreciate the style, balance, and complexity of beers. During the food revolution of the last twenty years, we've been slowly but surely educating our palates. The stylish cities of northern Europe—Prague, Berlin, Brussels, and London—have their traditions firmly steeped in the grain, but once you scratch below the surface of the more populist brands, you uncover a range of artisan beers to rival the finest châteaux and the best brandies. From floral, honeyed, and buttery pilsners to herb-infused, sweet and sour, zesty wheat beers, these are beverages with a gastronomic value to die for.

Herbs, spices, and other adjuncts such as honey have traditionally been employed in the revered art of brewing. With their variety of color, flavor, texture, balance, and suitability for different cuisines, these beers never disappeared, they just got lost amid the overwhelming volume of cheap, tasteless lager. However, after a marketing assault by the wine trade in the 1980s that made the Charge of the Light Brigade look like a playground fracas, beer in the world of fine dining appeared to have received its marching orders. Fortunately, you can't keep a good thing down forever.

Recent food scares have resulted in serious questions being asked about the provenance of our food. As our understanding of intensive production methods and unethical handling procedures grows, so does our demand for locally produced, better quality food. Farmers' markets are burgeoning, the organic movement is gaining momentum, we want taste and flavor, and we don't mind if it takes a little longer to grow our produce. We're going back to the importance of flavor, rather than being dictated to by fashion—and this is where beer comes in. The beers that I'm talking about are artisanal products, made from recipes perfected over centuries. As consumers, we're getting back into seasonality and traditional local and regional cooking, and these beers have the credentials to elicit and enhance the food flavors they can be matched with. The spicy cuisine of Asia and India—which has now become part of Western food culture—is also far more suited to the grain than the grape.

In a world where there are as many beer flavors as food flavors, and a different beer for every occasion, it's now possible to enjoy beer with the same level of appreciation that first led the pharaohs to worship in its wake. Having unburdened ourselves of the restrictions of ignorance regarding wine—when we couldn't see past the lone bottle of liebfraumilch—it's time to don the "gastronaut" hat once again. For all lovers of taste, it would be nothing short of self-deprivation not to salivate, slaver, and slurp your way from beginning to end of this inspiring and informative book on beer.

Yorkshire, United Kingdom

INTRODUCTION

By Adrian Tierney-Jones

Are there really 1001 beers in the world worth drinking? It's a question I've been asked time and time again while compiling this book. The simple answer would be "yes," but of course I never leave it there, because for me each beer is a work of art. After an hour of my rhapsodizing on the glory of beer, the rich variety of brews available across the world, the styles, the hop varieties, the fermentation methods, the places they are drunk, and so on, most people wish they had never asked the question.

For beer fanatics, on the other hand, the burning questions are: What criteria did I use when making my list of beers? Did I include their favorite beer? And if not, why not? Beer lovers can be as passionate about their favorite suds as any sports fans are over their beloved baseball or soccer teams—and woe betide anyone who dismisses them!

I decided to put together a manifesto, a declaration of intent, both to entice and to explain why I and my excellent team of beer writers made the decisions we did. It was to be something that would satisfy the curious and hopefully encourage more debate (and some controversy). The reasons for choosing beer X over beer Y had to be as clear as a glass of Bavarian kristall or Bohemian pilsner, and just as refreshing. There could be no ambiguity, no reservation, and no regret. Sadly, despite what my friends think, I haven't tasted every beer within these pages—it's a wish list for me, too.

So I wrote the following: "My team of writers and I have chosen these beers because they are superb examples of brewing craftsmanship, are wonderful to taste, and will remind people time after time why beer is the best drink in the world: the drink that brings people together, inspires sociability, and quarries forth a whole new dimension of sensory contemplation. They have also been chosen because they represent the devotion, innovation, inspiration, and sheer *joie de vivre* that brewers bring to their beers.

"All of the beers have a story to tell. Some, far older and more venerable than others, have a history on a par with the grandest of noble families: they represent a continuity that runs through beer like a river threads its way through the land to the sea. They are supreme examples of their countries' brewing heritage, beers coming from great brewing nations such as Germany and Belgium, England and Scotland, and the United States—a country for so long blighted by the folly of Prohibition. And not forgetting the Czech Republic, where beer is less a way of life than a template for life. Many of the beers here are available near you, whether in a bar or pub, liquor store, or online. Others will encourage people to save up their carbon units and take a trip to brewing nirvana. This book is beer as travel.

"Some of these beers are here because they represent brewing innovation and imagination. There are beers matured in wood, as complex and concentrated in flavor as the finest single malt whiskey. There are beers aged and oxidized that have died and passed through the valley of shadows, emerging triumphant and born again. There are beers that shine like the sun in a glass, cheerful and life affirming, the bright chatter of hops and malt engaging and companionable. There are dark brooding stouts, porters, and dunkels, near-Shakespearean in their character. There are IPAs, beers that chime and clang with the sensual notes of the hop—that all-important piece in the jigsaw of brewing. There are fruit beers, which blossom when cherries or elderberries are added during maturation. There are beers with spice, beers with coffee, chocolate, even salt and pepper."

That's the poetic part, but as you travel through the pages of this book, you will also come across a smattering of best-selling beers, iconic brews that reach every corner of the world. These are beers now made on an industrial scale that cannot be called "crafted" or "innovative" by any stretch of the imagination. However, I really thought it would be wrong to ignore a stout that started off in Dublin and is now brewed across the world, or an American lager that was part of the German-led brewing wave that swept across the United States in the mid-19th century.

Even though this book is full of magnificent beverages, it is not a list of the world's "best" beers (like many who write on the subject, I believe that the best beer is the one that suits whatever you are doing at the moment of popping the cap). It is a list of the beers you really should try before you shuffle off this mortal coil—if only to discover what you dislike.

In the last thirty years, the world of beer has undergone a seismic change that has brought forth a whole new generation of brews and breweries. In the United Kingdom, cask-conditioned beer, seemingly destined for the graveyard in the 1970s, was revived by the Campaign for Real Ale, a movement that helped spawn a new wave of microbreweries (at the time of writing the figure stands close to 700). Brewing beer and selling it to discerning drinkers has never been more popular.

The selection of beers from the United Kingdom includes both well-established favorites, such as Adnams Broadside, Fuller's London Pride, and Theakston's Old Peculier, as well as recent newcomers such as BrewDog's IPA, Thornbridge's Jaipur, and Purple Moose's Snowdonia Ale. The British brewing scene, for so long rightly concerned with preserving traditional beer styles, is now spreading its wings: in some cases, approaching the United States in terms of innovation and flavor profile.

In the States, the British resurgence of ale and the legalization of home brewing in 1978 helped to kick-start a similar revolution. Old beer styles have been resurrected, new ones brought forth into the world, and the 1,400 or so breweries in the United States are some of the most exciting across the globe. The 2009 Great American Beer Festival had seventy-eight separate style categories—so whether you want an imperial pale ale, a brown porter, or an English-style summer ale, you will be spoiled for choice. Innovation is another keynote of North American brewing: beers like the immensely potent Angel's Share Ale from The Lost Abbey, or the magisterial Consecration from Majestic River, have slumbered within wood for months, developing new depths of flavor and aroma.

The resurgence of porter is a particularly striking success story of the craft beer revival. Guinness brewed its last batch in 1972—ironically, the year that San Francisco's Anchor Brewery first produced their coffeeish and chocolaty version. In the 1980s, British and American brewing pioneers went on to produce porters. Nowadays, this style of beer, which emerged in the 18th century, is part and parcel of many a brewery's portfolio, in North America and Europe alike.

When I first started discussing the book with the creative team working alongside me, the first question was: in what order should we put the beers? We first thought about grouping them in terms of beer styles, such as pale ales, doppelbocks, and fruit beers. This, however, seemed too inward-looking and potentially divisive. So, racking our collective brains, we thought about color: amber, blond, white, dark, and specialty. OK, so the last is not a color, but we needed a category for beers that didn't fit elsewhere! Here's how we grouped them:

Amber—the majority of top-fermenting ales (as opposed to bottom-fermenting lagers), the copper-colored, the bronzed, the ambers, the bitters and ales, the IPAs, the pale ales.

Blond—lagers, lighter golden ales, some IPAs, pale ales, and the like.

White—the majority of beers that we call white are wheat beers; some are blond and some are amber. This use of the word "white" has its root in a time when most beers were dark, but beers made with a significant amount of malted wheat in the mash were lighter and hence called "white."

Dark—dark beers including stouts, porters, some brown ales, and dark lagers.

Specialty—here we have put the lambics (due to their unique fermentation process), fruit beers, wood-aged beers, and any other beer that we couldn't fit elsewhere.

One other tricky issue was the naming of the beers. We decided to use the specific name of the beer as featured on the beer label unless the name of the beer was generic, such as "IPA," "Grand Cru," or "Kriek." In such cases, for clarity, we prefixed it with the name of the brewery. If we were ever in any doubt, we used the name preferred by the manufacturer. We then placed the beers in alphabetical order within each chapter.

This book is not the opinion of just one person; it represents the wisdom and opinions of over forty experts in their field. I know the passion and curiosity of my fellow British beer writers well. I hadn't, however, met many of the North American writers (though I had been reading their work for years); I was bowled over by their passion and knowledge about the revolution that is shaking the world of American craft brewing. Australia and New Zealand were represented by a brace of experts who unveiled a completely new world of craft brewers. Then there were the European experts who possess a near-gnomic knowledge of brewing on the Continent. The photography, too, deserves a special mention. The photographers—based all around the world—took great care to photograph the beers at the temperature suggested by the brewers, whether ice-cold or at room temperature, and where possible, they photographed each beer in the appropriate branded glass.

This is my third book on beer. Typing the last words feels like coming to the end of a journey. But for you it is just the start. I hope it's a journey that you'll enjoy and that will last a long and happy lifetime. As I said at the start of this introduction, the beers within are works of art—whether they are Leonardo da Vincis, Andy Warhols, or Jack Vettrianos, I leave up to you.

Index of Beers by Country

Maredsous 10 186
Mc Chouffe 739
Moinette Blonde 432
Monk's Café Flemish Sour Ale 909
Nostradamus 206
Oerbier 207
Oerbier Special Reserva 207
Orval 218
Oud Beersel Oude Geuze 911
Palm 221
Pannepot 777
Pauwel Kwak 223
Petrus Aged Pale 455
Petrus Oud Bruin 779
Piraat 228
Poperings Hommel Bier 465
Rodenbach 921
Rodenbach Grand Cru 922
Saison de Pipaix 476
Saison D'Erpe-Mere 477
Saison Dupont 477
Saison Voisin 244
Sara 797
Scotch Silly 256
Special De Ryck 265
St. Bernardus Abt 12 809
St. Bernardus Tripel 494
St. Bernardus Wit 604
St.-Feuillien Triple 496
Stille Nacht 497
Stouterik 814
Taras Boulba 509
Timmermans Framboise Lambic
    936
Tonneke 280
Trappistes Rochefort 10 825
Tripel Karmeliet 522
Urthel Hop-It 531
Urthel Samaranth 287
Vapeur en Folie 533
Westmalle Trappist Tripel 545
Westvleteren Abt 12° 294
Witkap-Pater Dubbel 295
Witkap-Pater Stimulo 547
XX Bitter 549
Zinnebir 554

Bosnia and Herzegovina
Sarajevsko Pivo 482

Brazil
1999 27
Baden Baden Stout 626
Bamberg Rauchbier 628
Belgian Ale 319
Demoiselle 873
Eisenbahn Dunkel 679
Eisenbahn Kölsch 370
Eisenbahn Pale Ale 112
Xingu Black Beer 841

Bulgaria
Stolichno Bock 811

Canada
Amnesiac Double IPA 314
Black Oak Nut Brown Ale 65
Blanche de Chambly 563
Boréale Blanche 568
Brockton IPA 334
Coup de Grisou 355
Dernière Volonté 359
Éphémère (Apple) 879
Garrison Imperial Pale Ale 136
Grand Baltic Porter 697
Granite Best Bitter Special 139
Humulus Ludicrous 157
Iron Duke 159
King Pilsner 406
MacKroken Flower 731
Maudite 191
McNally's Extra Ale 192
Mill Street Coffee Porter 908
Mitchell's ESB 197
Olde Deuteronomy Barleywine
    216
Palliser Porter 776
Phillips Original IPA 456
Propeller Extra Special Bitter
    232
Propeller IPA 233
Rosée d'Hibiscus 924
Route des Épices 924
St.-Ambroise Pale Ale 493
St.-Ambroise Oatmeal Stout
    808
Terrible 818
Trois Pistoles 826
Wild Rose Cherry Porter 840

China
Tsingtao 525
Zhujiang Beer 554

Croatia
Karlovačko Svijetlo Pivo 403
Tomislav Pivo 823

Czech Republic
Bernard Celebration 54
Bernard Dark 631
Bohemia Regent Prezident 331
Bohemian Wheat Lager 567
Bud Super Strong 339
Budvar Světlý Ležák 341
Budweiser Budvar Tmavý Ležák 651
Černá Hora Granát 653
Chodovar Zámecký Ležák Speciál 348
Chyne Rauchbier 87
Duchmaus Weissbier 570
Eggenberg Dark Lager 111
Eggenberg Pale Lager 369
Eliščino Královské 13° 877
Flekovský Tmavý Ležák 13° 687
Gambrinus Premium 379
Grošák 140
Herold Bohemian Black Lager 709
Herold Bohemian Blond 388
IPA Samuraj 158
Jihlavský Grand 402
Jubiler 402
Koutská Desítka 410
Koutská Nefiltrovaná Dvanáctka 410
Koutský Tmavý Speciál 18° 722
Krušovice Černé 724
Lipan Světlý Ležák 421
Master Polotmavý 191
Opat Bitter 444
Ostravar Premium 448
Pardubický Porter 778
Pilsner Urquell 462
Primátor Double 24% 782
Primátor Exklusiv 16% 230
Primátor Polotmavý 13% 231
Primátor Weizenbier 597
Richter Černý Speciál 14° 787
Rychtář Premium 475
Samson Budweiser Bier Premium 481
Staropramen Granát 266

Štěpán Pale Lager 496
Svijanský Rytíř 506
Troobacz, The 828
Velkopopovický Kozel 534
Vendelín Světlý Ležák 535
X-Beer 33° 299
Žamberecky Kanec Imperial Stout 844
Žatec 553
Žatec Xantho 945
Zvíkovský Rarášek 611

Denmark
Amager IPA 40
Bombay Pale Ale 67
Elephant Beer 114
Jacobsen Saaz Blonde 395
Jacobsen Sommer Wit 586
Julebuk 165
Limfjords Porter 728
Little Korkny Ale 180
Midtfyns Imperial Stout 743
Mikkeller Beer Geek Breakfast 744
Mikkeller Black 745
Mikkeller From To 746

Egypt
Sakara Gold 479

England
1698 26
Adnams Broadside 31
Adnams The Bitter 32
Arctic Global Warmer 622
Barnsley Bitter 50
Batemans Triple XB (XXXB) 52
Batemans Victory Ale 53
Bee's Organic Ale 854
Benedictus 320
Bishops Finger 62
Black Adder 634
Black Sheep Best Bitter 66
Blandford Fly 858
Brakspear Bitter 70
Brakspear Triple 71
British Bulldog 74
Brodie's Prime 647
Butcombe Gold 344
Combined Harvest 90

Cornish Knocker 92
Devonshire 10'der' 666
Dorothy Goodbody's Wholesome Stout 669
Double Maxim 102
East Street Cream 109
Espresso 684
Exmoor Beast 685
Exmoor Gold 373
Fuller's ESB 129
Fuller's Golden Pride 130
Fuller's London Porter 690
Fuller's London Pride 132
Fuller's Vintage Ale 133
Gale's Prize Old Ale 883
Greene King Abbot Ale 140
Harvest Pale 386
Harveys Christmas Ale 145
Harveys Imperial Extra Double Stout 706
Hereford Pale Ale 387
Highgate Old Ale 711
Hobgoblin 150
Hobsons Postman's Knock 151
Honey Dew 890
Honey Spice Triple 891
Hook Norton Double Stout 714
J. W. Lees Bitter 159
JHB 401
Little Scotney Pale Ale 180
Mackeson Stout 730
Manns Brown Ale 734
Martha's Mild 737
Meantime Coffee Porter 905
Meantime India Pale Ale 193
Meantime London Pale Ale 194
Meantime London Porter 741
Meantime London Stout 742
Moonraker 747
Moorhouse's Black Cat 749
Morrissey Fox Blonde 436
Newcastle Brown Ale 201
Nightmare 754
Nottingham Extra Pale Ale 441
O'Hanlon's Port Stout 762
Old Empire 443
Old Freddy Walker 766
Old Hooky 213
Old Peculier 768

Old Slug Porter 770
Old Tom Strong Ale 771
Otter Head 220
Pale Rider 454
Pedigree 225
Pendle Witches Brew 226
Proper Job 469
Ridgeway Foreign Export Stout 787
Riggwelter 239
Ripper 474
Samuel Smith's Imperial Stout 794
Samuel Smith's Nut Brown Ale 249
Samuel Smith's Old Brewery Pale Ale 250
Samuel Smith's Taddy Porter 796
Sarah Hughes Dark Ruby 798
Sharps Doom Bar 258
Sneck Lifter 263
St. Peter's Cream Stout 811
St. Peter's Fruit Beer (Grapefruit) 929
Strong Suffolk Vintage Ale 815
Summer Lightning 505
Sussex Best Bitter 271
Tanglefoot 272
Thomas Hardy's Ale 275
Thornbridge Alliance 934
Thornbridge Bracia 819
Thornbridge Jaipur 513
Thornbridge Kipling 515
Thornbridge Saint Petersburg 820
Tickle Brain 276
Timothy Taylor's Landlord 278
T'Owd Tup 824
Tribute 282
Union 286
Wadworth 6X 290
Wells Banana Bread Beer 940
Wells Bombardier 293
Wild Hare 545
Woodforde's Headcracker 548
Woodforde's Wherry 296
Worthington's White Shield 297
Yankee 551
Yorkshire Stingo 301
Young's Special London Ale 552

Estonia
A. Le Coq Porter 615
Saku Porter 794

Gulpener Korenwolf 575
Hemel & Aarde 707
Hertog Jan Grand Prestige 710
La Trappe Blond 417
La Trappe Dubbel 169
Lindeboom Pilsener 421

New Zealand
12 Gauge 307
Big John Special Reserve 60
Emerson's Old 95 117
Emerson's Pilsner 371
Enigma 681
Epic Mayhem 118
Fair Maiden Ale 119
Green Man Stout 699
Hop Rocker 391
Mammoth 185
Mata Artesian 427
Moa Original 431
Nor'wester 205
Smokin' Bishop 928
Stonecutter 269
Three Boys Wheat 606
Tuatara Indian Pale Ale 284

Nigeria
Guinness Foreign Extra (Nigeria) 703

Northern Ireland
Clotworthy Dobbin 656

Norway
Ardenne Blond 316
Dark Force 661
Dark Horizon 662
Nøgne Ø Imperial Stout 758
Norwegian Wood 759

Palestinian Territories
Taybeh Beer Golden 511

Peru
Cusqueña 357
Cusqueña Malta 658

Poland
Brackie 333
Łomża Export 422

Okocim Mocne 208
Perła Chmielowa 455
Strzelec Jasne Pełne 503
Strzelec Mocne 270
Żywiec 555
Żywiec Porter 845

Portugal
Sagres Bohemia 242
Sagres Preta 793
Super Bock Stout 817

Romania
Ursus Black 833

Russia
Baltika 4 49
Baltika 6 627

Scotland
1488 Whisky Beer 850
Bitter & Twisted 328
Broughton Old Jock Ale 77
Broughton Scottish Oatmeal Stout
    650
Caledonian 80 80
Dark Island 663
Deuchars IPA 359
Fraoch Heather Ale 882
Innis & Gunn Oak Aged Beer
    894
Midnight Sun 907
Ola Dubh 910
Old Engine Oil 765
Paradox 915
Punk IPA 470
Red MacGregor 237
Rip Tide 788
Róisin 923
Schiehallion 485
Skull Splitter 262
Tokyo* 937
Trade Winds 607
Traquair House Ale 282
Traquair Jacobite Ale 826

Singapore
ABC Extra Stout 616
Tiger Beer 516

Slovakia
Brokát Dark 648
Zlatý Bažant 12% 555

Slovenia
Union Temno Pivo 833

South Africa
Castle Lager 344
Castle Milk Stout 652
Durban Pale Ale 364
iJuba Special 893
Mitchells 90/- 197
Raven Stout 784

South Korea
Prime Max 467

Spain
Alhambra Negra 619
Bock Damm 642
Estrella Damm 371
Estrella Damm Inedit 571
Glops Torrada 138
+Lupulus 424
Mahou Negra 731
+Malta 184
+Negra 753
Reserva 1925 474
Voll-Damm 289

Sri Lanka
Lion Stout 729

Sweden
D. Carnegie & Co. Porter 660
Jämtlands Heaven 717
Nils Oscar God Lager 439
Nils Oscar Imperial Stout 756
Nils Oscar Kalasöl 202
Nils Oscar Rökporter 757
Pickla Pils 457

Switzerland
Bärni Dunkel 628
Bier-Bienne 57
Einsiedler Lager Hell 370
Hanfblüte 145
La Meule 897

AMBER BEERS

5 Barrel Pale Ale

Odell Brewing Company | www.odellbrewing.com

Country of origin United States
First brewed 1994
Alcohol content 5.2% abv
Serving temperature 44°F, 7°C

When Doug Odell opened his brewery in Colorado in 1989, it was only the second microbrewery in the state. Five years later, in 1994, Odell expanded his brewery and installed a fifty-barrel brewhouse. But to keep his creative juices flowing, a five-barrel pilot brewery was also installed for research, experimentation, and, perhaps most importantly, to have some fun.

The brewers immediately got to work on the new pilot brewery, and, for the very first brews, they created five experimental batches of a pale ale—one after the other in rapid succession—trying to get it to their exacting specifications. Since it was the first beer created at the new five-barrel pilot brewery, Odell decided it was only fitting that he name it 5 Barrel Pale Ale. As with all Odell beers at the time, it was only available on draft. But in 1996, the brewery added a bottling line, and 5 Barrel Pale Ale was among the first in the line-up of beers to be packaged.

The team says that its research has led to the discovery of new "hop exposure processes that Odell believes deliver the optimal flavor and aroma profiles." The way 5 Barrel Pale Ale is brewed involves eight different hop additions with a half-dozen different hop varieties. It also infuses whole hops in both the hop-back and the fermenter. The team believes that this imparts a uniquely fresh and lively hop flavor and aroma.

The 5 Barrel Pale Ale has won numerous awards at the Los Angeles County Fair, the Great American Beer Festival, and the Stockholm Beer and Whiskey Festival, as well as a gold medal at the North American Beer Awards in 2008. **JB**

Tasting notes

Odell's 5 Barrel is bright amber in color with a dense white head. It has a rich nose of spicy, citrus hops and warm bready malt aromas. With a creamy mouthfeel and zesty hop character, this beer really shines because of its biscuity malt backbone and sweet, dry finish.

V Cense

Brasserie de Jandrain-Jandrenouille | www.brasseriedejandrainjandrenouille.be

Country of origin Belgium
First brewed 2008
Alcohol content 7% abv
Serving temperature 44°F, 7°C

The V Cense—like the French *cinq sens* or just "fifth sense" if you prefer—gets its name from a few sources. If the IV Saison was the brewers' fourth child, this is the fifth. While the IV Saison has four ingredients, this one has five—adding a spice they prefer to keep secret for some reason. The name is also a play on words since *cense* is a French word for "farmhouse," like the 18th-century Wallonian Brabant farmstead where this beer is brewed.

The V Cense is what hopheads might call a "citrus bomb." The brewers, Stéphane Meulemans and Alexandre Dumont, manage to get a concentrated fruit aroma from the hops, including a period of dry-hopping with the Amarillo variety. The beer smells, above all else, like sweet mandarin oranges. Inspiration comes partly from hoppy American IPAs but without the often tongue-coating hop bitterness that can hinder drinkability. The V Cense has drinkability in spades, its stealthy 7 percent strength safely hidden behind its refreshingly bright hop flavor. When asked what type of beer V Cense is, Dumont answered: "It's a dangerous beer, that's what it is." It also gets a balancing touch of sweetness from Munich and caramel malts—despite the generous use of American hops, the brewers also wanted to make beers that were distinctly Belgian.

After IV Saison and V Cense . . . what next? The brewers joke that they plan to "do it like *Star Wars*," with episodes IV, V, and VI coming out before I, II, and III. Film buffs with a taste for beer will hope that their later efforts are even better than their early ones. **JS**

Tasting notes

This pours a lovely bright amber color. The nose is full of mandarin orange with added notes of grapefruit, lemon, and tropical fruit. The well-rounded flavor is lightly sweet and mildly hop-bitter, meshing well with that juicy aromatic backdrop. Lingering fruity aftertaste.

6-Korn Bier

Pyraser Landbrauerei | www.pyraser.de

Country of origin Germany
First brewed 2003
Alcohol content 4.7% abv
Serving temperature 46°–50°F, 8°–10°C

It is mild but not empty, sweetish but not sticky, subtle and yet complex. But most of all, it is unique among German beer styles. Made of six different malted grains, Pyraser 6-Korn Bier is designed to stand out among the crowd of mass-produced beers.

Brewmaster Helmut Sauerhammer used to experiment with multi-grain beers in his own Lindwurm Bräu in Heideck; he managed to succeed with a five-grain ale. Unfortunately he went bankrupt and so did his brewpub. With undiminished creativity and skill he began at Pyraser Landbrauerei, a brewery that, with its wide range of specialties and seasonals, such as a pils with fresh hops, has proved to be a master of innovation. With a commission to brew something new that could sell beyond Franconia, Sauerhammer set to work.

Pyraser 6-Korn Bier is made with 20 percent each of wheat and barley, with the former providing amino acids for a faster fermentation, while the latter serves as the most important starch supplier; 40 percent is spelt, which gives a fruity and nutty aroma. The rest of the grain bill consists of rye, which brings in a spicy crispiness, emmer for a full and round flavor, and oats for creamy, honey-like notes. Due to its residual sweetness, the beer undergoes gentle bottle fermentation and comes out astonishingly dry.

In Franconia, the beer has found a select base of fans, yet, as alternative cereals like spelt and emmer become more popular, this beer gains more admirers. Its northernmost point of sale is the town of Bremen, though it also travels to Austria, France, and China. **SK**

Tasting notes

Opalescent orange with pinkish tints; a beige foam of rather short retention. Expect a grainy nose with slightly sour, fruity esters; a creamy touch on the palate; honey notes combined with a pronounced graininess; and a subtle crispiness evolving. Mild yet dry finish.

90 Shilling

Odell Brewing Company | www.odellbrewing.com

Country of origin United States
First brewed 1989
Alcohol content 5.6% abv
Serving temperature 55°F, 13°C

When Doug and Wynne Odell moved from Seattle, Washington, in 1989 to open Colorado's second microbrewery, no one would have predicted that the city they chose would become a microcosm of U.S. brewing. As well as Odell Brewing, which has grown into a regional operation selling its ales in nine states, a beer tourist visiting Fort Collins can experience both the range of brewery sizes seen in the United States and the variety of styles.

Just outside of town, Anheuser-Busch InBev runs one of its five breweries open to visitors, its massive plant producing both mainstream Budweiser beers and Michelob specialty beers. Within the city, it's a short walk from Odell's to New Belgium Brewing, one of the largest craft breweries in the nation; the Fort Collins Brewery; and Coopersmith's Pub and Brewing, which remains a fixture on the town square.

The Odells located their first brewery in a grain elevator built in 1915, employing all four of its floors to install a traditional gravity-fed system that drew on British brewing heritage and employed open fermentation. They built the current fifty-barrel brewery in 1994, still selling only draft beer until installing a bottling line in 1996. When the brewery introduced its flagship 90 Shilling at its opening party, few drinkers in Colorado knew what to expect from a beer taking its unique name from the former Scottish method of taxing beer. The "90" is intended to refer to the quality of the beer rather than its weight, as it was designed from the beginning as a "lightened up" Scottish ale. **SH**

Tasting notes

Bright, rich copper colors in the glass, topped with a rocky tan head. Caramel aromas turn into richer toasted caramel flavors, with hints of chocolate and light fruitiness also joining in on the palate. Relatively dry at the finish, nuttiness lingering in the memory.

1612er Zwicklbier

Hofbräuhaus Traunstein
www.hb-ts.de

Country of origin Germany
First brewed 1612
Alcohol content 5.3% abv
Serving temperature 44°–46°F, 7°–8°C

Zwickel (or Zwickl) beers are in the same traditional style as Kellerbiers: unfiltered, served straight from the cask (or conditioning tank), and naturally cloudy in the glass. This style of beer almost seems at variance with the German brewing obsession for clarity and continuity, but a lot of breweries still produce a Zwickelbier, and the style is most commonly seen in the south of the country, especially Bavaria.

Hofbräuhaus Traunstein dates from 1612, when the Bavarian Duke Maximilian I founded a brewery solely for producing Weissbier. Today the brewery's range of beers also includes a pilsner and dunkel. Hops come from the brewery's own farm in the Hallertau area, whereas the malt is sourced locally, something in which the brewery takes great pride. 1612er is only available in the brewery's restaurants and beer halls, which offer the best conditions for maturing a beer. **WO**

Tasting notes

Naturally cloudy and amber colored; hint of floral hop on the nose; palate rings with clear malty notes plus a hint of spiciness from the yeast. The finish has a pleasant hop bitterness.

1698

Shepherd Neame
www.shepherd-neame.co.uk

Country of origin England
First brewed 1998 (relaunched 2005)
Alcohol content 10.5% abv (relaunched 6.5% abv)
Serving temperature 48°–52°F, 9°–11°C

In 1998, when Shepherd Neame marked its 300-year anniversary, it launched a commemorative beer, simply called 1698. It was packaged in tall, dark brown bottles and was fearsomely strong, at 10.5 percent. It sold for a year and was then withdrawn.

A few years later, a decision was made to resurrect 1698 with some subtle but important differences. The beer was chosen to be Shepherd Neame's new bottle-conditioned beer. The company had overhauled its bottling line and improved microbiological standards in the bottling hall. The new 1698 differs from the previous version in that it is "thrice hopped." This means Target hops go early into the copper for bitterness, Golding hops are added later for aroma, and then yet more Golding is hurled into the whirlpool as the beer is being strained and readied for fermentation. When 1698 resurfaced, it was to rave reviews. **JE**

Tasting notes

This big, smooth, copper-colored ale has an inviting aroma of malt, pear drop candies, and gently grassy hops. Bitterness develops in the drying finish with malt, hops, and fruit.

1999

Cervejaria Baden Baden
www.cervejariabadenbaden.com.br

Country of origin Brazil
First brewed 2004
Alcohol content 5.2% abv
Serving temperature 46°F, 8°C

The Baden Baden brewery did not try to reinvent English bitter ales: 1999 merely pays homage to this classic beer style, which is all too rare in South America. This brew is not pretentious, just refreshingly familiar and pleasingly simple. Head brewer Otto Siegfried Dummer is a graduate of Munich's Doeman's Academy, and he oversees the production of eleven beers. The reputation of the brewery is spreading quickly, not only in Brazil but worldwide, and 1999 is without a doubt one of the reasons for this continued success.

The brewery has come a long way very quickly, but high standards have not been compromised. Based in Campos do Jordão, the brewery boasts a restaurant where a range of traditional Swiss and German delicacies is served with the beer. The town has long been a favorite weekend resort for Brazilians but is becoming internationally famous for its microbrewery. **AH**

Tasting notes

Barley malt aroma with a touch of caramel and notes of wood on the palate gives way to dry bitter malt before finishing with a slightly sweet aftertaste. Accompanies red or white meats.

Aardmonnik

De Struise Brouwers
www.struisebrouwers.be

Country of origin Belgium
First brewed 2006
Alcohol content 8% abv
Serving temperature 54°F, 12°C

Flemish Old Brown ales can be some of the most satisfying sour ales on the planet; strangers to the style might be put off by the use of the word "sour," but it's a refreshing and complex style that deserves full consideration. These beers also boast an impressive lineage—this style of beer, which is usually a blend of brown ales aged in oak barrels, dates back hundreds of years. However, one of the most complex and most sour of these is a newcomer: Aardmonnik.

It is a blend of 30 percent old and 70 percent young beer and it is aged in French oak barrels (which formerly held Burgundy wine) for at least eighteen months. Brewer Urbain Cotteau says that the yeasts continue to devour all the sugars in Aardmonnik for a long time after bottling, which helps to produce a very dry beer. The carbonation of this brew is also likely to increase over time as these yeasts wave their magic wands. **CC**

Tasting notes

Pours a brownish red color with limited carbonation. Very tart and sour in taste, and very complex, with notes of cherries, figs, plums, and oak. Very dry with a hint of alcohol in the finish.

Abbaye des Rocs

Brasserie de l'Abbaye des Rocs | www.abbaye-des-rocs.com

Country of origin Belgium
First brewed 1979
Alcohol content 9% abv
Serving temperature 55°F, 13°C

When someone uses the generic term "Wallonian ales," the beers of Abbaye des Rocs may be just what they have in mind. Located in scenic Montignies-sur-Roc, a western Hainaut village near the French border, the beers of this brewery are strong, spiced, nice with food, and typically found in 25-ounce (75-cl) bottles that are ideal for sharing.

Its reddish brown ale, first brewed in 1979, is enough of a flagship that the word "Brune" is often dropped. This Belgian abbey beer is typical in that it has virtually nothing to do with a working abbey. On assessing such beers, if you are kind you say it was inspired by the strong Trappist ales that help make Belgium famous; if you are cynical you say it's just marketing. Of course it doesn't matter either way if the beer is worth it—and this one usually is (this is an artisanal product and can be inconsistent).

Unlike many other Belgian breweries, Abbaye des Rocs avoids the use of sugar, which is often added as an adjunct to lighten body and boost alcoholic strength. The Brune shows pleasant caramel malt flavors, richer than what is found in many other Belgian dark ales. That malt backbone is just about the only thing keeping this beer's heavy spicing from being over the top. The artisanal inconsistency means that some bottles show good complexity and balance; others are like licorice bombs. The yeast, meanwhile, can bring out the notes of figs, prunes, or other dried stone fruits. Abbaye des Rocs Brune is big enough for your steak but equally happy with some cheese and smoked sausage. The important thing is to share. **JS**

Tasting notes

Dark brown pour with red-orange highlights and tan head. Nose is heavy with anise, brown sugar, and notes of clove and dark fruits. Sweetish caramel flavor stops short of cloying, with moderate bitterness for balance. Big anise backdrop. Welcome alcoholic warmth.

Achel Bruin Bier Extra

Brouwerij der Trappistenabdij De Achelse Kluis | www.achelsekluis.org

Country of origin Belgium
First brewed 2002
Alcohol content 9.5% abv
Serving temperature 46°–50°F, 8°–10°C

An alcoholic strength of 9.5 percent is not out of the ordinary for Trappist ale—and yet Achel's decision to make this strong beer was a revolutionary one for them. Brewing had restarted at the remote Achel monastery, situated on the Flemish-Dutch border (the brewery and monastery are in Flanders, but much of the domain is in the Netherlands), in 1998, after a gap of eighty-two years. However, the small brewery in the cafeteria was different from its sister abbeys in that its beers were aimed at the numerous hikers and cyclists visiting the woodland area around the abbey.

For these people, exuberant alcoholic drinks were not really the ideal refreshment, and the brown and blond beers, served on draft, were a modest 5 percent. Gradually, bottling took a more prominent role in the production, especially when Father Antoine was joined by the quiet but workaholic young brewer Marc Knops, who didn't shy away from accomplishing three, or even four brews a day.

Bottled beer can use a bit more power, and so for Christmas 2002, the brewery made a special offering they christened De 3 Wijzen—referring to the three kings of Epiphany. It is not an exaggeration to say that the beer was a direct hit with connoisseurs, and pressure mounted on the brewery to make it into a permanent offering. Now known as the Extra, it remains the strongest beer emanating from the Limburg province cloister. Visitors to the cafeteria can also unashamedly watch their tipple being brewed, as the whole brewery set-up is behind tall glass windows—a true rarity, too, for a Trappist brewery. **JP**

Tasting notes

Dark, chestnut-colored beer with an amber shine and a luxurious yellowish head; lacy rings are left down the side of the glass. A nose of dark roasted malts, chocolate fondant, and pecan nuts. Tastes chocolaty, nutty, with hops at the end. Slight oily (walnut) mouthfeel.

Adelscott

Brasseries Fischer & Adelshoffen | www.heineken-entreprise.fr

Country of origin France
First brewed 1982
Alcohol content 6% abv
Serving temperature 48°F, 9°C

The tangled nature of the European brewing industry has no better example than Brasseries Fischer and Adelshoffen, situated in Schiltigheim near Strasbourg on the Franco-German border. Fischer was founded as Brasserie de l'Ors Blanc in 1821 in Strasbourg by Jean Fischer, then in 1854 it transferred to Schiltigheim, a town with a reputation for the quality of its water. In 1921, on its centenary, Fischer absorbed its neighbor Adelshoffen to create the brand Pêcheur ("the fisherman"), however, both plants were kept running. Over the years, Fischer and Adelshoffen acquired a reputation for enterprise and innovation in its beer range and marketing.

Adelscott Malt Whisky beer, which is also known as "the different beer," was conceived in 1982. Something of a slow-burner, it eventually became a huge success, growing in sales mainly through word-of-mouth rather than by advertising and marketing. The dark, burnished amber–colored Adelscott was the first beer to be flavored and colored by peat-smoked whiskey malt. Since then, the style has inspired so many other breweries that it now enjoys a sub-category among smoked beers.

Its near neighbor, Heineken, also with a brewery in Schiltigheim, absorbed the Groupe Pêcheur in 1996. Heineken announced the closure of Adelshoffen in September 2000 and in 2008 decided it would be closing the Fischer plant to transfer production to Brasserie de l'Espérance (also located in Schiltigheim) and Mons-en-Baroeul. Fortunately, despite all these changes, Adelscott has managed to survive. **AG**

Tasting notes

A cream-colored head unveils a dark, polished amber hue and reveals a smoky aroma. The palate begins intensely sweet with caramel notes developing and vague fruit flavors appearing, influenced by more smoked peat to a dry, slightly acid finish.

Adnams Broadside

Adnams | www.adnams.co.uk

Country of origin England
First brewed 1972
Alcohol content 6.3% abv
Serving temperature 50°–54°F, 10°–12°C

Back in 1672, the Royal Navy fought a disastrous engagement with its Dutch counterpart off the English coast near the Suffolk town of Southwold. Just as the Royal Navy was gearing up to rule the waves, the Battle of Sole Bay ended in defeat for them as ships were sunk, the Earl of Sandwich perished, and bodies washed ashore for weeks.

This battle was remembered in a less lethal fashion 300 years later when Adnams Brewery released the first edition of Broadside, an amber-colored beer full of fruity flavor with a deep, earthy hop expression. The beer was only bottled at the time and, as its alcohol content was 6.3 percent, it remained in bottles as a connoisseur's beer for the end of the evening. However, in 1988, a cask version of the beer appeared.

According to Fergus Fitzgerald, head brewer at Adnams, "The company believed it could become a much loved cask beer, but not at 6.3 percent, so the brewers set about creating a version that was lower in alcohol but still retained the fruitiness and malt character of the beer."

With locally grown pale ale malt and the English hop varieties Golding, Fuggle, and First Gold incorporated into the mix, this is very much a beer that chimes with Adnams's commitment to cutting down food miles. In 2008 this passion for sustainability saw the brewery produce the UK's first ever carbon-neutral beer—East Green—while its newly built distribution center, just outside the town of Southwold, has a "living" green roof and various other eco-friendly features. **ATJ**

Tasting notes

On draft, it's a tangy and complex strong bitter with plenty of citrus and spice on the nose, and a deep and satisfying palette of rich biscuity malt, high notes of citrus fruit, and a dry, spicy finish. The bottle version is richer and fruitier and is exquisite with a strong, mature Cheddar.

Adnams The Bitter

Adnams | www.adnams.co.uk

Country of origin England
First brewed 1960
Alcohol content 4.5% abv
Serving temperature 50°–55°F, 10°–13°C

Adnams is one of the best-loved cask-beer breweries in England. It lies in the center of Southwold, a pretty seaside town that boldly faces the uncertain charms and moods of the North Sea. Adnams's pubs are dotted around Southwold, all places where the brewery's beers can be enjoyed at their very best. The beers also have a cachet and reputation that many other breweries of a similar size would sell the family silver for. During the 1970s, when it looked as if cask beer would die out, Adnams's beers, along with the likes of Wadworth 6X and Ruddles County, were known and noted by connoisseurs. This was the sort of brewery that inspired many a pilgrimage.

Adnams Bitter is the jewel in the brewery's crown. A grandee of an ale, it first saw the light of day in November 1960, when Adnams was a small country brewery gearing up for the challenges of a new decade, as drinkers started to turn their backs on mild brews. The bitter is a mainstay of the brewery, a vigorous ale that showcases the qualities of the classic English hop varieties Fuggle and Golding; the beer is also dry-hopped with Fuggle. Into the mash tun goes Maris Otter pale ale barley, grown in East Anglia and malted locally—this helps to cut food miles and is just one aspect of the brewery's quest for sustainable brewing.

On the pump clip and bottle label a neat medieval figure with a sword craves the drinker's attention—this is Southwold Jack, a painted wooden figure dating from the Middle Ages who can be found inside the town's attractive St. Edmund's church. **ATJ**

Tasting notes

A muscular bitter whose earthy and scented orange hop characters are counterpointed by the rich and urgent biscuity maltiness. The finish is dry and grainy, inviting you to have another sip. A global classic and a benchmark for its style.

Aecht Schlenkerla Rauchbier

Brauerei Schlenkerla | www.schlenkerla.de

Country of origin Germany
First brewed 1678
Alcohol content 5.2% abv
Serving temperature 44°–46°F, 7°–8°C

"Tastes like ham!" The first sip of Aecht Schlenkerla's Rauchbier often induces such a statement. Some people are immediately turned off. Others are curious enough to have another sip, and another, and cannot stop savoring this vigorous dark beauty. At only 5.2 percent alcohol content, this is probably one of the weakest extreme beers in the world. It wins awards in categories ranging from "weirdest beer in the world" to "best culinary specialty." This beer is indeed the parting of the ways, and it's all due to a recipe that is 100 percent smoked malt.

It all comes down to what you expect. With Schlenkerla, expect the magical taste of fire: ashes, peat, leather, wood, and earthy notes mixed with caramel, chocolate, and roasted aromas—all due to the enigmatic depth of smoked malts.

Aecht Schlenkerla Rauchbier dates back to the 17th century, as does the origin of the brewery in Bamberg. Young owner Matthias Trum is eager to preserve this tradition. He still kilns his own malt over beechwood fire as brewers used to do before modern firing installations were available. The style only survived in the Bamberg region where, for the locals, smoked beer is a common drink, a session beer. Beyond the region it is more or less considered a curiosity. Abroad, the beer is appreciated as the Rauchbier benchmark, and serves as a reference for craft brewers who seek to experiment with smoked malt. It has also come to epitomize *the* German super specialty, even more than wheat beer. Schlenkerla is an all-time classic. **SK**

Tasting notes

Bright ruby-chestnut color, dense beige foam. A strong smoky nose: peat, leather, ashes, and earthy aromas. The palate offers a solid ground of roasted flavors with hints of chocolate and caramel balanced by bitterness. Velvet mouthfeel, medium body, dry, smoky-bitter finish.

Alaskan Amber

Alaskan Brewing | www.alaskanbeer.com

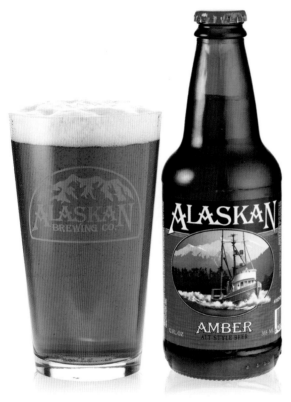

Country of origin United States
First brewed 1986
Alcohol content 5.3% abv
Serving temperature 48°F, 9°C

Alaskan Brewing uses a distinctively 21st-century approach to brewing a recipe that dates back to around 1900 for its flagship Amber Ale. To understand why probably requires a visit to Juneau, where Geoff and Marcy Larson opened the brewery in 1986. The city can be reached only by sea or by air, and the approach on water includes a stunning view of Mendenhall Glacier. The glacier is retreating about 30 feet (9 m) per year, a reminder to the residents of Alaska of the balance between man and nature.

Alaskan Brewing was the first craft brewery in the United States to install a carbon dioxide reclamation system and the first to use a mash filter press in brewing. By using the mash press, the brewery saves one million gallons of water annually and needs to ship 360,000 fewer pounds of spent grain to the mainland. The Larsons understood the consequences of the brewery's environmental footprint long before it was the subject of chic discussion, as well as the importance of brewing beer for the locals rather than one created for cruise ship tourists.

The recipe for Alaskan Amber is based on a beer from one of the five breweries operating in Juneau at the beginning of the 20th century. Marcy Larson did the research, using shipping invoices and newspaper articles, which Geoff Larson used for his test batches. They set out, in Marcy Larson's words, to "give it a sense of place." They rejected the first sixteen attempts, disposing of ten barrels at a time, before they came up with a batch that was both fit to sell and properly rooted in the history of Alaska. **SH**

Tasting notes

Bright copper in the glass, with a thick white head. Malty on the nose, with hints of fruit. Medium body, a bit of biscuit and caramel emerging on the palate. Dry and satisfying finish; a subtle beer that disappears with alarming speed.

Alaskan ESB

Alaskan Brewing | www.alaskanbeer.com

Country of origin United States
First brewed 1989
Alcohol content 5% abv
Serving temperature 50°F, 10°C

Although Alaskan Brewing has achieved international fame, some of its beers never leave southeast Alaska. Alaskan ESB, for instance, has won dozens of medals in national and international competition since it was first brewed in 1989 as a seasonal called "Autumn Ale." It became Alaskan Frontier Ale in 1995, a play on the state nickname "The Last Frontier," and then ESB in 1998 as U.S. consumers began to know the Extra Special Bitter style. It was sold in bottles "Down South" (what Alaskans call the continental United States) on a year-round basis until 2008. However, these days you have to head to the Juneau area to enjoy the beer, and hope your timing is right. In its most recent form, ESB was brewed as part of Alaskan's "Rough Draft" series for release in October 2009, so that the brewers could bitter it with fresh whole hop cones flown in from Washington's Yakima Valley.

Rough Draft beers are sold only in Alaska. Although Alaskan Brewing sells 70 percent of its beer outside the state (which has a limited number of potential beer drinkers), it is a distinctively local brewery. The brewery's employees regularly develop a dizzying number of new recipes on a one-barrel pilot system, with the results available only in the company break room. The best of these are later brewed on Alaskan's original ten-barrel system for limited distribution on draft. Considering that the brewery uses but one yeast strain for all its beers, the range is surprisingly diverse, including examples such as raspberry wheat beer, an IPA flavored with jalapeño peppers, and a coffee beer. **SH**

Tasting notes

The caramel and nutty aromas and flavors suggested by a deep amber pour are quickly balanced by an equal measure of spicy hops, then bitterness that lasts beyond the finish. Medium bodied, but ready to take on the spiciest of dishes.

AleSmith IPA

AleSmith Brewing
www.alesmith.com

Country of origin United States
First brewed 1999
Alcohol content 7.25% abv
Serving temperature 55°F, 13°C

AleSmith Brewing is one of several breweries started in the mid-1990s that helped turn the beer wasteland that was San Diego into an oasis in less than a decade. AleSmith's tasting room was an early gathering spot for area brewers, who would often bring in beers from around the world to sample.

Hops certainly have become part of San Diego's fame, with AleSmith's IPA a prime example. Brewer Tod Fitzsimmons first created IPA at home, adding massive amounts of hops in the final ten minutes of boiling, an inefficient way to extract bitterness but one that enhances hop flavor and aroma. "The beauty of this beer is how the components of malt and hops exert themselves separately and substantially, rather than working to balance each other," says owner and brewmaster Peter Zien, who bought the brewery from Skip Virgilio in 2002. **SH**

Tasting notes
Pure bright hops on the nose, pine, citrus, and pineapple.
Caramel and orchard fruit on the palate blends with hop
flavors that are much like the aromas, plus a solid bitter punch.

Alpha Dog

Laughing Dog Brewing
www.laughingdogbrewing.com

Country of origin United States
First brewed 2008
Alcohol content 8% abv
Serving temperature 44°F, 7°C

First brewed as a pilot beer in November 2008, Alpha Dog proved so popular that the second batch was brewed just a couple of months later, after customers continued to clamor for it.

Weighing in at a whopping 127 IBUs, Alpha Dog is a double entendre of sorts. On the one hand, the name refers to the high level of aromatic hops (also known as the "alpha acids" in hop bitterness); while on the other hand, the name indicates that this is a big, hefty beer. When he was first developing Alpha Dog, owner Fred Colby consulted closely with hop growers, asking their advice on which hops would help make his imperial IPA stand out from the growing crowd. He settled on using Columbus hops, together with Mount Hood hops to dry hop the beer as well as bitter it. This results in a unique flavor; Alpha Dog is "top of the pack" at Laughing Dog according to Colby. **LMo**

Tasting notes
Alpha Dog coats the mouth with a sticky blend of pine and
grapefruit and more than a hint of honey and apricot
sweetness. The aromatic hops finish off with a pleasant dryness.

The flower cones from this young crop of hops will be used in brewing. ➡

Alpha King

Three Floyds | www.3floyds.com

Country of origin United States
First brewed 1996
Alcohol content 6% abv
Serving temperature 39°F, 4°C

Nick Floyd lives in a world filled with monsters and aliens, mutant woodland creatures, and cannibalistic fairy princesses. It exists in the unique space-time that burps out every time a Three Floyds beer is released from its bottle or keg and was created with the help of brewers and artist friends because the real world just isn't strange enough for Nick.

Looking upon the Midwestern beerscape in 1996 from his scrappy brewhouse in a run-down part of Hammond, Indiana, Floyd found the region "lacking in hoppy beers" and set about to fix the situation "using the best malts we could buy: American two-row, German and Belgian aromatic malts, and the best British crystal malts. And above all, to highlight great American aromatic hops."

The "Alpha" refers to alpha acid, the hop's main bitter principle; as Floyd says, "Alpha King loosely translates into Hop King." Three Floyds (the other two Floyds are his father and his brother who were both instrumental in getting the brewery going) runs a contest called the Alpha King Challenge every year to find other breweries' beers that celebrate hops as enthusiastically as Alpha King. Alpha King is a true enthusiast's beer, an intimidating mouthful that is always very highly rated by the online beer-ranking sites. It's not your typical pale ale; it's deep blond, almost red and somehow finds room to be massively malty at the same time, despite the outrageous quantity of hops. Like one of Nick Floyd's creatures, it is exaggerated, strange even, but Alpha King manages to walk among us—and delight. **RM**

Tasting notes

Alpha King has a very complex malty-hoppy nose, with hints of marmalade and pine sap. Flavor is very rich and malty up front, with a big bitterness building into the mid-taste. The beer has a bitter, herby finish with thyme and burned-sugar notes.

Altbayrisch Dunkel

Brauerei Schönram | www.brauerei-schoenram.de

Country of origin Germany
First brewed *ca.* 1750
Alcohol content 5% abv
Serving temperature 46°–50°F, 8°–10°C

When Helga and Alfred Oberlindober, the owners of Brauerei Schönram in the Bavarian region of Chiemgau, employed Eric Toft as their new brewmaster in 1998, it was solely for his qualifications and craftsmanship. But the meeting of minds turned out to be a piece of luck. Toft is a brewmaster with a creative mind of his own, and his inspiration and inventiveness has matched well with the desire of the Oberlindobers to think out of the box and advance the business. All share an uncompromising dedication to quality.

When Toft began, Altbayrisch Dunkel, the dark lager that had been brewed for the past 250 years, had become a neglected niche product within the range of the brewery. Since the beginning of the 20th century, blond lager beers have come out on top. Toft, however, cast an eye on the style. The dark lager is one of his favorites, he is happy to say, and so he revived it. Where others were tinting their blonds with coloring malts to make them dark, Toft began using different kinds of dark and roasted malts to create a profound taste as well as color. Being the hophead that he is, he also went for delicate aroma hops such as the German varieties Tradition and Hersbrucker. With their flowery, citrus, and herbal notes, they lend an airy touch to the gloomy depth of the beer.

In short, Toft gave more of everything to the beer and it paid back: the Altbayrisch Dunkel has become a drink to remember and production has tripled since the relaunch. Toft is already developing new ideas for his next brew, like experimenting with old whiskey casks. **SK**

Tasting notes

Chestnut in color beneath a big, beige head. Altbayrisch Dunkel offers a grainy nose with aromas of dried fruit and bitter orange. The palate has dark caramel notes and roasted flavors, round and smooth, while a pronounced bitterness joins in.

Amager IPA

Amager Bryghus | www.amagerbryghus.dk

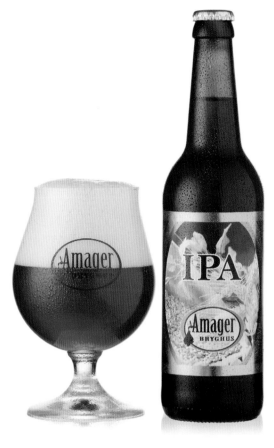

Country of origin Denmark
First brewed 2009
Alcohol content 7% abv
Serving temperature 41°–46°F, 5°–8°C

A brewery that is housed in a former air-raid shelter that has also been used as a bible warehouse should be safe from any possible calamity. So far Amager Bryghus has been able to avoid both man-made and divine disasters by the simple expedient of brewing great beer. The brewery is run by two college friends, Jacob Storm and Morten Lundsbak, who worked together on a brewing project and knew it had to end in a brewery at some point. Amager Bryghus was the result of ten years' dreaming and planning for the pair, who polished their skills as home-brewers until they could call themselves commercial brewers in 2007.

Their experience as home-brewers was used to the full in constructing the brewery, which they put together themselves with the motto "What we don't know, we can learn." The opening also brought brewing back to the island of Amager, which forms part of Copenhagen, for the first time since 1913. Known as Ama'rkaner, the locals have taken to the Amager Bryghus as one of their own, and it is from this local base that the pair has seen growing appreciation of Amager beers in Denmark and farther afield.

Jacob and Morten's style of brewing with big, hoppy ales, blonds, and stouts doesn't go to the same extremes as some of the newer microbreweries, though. The beers are brewed to ensure that "ordinary" beer drinkers aren't frightened off and still get to use all their senses. The United States rather than Britain is the source of inspiration for the brewery's IPA. The beer uses Simcoe, Amarillo, and Cascade hops. **AA**

Tasting notes

In the glass, the coppery color of a classic American IPA sits beneath an off-white head. The floral and citrus aroma is carried through into a well-balanced hoppy taste that doesn't bite too hard but stays for a lingering, full finish. The alcohol is well disguised.

Amber Shock

Birrificio Italiano | www.birrificio.it

Country of origin Italy
First brewed 1996
Alcohol content 7% abv
Serving temperature 43°–46°F, 6°–8°C

One welcome outcome of the world beer revival has been the rediscovery of unfiltered, unpasteurized lager. Once an unthinkable notion for beer enthusiasts who associated "real" only with "ale," and limited to a handful of obscure local producers in the German-speaking world, living lager has flourished in the hands of a select few craft brewers. Among them is Agostino Arioli of Birrificio Italiano, one of the longest established and most respected of Italy's new micros, situated at Marinone near Lake Como in Lombardy. A former home-brewer, he was inspired to turn professional through a visit to a Vancouver brewpub, and Amber Shock, loosely inspired by German bocks, is widely regarded as his masterpiece.

Amber Shock has built a cult following partly through its limited availability, necessitated by a particularly complex and time-consuming production process. It's brewed with pils and Munich malts, plus caramalt from Germany and France, and hopped with Hallertauer Magnum and Perle in three additions, with an ale-style decoction mash and a long boil to help bring out the caramel richness of the malt. A Bavarian cold-fermenting lager yeast is then used. The beer is later packed in distinctive liter bottles and conditioned for four weeks with the yeast continuing to ferment, with no addition of wort or sugar to help it along. The brewery says kegging the beer for draft sales would result in something completely different, and serves it only from the bottle even at its celebrated brewpub. Those drinkers who thought that only ales can offer true complexity are in for a delightful shock. **DdM**

Tasting notes

Hazy deep amber with a fine off-white head, this has a ripe fruit and caramel aroma with a buttery hint, a sweetish meaty palate with orange, herbal liqueur, and minerals. It has a subtly spicy refreshing finish with gentle roast notes.

Anchor Steam Beer

Anchor Brewing Company | www.anchorbrewing.com

Country of origin United States
First brewed 1896
Alcohol content 4.9% abv
Serving temperature 44°F, 7°C

Steam beers were once widespread across the American West: they were an attempt to re-create the lagers familiar to those coming from the East, where migrant German brewers held sway, but without ice cut from the rivers and lakes that abounded in colder climates. The resulting beer was a hybrid, lager yeast fermented at ale temperature. As for the term "steam," the old books refer to the high pressure of the beer and the cloud of "steam" released when they were tapped. Anchor is the last of this breed and owns the trademark on the word "steam."

When Fritz Maytag got involved with the ailing Anchor in 1965, the beer was in serious trouble. Brewed in a run-down facility, the beer was inconsistent and often sour. Maytag, now Anchor's president, threw himself into learning about brewing. "We got rid of the sugar, then a common thing in the industry, and went to all malt. We switched from caramel coloring to caramel malt, which we thought would give it more flavor as well. Then an industry friend told us about this new hop that had a 'distinctive' flavor, so we started adding Northern Brewer." Yeast was a big problem, and at one point the brewery was even using baker's yeast out of desperation. Eventually the problems were solved and the bottled product was released in 1971.

Asked how he feels about the beer now, Maytag replies: "It's not a radical beer, just mellow, pleasant, rich, and satisfying. On my world travels, I always find myself wondering how it will taste when I get home. I've always just been thrilled." **RM**

Tasting notes

Aromas of sweetish caramel malt and some dry woody-herbal hops. It's barely sweet on the palate, spritzy in mouthfeel, with nice caramelly notes, well balanced by the dryish bittersweet flavor of Northern Brewer hops. The finish is long, clean, and bittersweet.

Angry Boy Brown Ale

Baird Brewing | www.bairdbeer.com

Country of origin Japan
First brewed 2001
Alcohol content 6.2% abv
Serving temperature 46°–54°F, 8°–12°C

Baird Brewing founder and brewmaster Bryan Baird explains that Angry Boy Brown Ale began life as a seasonal beer. Although it has the classic color and rich maltiness of an English brown ale, certain features put it distinctly in the American style. Foremost among these features is the flavor turbulence beneath the surface. The malt body has been kicked up several notches, while the addition of Japanese brown sugar adds a certain tangy sweetness at the onset. Although it is robust and full in the mouth, it is dry in the finish.

With six varieties of malt (four barley malts and two wheat malts) going into the mash tun, plus the Japanese brown sugar, tempering this complex flavor profile requires several kinds of hops. At present, four are used: Amarillo, Columbus, Glacier, and Nugget. Because the beer itself has a 6.2 percent alcohol content, a hopping rate heavier than average is required. The result is a big, rich, and downright chewy beer with plenty of flavor and texture.

At present, the brewery produces some forty to fifty seasonal beers per year, including Baird's special beers, which are brewed with local produce such as mikan and other citrus fruits, apples, strawberries, green tea leaves, and whatever is in season and available in quantities sufficient for a batch of beer.

Baird Brewing will continue to expand in Japan through growth in pubs. Their initial taproom in Numazu was joined in the spring of 2008 with one in Tokyo, and another pub is slated to open in the summer of 2009. Baird believes that retail presence is essential in growing the craft beer market. **BH**

Tasting notes

Golden brown with a light tan head. Fruity and spicy aroma, with malt and hops in good balance. The palate has a full, tangy mixture of sweet spices and herbal hops. The malt recedes, and bitterness comes in. The finish is long, with fruit and spices.

ARROGANT BASTARD ALE

Arrogant Bastard Ale

Stone Brewing | www.arrogantbastard.com

Country of origin United States
First brewed 1997
Alcohol content 7.2% abv
Serving temperature 55°F, 13°C

What came first? The beer or the arrogance? Although Stone Brewing didn't start selling Arrogant Bastard Ale until sixteen months after opening its brewery in 1996 (then based in San Diego), co-founder and brewmaster Steve Wagner stumbled across the recipe while developing Stone's first beer, its pale ale. "We were doing single hop experiments, working on the grist bill for the pale ale," he said. One evening he and co-founder Greg Koch sat down to taste one of the batches three weeks after it was brewed. Wagner took a sip and realized that he needed to consult his copious brewing notes. "Oh, man, I screwed up," he told Koch. He'd added a far larger dose of hops than he had intended, and the beer was off the chart in terms of bitterness. Koch tasted the beer, then told Wagner it was the best beer he had ever drunk. They joked that it would be too good for others to appreciate.

No other craft beer in the United States sells as well in 22-ounce (650-ml) bottles as Arrogant Bastard. And no other label carries quite as bold a message: "This is an aggressive beer. You probably won't like it. It is quite doubtful that you have the taste or sophistication to appreciate an ale of this quality and depth. We would suggest you stick to safe and more familiar territory—maybe something with a multimillion-dollar ad campaign." **SH**

Tasting notes
Rich dark fruits in the aroma matched with piney hops.
More of the same in the mouth: fruit blending with caramel
sweetness always balanced by hop bitterness and flavor.

Artigian Ale

Birrificio Bi-Du | www.bi-du.it

Country of origin Italy
First brewed 2002
Alcohol content 6.2% abv
Serving temperature 50°–54°F, 10°–12°C

Beppe Vento is one of the most talented Italian craft brewers. In his career, he has brewed around twenty or more different beers. From his regulars to seasonals, his creativity seems to have no limits. Most of the beers are top-fermenting ales, stout, blanche, Kölsch-style, and barleywine. Some use the usual ingredients, such as malts and hops, whereas others are enriched with honey, heather, angelica, yerba maté, or mulberries. One of his more innovative beers is H10op5, an ale brewed with ten different hops added in at five different times in the process. Even if some of their beers sound a little odd, the result is always the same: a beer that has flavor and originality, and is easy to drink.

Artigian Ale lives up to this reputation. The Artigian in the name, which means "artisan" in Italian, suggests Vento was probably tempted to create a bitter ale or a strong ale. As a result, Artigian Ale has an alcohol content of 6.2 percent, but is closer to a bitter in terms of aromatic profile and flavor. The malts used include pale ale, crystal, and caramunich, while the hops are British except for Cascade.

Sometimes, on special occasions, Vento will adopt the Randall system (a hop-filled filter through which beer flows) for an even more hoppy Artigian Ale. This is definitely a pub ale and probably the best Italian answer to the British tradition of real ale. **MM**

Tasting notes
The nose starts with a citrus hoppy aroma, then fruit and
light caramel notes emerge. Sweetish on the palate, but then
progresses to a very clean and dry hoppiness on the finish.

← The devilish artwork of Arrogant Bastard Ale.

Asgaard Das Göttliche

Brauerei Schleswig | www.asgaard.de

Country of origin Germany
First brewed 1994
Alcohol content 4.8% abv
Serving temperature 46°F, 8°C

As Nordic mythology has it, Asgaard is the realm of the gods where the beer-drinking clan of the Æsir lives. The Æsirs were the gods of the Vikings, who also liked beer. In medieval times, these Germanic people lived in northern Europe and one of their most important settlements was Haithabu, which is said to have been the first and the biggest trade city in northern Europe. It was situated very near to the modern northern German town of Schleswig where brewmaster Ronald T. Carius opened his brewery and pub in 1994.

Asgaard Das Göttliche ("Asgaard the Divine") is connected to Viking culture and is marketed with Viking writing and symbols. Even though its style has little to do with the honey beer of the Vikings, this amber lager possesses the magic of the lucid North: its flavor combines fruity maltiness with a clear-cut yet harmonious bitterness, herbal head notes, and a fresh, tart bite. In order to create the distinct malty body, Carius uses Munich malt, a rare beast these days in many German brewhouses. Luckily a small local malthouse, which is still capable of slow and gentle kilning, manufactures it for him. On the hopping front, the German variety Tettnanger produces wonderfully herbal and fruity-bitter notes.

Carius moved from Lower Saxony to the far north next to the Danish border more than fifteen years ago to set up his brewery and took a chance to reconstruct and revive an old freight depot in Schleswig. Among the first people he met was the curator of the Viking Museum Haithabu, which is undoubtedly where the Viking spell was originally cast upon him. **SK**

Tasting notes

Amber to copper with golden-red tints; cream-colored foam. This beer offers a malty aroma with hints of dried fruit. The palate has mild roasted and caramel-like flavors balanced by a well-defined bitterness, herbal head notes, and tart bite. Dry and clean finish.

Autumnal Fire

Capital Brewery | www.capital-brewery.com

Country of origin United States
First brewed 1997
Alcohol content 7.3% abv
Serving temperature 48°–52°F, 9°–11°C

When craft brewing came to Wisconsin in the late 1980s, many of the brewers felt that high-quality lagers might be attractive to a local audience who probably had never heard of an ale, much less tasted one. While there are lots of different beer styles brewed in that state today, there are more small breweries laying down lagers in Wisconsin than anywhere else outside of Germany. Capital is among the best of these.

Part of Capital's success is due to their sizable tank farm of old stainless-lined dairy tanks used for lagering. As lager spends a lot of time in the tanks, picking up a big load of them for a song is a really good thing for a small brewery. Extended aging at low temperatures is essential for lager's clean and creamy smoothness. It can't be faked.

Spurred by the success of its Blonde Doppelbock, the brewery wanted something more fitting for fall, according to president and brewmaster Kirby Nelson. "The name is an interesting story," says Nelson. "September 8, 1996. There I was, in a picture in the *Milwaukee Journal Sentinel*, hat on backwards and lookin' like a dirtbag holding an Oktoberfest beer. The caption said 'Kirby Nelson holds a glass of autumnal fire.' Then the guys started calling me Mr. Autumnal Fire and that was it. We had our name."

Most craft-brewed lagers stick pretty closely to Bavarian styles, and the few examples that push the boundaries—as Autumnal Fire does—stand out. With an alcohol content of 7.3 percent, think of it as an Oktoberfest or Märzen gone haywire, but in a good way. This seasonal beer uses pilsner and Munich malts. **RM**

Tasting notes

Luscious caramelly aromas with toasty overtones and perhaps a hint of spiciness. The taste is big and sweet at first, then balancing out to a long, creamy finish with a clean bitterness, toasted toffee accents, and a lingering, warming sensation as the beer goes down.

Back Door Bitter

Birrificio L'Orso Verde | www.birraorsoverde.com

Country of origin Italy
First brewed 2006
Alcohol content 4.8% abv
Serving temperature 50°–59°F, 10°–15°C

Cesare Gualdoni made the best decision of his life when he left his old job to start a microbrewery in the hilly region of Brianza in Lombardy. Gualdoni opened L'Orso Verde in 2004 to dispense what were formerly his home-brewed beers to the public; they went down well. Since then he has built on his brewing skill, achieving good results in craft beer competitions throughout Italy. He takes inspiration from different styles and now brews almost ten beers, both top and bottom fermented. The most popular are the porter-style Nubia, the lager Chiara, and Back Door Bitter. The latter was inspired by Gualdoni attending a tasting of U.S. artisanal beers at the Pianeta Birra trade fair. Before this, he wouldn't have classed himself as a big hop lover, but he quickly fell in love with the aroma of the beers that he tasted and decided to brew something similar, although it would still have his personal approach.

Back Door Bitter is a real ale made with several malts: pale ale malt is the backbone, but there is also Munich, caramunich, and crystal, plus some wheat malt that helps to keep the foamy head consistent. There are five varieties of hop: First Gold, East Kent Golding, Styrian Golding, Chinook, and Cascade. The last two are added in the final minutes of boiling, then there is a dry hopping of Chinook and East Kent Golding that lasts for twenty days. The complete brewing process takes about six weeks, including the second fermentation in bottle.

Back Door Bitter is an articulate ale that shows a pleasant bitterness. It is at its best with cheese that is not too mature or pasta dishes with meat sauce. **MM**

Tasting notes

Deep amber color, lightly cloudy with a beige foam. Back Door Bitter is quite complex with hoppy and floral notes at the start, then fruit and caramel come out. The beer has a long-lasting, pleasant hoppy flavor, round body, and lingering aftertaste.

Baltika 4

Baltika Brewery | www.baltika.ru

Country of origin Russia
First brewed 1992
Alcohol content 5.6% abv
Serving temperature 48°F, 9°C

The rise of the company that today stands as the largest brewery in Eastern Europe began as recently as 1990, when the first factory opened in St. Petersburg. Beer had been a popular drink during the czarist regime, but beer production suffered during the Soviet era as the state-owned breweries turned to low-quality imports, such as rice, in the absence of barley. Unsurprisingly the results were dire, and vodka easily surpassed beer as the nation's favorite alcoholic drink.

The emergence of the Baltika brand in 1992 contributed to a rapid resurgence of beer consumption in Russia. Baltika 4, also referred to as "Baltika Original," was part of the first batch of drinks produced by the brewery that has since grown to several varieties. Produced with caramel and rye malts, Baltika 4 is a dark beer based upon a typical Vienna lager, and it gained instant favor with Russia's younger population.

From the outset, Baltika beer has been brewed along classic European lines, aided by an investment program for the development of the brewing process that included the installation of water purifiers and the utilization of beer-filtering machines. This brought the company up to speed with European practices and made it the country's largest beer producer within four years of the Baltika brand launch. This unparalleled brewing success story includes exports to more than fifty countries, accounting for 80 percent of all Russian beer exports, and ownership of eleven brewing plants and two malt houses. With Carlsberg now the majority shareholder, Baltika's international profile looks likely to continue to rise unabated. **SG**

Tasting notes

A clear copper coloring reveals itself with a bubbly tan head that simmers away after the first few sips. On the nose, lightly roasted malts and caramel with a faint hint of chocolate are evident and also appear on the palate alongside dark fruits, leaving a sweet finish.

Barnsley Bitter

Acorn Brewery | www.acorn-brewery.co.uk

Country of origin England
First brewed 2003
Alcohol content 3.8% abv
Serving temperature 50°–54°F, 10°–12°C

Place names are not valid as part of a registered trademark, which is one reason why there are currently two Barnsley Bitters available, brewed by two different breweries. A few years ago, there were three. Why such competition for the name?

The original Barnsley Bitter was a rich, malty ale that was revered across the north of England. However, in the 1960s, the Barnsley Brewery was bought by John Smith's. Production of Barnsley Bitter ceased, but the beer was not forgotten, and in 1997 the Oakwell Brewery opened on the site of the original Barnsley Brewery. Soon, alternative Barnsley Bitters were being brewed in nearby Elsecar, and even in the coastal resort of Blackpool. Both ventures failed, and brewer Dave Hughes left Elsecar to found Acorn, on the outskirts of Barnsley, in 2003. Now, both Oakwell and Acorn brew a 3.8 percent dark ale called Barnsley Bitter, each claiming a genuine lineage to the original. Oakwell tends to shun publicity and focuses on supplying a local market, whereas Acorn has ambitious plans and is rapidly gaining a national reputation.

Acorn's Barnsley Bitter is brewed with the original's two-strain yeast, to a recipe that resembles the vanished beer as closely as possible. It's a classic Yorkshire ale: sweeter, darker, and maltier than most beers from other parts of England, the kind of beer Yorkshiremen might use in an argument to prove that their simple approach to quality will always triumph. Acorn's perennial success at the Great British Beer Festival—held in London—suggests that even southerners may agree. **PB**

Tasting notes

A ruby, chestnut-colored ale with a light, malty aroma, Barnsley Bitter combines the drinkability of a true session bitter with a dark, well-rounded richness that includes hints of chocolate, coffee, and red berry fruit, with a long-lasting, bitter finish.

Barre Alt

Privatbrauerei Ernst Barre | www.barre.de

Country of origin Germany
First brewed 1962
Alcohol content 4.8% abv
Serving temperature 43°–46°F, 6°–8°C

About one-tenth of the beers that are poured in Germany's federal state North Rhine-Westphalia are of the Altbier style, a hoppy, top-fermented amber-brown beer. The stronghold of alt beer is Düsseldorf, the state capital, but one of the best alts is brewed 150 miles (242 km) to the north: Barre Alt, a specialty from Privatbrauerei Ernst Barre.

The family-owned brewery, which is situated in the small town of Lübbecke, launched the beer in 1962 when the style was fairly popular. Since its relaunch in 2004, the output of Barre Alt has remained stable and it has won more fans. According to technical director Dirk Stapper, the recipe was improved to make the beer more harmonious. The brewery plumped for the aroma hop Hallertauer Perle, which is fairly bitter but still contains enough polyphenols and aromatic substances to soften the edges. Furthermore, the beer is made with pilsner malt and roasted malt extract, which intensifies the color and provides dark flavors. Thus, Barre Alt is anything but mild. The beer has become a classy, award-winning specialty with lots of character. In the product range of a company that claims to be the oldest pils brewery in northern Germany, it naturally occupies a niche.

Privatbrauerei Ernst Barre was founded by Ernst Johann Barre and dates back to 1842. Today the brewery is run by a sixth-generation family member, Christoph Barre, who takes pride in keeping the company's independence. On-site visitors can tour the museum to discover the history of brewing or savor regional food in the ancient fermenting cellars. **SK**

Tasting notes

Copper brown in color, topped by beige foam. The nose offers a decent grainy aroma and hints of dark chocolate. Soft palate, light body, with a harmonious bitterness of roasted and hoppy flavors that evolve into a salty moment reminiscent of licorice. Dry, bitter finish.

Batemans Triple XB (XXXB)

Batemans Brewery | www.bateman.co.uk

Country of origin England
First brewed 1979
Alcohol content 4.8% abv
Serving temperature 52°F, 11°C

Records show that XXXB was first brewed at the end of the 1970s, but its heritage goes back to the earliest days of the brewery, when stronger beers, with robust overtones of graininess and malt, were typical of the region. The brewery's home county of Lincolnshire is far from England's hop heartlands of Kent, Herefordshire, and Worcestershire, which means that traditionally the sugary and nutty flavors from locally grown barley tended to dominate the palate, unlike the more aromatic, hoppier beers of southeast and west England. When XXXB was first produced, two hop varieties were used, Golding and Challenger, but nowadays small amounts of the American hop Liberty are also added to the boil. Bred from the Hallertauer Mirttelfruh hop, it adds a subtle spiciness and floral characteristics to the beer.

The name XXXB comes from an era when brewers marked barrels with an increasing number of "X"s to denote strength. The "X" itself doesn't indicate any particular strength, but a brewery's weakest beer was marked with a single "X." XXXB's style mimics the stronger pale ales from England's brewing capital in Burton-on-Trent. In Victorian times, when factory workers from the Midlands arrived in nearby Skegness for their annual vacations, they sought out beers similar to those they found at home.

In 1986, at a moment when the future of the brewery seemed in doubt, XXXB was awarded the title Champion Beer of Britain, an accolade that helped propel the brewery's name far beyond its traditional heartland to a national audience. **TH**

Tasting notes

A classic English, auburn-colored ale. The use of Maris Otter pale ale, together with a cocktail of Golding, Challenger, and Liberty hops, helps to produce a rich, robust beer with hints of spice and banana fruitiness on the nose and a chocolate maltiness on the palate.

Batemans Victory Ale

Batemans Brewery | www.bateman.co.uk

Country of origin England
First brewed 1987
Alcohol content 6% abv
Serving temperature 54°F, 12°C

Batemans is quite possibly one of Britain's most picturesque breweries. It has remained in family hands since the founding of the business in 1874 and now brews five core brands, which include Dark Mild, Salem Porter, and XXXB. It has also become renowned for specialist beer concepts using seasonal fruit, notably strawberries, along with vanilla and licorice to produce memorable ales. Much of Batemans's old Victorian brewhouse—now part of a visitor center and museum—is constructed in brass and copper, and it is a superb example of preservation and education. The Brewing Experience traces the history of the business and explains the brewing process. A custom-built brewhouse, nicknamed The Theatre of Beers, came onstream in 2002 to underline the brewery's commitment to "good honest ales."

All hasn't been plain sailing, however. A family dispute almost led to the brewery's complete closure in the 1980s. Victory Ale was brewed to celebrate the successful outcome of that bitter struggle and was revived in 2005 to mark the 200th anniversary of the famous Battle of Trafalgar, a pivotal moment of the Napoleonic War that was fought between the Royal Navy and the combined French and Spanish navies off the southwest coast of Spain. Victory Ale is brewed using Golding as well as Liberty, an American hop variety with a mild spiciness that is often used in wheat beers; meanwhile, into the mash tun go Maris Otter pale ale and crystal malt. The result is a beer that merits its triumphant name, especially because it was named as one of the world's fifty best beers in 2007. **AG**

Tasting notes

Rich amber in color, Batemans Victory Ale is full flavored and fruitily aromatic with a malt-laced palate and spicy hop character. The secret is in its fine balance of rich, malty toffee and shortbread piquancy complementing a warm hoppy afterglow.

Bell's Amber Ale

Bell's Brewery, Inc. | www.bellsbeer.com

Bernard Celebration

Rodinný Pivovar Bernard | www.bernard.cz

Country of origin United States
First brewed 1985
Alcohol content 5.8% abv
Serving temperature 39°–43°F, 4°–6°C

Country of origin Czech Republic
First brewed 1995
Alcohol content 5% abv
Serving temperature 44°F, 7°C

Bell's Amber is a throwback to the early days of craft beer, when things were a little less complicated. After half a century of watery yellow beers, the rich maltiness of Bell's Amber was a revelation in 1985.

The beer was a home-brew long before it was produced in a commercial brewery. It is brewed from four malts, with an emphasis on "caramel maltiness," according to founder Larry Bell. In addition to the very slight toasty taste of pale ale malt, Munich malt adds a clean caramel flavor, whereas crystal malt adds toffeelike, raisiny, and even slight burned-sugar notes. Hops are subdued, but plentiful enough for good balance. The soft but complex maltiness and lack of really aggressive or bitter flavors make Bell's Amber a food-friendly beer "that doesn't get as much love as it deserves," says Bell. It is unfiltered and bottle conditioned, often showing a rustic haze. **RM**

Rodinný Pivovar Bernard is an example of the many excellent new developments in the beer culture of the Czech Republic, but the brewery's history dates from 1597. Its current name comes from Stanislav Bernard, who purchased the brewery when it was privatized in 1991. After years of Communist control, the facilities were largely in a state of ruin. After extensive reconstruction, the brewery celebrated its return to form with this Sváteční Ležák, or "holiday lager," a seasonal brew that earned an award from the Czech beer consumers organization as the best special beer of 1995.

Bernard Celebration is brewed from choice Saaz hops and the brewery's own malt. When bottled, it receives a small dose of fresh yeast culture and the slight refermentation in the bottle gives the beer a marked vibrancy when poured, with much more carbonation than many Czech pale lagers. **ER**

Tasting notes
Caramel-like nose with a hint of spicy hops, fruitiness, and a bit of yeasty depth. Very malty up front, then building to a gentle toastiness with moderate bitterness for a pretty even balance.

Tasting notes
This excellent beer offers an aroma of biscuity malt and freshly baked bread with more rich barley notes in the body. The finish balances its sweetness with a bitter touch of Saaz.

"The Good Soldier Švejk" enjoys Czech beer culture on this Prague restaurant sign. ➡

Bibock

Birrificio Italiano | www.birrificio.it

Country of origin Italy
First brewed 1997
Alcohol content 6.2% abv
Serving temperature 46°–50°F, 8°–10°C

With this beer, creator Agostino Arioli showed his personal style in the brewing process by trying to create a beer that is rich in flavor and easy to drink in a pub but has an exact character that a beer lover will never forget. From the first brew in 1997, the recipe has changed quite a lot, both in malts and hops, following Arioli's desire to make an amber-colored, bottom-fermenting beer with a fairly hoppy personality but not as "heavy" as bock beers are usually supposed to be.

For Bibock, four kinds of malted barley are used in the recipe: carapils, pilsner, Munich, and caramel. The yeast comes, as is usual in Birrificio Italiano's beers, from Bavarian brewers Weihenstephan, whereas the hops used are Northern Brewer, Spalter Select, and Fuggle. This last is really a finishing touch, because for the first hopping Northern Brewer and Spalter Select are used; in the second it's Fuggle, while the third and decisive addition is made by dry hopping the fermenting beer with Fuggle.

The final result, after a few weeks of maturation, is a beer that has a very fresh character, thanks to the dry hopping. In a perverse way, the beer is not really hoppy in the aromatic sense that you would expect from this three-step hop infusion. Compared to traditional bocks, the genius of Arioli is such that Bibock has intense fruity notes and a dry finish on the palate, which you don't find in the traditional bock. But what's in a name? Bibock is splendid company for an evening with friends, and is an ideal accompaniment to mature cheeses, such as Parmigiano Reggiano, or grilled meat on the barbecue. **MM**

Tasting notes

Pale amber-colored with a very complex bouquet that begins with fresh notes but rapidly becomes dominated by citrus and spicy tones, chinotto and dried Curaçao orange peel, and a touch of flowers. Well-balanced body in the palate and very persistent aftertaste.

Bier-Bienne

Augenbrauerei Biel | www.bier-bienne.ch

Country of origin Switzerland
First brewed 2006
Alcohol content 5.2% abv
Serving temperature 50°F, 10°C

Visitors to Switzerland who dig beyond the usual clichés of cuckoo clocks, cheese, chocolate, and red penknives are often amazed by the harmonious cohabitation of four languages in the same nation. The city of Biel-Bienne is a living example of this collaboration: it stands north of Berne, on the German-French language border, and proudly proclaims its bilingual status—hence the hyphen in the name. Biel is the German form and Bienne the French, and over time, Biel-Bienne's inhabitants have developed a flair for self-deprecating humor and sublimely silly puns.

When Daniel "Trini" Trignani opened a beer shop in the city in the late 1990s, it just had to be named Bier-Bienne. Since then, the shop has moved a short distance down the road and is now partnered with an idiosyncratic bar, fittingly christened POOC because the premises used to be a Co-op mini-mart. In 2006, Trini decided to make a house beer for both Bier-Bienne and POOC, and chose a San Francisco-style steam beer. This is a style that could also be described as "on the border," being fermented with lager yeast at ale temperatures. Naturally the bottle label was written in "Biennetütsch," a humorous half-and-half mix of German and French.

Interestingly, Bier-Bienne is a house beer that is not contract brewed as regular as clockwork. Every month or so, Trini and his staff take over the Aare Bier brewery plant in Bargen and brew either a batch of Bier-Bienne or its softer, blond little sister Bier-Bienne 2 (launched in 2008 to lure local lager drinkers into craft beer territory). **LM**

Tasting notes

Bier-Bienne is a deep amber beer with a thin head. Crisp, sturdy, nutty malt backbone, peppery hop notes leading to a clean balanced finish, the discrete fruitiness nicely dodging the solvent notes sometimes found in steam beers. A nice session brew.

Bière de Brie Ambrée

Ferme-Brasserie de Gaillon | www.biere-de-brie.com

Country of origin France
First brewed 2001
Alcohol content 7.5% abv
Serving temperature 46°–50°F, 8°–10°C

Rarely can beer claim a *goût de terroir* of the sort boasted of in the upper echelons of the wine industry, where grapes are grown, juiced, and fermented and the results bottled all on the same estate. Although some brewers make a virtue of using local ingredients, very few offer finished products with such a direct connection to their local soil as Hugues and Geneviève Rabourdin at Ferme-Brasserie de Gaillon.

Their Gaillon farm is at Courpalay, east of Paris, in the heart of the old province of Brie. The area is famous, of course, for its soft rinded cheese, but it's also known as Paris's grain silo: farm brewing was once common but proved less tenacious here in the 20th century than in more northerly parts of France. Cereals had been the Rabourdin's business before they saw the opportunity to restore a local craft and create a product with a unique provenance by, in their words, "adding the rhythms of brewing naturally to the rhythms of sowing and reaping."

The Ambrée, one of Hugues's first recipes, is made from the farm's own malted barley, with hops only and no spicing. Brewing takes place in one of the barns, with an eight to ten-day warm fermentation using Belgian ale yeast. This is followed by several weeks of lagering in tanks at 32 degrees Fahrenheit (0°C), then at least four weeks of secondary fermentation. The result, which can be sampled in the farm's stables, is a big, honest, and rustic delight that rewards careful sipping. It has enjoyed considerable acclaim in a country that values food and drink highly, twice winning gold medals at the Concours Général Agricole in Paris. **DdM**

Tasting notes

A reddish amber beer with a white head, hints of smoky burnt rubber, cheese, barley sugar, and herbal liqueur on the nose. An intense biscuity palate with sweetish malt and tangy orange. A grainy finish that is mild on hops but with a chewy, dry roast bite.

Big Hoppy Monster

Terrapin Beer Company | www.terrapinbeer.com

Country of origin United States
First brewed 2004
Alcohol content 8.75% abv
Serving temperature 50°F, 10°C

After Prohibition ended in 1933, Georgia placed severe limitations on the sale and consumption of alcohol, just like many other states. Uncle Sam might have okayed booze with the passage of the 21st Amendment, but reform took generations: breweries were outlawed until 1993. Even after the emergence of craft beer in the United States, the Bible Belt held onto other regulations that limited the availability of specialty ales and lagers. Small breweries were prohibited from selling in many stores; no one could buy a cold one on Sundays; and malt beverages over 6 percent were banned from sale. The measures didn't simply block high-gravity beer, they stunted the growth of an entire beer culture. No Belgian Trappist ales, no barleywine, nothing "imperial." The South was widely dismissed as a beer wasteland.

Backward? Sure. But that didn't mean southern breweries and beer fans weren't eager for progress. When the alcohol limit in Georgia was finally lifted in 2004, Terrapin Beer barged through the door with its Big Hoppy Monster. The garnet-colored ale, with its hefty malt backbone, hoists an astounding load of citrus hops: Warrior, Centennial, Cascade, Ahtanum, and, for good measure, a dry-hopped dose of Simcoe. The beer seemingly created an entire new style category. A red barleywine? A double red ale? What occurred next was instant evolution. Out of nowhere, a craft brew scene emerged in the college town of Athens, and people in beer-rich places such as Colorado and Oregon began traveling to the South for a taste of its special ale. **DR**

Tasting notes

Cloudy and red with a long-lasting collar of off-white foam. The sweet, nutty, toffeelike character of crystal malt dominates the palate. Citrus hops are strongly present but never biting. Finishes with a pleasant, medium-bodied, creamy warmth.

Big John Special Reserve

Harrington's Breweries | www.harringtonsbreweries.co.nz

Country of origin New Zealand
First brewed 2001
Alcohol content 6.5% abv
Serving temperature 39°–41°F, 4°–5°C

Based in Christchurch, New Zealand's largest family-owned brewing company fired its first brew kettle in 1991. John and Val Harrington opened their first brewery on the site of the old Ward's brewery—the city's oldest—with the intention of brewing three times a week. Sales took off, and within a fortnight of opening John realized that he had underestimated demand for his beers. In 1993, a second brewery was opened, and a third was added in 1999, which expanded capacity by 30 percent. In recent years a modern packaging line has been installed, and the company now undertakes contract bottling for a number of Christchurch's smaller craft breweries.

The first Harrington's beers were simple lagers in the mainstream Kiwi styles of the time. They were brewed to be sold cheaply, primarily in working men's clubs and through the company's own chain of liquor stores. However, they differed from those of the country's two largest brewers in that they were brewed using all malt without added sugars. Today Harrington's produces an astonishing range of beer styles, including limited release and special editions.

Named after the man who started the company, Big John Special Reserve was first brewed in March 2001. The brewery used to age its famous strong dark lager in bourbon casks for around a year, but the casks became unavailable, and, since 2007, a measure of bourbon is added at the end of the boil. A frequent award winner, Big John Special Reserve was judged Supreme Champion at the 2002 New Zealand International Beer Awards. **GG**

Tasting notes

Pouring a deep copper hue beneath a wispy, tan-colored head, there's caramel, coffee, and chocolate on the nose, along with suggestions of molasses, dark fruit, and sweet bourbon. The mouthfeel is surprisingly slender, but there's plenty of alcoholic warmth and a balancing dry finish.

Bischofshof Zoigl

Brauerei Bischofshof | www.bischofshof.de

Country of origin Germany
First brewed *ca.* 17th century
Alcohol content 5.1% abv
Serving temperature 46°F, 8°C

In its purest form, Zoiglbier is more of a brewing attitude than a beer style, relating as it does to the efforts of a group of communal breweries located in the Oberpfalz, in the northeastern region of Bavaria. The word comes from *Zeiger* ("pointer"), a sign that is placed at the front of a Zoigl-producing house to indicate that the beer is ready. This pointer looks similar to the Star of David, but it represents the elements of brewing: fire, water, and air; and the ingredients: water, malt, and hops.

When a traditional Zoiglbier is brewed, the first process of the boil takes place in the communal brewhouse of the particular town. For fermentation, the boiled and hopped wort is then taken to one of the brewers' cellars, where fermentation lasts ten days. The beer is produced pretty much the same way by each brewhouse, although it tastes different because the various families have their own recipes.

There is no Zoiglbier appellation, so even though this beer has been traditionally produced in five small towns in the region, several bigger breweries such as Bischofshof also make a Zoiglbier. Based in Regensberg, Bischofshof has an up-to-date brewhouse that was constructed in 2006, and it is here that its Zoigl is made in a more modern way, although it is very much to the brewery's credit that it hasn't neglected such a historic brew. After all, the brewery has its own sense of history, having been founded by the prince-bishop Wilhelm Graf von Wartenberg in the middle of the 17th century, when it is believed that its Zoiglbier made its debut. **WO**

Tasting notes

Bischofshof Zoiglbier is a typical unfiltered Kellerbier with a light cloudy dark-gold color; it is very fresh and spicy on the nose. The palate echoes the nose's gentle spicy notes with a sweetish undercurrent, before descending to a light hoppy finish.

Bishops Finger

Shepherd Neame | www.shepherd-neame.co.uk

Country of origin England
First brewed 1958
Alcohol content 5.4% abv
Serving temperature 48°–52°F, 9°–11°C

Customs and tradition play a large part in the world of brewing, but few beers are as anchored in history or ritual as Bishops Finger. Taking the history first of all, this satisfying, strong ale from Shepherd Neame was created in 1958, but its name harks back to a time many centuries earlier when pilgrims made their slow progress across the English county of Kent to the shrine of St. Thomas Becket at Canterbury Cathedral. On their journeys, they relied for directions on road signs shaped like a finger, a distinctive piece of wayside furniture that still exists in rural parts of the county today. The "bishop's finger," as it became known, helped many a traveler reach his holy destination.

Ritual plays a part in the way in which the beer is brewed, with rules for production governed by a special charter issued by the brewery in 2003. These ensure that the beer is only ever brewed on a Friday, and only by the head brewer, with ingredients sourced wholly from Kent: water from the brewery's artesian well, barley from local fields that has been turned into pale and crystal malts, and an abundance of fine hops—Target and East Kent Golding—from the county's world-famous farms to bring fruit and bitterness to the palate.

Rigid adherence to these parameters has allowed Shepherd Neame to acquire Protective Geographic Indication status for Bishops Finger from the European Union. This is the badge of authenticity that has been secured by the likes of Parma ham and Camembert cheese, and it means, in practice, that no other beer can legally describe itself as a Kentish strong ale. **JE**

Tasting notes

A deep amber-colored ale, with gentle pear drop candy, buttery malt, and a hint of licorice in the aroma. Perfumed pear and vinous fruit join dry, peppery hop notes in the taste, overlaying silky, malty sweetness before a notably dry, hoppy, bitter finish.

Bitch Creek ESB

Grand Teton Brewing Company | www.grandtetonbrewing.com

Country of origin United States
First brewed 1989
Alcohol content 5.5% abv
Serving temperature 55°F, 13°C

The brewery began life in Wyoming but moved to Idaho. Founders Charlie and Ernie Otto first called their business Otto Brothers Brewing, but today it goes by the name of Grand Teton Brewing. One of its best known beers is called Bitch Creek ESB, and almost everybody agrees that it is a fine and hoppy example of what's become known as an American brown ale.

The brothers opened Wyoming's first microbrewery in Charlie's backyard in Wilson, Wyoming, in 1989. After lobbying to get brewpubs legalized, they began running the state's first brewery restaurant in 1992. By then, they'd introduced the modern-day growler that went on to become a staple in U.S. brewpubs. At the end of the 19th century, beer drinkers would carry beer home from the pub in a pail known as a "growler." Lacking a bottling line and looking for a way to sell beer for his customers to take home, Charlie Otto hit on the idea of putting a brewery label on a half-gallon glass container, calling it a "growler," and telling customers they could return empties to be refilled. Brewpubs across the country soon copied the idea.

Otto Brothers moved to its new home in Victor, Idaho, in 1998 and took on the name Grand Teton Brewing in 2000. Like Old Faithful Ale, the official beer of Yellowstone National Park, Bitch Creek takes it name from a local landmark. Bitch Creek flows down the west side of the Tetons and is a favorite destination of fly fishermen. To celebrate the brewery's 20th anniversary, brewmaster Rob Mullin created an XX series of stronger beers, including XX Bitch Creek Double ESB. **SH**

Tasting notes

Dark mahogany in the glass. The initial aromas of grapefruit and pine from Northwest hops mostly overwhelm caramel notes. More caramel sweetness emerges on the palate, some nuttiness and toffee, as well as citrus from the hops. Finishes solidly bitter.

Bittersweet Lenny's RIPA

Shmaltz Brewing | www.shmaltz.com

Country of origin United States
First brewed 2006
Alcohol content 10% abv
Serving temperature 50°F, 10°C

Throughout his controversial career, Leonard Alfred Schneider was better known by his stage name, Lenny Bruce, and he was only forty years old when he died penniless of a drug overdose. But he left his mark. As a result of his many arrests and trials for obscenity, Bruce became a symbol for free speech, inspiring countless others to push the boundaries of artistic expression.

In 2006, another upstart was also pushing the boundaries, not of free speech, but of beer. Jeremy Cowan had founded Shmaltz Brewing in 1996 with a knowing wink. Since then, his brand He'Brew—The Chosen Beer—has been stirring up its own controversy with its tongue-in-cheek marketing. So it was almost a forgone conclusion that He'Brew would create a rye double IPA dedicated to the late Jewish comedian Lenny Bruce.

Like its namesake, Lenny's RIPA communicates with bitterness using "an obscene amount of hops," including Amarillo, Cascade, Centennial, Chinook, Crystal, Simcoe, and Warrior. It's also dry hopped with Amarillo and Crystal hops, but to get that perfect balance, five traditional malts are used, including four barley and one wheat, plus three rye varieties: rye ale malt, torrified rye, and crystal rye 75.

Advertised as having "shocking flavors—far beyond contemporary community standards," the brand is as wry as it is rye. Beyond the hype, it's the first beer of its kind, a double IPA made with rye, a giant of a beer that manages to be as balanced as it is wild, a stunning performance worthy of the comedian who challenged the United States's moral hypocrisies with words. **JB**

Tasting notes

A beautiful ruddy copper color with a thick tan head. The nose is a complex mix of big hops, sweet malt, and rye. Thick, creamy, and chewy, it's an amazing array of changing flavors, from omnipresent rye to piney hops, peppery spices, sweet malt, and warming alcohol.

Black Oak Nut Brown Ale

Black Oak Brewing Company | www.blackoakbeer.com

Country of origin Canada
First brewed 2000
Alcohol content 5% abv
Serving temperature 46°F, 8°C

Black Oak Brewing has, in its relatively short existence, firmly embedded itself in the provincial beer scene. Owner Ken Woods conceived of his business while working as a server at a now-defunct Toronto brewpub. He built the brewery in Oakville because of its location within the southern Ontario region in which he intended to sell, plus the lower rents he found there. He and then-partner John Gagliardi shipped their first keg of the brewery's other flagship brand, Black Oak Pale Ale, on January 10, 2000—a good start to the millennium.

A curiosity of the Greater Toronto Area, however, is that support for craft breweries outside of the borders of the metropolis has been notoriously weak, even when said breweries are located within the very communities they serve. So, after years of shipping the bulk of his beer from suburb to city, Woods finally found a location in an industrial zone on Toronto's west side and moved his brewery in 2009.

Although Black Oak's two main brands are crafted in styles of English origin, both are unapologetically modernist interpretations. The Black Oak Pale Ale is blond enough to be viewed from a distance as a pils, whereas the Black Oak Nut Brown Ale has considerably more sweetness than one would expect from a Yorkshire brown ale. As the brewery's only year-round offerings, they make up the bulk of production, supplemented seasonally by more unconventional brews, such as the Belgian-inspired Summer Saison, the spiced Christmas beer Nutcracker Porter, and wintertime's Double Chocolate Cherry Stout. **SB**

Tasting notes

"Nut Brown" is certainly an apt moniker for this ale, with its light mahogany hue and notably nutty character. Sweetish malt dominates the palate, while drying rather than bittering hops set it up as a fine complement to rare roast beef.

Black Sheep Best Bitter

Black Sheep Brewery
www.blacksheepbrewery.com

Country of origin England
First brewed 1992
Alcohol content 3.8% abv
Serving temperature 52°F, 11°C

Black Sheep Brewery was founded in 1992 by Paul Theakston, a member of the illustrious brewing family that first started making beer in north Yorkshire in 1827. Paul had left the family business in 1987 to start his own brewery, and this was Black Sheep's debut beer.

As with all their beers, its base is liquor from the brewery's own wells, Maris Otter pale ale malt, a little crystal malt, torrefied wheat—this is 10 percent of the grist and helps to give the beer its distinctive, full, and lasting white head—the English Golding and Fuggle hops, and a multi-strain Yorkshire Square yeast. The beer is fermented in Yorkshire Squares, a method of fermentation once used by brewers in the area. The top of the square acts as a yeast collector, which separates the fermenting beer from the rigorous yeast head that forms on the top of the liquid; this is said to soften the beer's taste. **TH**

Tasting notes
Well hopped, the beer exudes tangy, citrus fruit and pepper flavors. A handful of roasted malt is used, which imparts a biscuit flavor. Its finish is long and refreshingly vital.

Black Wattle Original Ale

Barons Brewing Company
www.baronsbrewing.com

Country of origin Australia
First brewed 2005
Alcohol content 5.8% abv
Serving temperature 43°F, 6°C

Early Australian brewers were known to try to improve their beers by adding all sorts of ingredients. This was often done in an attempt to fix "crook" beer and mask undesirable flavors caused by wild yeasts and scorching temperatures. Largely, such experiments failed, and for the last century the ingredients list for Australian beers has been much the same as any country in the world.

At least, this was the case until Richard Adamson decided to launch a range of beers making use of uniquely Australian ingredients. Barons Black Wattle Original Ale has the addition of roasted wattleseed, a seed native to Australia that forms part of the bush tucker eaten by Aboriginal Australians. The use of local ingredients proved a stroke of marketing genius. Barons now has a distribution network into the United States, Russia, and the United Kingdom where it offers "a little bit of Australia in every bottle." **DD**

Tasting notes
Pours with a strong head and a ruby color that is supported by an aroma hinting at toffee and flowers. Roasted wattleseeds add an intriguing twist to the caramel malt flavors.

Boltens Ur-Alt

Privatbrauerei Bolten
www.bolten-brauerei.de

Country of origin Germany
First brewed 1991
Alcohol content 4.9% abv
Serving temperature 46°F, 8°C

Privatbrauerei Bolten prides itself on being the oldest Altbier brewery in the Lower Rhine area—and hence in the world. It is documented that the site, called Kraushof, has been entitled to brew since 1266.

This beer is the unfiltered version of the brewery's regular alt beer with pilsner, Munich, roasted malts, and a tiny share of wheat malt going into the grist. Depending on the quality, three to five different kinds of hops are used, ranging from the bittering variety Hallertauer Nordbrauer to the aromatic varieties Hallertauer Perle and Spalter Select. This selection gives a harmonious, rounded bitterness that blends in with the caramel and roasted flavors of the malts. After warm fermentation, Bolten Ur-Alt matures in cold temperatures for three to four weeks. This is an unusually lengthy period, but it gives most of the yeast cells enough time to settle, preventing cloudiness. **SK**

Tasting notes
Herbal hop aromas with hints of malt and citrus. On the palate, a fresh, fluffy feeling that evolves into a brilliant roasted malt character. An aromatic bitter finish.

Bombay Pale Ale

Nørrebro Bryghus
www.noerrebrobryghus.dk

Country of origin Denmark
First brewed 2003
Alcohol content 6.5% abv
Serving temperature 41°–50°F, 5°–10°C

When Anders Kissmeyer left Carlsberg to create his own brewery, his inspiration was the U.S. craft brewery scene. Kissmeyer adored East India Pale Ale from the Brooklyn Brewery, and when it came to brewing his own IPA, he asked Brooklyn's Garret Oliver for help. Oliver commented on Kissmeyer's recipe ideas and helped to develop a truly transatlantic IPA—an English beer style, reborn in the United States, brewed in Denmark with U.S. guidance, using malt and hops from England, the United States, and continental Europe.

Perle and Willamette hops add bitterness, but the reliance on English hops for aroma produces a beer that's instantly recognizable as being in the U.S. IPA style. With a full malt character balancing out IPA hop levels, it's a brewpub favorite served with spicy Asian food and strong cheeses, but the caramelization also makes it a fine match for roast or barbecued meat. **PB**

Tasting notes
Pours with a deep suntan color and a thick, creamy head. A spritzy aroma of lemon and buttery sweetness, followed on the palate by citrus hops held in check by creamy caramel malt.

Boont Amber Ale

Anderson Valley Brewing Company | www.avbc.com

Country of origin United States
First brewed 1987
Alcohol content 5.8% abv
Serving temperature 44°F, 7°C

Anderson Valley Brewing Company was founded in Boonville, a small northern Californian town of barely 700 residents. Its isolated location led its residents to create their own local dialect, known as "Boontling," with more than 1,000 unique words and phrases. It has its origins in English, Irish, Pomoan (a local Native American language), Scottish Gaelic, and Spanish.

The very first beer brewed in Boonville, the Boont Amber Ale, was named in honor of the quirky town. Its early popularity led it to win four medals at the Great American Beer Festival and helped Anderson Valley to be declared one of the Top Ten Breweries in the World in both 1997 and 1998. Boont Amber is made with all-American ingredients, including two-row pale malt and several varieties of crystal malts. Three different hops are added in three separate additions: Horizon, Northern Brewer, and Liberty, which are all from the Pacific Northwest.

The original brewery was in the basement of the Buckhorn Saloon and was a small ten-barrel system built to provide beer for the brewpub upstairs. But due to increasing demand, production was moved in 1996 to a new Bavarian-style, thirty-barrel brewhouse. Today the grounds include a tasting room, bottling line, and stables for the Shire horses that are used to pull an old-fashioned wagon to and from town. Anderson Valley Brewing describes its annual beer festival as "The bahlest steinber hornin', chiggrul gormin' tidrick in the heelch of the Boont Region!" ("The best beer-drinking, food-eating party in the entire of the Boonville region!") **JB**

Tasting notes

Bright, clear brown in color with a very thick tan head. The nose is sweet and fruity, with a creamy mouthfeel. Soft malt and a subtle rich, roasted quality make this amber ale clean, simple, and easy drinking. The finish is tart and lingers a long time.

Brains SA

SA Brain & Company | www.sabrain.com

Country of origin Wales
First brewed 1958
Alcohol content 4.2% abv
Serving temperature 52°F, 11°C

The game of rugby in Wales is not so much a sport as a religion. Match days in the capital, Cardiff, are epic events, with the city's streets teeming with fans, many of whom have no hope of attending the event, such is the clamor for tickets. Their consolation is to find a corner in a bustling pub to watch proceedings on the television and enjoy the local ale.

Cardiff's major brewery—indeed the major independent brewery in Wales—is Brains, a company founded in 1882. The business today turns out a wide range of intriguing ales, but the flagship beer remains a brew known only by two letters: SA. The initials reflect the name of the brewery's founding father, Samuel Arthur Brain. However, the abbreviation has been humorously twisted by rugby followers, who claim it stands for "skull attack." This unfortunate, though affectionate, nickname somewhat exaggerates the beer's strength because, at 4.2 percent, SA is not particularly potent. It is, in fact, a very suppable pint, with the balance of flavor tipped more toward pale and crystal malts than the featured Challenger, Fuggle, and Golding hops. If, however, you prefer your ales more hoppy and your malt less prominent, there is an alternative. In 2006, a lighter, more bitter, sister brand, SA Gold, was launched and has proved very successful across the border in England.

The Wales–England border features on a famous advertisement for Brains beer. It depicts a road sign with two important letters missing from the name of the principality. "It wouldn't be Wales without SA," declares the strapline. Many drinkers could not agree more. **JE**

Tasting notes

A full-bodied, amber-colored best bitter with malt leading the way in both the aroma and the lightly fruity taste, but with hops providing a firm bitterness throughout to counter the sweetness. The drying finish adds to the easy-drinking character.

Brakspear Bitter

Brakspear Brewing Company | www.brakspear-beers.co.uk

Country of origin England
First brewed 2004
Alcohol content 3.4% abv
Serving temperature 52°–55°F, 11°–13°C

Brakspear was one of the most revered breweries in England. It is hard to fathom how a business established in the 18th century, and as much a part of the Oxfordshire town of Henley-on-Thames as its famous rowing regatta, could be allowed to slip away, but it happened. The board of directors sold off the brewery site for redevelopment and leased out the rights to brew and market the beers elsewhere.

The company that took up the challenge of re-creating Brakspear's distinctive ales was Wychwood Brewery at Witney, Oxfordshire. It constructed a new Brakspear brewery alongside the Wychwood site, piecing together the original brewing plant to re-create the previous Brakspear system as accurately as possible, including the "double-drop" fermentation process, in which beer is partly fermented in one vessel and then dropped to a lower tank, leaving dead yeast and proteins behind.

The feeling is that the new Brakspear brewery has come as close as any brewery could to reviving the flagship beer, Brakspear Bitter. At 3.4 percent, it is remarkably quaffable and refreshing, yet packed with flavor: a traditional English ale in every sense, from the pale and crystal malts in the mash tun to the Fuggle and Golding hops in the copper. What's also impressive is the way in which other characteristics of Brakspear beer have been retained, such as the slightly salty finish and, more significantly, a prominent butterscotch note from fermentation with the original Brakspear yeast. The Henley brewery, sadly, cannot be brought back, but Brakspear's beer, at least, lives on. **JE**

Tasting notes

A classic amber bitter, packed with a lot of character for its low strength. Fruity, floral, butterscotch notes fill the aroma. In the mouth, there's a hint of orangey fruit, but generally the taste is dry and bitter, rounding off hoppy and slightly salty with more butterscotch.

Brakspear Triple

Brakspear Brewing Company | www.brakspear-beers.co.uk

Country of origin England
First brewed 2005
Alcohol content 7.2% abv
Serving temperature 52°–55°F, 11°–13°C

After the much-loved Henley-on-Thames brewery closed in 2002, the future of Brakspear's wonderful beers seemed bleak, until the old brewing equipment was reassembled alongside Wychwood Brewery in Witney. To mark the successful revival of a great brewing name, a new beer was launched.

Brakspear Triple is the creation of Wychwood brewer Jeremy Moss, who devised a strong, special beer full of the familiar Brakspear character. It is called Triple for two reasons. Firstly, the beer is triple hopped, with Northdown hops and Cascade in the copper, and then more Cascade in the fermentation vessel. Secondly, the beer is triple fermented, using the original Brakspear yeast. After primary fermentation, there's a long, slow, secondary fermentation in conditioning tanks and finally, because the beer is packaged with live yeast, there's a third fermentation in the bottle.

It's a stunning drink. The crystal malts used alongside pale malt in the mash tun really show through, bringing sweet barley flavors to the palate. These are contrasted by pronounced citrus notes from the Cascade hops and also by tropical fruit flavors generated by the action of the yeast.

Brakspear Triple has little in common, stylistically, with the triples brewed by Belgian and Dutch Trappist monks, but there are some religious links to be found. A distant ancestor of the brewery's founding family is one Nicholas Breakspear, who grew up to be the only English pope. When you pour yourself a glass of Triple in the specially designed chalice glass, the ecclesiastic connections become even more tangible. **JE**

Tasting notes

A red-brown ale with rich malt and tropical fruit in the aroma. Sweet, lightly toffeeish malt in the taste is soon joined by juicy pineapple and grapefruit flavors and an enjoyable butterscotch note. The same flavors return in the drying, slightly salty finish.

BridgePort India Pale Ale

BridgePort Brewing Company | www.bridgeportbrew.com

Country of origin United States
First brewed 1996
Alcohol content 5.5% abv
Serving temperature 50°F, 10°C

The Columbia River Brewery was arguably the first modern microbrewery in Oregon when it opened its doors in 1984, and it has successfully trademarked the phrase "Oregon's oldest craft brewery." Two years later, it acquired its present moniker, the BridgePort Brewing Company, when its brewpub opened to the public in Portland's historic warehouse district. A dozen years after that, in 1996, award-winning brewer Karl Ockert first brewed BridgePort's India Pale Ale.

The idea came from an offhand remark made by one of Ockert's friends, who pointed out that the brewery was located close to one of the biggest hop-growing areas in the United States. Ockert then set about to make a traditional English IPA with American hops. At the time, brewing a beer that was 50 IBUs was considered crazy, and many fellow brewers told Ockert that they didn't believe anyone would drink or buy such a bitter beer. But the brew's popularity was almost immediate. The year after it debuted, BridgePort India Pale Ale was awarded a gold medal at the Great American Beer Festival, the first of many accolades it has received. The most impressive is undoubtedly being the first beer from the United States to be named the Champion Beer at the venerable Brewing Industry International Awards in 2000, besting more than 750 beers.

BridgePort India Pale Ale uses a process called natural-conditioning, in which the beer is fermented a second time in its respective bottle, keg, or cask. A unique blend of five hops is used, but the specific varieties are a closely guarded secret. **JB**

Tasting notes

BridgePort's IPA is a golden amber color with a rich tan head and great lace. The nose is redolent of citrus and pine hop aromas. With a rich, creamy mouthfeel, biscuity malt, and terrific hop bittering, the complex flavors never overpower, but remain smooth and very drinkable.

BridgePort Old Knucklehead

BridgePort Brewery | www.bridgeportbrew.com

Country of origin United States
First brewed 1989
Alcohol content 9% abv
Serving temperature 55°F, 13°C

Beer lovers understand that a true appreciation of the craft and culture of beer calls for veneration and irreverence in equal measure. That's why, if a thriving brewery decides to create a special, limited edition, vintage brew in honor of the people who have helped it achieve success, it's entirely appropriate to name the beer Old Knucklehead and to put a picture of the person they are "honoring" on the label directly beneath this honorific. Since 1989, BridgePort has insulted/complimented a number of influential figures in this way, including legendary beer writer Fred Eckhardt. Each time a new vintage is created and a new Knucklehead named, the brewery hosts a "changing of the Knucklehead" ceremony that involves the "knuckling in" of the new title holder and the tapping of a cask-conditioned firkin of the new beer.

Old Knucklehead is an English barleywine-style ale, brewed at the onset of winter with double the amount of malt and hops of a normal beer. Traditionally, the beer has topped out around 9 percent, but in 2008 the brewery went a little further. A portion was drawn off and aged for three months in American oak bourbon barrels, then blended back in to produce a 10 percent ale that was both richer and more complex in flavor and yet less heavy than other beers of this strength. Only seventy-five barrels of the beer were produced.

So what does it take to become a Knucklehead? A BridgePort brewer diplomatically says you have to be "eccentric in an amusing way." One past winner thinks this is overpolite: "I think you have to be a certified curmudgeon to be an Old Knucklehead." **PB**

Tasting notes

A resiny, rich mahogany appearance. Vanilla, bourbon, and oak dominate on the nose, with flavors of toffee, toasted malt, sherry, raisins, plums, and molasses joining in on the palate. Somehow, with so much going on, it remains smooth and easy to drink.

British Bulldog

Westerham Brewery Co. | www.westerhambrewery.co.uk

Country of origin England
First brewed 2004
Alcohol content 4.3% abv
Serving temperature 44°–50°F, 7°–10°C

There's nothing more British than a bulldog: its ugly curled-up chops and stumpy legs no match for an unfaltering tenacity in the face of catching sticks. So it will please all British beer fans to find a proud patriot of the same name in this book. British Bulldog beer, though, is far from ugly; instead it is a fine specimen of beer: quite full bodied with plenty of bite.

It should come as no surprise that Westerham has produced something so enjoyable because it is a brewery with plenty of pedigree. Although a relative newcomer, only opening its doors in 2004, it has picked up the heritage left by Black Eagle Brewery (a much-loved local brewery that shut its doors in 1965) and produces a host of excellent brews.

British Bulldog is a traditional Kent bitter, with plenty of Maris Otter pale ale malt and crystal malt for color and richness, with local hops Northdown and Finchcocks's Whitbread Golding for a full flavor and aroma. Its low carbonation and alcohol levels mixed with the careful balance of the hops and malt mean it is wonderfully sessionable. The beer also delivers a fine amber-gold color and fruitiness that is subtle but apparent to those with a discerning palate.

Westerham is run by Robert Wicks, who gave up a lucrative life in the financial sector to follow his brewing dream. Now firmly established as a brewer of repute, he also possesses a firm commitment to acting in an environmentally sound way and sourcing locally produced quality ingredients. It's no surprise, therefore, that Westerham has produced a sterling beer that the British can be proud of. **TS**

Tasting notes

Pours medium amber color and has plenty of frothy head to enjoy. The nose shows off the fruity qualities, whereas on the palate the sweet malts are beautifully complemented by the hops to make the beer a great match with a tangy cheese.

Brooklyn Lager

Brooklyn Brewery | www.brooklynbrewery.com

Country of origin United States
First brewed 1988
Alcohol content 5.2% abv
Serving temperature 46°–48°F, 8°–9°C

It comes as a surprise to many beer enthusiasts to learn that mainstream U.S. lager, dismissed by many as lacking in beery character, wasn't always the way it is today. In the late 19th century German brewers fleeing unrest in their home country landed in America by the thousands, and built the U.S. brewing industry as a copy of the one they had left behind. Some of the most popular beer styles were Viennese and Bavarian lagers, darker and more characterful than blond pilsner. Then came Prohibition, and over fourteen years, Americans forgot the taste of beer and switched to soft drinks. When Prohibition was repealed, they found the taste of dark lager had become too harsh and full, and brewers quickly switched to lighter beers to rebuild their businesses.

More than fifty years later, two New York beer fans decided to revive Brooklyn's place in the history of U.S. brewing, and gained access to brewers' notebooks and recipes that predated Prohibition. Brooklyn Lager was very different from most other beers at the time: all malt, with no adjuncts, such as rice, and seasoned with Hallertauer Mittelfrueh, Vanguard, and Cascade hops, it has far more flavor than Americans were accustomed to. Unusually for a lager, it's dry hopped—a practice normally associated with English cask ales whereby fresh hops are added to the beer as it matures, in this case in the lagering tanks. This is what American craft brewers do best—taking old traditions from Europe, reviving them, and giving them a twist to create something truly American. This modern old-fashioned beer proves that history is often circular. **PB**

Tasting notes

A warm amber color. Spicy, floral hops mingle with toasty malt on the nose. On the palate, that balance continues with sweet caramel malt at the base and perfumed hops hovering just over the tongue, uniting in a smooth, dry, crisp whole.

Broughton Old Jock Ale

Broughton Brewery | www.broughtonales.co.uk

Country of origin Scotland
First brewed 1985
Alcohol content 6.7% abv
Serving temperature 50°–54°F, 10°–12°C

Broughton Brewery opened in 1980 in a former sheep abattoir in the Scottish Borders. Its founders were David Younger and James Collins—Younger was from the seventh generation of the famous Younger brewing dynasty, and Collins was a member of the renowned Scottish publishing firm. The brewery was one of the first enterprises to ride the wave of the Scottish real ale revival and watched many of its peers go under. Tough times eventually caught up with Broughton, too, and in 1985, Giles Litchfield of Derbyshire-based Whim Ales acquired it; he saw the value in making its beers more widely available.

Soldiers of the Highland and Lowland Regiments of Scotland have long been referred to as "Jocks." The beer label depicts a fierce-looking infantryman with red hair. Old Jock Ale, typical of the Scottish "wee heavy" ales, reflects that strength and character. **AG**

Tasting notes
Full bodied and warming, with the estery, fruity flavor of strong Scottish ale. A balance of hop bitterness with sweet malt and licorice, plus its strong alcohol, makes a formidable creation.

Buddy Marvellous

Bryncelyn Brewery | www.bryncelynbrewery.org.uk

Country of origin Wales
First brewed 1999
Alcohol content 4% abv
Serving temperature 52°–54°F, 11°–12°C

Beer and rock 'n' roll are soul mates—not just on the gig circuit but often in the brewhouse, too. Cream, Led Zeppelin, and Frank Zappa are just a few performers to have had beers named in their honor. Another is Buddy Holly, whose work left a lasting impression on a publican from South Wales. Will Hopton, licensee of the Wern Fawr pub, near Swansea, was captivated by Holly's music at an early age. When Hopton decided to open a brewery in his pub cellar in 1999, it seemed only natural that Buddy Holly should be the inspiration.

Will and his brewer, Robert Scott, created a catalog of Holly-inspired beers. They include Oh Boy, Rave On, and a Christmas beer, That'll Be the Sleigh. The beers are regular award winners, none more so than Buddy Marvellous, a ruby ale that was Champion Beer of Wales in 2002. The success of the brewery has led to expansion, and there are plans to bottle the beers. **JE**

Tasting notes
A ruby beer with an aroma of malt and fruit. Bitterness is kept on the low side, but fruity hops and roasted grain are in evidence in the taste. Plenty of body and a pleasant, dry finish.

← One of Broughton's session ales: The Reiver (meaning "border raider").

Bush Ambrée Triple

Brasserie Dubuisson | www.br-dubuisson.com

Country of origin Belgium
First brewed 2008
Alcohol content 12% abv
Serving temperature 48°–54°F, 9°–12°C

Like many breweries in this fertile region of Hainaut Province, Brasserie Dubuisson started as a farm that brewed beer. Commendably, Dubuisson ("bush" in English) still manages to distinguish itself from its neighbors by the kind of beer it produces.

In 1933, Dubuisson's brewer brought forth an amber-colored strong beer in a loosely British style, which was very much against the grain of other local brewers who kept to the traditional, light, saison style. The brewer also thought that it was a good idea to stress the beer's British links by using the translated name, Bush. This Bush Ambrée proved so popular that Dubuisson remained a single-beer brewery until 1991.

However, when the brewery tentatively started to export abroad, to its amazement, it learned that only seven countries in the world would accept the Bush name. The largest brewer at the time, Anheuser-Busch, prevented the use of the Bus(c)h name, apparently fearing that its altogether different flagship beer might be tarnished by this flavorful amber ale. This is the reason why Bush is known as "Scaldis" in most countries.

Gradually Brasserie Dubuisson started to experiment and used oak aging with some success (try Bush Prestige). This sense of adventure saw the brewery's beers packaged into elegant champagne-sized bottles. Inevitably, these larger bottles began to be used for the non-oaked beers, too, which resulted in an amber, as well as a blond, Triple. Cynics might think that there is little to choose between the two, but the Triple gets an extra three weeks' lagering, strengthening the nutty, malty aromas, and it is not filtered. **JPa**

Tasting notes

Very lively carbonation and a cream-colored head over hazy red-amber beer. Warm alcohol nose, plus cookies and roast notes reminiscent of cake flambéed with brandy. Honey, amber malts, almonds, and dried apricots on the palate. Much livelier than the filtered version.

Caldera IPA

Caldera Brewing | www.calderabrewing.com

Country of origin United States
First brewed 1997
Alcohol content 6.1% abv
Serving temperature 50°F, 10°C

Caldera Brewing is located in Ashland, Oregon, near the southern border of the state. Founded by head brewer Jim Mills, for the first eight years it produced only draft beer, and for most of that time self-distributed it, too. After six years of delivering its own beer, the brewery expanded its market by working with more traditional beer distributors and turned its attentions to introducing packaged beer. For this enterprise, it chose to put its beer in aluminum cans.

In June 2005, Caldera became the first brewery in the State of Oregon to put its beer in cans. Years later, it remains Oregon's lone micro-canning brewery. Decidedly small, Caldera produced only around 3,000 barrels in 2008 (by contrast, Anheuser-Busch made more than 24 million barrels in the same year). Caldera is focused on being just a production brewhouse, with no pub, restaurant, or even tasting room. Everything is brewed on a small ten-barrel system, with varying size fermenters allowing the brewery to do single, double, and triple batches.

Brewed with premium two-row pale, Munich, and crystal malts, the flagship IPA has a big malt backbone. And that's for good reason, because Mills uses three big aroma hop varieties in his beer: Amarillo, Centennial, and Simcoe. Unlike many other breweries in the Pacific Northwest, Caldera uses fresh whole flower hops in every step of the brewing process, which it believes imparts cleaner flavors than hop pellets. The Caldera IPA was honored with a gold medal at the Stockholm Beer and Whiskey Fest in Sweden in 2008, one of several awards the IPA has garnered. **JB**

Tasting notes

Clear amber golden color with a rich tan head, Caldera's IPA has a big hop nose thick with a complex mélange of grapefruit, grassy, and herbal aromas. The flavor is also a big hop wallop with oniony, bitter notes and a dry, lingering finish.

Caledonian 80

Caledonian Brewing Company | www.caledonian-brewery.co.uk

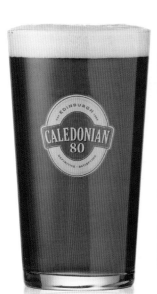

Country of origin Scotland
First brewed *ca.* 1870s
Alcohol content 4.1% abv
Serving temperature 50°F, 10°C

At the time of its construction in 1869, Lorimer and Clark's Caledonian Brewery had more than forty brewing neighbors in Edinburgh. This was largely due to the quality of the water from wells under the city, which coined the nickname "the charmed circle." Nowadays, "the Caley" is Edinburgh's sole survivor.

Caledonian 80 has been Champion Beer of Scotland on several occasions, and it is a fine example of the robustly malty, richly sweet beers with a relatively low hop content that are the signature of Scottish brewing. Its name is actually Eighty Shillings, a legacy of the days when Scottish beer was loosely categorized by the amount of tax payable on a hogshead (504-pint barrel). The system progressed through 60/-, 70/-, and 80/- to the full-flavored and alcohol-hefty 90/- and it was legally recognized in 1914.

Caledonian's Victorian brewhouse design allows each stage of the process to be shifted around by the force of gravity (grain goes in on the top floor), and it is the United Kingdom's only remaining brewery that uses direct-fired coppers. Its hand-beaten inner dome concentrates heat and develops a constant churn and roll. The method is particularly effective because the beer is boiled quickly rather than being "stewed" in stainless steel vessels. This has its disadvantages, however, and major fires in 1994 and 1998 came close to shutting down the operation for good. The first reconstruction took two years and millions of dollars to complete. The second blaze destroyed one of the original coppers, but luckily the local company that made them still had the engineering drawings. **AG**

Tasting notes

A smooth, well-balanced, malty ale, now with noticeably more hop content that has improved and streamlined it. It is russet brown—like autumn leaves—in color, with a firm body, some ripe fruit flavor, and a satisfying vegetablelike late hop finish.

Cane and Ebel

Two Brothers Brewing Company | www.twobrosbrew.com

Country of origin United States
First brewed 2006
Alcohol content 7% abv
Serving temperature 50°F, 10°C

"This was supposed to be a 'one and done' beer," says one of the founding brothers Jason Ebel about Cane and Ebel. From the start, though, people responded to this luscious mouthful of a beer, and it is now produced year-round. The brothers take input from all corners of the company for the artisan beers, and, in this case, "one of the sales guys really wanted a rye ale," says Ebel. "I had seen a travel show where they were harvesting Thai palm sugar, and I really wanted to try that, to see if it would cut the sharpness of the rye."

Rye "is a pain in the butt" for brewers because it can be a bit gluey in the mash tun. But it offers a bright, peppery spiciness as well as some oily creaminess on the palate. On top of that, there is a delicious burned-sugar character from the caramel malt that also gives Cane and Ebel its mahogany color. Seventy pounds of fairly pale Thai palm sugar per fifty-barrel batch adds vanilla, mango, and papaya aromas for a hint of the exotic. Finally, hop varieties like Summit add citrus, even oniony notes.

Sugar has been used in brewing for hundreds of years. It always lightens the body, a good thing for stronger beers. Varietal sugars like this one harvested from palm blossoms add layers of complex aroma as well. This is a big, bold beer, but because of the sugar, it is lighter on the palate than you would expect from its 7 percent strength. At 68 IBU, there is plenty of bitterness here for any hophead, but because there is so much going on, the beer never feels lopsided. It is a very flavorful beer, so naturally it pairs best with "big, assertive food like barbecue," says Ebel. **RM**

Tasting notes

Heady aromas of spice, citrus hops, burned sugar, and a touch of tropical fruitiness. Palate is sweet up front, building to a bitter middle, drying a little, but with a creamy, oily texture from the rye. Finish is long and bitter, with the burned-sugar flavors lingering.

CascaZilla

Ithaca Beer Company | www.ithacabeer.com

Country of origin United States
First brewed 2004
Alcohol content 6.5% abv
Serving temperature 46° F, 8° C

In 1995, Dan Mitchell recognized that the Finger Lakes region around Ithaca, New York, was loaded with local wineries but that the city did not have its own brewery. He felt that Ithaca could support a local craft brewery, so he bought a brewing system from a disused brewpub in Austin, Texas, in 1997. After months of installation work, the Ithaca Beer Company was officially ready to open in December 1998.

Ithaca is a college town that has a somewhat counter-establishment vibe. The mood fits perfectly with the idea of supporting locally produced products. Among the beers Ithaca makes are Flower Power IPA, Apricot Ale, Pale Ale, Nut Brown, and Partly Sunny Wheat Beer. Ithaca now sells beer in New York, Connecticut, Massachusetts, Rhode Island, and Ohio. It also makes highly regarded gourmet root beer and ginger beer soft drinks.

The label says that CascaZilla is a "Monstrously Hoppy Red Ale," and the description is spot on. The beer was first brewed in 2004 as a season beer for the autumn and it was the brewery's first beer to have hops in the driving seat. The name is a play on Cascadilla Creek and Gorge, which flows through the city of Ithaca, and Cascade hops, one of the hop varieties used during the brewing and also for dry hopping. CascaZilla is brewed with British crystal malt and a mix of American hops such as Chinook, Crystal, Amarillo, and Cascade, all of which set the pace for the flavor profile. This beer has a cult following among hopheads in upstate New York and has won medals at regional and national competitions. **RL**

Tasting notes

CascaZilla opens with an immediate intense floral hop aroma, rich thick head, and a glowing tarnished penny color. Spicy, herbal hop flavors abound throughout this well-built brew. The beer finishes with a Scotch Pine note and a hint of dryness.

Celebration Ale

Sierra Nevada Brewing Company | www.sierranevada.com

Country of origin United States
First brewed 1981
Alcohol content 6.8% abv
Serving temperature 48°–55°F, 9°–13°C

Celebration Ale was first brewed as a Christmas beer and is still released every holiday season. Each year, the brewers eagerly await the first shipment of a new crop of hops from Yakima, Washington, one of the major (if not the major) hop-growing areas in the United States. Once the freshly dried hops have made the trip about halfway down the West Coast to Sierra Nevada Brewing, in Chico, California, Celebration is brewed nonstop for about one month in order to meet the growing demand for this popular beer.

There has been debate over the years about what kind of beer Celebration Ale really is. Some say it's a Christmas spiced beer while others argue that it is an IPA or a strong ale. "Celebration is one of the nation's first American-style IPAs, and it is, simply, an IPA," says the brewery's communications coordinator, Bill Manley. "Despite what people think, no spices are used to brew the beer. To achieve the distinctive aroma and flavors, the brewers utilize a traditional dry-hopping technique that involves hanging nylon sacks stuffed with whole cone hops inside fermenting tanks along with Sierra Nevada's unique "hop torpedo," which is stuffed with 80 pounds (36 kg) of hops.

Celebration Ale aficionados eagerly await the beer like children before Christmas. A black market even exists for saving and trading past vintages, despite the unorthodoxy of aging an IPA. Aging Celebration Ale allows the hops to mellow a bit, letting the rich and creamy malt body move to the front, and creating a unique range of flavors that transform through the years. **LMo**

Tasting notes

Featuring the first hops of the growing season, this pioneering IPA is full of complex flavors and aromas from the generous use of whole-cone American hops. Expect hints of floral hops, pine, malt, orange peel, and sweet caramel that fade to a spicy cinnamon finish.

Chouffe N'ice

Brasserie d'Achouffe | www.achouffe.be

Country of origin Belgium
First brewed 1998
Alcohol content 10% abv
Serving temperature 39°–50°F, 4°–10°C

Achouffe is one of the most familiar Belgian craft brewers, distinguished by its cheerful trademark *"chouffes"* (gnomes) grinning out from the shelves in more than twenty countries. This success must have seemed unthinkable back in 1982 when Pierre Gobron and Chris Bauweraerts set up shop on a shoestring in the village of Achouffe, deep in the Ardennes. But the pair knew a thing or two about marketing—the rosy-cheeked *chouffe*, drawn from local folklore, formed the core of a regional brand identity that now encompasses a fan club and an annual event, La Grande Choufferie, based at the well-regarded brewery tap in the village. In 2006, the business was sold to expanding Belgian national Duvel Moortgat, although so far little has changed except improved access to the market.

Achouffe has concentrated on its flagship blond ale La Chouffe and the vaguely Scottish-accented Mc Chouffe. However, in the 1990s, it began to experiment with seasonal releases, of which Chouffe N'ice is a survivor. The name indicates this is a winter beer, available from the beginning of December until stocks run out. It's not a proper ice beer, with alcohol concentrated by freezing, though at 10 percent it's the heftiest of the brewery's regulars. Brewed with Belgian pilsner malt, dark candy sugar, and Tomahawk, Styrian Golding, and Czech Saaz hops, it is also flavored with spices, including bitter orange peel and thyme, and bottle-conditioned in Wallonian fashion in 25-ounce (750-ml) bottles. It's arguably the star of the brewery's range and on a cold winter day can be relied upon to make your cheeks as rosy as a *chouffe*'s. **DdM**

Tasting notes

A deep reddish-brown beer with a yellowy head and a slight detergent note on a fruit, nut, and herb aroma. The generous honey-sweet palate has subtle herbs, and there are more nuts with chewy fruit and burned sugar on a warming, sweetish finish.

The cheeky *chouffe* that identifies the brewery's brand. ➡

Christmas Ale

Red Hill Brewery | www.redhillbrewery.com.au

Country of origin Australia
First brewed 2005
Alcohol content 7.5% abv
Serving temperature 46°–54°F, 8°–12°C

It was during a 1995 trip to Bruges that Australians David and Karen Golding first became fascinated by strong Belgian ales. During a trip to New Zealand in 2001, they came across a beer that excited them as much as the Belgian ales. Even better, it came with a brewer who was prepared to share what he knew. The beer was Benediction of the Australis range, and their brewer and soon-to-be mentor was Ben Middlemiss.

The beer is very challenging to brew. Thankfully, the Red Hill Brewery is a family affair. David is up to his elbows in malt while his father tends to the hop garden and Karen runs the restaurant. Even David's mother makes the muslin bags used in the extended dry hopping that is so important to the process. Middlemiss catches up with the Golding every now and then, and David and Karen enjoy Ben's look of approval whenever he tastes their Christmas Ale. **DD**

Tasting notes
Glows a deep orange-amber in the sun and releases a spicy, hop-driven aroma over a lush, lingering head. Slow, deliberate consideration should reveal some caramel malt sweetness.

Christoffel Bok

St. Christoffel | www.christoffelbeer.com

Country of origin Netherlands
First brewed 2005
Alcohol content 6.5% abv
Serving temperature 46°–50°F, 8°–10°C

Back in the early 1980s, when pale lager from Heineken and other big brewers dominated the Netherlands' beer scene, the few remaining strong, dark specialties that had been brewed as winter warmers since the late 19th century became the principal cause célèbre for PINT, a new beer consumers' organization set up on the model of Britain's Campaign for Real Ale.

The movement also spawned a new generation of innovative microbreweries, such as St. Christoffel. For years Christoffel's range lacked a seasonal bokbier, effectively excluding itself from PINT's flagship annual event, the Bokbierfestival in Amsterdam. Finally, in 2005, the brewery unveiled a cold-fermented interpretation of this fascinating and historic style, which has since been joined by a stronger bottled Winterbock. The wait was worthwhile, as the beer won top prize in its class at PINT's 2008 event. **DdM**

Tasting notes
Clear, deep red-amber beer with a big bubbly foam head and balsamic traces on a light aroma. A notably dry, malty, and nutty palate with emerging hops and burned-malt finish.

Ch'ti Ambrée

Brasserie Castelain | www.chti.com

Chýně Rauchbier

Pivovarský dvůr Chýně | www.pivovarskydvur.cz

Country of origin France
First brewed 1978
Alcohol content 5.9% abv
Serving temperature 46°F, 8°C

Country of origin Czech Republic
First brewed 2007
Alcohol content 4% abv
Serving temperature 46°F, 8°C

In the Nord Pas-de-Calais region of France, the classic beer style has long been a rustic, farm-based bière de garde (although the influence of Belgian breweries just over the border is also starting to seep through), and this is the tradition that Yves Castelain and his sister Annick revived in 1978 when they took over their parents' brewery at Benifontine.

Ch'ti Ambrée is, like the rest of the range, bottom fermented and filtered, but it is unpasteurized, which helps to maintain freshness and character in the mouthfeel. It also sings with the distinct sour oak and spicy malt flavors that characterize bières de garde. Hops come from nearby Flanders, and water is drawn from a well directly beneath the brewery. Fiercely proud, Castelain insists on using the spring-grown Scarlett malted barley—France's number one variety—alongside the winter-grown esterel. **AG**

Among the first new brewpubs to appear in the wake of Czechoslovakia's Velvet Revolution was Pivovarský dvůr Chýně in the village of Chýně, just outside Prague. It was fifteen years after its founding in 1992, however, before brewmaster Tomáš Mikulica decided to produce a Rauchbier, after the typical smoked malt style of Bamberg in northern Bavaria.

For the grist, Mikulica uses three-quarters' Weyermann's beech-smoked malt, with the remainder being pilsner and caramel malt. His Rauchbier is brewed to an original gravity of 12 degrees Plato, but beers from Chýně are moderately attenuated, with a substantial amount of malt sugars remaining, and the Rauchbier results in only 4 percent abv. It is hopped three times with Saaz and lagers for about six weeks before being served. The result is a slightly sweeter Rauchbier than many Bamberg versions. **ER**

Tasting notes
Deep reddish amber color with an attractive creamy head. The nose is a touch woody with some ripe fruit apparent while the palate is rich, full, and warming with a bitter finish.

Tasting notes
An expansive aroma of wood fire and syrupy notes in the nose. In the mouth, it's smoke in the front, sugary malt in the back, with the finish brightened by a healthy dose of bittering hops.

Clemens Ohne Filter

Brauerei Clemens Härle | www.haerle.de

Country of origin Germany
First brewed 1897
Alcohol content 5.4% abv
Serving temperature 46°F, 8°C

When Clemens Härle founded his brewery in the Allgäu village of Leutkirch in 1897, one of the first beers he released was this unfiltered lager. It was brewed in the predominant style of the times: amber to light brown in color with a pronounced malty character. Beers like this were called Braunbier ("brown beer") in Germany. The style persisted until the 1920s before more elegant, pale lager styles, such as pilsner or export, put them out of the market.

Ninety years after the brewery's foundation, Gottfried Härle took over the business and decided to revive the brewery's inaugural beer and to adapt it to modern tastes. Clemens Ohne Filter was thus created, an unfiltered lager with a fantastic orange hue, less malty than its predecessor and with a spicy, clean finish. For the grist, Härle uses Viennese, roasted and light colored malts of locally grown barley that bring in a pleasant fruity maltiness and the amber color. Aroma hops from nearby Tettnang are used in pellet form, with two additions during the boil and the third being added toward the end of the process consisting of dried hop flowers, hence the elegant top notes on the nose. Most crucial of all to the flavorsome character of this bottom-fermented beer is the slow, cold fermentation process. At low temperatures, lager yeast develops most of the taste components. Even though this procedure takes seven days and is quite costly, Härle holds on to it for the sake of quality.

While the German beer market is losing volume, Clemens Ohne Filter is bucking the trend and becoming increasingly popular. **SK**

Tasting notes

Amber with orange tints and beige foam. Citrus aromas and decent floral notes enchant the nose; there are also hints of red currant and pear. Soft and full bodied at first taste before coffee flavors emerge. A harmonious bitterness on the palate and a dry and velvety finish.

Collaboration Not Litigation

Avery Brewing Company | www.averybrewing.com

Country of origin United States
First brewed 2007
Alcohol content 8.7% abv
Serving temperature 59°F, 15°C

American brewers have turned to collaborative beers with particular enthusiasm, partnering with other Americans as well as brewers from further afield such as Scotland's BrewDog and Italy's Birrificio Italiano. Most collaborations involve two or more brewers getting together to formulate a recipe and make a beer that more than likely has never been seen before and will probably be brewed only once. Collaboration Not Litigation is altogether different: it is a blend of two established beers, both called Salvation.

It all began when Adam Avery of Avery Brewing in Colorado and Vinnie Cilurzo of Russian River Brewing in California discovered they were using the same name for two different Belgian-inspired beers. Avery's Salvation is strong and golden whereas Russian River's Salvation is strong and dark, brewed after the latter established a strong, golden beer called Damnation. The brewers tasted their beers mixed in several different proportions before settling on the blend.

When it came to brewing Collaboration for the first time, Cilurzo shipped all the ingredients he uses in his beer to Boulder, where Avery is based. Then he joined Avery in the Colorado city to brew a batch of each beer, the sizes based on the needed proportions. The beers were fermented separately, Russian River's remaining unfiltered and Avery's filtered because that's the way each brewery typically treats its beers. They were blended and first packaged for release early in 2007. Now Avery brews the beers every January and although Cilurzo does not go to Colorado, he still ships the ingredients to Avery Brewing. **SH**

Tasting notes

In a young batch of Collaboration, nutty caramel sugar and dark fruits from the Russian River contribution dominated. As the beer spends time in the bottle, orchard fruits and spicy hops (seemingly from Avery) assert themselves and an integrated beer emerges.

Combined Harvest

Batemans Brewery | www.bateman.co.uk

Country of origin England
First brewed 2001
Alcohol content 4.7% abv
Serving temperature 54°F, 12°C

The wide expanses of the south Lincolnshire fens are broken only by the sight of church towers. However, when you disembark from the train at the station of Wainfleet All Saints, the first thing you'll see is a building celebrating John Barleycorn rather than the Almighty. A couple of hundred yards away from the station, the old redbrick windmill stands as a symbol of the enduring appeal of Bateman's Brewery, one of the best-loved English family breweries.

Tradition and heritage is at a premium with Bateman's, with regard to its pubs and its best-selling beers, but this hasn't stopped the brewery from experimenting with different styles of beers, such as the fruit-flavored range it produced at the turn of the millennium. Combined Harvest is another example of the brewery's sense of adventure. According to Jaclyn Bateman at the brewery, "Combined Harvest comes into this category. It is different as it is brewed using four different grains: malted oats, malted rye, malted wheat, and barley, hence the name Combined Harvest. It has a subtle smooth bitterness which appeals to both men and women."

This beer was first brewed in 2001, when the brewery's bottled ale sales were increasing dramatically. With this in mind, head brewer Martin Cullimore was asked to brew a completely new style of beer for bottling that would be based on a selection of grains rather than just concentrating on barley. The result was Combined Harvest. It is only available in bottles and is an ideal drink with most food because of its well-balanced, delicate flavor. **ATJ**

Tasting notes

Dark gold in color. An astoundingly complex nose with rich citrus and toasty malt notes, and a slightly sweet undercurrent in the background. The palate has fruity bubblegum flavors before it descends to a bitter and dry finish, bolstered by lingering fruit and hop flavors.

Coopers Extra Strong Vintage Ale

Coopers Brewery | www.coopers.com.au

Country of origin Australia
First brewed 1998
Alcohol content 7.5% abv
Serving temperature 39°F, 4°C

Coopers is a brewery steeped in tradition. Its two flagship products, Sparkling Ale and Best Extra Stout, have been produced by the same family for more than 140 years. A healthy fear of change has meant that any upgrades to the brewery have been performed in such a way as to ensure that the flavor profile of Coopers' beers remains constant. A special panel of experienced Coopers drinkers who recall the beers of decades past is commissioned regularly to ensure that the brewery remains true to its history.

Coopers Extra Strong Vintage Ale is not subject to such restraints. It is a relative newcomer, first produced in 1998 with the involvement of current chief brewer, Dr. Tim Cooper. The first batch sold out within five days. Subsequent batches were not produced with the intention of replicating the flavor profile of the first, but rather improving it. This is the reason why each batch (or vintage) of Extra Strong Vintage Ale is unique and identified by its year in the same way as are the wines from the famous regions surrounding the South Australian brewery.

One unique feature is that the bottles have a "best after" date rather than a "best before" date. Beer that is not bottle conditioned is best consumed fresh. Being bottle conditioned and unpasteurized, Coopers beers contain live yeast, which mops up the excess oxygen and prolongs shelf life. Although delicious upon first release, Extra Strong Vintage Ale has an even longer shelf life than other Coopers beers due to its high alcohol content and will become less bitter and more malty over two to three years of careful storage. **DD**

Tasting notes

Coopers Vintage Ale presents itself with a reddish brown hue, dotted by yeast, and pours with a lingering head. Note the caramel and toffee flavors and aromas that intensify with careful cellaring. Consider savoring with strongly flavored cheeses.

Coreff Ambrée

Brasserie des Deux Rivières | www.coreff.com

Country of origin France
First brewed 1985
Alcohol content 5% abv
Serving temperature 50°F, 10°C

Coreff beers are widely identified as traditional Breton products despite the fact that their origins lie in the English county of Hampshire. Brasserie des Deux Rivières owners Christian Blanchard and Jean-François Malgorn spent two years there working at Ringwood Brewery under the tutelage of microbrewing pioneer Peter Austin before returning to Brittany in 1985.

The brewery is now situated in a former rope works in Morlaix at the confluence of the rivers Jarlot and Queffleuth (hence the name Deux Rivières). The brewery building is long and narrow and has a bar at the front featuring glass panels through which the brewing process can be observed.

The Ambrée is beautifully hop-accented, top-fermented, unfiltered, and unpasteurized in the manner of British real ales. It is also served from hand pumps, still a fairly uncommon sight in France. **AG**

Tasting notes
The aroma is of delicate hop, and the color of deep orangey gold is simply an invitation to sip. It is apple-fruity and malty on the palate with a dry finish.

Cornish Knocker

Skinner's Brewery | www.skinnersbrewery.com

Country of origin England
First brewed 1997
Alcohol content 4.5% abv
Serving temperature 54°F, 12°C

With its irreverent branding and eminent drinkability, Skinner's Cornish Knocker has been winning awards for this Truro-based brewery since 1998. Steve and Sarah Skinner started their brewing career at the Tipsy Toad brewpub on the island of Jersey in the early 1990s before they decided to become full-time brewers.

Knocker was the first beer that Steve Skinner brewed, and he was inspired by the new wave of lighter, more refreshing beers coming to the fore at the time such as Summer Lightning and Stonehenge Danish Dynamite. Made with Cornish-grown pale ale malt, a little bit of crystal, and a sprinkling of torrified wheat for body and head retention, plus the addition of Slovenian Styrian Golding for aroma and English Northdown for bittering, Cornish Knocker is fermented with a yeast from the now defunct Stone's brewery—in fact it was harvested just before the brewery was closed. **MC**

Tasting notes
A distinctly floral aroma. Initial tropical fruit flavors lead into a fresh "bread and butter" flavor and a pleasantly creamy mouthfeel, before moving to a gently bitter finish.

Cucapá Barley Wine Ale

Cerveceria de Baja California | www.cucapa.com

Country of origin Mexico
First brewed 2002
Alcohol content 10% abv
Serving temperature 59°F, 15°C

Finding a name for the beer brewed at the Cucapá microbrewery was a relatively simple affair. It derives from the Cucapá tribe, the first people to settle in the region of the city of Mexicali, thousands of years ago.

Cucapá began brewing in 2002, when the two brewing giants, FEMSA and Grupo Modelo, dominated the domestic market. Cucapá's pioneering spirit is most evident in the decision to brew barleywine: a drink never before brewed in Mexico.

Barleywine has its roots in England, is brewed typically to an alcoholic strength of 8 to 12 percent, and is consumed at a time when winter is at its most unforgiving. The brew has undergone something of a renaissance in recent years through the efforts of U.S. craft brewers, and Cucapá has followed suit with its own interpretation, wowing drinkers who previously only associated Mexico with pale lagers. **SG**

Tasting notes
A comforting nose of roasted malt, dark caramel, citrus fruits, and floral hints, while the palate is caressed with sweet malts, chocolate, and citrus to finish with a mild bitter taste.

Cucapá Chupacabras

Cerveceria de Baja California | www.cucapa.com

Country of origin Mexico
First brewed 2002
Alcohol content 5.8% abv
Serving temperature 44°F, 7°C

Cucapá's Pale Ale is arguably the finest example of master brewer Roberto Gonzales's ability to combine the best elements of his U.S. craft brewing experience with the natural resources available to him in Baja. Brewed using American two-row and caramel malts along with Centennial and Cascade hops from the Pacific Northwest, the Mexican influence comes from the water of the Colorado River, a feature of which is the very high mineral content that makes it perfect for extracting sugars from the malt.

The beer's name is unusual—the literal translation of *chupacabras* is "goat sucker." In 1995, Puerto Rico reported a series of attacks on various farm animals in which the carcass was apparently bled dry. Sightings described a demonic, large-fanged creature with the ability to hop like a kangaroo. The pale ale's name has so far failed to deter drinkers or beer judges. **SG**

Tasting notes
The aroma bounces with roasted nuts, dark chocolate, and stone fruits, giving way to a palate of earthy hops with chocolate and caramel malts before a long hoppy finish.

Dale's Pale Ale

Oskar Blues Brewery | www.oskarblues.com

Country of origin United States
First brewed 1998
Alcohol content 6.5% abv
Serving temperature 55°F, 13°C

A lack of money for promotion in the early years of the U.S. craft-brewing revolution saw smaller breweries asking drinkers to consider the importance of what is in the bottle rather than what is in the advertisement. This changed in 2002 when a tiny brewery in the Colorado town of Lyons began canning its beer—by hand in a barn beside the brewpub where Dale's Pale Ale was produced. Cans, previously shunned by craft beer drinkers, became hip. Oskar Blues grew thirtyfold in six years, and now produces a variety of flavors that are shipped all over the United States.

Many other smaller breweries soon also began canning, but Oskar Blues owner Dale Katechis quickly became a spokesman, assuring consumers that there would be no "can taste" to the beers. "People see the can and think they need to drink right from it," he said. "You'd never drink a full-flavored beer from a bottle. This is a better, safer package than a bottle." Cans proved particularly popular in the West, selling well at golf courses and to outdoors lovers because they are lighter to carry and easier to recycle. Katechis is an avid cyclist, and one of the brewery's first promotions was to give away a top-of-the-range bicycle to the first three customers who recycled 3,501 cans.

Of course, Dale's Pale Ale, and the beers that followed, thrived because of what was "in the can" rather than because of convenience. Dale's Pale Ale is particularly bold, with four varieties of American hops aggressively deployed, but properly balanced. In 2005, it topped twenty-four other top-notch U.S. pale ales in a blind tasting conducted by the *New York Times*. **SH**

Tasting notes

Pours copper with a fluffy white head; pine and citrus burst to the fore as soon as the can is popped. Additional sweet and bready notes on the nose, with more biscuit on the palate, as well as juicy-fruity hop flavors and balancing bitterness. Long, not quite dry finish.

Daü

Birrificio Troll | www.birratroll.it

Country of origin Italy
First brewed 2004
Alcohol content 3.9% abv
Serving temperature 46°–50°F, 8°–10°C

Hidden in a small Alpine valley is the Troll brewpub. It is a must-see microbrewery, founded in 2003 by Daniele Meinero and Alberto Canavese. Together they specialize in original brews, which are always very personal and never banal. Shangrila, for example, was their first beer and it's produced with some Himalayan spices; Febbre Alta contains aromatic herbs and other spices. They obviously produce "easier" beers, too, using just malts and hops, but to each brew they are able to add their personal touch.

Daü takes inspiration from Belgian saisons: more from how past saisons were, rather than how modern saisons are now. Meinero and Canavese knew that they wanted a refreshing, thirst-quenching beer, low in alcohol strength but flavored and spiced, and definitively tasty. So Daü is only 3.9 percent abv and features pils malt plus some caramel varieties, as well as a pinch of raw rye. Hops come from Germany and Belgium, with the Mittelfruh added in the late boiling for the aroma. But the aromatic profile is surely shaped more by the spices: coriander, ginger, and two different kinds of pepper. The younger this beer is tasted, the more peppery it will be. The brewing process usually lasts four months, with two months in bottle for the last fermentation and the necessary maturation. Daü is a beer that can last quite long in the cellar, evolving its flavors and aromas over time, which is quite a rare thing for a beer so comparatively low in alcohol.

This Italian tribute to the saison tradition makes a fine match with fish dishes, fresh goat cheese, or with the typical Roman pasta *cacio e pepe*. **MM**

Tasting notes

Cloudy golden color, with light amber tints, this beer has a wide and rich aroma with plenty of spicy and citrus notes. On the palate, a whisper of spices with a peppery note toward the end of the mouth. Very refreshing and drinkable session beer.

De Koninck Amber

Brouwerij De Koninck | www.dekoninck.be

Country of origin Belgium
First brewed 1930
Alcohol content 5% abv
Serving temperature 43°–46°F, 6°–8°C

One does not drink De Koninck Amber from a glass. This essential and original ale is served in a stemmed bulbous *bolleke*—cue giggles from the Anglo-Saxon side of the bar—and has been since the 1930s. These days, brewing takes place in a hypermodern brewhouse that was built in the 1990s. Here various other beers, including Blond, Tripel, and Winterkoninck, are also brewed, no doubt to the bemusement of older residents of the city, who grew up with the amber liquid in the stemmed *bolleke* bowl.

De Koninck is an ancient family brewery, and the Van den Bogaert family took over from the one that gave the brewery its original name. Tradition is still kept in high regard; for example, even in the days of Communism, the Zlatec hops were always original Czech. Malts (often French) are carefully selected and tested by the brewmasters themselves. More recent research has been conducted on the level of high-quality primings.

Traditionalist doesn't mean backward, though: De Koninck was probably one of the first Belgian breweries to have a fully continuous yeast propagator. The new brewhouse also marked the end of an overstretched production line, and environmentally friendly practices were introduced long before they became fashionable. De Koninck is well known abroad and you'll have no problem tracking it down. However, if you find yourself in Antwerp, join the trail of aficionados who dash to sample this beer in its original surroundings at the brewery tap, where it is served unpasteurized and fresh. **JPa**

Tasting notes

Foxy amber beer under a thick creamy head. A malty nose with some rubberlike sulfur touches and freshly gristed malt. The malt offers a biscuity sweetness, the noble hops give a restrained bitterness, and there is also a spritzy zestful sourness. Serve very fresh.

Dead Guy Ale

Rogue Ales | www.rogue.com

Country of origin United States
First brewed 1989
Alcohol content 6.5% abv
Serving temperature 43°–48°F, 6°–9°C

"I just look around at what everybody else is doing and do the exact opposite," says Rogue founder Jack Joyce. He's not kidding. Rogue focuses on big, personality-driven beers packaged in enameled bottles. Smoke, buckwheat, hazelnuts, and, of course, great wads of hops define the Rogue house style. The Altbier Dead Guy may be a bit of an outlier, even for such an iconoclastic enterprise.

With one foot in the orthodox world of German lagers, Dead Guy started as a straight-up Maibock called Maierbock, named for brewmaster John Maier. "We were brewing it at our Bayfront brewpub, and of course we didn't have a lot of tank space," says Maier, referring to the extended aging time that ties up tanks with conventional lagers, "so we thought we'd give it a try with our Pac-Man yeast. People liked it." Fermentation with ale yeast added complex, fruity aromas that tickled thrill seekers on the Oregon coast. Today Dead Guy accounts for about forty percent of Rogue production.

The beer contains a fair portion of Munich malt, which adds soft, toasted caramel notes, plus some pale caramel malt for some lingering sweetness. Hops are American—Perle and Sterling—and provide some elegant, German-style hop flavor and aroma. Dead Guy is also the only beer that is available in a glow-in-the-dark bottle, which fits the generally spooky theme of the product. This makes it the perfect beer for drinking during power outages, spelunking, or any time you want to switch off the lights and stare into the deep, dark mysteries of life. **RM**

Tasting notes

Malty nose with a dual personality: caramelly and toasty, plus a little bit of herby, almost minty, hop character. On the palate a mouthful of deep caramel sweetness, but well met by substantial hops. Finish is long and bittersweet, with peachy overtones.

Demon Hunter

Birrificio Montegioco | www.birrificiomontegioco.com

Country of origin Italy
First brewed 2006
Alcohol content 8.5% abv
Serving temperature 46°–50°F, 8°–10°C

Montegioco is a small village close to the wine-growing area of Tortona, in the south of Piedmont. Here, in 2006, Riccardo Franzosi, the brewer of Birrificio Montegioco, decided that after spending years as a home-brewer he would open a brewery. He had found an area where he felt he could produce beers closely linked to the terroir of where he lives. One of Franzosi's main aims is to make use of the products that grow in the valleys around him, such as peaches and chestnuts, and use them in his beers.

The brewery, which is in a factory that is a great example of 1930s industrial archaeology, produces an enormous number of beers—more than twenty—following many different styles. Demon Hunter is one of the most important products of this brewery: it is one of the first that Franzosi produced when he was a home-brewer, and it is also one of his favorites. As for the name, Demon Hunter comes from another passion of his: Celtic myths and culture.

This beer could be considered to be a strong ale, even if the alcohol content is higher than is usually seen in such beers, and it is produced using English malts, hops (Fuggle and Golding), and yeast, in order to give it a British soul (although Franzosi has a passion for specialty beers, this one is fruit free). After a first period of maturation in steel, the beer is refermented in the bottle and then matured for at least fifteen weeks. Demon Hunter is a classical Montegioco beer: complex and full of body, with the high alcohol content making it very warm and easy to drink. It is perfect with cheese or a strong-flavored meat dish. **ES**

Tasting notes

Copper color that sparkles with brilliant golden tints. The foam is very fine and persistent. On the nose, it is incredibly rich, with red fruit such as cherry and the warmth of alcohol making their presence felt. The mouthfeel is smooth, warming, and long in the finish.

Domaine DuPage

Two Brothers Brewing Company | www.twobrosbrew.com

Country of origin United States
First brewed 2001
Alcohol content 5.9% abv
Serving temperature 39°–44°F, 4°–7°C

"When we started this brewery," says founder Jason Ebel, "we wanted to do two things to differentiate us from everybody else. First, we would not brew a pale ale. Second, we would make this a Brabant-style ale." The Brabant region, which includes Brussels and historically extended into France, has a long history of rustic, top-fermenting beers.

Although this suburban Chicago brewery did eventually respond to marketplace pressure and brewed a pale ale, Domaine DuPage remains its flagship beer by a large margin. "It took people a while to figure out what it was," says Ebel of the smooth and softly toasty amber ale, "but once they did, it took off." The notion of this beer began when Ebel lived in northern France. "We took a side trip to a farmhouse in Aibes. There was a communal brewhouse in the village which several families shared. What fascinated me was that they all brewed the same recipe."

The beer is easy to love, but there is considerable depth beneath its easy-going charms. Brewed from a complex mix of malts, neatly balanced by just the right amount of hops, fermentation adds another layer of spicy, fruity perfume. Domaine DuPage has a slight sweetness up front that dries out to a smooth, slightly cocoa bitterness. This delicate balance and an alcohol strength of 5.9 percent makes it "our most food-friendly beer," says Ebel. "It works with everything from Thai cuisine to grilled meats." If you can get to northern France to enjoy this kind of beer in situ, by all means do so. The rest of us can pour a Domaine DuPage and imagine a little trip right here on our couches. **RM**

Tasting notes
Soft, malty notes on the nose, neither roasty nor caramel, but kind of cakelike. A reasonable amount of spicy yeast character and fruitiness. Soft and slightly sweet on the palate, drying to a very faint roasty-toasty finish with a dab of bittersweet hops.

CERVEZA CLARA
DOS EQUIS

Lager Especial

Dos Equis XX Amber

Cuauhtemoc Moctezuma Brewery
www.femsa.com/en

Country of origin Mexico
First brewed 1900
Alcohol content 4.5% abv
Serving temperature 39°–44°F, 4°–7°C

The story of Cuauhtemoc Moctezuma Brewery is a tale of revolution, assassination, takeovers and mergers, industrial and social innovation, and some very fine beers. The brewery was founded in Orizaba, Velacruz, by the German master brewer Wilhelm Hasse in 1894. Hasse wanted to meld German brewing heritage with Mexican traditions, and one of the company's earliest beers was Siglo XX (launched in 1900 to mark the new century), a dark, full-bodied beer modeled on the Vienna style that Hasse knew so well.

Dos Equis became Moctezuma's best-selling brand in the 1940s and 1950s before undergoing a period of relative anonymity. Then Moctezuma merged with Cuauhtemoc brewery, which in turn became part of FEMSA, Mexico's largest beverage company. Dos Equis (XX) Amber is now the biggest-selling imported dark beer in the United States. **SG**

Tasting notes

Deep amber with a thin white bubbly head. Traces of caramel and hops on the nose become clear on tasting with a sweet, toasted malt flavor and a lingering, slightly bitter finish.

Double Barrel Ale

Firestone Walker Brewing
www.firestonewalker.com

Country of origin United States
First brewed 1996
Alcohol content 5% abv
Serving temperature 50°F, 10°C

Cofounders David Walker and Adam Firestone first tried to age their beers in Chardonnay barrels in a corner of the Firestone family vineyards, ending up with beer not "even as good as shampoo." Yet, that hitch led to the Firestone Union, a patented use of new oak barrels that makes Firestone Walker beers unique.

The Firestone Union takes inspiration from the Burton Union system once common in Burton-on-Trent in England and still used by Marston's for Pedigree. The Burton system, developed in the 1840s, linked wooden casks to manage yeast during fermentation. It was not designed to take flavors from the wood, while the sole purpose of the Firestone system is to add wood character. Firestone blends a stainless steel-fermented beer with one that has been fermented in the oak barrels. The wood-fermented beer accounts for about 15 percent of Double Barrel. **SH**

Tasting notes

Attractive, bright copper in the glass, with an off-white head. Oak and vanilla are apparent on the nose. Rich, but clean on the palate, with citrusy hops and spicy, woody tannins.

← Siglo XX was dubbed "Dos Equis" (meaning "two Xs") by drinkers.

Double Maxim

Double Maxim Beer Company | www.dmbc.org.uk

Country of origin England
First brewed 1901
Alcohol content 4.7% abv
Serving temperature 52°F, 11°C

Double Maxim was first brewed in 1901 by the Vaux Brewery in Sunderland, England, and was initially called Maxim Ale. It was created in tribute to a detachment of local soldiers from the Northumberland Hussars, who had returned home safely from the Boer War in South Africa. In combat with the Boers they had been using the deadly Maxim, the world's first automatic machine gun, which was capable of firing 600 rounds a minute. The troops were commanded by Major Ernest Vaux, whose grandfather Cuthbert Vaux founded the brewery in 1837.

Double Maxim is a classic brown ale with a smooth and fruity taste. There is a tale that not long after its debut in the local pubs, landlords were complaining that it was too strong and was putting their customers to sleep. In 1938 it was renamed Double Maxim and the alcohol content changed. The beer was a local success and was regarded as Sunderland's version of Newcastle's eponymous Brown Ale. As a style, the brown ales of the northeast of England were regarded as different from the sweeter and weaker brown ales of southern England.

The Vaux brewery survived for more than 160 years, but it was sold, closed, and demolished in 1999. However, the Double Maxim Beer Company was set up in 1999 by two former Vaux directors—Doug Trotman and Mark Anderson—with the support of ex-Vaux head brewer Jim Murray. In 2007, the beer, like the Maxim gunners, returned to its hometown and to the highly efficient, purpose-built Double Maxim Brewery in Hughton-le-Spring. **TH**

Tasting notes

Maris Otter pale ale malt, crystal malt, and aromatic Golding hops go into the blend, making for a sweet caramel nose with a hint of fruity spice; on the palate, it is well balanced and smooth, with a distinct but delicate sweetness in the background.

Double Simcoe IPA

Weyerbacher Brewing | www.weyerbacher.com

Country of origin United States
First brewed 2006
Alcohol content 9% abv
Serving temperature 46°F, 8°C

High alpha acid is the holy grail of beer making, sought by industrial giants to cheapen the cost of their hop supplies and worshipped by a number of small brewers seeking to craft outrageously bitter beers. There's a dark side to this almost religious fervor for the grail, however, and it's cohumulone—the harsh substance that crops up in large amounts in hops with high alpha acids. Leave it to science to give us the perfect hop, Simcoe.

Introduced in 2000 by Select Botanicals Group in Washington state, Simcoe is high in alpha acids but low in cohumulone. For big brewers, it is a godsend; a little goes a long way. Craft brewers love it for its distinctive citrus aroma and its strong but pleasurable bitterness. Brewer Dan Weirback discovered it when he reformulated his popular India Pale Ale, Hop Infusion. It gave the beer a fresher, earthier flavor, and, he said, "I got to thinking: What would happen if you brewed a beer with nothing but Simcoe?"

A varietal beer—not unlike a wine that depends on one variety of grapes—wasn't completely unheard of, especially for U.S. craft brewers whose ales typically champion hops. When Weyerbacher introduced its new imperial IPA in 2006, however, it was the first that was wholly dependent on Simcoe. As you would expect, Double Simcoe is intensely bitter. Yet, the hops bring a variety of flavors to this strong ale: pineapple and pine, with a certain earthiness that is reminiscent of trekking through a forest, in search, perhaps, of that holy grail. Importantly, the trademark harshness is absent. Good riddance, cohumulone. **DR**

Tasting notes

Citrus fruits—grapefruit and orange—dominate, while some herbal and grassy notes emerge in the nose. A thick head promises a creamy quaff, and the first gulp is decidedly sweet with biscuity malt. Intense bitterness dominates, then it finishes clean and dry.

Downtown Brown

Lost Coast Brewery | www.lostcoast.com

Country of origin United States
First brewed 1991
Alcohol content 5% abv
Serving temperature 44°F, 7°C

The Lost Coast Brewery was founded by pharmacist Barbara Groom and family counselor Wendy Pound, who in 1986 had their own Eureka moment: Eureka, California, that is. After traveling throughout England, researching and studying what it would take to start a brewpub, they purchased the one hundred-year-old Pythian Castle in 1989. After extensive remodeling, a year later, they launched the Lost Coast Brewery and café.

Downtown Brown Ale was one of the first beers conceived by brewmaster Barbara Groom, who had concocted the brew with an eye toward making it ideal for pairing with food. She eschewed style guidelines in favor of simply the characteristics she wanted. The result is not a traditional brown ale, but instead a beer that is less hoppy and more full bodied than most North American brown ales and more balanced than many English brown ales. It's almost a blend between a porter and a traditional brown ale, with strong chocolate notes and a hint of roasted coffee. It's brewed with Willamette and Mount Hood hops along with crystal malt and, naturally, some chocolate malt.

Groom also discovered that the cool maritime climate of Eureka is ideal for top-fermenting ale yeast. To these English brewing traditions, Groom added Western Plains barley and wheat and the exceptionally clean water of Humboldt County to give her beer a distinctive flavor profile. Local artist Duane Flatmo created the artwork for the label, which is reminiscent of Picasso. The original brewpub location is still there, serving food and Lost Coast beer, but packaged beer production was relocated in 2000 to a larger facility. **JB**

Tasting notes

A thick, rich tan head and a beautiful copper brown color. With nutty aromas and a hint of chocolate notes, the flavors are malty and rich, with coffee and American bittering hops contributing to a chewy, complex brew. The finish is clean, with some lingering nuttiness.

Drake's IPA

Drake's Brewing Company | www.drinkdrakes.com

Country of origin United States
First brewed 2002
Alcohol content 7% abv
Serving temperature 50°F, 10°C

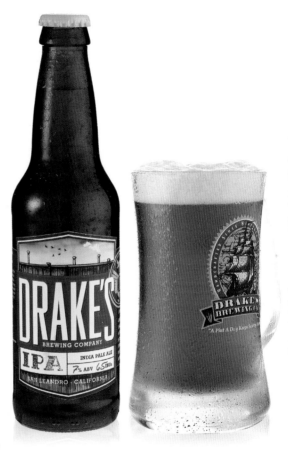

Drake's Brewing is a tale of Rogers. The first one, Roger Lind, founded what he originally called the Lind Brewing Company in 1989 and used a nautical theme for his beers, drawing on the exploits of British explorer Sir Francis Drake. One of Lind's relatives created the brewery logo and labels with its distinctive sailing ship, the *Golden Hind*.

A decade later, in 1999, the brewery was bought by the Rogers Family Company. They were next-door neighbors whose primary business had been selling coffee. The Rogers family took the brand names that Lind had been using and renamed the brewery Drake's Brewing. Lind had called the original IPA simply Drake's Ale, and, in its original form, the yeast he used emphasized its malt qualities.

After a few years, in 2002, the new owners brought in a new brewer to shake things up, yet another Roger (nearly), in this case local brewer Rodger Davis. This was at the same time that hoppy beers were just beginning to become much more popular. Davis switched to a yeast that better emphasized the beer's hop qualities and added, as he puts it, "a boatload of hops," also increasing the amount used to dry hop the beer. The beer features both Cascade and Columbus hops, yielding a hefty 65 IBUs, which placed it just above the upper limit that defined an India Pale Ale at that time. Rodger Davis's new Drake's IPA was an immediate hit with both beer drinkers and judges alike. That same year, Drake's IPA won a gold medal at the Great American Beer Festival, and captured several other awards over the next few years. **JB**

Tasting notes

With a deep amber golden color that is slightly cloudy, Drake's IPA is a big American West Coast interpretation all the way, thick with citrus, grapefruit, and herbal hop aromas. The flavors are likewise big and hoppy, though it's well balanced with a long, lingering tart finish.

Drop Top Amber Ale

Widmer Brothers Brewing | www.widmer.com

Country of origin United States
First brewed 2003
Alcohol content 5% abv
Serving temperature 44°F, 7°C

Widmer Brothers is most widely known for its flagship Hefeweizen, but it also makes the best-selling amber ale in the State of Oregon. The Drop Top Amber was originally a seasonal offering when it debuted in 2003, but proved popular enough for the brewery to make it available all year long. This is not as surprising as it initially seems, because the very first beer Widmer brewed was a Düsseldorf Altbier, one of the few German beers using top-fermenting ale yeast, and Altbier and amber ales share many similarities.

Drop Top Amber is brewed with pale, caramel, and extra special malts, but what sets it apart is a unique honey malt with "just a touch of unfermentable milk sugar." This gives the beer a velvety texture and smoothness, while the American ale yeast adds fruity esters in both the nose and flavor profile. Drop Top Amber is brewed with two Pacific Northwest hop varieties: Alchemy and Simcoe. Alchemy provides a soft bittering whereas Simcoe imparts its signature herbal, oniony aromas.

The name of the beer comes from a slang term for a convertible automobile, based on the fact that the top can be "dropped," or folded, into the back or trunk of the car. The inspiration for the dog that is featured on Drop Top's label was cofounder Rob Widmer's golden retriever, who, like most dogs, loves to go for a drive in a convertible. Drop Top has twice been awarded a gold medal at the Great American Beer Festival, in 2004 and again in 2008. It's an ideal complement to rich, heavy foods such as barbecue, hamburgers, grilled steaks, and pizza. **JB**

Tasting notes

Drop Top Amber Ale is amber in color with a thick tan head. The nose is fruity with a honeyed sweetness. The flavors are malty and sweet with a honey-smooth mouthfeel. Hop character is evident only on the back end, and the finish is sweet and clean.

Unusually, this artwork features the Drop Top dog accompanied by his master.

Dunkles Vollbier

Brauerei Drummer | www.europeanbeerguide.bambbrew.htm

Country of origin Germany
First brewed 1763
Alcohol content 4.8% abv
Serving temperature 46°F, 8°C

Anyone who has any interest in beer has to make their way to Franconia at least once during their lifetime to sit in one of the many brewpubs in the area and drink the beer. Chances are the beers sampled will be fresh, balanced, and full of character: it will be the right beer at the right time always.

This northern part of Bavaria is said to have the highest density of breweries in Germany, if not in the world. Indeed, about half of Bavaria's 600 breweries are situated in the region. Almost every village has one brewhouse at the very least. Towns such as Bamberg, Bayreuth, Kulmbach, or Forchheim are characterized by a long tradition of brewing. This has meant that a local culture of beer cellars, festivals, and beer styles has evolved over the centuries and is still very much alive. *Ungespundetes* (unbunged beer), *Rauchbier* (smoked beer), and *Märzen* (the typical dark or black lager) are available in many individual varieties. At the foot of the Walberla, a mystic Franconian table mountain near Forchheim, you can experience one such perfect moment when you order a Dunkles at Brauerei Drummer's brewpub in Leutenbach.

The beer's traits probably date to the brewery's origins in the 18th century. The recipe includes Munich malt and the aromatic hop variety Spalter Select. Peter Drummer, who took over the business after his father's death, in 1997, has altered the style a bit, and made it less harsh. Either drink the beer solo or with a schnitzel; that tapping sound coming from the kitchen will be Mrs. Drummer tenderizing the schnitzels to be served with the Dunkles. Enjoy. **SK**

Tasting notes

Copper to light brown with a firm beige foam. A spicy-sweet aroma of peat and roasted malts. On the palate, the first taste is dry, followed by roasted malts with hints of chocolate, coffee, and dried fruit. A well-toned body and a dry finish with spicy roasted flavors.

East Street Cream

RCH Brewery | www.rchbrewery.co.uk

Country of origin England
First brewed 1995
Alcohol content 5% abv
Serving temperature 50°–55°F, 10°–13°C

When it comes to thinking about drink in the west of England, many people consider cider to be king. The area, especially the county of Somerset, is dotted with ancient orchards and cider makers abound, with the odd farmer still producing it every autumn on an old cider press for personal consumption. Yet, beer brewing also has a strong position in the same area. Bristol was a major beer town and there are plenty of craft brewers, and it's entirely appropriate that RCH, one of the West Country's most successful brewers, is located on a site that was once used for cider making.

Originally founded in a seaside hotel—the Royal Clarence Arms—in the coastal resort of Burnham-on-Sea, the brewery moved to their current home in the village of West Hewish during the mid-1990s. This is very much a dedicated cask beer brewery with a portfolio of ales that are more often than not named after railway engines (e.g. Double Header and Firebox); both head brewer Graham Dunbaven and brewery founder and owner Paul Davey are steam engine enthusiasts. However, the naming of East Street Cream has different origins. According to Davey, "East Street Cream was first brewed in 1995 as a one-off for the 500th guest beer of the Dartmouth Inn, which was in East Street in Newton Abbot. The beer was named by one of the pub's customers in a competition run by the landlord of the time." The beer has many fans and has won plenty of awards. In 2009, it was named Champion Beer at the prestigious Tuckers Maltings Festival in Newton Abbot, a neat accolade for a beer with such strong links to this Devon town. **ATJ**

Tasting notes

Chestnut brown with a fragrant nose of fruitcake, plus a tingling hint of Muscat grape and dark stone fruit, such as raisins and currants; the Muscat theme continues on the palate and is also joined by more fruit. The finish is dry and grainy with tantalizing fruit notes.

Eggenberg Dark Lager

Pivovar Eggenberg | www.eggenberg.cz

Country of origin Czech Republic
First brewed 1993
Alcohol content 4.3% abv
Serving temperature 46°F, 8°C

The brewery in the South Bohemian town of Český Krumlov dates back to at least 1347. It was assigned to the Eggenberg noble family in 1622 as partial payment for debts incurred in war. In 1625, the family expanded the brewery into the buildings where it stands today.

Pivovar Eggenberg brewery produced a number of beers, including pale lagers at high strength and the region's charismatic dark lagers that were extremely popular before the wider growth of the pilsner style. Thus the arrival of Eggenberg Dark Lager in 1993 was welcomed as a return to form, rather than a new invention. As is traditional with Bohemian *tmavé pivo*, or dark beer, it finishes on a bittersweet note, rather than the slightly astringent finish of many German Schwarzbiers. It is only rarely seen outside of its home region, although it remains quite popular in the many historic pubs and restaurants in Český Krumlov. **ER**

Tasting notes
Less black than it is amber, medium bodied, and topped with a thick-set tan foam. In the mouth, it has very nice cold coffee and ginger flavors finishing with a pronounced sweetness.

Einbecker Mai-Ur-Bock

Einbecker Brauhaus | www.einbecker-brauhaus.de

Country of origin Germany
First brewed 1378
Alcohol content 6.5% abv
Serving temperature 54°–57°F, 12°–14°C

When applied to beer, the word "bock" is said to be a corruption of the city name Einbeck. The brewing of bock beer was originally a community affair. On May 1, since 1240, 700 citizens of Einbeck were chosen by lot to brew the beer. However, the citizen brewers were only supposed to brew enough beer for their own consumption. Those who brewed more sold the excess beer to the town council who then sold it to other towns. By 1492, beer was being shipped to the Baltic States, Stockholm, Denmark, and Amsterdam.

In Einbeck, three types of bock beer are made: dark, light, and amber. Mai-Ur-Bock is an amber beer made for springtime. It is intended as a warming drink in the period when the cold of winter is yielding to the first warm temperatures of spring. In 1851, the first bottling plant was installed and the type of bottle then chosen still remains in use today. **RP**

Tasting notes
The aroma is malty with some fruity notes. Tasting reveals considerable complexity with some malty sweetness, warmth from alcohol, and, finally, a bitterish finish.

Malting barley stored at the Eggenberg brewery in Český Krumlov.

Eisenbahn Pale Ale

Sudbrack Brewery | www.eisenbahn.com.br

Country of origin Brazil
First brewed 2002
Alcohol content 4.8% abv
Serving temperature 37°–41°F, 3°–5°C

The Eisenbahn brewery (meaning "railway" in German) was established in July 2002 by Juliano Mendes and his family in the town of Blumenau in Brazil's southern state of Santa Caterina. Dissatisfied with the mass-produced beers on offer, Mendes embarked on an ambitious venture to challenge the established breweries by producing high-quality beers following traditional recipes and using traditional methods.

Eisenbahn Pale Ale is brewed in the tradition of classic Belgian pale ales. One of very few pale ales produced in not only Brazil but also the whole of South America, Eisenbahn Pale Ale is unquestionably the finest. As with the brewery's other creations, this beer adheres to the Bavarian Purity Laws of 1516. This demonstrates that even in a subtropical climate, additional additives, such as preservatives and stabilizers, are simply not necessary and in fact often serve commercial rather than consumer interests.

A combination of three malts and a secret blend of Old and New World hops gives this beer much of its unique character and sets it apart from its contemporaries. The fact that Eisenbahn is located in Blumenau is not an accident either. The town attracted many German immigrants in the past, and they brought with them their traditional brewing methods and expertise. Sadly, many of these small, traditional breweries were eventually forced out of business by the large brewers who were more interested in the sheer quantity of sales rather than the quality of production. Eisenbahn represents a welcome return to the traditions of purity in brewing. **AH**

Tasting notes

With its blond body and white head, Eisenbahn Pale Ale offers a spicy aroma resulting from the blend of hops. Well balanced and malty on the palate, it has a refreshingly dry and bitter finish. Excellent with sausage, Emmental, or Gouda cheese.

EKU 28

Kulmbacher Brauerei | www.kulmbacher.de

Country of origin Germany
First brewed 1954
Alcohol content 11% abv
Serving temperature 59°–64°F, 15°–18°C

EKU 28 was the strongest beer in Germany for years until another—much smaller—brewery produced a 13 percent blockbuster. Nevertheless, this is still a beer to be treated with care, a true Doppelbock that is produced throughout the year and is somewhat of a cult beer among fans in Germany. It was first produced in the postwar recovery years, possibly conceived as a statement of brewing intent by the then independent EKU brewery. During these years, economic confidence was growing in West Germany, so a big beer would mirror that sense of self-assurance.

The Bavarian Purity Law of beer was strictly adhered to, although fermentation was another story given that beer yeast can give up the ghost when asked to ferment beers approaching 12 percent strength. The brewers solved the problem in their own inimitable way, by having two to three separate mashes of pale malt (this is the sole malt used, although the exact process remains a closely guarded secret), thus making a highly concentrated wort with plenty of sugars for the yeast to snack on. The beer is also given a lot of time to ferment and then mature.

EKU (meaning "Erste Kulmbacher Brauerei") is no longer independent, having merged with several other local breweries under the name Kulmacher, after their northern Bavarian home city of Kulmbach. One could say that EKU 28's sister brew is Kulmbacher Eisbock, another monster of a beer that weighs in at 9.2 percent abv. As for the number 28, this refers to the beer's original gravity (in German degrees), rather than its alcoholic strength. **WO**

Tasting notes

Amber near-reddish in the glass beneath a light yellow head of foam; on the nose there is an intense aroma of malt and fruit. EKU 28 is full bodied in the mouth, sweetish, but also clean and fresh, before reaching a long, rich, and warming finish.

Elephant Beer

Carlsberg | www.carlsberg.com

Country of origin Denmark
First brewed 1959
Alcohol content 7.2% abv
Serving temperature 44°F, 7°C

The name Carlsberg can't have escaped the attention of many beer drinkers around the globe. The Danish company has 45,000 employees producing and selling beer in 150 markets across the world. In 2008, its output equated roughly 100 million bottles of beer daily, placing it as the fourth largest brewing group in the world.

Carlsberg was founded in 1847 by J. C. Jacobsen, who was intent on introducing modern scientific techniques to the ancient art of brewing. He named his company after his son Carl, who later founded his own brewery—"New Carlsberg"—in 1882. This later merged with his late father's "Old Carlsberg" in 1901.

Carlsberg provided the world with two scientific breakthroughs: the development of the pH scale and the isolation of single strains of yeast. In 1883, Carlsberg successfully separated yeast strains; *Saccharomyces carlsbergensis*, the strain most commonly used for pale lagers, was isolated and the knowledge was made available to other brewers.

In 1955, Carlsberg started to brew a special strong pilsner for export to the Gold Coast (Ghana from 1957) and Nigeria, a region where 7.6 percent Guinness Foreign Extra Stout has long been popular. The new strong pilsner was known as Carlsberg Export but, due to its African popularity, gained the nickname Elephant. In 1959, Carlsberg decided to launch it on its domestic market with an official name change to Elephant Beer. The image on the beer's label was inspired by the life-sized elephant statues that form part of the main entrance to the Carlsberg brewery in Copenhagen. **JP**

Tasting notes

Pours a dark gold color with a rapidly diminishing head and a sweet honey and lemon aroma. The flavor is of honeyish malt with a woody, earthy quality. It possesses a subtle hop character and a spirituous alcohol quality. Some estery fruit notes are evident.

Danes regard the swirl under "Carlsberg" in its logo as an elephant's trunk. ➡

Ellie's Brown Ale

Avery Brewing Company | www.averybrewing.com

Country of origin United States
First brewed 1994
Alcohol content 5.5% abv
Serving temperature 50°F, 10°C

When a worldwide hops shortage in 2006 sent prices rocketing sky high and U.S. brewers started to worry whether they would still be able to make their traditionally hoppy beers, Adam Avery of Avery Brewing announced he would be putting more hops in some of his beers. Given the reputation Avery holds for creating bold beers nobody was shocked at this bullish attitude. They might instead have been surprised to learn that the third best seller, and for many years previously the best seller, for the Colorado brewery that created an ultra-strong series of beers called the Demons of Ale, was Ellie's Brown Ale. This 5.5% beer with a modest seventeen units of bitterness was named after Avery's chocolate Labrador dog Ellie. The acclaim continued in 2007 when the *New York Times* featured brown ales, and its tasting panel picked Ellie's as their favorite.

Ellie's was typical of the early beers from Avery in the mid-1990s—technically excellent and sometimes bold by Colorado standards, but nothing that created a buzz with aficionados. "I would say, looking back," recalls Avery, "that I was more in tune with the thinking of the you-can't-be-too-crazy crowd."

Most Colorado breweries' best-selling beer was amber in color and not particularly hoppy at the time; this is something that has only started to change in the 21st century. Avery broke the mold in 1996 with its aggressive India Pale Ale. This became the brewery's top seller in 2000, but, according to Avery in 2009, "Even three years ago, people would send our beer back to the bar saying it was too bitter." **SH**

Tasting notes

Ellie's Brown Ale is brown and bright in the glass, topped by a tan head that lingers. Rich aromas, flavors, and mouthfeel—sweet chocolate and caramel malt throughout—which is offset early on by a roasty and toasty character and later by earthy hops.

Emerson's Old 95

The Emerson Brewing Company | www.emersons.co.nz

Country of origin New Zealand
First brewed 1995
Alcohol content 7% abv
Serving temperature 50°–54°F, 10°–12°C

In 1990, having visited and worked at breweries in Britain, Germany, and Australia, Richard Emerson returned home to New Zealand armed with recipes, brewing knowledge, and a burning desire to introduce New Zealanders to some of the world's great beer styles. Within two years, he had started his own brewery; ever since, Emerson has produced some of the country's most flavorsome and acclaimed beers.

Back in the early 1990s, Kiwi drinkers had little choice of genuine ales, let alone strong examples that were bottle-conditioned with the potential to be cellared. Emerson's Old 95 evolved from a beer called "Old Ale," which first appeared in October 1993 as a limited-edition Christmas release. The following year, the grist was adjusted and the name changed to "Old 94." The result was an improvement but still not exactly what Emerson was aiming for, so, in September 1995, the recipe was tweaked once again and the beer christened "Old 95."

In 1999, a London ale yeast was introduced that, Emerson reckons "brought forth heaps more flavor earlier into maturation yet improved with age," and a year later, the grist was changed to emphasize malt aroma. Little changed for almost a decade, the beer's hopping was reformulated in 2009 to include three New Zealand-grown varieties: Pacific Gem, Styrian Golding, and Cascade. In order to maximize the production of fruity esters, fermentation of Old 95 is at a high temperature, up to 82 degrees Fahrenheit (28°C). It is often so powerful that the yeast head forces the vat's heavy stainless steel lids wide open! **GG**

Tasting notes

Old 95 pours an orangey amber hue beneath a cream-colored head. The aroma and palate offer a marmaladelike combination of sweet, toffeeish malt and racy, citrus-zest hop notes. Chewy sweet malt and grassy hops lead into an emphatic, bittersweet finish.

Epic Mayhem

Epic Brewing | www.epicbeer.com

Country of origin New Zealand
First brewed 2006
Alcohol content 6.2% abv
Serving temperature 43°F, 6°C

Luke Nicholas gained an appreciation for hops while living in California in the early 1990s. On returning to his native New Zealand, he was keen to re-create some of the hoppy West Coast U.S. beer styles that he'd come to love, but he couldn't find a job within the country's fledgling craft-brewing industry. Desperate times called for desperate measures, and he offered his services for free to his local Cock and Bull brewpub.

Nicholas progressed to the position of head brewer, as the pub's beers won plaudits from customers and a raft of medals in brewing competitions. Having shown what he could do, Nicholas was ready to take his beers to a wider audience, and, in May 2006, the first Epic beer, an American-style pale ale, was launched in bottles. At New Zealand's annual beer competition, Epic Pale Ale beat off almost 200 beers to take the supreme award.

Nicholas purchased the Epic brand in October 2007 and resigned from the brewery to concentrate on promoting his own beers. He has since developed the Epic brand online by using well-known social networking applications. Nowadays, Epic's full-time range is headed by Mayhem, a hugely hopped Kiwi interpretation of an American IPA. Although Nicholas is a fan of American Cascade hops and uses them in abundance in Epic Pale Ale, when making Mayhem, he blends them with Riwaka, a strongly aromatic New Zealand variety. The beer's grist, which includes British pale ale malt, Munich, and crystal malts, provides a luscious rich malt base that balances out the beer's challenging—some might say extreme—bitterness. **GG**

Tasting notes

This award-winning brew pours a brilliant amber hue beneath a deep, cream-colored head. The aroma and palate scream out tropical and stonefruit hop notes over a sweet, biscuity malt background. Savor this massive but delightfully balanced beer from a stemmed glass.

Fair Maiden Ale

Founders Organic Brewery | www.biobrew.co.nz

Country of origin New Zealand
First brewed 2006
Alcohol content 5.2% abv
Serving temperature 46°–50°F, 8°–10°C

Today the Duncan family is probably New Zealand's oldest and only continuous brewing family. It was 1854 when Joseph Dodson arrived in New Zealand from Australia and began brewing in Nelson. Joseph's daughter married Robert Duncan, and the two families owned and operated a brewery until 1969.

Thirty years later, John Duncan opened Founders Brewery in the city's Founders Historic Park. With a decade of experience at Nelson's Mac's brewery, John was aware of the public's growing interest in "naturally brewed" beers and decided to take his own beers to the next level. Founders became the first fully certified organic brewery in the southern hemisphere and one of only six in the world. These days the three brewing Duncans—John and sons Callum and Matt—craft a range of five full-time beers as well as occasional short-run, tap-only specialties in their compact brewhouse.

As John Duncan hands over the brewing to his sons, Founders has responded to the public's increasing thirst for more robust styles. The first of these was Fair Maiden Ale. The name works on several levels: "Fair" is another word for "pale," and the beer is a pale ale; and "Maiden" because the beer was Matt's first solo project. The depiction on the bottle label of the fair maiden as the figurehead on a ship is also apt: apart from brewing, Matt is interested in the history of sailing.

Aside from its organic status, the Founders brewery has a kosher certificate and the beers are GM free. Extended conditioning and maturation avoid the necessity for the fish- or egg-based clarifying agents, so the beers are also suitable for vegans. **GG**

Tasting notes

Pours an appetizing, bright amber hue beneath an off-white head. The aroma and palate are full of toffeelike sweetness, citrus, and tropical fruit notes, with a hint of grassiness that's typical of New Zealand hops. Best paired with crumbly, mature English cheeses and cold meats.

Fat Tire Amber Ale

New Belgium Brewing | www.newbelgium.com

Country of origin United States
First brewed 1991
Alcohol content 5.3% abv
Serving temperature 55°F, 13°C

Coors's beers and Fat Tire Amber Ale do not look or taste alike, but they share more in common than the fact that they are both brewed in Colorado. During the 1970s, Coors became a cult beer because its products were not available east of the Mississippi. Thirty years later, beer drinkers east of the Mississippi begged friends to bring them Fat Tire.

Fat Tire has been at the center of an amazing success story. When Jeff Lebesch and his wife Kim Jordan started the brewery in their basement in 1991, they expected the Abbey beer to be the flagship, but Fat Tire was an instant hit. Within a dozen years, New Belgium had grown into the third largest craft brewery in the nation, producing a dizzying range of beers. Walking through the brewery several years ago brewmaster Peter Bouckaert commented, "Luckily, we have Fat Tire, and that allows us to do all these other things." **SH**

Tasting notes
The flavors are biscuit and malt up front, with toasted caramel, nuts, and even molasses on the palate. Earthy hop character, well balanced, and finishes on the sweet side of dry.

Finlandia Sahti Strong

Finlandia Sahti Ky | www.finlandiasahti.fi

Country of origin Finland
First brewed 1992
Alcohol content 10% abv
Serving temperature 46°–50°F, 8°–10°C

There is nothing subtle about drinking sahti: some people adore the rugged complexity, whereas others are bemused, shrug their shoulders, and turn away. Finland has some of the most restricted alcohol policies in the world, and for generations many people made alcohol illegally. A change of the law allowed Antii Vesaka to set up a small brewery in 1992, and he was one of the first brewers to make sahti for commercial sale.

As a beer style, sahti was probably first made in medieval times. It was mashed in old wooden troughs that contained a bed of juniper twigs; this acts as a filter and is also said to contain many mysterious wild yeasts, which add to the visceral complexity of the beer. The beer is unhopped; it is full of protein, with the yeast helping to create a cloudy unfiltered beer. Finlandia has twice been chosen as the beer of the festival at the Helsinki Beer Festival. **TH**

Tasting notes
Protein-hazy amber topped by a rough white head. Earthy aroma with billowing notes of juniper. It tastes of bubblegum and bananas. Full bodied on the palate with a hint of oiliness.

First Harvest Ale

Cascade Brewery | www.cascadebrewery.com.au

Country of origin Australia
First brewed 2002
Alcohol content 5.5% abv
Serving temperature 46°F, 8°C

Built in 1824, the Cascade Brewery is situated at the foot of Mount Wellington, whose pure mountain streams have aided the brewery's success, along with the colder Tasmanian climate, which is so suited to the craft, and the strength of the local hops. Many colonial Australians had difficulty growing this essential flower, but the settlers in Van Diemen's Land had considerable success, and Tasmanian hops are now used worldwide.

The proximity of the brewery to the great hop fields of Tasmania allows Cascade to use hops within hours of them being picked. These special green flowers are moist to the touch and bursting with a freshly picked flavor and aroma that would bring the most experienced of brewers to his knees. Tasmanians like to keep things local, so it's no surprise that First Harvest Ale also makes use of the first Tasmanian barley of the season—malted at the brewery, of course. **DD**

Tasting notes
Expect a modest head in this copper beer supported by a leafy, herbacous aroma from the late addition of fresh hops. You may experience caramel and toffee flavors followed by a spicy finish.

Fish Tale Leviathan

Fish Brewing Company | www.fishbrewing.com

Country of origin United States
First brewed 1995
Alcohol content 10% abv
Serving temperature 48°–52°F, 9°–11°C

Situated at the southern tip of Puget Sound, a large inland waterway in the northwest corner of the United States, marine-themed beer names are to be expected from Fish Brewing. This American barleywine-style ale was named after the mythical sea monster.

In the late 1990s, the brewers tinkered with the recipe to better fit the region's progressively assertive palate, and Leviathan increased to the current 10 percent strength. At the same time general manager Martin Bills began experimenting with barrel-aging beer. Instead of utilizing whiskey or bourbon barrels, as did many of the early barrel-aging brewers, Fish Brewing chose to age Leviathan and Poseidon, an imperial stout, in wine barrels that it had obtained from an undisclosed winery. Continuing the wine theme, Fish began bottling the beers in standard-sized wine bottles—another practice that was not customary at the time. **LMo**

Tasting notes
Threads of caramel, brown sugar, and dried fruits marry with a sticky, sweet, and smooth mouthful of hops and caramel malt. The 10 percent strength is well masked and can sneak up on you.

Flying Fish Belgian Style Dubbel

Flying Fish Brewing Company | www.flyingfish.com

Country of origin United States
First brewed 1997
Alcohol content 7.2% abv
Serving temperature 50°F, 10°C

Gene Muller created Flying Fish Brewing in 1995 as a "virtual brewery" on the Internet. The plan was to get publicity for the web-based brewery in order to attract investors and turn the virtual brewery into a real beer-producing operation. The website gave beer lovers the chance to help "build" the brewery, name the beers, design labels and merchandise, and even apply for the job of head brewer.

By late 1996, Muller had opened a real-life brewery in southern New Jersey, and Flying Fish Brewing was born. Flying Fish produces four year-round beers, including the Belgian Style Dubbel, Extra Pale Ale, ESB Ale, and HopFish IPA. The brewery's range of seasonal beers includes OktoberFish, Farmhouse Summer Ale, and Grand Cru Winter Reserve. The company's Exit Series is a collection of limited release beers that uses the New Jersey Turnpike to celebrate the unique aspects of the Garden State. The first two releases were Exit 4, a Belgian trippel finished with American hops, and Exit 11, a hoppy American wheat ale.

Flying Fish's aim is to brew balanced beers that match well with food. Flying Fish Belgian Style Dubbel is made with two-row pale, Munich, Special B, and chocolate malts, demerara sugar, Styrian Golding hops, and Belgian ale yeast. The brewery makes versions of the ale for special occasions, including the cherry-infused Love Fish for St. Valentine's Day and Bourbon Dubbel, which is aged in whiskey casks. Flying Fish regularly appears at major beer events, such as the Great British Beer Festival, Oregon Brewers Festival, and Biere de Mondial in Montreal. **RL**

Tasting notes
This copper-colored ale pours with a decent-sized off-white head that coats the glass. The Belgian Style Duppel starts off with a fruity nose and the first sip delivers an appealing malty up-front flavor. The brew then turns slightly tart and finishes dry.

Forester Pale Ale

Two Metre Tall Company | www.2mt.com.au

Country of origin Australia
First brewed 2005
Alcohol content 5.5% abv
Serving temperature 46°–50°F, 8°–10°C

In essence, Ashley Huntington of the Two Metre Tall Company views brewers as farmers who add value to the ingredients grown on their land. This may sound extreme, but it is how winemakers have always seen themselves—a winery that did not tend to its grapes would not be treated seriously. Similarly, if a brewer wishes to have control over the attributes of his beer, he should plant, nourish, and harvest the raw ingredients that are used to produce it.

If you take this food production role a step further, you begin to question another mantra of commercial breweries, which is consistency. Brewers pride themselves on being able to produce the same beer under the same brand for years, hundreds of years in some cases. But if you accept beer as a product of the land, then by its nature it must change with the seasons and with the vagaries of nature. Some years have more sun and rain than others. Hop flowers harvested once a year are fresher the day they are picked than they are in the brew put down ten months later. As with wine, a beer that is a genuine product of its environment is likely to have subtle or even significant differences from batch to batch.

It is because of this approach that the Two Metre Tall Company is one of the only breweries in the world to grow its own hops and grain. The water it uses is unfiltered and collected from the local river or the sky. Like lambic beers, its ales are not for everyone, but trying one is like stepping back to a period when people brewed natural beer by sight and smell using nothing but their wits and the fruits of their labor. **DD**

Tasting notes

The character of this beer will depend on the vagaries of the season in which it is brewed. You may encounter a cloudy orange body embraced by a fluffy white head, perhaps followed by some engaging reminders of the land and a strong bitter finish.

Formidable

Birrificio Cittavecchia | www.cittavecchia.com

Country of origin Italy
First brewed 2001
Alcohol content 8% abv
Serving temperature 59°F, 15°C

Formidable was Inspector Maigret's favorite beer in the stories created by Georges Simenon. Michele Barro, founder and brewer of Birrificio Cittavecchia, is a great fan of the novels and named his strongest beer after the Inspector's tipple.

Like many a craft brewer, Barro started making beer at home. In 1999, he decided to take his hobby further and opened Birrificio Cittavecchia near Trieste. The area has a long tradition in brewing; for example, locals used to drink beer with dishes of traditional *bollito* (boiled meat) and *cren*, a sauce made with horseradish. Barro revived this old tradition with his brewery, producing both top and bottom-fermenting beers. Originally, Formidable was a special Christmas beer made in the winter; but its immediate success persuaded Barro to produce it all year around. The style is difficult to define: the yeast is British; the malt profile includes pils, Munich, Vienna, and some toasted barley malt. Hops are Hallertau Perle for bitterness and East Kent Golding and Saaz, mainly for aroma. Some sugar and a drop or two of coriander are also added to the recipe. The beer is matured for a couple of months, with an extra month of maturation in the bottle.

Formidable is the perfect nightcap, but Barro also recommends it with matured cheese or with the world-famous Vienna cake, *Sachertorte*. **MM**

Tasting notes

Gorgeous mahogany color, lightly cloudy with a thick, white, and persistent foam. Very rich and deep aroma, with lots of cherry fruit then licorice and a hint of smoky notes.

Fred

Hair of the Dog Brewing | www.hairofthedog.com

Country of origin United States
First brewed 1997
Alcohol content 10% abv
Serving temperature 50°F, 10°C

Fred is an elusive beer. Some call it a Belgian-style tripel and others say it is a strong ale; another camp argues that Fred is a double IPA or a barleywine-style ale. Hair of the Dog owner Alan Sprints appreciates the indefinable quality of the beer, and lets fans decide for themselves on the style. However, he does say that Fred was inspired in part by Belgian tripels.

The beer, which is the best-selling of all the Hair of the Dog beers, was inspired also by U.S. beer writer Fred Eckhardt. Now in his eighties, Eckhardt has been writing about beer from his home in Portland, Oregon, since before many of today's brewers were born, and he played an influential role in the birth of the modern craft beer movement in the United States. "Fred was a big inspiration to me as a home-brewer. He came to our home-brew club meetings, helped us out, and spoke with us about different beer styles we hadn't even heard of before," Sprints says. "I wanted to brew a beer as a thank you to him. I made Fred to honor him."

Sprints discovered that Eckhardt enjoyed the flavor of rye and that he was a big fan of hoppy beers. So, Sprints added ample amounts of both ingredients when designing Fred. "It really is the embodiment of the man in a beer," he says. "I pretty much stuffed as much as I could into the brew kettle and out popped Fred." **LMo**

Tasting notes

Deep, golden color. Spicy, with huge amounts of hops and malt, Fred can be enjoyed immediately. But it also can be cellared, taking on different flavors with time.

One of the Hair of the Dog logos featuring Roswell Barker the dog.

Freiställter Rotschopf

Braucommune Freistadt | www.freistaedter-bier.at

Country of origin Austria
First brewed 2009
Alcohol content 5.6% abv
Serving temperature 46°F, 8°C

The literal meaning of Freistadt is "free town," and, in the Middle Ages, this freedom included the burgher's right to brew. In Freistadt, this right was linked to the ownership of a building located inside the city walls. Depending on the size of the building, the annual allowance was between 15 to 140 "Eimer" (an old volume measure equaling about 15 gallons [56 l]).

Brewing must have been quite profitable here. Located on a merchant's route between the Alps and Bohemia, the so-called *"Zlatá stezka"* ("Golden Road"), Freistadt was granted the right to impose a tax on goods sold or bought here—with salt, fish, and beer being among the most prominent goods on sale. There were twelve breweries active in 1525, but in the course of the following one and a half centuries, the number declined to two in 1687—one for white (supposedly wheat) and one for brown beer. In 1777, these two were merged to form the Braucommune (community brewery). The capital stock of the brewery is still linked to the ownership of city buildings, and the denomination of the shares is still Eimer.

While the ownership of the brewery is organized traditionally, the plant itself has seen major technical upgrades in recent years. It has also been quite courageous in developing new beers from local ingredients including hops from the region. One such product was a Rauchbier—it was discontinued at the same time that the Rotschopf was released. Freistädter beers can be found primarily in the region north of Linz called Mühlviertel and, of course, in the bars and cafés of the city center of Freistadt. **CS**

Tasting notes

Reddish amber as the name suggests, this Vienna-style lager forms in the glass beneath a big white head. It is full bodied with a malty sweetness that underlines the hearty character, but soon gives way to a distinct bitterness from local hops for balance.

Füchschen Alt

Brauerei im Füchschen | www.fuechschen.de

Country of origin Germany
First brewed 1848
Alcohol content 4.8% abv
Serving temperature 46°F, 8°C

The center of the Altbier brewing universe is in the city of Düsseldorf, in the Altstadt (old town) where the four Düsseldorf Altbier brewpubs can be found. This small district along the banks of the Rhine has 300 pubs and clubs and calls itself "the longest bar in the world."

Since 2001, Brauerei im Füchschen has gained something of a cult status among young consumers, helping to triple the brewpub's output in just a decade. Yet, the beer has remained the same, as brewmaster Frank Driewer happily points out. Renowned as the mildest of the Düsseldorf Altbiers, Füchschen ("Little Fox") Alt nevertheless offers a pronounced bitterness along with a decent bite. The brewing is still done in a traditional, handcrafted way: employing four kinds of malts, the noble German hop Hallertauer Tradition, top-fermentation in open vessels, and three weeks of lagering. As Driewer reveals, they still apply the traditional method of putting wooden chips into the tanks. These chips provide substantial surface area for the yeast cells to settle and thereby clarify and harmonize the beer.

Füchschen's revitalization came along with fourth-generation owner Peter König, a trained cook, brewer, and maltster. He took over the business in 1995, upgraded the menu with light meals, modernized the brewhouse, relaunched the brand, and set up a fresh program of events. Regarding the nature of the locals (known as "Rhenish cheerfulness") it does not seem too far-fetched to suggest that König's nomination as Prince Carnival in 2001 also helped to spur good old Füchschen's rise. **SK**

Tasting notes

Amber with an orange hue; big beige foam mountain. This beer offers a malty nose with hints of caramel. The first taste reveals a soft mouthfeel evolving into a pronounced bitterness and complemented by a decent sour bite; a dry and mild finish.

Fujizakura Heights Rauch

Fujizakura Heights Beer | www.fuji-net.co.jp/beer

Country of origin Japan
First brewed 1998
Alcohol content 5.5% abv
Serving temperature 43°–46°F, 6°–8°C

Located near the northern side of Mount Fuji, this small brewery specializes in German-style beers. To learn how to make them, brewmaster Hiromichi Miyashita spent two months in western Japan and another two months in northern Japan, learning from expatriate German brewers. Between the two periods, he also studied in Germany for a six-week stretch. However, it turned out that sanitation was the most difficult thing for Miyashita to grasp. The brewery is designed with open fermentation tanks, which makes routine sanitation tasks an extremely important part of operations.

The most distinctive beer Fujizakura brews is this Rauchbier, a German-style smoked lager. It is brewed with smoked malt, Munich malt, caramel malt, and roast malt, and bittered with a one-time addition of Perle hops. It is the smoked malt that makes this such a difficult beer to brew, but it is also responsible for creating its unique flavor. Each batch of smoked malt varies in flavor intensity, so its quantity, along with the quantity of caramel malt, must be adjusted each time to achieve consistent results.

Miyashita admits that it took a while for customers to become accustomed to the unusual flavor of smoked beer. Gradually, though, it caught on after many customers found that it was superb when accompanying smoked sausages and fresh cured ham, not to mention other rich meat dishes. With a strong identity in German-style beers, Fujizakura continues to do well in Japan, where beer is essentially considered a German beverage. **BH**

Tasting notes

The color is deep auburn, with a light tan head. There is a clean aroma of malt and smoke flavors, which is light overall with a faint tartness. It is interestingly fruity, offset by a fine, crisp carbonation. The smoke flavor does not linger long.

Fuller's ESB

Fuller, Smith & Turner | www.fullers.co.uk

Country of origin England
First brewed 1969
Alcohol content 5.5% abv (5.9% in bottle)
Serving temperature 52°F, 11°C

Extra Special Bitter was launched in 1971, although it had first appeared in 1969 as a seasonal beer known as Winter Beer, replacing a beer named Old Burton Ale. A strong, highly complex beer, it is brewed from pale ale and crystal malts and a heady cocktail of Target, Challenger, Northdown, and Golding hops.

ESB was a continuation of the tradition of many British brewers who produced a stronger, richer, mouth-warming beer for drinking during the winter months. However, it quickly became established as a bottled beer available year-round. Drinkers loved it, and it has won many awards, including the prestigious Champion Beer of Britain, a title Fuller's has also gained for two of its other beers—Chiswick Bitter and London Pride—a record unmatched by any other brewer.

In the United States, Extra Special Bitter has come to denote a class of beers that are high in alcohol and full of hop flavoring, but without the assertive hop character of India Pale Ale. It is said that many of the United States's craft brewers were inspired to make beer because of Fuller's classic brew. As an experiment Fuller's current brewer John Keeling has been storing ESB and other beers in wooden whiskey casks, which produce luxurious, smoky, peaty flavors.

Situated near to one of London's busiest road junctions, brewing has taken place on the site of the Griffin Brewery, in the west London borough of Chiswick, for more than 350 years. John Fuller became involved in the brewery in 1829, and Henry Smith and John Turner joined him in 1845—thus forming Fuller, Smith and Turner as it is still known today. **TH**

Tasting notes

Deep bronze in color. With a rich hop nose, Fuller's ESB has a complex taste that is dominated by a tangy marmalade note and other sugar-rich citrus flavors. This is softened by the slightest hint of sweet fudge. Full in alcohol and it warms the tongue.

Fuller's Golden Pride

Fuller, Smith & Turner | www.fullers.co.uk

Country of origin England
First brewed 1967
Alcohol content 8.5% abv
Serving temperature 54°F, 12°C

As the benchmark for many barleywines, Fuller's Golden Pride has certainly stood the test of time. Originally developed in 1967, the beer was designed to replace the brewery's then strong ale, a 7 percent dark beer, the sales of which had started to fade away. The plan was always to make it clear that it was part of the London Pride family, still the company's flagship brand, and it was originally based on a grist mix from London Pride, ESB, and a pale ale. Hops remain Target for bitterness and Northdown and Challenger for aroma—quite modern varieties for the time.

The hops and the full fermentation process that ensured excellent attenuation (conversion of as many sugars as possible to alcohol) meant that the beer was a lot less sweet than many of its contemporaries, which could account for its popularity. One of the brewers, Reg Drury, recalls that the team was trying to achieve a pale, yet strong, beer and although it was initially brewed as a 9 percent, it was trimmed down in the late 1980s to its current 8.5 percent strength and, he says, it became a better beer because it was more balanced.

Despite no longer being marketed as a barleywine, Golden Pride's popularity has seen it become almost a lone survivor of its style as well as provide a beacon and an inspiration for the new wave of barleywines that are emerging from British craft brewers. This is a beer that is not only meant for savoring on its own, but it is also great with food, as an ideal partner to salty blue cheeses or even a crème brûlée—all of which is testament to Golden Pride's quality, versatility, and wonderful drinkability. **MC**

Tasting notes

A heady aroma of malt loaf, golden syrup, and caramel pours off this beer from the minute it is decanted into the glass, showing off its rich, deep amber color. The flavor is a richly satisfying figgy orange with a hint of roast, balanced with a slightly dry bitterness.

Fuller's celebrates the sporting life in this classic advertisement from *ca.* 1930.

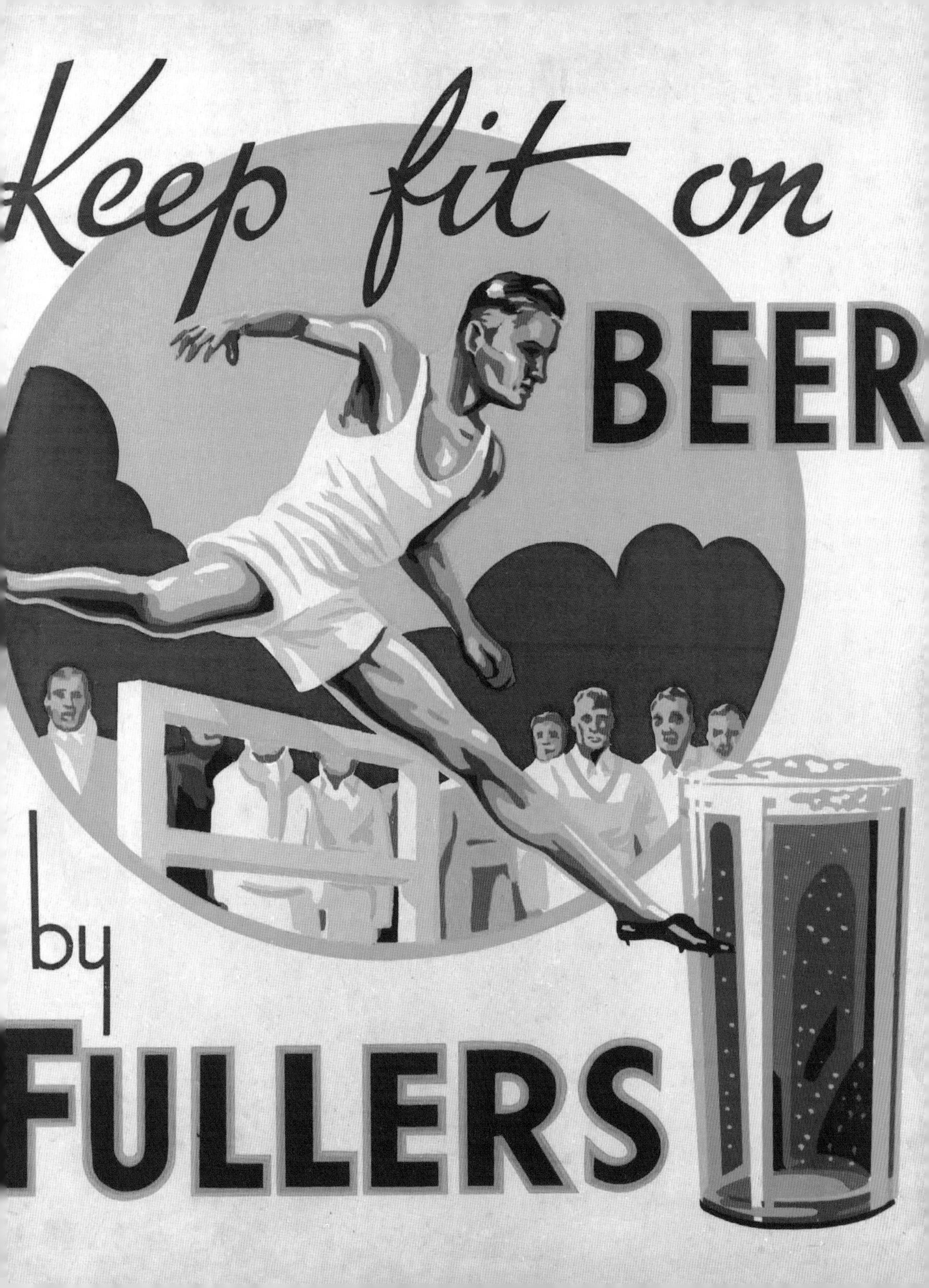
Keep fit on
BEER
by
FULLERS

Fuller's London Pride

Fuller, Smith & Turner | www.fullers.co.uk

Country of origin England
First brewed 1959
Alcohol content 4.7% abv
Serving temperature 52°–57°F, 11°–14°C

Although it was officially launched on St. George's Day, 1959, Britain's leading premium ale has a legacy that is much older. London Pride was born out of an earlier Fuller's beer called Special Pale Ale, and a recipe that dates back to the 19th century or even earlier.

Beer has been made by Fuller's in west London for more than 350 years, and many of the old brewing books are now in the stewardship of head brewer John Keeling. It's possible to look back through these books and trace the "family tree" of a beer such as Pride. Many Fuller's beers have been developed from older recipes in a similar way. Whereas today brewing folk will sit around a table and create a beer from scratch to fill a gap in the market, beers back then were created from recipes that the brewery already had.

London Pride is Fuller's most popular beer. The brewery currently produces around 200,000 barrels of beer per year, three-quarters of which have London Pride in them. For such a successful brew, however, London Pride is a simple one: it uses only two malts—crystal and pale ale. There are also relatively few hops: Target for bittering, and Challenger and Northdown are added late to the copper.

Keeling says the beer's popularity is down to its drinkability, which he attributes to the almost perfect balance between the zesty hop and biscuity malt character. It's possible to measure the drinkability of a beer. To do so, you simply give it away to some sports club or other, and measure how much they drink. It may not sound scientific, but the companies that offer this service take it very seriously. **ST**

Tasting notes

An extremely well-balanced brew. Its malty, biscuity nature is firmly underpinned by fruity hops on the nose, with a touch of treacle toffee in the mouth. The refreshingly bitter finish lasts a long time. A perfect accompaniment to a British pub lunch.

Fuller's Vintage Ale

Fuller, Smith & Turner | www.fullers.co.uk

Country of origin England
First brewed 1997
Alcohol content 8.5% abv
Serving temperature 48°–50°F, 9°–10°C

This extraordinarily complex beer started life as a very simple idea: to brew a special, commemorative beer that utilized the very best ingredients the brewery had bought that year.

Everyone at Fuller's agreed that the beer should be strong and bottle conditioned. It was brewed as a limited edition, with bottles individually numbered. It was 1997, and the best malt and barley from that year went into a beer that became much bigger than the ideas that originally inspired it. After six months, there was unanimous agreement that the ale had improved. Six months later, it was better still. Aging beers has now become popular across the world, but in the final years of the last millennium, Fuller's felt that they were rediscovering some very old, forgotten principles of brewing.

Vintage Ale has been brewed by Fuller's every year since. The recipe changes annually, depending on what the best ingredients are, and it occasionally reflects contemporary themes—there was even an organic version in 2000. Younger expressions of the beer have a pronounced hoppy character, which is the first characteristic of the ale to change. A few years later, the malt character softens and becomes fruitier. Head brewer John Keeling personally prefers a four- to five-year-old ale, but he is quick to add that this is entirely subjective.

This is a beer that takes five months to brew and only sells between 100 to 200 barrels a year. However, it is a beer that continues to surprise, delight, and educate drinkers and brewers the world over. **PB**

Tasting notes

Serve in a brandy balloon glass, at the low end of cellar temperature so that the aromatics are released as the beer warms. Character develops with age, but expect powerful malt and fruit characters to give way to complex spicy and sherrylike notes.

Furthermore
Knot Stock

Furthermore Beer | www.furthermorebeer.com

Country of origin United States
First brewed 2006
Alcohol content 5.5% abv
Serving temperature 44°F, 7°C

Chris Staples and Aran Madden formed Furthermore Beer in 2006, in the Wisconsin town of Spring Green, but the inspiration for their Knot Stock Pale Ale came five years earlier. Madden was working at a brewpub in Pittsburgh when he tasted a black pepper cookie from the Enrico Biscotti Company. He recalled that it was definitely odd, but made for a very memorable flavor combination. Almost immediately, the idea occurred to him to pair black pepper with a well-hopped American pale ale.

At the roots of Knot Stock is a 65-IBU American pale ale that uses Northern Brewer hops and has a healthy amount of caramel malt to soften the overall palate. Cracked black pepper is stuffed in a sack, boiled, and cold-infused. The result is a tangled set of flavors that is dominated by the uniqueness of the liquefied peppercorns. Knot Stock is not the only offbeat flavor combination from Furthermore. It makes Fallen Apple, a cream ale and cider combination; Three Feet Deep, a stout with a touch of peat-smoked roasted malt; and Oscura, a coffee lager that uses fresh roasted Nicaraguan beans. Furthermore is not shy when it comes to naming its beers. Fatty Boombalatty is a Belgian-style white beer that is hopped like an IPA. **RL**

Tasting notes
Amber gold beer with a thick off-white head. There is an immediate cracked peppercorn nose. It delivers a coating mouthfeel with a hefty amount of hop bitterness.

Galway Hooker
Irish Pale Ale

Hooker Brewery | www.galwayhooker.ie

Country of origin Ireland
First brewed 2006
Alcohol content 4.4% abv
Serving temperature 44°F, 7°C

Ireland's microbreweries took their first tentative steps in the mid-1990s with the opening of a collection of small independent breweries. The likes of Biddy Early in County Clare and the Porterhouse in Dublin were well aware of the hill that they had to climb in order to wean the Irish public off the factory-made beers that the large breweries had been serving up for a generation or more. As a result, these vanguard craft brewers stuck closely to the popular traditional Irish styles, with a stout, a red ale, and a pale lager being the typical lineup.

In the summer of 2006, Hooker Brewery arrived. Instead of the standard trilogy, there was just one beer and two secret weapons: a local focus on the lively pubs of Galway and a style of beer unfamiliar to the Irish palate—a pale ale dosed with intensely bitter and fruity Saaz and Cascade hops. Since then, Aidan Murphy and Ronan Brennan, who own and manage the tiny brewery, have built up a national following for their beer (named after the local fishing vessel, in case you were thinking something less wholesome), distributing to dozens of pubs all over the country. Galway Hooker has a cult following among Irish beer fans and has won multiple awards, including two stints as Ireland's Beer of the Year. **JD**

Tasting notes
Galway Hooker is complicated by a base of very Irish crystal malt, giving it a deliciously sweet biscuity character against the zingy grapefruit of the Cascade hops. Great with spicy food.

← Erin Fuller's beer label designs won an award from *Print Magazine* in 2007.

Garrison Imperial Pale Ale

Garrison Brewing Company | www.garrisonbrewing.com

Country of origin Canada
First brewed 2007
Alcohol content 7% abv
Serving temperature 46°F, 8°C

Exept for pioneering Halifax brewpub the Granite Brewery, craft beer was slow to come to Canada's maritime provinces. There were misfires, as was the case almost everywhere when small-scale brewing was re-established in North America, but nothing long-standing arrived in Nova Scotia, New Brunswick, and Prince Edward Island until the mid-1990s, a decade after craft brewing was firmly planted in Ontario.

One of those early arrivals was Garrison Brewing, founded by a retired naval officer named Brian Titus. As many ex-service personnel had done before him, Titus pondered why the great beer styles that he had encountered during his travels were not available in his hometown. He decided to open a brewery that would make them. As maritimers can be very stuck in their ways, the early days were not easy for Titus and neighboring Propeller Brewing, which opened at about the same time. He persevered and achieved widespread acceptance of his core brands, before pushing the boundaries.

The result was Garrison's Imperial Pale Ale, a hugely hoppy beer styled after the double IPAs that had become popular recently in the United States. Still, creating and marketing an ale so dramatically different in a region well known for its conservatism in beer must have been daunting. Imperial soon found its niche, helped along by successive Canadian Beer of the Year awards. The year after its introduction, Titus was inspired to add three new beers to his seasonal offerings, including Grand Baltic Porter, one of only a few beers of its style brewed in Canada. **SB**

Tasting notes

As an IPA of "imperial" pedigree, hoppy bitterness obviously figures prominently in the character of this ale. But it is the biscuity malt and warming, almost chewy, finish that gives it its style and character, and provides support for all those piney, citrusy hops.

Gavroche

La Brasserie de St.-Sylvestre | www.brasserie-st-sylvestre.com

Country of origin France
First brewed 1997
Alcohol content 8.5% abv
Serving temperature 50°F, 10°C

The French Flanders village of St.-Sylvestre-Cappel is but a strip of houses, shops, and bars straddled along the main road. However, down a side road in the center of the village is St.-Sylvestre brewery, whose beers are exported throughout the world. Although best known for its world classic Trois Monts, the brewery has an excellent selection of beer, one of which is Gavroche. When it was released, Gavroche represented a change, a challenge, and also something of a quandary: what constitutes bière de garde?

Much has been written about the bières de garde of this region of northern France, but a fair selection of them nowadays seem to owe a lot to their northern cousins in Belgium. See, for example, Cuvee des Jonquilles and Gayant's Goudale. Gavroche is another beer that would fit very easily into a Brussels specialty beer bar, with its handsome brown looks and a spicy, rich compendium of aromas more often found on a dubbel. That said, it's most definitely a French beer, as what could be more Gallic than a beer that was named after the sprightly and life-affirming street urchin in Victor Hugo's *Les Miserables*. Look at the silhouette on the bottle label: it is Gavroche.

Even though the beer was first released in 1997, it was originally slated for release during 1989 when the French Republic celebrated the bicentennial of its revolution. It was delayed because the brewery was said to be unhappy with the finished product at the time, and it took a few more years for it to be released. Whether traditional bière de garde or French dubbel, the wait was definitely worthwhile. **ATJ**

Tasting notes

This bottle-conditioned beer pours a dark amber in color and sits beneath a creamy, cappuccino head. On the palate, hop spice, dark fruit, and roast hints vie for attention; full bodied, it finishes with a flourish of alcohol warmth, malt dryness, and hop bite.

Glops Torrada

Llúpols i Llevats | www.llupolsillevats.com/cat07

Country of origin Spain
First brewed 2005
Alcohol content 4.8% abv
Serving temperature 55°F, 13°C

Àlex Padró Ruiz was eighteen when he first came face to face with the world of brewing in Germany. He decided that on his return to Spain he would do something similar. At college he came across Steve Huxley, a Spain-based, English brewmaster who is now part of the famed Barcelona beer shop La Cerveteca. Thanks to this fortuitous meeting Ruiz was taught how to brew by Huxley and, along with him and others, was a founder member of Humulus Lupulus–Cultura de Cerveza, a Spanish beer association. In 2005 he set up Spain's first microbrewery outside Barcelona.

The brewery's name, Llúpols i Llevats, translates as "hops and yeast." Faithful to the country where he first fell in love with brewing, Ruiz produces lager-style beers that are sold under the brand name of Glops. His beers are made in accordance with the Reinheitsgebot, and avoid any filtration or pasteurization. Glops Torrada is a bottom-fermenting dunkel-style lager, produced with Munich malts and Saaz hops. It matures and mellows out for at least three weeks in tank, after which it is bottled using isobaric pressure. The entire production is almost handmade, except for several operations that require mechanical tools.

Being the first Spanish microbrewery, it was hard at the beginning for Llúpols i Llevats to convince the public that they should try this new beer. Yet, by promoting local festivals and with good distribution, it is has beome well known and appreciated. Ruiz recommends drinking it alongside a local specialty— *coca* (toasted bread) seasoned with figs and foie gras—the perfect marriage in his opinion. **SS**

Tasting notes

Amber-honey in color, with a creamy head that doesn't stay long, plus gentle carbonation. On the nose there is a gentle breeze of yeast and bready notes, while in the mouth malt is omnipresent together with a slight hint of bitterness.

Granite Best Bitter Special

Granite Brewery | www.granitebrewery.ca

Country of origin Canada
First brewed 1992
Alcohol content 4.5% abv
Serving temperature 55°F, 13°C

The original Granite Brewery brewpub was, oddly enough, born out of a real estate venture. Having spent some years buying, restoring, and selling properties in Halifax, Nova Scotia, brothers Wilfred and Kevin Keefe decided to renovate the city-center Gainsborough Hotel and open a bar on the premises. Thus Gingers Tavern was born.

In 1984, Kevin Keefe became serious about learning to brew and decided to build his own brewery within Gingers. A year later, the brewery was in place, and Nova Scotia had its first craft-brewed beer. However, it was not until 1992 that the wonderful, dry-hopped and cask-conditioned Best Bitter Special emerged into the world. This happened after a third brother, Toronto-based Ron, was brought into the brewing fold following Wilfred's unfortunate death. With Kevin, Ron opened the Toronto outpost of the Granite in 1991, initially brewing the same ales as sold at its Maritime elder, but eventually expanding into cask conditioning with the Special.

For many a year, all of the Toronto Granite's beers, including the Best Bitter Special, were available solely on the premises of the brewpub. In 2004, a change in Ontario law allowed Keefe to shift his operating license to that of a brewery and treat his existing location as a tied house. Free from the restrictions of a brewpub permit, he opened a small store at one end of the bar and began selling growlers to thirsty local residents and also to the occasional beer devotee arriving from regions much farther afield. Thus was born a memorable beer legend. **SB**

Tasting notes

As a keg bitter, the beer is light amber in color with a fresh, dried-leaf aroma and a dry, gently caramel flavor.
In its cask-conditioned form, it is far more aromatic and considerably drier, but still with a robust, faintly orange-accented maltiness.

Greene King Abbot Ale

Greene King | www.greeneking.co.uk

Country of origin England
First brewed 1955
Alcohol content 5% abv
Serving temperature 50°–55°F, 10°–13°C

The link between beer and the church is a long one in England. Before they were despoiled on the orders of King Henry VIII, most monasteries brewed their own ale, and in the Suffolk town of Bury St. Edmunds, the brewers of the Abbot of the Great Abbey of St. Edmundsbury were noted in the Domesday Book.

In 1799, Benjamin Greene established a brewery next door to the home of the former abbot. The company became known as Greene King during the 19th century, after it merged with Frederick King in 1887. Greene King is now one of the biggest breweries in the United Kingdom, and its Abbot Ale enthrals beer connoisseurs. This is a strong best bitter and it has always been represented by the image of a rosy-cheeked abbot, but according to legend, the image of this holy man is based on a painting of an English earl who had no connection with the church. **ATJ**

Tasting notes
The nose is caramel with a hint of citrus fruit at the back. Hazelnuts, caramel, and malt sweetness clamber on the palate with a hoppy and citrusy fruitiness. The finish is dry and bitter.

Grošák

Minipivovar Koníček | www.minipivovarkonicek.cz

Country of origin Czech Republic
First brewed 2006
Alcohol content 6.3% abv
Serving temperature 46°F, 8°C

The rather remote Moravian-Silesian region of the Czech Republic is home to one of central Europe's most dynamic brewpub scenes. The region's brewing community seems to favor neighborly competition, and the well-loved brewpub in Hukvaldy is said to have inspired the Koníček microbrewery in Vojkovice, which appeared at the end of 2006. Soon after its founding, Koníček created an amber beer to complement its Ryzák pale lager and Vraník dark lager. Called Grošák, it was brewed originally as a Christmas special, but it proved so popular that the brewery added it to its permanent line.

Brewer Mojmír Velké uses malt from Moravamalt in the nearby town of Brodek and purchases pure yeast from the large Zubr brewery in Přerov. Grošák is only available on tap and has won several accolades at the Czech brewmasters' awards. **ER**

Tasting notes
Topped with thick beige foam, this cloudy, amber lager hides its strength behind honeylike notes of rich malt and a perfectly balanced hop bitterness, finishing with a slightly acidic, dry gulp.

Grottenbier

Brouwerij St. Bernardus | www.sintbernardus.be

Country of origin Belgium
First brewed *ca*. 2000
Alcohol content 6.5% abv
Serving temperature 43°–52°F, 6°–11°C

Long before the breweries in Buggenhout began making "champagne beers," Pierre Celis had the idea of conditioning beer in the Champenoise way. This meant that instead of filtering the beer at the bottling stage, it would be dosed with fresh yeast and sugar, turned on specially built racks (*pupitres*), and finally have the neck frozen to remove the yeast.

He wanted to mature the beer in caves and found a suitable location at Kanne, close to Maastricht. He then searched for a brewery to make the basic beer. He eventually found one in St. Bernardus, and the brewery started making this dark, enigmatic beer. Experience has shown that Grottenbier should not be cooled too much or it will lose its incredible complexity. Grottenbier has became so successful, that a lighter-colored version was also created, but many drinkers still prefer the original. **JPa**

Tasting notes
Fruity and yeasty nose, not unlike cola. Dark fruit and mushrooms determine the slightly tart flavor that ends on burned, roasted notes, dwindling to the more plain sweetness of rose water.

Gulpener Dort

Gulpener Bierbrouwerij | www.gulpener.nl

Country of origin Netherlands
First brewed 1953
Alcohol content 6.5% abv
Serving temperature 44°F, 7°C

More than 125 years after the founding of the brewery, Gulpener decided to produce its first special beer. The brewmaster was Joep de Kroon, and his inspiration was Meibier, a beer especially produced for May.

Gulpener Dort is made with pale malt, maize, and caramel, and Hallertau hops. Bottom-fermenting yeast is used and the Dort is lagered for ten weeks. The brewery tries to keep production as sustainable as possible, using locally grown hops and malt. The fact that a non-Dutch beer has been made and sold successfully in the Netherlands for fifty-five years makes it noteworthy. The brewery recognizes that the current version of Dort is not the same as the one brewed during the 1950s and 1960s, and attributes these changes partly to the legal requirements of the European Union and partly to changes in brewing techniques and technology over the years. **RP**

Tasting notes
Light brown to dark gold in the glass. The aroma is malt-driven, while the palate rings with a definite sweetness, although dry grainy notes help to balance any overdrive toward sweetness.

Hadmar

Weitra Bräu Bierwerkstatt | www.bierwerkstatt.at

Hampshire Special Ale

D. L. Geary Brewing | www.gearybrewing.com

Country of origin Austria
First brewed 1994
Alcohol content 5.2% abv
Serving temperature 48°F, 9°C

Country of origin United States
First brewed 1989
Alcohol content 7% abv
Serving temperature 50°F, 10°C

This Vienna-style lager is named after Hadmar von Kuenring, who founded the small town of Weitra in 1201. The town received its charter in 1321, enabling the burgher to brew and sell beer, and Weitra soon became an important brewing town. In its heyday, Weitra had twenty-two breweries, two of which still survive today.

The Vienna style had virtually disappeared in Austria, but its reintroduction in 1994 proved to be an immediate success. Today the brewing recipe has changed slightly—to replace standard malts with those from organic production—but the production methods remain unchanged: the wort is boiled in a directly fired copper kettle built in the early 1960s. The Bierwerkstatt still uses open fermenters and matures its beers (apart from Hadmar there is a small amount of Helles) in horizontal lager tanks. **CS**

David Geary modeled his strong English ale after the many cask-conditioned ales that he'd sampled while learning the trade in Scotland. When English beer critic Michael Jackson visited his brewhouse, Geary showed him what he'd learned. Could this magnificently malty ale from Maine stand up to those served in the traditional pubs of London? "I remember him sitting in the tasting room. I poured him a cask-conditioned Hampshire. He smelled it and did all the beery things. And he looked up at me and said, 'This is a very special beer.' I felt giddy."

Initially Hampshire Special Ale was available only in December, and its distribution was hotly anticipated. Its long, lingering flavors of majestically balanced malt and hops made it a special Christmas treat. Geary said it was "just nuts" to make fans wait all year for a taste. Today, this special ale is a year-round specialty. **DR**

Tasting notes
The copper color and the slightly sweet nose are characteristics of the Vienna style—as is the balanced bitterness and intense toasty malt character. Low carbonation and extremely smooth.

Tasting notes
A rich copper hue, a big malty aroma, and a dense fruity character. A spike of hop bitterness on the palate is quickly countered by lightly sweet caramel. Smooth finish.

Miniature showing Hadmar (right), namesake of Weitra's Vienna-style lager.

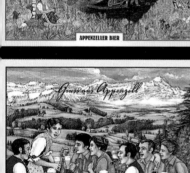

Hanfblüte

Brauerei Locher | www.appenzellerbier.ch

Harveys Christmas Ale

Harveys Brewery | www.harveys.org.uk

Country of origin Switzerland
First brewed 2000
Alcohol content 5.2% abv
Serving temperature 46°–54°F, 8°–12°C

Country of origin England
First brewed 1971
Alcohol content 8.1% abv
Serving temperature 55°–64°F, 13°–18°C

Brauerei Locher produces seven different beers. Most of them are sold under the Appenzell brand, the canton where the brewery is based. A family-run business since 1886, it has earned a reputation for high quality and an innovative approach. It is one of only a few Swiss breweries producing lager matured for a full year in wooden barrels; it still uses open fermenters and classic horizontal lagering (storing) vessels.

Karl Locher, who runs the operation with his cousin Raphael, admits that Appenzeller Hanfblüte was a difficult beer to produce. "We have three parts of the hemp introduced at different times," he says. "We don't get the THC (tetrahydrocannabinol), the thing that makes you hallucinate, but some think they can feel it." The beer's original label showed a harvest scene with one character sitting under a tree smoking the traditional Appenzell pipe. The local trading standards office took a dim view and threatened to cease production. The brewery rubbed out the pipe and the figure now has his thumb in his mouth.

Brauerei Locher brewed Switzerland's first organic beer—Vollmond. Other beers in the portfolio include Appenzeller Swiss Mountain and Castegna, a chestnut beer with a musty aroma and slightly sweet nuttiness that takes more than three months to mature and two sips to appreciate. **AG**

Harveys is a brewery rich in heritage, which has been active in the English town of Lewes for around two centuries. Started by John Harvey back in the 1700s, it remains a family business and represents a fine example of historic British brewing.

The brewery has long enjoyed a love affair with fine cask beers, but Christmas Ale is proving that the firm's bottled beers are equally good, and this seasonal winter warmer is deservedly popular. At slightly more than 8 percent abv, it's a barleywine-style beer that is best savored rather than swigged. Beware if you are unaccustomed to the style because it can be a challenge to the palate, being relatively thick and sweet. Heavily hopped, it is expressive of the breweries artisan approach and contains ingredients locally sourced from Sussex and the neighboring counties of Kent and Surrey. Meanwhile the water for the beer is drawn from the on-site well.

All these factors combine to make Christmas Ale a genuine drinking experience as well as a great accompaniment to a good juicy steak. Although it's a seasonal, the brew is so popular that Harveys has always produced enough to last throughout the year. The brewery also produces a golden barleywine called Elizabethan Ale, which made its first appearance in 1953, the year of Elizabeth II's coronation. **TS**

Tasting notes

Hemp leaves and hemp flowers give a distinctive herb and floral aroma and a flavor bordering on ginger with hints of fresh vegetation. Made with Vienna malt and Stammheim hops.

Tasting notes

So velvety it slips down the throat, but not before you marvel at its deep amber color and woody aroma. The sweetness is like molasses sugar, and there's plenty of cinnamon to match.

Original artwork commissioned by the brewery for their large range of beers.

Hercules Double IPA

Great Divide Brewing | www.greatdivide.com

Country of origin United States
First brewed 2004
Alcohol content 10% abv
Serving temperature 50°F, 10°C

Aptly named, Hercules is, arguably, a strongman in the beer world, weighing in at 10 percent and possessing 85 IBUs. But like many big, tough guys, Hercules Double IPA is really a sweet pussycat deep inside, a secret that belies its forceful and bitter exterior.

"Hercules is very hoppy. But many people perceive more bitterness in our regular Titan IPA, which is 65 IBUs—a full twenty units less than Hercules," says Great Divide founder Brian Dunn. "Hercules has a huge malt base, making it extremely well balanced, and all that malt does a great job of balancing out the bitterness. We developed this beer to be a well-balanced double IPA, not a one-dimensional hop bomb."

Made with Columbus, Centennial, and Simcoe hops, Hercules is a completely different beer to Titan, unlike some double IPAs in which the brewer simply boosts the hops and malt profile of their regular India Pale Ale. A multiple award winner, Hercules has not been tweaked since it was first developed.

"At the time Hercules was created, we didn't do test-batch beers; we just didn't have the people or the space," Dunn says. "So, I wrote down the parameters on what we wanted to achieve in this beer—the abv, the IBUs, the flavor profile, and such—and then we sat in the brewery and tweaked it on paper. . . . We really haven't changed the recipe since then."

Dunn says Hercules is balanced enough to go with a great variety of food, but he recommends pairing it with grilled fish tacos or Roomano, a hard, Dutch cheese that is not the same as the ubiquitous Italian Romano cheese. **LMo**

Tasting notes

A massive hop hit of resinous pine, citrus fruits, and grassiness balances out what could be an overbearing sweetness if this big boy got in the wrong hands. But Great Divide handles Hercules with finesse. A slight booziness rounds out the flavor experience.

Hibernation Ale

Great Divide Brewing | www.greatdivide.com

Country of origin United States
First brewed 1995
Alcohol content 8.1% abv
Serving temperature 55°F, 13°C

In the late 1990s, several Colorado breweries attached the suffix "-ation" to beers released for winter drinking (no doubt in homage to the German practice of adding "-ator" to the names of their cold weather beers). Colorado examples included Old Jubilation from Avery Brewing, Odell Brewing's Isolation Ale, and the particularly successful Great Divide Hibernation Ale. The Denver-based brewery makes Hibernation each July but does not release it until the beginning of November. Many of its fans will further age it for a year or more in their own cellars to give it a richer and deeper flavor.

When Brian Dunn started Great Divide Brewing, he was the only full-time employee. After earning an undergraduate degree in soil science and a masters degree in environmental policy, he lived overseas for five years running large-scale farms or researching start-up farm export operations. Unhappy with the job prospects, he wrote a business plan to start the Denver microbrewery. He raised money, rezoned the building, and installed the equipment. The first brew was in May 1994. His beers quickly earned praise for their thoughtful balance, including the Denver Pale Ale, St. Bridget's Porter, and the much stronger Hibernation Ale, at times described as an old ale and others as a strong ale.

The brewery has expanded several times since it opened. In 2007, Great Divide renovated the building to include a taproom so that beer tourists could sample the widening range of beers it now offers right at the brewery. **SH**

Tasting notes

Plenty of noticeable chocolate and spice early on, plus a good roasty character (both nuts and hints of coffee beans) on the nose and in the mouth. Caramel and dark fruit flavors, as well as their sweetness, are nicely balanced by an earthy, husky mouthfeel.

Hightail Ale

Mountain Goat Brewery | www.goatbeer.com.au

Country of origin Australia
First brewed 1997
Alcohol content 4.5% abv
Serving temperature 46°F, 8°C

It has only been in the last thirty years that Australians have had access to beers other than icy cold pilsner derivatives (apart from the odd stout). For many, their exclusive relationship with this style of beer was a product of necessity and ignorance, rather than any genuine selection based on merit. There are still those who remember the dark days of the 1980s, when most pubs had one or two beers on tap, and it was considered a scandal among your mates if you selected the one that was from interstate. This was especially so if you were "shouting" pitchers for sharing. Looking back, it is little wonder that the focus on Australian beer drinking has until recently been on the culture and rituals of mateship rather than the presentation and flavor of the beer.

Those who did have a wider perspective had either drunk beer overseas or were home-brewers. Between them, the two founders of Mountain Goat Brewery have engaged in both activities. Dave Bonighton was brewing in his Melbourne backyard in the early 1990s when he received a postcard from Cam Hines, who was backpacking in Canada. Hines's beer experiences had been a revelation and his postcard suggested that they start their own brewery.

By all accounts the early years were very difficult, with Hines and Bonighton (and their mates) drinking most of the Hightail Ale that they managed to get publicans to stock. Over time though, the food and wine savvy Melbourne drinkers have warmed to this locally produced amber ale, and it has now firmly established its place as a Victorian icon. **DD**

Tasting notes

Hightail Ale announces its presence with a strong, creamy head and deep copper exterior while lightly emitting an aroma of floral hops and sweetness. A well-balanced caramel malt flavor and a refreshing finish follows. This ale is perfect with braised short ribs.

Hitachino Nest Beer XH

Kiuchi Brewery | www.kodawari.cc

Country of origin Japan
First brewed 1997
Alcohol content 8.3% abv
Serving temperature 54°F, 12°C

The name XH stands for "extra high" and reflects the high alcohol content of this rich and flavorful beer, which is brewed in the style of a strong Belgian ale. XH begins with pale, Munich, and crystal malt, and is fermented with a Belgian high-alcohol yeast, similar to those used in abbey beers, which also contributes a strong, sweet aroma. Chinook hops are used for bittering and Styrian Golding for aroma. Brewmaster Koichi Taka explains that since the flavor changes as the beer ages, it is difficult to explain when it should be consumed. He also says that the sheer quantity of malt used, roughly 1.5 times more than conventional beers, makes the beer difficult to brew, particularly during the sparging stages. Owing to the higher alcohol, the head is smaller and dissipates more quickly. However, high alcohol allows it to be aged longer, up to five years in ideal storage cases. A special version in which the beer is aged for six months in oak casks before bottling is produced for the U.S. market.

The creation of XH by Kiuchi is a reflection of the continued popularity of Belgian beers in Japan, which started in the mid-1980s in the major cities of the country. In central Tokyo alone, there are more than thirty Belgian beer specialty bars. The popularity of these beers in Japan can be explained by comparing them to sake, Japan's native fermented rice beverage that is both sweet and high in alcohol. XH is a favorite of those who enjoy strong Belgian beers and is good with many rich, meaty dishes. Brewmaster Taka notes that it is particularly popular with Westerners living in Japan, who frequently order it by the case. **BH**

Tasting notes

Hitachino Nest Beer is a deep reddish amber, with a light tan head. The aroma of sweet fruitcake with herbal hop notes greets you, while it has a rich and tangy malt profile with dried fruit sweetness. It is a bit like port wine, with a tangy, sweet finish.

Hobgoblin

Wychwood Brewery | www.wychwood.co.uk

Country of origin England
First brewed 1988
Alcohol content 4.5% abv
Serving temperature 52°F, 11°C

Did hobgoblins ever live in the medieval Wych Wood, a forest that borders the historic town of Witney in Oxfordshire? Nobody knows, but former head brewer Chris Moss certainly created a magical potion when he took some pale, crystal, and chocolate malts and mixed them with Fuggle and Styrian hops to make the first Hobgoblin. At the Wychwood Brewery in 1988, Moss was asked to brew a celebratory ale for the wedding of a local publican's daughter. It was a huge success, and as the bride and groom's health was toasted, the idea grew that this ale, a deliciously dark and rich brew, could become a commercial success.

Wychwood had a reputation for its quirky and imaginative packaging. Many of the beer labels took their inspiration and artwork from myths and legends associated with Wych Wood. The brewery gained a growing fan base, as keen on the beers as they were on the artwork of the labels. In 1996, the beer was bottled and sold in British supermarkets for the first time, at a time when most bottled beers were packaged and labeled in a very traditional way. However, the image of a hobgoblin roaming the Wych Wood captured the imagination of a new generation of beer drinkers who helped to make it the fifth best-selling bottled ale in the United Kingdom.

In recent years, the strength of the draft version of the beer has been reduced to 4.5 percent, a decision that has helped increase sales. The company is now owned by the national brewery Marston's, who says it has no plans to move the production away from the Witney home, close to the magical wood. **TH**

Tasting notes

Ruby red in color, Hobgoblin is a full-bodied beer with heaps of malt flavor. It has a delicious chocolate-toffee-malt character on the palate, which is balanced with a rounded moderate bitterness and an underlying fruitiness. The beer's finish is full of dark fruit.

Hobsons Postman's Knock

Hobsons Brewery | www.hobsons-brewery.co.uk

Country of origin England
First brewed 2006
Alcohol content 4.8% abv
Serving temperature 46°–50°F, 8°–10°C

Postman's Knock is a tribute beer. It is dedicated to the memory of Simon Evans, a writer and broadcaster who relocated to Shropshire in the years following World War I and immortalized the county in his later stories. Evans had been a casualty of the war. Gassed in the trenches, he was advised for his recuperation to seek the fresh, pure air of the countryside. He moved from Liverpool to the rural town of Cleobury Mortimer, where his job as a postman saw him walking many miles a day. Along the way, he encountered many colorful characters, people whom he placed, with all their charming eccentricities, into his engaging short stories and broadcasts in the 1930s.

Cleobury Mortimer is today home to Hobsons Brewery, which decided to honor Simon Evans with this beer in 2006. The business was founded by the Davis family in 1993 and has relocated and expanded since. The beer range incorporates a fine best bitter, a golden ale, an old ale, and Hobsons Mild, which won Champion Beer of Britain in 2007. Postman's Knock is also a mild, but a strong one with vanilla pods thrown into the copper to add creaminess to the coffee and chocolate notes developed by crystal and chocolate malts in the mash tun. Fuggle and Golding are the hops, but their impact is restricted to providing balancing bitterness rather than giving extravagant fruit flavors. Postman's Knock is a fine tribute to a man who helped place Cleobury Mortimer on the map, but it is also worthy in its own right. A small donation from every bottle sold also goes to provide funds for a children's hospice. **JE**

Tasting notes

A bright ruby mild, with chocolate, nut, coffee, and treacle in the nose. The gentle bitter taste is filled with smooth chocolate, biscuity malt, nuts, and freshly ground coffee beans. There are more nuts and coffee in the dry, pleasantly bitter finish.

Hoepfner Maibock

Privatbrauerei Hoepfner
www.hoepfner.de

Country of origin Germany
First brewed *ca.* 1920s
Alcohol content 6.6% abv
Serving temperature 46°F, 8°C

One of the most famous of all bock beers is the Maibock, a springtime treat that is only available between March and the start of May each year. This is a beer that acts as a bridge between the strong, dark doppelbocks of Lent and the lighter and friskier golden beers that are so welcome in the summer sun.

Hoepfner's contribution to the Maibock cause is one of the best known of its kind in Germany, and the beer won a gold medal at the World Beer Cup in 2008. This acclaim could have something to do with the care with which the brewery picks its raw materials. Barley is malted at Hoepfner's own maltings close to the brewery, while the beer is hopped with Tettnang (grown close to the Bodersee area) and Hallertau. Following fermentation, the beer is stored for up to twelve weeks in steel tanks before being sent out to eager Maibock drinkers. **WO**

Tasting notes
Deep gold in color with a strong aroma of malt followed by a well-balanced hop character. On the palate initial sweetness is tempered with a light, pleasant bitterness.

Hofbräu Maibock

Staatliches Hofbräuhaus in München
www.hofbraeu-muenchen.de

Country of origin Germany
First brewed 1614
Alcohol content 7.2% abv
Serving temperature 41°–54°F, 5°–12°C

The Staatliches Hofbräuhaus was founded in 1589 by Wilhelm V, Duke of Bavaria, the brewery founder who imported beer (what today is called bockbier) from Einbeck. His son Maximilian I preferred Weissbier, but in 1614, brewmaster Elias Pichler decided that brewing only dark and Weissbier was not enough—something stronger had to be added. He unveiled a new beer: Maibock, a Bavarian interpretation of a bock beer.

Some 200 years later, at the festival to celebrate the marriage of Prince Ludwig of Bavaria and Therese von Sachsen-Hildburghausen, the brewer of the now-royal Hofbräuhaus wanted to make something special for the occasion. That beer (and event) became known as Oktoberfestbier. In 1896, after several hundred years in the same location, a new brewhouse was built and occupied. After near-destruction in World War II, the brewery was rebuilt and still stands today. **RP**

Tasting notes
Somewhat dark—near copper—with a small white head. The aroma is malty with some fruit notes. The taste is quite malty though well balanced, closing with some bitterness.

A vintage color print of Munich's celebrated Hofbräuhaus during Oktoberfest. ➡

Hoftrol

Brouwerij 't Hofbrouwerijke
www.thofbrouwerijke.be

Country of origin Belgium
First brewed 2005
Alcohol content 6.2% abv
Serving temperature 54°F, 12°C

There is much local pride in this small brewery. Jef Goetelen opened 't Hofbrouwerijke in 2005, and the brewery and its beers have steadily grown in quality and production. 't Hofbrouwerijke translates into English as "The Little Garden Brewery," a name that refers to the small garden in Goetelen's backyard.

Most of the beer names begin with the prefix "hof," which can either mean garden or courtyard in Dutch. Hoftrol is an amber-colored brew of medium strength that has a mild sourness and bitter character, due to the use of *Brettanomyces* yeast strains and fine hopping. Trappist beer lovers may find that it reminds them of a certain brew of high regard originating in the Luxembourg Province. Goetelen brews beers that he enjoys drinking, such as Orval, which is loved by him and many others. Like Orval, Hoftrol is unfiltered, unpasteurized, and refermented in the bottle. **CC**

Tasting notes
Hazy amber red brew that pours with a big tan head. Aroma is fruity, yeasty, and malty, with definite Brettanomyces notes. Flavor is malty, mildly sour, woody, with notes of apples.

Hog Heaven

Avery Brewing Company
www.averybrewing.com

Country of origin United States
First brewed 1998
Alcohol content 9.2% abv
Serving temperature 55°F, 13°C

The notion of what a barleywine should taste like has been reinvented many times since San Francisco's Anchor Brewing revived the style with its Anchor Foghorn. In retrospect, Avery co-founder Adam Avery might not have included the words "Barleywine-Style Ale" on his label, but in 1998, it seemed appropriate. "Now most people want to call it a double IPA," Avery says. "Back then I'd never heard the term 'double IPA.'"

Avery wanted to make an aromatic beer using not too much crystal malt. On the hop front, he liked Columbus, a high-alpha hop that was still relatively new in 1998; it is rich in piney aromas although a little coarse. He uses only Columbus in brewing Hog Heaven, pumping enough into the recipe to finish with a calculated 100-plus IBUs, and the malts are two-row barley and caramel. The beer improves with age and is cellarable for three years. **SH**

Tasting notes
A blast of citrus (particularly grapefruit) on the nose is quickly followed by sweet notes of cotton candy. There is a menagerie of fruit on the palate, complex and layered. Cleverly bitter.

Hop Rod Rye

Bear Republic Brewing
www.bearrepublic.com

Country of origin United States
First brewed 2000
Alcohol content 8% abv
Serving temperature 50°F, 10°C

From the time its Healdsburg brewpub opened in 1996, Bear Republic started earning a reputation for beers that were rich in hop flavor as well as possessing no small measure of bitterness.

Perhaps not surprisingly, Hop Rod Rye defies categorization. At 8 percent abv and with more than 90 IBUs, it is somewhere between an India Pale Ale and a double IPA. However, there is also 20 percent rye in the grist, which adds a rich, bready texture. Brewing beers with rye is particularly difficult because, like wheat, rye has no husk. It grows thick during mashing and can turn rock hard if a brewer is not careful. The brewers at Bear Republic, though, seem to be comfortable using the grain because they've also made a beer, not nearly as potent at 5 percent abv, with 100 percent rye malt. The brewpub celebrated its tenth anniversary in 2006 and also opened a separate production brewery. **SH**

Tasting notes
Bright piney, citrus hops and spicy notes on the nose. The dark bready character blends smoothly with citrusy hop flavors on the palate, while there is a powerful bitter bite in the finish.

Hopleaf Extra

Simonds Farsons Cisk
www.farsons.com

Country of origin Malta
First brewed 2006
Alcohol content 5% abv
Serving temperature 46°–50°F, 8°–10°C

In the 1880s, British brewer H. and G. Simonds of Reading set up business on Malta to bottle beer that had been brewed in England. Brewing began on the island in the 1920s, with the current brewery being constructed in 1946. Simonds Farsons Cisk continues to produce a range of dry, hoppy beers bearing the Hopleaf name.

For years the brewery's ales were produced the English way, in open-topped square fermenters, but in 1998, closed conical ones were installed. As Malta has no tradition of growing hops and barley, all the ingredients for these English-style beers are imported. Hopleaf Extra was introduced in 2006—a stronger companion to its sibling Hopleaf, which is a rather modest 3.8 percent in alcohol. Hopleaf Extra has a strong, fresh character and is robust enough to be chilled, which is essential on an island where the summertime temperatures can soar. **TH**

Tasting notes
An English-style strong pale ale. Challenger and Target hops produce a beer of great intensity and complexity, with overlays of citrus flavors giving way to a sudden dryness.

Hövels Original

Hövels Hausbrauerei | www.hovels-hausbrauerei.de

Country of origin Germany
First brewed 1893
Alcohol content 5.5% abv
Serving temperature 44°–48°F, 7°–9°C

This reddish-colored beer appears to combine the qualities of many styles, and so it is fitting that it is the sole beer on the beverage list of the union of German wine sommeliers. Furthermore, it is perhaps the most elaborate creation of Germany's former "beer capital," Dortmund. Situated in the Ruhr, the coal and steel region, Dortmund's big breweries quenched the thirst of the miners and workers who labored there. The main product since the 1850s was a pale lager, which became known as Dortmunder Export because of its success beyond the Ruhr boundaries.

Brauerei von Hövel, Thier and Company was a medium-sized lager brewery of that period, whose new owner in 1889 invested in the most up-to-date technology, such as refrigerating machines and coppers with an accurate temperature control. Thus it was able to mash after the infusion method, a routine process today, but at that time an innovation. As was also unusual in those times, in 1893, it began producing a second brand. While the Export remained the workers' beverage, Bitterbier, as Hövels was called back then, was intended to answer a demand for more ambitious beers. A mixture of four malts, it is complemented by Hallertau hops.

The beer lost favor after World War I, but was reintroduced in 1984. Today, it is produced in the Dortmunder Actien-Brauerei plant that belongs to the Radeberger group. In 2009, builders tore down the historic Hövel, Thier and Company brewery, with only the Hövels Hausbrauerei brewpub surviving—and, most importantly, the unique Hövels Original. **SK**

Tasting notes

Light brown with a red hue and creamy beige head. This beer offers a citrus fruit nose with hints of caramel and breadlike aromas. On the palate, expect dry, bready, and caramel flavors accompanied by a fresh bitterness. The finish is clean, velvety, dry, and bitter.

Humulus Ludicrous

Half Pints Brewing Company | www.halfpintsbrewing.com

Country of origin Canada
First brewed 2007
Alcohol content 8% abv
Serving temperature 46°F, 8°C

Although the region grows a considerable amount of the barley used to craft beers, the Canadian Prairies have not proven to be fertile ground for breweries. Since the Big Rock Brewery opened in 1984, there have been few successful brewery start-ups in Alberta (save for Wild Rose and Alley Kat); Saskatchewan has witnessed a boom in largely forgettable brewpubs; and Manitoba, well, the easternmost province on the Prairies has been a bit of a desert for craft beer. Until, that is, David Rudge headed to Winnipeg in order to start Half Pints Brewing. In so doing, he not only brought a new beer aesthetic, but he also added a wonderful note of irreverence to the local beer scene.

Manitoba had seen very little of craft brewing, or brewing in general, for that matter. Both Molson and Labatt closed operations in the province in 1998, leaving only the Fort Garry Brewing Company as a provider of locally brewed beer. The young craft brewery was joined by two others the following year, but both struggled to survive into the new millennium, along with one ultimately ill-fated brewpub. Into this tumultuous market, Half Pints was born.

Perhaps it is Rudge's sense of humor that keeps the company afloat, evident in brand names such as Little Scrapper IPA—presumably a self-reference for the height-challenged Rudge—and Weizen Heimer. But more likely it is the brewer's faith in the "If I brew it, they will come" ethic, which has resulted in the creation of numerous palate-challenging beers, such as the big-bodied, barleywine-style Burley Wine and the seasonal double IPA, Humulus Ludicrous. **SB**

Tasting notes

A big hoppy beer, Humulus Ludicrous starts with a perfumey aroma holding notes of burned orange peel. In the body, it carries plenty of hoppiness on a solidly malty base, ending in a modestly bitter, toffee-accented finish. Strong yet subtle.

India Pelican Ale

Pelican Pub & Brewery
www.pelicanbrewery.com

Country of origin United States
First brewed 1997
Alcohol content 7.5% abv
Serving temperature 44°–50°F, 7°–10°C

India Pelican Ale was first brewed as a seasonal beer. After the second batch was brewed a year later, demand for it was so overwhelming that India Pelican Ale was moved into regular production.

At this time, brewer Darron Welch got feedback from customers who wanted the IPA to benefit from even more hops. Welch had recently engaged the services of an outside laboratory to help to maintain quality and consistency in his beers, and he learned through them that the actual bitterness of India Pelican Ale was substantially lower than he had designed it to be. "So my customers were right!" Welch says, and he began adding more hops to the beer batch by batch to slowly bring up the actual specification of the beer to the intended levels. "And a funny thing happened. The more hops I added, the faster the beer sold." The IPA reached its current specifications by late 2003. **LMo**

Tasting notes
Flavors of pine, lemon, grapefruit, orange, and even pineapple dance gracefully with caramel and malt notes. The finish is punctuated with bright, crisp, citrusy bitterness.

IPA Samuraj

Pivovar Kocour Varndsorf
www.pivovar-kocour.cz

Country of origin Czech Republic
First brewed 2008
Alcohol content 4.8% abv
Serving temperature 48°F, 9°C

The Czech Republic's burgeoning craft breweries still remain largely focused on traditional pale and dark lager styles. But Pivovar Kocour has earned a name for a more innovative lineup, offering several remarkable ales, many of which are developed with guest brewers.

Perhaps the most remarkable is the IPA Samuraj, a U.S.-style India Pale Ale guest brewed by Japan's itinerant brewmaster Toshi Ishii. The combination of a Japanese brewer and U.S. hops might sound unusual, but Ishii spent several years at San Diego's Stone Brewing Company before moving on to brew his own U.S.-style craft beers at Japan's Yo-Ho Brewing Company. His IPA Samuraj is produced from Bohemian pale malt. Centennial, Amarillo, and Columbus hops are used, along with a top-fermenting yeast of the California Ale strain. The result is a very American style of pale ale, with nary a Japanese or Czech influence in sight. **ER**

Tasting notes
Big, citrus-scented hop aroma, though the image of its clear deep gold is equally arresting. Despite the intense hoppiness, this is an elegant, well-balanced beer.

Iron Duke

Wellington County Brewery
www.wellingtonbrewery.ca

Country of origin Canada
First brewed 1986
Alcohol content 6.5% abv
Serving temperature 50°F, 10°C

In the mid-1980s, three breweries vied to become the first modern craft brewery in the province of Ontario. Wellington County came in third, opening in the fall of 1985. Of the trio, and the dozen or so small breweries that followed, the plans for Wellington were by far the most ambitious and optimistic: bringing cask-conditioned ale to a marketplace that was awash in draft lagers. Things didn't work out quite that way.

Publicans did not rush to Wellington in search of their cask ale, and so the brewery had to develop contingency plans. The solution was to sell the beer in 34-ounce (1-l) plastic bottles. Over time, new brands were added to the brewery's portfolio, including the winter warmer, Iron Duke. Although the company has remained small, particularly relative to its rapidly expanding co-pioneering breweries, it has developed a solid reputation and dedicated following. **SB**

Tasting notes
A malt-led ale, with a rich and toffeelike nose holding dried fruit notes and a winey body with chocolate caramel, stewed fruit, hints of raw cocoa, and just a touch of coffee on the finish.

J. W. Lees Bitter

J. W. Lees
www.jwlees.co.uk

Country of origin England
First brewed 1828
Alcohol content 4% abv
Serving temperature 54°F, 12°C

Manchester, England, has a dynamic brewing scene that threads back to the earliest days of the industrial revolution. Lees is one of the four breweries in the city that is left from that time. The company can trace its roots back to 1828, although it did not become J. W. Lees until 1876. However, it is likely that Lees has always brewed a version of its dry clean pale bitter.

J. W. Lees Bitter is typical of beers from this region of England—where dryness and sweetness vie for attention on the palate. It is a pale amber beer, with a malty and fruity aroma, a distinctive malty taste, and a fresh finish. Not surprisingly, it is the brewery's most popular beer and it is sold in every one of its 170 pubs.

The beer is marvelous with food such as traditional Lancashire hotpot or crumbly Lancashire cheese, with the creamy, nutty flavors of the cheese marrying well with the fruity, sweetness of the beer. **TH**

Tasting notes
An amber and copper-colored bitter. It has multiple layers of sweet maltiness and a fruity, lemon, citrus finish. It is very dry. Its strength makes it a perfect session beer.

James Squire Golden Ale

Malt Shovel Brewery | www.malt-shovel.com.au

Country of origin Australia
First brewed 2005
Alcohol content 4.5% abv
Serving temperature 39°–44°F, 4°–7°C

The quintessential image of Australian beer is a round of icy cold glasses of lager being consumed by a group of mates in an outdoor, sun-drenched setting. While not all beer is drunk this way Down Under, it is true that Australia's climate has driven certain behavior and preferences in its beer drinkers. The long hot summers and mild winters did not do the heavy, traditional beers of the Mother Country any favors, and Australia embraced the pilsner-style lager almost a century before England gave it a second look.

It is likely that this is why the craft beers of Australia still represent a small fraction of the volume of crisp, refreshing lagers that are consumed by Australians each year. Another factor at play is the important role of beer in the rituals of mateship, which are intended to reinforce the bond between the drinkers over an extended period. For many Australians engaging in this tradition, sessionability is an even more important quality than refreshment.

It is perhaps for these reasons that Golden Ale (Australia's answer to English summer ales) is the most popular of the James Squire range. The beer has all the flavor and aroma of a craft beer, while retaining the drinkability that many Australians cherish. Chuck Hahn of the Malt Shovel Brewery used the ale yeast from its popular Amber Ale but fermented it at slightly reduced temperatures and used 30 percent wheat malt to produce a tartness on the finish more like the dry finish of a lager. This delightful hybrid is also popular with Australian women, who enjoy the pleasant tropical fruit aroma and mild bitterness. **DD**

Tasting notes

The orange amber color of this beer will sparkle in the sunshine in which it is intended to be consumed. Take the time to enjoy the tropical fruit aroma on the nose before quenching your thirst with this mildly bitter, highly sessionable ale.

James Squire Original Amber Ale

Malt Shovel Brewery | www.malt-shovel.com.au

Country of origin Australia
First brewed 1998
Alcohol content 5% abv
Serving temperature 44°F, 7°C

Australia is not known for its brown ales, although the style was popular back in the time when James Squire (the brewer that the beers from Malt Shovel Brewery are named for) was still alive. James Squire was transported to Australia as a convict in 1788 as part of the First Fleet. At that time, rum was the favored drink (and even the unofficial currency) of the colony, however, it was regarded by government officials as being destructive and corrupting. It was for this reason that, possibly for the first and last time in Australian history, the brewing and consumption of beer was officially encouraged.

James Squire was one of the first to take up the challenge, commencing brewing in the 1790s. This was not a simple endeavor, with Australia's long hot summers, wild yeasts, and a lack of basic ingredients making the brewing of quality beer difficult. However, James Squire persisted and in 1806 was awarded a cow from the governor's herd for being the first in the colony to successfully grow hops.

The Original Amber Ale is said to be a tribute to the brown ale James Squire would have brewed for his fellow convicts and free settlers. It is likely though that his beer would have been a lot thicker than the modern version and certainly unfiltered. The real appeal of the present-day version is that it is complex while being accessible. For many Australians, the Original Amber Ale is a first step in a broader move from an exclusive relationship with crisp pilsner derivatives to a more considered selection of beers of varying complexity and styles. **DD**

Tasting notes

Once poured, a thick foamy head should envelop a nut brown beer giving off aromas suggestive of the caramel, malt sweetness to follow on the palate. Surprisingly refreshing, the lingering finish perfectly complements Italian meat dishes.

Jenlain Ambrée

Brasserie Duyck | www.duyck.com

Country of origin France
First brewed 1968
Alcohol content 7.5% abv
Serving temperature 43°–46°F, 6°–8°C

Take a trip through northern France and you are in beer country—from the Channel coast to its eastern border, in this region Bacchus gives way to Jean Barleycorn with the world-renowned bières de garde. Travel to the small village of Jenlain and you will see Brasserie Duyck (pronounced *dweek*), long considered to be the brewery that kicked off the whole bières de garde revival with its pioneering Ambrée. This was a rugged and rustic beer that has been packaged in corked and wire-fastened champagne bottles since 1950 (though it is also available in conventional bottles). It was sold as "Old Beer" then, but in 1968, Robert Duyck made the decision that would change the brewery's fortunes and named the beer after the village in which he brewed.

Just as French brewing seemed about to throw in the towel and capitulate to cold-fermenting lager styles in the 1970s, students in the city of Lille made a cult out of this top-fermented amber-colored ale. "It was the beginning of a lift in sales," says brewery boss Raymond Duyck, who is the fourth generation of the family to brew, a line that started with his great-grandfather in Dunkirk and came to Jenlain in the 1920s.

The current brewery is a modern, slick operation, with mechanization at the fore of things: bottles whiz about on conveyor belts, packaging emblazoned with the brewery's logo is tucked around packs of bottles, and robotic arms shift pallets of beers around the bottling hall. Meanwhile, in the maturation room, tanks of Jenlain's Ambrée (as well as the brewery's other beers) sleep the sleep of the just, keeping faith with an older way of brewing. **ATJ**

Tasting notes

Jenlain's Ambrée has what is considered to be the classic bière de garde profile. It is amber in color and has an aromatic and earthy nose. On the palate, it is spicy, herbal, and smooth with an earthy undercurrent before its bighearted, malt-accented finish.

Jenlain Noël

Brasserie Duyck | www.duyck.com

Country of origin France
First brewed 1950
Alcohol content 6.8% abv
Serving temperature 48°F, 9°C

Christmas beers became a tradition in northern France in the years after World War II. They were usually produced as a seasonal gift for a brewery's regular customers. Given that the weather was colder and drinkers needed something warming, these beers were darker and stronger in alcohol content. Most breweries of this French beery heartland have stuck to this admirable Yuletide tradition, with examples including Cuvée de Noël from Brasserie Bailleux and Brasserie St.-Sylvestre's La Bière de Noël—both of them over 7 percent abv. Jenlain's Bière de Noël is no different, a spicy souped-up version of the same brewery's Ambrée with a blend of aromatic Alsace and Hallertau hops and a malting regime that coaxes the best characteristics out of three varieties: Plaisant, Cambri, and Prisma.

When Léon Duyck got brewing off to a great start in 1900, passing it down through the generations seemed natural. Now, Raymond Duyck (Léon's great-grandson) is at the helm, and the reputation of the brewery continues to soar with successful new brands, such as Jenlain Blonde, being introduced and the brewing plant undergoing much needed modernization. Further investment in 2007 replaced the brewery's spartan appearance with stained glass windows and an attractive courtyard. As Christmas draws near, there's no better place to enjoy the annual treat of Bière de Noël than on tap in a bar in Jenlain. Once inside, drinkers are faced with an array of beers, so if you ask for a Jenlain, the likely response will be "which one." Come December, it's got to be Noël. **AG**

Tasting notes

Deep copper in color with an impressive head. Some earthy hop on the aroma overtaken by spice and herb nuances. The palate is fruity and malty before a spice hop character builds up along with an alcohol warmth. Alternately floral and caramel on the finish.

John Barleycorn Barleywine Ale

Mad River Brewing Company | www.madriverbrewing.com

Country of origin United States
First brewed 1991
Alcohol content 9% abv (but varies slightly)
Serving temperature 55°F, 13°C

Blue Lake, California, is a small town of just over 1,000 people located in the idyllic beauty of Humboldt County in the northern part of the state. There, in 1989, near the north fork of the Mad River, Bob Smith founded Mad River Brewing, realizing a dream he'd held since the 1970s. His first beer was Steelhead Extra Pale Ale, which is still the brewery's flagship.

In 1991, Mad River began brewing a winter warmer for the holidays, a traditional barleywine-style ale. As it says on the bottle, the beer is "brewed to celebrate the joy of the harvest", and traditionally it is released during the harvest moon, which is the full moon nearest to the autumnal equinox. The name John Barleycorn is based on an old English folksong from the 16th century. John Barleycorn is the personification of barley who is attacked and made to suffer indignities and eventually death. These correspond roughly to the stages of barley growing and cultivation. After John Barleycorn's death, he is resurrected as beer, bread, and whiskey.

Each year, local artist Janis Taylor creates a new woodcut label based on the tale of John Barleycorn. In the early years, new spices were added to the beer. In 1991, molasses, anise, and honey were used; the next year, ginger-root and honey. Since 1998, 100 percent organic malt has been part of the recipe, with only the hops changing each year along with small variations to the brewing process. The beer is brewed in ten-barrel quantities and because of its strength can be laid down and aged. The 2007 version won a gold medal at the Great American Beer Festival. **JB**

Tasting notes

A generous tan head and deep amber color flecked with red presents an enticing beginning for the 2008 version. The nose is all malty sweetness, but the flavors are warming with a wonderful subtle spiciness. Mouthfeel is thick and chewy, and the spicy finish lingers long.

Julebuk

Søgaards Bryghus | www.soegaardsbryghus.dk

Country of origin Denmark
First brewed 2007
Alcohol content 6.3% abv
Serving temperature 46°F, 8°C

When craft brewing finally arrived in the land of Carlsberg, it did so with a vengeance. It mushroomed from handfuls of breweries to dozens and then to a number somewhere well above a hundred (it's hard to get a precise number at any time because new breweries open regularly). This wave of craft brewing even made it to the northern port town of Aalborg, much better known for aquavit than for ale and lager.

The man behind the beer in this case is Claus Søgaards, who was raised in Aalborg and trained first as a butcher, then a chef, and finally a brewer. In 2004, he and his wife and partner, Lisa, set up their brewery on the town square known as C. W. Obels Plads. As both of them had extensive backgrounds in the hospitality trade, a 125-seat restaurant and 50-seat bar was also incorporated into the facility. Julebuk is the brewery's Christmas beer, named both for an old dressing-up game and the German style of beer known as bock, or *buk* in Danish. Unlike its Teutonic counterparts, however, this bock is seasoned with Christmas spices, something that would never be allowed in the land of the Reinheitsgebot.

In 2008, Søgaards made news in advance of the first ever European Beer festival by introducing what was at the time the world's most expensive beer, Egtvedpigens Bryg. It is based on a recipe developed through the analysis of a bowl unearthed from a grave dated to 1357 B.C., which also contained the bones of the "Egtved Girl" for whom the beer is named. It sold for 2,021 Danish kroner per bottle, which at the time converted to more than U.S. $400. **SB**

Tasting notes
Deep brown with a nose of sherry and port wine, accented by allspice, this sweet bock starts with a light fruitiness before developing chocolate, cinnamon, dried fruit, and vanilla notes and drying to a warming finish. A marvelous winter lager whether fresh or aged.

Krampus Imperial Helles Lager

Southern Tier Brewing | www.southerntierbrewing.com

Country of origin United States
First brewed 2008
Alcohol content 9% abv
Serving temperature 48°F, 9°C

Ah, Christmas. Brewers have made special beers to commemorate the holiday for centuries: strong, often spiced brews whose labels frequently depict the joy and innocence of this child fantasy.

Meet Krampus. He's the fanged, goat-horned creature of old German myth who accompanies St. Nick and stuffs naughty kiddies into a bag and drags them off to the underworld. Krampus is the anti-Claus, the dark embodiment of evil who would come down your chimney with a bound—if *The Night Before Christmas* had been penned by Wes Craven.

Krampus is also the beer that the warped characters at Southern Tier Brewing in New York have chosen as their holiday treat. It's an especially fitting name, for the brewers have taken a completely innocent beer style, German Helles, and twisted it into its evil twin: Imperial Helles. Yes, it's a contradiction of terms: an amped-up mild lager. Brewer "Phin" DeMink said that he chose the style because the name, Helles (which means "bright" in German), seemed appropriate for a hellish character. Despite its high gravity, Krampus's Helles roots are properly evident. The Munich malt is both biscuity and lightly sweet; the Chinook and Willamette hops provide a balanced, fruity finish. The cold lagering seems to have mellowed the beer just a bit, giving it an almost quaffable feel.

But isn't that the true sign of the evil? Rather than storming in like a fire-breathing malt bomb, Krampus is clever and subtle; you won't know what hit you until they carry you off in a bag. **DR**

Tasting notes

Reddish amber with a grapefruitlike nose and a touch of honey and clover. Rich caramel notes emerge swiftly and threaten to overtake the palate, only to be balanced by exceptionally resiny hops. Never overbearing, its medium body finishes sweet and satisfying.

Krinitsa Porter

Krinitsa | www.krinitsa.by

Country of origin Belarus
First brewed 2008
Alcohol content 8% abv
Serving temperature 46°F, 8°C

Belarus is a new country to appear on the radar of beer drinkers. Despite the fact that distilled spirits have always been secondary to beer (it is still legal to have your own still), there has been brewing in the region for the past two centuries.

Krinista is a fairly new kid on the brewing block, having been set up in an industrial area on the outskirts of Minsk in 1973, with the first beers flowing out two years later. It is the largest brewery in Belarus and is jointly owned by the state. In 2006, Baltic Beverage Holdings and Carlsberg looked set to purchase a 51-percent share in the brewery, but Belarus's controversial leader President Lukashenko stepped in to foil the move.

Krinista Porter is a recent addition to the brewery's portfolio, although a beer of the same name was first brewed a few years previously (and indeed won an award in 2004). This, however, is a totally different brew that was intended for Christmas 2008; it is said that the brewing team was unhappy with the result so they brewed it again—with new labels. The result is a strong and dark variation on the Baltic Porter theme: just right for winter nights when the wind blows and the rain comes down like sharp pine needles.

It's not surprising to learn that Krinista's best-selling beer is a pilsner, but what is slightly different is that it is called Aleksandria and supposed to have been brewed for and named for President Lukashenko. Whether this was produced as a "thank you" for his intervention in the dispute with Baltic Beverage Holdings is not known. **ATJ**

Tasting notes

In the glass, amber beneath a caramel-white head; nose is earthy with hints of citrus and even faint scents of the hop store. On the palate, licorice, dark malts, treacle toffee, cough mixture, and alcohol turn up; it has a very spirituous character, and there is a lasting medicinal finish.

La Bavaisienne

Brasserie Theillier
www.bottledbeer.co.uk

Country of origin France
First brewed *ca.* 1980s
Alcohol content 7% abv
Serving temperature 48°F, 9°C

Traditional northern French bières de garde came into their own in the 1980s with a new surge of interest among the farmhouse producers and consumers. La Bavaisienne Ambrée was one of the beers that benefited from this curiosity in what had been seen as an unfashionable old style of beer. It is brewed using one malted barley, Escourgeons, which is a winter variety grown locally, and a single hop variety, Alsace, which is prized for its spicy and herbal aroma qualities. The brew draws favorable comparisons with strong, well-hopped British cask-conditioned ales.

The coolness of northern France means that the fertile land is perfect for beer's raw ingredients: cereals and hops. Theillier is reputed to be the oldest brewery in the Nord Pas-de-Calais region, and it has survived turbulent times in an area that once supported 575 breweries. Today, there are fewer than thirty. **AG**

Tasting notes
Dark red to amber in color, it has a good fruity and herbal malt nose and inviting winelike suggestions. Citrus, grass, and bready yeast enter the flavor profile in a bittersweet surge.

La Binchoise Spéciale Noël

Brasserie La Binchoise
www.brasserielabinchoise.be

Country of origin Belgium
First brewed 1993
Alcohol content 9% abv
Serving temperature 50°F, 10°C

Bruno De Ghorain has served as brewmaster at La Binchoise since 1989, when it opened in Binche. The brewery is a family affair: Bruno's cousin, Benoit de Ghorain, handles sales and marketing, and helps with brewing as well. Spéciale Nöel, which is labeled as Reserve Speciale for export to the United States and the United Kingdom, is the strongest and most assertive beer in the brewery's line-up. With the increasing popularity of Christmas beers in Belgium in the 1990s, La Binchoise saw this beer as a logical extension of their product range. As the name suggests, it began as a seasonal brew but is now available all year around.

All La Binchoise beers are bottle conditioned, unfiltered, and unpasteurized, and some can be found on draft, too. The very hard water in the area is perfect for brewing many styles of Belgian ales, and Binchoise produces seven beers throughout the year. **CC**

Tasting notes
A chestnut-colored beer, with a pleasant fruity and spicy character. Notes of nutmeg and cinnamon are evident. A full-bodied, malty brew with a somewhat sweetish finish.

La Moneuse

Brasserie de Blaugies
www.brasseriedeblaugies.com

Country of origin Belgium
First brewed 1988
Alcohol content 8% abv
Serving temperature 43°F, 6°C

In the late 18th century, a bandit named Antoine-Joseph Moneuse led a gang who terrorized villagers across northern France Their fun ended in 1798 when authorities in Douai put them to the guillotine, but the highwayman's name lives on with this strong, dry blond ale made near the French border.

Marie-Noelle Pourtois, a descendant of Moneuse, started brewing at Blaugies in 1988. As farmhouse breweries go, this is the genuine article. The family still makes its world-class beers using a kit in the garage, and bottling takes place in the barn across the road. In theory, son Kévin has taken over brewing, but Marie-Noelle is rarely far from the kettle. Moneuse is ideal for sharing over a meal, offering honest flavors of cereals and noble hops. In good condition, it tastes like the brewers grew the ingredients themselves in the backyard and threw them fresh into the pot. **JS**

Tasting notes
An opaque light amber beer with a rocky white head and sticky Belgian lace. Smells hoppy and bready with some orange fruit esters in the background. Fairly dry on the finish.

La Trappe Dubbel

Bierbrouwerij de Koningshoeven
www.latrappe.nl

Country of origin Netherlands
First brewed 1982
Alcohol content 7% abv
Serving temperature 54°–61°F, 12°–16°C

Abdij Onze-Lieve-Vrouw van de Koningshoeven is the only Trappist brewery outside Belgium. In 1999, after the monks signed a production agreement with Bavaria, a commercial Dutch brewery that specializes in mass-market beers, the International Association of Trappists withdrew permission for Koningshoeven's beer to carry the association's logo. This logo is meant to designate a beer as an authentic Trappist product. The brewery continued labeling (minus the logo) their beers as Trappist regardless. In 2005, the agreement between the monks and Bavaria was modified so that the brewery could stand again as an officially recognized Trappist brewery.

The Dutch abbey has long outpaced its Belgian brothers in the commercialization of its beers. In the early 20th century, Koningshoeven produced many drinks in addition to beer and even bought several pubs. **RP**

Tasting notes
This beer differentiates itself from several Belgian Trappist dubbels by toning down the chocolate and coffee notes. It is sweeter on the palate with slight aromatic hop notes on the nose.

Lagunitas Brown Shugga

Lagunitas Brewing Company | www.lagunitas.com

Country of origin United States
First brewed 1996
Alcohol content 9.5% abv
Serving temperature 44°–50°F, 7°–10°C

Lagunitas founder Tony Magee describes Brown Shugga as a "strange and irresponsible beer." This seasonal ale was born as a result of a series of mishaps on the night shift back in 1996. "I got a call at home from the brewer, telling me that the original gravity of the Gnarleywine he was brewing was too low. I had miscalculated the recipe." This is a test of the skill and creativity of a brewmaster. "I told him to go to every grocery store in Petaluma and buy all the brown sugar that he could find and stick it into the kettle until he got the beer to the right strength. On Monday morning, I came into the brewhouse early and there were about 200 boxes of C and H Brown Sugar scattered on the floor." Progress was dicey in the fermenter, but after some weeks, a beautiful creature emerged from the aging tanks.

Sugar has a history in beer dating back to mid-19th-century England. Cheap sugar from the colonies and a few bad barley crops led to its adoption in beers such as India Pale Ales. Contrary to what one might expect, sugar thins out the body of a beer and makes it less sweet because sugar ferments completely, which is not the case with malt. It can serve to increase drinkability in strong beers such as Belgian dubbels and tripels, and that is the role it serves in Brown Shugga. Brown sugar contains molasses, and this adds a layer of flavor even as it lightens what would otherwise be quite a chewy beer.

By the way, if you know your Frank Zappa, you may have figured out that the quick-thinking salvage job that created this beer holds a secret message: Necessity really is the Mother of Invention. **RM**

Tasting notes

A complex nose of deep toasted notes and rich burned sugar aromas, along with some resiny hoppiness and pruney fruitiness. Sweet on the palate, complex fruity, malty, sugary flavors with some sharpness. Aftertaste similar, with some alcohol evident.

The C and H refinery in the small town of Crockett, California. ➡

Lagunitas Maximus

Lagunitas Brewing Company | www.lagunitas.com

Country of origin United States
First brewed 1996
Alcohol content 7.5% abv
Serving temperature 50°F, 10°C

The Lagunitas Maximus is one of the earliest known examples of an imperial, or double, IPA and has been in continuous production since it was first brewed in 1996. This may make it a contender for the oldest continuously brewed double IPA in the United States, or indeed the world. It was the fifth seasonal made by Lagunitas, only one of which it never made again. The Maximus proved so popular that when the season was over, Lagunitas kept brewing it and hasn't stopped yet.

It was originally going to be called "Hair of the Dog Ball Ale," which would have been in keeping with some other beers being made at the time: Hairy Eyeball and Eye of the Hairball. The next choice for a name was "Eye of the Dog," but eventually it was called "Maximus" instead. Lagunitas's brewmaster and founder Tony Magee originally created Maximus by taking his IPA recipe, which has since become the flagship beer, and increasing all of the raw materials by 35 percent. The hops used are Cascade, Centennial, Horizon, Liberty, and Willamette, all in the first edition and then used again for dry hopping, too.

The malt build includes two-row malt from Rahr, a touch of wheat malt, and, as Magee puts it, "a handful of crystal malt." He adds, "The mash temp is also a bit high so that there is a strong malt backbone to pile all of the hops against. I think it is called balance. Some think balance is overrated." The beer has never won any awards because Lagunitas has never entered it into any contests. In keeping with the overall ethos of the company, the beer speaks for itself. According to Lagunitas, "Beer speaks, people mumble." **JB**

Tasting notes

Bright amber in color, the Maximus wallops you on the nose with a big howitzer of hops. Strong citrus, grassy, and vegetal aromas dominate. Equally mammoth hop flavors are buoyed by a malt backbone that ultimately balances the beer. The finish is tart and lingers.

Le Merle

North Coast Brewing | www.northcoastbrewing.com

Country of origin United States
First brewed 2007
Alcohol content 7.9% abv
Serving temperature 39°–44°F, 4°–7°C

This beer started, like so many, as a one-off. "We had been wanting to do a saison for a while," says North Coast's president and brewmaster Mark Ruedrich. "So when Whole Foods approached us to do a twenty-fifth anniversary beer in 2006, we thought a farmhouse beer would work perfectly for them."

Saison is a complex style with obscure origins, but it seems to be most associated with the agricultural areas of Wallonia, or French-speaking Belgium. Pale, hazy, and hovering between weak and strong, the rustic charms of saison have been rediscovered over the last few years.

Like all saisons, Le Merle is a highly yeast-dependent beer. "Some of the yeast strains scared the hell out of us," says Ruedrich, referring to their odd behavior and strange ways in the brewery. "The one we use just percolates along, down, down, down." Ever keen to explore the fine points of beer balance, the crew at North Coast has recently been paying attention to the role of acidity in beer. "Our yeast creates a beer with a tang at the end, which allows us to play with the hop balance." The yeast contributes some lush pineapple fruitiness that is mixed in with similar tropical aromas from Simcoe hops. The base for the beer is nothing very exotic, just pilsner malt and a bit of sugar to lighten the body. All the magic is in the yeast and hops.

The beer is named for Ruedrich's wife, Merle, who "has toiled at my side for twenty odd years, while I got to do the fun stuff," says Ruedrich. "Honestly, I think I got off cheap for just naming a beer after her." **RM**

Tasting notes

Complex aroma of citrus, pineapple, and a touch of gumdrop (allspice) spiciness on the nose. Full bodied and very creamy on the palate, but with a bright tanginess that livens it up, it is all balanced by a soft bitterness. Long, spicy-fruity finish.

Leafer Madness

Beer Valley Brewing | www.beervalleybrewing.com

Country of origin United States
First brewed 2008
Alcohol content 9% abv
Serving temperature 50°F, 10°C

The one thing that people ask Beer Valley Brewing's owner and brewer Pete Ricks more than anything else is if Leafer Madness Double IPA is named for the cannabis exploitation film and cult classic *Reefer Madness*. It is not.

The moniker actually pays homage to a very dark time in the early days of Beer Valley's existence. It was 2007, and prices for hops had started to skyrocket thanks to a worldwide shortage. After many sleepless nights worrying about where he would find hops for his fledgling brewery, Ricks got a telephone call from a local hop farmer who said that they were going to have to plow under a large field of hops because some of the plants had been damaged in a nearby fire. The farmer told Ricks that he could have all the hops he could salvage before the equipment started to roll.

With a mighty storm brewing, Ricks grabbed some big boxes of plastic garbage bags and headed for the hop field 40 miles (64 km) away. "By this time, it was dark, and the storm had moved in," Ricks says. "So there I was, standing out there in a pile of hops up to my knees, in front of my truck with the headlights on, scooping up as many hops as I can into trash bags with a five-gallon bucket." He took the first load back to the brewery and returned for more. "When I had gathered as many bags as I could fit in my truck, I was sitting there thinking to myself that this was totally mad," he says. "Never did I imagine when I started this company that I'd be out in a driving rainstorm at night scooping up hops. That was really the beginning of the name Leafer Madness." **LMo**

Tasting notes

Brewed with a variety of hops, Leafer Madness is a hop bomb, but is still nicely balanced with a sturdy malt backbone. Earthy hops begin the dance with citrus and pine notes following. A pleasantly boozy aftertaste only adds to the enjoyment.

Left Hand Sawtooth Ale

Left Hand Brewing | www.lefthandbrewing.com

Country of origin United States
First brewed 1994
Alcohol content 4.8% abv
Serving temperature 54°F, 12°C

The story of how Left Hand Brewing got started in Colorado is similar to many told about the early days of U.S. craft brewing. Eric Wallace and Dick Doore met as cadets at the U.S. Air Force Academy in Colorado Springs in the early 1980s. Wallace went on to spend eight years in Italy and Turkey as a communications officer, meeting his Italian wife along the way. They moved to Colorado in 1993, by which time the craft-brewing movement was in full swing. Doore, meanwhile, earned a master's degree in mechanical engineering before heading to Colorado.

The pair soon began home-brewing together and were living in the town of Niwot—called after Chief Niwot, whose name translates to "Left Hand"—when they decided to start a microbrewery. They found a building nearby: a former sausage factory (the original mash tun sat over the pig-killing floor) that had sloped floors with drains perfect for a brewery.

Sawtooth Ale, based on one of Doore's favorite home-brew recipes, quickly established itself as a flagship beer. Although Longmont's glacier-melt soft water is ideal for brewing many styles of beer, the brewers harden it to simulate the water from Burton-on-Trent. Sawtooth is made with five malts and English hops. It is at its best when properly cask-conditioned. The brewery also makes a heavyweight version of the beer, although not regularly. Chainsaw Ale is packed with extra malts and hops, essentially making it a "double" at 9 percent alcohol. More suited for a snifter than a 20-ounce (59-cl) Nonic glass, it's rich with caramel, toffee, and dark cherry flavors. **SH**

Tasting notes

Pours bright amber with an off-white head. Lively floral nose includes sweet caramel notes. Caramel also blends with apple fruitiness on the palate, the flavors enhanced by a creamy mouthfeel. Hop bitterness is restrained but persistent and balancing.

Ley Line

Birrificio Bi-Du | www.bi-du.it

Country of origin Italy
First brewed 2005
Alcohol content 5% abv
Serving 50°–54°F, 10°–12°C

Bi-Du's founder Beppe Vento has no shortage of imagination when it comes to firing up his brewing kettle. Every year, he creates several different beers that provide fans with ample reason to try, and to buy, his brews. His choice of original ingredients is very open-minded. There is the beer Saltinmalto for instance. As a word, Saltinmalto is difficult to translate but think of it as a composition of "salt" and "malt"; with probably a teaspoon of black salt from Hawaii, this beer is personalized by Vento. He argues that salty food makes people thirsty, so with a salty beer you'll never stop drinking! Joking aside, maybe the real reason for this beer is that Vento had discovered the beer style Leipziger Gose, where salt goes into the brew.

Ley Line takes its name from a mystical theory created by English antiquarian (and brewer) Alfred Watkins at the end of the 19th century. The theory of ley lines supposes that lines of energy cross the earth and can be used to discover water, ancient sites, and even treasure, a theory that inspired Vento to produce a beer that crosses different beer cultures: England provides the malts and some hops; Belgium, some more malts and yeast; and Germany even more malts and hops. As for the Italian component, Vento added *corbezzolo* (strawberry tree or *Arbutus unedo*) honey to the recipe. **MM**

Tasting notes
Cloudy in the glass. Intriguing and delicate aroma, floral and fruity (apple). Well-measured body, elegant and persistent in the finish. The touch of honey is perceptible but not intrusive.

Liefmans Goudenband

Liefmans Brouwerij | www.liefmans.be

Country of origin Belgium
First brewed 1956
Alcohol content 8% abv
Serving temperature 48°–54°F, 9°–12°C

The origins of Liefmans go back as far as 1679. Since World War II, the brewery has had several owners: Sunderland brewery Vaux; then Belgolaise Investment; and, in 1990, the Riva brewing group, who decided that the age-old brewing equipment was beyond repair. It transferred brewing to its own Dentergem plant and kept the Schelde-side site as a lagering place.

Lagering is crucial for the Liefmans beers, as they have always proudly carried the caption "Provisiebier" (aging beer), whether on the label or, later, on the famous paper wrappers known as "pajamas." Goudenband, which uses several pale and dark malts, is lagered for a year before being blended with a younger beer to restart fermentation; this makes for a classical example of Flemish blended beer. Some batches are lagered for more than two years, and Goudenband is given a keeping date of ten years.

This century, Riva got into serious trouble, and its new management was the first to see the importance of the Liefmans heritage, changing the name to Liefmans Breweries. However, the Duvel-Moortgat group took over in 2008. Moortgat never made any secret of the fact that all it was interested in was the original Liefmans beers. It has reduced the number of beers produced to four, and added one new one. Goudenband is by far the strongest beer. **JPa**

Tasting notes
Roasted and sweet notes on the nose; a hint of earthy mushroom. Goudenband is pretty complex: young it has sweet, sourish, and roasted bitter notes.

The bottles are stored in crates before being individually wrapped in tissue paper. ➡

Ligera

Birrificio Lambrate | www.birrificiolambrate.com

Country of origin Italy
First brewed 2007
Alcohol content 5% abv
Serving temperature 43°F, 6°C

Birrificio Lambrate, which is also known as the "Skunky Pub," was the first brewpub to be established in Milan and was created in 1996 by friends Davide and Giampaolo Sangiorgi and Fabio Brocca. Although they only started brewing small amounts, solely for the pub, they had to grow quickly because the beer kept running out in a few days. Lambrate now produces a wide range of beers, which are found in its lively and atmospheric brewpub, as well as in several other discerning beer bars in Milan (such as Hop, a small, funky bar opposite the historic Rotonda della Besana).

Ligera is one of the latest "brewing ideas," and the name comes from the nickname of a local gangster who operated in the 1920s. Head brewer Fabio Brocca, working in tandem with assistant Stefano Di Stefano, decided that they wanted a sort of American pale ale, rich in hop flavor but still very easy to drink: a beer that would wipe out thirst on a hot summer day.

Ligera uses German malts, a British yeast, and different varieties of hops: just a drop of Cascade, lots of Chinook, mainly for the bitterness, plus Amarillo and Willamette. Bitter indeed, but not too much, the IBU count for Ligera is 47; strong, yes, but not enough to wipe the enamel off drinkers' teeth. There is also a final dry hopping of Amarillo and Willamette that can last for the two to three weeks that the beer sits maturing. Alhough this is a beer that plays on the hoppy profile, it is also easy to approach and drink. Sold mainly on draft at the Skunky Pub, Ligera is an ideal beer with which to start the night: cool and refreshing, just like Birrificio Lambrate. **MM**

Tasting notes

Pale amber color, lightly cloudy, white foam not too abundant. An intriguing aroma of fresh hops, citrus, and floral tones. Nice body with a pleasant return of sharp hoppiness that lasts long and creates the desire for another sip. A true thirst quencher.

Little Creatures Pale Ale

Little Creatures Brewery | www.littlecreatures.com.au

Country of origin Australia
First brewed 2000
Alcohol content 5.2% abv
Serving temperature 43°F, 6°C

Little Creatures Brewery was formed in 2000 after Phil Sexton, Nick Trimbole, and Howard Cearns lamented the state of the industry during the 1990s. To Cearns, it was a time when drinkers valued style over substance. For Sexton, there was unfinished business following the sale of his brewery to Carlton and United. It was a good match of skills. Sexton was a master brewer and founder of Matilda Bay Brewery. Cearns had a background in creative marketing in the beer industry. Along with funding from some university mates (and eventually Lion Nathan), the founders were in a good position to lead the second wave of Australia's microbrewery revolution.

What of the beer, however? At the time, apart from the odd skirmish, the preferred beers of Australians were icy cold, refreshing, and somewhat plain. The style that was exciting Sexton and Cearns (and, in time, much of the world) was the U.S. interpretation of traditional English India Pale Ale. It was a style Sexton could claim some credit for, having worked in the United States and been involved in the development of the famous BridgePort IPA.

Little Creatures put its own spin on it, of course, using a range of Australian malts to balance the frenzy of hops imported from the United States. Cearns came up with the brewery's name after reading about little creatures wandering from ale house to ale house in *The Hobbit* by J. R. R. Tolkien and thinking it sounded a little bit like fermenting yeast. It was not long before both brand and beer became well known to drinkers throughout Australia. **DD**

Tasting notes

Take the time to draw deeply from the hop-driven aromas of passion fruit, oranges, grapefruit, and lychee. Citrus and honey flavors should be balanced by a mild sweetness and a dry finish that lingers just long enough to complement your Bucatini all'Amatriciana.

Little Korkny Ale

Nørrebro Bryghus
www.noerrebrobryghus.dk

Country of origin Denmark
First brewed 2006
Alcohol content 12.25% abv
Serving temperature 50°–54°F, 10°–12°C

The Nørrebro Bryghus in Copenhagen turns out new beers at a remarkable rate. Since it opened in 2003, the brewery has won acclaim by taming the "wild" U.S. styles without losing drinkability or balance. Its success is in no small part down to the founder and brewmaster Anders Kissmeyer. He learned his trade as one of Carlsberg's "flying brewers," traveling to various countries to troubleshoot problems. It gave him an appreciation of British brewing and introduced him to the U.S. microbrewing revolution.

Little Korkny Ale is the first barleywine produced by Nørrebro Bryghus and is typical of the brewery's ability to mix complex flavors without compromising drinkability—a challenge in a 12 percent brew. Brewed with pale ale and crystal malts, it is aged in barrels for two years. In 2008, the beer won bronze in the Aged Beer category in the World Beer Cup. **AA**

Tasting notes
Dark, coppery brown beer with a rich aroma of caramel and dried fruits. The taste is hoppy, with more caramel and plum fruit, and a long warming aftertaste. Distinctly sweet.

Little Scotney Pale Ale

Westerham Brewery Co.
www.westerhambrewery.co.uk

Country of origin England
First brewed 2004
Alcohol content 4% abv
Serving temperature 54°F, 12°C

Once the hop garden of Britain, Kent has seen many crops replaced and its coned oast houses turned into weekend homes. In the golden age of British brewing, Scotney Castle, near Tunbridge Wells, was where the Fuggle family farmed the world-famous hop that now bears its name. The castle is now the only hop garden run by the National Trust, a conservation group.

Westerham Brewery created Little Scotney Pale Ale using Target hops from Scotney, and a percentage of the sale of each bottle is donated for reinvestment in the hop gardens. Generous doses are added late in the boil, with more added for dry hopping, producing an intense floral character. This beer is a hymn to the hop, not in an intense, hop-explosion way, but in that it evokes this miraculous plant as surely as if you had fresh hop flowers cupped in your hands. Hops are certainly center stage in this mouthwatering ale. **PB**

Tasting notes
Resiny, floral aroma of fresh hops on the nose. Sweet malt hits the palate first, opening up with a hint of light caramel. An explosion of floral sweetness before a long dry finish.

Mad Elf Ale

Tröegs Brewing
www.troegs.com

Country of origin United States
First brewed 2002
Alcohol content 11% abv
Serving temperature 52°F, 11°C

Tröegs Mad Elf Ale is a singular phenomenon in the eastern United States, attracting queues of anxious fans at local stores upon its arrival every autumn. Some of its most manic followers preorder as many as ten cases of the Christmas beer to cellar and ration out through the year. This is beer as liquid treasure.

Each season the tiny brewery increases its production, and every year it still manages to sell out before Christmas. Although cherries and honey certainly produce distinct flavors, the deeper character of this hugely flavored ale comes from neither of these ingredients. Instead, it's the Belgian yeast—a Duvel clone—that does the work, slowly fermenting over two months at a relatively high temperature to produce exceptional spiciness. Think pepper, clove, and ginger. Together, it's very reminiscent of fruitcake, or perhaps a glass of Malbec. **DR**

Tasting notes
The bright ruby color points clearly to the cherries added after fermentation. A fresh honey aroma hits the nose before spicy pepper and clove bite the tongue for a palate-cleansing finish.

Mad Hatter

New Holland Brewing Company
www.newhollandbrew.com

Country of origin United States
First brewed 1998
Alcohol content 5.25% abv
Serving temperature 36°–37°F, 2°–3°C

"This was the brewery's first dry-hopped beer, back in 1998," says New Holland's "beervangelist" Fred Bueltman. At the time, co-founder Brett VanderKamp had been experimenting with dry hopping, a technique of adding hops to the fermenter for aroma. The lightning-strike moment came when he dumped the hop cones loose into the tanks. The beer's aroma just jumped out of the glass after that.

India Pale Ales have a long history, and over the centuries the recipes have been the same: high-quality pale malt, perhaps a dash of other malts for character, and a boatload of the best hops that can be found, with a special emphasis on aroma. Mad Hatter fits into this mold, although, at 5.25 percent, it is light enough to be enjoyed a few pints at a time. This refreshing and balanced beer is versatile with foods. The brewery recommends it particularly with bitter salad leaves. **RM**

Tasting notes
Potent nose of citrusy and slightly resiny hops. Some bready maltiness, with vague fruit and honey notes. Softly malty on the palate, building to a long, characterful hoppy finish.

Magnumus Ete Tomahawkus ESB

Rock Art Brewery | www.rockartbrewery.com

Country of origin United States
First brewed 2006
Alcohol content 8% abv
Serving temperature 50°F, 10°C

Even if one chose to ignore the obligatory government advisory against drinking while pregnant, this bottle's label has enough warnings to scare off all but leather-livered beer drinkers. Its name sounds like a battle between bloody Roman gladiators. In bold letters it alerts: "EXTREME." And, if you missed that, it adds, "This ain't for no Momma's Boy or Daddy's Girl!"

Brewer Matt Nadeau chuckles at the cautionary language and explains, "Well, we wanted our regular customers to know that this beer is completely different from everything else we were making." Indeed, for the first several years after Rock Art began business in Vermont, it was known mainly for very competent but classical styles. Nadeau ran the one-man, small-batch brewery out of his basement, finishing long days by lugging filled kegs up a flight of stairs. His most "extreme" beer was Ridge Runner, an English-style barleywine that was 7.5 percent abv—a bit low by modern U.S. standards.

Moving into a larger facility allowed Nadeau to experiment with stronger brews. Magnumus Ete Tomahawkus ESB was the first of his Extreme series, an extra special bitter, squared: that is to say, double the malt bill, double the alcohol. The bitterness is way up there, too, thanks to an ample addition of bold Tomahawk hops. "I wanted to make an ESB-cubed, but I would've run into problems with distribution," Nadeau said, noting that local regulations required beers over 8 percent to be distributed in state-run stores. The limit has since been raised, but Nadeau is quite happy with leaving this decidedly extra special beer as is. **DR**

Tasting notes

Poured into a pint glass, the lightly orange/amber body creates a generous head of foam with a firm, enticing aroma of citrus. Some sweet, biscuitlike malt arrives on the palate first, but this is quickly swamped by pinelike hop notes. The finish is smooth and dry.

The Maharaja Imperial India Pale Ale

Avery Brewing Company | www.averybrewing.com

Country of origin United States
First brewed 2004
Alcohol content 10.2% abv
Serving temperature 44°–50°F, 7°–10°C

According to the dictionary, "Maharaja" is derived from two Sanskrit words: *mahat*, meaning "great" and *rajan*, meaning "king"—and much like a beloved ruler, Avery Brewing's Maharaja Imperial IPA is held in high regard. The Maharaja lords over both hops and malt with a heavy hand. Although it can be intense and imposing, the Maharaja rules with balance, making for a surprisingly approachable beer.

The beer has only been around since 2004, but the idea behind it was inadvertently being planned at the brewery for several years before it came into existence. "The journey toward the Maharaja was actually a long time coming, probably dating all the way back to late 1997 when we first produced Hog Heaven barleywine-style ale," says Avery's marketing director. "Years of brewing and enjoying Hog Heaven made us start asking what the next step was. While Hog Heaven was delicious, we wanted to see if we could make an even more robust, in-your-face hop aroma and a bigger, yet balanced, hop flavor in a beer."

Avery's brewers got their imperial IPA initiation when they brewed their Eleventh Anniversary Ale. The Maharaja took over the throne shortly after that inaugural brew. "We loved Eleven, and decided that we needed to make an imperial IPA every year, and the Maharaja was that beer." Produced March through August, the Maharaja greets its followers every summer and is part of Avery's Dictator series, which also includes Kaiser Imperial Lager and Czar Imperial Stout. Maharaja's summer release makes it a perfect pairing for barbecues and picnics. **LMo**

Tasting notes

Vibrant and forceful, the Maharaja rules over an enormous amount of floral and citrus hops that are confidently bolstered by a sturdy frame of toasted malt. The finish is viscous and smooth, with a softly gloved alcohol presence that belies its strength.

+Malta

Companyia Cervesera del Montseny | www.ccm.cat

Country of origin Spain
First brewed 2007
Alcohol content 5.1% abv
Serving temperature 48°F, 9°C

"Más Malta" is the Companyia Cervesera del Montseny's pale ale, and it is produced with a nod toward the traditional English style, rather than the North American favorite that single-handedly propelled the U.S. craft brewing revolution. Pale, crystal, and wheat malts make up the grain bill, while Challenger, East Kent Golding, and Fuggle in whole-flower form are the hops responsible for the pleasant bitterness. The beer goes through a secondary fermentation in the bottle, a process that helps the formation of its sturdy yet mouth-pleasing carbonization.

Brewmaster Pablo Vijande likes to emphasize that his beers are "natural and integral." All the beers are unpasteurized and unfiltered, and he also only uses whole-flower hops. Such practices are taken for granted within the craft beer community in the United Kingdom and North America, but in Spain, where the majority of beer lovers drink cold and crisp lagers, the same thought is not necessarily given to their production and aesthetic. To inform the public's opinion of craft beers, Vijande and his staff organize mini beer festivals, together with other local microbreweries, in which people have the opportunity to talk with the brewers and get a chance to learn about craft beer.

In spring 2009, a new version of +Malta was released by Companyia Cervesera del Montseny— +Malta Cuvée, a reserve beer that mellows in oak barrels for almost a year. This gave Vijande yet another opportunity to push the versatility and innovation of craft brewing to a wider Spanish audience. **SS**

Tasting notes

Amber red in color sitting beneath a firm white head. On the nose, it has sweet, malty, almost fruity notes. The palate maintains a similar fruity sweetness, although the clean bitterness and roasted hints balance this out. +Malta is bottled unfiltered.

Mammoth

Pink Elephant | homepages.paradise.net.nz/pinkelep/index.html

Country of origin New Zealand
First brewed 1990
Alcohol content 7% abv
Serving temperature 54°–57°F, 12°–14°C

In 1990, a decade after migrating from England, Roger Pink started brewing commercially near Nelson, in New Zealand's South Island. From day one, Pink was determined to brew traditional English-style ales; this was a remarkably brave move in a country whose beer scene was, and to some degree still is, dominated by sweet, fizzy lagers. Pink's robust brews were never going to be an instant hit with the average Kiwi beer drinker, and demand remained limited. Looking for a more discerning and open-minded clientele, and noticing a growing interest in wine tourism in New Zealand, Pink shifted the brewery to Marlborough in 1996, opening a beer-tasting facility and café in the heart of the famous wine region.

After picking up a raft of brewing awards and attracting many favorable reviews, Pink was tempted to produce ever more exotic styles, and the Pink Elephant range gradually increased. But brewing up to ten different beers while also welcoming visitors to the brewery proved too much for a one-man operation, and the tasting room was closed and the beer range rationalized.

Now located in a rural area, Marlborough's oldest established craft brewery concentrates on producing high-strength specialty beers and short-run, limited-release seasonal brews. Mammoth Strong Ale was one of the brewery's first brews and is now the only representative of the original range. It has since been superseded in potency by limited-release specialties such as Trumpet, a honey-infused barleywine, and the intense, roasty Imperious Rushin Stowt. **GG**

Tasting notes

Pouring the color of cola beneath a wispy tan head, there's a sweet confected aroma of toffee and berry fruit. On the palate, caramel and fruit flavors lead to a tart finish, with a lingering hop bitterness. Deceptively quaffable and perfect with aged cheddar cheese.

Maredsous 10

Duvel Moortgat | www.duvel.be

Country of origin Belgium
First brewed 1963
Alcohol content 10% abv
Serving temperature 46°F, 8°C

Any sister brew to the strong golden ale giant Duvel is pretty much by definition going to be sometimes overlooked. More is the pity, especially when said sisters are the Maredsous line of abbey ales produced by Duvel Moortgat. The Benedictine abbey at Denée is still involved in decisions affecting the three Maredsous beers, and the brewery proudly notes that a significant part of the profits from the brand is directed toward the charitable works of the abbey. (Like several other religious houses connected to brewing beer, whether on the premises or not, Maredsous Abbey also produces its own cheese.)

Maredsous ales come in a threesome, each bearing a number. The original reference was to the gravity of the unfermented beer expressed in degrees Belgian—essentially a measurement of how much fermentable sugar was available to the yeast. Although this number quite often matched up with the final alcohol content, this wasn't always the case, particularly where stronger beers were concerned. So the Maredsous 10, for example, with an original gravity of 10 degrees Belgian emerged from fermentation with an alcohol content of just over 9.5 percent.

In order to simplify matters, the brewery tweaked the recipes so that now each number refers directly to strength. The 6 is a gentle but fulfilling ale with a perfumey character and appetizingly dry finish, the 8 is a dark and chocolaty dubbel, and the 10, although billed as a tripel, doesn't seem quite suited to the description. There was also a Maredsous 9, but it was dropped for reasons known only to the brewery. **SB**

Tasting notes

Amber gold in color, the biggest beer in the Maredsous range offers notes of orange marmalade on the nose and a body that is rich, balanced, fruity, and even a bit creamy. Its significant strength is most obviously apparent in the lengthy, warming finish.

The neo-gothic Maredsous Abbey was founded in 1872. →

Märzen

Staffelberg Bräu | www.staffelberg-braeu.de

Country of origin Germany
First brewed 1949
Alcohol content 5.5% abv
Serving temperature 46°F, 8°C

Even though Karl-Heinz Wehrfritz trained as a butcher and did not aspire to be a brewer, it was clear that his future would be in brewing when he married Helga, daughter of Staffelberg-Bräu owners Anton and Maria Geldner. Together with his wife and in-laws, Wehrfritz now leads the 150-year-old family business. However, Wehrfritz hasn't forgotten the trade that he originally trained for: besides the brewhouse, the company also comprises a butchery and a cozy tavern, and Wehrfritz often switches from making sausages to boiling wort and back, all in one day. Thus, visitors eat and drink well at this brewpub in the heart of Franconia.

How about a fresh meat platter with a Staffelberg Märzen? The latter is a Franconian amber lager of the traditional style that is rarely to be found these days. It seduces with its caramel body and balances its malty riches with a proper but not too dominant bitterness. In brewing, Wehrfritz uses Munich and pilsner malts in a decoction mash. Part of the mash is taken out and boiled in a separate vessel, then reintroduced in the mash tun to heat the remainder. The boiling vessel is directly heated, which contributes to the caramelization effect. With a final attenuation of about 75 percent, this beer is rather sweet, one of the reasons why most of the breweries have abandoned the style.

The brewery is situated north of Bamberg in the scenic village of Loffelden at the foot of the impressive Staffelberg mountain. The nearby baroque complex of the monastery Banz and the renowned Franconian rococo building of Basilika Vierzehnheiligen also bring culturally aware visitors to the area. **SK**

Tasting notes

Brilliant amber with orange tints, steady off-white head. The nose offers a delicious caramel aroma and some herbs. On the palate expect a sweet, bready maltiness with toasted flavors and topped by caramel notes. Full bodied with a discreet hoppy finish.

Märzen Export Eiszäpfle

Badische Staatsbrauerei Rothaus | www.rothaus.de

Country of origin Germany
First brewed *ca.* 19th century
Alcohol content 5.6% abv
Serving temperature 46°–50°F, 8°–10°C

March is a time to bid farewell to the season of darkness, cold, and inactivity. In the old calendars, it was the start of a new year. For one industry, however, before technology changed things, March used to mark the end of labor: the brewing of beer came to a halt.

After all, brewing is a process that depends on cool temperatures. After the mash, the temperature of the brew has to be brought down quickly—otherwise fermentation kicks off resulting in a sour mess. For the same reasons, beer that is stored in too warm an environment becomes undrinkable after a short time. This is why brewers used to build huge wooden racks where they "grew" big icicles. These served as cooling components and, buried deep in the earth or stored in ice cellars, sometimes stayed intact until the end of the following summer. Deep in the ground, beneath the old town of Nuremberg, for example, there is a cavernous system of hundreds of beer storerooms.

Called "Märzen" after the name of the month, the lager was boiled for a long time, and its original gravity was high. Traditionally, the malty flavors dominated, and, in order to help with stability, the amount of hops added was high, even though by March the hops in the storeroom would see a muting of their aromatic properties. Luckily, Badische Staatsbrauerei Rothaus can count on its extraordinarily soft water to enhance every hint of the Tettnang and Hallertau aroma hops used in the brew. Nobody knows when Rothaus first brewed Märzen, since its archives were destroyed in World War II, but the beer probably emerged sometime in the 19th century. **SK**

Tasting notes

Amber with golden tints and a fine volatile foam. This beer offers a malty nose with hints of hop spices. The first taste is sweet, followed by hoppy notes; the predominantly malty character is balanced by bitter flavors. Medium body and bittersweet finish.

Master Polotmavý

Plzeňský Prazdroj | www.pivomaster.cz

Country of origin Czech Republic
First brewed 2007
Alcohol content 5.2% abv
Serving temperature 46°F, 8°C

In 2007, senior brewmaster Václav Berka presented a new line of beers to a small group of beer lovers in Prague. Unlike the brewery's other brands, many of which are most commonly seen in bottles, the new line would only be available on tap, from small kegs, to ensure maximum freshness, and only at selected pubs. Called "Master," the line included a very strong dark lager resembling a Baltic porter and Master Polotmavý, a remarkable amber lager.

While some particularly smitten fans might have assumed that both beers had fallen from heaven, the amber Master Polotmavý has a source a little closer to home. A clear influence is the celebrated Vienna lager of Anton Dreher, first produced around 1840. Although Vienna lager went extinct in its homeland, across the border in today's Czech Republic many brewers make a *polotmavý* (half-dark) lager of similar color, aroma, and flavor, and Master Polotmavý appears to come straight out of that amber lager tradition. It is a beer that pairs especially well with food, in particular pasta dishes and pizza, whose sweet notes are well matched by the sugary malt. Although Master Polotmavý continues to be available only on draft, and generally only in the Czech Republic, the brew has occasionally turned up at beer festivals outside of its home country. **ER**

Tasting notes
This rich amber lager is extremely full in malt flavor, balancing its sweetness with a moderate bitterness complemented by vanilla, caramel, and candied-orange notes.

Maudite

Unibroue | www.unibroue.com

Country of origin Canada
First brewed 1993
Alcohol content 8% abv
Serving temperature 46°F, 8°C

In the early 1990s, when craft beer was still a bit of a curiosity, it was a brave entrepreneur who decorated the label of his brewery's second brand with a picture of a canoe flying through a fire-red sky while the devil grinned below. Braver still was the man who named such a beer Maudite (meaning "damned" in French). But that's the kind of person André Dion is, or at least was when he launched Unibroue.

Dion's first brew, Blanche de Chambly, was a Belgian-style wheat beer. As surprising as the Blanche was to Québec's beer drinkers, who were used to more pedestrian golden ales and lagers, the arrival of Maudite also challenged their sensibilities. In addition to the surprising name and graphics, both lifted, incidentally, from a well-known Québécois fable of a group of canoeing lumberjacks getting in trouble with the Devil, when Maudite first appeared, it was dark, spiced, strong, and utterly unlike anything previously seen on the domestic market. It has remained a flagship brand for the Québéc brewery ever since. Although Maudite is often referred to as a Belgian-style beer, it would arguably be better dubbed a Belgian-inspired ale, since its idiosyncratic spicing, well-promoted food friendliness, and use of Québécois lore positions it firmly as a product of its home province. **SB**

Tasting notes
Expect a full nose from this ale, with ample notes of coriander, allspice, and other spices. A rich, dryish, and faintly earthy mix of chocolate, citrus, red fruit, and cinnamon spice in the body.

Polotmavý was inspired by a historic recipe dating back to 1585.

McNally's Extra Ale

Big Rock Brewery | www.bigrockbeer.com

Country of origin Canada
First brewed 1986
Alcohol content 7% abv
Serving temperature 50°F, 10°C

Back in the mid-1980s, strong beer in Canada was almost exclusively of an adjunct-laden, at times almost syrupy style known as "malt liquor." So, for a small brewery, the release of a strong Irish-style ale was an act of faith and more than a little hope. Thankfully, for Alberta's original craft brewery, it was successful.

As the first Canadian craft brewery to be opened between the Rocky Mountains and the Greater Toronto Area, Big Rock had pretty much a blank canvas on which to paint its notions of what beer should be. And despite having hired a Teutonic brewer by the name of Bernd Pieper, Ed McNally foresaw English and Celtic beer styles. First off the mark was the now-iconic Big Rock Traditional Ale, known to its admirers far and wide as simply "Trad." This was followed by a best bitter, later renamed Classic Ale, and a porter. The release of the last beer was a particularly gutsy move, because the Alberta market was at the time populated almost exclusively by golden lagers and had not seen a domestically brewed black ale for a long, long time.

Still, the porter's launch was nothing compared with the release of McNally's Extra Ale. Strong ales simply did not exist on the prairies, and the acceptance of beer as a winter warmer or after-dinner drink was still a good decade away, so there was not even a context in which to place this beer. Fortunately, accolades were quick to come, including praise from famed beer writer Michael Jackson, who deemed it "a classic." This seemed to be enough for even wary Albertans, and the beer's success spread rapidly, eventually becoming one of Big Rock's most recognizable brands. **SB**

Tasting notes

One characteristic of "old school" Irish ales is a slight buttery character, which McNally's Extra Ale freely presents, along with a caramel apple nose and malty, plummy notes throughout the body of the palate, before leading to an off-dry, warming finish.

Meantime India Pale Ale

Meantime Brewing | www.meantimebrewing.com

Country of origin England
First brewed 2005
Alcohol content 7.5% abv
Serving temperature 46°–54°F, 8°–12°C

There are two styles that gave birth to almost all modern beer: porter, which gave us stout, and India Pale Ale, which led to pale ale, bitter, real ale, and, arguably, blond lager. When Alastair Hook set up the Meantime Brewery, his first ambition was to create authentic versions of both beer styles. The history of IPA weighed on his thoughts particularly heavily, given that in the 19th century, the original beer was loaded onto the East Indiamen fleet just half a mile upriver from Meantime's Greenwich brewery.

Hook felt that it was crucial to understand not only the recipe but also the cultural context of the original beer, and Meantime IPA was developed with the help of a huge amount of detailed historical research. At the time, most contemporary IPAs were 3.5 percent to 4 percent abv and drunk as light session beers. The beer that Hook wanted to re-create was much stronger, at 7 percent to 8 percent, and as expensive as French claret. Meantime IPA's champagne bottle with cork and wire seal reflects this sense of worth.

The beer is packed with as many Fuggle and Golding hops as can physically be added into the copper. The lauter tun is filled with more hops, and the beer is then dry hopped to give a historically accurate hopping rate of 2 pounds (910 g) per barrel.

IPA evolved from strong country-house ales that were cellared for several years before being drunk. The famous maturation on the six-month voyage to India was an accelerated version of this cellar aging. Without that journey, Meantime recommends that the beer is even better when stored for a few years. **PB**

Tasting notes

A copper-colored beer with a spicy, orange zest aroma. On the palate, there's no mistaking the hops, but an earthy character complements the citrus and floral hit. Stunning with cheese, perfect with curry—it does everything that lager can, and much more.

Meantime London Pale Ale

Meantime Brewing | www.meantimebrewing.com

Country of origin England
First brewed 2007
Alcohol content 4.7% abv
Serving temperature 50°F, 10°C

The thing to know about Meantime beers is that they are wonderfully English and originated in London. This is something that the brewery is very proud of because, as master brewer Alastair Hook will happily point out, most British beer styles were invented in London, or a Londoner had at least something to do with them. Stout? London. Porter? London. Pale ale and IPA? You guessed it, London. The gypsum-rich waters of Burton were more suited to the brewing of pale ale, and it was this town that would go on to make the style famous, but, as Hook will testify, it was a Londoner who thought of it first.

Developed some decades after IPA, pale ale had taken the British Empire by storm, as people demanded stronger and less heady beers that were quicker to produce and required no aging. These beers did not have to withstand the long and violent sea journeys to and from India, so a lower alcohol content and hopping rate made a lot of sense. The new, light, hoppy ales became popular with the English middle classes of the Victorian age. But beer is subject to the whims of fashion, and by the 1880s, pale ale had dwindled out of favor. However, a century later, it was picked up and kept alive by a new generation of U.S. brewers.

Meantime London Ale is a traditional English pale ale and yet, with the use of some powerful American hops, it makes a respectful nod toward the U.S. chapter in the history of this great beer style. During the 19th century, demand for hops exceeded domestic supply, and it was not unusual for Californian hops to be used in English brewing. **ST**

Tasting notes

Meantime London Pale Ale has a complex nose with a heady mix of spearmint, grass, and "hop sack" aromas. The fruit on the palate gives way to a very dry finish with a lingering bitterness. Great alongside mature cheese, penne arrabiata, or a bitter-leaf salad.

Minoh Double IPA

Minoh Beer | www.minoh-beer.jp

Country of origin Japan
First brewed *ca.* 2006
Alcohol content 9% abv
Serving temperature 50°–55°F, 10°–13°C

Imagine that your father decides to give you a brewery for Christmas. Sound like a dream? Well, that's pretty much what happened to Kaori and Mayuko Oshita in 1997, when their father, Masaji, a prosperous liquor wholesaler looking to branch out, decided to build a brewery and put his daughters in charge of brewing.

It was obviously a good idea, because since its founding the brewery has produced a lot of interesting beers. Most unusual might be the Cabernet Ale, made with the juice from Cabernet Sauvignon grapes, or perhaps the hemp beers, Hemp High and Ganja High, brewed in collaboration with another retailer. The latest in this parade is Minoh Double IPA, which features both high alcohol and extreme bitterness.

Brewmaster Kaori Oshita relates that the Double IPA wasn't without its difficulties in the brewing process. The beer requires lots of malt, so it was hard to get the gravity high enough. The sparging process was also very involved and time consuming. However, the most difficult aspect came with the supply of hops. The beer uses Cascade, but when it was released as a regular offering in 2008, Cascade hops were in short supply. Matters improved in 2009, however, and it became easier to get a stable supply.

Since the beer is extremely bitter and high in alcohol, Kaori Oshita says the brewery staff was not sure that it would sell in great quantities, although they knew there were regular customers for it. Still, shipments are increasing, exceeding all expectations. Surprisingly, the beer seems to be particularly liked by female and older customers. **BH**

Tasting notes

The beer is a deep bronze orange, with an off-white head. There is a malty aroma with sweet vanilla notes on top of a hop background. A very strong malt flavor comes through at first, while the hops are understated with very little forward flavor. The gentle finish is smooth and malty.

Mitchell's 90/-

Mitchell's Knysna Brewery
www.mitchellsknysnabrewery.com

Country of origin South Africa
First brewed 1990
Alcohol content 5% abv
Serving temperature 55°F, 13°C

Named after an old British currency, the number of shillings in the beer's name denotes its strength. Such beers were traditionally brewed in Scotland, with 60/- meaning light and 70/- heavy; the most robust were 90/-, of which Mitchell's ale is a shining example.

The beer undergoes a longer than usual boil in the kettle, which helps to draw out its rich brown sugar and caramel flavors, which can be savored in the finished beer as unfermented sugars. These extra sugars also help to give this beer its darkish amber color. As was the tradition with most Scottish-style beers, it is not heavily hopped, and malty aromas dominate the nose and palate rather than resinous or floral hop characteristics. In the bottle, it is unpasteurized, which adds a further dimension to its flavor.

Mitchell's Knysna Brewery was set up in 1983 by Lex Mitchell in a small building in the center of Knysna. In 1985 it moved to the Knysna industrial area, where it employs a mixture of British mashing and German lagering technology to make its beers. It expanded its operation in 1989 with the opening of a brewpub in Cape Town, which also brews a 90/- Ale that is different to its Knysna cousin. In 1989 the company was bought by the U.K. brewery Scottish and Newcastle, and in 2002 a consortium of local businessmen brought the company back into South African ownership. **TH**

Tasting notes

Bold, spicy notes dominate the taste—well rounded with complex aromatic notes of Christmas pudding, backed up with hints of cinnamon and caramel. Full bodied in the mouth.

Mitchell's ESB

Spinnakers Brewpub
www.spinnakers.com

Country of origin Canada
First brewed 1984
Alcohol content 5.2% abv
Serving temperature 50°F, 10°C

The first modern brewpub to open in North America was the Horseshoe Bay Brewing Company, which beat its U.S. counterparts to market by mere months. Due to a quirk in British Columbia's nascent brewpub law, however, both Horseshoe Bay and the province's second brewery, the Prairie Inn, were forced to house their breweries in separate facilities outside of the pub. Thus, the honor of being Canada's first brewpub with its brewery located in-house became the property of Victoria's Spinnakers.

For Paul Hadfield and his partners, who included British Columbia's craft brewing pioneer John Mitchell, the opening of the pub was a leap of faith, since even as construction progressed the amendment allowing the brewery to be part of the pub had not been passed. Fortunately, passed it was, and Spinnakers was able to commence its business on schedule in May 1984.

"First in-house brewpub" was but one of many firsts for Hadfield and Spinnakers. First modern cask-conditioned ale commercially brewed in Canada, first brewery to use a yeast that had traveled into space (aboard the Space Shuttle), first Canadian brewery with an on-site vinegar production house, and first British Columbia brewpub to get its bottles into the provincial liquor stores are but a few of the groundbreaking moments that have followed. **SB**

Tasting notes

Amber copper in color, with a rich and malty floral aroma leading into a toasty, fruity body accented by a moderately bitter and faintly nutty hoppiness. A dry finish.

Mitchell's brewpub enjoys a great waterfront location in Cape Town.

Moose Drool Brown Ale

Big Sky Brewing Company | www.bigskybrew.com

Country of origin United States
First brewed 1995
Alcohol content 5.3% abv
Serving temperature 55°F, 13°C

In the same year (1995) that Big Sky Brewing began producing beers with names like Whistle Pig Red Ale and Moose Drool Brown Ale, another brewery won a medal at the Great American Beer Festival for an ale called "Dog Spit Stout." By choosing such names, even ones that many find unappetizing, small-batch breweries signaled that they were making something different from the mainstream lagers that dominated the U.S. beer scene. Moose Drool is, in fact, brewed in the tradition of English brown ales and hopped in moderation, forgoing the citrus-dominated Northwest hops that have become a hallmark of U.S. brown ales.

While developing their first recipes, the brewery founders asked the mother of one of the brewers to paint pictures of a variety of animals. One painting depicted a moose lifting his head from a pond, and upon seeing it, one of the founders said, "It's a moose, he's drooling, let's call it 'moose drool.'" The name has served Big Sky well, although the brewery has been to court several times to defend trademark infringement charges by Canadian brewer Moosehead. The flagship Moose Drool has helped the brewery grow into one of the forty largest craft producers in the country, selling its beers across the West and upper Midwest.

Missoula, where the brewery is based, is a magnet for outdoors enthusiasts: attracting hikers, mountain bikers, white-water enthusiasts, and those tracing the Lewis and Clark Trail. By first packaging beer in aluminum bottles in 2003 and by installing a canning line in 2009, Big Sky made its beers more portable for such consumers. **SH**

Tasting notes

Brown at the pour with added copper highlights. Dark fruits and chocolate mingle in the aroma, with the same flavors joined by toasted nuts on the palate. The beer is malt accented with hops providing a hint of spice and earthy impressions.

Mythos Red

Mythos Brewery | www.mythosbrewery.gr

Country of origin Greece
First brewed 2007
Alcohol content 5.5% abv
Serving temperature 39°–43°F, 4°–6°C

Mythos Red comes out of a brewery with a mixed history: it is located in Thessaloniki but has German roots that date back to 1968 and the Henninger Brau Frankfurt. Subsequent buyouts over the following three decades led to the Mythos name emerging in 2000 and, after a brief spell with Scottish and Newcastle, it is now owned by Carlsberg.

Mythos beer is the dominant brand. It is also known as Mythos "green" because of its label color, and its popularity has transformed Mythos Brewery into the second largest brewery in Greece, exporting to thirty countries. More recently, British brewers Adnams signed up to distribute the beer in the United Kingdom, and it is thought that the British love affair with the Greek Islands will make it a hit.

Mythos Red is a later addition to the Greek party and is a concoction of water, barley malt, hops, and yeast as expected, but also glucose syrup, which undoubtedly contributes to its caramel quality. The brewing team behind it took a bit of a chance on something rather different to the "green," and Mythos Red was apparently created for "people who search for alternative choices in their life and new ways of expressing these choices." The team has achieved the unusual, simply because the beer is a surprising choice of variety for a commercial brewery and a success in terms of quality as well. Indeed the beer is a lovely premium red, pouring a lively amber but with an incredibly appealing foamy head. There's a faint fruity nose to it, and it is a great alternative for those who are tired of the lagers. **TS**

Tasting notes

Well, it is red, obviously, and thanks to the glucose has a fine caramel profile on the palate. The head is long-lasting when poured correctly, and the hops are potent enough to balance sweetness up front with bitterness at the back.

Negra Modelo

Grupo Modelo | www.gmodelo.com.mx

Country of origin Mexico
First brewed 1926
Alcohol content 5.4% abv
Serving temperature 50°F, 10°C

In Mexico City, the Cervecería Modelo opened in 1925, and in just three years was selling 8 million bottles of its still-popular Modelo and Corona beers. Modelo spent the next eight decades acquiring other Mexican beer brands, opening up additional breweries, and changing its name to Grupo Modelo. In 2005, when it celebrated its eightieth anniversary, it was operating seven brewing facilities throughout Mexico. Two years later, it broke ground on its eighth brewery and owned 63 percent of Mexico's total beer market.

Most beers brewed in Mexico are a variation on pilsners or the Vienna lagers of Austria. This is because the man who proclaimed himself emperor of Mexico in 1864, Maximilian, was a Hapsburg prince whose father was Archduke Franz Karl of Austria. Even though he was ousted from power after only three years, the culture he introduced to Mexico, including the beer, has remained and been adapted by the Mexican people.

A year after the brewery opened, Negra Modelo was introduced on draft only and by 1930 was being bottled. It remains one of the few dark beers brewed in Mexico and is not surprisingly the nation's best-selling dark beer. However, there is still some debate about exactly what style of beer Negra Modelo is. Many believe it is a dark Vienna-style lager whereas others insist it is closer to a Munich-style dunkel. It is, in a sense, its own beer, so its taste profile doesn't fit either style very well. Nevertheless, it is a thin-bodied beer with lots of flavor and able to fulfill the double duty of being not too heavy for Mexico's hot climate yet flavorful enough to pair with spicy Mexican food. **JB**

Tasting notes

The color is bright amber brown. The nose is mostly malt sweetness with nutty aromas. The flavor profile is likewise sweet and malty with hints of vanilla, caramel, and a touch of nuttiness, like almonds. The mouthfeel is thin, but good balance and full flavors make it refreshing.

Newcastle Brown Ale

Newcastle Federation | www.scottish-newcastle.com

Country of origin England
First brewed 1927
Alcohol content 4.7% abv
Serving temperature 52°F, 11°C

For a beer that was originally brewed for Tyneside shipyard workers in the northeast of England, the global popularity of Newcastle Brown Ale has risen to great heights over the past seventy years. "Newkie Broon," as it is known to its myriad fans, was introduced initially to counter the growing sales of beers from Burton-on-Trent and the Midlands. These beers were brought northward by rail to Newcastle on the north bank of the Tyne and to Gateshead on the south.

Newcastle Brown Ale was first produced in an era when most British beers were measurably darker than their contemporary ancestors—the beer is translucent and appealing, a glowing reddish-brown ale, normally sold in a clear, glass bottle. It quickly became a favorite on Tyneside, but its fame only truly started to spread nationally when it was discovered by a generation of university students after Newcastle Breweries won a contract to supply beer to hundreds of student bars across the United Kingdom. This beer from the industrial northeast suddenly acquired middle-class student chic. Rarely sold on draft, Newcastle Brown is a natural beer for exporting.

For many years, the beer was brewed in the heart of Newcastle. However, this site closed in 2004, and production moved to the former Federation Brewery in Gateshead, where the beer is brewed to an alcohol strength of 7.5 percent before being diluted to the strength at which it meets its drinkers. Traditionally, the beer should be drunk from a half-pint schooner—with the drinker taking several small sips before pouring a little more of the cooled beer into the glass. **TH**

Tasting notes

This is a full-bodied beer with a palate that is dominated by brown sugar and candy caramel flavors; fruit notes follow on mid-palate, before the lingering sweet finish. The beer is well balanced and although hoppy notes are low, they are definitely in the mix.

Nils Oscar Kalasöl

Nils Oscar Brewery | www.nilsoscar.se

Country of origin Sweden
First brewed 1997
Alcohol content 5.2% abv
Serving temperature 50°–57°F, 10°–14°C

Sweden has long had a deeply ambivalent relationship with alcohol. Although a vote on Prohibition in 1922 went narrowly against an outright ban on alcohol, for years afterward drinking was deeply unfashionable.

Things changed in 1995 when Sweden joined the European Union, and the state monopoly on alcohol was removed. New breweries were established, and pubs were opened across the country. But with no indigenous pub culture, these places took their cues from elsewhere: Stockholm has plenty of English, Irish, and Czech-themed pubs, but none that feel quintessentially Swedish.

Given this reliance on foreign drinking culture, it's no surprise that a craft brewery such as Nils Oscar should brew a range of European beer styles. But Kalasöl, an Oktoberfest beer, is more than just another copy of a foreign beer. Oktoberfest is held in deep affection across Scandinavia. Every autumn, bars up and down Sweden and Denmark are festooned with Bavaria's blue and white checks and serve plenty of Oktoberfest beers. Kalasöl is a direct translation of the German word "Festbier," and it is brewed in true Oktoberfest style. It's a bottom-fermented, amber-colored lager beer with caramel and roast malts added to a base of pale and Munich malt. The hops are a little more eclectic than a traditional Festbier, with Cascade and Fuggle joining the more traditional Saaz and Hallertau. First brewed as a seasonal beer, Kalasöl has proved so popular that it is now available all year around. It is at its best with hearty fare such as roast meat, spicy stews, broiled meat, and fowl. **PB**

Tasting notes

This beer pours a deep coppery amber with a thick beige head and an aroma that is full of toffee, toasty malt, and fresh bread. Complementary flavors of bread, biscuit, nut, and caramel on the palate are rounded off perfectly by a spicy, citrus hop character.

The iconic Nils Oscar logo features the grandfather of the company's current owner. ➡

Nils  *Oscar*®

Nivura

Birrificio Scarampola | www.birrificioscarampola.it

Country of origin Italy
First brewed 2004
Alcohol content 6.5% abv
Serving temperature 50°–54°F, 10°–12°C

Maurizio Ghidetti started to brew in 2002 in Osteria del Vino Cattivo (Osteria of Bad Wine) and immediately decided to show his passion for unfiltered and unpasteurized beers. From the beginning Ghidetti was really fascinated by local and quite unusual ingredients: one of his first brews, which is still in production, was IPA. In most cases, these initials are understood to stand for India Pale Ale, but in Ghidetti's case the "P" instead stands for *pompelmo*, the Italian word for "grapefruit."

Nivura follows the same principles of Ghidetti's philosophy. It is a top-fermenting Belgian-style pale ale, which is enriched with chestnuts—the addition of these is reflected in the beer's name. Nivura is a local area where chestnut trees are traditional and remain a source of work for the small community. Alongside the chestnuts, pale ale malt is joined by a pinch of black malt, which helps to give more color to the beer. The chestnuts are picked up from September to October, then are laid down on the first floor of small houses that function as a drying room (in local dialect they are called *tecci*). A fire burns below very slowly, for three weeks, and dries the chestnuts to give them the smoked aroma.

Chestnut beers are quite popular in Italy; it is a sort of Italian style developed for the historic reasons that chestnuts were a traditional food for people living in the mountains during the last war. Nivura is one of the best examples of this style, a beer with an original flavor, smooth and drinkable, and very good when matched with soft cheese. **MM**

Tasting notes

Cloudy amber color, with a thick and refined foam. The aroma is complex and articulated with smoky chestnut, honey, and floral notes. Well balanced in the palate, this beer reveals immediately an elegant sweetness and finishes with an aftertaste underlined by chestnuts again.

Nor'wester

The Dux Brewing Co. | www.thedux.co.nz

Country of origin New Zealand
First brewed 1993
Alcohol content 6.5% abv
Serving temperature 50°–54°F, 10°–12°C

Founded in 1978 in Christchurch, Dux de Lux was the city's first vegetarian restaurant. A year later, the Dux fired its first brewing kettles, and it is now one of New Zealand's longest-established brewpubs. In late 2003, a second brewpub in the tourist resort of Queenstown was acquired, and production of the group's excellent range of beers is now split between the two sites.

Having begun with just two beers—the malty Dux Lager and roasty Hereford Bitter—brewer Richard Fife has expanded the range and now oversees production of seven permanent beers as well as regular seasonal releases. With a background as a chef and a passion for brewing, Fife loves to experiment with flavors, and beers aged in wine barrels that previously held Pinot Noir are an occasional specialty.

The Dux's range caters for most palates, with crisp, golden pilsners; darker, maltier Vienna and Munich-style lagers; a creamy, Irish-style dry stout; real ginger beers (both alcoholic and nonalcoholic); and the legendary Nor'wester, a strong pale ale, and Sou'wester, a sweet winter stout. Until recently, the beers were only offered on draft at the brewpubs, but since mid-2008, a selection has been offered in bottles.

Over the years, the two brewpubs have won a hatful of awards, but the supreme accolade came in 2003 when Nor'wester won Grand Champion Beer at the Australian International Beer Awards. Named after the dry winds that parch the Canterbury Plains, this complex brew is made with a grist of six British and German malts, hops from both sides of the Pacific, and an ale yeast sourced from Truman's of London. **GG**

Tasting notes

Pours an attractive orange marmalade hue beneath a tan head. The beer's punchy aroma combines toffee, caramel, chocolate, smoke, dark fruit, and citrusy hops, while the palate is creamy and mouthfilling, with malt, fruit, and resiny hops merging into a long, bittersweet finish.

Nostradamus

Brasserie Caracole
www.brasserie-caracole.be

Country of origin Belgium
First brewed 1993
Alcohol content 9.5% abv
Serving temperature 50°–59°F, 10°–15°C

Nostradamus is dark, rich, complex, alcoholic, and enticing—descriptions that work both for Christmas ale and for many Wallonian ales. The beer is, actually, both of these, having started its life as Cuvée de l'An Neuf. An array of roasted and colored malts helps to give it a rich and roasty character, and the hops include Saaz and Hallertau. Many tasters find licorice in this beer, but the brewery denies the use of the spice. In fact, it is very particular on the selection of the ingredients that it uses, and it comes as no surprise that a number of the beers are organically certified.

Aesthetics play a role in the image of the beer, too. Take a look at Nostradamus: the French medieval soothsayer looks out at the world, in the shape of a snail (*caracole*). These attentions to detail only make the beer even more inviting, and it is now available to be enjoyed all year around. **JPa**

Tasting notes
Nutty, perfumey, and sweetish on the nose; alcohol notes also make their presence felt. On the palate, there's sweet caramel, a slightly roasted touch, and a fruity presence. Very full bodied.

Obliteration V

Midnight Sun Brewing Co.
www.midnightsunbrewing.com

Country of origin United States
First brewed 2009
Alcohol content 8.2% abv
Serving temperature 41°F, 5°C

Obliteration V is the fifth in a series of experimental beers brewed by Midnight Sun, an award-winning brewery based in Anchorage, Alaska. In each of the Obliteration brews, Midnight Sun uses different hop varieties so that the imbiber can experience the character that each hop variety contributes to the beer. Obliteration V is brewed with the high alpha-acid hops, Warrior and Nugget, and Amarillo is added to the mix in the dry-hopping stage. "We list the hops that we use on each brew's bottle so everyone can get a feeling of what these hops taste like at such extreme levels," says head brewer Gabe Fletcher.

Midnight Sun has been brewing in Alaska since 1995. The brewery's name comes from the long hours of sunlight that Anchorage residents relish during the summer months, thanks to the city's close proximity to the North Pole. **LMo**

Tasting notes
Resinous pine and grapefruit aromas blast out on pouring. The first sip delivers another hop jolt, but hints of malt and fruity sweetness keep the bitterness delightfully in check.

Oerbier

De Dolle Brouwers
www.dedollebrouwers.be/en/index.html

Country of origin Belgium
First brewed 1980
Alcohol content 9% abv
Serving temperature 54°F, 12°C

Back in the 1970s, the three Herteleer brothers brewed beer enthusiastically in their mother's bathtub. Their aim was to create an essential beer seen through a west Flanders eye, the province that carries so much of Belgium's beer heritage. They clearly knew what they were doing because they entered a brewing competition and won. Next, they found a brewery in the town of Esen near Diksmuide that had gone out of business and began brewing.

Four malts, dark candy sugar, and locally grown Golding hops are used to ensure the beer's typical Oerbier character. The brewery recommends aging the brew for a couple of years before drinking, preferably at 46 degrees Fahrenheit (8°C), as it does in its own cellars. This is quite a turnaround in attitude, since the first editions of Oerbier carried a best-by date of one hundred days. **JPa**

Tasting notes
Offers a very fruity nose with plums, grapes, and dark and light malts. On the palate is a bitter beginning, leading to a sweet undercurrent, fruity and grapelike, that lasts to the finish.

Oerbier Special Reserva

De Dolle Brouwers
www.dedollebrouwers.be/en/index.html

Country of origin Belgium
First brewed 2002
Alcohol content 13% abv
Serving temperature 57°F, 14°C

The "mad brewers" of Esen were making extreme beers long before it was cool among U.S. craft brewers. Their first was Oerbier in 1980. The more recent and rare Oerbier Special Reserva, which is aged eighteen months in French Bordeaux wine casks, owes more to the Flemish sour ale tradition than it does to the recent craze for barrel-aging craft beers. Yet the scale and complexity of this brew leave most other Flemish ales in the dust, for this is a beer that inspires deep contemplation.

In this case, the barrel aging adds layers of flavor to what is already one of the world's most interesting beers. Oerbier is pretty potent to start with, checking in at 9 percent alcohol. However, the final product is in the ballpark of 13 percent. It's as big as wine, yet wine rarely if ever has flavor this intense and ponderous. This is not a drinking beer; this is a sipping beer. **JS**

Tasting notes
Nose brings to mind sour cherries, balsamic vinegar, dark rum, and hints of chocolate. Moderate bitterness arrives late and joins some alcohol and tart fruit in the lingering aftertaste.

O'Hara's Irish Red

Carlow Brewing Company
www.carlowbrewing.com

Country of origin Ireland
First brewed 1998
Alcohol content 4.3% abv
Serving temperature 50°F, 10°C

In recent years, Ireland's large breweries have cut back on the amount of red ale they brew in favor of the lagers that now dominate the country's beer market. This has left a niche for the handful of microbrewers almost all of whom have a successful Irish red in their lineup. O'Hara's Red, formerly known as Moling's Irish Red after the Carlow brewery's local saint, is among the best of the genre. The lynchpin ingredient for the style is crystal malt, offering a distinctive caramel and toffee flavor and aroma with a dusting of summer fruits.

A cozy, comforting beer at a very sessionable strength, O'Hara's Red is best enjoyed from the bottle at cellar temperature, although it is occasionally available cold on draft keg. While its stylistic roots lie in the dumbing-down of Irish ale, it stands out as a testament to the indefatigable talent and enthusiasm of Ireland's smaller-scale brewers. **JD**

Tasting notes
A deep rich red color with light sparkle and a firm white head. The sweet caramel and roasted flavors make it the perfect accompaniment for meat dishes such as roast pork or Irish stew.

Okocim Mocne

Browar Okocim
www.okocim.pl

Country of origin Poland
First brewed *ca*. early 1900s
Alcohol content 7% abv
Serving temperature 39°–44°F, 4°–7°C

Poland's brewing heritage has long been overshadowed by its central European neighbors Warsaw or Krakow may not have the beer history and culture of Munich and Prague, but the 21st century looks likely to redress that imbalance.

Okocim is one of the country's oldest breweries and it dominates the national market alongside Zywiec and Kompania Piwowarska. Johann Evangelical Gotz founded the brewery in the town of Brzesko in 1845, having been inspired by Joseph Groll's creation of Pilsner Urquell three years earlier in western Bohemia. The impressive building remains largely as it did when beer production first began.

Translated as "strong," Mocne more than lives up to its name with an intense malt flavor that is popular with drinkers who want something with more bite to appease a palate that is acclimatized to vodka. **SG**

Tasting notes
Pours a pale amber color with a healthy head that diminishes to a thin coating, emitting a hoppy, floral nose. The palate is struck by a sweet caramel malt taste with subtle hints of fruit.

Vintage scenes from the historic Okocim brewery. ➡

Old Boardhead Barleywine Ale

Full Sail Brewing | www.fullsailbrewing.com

Country of origin United States
First brewed 1990
Alcohol content 9% abv
Serving temperature 44°F, 7°C

Old Boardhead is a bit of a contrarian brew. Like many barleywines, its name includes the word "old," but this ale is far from mature, being aged only for one month in the brewery before it is released to the public. Many barleywines are designed to be aged or cellared, but, at a relatively light 9 percent alcohol content, Old Boardhead is meant to be enjoyed fresh from the brewery—although aging the beer does bring about some interesting and desirable flavors. In fact, Old Boardhead is often the subject of vertical tastings from different vintages.

Unlike many other barleywines, which are brewed once a year for the winter season, Old Boardhead is brewed a number of times throughout the year to meet ongoing demand, and to assure that the beer is as fresh as possible, as well. The recipe for the beer changes each year and is mostly dependent on what varieties of hops are available at the time when the beer is first brewed in autumn.

It started out as a one-off draft beer when former brewer Greg Knutson, now human resources director at Full Sail, decided to make a barleywine. The beer was brewed again in the early to mid-1990s after Full Sail opened a small brewing operation adjacent to the McCormick and Schmick's Harborside restaurant in Portland, Oregon. "The opening of the Portland brewery allowed us to take the original Full Sail brewery out of mothballs and do some small batches," says brewmaster John Harris. Old Boardhead was one of those, and then, eventually, in 1998, it became an annual brew to meet year-round demand. **LMo**

Tasting notes

Rich, malty aromas of sugar and caramel dance with strong alcohol and citrus. An initial sweetness of brown sugar and caramel is underplayed by hops and spice as the alcohol blooms with a warming glow in this silky smooth brew.

Old Crustacean

Rogue Ales | www.rogue.com

Country of origin United States
First brewed 1989
Alcohol content 11.5% abv
Serving temperature 50°F, 10°C

Old Crustacean is a hefty brew, weighing in at 11.5 percent alcohol content and verified as having 120 IBUs by the Siebel Institute of Technology. The recipe comes from a barleywine-style ale that was first brewed in 1986 by Rogue's long-time brewmaster John Maier, when he was still a home-brewer. (Maier won Home-brewer of the Year from the American Home-brewers Association in 1988 before turning pro.) He says his inspirations for those first batches of his home-brewed barleywine included Sierra Nevada's Bigfoot and Anchor's Old Foghorn.

Shortly after he began working for Rogue, Maier and assistant brewer Nate Lindquist scaled up Maier's award-winning barleywine recipe for commercial production. Lindquist suggested the name, Old Crustacean, in honor of the deep-sea denizens that dwell in the Pacific Ocean, just a few steps outside the door of Rogue's brewery in Newport, Ore. Brewing such a big beer on a small start-up brewing system, however, proved to be a challenge.

While fresh from the brewery, "Old Crusty," as it is often called, is designed to be cellared, and, like a fine wine, will take on different nuances throughout time if handled properly. "We recently held a tasting with Old Crustacean in bottles from as far back as 1993 going all the way up to 2006," Maier says. "It was amazing how well those older bottles held up. There was a pleasant, smooth sherry character to the older ones that was really quite nice." Meant to be sipped and savored slowly, Rogue calls Old Crustacean the cognac of beers. **LMo**

Tasting notes

Intense and robust with a huge, citrus, and piney hop presence and a strong, but not overly sweet, malt backbone. A touch of fruitiness and a warm wallop of alcohol are a welcome addition to this barleywine, adding to Old Crustacean's complexity.

Old Foghorn

Anchor Brewing Company | www.anchorbrewing.com

Country of origin United States
First brewed 1975
Alcohol content 8.8% abv
Serving temperature 48°F, 9°C

During the 1970s, North American beer culture was vastly different from what we know today, and in those years, Fritz Maytag worked hard to save his Anchor Brewing from imminent bankruptcy. With the exception of a few imports on beer shelves, the brews available were quite homogenous, and Maytag's hard work helped to build up his reputation for making distinct and high-quality beers.

In 1975, Maytag traveled to England in search of inspiration from the country's brewing tradition. To his surprise, he found more conventional brewing techniques than traditional, but there was one thing that he discovered of interest: barleywine. He had never heard of the style and was intrigued by it—an ale that maintains some of its sweetness because the fermentation had stopped due to high alcohol. Nothing resembled it in the United States; it was even rare in England.

As soon as he returned home, Anchor brewed Old Foghorn in November 1975. It was all-malt and brewed using only the first runnings from the mash tun and highly hopped with Cascade hops (one of the first instances in a commercial beer). The brewery even dry hopped it, a process that was unheard of at the time. It was finally bottled in spring 1976.

Maytag was thrilled with the result, but it took a long time to sell the first few batches of Old Foghorn, it being so unique. However, over time people have come to understand the tradition behind it. Today, with its nine to eighteen months of dry hopping, it is one of the world's best-known barleywines. **MO**

Tasting notes

The nose is full and balanced, reminiscent of dark caramel, with some piney hop aroma and a subtle rum character. Rich, it starts with a substantial sweetness suggesting a sticky mouthfeel. The resiny hops sneak in quietly, with dried fruit aromas lingering on the finish.

Old Hooky

Hook Norton Brewery | www.hooky.co.uk

Country of origin England
First brewed *ca.* 1900
Alcohol content 4.6% abv
Serving temperature 52°F, 11°C

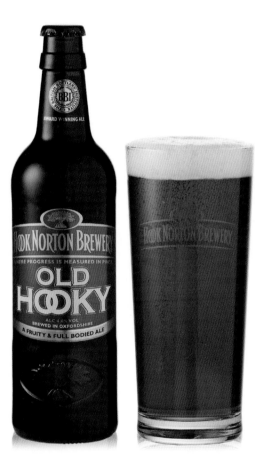

No one seems to know how or why Old Hooky got its name, as it is not actually an old ale. Instead it is a full-bodied, strong bitter. This is a style that was traditionally brewed by many British brewers as a stronger version of their ordinary bitter, which would normally have a strength of around 3.6 percent.

Maris Otter pale ale malt and crystal are used in the mash tun together with some malted wheat (good for head retention), with the spent grains going as animal feed to a local farmer. The unfermented wort is then boiled with a cocktail of Challenger, Fuggle, and Golding hops, which gives the beer its depth of aromatic flavor and bitterness. Dry hops are then put into the casks and add a final flourish of floral notes.

Much of the historic Oxfordshire brewery remains as it was more than a century ago, when the top architect William Bradford designed it, although new mash tuns, fermenters, and a malt silo have all been installed in recent years. The brewery might celebrate heritage and tradition, but it is not stuck in an old-fashioned time warp. Brewer and current chief executive James Clarke says that his great-great-grandfather John Harris, the founder of the brewery, would have used stainless steel vessels to brew Old Hooky, too, had they been available.

A visitor center is housed in the brewery's old maltings. The building is also home to the brewery's museum and a collection of village memorabilia telling the tale of Hook Norton's ales. Those with a keen nose and eye for brewery history can also book tours of Hook Norton. **TH**

Tasting notes

In the glass, a deep copper color, this wonderfully balanced beer has a rich aroma of Maris Otter maltiness. Its taste is fruity by nature—with hints of tangerine and fruitcake, well balanced by hop bitterness. The finish is long and deeply satisfying.

Old Stock Ale

North Coast Brewing | www.northcoastbrewing.com

Country of origin United States
First brewed 2000
Alcohol content 12.5% abv
Serving temperature 55°F, 13°C

With an alcohol content that rivals many wines, plus a more than generous measure of hops, which acts as a natural preservative, North Coast's Old Stock Ale was not meant to be enjoyed immediately after purchase (even though the beer is quite tasty fresh from the brewery). This beer was designed to spend time in the cellar, languishing in the bottle much like a port, until the sweet nectar inside flourishes with a symphony of flavors that rivals anything produced from the grape. The bottles are vintage-dated to help keep track of when the beer has reached its prime.

North Coast's president and brewmaster Mark Ruedrich says, "We encourage vertical tastings of Old Stock." Ruedrich, who lived in Devon, England, for a few years in the 1970s, says Old Stock is brewed with classic Maris Otter pale ale malt and Fuggle and East Kent Golding hops, all of which are imported from England. "Old Stock, the most English-inspired of our beers, is my homage to the southwest—of England, that is," he says, adding that, for pairing with cheese, Old Stock is unparalleled. Keeping to the English theme, he says, "It's a natural with farmhouse Cheddars like Montgomery or Keen's (both of which are made in southwest England) or Lincolnshire Poacher. Ditto with Reggiano Parmigiano—my favorite pairing."

A pioneer in the craft beer movement, North Coast opened in 1988 as a local brewpub in Fort Bragg on California's Mendocino Coast. In addition to its North Coast brands, the brewery has resurrected the brand of Acme, a historic San Francisco brewery with a heritage that dates back to the 1860s. **LMo**

Tasting notes

Aromas of toffee, oak, and dark fruit announce the flavors in this rich beer. A strong caramel backbone leads the way as dessertlike nips of chocolate, rum, and dates take flight. A boozy, bourbonlike presence makes Old Stock Ale a pleasant nightcap.

Old Thumper Extra Special Ale

Shipyard Brewing | www.shipyard.com

Country of origin United States
First brewed 1994
Alcohol content 5.9% abv
Serving temperature 50°F, 10°C

The story of how Old Thumper Extra Special Ale came to be brewed at Shipyard Brewing in Maine is a rather unusual one. British brewer Peter Austin, the founder of Ringwood in Hampshire, England, first produced the ale in 1978 (Austin is often seen as the father of the microbrewery revolution in the United Kingdom). It was known as "No Name Bitter." A radio promotion was held to name the beer, and the winner told the story of enjoying the beer so much in his local pub that he overindulged. He said he woke up the next morning with a thumping headache, so the beer should be called "Old Thumper." As a prize, he received two gallons of Old Thumper each year for life. A decade later, Old Thumper Extra Special Ale was named Grand Champion at the Great British Beer Festival.

Alan Pugsley, Shipyard's brewmaster, trained under Austin at Ringwood. In 1992, Pugsley and entrepreneur Fred Forsley started brewing beer at Federal Jack's Restaurant and Brewpub in Kennebuck, Maine. The pair soon opened a brewery in the waterfront area of Portland, Maine, in the former Crosby Laughlin Foundry. It was natural for Pugsley to start brewing Old Thumper under license at Shipyard in October 1994. The U.S. launch featured a "simultap" at thirty-five New England taverns connected by phone to Shipyard in Maine and Ringwood in England.

Today, Shipyard ships beer to more than thirty states and makes a range of twelve brews, including Summer Ale, made with wheat; Pumpkinhead, made with pumpkin and spices; and Longfellow Winter Ale, a porter-Scotch Ale hybrid. **RL**

Tasting notes

This rich amber-copper-colored beer pours with a generous off-white head. The nose features a flurry of light hop notes, while fruity flavors dance on the palate. Overall, Old Thumper has a very smooth mouthfeel with a pleasant hop note in the finish.

Olde Deuteronomy Barley Wine

Alley Kat Brewing | www.alleykatbeer.com

Country of origin Canada
First brewed 1995
Alcohol content 10% abv
Serving temperature 55°F, 13°C

Alley Kat co-founder Neil Herbst was teaching a home-brewing course in a University of Alberta campus near Edmonton when the idea struck him to open his own craft brewery. Luckily, it occurred at the same time that he lost his job, and he was able to fund the new project with his redundancy payment. Even more fortunate, one of his students, Richard Cholon, also saw the potential in an Edmonton-based craft brewery.

Opening shortly thereafter, in 1995, the two men styled their brewery's image in a quirky fashion, using sometimes comical images of cartoon "kool kats" on its labels—a style nowadays featured on only the Olde Deuteronomy packaging—and emphasizing the feline imagery at every turn. Yet, the beer behind the "kats" was anything but gimmicky, with numerous awards bestowed upon the brewery even within its first few years of operation.

Cholon eventually left to be replaced by Herbst's wife, Lavonne, and the brewery continued its slow but steady penetration of the tough northern Alberta beer market. Beers were added and subtracted from the brewery's portfolio through the ensuing years, but the mainstays that hung in helped cement what remains a still-growing national reputation for quality.

Oddly enough for a country you would think would welcome a proliferation of winter warmers for when the cold winds blow, Canada has not been fertile ground for the potent beer style known as barleywine, and so Herbst's decision to maintain one in his portfolio, however sporadically brewed, is most welcome. **SB**

Tasting notes

The nose of Olde Deuteronomy is almost as fascinating as the taste, offering a complex blend of spice, chocolate-caramel, and dark, dried fruit. In the body, toffee and spice flavors lead to rich fruitiness before ending with a lengthy, warming finish.

OMB Copper

Olde Mecklenburg Brewery | www.oldemeckbrew.com

Country of origin United States
First brewed 2009
Alcohol content 4.8% abv
Serving temperature 43°F, 6°C

The Olde Mecklenburg Brewery is located in a rehabilitated brick building on the south side of Charlotte, North Carolina. The brewery, a partnership between Jon Hayward, Carey Savoy, and John Marrino, made its first beer for public consumption in 2009.

Marrino fell in love with German beer styles while living in Bielefeld, Germany. After he left his job in the United States with a water treatment company, Marrino took his family on a three-month trip around the country. One day, he read a newspaper story about the revival of Rhode Island's Narragansett Brewery, and it occurred to Marrino that he should get into brewing.

Marrino started home-brewing, attending beer festivals, and visiting breweries. All of this research confirmed to him that there was an opportunity to make traditional German styles in the United States. He put together a business plan, located partners, and found the financing to launch Olde Mecklenburg Brewery. The company brought in an experienced Altbier brewer from Germany as a consultant.

OMB Copper is a Düsseldorf-style Altbier, lagered made using a decoction brewing process, where the brew is split during mashing, boiled separately, and then reconstituted. The results are a refreshing beer that has subtle sweetness and complexity. The complicated brewing process means that when the Altbier is made, the day starts around 5:30 A.M. and lasts until around midnight. Olde Mecklenburg also produces a Kölsner—a Kölsch-pilsner hybrid that is lighter in color and much hoppier in flavor—and a fall seasonal, Mecktoberfest. **RL**

Tasting notes

This beer pours a glowing amber color with a fluffy head. There is a slightly sweet initial aroma. The beer offers a full flavor profile that is not overly heavy, opening with a satisfying malty character that eventually travels to a clean, crisp finish.

Orval

Brasserie de l'Abbaye Notre-Dame d'Orval | www.orval.be

Country of origin Belgium
First brewed 1932
Alcohol content 6.2% abv
Serving temperature 44°–50°F, 7°–10°C

One brewery, one name, one beer—how many brewers are content to be this single-minded these days and still remain successful? The Trappist monks at Orval, in the southeastern nook of the Luxembourg province, manage very well. Business is good for this magnificent abbey and its inhabitants, especially since the brewhouse was installed in 2008.

Jean-Marie Roc is the emblematic brewmaster, and he is happy to serve guests a true exclusive: Orval on tap. It's different from the bottled beer, of course, but still essentially the same. And then there is Petit Orval, the monks' own table beer. Again, it's the same thing, just diluted. Some people will say that no two bottles of Orval are ever the same, perhaps because the beer travels badly. It ages, however, remarkably well, and it is hard to pick what is best: a freshly opened bottle at the brewery or a dusty one that has remained for years in the cellar.

The first beers, brewed by monks with some outside help, were pretty different from what we know now. The German Braumeister Pappenheimer and the world-famous professor of brewing techniques, Jean De Clerck, both imprinted their stamps on the beer. Maybe that is why it is incomparable. The alcoholic strength given on the bottle will vary depending on where you buy it—the reason being that no one can tell when the *Brettanomyces* yeasts that are added for bottle conditioning will stop fermenting. Dry hopping with East Kent Golding also adds to the allure. The art deco–influenced bottle design and elegant glass round off this magnificent beer. **JPa**

Tasting notes

The nose has the bitterness you get from vegetables, spices, and flowers. The taste starts very bitter, then is balanced by malt, just short of sweetness; finally there are hints of mandarin zest, hop shoots, and olives. Light, champagne-like carbonation with a lingering bitterness in the finish.

Ostfriesen Bräu Landbier Dunkel

Ostfriesen Bräu | www.ostfriesenbraeu.de

Country of origin Germany
First brewed 1999
Alcohol content 4.8% abv
Serving temperature 46°F, 8°C

Mudflats, dikes, marshland, and moors—East Frisia is flat, rural, and sparsely inhabited. Many tourists flock to this northern German region, some by bike and others by boat. They enjoy the seaside, build sand castles on the beach, and take a swim in the North Sea, if the weather plays along. For many of those who have to cope with gray clouds, rain, and wind, the Landbier Dunkel of Ostfriesen Bräu saves the day.

There are only a few breweries in northern Germany. Apart from a small brewpub in Werdum, Ostfriesen Bräu is the only brewery in the region; based in the small village of Bagband, it stands out like a lighthouse. And its beer is certainly one to remember, being a light-hearted dark with a delicious caramel body.

Owner and brewmaster René Krischer opened the site in 1999 and made the community of Bagband a "beer village" overnight. Besides establishing the brewhouse in an ancient dairy, he set up a pub, restaurant, and beer museum where people can hold seminars and also brew their own beer. Since beer, especially in northern Germany, is a blond and bitter drink, Krischer was sure to brew a decent dark lager just to make a difference. For the Landbier Dunkel, he only uses dark and roasted malts in a labor-intensive decoction mash, where part of the mash is taken out and boiled in a separate vessel, then reintroduced in the tun to heat the remainder. The boiling in this process further intensifies the color. The beer is unfiltered and unpasteurized, while a long period of cold lagering makes it rounded and harmonious. **SK**

Tasting notes

Copper brown with ruby hints, the nose is sweet-sour with a whisper of berries and caramel. Expect a mild drink that builds up a medium body with caramel and roasted flavors. A gentle bitterness joins in and takes the beer to a flowery finish.

Otter Head

Otter Brewery | www.otterbrewery.com

Country of origin England
First brewed 1991
Alcohol content 5.8% abv
Serving temperature 54°F, 12°C

Back in the 1980s, David McCaig was working for the British brewing giants Whitbread at their Liverpool plant. A closure was on the cards and McCaig took retirement; he settled in Devon where he started making furniture. However, once a brewer always a brewer. In 1990, he set up Otter Brewery on an old farm high up in the hills north of the small market town of Honiton. As the headspring of the River Otter was very close, there really could be only one name for the enterprise. The otter—the animal that is—also become integral to the brewery's branding, although one look at a bottle or beer mat shows that its representation owes more to Picasso than Henry Williamson's novel *Tarka the Otter*.

Otter Brewery is very much a family concern. The ancestors of McCaig's wife Mary-Ann once ran the Oak Brewery in Westbury, Wiltshire. "Beer is in the blood" she says. One of their sons Patrick is in charge of marketing, while another, Angus, is head chef at the brewery's tap, the Holt, in Honiton. Their beers are distributed across England's West Country and beyond.

The first beers to emerge from the brewery were Otter Ale and Bitter, but not long afterward, Otter Head was released, a strong chestnut-colored beer that has remained a cult favorite of the brewery's fans ever since. While the Bitter gets six to seven days of fermentation and maturation, Head gets at least ten days. This time period allows them to produce a rich and soothing beer that, although available year-round, is particularly satisfying during the dank and dark days of winter. **ATJ**

Tasting notes

A big-tasting, flavorsome strong ale with toffee, rich malt, and resiny hop aromas on the nose. On the palate, there's rich malt, fruitiness, nuttiness, vinous fruit, and even a trace of chocolate that is balanced by a resiny hoppy finish with a lasting dryness.

Palm

Brouwerij Palm | www.palmbreweries.com

Country of origin Belgium
First brewed 1904
Alcohol content 5.4% abv
Serving temperature 54°–57°F, 12°–14°C

Belgian beers are famous worldwide for their quality, but the common perception is that most of them are strong and rich ales, usually created by Trappist monks. This makes it all the more surprising to discover that the best-selling ale in Belgium is Palm, a light and drinkable high-quality, mellow, amber ale, perfect for sipping on a summer's evening in the garden.

This is no Johnny-come-lately either; it was first brewed by Arthur Van Roy in 1904 for a competition held by Belgian brewing colleges to increase the alcoholic content of lighter Belgian beers to more than 5 percent. The contest was conceived to challenge the new lagers and pilsners that were flooding the Belgian market and crowding out the traditional ales. These new amber beers—"speciale Belge"—were saturated with carbon dioxide to make them as effervescent as the pilsners they were competing against.

Palm is a top-fermentation beer, produced by three specially chosen yeast strains to provide its distinctive fruity banana taste. Roasted malt is used to give it its color and honeyed mellowness, while the hops are sourced from Kent in England for their subtle aroma. Palm Brewery itself, located in Steenhuffel, Belgium, dates back to 1747 when it was called De Horne brewery. The brewery was destroyed in World War I, but Van Roy rebuilt it, and by 1929 he had added the name Palm to his beer to celebrate its award-winning success. It is now the largest independently run brewery in Belgium. As with many Belgian beers, Palm should be served in a snifter, so the full bouquet can be enjoyed. **JM**

Tasting notes

A clear golden amber ale with a creamy white head and only a mild aroma. On the palate, it displays a balanced mellow mixture of caramel flavors, banana, toasted malts, orange, and crisp hop notes with a refreshing clean, dry finish.

Paulaner Salvator

Paulaner Brauerei | www.paulaner.de

Country of origin Germany
First brewed 1773
Alcohol content 7.9% abv
Serving temperature 44°–50°F, 7°–10°C

Paulaner is the biggest brewery in Munich and today belongs to the Schörghuber group. It was founded in 1634, when it was a monastic brewery. The monks then were allowed to produce beer, but only for their personal needs; it wasn't until 1780 that they could sell their beer officially. Paulaner's Salvator is the most famous of the Bavarian strong Lent beers, sustaining and nourishing brews that kept monks going through the period of fasting. It was originally brewed in 1773 when Frater Barnabas, a Paulaner monk, became master brewer, and the brewery claims that the recipe is virtually unchanged since the beer's debut.

It was initially called Sankt-Vaters-Bier, but after the demise of the monastery in 1799 and the emergence of a secular brewing operation, it was renamed Salvator (meaning "savior"). One of Salvator's biggest fans was King Ludwig I, who declared: "Salvator is a luxury article." This royal approval, along with its simple but successful early form of branding, caused a rush of Munich copycat beers with the same name until the brewery successfully applied for a protective patent in 1896.

Devotees of Salvator make a beeline to drink it at the Nockherberg, Paulaner's great beer hall, which has been rebuilt after a devastating fire in 1999. Each year, a day before the official beginning of the strong beer season, it is customary for actors to go on stage and satirize politicians in Berlin and Munich. It is thought that during the two weeks of the strong beer festival in Munich thousands of gallons of Salvator are ordered and drunk at the Nockherberg alone. **WO**

Tasting notes

Salvator is dark amber in color with a strong, malty taste on the palate. There is also, however, a sweetness that is well balanced by a light and fine hop character. The alcohol is shy to emerge, which makes it very drinkable but also dangerous after more than a few pints.

Pauwel Kwak

Brouwerij Bosteels | www.bestbelgianspecialbeers.be

Country of origin Belgium
First brewed *ca*. 1980s
Alcohol content 8% abv
Serving temperature 50°F, 10°C

A beer that is perhaps better known for its unusual glass than for the liquid contained within might seem to be more style than substance. However, just as the Kwak "stirrup cup" is no ordinary glass, Kwak is no commonplace ale. Named after a Napoleon-era innkeeper, Pauwel Kwak, who is said to have run a tavern called De Hoorn in the town of Dendermonde (the brewery's current home), Kwak is the modern product of Bosteels. This is a traditional family brewery, founded in 1791, which is currently run by the father-and-son team, Ivo and Antoine Bosteels.

The style of amber strong ale that claims Kwak as a charter member was formerly well liked in east Flanders according to several sources, but over the years it fell out of favor (ironically it may even have been replaced by the Bosteels pils popularized by the first Antoine Bosteels). In resurrecting it, however, the current Bosteels generation hit upon the neat marketing strategy of using a stirrup glass as their signature vessel. Coachmen once hung the glass from a C-shaped clasp built into the side of their carriages. In a more modern context, the practice might be compared to a smaller version of the yard ale glass.

As much as it added cachet to the beer—travelers' tales abound of being forced to surrender a shoe as a guarantee against the glass—it also prompted some to diminish Kwak as a gimmick brew. It is not. As with the brewery's other two products—DeuS and Karmeliet Tripel—Kwak is a serious beer deserving of attention and contemplation but, as with its glass, never to be taken too seriously. **SB**

Tasting notes

Caramel or toffee are likely the flavors that first-time tasters will take away from this beer, but closer contemplation reveals much more—from a toasty, earthy aroma to notes of orange and spice in the body and a lengthy, drying finish. Would rejuvenate even the weariest coach driver.

Pedigree

Marston's | www.marstonsbeercompany.co.uk

Country of origin England
First brewed 1952
Alcohol content 4.5% abv
Serving temperature 52°–55°F, 11°–13°C

In its heyday, Pedigree was regarded as one of the most sublime of British ales. Brewed using the uncompromising hard waters from Burton-on-Trent in Staffordshire, England, it has a nutty delicateness, which vied for attention on the nose with the famous "Burton snatch," a waft of struck-match sulfur that was a by-product of the mineral-rich waters of the area.

The beer first reached the public as Pedigree in 1952, when Marston's named its best ale Pedigree pale ale, a sign that the austere years after World War II were ending. Branding was being put on hand pumps and consumers were showing a liking for bottled beers with good labeling. At this time, bottled beers were usually served in better condition than draft beers, as restrictions on building materials meant that for years many pub cellars had not been refurbished.

The brewery uses the classic Burton Union system, which was introduced in the 1840s and was at one time widely used for the production of "better" ales. At the start of fermentation, the beer is transferred into 264 linked oak barrels, with carbon dioxide, a by-product of fermentation, helping to expel the yeast off the beer through swan-necked pipes into troughs. Brewers regarded the system as unparalleled for the production of bright, clean, strong-tasting pale ales. Marston's is the sole survivor of this expensive system.

In 2009, Pedigree's bottle strength was increased by 0.5 percent. This was a recognition that bottled beers often need a little more strength than their cask-conditioned brothers to ensure an appetizing flavor and mouthfeel. **TH**

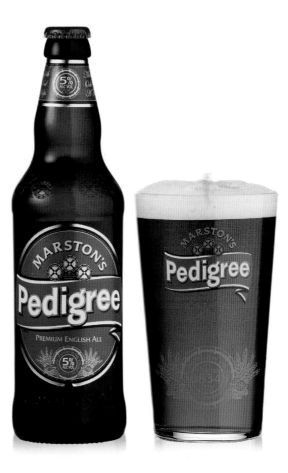

Tasting notes

Gentle caramel notes on the nose with a hint of the "Burton snatch"; toasted biscuity maltiness also in the background. The mouthfeel is rounded and voluptuous, with interplay between spicy hop and a soft billowing of malt sweetness, before a lasting and dry finish.

Marston's branding features a distinctive three-barrel graphic.

Pendle Witches Brew

Moorhouse's Brewery | www.moorhouses.co.uk

Country of origin England
First brewed 1982
Alcohol content 5.1% abv
Serving temperature 52°F, 11°C

Pendle Witches Brew, a marvelous amber-colored beer crammed with malt flavors, was first brewed to satisfy the thirst of bingo players and late-night carousers. Its origins lie in 1982, when local businessman Alan Hutchinson, who had a chain of hotels, bingo halls, and nightclubs, bought the brewery. He was persuaded by his new head brewer to produce another beer to accompany Premier, the company's first brew. The name for Pendle Witches Brew is inspired by the infamous witches of the Pendle countryside around the brewery's hometown of Burnley—today the witch theme casts a spell across many of the company's beers, such as Blonde Witch and Witchfinder General.

The two-beer business strategy was successful, and production grew steadily. Sadly, Alan Hutchinson died suddenly in 1985, and an entertainment company called Apollo Leisure bought his business empire. The hotels and bingo halls fitted in quite neatly with the new owner's existing business, but there was little desire to run a small brewery. Local businessman Bill Parkinson now owns Moorhouse's (having famously bought the brewery just days before it was due to close), and the brewery has thrived under his ownership.

For a beer of its strength, this is an easy drinking beer. Indeed some might say that it is too easy to drink. It is full bodied and well balanced, with the great English aromatic hop Fuggle working in tandem with a grain grist of Maris Otter and Pearl pale ale malt plus some crystal malt for color and body. The beer is an ideal companion with food, and its sweetness makes it a good partner to a hot Indian curry. **TH**

Tasting notes

A robust but easy-drinking beer. On the nose, gentle citrus and a hint of ripe plums; the palate is full of soft malt flavors that are balanced with distinct aromatic, citrusy hop flavors and a bittersweet character. This all helps to lead to a satisfying bitter, dry finish.

Pietra

Brasserie Pietra | www.brasseriepietra.com

Country of origin France
First brewed 1996
Alcohol content 6% abv
Serving temperature 44°F, 7°C

Corsica is the fourth largest island in the Mediterranean after Sicily, Sardinia, and Cyprus. It lies about a hundred miles (160 km) from Italy's western coast, although the island has been French since it was bought from the Genoese in 1764. Much of the mountainous, forested terrain is *maquis*—the harsh rocky scrubland that gave its name to the guerrillas of World War II's French Resistance.

In 1992, Dominique and Armelle Sialelli decided to create a beer brand for Corsica, which—unsurprisingly, given its position between France and Italy—was otherwise a wine-drinking island. The couple was determined to utilize typically Corsican ingredients and flavors. After four years of planning and research, Pietra, a dark lager, was launched in 1996. The beer is described as a chestnut beer. Chestnut flour is not merely a flavoring—it is actually incorporated into the mash to provide fermentable sugars. As little of the island of Corsica is suited to arable farming, chestnuts have long been milled into flour. In fact, 85 percent of the yearly harvest is made into chestnut flour. The rest is cooked for consumption or preserved in sugar syrup as *marron glacé*.

The brewery also produces Serena, a 5 percent pale lager, and Colomba, a wheat beer of the same alcohol content. Although Colomba resembles a wheat beer in the Belgian style, it is spiced with flavors typical of the *maquis*: myrtle, juniper, and tree strawberry (*Arbutus unedo*). Pietra is ideally suited to pairing with typical Corsican food, particularly partridge, roast woodcock, game stew, and wild boar. **JP**

Tasting notes

Pours a deep copper color with a thick white head of large bubbles. The aroma is malty. The flavor is primarily malty with some integral nutty sweetness and low bitterness. It is well balanced and has a smooth mouthfeel. Some fruitiness is evident in the finish.

Piraat

Brouwerij Van Steenberge | www.vansteenberge.com

Country of origin Belgium
First brewed 1986
Alcohol content 10.5% abv
Serving temperature 46°F, 8°C

The Van Steenberge brewery waxes lyrical about its golden ale, Piraat. In promoting the nautically themed beer, the brewers recall the days when water was not available on ships. (People didn't drink it on land because it was mostly contaminated.) The company's website declares that it was beer that refreshed travelers on the oceans.

Piraat is a relatively new creation, one of a number of strong blonds that have arrived on the Belgian beer scene following the great success of the world-famous Duvel. Like that beer, which is named for the Devil, this one conjures up adventure and wickedness. With plenty of alcohol in the mix, there's good reason.

There are, in fact, a pair of Piraats in the Van Steenberge range. The first weighs in at 9 percent; its brother packs a bigger punch at 10.5 percent. But, despite such potency, both remain rather slight in body—a trick achieved by packing the mash tun with rice and sugar as well as barley malt to provide plenty of fermentable sugar. Perfumed citrus notes are supplied by the double hopping of Saaz from the Czech Republic and Hallertau from Germany. Both versions are sold in bottle- and keg-conditioned forms, which ensures a lightness of texture that makes the beer very drinkable for its strength. A fine beer to sip with respect. **JE**

Tasting notes
Crisp but warming golden ale with a zesty orange aroma. Sweet, spicy, perfumed notes join citrus sharpness and gentle herbal notes on the palate. The finish is dry, bittersweet, and hoppy.

Premier Cru

Brasseries Kronenbourg | www.k1664.co.uk

Country of origin France
First brewed 1997
Alcohol content 6% abv
Serving temperature 46°F, 8°C

Brasseries Kronenbourg is the best known of France's brewing companies, and the journey to success began in 1664 when Jérôme Hatt brewed his first beer in Strasbourg in the Alsace region. The original brewery was in the center of the city, but it suffered regular damage when the River Ill flooded. In 1850, it was moved to higher ground in Cronenbourg. The spelling of the name reflects its Alsace heritage.

Kronenbourg has consistently taken the lead in innovation and enterprise in the industry, particularly in developing packaging. In 1947, it became the first brewery to release its products in an 11-oz (33-cl) bottle; in 1953, it was an early adopter of can technology; and, in 1963, it introduced the six-pack. Another groundbreaking development was the 1964 introduction of alcohol-free beer.

Premier Cru, with its distinctive and revolutionary frosted blue bottle, won a gold medal in the strong lager category at an international beer competition in 2005. Its flavor is more robust than most of its contemporaries, whereas its dark golden, almost amber color, derived from a clever roasted barley regime, complements a velvety smooth texture. Premier Cru also highlights the features of the noble Strisselspalt hop—the "caviar" of hops—grown locally for their aromatic qualities. **AG**

Tasting notes
Deep gold in color with some light spice and apple aroma. The toasted grain, nutty palate continues to a sharp and dry finish. Ideal with red meats, game, fish, and cheese.

A print of hop-gathering in Alsace for Kronenbourg, *ca.* 1880. ▸

Primátor Exkluziv 16%

Pivovar Náchod | www.primator.cz

Country of origin Czech Republic
First brewed 1996
Alcohol content 7.5% abv
Serving temperature 44°F, 7°C

For many, the term "lager" is equivalent to "pils," but European lager traditions include dozens of styles beyond pilsner. As if to demonstrate this sense of lager's broad church, the now defunct British magazine *Beers of the World* selected Primátor's Exkluziv as its best overall lager in 2008. A strong beer, it is roughly akin to a maibock or a pale doppelbock.

With 7.5 percent alcohol, the beer is hardly a pilsner-style daily drinker. It is brewed to an original gravity of 16 degrees Plato and is exclusively from Czech pale malt. Two varieties of Czech Saaz hops are used, in pellets as well as extract form, following a recipe said to have been found in the brewery's archives. The result is a bittersweet beer with a fine Saaz hop aroma and finish.

Originally, strong beers of this type were rarely brewed at the Náchod brewery: founded in the east Bohemian city in 1872, its primary output was composed of table beers brewed at 10 and 11 degrees, with occasional strong pale lagers produced for holidays and special events. Only in 1935 did the brewery begin using the Primátor brand name, at first only in conjunction with its dark lager before extending it to its entire line. All beers were only on draft until 1937. Today, all thirteen of its beers are available in bottles. It regularly wins awards from the Union of Friends of Beer, the Czech beer consumers' organization, which named Primátor Exkluziv Best Special Beer in 2008. The beer is said to make an excellent pairing for the country's beloved pickled cheese. **ER**

Tasting notes

Pouring a clear deep gold with a loose white head, this strong lager could be called an imperial pilsner: loaded with rich, sugary malt, lots of peppery Saaz hop presence and a well-balanced bittersweet finish. Be careful, as this doesn't taste anything like 7.5 percent.

Primátor Polotmavý 13%

Pivovar Náchod | www.primator.cz

Country of origin Czech Republic
First brewed 2005
Alcohol content 5.5% abv
Serving temperature 46°F, 8°C

When brewmaster Pavel Kořínek released Primátor's new amber lager in 2005, it created quite a splash among beer drinkers in the Czech Republic. With an original gravity of 13 degrees Plato, the beer had a gulpable sweetness in the mouth followed by a lasting, caramel finish. Containing 5.5 percent alcohol, it qualified as a "special" in Czech brewing terms, but wasn't so strong as to be sipped in tiny amounts.

The beer's history could be traced back a century or more. The amber lagers known as "the Vienna style" are perhaps most famous for their almost total disappearance, although they have remained in vestigial forms in faraway countries, such as Mexico. Many, however, kept being brewed in the Czech lands, just across the country's border to the north. With time, however, Czech beers that were brewed as amber lagers were confused with the half-and-half "cut" pints served in the country's bars, a cocktail composed of half Munich-style dark lager and half pilsner-style pale lager in the same glass. Though the colors of "cut" beer and Vienna lager are similar, the taste is quite different.

Therefore Primátor's new amber turned heads, especially in comparison to its earlier take on the style: brewed at 15 degrees Plato, with 6 percent alcohol by volume, it had been discontinued in 2001. Four years later, the new 13 degrees could be viewed as a continuation of the earlier beer, though it seems far more malty and sugary in the mouth, with more Vienna character than almost any other amber brew in Bohemia. **ER**

Tasting notes

With Czech, Bavarian, and caramel malts going into the brew, as well as just a touch of wheat malt, this amber lager is refreshingly crisp and sweet on the palate, with the sugary notes being well balanced by a gentle touch of Saaz hops.

Propeller Extra Special Bitter

Propeller Brewing Company | www.drinkpropeller.ca

Country of origin Canada
First brewed 1997
Alcohol content 5% abv
Serving temperature 50°F, 10°C

While some might say that nearly every craft brewery of the modern age is the product of a flight of fancy, and a home-brewer's dream of "turning pro," the story of Propeller is a little more literal in that sense than most. For prior to turning professional brewer, owner John Allen's job as a prop master for movies and television was to weave complex tapestries of fantasy and make them seem real. So, when he finally "burned out," as he describes it, his desire to create something of greater substance led him to open the John Allen Brewing Company in Halifax, Nova Scotia.

While Allen notes that naming his business after himself seemed like a good idea at the time, when it came to naming his beer, even he had to admit that John Allen Extra Special Bitter didn't exactly roll off the tongue. Opting for a nautical theme, he decided on the propeller as an emblem even before he discovered that the inventor of the marine screw propeller, John Patch, had been a Nova Scotian. Allen harmonized his trademarks and Propeller Brewing was born.

Since his home-brewing background had already schooled him in British-style ales, and the already well-established Granite Brewery had built a local taste for flavorful ales, Allen opted to build his business on the back of such classic styles, making the Extra Special Bitter (ESB) and Pale Ale his flagship brands. These beers were followed by a short-lived hemp beer and a successful porter, and later by a more populist Honey Wheat and a hoppy IPA. Ultimately, none could dethrone the ESB as the brewery's defining beer, all fantasy aside. **SB**

Tasting notes

Hopped more to dryness than bitterness, this ale offers a soft and cocoa-accented aroma, while the body is mildly roasty with notes of chocolate, caramel, and roasted chestnut, before it descends to a dry and mildly bitter finish. Profoundly sessionable.

Propeller IPA

Propeller Brewing Company | www.drinkpropeller.ca

Country of origin Canada
First brewed 2005
Alcohol content 6.5% abv
Serving temperature 46°F, 8°C

From time to time, a beer bubbles to the surface that for many people defines its style. Sierra Nevada Pale Ale, for example, is to many the definitive U.S.-style pale ale, just as Westmalle Tripel can be said to be the archetypal tripel. What happens, though, when the beer seen to illustrate its style is not actually at all typical? Then you have the curious case of the Labatt-brewed Alexander Keith's India Pale Ale.

Famous across Canada as a beer from the east, Keith's is by far the best-known IPA in the land, despite having little significant hop character, no real fruitiness in its malt profile, and a quite average alcohol content of 5 percent. It's not exactly a standard IPA, but a popular enough beer throughout Canada, and it's widely regarded as what an IPA should be.

It was in this environment that John Allen chose to produce an IPA of his own, a beer the brewery website describes as "bracing, bitter, and higher in alcohol." In other words, given the prevalence of Keith's example, the polar opposite of what most in his market would expect of an IPA. In order to counter any possible confusion and to bring people into the brewery's new store, Allen says Propeller IPA was originally sold only from the brewery, "We sold it from the brewery in 650-ml bottles for a year, until most people understood what we were doing," he says.

Later, the beer was moved into six-packs, although again only from the brewery store at first. It's a strategy that has proved quite successful, as Allen reports that the IPA has vaulted to Propeller's number-two-selling beer, behind only the Extra Special Bitter. **SB**

Tasting notes

Blending the smoothly balanced quaffability of the British style of IPA with the spicy, citrusy hoppiness of the U.S. interpretation, this beer effectively and impressively blurs the line between the two. At the table, this is a fine choice with a curry.

Pure Hoppiness

Alpine Beer Company | www.alpinebeerco.com

Country of origin United States
First brewed 2000
Alcohol content 8% abv
Serving temperature 50°F, 10°C

A true cult favorite, Pure Hoppiness is made in very small batches, and it sells out every time it's released. The hard-to-find double IPA is known for its heaps of hops. As Alpine founder Patrick McIlhenny likes to say about his beer: "So mega-hopped it will take you to hop heaven." The brewery uses hops in the boil, of course, but also adds additional hops in a giant hop-back and, at the end of the process, also includes "an incredible amount of dry hopping for that cutting-edge 'hop bite.'"

McIlhenny was originally a fireman when he took up home-brewing in 1983. After winning numerous competitions, he got a part-time job at his local home-brew supply store and started teaching home-brewing. His early recipes taught him that some flavor components were desirable and others weren't, like too much bitterness. When McIlhenny first made Pure Hoppiness, there wasn't yet a recognized double IPA category. Its original purpose was his attempt to make an IPA that was too hoppy for his wife, a self-avowed hophead. He failed, apparently, as she loved it. Pure Hoppiness is made with both Canadian and premium English malts. The hop varieties come from the Pacific Northwest and the Hallertau region of Germany.

The seeds of Alpine Beer were first sown when McIlhenny volunteered at a local craft brewery and persuaded them to let him make his own beer there on its equipment. In 2001, he bought a small brewing system and stored it while he tried to find a location to build a brewery. The following year, he self-funded, self-designed, and constructed his brewery. **JB**

Tasting notes

Pure Hoppiness is honey amber with a generous ivory head. Its nose is thick with citrus, grassy hop aromas. The double IPA is a creamy hop bomb that just oozes intense hop goodness throughout but still manages to be balanced and very drinkable: a remarkable feat.

Rajah

Stazione Birra | www.stazionebirra.biz

Country of origin Italy
First brewed 2006
Alcohol content 5.2% abv
Serving temperature 43°–46°F, 6°–8°C

If you name a beer Rajah, it's not difficult to guess that it is an India Pale Ale, which was probably what Fabio Verzieri thought when he brewed this ale for the first time. Rajah has a fairly simple recipe, and, given its style, it veers more toward a hoppy profile than a malty one. Into the mash tune goes pils and caramel malts, while the hops are Hallertau Magnum, Spalter Select, and Hersbrucker; some Cascade is also used for aroma and is added ten minutes, or so, before the end of the boil. The fermentation process takes place all in tanks. The beer is mostly sold in the brewpub, but when bottled it rests for at least a week before being sold.

Rajah, which is just one of the six regular beers made at Stazione Birra, was an immediate success with beer drinkers, something that surprised even Verzieri. It is currently one of the blockbusters of the brewery's entire range, probably for two reasons: it's a tasty, easy-to-drink, beer, and it also goes well with spicy food such as chestnut gnocchi with pumpkin sauce and provolone cheese or turkey in beer with almonds and pineapple, just two of the dishes that are sold in Birra's brewpub restaurant.

Verzieri opened Stazione Birra with some friends in 1998, and, as well as being somewhere to drink unpasteurized beers, it has become a well-known venue in which to listen to live music. Verzieri occasionally gets worried that the brewpub might be seen solely as a music hall, rather than somewhere noted for its beer. However, it has been pointed out to him that there's nothing wrong with putting live music and good-quality beer together. **MM**

Tasting notes

Rajah is deep amber color with a white fine foam. The aroma is quite complex with toasted notes and a hint of black tea leaf. On the palate, the hoppy flavor is immediate, very pleasant and long lasting. Lightly astringent in the aftertaste.

Re Ale

Birra del Borgo | www.birradelborgo.it

Country of origin Italy
First brewed 2005
Alcohol content 6.4% abv
Serving temperature 54°–57°F, 12°–14°C

Leonardo Di Vincenzo started his brewing career with a tribute to the first style of beer he ever loved: an English ale served in a pub on a visit he made to England. Given this beer's name, Re Ale, it's not hard to guess that the English pint was a cask-conditioned real ale. The brewing, however, was still in the future because Di Vincenzo was taking a degree in biology at Rome University. His passion for brewing remained strong, eventually taking precedence over his studies. In 2005, Di Vincenzo opened a microbrewery in the village of Borgorose, not far from Rome.

On his debut, his brewing ideas remained strongly focused on the British influence of top-fermenting ale, especially with the first trial brews for beers such as Duchessa or DucAle. However, Re Ale is the beer that made him famous in the passionate world of Italian brewing. With its well-rounded body and rich flavor and aroma, this beer was what Di Vincenzo had been searching for. Munich and crystal malts, plus some caramelized wheat malt, provide the malt base for Re Ale, while the hop regime is a mixture of Cascade, Amarillo, and East Kent Golding put in together during the boil at intervals of fifteen or twenty minutes. The brewing process is quite quick: twenty days of primary fermentation followed by more or less two weeks in the bottle.

Re Ale is a very enjoyable and truly inspired ale, as well as being a great companion to food. In Italy it is excellent with spicy pasta dishes or a well-ripened sheep's cheese. However, it is just as pleasing when drunk and contemplated on its own. **MM**

Tasting notes

Brilliant amber color with a fine white foam. On the nose, the aroma starts very citrusy (grapefruit and orange), with a hint of spices and pepper. On the palate, there is a low carbonation, with a good balance between crisp maltiness and citrus fruits, before a final flourish of hop bitterness.

Red MacGregor

Orkney Brewery | www.orkneybrewery.co.uk

Country of origin Scotland
First brewed 1996
Alcohol content 4% abv
Serving temperature 50°F, 10°C

Roger White, the original owner of Orkney Brewery, claimed to be a descendant of Scotland's MacGregor clan and consequently named this distinctive beer in its honor. The most famous MacGregor was Rob Roy (1671–1734)—the rustler, freebooter, Jacobite sympathizer, and warrior. Red MacGregor, the beer, is as distinct in color and as robust as its namesake, yet it is also delicate and sophisticated.

The cask version was the first Scottish beer to win a gold medal at the British Institute of Innkeeping World Cask Beer awards, and it came second only to another Orkney beer, Raven Ale, in the Champion Beer of Scotland competition in 2009, a feat that confirms the archipelago's reputation as a producer of exceptional food and drink, such as malt whisky, cheese, beef, salmon, lobster, crab, and mussels. All of the above are fine table companions to Red MacGregor.

Orkney Brewery was set up in 1988 in a former schoolhouse in Quoyloo on Orkney. It merged with Atlas Brewery in 2004 under the name Highland and Islands Breweries, which was later taken over by Sinclair Breweries. The business operates under strict ecological lines with waste water filtered through two neighboring lochs supporting fish and waterfowl.

Orkney has some of the finest archaeological sites in Europe, including 5,500-year-old Neolithic burial tombs and stone circles that have UNESCO World Heritage status. The brewery considers this link and its location as being influential on its enterprise, rather like the indefinable terroir of French wine-making. Indeed, its slogan is "5,000 Years in the Making." **AG**

Tasting notes

Brilliant ruby red with contrasting smooth, white head. Deliciously perfumed, its floral, lychee aromas unveil notes of violets and rosewater with hints of spiciness and toasted malts. On the mouth, rich summer berries and toffee-tinged malt give way to a dry, floral hop bitterness.

Rejewvenator

Shmaltz Brewing | www.shmaltz.com

Country of origin United States
First brewed 2008
Alcohol content 7.8% abv
Serving temperature 48°F, 9°C

What started off as a high school joke became reality when Shmaltz Brewing was founded by Jeremy Cowan in 1996 and the He'Brew brand was launched. Its slogan is "The Chosen Beer." At first, the operation consisted of just one hundred cases of a beer brewed with pomegranate, hand-bottled and delivered by Cowan himself around San Francisco. They sold like hot knish and, in 1997, Shmaltz officially became a contract brewery.

Cowan was looking to create a beer that reached out to the Jewish community—a high-quality product that maintained Jewish humor and culture. Each fall, to celebrate Shmaltz's anniversary and the holy days of the Jewish faith, it brews a new beer in their Jewbelation series. In 2007, it launched the Sacred Fruit range for spring release, each beer featuring a certain fruit. The fruits used have some sort of biblical reference that is shown on the label. The Rejewvenator was first brewed in 2008 as part of this series.

It is a mixed style bringing together elements of a doppelbock and a Belgian dubbel. The fermentation starts at cold temperatures with a lager yeast. The beer is then allowed to warm up, and a top-fermenting abbey yeast strain is pitched. Lastly, fresh-pressed fruit juice is added to the fermenter and, after a month-long maturation period, the beer goes through a centrifuge filter and is bottled. In 2008, it was brewed with figs and, in 2009, it came back after popular demand with fresh crushed date juice added to the tank. It has met with so much success that it looks like this He'Brew beer will be back in years to come. **MO**

Tasting notes

Mahogany with a beige head. The nose is full with notes of red fruit, candy sugar, and earthy tones. The mouth has a subtle sweetness that turns dry, leaving the malt to step forward. The finish has a substantial bitterness while aromas of dried fruits and dates linger. Warming.

Riggwelter

Black Sheep Brewery | www.blacksheepbrewery.com

Country of origin England
First brewed 1995
Alcohol content 5.7% abv
Serving temperature 52°F, 11°C

Humor is never far away from Paul Theakston, the founder of Black Sheep Brewery. In English, the idiom "the black sheep" refers to a member of a family who is deemed undesirable. The name reflects the Theakston family brewery schism, now long healed, that took place when he broke away to open his own business. Sheep are also the main source of income in this rural community. The theme continues with Riggwelter; in the local Yorkshire dialect it means a sheep that is lying on its back and cannot get up. The beer's creator, former head brewer Paul Ambler, said that devising the beer was easy, but persuading Paul Theakston it should go into production was the hard part. While Ambler's brief was to make a beer with a distinctive taste, Theakston is not a fan of strong roasted flavors, which Riggwelter is packed with.

For the grist, Ambler took Maris Otter pale ale malt, crystal malt, and torrified wheat, which helps give the beer its glorious white collar when poured, and then added pale chocolate malt. The stronger alcohol content comes from the use of sugar in the grist. To balance the alcohol and roasted flavors from the pale chocolate malt, a double amount of Golding is used as late hops, adding extra aroma and bitterness.

Black Sheep beers are fermented in vessels called "Yorkshire Squares"; today they are circular in shape and made of stainless steel, but the process is the same. The unfermented wort is poured into the bottom of a two-tiered chamber, and, as the beer ferments, the yeast rises up into the second chamber where it is collected, allowing the beer below to drain away. **TH**

Tasting notes

A wolf in sheep's clothing, this is full of roasted malt, hops, and banana flavor. The palate is dry and a complex mixture of hops, fruit, and roasted malt with a dry refreshing finish. Like a rich Burgundy wine, Riggwelter pairs well with red meats.

Rising Sun Pale Ale

Baird Brewing | www.bairdbeer.com

Country of origin Japan
First brewed *ca.* 2001
Alcohol content 5% abv
Serving temperature 46°–54°F, 8°–12°C

Baird Brewing has literally been built from the ground up in the small fishing town of Numazu, about two hours south of Tokyo by train. Founded by Ohio-native Bryan Baird and his wife, Sayuri, the brewery began life in 2001 on an 8-gallon (30-l) brewing system. Brewing on such a small system kept Baird quite busy for just over two years, when he was finally able to move up to a larger, two-barrel system. Still, it was a challenge relished by the energetic Baird, who has built his lineup of regularly brewed ales to seven. In 2006, he finally installed an eight-barrel system, but still keeps the two-barrel system for seasonals.

Perhaps his most representative beer is Rising Sun Pale Ale. He says that since he was already brewing an IPA, he hoped to distinguish this beer by using American West Coast pale ales as an inspiration. Naturally, this depended mainly on the hop profile. Initially, Baird used Amarillo, Centennial, and Perle, but over the years the brewery began to experiment with other hops. At present, the beer is brewed with Simcoe, Centennial, Amarillo, Cascade, and Ahtanum. Baird admits Rising Sun has not been an easy beer to brew. The biggest challenge, and the one key to the beer's success, has been combining the citruslike hop flavors to get the desired result.

Although Rising Sun Pale Ale is the best selling of Baird's seven regular beers, it still doesn't surpass 25 percent of overall sales. Current plans are for two new regular beers, one probably a lager and the other based on Belgian yeast. With a regular parade of seasonal beers, Bryan Baird will certainly stay busy. **BH**

Tasting notes

It is golden bronze with an ivory head. There is a well-defined U.S. hop aroma with faint malt in the background. The brisk, hop-dominated flavor is backed by creamy textured malt. There is a strong and brisk quenching finish with lingering hops.

Rogers' Beer

Little Creatures Brewery | www.littlecreatures.com.au

Country of origin Australia
First brewed 2001
Alcohol content 3.8% abv
Serving temperature 39°F, 4°C

Little Creatures Brewery had to work hard to have its flagship pale ale accepted by both publicans and drinkers after its release in 2000. Like other beers of its style, it was quite shocking to many, and at that time, Australians were not generally used to there being that much flavor in their beer. Although pale ale was eventually embraced around the country, the Little Creatures founders wanted to develop a beer that was an easy drinking ale. Not that Australians were used to this concept at the time, either.

Rogers' is one of the smartest beers available. Carefully designed, it uses at least five specialty malts to give it its amber color, caramel notes, and smooth mouthfeel. In contrast to the pale ale, it has only been lightly hopped, making it less bitter and more sessionable. However, the real genius of the beer is that it manages to do all of this and only be 3.8 percent in its alcohol content. Australia has a wide selection of mid-strength beers, but the view of those who tend to think about such things is that life is too short to drink any of them. Rogers' is the single, striking exception.

So impressed were the staff of Little Creatures with the design of this beer that they decided to name it after the people who made it. Roger Bussell knew a lot about malt, and was reportedly as good as you could get when it came to ale brewing. Roger Bailey was an experienced brewing engineer. The prolific Phil Sexton assisted as a technical adviser. The best place to enjoy Rogers' is at the brewery itself in Fremantle, western Australia, which is set in an old crocodile farm and is as welcoming as a cellar door. **DD**

Tasting notes

Best served cold, this beer presents itself with a light amber body and pillowy head. A combination of floral and caramel aromas follow through with a nutty, fruity body and a firm, bitter finish. An extremely sessionable beer that is perfect for a week night's ale or two.

Sagres Bohemia

Sagres | www.sagresbeer.com

Country of origin Portugal
First brewed 2005
Alcohol content 6.2% abv
Serving temperature 48°F, 9°C

Given that Portugal is better known for wine and port, the really surprising thing about Sagres Bohemia is that it is as good or better than many of the amber beers from Bavaria and Austria. Its color and flavor have much in common with the lagers of Vienna, or the seasonal Märzen and Oktoberfest beers of Germany.

The classic place to drink this beer is probably the Cervejaria Trindade in Lisbon, a restaurant owned by Central de Cervejas. Think of a Portuguese steak and fish house with a splash of Munich beer hall, and you've got it. Although the restaurant is packed with tourists, it's hard to deny the bustling atmosphere and tiled walls depicting happy beer-gulping monks. Trindade celebrated its 170th anniversary in 2006, and Centralcer marked the occasion by releasing a special version of Sagres Bohemia.

The company says that the beer was made to accompany food, and it does this well. Its bready aroma and mildly sweet flavors can bring out the best in seared meat or sausage, whereas the bitterness and carbonation are reasonable enough to cut through the fat. Despite its bocklike strength, the beer remains light enough to be refreshing. It's no wonder that this is one of the few Portuguese beers that is also available in 25-ounce (75-cl) bottles, ideal for sharing.

At the Trindade, the beer is served in a frosted tulip glass, perhaps next to a sampler of farmhouse sausage. When the food and drink and ambiance all come together, there is no need to close your eyes and pretend you're in Munich. Portugal is a fine place to be in its own right. Even for beer lovers. **JS**

Tasting notes
Pours dark, reddish amber into the glass beneath an off-white cap. Nose is caramel-sweet and bready. On the palate, it is not as sweet as feared; instead there's a mild, grassy bitterness. Tinges of alcohol do not interfere. Refreshing despite its strength.

Saison Rue

The Bruery | www.thebruery.com

Country of origin United States
First brewed 2008
Alcohol content 8.5% abv
Serving temperature 50°F, 10°C

This is one of a new breed of U.S. beers that takes its inspiration from Belgium yet seeks to create something uniquely American. Patrick Rue, the young founder of The Bruery, focuses on adventurous, large-format, bottle-conditioned beers: a rapidly growing segment of the U.S. craft beer market.

Saison Rue is an intersection of several interests, according to Rue. "I'm a big fan of Dupont Avec Les Bon Voeux because it is complex, spicy, big, yet easy on the palate. I'm also a fan of beers that contain *Brettanomyces* yeast because it brings another dimension to the beer and noticeably changes it over time. Rye is the perfect ingredient in a beer that is going to become extremely dry as it adds mouthfeel and texture." Rye is a challenging ingredient to brew with as it can be gluey in the mash tun, making it difficult to run off the wort. But its unique pepperiness and creamy texture make the effort well worthwhile.

Historically, saison's origins are rather obscure. One meaning of the term is used to designate the stronger, full-strength beers that were brewed only in the proper winter brewing season or *en saison*. The style is highly dependent on yeast character. Some, but not all saisons add *Brettanomyces*, which adds a range of earthy and fruity flavors plus a bit of acidity. Like all bottle-conditioned beers, Saison Rue is a living thing. "We typically warm-condition the beer for two months before we release it to allow the *Brettanomyces* to come through," says Rue. "I enjoy Saison Rue the most after six months in the bottle when the *Brett* is especially prevalent." **RM**

Tasting notes

Saison Rue is characterized by a nose that is full of bright, fruity flavors with some big herbal and spicy notes. A sharp palate with a fair bit of acidity and a kind of peppery bite, balanced by an element of sweetness and the mouth-coating creaminess of rye.

Saison Voisin

Brasserie des Géants (Légendes) | www.brasseriedesgeants.com

Country of origin Belgium
First brewed 2001
Alcohol content 5% abv
Serving temperature 54°F, 12°C

An old castle with a brewery inside: what could be better? Géants opened in 2000 at the Château de Irchonwelz, near the Hainaut town of Ath. The area is famous for its annual parades of gigantic puppets, hence the brewery name. Inside the castle, the small brewery is surprisingly modern. The doors open to the public on certain days of the year for small medieval fairs, during which the Saison Voisin is invariably available on draft. It is a great challenge to drink only one, especially from a curvy tumbler glass that encourages real gulping rather than dainty sipping.

The Saison Voisin is a bit of an unsung hero, not only among Géants beers but also among saisons in general. It's less complex than the famous Saison Dupont and less alcoholic than some of the so-called super saisons. It is supposedly made from a recipe that dates to 1883. A few generations of the Voisin family made a version of this beer in nearby Flaubecq until the Brasserie Voisin shut in 1989. Géants later bought the equipment, and old Léon Voisin was so impressed that he passed on the Saison Voisin recipe.

The beer has improved with seemingly greater hop bitterness during the last couple of years. The biscuit malt flavor is still there but less pronounced. Meanwhile, its relatively low strength makes the Voisin sessionable by Belgian standards, almost a throwback to the traditional low-strength saisons from which it descended. The current result is an honest, bone-dry, refreshingly bitter amber ale that deserves more fame. In 2006, Géants merged with Ellezelloise to become the Légendes brewery. **JS**

Tasting notes

Pours a lovely copper color with a soapy-beige head. In the nose, grassy hops find biscuity maltiness, and notes of pear and tart cider. There is almost no sweetness, mainly a dry and grassy bitterness that envelops the tongue. Very dry finish and lingering bitter aftertaste.

Samichlaus Bier

Castle Brewery Eggenberg | www.schloss-eggenberg.at

Country of origin Austria
First brewed 1979
Alcohol content 14% abv
Serving temperature 50°F, 10°C

The story of one of the world's strongest lagers begins beneath the mountains of central Switzerland, where, in the 1970s, the Hürlimann Brewery made a name for itself through adventurous experiments with yeast. The Swiss brewers discovered a way of fermenting wort to create a beer of 14 percent abv, comfortably above the levels normally achieved by brewers' yeasts. Sensibly, they decided to make the fruits of their labors a celebratory beer, with Christmas providing the ideal occasion for rolling out their creation. The beer, which they called Samichlaus, from the Swiss-German for Santa Claus, took the brewing world by storm and earned a place in the *Guinness Book of World Records*.

The fate of Samichlaus looked to be bleak by the late 1990s, when Hürlimann was taken over by its local rival Felschlössen, and the beer was cut from the portfolio. Fortunately, help was at hand in the form of Austrian brewery Eggenberg. This family business also specialized in strong, specialty beers, and in 1999, it seized the opportunity to take on the brewing and marketing of such a special product.

Samichlaus is brewed annually on December 6, St. Nicholas's Day. It ferments for three weeks and is then cold-conditioned for ten months before being packaged and released in time for Christmas. The malts in the mash are pilsner, Munich, and roasted, with local Muehlviertler hops joining Perle, Magnum, and Spalter Select for balance. But it is the yeast that gives this beer its uniqueness, raising the strength to giddy heights and gifting the world a comforting brew with which to ease into the spirit of Christmas. **JE**

Tasting notes

Malt, sherry, and vine fruits fill the aroma of this dark amber beer. The taste is equally full and sweet, with raisins, plums, and flashes of orange topping smooth, creamy malt. The same fruitiness features in the creamy, warming, dry, and tangy finish.

Samuel Adams Boston Lager

Boston Beer | www.samueladams.com

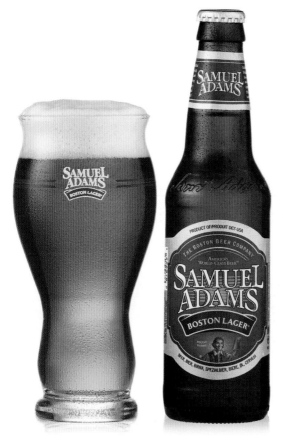

Country of origin United States
First brewed 1985
Alcohol content 4.9% abv
Serving temperature 41°F, 5°C

Twenty-five years after it was first brewed, Boston Lager has a strange grip on beer enthusiasts. It is now old hat, a beer that is so commonplace that it appears in the coolers at takeout restaurants and on tap at ballparks. Some beer snobs—looking for the next best thing—shrug it off without a second thought. Even the brewery seems to have progressed beyond its flagship, regularly producing more than thirty different varieties, some of them highly praised experimental styles brewed in small batches with exotic flavors.

When Boston Lager was first introduced, there was nothing like it in the United States. Mass-produced lagers were fizzy, yellow, and characterless; the few available microbrews were mainly hoppy ales. Here was an amber lager that was proud of its distinctive ingredients: two-row barley and German "noble" aroma hops. A decoction mash and krausening gave it a smooth finish; dry hopping—then unheard of in U.S. lagers—gave it a distinct nose.

As the American craft beer renaissance moves into its second generation, it is tempting to toss this groundbreaking brand a bouquet for old time's sake. There's no need. Anyone who takes an honest pour today will recognize why this beer is still such a pleasure. Sweet, lightly roasted malt and fresh gardenlike hops dance across the palate in comfortable harmony. A refreshing and reliable thirst quencher, Boston Lager is nonetheless a full-bodied complement to an array of dishes. If this is the modern version of a go-to beer, a standby that one can always depend upon, we live in a wondrous world. **DR**

Tasting notes

This bright amber copper beer has a proud firm head of foam; solid hop aroma of freshly cut grass. Although exceptionally well balanced, distinctly sweet malt and hop bitterness provide an outstanding complexity and a smooth, mellow finish.

Samuel Adams Double Bock

Boston Beer | www.samueladams.com

Country of origin United States
First brewed 1988
Alcohol content 9.5% abv
Serving temperature 44°F, 7°C

When Jim Koch shows up to pour a few rounds at the Boston Beer booth at the Great American Beer Festival, the crowds surge forward and glasses are thrust in his direction. But Koch did not get into brewing until he discovered a recipe for his great-great-grandfather's Louis Koch Lager in his parents' attic when he was thirty-five years old. In 1984, he made the first home-brewed batch of Samuel Adams Boston Lager, one of the most successful new beers launched in the United States during the craft beer era.

Boston Beer has a small brewing operation in the former Haffenreffer Brewery in the Jamaica Plain section of Boston, but most of its beer is turned out at breweries that it has acquired in Cincinnati (the former Hudepohl-Schoenling Brewery) and outside of Allentown (originally the F and M Schaefer Brewery). With all of the industry consolidation that has taken place, when InBev took over Anheuser-Busch in 2008, Boston Beer became the largest U.S.-owned brewer to have its own brewhouse (Pabst Brewing turns out more beer, but does so under contract with other brewers).

The Samuel Adams Double Bock is part of the brewery's Imperial Series, and you can taste the half pound per bottle of Harrington Metcalfe and caramel 60 malt that goes into the recipe. Double Bock is brewed using only first wort—wort that has not been sparged in the lauter tun—delivering a very high-gravity liquid. The beer is aged for more than four weeks, which helps to intensify the flavors. The result is a classic German-style doppelbock. **RL**

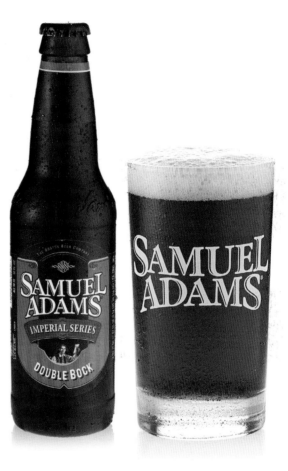

Tasting notes

This beer pours a tarnished penny color with a relatively thin, but long-lasting, tan head. There is an immediate sweet malty nose that lingers. You can certainly taste the alcohol, but the caramelized malt builds a silky mouthfeel and long satisfying finish.

Samuel Adams Irish Red

Boston Beer | www.samueladams.com

Country of origin United States
First brewed 2007
Alcohol content 5.5% abv
Serving temperature 41°F, 5°C

"When you're the little guy," says Jim Koch, Boston Beer's founder, "you can't do bar promotions with pretty models, or ticket giveaways, or inflatable sumo wrestlers, or all the other things that big guys do. . . . When we go into bars, we want to educate people, and the best way we can do that is with our beers. Give them a taste and explain how they're different."

And then, some genius in the Boston Beer marketing department decided to create the Beer Lovers Choice campaign to pit two prototypes against each other in a winner-takes-all contest. Barflies and aficionados taste both varieties at hundreds of events each year and vote for their favorite. The winner goes into full production the following year. This fine Irish Red was the overwhelming favorite in 2007, and it quickly emerged as one of the best ever to wear the Samuel Adams label.

Irish red ale is a scary notion these days, its name being applied to anything that has even a hint of rose behind the amber. Poseurs and wannabes latch onto the style knowing that anything called "Irish" will attract the guzzlers, regardless of quality. "When Boston Beer designed this one," says Koch, "it took a step backward, to the style's 18th-century origins as a malt hero." Credit the Harrington and Metcalfe malted barley for the body; meanwhile caramel 60—the malt that frequently shows up in bock or Vienna lager—provides the deep-red color and long-lasting head. It's all balanced by earthy East Kent Golding and Spalt Spalter hops. Of course, the thousands of beer lovers who made Irish Red their champion don't know its pedigree. Sip for sip, they just love how it tastes. **DR**

Tasting notes

The deep red color that defines this style sparkles like the clearest ruby gem. Sweet malt with a touch of fruit is matched by an earthy hop aroma. Its man-sized portion of malt is biscuitlike, but not overly sweet: a triumph of superb, full-bodied balance.

Samuel Smith's Nut Brown Ale

Samuel Smith | www.tadcaster.uk.com/breweriesSamuelSmith.htm

Country of origin England
First brewed *ca.* 1900
Alcohol content 5% abv
Serving temperature 55°F, 13°C

Brown ale is a style of beer that has a strong regional association with the north of England. The widely known archetype, Newcastle Brown Ale, is a pretty good representation of the style, and although it may not be what it once was, enough of the original remains to give an exemplar for the style—medium to dark brown in color, only lightly hopped, with some toffeelike malt character. It is something of a paradox—the beers are fairly sweet and full-flavored, but somehow have a slightly dry, nutty austerity.

Samuel Smith's example, which possibly predates the presumed original from Newcastle, is much more robust. It is bigger bodied, with a toasted nutty malt character and a chewiness that isn't really found in any other example of the style. This quality is said to come from Smith's use of an old system of fermentation, the Yorkshire Square—a huge double-decked stone vessel that is said to produce a more rounded style of beer.

The beer ferments in the lower chamber, and the frothy, yeasty head gains access to the top deck through a manhole-sized aperture. This necessitates frequent "rousing"—the fermenting beer is sprayed through the rocky yeast cap to encourage fermentation. It has been suggested that this system has encouraged a more vigorous strain of yeast over time, and certainly Smith's ales all have an unusually full-bodied character.

Sam Smith is one of the last breweries to use this system, and it preserves its huge Welsh slate squares with pride. Although modern drinkers are dazzled by ever brighter and more intense hop characters, Sam Smith's Nut Brown is a paragon of tradition. **ZA**

Tasting notes

This ruddy brown beer is exceptionally clear in the glass, with a fine, persistent carbonation. The aroma really does have a nutlike quality, some toffee, and an earthy hop note. Medium dry, with nutty malt dominating, and a slightly woody quality to the finish.

Samuel Smith's Old Brewery Pale Ale

Samuel Smith | www.tadcaster.uk.com/breweriesSamuelSmith.htm

Country of origin England
First brewed *ca.* 1980s
Alcohol content 5% abv
Serving temperature 52°F, 11°C

This is a beer whose reputation stretches from New York to California and from Perth to Brisbane, yet ironically it comes from an enigmatic and secretive brewer in a small North Yorkshire town. Its popularity may be something to do with the fact that it is a sublime example of a stronger English bitter. On draft, the beer is full of smooth malty biscuit character, and it has the crisp, clear taste that one would expect from a beer fermented in Yorkshire Squares.

Other brewers have stainless steel squares and some are even round, but tradition means much at Sam Smith's and its squares are not only square but made with Yorkshire stone, too. Other aspects of the brewery's tradition means that the grist of pale and crystal malts is boiled in traditional mash tuns and the hops are Golding and Fuggle; added late these bring a dash of spice to the beer. The yeast has been used at the brewery for more than one hundred years, and its vigor and vitality create the beer's rich, frothing, foaming head in the fermenting room. The original well at the brewery, sunk in 1758, is still in use, and the brewing water for Old Brewery Pale Ale is drawn from deep underground. The brewery even has that rare unicorn of brewing, a cooper, who still makes and repairs all the wooden casks that are used to serve a cask-conditioned version of Old Brewery Pale Ale in many of the company's pubs.

The Samuel Smith brewery was founded in 1758, although the Smith family didn't take it over until 1847. The family is also responsible for founding the John Smith brewery next door. **TH**

Tasting notes

Old Brewery Pale Ale is a traditional Yorkshire-style bitter—dark tan in color with the effervescence in the beer helping to form a brimming white head on top. It is malty to taste with a hint of butterscotch, nuts, and fruit, and a dash of spicy hops.

The Old Brewery in Tadcaster, North Yorkshire, England.

Münchener Farbmalzfabrik
· Emil Gunßer ·
Reichenbachstr 39 Tel · 5334
Münchener Farbmalz entspricht den
steueramtlichen Vorschriften ·

·Franz Roth· 1912·

Schäazer Kronabier

Brauerei Drei Kronen | www.kronabier.de

Country of origin Germany
First brewed 1837
Alcohol content 5.1% abv
Serving temperature 46°F, 8°C

Knock, knock. Be prepared to knock on the table when you enter the Drei Kronen brewpub. This is what locals used to do in Franconian taverns to greet guests, and Drei Kronen (Three Crowns) has become known for it. The brewery's standard lager offers a fabulous fruity maltiness, floral head notes, and a balanced interplay of sweet and bitter flavors. It has been brewed since brewmaster Josef Lindner's family business was founded in 1837, and probably even before. Lindner uses pilsner and Munich malts to create the warm color. He worked on the bitterness to make it more harmonious and switched from bittering hops to the German noble breed Hallertauer Tradition.

In homage to Lindner's grandfather whom the locals called "Kronawirt" (crown landlord), the brewery relaunched the brand at the beginning of the 1990s, naming it Schäazer Kronabier. **SK**

Tasting notes
This lager smells like honey; the first taste is sweet, fruity maltiness, medium bodied with elegant floral notes. Balanced by a moderate bitterness that only emerges at the end.

Schlägl Doppel Bock

Stiftsbrauerei Schlägl | www.stift-schlaegl.at

Country of origin Austria
First brewed 1580
Alcohol content 8.3% abv
Serving temperature 50°F, 10°C

The White Canons of the Premonstratensian order started brewing beer well before 1580 in a remote village on the southern edge of the Bohemian Forest. The monastery was founded in 1202, but there are no records of the brewery until the late 16th century.

Although the "doppel" in the doppel bock means "double," this beer is not twice as strong as standard bocks. However, it is a little stronger; German bock beers are typically around 7 percent abv.

As is the case in most other Austrian breweries, Schlägl's bock beer is brewed in time for Christmas and is available only from November to late December. Schlägl is the only brewery in Austria that is wholly owned by a monastery, and it is across the street from the actual baroque monastery buildings. These comprise a church with a Romanesque crypt, which legend has it was used to store beer for some time. **CS**

Tasting notes
The nose is sweet and fragrant, resembling violets. Carbonation is rather low, so the potent body and the sweetness can tend to dominate the overall impression.

Stamp from 1912 showing the Emil Gussner malt factory in Munich.

Schumacher Alt

Brauerei Schumacher | www.schumacher-alt.de

Country of origin Germany
First brewed 1838
Alcohol content 4.6% abv
Serving temperature 46°F, 8°C

Heavily bombed in World War II, the city of Düsseldorf has been completely rebuilt, and to walk around the old town (or "Altstadt"), you wouldn't think that most of it is only fifty years old or less. This is a lively, beery area, full of bars and restaurants, known as "the longest bar in the world." This is an Altbier city and adverts for Diebels, the best-selling of its style, crop up everywhere, run a close second by one of its rivals, Frankenheim. However, it's the quartet of small brewpubs that connoisseurs of alt come to investigate: Schüssel, Fühschen, Uerige, and Schumcher. Uerige might be the best known of the bunch, but Schumacher runs it a pretty close second.

Schumacher Alt has been brewed since 1838, when Johann Matthias Schumacher took over an already existing brewery. Thirty-three years later, the brewery moved out of the Altstadt to the nearby Oststrasse, where it and its restaurant are still situated today. Here this beer comes as fresh as possible from wooden casks. However, it still maintains an important and traditional place within the Altstadt at the Golden Kessel. A visit to both Oststrasse and the Golden Kessel (as well as the other three Altstadt brewers) will see drinkers being served by blue-shirted beer waiters called "Kobes" bustling their way through the crowds, looking for empty glasses to be replenished. They wander round, tray in hand, topping up the thirsty and posing for pictures. When you order a beer, they make a mark on your beer mat and use that to create the bill, so beware of adding extra doodles to beer mats and upping the price. **WO**

Tasting notes

The dark mahogany color of Schumacher Alt is typical, as is the fine foam at the top of the small glasses. Schumacher Alt tastes very fresh with a light bitterness from hops at the palate and a fresh hop finish with light and pleasant notes of fine yeast.

Scotch Ale

Red Hill Brewery | www.redhillbrewery.com.au

Country of origin Australia
First brewed 2005
Alcohol content 5.8% abv
Serving temperature 46°–54°F, 8°–12°C

Although brewers are often loath to admit it, the tax and laws that regulate the brewing industry have driven decisions about beer that would not have been made otherwise. Rarely have these changes been for the better from the beer's perspective. Taxation, for example, is the reason why most beers in Australia are 5 percent abv or less. In most cases, the brewer brews the beer in the way that he or she would like, and then, after a wistful taste, pours water into the vat until the alcohol drops below the percentage required to keep the tax man at bay.

However, in the case of Red Hill Brewery in the Mornington Peninsula, Victoria, the law has unexpectedly resulted in what can only be described as a win-win situation. After spending seven years planning a brewery and mortgaging their home for funding, David and Karen Golding discovered to their horror that they were prohibited from opening one unless it had some agricultural connection to the land. After much deliberation, David and Karen decided to become hop farmers and to operate a brewery to support their bountiful crops of hops.

And farm they did. The Red Hill Brewery is now the only brewery in Australia that grows its own hops. Once a year, a group of volunteers from the local community lends a hand to harvest the five different varieties of hops in return for a few high-quality samples. This means that the hops are grown to order and are as fresh as a beer could hope for. It's no wonder that the locals are known to raise a glass of Scotch Ale to the Mornington Peninsula's favorite farmers. **DD**

Tasting notes

This ale pours an inviting scorched red color and entices with a strong carmalized aroma before delivering a well-balanced toffee malt sweetness. Local hop flowers subtly contribute to a mildly bitter finish. A perfect match to fricassee chicken in red wine.

Scotch Silly

Brasserie Silly | www.silly-beer.com

Country of origin Belgium
First brewed 1919
Alcohol content 8% abv
Serving temperature 46°F, 8°C

Brasserie Silly is a family-owned brewery that first opened in 1850 in the little town of Silly in Hainaut Province. Up until World War II, the area's inhabitants mainly worked in farming, and the brewery was a farm when it first opened. During the 1970s, the brewery underwent a series of changes, first of all changing from Meynsbrughen (the family name) to Silly, then expanding its range of beers with a view to becoming better known in Belgium and beyond.

Scotch de Silly is one of the brewery's great survivors, a Scottish style of beer with an intriguing history. It is said that a Scottish regiment was stationed in Silly just after World War I and that the troops desired something that reminded them of home: in other words beer. The officers asked the brewery owner to brew a strong Scotch ale for them, a style of beer that would have been darkish, malty, and slightly sweet. He agreed and experimented with a number of different recipes, always testing each one by bringing a keg or two to be sampled by the troops at a tasting party. As Belgium's hop fields had been decimated by four years of war, East Kent Golding were imported from England, courtesy of the British army (the same hops are in use today, although they arrive by more conventional means). They were given to the brewery at no charge. Eventually, it was decided which of the recipes the troops liked best, and, according to the brewery, this is the one that is still used today. One delightful coda to the tale of this beer is the story that a son of one of the Scottish soldiers ended up working at the brewery. **CC**

Tasting notes

Pours an amber brown color and settles in the glass beneath a mild tannish head. There are notes of sweet caramel malt, dark fruits, and molasses in the nose. Flavor is sweet dark chocolate and brown sugar, with hints of spice and a mild alcohol burn.

Sella del Diavolo

Birrificio Barley | www.barley.it

Country of origin Italy
First brewed 2006
Alcohol content 6.5% abv
Serving temperature 54°F, 12°C

Sella del Diavolo (Devil's Saddle) takes its name from a promontory close to the famous Poetto beach near Cagliari. Legend has it that, after a battle with the angels, the devil fell from his horse and lost his saddle, which is now this promontory on the beautiful sea of Sardinia. The beer brewed by Nicola Perra is not as devilish as the name might suggest, but it is full of temptation. Unlike the brewery's BB10 or Zàgara (which has orange flower honey in the recipe), this beer looks to malted barley and hops alone to weave their magic—as well as the spring water with which all Birrificio Barley's beers are made.

Sella del Diavolo is a beer that Perra first created when he was still a home-brewer, with two years of experimentation needed to take it to perfection. Five different malts (three German and two caramel from Belgium), plus two German hop varieties from the Hallertau region (Tradition and Hersbrucker) go into the brewing kettle. The first hop is added for the bitterness while the wort is boiling, whereas the second is mainly for the aroma and is put in during the last minutes. The beer also undergoes two weeks of fermentation in the bottle.

Even though Sella del Diavolo is a top-fermenting beer, it can be difficult to define: the malty profile is comparable to German bocks, but the hoppy side of the beer is more reminiscent of a British beer. Besides, Perra doesn't like to classify his beers and is happy for drinkers to take Sella del Diavolo for what it is: a very tasty ale that is easy to drink. It's wonderful with roasted meat, or with cheese that is not too mature. **MM**

Tasting notes

Sweet and fruity aroma, morels and plums, at the beginning, followed by fresh notes that are lightly peppery. Sella del Diavolo is well balanced in the palate with the return of fruitiness and sweetness; pleasant aftertaste that doesn't linger for too long.

Sharp's Doom Bar

Sharp's Brewery | www.sharpsbrewery.co.uk

Country of origin England
First brewed 1995
Alcohol content 4.3%
Serving temperature 54°F, 12°C

Doom Bar is a sandbank off the north Cornwall coast. It protects the estuary of the River Camel from the wild Atlantic Ocean, but over the centuries it has been a major handicap to shipping, causing many vessels to run aground. Since 1995, however, a beer named after the underwater menace has provided the bedrock for a hugely successful brewing enterprise.

Bill Sharp was the founder of Sharp's Brewery, based just across the estuary from Padstow harbor. He took to brewing for his own pleasure but found that there was a ready market for his beers locally and turned professional in 1994. Doom Bar was one of his earliest beers. Initially it was a blend of two other brews—Cornish Coaster and Sharp's Own—but today it is an authentic beer in its own right, carefully constructed from pale and crystal malts and spiced with Northdown and Northern Brewer hops.

Sharp sold his brewery to new owners in 2003. They have moved the business forward, targeting the U.K. national market with Doom Bar. Head brewer Stuart Howe enjoys experimenting with intriguing bottle-conditioned ales such as Chalky's Bite (laced with fennel), Honey Spice Wheat Beer, and the potent but mellow barleywine, Massive Ale. But it is Doom Bar that remains the customers' favorite: its easy-drinking nature attracts a wide-ranging clientele—in fact, Doom Bar is responsible for 70 percent of the brewery's activity. Cornish seafarers have always had to look out for Doom Bar. Now it seems that the rest of the country—and, with exports rising, the wider world—will soon be aware of its presence. **JE**

Tasting notes

A well-balanced, amber ale with creamy, nutty malt and some spicy hop in the aroma. The same maltiness leads on the palate, with a hoppy sharpness and some bittersweet fruit, and continues to feature in the dry finish along with a pleasant, building bitterness.

Shipyard IPA

Shipyard Brewing | www.shipyard.com

Country of origin United States
First brewed 1997
Alcohol content 5.8% abv
Serving temperature 50°F, 10°C

Alan Pugsley, co-founder of Shipyard Brewing, is one of the most influential persons in the U.S. craft beer industry. Before coming to the United States, he was an apprentice at the Ringwood Brewery under Peter Austin, who is considered to be the "grandfather of the microbrewery movement." Since arriving in the United States in 1992, Pugsley has helped to establish numerous craft breweries and brewpubs. The Ringwood yeast he brought with him has become one of the most popular ale yeasts used by microbreweries. It's also the yeast used to create this IPA.

Shipyard IPA is brewed with two-row British pale ale malt, along with crystal malt and malted wheat. But it's the hops that really make this beer. Most beers use a combination of two or more hop varieties, but Shipyard uses only one. Such beers are known as single-hop beers. They are often brewed as experimental beers, so that brewers and beer lovers can enjoy how individual qualities can be realized by a specific hop variety. Few are versatile enough to be used alone to create a commercial beer.

The hop used for this beer is Fuggle. It is popular with brewers because of its mildness and spicy aromas, especially when used in making a number of English-style ales. Although often too mild for bigger India Pale Ales, Pugsley managed to get 50 IBUs out of the Fuggle hop, using a "hop percolator," which is packed with hops and floated in the brew kettle to impart the requisite hop intensity. Originally known as "Shipyard Fuggles IPA," the beer been recently rebranded as simply "Shipyard IPA," but it's the exact same brew. **JB**

Tasting notes

Shipyard's IPA is bright orange amber in color with a dense, tight ivory head. The hops impart grassy, herbal aromas to a primarily malty sweet nose. With a creamy, effervescent mouthfeel, the bitter flavors stand out prominently and the finish is very dry and tart.

Sierra Nevada Bigfoot Barleywine Style Ale

Sierra Nevada Brewing Company | www.sierranevada.com

Country of origin United States
First brewed 1982
Alcohol content 10.4% abv
Serving temperature 55°–61°F, 13°–16°C

Bigfoot is appropriately named because this beer is a legendary monster. It started as a quest. "I was traveling to England occasionally, buying all the strong ales I could get my hands on," recalls Sierra Nevada's founder Ken Grossman. "Fritz [Maytag, of Anchor] had just come out with Old Foghorn, and I had a home-brew shop so I had access to all kinds of ingredients. It just felt right to attempt a strong barleywine."

Bigfoot was an extreme beer in its day; it's still a formidable mouthful. "The goal in this 10.4 percent beer," says Grossman, "is to balance the hops and malt to make something drinkable." The grain bill is relatively simple—two-row pilsner and English caramel malts—but at 10.4 percent abv, everything is magnified. The toasted caramel and burned sugar aromas from the caramel malt come on strong. Good thing, because this beer has a load of resiny hops added to the tune of 90 IBU; it is then dry hopped with Cascade, Centennial, and Chinook.

Sierra Nevada is famous for its yeast, a robust and adaptable strain used by the old Ballantine brewery. It is fairly neutral, but adds a soft round fruitiness to all the Sierra Nevada beers. It's alcohol tolerant: a good thing for this beer. Grossman feels that the beer is best when the bright resiny hop flavors are fresh and right up front. Some aficionados like a little time on it. Beers along these lines were often aged a decade or more in 18th-century England. Bigfoot holds up well for four to ten years, but the character changes, becoming more vinous and malty, sometimes showing a bit of old leather in the nose. **RM**

Tasting notes

Aromas of toffeelike malt plus spicy, slightly resiny hops, with a kind of woody complexity. Alcohol and estery fruit are evident. Very sweet and full bodied up front, building to massive bitterness with caramel and orange overtones. Long, warming, bittersweet finish.

Sierra Nevada Harvest

Sierra Nevada Brewing Company | www.sierranevada.com

Country of origin United States
First brewed 1996
Alcohol content 6.7% abv
Serving temperature 48°–50°F, 9°–10°C

This is a review of a series of three beers, and the concept behind them. For a long time, wine has stubbornly owned and held on to the concept of terroir: the influences of soil, climate, and other factors that can be tasted in the glass. For a couple of hundred years, beer has been an industrial product, cut off from the land. Now that brewing has gotten more hands-on again, it's useful to remind people that it is fundamentally an agricultural product.

The Sierra Nevada brewery is very near to some of the old hop-growing areas in Northern California, and this beer was intended to combine this heritage with the new enthusiasm for hops that the craft beer market was showing. "We wanted to show people what goes into the beer," says Sierra Nevada's chief executive Ken Grossman. The first in the series of three Sierra Nevada Harvest beers is the Wet Hop Harvest Ale. With this beer, the hops are fresh from the fields and not dried as is normal. This means that the hops have to get into the kettle within a couple of days, or they will start to decompose.

The brewery now has its own plantings of 9 acres (6.4 ha) of hops, which are used in the Chico Estate Harvest Ale. At the time of writing, Grossman was hopeful that the company's 26 acres (10.5 ha) of barley would be malted and ready to be used in the batch that would be brewed in the autumn of 2009. The third beer in the Sierra Nevada's series is the Southern Hemisphere Harvest Ale, which comes out in the spring, and, as the name might suggest, features hops from New Zealand. **RM**

Tasting notes

Southern Hemisphere has a beautiful orange-tinged hop nose, very fragrant and slightly herby, and melding with caramelly malt. Sweet and malty up front, then very clean bitterness takes over. Big flavors on the palate, but not heavy. Long bitter finish, but fresh and elegant.

Skull Splitter

Orkney Brewery | www.orkneybrewery.co.uk

Country of origin Scotland
First brewed 1988
Alcohol content 8.5% abv
Serving temperature 55°F, 13°C

Skull Splitter gets its name from the nickname given to Thorfinn "Hausakluif" Einarsson, who was the seventh Viking Earl of Orkney around 950 C.E., and, as the name might suggest, he was renowned for his prowess with a battle-ax. It's a beer that sits firmly in the Scottish "Wee Heavy" range of beers and won Supreme Champion Winter Beer of Britain in 2001. "Wee Heavy" is another name for strong Scotch ale, which is brewed between 5.5 percent and 6.5 percent abv. Beers in this strong and sturdy category—barleywine is another—tend toward sweetness and a full body, with a low hop content.

Skull Splitter is hefty on pale ale malt, while the addition of crystal and chocolate malts provides a rich, fruity backbone perfectly balanced by the spicy herbal character of East Kent Golding hops. The rich and complex nature of the beer's palate makes it an ideal late-night beer, yet it is also ideal at the table, working well with paté, red meat dishes, and strong cheese.

Orkney Brewery was set up in 1988 on Orkney, which lies off the north coast of Scotland. In 2004, the business merged with Atlas Brewery in Argyll under the name Highland and Islands Breweries. Two years later, it was taken over by Sinclair Breweries. Rather belatedly, after twenty years of production, Skull Splitter found itself at the center of some controversy in 2008 when the British alcohol "watchdog," The Portman Group, carried out an investigation into complaints that the ale had an "aggressive" theme and that it should be renamed. The brewery immediately launched a very public campaign to save it, eventually forcing the advisory organization to climb down. **AG**

Tasting notes

Rich tawny red in color. A juicy, almost fruity malt character with an aroma range of dried fruits—dates and figs—hints of ginger, cinnamon, and a veil of vanilla. Its rich, fruity, winelike complexity on the palate includes fresh citrus and dried fruits and exotic spices.

Sneck Lifter

Jennings | www.jenningsbrewery.co.uk

Country of origin England
First brewed 1990
Alcohol content 5.1% abv
Serving temperature 52°F, 11°C

Sneck Lifter was first produced in 1990 as a seasonal winter beer, traditionally a strong dark ale that is intended to warm the cockles of beer drinkers' hearts (although some might argue that Sneck Lifter's comparatively low alcohol content makes it more of a strong bitter than a winter warmer). It has its genesis in a time of turbulent change in the British brewing industry: a time when the government changed competition law and allowed the licensees of more than 10,000 pubs owned by national brewers to buy a guest cask ale of their choice from any brewer.

Enterprising brewers recognized this as an opportunity for increasing the sale of beer beyond their own pubs—and, as it happened, it was the stronger, more intriguing and flavorsome beers that proved a hit in this new market. Sneck Lifter was one of these fortunate beers; it was so successful that, from 1995, it began to be produced all year-round.

Jennings is a traditional English ale producer situated in the picturesque Cumbrian market town of Cockermouth, which lies on the edge of the English Lake District. The brewery can trace its roots back to 1828, when John Jennings, who was the son of a maltster, opened a small brewery in the village of Lorton. The company often gives its beers humorous names that are derived from local dialect. A "sneck lifter" is a cunning person who quietly tries to lift the latch of a pub's door—the sneck—to sneak in and spend his last coin on a glass of beer, in the hope that he will start a conversation with someone who will buy him a second or even a third. **TH**

Tasting notes

Reddish dark ale in the glass, with a complex balance of sugar, malt, and hops on the nose. The dry, biscuit flavor of the malt gives way to chocolate and coffee notes that dance in harmony with the peppery, bittersweet character of the Golding and Fuggle hops.

Snow Cap

Pyramid Breweries | www.pyramidbrew.com

Country of origin United States
First brewed 1986
Alcohol content 7% abv
Serving temperature 55°F, 13°C

Pyramid Breweries began in 1984 as the Hart Brewing Company, originally named for founder Beth Hartwell. When an investment group bought the Washington-based Hart Brewing and Bainbridge Island's Thomas Kemper Brewery in 1989, it moved both brewery and business operations to Seattle and renamed the company Pyramid Breweries after the Pyramid beer brand that Hart Brewery had created.

The first Pyramid beer was a pale ale. Although it evoked imagery of ancient Egypt, the appellation in fact came from Pyramid Peak, a 7,182-foot (2,189-m) mountain in the Cascade Mountain Range. It is located in the North Cascades National Park and is one of several peaks that form a crescent around Colonial Glacier. When Hart Brewing decided to create a holiday beer, it added snow to the peak of the pyramid motif so that it resembled its namesake's snow-capped peak, and thus Snow Cap ale was born. It is a winter warmer beer in the British tradition, which is a type of English strong ale, or old ale, with a big malt presence. These beers are normally sweet, but without any spices.

Snow Cap is brewed with two-row barley, caramel 80L, and chocolate malt plus three hop varieties: East Kent Golding, Nugget, and Willamette. A flocculent—meaning the yeast clumps together, sinking to the bottom to help clarify the beer—English yeast is used to give a rich, full-bodied mouthfeel. Pyramid Snow Cap is a good sipping beer that can be enjoyed on its own; it can also be paired with shellfish, rich game, and chocolate desserts. **JB**

Tasting notes

Pyramid's Snow Cap is a deep chestnut color with a snowy off-white head. Its nose is complex with aromas of caramel, ripe bananas, and fruits such as black currants, strawberries, and cherries. Soft malt flavors with hints of toffee and hazelnut and warming, long spicy finish.

Special De Ryck

Brouwerij De Ryck | www.brouwerijderyck.be

Country of origin Belgium
First brewed 1920
Alcohol content 5.5% abv
Serving temperature 43°F, 6°C

The De Ryck brewery is one of those family-run outfits that is not supposed to exist anymore. Despite its local success—its beers are popular and widely available around the village of Herzele and nearby towns—the big fish have not gobbled it up yet. Thankfully.

Brewer An De Ryck is the great-granddaughter of founder Gustaaf De Ryck and, like her ancestor, learned the trade in Germany. The Altbier house where Gustaaf worked was called Zum Goldenen Adler (The Golden Eagle). The brewery he opened in 1886 had the same name, essentially, but in bilingual fashion was called either l'Aigle D'Or or De Gouden Arend (these days it's tough to imagine a Flemish brewery taking a French as well as a Dutch name). The brewery's current line of abbey-style Arend beers pays homage to its 19th-century roots.

In 1920, the brewery renamed itself De Ryck and launched the Special, a type of English-inspired pale ale that was especially popular in Belgium between the world wars. Interestingly, De Ryck's version predates the more famous Palm (1928) and De Koninck (1939)—although there are several references to Belgian "special" pale ales going back to 1900. The Special remains a simple beer of character. Its strength has inched upward from around 4 percent to about 5.5 percent, but it remains thirst-quenching and sessionable. Although its malt backbone and classy hopping keep a certain Englishness, its light body and crisp sparkle are distinctively Belgian. Like the brewery itself, the Special has no doubt evolved over the years, but probably not much. Again, thankfully. **JS**

Tasting notes

Special De Ryck pours a bright and clear amber whether from bottle or tap. Light floral hops and biscuit in the nose. These days, its hop bitterness is more noticeable than the lightly sweet maltiness, especially when fresh. Begs to be gulped in quantity.

Spezial Rauchbier

Brauerei Spezial
www.brauerei-spezial.de

Country of origin Germany
First brewed 1550
Alcohol content 4.7% abv
Serving temperature 46°F, 8°C

Rauchbier—smoked beer—is the famous signature beer of Bamberg, and the one produced by Brauerei Spezial is supposedly the oldest one. These days, malted barley is dried in kilns and the heat can be controlled, but once upon a time, master brewers often dried their malt over open fires. The taste of the beer depended in part on the wood used, and some of the beers would probably have tasted like smoked ham; this is still one flavor characteristic that has survived. Spezial is one of few breweries that malt barley for their own use, with beech the chosen wood.

Although beer has been produced free of smoky taints for nearly two centuries, there is still demand for old-fashioned tastes, and Rauchbier meets that demand in Bamberg. The biggest problem for the brewer is to make sure that the bitterness of the smoke combines successfully with the bitterness of the hop during production. Without this balance, the beer can become undrinkable.

The Brauerei Spezial site is said to have first housed a brewery in 1535, when a certain Linhard Großkopf started making beer. In 1900, the Merz family bought the brewery, and it still remains in their hands today. Spezial also owns a popular brewery-restaurant that is noted for its fine dishes, which are well matched with the Rauchbier. **WO**

Tasting notes

Fine and mild smoky touch on the nose and in the mouth. The malt aroma is very clear and it is well balanced between the bitterness of the hop and the bitter aroma of smoke.

Staropramen Granát

Pivovary Staropramen
www.pivovary-staropramen.cz

Country of origin Czech Republic
First brewed 1884
Alcohol content 5% abv
Serving temperature 48°F, 9°C

When the brewery was founded in 1871, it was known as the Smíchov Joint Stock Brewery and had an original capacity of just 594,000 gallons (22,500 hl). By 1889, production had more than quadrupled, and by 1939, the brewery was among the largest in central Europe. Today, it produces more than forty times its original capacity, and its beers are exported worldwide. When the brewery's board of directors registered its trademark in 1911, they booked seventeen possible names, including Pračep (Original Tap), Starozdroj (Old Source), and Starosmíchovský (Old Smíchov) Fortunately, it stuck with Staropramen, or Old Spring.

Less well known than the brewery's pale and dark lagers is the unusual Granát, or garnet, a semidark beer. It was out of production for many years until 1999, when it reappeared as a special beer called Millennium, regaining its original name of Granát a couple of years later. Inspired by the amber Vienna lagers developed by Anton Dreher, Granát is credited with reintroducing the half-dark or amber lager style to a wider commercial audience. In its current incarnation, Granát is served most commonly in a small glass, as if the beer's rich maltiness would be too much to handle in the full pour. It is brewed from a mix of pale and dark malts, with a taste that bridges a pale lager's crisp hoppiness and a dark lager's rich body. **ER**

Tasting notes

Deep amber with glinting reddish notes and topped with a thick sandy mousse, this special lager has lovely caramel and cola notes on the nose, a full, malty mouthfeel, and sugary body.

Original sign from the Staropramen brewpub in Prague, Czech Republic.

Registrovaná slovní i obrazová ochranná známka.

Starosmíchovské, Pračep, Starozdroj.

„SMÍCHOVSKÝ

STAROPRAMEN"

z PRVNÍHO

AKCIONÁŘSKÉHO PIVOVARU

NA SMÍCHOVĚ Č.P.43.

ZALOŽENÉHO R.1869.

Vyznamenán prvními cenami na všech obeslaných výstavách.

Stern-Bräu Festbier

Stern-Bräu Günter Scheubel | www.landgasthof-sternbraeu.de

Country of origin Germany
First brewed 2004
Alcohol content 5.5% abv
Serving temperature 46°–50°F, 8°–10°C

For those drinkers who pine for a lager of the lighter kind, elegant and refined but also with a good nose, Stern-Bräu Festbier is just the job. This unfiltered beer is clean and straight, complex and subtle at the same time. It has a medium body, enchanting hop aroma, and 10 percent smoked malt. Yet its color is shiningly brilliant due to a slow, cold fermentation and twelve to fourteen weeks of cold lagering in maturation tanks.

Günter Scheubel, brewmaster, owner, and junior boss of the small Franconian brewery Stern-Bräu in Schlüsselfeld, created the beer by experimenting time and time again. He spent his period of apprenticeship at Brauerei Greifenklau in Bamberg, where he first learned about the art of using smoked malt. Working with internationally renowned maltsters, he found out more about specialty malts and their effect on color.

Of course, he appreciates Schlenkerla Smokebeer, but Scheubel has made something different; he has made a beer the way he prefers it. This certainly has a lot to do with his choice of hops; one of the best hops for light lagered beer, he says, is Tettnanger, with its gorgeous aroma.

Scheubel loves his profession and he is the latest brewmaster in a long family tradition. The family began brewing in 1828, yet he does not seem to be trapped by this heritage. Neither tradition nor inspiration are relevant issues: simply put, he is a Franconian craftsman, down-to-earth, with absolutely no high-flown aspirations, but possessed of skill and a single-minded passion: to make a good beer. With Stern-Bräu Festbier, he has succeeded. **SK**

Tasting notes

A lustrous orange color in the glass beneath a soft foamy head. Flowery, creamy, and smoky aromas enchant the nose. On the palate, expect a decent bready sweetness, balanced by dry bitterness, inspired by flowery hop notes and pleasant smoky tastes. Dry, bitter finish.

Stonecutter

Renaissance Brewing | www.renaissancebrewing.co.nz

Country of origin New Zealand
First brewed 2005
Alcohol content 7% abv
Serving temperature 50°–54°F, 10°–12°C

Established in Blenheim in 2005, Renaissance Brewing is the brainchild of two beer-loving brothers-in-law, from California—Andy Deuchars and Brian Thiel. As well as a shared passion for craft beer, the two have complementary skills: Deuchars has a wealth of brewing experience, and Thiel is a well qualified motor mechanic with the engineering nous to maintain a modern brewery.

Sharing a surname with one of Scotland's famous brewing families, it is hardly surprising that Deuchars has ale brewing in his blood. With brewing experience at Brewski's Gas Lamp Pub and Brewery in San Diego and the highly respected Anderson Valley Brewing in northern California, Deuchars is emphatic about his philosophy: "As you can see, all of my experience is in ale brewing, and I really have no interest in doing lagers, especially a light or golden one!" In a country such as New Zealand, whose mainstream beers are golden and amber lagers, it's a brave approach, but one that's paid off; the brewery has won a raft of awards and is experiencing sustained growth.

Easily recognizable from their classy packaging, the Renaissance beers are also available on draft. If ever there was a beer with a truly international pedigree, Stonecutter Ale must surely be it. Brewed by two Americans with a grist of malts from Australia, Germany, and the United Kingdom, plus two varieties of New Zealand hops and a London ale yeast, it is the brewery's interpretation of a Scotch Ale. A small addition of peated malt—the type commonly used in whisky—gives this rich, warming ale a pleasing hint of smokiness. **GG**

Tasting notes

Dark amber with ruby highlights beneath a tan head. Toffee, caramel, chocolate, raisins, alcohol notes, and a hint of smokiness combine in the aroma and palate. Full bodied, warming and luscious, with a long finish, it's a fine match for hearty casseroles or shortbread.

Strzelec Mocne

Browar Jędrzejów | www.piwostrzelec.pl

Styrian Ale

Handbrauerei Forstner | www.forstner-biere.at

Country of origin Poland
First brewed 1995
Alcohol content 7% abv
Serving temperature 50°F, 10°C

Country of origin Austria
First brewed 2005
Alcohol content 6.2% abv
Serving temperature 50°F, 10°C

Jędrzejów is a small town in central Poland and it is famous for its astronomical museum, its medieval Cistercian monastery, and beer. The museum has one of the world's best collections of astronomical clocks and sundials, and the local brewery was named after the constellation Strzelec, or Sagittarius.

Why not Leo or Orion? The answer lies in Jędrzejów's town crest, conferred on the town in the 13th century. It resembles a large white arrow on a red background. It is almost identical to the astronomical symbol for Sagittarius, and the label of Strzelec Mocne features an image of this archer. As the second part of the beer's name would suggest, this is a strong beer. Mocne is the Polish word for "strong," often seen as a class, or style, of Polish beer. However, fans of U.S. extreme beers and some of Belgium's tripels might find the alcohol content of 7 percent a mite sessionable. **RZ**

Gerhard Forstner started his brewpub in 2001 in the small village of Kalsdorf, south of Graz. In 2004, he was invited to participate in a Styrian beer festival and faced a challenge that none of the brewpubs in the province were willing to accept: to supply a festival ale.

Forstner had very little experience with ales, but he had brewed an Irish Red before. He researched recipes for strong ales and brewed the festival ale. It proved to be an instant success, so much so that Forstner decided to make a beer of the same style as a regular part of his portfolio. Styrian Ale became the first bottled ale from an Austrian brewpub—and it is still brewed in limited quantities. The "Styrian" in its name refers to the use of local Styrian water, not Styrian hops: the recipe calls for Cascade. Malts are pilsner, wheat, caramel, and chocolate, whereas the yeast is the well-known Nottingham yeast strain. **CS**

Tasting notes
Light amber color beneath a creamy white head. A delicate malty aroma leads to a sweet palate followed by delicate bitterness. Ideal for duck roasted with apples.

Tasting notes
Pours dark amber to reddish brown, shows little head, but has a rich, fruity aroma with hints of cocoa, blueberry, and wild strawberry. Full bodied in its mouthfeel; light, bitter finish.

Surly Furious

Surly Brewing | www.surlybrewing.com

Sussex Best Bitter

Harveys Brewery | www.harveys.org.uk

Country of origin United States
First brewed 2006
Alcohol content 6.2% abv
Serving temperature 50°F, 10°C

Country of origin England
First brewed 1955
Alcohol content 4% abv
Serving temperature 54°–55°F, 12°–13°C

From the very beginning of Surly Brewing's history, head brewer Todd Haug told founder Omar Ansari, "One of these days, I'm going to put our beer in cans." Ansari initially laughed but kept an open mind. When he looked at the technical specs more closely, he realized that the idea wasn't all bad. However, he wasn't quite convinced until Haug's wife suggested that they put their beer in "tall boys." "When she said that, something just clicked," Ansari reminisces. "People don't think of Guinness or Boddington's as canned beer; they think of it as good beer in a can."

However, Surly didn't want just any canned beer, they wanted it to be a big beer. Their first beer to be canned turned out to be Furious, described as a "tempest on the tongue." It's an American IPA weighing in at 99 IBUs and uses big American aroma hops balanced with Scottish malt. **JB**

The best British bitters are about a balance between cereally maltiness and a citrus and fruity hop character, with the bite of bitterness in the mix. Cask-conditioned bitter remains the mainstay of many a British pub, and in the south of England, especially in the county of Sussex, this eloquent yet feisty bitter from Lewes-based brewery Harveys is a classic English bitter.

The beer is more than fifty years old now. Prior to its emergence, the brewery's main sellers had been two beers, a mild and a bitter called IPA. According to managing director Miles Jenner, "The 1950s was when we stabilized our beer flavor profile with a good hop character and a slight sweetness which is very moreish. The sweetness happened because there was a postwar liking for slightly sweet things." Needless to say, Sussex Best Bitter is a beer that has been showered with countless awards. **ATJ**

Tasting notes

Deep copper in color with a thick ivory head. The complex nose has floral aromas with grapefruit, citrus, and pine notes. A big hop presence with a touch of caramel and a dry, bitter finish.

Tasting notes

On the nose, a muscular and musky hop presence, thanks to a hop grist of Fuggle, Golding, Progress, and Brambling Cross. The palate is full bodied with a slightly sweet background.

Tanglefoot

Hall & Woodhouse | www.hall-woodhouse.co.uk

Country of origin England
First brewed *ca.* 1985
Alcohol content 5% abv
Serving temperature 52°F, 11°C

In common with many long-established breweries Hall and Woodhouse has a sampling room, where the head brewer can taste the latest beers in the company of the brewing staff—some prototype beers never make it past this stage. In the mid-1980s, the brewery were keen on producing a pale-colored ale that mimicked some of the attributes of a yellow English lager but had the strength of a continental beer. It was a time of change in the drinking tastes of England as people moved from darker ales to lighter-colored lagers.

A number of test brews were prepared, some of which were sold in local pubs, though others only got as far as the tasting room. One brew stood out—but what should it be called? In a moment of serendipity, the name came: after several glasses in the sampling room one day, the head brewer, the redoubtable John Woodhouse, struggled to his feet and promptly fell over them—Tanglefoot was born. It was obviously the correct decision, as the beer proved an instant hit and was voted the Best Beer in the World at the Brewing Industry's International Awards in 1987.

The origins of Hall and Woodhouse go back to 1777, when Charles Hall founded a small brewery in the nearby Dorset village of Ansty. Business boomed, with both farm laborers and soldiers, billeted at nearby Weymouth for the Napoleonic Wars, providing custom. The company's Badger image was adopted in 1875 and the brewery moved to its present site on the banks of the River Stour at Blandford St. Mary in 1899. It is a fixture on the southern England brewing scene, owned by the fifth generation of the Woodhouse family. **TH**

Tasting notes

A light, amber-colored ale with a light touch of peardrop candy and melon fruit on the nose, and hints of toffee. The fruitiness (more peardrop candy, lemon) continues onto the palate, together with whispers of caramel voluptuousness. A fruity finish with hints of warming alcohol.

A Hall & Woodhouse pub sign in the village of Widecombe-in-the-Moor, Devon, England. ➡

17 77

Independent Family Brewers

THE OLD INN

THE OLD INN

HALL & WOODHOUSE

FOOD ALL DAY

Theresianer Strong Ale

Theresianer | www.theresianer.com

Country of origin Italy
First brewed 1999
Alcohol content 8.5% abv
Serving temperature 54°F, 12°C

This is the story of Martino Zanetti, an Italian coffee entrepreneur who decided to go on an adventure into the beer world. The owner of the Hausbrandt coffee brand fell in love with beer some years ago and decided to start his own brewery. He chose the name after Borgo Teresiano, a quarter in the city of Trieste where the first Austrian brewery opened in 1766. It was then the most important port on the Adriatic Sea and under the dominion of the Hapsburg Empire.

With the collaboration of Tullio Zangrando, a brewmaster who graduated from Weihenstephan, and Christian Romano, his young but clever pupil, Theresianer brews a large variety of beers, including a Vienna-style lager, a pale ale, and a Weizen. Every beer is made with pure water from the Dolomites, the mountains that tower over the town of Nervesa della Battaglia where the brewery is located.

Theresianer Strong Ale uses top-fermenting yeast and is made with a large addition of pilsner malt, plus some Munich for color and a drop of black malt to help develop the light roasted notes that are so apparent during tasting. The malt and hops come from Germany; the brewer's choice—when they are available—include Spalter Select, Saaz, and Tettnang. Fermentation is for five days, and the ale then matures for at least six weeks before it is ready.

Top-fermentation beers are quite an unusual choice for medium-sized breweries in Italy, but this ale is definitely a good effort. It matches well with mature or blue cheeses, but the brewer's favorite choice is to have it with chocolate cakes such as *Sachertorte*. **MM**

Tasting notes

Deep amber color with tawny reflections, intense fruity nose with notes of apricots and pineapple. On the palate, it reveals a warm feeling surrounded by honey notes and hints of licorice and dry fruits. In the aftertaste, it's easy to recognize an undercurrent of roasted coffee.

Thomas Hardy's Ale

O'Hanlon's Brewery | www.mythbirdbeer.com/thomashardysale.shtml

Country of origin England
First brewed 1968
Alcohol content 11.7% abv
Serving temperature 55°–64°F, 13°–18°C

Thomas Hardy's Ale is one of the most celebrated British beers of the past few decades, a venerable and venerated barleywine that once held the accolade of being the strongest beer brewed in the British Isles. It first appeared in 1968 and was brewed to celebrate the fortieth anniversary of the death of English writer Thomas Hardy.

The beer was brewed once a year and the brewery stated that each vintage would last up to twenty-five years. At the turn of the century, Eldridge Pope brewery (which had renamed itself Thomas Hardy) stopped brewing, and Thomas Hardy's Ale seemed to have come to an end. However, with the rights to the brand bought by a U.S. beer importer, it fell to a small West Country craft brewery called O'Hanlon's to brew the beer, with the first vintage appearing in 2003. According to the brewery's co-owner and founder John O'Hanlon, "This was a real challenge for us and it changed the complexion of the brewery."

O'Hanlon's was rightly lauded for its care and attention to this British brewing icon, and Thomas Hardy's Ale won many awards. However, in 2009, the story of Thomas Hardy's Ale took another twist when O'Hanlon's announced that it would stop producing it: "It wasn't an easy decision," said O'Hanlon, "but in the end, it just wasn't worth it. Our regular beers take about two weeks to brew. With Thomas Hardy, we'd start brewing in January and it was September before we could start bottling it." However, with the right to brew the beer owned by U.S. importer George Saxon, there's every chance that it will reappear again soon. **ATJ**

Tasting notes

On the nose, suggestions of dark stone fruits, roast malt, alcohol, a peatlike smokiness, and a floral hoppiness. Portlike on the palate with notes of Stollen cake, brandy, baked bananas, and ripe apricots; a spicy, peppery hoppiness keeps inclinations to oversweetness in check.

Tickle Brain

Burton Bridge Brewery
www.burtonbridgebrewery.co.uk

Country of origin England
First brewed 2006
Alcohol content 8% abv
Serving temperature 55°F, 13°C

Burton Bridge Brewery takes its name from a bridge over the River Trent at England's Burton-on-Trent, arguably the most famous beer town in the world, with past and present breweries including Bass, Allied, Marston's, and Everards. It was established in 1982 by Bruce Wilkinson and Geoff Mumford in the old Fox and Goose pub, with the two of them working on a tight budget and doing practically everything themselves for the first seven years of the brewery's existence. They even handled much of the brewery construction themselves, for example, hand-drilling 9,000 holes into the false bottom of the stainless steel mash tun.

Tickle Brain is a deliberate replica of a Belgian abbey-style beer. The name of the beer, however, refers to a Tudor description of strong ale, and the label and pump clip feature the most recognizable of all Tudors, King Henry VIII, remembered for separating the English church from Rome and for his six wives (two of whom he famously had beheaded). Tickle Brain uses Northdown hops and pale and chocolate malt to achieve its flavorful, well-balanced character. The brewery, which on average has been a finalist in national beer competitions for every year of its existence, owns five pubs in the Burton area, all with freehold tenants and each with its own identity. **AG**

Tasting notes
Malty-sweet nose with some roasted barley and appreciable alcohol notes. Caramel, more roasted malt, and sweet dried fruits develop for a full-bodied, sweetish, and warming flavor.

Tijuana Morena

Consorcio Cervecero de Baja California
www.tjbeer.com

Country of origin Mexico
First brewed 2000
Alcohol content 4.8% abv
Serving temperature 39°–44°F, 4°–7°C

Tijuana is an intoxicating and maddening metropolis that sits on the Mexico–United States border, opposite its sister city of San Diego in California. Located on the outskirts of this bustling frontier city is Cerveza Tijuana, a fine example of Mexico's flourishing craft beer scene. Cerveza Tijuana founder Jose Gonzalez Ibarra, whose father had worked in the Mexican beer industry, was inspired to try and create a new type of Mexican beer. He subsequently packed his bags for Europe to study their traditions and methods and later came back to make his dream become reality when he set up Cerveza Tijuana (known as "TJ") in January 2000.

Tijuana Morena is one of three beers made by the TJ brewmaster David Masa, a man from a long line of master brewers who perfected their craft in some of the Czech Republic's most prestigious breweries. A dark beer made using four different types of European malt, it carries a smooth caramel flavor that has, thanks to word of mouth, gained a popular following in a country overrun with a series of bland lagers. TJ is now a leading figure in the Mexican microbrewing revolution and has started exporting across its nearby border to the United States. Visitors to the brewery in Tijuana can take a tour of the production plant and also taste its excellent Mexican beers with a Czech twist in the on-site tavern. **SG**

Tasting notes
An aroma of rich, sweet malt fills the glass, with the palate struck by caramelized malt and slightly roasted notes releasing a sweet aftertaste.

Morena and Güera are both 4.8 percent abv. The brewery's other beer is a light.

CERVEZA

Tijuana

-T·J-

BEER

Timothy Taylor's Landlord

Timothy Taylor | www.timothy-taylor.co.uk

Country of origin England
First brewed 1953
Alcohol content 4.3% abv
Serving temperature 52°–57°F, 11°–14°C

Every beer worth its malted barley gains endorsements, but few can match the great celebrity pull of Timothy Taylor's Landlord. Back in 2003, when Madonna was infatuated with all things British (including her then new husband Guy Ritchie), she confided her love of British beer on a national chat show: "I have learned to love real ale. Timothy Taylor is the best." Subsequently an endorsement came from Hugh Grant, who at an art gallery opening quipped for the paparazzi that he had only come for the Landlord.

The Yorkshire beer's fame is justifiably widespread. It is unrivaled as a four-time Champion Beer of Britain, the Campaign for Real Ale's ultimate accolade. Timothy Taylor boasts—in characteristically subdued fashion—that Landlord has won more awards nationally than any other beer.

Surprisingly, given its status as a cask ale favorite, Landlord started life in 1952 as a bottled product; it became available on draft in 1953. Landlord's unmistakable iconic label is a family affair. Roberta, the daughter of then managing director Philip Taylor, was an art student who devised the eye-catching jovial landlord that remains front and center to this day.

The beer's base is 100 percent malted barley, Golden Promise, and it is made exclusively with spring water. Only whole hops are used, a combination of Whitbread Golding varieties, Fuggle, Golding, and Styrian Golding. Head brewer Peter Eells is passionate about whole hops, comparing their flavor contribution to the difference between dressing a pizza with fresh rather than dried herbs. **LN**

Tasting notes

The nose is citrus and floral hop perfume. The color is light amber, recalling the rich orangey brown of a Halloween pumpkin. The taste is balanced; hop fruitiness to the fore against underlying nutty maltiness. A long warming finish with a moreish bitter linger.

Tommyknocker Butthead

Tommyknocker Brewery | www.tommyknocker.com

Country of origin United States
First brewed 1995
Alcohol content 8.2% abv
Serving temperature 44°F, 7°C

Tommyknocker Brewery is located in the town of Idaho Falls, Colorado, which can be found 25 miles (40 km) outside Denver. Their brewpub is in the Placer Inn, which dates back to 1859 and is close to the spot where the discovery of gold first sparked the Colorado gold rush. The brewery's name and logo reflect the area's mining heritage. A Tommyknocker is a legendary elflike being that some immigrant miners from Cornwall claimed lived in the gold and silver mines. The Tommyknockers were said to be pranksters, dumping lunch pails or hiding tools, while at other times they would knock on the walls of the mine to alert miners to where they could find the richest veins.

Today, Tommyknocker is popular with locals and visitors passing through the town en route to Rocky Mountain ski resorts. In 2008, the company produced 9,000 barrels, with its Maple Nut Brown Ale being the most popular bottled beer and Pick Axe Pale Ale the leading seller on draft in the pub. The company makes a variety of beers, including an oak-aged version of Butthead Doppelbock, Jack Wacker Wheat Beer, Black Powder Stout, and Cocoa Porter Winter Warmer.

Tommyknocker Butthead was one of the first beers made by the brewery, though it was originally pegged as a fall seasonal. It soon had a loyal following and became Tommyknocker's most decorated beer, taking medals at several competitions, including five times at the Great American Beer Festival. It quickly joined the brewery's regular lineup. Brewed with Munich, caramel, and chocolate malts, and balanced by Hallertau hops, it adheres to the Reinheitsgebot. **RL**

Tasting notes

This beer opens with a sweet and slightly fruity alcohol aroma, with a rich mahogany color and tan head. The flavor is dominated by caramelized malt and vanilla that surrounds your taste buds, but the finish twists to a slightly tart, dry note.

Tonneke

Brouwerij Contreras
www.contreras.be

Country of origin Belgium
First brewed 1920
Alcohol content 4.8% abv
Serving temperature 48°F, 9°C

This historic brewery near Ghent was first established in 1818 under the name Latte. The Contreras family purchased it in 1898, added a number of new beers, and increased production in the 1920s; they also changed the name to Brouwerij Contreras. The amber session ale Tonneke was named after the small oak barrels it was served from—*tonnen* in Dutch. Tonneke was essentially similar to the cask ales of Britain. Belgium has a few top-class, amber-colored, mildly hopped, aromatic session beers, and Tonneke is among the best of these.

Contreras had been in decline for some years, when former architect Frederik de Vrieze, who married owner Willy Contreras's daughter, took over. Under de Vrieze's direction, the output of Contreras has increased, with 2008 seeing 75,000 gallons (3,000 hl) being produced, three times the 2004 output. Several new beers have been added, and exports have begun to reach both the United Kingdom and the United States. Contreras is a very photogenic brewery and one of its rarities is an old copper heat exchanger, which is still in use, alongside an open mash tun, copper brew kettle, and a series of short and squat fermenters. The beer is made in a highly labor-intensive way, and it can be very honestly described as hand-crafted, a phrase that's all too often misused by some breweries. **CC**

Tasting notes
Hazy amber-colored beer. Aroma is light, with sweet caramel malts and some fruitiness. Taste is sweet toasted malts, mild hops, and toffee, with a bittersweet finish.

Torpedo Extra IPA

Sierra Nevada Brewing Company
www.sierranevada.com

Country of origin United States
First brewed 2009
Alcohol content 7.2% abv
Serving temperature 48°–50°F, 9°–10°C

Torpedo Extra IPA tastes good, as long as you like hops, but most drinkers would never guess that rather extreme means had been used to give the beer such aromatic intensity. "We'd been dry hopping for thirty years," says Sierra Nevada's founder Ken Grossman, referring to the process of adding hops to the fermenter for additional aroma. "We started to think about how we could get a little more out of the hops by keeping the liquid moving through the hops. We ended up playing with designs where the beer was actually flowing through a bed of hops outside the fermenter for a period of days or weeks."

The torpedolike shape of the stainless steel vessel they created for the hop infusions gave rise to the name of the beer. Grossman prefers whole hops to pellets, because the pulverized hops leak all kinds of stuff into the beer. The focus of Torpedo is hops, hops, and more hops. The brewery has been showcasing some unusual varieties: Citra, which has citrusy notes as the name suggests and the Germanic high-alpha hop, Magnum, specially selected for its high oil content.

The determination of the brewery to achieve a particular flavor demonstrates the fact that Grossman has one of the keenest technical minds in craft brewing. You can see it in the impressive solar power arrays, but it's wonderful to be able to taste it in the glass. **RM**

Tasting notes
Very bright nose, green aromas of grass and hay with lemony overtones. A soft caramel malt up front, then hops. Bitterness dominates, but it is refined, not tarry. A clean bitter finish.

The rustic label belies the technical skill that goes into making Torpedo.

Purest Ingredients

Finest Quality

SIERRA NEVADA ®

TORPEDO™

EXTRA IPA
ALE

12 FL OZ

BREWED & BOTTLED BY SIERRA NEVADA BREWING CO., CHICO, CA

Traquair House Ale

Traquair House Brewery | www.traquair.co.uk

Tribute

St. Austell Brewery | www.staustellbrewery.co.uk

Country of origin Scotland
First brewed 1965
Alcohol content 7.2% abv
Serving temperature 54°–59°F, 12°–15°C

Country of origin England
First brewed 1999
Alcohol content 4.2% abv
Serving temperature 52°–55°F, 11°–13°C

Traquair House at Innerleithen, near Peebles in the Scottish Borders, was built as a royal hunting lodge 900 years ago and is Scotland's oldest inhabited house.

The brewery had fallen into disuse by the early 1880s but was stumbled upon in the 1960s by Peter Maxwell Stuart, father of Traquair's twenty-first and present laird, Lady Catherine Maxwell Stuart. The brewhouse was intact, still with its original Russian memel oak open brewing copper, mash tun, coolers, and fermenters. Traquair House Ale was Peter Maxwell Stuart's first beer and determined the style of the strong dark ales that were traditional in Scotland centuries ago. "It's based on a recipe that the lady of the house would have brewed many centuries ago," says head brewer Ian Cameron. "Around 1745, they would have used orange peel to spice the beer up, but now we use coriander." **AG**

At 11 A.M. on August 11, 1999, an eerie silence took hold of the United Kingdom for the first total eclipse of the sun visible in Britain for seventy-two years. Totality was only achieved in Cornwall, however, which saw thousands of visitors.

Local brewers were quick to spot the potential of this rare event. The most successful beer was from Cornwall's St. Austell Brewery: the cleverly named ale Daylight Robbery. After the eclipse, though, a name change was needed. So "Daylight Robbery" became Tribute, which soon became St. Austell's most popular beer. One reason for its success is the citrus character from the Willamette, Fuggle, and Styrian Golding hops, but most important is its malt base. For Tribute, St. Austell created a new type of malt, a darker grain: Cornish Gold. Alongside Maris Otter pale malt, it deepens the golden color and adds a gentle toffee note. **JE**

Tasting notes
One of the most memorable winter beers on the market with an oak-influenced and fruity malt aroma and spiced fruit flavor unveiling traces of vanilla and sweet sherry.

Tasting notes
A refreshing, dark golden beer with citrus notes that extend from the aroma through to the drying, bitter finish. Hints of toffee and biscuit contribute depth to the character.

Triple 22

Handbrauerei Forstner | www.forstner-biere.at

Troegenator Double Bock

Tröegs Brewing | www.troegs.com

Country of origin Austria
First brewed 2007
Alcohol content 9.5% abv
Serving temperature 54°F, 12°C

Country of origin United States
First brewed 2002
Alcohol content 8.2% abv
Serving temperature 46°F, 8°C

In 2006, Gerhard Forstner went to Belgium and spent time studying the local beers and breweries. When he returned to his small brewpub in Styria, Austria, he began to brew experimental batches. At 9.5 percent, Triple 22 is the beer with the strongest Belgian character that is produced by Forstner's Handbrauerei.

"Handbrauerei" means that the beers are brewed by hand. They are brewed in extremely small batches with a generous grain bill of barley and wheat malts plus Perle, Magnum, and Cascade hops. Fermentation and maturation take more than six months. For Triple 22, Forstner uses three different strains of Belgian yeast, adds candied sugar, and hand-bottles the beer in a limited run of 700. In these, it undergoes a fourth fermentation using a champagne yeast. Forstner is confident the beer matures well in the bottle, but few remain undrunk for long enough to check. **CS**

Chris and John Trogner, the brothers behind Tröegs Brewing, dreamed of a rich, malty, thirst-quenching double bock like the one that is brewed at the Andechs monastery brewery, southwest of Munich. Before they even bought their first brew kettle in the mid-1990s, they named their imaginary first brew. "The family nickname, what everyone used to call us," said Chris, "was 'Troeg' (rhymes with rogue). It was only natural that if we added the traditional double bock '-ator' suffix we had to have a beer called Troegenator."

Troegenator is slightly bronze, a little less dark than the typical double bock. Its bill of Munich malts tends to produce a bit less licorice bite. Smooth and silky, the lager is a sneaky one, its sweetness balanced by Saaz and Hallertau hops and its alcohol well hidden. Because it's so easy to drink, this medal-winning beer has become the brewery's second-biggest seller. **DR**

Tasting notes

Expect a very sweet nose with hints of very ripe apricot. The taste is sweet and fruity, but the heavy bitterness is present right from the start. Balanced with a chocolaty finish.

Tasting notes

Bronze with a big, fluffy head and bready aroma. Sweet malt washes lightly across the palate for a slightly spiced hopped finish. Chocolate and molasses emerge as the glass warms.

Tuatara Indian Pale Ale

Tuatara Brewing
www.tuatarabrewing.co.nz

Country of origin New Zealand
First brewed 2002
Alcohol content 5% abv
Serving temperature 46°–50°F, 8°–10°C

Following his first commercial brewing position at Wellington's Parrot and Jigger brewpub, Kiwi Carl Vasta started his own brewery in a local workingmen's club. After working as a brewing consultant in Australia, he came home and formed Tuatara Brewing together with two Wellington publicans. Having set up home on a farm in the foothills of the Tararua mountains, he also started brewing Tuatara's beers in his small lifestyle brewery. It is now one of New Zealand's largest craft breweries.

Aside from a crisp, fruity pilsner with the grassy, citrusy signature of New Zealand hops, Vasta uses imported yeasts and water treatments to achieve the authentic aromas and flavors of the European styles he makes. The range includes a Bavarian-style Hefeweizen and Helles, a strong golden Belgian-style ale, and a very English-tasting porter. **GG**

Tasting notes

Pours amber to pale copper. There's plenty of toffeeish malt, with hints of butterscotch and citrusy hops in aroma and palate. Creamy and smooth, it finishes with an earthy, herbal dryness.

Uerige Alt

Uerige Obergärige Hausbrauerei
www.uerige.de

Country of origin Germany
First brewed 1862
Alcohol content 4.7% abv
Serving temperature 46°F, 8°C

This beer is a true legend. Top-fermented Altbier is one of the most famous beers in the region around Düsseldorf, the capital of Nordrhein-Westfalen. Alt is the beer with which this city is most associated. It gets its color from an addition of dark roasted barley malt. Reportedly, the recipe has not changed in 147 years. It is a secret: people know the ingredients—barley malt, roasted malt, caramel malt, hops, and water, plus the special yeast of Uerige—but not the proportions.

In the 17th and 18th centuries, the brewhouse building was a family residence, then it became a bakery, and finally a restaurant with a small hotel. In 1862, the owner sold the house to the brewer Wilhelm Cürten. His widow passed it on to the master brewer Jean Keller. After World War II, when the Uerige was destroyed, Rudolf Arnold built a new brewery, which today produces this peerless Uerige Alt beer. **WO**

Tasting notes

Good malty nose, underpinned by a subtle resiny hop character; on the palate fragrant and fruity, hints of caramel-like sweetness leading to a dry, spicy, and hoppy finish.

Ulmer Maibock

Familienbrauerei Bauhöfer
www.ulmer-bier.de

Country of origin Germany
First brewed 1893
Alcohol content 7.3% abv
Serving temperature 44°–50°F, 7°–10°C

Ulmer Maibock is a renowned delicacy in the Ortenau region of the Upper-Rhenish lowlands. It has been brewed in the village of Renchen-Ulm since 1893, and brewmaster and fourth-generation owner Gustav Bauhöfer has long known that standard beers are not enough to satisfy the local palate.

Ulmer Maibock combines lightheartedness with depth, character with drinkability. It is made of pilsner malt and slowly fermented in open vessels. It matures for about six weeks. Bauhöfer assigns the beer's popularity to a certain Frau Schindler, a waitress at the brewery's tavern during the postwar era when there were only Export and Maibock on the list. Before taking orders, Frau Schindler described the Maibock to the innocents, a dedication to beer passion that is hard to find in today's taverns, and one that made Ulmer Maibock the must-have beer. **SK**

Tasting notes
An almost neutral aroma with hints of rubber. The first sip is full bodied yet straight, evolving into a voluminous bitterness: herbal and floral notes. Dry, bitter, but warming finish.

Ulrichsbier

Berg Brauerei Ulrich Zimmermann
www.bergbier.de

Country of origin Germany
First brewed 1911
Alcohol content 5.3% abv
Serving temperature 46°F, 8°C

First brewed in 1911, Ulrichsbier is arguably the oldest brand of beer still being brewed in Upper Swabia. Made with a mix of light-colored and roasted malts, plus German-grown Hallertauer Magnum for bitterness and Tettnanger Perle for aromatic notes on the nose, this amber-golden brew is a classic representative of the bottom-fermented beers that were common before light-colored lagers.

Originally, Ulrichsbier was released for a festival at the brewery site that is held each year on the occasion of the Saint Ulrich celebration on July 4. Curiously, it used to come out with differing original gravity. Very often it was brewed like a bock. Following this tradition, the Berg Brauerei brings out a stronger version of 7.1 percent alcohol content during the winter season. Family-owned since 1757, the brewery uses high-quality local ingredients and traditional brewing methods. **SK**

Tasting notes
A moment of sweetness, medium body, moderate but lasting bitterness balanced by decent roasted malt and coffeelike flavors, acid freshness. Pleasantly bitter, tartish finish.

Union

Meantime Brewing | www.meantimebrewing.com

Country of origin England
First brewed 2000
Alcohol content 4.9% abv
Serving temperature 46°F, 8°C

Meantime's founder and brewmaster Alastair Hook has never been someone who does the obvious. Even though his introduction to beer came from visiting real ale festivals, a trip around Europe awakened his eyes and palate to the glories of lagered beers, as did his time studying brewing in Bavaria. During the 1990s, he became known as an advocate of lager, working both at the Freedom brewery and Mash brewpub. So it was no surprise that one of his earliest beers at his own brewery Meantime was a lager. Even though it was dark and deep copper in color, Union was most definitely a lager, but not as most people knew it.

The brewery's communications director Peter Haydon says: "Meantime is all about challenging people's perceptions, and one of the great common misconceptions about beer is that lager is cold, yellow, and fizzy. It seemed an obvious thing to do to produce a lager that wasn't what people thought lager was. That meant, as soon as you gave it to them, they were intrigued to know why it was different, meaning you could tell them two stories at once, one about Vienna-style lagers, and one about Meantime."

Hook looked toward Vienna for inspiration for Union, producing a luscious and full-bodied beer that is available both bottled and served on draft. As for the beer's somewhat functional name, this was thought up by an old friend of Hook's: "The thinking was that Meantime was a union, a coming together of friends, in order to achieve a goal, while the beer was a coming together—a union—of malt, water, and hops for a similar purpose." **ATJ**

Tasting notes

Amber brown in the glass, sleek and sensuous. On the nose, coffee and chocolate and resiny hop notes invite further exploration; the palate is smooth and full bodied with further chocolate and coffee, plus a hint of smoke and a slight tingle of fruit before the crisp and dry finish.

Urthel Samaranth

Brouwerij De Leyerth | www.urthel.com

Country of origin Belgium
First brewed 2002
Alcohol content 11.5% abv
Serving temperature 50°–54°F, 10°–12°C

Yes, Urthel beers *are* Belgian beers. They're brewed, however, at the Koningshoeven Trappist brewery, just over the Dutch border and home to the La Trappe beers. Their creator, brewmaster Hildegard van Ostaden is Flemish to the core and lives in Ruisled in West Flanders. She also studied brewing in Gent, before taking up teaching brewing in her old school.

During the first years of the De Leyerth brews, the beers hailed from the East Flemish Van Steenberge brewery, but in 2007, production was moved to Koningshoeven in the Dutch North Brabant province. Finding out when a beer was first brewed is not always easy, but Samaranth is the exception confirming the rule. The first pouring can even be narrowed to a single date: September 5, 2002, when van Ostaden got married. Samaranth is thus a marriage ale: a marriage made in heaven, of exceptional strength, if the beer is any indication. It can be described as a barleywine with a Belgian touch, albeit unspiced, which distinguishes it from the usual Belgian holiday ales.

None of the Urthel beers can be totally dissociated from the bulbous-nosed dwarfs, known as "Erthels," who feature on the artwork that graces the bottle labels. This lightness of touch might irk some serious beer explorers, who would rather learn more about types and specifications of malts and hops used in the brew, but it has proved to be a good selling point for the beers. The artwork is the specialty of husband Bas, a gifted illustrator whose inspiration could all too easily be taken from the Efteling fairy-tale theme park in Holland, which he used to live close to. **JPa**

Tasting notes

Fruity and leafy with the first pass of the nose, turning into preserved orange, strawberry syrup, and dried figs. The taste is yeasty, nearly meaty, also bitter with hints of walnut peel; a sweetness as in Mandarine Napoléon. Very creamy, velvety, and rich on the palate.

Victory HopDevil

Victory Brewing | www.victorybeer.com

Country of origin United States
First brewed 1995
Alcohol content 6.7% abv
Serving temperature 44°F, 7°C

After brewers Bill Covaleski and Ron Barchet trained at Germany's Weihenstephan Institute, they seemed destined for a career dominated by German-style lagers. Traditional, malty, and decidedly Bavarian characterizes the beer they brew in a former bakery on the outskirts of Philadelphia.

A funny thing happened on the way to lager fame. While the two young brewers were setting up their brewery's restaurant in 1995, they got their hands on a long-awaited supply of Sierra Nevada Celebration, the famously hoppy beer from California released just once a year for the Christmas season. "It hit us like a ton of bricks," Covaleski said. "We looked at each other and said, 'We have our own brewery! We don't have to wait once a year for a hoppy beer.'" Thus was born HopDevil, Victory's homage to hops.

The restaurant workers loved it at first sip, and so did adoring fans. Quickly, it leapt past Victory's highly regarded lagers to become its top seller. This is no Celebration clone, though. Instead, HopDevil is the kind of beer they'd make in Munich if they gave up the Hallertauer and converted to Cascade: lots of whole flower Cascade, plus Centennial and a third hop variety that, Covaleski says, "We simply don't talk about." Nor is it one-dimensional hop juice. Those much-beloved German malts provide a unique backbone and complexity to this India Pale Ale. Copper colored and subtly sweet, a sip fills the palate with a surprising softness for such a bitter beer style. Over the years, HopDevil's fame has spread. In 2002, it was named the top U.S. beer at the Great British Beer Festival. **DR**

Tasting notes

On the nose, huge pine and citrus aromas rise above a creamy head. Malt sweetness dominates the palate at first, followed by grassy, citrusy hops with a tight spiciness, then there's a sweet, smooth, satisfying finish that is never cloying.

Voll-Damm

S. A. Damm | www.volldamm.es

Country of origin Spain
First brewed 1953
Alcohol content 7.2% abv
Serving temperature 43°–46°F, 6°–8°C

Following the great success that Damm achieved with Estrella Dorada (which was renamed Estrella Damm), it decided that it was time to bring out a new beer. So, in February 1953, Voll-Damm was brewed for the first time, with the tag "Das originale Märzenbier"; this referred to Oktoberfest beers, the unique kind of beer that was developed in Munich and originally produced in March toward the end of the brewing season.

This Spanish version perfectly fitted the category by respecting the production period and being seasonal; however, public demand and appreciation were such that, two years after the beer's first production, the company decided to make it available all year around. As the German name "Voll" suggests, this beer is very full bodied, thanks to the extra malt used in a typical Märzen recipe. Times have changed though, and nowadays the recipe is no longer full malt: barley malt extract, rice, and maize also go into the mix. However, this hasn't diminished its appeal: in 2004, it received the gold medal in the strong lager category at the International Beer Competition Awards, and in 2007, it was named the World's Best Strong Lager in the World Beer Awards.

Due to its robust and full-bodied characteristics, Voll-Damm is a beer that is best with seafood, meat, and grilled vegetables. It is the only Spanish double-malt beer. It is less popular then its ancestor Estrella Damm so is a little harder to find in bars and pubs, especially out of its Catalonian home territory. There, it is the third most popular beer, but once it travels out of the region, its appeal seems to drop. **SS**

Tasting notes

Amber gold in color, topped by a white foam head. The nose produces some light hop aromas while the taste and mouthfeel is more intense, characterized by a hopped body with gentle carbonation. The finish is a light sense of hop and alcohol.

Wadworth 6X

Wadworth | www.wadworth.co.uk

Country of origin England
First brewed 1928
Alcohol content 4.3% abv
Serving temperature 52°–55°F, 11°–13°C

There are few beers so closely related to the concept of traditional cask ale in the United Kingdom as Wadworth 6X. Back in the 1970s, when "real ale"—as the newly founded consumer group, the Campaign for Real Ale, dubbed it—was in danger of falling into extinction, 6X was seen as one of the great flag wavers for this dying breed. Along with the likes of Marston's Pedigree, Ruddles County, and Theakston's Best Bitter, it was a beer whose reputation transcended its natural trading area, making it known to beer lovers across the United Kingdom.

The British real ale scene has improved greatly since those dark days, but 6X is still waving the flag for traditional beer. Everything about it is stamped with brewing heritage, from the historic Victorian brewhouse in Devizes, Wiltshire, where it is produced, to the typically British ingredients that create such a distinctive, malty, fruity flavor.

6X first saw the light of day back in December 1928. At first it was a blended bottled beer, part of a series of ales that also included 2X and 3X. Today it is Wadworth's best-selling beer, hogging most of the production capacity at the redbrick, town center brewery. Pale malt is combined with a little crystal malt and some cane sugar in the mash tun, whereas the hops are 85 percent Fuggle and the rest Golding: the great British double act that provides a smooth, rounded bitterness and a mellow, fruity flavor. There is also a third ingredient, if you are lucky to find it, and that is oak. Wadworth still maintains its own cooper, and selected pubs serve 6X from wooden casks. **JE**

Tasting notes

This deep amber beer exemplifies the malt profile that defines most of Wadworth's beers. Malt fills the aroma and then leads in the bittersweet taste, where it is joined by slightly perfumed, raisin-fruity notes, with hops building in the drying, bitter, yet still malty, finish.

A cooper repairs the brewery's traditional wooden barrels.

Wailing Wench

Middle Ages Brewing | www.middleagesbrewing.com

Country of origin United States
First brewed 2003
Alcohol content 8% abv
Serving temperature 50°F, 10°C

There may be no sadder—nor delightful—commentary on the hedonistic nature of alcohol consumption than the presence at some U.S. sporting events of the beer wench. She's the attractive woman who is employed to fetch you a beer so that you don't miss a single play while standing in line. With a bit of luck, your woman will bring back a pint of her own namesake, Wailing Wench, a dark and robust ale that, according to the label, is "screaming with hops."

Before you raise objections over this mild bit of political incorrectness, you should know that it was a woman who dreamed up the name and its slogan. Mary Rubenstein runs the small Middle Ages Brewery in Syracuse, New York, with her husband Marc. And it's all done with a playful nod to the days of yore. "We're big Monty Python fans, and a lot of the ideas for our brewery came from the movie," says Marc, referring to the classic Monty Python and the Holy Grail. The brewery's beers, with names such as Dragonslayer, Druid Fluid, and Wizard's Winter, sound like something on the round table of King Arthur and his knights.

Indeed, there's a very strong influence of Merrie England at Middle Ages. Marc was trained by Alan Pugsley, the British expatriate who spread the gospel of fellow Brit and master brewer Peter Austin throughout the United States. Middle Ages uses Austin's classic Ringwood yeast, known for adding a nutty flavor to ale. "I think it's an awesome yeast," says Marc. "It drops quickly to the bottom of the fermenter, which makes it perfect for cask ale." That's right, Wailing Wench is that rare thing on the U.S. bar-top: real ale. **DR**

Tasting notes

It may not be screaming with hops, but this strong, dark amber ale loudly states its case as a massively dry hopped strong ale. Strong herbal and floral hops balance toffeelike malt on the palate, then finish bitter with a smart, warming alcohol rush.

Wells Bombardier

Wells & Young's | www.wellsandyoungs.co.uk

Country of origin England
First brewed 1980
Alcohol content 5.2% abv
Serving temperature 50°–54°F, 10°–12°C

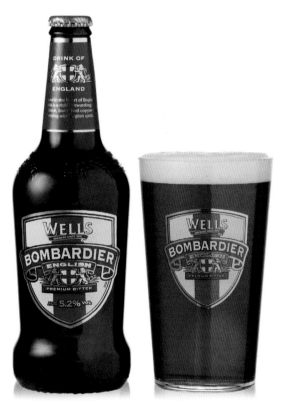

As English as bowler hats, umbrellas, and cricket, Wells Bombardier is "the drink of England" and the top brand of Wells and Young's. It is a fruity-tasting bitter that has developed a strong connection to St. George's Day, the day that celebrates the patron saint of England. While the Irish have Guinness with which to toast each other on St. Patrick's day, if Wells and Young's gets its way, the English will be exclusively supping Bombardier on April 23 each year—no bad thing.

The beer is brewed in the heart of middle England, with pure mineral water pulled from a well sunk in Bedford by Charles Wells, the brewery's founder, in 1902. Wells Bombadier was introduced to celebrate the company's receipt of the Queen's Award for Export Achievement and it quickly went from a popular regional brew to a worldwide success.

Head brewer for the last ten years, Jim Robertson ensures that only the best ingredients are used in the brewing process. The hops are hand-sampled to ensure their quality, with only the ripest English Challenger and Fuggle hops being used. The brewery also adds a lot more malt per pint than many other beers, and to help give Bombardier its full flavor and deep copper red color, the crystal malt is crushed rather than ground. The beer is then fermented for at least seven days, and the result is a wonderfully bitter brew that is very satisfying indeed. Another great thing about Bombardier is the fact that it is the Official Beer of English Heritage. Therefore, sitting back and relaxing with a pint of it is helping to protect England's historic environment. Top hole, what! **JM**

Tasting notes

An appealing deep copper-colored ale, that immediately attracts with a tempting aroma of dark fruits and an underlying hop spiciness; on the palate, luscious malty notes and a hints of fruit combine before leading to a bitter finish.

Westvleteren Abt 12°

Brouwerij der Abdij van St. Sixtus
www.sintsixtus.be/eng/brouwerij.htm

Country of origin Belgium
First brewed *ca*. 1941
Alcohol content 10.2% abv (minimum)
Serving temperature 54°F, 12°C

What might characterize Westvleteren abbey more than most Trappist breweries is that the beer is made exclusively by the fathers. According to the monks, this is the main reason for the strict limitation on output. Were they to give in to the demand for the beer (a demand that grew phenomenally after the beer was dubbed the best in the world by an online rating site), they would be forced to hire outside employees.

Until 1992, the brewery allowed the nearby St. Bernard brewery to use the name St. Sixtus for its beers. The divorce was rather bitter, and courts decided that the Sixtus name was off-limits to both, hence the name change to Westvleteren. The 12 degree beer is definitely the top product. Beer aficionados from the whole world flock to the brewery for this most venerated beer. **JPa**

Tasting notes

Dark malt, blue cheese, wood, plum, and raisin nose. Roasted malts with an outspoken sweetness when young, turning to Sauternes or sherry, chocolate, and overripe fruit with age.

The Wise ESB

Elysian Brewing
www.elysianbrewing.com

Country of origin United States
First brewed 1997
Alcohol content 5.9% abv
Serving temperature 50°F, 10°C

Founded in 1996, Elysian Brewing owns and operates three brewpubs in Seattle. Since opening, brewmaster Dick Cantwell has created over sixty different beers, on a modest 200-barrel brewing system, including six year-round standards, of which The Wise ESB was the very first beer Elysian brewed. They all feature themes taken from Greek mythology, and the reference to wisdom in the ESB's name is an allusion to the Greek goddess Athena, the goddess of wisdom, peace, warfare, strategy, handicrafts, and reason.

Elysian's ESB starts with traditional malts, such as pale, Munich, crystal, and Belgian Special B, but hops from the Pacific Northwest put an American stamp on it. The beer's primary hop variety is Chinook, but is finished with both Cascade and Centennial hops, and has won three gold medals from the Great American Beer Festival (GABF) since 2003. **JB**

Tasting notes

The nose is complex and malty, with aromas of toffee, citrus, and grapefruit. The ESB has a creamy mouthfeel with malty sweetness nicely balanced with American hop character.

Witkap-Pater Dubbel

Brouwerij Slaghmuylder
www.witkap.be

Country of origin Belgium
First brewed 1929
Alcohol content 7% abv
Serving temperature 46°–50°F, 8°–10°C

Although Witkap has never been linked officially to any religious institution, it can claim a lineage going back to the famous Trappist brewery of Westmalle. Here the creator of the Witkap beers, Hendrik Verlinden, perfected his brewing skills before World War I. After striking out on his own, he began work on his own Trappist-style beer and named it Witkap (White Cap), cleverly linking a reference to the white cowls of the Cistercian order of monks with the luscious head of the beer itself.

Drie Linden later contracted the brewing to Slaghmuylder, an 1860s-vintage family brewery in East Flanders, which gained full rights to the brand two years later and extended the range to include a double, triple, and a blond. The brewery recommends pouring the dubbel carefully to leave the yeast in the bottle then tasting with a Belgian chocolate dessert. **DdM**

Tasting notes
The powerful palate has sweet-sour fruit, cedar, fresh marmalade, tobacco, licorice and toffee, with a long, rounded, lightly drying angelica, and smoke-tinged finish.

Wodan

Brauerei Ganter
www.ganter.com

Country of origin Germany
First brewed 1898
Alcohol content 7.5% abv
Serving temperature 50°–54°F, 10°–12°C

Freiburg in Breisgau is one of southwest Germany's most scenic cities, an easy-going student community with a taste for bicycling, eating great Swabian food, and a pretty nice beer scene. Should you ever visit, make your way to the Dom, the cathedral in the old town, and look for a blue house front: Ganter's Brauereiausschank. This fine establishment offers solid local fare and the whole Ganter range served in tip-top condition at decent prices. Especially worthy of note are Urtrunk, a crisp, very subtle, and surprisingly complex unfiltered pale lager, and Wodan.

Named after the Saxon counterpart to the chief Norse god Odin, officially Wodan is a seasonal doppelbock, available in bottles from November to February, but you can sample it pretty much all year around on draft at the brewery tap in Freiburg. It's splendidly warming and dangerously drinkable. **LM**

Tasting notes
The nose and palate are dominated by dark fruit with hints of blackcurrant, prunes, and raisins; little residual sweetness, a solid nutty malt backbone, and final bitterness for balance.

Woodforde's Wherry

Woodforde's | www.woodfordes.co.uk

Country of origin England
First brewed 1981
Alcohol content 3.8% abv
Serving temperature 52°F, 11°C

In 1981, Wherry was the first commercial beer brewed by home-brewers Ray Ashworth and Dr. David Crease. Their brewery was part of a new age of aspirant brewers in the United Kingdom, many of whom had been inspired by the actions of the Campaign for Real Ale (CAMRA). These brewing pioneers wanted to rebel against what they saw as the "relentless blandness" of larger brewers' products. At the time when Ashworth and Crease went to work, the area of Norfolk in which they lived was often described as a "beer desert." All the brewers had closed, and there was a lack of choice of cask beers in local pubs. Enthusiastic home-brewers, both men realized that their hobby could be turned into a viable business.

Ashworth and Crease named their brewery after Parson Woodforde, an 18th-century Norfolk clergyman who enjoyed good food and beer, which he often brewed himself. The first beer was Wherry, named after a type of sailing boat that had been in the past used to transport people and goods on the Norfolk Broads. Wherry is made with Maris Otter pale ale malt plus a generous variety of colored malts and Golding hops that impart marvelous zesty flavors. Among its many awards, Wherry was chosen as the Champion Beer of Britain in 1996.

In 2009, Neil Bain joined the team as head brewer. All too often, a new head brewer likes to change things, but Bain said that his role at Woodforde's would not be to change the outstanding range of beers, but to ensure consistency and to promote the best possible brewing practices. **TH**

Tasting notes

Woodforde's Wherry is a clean, zesty, refreshing bitter. It is amber gold to the eye and has a tingling hoppy floral aroma with hints of lemon, grapefruit, and other citrus fruits. Underlying it all are sweet malt flavors, which tickle the taste buds.

Worthington's White Shield

White Shield Brewery | www.worthingtons-whiteshield.com

Country of origin England
First brewed *ca.* 1820s
Alcohol content 5.6% abv
Serving temperature 50°–54°F, 10°–12°C

While it's arguably the world's most authentic IPA, White Shield stopped calling itself "Worthington India Pale Ale" about a century ago. William Worthington originally turned up in Burton-on-Trent looking for a piece of the lucrative Baltic trade in the 18th century, and he was in prime position when Burton brewers broke into the Indian market in the 1820s and 1830s.

Worthington's IPA never rivaled the legendary names of Bass and Allsopp, but it was popular in India and increasingly so at home in the 19th century. When the arrival of lager, higher duties on higher strength beers, and an anti-alcohol climate conspired to sound the death knell for strong, hoppy IPAs, Worthington's changed the name of theirs to White Shield—a nickname it had had for years thanks to the label.

Worthington's merged with Bass in 1926. Only normally available in bottles, White Shield spent the next seventy-five years as a drink beloved of ale connoisseurs, who debated whether or not you should leave the sediment in the bottle or add a little extra yeasty body to the glass. In the 1970s, White Shield was a rare beacon keeping alive the flame of bottle-conditioned beers. But Bass farmed it out for contract brewing, and each successive caretaker loved the beer a little less, until it looked set for oblivion. Brewer Steve Wellington of Burton's Museum Brewery stepped in and asked the board of Bass (now Molson Coors) if he could bring White Shield back home. He's tended it for about ten years now, and restored it to its former glory—a remarkable beer that brings the true taste of 19th-century India Pale Ale to new generations. **PB**

Tasting notes

A stunning beer with bags of fruit, loads of spice, a hint of freshly baked bread, some treacle, caramel and toffee, all suspended in a fine balance with no one flavor overpowering the other. Wonderful in particular with either Stilton or mature Cheddar.

X-Beer 33°

U Medvídků | www.umedvidku.cz

Country of origin Czech Republic
First brewed 2005
Alcohol content 12.6% abv
Serving temperature 59°F, 15°C

Prague's U Medvídků pub has gone through several incarnations since first opening back in 1466. Once a legendary brewpub, then a famous cabaret, in recent years it has been known as one of Prague's favorite sources for Budweiser Budvar, served in the cavernous beer hall along with classic Bohemian cuisine.

However, in 2005, U Medvídků began brewing its own beer in the tiny on-site microbrewery run by brewmaster Ladislav Veselý. All the beers are brewed and fermented in oak barrels, a practice that was discontinued by even the most traditional Czech breweries, in part due to the time-consuming nature of cooperage: at least once a year, all of U Medvídků's oak barrels must be relined with brewer's pitch.

There is something slightly oaky and pitchlike about U Medvídků's brews, especially the remarkable X-Beer 33. First brewed at 30 degrees Plato and called X-Beer 30, the beer was strengthened to 33 degrees Plato and correspondingly renamed. It claims to be the strongest lager beer in the world, at least in terms of original gravity, as it is made without any addition of alcohol, sugar, or wort. Instead it is slowly fermented from its extremely high gravity using two types of yeast and conditioned for at least seven months. X-Beer 33 is the Czech beer that most resembles an English barleywine, and it pairs well with desserts and cheese courses. **ER**

Tasting notes

A pronounced nose of forest strawberries and plum compôte. Leathery tannic notes support a sweet and viscous malt body with orange peel and honey, with a lightly peppery finish.

XS: Imperial India Pale Ale

Rogue Ales | www.rogue.com

Country of origin United States
First brewed 1996
Alcohol content 9.2% abv
Serving temperature 44°–50°F, 7°–10°C

Rogue's Imperial India Pale Ale is one controversial beer. Part of the brewery's XS series of exceptionally strong beers, I2PA, as it is sometimes called, is believed to be one of the first imperial IPAs ever brewed. And it might even be the original, claims brewmaster John Maier. "We certainly thought it was the first imperial IPA," Maier says. "But then I got a phone call from Vinnie (Cilruzo, of Russian River Brewing) who said that he had brewed one before I2PA." Maier says it would be hard to determine which brew came first, because the brewers had the inspiration to make an imperial IPA within a few months of each other—and without knowledge of the other beer. Either way, I2PA played a hand in launching the imperial IPA style, which has exploded on the craft beer scene.

I2PA is the brainchild of Nate Lindquist, who worked as a brewer at Rogue in the early years. His first imperial IPA was slightly different to the current commercial version. "I tasted it and told him there weren't enough hops; it needed more 'oomph,'" Maier says. "We doubled the hops and changed some of them to American hops for that Cascade aroma." And the rest is controversial history. Even the name is the subject of debate, with some fans calling it "I-Two-P-A" as though it's a new droid in a *Star Wars* movie, and others calling it the more math-oriented "I-Squared-P-A." **LMo**

Tasting notes

I2PA is aged for nine months. Enjoy the aromas of pine and citrus hops, caramel, and even vanilla bean notes that seem to leap out of the bottle when poured.

An U Medvídků brewery sign on a wall in Prague, Czech Republic.

Amber 299

Yorkshire Stingo

Samuel Smith | www.tadcaster.uk.com/breweriesSamuelSmith.htm

Country of origin England
First brewed 2008
Alcohol content 8% abv
Serving temperature 52°F, 11°C

"The miller he bought him a barrel of ale, and called it right good Stingo," declares the traditional English folk song. Depending on where the song is sung, it may be rendered as "stingo" (in Yorkshire) or "spingo" (in the West Country), but the meaning is the same—strong ale.

It would be tempting to view the release of Smith's Yorkshire Stingo as a commemorative beer, because it coincidentally appeared exactly 250 years after the founding of The Old Brewery. Smith's insists that this wasn't the plan, but nevertheless, it has all the elements that one might expect of a celebratory beer: it is strong, it has cellaring potential, and it has an interesting production process.

Although this is clearly a beer that has potential to develop with age, Smith's insists that this is not its intent. Unusually, it ages this bottle-conditioned beer for a year at the brewery, and say that it is ready for consumption on release. The beer undergoes a period of wooden cask aging as well as a period of bottle conditioning. After a year of combined cask and bottle aging, the beer is ready to drink. Only time will tell if Yorkshire Stingo gets better with age, but it is clear that it doesn't necessarily require aging: it's a fruity delight fresh from the bottle.

Had this beer come from any other brewery, it would have been launched with a fanfare and a splash of publicity. In typically understated fashion, Smith's ushered Yorkshire Stingo out through the back door with a blanket thrown over its head, away from prying eyes. Almost despite themselves, the brewers seem to have created a classic. **ZA**

Tasting notes

Deep burnished copper-brown in color. Lots of dried fruit in the malt-driven aroma, alongside some interesting leathery notes. Sweetness on the tongue turns into a woody, almost vinous dryness, with a creamy texture and followed by a malty, dried-fruit finish.

Watercolor of the Yorkshire Stingo Inn, Marylebone Road, London, 1770.

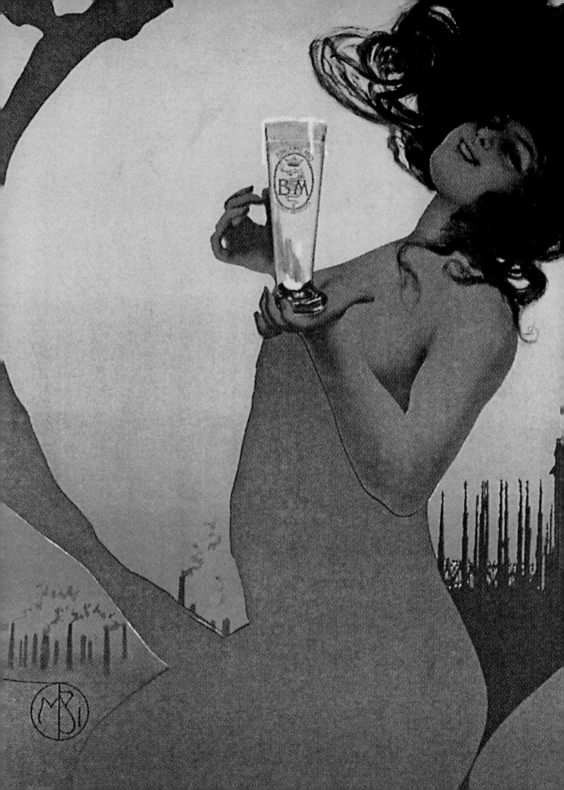

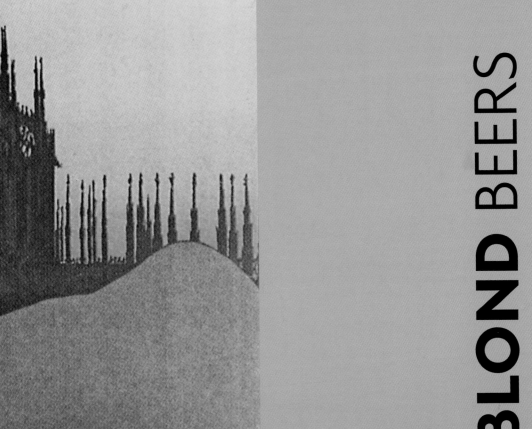

BLOND BEERS

3 Monts

La Brasserie de St.-Sylvestre | www.brasserie-st-sylvestre.com

Country of origin France
First brewed 1984
Alcohol content 8.5% abv
Serving temperature 50°F, 10°C

The Ricour family has owned La Brasserie de Saint-Sylvestre since 1920 when Rémy Ricour, the grandfather of current owners François and Serge Ricour, took over an existing brewery in this village at the center of French Flanders's hop country. The tale is told how when the brothers' grandfather was taken as a prisoner of war in World War II, their sixteen-year-old father had to take over the running of the brewery. By the end of the war, the hop and malt shortages meant that they were making a beer that was 5 percent. Add a further 3.5 percent alcohol content and you will get to the strength of the brewery's famed 3 Monts, a beautiful beer that takes its name (with a big pitch of irony given the area's flatness) from three neighboring hills.

3 Monts first saw the light of day in 1984, in the wake of the brewery swapping its main business of lagers for top-fermenting beers, such as Bière de Mars (now Bière Nouvelle) and a Christmas beer. For 3 Monts, hops from the region and barley from an area north of Paris go into the mix. Fermentation takes place over several days and the beer is then "garded" for between three to four weeks. Even though the beer spends a respectable time maturing, when next seen in the glass, the question about what constitutes a bière de garde crops up. 3 Monts is golden in color and seemingly has more taste and aromas in common with Belgian tripels than the classic amber malt bombs that constitute bière de garde. Ricor says that he sees 3 Monts more as a Flemish beer than a French beer, which perhaps implies it has a close link with the beers produced over the border to the north. **ATJ**

Tasting notes

A blond stunner with a blast of fruit on the nose, underwritten and kept in line by a hint of grainy cereal. The palate resonates with its rich, ripe fruitiness, almost like a rich white wine, while the finish roars with alcoholic warmth and hints of bitterness.

IV Saison

Brasserie de Jandrain-Jandrenouille | www.IVSaison.be

Country of origin Belgium
First brewed 2007
Alcohol content 6% abv
Serving temperature 44°F, 7°C

Like many of Belgium's more interesting craft brewers, Stephane Meulemans and Alexandre Dumont have day jobs. Respectively, they are the senior vice-president of worldwide sales and a business development manager for Yakima Chief, the Washington state hop producer that accounts for more than one-fifth of all hop acreage in the United States. They know a thing or two about hops.

American hops have become more fashionable in Belgium in recent years, with some brewers prizing the fruity, floral aromas of varieties such as Amarillo and Cascade. From their Yakima Chief office in Louvain-la-Neuve, Meulemans and Dumont have watched these efforts with interest, and in summer 2007, they decided to set a new example.

The IV Saison ("*Quatre Saison*," or "Four Seasons") is so named for a few reasons. Both its fathers have three kids, so this was the fourth child for each of them. Also the beer has four basic ingredients: water, malt, hops, and yeast. The beer's principal traits are a distinctive lemony hop aroma and a restrained bitterness; the brewers seem to be aiming to promote drinkability rather than to coat the tongue with resin. It is also clean tasting for a Belgian ale, avoiding yeasty esters to accentuate the beer's natural ingredients.

Rarely do new breweries make the sort of impression among local aficionados that the IV Saison made in 2008, as the Jandrain-Jandrenouille debut gradually became more widely available in Belgium. It's still hard to find, as production remains small, but the brewers plan to expand a great deal in the next few years. Buzz is growing and exports are imminent. **JS**

Tasting notes

Bright, yellow gold beer with fluffy white head and sticky lace. Smells like fresh, lemony hops, lemongrass, grapefruit, and cereals. Crisp grassy hop bitterness is moderate but lasts into the aftertaste, cradled by that citrus backdrop. Lively beer, dry on the finish.

#9

Magic Hat Brewing Company | www.magichat.net

Country of origin United States
First brewed 1995
Alcohol content 4.6% abv
Serving temperature 44°F, 7°C

Vermont's Magic Hat Brewing is all about fun and being unconventional. Imagine if Willy Wonka had chosen to become a brewer instead of a candy maker and you have some idea of the gentle madness behind Magic Hat. With beer names like Chaotic Chemistry, Circus Boy, Hocus Pocus, Jinx, Odd Notion, and Wacko, a beer named #9 sounds almost normal. The name is perhaps even more mysterious than the beer. Whenever co-founder Alan Newman is asked why the beer is called #9, he always replies the same way: "Why, indeed!"

Magic Hat has taken the same enigmatic approach to marketing what has become its most popular beer, preferring to fan the flames of befuddlement with advertising copy such as: "It is the ale cloaked in secrecy. A mystery of malts and hops that swirls across the palate to ask more questions than it answers." #9 was originally a summer seasonal beer, but its unanticipated popularity magically turned it into a year-round flagship. It proved so popular, in fact, that three years later, the brewery was forced to move to its present, and much larger, location near Lake Champlain's Bartlett Bay.

#9 is essentially a pale ale with essence of apricot added, although Magic Hat describes it as a "not quite pale ale." It is brewed with pale and crystal malts together with Cascade and Columbus hops. The apricot essence gives it an unusual nose and palate, quite unlike anything else. Its sweet malt and fruitiness makes it an ideal match with a variety of spicy dishes, such as Indian, Thai, and Szechwan cuisine. **JB**

Tasting notes

Magic Hat's #9 is cloudy golden in color with a perfumey nose of candy sweet, apricot, and other fruit aromas. The taste profile is also quite sweet with malt and fruit character dominating. The finish is dry with thick apricot flavors that linger a long while.

12 Gauge

Leigh Sawmill Brewing | www.sawmillbrewery.co.nz

Country of origin New Zealand
First brewed 2008
Alcohol content 6.5% abv
Serving temperature 39°–44°F, 4°–7°C

With a plentiful supply of native timber and a natural deep-water port, Leigh once boasted a thriving logging industry. Today the picturesque fishing village and neighboring coastline are more of a playground for visiting holidaymakers and eco tourists.

The brainchild of English immigrants Peter and Decima Freckleton, Leigh Sawmill Brewing was established in 2004 to complement the adjacent café and accommodation with a range of hand-crafted, premium beers. The brewhouse features a traditional copper kettle, timber-clad fermentation vessels, and stainless steel conditioning tanks. While tours, tastings, and off sales are available from the brewery, the beers are available on tap at the café and in a handful of local outlets. Asked if he plans to send them farther afield Peter says, "Watch this space."

The Freckletons' brewery is unusual in that it is New Zealand's only microbrewery that has its own canning facility. It produces four beers, a wheat beer, pale ale, dark ale, and pilsner (all 4.5 percent) that are sold in the stylish silver cans; and a further two, a dark ale and a strong pilsner, both 6.5 percent, that are available in attractive swing-top bottles.

Originally known as "El Grande"—a reference to the big prize in Spain's national lottery—and now named after a shotgun, 12 Gauge is a rare example of a strong, pilsner-style lager. Made with a blend of pale and pilsner malts, New Zealand Green Bullet and Motueka hops, and filtered soft rainwater, this refreshing but hefty brew is fermented cool and given an extended cold maturation. **GG**

Tasting notes

Pouring a bright yellow gold hue beneath a dense white head, there's a sweet candylike aroma with lemony notes and a hint of alcohol. The palate is delightfully rich and mouth-filling, with sweet, biscuity malt and crisp, citrusy hops leading into a lingering, grassy finish.

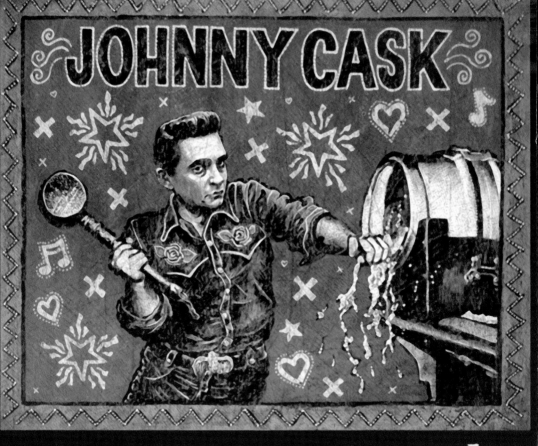

JOHNNY CASK

Dogfish Head 75 Minute IPA

90 Minute
Imperial IPA

Dogfish Head
www.dogfish.com

Country of origin United States
First brewed 2001
Alcohol content 9% abv
Serving temperature 50°F, 10°C

After centuries of following recipes, brewers have pretty much settled into a routine when it comes to hops: boil them at the beginning of the brew to extract bitterness, toss them in at the end for aroma. What would happen, Dogfish Head founder Sam Calagione mused, if you added hops throughout the brewing process? Well, for one thing, you might have a brewhouse mutiny on your hands. Try convincing a brewery assistant to stand atop a steaming brew kettle to toss handfuls of hops into a boiling batch for an hour or more. Calagione's solution: an electric vibrating football game board. With less than mechanical precision, the board was used to shake the hops gently into the kettle, before a splash of wort shorted it out.

One taste of the finished product, however, told Calagione that he was on to something. The brew was bitter, yes, but intensely complex with an exceptional malt balance that provided unusual fruitlike flavors. That brew evolved into 90 Minute Imperial IPA, its name derived from the length of time that the hops are infused in the boil. Today the brewery uses a giant, computer-controled pneumatic cannon. The contraption automatically fires hops into the brew kettle so there is no need for anyone to get fed up. **DR**

Tasting notes
The aroma that rises from the creamy head is of dried fruit with a touch of citrus. A full-bodied sip assaults the palate with a balance of teeth-chattering hops and smooth, caramel-like malt.

Abbaye D'Aulne
Triple Blonde

Brasserie du Val de Sambre
www.valdesambre.be

Country of origin Belgium
First brewed 2000
Alcohol content 9% abv
Serving temperature 46°F, 8°C

Val de Sambre is located in a beautiful hidden valley, near Charleroi in the Hainaut province. The brewery is housed inside part of the D'Aulne Abbey, which dates back to the Middle Ages. The abbey was founded in the 7th century, then Cistercian monks took over in the 12th century, before French revolutionary forces burned it down in 1794.

Brewing has taken place on-site for hundreds of years, although the current operation only swung into action at the start of the millennium. Previous to that, the Abbey D'Aulne brands had been brewed by Affligem. Old adverts for the beer, which feature jolly monks, are dotted about the tasting room. Brewer Frederick Collinet oversees the production of a dozen different beers, of which this Triple Blonde is an excellent example of his skill. This beer was already being brewed at Affligem before Val de Sambre fired up its coppers. It is available both in bottle-conditioned form and on draft. It is instructive to compare the beer from both bottle and tap, with the latter coming across as more earthy and maltier. Tourists are welcome to contemplate the beers in the tasting room. Pâté, artisanal bread, and cheese, plus the local specialty *esceveche,* can be sampled alongside the beers. **CC**

Tasting notes
Pale, lightly hazy, gold-colored brew that pours with a big foamy head. Aroma has notes of citrus, pear, and spices. Taste is fruity, spicy, and mildly sweet, with a light touch of alcohol.

A special cask-conditioned ale that is a blend of the 60 and 90 Minute varieties.

Achel Blond 8°

Brouwerij der Trappistenabdij De Achelse Kluis | www.achelsekluis.org

Country of origin Belgium
First brewed 2001
Alcohol content 8% abv
Serving temperature 50°–57°F, 10°–14°C

Given the origins of the strict Trappist order of monks at La Trappe, Normandy, it's not surprising that they once produced cider as part of their commitment to self-reliance. When Trappists settled in Belgium in the mid 19th century to help re-establish monasticism in the newly independent Catholic state, they adapted to local traditions and ingredients and switched to brewing complex and fruity Trappist beers.

The abbey of St. Benedict at Hamont-Achel first opened its own brewery in 1850, producing beer almost entirely for its own consumption. Brewing ceased when the occupying German army confiscated the copper kit during World War I, and it didn't restart after the war because the abbey was registered to two monks of Dutch nationality and therefore was not entitled to reparations. In fact, production didn't restart until 1998, with the abbey initially brewing beer only for its new café, the first Trappist brewpub. Bottle-conditioned beers appeared five years later.

The wider Trappist fraternity pulled together on the project, and the legendary Brother Thomas of Westmalle was called out of retirement to help develop the recipes. Thomas's love of hops, which influenced the celebrated Westmalle Tripel, is highly evident in this blond, which is a stronger variant of the 5 percent draft blond that was developed for the café, with 27 IBUs worth of Saaz and Tradition hops added to a grist of pils malt and brewing sugar. However, this is no clone of established Trappist brands—top quality and made with real attention to detail, it's a distinctive and very modern-tasting beer. **DdM**

Tasting notes

A rich, deep-gold beer with fruity banana, pear, and herbal hints on the aroma, and a smooth fluffy malt palate with rooty, slightly vegetal hops and mirabelle fruit. There's lingering spice over firm sweetish malt and a touch of alcohol on the finish.

Advents-Bier

Brauhaus Schweinfurt | www.brauhaus-schweinfurt.de

Country of origin Germany
First brewed 1998
Alcohol content 5.4% abv
Serving temperature 43°–46°F, 6°–8°C

Grilled pork shoulder, tender T-bone in horseradish cream, or marinated braised beef? Brauhaus am Markt in the center of Schweinfurt serves tasty Franconian-style dishes. Be prepared for a hearty meal that comes with potato dumplings and a lot of sauce—regular features of the indigenous cuisine. The beer is typically Franconian, too. It offers a rich maltiness inspired by decent hoppy top notes. One such beer is a seasonal: Brauhaus Advents-Bier is only available from November to January, as the advent in its name suggests.

Since 1998, Brauhaus Schweinfurt's golden lager has lightened up the gloomy days of winter. Brewmaster Johann Weichert brews it with pilsner malt plus a special variety in a labor-intensive two-step decoction mash, where a portion of the mash is pumped to the copper, brought to the boil, and then returned to the main mash. This method intensifies the color and character of the beer. Furthermore Weichert uses the German aroma hop Tettnanger twice to give the beer a decent herbal bitterness. Reminscent of a Franconian Märzen, Brauhaus Advents-Bier offers a predominantly malty nose. Being an ambitious, passionate brewer, Weichert refined the Advents-Bier recipe when he realized that customers found it a bit too harsh; to this end he slightly decreased the bitterness, but most of all sought to make the beer more rounded.

Brauhaus Schweinfurt was founded as a private limited company back in 1903, but before that it was a family-owned brewery with the brewhouse situated downtown at the exact same place where today the tavern is located. **SK**

Tasting notes

Golden color with a warm hue and festive white head. This beer offers a rather sweet, malty nose. The palate is initially greeted by sweetness completed by grainy notes and hints of caramel, well-balanced bitterness with floral and herbal moments. Dry, mild finish.

Allagash Tripel Reserve

Allagash Brewing | www.allagash.com

Country of origin United States
First brewed 1998
Alcohol content 9% abv
Serving temperature 50°–61°F, 10°–16°C

Allagash Brewing boasts one of the most innovative gourmet beer ranges available in the United States. Wild *Brettanomyces* yeast, multiple hop regimens, postfermentation blends, and unusual ingredients, including grapes, yarrow, raspberries, and ginger, have all found their way into brewery founder Rob Tod's exotic (and occasionally pricey) bottles.

This classic Belgian-style tripel—one of Allagash's original core brands made without funky ingredients—earns undying praise from beer fans. No unconventional brewing processes and no secret ingredients—unless you count the yeast. Tod won't divulge any details about the strain, possibly because it is clearly vital to the golden ale's complex layers of flavor. The brew kettle sees only two-row malt, candy sugar, and light, unassuming hops—the same base any practiced brewer from Flanders would employ. Surely, they alone are not responsible for the sweet, honey and fruit flavors that roll across the palate.

The ale ferments in tanks for two to three weeks, then is filtered and bottled with a second strain of yeast for an important second stage of conditioning. Bottle conditioning is expensive: It takes extra time and it can be unstable. Allagash has experimented in-house with forced carbonation of its tripel, but with unsatisfactory results. "Secondary fermentation in the bottle brings the beer to a new level in terms of complexity, subtle flavors and aromas," Tod says.

Yeast, simple yeast. Compared to Allagash's fanciful, envelope-breaking variety of "extreme" beers, its Tripel is as basic as it gets … and yet entirely mysterious. **DR**

Tasting notes

Golden with a billowing pillow of foam that wafts mellow notes of honey, pear, and apple with a hint of herbal hops. Crisp, tingling, but not overwhelming yeast character enhances the sweet, fresh fruitlike flavor. The finish is sweet and warming, but not overly alcoholic. A true tripel.

Alpha Pale Ale

Matilda Bay Brewing Company | www.matildabay.com.au

Country of origin Australia
First brewed 1999
Alcohol content 5.2% abv
Serving temperature 39°F, 4°C

Australia does not have a history of highly hopped beers. Until recently, India Pale Ales had not been brewed commercially for more than a century, if at all. American Pale Ales were a rare import. Then Little Creatures from Western Australia turned to the United States for inspiration before releasing a fantastic pale ale. Some time later, the craft branch of the country's largest brewery, Matilda Bay Brewing, re-released Alpha Pale Ale after acquiring it from the Masthead Brewery where it was first brewed by Brad Rogers.

Alpha Pale Ale is, of course, all about the hops. Reportedly no fewer than five varieties are responsible for its complex character. The "Alpha" is a reference to the alpha acid in the bittering hops; these are added at the start of the boil and contribute to the bitterness and overall flavor of the beer. This is what gives Alpha Pale Ale its tremendous hoppy kick after the initial taste. Aroma hops are also added late in the boil to develop the beer's enticing aroma. Just to be sure that things are aromatic enough, more hops are added after the beer has fermented before a month of conditioning.

The result is a well-balanced, striking beer that is about as far away from Australia's stock lagers as could be imagined. To some, this beer confronts and confuses; to others, it is a world-class offering that uses its intense hop complexity to lure and reward. It is appropriate that this beer is sold by Australia's first craft brewery. Its founder, Phil Sexton, was involved in the development of both Bridgeport IPA and Little Creatures Pale Ale. One imagines he would approve of this addition to the Matilda Bay stable. **DD**

Tasting notes

Alpha Pale Ale pours with a burned-orange tinge and a generous off-white head. Linger over the intense citrus hop aromas as the beer warms slightly before embracing the sweet fruit and honey flavors and finishing with a bitter triumph.

Amnesiac Double IPA

Phillips Brewing Company | www.phillipsbeer.com

Country of origin Canada
First brewed 2004
Alcohol content 8.5% abv
Serving temperature 50°F, 10°C

When he first started his brewery in 2001, Matt Phillips worked hard to position himself as a renegade of sorts, ferrying beer around Vancouver Island in his beat-up Subaru, expanding distribution to the lower mainland via a series of rented trucks and sleepless delivery runs, and starting up his business in what was still a fairly conservative market by brewing a raspberry beer, an unapologetically hoppy IPA, and a stout flavored with espresso beans. And so it only made sense that he would also add to his portfolio one of the biggest and hoppiest beers brewed to that point in Canada, crafted in the style that Americans were already calling double IPA, or occasionally imperial pale ale.

Phillips enjoyed an element of good fortune. On the distribution front, the provincial liquor authority was being quite generous with providing listings to local brewers, and so Phillips applied for, and received, three of them. Additionally, the brewery had just moved from its original, cramped location into a significantly larger space, which allowed for a doubling and, eventually, quadrupling of production capacity.

So, with new listings for brands and space in which to create them, Phillips and his team got to work on crafting a new set of beers, turning first to the highly hopped, high-strength style that was rapidly gaining ground south of the border. "I have a small addiction issue with hops," says Phillips, "so everything we were doing at the time was pretty hoppy." Phillips was also intent on creating a beer that had malt structure in addition to hoppiness—"more than simply a hop bomb," in his words. **SB**

Tasting notes

For such a big beer, Amnesiac is almost frighteningly accessible, with a highly fragrant aroma accented by citrus, pine, and caramel notes, and a bitter but hardly overwhelming body of round and fruity malt mixed with citrusy hops. A lovely nightcap ale.

Arabier

De Dolle Brouwers | www.dedollebrouwers.be

Country of origin Belgium
First brewed *ca.* 1985
Alcohol content 8% abv
Serving temperature 50°F, 10°C

When the Herteleer brothers started brewing in Esen, they pretty much single-handedly started the microbrewery revolution in Belgium; soon afterward Achouffe and Abbaye des Rocs would follow. From the beginning, Oerbier always led the way, but the brothers' curiosity and expanding knowledge led to new additions to their portfolio. A special place was soon reserved for this blond, strong ale, which replaced a basic blond ale known as Oeral. According to Els Herteleer, Arabier was a bit more typically in style for the Dolle Brouwers (Mad Brewers).

As for the name, Arabier not only means "Arab," but also "beer from the ara parrot," as a cartoonlike bird on the label proclaims. Once upon a time, Arabier-on-tap was known as Arafat, but that would seem a tad too bitter these days. . . . Talking of which, bitterness is important for Arabier. Abundant use is made of the flowery and fragrant Nugget hop (from the local hop-growing area of Poperinge), an effect that is intensified by dry hopping the lagering beer in tank for a month. This pronounced hop character also explains why the brewery, in steep contrast to the Oerbier, recommends the consummation of Arabier well before the "Best by" date, in order to appreciate the effect of this hopping.

Arabier is available sporadically on tap, and a very good place to sample it is the brewery tap during the summer months. Don't hesitate to enjoy it on the outside terrace, which overlooks a peaceful rural scene: the quiet is only broken by the chickens next door, the lowing of the cows, and, of course, the merry sounds of a full house of dedicated drinkers. **JPa**

Tasting notes

Clear yellow blond beer beneath a robust white head. Young, the beer smells of honey and hops; later becoming nutty, alcoholic, and mushroomlike. Dry hopping returns in the taste, accompanied by citrus and other fruity flavors. A slight lactic streak may show up with age.

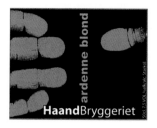

Ardenne Blond

HaandBryggeriet | www.haandbryggeriet.net

Augustiner Lagerbier Hell

Augustiner-Bräu Wagner | www.augustiner-braeu.de

Country of origin Norway
First brewed 2005
Alcohol content 7.5% abv
Serving temperature 43°–46°F, 6°–8°C

Country of origin Germany
First brewed *ca.* 19th century
Alcohol content 5.2% abv
Serving temperature 46°F, 8°C

Haandbryggeriet: "hand brewery." The name says it all. This small enterprise, based in the town of Drammen, just south of Oslo, sums up what small-scale craft brewing is all about, and the passion that goes into it.

Ardenne Blond is a skillful interpretation of a saison from the French-speaking region of Wallonia in Belgium. Lager malt, caramalt, and wheat malt provide the cereal base for the brew, with candy sugar topping up the fermentable material, raising the strength without adding too much body. The hops in the copper are fragrant Styrian Golding, but coriander is also added to enhance the beer's spicy citrus character. What really defines the brew, however, is the yeast. Initially, a conventional brewing yeast was used for fermentation but, in 2008, the decision was made to try a yeast called *Brettanomyces clausenii*, producing what the brewers describe as "a nice grapefruity aroma." **JE**

Established in 1328 and thus Munich's oldest brewery, Augustiner-Bräu has become an institution in Bavarian beer culture. A joke about Munich brewers says it all: the brewmaster of Augustiner-Bräu and two colleagues from other Munich breweries go to a pub. His fellow drinkers each order a glass of their own brand. The Augustiner brewmaster takes a soft drink. "Why don't you get yourself a beer?" comes the question. The Augustiner brewmaster replies, "I thought that since you weren't having one, then I wouldn't either."

Lagerbier Hell is a wonderful example of the Munich Helles style, a malt-accentuated pale lager with underlying hop bitterness. Due to its prolonged secondary fermentation, the Augustiner Helles is very complex and round. It is the most popular Augustiner brand and lovingly nicknamed "Grüner August" (Green August), a reference to the monk on the green label. **SK**

Tasting notes

A perfumed aroma, laced with bitter orange, leads to sweet malt in the full-bodied taste of this blond, offset by perfumed, orange-citrus notes, a gentle bitterness, and a spicy warmth.

Tasting notes

Brilliant light lager with a shiny, moist, white head. The beer offers a malty aroma with hints of hoppy notes. The first taste is sweet. A voluptuous carbonation flatters the palate.

Avatar Jasmine IPA

Elysian Brewing | www.elysianbrewing.com

Country of origin United States
First brewed 2005
Alcohol content 6.3% abv
Serving temperature 43°–48°F, 6°–9°C

The idea of a Jasmine IPA was inspired by a comment at an IPA judging panel by the English beer luminary Mark Dorber who noted that a beer had an aroma of "jasmine tea." The notion intrigued Dick Cantwell (who founded the brewery along with David Buhler and Joe Bisacca). He let idea steep for several years before brewing the beer as a seasonal. "We took it to the Washington Brewers Fest and had a line of about fifty people, many of whom were women, a demographic, as you know, not always enamored of beers as bitter as IPA. Still, the guys liked it." Avatar has since won a number of awards and is now a year-round product.

The beer uses Amarillo hops in the finish, plus a newish hop variety called Glacier for what Cantwell terms a "less fierce hop flavor, so the jasmine can come forward." Fifteen pounds (7 kg) of flowers are added at the end of the boil for each twenty-barrel batch. **RM**

Tasting notes

Full of the complex, musky aromas of jasmine and hops, with a little sweet caramel. Off-dry on the palate, ramping up to a sharp bitter middle. Finish is bitter, with exotic floral overtones.

Baffo d'Oro

Birra Moretti | www.birramoretti.it

Country of origin Italy
First brewed *ca.* 2006
Alcohol content 4.8% abv
Serving temperature 37°–41°F, 3°–5°C

Moretti is one of the great breweries of Italy. It was founded in 1859 by Luis Moretti in Udine, which is in the northeast of the country. The first beer emerged in 1860, and Moretti went on to become one of the top breweries, famously symbolized by the mustachioed man who appeared on their labels from the 1940s on. Lao Menazzi Moretti, then the owner of the brewery, apparently saw someone seated outside a trattoria who he thought perfectly represented everything that the beer was: genuine, authentic, and traditional. He took a photograph and, from that moment, on the image became inseparable from the beer itself.

Baffo d'Oro is an all-malt lager that gets its name from the iconic figure (*baffo* is mustache in Italian). A luxury beer, it is excellent with food. In 2008, chef Claudio Sadler created a menu that brought together several of Moretti's beers, including Baffo D'Oro. **ES**

Tasting notes

A gold colored beer beneath a white head. On the palate, it is crisp with sweetish malty notes followed by a slight hoppy finish. If no sea urchins are available, try with pizza.

Beerlao

Lao Brewery | www.beerlao.la

Beersel Lager

Proefbrouwerij | www.proefbrouwerij.com

Country of origin Laos
First brewed 1973
Alcohol content 5% abv
Serving temperature 39°F, 4°C

Country of origin Belgium
First brewed 2005
Alcohol content 5.2% abv
Serving temperature 46°F, 8°C

Sitting on the banks of the River Mekong in Vientiane, Laos's capital city, is said to be the perfect place to enjoy a glass of Beerlao. Typically, the beer is served from striking green bottles; indeed it is unusual to see Beerlao served on draft—if it is, it is called "fresh." It is best enjoyed well chilled but is often served warmed from the sun with ice cubes added to the glass.

Rice has been grown in Laos since ancient times, and it is no surprise that jasmine rice grain is used in the beer's grist—the rest, malted barley, comes from France. German Hallertau hops add soft, floral, buttery qualities, and the origins of the yeast are German, too. The water for the beer originates in the foothills of the Himalayas. Beerlao's soft bitterness, with its hints of sweetness, makes it an ideal companion to local dishes, and its alcoholic strength means that it is able to cope with the fiery spices that feature in the cuisine. **TH**

Beersel Lager is made from organic barley malt, plenty of Saaz hops, and a touch of beet sugar. It is unfiltered, unpasteurized, and well hopped, and, unlike most lagers, it gets a secondary fermentation in the bottle. This is a full-flavored and refreshingly bitter beer with refined cereal taste. But, most importantly, it has a serious, dry, floral hop character that starts with the nose and carries long into the aftertaste. If only more lagers had this much class.

Unbeknown to most beer lovers who know Belgium for its ales, lager is by far the country's most popular drink. It usually goes under the pseudonym "pils" and fits the mold of other international lagers: made in vast quantities, yellow, and lacking complexity. The typical Belgian sees flavorful ales as "special" beers meant for special occasions—Fridays, for example— whereas pils is the everyday beer of choice. **JS**

Tasting notes
Darkish yellow in color with a pleasant, uncloying, honey-flavored sweetness, balanced by a light, refreshing bitterness. The alcoholic strength contributes to a long, satisfying finish.

Tasting notes
Slightly hazy gold with a few fingers of white foam. Nose mostly entices with floral, grassy hops. Moderate bitterness takes charge of flavor, with faint cereals in backdrop.

Bel Pils

Duvel Moortgat | www.duvel.be

Belgian Ale

Dado Bier | www.dadobier.com.br

Country of origin Belgium
First brewed 1930
Alcohol content 5% abv
Serving temperature 41°–43°F, 5°–6°C

Country of origin Brazil
First brewed 2007
Alcohol content 8.5% abv
Serving temperature 46°–54°F, 8°–12°C

Bel Pils has been a regular feature of the Duvel Moortgat brewery since its first outing in 1930, when it was called "Extra Blonde" (from 1976–1993 it was called "Extra Pilsner" before Bel Pils became its regular name). Head brewer Hedwig Neve laments that few places have enough turnover of this beer to let it be served at its very best. "A pilsner tap ought never to stop, but pour continuously!" he says. Still, real quality cannot be hidden, and to find this beer either on tap or in bottle is like coming across hidden treasure.

The ample use of Saaz, a hop used in other Moortgat beers, explains a lot of the beer's appeal. This pils is more bitter than most of the indifferent yellow liquids pouring from Belgian taps. It might also explain why, sadly, the brewery has had more success in recent years with young drinkers of Bel's younger sibling Vedett, which is slightly stronger and far sweeter. **JPa**

Dado Bier is Brazil's pioneer craft microbrewery. Based in Porto Alegre in the very south of the country, it opened in 1994 and was the first of its kind.

Yeast is imported from Belgium, and five different malts and a selection of imported hops go into the mix, which involves a double-fermentation process. After the initial fermentation period, the beer is moved into a separate vessel to continue its transition; this way sediments and other undesirable residue are left behind in the primary vessel. For its time in the bottle, the beer is left unfiltered, which means that the yeast carries on working, allowing the beer to change and mellow over time. Despite its name, this is not a carbon copy of a Belgian-style beer. Dado's brewing team carried out extensive research in order to bring an original and interesting edge to a New World version of an Old World favorite. **AH**

Tasting notes
Straw colored and crystal clear beneath a huge white head. Faint bitter hop nose, flowery and grainy. On the palate, a fine hoppiness, good malt base, and just enough sweetness.

Tasting notes
A hazy golden body glimmers beneath a creamy white head. A spicy citrus aroma continues on the palate, where it is joined by caramel and lots of malt. Well balanced with a warming finish.

Benedictus

Durham Brewery | www.durham-brewery.co.uk

Country of origin England
First brewed 2000
Alcohol content 8.4% abv
Serving temperature 57°F, 14°C

Steve Gibbs was a dedicated full-mash home-brewer and started up Durham Brewery in 1994 when he and his wife Christine were made redundant.

He has created modern interpretations of classic beer styles, incorporating traditional brewing methods with an almost fanatical attention to hygiene and quality control. High standards have always been number one priority in the brewhouse, which is situated only a few miles from the city of Durham and its World Heritage site cathedral. Most of the twenty-strong portfolio of ales are named in honor of Durham's centuries-old religious heritage: Magus, White Friar, Bishop's Gold, and Sanctuary. In contrast to Durham's tendency to hark back to medieval times, the brewery's systems of cask tracking, recipe formulation, stock control, traceability, and accounting are as up to date as any high-tech business.

The portfolio is divided into the White Range, Gold Range, and Coloured Range with many of the beers being complex arrangements of English, U.S., Czech, and Slovenian hops. Benedictus falls into the Gold category; its smooth barleywine structure and aromatic headiness make it extremely easy to drink. "The idea was to make a series of classic styles," says Steve, "as barleywine is one we knew, we had to make one. Historically, beers of this strength were normally sweet, the yeast not being able to process all the sugars in the wort. So we use an extremely active yeast that renders the finished beer drier than would be expected. Even so, there are still enough unfermented malt sugars that fill out body and mouthfeel." **AG**

Tasting notes

Benedictus is golden in color with a notable ripe, fruity malt body. A complex blend of hops extends its depth of flavors and its aromatics to help create a balancing bitterness before the satisfying finish settles down to a rich warmth.

Durham Brewery takes its iconography from the city's famous cathedral.

By faith moses refuses to be called the son of Pharaoh's
daughter. Choosing rather to suffer affliction with the
people of God than to enjoy the pleasures of Sin for a season.

To the Glory of GOD and in loving memory of
one of the JUDGES of the HIGH COURT of

the HONOURABLE SIR HENRY MANISTY
JUSTICE who died 31st JANUARY 1890

Big Daddy

Speakeasy Ales & Lagers | www.goodbeer.com

Country of origin United States
First brewed 1998
Alcohol content 6.5% abv
Serving temperature 50°F, 10°C

Back in the dark days of Prohibition, an illegal bar was widely known as a speakeasy. Before and during Prohibition, the nation was split along urban and rural lines. At that time, America was still predominantly agrarian, so a rural majority was able to get Prohibition passed. In the big cities, however, where almost everyone opposed it—including police, judges, and government officials—speakeasies were tacitly allowed to exist. By one estimate, as many as 100,000 flourished in New York City alone.

San Francisco had a particular reputation for its speakeasies, and this was the inspiration behind the opening of Speakeasy Ales and Lagers, one of only two production breweries in the city—and, as they market it, the second-largest, too (the largest is, of course, Anchor). The steam-fired brewhouse is located in the Bayview District. All of Speakeasy's beers are named with tongue firmly in cheek and a nod toward the seamier side of the underground bar scene: Prohibition Ale, Untouchable Pale Ale, Old Godfather, and Rum-Runner Rye.

But by far their most popular beer is Big Daddy, an India Pale Ale loaded with big West coast hop varieties. Big Daddy was named after Dave Keene, the owner of San Francisco's best beer bar, The Toronado. His nickname is "Big Daddy" and he is the unofficial "godfather" of the San Francisco beer community. In that spirit Speakeasy refers to their fans as "the mob."

Big Daddy is brewed with three Pacific Northwest hops and generously dry-hopped. It's balanced with Pale Ale Malt and German Munich Malt. **JB**

Tasting notes

The beer pours a bright golden blond with a pillowy white head. Citrusy hops dominate the nose, and these are accompanied by grapefruit, floral, and grassy aromas. The beer has a creamy, rich mouthfeel, and has a huge hop character.

Bikini Blonde Lager

Maui Brewing Co. | www.mauibrewingco.com

Country of origin United States
First brewed 2006
Alcohol content 4.5% abv
Serving temperature 44°F, 7°C

When Garrett Marrero and Melanie Oxley opened Maui Brewing in 2005, it was originally just a brewpub, but the following year they made it into the first microbrewery on the island, a distinction that's still true four years later, in 2009. It's also been one of the fastest growing businesses in Hawaii. The brewery is located next door to one of Maui's biggest tourist attractions, the train depot for the Sugar Cane Train, Lahaina Kaanapali and Pacific Railroad.

By 2007, they were offering three of their beers in cans, and less than two years later had doubled their production. They chose cans precisely because of the environmental concerns of being on a tiny island, in an effort to keep broken glass off the thirty miles of Maui's beaches. Maui is the second largest of the Hawaiian Islands. Beginning with the Polynesians centuries ago, sailors have been frequent visitors to the island. According to the newest island legend, created by Maui Brewing, the real reason that sailors come to shore is to drink their Bikini Blonde Lager.

Maui Brewing's Bikini Blonde Lager is a Munich-style Helles that is filtered and canned. It's the lightest beer the brewery makes and uses 100 percent malted barley. At only 18 IBUs, it's modestly hopped with Tettanger, a hop of noble character, but also with Liberty and Sterling, both of which are American varieties. Sterling is similar to the popular Saaz hop, which is another of the four noble hops. Bikini Blonde is ideal for Hawaii's tropical weather and is a perfect match with Hawaiian barbecue, eggs, and the canned meat, spam, which is highly popular on the island. **JB**

Tasting notes

The Bikini Blonde wears slightly cloudy straw gold and a thick white headdress. The subtle nose is briskly sweet with grassy, haylike hop aromas. With a refreshing effervescence, the flavor profile is lightly sweet with good balance, noble hop character, and a dry finish.

Bintang

Multi Bintang | www.multibintang.co.id

Country of origin Indonesia
First brewed 1930
Alcohol content 4.8% abv
Serving temperature 39°F, 4°C

Multi Bintang is Indonesia's most popular brewer, but none of the ingredients are sourced locally, other than the water. Malt and hops come from Australia and Europe, while the yeast is from the Netherlands. Even though Indonesia is an Islamic country, beer is available in most cities, towns, and tourist areas, though less than 3 percent of Indonesians drink alcohol.

Bintang is an unassuming beer that goes well with simple foods, especially those freshly cooked from the barbecue. There is no single Indonesian cuisine: the food on the islands is an eclectic mix, with inspiration drawn from many cultures across the world. The success of Bintang is that it will work with most things, though the pairing might not be inspirational. Many visitors to Indonesia enjoy drinking it with rijsttafel—an elaborate, traditional meal of up to forty different spicy dishes served with small side portions of rice. **TH**

Tasting notes

Light gold in color, it has a fresh, malty aroma that gives way to hoppy bitterness. A light head quickly forms, which then disappears. A satisfyingly dry finish at the end of the palate.

Biolégère

Brasserie Dupont | www.brasserie-dupont.com

Country of origin Belgium
First brewed 1992
Alcohol content 3.5% abv
Serving temperature 50°F, 10°C

Biolégère is a standout session beer in a country known for strong, assertive brews. This is possibly the best "table" beer in Belgium and earns additional kudos for being an organic beer. It is one of several organic beers that Dupont produces, including one made with honey—Bière de Miel Biologique. Brasserie Dupont is a very enjoyable place to visit, though it only opens its doors to the public on the last weekend of September, when its home village of Tourpes has an open house.

Dupont's delight in its artisanal character extends to its bakery, which was opened in 1994, and a year later it began to make cheeses. Several fine cheeses are made, three being washed with the brewery's Moinette and one with Saison Dupont. All the brewery's beers can be tasted at Caves Dupont, a pub across the road that always has the brewery's sole bottom-fermented beer Redor pils plus Saison Dupont on draft. **CC**

Tasting notes

Hazy yellow brew that pours with plenty of carbonation. There are notes of citrus and herbal yeastiness in the nose and lemon, malty sweetness, and earthy farmhouse character in the taste.

Bintang merchandise on sale in Kuta, one of Bali's popular tourist resorts.

Birra Dolomiti Doppio Malto

Birreria Pedavena | www.birrapedavena.it

Country of origin Italy
First brewed 2008
Alcohol content 6.7% abv
Serving temperature 46°–50°F, 8°–10°C

Birreria Pedavena has a long pedigree. It was founded in 1897 in the town of Pedavena, close to the Dolomites. Over the years, it became a reasonably big company in the Italian beer market, remaining independent until 1974 when Heineken Italia bought it. Heineken owned the company for thirty years and then in 2004 announced plans to close this historic brewery. But Birreria Pedavena survived, after being acquired by independent Italian brewery Gruppo Castello. Currently, the brewery specializes in producing pilsners, but it also brews an unpasteurized and unfiltered lager called Centenario. This can be drunk only at the brewery's renowned tap.

In the last few years, Pedavena has been keen to source local ingredients, and it started collaborating with barley growers within the neighboring area, in a project that was partly financed by the local government. The first result is Dolomiti Doppio Malto, a strong lager with a full body that is very drinkable. The beer uses a high percentage of local barley plus some pale malt from Germany and France (although future plans aim to increase the amount of local barley). A drop of caramel malt, again from Germany, gives greater body to the beer. Hops are Hallertau Magnum and Perle, which are added for bitterness during the boil, and a final, generous pinch of Saaz for aroma. Two months are needed to complete this beer with double fermentation in tanks and one month, at least, of lagering. All this attention to detail means that Dolomiti Doppio Malto is much richer in flavor and aroma than the brewery's other lagers. **MM**

Tasting notes

Pours a brilliant golden color beneath a white and persistent foam. Immediate light hoppy aroma underlined by sweet notes of malt. Well-balanced, rounded body on the palate with fruity notes (apple) making an appearance. On the finish, a good hoppy character that lingers.

Bitburger Premium Beer

Bitburger Braugruppe | www.bitburger.com

Country of origin Germany
First brewed 1909
Alcohol content 4.8% abv
Serving temperature 41°F, 5°C

"Bitte, ein Bit"—"A Bit, please"—is one of the best-known slogans in German brewing and it has helped propel a pilsner from a family brewery on the border of Luxembourg to the top of the country's beer list.

The town of Bitburg stands north of Trier, in the Eiffel region of Germany. Its famous brewery was established in 1817 by Johann Peter Wallenbronn and has grown steadily in the hands of his descendants, the Simon family. In 1980, a state-of-the-art, energy-efficient new production base was unveiled, which is connected to the central plant by underground pipeline.

In recent decades, Bitburger has really pushed on; sporting sponsorships and smart advertising have raised the brand from a regional brew to a national, and now international, brand. The trade name has been boosted by the success of the low-alcohol Bitburger Drive, but really there is only one beer that people associate with the brewery and that is the pilsner Bitburger. For an international brand, it is remarkably flavorsome, brewed with German and French barley malt and naturally soft well water. It is laced with hops that come from the famous Hallertau hop gardens in southern Germany and from local farms, too. The tangy, herbal bitterness that they bring to the beer lasts long into the smooth, clean finish. The added bonus with Bitburger is that—apart from the canned product—the beer is never pasteurized. Even bottled beer created specifically for export escapes the flavor-tarnishing heat treatment, with rigorous filtration the more drinker-friendly answer to endowing the beer with a good shelf life. **JE**

Tasting notes

A golden pilsner-style beer with an aroma of perfumed hops and sweet, pale malt. The soft, malty palate is overlaid with lightly lemony, herbal hop notes and rounded off by a satisfying, dry, bitter and tangy finish as herbal hop flavors really take over.

Bitter & Twisted

Harviestoun Brewery | www.harviestoun.com

Country of origin Scotland
First brewed 1998
Alcohol content 4.2% abv
Serving temperature 54°F, 12°C

Founded in 1984 by Ken Brooker on a farm just outside Dollar in central Scotland, Harviestoun has been a real Scottish success story. In 2004, due to the growing demand for Harviestoun's beers, the brewery moved to a new purpose-built, fifty-barrel plant, a few miles away in Alva. This location allowed the brewery to continue using the outstanding soft water from the Ochil Hills. After twenty-two years, Brooker decided to retire from the brewery but not before winning numerous awards for his beers, including Champion Beer of Britain for Bitter and Twisted in 2003.

Bitter and Twisted has been a cornerstone of Harviestoun's success. It was first brewed in 1998 as a monthly special, and was so well received that the pub trade and consumers continually demanded it be brewed again until it was made a permanent fixture. Originally called "Buchanan's IPA," the name was soon changed to "Brooker's Bitter and Twisted" (Brooker's was later dropped). The name came about in response to Ken complaining about his harsh penalty for speeding compared to others. Brooker's wife, Ingrid, declared that "we should call it Bitter and Twisted because that's what you're becoming," to which all the brewery staff promptly agreed.

Like many small breweries, Harviestoun caught the eye of a larger company, and it became a subsidiary of the Caledonian Brewing Company in 2006, though in 2008 it once more regained its independence. These days the beer is brewed by Stuart Cail, and Harviestoun continues to innovate with its Highland Park whisky barrel-aged series, Ola Dubh. **MC**

Tasting notes

This beer is all about the hops and carbonation mingling to provide a truly refreshing beer. The pour releases a grapefruit nose with just a hint of something herbal and spicy, then on the tongue it's tingly and thirst quenching, ending in a pleasant spike of citrus twist.

Blonde Doppelbock

Capital Brewery | www.capital-brewery.com

Country of origin United States
First brewed 1994
Alcohol content 7.8% abv
Serving temperature 48°–52°F, 9°–11°C

This beer started as "an absolute failure" according to Capital's president and brewmaster Kirby Nelson. "I had been in Germany tasting these sort of beers fresh, which was an absolute revelation." When he returned home to Wisconsin his intent was to create a strong lager with a unique personality. Furthermore, since the brewery had the capability to do "an upward step decoction," Nelson was eager to see if it would add the rich, clean maltiness that German malts were famous for. It turns out not to be the case, hence the "failure," but the decoction, where a portion of the mash is boiled, caramelizing some of the malt flavors, still "made for a pretty good beer."

Decoctions used to be the only way to brew most styles of lager, but because of the high cost in time and energy, along with modern malt that seldom needs such extreme treatment, few breweries decoct today. Done right, decoction adds a layer of caramelly flavor that is nearly impossible to achieve any other way. Like most lagers, the recipe is pretty simple, just pale and light caramel malt. Bitterness and a tiny amount of aroma come from Liberty hops, one of the newer U.S. varieties that have been bred to have aromas similar to the prized German noble hops, particularly Hallertau.

Historically, bocks are blond in color, with the stronger doppelbocks leaning toward brown. Pale bocks are the norm, and they tend not to be of the stronger doppel sort. Pale doppelbocks are rare but, as this example demonstrates, the style is well worth seeking out and is especially great for drinking in the chilly spring sunshine. **RM**

Tasting notes

Bready and honeyish caramelized malt notes in the aroma, along with just a touch of spiciness from hops. Flavor is sweet on the palate, rich in lightly caramelized malt character, with just enough hops to balance it out. Aftertaste very smooth, clean, and creamy.

Bluetongue Traditional Pilsener

Bluetongue Brewery | www.bluetongue.com.au

Country of origin Australia
First brewed 2006
Alcohol content 5.8% abv
Serving temperature 37°–39°F, 3°–4°C

There actually is a blue-tongued lizard that roams the vineyards of the spectacular Hunter Valley, New South Wales, where the Bluetongue Brewery is based. When threatened, it pokes out its strikingly blue tongue in the hope of putting off predators. Putting off Australians certainly was not the goal of the four local entrepreneurs who established the Bluetongue Brewery in 2003. Instead, their aim was to develop a premium beer range that was appealing to the Australian palate and able to be profitably marketed and sold both locally and nationally.

The first beers developed by the Bluetongue Brewery were high-quality versions of the classic Aussie lager, as well as its pilsner ancestor. They also adopted an easy-drinking ginger beer similar to one that had been traditionally enjoyed in the Newcastle and Hunter Valley region. The strategy worked, with the Bluetongue Brewery experiencing rapid growth, in part due to the input of Australian marketing legend and renowned beer drinker John Singleton. He purchased a large share in the brewery in 2006, and famously remarked that "if you take rugby league and beer out of life there is nothing left." The brewery promptly announced a multimillion-dollar five-year sponsorship with the local rugby league team.

In what was perhaps a wake-up call for some of Australia's more esoteric microbreweries, Bluetongue Brewery was acquired by Coca-Cola Amatil in late 2007 and is now planning to expand production with a new brewery and tourist attraction to complement the vineyards in the Hunter Valley region. **DD**

Tasting notes

This brilliantly golden beer sparkles like a jewel in the Hunter Valley sun. Floral, spicy aromas follow through with a balanced sweetness and crisp, bitter finish. Bluetongue Traditional Pilsner is perfect for a day of watching the big game with your mates.

Bohemia Regent Prezident

Pivovar Regent | www.pivovar-regent.cz

Country of origin Czech Republic
First brewed 2000
Alcohol content 6% abv
Serving temperature 44°F, 7°C

Although this super-premium pale lager dates only from the year 2000, it is said to be based on earlier recipes from the archives of the Bohemia Regent brewery. The Třeboň brewery's past is long enough to include dozens, if not hundreds, of original recipes, and records date back to 1379. In 1482, it was enlarged by the local lord to include lagering cellars next to Třeboň Castle. The brewery stands in the same location today, overlooking the town's famous carp ponds; not far away is the tomb of the Schwarzenberg noble family, the brewery's last aristocratic owners.

Dating from the second half of the 19th century, the current building is among the most unusual in Bohemia, ornately decorated with castlelike crenelles and ramparts. Above an archway in the brewery's court is written *"Chmelovina naše ta božskou má sílu, všechny nás rozehřívá k radostnému dílu,"* which could be translated as "Our hop-brew has divine powers, it warms us up for joyous hours."

It is the warming nature of strong pale lagers that makes them the traditional brews of Christmas and New Year in Bohemia. Prezident has much in common with many Bohemian Christmas beers, and it is easy to imagine that an earlier version of this beer might have graced a feudal lord's holiday table. Brewed at 14 degrees Plato, Prezident is two degrees stronger than most premium beers in Central Europe, resulting in a rich, malty body. Brewmaster Ivan Dufek gives much of the credit to the use of top-shelf raw ingredients: hops from Saaz, rich Czech malt, and, in particular, the brewery's own excellent water. **ER**

Tasting notes

A classic continental strong lager, this malty brew pours clear, deep gold with a loose, chalk-white head. Like many traditional pale lagers in Bohemia, it has some butterscotch in the mouth, with traces of vanilla and caramel, followed by a rich, lasting finish.

Bons Voeux

Brasserie Dupont
www.brasserie-dupont.com

Country of origin Belgium
First brewed 1970
Alcohol content 9.5% abv
Serving temperature 54°F, 12°C

In 1970, Brasserie Dupont came up with a strong holiday ale, complex in flavor and long lagered, intended to be a gift for customers. This beer was aptly named "With best wishes from Brewery Dupont" ("Avec les Bons Vœux de la Brasserie Dupont"). What brewer Marc Rosier didn't expect was that Bons Vœux would become so sought after he would have to make it a year-round brew, and even let it appear on tap.

Today, Bons Vœux is one of the highest-profile beers from Dupont, and head brewer Olivier Dedeycker tries to concentrate on these regular beers, "Better a couple of excellent beers," he once said, "than a whole range of mediocre offerings." Not only is quality a priority, but the brewery has also returned to its farming roots and opened a farm shop that sells its own cheeses, some of which are washed with beer, and bread, made with the grist for the brewing. **JPa**

Tasting notes
Hazy, peach-orange color. Earthy aromas on the nose joined by leather, citrus zest, and faint spices. Leafy flavors, with a faint sweetness. Refreshing despite its full, chewy mouthfeel.

Brackie

Bracki Browar Zamkowy
www.brackibrowar.neostrada.pl

Country of origin Poland
First brewed *ca.* 1850s
Alcohol content 5.5% abv
Serving temperature 46°F, 8°C

Cieszyn is a Polish town close to the border with the Czech Republic. It has been home to a brewery on the same site since the 1840s, when it was built by Albrecht Frederick Habsburg, a prince of the Austro-Hapsburg empire, making it one of Poland's oldest breweries. Wheat beer would have been the original brew under royal perogative, however, influences from Prague and, especially, Pilsen, would have been hard to resist, and Brackie dates from this time.

Brackie remains very much a popular local beer. Pils malt is used from the Czech Republic, caramalt comes from Poland, and Polish hops are used wherever possible. The beer is fermented in the ancient lagering cellars built into the hillside near the town, all of which helps to produce a remarkably hoppy pilsner for its style. You will have to travel to Poland to try it—which is no bad thing. **ATJ**

Tasting notes
On the nose, hints of toasted grain with a lemony, citrusy hop undercurrent. On the palate, more toasted grain, a sherbet lemon center, and a bitter tang that lingers in the finish.

Brockton IPA

Granville Island Brewing | www.gib.ca

Country of origin Canada
First brewed 2009
Alcohol content 6% abv
Serving temperature 46°F, 8°C

The opening of Granville Island Brewing, Canada's first craft brewery of the modern era, in 1984, signaled a prosperous start to Canada's craft beer renaissance. First, however, founder Mitchell Taylor, like all brewing pioneers, needed to convince his provincial legislature to modify existing brewing regulations to allow for his micro-sized operation.

The life of Canada's ground-breaking packaging craft brewery—the three operations that came before it were strictly brewpubs—has not been without its problems. To begin with, only one year into its life, the company made the decision to go public on the Vancouver Stock Exchange, thus beginning an extended period of structural turmoil. Several further changes took place, including the moving of Granville Island's main brewing and packaging facilities to the town of Kelowna, and the conversion of the original facility to a specialty brewery and taproom. Still, the brewery has persevered throughout and, in 2009, it celebrated its twenty-fifth anniversary with a complete redesign of its labels and imagery, and the addition of a new beer to the company portfolio: Brockton IPA.

Although the brewery states that Brockton is crafted in the style of a Pacific Northwest IPA, that claim will come as a surprise to fans of the intense, resinous IPAs of Washington and Oregon. Rather, the anniversary ale offers a more muted and broadly accessible interpretation, with obvious U.S. hop influence but little in the way of bold aggression: less "hop bomb" than "hop firecracker." **SB**

Tasting notes

Rich honey gold in color, this tasty IPA combines aromas of canned peach and nutty hop with light, fresh citrus notes. In the body, it offers beautiful balance between caramelly, fruity malt and hoppy bitterness that culminates in a dry, appetizing finish.

Brooklyn Local 1

Brooklyn Brewery | www.brooklynbrewery.com

Country of origin United States
First brewed 2007
Alcohol content 9% abv
Serving temperature 50°F, 10°C

If you open a bottle of Local 1, you'll find yourself at a wondrous crossroads, where Brooklyn meets France, and beer meets wine. This uniquely styled ale is almost impossible to classify; it's refreshing and spicy, like a saison, yet its strength and yeast bite will remind you of a Belgian tripel. Its brewer calls it a "Brooklyn original," though he readily acknowledges its character is largely the product of an ancient fermentation process made popular by certain French winemakers.

Start with the ingredients: German malt gives it sweetness, Perle hops from Austria provide snappy bitterness, demerara sugar from Mauritius imparts a creamy mouthfeel and smoothes out the rough edges. The flavors are brought together by a softly tingling, delicately spicy, fruitlike effervescence that can only be described as champagne-like, for good reason. This fine beer is entirely refermented in the bottle, in the manner of a fine magnum of Moët. After its initial fermentation, the yeast is filtered out and the beer goes into the bottle completely flat. New yeast is added, along with a dose of sugar, and the beer is refermented for several weeks at a relatively warm 77 degrees Fahrenheit (25 degrees Celsius). The bottles are then cold stored for a few more weeks of further conditioning.

The brewery claims that Méthode Champenoise was invented by early French and Belgian beer makers as a means of achieving high carbonation. Whatever the truth, the complex fermentation regime produces a swarm of aromas that tickle the nose after the cork is popped. Peach, citrus fruit, rum—it's what champagne would taste like if made by Belgian monks. **DR**

Tasting notes

Poured into a goblet, a tight, white head forms above a bubbly golden body. A sweet, herbal aroma rises with just a touch of hops, boosting its subtle flavors of fruit, spice, and rum. A slight peppery bite gives way to a smooth dry finish.

Brugse Zot

Huisbrouwerij De Halve Maan | www.halvemaan.be

Country of origin Belgium
First brewed 2005
Alcohol content 6% abv
Serving temperature 46°F, 8°C

The story of the Halve Maan brewery is both old and new, long and short, and, not surprisingly, rather complicated. To begin with, the brewing history of the building in which the Half Moon is housed dates back to the era when Bruges was a great European port, roughly the mid 1500s. It fell into the hands of the Maes family in 1856, after which, like many breweries of its time, it cycled through the production of traditional ales and modernist pilsners, eventually landing in the 1980s at a strong blond ale known as Straffe Hendrick, or Strong Henry.

So successful was Straffe Hendrick that the Riva brewery acquired the brand, and production ultimately moved out of the city, leaving the brewery dark for a period of three years. The descendents of the Maes family, the Vanneste family, maintained control of the structure, though, and in 2005, surprised one and all by reopening the building as a production brewery. Cleverly, it started out with a series of beers called "Dilemma," and drinkers were asked which version of the test brews they preferred. Brugse Zot was victorious.

The name refers to an episode that took place during the Austrian rule of Bruges, when the emperor was paying a visit to the city. Asked what the city would like as a gift, city elders replied that a new madhouse was needed. The emperor replied simply that if the city gates were bolted shut, the entire place could serve as a madhouse. Thus, the Brugse Zot, or Fool of Bruges, was born. Also produced under the Brugse Zot name is a sweetish, cocoa-spicy dubbel. **SB**

Tasting notes

There is plenty of peppery spice on the attractive nose of this beer, indicative of the spice notes found also in the zesty, citrusy body and mildly bitter finish. Despite its strength, this entirely quaffable ale is perhaps the epitome of a Belgian session beer.

Sign for the Henry Maes Brewery in Bruges, Belgium. ➡

BROUWERIJ

ENRI MAES

Brunehaut St. Martin Blonde

Brasserie Brunehaut | www.brunehaut.com

Country of origin Belgium
First brewed 1999
Alcohol content 7% abv
Serving temperature 44°F, 7°C

This forward-thinking brewery has survived two world wars and a bankruptcy, but its new owner Marc-Antoine de Mees has his foot set firmly in the 21st century, while still managing to preserve the traditions of the past. Brasserie Brunehaut opened in 1890. Luckily, it was so far out in the middle of nowhere that the German army did not discover its beautiful copper kettles during World War I, and it is these venerable kettles that are at the heart of today's brewery. In 1990, Brunehaut was bought by two brewers, but after fifteen years, bankruptcy loomed, and De Mees stepped in.

Strong blond ales are one of the mainstay beers of Belgium, and nearly every brewery has one in its portfolio. St. Martin Blonde is an officially recognized abbey beer, named after the St. Martin Abbey in Tournai. Having a beer with the recognized abbey seal is important to beer drinkers in Belgium, as well as abroad, hence Brunehaut's desire to have such a beer.

The brewery exports about sixty percent of its yearly production to around ten different countries, including Japan and the United States. Since De Mees took over in 2006, output has increased by two-thirds, and Brunehaut is clearly a brewery on the move. Environmental considerations are also important: Special, recyclable kegs (which have thirty times less carbon footprint then their stainless steel brethren) have been used since early 2008. There are other commendable green characteristics in play at the brewery: De Mees's wife is a farmer, and she grew 25 acres (10 ha) of organic barley at her farm in 2008. There are plans to grow hops, too. **CC**

Tasting notes

Hazy orangey golden-colored brew that pours with a very big head. Aroma is yeasty, spicy, with some fruitiness and hop character. Flavor is light citrus—with a fruity, honey, and mild bitterness. A good beer to pair with funky cheeses such as Brie and Camembert.

Bud Super Strong

Budweiser Budvar | www.budweiser-budvar.cz

Country of origin Czech Republic
First brewed 1997
Alcohol content 7.6% abv
Serving temperature 46°F, 8°C

Although its founding in 1895 makes it a fairly recent arrival in the history of Czech brewing, the Budvar brewery remains one of the country's most conservative. One of its sole concessions to modernization was to change from the older, open-style fermentation vessels to upright cyclindroconical fermenters in 1996. The rest remains largely as it has been for more than a century. Budvar continues to use whole Saaz hop cones in its lagers, rather than pellets or extracts, and it conditions its beers for far longer than many of its competitors.

Nevertheless, this highly traditional brewer is hardly tradition bound. In 1997, brewmaster Josef Tolar introduced an unusual product: Bud Super Strong, a higher-octane version of a golden lager, brewed at 16 degrees Plato and initially containing 7.2 percent alcohol. It is hopped with 100 percent Saaz and conditioned for at least 200 days, leaving the cellars with a thick, slightly viscous body and rich vanilla and caramel notes. At the time of its release, reaction among beer fans was mixed, especially with regard to the name. As such, the beer was occasionally dismissed as one for quick intoxication, rather than a quality lager for connoisseurs. With time, however, it began to earn recognition as a great lager of distinctive flavors: not complex so much as crisp, refined, and focused.

Now brewed at a slightly stronger 7.6 percent alcohol, Bud Super Strong is a dessertlike treat and an excellent winter warmer. In Bohemia and Moravia, there is a tradition of serving strong pale lagers for Christmas and New Year's Eve, and it is easy to see Bud Super Strong as the modern-day descendant of that line. **ER**

Tasting notes

A highly focused flavor profile concentrates on the richness of Moravian malt, with less of a Saaz hop presence than Budweiser Budvar's traditional strength pale lager. Expect slight caramel, orange peel, and honey notes in the mouth, with a slightly astringent note in the finish.

Budels Pilsener

Budelse Brouwerij | www.budels.nl

Country of origin Netherlands
First brewed 1884
Alcohol content 5% abv
Serving temperature 44°F, 7°C

Budelse Brouwerij was founded in 1870 by Gerardus Arts, when it was originally called "de Hoop" (the Hope). The current name comes from its home village Budel, which can be found in the southern Dutch province of North Brabant. Despite the consolidation in the postwar Dutch brewing industry, as Heineken and Bavaria hoovered up smaller, independent breweries, Budelse has stayed small (less than ten employees) and remains family owned.

In the beginning, as was common with several other Dutch breweries of the period, Budels combined brewing with an agricultural business. When, in 1879, a railroad station was opened in the village, Gerardus Arts set up the hotel-pub-restaurant Het Brouwershuis. However, this branch of the business ended in the 1920s, though the brewery continued its policy of diversification by continuing to produce lemonades and other soft drinks. Up until World War I, Budel was also home to two other breweries, but a shortage of raw materials saw Budels emerge as the sole survivor.

Of the current range of beers, the Pils is the longest in production by more than fifty years. It has won several awards in Belgium and the Netherlands and is lagered for six to eight weeks at a temperature just above freezing, thus making a smooth and clean beer. As well as the Pils, Budels produces a range of several organic beers, plus several German styles such as an alt and a Kölsch. They also produce an organic lager for British brewery Bath Ales, which is sold as Natural Blonde. The anchor in the current company logo harkens back to the days when the brewery was called de Hoop. **RP**

Tasting notes

This is a clear, golden beer with a short-lived white head. The nose is light, pleasant, and sweetish with a hint of lemons and a faint green grassiness. Soft on the palate with a light maltiness kept in balance with an equally featherweight hop fruitiness. A clean and refreshing beer.

Budvar Světlý Ležák

Budweiser Budvar | www.budweiser-budvar.cz

Country of origin Czech Republic
First brewed 1895
Alcohol content 5% abv
Serving temperature 44°F, 7°C

Brewed in the town of České Budějovice—known as "Budweis" in German—the Czech Republic's iconic Budvar has long fought for its right to use the Budweiser brand made famous by the U.S. Anheuser-Busch. Budvar's location gives its claims substantial weight.

Of key importance is Budvar's founding story as a Czech-owned brewery in a town whose brewery was controlled by a minority of ethnic Germans. In the era of the so-called Czech National Awakening at the end of the 19th century, such divisions began to have great significance. Much as the Czech National Theater was founded in Prague to present opera in the language of the people, rather than that of the ruling German-speaking aristocracy, the majority of Czech citizens in České Budějovice founded Budvar brewery as a joint-stock company. Within only a few years, the nationalist fervor of Czech beer fans meant that Budvar's production had greatly surpassed the earlier brewery.

There was perhaps more to the beer's popularity than mere patriotism. Brewed at 12 degrees Plato, Budvar's flagship *světlý ležák*, or pale lager, is a truly remarkable pint. Just as in earlier days, it is still hopped with whole cones of the premium Saaz hop varietal and conditioned for at least ninety days. The result is a well-attenuated golden beer with less malt heft than many Bohemian pilsners, as well as a flowery Saaz nose of remarkable complexity. The brewery remains among the most traditional in the country, still taking its brewing water from classic artesian wells. Although it has long been considered a prime candidate for privatization, it remains the proud property of the Czech nation. **ER**

Tasting notes

A world-class pilsner: clear, deep gold with a thick, long-lasting, creamy head. The Saaz hop aroma is spicy, peppery, and tinged with notes of citrus blossoms; in the mouth, it is full without being heavy, finishing with a lasting Saaz bitterness.

Because it fits so gracefully and so gaily into the scheme of good living, BUDWEISER is recognized as the King of Bottled Beer. Millions who welcomed beer back, are finding there is only one BUDWEISER — brewed and fully aged in the world's largest brewery.

Budweiser
KING OF BOTTLED BEER

ANHEUSER - BUSCH ~ ST. LOU

Budweiser

Anheuser-Busch | www.budweiser.com

Country of origin United States
First brewed 1876
Alcohol content 5% abv
Serving temperature 39°–41°F, 4°–5°C

You'd have to have been living in a cave not to have heard of Budweiser. Sponsorships of the Olympics, football's World Cup, and block bookings of Super Bowl telecasts, which is still the most watched event in the United States, make Bud a global property.

Yet there's not a lot of love among aficionados for what has been until recently the world's perennially best-selling beer brand (along with Bud Light). It is derided in some quarters as unchallenging and unrewarding, the brewing version of sliced white bread. Perhaps this is to miss the point. Budweiser is, politely, a delicate beer, its slight body readily revealing any defects in the brewing process. But if you want to observe the unrelenting dedication to producing quality beer, shadow an Anheuser-Busch brewmaster.

This commitment to quality begins with the raw materials: while other brewers operate malthouses, Anheuser-Busch is one of the few to own outright barley farms and hop gardens. Until a few years ago, it was the only multinational brewer to persist with whole hops, finally conceding that industry norm hop pellets offer storage savings and longer-term freshness. Each day the brewers make teas of the ingredients and taste them to ensure flavor consistency. There's also Bud's insistence on freshness, with its idiosyncratic "born on" labeling of its beers.

Yet the niggle remains. Surely there are more challenging, rewarding beers? Yes, certainly, but Bud never pretends to be something that it isn't: this is a beer about refreshment and drinkability, not for sipping out of a china teacup with a pinkie extended. **LN**

Tasting notes

Faint aroma, offering clean dry biscuit maltiness and a light citrus hop fragrance. Color is of straw, pale and bright, with gentle effervescence producing a soft, delicate foam head. Bud's stock-in-trade is its drinkability—a clean, crisp taste making its alcoholic strength deceptive.

Budweiser: light but refreshing—and a world best seller.

Butcombe Gold

Butcombe Brewery | www.butcombe.com

Country of origin England
First brewed 1998
Alcohol content 4.7% abv
Serving temperature 50°–55°F, 10°–15°C

What do you do if you've a long history of helping others make beers but fancy starting out on your own? Easy, use the redundancy money from your old job to convert some old farm buildings at your family home into your own brewery. At least that's what Simon Whitmore did when he set up Butcombe Brewery in 1978.

Starting with just a ten-barrel kit, initially he produced only one ale—Butcombe Bitter—which was received warmly by the beer drinkers in his home territory of Bristol. At the time, it was the vogue for small brewers to produce a variety of novelty beers, but Whitmore chose to put all his efforts into producing one to the best of his ability. This decision paid dividends as the 1990s saw Butcombe Brewery become one of the fastest-growing craft breweries in the southwest of England. It took nearly twenty years before Whitmore could be persuaded to diversify, but it turned out to be worth waiting for: Butcombe Gold was released to great acclaim in 1998. Made with English pale ale malt and hopped with English Fuggle hops, the beer has joined the brewery's Bitter as one of its favorites.

The brewery has maintained its rate of growth and also owns fifteen pubs; there are now a total of four Butcombe beer brands, too. **JM**

Tasting notes
Butcombe Gold is dry, zesty, and slightly sweet on the tongue, with a distinctive Fuggle hop flavor. The hop taste builds noticeably on the palate and provides a full, bittersweet finish.

Castle Lager

SABMiller | www.castlelager.co.za

Country of origin South Africa
First brewed 1895
Alcohol content 5% abv
Serving temperature 39°–46°F, 4°–8°C

In the 1890s, many immigrants to South Africa believed that they would find their own El Dorado. But one man, Englishman Charles Glass, spent his time perfecting his brewing skills rather than panning for gold. He was widely traveled; there are some suspicions that he had perhaps seen at first hand the blond beers of Bohemia. His first beers were dark in color, but the thirsty miners developed a taste for his pale, golden beer, and Castle Lager was born.

At first, life was hard: the brewery was ramshackle, and the beer ingredients faced a long journey from England. Charles was often seen wheeling a barrow of beer through the mining encampments selling his brews. Many miners were accustomed to drinking "hard tack"—a raw potato spirit mixed with tobacco juice and pepper—which was very cheap. Over time, they developed an appreciation for golden beer with its "somewhat bitter; somewhat dry but never sweet" taste, and Castle Lager became very popular. Around this time, South African Breweries was founded, with its registered offices at the Castle Brewery.

Castle Lager is an easy beer with few rough edges—it pairs with most things, and soft cheeses such as Brie or Camembert are ideal. Given the South African love of the barbecue, or *braai*, it is a perfect, if gentle, partner for food cooked over hot coals. **TH**

Tasting notes
The aroma is fresh and dominated by floral hops with a hint of citrus. The taste is primarily refreshing—with a nice malt sweetness and a slight bitterness.

South African Breweries is now one of the biggest breweries in the world.

Chang

Thai Beverage Plc | www.changbeer.com

Tasting notes

Golden straw in color, with pleasing carbonation. The head dissipates quickly with little to no lacing. The nose offers sweet light malt with a smidgen of floral hop notes. The mouthfeel is sweet malt with a hint of bitter hops. The finish is brief.

Country of origin Thailand
First brewed 1995
Alcohol content 6.4% abv
Serving temperature 37°–41°F, 3°–5°C

You pay your money and take your chances with sports sponsorships. When English football team Everton FC unexpectedly made the finals of the FA Cup in 2009, ThaiBev gained global exposure for its flagship lager, Chang, which appeared on the players' shirts. This is to digress: Chang is, as its label makes clear, the Thai word for "elephant," an evocative image for the populace. The beer was born in the mid-1990s as its spirits-and-hospitality-conglomerate parent rushed into the beer market, bringing to an end the virtual monopoly enjoyed by rival Boon Rawd Brewery.

Within three years, the lower-priced Chang claimed to have taken an astonishing 60 percent of the entire Thai market. Boon Rawd, of course, responded in kind, launching Leo, an economy brand that is today the Thai market leader, pushing Chang into second place (Singha is a distant fourth, but competes in a different segment, positioned as a premium beer). Chang is, in fact, two different beers. The internationally marketed 5 percent abv premium lager is an all-malt brew. In Thailand, Chang is best known as a stronger, economy-priced beer, at 6.4 percent abv with an addition of rice to the grist.

In common with rival Boon Rawd, ThaiBev is building its international presence (both brewers remain relatively untangled in the global brewing industry consolidation, though ThaiBev's joint venture with Carlsberg ended in acrimony). ThaiBev has made its first acquisition in China and already owns a Scottish distillery. Expect to see more of Chang soon, bulling its way into venues beyond football stadiums. **LN**

Chimay Triple/Chimay Cinq Cents

Bières de Chimay | www.chimay.com

Country of origin Belgium
First brewed 1968
Alcohol content 8% abv
Serving temperature 46°F, 8°C

Unexpectedly, the brothers at the Abbaye de Notre-Dame de Scourmont, better known as Chimay, have found themselves at the heart of some controversy. More predictably, for one of seven existing Trappist breweries, most of it has centered around the beer.

It began with the "revelation" that the brewery was using nontraditional brewing ingredients, specifically malt and hop extracts and wheat starch. If you believe the monks who oversee operations and Paul Arnott, who for years led the brewing at Chimay, nothing in the brewing process has changed, save for a switch to conical as opposed to open square fermenters. It was the addition of the ingredients to the labels, plus an error in translation, that led to the controversy, they say. Where the hop extract is concerned—and a significant hop character is apparent in the White, so this is no small issue—Arnott says that hop concentrate has been in use for decades and is a pure and natural product. Of the malt extract, brewery management told the British beer writer Roger Protz that the quantity used amounts to 0.1 percent for color correction, and the wheat starch was a translation slip, they say; it should have read "wheat flour," which is used for foam retention.

Then there was the controversial launch of Chimay White—also known as Cinq Cents—as a draft product. The rebranding of the beer as a tripel likely didn't help matters, either, making a singular ale with decades of history appear, in the words of beer writer Michael Jackson, "like a 'me, too.'" Still, the beers continue to sell well and make the distinctive Chimay chalice one of the best-known beer glasses globally. **SB**

Tasting notes

Sitting between gold and amber in color, Cinq Cents is unquestionably the driest and hoppiest of Chimay's beers, with a firm but rather austere maltiness supporting spicy, bitter hops and dry fruitiness, ending in an appetizing mix of faint acidity, bitterness, and alcohol.

Chodovar Zámecký Ležák Speciál

Pivovar Chodovar | www.chodovar.cz

Country of origin Czech Republic
First brewed 1973
Alcohol content 5.1% abv
Serving temperature 44°F, 7°C

When the brewery in the western Bohemian town of Chodová Planá celebrated its 400th anniversary in 1973, it decided to create a special festive lager, brewed at a slightly higher original gravity of 13 degrees Plato to stand out among the ubiquitous 10 degree pale lagers and less common 12 degree premium beers of the era.

Unfortunately, the brew was discontinued for several years afterward. However, once the formerly state-run enterprise had been successfully privatized in 1992, the special beer was given a second life. Now known as Chodovar, the brewery released the 13 degree beer as its Zámecký Ležák Speciál, or "Special Chateau Lager," in 1995.

Chodovar has its own maltings, processing 1,700 tons of barley from Bohemian and Bavarian farms each year, and the beer is made from its own pale malt, which could account for the emphasis placed on the beer's rich graininess and sweet notes, rather than aroma hops and bitterness. It is given an exceptionally long conditioning, approaching ninety days, in the brewery's cavelike stone cellars, carved into the rock below the brewhouse.

Although Zámecký Ležák Speciál is exported in bottles and kegs to several countries, there is nothing quite like paying a visit to the brewery itself. In addition to sampling the beer inside the stone cellars, guests can stay in the on-site hotel. The big draw, however, is the chance to bathe in beer in Chodovar's own beer spa, which combines Bohemia's brewing traditions with its long history of therapeutic hot springs. **ER**

Tasting notes

Zámecký Ležák Speciál is a showcase for the brewery's own malt. This deep gold brew has a nose of whole grains, biscuity notes, and floral Saaz hops. In the mouth is a touch of honey, apricot, and caramel followed by a very mild bitter backbite.

Christoffel Blond

St. Christoffel | www.christoffelbier.com

Country of origin Netherlands
First brewed 1986
Alcohol content 6% abv
Serving temperature 44°F, 7°C

Although referred to as "Christoffel Blond," the label on the bottle simply reads "Christoffel Bier," which was the name of this beer before its red-headed brother—Christoffel Robertus—was born seven years later. On its debut in a country where lager rules supreme, the Blond made an immediate statement of difference by being double hopped and having a bitterness of 43 IBUs. That the first and main product of this brewery is a strong-tasting blond beer is no surprise given that founder Leo Brand studied brewing at the Weihenstephan brewing university near Munich. After completing his studies, he spent ten years working at German breweries and malting plants. On returning to the Netherlands and starting this brewery, his first beer was what went on to be called Christoffel Blond.

Despite the saintly tone of its name, Bierbrouwerij Sint Christoffel is neither an old nor an abbey-related brewery. Instead its name comes from the patron saint of the town in which it is based. However, one might say that there is something "royal" about it as the founder is a member of the Dutch Brand family, which has had a family brewery since 1871. Since 1989, however, it has been part of the Heineken family.

Christoffel remains independent. Founded in 1986 by Brand in the town of Roermond, it has taken to heart the Bavarian Reinheitsgebot of 1516 and still uses only the ingredients listed in the original ordinance. In 2001, the company was taken over by Hillenaar Outdoor Advertising and Brand stepped aside. The selection remains the same and, many would say, the quality as well. **RP**

Tasting notes

A clear blond beer with a stable white head, the aroma is somewhat hoppy. The beer, while reminiscent of Bohemian pils, is clean and presents a forceful bitterness, especially in the aftertaste. It is not, however, a lingering bitterness, but rather an integrated part of the full taste.

Ch'ti Blonde

Brasserie Castelain | www.chti.com

Country of origin France
First brewed 1978
Alcohol content 6.4% abv
Serving temperature 44°F, 7°C

Brother and sister Yves and Annick Castelain took over their parents' brewery in 1978 intending to retain its independence and traditional methods while remaining commercially viable. The brewery remains a champion of the indigenous bières de garde, but Yves Castelain saw that there was scope for different styles; the organic ale Jade was a brave move into uncharted territory, and is now France's best-selling organic beer.

Ch'ti beers were given a boost in 2008 by the success of the film *Bienvenue chez les Ch'tis* (*Welcome to the Ch'tis*). (Ch'ti is the nickname for the people of this region, supposedly because of the predominance of "ch" sounds in their dialect.) The Blonde was featured heavily in the film, which tells the story of a southern French postal worker who falls for the charm of the Ch'ti. **AG**

Tasting notes
Four different hop varieties give this honey gold beauty a peppery and tropical fruit nose in turn. Starts sweet but develops some malt and a significant bitterness.

Cisk Lager

Simonds Farsons Cisk | www.farsons.com

Country of origin Malta
First brewed 1928
Alcohol content 4.2% abv
Serving temperature 41°–46°F, 5°–8°C

Giuseppe Scicluna set up Malta's first private bank in 1840. Some of the locals had difficulty pronouncing the English word "check" and corrupted it to "*cisk*." Soon, Scicluna became known as *ic cisk*—"the check." In 1928, the bank took over the operations of one of its clients, the Malta Export Brewery, which had trading links with Augustiner brewery in Munich, Germany.

Malta Export was in a race with local rival Farsons, which had English links, to brew the island's first beer. The nickname of the bank's founder was appropriated, and Cisk Muncher was born. Unsurprisingly, with the onset of World War II, the link with Bavaria in the beer's name was dropped. In 1948, the companies merged creating one that melded English and continental brewing styles. It is a formula that works well. **TH**

Tasting notes
A golden, orange-colored, sparkling beer. Its rich hop aroma and pleasant bitterness, combined with a mild astringency and lemon citrus overtones, make it a fine thirst quencher.

Commerzienrat Riegele Privat

Brauhaus Sebastian Riegele | www.riegele.de

Country of origin Germany
First brewed 1911
Alcohol content 5.2% abv
Serving temperature 46°–48°F, 8°–9°C

Commerzienrat Riegele Privat approaches you unobtrusively, yet with remarkable character. The first impression is all about smoothness, but the palate also takes pleasure in elegant as well as complex flavors.

The sophisticated character of this blond lager is based on water from the brewery well, noble hops, and refined barley malts. The latter have been separated from their husks at the process of crushing. With only the grits added to the mash, the beer remains clean of husk tannins, which usually bring in a more edged sensory impression. Furthermore, the Hallertauer hop breed Hersbrucker provides for a harmonious bitterness. All of this, together with long lagering at cold temperatures, makes Commerzienrat a complex and balanced beer. **SK**

Tasting notes

The nose offers a crisp maltiness and fruity acidity, with floral and citrusy moments. A creamy softness imbues the palate; decent sweetness dances with delicate acidity. Smooth finish.

Coopers Sparkling Ale

Coopers Brewery | www.coopers.com.au

Country of origin Australia
First brewed 1862
Alcohol content 5.8% abv
Serving temperature 39°F, 4°C

Yorkshireman Thomas Cooper first brewed his Sparkling Ale in 1862 in South Australia. Notwithstanding the challenging environment for brewing, and stiff competition from imported English beers, Coopers's ales and stouts quickly proved popular. Remarkable for a time when hundreds of small brewing operations came and went, the Coopers Brewery survived for Thomas's lifetime, and beyond. In fact, one of his great-great-grandchildren, Dr. Tim Cooper, is the current managing director and chief brewer.

Unlike most Australian beers, Coopers Sparkling Ale is bottle fermented, which means there is often a healthy dose of yeast sediment at the bottom of the bottle. Consequently, some drinkers roll or tip the bottle to distribute the yeast evenly before the beer is poured. **DD**

Tasting notes

Light blond body, clouded by yeast and complemented by a solid head and subdued floral aroma. The fruity overtones and mildly bitter finish make this beer a perfect pairing with steak.

SIGILLVM · MONASTERY · B · MARIE · DE · CORSSENDONC · CORSSENDONC

Corsendonk

Corsendonk Agnus Tripel

Brouwerij Corsendonk | www.corsendonk.com

Country of origin Belgium
First brewed 1982
Alcohol content 7.5% abv
Serving temperature 50°–57°F, 10°–14°C

Corsendonk abbey beers are sometimes overlooked by beer enthusiasts. They are contract brewed and not linked to a functioning religious institution, so perhaps they are perceived to lack authenticity. On the other hand, they are also well-made, flavorful, and superbly marketed beers that have been responsible for opening up the world of Belgian monastic-style brews for legions of drinkers.

Corsendonk was an Augustinian priory, founded in 1395 by the daughter of the duke of Brabant at Oud Turnhout, now in the province of Antwerp. It was closed in 1785 by Austrian Emperor Joseph III and lay derelict until 1968, when a new owner began to rebuild it as a restaurant, hotel, and conference center, a function that it still fulfills today. Corsendonk beer appeared in 1982, when the tourist office approached local beer distributor De Keersmaekers. Although formerly a brewer that had produced its own abbey beer in the 1960s, the company no longer had brewing capacity so outsourced the beers to Du Bocq.

The blond tripel-style Agnus, short for "Agnus Dei" (the "Lamb of God" prayer from the Roman and Anglican mass) and also known as "Abbey Pale Ale" in North America, was one of a pair of bottle-conditioned beers that first launched the Corsendonk brand. It has been brewed from the start by Du Bocq of Purnode in the province of Namur. It's a spicy and perilously drinkable beer that's the perfect accompaniment to Flemish asparagus. Or try matching it with the mild, creamy Corsendonk semisoft cheese, commissioned from a dairy in nearby Gierle. **DdM**

Tasting notes

A classic hazy blond color with a fine white head, this beer has a spicy coriander and cream-tinged aroma and a thick citric palate with a hint of cloves. There's some notable vanilla and alcoholic weight in a creamy but tart and quite hoppy finish.

The design of the Corsendonk trademark recalls the early Middle Ages.

Coup de Grisou

Les Brasseurs RJ | www.brasseursrj.com

Cucapá Clásica

Cerveceria de Baja California | www.cucapa.com

Country of origin Canada
First brewed 1989
Alcohol content 5% abv
Serving temperature 46°F, 8°C

Country of origin Mexico
First brewed 2002
Alcohol content 4.5% abv
Serving temperature 46°F, 8°C

In 1998, a three-way merger resulted in the birth of Les Brasseurs RJ. Two of the companies, Les Brasseurs GMT and Cheval Blanc, were among the pioneers of Québec's craft brewing industry. The former was the province's first commercial craft brewery; the latter emerged from the landmark Montréal brewpub, which was the first to open in the city. The third, and the one that initiated the merger, was Les Brasseurs de l'Anse, a small brewery from the Saguenay region formed in 1995.

The Cheval Blanc had been a traditional, family-owned tavern for three generations until Jérôme Denys introduced house brewing. He separated the two businesses and opened a stand-alone brewery. Among the original creations that Denys took from brewpub to brewery was Coup de Grisou, a buckwheat beer. A "coup de grisou" is a fatal gas explosion in a mine, which explains the rather dramatic beer label. **SB**

In 2002, the Garcia family opened one of the country's first microbreweries in the city of Mexicali, specializing in quality, fresh ales. Producing a beer that refused to correspond with the pale lagers that were saturating the Mexican market was a huge leap of faith. However, Cucapá has forged a strong following in the local community. The company settled upon its current output of seven varieties by continually experimenting with recipes, but the Clásica has remained a constant presence. A blond ale in the pilsner style, medium-bodied with a distinctive malt character made with ingredients from the region, Cucapá Clásica is a gentle introduction to the Cucapá taste. By 2007, demand was so great that a new production plant was built, and packaged beer was being sold across Mexico and in the southwest of the United States, taking on the original craft beers in their own territory. **SG**

Tasting notes

Coriander and buckwheat combine to give an explosively spicy aroma, while the grain adds a faintly roasted, earthy note to the flavor. A complex but subtle flavor and dryish finish.

Tasting notes

A gentle golden color with a thin white head releasing a sweet aroma of fruit and flowers while the palate picks up malt and sweet, citric flavors leaving a smooth aftertaste.

Curieux

Allagash Brewing | www.allagash.com

Country of origin United States
First brewed 2004
Alcohol content 10.5% abv
Serving temperature 55°F, 13°C

"I wouldn't call it a mistake," Rob Tod, the founder of Allagash Brewing, says of his groundbreaking barrel-aged tripel Curieux, "but it was a total accident." For reasons that only a brewer can appreciate, Tod insists on bottling his tripel reserve in special corked bottles imported from Belgium. When a bottle shipment was delayed in mid-2004, the brewery found itself with a supply of the strong golden ale that would either have to be moved or tossed. He scanned the brewery floor and his eyes fell upon some used wooden Jim Beam bourbon barrels that he'd planned to save for a batch of his dark and malty dubbel. "We didn't think a tripel would be a good fit at all," Tod says. "For some reason, you think of a dark beer as a better match with a barrel."

Indeed, Belgian red ales, American imperial stouts, and English barleywines—these are beers that seem prime for the oaky influence of wine and whiskey barrels. A tripel, though? Too delicate, too complex, too light . . . and then Tod and his co-workers took a sip. "Wow," he said. "It totally transformed the tripel and turned it into a new beer. Coconut, vanilla, herbal character, and, of course, charcoal and bourbon."

When Allagash went forward with production, Tod figured it would a one-off. It was a costly, time-consuming, and labor-intensive process so he decided to brew 200 cases. The batch sold out in two weeks. Five years later, the brewery still can't make enough. Curieux gave Tod the inspiration to continue experimenting with other beers on wood: a strong pale ale, a stout, a wheat called "Odyssey," and a wee heavy known as "Musette." **DR**

Tasting notes

Color is hazy orange/blond topped by a solid foamy head; the nose throws off volumes of honey, fruit, and almond. The first sip is of a typical tripel, with a sweet but not cloying honey and tingly yeast bite, followed by rivers of complex flavors of oak, vanilla, and bourbon.

Cusqueña

Backus and Johnston | www.cusquena.com.pe

Country of origin Peru
First brewed 1908
Alcohol content 5% abv
Serving temperature 28°–36°F, -2°–2°C

Cusqueña (pronounced cus-ken-ya) is brewed high in the Peruvian Andes, in the city of Cuzco, and is known among the locals as the "gold of the Incas." This fortuitous and stunning mountain location allows the brewery to make use of the purest glacial melt waters that tumble down from the heights of the Andes. When combined with Saaz hops and 100 percent malted barley (including the varieties Metcalfe and Scarlett), the essential elements of a classic premium lager beer of the pils style are correct and present. Cusqueña's brewmasters are trained in Germany, and all the beer they brew is bottled at source and never made elsewhere. In Peru, the beer is also available on draft.

Cuzco was formerly the capital city of the Incas. Nearby is the UNESCO World Heritage site Machu Picchu. From the 13th to 16th centuries, the Incas oversaw a huge empire, and Chicha beer, brewed from corn or Peruvian pepper-tree berries, was the order of the day. The Cuzco plant celebrated its centenary in 2008 and so is no newcomer to the world of brewing either. Cusqueña is popular throughout not only Peru but also Chile and other South American countries. It has now spread far beyond the old frontiers of the Inca empire to enjoy worldwide recognition.

Cusqueña was served at the 2005 Live 8 Concert in Scotland. George Clooney and U2's Bono were so taken with the beer that they ordered crates of it to be delivered to their hotel rooms. Cusqueña was even served at a Christmas reception at the House of Commons in London, England, after being requested by the All-Party Parliamentary Beer Committee. **AH**

Tasting notes

Cusqueña is gold in color and pours with a medium white head that laces the glass. Classic pils in style, the beer has a malt and honey aroma. Clean and crisp, the malt is also present on the palate. Try as an accompaniment to fresh swordfish steak or grilled tuna.

Cuvée des Jonquilles

Brasserie Bailleux
www.sheltonbrothers.com

Country of origin France
First brewed 1990
Alcohol content 7% abv
Serving temperature 50°F, 10°C

Brasserie Bailleux is one of the best-kept secrets of the bière de garde region of northern France. Located in the idyllic hamlet of Gussignies, it is a small microbrewery attached to the restaurant Au Baron that Roger Bailleux opened in the 1970s.

The excellent food and brilliant beers have drawn beer hunters from across the world, many of them attracted by the brewery's signature beer, Cuvée des Jonquilles. "We started it off as a spring beer," says Bailleux, who is actually Belgian, "and called it after the daffodils which cover the area in the spring. It became so popular that people wanted it all year around."

Bailleux is a small operation, located at the back of the restaurant, where summer barbecues are cooked within an old copper. As befits an area steeped in beer culture, rabbit cooked in beer and coq au bière are on the menu. On brewing day, the warm fug of mashed barley malt hangs in the air. Cuvée des Jonquilles has an all-malt mash with hops, including Brewers Gold, Hallertau, and Stisselspalt; the yeast is top fermenting. After a week's fermentation, the beer spends two weeks cooling and maturing, then is bottled where a secondary fermentation takes place. The beer is then kept back for a month before being sold. **ATJ**

Tasting notes
A luscious blond bombshell with plenty of nods to the saisons of neighboring Wallonia. On the palate, it is refreshing and zesty, with bags of tropical fruit before an assertive bitter finish.

Delirium Tremens

Brouwerij Huyghe
www.delirium.be

Country of origin Belgium
First brewed 1989
Alcohol content 8.5% abv
Serving temperature 46°F, 8°C

Brouwerij Huyghe has an odd reputation in Belgian brewing—it gets no respect. One reason for this is its pursuit of off-the-wall beers, such as Mongozo Coconut Beer, served in a glass styled after a half coconut shell, of course, and the Floris line of fruit beers, which includes one flavored with cactus and another with chocolate. Then there is the Rubbel Sexy Lager, whose label sports female models adorned with scratch-off swimsuits, about which the less said the better. But behind the gimmicks, smoke, and mirrors is a serious brewery with some seriously enjoyable beers, such as their flagship Delirium Tremens.

Because this, too, is a bit of a gimmicky beer, with a provocative name and cartoons of pink elephants and dancing alligators on the label, many tasters are tempted to write off this blond ale as one of the brewery's line of oddball productions. However, what sits inside the slate-gray bottle is anything but a joke.

Although once denied entry to the United States because of its name, and pulled off the shelves in Ontario, Canada, for the same reason, Delirium Tremens has thrived, establishing itself in international markets and spinning off two sister brands, Delirium Nocturnum and Delirium Noël. **SB**

Tasting notes
Bright gold in color, this is a powerfully fruity brew, with a sweet aroma and palate accented by notes of spice and apparent, even insistent, alcohol. A rewarding nightcap.

Dernière Volonté

Brasserie Artisanale Dieu du Ciel!
www.dieuduciel.com

Country of origin Canada
First brewed 2004
Alcohol content 6.5% abv
Serving temperature 41°F, 5°C

In the Plateau de Montréal neighborhood that the Dieu du Ciel! brewpub calls home, it is quite common to witness the mingling of cultures, whether it be Québécois and Haitian, Jewish and Catholic, or hipster and punk. So it follows logically enough that one of the things that the brewing team does very well at the brewpub is mix up brewing cultures.

In truth, the Québec beer scene is a bit of a mash up of influences. As far back as the mid 1980s, Belgian beer and brewing influences have found enthusiastic acolytes in "la belle province"; however, British beer styles have also held a firm grip on many brewing traditions, as witnessed by the pre-craft brewing taste for moderately well-hopped ales when all others had changed over to lagers. The American styles, too, have been generally well-received in Québec, whether as craft-brewed IPAs or the more lamentable high-alcohol malt liquors, and even the northern French have had a brewer's foot in the Québécois door for many a year. All of which may explain the cross-pollination of styles that has resulted in Dernière Volonté (Last Will), one of the first four beers Dieu du Ciel! elected to bottle as a year-round offering once it opened its production brewery north of the city. **SB**

Tasting notes

On the nose, a fresh and floral fruitiness features notes of ripe melon and peach, backed by leafy hop. On the palate, it starts sweet before developing a more severe hoppiness.

Deuchars IPA

Caledonian Brewing Company
www.caledonian-brewery.co.uk

Country of origin Scotland
First brewed 1987
Alcohol content 4.4% abv
Serving temperature 48°F, 9°C

Deuchars IPA is Scotland's best-selling cask ale and is produced in a brewery steeped in tradition. The Victorian home of the Caledonian Brewing Company, located in Scotland's capital city Edinburgh, is known affectionately as The Caley. It's an imposing brewhouse where gas-fired open coppers give the hopped wort a vigorous rolling boil, which, it is claimed, helps to make the brewery's beers so unique. (The use of whole hop flowers instead of oils or pellets also helps provide its distinctive flavor.)

Edinburgh was once known as a city of beer, books, and bibles. It even gained the insalubrious nickname of "Auld Reekie," thanks to the number of breweries that drenched its air with the smell of "the boil"; regardless of the reek, all of them were attracted by the pure supply of hard water. Today, Edinburgh's sole surviving brewery is Caledonian.

Scottish traditional "heavy" is a beer that is best known for its sweeter, more malty character. Deuchars IPA is closer to a fruity golden ale than any heavy. The beer is made using Pipkin pale ale malt, crystal, and wheat malt, along with Fuggle and Super Styrian hops. In 2002, it became the first Scottish beer to be crowned Champion Beer of Britain. **JM**

Tasting notes

A tasty, clear, crisp, and light beer, dark gold in color. Its dry palate is tempered by a soft and silky maltiness and balanced with quenching citrus fruit. Long, deep, bitter, hop finish.

Deus

Brouwerij Bosteels | www.bestbelgianspecialbeers.be

Country of origin Belgium
First brewed 2000
Alcohol content 11.5% abv
Serving temperature 46°F, 8°C

Deus was created by Brouwerij Bosteels, which has been making beer in the village of Buggenhout since 1791 and is still in family hands. Deus may have its imitators (such as Brazilian brewers Eisenbahn's very tasty effort Lust) and it may have its hometown competitors (the amazing Malheur Bière Brut), but it still ranks as one of the most complex beers in the Belgian beer canon.

It is a beer that goes through a lengthy and creative process to produce its intricate nature, which includes a journey from Belgium to France and back again in order to create the very finest of vintages. Brewed using summer two-row barley, Deus is fermented in a fairly normal way. The brew then goes through a secondary fermentation in conditioning tanks before being shipped by tanker to a cellar near Epernay in Champagne, France, where it is refermented with champagne yeasts in the bottle and kept at a steady temperature for nine months.

Then, something particularly unusual is done—the bottles are tilted and rotated for a week (a process traditionally called *remuage*) and then the yeast that gathers in the neck of the bottle is frozen and removed (termed *degorgement*) before the bottle is corked and put on sale, in the same way that a champagne wine would be. This incredible beer is a genuine salute to the creativity and craft of the modern-day brewer. Absolutely outstanding as an aperitif or as a celebratory tipple, it utterly outstrips any low to mid-level champagne for complexity, moreishness, and tongue-tingling entertainment. **MC**

Tasting notes

After carefully opening the bottle, you will be assaulted by floral orange tones with underlying caramel notes; on tasting, you can expect an initial fizzy flourish followed by gloriously rich marmalade and rye bread notes with a hint of cedar and a lingering herbal note.

Doctor Okell's IPA

Okells | www.okells.co.uk

Country of origin Isle of Man
First brewed 2003
Alcohol content 4.5% abv
Serving temperature 50°–55°F, 10°–13°C

Doctor Okell's IPA was first introduced when the brewery, whose main beers at the time were bitter and mild, realized that there was a growing market for guest beers and that more bottled beers were being drunk at home. Named after Doctor William Okell, who started the brewery in 1850, this is a low-strength IPA that majors on Cascade for aroma and Target for bitterness; there are also four other hops in the mix. The beer has an impressive 43 IBUs and is the brewery's best seller on the British mainland. There is also a stronger and hoppier version, Doctor Okell's Elixir, which is brewed occasionally.

Okells's beers are long-established favorites in the island's pubs; in fact the brewery owns fifty percent of the one hundred or so on the island. Its beer is part of the Manx lifestyle that is promoted in tourist literature. Okells's beers are still brewed according to the Manx Beer Purity Law. This is the Reinheitsgebot of the island, which only allows beer to contain malt, hops, sugar, and water. Ingredients that are not permitted include raw cereal, corn syrup, and opium. "It doesn't hinder us in any way," says the brewery's affable head brewer Mike Cowbourne, who has been with the company for more than twenty years. "If you want to do a non-Purity Law beer, then you have to ask the Tynwald (the Manx Parliament) for permission. We have had to do it for our wheat beer, MacLir, which took six months to be approved, while we also had to get permission to do fruit beers." The brewery is currently based in Kewaigue, just outside the Manx capital of Douglas, where it moved in 1994. **MC**

Tasting notes

Light in color, with bags of citrus fruit on the nose, joined by the characteristic hopsack aroma. Meanwhile, in the mouth, a soft maltiness opens the proceedings before the hops belt out fruit and bitterness; it finishes off with a zingy bitterness that makes the beer eminently drinkable.

Dom Kölsch

Dom-Brauerei GmbH | www.dom-koelsch.de

Country of origin Germany
First brewed 1894
Alcohol content 4.8% abv
Serving temperature 46°F, 8°C

Dom-Brauerei is one of roughly twenty breweries and brewpubs remaining in and around Cologne that still produce this highly localized top-fermenting beer. It has been awarded its own appellation contrôlée, which means that anyone producing Kölsch outside the city has to call it a Kölsch-style beer, although some surrounding villages have been granted special approval. Dom, which was established toward the end of the 19th century and is named after the famous gothic Dom cathedral in the center of the city, is not the biggest Kölsch producer—that honor belongs to Küppers—however, Dom's Kölsch does have a reputation in the wider world. It is seen as one of the spiciest of the beer style and is not as smooth tasting as many of its competitors.

The brewery was established in 1894, when Carl Goeters and the Steingroever brothers acquired two home breweries in Cologne. The company's rate of growth remained healthy over the years up until World War II, which led to the widespread devastation of Cologne and the disruption of brewing operations. It wasn't until 1956 that the destroyed buildings were finally reconstructed and the brewery started producing beer again. Since 1974, Dom-Brauerei has only brewed Kölsch. During the 1970s, Dom was integrated with the Stern brewery in Essen, but thirteen years later it became an independent company again. In 1998, Stern became the Dom-Brauerei. In 2000, Dom moved their brewing production a short distance down the road to the former home of Küppers, who had also moved location. **WO**

Tasting notes

Golden yellow in the glass, glistening and glittering beneath a fine foamy head. Fruity on the nose, which follows through to the palate; not a bitter beer, but there is a discernible hop character in the mid-palate. Pleasant and spicy, with a long finish.

Dortmunder Gold

Great Lakes Brewing Co. | www.greatlakesbrewing.com

Country of origin United States
First brewed 1988
Alcohol content 5.8% abv
Serving temperature 36°F, 2°C

With its significant German immigrant population, Cleveland was a lager town almost from the day in 1832 when the Erie Canal was finished. Leisy, Gehring, Müller, Eilert, Schlather—the brewers' very names foretold the light, crisp, and refreshing German-style lagers that locals would drink for the next 150 years, until the last one—Schmidt's—closed in 1984. It is only appropriate, then, that when Great Lakes Brewing opened in 1988 in the historic Market Tavern, as Ohio's first microbrewery, it would specialize in lagers.

At the start, the founders—brothers Patrick and Daniel Conway—turned to a longtime Cleveland pro for advice: Thaine Johnson, the former master brewer at the defunct Schmidt's brewery. It was Johnson who developed the recipe for this exceptionally balanced, golden Dortmunder-style lager, the new brewery's first product. As with any pale lager, achieving the perfect balance is a product of expert yeast fermentation. The brewery doesn't reveal much about its proprietary strain, but its telltale sign is a slight bit of fruitiness in the finish.

The brewery—known for witty brand names honoring local legends—originally named this beer The Heisman, after storied college football coach John Heisman, who was born near the brewery's site. New York's Downtown Athletic Club objected to the use of the name, however. Uncertain what to rename the beer, the Conways found their answer after winning their first gold medal at the Great American Beer Festival in 1990. A photograph of their medal is displayed on the label of Dortmunder Gold. **DR**

Tasting notes

A tight head skates across a pilsner glass's clear, golden pool. Upon the first sip, its light honey aroma is countered by apple tartness. A delicate balance between sweet malt and light hoppy bitterness is enhanced by a tart, clean, somewhat dry finish.

Durban Pale Ale

Shongweni Brewery | www.shongwenibrewery.com

Country of origin South Africa
First brewed 2007
Alcohol content 5.7% abv
Serving temperature 46°F, 8°C

Passion is a thing that unites craft brewers across the world, and it's as essential as having the means to bring beer into the world. Stuart Robson, who set up Shongweni Brewery in KwaZulu-Natal in 2007, has had to show that passion. He says: "The red tape to establish a brewery here can be significant, mainly due to a misunderstanding by planners and the like that all breweries are going to be huge concerns like SABMiller."

Despite these obstacles, Robson's beers are getting a name for themselves, both in South Africa and in the wider world. His Durban Pale Ale was one of his debut beers and according to Robson was "inspired by the original IPAs sent to India. The Durban link came from a little research and perhaps a little folklore. The original IPAs spent some time in transport and that route took them around the Cape. At the time, the British Empire had outposts, one of which was the port of Durban, and it is believed that not all of the beer destined for India actually made it there, with some being 'liberated' by thirsty soldiers stationed in the port." A proportion of each brew is kept back and released to the trade after twelve months. This was initially done to show consumers that not all beer will "go off" after thirty days. Robson found that people actually liked the matured taste.

Local pale ale malt and hops imported from Kent go into the mix, and the beer is then fermented and matured for a total of a hundred days to try and get as close as possible to the taste of the original IPAs. It is bottle conditioned, and Robson recommends that it be served with barbecued meat or a spicy curry. **ATJ**

Tasting notes

Dark gold in the glass with the nose offering up rich orange notes plus hints of caramel and a hoppy spiciness. On the palate, it's a full-bodied presence, with an excellent balance between the malt-accented sweetness and luscious orangelike tanginess. Dry finish with hints of fruit.

Duvel

Duvel Moortgat | www.duvel.be

Country of origin Belgium
First brewed 1923
Alcohol content 8.5% abv
Serving temperature 44°F, 7°C

This is the classic Belgian strong golden ale, and it has achieved much fame and acclaim. In fact, such has been the success of Duvel that Moortgat, which opened in 1871, recently renamed itself Brouwerij Duvel Moortgat. Meanwhile, Duvel ("Devil" in Flemish) is the one beer that can be found in most Belgian cafés.

This flagship beer was originally a dark beer called "Victory Ale." As the name might suggest, it was brewed to celebrate victory over the Germans in World War I. In 1970, the beer was reformulated as a blond ale. These wispy colored ales were gaining in popularity at that time, and Moortgat wanted to take advantage of the trend. The Moortgat family has always been adept with their marketing. The new Duvel Depot is an impressive and atmospheric tasting café where all the beers of the Duvel Moortgat group (it also owns Ommegang in the United States as well as others in Europe) are showcased. The walls of the Depot are filled with the very best of Moortgat breweriana.

Despite its size, the brewery still experiments. A dry-hopped brew, Duvel Tripel Hop, was released in 2007 and was well received. As the name suggests, it uses three hops in its recipe, while the alcohol was bumped to 9.5 percent abv. Hopefully, there will be more experiments like this.

The brewery's success has spawned a plethora of beers with devilish names, but Duvel remains the benchmark. One of its gifts is that there are few beers that have such a high level of carbonation, and the classic Duvel tulip glass is a practical as well as an iconic container for this golden brew. **CC**

Tasting notes

Golden straw-colored brew with notes of candi sugar, fruits, alcohol, hops, and yeast in the nose. Light bodied, but with plenty of backbone to balance the hops and alcohol. Taste is dry with a warming alcohol, sweet malts, and a dry, semibitter aftertaste.

Echigo Pilsner

Echigo Beer | www.echigo-beer.jp

Country of origin Japan
First brewed 1999
Alcohol content 5% abv
Serving temperature 44°F, 7°C

In early 1995, Echigo Beer opened Japan's very first brewpub, producing primarily ales and other specialty beers that were largely unknown to the Japanese public. It wasn't until 1999 that it began to produce lager. Its first was a pilsner, the style on which most mainstream Japanese beer is based.

Founder Seiichiro Uehara explains that the brewpub needed more variety in its beer lineup, so decided to expand with lagers. Initially it produced a pilsner, then a Munich-style lager, with bocks and other lager styles brewed as seasonals. Although the pilsner was comparatively easy to brew, it was the Munich lager that initially caused difficulties. After two to three batches, the brewers were finally satisfied with the results. Although the Munich lager is no longer brewed on a regular basis, the Echigo Pilsner has turned out to be the best seller, and now accounts for some two-thirds of sales.

Such a clean beer with exacting characteristics is no surprise, since the parent company is a premium sake brewer, Uehara Shuzo, based in Niigata. Indeed, its sake brand Tsurukame is strongly revered throughout Japan, and is even supplied regularly to the Japanese imperial household.

Echigo offers several versions of pilsner beer, from expensive bottled and unfiltered versions produced at its original brewpub, to less-expensive canned versions. Echigo even produces a low-cost beer called "Reijoh" for a Tokyo-based supermarket chain, which sells it for far less than equivalent lagers brewed by the four major breweries. **BH**

Tasting notes

It is a bright medium yellow with remarkable clarity. The aroma is clean and brisk, with a slight hop emphasis, while the flavor reflects a good balance of malt and hops. Very well made, it is clearly in the Japanese premium lager style, with minimal aftertaste and a quick finish.

Edelstoff

Augustiner-Bräu Wagner | www.augustiner-braue.de

Country of origin Germany
First brewed 1927
Alcohol content 5.6% abv
Serving temperature 46°F, 8°C

Augustiner Edelstoff is an export beer, a style that is traditionally brewed for exporting and so has a little bit more alcohol to make it more durable for the journey. It is also sold in its home country, and is a beer that is brewed to mark a special event or celebrate an important personage connected with the brewery. Edelstoff translates as "precious substance," and the beer first saw the light of day in 1927, when the Weimar Republic was coming out of a catastrophic currency and political crisis.

Edelstoff has a strong fan base in its home city of Munich, where Augustiner Bräu München is the oldest such establishment (founded in 1328). Naturally, Edelstoff has its own little world of words and culture —because its foam is so fine it is ordered as *schaumige* (loosely translated as "frothy"). When served, more than one-third of the glass is creamy foam, which perfectly preserves the freshness of the beer. Every waiter in every restaurant or beer hall that belongs to the brewery knows this secret.

Augustiner monks initially founded the brewery in a monastery in the middle of Munich, but today it is near the Theresienwiese, where the Oktoberfest takes place every year. This event plays an important role for all breweries in Munich, and Augustiner is the most traditional of all. It is the last one still to have its beer in wooden casks and not steel containers. Throughout the year, in all the brewery's restaurants and beer halls, the breeching of each new cask is announced with the loud ringing of a bell so that everybody can finish their glass of beer and order a fresh Edelstoff. **WO**

Tasting notes

Clear and golden in the glass with fine hop notes on the nose and delightfully smooth on the palate; it is also sparkling and fresh. A light sweetness and similarly light citrusiness vie for space on the palate; a very malty finish accompanied by a light, but gentle, bitterness.

Edelweiss Gamsbock

Hofbräu Kaltenhausen | www.edelweissbier.at

Country of origin Austria
First brewed 1997
Alcohol content 7.1% abv
Serving temperature 48°F, 9°C

The location of Hofbräu Kaltenhausen, founded in 1475, was chosen carefully: the cellars are built into a mountain with natural chasms that provide cooling with extremely cold air. This cooling system is still in operation. In 1921, the brewery became a founding member of Österreichische Brau—the nucleus of BrauUnion that was later taken over by Heineken.

In 1986, the Edelweiss brand was introduced—starting with a filtered Kristallweizen—but soon the unfiltered Hefeweizen became more popular. It is now Austria's best-selling wheat beer. The strong Gamsbock, named after the chamois buck that is common in the local mountains, covers a small niche in the brewery's portfolio, but it is still the most popular Weizenbock in Austria. Brewmaster Günther Seeleitner recommends pairing the silky smooth Gamsbock with cakes and desserts. **CS**

Tasting notes
This straw-colored, very cloudy beer pours with a big head. The aroma is fruity with hints of banana peel and orange zest. Very full bodied, even sweet, with a flavor of banana and bubble gum.

Efes Pilsen

Efes Beverage Group | www.efesbev.com

Country of origin Turkey
First brewed 1969
Alcohol content 5% abv
Serving temperature 44°–50°F, 7°–10°C

Although not necessarily famed in beer circles for their pilsner, the Turkish take pride in being associated with a beer-making region, thanks to their close proximity to Mesopotamia, the site of the first brew around 9,000 years ago. This historic pedigree underlines the heritage of Efes (named after the old port of Ephesus) and also makes it the best-selling beer in the country.

The Efes group brews the beer and is the fifth biggest brewer in Europe. Efes Pilsen first appeared in the 1960s, when the emerging Turkish middle classes were turning their backs on the national beverage, raki, which they saw as the drink of peasants. Raki has made a bit of a comeback, but Efes Pilsen is still the beer that Turkish drinkers (especially those with nationalist sentiments) call for. Naturally it's a bottom-fermented beer, and it is brewed using Hallertau hops and a pils malt from Turkish soil. **TS**

Tasting notes
The beer has a sweet profile up front, but there's an interesting tang off the malt, and the Hallertau hops help counterbalance with a bit of bitterness. Very refreshing in the finish.

Eggenberg Pale Lager

Pivovar Eggenberg | www.eggenberg.cz

Einhundert 100 Bitterpils

Pivatbrauerei Vitzthum | www.einhundert.be

Country of origin Czech Republic
First brewed 1979
Alcohol content 5% abv
Serving temperature 44°F, 7°C

Country of origin Austria
First brewed 2007
Alcohol content 5% abv
Serving temperature 41°F, 5°C

Even before the Velvet Revolution, a large number of the strictures placed upon Czech breweries by communism had been loosened. In 1973, the brewery in Český Krumlov was allowed to add an 11 degree pale lager called Zámecké (or Chateau), and from 1979, Eggenberg made a pale lager brewed at 12 degrees Plato, inspired by the classic pilsners.

It was then known as the Schwarzenberg Brewery, after the Bohemian noble family who had acquired the property in 1719. At the time, there was great rivalry between barley beers, meant for the masses, and more costly wheat beers; the brewery ceased making barley beers in 1800. By 1937, however, it had returned to using barley, at which point it began making lager beers in the Bavarian style. Today the 12 degree pale lager is the brewery's flagship beer. Brewed from two-row Czech pilsner malt, it is at its best on draft. **ER**

German pilsner is usually defined as a pale golden, bottom-fermented beer with a bitterness beyond 30 IBUs. Yet many beers that are labeled pils, pilsner, or pilsener in German-speaking countries now have a bitterness level below 25 IBUs. These bland beers are easy to drink and easy to sell.

Marcus Hertel was studying at the Weihenstephan brewing academy when he decided to create a beer with a record-breaking 100 IBUs. To get it brewed, he turned to a friend who ran the small family-owned Privatbrauerei Vitzthum in Uttendorf. Hertel and Vitzthum decided that Einhundert Bitterpils should be brewed with 100 IBUs but should avoid picking up too much hop aroma. Hertel believed that the use of aroma hops in the quantities necessary to achieve 100 IBUs might make the beer too perfumey on the nose. The final result was a quite unique brew. **CS**

Tasting notes

This classic pale lager is refreshingly crisp and sweet, balancing its sugary notes with a gentle touch of Saaz hops. When poured correctly, it should support a small coin on its thick foam head.

Tasting notes

A straw color and a huge head. On the nose, there is a slight grassiness plus a slight burned-malt note. Refreshing, there is just enough body to balance the intense, long-lasting bitterness.

Einsiedler Lager Hell

Brauerei Rosengarten
www.einsiedlerbier.ch

Country of origin Switzerland
First brewed *ca.* 1930s/1940s
Alcohol content 4.5% abv
Serving temperature 46°F, 8°C

Eisenbahn Kölsch

Sudbrack Brewery
www.eisenbahn.com.br

Country of origin Brazil
First brewed 2005
Alcohol content 4.8% abv
Serving temperature 37°–41°F, 3°–5°C

Rosengarten in Einsiedeln is one of the many Swiss breweries that opened during the 1860s when the Swiss wine industry was suffering the effects of the phylloxera plague. Many master brewers from south Germany, and especially Bavaria, were brought in to help start breweries across Switzerland. As a result, Schweizer Lager Hell (pale Swiss lager) owes a lot more to the Bavarian Helles style than to Bohemian pilsner.

From 1936 to 1991, the Swiss beer market was ruled by a brewer's convention that dictated which styles of beers could be brewed (pale lager, special lager, dark lager, and strong lager), and also set the bottle sizes at a slightly unusual 10 ounces (290 ml) and 20 ounces (580 ml). Lager Hell conforms to this dictat and is a must-try beer for scholars of the Swiss beer landscape. **LM**

Eisenbahn Kölsch came into being after the founders of this Brazilian brewery made several trips to Germany to research beer styles and were delighted by the light and refreshing taste of the Kölsch on offer.

Eisenbahn is based in Blumenau in the south of Brazil, and the brewers are very much traditionalists in their approach to beer. They re-create classic beer types just as they were intended to be, and their Kölsch-style beer is no exception. Brewed with a combination of four different malts including wheat malt, the ingredients and cold-filtering process result in the distinctive pale color and light delicate flavor. This is an exceptional New World take on an Old World classic, and it won the Best Standard Pale Ale category at the World Beer Awards in 2008. **AH**

Tasting notes

A prototype Swiss pale lager, straw colored, with a soft, rather full, malty base, flowery hopping reminiscent of fresh hay, and a tiny hint of sulfur. A crisp finish with a moderate bitterness.

Tasting notes

Light fruit aroma and a hint of caramel, followed on the palate by a fragile malty character and just a tang of lemony citrus. Combines with smoked salmon, shrimp, or omelette.

Emerson's Pilsner

The Emerson Brewing Company
www.emersons.co.nz

Country of origin New Zealand
First brewed 1995
Alcohol content 5% abv
Serving temperature 43°–46°F, 6°–8°C

When The Emerson Brewing Company launches a new beer, the New Zealand beer industry sits up and takes note: such is the high regard for Richard Emerson and his Dunedin-based craft brewery.

Emerson's first commercial release was its London Porter, launched in 1993. A robust, roasty brew, it was an exceptionally brave move in a Kiwi beer market that at the time was totally dominated by bland, sugary lagers. In 1995, the brewery released Pilsner, an organic beer that became its flagship and best-selling bottled beer. Bursting with passion fruit, spice, and citrus flavors, New Zealand's first organic beer is a showcase for locally grown Riwaka hops. Rated one of the top ten beers by Kiwi beer writers, it is the beer equivalent to the country's world-beating sauvignon blancs. **GG**

Tasting notes
Sweet vanilla biscuits and toast with hints of passion fruit, citrus, spice, and grassiness on both the nose and palate, leading into a lingering, dry, quenching finish.

Estrella Damm

S. A. Damm
www.damm.es

Country of origin Spain
First brewed 1876
Alcohol content 5.4% abv
Serving temperature 41°–44°F, 5°–7°C

You know that a beer is successful when there's no escaping its branding, whether it is a bright and breezy billboard-sized advert or a smaller, more homely sign that hangs outside local bars. Estrella Damm is one such beer and it's hard to escape its success. It is a top brand of beer in Spain and can be found throughout Europe. Obviously, this beer is Estrella (Star) by name, Estrella by nature.

Back in 1876, when the brewery was started and Estrella Damm was first brewed, did its founder and Alsatian brewmaster August Kuentzmann Damm think that his creation would travel so far and see the turn of two centuries? Probably not, but later, in 1910, the brewery's name was changed to "Damm" as a tribute to its founder. **SS**

Tasting notes
Fruity nose has hints of grape and oranges, as well as a whisper of grainy malt. Crisp start on the palate before being joined by caramel, vanilla, and fresh floral notes. Clean, light finish.

Etoile du Nord

Brasserie Thiriez | www.brasseriethiriez.com

Country of origin France
First brewed *ca*. 2003
Alcohol content 4.5% abv
Serving temperature 46°–54°F, 8°–12°C

Brasserie Thiriez was set up in 1996 by Daniel Thiriez in the hamlet of Esquelbecq, a few miles inland from Dunkirk. He brews in a former brewery, attached to which is a bar-cum-shop where his beers can be purchased. "I was a human resource manager for a large supermarket for ten years," he says. "I had always been interested in beer and brewing and started home-brewing when I was a student with kits brought from England. I wanted to be independent and live in the countryside."

When he bought the old brewery, there was nothing left to remind anyone that beer had ever been made there, but some of the older folk told Thiriez that they remembered it before it closed in 1945. "One of my biggest influences was Moinette," he says, "and I also like the bitterness that hops give and I suppose I brewed the beers I wanted to drink."

Thiriez calls Etoile du Nord a pale ale (which he emphasizes by using Kentish hops). Several years after starting the brewery, he was corresponding with an English brewery in Kent and had the idea of brewing a mix between an English ale and his own style of beer. "Les Frères de la Bière" was the original name but, after the English brewery closed, the beer was rechristened "Etoile du Nord." Top fermented and bottle conditioned, it is one of the brewery's best sellers (alongside La Blonde d' Esquelbecq) and is sold in the United States under the name of Thiriez Extra. Daniel Thiriez is an excellent example of how the passions and devotions of the last couple of decades of the craft beer revolution have influenced people across the globe. **ATJ**

Tasting notes

Blond in the glass beneath a snow-white head that can be rocky. Nose has a hint of banana and strawberry, plus fresh bubblegum aromas. A hoppy bitterness kicks in midway down the palate; a fruity, dry, bitter finish with the bitterness staying for a while.

Exmoor Gold

Exmoor Ales | www.exmoorales.co.uk

Country of origin England
First brewed 1986
Alcohol content 4.5% abv
Serving temperature 48°F, 9°C

It's a mantra in the brewing industry that people drink with their eyes, which could partly explain the enduring global success of gold-colored lagers. Back in the United Kingdom, this recognition of the visual appeal of a glass of beer has been acknowledged with the sweeping success of golden ales: pale and winsome beers that look like lager but are most definitely ales. The first golden ale is always reckoned to be Exmoor Gold, which appeared in 1986, when the majority of British beers were amber in color.

"It was first brewed as a celebration brew to mark the 1,000th brew of Exmoor Ale," recalls Peter Turner, who was a director of the brewery at the time. "As far as I can remember, it was meant to be an extremely different single malt ale. It must be recalled that it encountered great resistance in its first few years as it was so different to any of the 'traditional' (colored) ales then on the market. Slowly though it was accepted by the market, and then all breweries from then onward realized that they needed a single malt ale in their portfolio." As Turner says, this is a single-malt beer with pale ale malt going into the mash, while the hop regime includes Golding, Challenger, Styrian Golding, and Fuggle.

Exmoor Ales started in 1980. It was originally called Golden Hill, after its hilltop location in the small Somerset town of Wiveliscombe. Almost immediately, Golden Hill made its mark on the beer world when Exmoor Ale was voted Best Bitter at the Great British Beer Festival in 1980. Since then an impressive number of brewing awards have come the brewery's way. **ATJ**

Tasting notes

Enticingly golden in color. The nose interplays between a fresh bouquet of grassy and floral hop and a subtly soft, fluffy, caramel-tinged maltiness. The palate sees more balance between gentle grainy maltiness and sprightly floral, citrusy fresh, hop fruitiness. The finish is bittersweet.

Fancy Lawnmower

Saint Arnold Brewing | www.saintarnold.com

Country of origin United States
First brewed 2000
Alcohol content 4.7% abv
Serving temperature 39°–44°F, 4°–7°C

One doesn't think of Texas as a hotbed of craft brewing, but pockets of fine beer exist there. Surprisingly, there is a large group of wild home-brewers, but even so, brewers have to use every trick in the book to sell great beer to a public reared on Lone Star and Pearl.

The name Fancy Lawnmower "comes from the old home-brewers' term for crappy light beer," says Brock Wagner, a former investment banker who started Saint Arnold Brewing—named after the patron saint of brewing—in 1994. "I remember walking around the brewhouse asking people what adjective they liked that had the tone I was after (indicating it was upscale but clearly tongue-in-cheek). 'Fancy' won over 'gourmet.'"

Fancy Lawnmower beer is a Kölsch-style creation, tipping its hat to the German top-fermented style that originates in the city of Köln (Cologne). Stylistically, Kölsch has a lot in common with pale lagers such as pils, but it is softer and creamier, and has a fruity perfume that comes from an ale fermentation. It is also lagered at cold temperatures, which adds smoothness, appealing to mainstream drinkers. Whatever it is, this style of beer works for Saint Arnold, according to Wagner. "We have seen tremendous growth recently, and it now outsells our blond in all markets except Houston."

So how do you make Fancy Lawnmower? Plenty of German and domestic pilsner malt and a little malted wheat for a creamy texture and a great head. Hallertau, one of the "noble" hops, is used throughout. "It is the floral finish combined with the nutty malt character that I think makes it so interesting while still being a thirst quencher," says Wagner. Neat trick. **RM**

Tasting notes

Fresh, bready malt aroma with a slight hop character and some fruitiness. It is creamy in the mouth without being oversweet, and a gentle bitterness gradually builds up for balance. The finish is creamy and pleasantly yeasty, with a soft peachy fruitiness.

Farrotta

Almond '22 | www.birraalmond.com

Country of origin Italy
First brewed 2005
Alcohol content 5.7% abv
Serving temperature 39°–43°F, 4°–6°C

Jurij Ferri's Swedish grandfather was a character who could have come straight out of the novels of Joseph Conrad. He started his career as a ship's boy and ended it as the maître d' of the world famous Moulin Rouge in Paris. Thankfully, for Italian beer lovers that is, Ferri inherited the old man's love of food composition and the alchemy of the ingredients rather than the passion to wander off to sea. This sense of epicurean affection naturally helped quite a lot when the Swedish-Italian Ferri began to develop his personal philosophy in the art of brewing. He spent years home-brewing, focusing on the Weizen style, until he got bored. Then he opened his microbrewery in 2003 in an old 19th-century building where the local women used to work at peeling almonds to produce the famous sugar-coated nuts known as "confetti" (hence the brewery's name). This was the first in the Abruzzo region, and he began his trade without knowing a lot of what other brewers were doing up in the north.

Ferri is a self-made brewer who is now recognized as one of the most talented on the Italian scene. His personal approach to malts, hops, and spices has made him produce a wide range of different beers. In Farrotta, a traditional local ingredient—organic spelt—plays a strong role in the recipe. Other malts are pilsner malt, which makes up 60 percent of the grist, and Vienna malt, which is 10 percent. Hops are Styrian Golding for the bitterness and Cascade for the aroma, and locally produced acacia honey is added to the wort while it's cooling. The final result is a beer with an elegant flavor. Try it with white meat or pasta. **MM**

Tasting notes

Deep golden color with attractive orange tints. Opalescent with a good strong foamy head. The aroma starts off with dominant notes of raw grain, but is joined by a definite undercurrent of tangerine peel and acacia honey. Well balanced in the palate, with a pleasant rustic hint.

Faust Kräusen

Brauhaus Faust | www.faust.de

Country of origin Germany
First brewed 1996
Alcohol content 5.5% abv
Serving temperature 46°F, 8°C

As early as 1885, the founder of the Faust brewery dynasty, Adalbert Faust, was experimenting with fermentation methods. A graduate of Weihenstephan, Germany's renowned university for agriculture and brewing near Munich, he elaborated the procedure that involves kräusening (carbonating) the beer.

Inspired by this research, current owners Cornelius and Johannes Faust created a new, unfiltered lager that comes out remarkably fresh and tasteful. The two brothers released Faust Kräusen in 1996, the year they took over the family business. Basically, what they do is add freshly fermenting wort to the lagering tanks in which the young beer matures for no fewer than six to seven weeks. Kräusening revives the remaining yeast cells, cleaning up the flavor, carbonating the beer, and providing a high attenuation. As the brewery has open fermentation vessels, the brewers can see by the formation of the foamy head—kräusen—when to call a halt to the fermenting wort. When the white head has reached its peak—high kräusen—the yeast is at its most active and powerful. All this attention to detail is important because Faust Kräusen has many fans, even outside its home region of Bavaria. Some cases have even been exported to places as far away as Taiwan and Singapore.

Brauhaus Faust has an interesting history. The brewery has changed hands several times, and in the 19th century it belonged to a family named Krug. The Krugs went on to found the Schlitz brewery in Milwaukee, which was the second biggest brewery in the world during the first half of the 20th century. **SK**

Tasting notes

Golden to orange and opalescent, with a big off-white head. This beer offers a slightly sour, fruity nose with hints of ripe pear. On the palate, expect a fluffy, soft mouthfeel and toasty flavors with decent fruity notes. Bitterness remains in the background. Dry, slightly sour finish.

Flensburger Pilsener

Flensburger Brauerei | www.flens.co.uk

Country of origin Germany
First brewed 1922
Alcohol content 4.8% abv
Serving temperature 42°–46°F, 6°–8°C

"Plop." This sound is music to many a German beer lover's ears, especially in northern Germany where it marks the overture to a refreshing pleasure. Until about twenty years ago, whenever you heard the "plop" sound, you could almost be sure that it was the swing top of a Flensburger Pilsener. As crown caps emerged in the 1960s in Germany, gradually all breweries converted their packaging. Only in Schleswig-Holstein were things different: Flensburger and the nearby Dithmarscher Brauerei stuck to their old-fashioned bottles. Some say it was for marketing considerations; others claim that they could not afford a change. Whatever the truth, the swing top actually became their USP. The marketing department of Flensburger even secured the sound as a trademark.

The beer was first brewed in 1922 when the outstanding quality of the local spring water induced Flensburger to satisfy the increasing demand for pilsener with a brew of its own. The beer gets a good dose of bittering hops, Magnum or Herkules, and some additional aroma hops, Spalter Select and Hallertauer Tradition. From 1983 to 1993, the Pilsener was the only beer that Flensburger Brauerei produced.

Flensburger Pilsener became a cult brand in the 1980s, thanks to a cartoon about a crooked underdog biker named Werner. Young consumers were eager to get hold of one of these outdated bottles, and what they discovered was a beer with a surprisingly distinctive, north German character, a bone-dry, straightforward, extra bitter pils. It was for these uncompromising features that the regional brand became a national celebrity. **SK**

Tasting notes

Straw colored; impressive white head. This beer offers a decent grainy nose. The palate does not distinguish any noteworthy maltiness. Bitterness is prominent. Around a floral and herbal heart, it builds up to a grapefruitlike finish where it lingers for a long time.

Früh Kölsch

Cölner Hofbräu Früh | www.frueh.de

Country of origin Germany
First brewed 1904
Alcohol content 4.9% abv
Serving temperature 46°F, 8°C

Today Früh is the third largest Kölsch brewer in Cologne. However, the brewery's beginnings were not so auspicious. Within a short time of starting the brewery, Peter Josef Früh died. His wife and daughters took over the brewery, but then came World War I, the collapse of the economy, and then World War II. Unlike the rest of the city, the brewery survived bombing raids relatively undamaged. Many brewery buildings were hit, but not the brewhouse. Since many of the other breweries in the city were either destroyed or damaged, Früh earned extra revenue by brewing for its competitors. In the 1950s, the brewery and pub were rebuilt and a decade later, the third and fourth generations of the family took control of the brewery.

In 1969, bottled Früh Kölsch was introduced. In the early years, Früh attempted to produce and offer a "different" Kölsch. By using a different filtering system and brewing technique, the brewery was able to offer a beer that was lighter in color and less bitter. In fact, it was, and remains, the lightest Kölsch in the family. Perhaps it is fitting then that the current management of Früh considers women and young people their target market. Going one step further, in 1991, Früh became the first Kölsch brewer to offer an alcohol-free version of the beer.

Visitors to the P. J. Früh tavern, which sits on a small square in the shadow of Cologne's vast cathedral (or "Dom"), can stay in rooms on the brewpub's first floor. The brewery used to be on this site before it moved to a more spacious one. These rooms were where Peter Josef Früh and his family originally lived. **RP**

Tasting notes

The beer is clear and golden with a soft white head. The aroma is malty and fruity. Unlike in the brewpub, where it is served by gravity from keg, the bottled version is highly carbonated. However, the taste is softly malty with a clean, dry finish and aftertaste.

Gambrinus Premium

Gambrinus | www.gambrinus.cz

Country of origin Czech Republic
First brewed 1869
Alcohol content 5% abv
Serving temperature 46°F, 8°C

There are several versions of the origins of the name Gambrinus, but they all trace back to beer, brewing, cellars, and hops. It is one of the most overused of the world's beer names, and Gambrinus breweries exist in France, Canada, and the United States. The reason? Gambrinus is the unofficial patron saint of beer and was, depending on which story you believe, a legendary king of Flanders, a cup-bearer in the court of Charlemagne, or a nickname of John the Fearless, who was believed to be the inventor of hopped beer. The favorite story, however (and the one told by Plzeňský Prazdroj, the company that brews the beer), relates to Jan Primus who was more formally known as John I, Duke of Brabant (1267–1294). He is said to have been a perfect example of a feudal prince: chivalrous, brave, adventurous, and even-tempered, all of which made him a popular character in medieval literature.

The two Gambrinus brands, Světlý and Premium, enjoy 25 percent of the Czech market (there is another pale lager in the portfolio, Gambrinus Excelent) and they are everyday, quaffing beers. Nowadays, Gambrinus is a subsidiary of Plzeňský Prazdroj (also the producer of Pilsner Urquell), which is owned by global giant SABMiller. Pilsner Urquell is the only major Czech brewery still with its own maltings, buying raw Moravian barley from selected farmers. Gambrinus and Pilsner Urquell share the maltings along with filtration facilities and filling lines, but their brewhouses are quite separate, as are their yeast strains: Gambrinus uses the company's W strain; Pilsner Urquell the H strain. **AG**

Tasting notes

On the nose, a fresh, grassy, and lemonlike aroma with hints of butter appearing at intervals throughout a full malt palate. Beautifully golden in color, it accompanies chicken and pork dishes particularly well and is also a formidable table companion to cheese.

Geary's Pale Ale

D. L. Geary Brewing | www.gearybrewing.com

Country of origin United States
First brewed 1986
Alcohol content 4.5% abv
Serving temperature 48°F, 9°C

Sometimes a dream takes a bit of time to come to fruition. Although the D. L. Geary Brewing Company was incorporated in October 1983, it was three years before its first beer flowed. David and Karen Geary wanted to produce a world-class beer and sell it around New England. At the time, a small number of microbrewers were gaining a toehold, mostly along the West Coast of the United States.

Thanks to introductions made by Scottish brewer Peter Maxwell Stuart of Traquair fame, David Geary began to train at breweries in the United Kingdom. He spent time at several small Scottish and British commercial brewhouses and then returned home to work with Karen on the business plan for the new company. Finding a location for the brewery, deciding on recipes, designing packaging, and generating capital consumed most of the next two years.

In the autumn of 1986 the brewery was ready, and on December 10th the first pints of Geary's Pale Ale were sold. Today the company's brands are sold in seventeen states. In addition to the Pale Ale, Geary's makes a London Porter, Imperial IPA, Wee Heavy Scottish Ale, and Hampshire Special Ale, which started its life as the brewery's winter seasonal. It also makes an Autumn Ale, Winter Ale, and Summer Ale.

Geary's apprenticeship in the United Kingdom shows through in the company's ales. Geary's Pale Ale is brewed with pale, crystal, and chocolate malts; Cascade, Mount Hood, Tettnang, and Fuggle hops; and Hampshire yeast. In a blind tasting, it would be difficult to separate the ale from one of Burton-on-Trent. **RL**

Tasting notes

Classic pale ale glow with a rich, creamy, off-white head. Slight hop aroma and the beer opens with a touch of fruitiness before the hops take control. There's a nice level of hop bitterness throughout with hints of roasted malt around the edges.

Göller Kellerbier

Brauerei Göller | www.brauerei-goeller.de

Country of origin Germany
First brewed *ca.* late 1980s
Alcohol content 4.9% abv
Serving temperature 46°F, 8°C

Kellerbier (also known as "Zwickel" beer) is a traditional style of beer that has become popular in the last couple of decades. Beer drinkers now expect their favorite breweries to produce a Kellerbier, although not everyone finds it easy to fulfill such expectations. Kellerbier is difficult to produce and to distribute, but it is one of the most traditional kinds of beer that still exist in Germany. It is unfiltered and unpasteurized and, therefore, in the glass it can be hazy. However, a decent Kellerbier offers a sense of something with a history to it: a beer style that swims against the ubiquitous tide of clear golden pils.

Göller is a traditional Franconian brewery based in the beautiful town of Zeil, and it produces a variety of beers including a Rauchbier, which is one of the cleanest tasting, especially when compared with the fiery ones of Bamberg. The Göller Kellerbier is unfiltered, bottled when rather young, and less carbonated than a pilsner—it is a classic example of the style. Since 1999, the beer has been sold in a swing-top bottle, another little detail that perhaps sets it apart and says, "Here is a special beer."

Brauerei Göller was founded in the year 1514 (two years before the Purity Law became effective). The Göller family acquired the company in 1908 and has been in charge ever since. Local barley is bought from a group of farmers who have supplied the brewery for some time; whereas hops come from traditional German hop-growing areas. One of the highlights of a visit to Zeil is Göller's own restaurant and beer tap, where the brewery's many beers can be appreciated. **WO**

Tasting notes

Orange gold in color and lightly cloudy in the glass. The malt aroma in the nose is clear and has the same intensity on the palate. There are hints of fresh bread on the palate as well. The bitterness of the hop is not obtrusive and the finish is spicy.

Goose Island India Pale Ale

Goose Island Beer Company | www.gooseisland.com

Country of origin United States
First brewed 1993
Alcohol content 5.9% abv
Serving temperature 50°–55°F, 10°–13°C

Goose Island is an embodiment of all the virtues that Midwesterners like to see in themselves: integrity, modesty, a willingness to work hard, and do a lot with a little. Goose is solid. It has had its share of classics, of which the IPA is one, but the low-key brewery has produced some real dazzlers, too, such as Matilda and Bourbon County Stout. Year after year, one great beer after another, it pulls it all off without a lot of fanfare.

Goose Island started off as a brewpub in 1987, run by John Hall, a packaging executive looking to do something interesting with his life. His son Greg now serves as brewmaster and as the highly visible promoter of all things Goose. The IPA reflects the Goose gestalt perfectly: a great example of a beer that's only as complicated as it needs to be. Just a single malt, mashed with a simple infusion, brewed similarly to the English examples that inspired it. It's a testament to the amazing nature of well-made malt that such a simple recipe could result in this kind of depth. Aroma is provided by four hops: Styrian Golding, Fuggle, and Cascade, then the brew is dry hopped with Centennial for a bright and fresh hop aroma. The yeast is an English strain that brewed more than 200 batches before being recultured. As a result, it developed its own unique character and is the workhorse for Goose Island's ale production.

The beer fits with the English notion that beer is for drinking, not for sipping. "We wanted more of an English-style IPA," says Greg Hall. "We are not anti-hop," as some online beer raters have claimed. "It's about making a balanced, drinkable beer." **RM**

Tasting notes

A noseful of fresh floral hops, spicy and just a bit resiny, along with some light malt notes. Goose Island India Pale Ale is sweet and malty on the palate at first, building to a solid, spicy bitter middle. Finish is malt-tempered bitterness, again with a little more spice.

Gouden Carolus Hopsinjoor

Brouwerij Het Anker | www.hetanker.be

Country of origin Belgium
First brewed 2008
Alcohol content 8% abv
Serving temperature 48°F, 9°C

Belgian brewers are canny creatures. It has not gone unnoticed that recent years have seen the growing popularity of hop-driven beers, both at home and abroad. This has naturally led to various brewers (think Achouffe's Houblon for a start) releasing beers where hops have led the charge on the palate. Gouden Carolus Hopsinjoor is one of these creations, and it comes from a brewery that already had a number of very complex, malty beers.

Het Anker occupies one of the oldest brewing sites in Belgium with records of brewing in Mechelen dating back to 1369. In fact, much of the Het Anker complex could be regarded as a living museum. It is a UNESCO World Heritage site and several of the buildings date to the 14th century. The brewhouse has beautiful copper kettles dating from 1947, and there is a replica pub located above the brewhouse.

When Charles Leclef purchased the brewery in 1998, things were not going so well. Sales and production were way down from previous decades, and the brewery was in need of a major upgrade. Since then, Leclef has led a major resurgence of Het Anker, and it now produces more than 250,000 gallons (10,000 hl) of beer per year. It also exports to twenty-five different countries—approximately 65 percent of the brewery's output is sent outside Belgium. Beer quality and consistency have been key factors.

The name "Hopsinjoor" is a play on words. Several hops are used in the beer (Golding, Hallertau, Saaz, Spalt), but Op Sinjoorke is also the name of a playful vagabond allegedly linked with Mechelen's history. **CC**

Tasting notes

Pours a hazy yellow straw color and is topped with a big rocky head. Nose is spicy, yeasty, and herbal, with a noble hop presence. Taste is fruity and spicy, with some sweet malt, and a fine hop bitterness that works well with the other flavors.

Grolsch Premium Pilsner

Koninklijke Grolsch | www.grolsch.nl

Country of origin Netherlands
First brewed 1897
Alcohol content 5% abv
Serving temperature 44°F, 7°C

Grolsch Premium Pilsner is popular with connoisseurs because, even though it is a mass-market pilsner, it is unpasteurized and is lagered for ten weeks, which gives it more credibility (and taste) than its competitors.

It is brewed in the city of Enschede, although it gets its name from the small Dutch town of Grol. The brewery first appeared in the 17th century and used the name "de Klok" (the Clock). In 1897, the founding family sold it to the Theo De Groen family, and the introduction of the swing-top bottles a year later suggests that the new owners brought new energy to the business. Bierbrouwerij de Klok used ice cut from the local canals during the winters to keep its beers cool in insulated cellars, and it distributed the beers locally by horse and wagon. In 1954, the success of the Grolsch brand saw the name of the brewery change to Grolsch Bierbrouwerij. In 1995, in recognition of its long history, Grolsch was given permission to add "Royal" to its name (thus becoming Koninklijke Grolsch).

The Premium Pilsner uses a yeast strain developed by Grolsch long ago and is brewed using two-row European spring barley, a small amount of maize, and Hallertau and Saaz hops. The beer is also brewed under license in the United Kingdom. **RP**

Tasting notes

On the nose, soft and fragrant notes of grassy hops. Gentle carbonation on the palate, good body, light graininess, and hints of herbal and spicy hop leading through to a bitter finish.

Gubernijos Ekstra

AB Gubernija | www.gubernija.lt

Country of origin Lithuania
First brewed 2001
Alcohol content 5.5% abv
Serving temperature 46°F, 8°C

They know all about history at the Gubernija Brewery in the northern Lithuanian city of Šiauliai. It is reputed to be the oldest brewery in the country, with brewing on site kicking off in 1665, but it wasn't until the end of the 18th century that the name "Gubernija" was first used. During World War II, history rolled over the brewery with devastating consequences, totally destroying it in the process, although it was rebuilt when peace came along.

In the mid-1990s, the brewery was privatized and sold, a process that enabled a lot more investment to be made into a new brewhouse and other equipment. This was a time of great change in the Lithuanian brewing industry when breweries started to spend more on advertising and also bringing out new beers. Gubernijos Ekstra dates from this period, a pale lager style that is easy-drinking and refreshing. Pale malt and aromatic hops are used in the brew, along with a small amount of corn, which the brewery says is an essential addition for the taste and mouthfeel. For a true Lithuanian beer experience, enjoy this beer alongside a plate of *Kepta Duona*, fried black bread with a powerful garlicky mayonnaise dressing. *Isveikata* (Cheers) as they say in Lithuania. **ATJ**

Tasting notes

Straw gold in color. The nose has light malt-edged notes with floral hints. Well rounded and light on the palate with a sweetish graininess and a hint of hop fruitiness.

Grolsch Premium Pilsner is known internationally for its distinctive swing-top bottles.

Guldenberg

Brouwerij de Ranke | www.deranke.be

Harvest Pale

Castle Rock Brewery | www.castlerockbrewery.co.uk

Country of origin Belgium
First brewed 1994
Alcohol content 8.5% abv
Serving temperature 55°F, 13°C

Country of origin England
First brewed 2003
Alcohol content 4.3% abv
Serving temperature 46°F, 8°C

Guldenberg is not a Belgian abbey-style tripel, rather a big and strong golden ale that suggests what tripels could be. These days in Belgium there is a small but thankfully growing movement of small brewers who are opposed to a long-standing trend of overspiced, overly sweet, specialty ales. Nino Bacelle and Guido Devos of De Ranke are at the forefront of this cadre.

Guldenberg's malty sweetness is relatively mild, taking a backseat to robust bitterness from plenty of earthy, herbal Hallertau hops. The brewers add more during fermentation via dry hopping in order to increase the hop aroma and flavor. The impression of herbs and spices in the flavor comes from the hops and the yeast, not from ingredients better reserved for soup. The beer can be found on draft or in bottles. Its hoppy flavor tastes fresher on draft, but the bottle-conditioned version is arguably more complex. **JS**

Chris Holmes had long nurtured a desire to run his own brewery, and the opportunity presented itself in the late 1990s, when his pub company went into partnership with the former Bramcote Brewery. The business was renamed the Castle Rock Brewery after the nearby landmark of Nottingham Castle.

Harvest Pale has become the company's flagship beer and now accounts for almost two-thirds of total production. It was solely intended as a special brew for the city's beer festival in 2003. However, the beer was an instant success and rapidly found favor with local drinkers. Not surprisingly, the beer soon gained a permanent slot in the brewery's portfolio. It is fashioned from gently kilned malt and flavored with a skillful blend of U.S. hops. It has gone on to win many awards, not least the ultimate accolade of Champion Bitter of Britain in 2007. **JW**

Tasting notes
Cloudy, almost opaque golden-orange color. Nose is hoppy and herbal. On the tongue, a mild sweetness is enveloped by a serious bitterness, grassy and dry—and still drier at the finish.

Tasting notes
A deep straw-colored beer of great character with an aroma that bursts with citrus fruit, echoed on the tongue with just the slightest hint of toffee. Full bodied and utterly refreshing.

Haywards 5000

SABMiller | www.sabmiller.in

Hereford Pale Ale

Wye Valley Brewery | www.wyevalleybrewery.co.uk

Country of origin India
First brewed 1983
Alcohol content 7% abv
Serving temperature 44°–48°F, 7°–9°C

Country of origin England
First brewed 1987
Alcohol content 4% abv
Serving temperature 50°–54°F, 10°–12°C

India may be linked inextricably with IPA, but few drinkers in the subcontinent today have ever heard of it. Indians never got to try it in its heyday. When India gained independence in 1947, the tastes of Indian society developed from the habits of the Raj over the latter half of the century. Today, the Indian beer market is one of the fastest growing in the world. It consists entirely of lager, split into strong and mild categories.

Haywards 5000 leads the strong lager market. First brewed when SABMiller took over Shaw Breweries in 1983, it is the only national brand in a fiercely regional market. Using quality Indian malts and German hop extract, the fermented brew is taken through an "ester-balancing" process to ensure a smoothness and pleasant aftertaste not often associated with lagers at this strength. It's the only strong Indian lager exported to Europe, the Middle East, and Southeast Asia. **PB**

The timing seemed pretty bad when Peter Amor founded the Wye Valley Brewery in 1985 with the intention of creating some fantastic ales, only to realize that his target audience was switching in droves to lager. Two years later, the brewery went after a piece of that action by creating a pale golden beer of its own: Hereford Pale Ale (HPA). The beer is brewed with 100 percent pale malt. Some of the bittering hops are Target, but most of them—and all the late addition aroma hops—are Styrian Golding from Slovenia: hops that create a very distinctive floral, refreshing ale.

For fifteen years, HPA was a bit player in the Wye Valley portfolio. Then the ale market caught up with Wye Valley, and blond ales started winning prizes at beer festivals across the United Kingdom. With no change at the brewery, sales of HPA began to pick up, and it is now Wye Valley's best-selling beer. **PB**

Tasting notes

Darker than most lagers, malty sweetness and fruit on the nose give way to a full-bodied, caramel malt flavor with little bitterness. A smooth finish comes with a hint of alcohol burn.

Tasting notes

As pale as a golden pilsner. A pronounced citrus and floral hop aroma leads into a quenching flavor on the palate, with hints of grapefruit and lime, before a long, dry, refreshing finish.

Herold Bohemian Blond

Pivovar Herold | www.pivovar-herold.cz

Hoegaarden Grand Cru

Brouwerij van Hoegaarden | www.hoegaarden.com

Country of origin Czech Republic
First brewed *ca.* 1860
Alcohol content 5.2% abv
Serving temperature 44°F, 7°C

Country of origin Belgium
First brewed *ca.* 1969
Alcohol content 8.5% abv
Serving temperature 43°–46°F, 6°–8°C

The pilsner style has conquered the world with its popularity. However, the versions produced in its homeland of Bohemia are noticeably different from pilsners elsewhere. A highly traditional example, Herold Bohemian Blond Lager is brewed at a full 12 degrees Plato, then cold conditioned for around seventy days. The malt is produced at the brewery's own maltings using barley purchased from the surrounding farms, which might explain its prominence in the beer's flavor profile. Water comes from the brewery's own artesian springs. The beer is filtered through diatomaceous earth, then pasteurized before bottling.

Brewmaster František Pinkava credits his success to the use of such time-tested methods as a decoction mash and traditional open fermentation vessels. This beer could be dated as far back as 1780, although the style indicates mid-to-late 19th century. **ER**

Hoegaarden Grand Cru belongs to the tripel tradition, echoing monastic beers that are strong, pale in color, and well hopped, but it also doffs a cap to its better known stablemate, being laced with the same mix of coriander and orange peel. There is one main difference, however: Hoegaarden Grand Cru is not a wheat beer. There is no wheat in the mash tun, just barley malt. The hops, playing second fiddle to spices when it comes to taste, mostly provide a bitter balance and preservative qualities, leaving the other major flavor influence to the fermentation, which generates tropical fruit notes and a whiskeylike character.

Anheuser-Busch InBev divides its marketing budget between three sectors: global brands, multicountry brands, and local champions. Sadly, the Grand Cru doesn't feature in any of the lists, so it seems destined to stay—unjustly—in the shadows for some time. **JE**

Tasting notes

Pours a gorgeously deep, clear gold with a nose of fresh hops, honey, and fruit. The emphasis is on hearty malt, balanced by a refreshing hop bite in the finish. Good dry aftertaste.

Tasting notes

Golden in color with a spicy, fruity aroma and a bittersweet taste that blends spices with melon, mango, peach, and orange notes, all underscored by a whiskeylike warmth.

Hommelpap

Brasserie Ferme-Beck | www.fermebeck.com

Hop-Head

Bend Brewing Company | www.bendbrewingco.com

Country of origin France
First brewed 1994
Alcohol content 7% abv
Serving temperature 50°–54°F, 10°–12°C

Country of origin United States
First brewed 2004
Alcohol content 8.7% abv
Serving temperature 50°F, 10°C

Brasserie Ferme-Beck is close to the French-Flemish town of Ballieul. It's a family-owned farm brewery in the bière de garde region. As the farm is approached, hop poles are an obvious clue as to what the Beck family farm does. They focus on Challenger, Magnum, Nugget, and Brewers Gold hop varieties, but they also grow barley, some of which is used for brewing, raise animals, and have a couple of *gites*. Even the water for brewing comes from a spring beneath the farm.

Brewing began here in 1994 and the main beer they produce is the robustly hoppy Hommelpap (or hop juice). It is mainly bottled (by hand) and the brewery recommend that it be drunk fresh to enjoy its hop character to the full. Visiting this place is very much a way of plugging into the heart of the bière de garde tradition, and there is a bar above the brewery where this unique artisanal beer can be sampled. **ATJ**

Hop-Head came about when brewer Tonya Cornett finally gave in to a loyal customer and brewed an imperial India Pale Ale. "Imperial IPAs were just beginning to spread and (the customer) kept bugging me to make one," she says. She attended a symposium on the making of imperial IPAs and came home feeling like she was armed with enough knowledge to finally brew one. "I had the technique, but I didn't know what hops I was going to use," Cornett says. "In the end, it wound up being a process of elimination—what hops did I have enough of to make this beer?"

Cascade and Nugget hops eventually made the cut. Hop-Head was meant to be a one-off brew, but the beer was an instant hit, garnering several awards and making more than just one customer happy. However, Cornett is reluctant to make Hop-Head a standard beer because she fears it would make it less special. **LMo**

Tasting notes
Ferociously hoppy with plenty of burly hop resins on the nose, joined with a touch of grapefruit. It's dry and spritzy on the palate, with a hint of citrus lemon. The finish is long and bitter.

Tasting notes
Citrusy hops take center stage with a nimble malt backbone for balance. For a big, burly IPA, Hop-Head is light on its feet, with an unusually crisp finish and a coy suggestion of alcohol.

Hop Monkey IPA

Laurelwood Brewing Company | www.laurelwoodbrewpub.com

Country of origin United States
First brewed 2008
Alcohol content 6% abv
Serving temperature 48°F, 9°C

Hop Monkey IPA was originally going to be called "Cellarman," in honor of the people who work the physical, entry-level job at breweries. But the name needed too much explanation for the layperson and became awkward on the bottle's label. Laurelwood, the original organic brewery in Portland, Oregon, has many beers named after animals, so the brewers turned once again to the animal kingdom for this IPA's moniker. "In the brewing industry, the entry-level brewery employee is often called a 'brew monkey' or 'keg monkey,'" says head brewer Chad Kennedy. "We went for a variation on that theme with a nod toward our affinity for hops in our brewery."

Hop Monkey IPA was developed in response to customers' changing tastes. It replaced both an earlier IPA and a pale ale and was designed to appeal to both the IPA and pale ale drinker. Not wanting to brew a dulled-down IPA—especially in the hop-growing region of the Pacific Northwest—Laurelwood brewers created Hop Monkey IPA as a more balanced complement to its award-winning, hoppier Workhorse IPA, which is not available in bottles.

The beer is brewed with regionally grown two-row pale and crystal malts and four different varieties of hop: Cascade, Centennial, Columbus, and Ahtanum. Hop Monkey also takes advantage of the brewery's hop-back to capture all the hops' aroma and flavor compounds that can often be boiled away during the brewing process. If you happen to be flying out of Portland, you can pick up a bottle at one of two pubs the brewery has at Portland International Airport. **LMo**

Tasting notes

Pine and citrus notes take center stage with a bready backbone in Hop Monkey IPA. The body is fuller than expected, with a lush mouthfeel and smooth carbonation, making this a well-balanced beer with a full, but not over-the-top hop flavor.

Hop Rocker

Mac's Brewery | www.macs.co.nz

Country of origin New Zealand
First brewed 2006
Alcohol content 5% abv
Serving temperature 36°–39°F, 2°–4°C

From the unique ribbed bottle with its rip-tab cap to the chunky, almost childlike font used on the labels, Mac's Brewery has always tried to do things differently. When former All Black team member Terry McCashin and his wife Bev opened their Nelson brewery in 1981, they broke the stranglehold of New Zealand's two major brewers by creating a portfolio of beers that were brewed according to the Reinheitsgebot, the famous German beer purity law of 1516.

At a time when the country's mainstream brews were laden with sugars and caramel coloring (some still are), the first McCashin's beers, Mac's Gold (a golden lager), Black Mac (a dark lager), and Mac's Real Ale (a blend of the other two), were made with just four ingredients: malted barley, hops, yeast, and water. Kiwis embraced the idea of these so-called "natural" beers, and they soon attracted a cult following. They continue to be regarded as something out of the ordinary, with good reason.

Although Mac's offers a range of easy-to-drink golden lagers, brews like Sassy Red, a nod toward an English best bitter; Black Mac, a roasty, porterlike brew; and Great White, a quenching, Hoegaarden-like, spiced wheat beer, are widely appreciated by those seeking more flavor and interest in their glass. Mac's head brewer once described Hop Rocker as "New World Pilsener" and he's got a point. Two tangy and aromatic New Zealand–grown hop varieties, Nelson Sauvin and Cascade, are responsible for the distinctive grapelike and citrus-zest signature of this Kiwi interpretation of a classic European lager style. **GG**

Tasting notes

Pours a rich golden hue beneath a brilliant white head. The aroma and palate offer a combination of grainy malt sweetness and grassy and citrusy hop notes. The invigorating carbonation, crispness, and cleansing finish make it an ideal partner for pâtés or battered fish and chips.

Houblon Chouffe

Brasserie d'Achouffe | www.achouffe.be/en

Country of origin Belgium
First brewed 2006
Alcohol content 9% abv
Serving temperature 43°–50°F, 6°–10°C

These days, Brasserie d'Achouffe, which is hidden away in the small Ardennes village of the same name, is a subsidiary of the Duvel Moortgat brewery, as well as being a historic landmark. Founders and brothers-in-law Pierre Gobron and Fleming Chris Bauweraerts began brewing in 1982, at a time when the Belgian microbrewery revolution had just begun. Although Pierre was the driven brewer and technician, always motivated to search for something better, Chris was a born tradesman—and didn't he do well? These days, nobody in Belgium would consider describing Brasserie d'Achouffe as a small brewery! It's all a far cry from the origins at what was then called Brasserie de la Vallée des Fées (Brasserie of the Valley of Fairies), a name that was the full responsibility of the American importer...apparently.

Not only does Achouffe export a lot abroad, but the founders' curiosity has never been restricted to the cramped Belgian borders. Visits to the United States have resulted in collaboration, not only with another Duvel Moortgat subsidiary Ommegang, but also with the charismatic Garrett Oliver at Brooklyn Brewery. No wonder the typical American IPA tickled the Chouffe brewers' imagination (and their palates), and this was the result.

Three different types of hops are used in the brew, producing 59 International Bitterness Units (IBUs measure the strength of a beer's bitterness). Given that some American IPAs have an IBU of 90 or even 120, this beer is nowhere near one of those hop monsters, but it's pretty powerful all the same! **JPa**

Tasting notes

Hazy yellowish beer with a head like whipped egg white. Hops waft up in a way that is more European than American; there is also a hint of dried mandarins. On the palate, some citrus, dry hops, tannins, and even pine. Resiny-oily mouthfeel and medium to well-bodied, dry aftertaste.

Hue Beer

Hue Brewery | www.huda.com.vn

Country of origin Vietnam
First brewed 1994
Alcohol content 5% abv
Serving temperature 46°–54°F, 8°–12°C

This refreshing lager has quickly gained popularity among fans of Asian produce and beer drinkers looking for a dry and light tipple with which to while away a hot evening. Hue was one of the first products to be exported to the United States after the end of the thirty-year U.S. embargo on Vietnamese goods that was enforced after the Vietnam War. It was happily received and is now garnering fans worldwide for its lightness and sweetness.

The Hue Brewery was set up in 1990 to brew fine-quality local beer. The brewery was founded by local businesses, the state, and a subsidiary company of the Danish brewer Carlsberg. One of its first products was Huda—the name is a contraction of Hue and Danish, to honor the brewery's partnership—and it is now the most popular beer in Central Vietnam. Hue itself was launched especially for export in 1994 to coincide with the lift in U.S. trade restrictions. The name Hue was chosen because the brewery felt it would be recognizably Vietnamese on the foreign markets.

Hue is made with barley, rice, hops, and yeast. The malts and hops are brought in from recommended worldwide suppliers and extensively checked for quality. The water used in the brewing process comes from the local Perfume River, which is fed by two natural springs and is named after the scented medicinal plants and flowers that grow along its banks. If you have a penchant for Vietnamese food, Hue beer is the perfect accompaniment; it's equally good on its own and is a great beer to enjoy on a balmy sunny evening. **JM**

Tasting notes

Pouring a translucent yellow color and sporting a thin white head, Hue has a slight hoppy aroma, with notes of rice flour and corn. It's light and slightly sweet tasting with a medium body, hints of straw and light malts, and a gentle hop finish.

Irie

Almond '22 | www.birraalmond.com

Country of origin Italy
First brewed 2004
Alcohol content 5% abv
Serving temperature 46°F, 8°C

Jurij Ferri's favorite part of the brewing process is developing the initial creative idea. Sitting at his desk, he loves to think about different ingredients and imagine how they might mix together and when to use them. Rather like a sorcerer's apprentice, Ferri first designs the beer in his mind, then starts to brew, all without producing small batches or undertaking quantity trials. This means that there is a wide range of beers, nine at the time of writing, but all of them share a clear Almond '22 style.

Malt and hops obviously provide the backbone of Almond '22's beers, but it seems that Ferri also enjoys playing about with herbs, spices, and honey. Many of his beers are enriched with unusual ingredients. Blanche de Valerie, for example, is enlivened by the addition of Sarawak black pepper cultivated in Borneo. Irie is a kind of paradigm of this sort of beer. It is 100 percent pilsner malt while the hops are Saaz and Fuggle in the first stage and Saaz is added again for the final aromatic hop. This is all fairly straightforward, but then the imagination of the brewer really starts to run wild: coriander, sweet and bitter orange peel, orange flowers, and rose buds are all added.

With the beer resting for sixty days (fifty for the second fermentation and maturation in the bottle), the end result is an elegant and charming unfiltered and unpasteurized ale, which is typical of Almond '22's beers. It is ideal to take out for a picnic with focaccia and Parma ham or perhaps a pasta dish with asparagus, a typical Milanese cutlet, or vegetables fried in batter. **MM**

Tasting notes

Pale golden and opalescent with thick and persistent foam. Very elegant aroma, which is rich in citrus notes, coriander, and rose petals. Dry and drinkable in the palate, with a nice long aftertaste that harks back to the floral notes on the nose. A real thirst-quenching beer.

Jacobsen Saaz Blonde

Husbryggeriet Jacobsen | www.jacobsenbryg.dk

Country of origin Denmark
First brewed 2005
Alcohol content 7.1% abv
Serving temperature 41°–44°F, 5°–7°C

There is something refreshing about Husbryggeriet Jacobsen, and it's not just its range of interesting specialty beers, which include an apple-flavored wheat beer, Bramley Wit (now discontinued), as well as Jacobsen Saaz Blonde. It's the fact that a global beer giant such as Carlsberg—currently the fourth biggest brewery group in the world—still devotes some of its energies to experimentation.

Such experiments are overseen by master brewer Jens Eiken in the brewery's pilot brewery in Valby, Copenhagen. Just like the aforementioned Bramley Wit, this beer is the creation of former brewer Morten Ibsen. It is a Belgian-style blond ale that takes its name from the distinguished Saaz hop from the Czech Republic. This hop has a famously herby, piney aroma. Extract of angelica, also known as "Nordic Ginseng," adds a distinct herb bitterness that complements the fruity taste of the yeast. The rich color is typical of a Belgian blond and comes from the use of pilsner malt and a bit of caramel malt, for sweetness. The result is a deliciously fruity, blond beer that makes a great alternative to white wine as an aperitif.

Like all Scandinavians, the Danes love to drink beer with food, a habit that should be more widely accepted in other parts of the world. All the Jacobsen beers come in larger-sized bottles that can be shared over lunch or dinner. The shape of the bottle was inspired by the old Carlsberg lighthouse next to the old brewery entrance, which was built to celebrate the installation of electric lighting in 1883. **ST**

Tasting notes
Fragrant tropical fruit and a touch of pine on the nose, followed by a dry and chewy palate with some spicy clovelike bitterness. Full flavored and mellow, it is very easy to drink for its strength. Try it with scallops and meaty fish dishes.

James Boag's Premium Lager

James Boag and Son | www.boags.com.au

Country of origin Australia
First brewed 1994
Alcohol content 5% abv
Serving temperature 39°F, 4°C

In 1999, headlines of Australian newspapers expressed a nation's fury at comments by the world's most famous beer writer, Michael Jackson. Not one to pull punches, the late Mr. Jackson had claimed at a beer tasting that Australians had a particular attachment to "very cold, very bland beer that is perhaps even colder and blander than the coldest and blandest of American beer."

While to some at that time these comments may have had a ring of truth about them, Philip Adkins, who was then the major shareholder and chief executive of James Boag and Son (and American to boot), leaped to the nation's defense and publicly accused Mr. Jackson of not having the nose or the palate to understand what he was drinking. Jackson responded by pointing out that he had recently praised James Boag's Premium Lager at a tasting, that Adkins was taking himself way too seriously, and in any event the comment was correct.

Adkins was outraged because he felt his brewery's flagship beer was being maligned. He was a very successful international merchant banker who had bought 10 percent of J. Boag and Son in 1992; in 1994, he set out to develop a world-class lager. To do so, he assembled a team of expert judges and asked them which attributes they would rank highly in a tasting. He worked backward from their findings to develop a beer that would match the criteria. James Boag's Premium Lager was the result. It continues to be a widely distributed, high-quality example of the type of beer most enjoyed by Australians. **DD**

Tasting notes

This golden lager offers the sweet smell of hops as it glistens beneath a vibrant white head. It follows through with a pure, clean taste and a crisp finish. This refreshing beer is perfect for a barbecue with a few mates.

James Squire Pilsener

Malt Shovel Brewery | www.malt-shovel.com.au

Country of origin Australia
First brewed 2000
Alcohol content 5% abv
Serving temperature 39°–44°F, 4°–7°C

With its climate, the move toward an icy cold lager in Australia was a natural one. Lager was first successfully brewed and promoted in Australia on a notable scale by the U.S. Foster brothers in 1888, one hundred years after the establishment of the colony of New South Wales. Although there was considerable debate among brewing circles as to the desirability of this new style of beer, within forty years the hardworking Australian public had eagerly adopted its new love, and, apart from the odd stout, porter, or ale, the transformation was complete.

It would be fair to say, however, that the beers that became entrenched during that period were more famous for their refreshing qualities than the classic aromas and delicate mouthfeel associated with the pilsners on which they are based. Although a strong beer drinking culture developed, for a long time beer diversity and quality in Australia was looking somewhat dire. This began to change in the 1980s, when microbreweries challenged the Australian public to think more about flavor rather than volume and temperature. American-Australian Chuck Hahn was at the forefront of these efforts, startling the Australian public with his first premium lager in 1988.

Hahn has probably done more to educate the Australian public about beer than anyone in the country's history. It is fair to say that most Australians' first premium beer experience would be through one of his brews. James Squire Pilsener is a good place to start as it is familiar while being a top example of the most competitive beer style in the world. **DD**

Tasting notes

Brilliantly golden, this beer offers up spicy and floral aromas before rewarding with a crisp mouthfeel and a tight, bitter finish. James Squire Pilsener can be enjoyed with oysters but also excels in playing a supporting role to the traditional Australian barbecue.

Jenlain Blonde

Brasserie Duyck | www.duyck.com

Country of origin France
First brewed 2005
Alcohol content 7.5% abv
Serving temperature 43°–46°F, 6°–8°C

The accepted wisdom about northern France's bières de garde is that they are malt accented and amber hued, but a tasting trip around the area will uncover many different shades of color, including a lot of blonds. It could be the influence of Belgian tripels and golden ales to the north, or it might be the effect of what is generally seen as the beer drinker's preference for a lighter-colored beer in the glass (hence the success of lagers). Maybe this was what Brasserie Duyck had in mind in 2005 when it brought Jenlain Blonde Bière de Garde into the world (although it had launched a now discontinued golden ale called Sebourg in 1993, which was named after a nearby village that had a tradition of blond bières de garde). Or maybe it looked at the success of fellow northerners, such as 3 Monts and Cuvée des Jonquilles, and thought it time to push the blond boat out (Sebourg was a mere 6 percent compared to the usual 7.5 percent of many beers in the region). Whatever the reason, this new entry to Duyck's portfolio was an immediate success, winning several awards in the wake of its debut.

Like its dark sibling, the blond is also "garded," laid down for forty days and nights in the massive maturing tanks that are such a feature of the brewery; the temperature is kept low during this time, and some of the beer is packaged in traditional champagne-style bottles with a cork and wire cage. For a genuine biére de garde experience, enjoy the beer in the local bar in Jenlain, just down the road from the brewery, or perhaps at a beer café in the city of Lille. **ATJ**

Tasting notes

Bright gold in the glass. Fresh and fruity nose with hints of lemon. The palate reverberates with slightly sweet and tart citrus notes, followed by hints of toffee and caramel. There is lemon in the finish plus breakfast cereal and a peppery hoppiness that lingers.

Jennas

Birra Ichnusa | www.birraichnusa.it

Country of origin Italy
First brewed 2006
Alcohol content 4.9% abv
Serving temperature 37°F, 3°C

In the Sardinian dialect, which is a different linguistic beast from Italian, Jennas means "door." In a certain way you could argue that Birra Ichnusa's beers are the doors to this beautiful island, a sort of entrance to the local way of life that involves sharing a beer among friends, as it does in most of Italy.

Amsicora Capra founded Birra Ichnusa in 1912 near Cagliari. He was a respected entrepreneur who was also involved in the wine business, and, thanks to his talent and experience, the brewery was soon doing extremely well in the regional market. This success has remained constant, and the beers brewed by Ichnusa are popular among Sardinians and the thousands of tourists that land on the island every year. Even after 1986, when Heineken Italia bought the brewery, Ichnusa remained a regional label, which is still regarded with great affection.

The brewery now produces three different beers, all bottom-fermented lagers: the classical Ichnusa, the stronger Ichnusa Speciale, and Jennas. At the moment, Jennas is the only beer produced in Italy by a large brewer that is unpasteurized. Outside Sardinia you can find it only in a few selected pubs.

Jennas is brewed with pale malt and Saaz hops. Microfiltration is a special technique that adds to the character of the beer and results in an honest and fresh lager, with a nice, delicate, hoppy aroma that is truly thirst quenching in the palate. It's definitely a beer to drink on it own, an all-day-round refreshing drink, but in Sardinia it also remains a good choice with local traditional food or pizza. **MM**

Tasting notes
Brilliant golden color with a thick, white foam. Delicate and fresh hoppy aroma and, after a while, some fruity notes of honey and malt. Light body and thirst quenching, Jennas leaves a nice but not too long hoppy aftertaste. Very pleasant to drink on a sunny afternoon.

Jever Pilsener

Friesisches Brauhaus zu Jever | www.jever.de

Country of origin Germany
First brewed 1934
Alcohol content 4.9% abv
Serving temperature 44°F, 7°C

To those drinkers who are used to the softer and cleaner flavored pilsners of the rest of Germany, this popular beer from the Freisland region, in the north of the country, can often come as a surprise: it is dry and bitter in a way that few German lagers are. For that reason, it has developed a cult following and large fan base not usually seen by breweries that are part of a big brewing group.

The brewery has had a checkered history since its foundation in 1848 in the town of Jever. In 1867, the founder died and his son sold it on. The second owner was succeeded by his son who was killed in World War I. Shortly after the war, the brewery was sold again, this time to the Hamburger Bavaria-St. Pauli-Brauerei. By 1934, the brewery entered a period of relative tranquillity, and its products became well known beyond the area where the brewery is located. Since 1994, the brewery has been sold twice and is now owned by the Radeberger Gruppe.

In 1887, a natural spring was found close to the brewery, which became the source for all Jever beers. In the years after World War II, the brewery's most popular beer was Jever Export. However, from the 1960s, Jever Pilsener began to grow in popularity and sales, and eventually overtook the Export, nudging it into the dustbin of beer history.

Jever Pilsener is made from pale malt and hopped with Hallertau and Tettnang. It is lagered for three months and is the flagship product of the brewery, whose other range of beers includes an alcohol-free pilsner, a beer pre-mixed with lime, and a dunkel. **RP**

Tasting notes

Clear gold in color, this beer sits beneath a modest white head. The aroma is of hops and crisp malt. The accented bitterness is immediately noticeable on tasting but is well balanced against the crisp, drying maltiness. Despite the dry and bitter aftertaste, drinkers should take another sip.

JHB

Oakham Ales | www.oakhamales.com

Country of origin England
First brewed 1993
Alcohol content 4.2% abv
Serving temperature 52°F, 11°C

Possibly the most significant trend to affect British brewing in recent times has been the development of the golden ale. In a country where brown has been best for centuries, the arrival of bright blond beers has offered a welcome change, and now there's barely a brewery in the land that does not have a lighter alternative in its portfolio.

One of the most successful of this new breed of refreshing, pale creations comes from Cambridgeshire. The bedrock of the Oakham Brewery business in Peterborough has been its award-winning golden ale, known usually by its initials of JHB. Spelled out in full, the name appears as Jeffrey Hudson Bitter. The said Mr. Hudson was a 17th-century royal courtier and a favorite of King Charles I and his queen, Henrietta Maria. What endeared Hudson to the monarchs was the fact that he was a midget (first impressions count for a lot, and Hudson made his in startling fashion by leaping out of a pie). He became a loyal companion and fought on the Royalists' side during the English Civil War.

The beer named in Hudson's honor is produced using low color Maris Otter malt, plus wheat malt, in the mash tun. Seasoning in the copper is provided by Mount Hood hops from the United States and English Challenger, both of which contribute in their own way to the spicy, zesty fruit character of the beer. The fact that JHB claimed the top prize in the Campaign for Real Ale's Champion Beer of Britain contest in 2001 testifies to both its quality and the ever-increasing popularity of golden ales in the United Kingdom. **JE**

Tasting notes

This pale, straw-colored ale is crisp, firmly bitter, and hoppy with plenty of zesty, peppery, grapefruit, and tangerine notes in both the enticing aroma and spritzy taste. Fruity hops continue to work their magic in the dry, bitter, long-lasting finish.

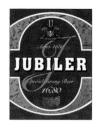

Jihlavský Grand

Pivovar Jihlava | www.pivovar-jihlava.cz

Jubiler

Pivovar Vyškov | www.pivovyskov.cz

Country of origin Czech Republic
First brewed 2001
Alcohol content 8% abv
Serving temperature 44°F, 7°C

Country of origin Czech Republic
First brewed 2004
Alcohol content 7.5% abv
Serving temperature 46°F, 8°C

Located in the woody highlands that form the boundary between Bohemia and Moravia, in the very middle of the Czech Republic, the town of Jihlava has a recorded brewing history dating back to at least 1348. It was famed as a center of medieval brewing.

The current brewery dates to 1860. Inspired by the strong brews in the town's heyday of silver mining in the Middle Ages, Jihlavský Grand was created by brewmaster and former owner Jan Kylberger in 2001. It is fermented in modern cyclindroconical vessels and brewed at 18 degrees Plato, a common strength for dark lagers in the Czech lands, though being orangey gold, it is closer to a German Maibock in color. It is cold conditioned for at least sixty days, sometimes longer.

K. Brewery Trade bought the Jihlava brewery in 2008. It remains noted for its pale and dark lagers under the Ježek brand that sell around the world. **ER**

One of the Czech Republic's last remaining state-owned breweries, Pivovar Vyškov is located in wine-loving South Moravia, not far from the borders with Austria and Slovakia. This unique brewery has little exposure beyond its home region; it is almost never seen on draft in Prague and global exports are minimal.

Created by brewmaster Dušan Táborský to celebrate the 325th anniversary of the brewery's founding, Jubiler's original gravity is set at 16.8 degrees Plato, putting it in the territory roughly between a German Maibock and a doppelbock. Unlike most bock beers, however, this Moravian strong lager has a pronounced Saaz hop presence to counterbalance its sweet Haná malt body, said to be due to a blending with the brewery's pale lager, Generál. Jubiler is conditioned for more than three months and ages well in the bottle, mellowing in hoppiness. **ER**

Tasting notes

A fine match for curries and other spicy fare, this unusual lager has a very fine carbonation. Look for slight spicy notes on the nose with a sweet, full mouthfeel, followed by a crisp finish.

Tasting notes

The alcohol is barely noticeable, making it very drinkable despite a richer body than the clear, deep gold might lead you to expect. Expect strong hop bitterness in the finish with a peppery aroma.

Juniper Pale Ale

Rogue Ales | www.rogue.com

Country of origin United States
First brewed 2001
Alcohol content 5.3% abv
Serving temperature 50°F, 10°C

Juniper Pale Ale was first brewed to commemorate the 2002 Winter Olympics in Salt Lake City, Utah. This pale ale is made with juniper berries, the same berries used to make gin, and Rogue Ales actually operates a gin distillery at its Newport, Oregon, brewery. Brewmaster John Maier liked the idea of adding the berries as they are a product indigenous to Rogue's home state.

The annual winter ale is touted as the perfect beer for the quintessential Thanksgiving dinner. "The juniper berries provide a dry, spicy finish that is a great complement to the relatively neutral flavor of most turkey dishes," says Brett Joyce, president of Rogue.

Rogue collectively calls its breweries, distilleries, retail outlets, fans, and workers by the title "Rogue Nation." In 2007, the turkey was named the official bird of Rogue Nation. To reflect this, the ale is dedicated on every bottle to "the turkey in each of us." **LMo**

Tasting notes
Golden yellow color. On the nose, it is fresh, grassy, and fruity with hints of toffee. A rich mouthful of maltiness is balanced by citrus fruit, with peppery notes. A dry, bittersweet finish.

Karlovačko Svijetlo Pivo

Karlovačka Brewery | www.karlovacko.hr

Country of origin Croatia
First brewed 1854
Alcohol content 5.4% abv
Serving temperature 39°–43°F, 4°–6°C

Croatia was once a land of wine, but now you're much more likely to see people raising a pint glass than studying the wine list. One can't help thinking that it is Croatian beers such as Karlovačko that have helped to end the grape's reign. Located in the city of Karlovač, which lies on four rivers, the brewery draws on the area's rich source of natural mineral springs to get high-quality water to use in its beers.

Initially, the beer produced at Karlovačka Brewery was solely for the enjoyment of the army's top brass, but at the turn of the 20th century the brewery was modernized and production increased. The man behind stabilizing the brew quality to allow for the higher output was Austrian Vilim Wambrechtshamer. His techniques were clearly successful. Today Karlovačka is the second largest brewery in Croatia and was bought by Heineken in 2003. **JM**

Tasting notes
A clean, crisp pilsner with a sweet malt aroma showing notes of floral hops. On the tongue, grainy malts and spicy hops balance sweet and biscuity flavors. Bitter and hoppy aftertaste.

Kasteel Cru

Brasserie de Licorne | www.kasteelcru.co.uk

Country of origin France
First brewed 2001
Alcohol content 5.2% abv
Serving temperature 44°F, 7°C

Kasteel Cru is brewed by Brasserie de Licorne (Unicorn Brewery) in the town of Saverne in the Alsace region of France, an area where German brewing know-how and French inspiration combine to good effect. The light, sweet maltiness of the beer comes from its locally sourced spring barley mashed with water from the Vosges Mountains. Hallertau hops from Germany create a subtle bitterness, but the undoubted *pièce de resistance* is the use of champagne yeast for a balanced natural acidity with no astringency, which also creates its distinctive rising bubbles and sharply defined white foam in the glass. It is the only beer in this style made entirely in France, and even its bottle is produced by glass moulders in Reims, deep in champagne country. Take-off occurred in 2001, after the company had identified a gap in the market for a premium lager that appealed as much to women as men.

La Brasserie de Licorne was established in 1845 and was taken over by the German Karlsbräu in 1989, which totally modernized its plant and production methods. Coors Brewing Company now owns it, under whose guidance annual production has reached 22 million gallons (1 million hl), with a turnover of more than U.S. $200 million.

The bright, crisp, and lively Kasteel Cru makes the perfect aperitif—those champagne-style bubbles animate the appetite—and it delivers well while sipping in summer when work is at an end for the day. It accompanies light meat dishes—chicken and pork—while a lager of this exuberance would also be a perfect match for most types of fish. **AG**

Tasting notes

Delicate on the eye and pale straw in appearance, with streaming bubbles rising into a sharp white foam. The aroma is light and has slightly fruitlike characteristics. It delivers a light mouthfeel with a sweet-sour balance and a clean, crisp finish.

King Cobra

Cobra Beer | www.cobrabeer.com

Country of origin Belgium
First brewed 2005
Alcohol content 8% abv
Serving temperature 46°F, 8°C

An Indian lager, brewed in Poland, bottled in Belgium, and marketed around the world by a British company is a pretty intriguing mix of factors with which to launch a new beer. King Cobra is essentially a stronger, classier version of the standard, 5 percent Cobra lager, a beer devised by Karan Bilimoria, the Oxbridge-educated son of an Indian army general, who saw a gap in the market for a "less bloating" beer for washing down spicy curries. Cobra was devised together with the help of a Czech brewmaster and was brewed first in India for export to the United Kingdom. Later, production switched to Charles Wells in Bedford, England, but the brand is once more brewed in India today, as well as elsewhere around the world.

Initially King Cobra was brewed at Brouwar Belgia, an offshoot of Palm Breweries in Poland, and, after primary fermentation, was trunked to Rodenbach in Belgium for bottling in champagne-style glassware. Today, both brewing and bottling takes place at Rodenbach, producing a beer that combines the grainy sweetness of an Asian lager (from its grist of rice and maize as well as barley) with tropical fruit notes from the fermentation process. German Hallertau hops add a balancing bitterness. The beer is bottled flat, but thanks to the addition of a Belgian yeast strain used by Trappist monks and two weeks of warm storage at the brewery before release, it undergoes a secondary fermentation in the bottle that adds a natural sparkle of carbonation. The lightness of touch of this process helps keep the beer crisp and quaffable, despite the 8 percent alcohol. **JE**

Tasting notes

Sweet cereals and juicy melon in the aroma follow through into the crisp, bittersweet taste of this golden beer that also offers hints of pear. Hops and bitterness develop more in the dry, warming finish, with fruit lingering. Easy to drink and well carbonated.

King Pilsner

King Brewery | www.kingbrewery.ca

Country of origin Canada
First brewed 2002
Alcohol content 4.8% abv
Serving temperature 41°F, 5°C

Just north of Toronto in the southern part of the province of Ontario lies the small hamlet of Nobleton, a part of King Township. And, on an otherwise unremarkable stretch of road just outside the modest town center you will find the King Brewery, one of a third wave of craft breweries that arrived on the local beer scene following the turn of the millennium.

The labor of love of former home-brewer Phil DiFonzo, King is a traditionalist's delight, crafting as it does only two regular brands, both lagers brewed according to strict ingredient and stylistic controls. A notorious perfectionist, DiFonzo personally oversees virtually all aspects of the operation, scheduling, maintaining, brewing, and occasionally delivering the beer personally.

For his first flagship product, DiFonzo wanted to brew a beer style the province had not yet seen domestically produced—the Czech-style Bohemian pilsner. To this end, he imported all his ingredients, even sourcing a special pilsner malt, and played with his recipe until he felt he had it just right. Somewhat unusually for his home market, he even distills his brewing water and remineralizes it so that it resembles the water of the town of Pilsen, where this style of beer was born in the 19th century.

Launched as a draft-only brand, King Pilsner was bottled slightly more than a year later and then went on to find a strong foothold in the Greater Toronto area market. In particular, it is favored by many of the region's finer dining establishments, often as one of only a handful of beers carried. **SB**

Tasting notes

Following a perfumed, almost floral arrival on the nose, this lager offers a quenching mix of well-balanced, faintly butterscotchy malt and firm, drying hoppiness. While just off-dry in the body, it finishes with an appetizing smack of almost dusty bitterness.

Kirin Ichiban

Kirin Brewery | www.kirin.com

Country of origin Japan
First brewed 1990
Alcohol content 5% abv
Serving temperature 37°–41°F, 3°–5°C

Kirin Ichiban Shibori boasts a unique claim to fame, one happily uncontested by the majority of beers in the world. It is, say its brewers, the world's most expensively produced beer. Unlike other beers that sparge the mash with hot water to extract lingering fermentable sugars, for Kirin Ichiban this practice is eschewed. Instead, there is only one draining of wort from the mash. This wort should contain less bitter tasting tannins, arguably resulting in a beer that is mild and smooth to taste.

This production process is front and center in the marketing of the brand in Japan: the literal translation for Ichiban Shibori is "first press." This process results in a not inconsiderable loss of fermentable extract, estimated at 15 to 20 percent less than the achievable total from the sparging norm. Given that Kirin Ichiban doesn't command a higher price point compared with its traditionally sparged super-premium competitors, it takes real commitment on the part of Kirin to maintain this process.

Ichiban's grist is made up largely of malted barley. To be described as a "beer" in Japan, thanks to the country's absurd system of beer taxation based on the composition of its base raw material, malted barley content must comprise in excess of two-thirds of the grist. There are also additions of rice and maize. Its hop bill includes Saaz from the Czech Republic and three varieties from Germany's Hallertau region.

Does an expensive brewing process result in a demonstrably better-tasting beer? There's only one way to be certain. **LN**

Tasting notes

The color is of lightly shaded straw. The nose offers faint citrus hops and hints of green apple. Vigorous carbonation generates sparkle, a soft meringue of foam, and pleasing white lacing. Ichiban delights with full-bodied chewiness and is a beer to be savored with rapturous slow intensity.

Kiwanda Cream Ale

Pelican Pub & Brewery | www.pelicanbrewery.com

Country of origin United States
First brewed 1996
Alcohol content 5.2% abv
Serving temperature 44°F, 7°C

While the Pelican Pub and Brewery was still in the planning stages, brewmaster Darron Welch was trying to decide what he should brew as the lightest beer they would offer at the brewpub. He recalled the cream ales of the 19th century, which were essentially the American ale brewer's response to the new influx of lagers being brewed by countless new German-American brewers who were settling in the United States. In his estimation, they were like "ale-fermented pre-Prohibition American Pilsner, with a lagering period added to the post-fermentation maturation, which gave the beer pilsner characteristics." Welch loved the idea of making a hybrid-style beer and also one of the few "historically American beer styles."

Kiwanda Cream Ale was named for Cape Kiwanda State Natural Area, which is located in the same town as the brewpub, Pacific City, Oregon. The beer has garnered numerous awards, including three gold medals at the Great American Beer Festival, together with a gold and silver medal at the World Beer Cup. Such success helped propel Pelican into the spotlight; they have been named Brewpub of the Year at the Great American Beer Festival three times—the only brewery to achieve that accolade.

Kiwanda Cream Ale is actually a single-hop beer, with only Mount Hood going into the mix, but that's done strictly to get the specific character of the aroma, flavor, and bitterness that the beer calls for. Three malts are used: two-row pale, Carapils, and flaked barley. The result is a rare beer: light in color and body, but full of flavor, texture, and character. **JB**

Tasting notes

Kiwanda Cream Ale has a bright golden hue and a fluffy white head with great lace. The nose is filled with fruit and floral aromas. The taste starts out creamy and very refreshing, with clean malt flavors balanced by fruity hop character. It's effervescent throughout, with a sweet finish.

Knappstein Reserve Lager

Knappstein Enterprise Brewery | www.knappstein.com.au

Country of origin Australia
First brewed 2006
Alcohol content 5.6% abv
Serving temperature 46°F, 8°C

While Australian lawmakers have never prohibited the sale of beer, World War I and the agitation of the temperance movements saw the introduction of six o'clock closings of pubs in most Australian states. The rationale varied from supporting the war effort to improving public morals. While it is doubtful that either of these aims was achieved, the laws did result in the growth of an infamous drinking culture known as the "six o'clock swill" in which men stood shoulder to shoulder in crowded pubs, ordering and drinking as many beers as could be physically consumed during the time from when they finished work to six o'clock.

Another, less considered consequence of these laws was the effect on Australia's small breweries. One casualty was the Enterprise Brewery in Clare, South Australia, which had been brewing beer to support the local copper miners since 1878. It closed within twelve months of the reduced trading hours coming into effect. To the surprise of many overseas visitors, South Australia kept its World War I trading hours until 1967. The Enterprise Winery was established at the brewing site by Tim Knappstein in 1969, and in 2006 the Enterprise Brewery was brought back to life after an absence of almost a century. By this time, Clare and the surrounding region had become famous for its Riesling in particular; Knappstein Reserve Lager was designed by winemakers as a sophisticated alternative. Beautifully presented, the beer is only available in bottles and is clearly targeted at those who would prefer to drink their lagers in the same considered manner in which they drink their wine. **DD**

Tasting notes

You will be greeted with a spectacular fruit aroma of lychee and passion fruit followed by citrus and pine notes on the palate reminiscent of a Sauvignon Blanc. A bitter finish is perfect for washing down the remnants of seared scallops and a seasonal salad.

Koutská Desítka

Pivovar Kout na Šumavě | www.pivovarkout.cz

Country of origin Czech Republic
First brewed 2006
Alcohol content 4% abv
Serving temperature 44°F, 7°C

The medium-to-low-alcohol beers known as *výčepní pivo* in Czech and Schankbier in German are rarely considered flagship brews. Instead, these lagers are the traditional session beers and table brews of central Europe—a step down in prestige, strength, and heft from the richer, stronger lagers. However, this is not quite the case with Koutská Desítka. This beer displays many of the features of a great flagship pilsner, including a pronounced Saaz hop aroma, a rich malt body that belies the high-volume session beer concept, and a stark bitterness in the finish.

Although the producer, Pivovar Kout na Šumavě, is a relative newcomer, it is among the region's most traditional. The brewery does not pasteurize its beers, and eschews grain adjuncts and hop extracts, instead using 100 percent Czech barley malt and the great Saaz semi-early red hop varietal from Bohemia's Žatec region. Water comes from two underground lakes in the thick Šumava forest, often referred to by the German name of Böhmerwald. All beers lager for at least two months under the watch of brewmaster Bohuslav Hlavsa, who came to Pivovar Kout na Šumavě after thirty years at the region's now-defunct Domažlice brewery. **ER**

Tasting notes
Pours a clear, deep gold topped by a thick white crown. There is a pronounced Saaz hop aroma in the nose with hoppy notes in the finish surrounding a hearty malt corpulence.

Koutská Nefiltrovaná Dvanáctka

Pivovar Kout na Šumavě | www.pivovarkout.cz

Country of origin Czech Republic
First brewed 2006
Alcohol content 5% abv
Serving temperature 44°F, 7°C

The reappearance of Koutská Nefiltrovaná Dvanáctka marks a minor miracle in the history of Czech brewing. The brewery, located in the tiny forest town of Kout na Šumavě, is believed to date at least from the end of the Thirty Years' War, though the building's earliest written reference is from 1736. As with all Czech breweries, it was nationalized after World War II. For twenty-five years, the brewery was part of various Communist-era production groups, until the central planners shuttered it in 1971. It was mostly a ruin when purchased in 2001 by Jan Skala. However, the original chimney was still intact, and one of the two boilers, dating from 1908, was discovered to be in working condition.

The first few years were spent clearing away rubble and trash. During the reconstruction of the brewery's boiler room, an original recipe for the beer was discovered. Written by hand in the ancient Schwabach style of black-letter script, it was largely unintelligible, but after repeated efforts, the old recipe was deciphered. Today, both clear and cloudy versions of the beer are produced, but it is the semi-opaque Nefiltrovaná Dvanáctka ("unfiltered twelver") that seems to transcend the limits of the genre. **ER**

Tasting notes
This traditional unfiltered beer pours a cloudy deep gold, with more malt and a bit less hop aroma than Koutská Desítka. It has moderate carbonation and a prickly finish.

La Chouffe

Brasserie d'Achouffe | www.achouffe.be

Country of origin Belgium
First brewed 1982
Alcohol content 8% abv
Serving temperature 46°F, 8°C

When brothers-in-law Christian Bauweraerts and Pierre Gobron opened their small "hobby brewery" in the Ardennes region of Belgium in the early 1980s, they decided to play on the name of their home village of Achouffe and invent a mascot of sorts for their beers in the form of a white-bearded elf, henceforth known as a "chouffe." The word for beer is feminine in French, so their first brand was christened "La Chouffe."

What made d'Achouffe's success that much more remarkable was that the brewery's flagship brand was not only strong and spiced, but also available exclusively in a 25-ounce (750-ml) bottle. Then again, such characteristics may also have been why La Chouffe and its sister brand, Mc Chouffe, stood out on beer store shelves as they did. Having grown their business through close to a quarter century, Bauweraerts and Gobron decided in the summer of 2006 to sell to the much larger brewing company Duvel Moortgat. While the move made some Chouffe fans understandably nervous, for fear the beers would be altered, or worse, the subsequent years proved Duvel Moortgat to be able guardians of the elves, if anything improving the overall character and quality of the quirky ales. **SB**

Tasting notes
Refreshing despite its strength, the sometimes overwhelming coriander spicing of this golden ale seems to be more in balance with the honeyish malt since Duvel purchased the brewery.

La Choulette Des Sans Culottes

Brasserie La Choulette | www.lachoulette.com

Country of origin France
First brewed 1983
Alcohol content 7% abv
Serving temperature 46°F, 8°C

Alphonse Dhaussy brewed the first La Choulette beer in 1981, four years after he had taken over the Brasserie Bourgeois-Lecerf in Hordain. Brewing know-how had been handed down to him by his grandfather Jules, who had been producing traditional farmhouse beers since 1895. The name change to La Choulette came from Alphonse's son Alain, as a homage to an almost-forgotten local sport that is similar to golf. The Sans Culottes part of the name refers to the French Revolutionaries of 1789 and their mode of dress, which set them apart from the culottes-wearing ruling class. The Republican Guard later took up the garb and their striped leg-wear is depicted on the beer's label.

All of La Choulette's products are top-fermented, unpasteurized, and filtered. They are also fermented with a specially developed yeast that works well at temperatures of 60 to 65 degrees Fahrenheit (16°–18°C). Fermentation takes between five and eight days, with beers conditioned for up to six weeks.

Aficionados advise drinking La Choulette beers young as they develop a strong and hefty maltiness within a year; fans of strong malty beers might disagree. La Choulette Des Sans Culottes won a gold medal at the 1995 World Beer Championships. **AG**

Tasting notes
A deep golden hue unveils rich fruit aromas that continue in the flavor before being layered with sweet malt. It works through levels of bittersweetness, mellowness, and vinous depth.

La Gauloise Blonde

Brasserie du Bocq | www.bocq.be

Country of origin Belgium
First brewed 1994
Alcohol content 6.3% abv
Serving temperature 41°–54°F, 5°–12°C

Farmer Martin Belot first built a brewery on his property at Purnode, in the rolling countryside of the Condroz region in Namur province, in 1858, mainly to have something productive to do during winter. Belot named it after the Bocq River, a tributary of the Meuse that runs nearby. The first Gauloise beer, a strong brown ale, appeared in 1920, the name referring to the area's Celtic, pre-Christian past. For a while, the labels depicted Ceres, the Roman goddess of agriculture.

For decades the brewery remained a sideline, albeit with a strong local reputation. Then in 1960 Belot's descendants closed the farm to concentrate on brewing. In 1967, they acquired the Saison Régal brand and began to focus on traditional, bottle-conditioned ales rather than competing in the rapidly expanding market for pils-style lagers. This decision placed them well for when the international market for fine Belgian ale began to boom. Today the family-owned du Bocq is one of the bigger specialist producers, exporting its beers to the rest of Europe and Japan, and handling a long list of contracts and custom-labeled beers.

Part of its recent success has been a canny brand extension of its oldest beer, the venerable brown ale, La Gauloise. First produced in 1994, La Gauloise Blonde was an overdue response to the growing popularity of lighter-colored beers. Like its companions, it is cold matured in tanks, filtered, retanked at a warmer temperature, then bottled with a fresh dose of yeast and sugar. The result is a relatively light but well-made ale, broadly in the abbey style, and recommended to accompany fish, white meats, and poultry. **DdM**

Tasting notes

Hazy yellow gold with a loose white head and a toffee vanilla aroma with some hops and yeasty esters, this has a clean but full citric, banana-tinged palate with restrained leafy hops leading to more citrus and mild hops in a pleasantly rounded finish.

La Goudale

Les Brasseurs des Gayant | www.brasseurs-gayant.com

Country of origin France
First brewed 1994
Alcohol content 7.2% abv
Serving temperature 50°–55°F, 10°–13°C

Gayant is one of the biggest brewers in the bière de garde region of northern France. It is a business with a history going back to 1919, when several of the local brewers got together to form one brewery after the town of Douai was severely damaged in World War I. "Gayant" is French for "giant," and the name celebrates the town's annual procession of giant figures, an old Flemish tradition that harks back to the days when the area was part of the Spanish Empire.

Giant by name, giant by nature, Gayant is brewing on an industrial scale; nearly 4.8 million gallons (180,000 hl) of various beers, including the superstrong La Bière du Démon; a beer-and-tequila mix called Tequieros; and a spicy Christmas beer, St. Landelin, are produced annually. It is at the opposite scale of, for example, fellow bière de garde producer Brasserie Thiriez. The brewery also has a small pilot microbrewery where the company's brewing supremo Alain Dessy tries out new recipes.

Gayant's best seller is La Goudale, which the brewery claims is brewed to an ancient medieval recipe that was found in an equally ancient library, although it only emerged in 1994. A pale, aromatic beer that has the feel of an abbey beer, it has French-grown barley in the mash (a certain amount of malted wheat is also used), while hops also come from France. After the brew, the beer undergoes a week's top-fermentation and then is conditioned for between two to three weeks. It is packaged in the traditional bière de garde corked bottle, though it is also available in the less romantic form of cans. **ATJ**

Tasting notes

Dark gold, apricot yellow in color. Nose has crisp malt and aromatic tropical fruit notes. On the palate, there are malty, bready, toffee, caramel, and peppery notes, plus a hint of malt loaf sweetness. Its strength means that there is also alcoholic warmth. Finish is dry with citrus in the background.

La Rulles Blonde

Brasserie Artisinale de Rulles | www.larulles.be

Country of origin Belgium
First brewed 2000
Alcohol content 7% abv
Serving temperature 46°–50°F, 8°–10°C

La Rulles proudly labels its products "Bière de Gaume," establishing instant provenance for beers that are surprisingly new arrivals. The Gaume is part of the Belgian province of Luxembourg in the far southeast of the country, a rolling, rocky landscape that spills south from the Ardennes massif. It once boasted a rich brewing tradition. At the end of the 19th century, there were around fifty breweries, many of them farm-based, slaking the thirst of a largely agricultural population. By 1990, only two—the tiny Gigi and the Trappist brewery of Orval—survived.

It is gratifying, then, that the recent surge of interest in Belgian beer has also swept through this remote corner, with three excellent newly established microbreweries busy re-creating a regional beer culture. Of these, Rulles is arguably the leading light. Its founder, former chemist Grégory Verhelst, isn't Gaumais by birth, but his wife is, and it was in an old farm in the Gaumais village of Rulles that he began developing his recipes. His first plan was to work on only one beer—this blond—until it had reached perfection: rejecting spices and opting for bottle conditioning in 25-ounce (750-ml) bottles.

With one eye on contemporary international trends, the blond is much more aromatic and hoppy than is typical in Belgium, with amber malt giving a fuller body than usual for this style. There's also a detectable dose of aged, sour flavors. It remains one of the more distinctive beers to have emerged from the country in the past decade, rocketing its creator to a well-deserved reputation almost overnight. **DdM**

Tasting notes

La Rulles Blonde is a deep gold beer with a creamy off-white head, honey and peaches in the aroma, and a fresh, perfumed, seedy palate with sweet fruit turning drying and chewy. A notable dose of hops turns bitterish over biscuity malt in the finish.

La Rulles Estivale

Brasserie Artisanale de Rulles | www.larulles.be

Country of origin Belgium
First brewed 2004
Alcohol content 5.2% abv
Serving temperature 43°–46°F, 6°–8°C

Is being a brewer in Wallonia fun? One would think so, considering the number of microbreweries that have sprouted up in the region over the past twenty years. It certainly has its drawbacks, though. Of course there is the crushing grasp the big brewers and distributors have, but beyond that, being a microbrewer seems to come with a few requirements, such as having a full range of beers: blond, blanche, ambrée, and brune. There's a degree of flexibility in that one of these can be exchanged for a triple, but these unspoken rules can lead to some predictability in a brewery's range.

This was the route that La Rulles's founder Grégory Verhelst seemed to be taking, but fate, thankfully, has led him in other more inspirational directions. One of the first changes from the usual range of beers was the creation of a Cuvée de l'Anniversaire starting in 2000; this was intended to be an annual anniversary beer. The fourth in that list in 2004, which was made as a light refreshing ale for the summer months, proved such a success that it returned the following year. It was named Estivale—effectively "summer ale"—and since then has been a permanent offering.

The ale gained enormous popularity seemingly overnight. This could well be said about most beers brought into the world by Verhelst, but Estivale had an extra boost when the famous Delirium Café (whose beer list boasts well over 2,000 beers) in Brussels put it on tap and people raved about it. The brewery uses pale and blond malts in the mix and American hops; the brewery describes it as "pretty bitter" and recommends drinking it rather cool. **JPa**

Tasting notes

Veiled orange golden beer with a wild head. A fine hop nose, combined with honey and nectar-laden blossoms, invites sampling. The palate will yield more honey, with a very hop-bitter finish and citrusy hints. The balance is just perfect, and you'll end up more than refreshed.

La Rulles Triple

Brasserie Artisinale de Rulles | www.larulles.be

Country of origin Belgium
First brewed 2003
Alcohol content 8.4% abv
Serving temperature 46°–50°F, 8°–10°C

Grégory Verhelst, founder of Brasserie Artisinale de Rulles, started experimenting seriously with brewing in 1998. His first commercial brew was in 2000, and three short years later he had to open up a new generously sized storage space behind his house (this was in full use as early as 2006). A fair share of his beers travel across the globe. All of this is achieved with the aid of two friends and his father-in-law. Incidentally, he operates a 750-gallon (30-hl) plant.

Despite his devotion to going his own bittersweet brewing way, he also felt the need to brew some classics. A tripel is never amiss from a brewery's range, and there's always place for a good one—like this. Verhelst aimed for something with a bit of body, but without abandoning his own ideas about bitterness; it is doubtful if there is a more bitter tripel in Belgium.

La Rulles's Triple has a fuller body than most tripels, which is not that surprising, given that no pure sugars are added; used with other tripels it gives a higher degree of fermentation and a thinner body. Fermentation takes twelve days, with lagering for one week. Unlike many of his compatriots, Verhelst uses American hops—Warrior, Cascade, and Amarillo—and in pellet form. The beer is unpasteurized and refermented in the bottle, which helps add to its lustrous quality.

The distinctive label of La Rulles Triple carries an image of the brewery's mascot—the flat-capped, slightly mischievous-looking Marcel le Rullot. On it he contemplates a glass of the tripel that just might be the Holy Grail. **JPa**

Tasting notes

Peach-colored beer. Herbal nose, with touches of ginger, laurel, and leafy herbs adding to the bouquet. Fresh, lively taste with mint and even camphor on the palate, becoming dry-hoppy and ending with more fruity, citrusy notes. Well bodied for a tripel.

La Trappe Blond

Bierbrouwerij de Koningshoeven | www.latrappe.nl

Country of origin Netherlands
First brewed 1928
Alcohol content 6.5% abv
Serving temperature 54°–61°F, 12°–16°C

A beer called La Trappe Blond was first brewed in 1928, when like other European countries, the Netherlands had seen the rise of a vociferous prohibitionist movement. The monks had settled on land near Tilburg on the Belgian-Dutch border in the 19th century after leaving their original home in Normandy. Yet, no one should have underestimated the hardnosed commercialism at the heart of Koningshoeven (or "de Schaapskooi," as it was called then). This was, after all, a brewery that produced many other drinks, such as lemonade, in addition to beer.

At the time the Blond was introduced—called a "light" beer, it had an alcohol content of 4 percent—the brewery was mainly making bottom-fermenting beers, a situation that after World War II saw pils production at the heart of the brewery—the beer was given the name Trappist Pils. The revival of Trappist brewing south of Belgium led to a change of heart in the 1980s and the monks created the La Trappe range.

In 1999, La Trappe Blond was relaunched in the Trappist style with top-fermenting yeast, English hops, and pale malt. It replaced a beer called Enkel, which was seen as the monks' everyday beer (they drank a bottle daily). Again, this was not the most favorable time to launch a beer, given that this was the year when Bierbrouwerij de Koningshoeven lost its Trappist beer status due to the involvement of Bavaria, a Dutch brewery dealing in mass-market beers. In 2005, the agreement between the monks and Bavaria was modified so that the brewery could stand again as an officially recognized Trappist brewery. **RP**

Tasting notes

As the name might suggest, a light-colored blond ale with a soft fruity nose. On the palate, slightly sweet with floral and citric notes. The aftertaste is softly bitter. The mildness of the flavors makes this beer ideal for pairing with stronger-flavored foods.

Lagunitas Pils

Lagunitas Brewing Company | www.lagunitas.com

Country of origin United States
First brewed 1996
Alcohol content 5.3% abv
Serving temperature 39°–44°F, 4°–7°C

"I think this is our best beer," says Lagunitas founder Tony Magee. This may seem like a surprising statement for a brewery that has built its reputation mostly on crunchy, counterculture ales with Frank Zappa-referenced names. But, as he says, "Big IPAs are comparatively easy to make, like chili or jambalaya. But making a light broth is perilous. . . . A well-made lager is about the most difficult thing there is to brew." That doesn't mean that this is a shy, retiring beer. "I wanted to formulate the lager equivalent of our IPA. Comparing the malt bill and hop bitterness, the two beers are very close in structure, but they could not be more different," says Magee.

Pilsner is a style that sprang to life in Bohemia in 1842, driven by the craze for pale beer that IPA ignited. So it's not crazy to draw comparisons between the two. "I wanted to use the essential ingredients of Pilsner Urquell (their yeast and Saaz hops), but wanted to use American malt and water, to give it our own 'local' characteristics and make it our own."

When fresh, pilsner is a glorious beer, which helps one understand why its Czech homeland has one of the highest per capita rates of beer consumption on earth. Successful pilsner brewing is highly reliant on using the best quality ingredients, plus relentless attention to details. It is a fleeting pleasure. Once brewed it is vulnerable to the ravages of time. The weeks required to cross an ocean suck the life out of lighter beers like pilsners, so you're better off sticking with examples brewed on your own continent. Which makes Californians grateful for Lagunitas. **RM**

Tasting notes

Super-bright, spicy, Saaz hops with hints of grassiness and a clean maltiness on the nose. On the palate, a moderate body, but not particularly sweet, with a robust bitterness building. Finishes with a long, elegant, and herbal sort of bitterness.

L'Angelus

Brasserie d'Annœullin | www.top-biere.com

Country of origin France
First brewed 1988
Alcohol content 7% abv
Serving temperature 48°F, 9°C

Farmer Auguste Maille had long been brewing in the village of Annœullin, midway between Lille and Lens in northern France, before he decided to make it a business venture in 1905. Despite the Nord-Pas-de-Calais region being close to the frontline in two world wars, with the enormous upheavals that resulted, the brewery is still owned by Monsieur Maille's direct descendants. Continuing the passionately traditional craft are Bertrand and Yolande Lepers and their son Charles, who represent the fifth and the sixth generations of the family. Understandably, the business is better known after the village it is situated in rather than its official title of Brasserie Lepers.

All their beers undergo a week's fermentation in horizontal tanks and up to five weeks of "garde," prior to bottling. L'Angelus's label and voluptuously shaped glass depict a peasant couple working in a field and offering thanks to God. The image was inspired by Jean-François Millet's iconic trio of 19th-century realist paintings, *The Sower*, *The Gleaners*, and *The Angelus* (originally called *Prayer for the Potato Crop*). This top-fermented beer, which is packaged in a distinctive corked bottle, won a gold medal in the Concours Général Agricole de Paris in 2007 and 2009.

Among the brewery's other offerings is their springtime beer, L'Angelus de Mars (5.5 percent), golden amber in color with an aromatic nose, a surprising dark malt character, and a light citrus hop touch. Another seasonal is L'Angelus de Noel (7.5 percent), a full, sweet, and malty Christmas beer with lingering caramel notes on the palate. **AG**

Tasting notes

L'Angelus is pale gold in color and has a creamy head. The beer is lemony and floral on the nose, which allows the herbal hops to temporarily take control on the palate before ending in a complex, orange-tinged, malt finish.

Le Freak

Green Flash Brewing
www.greenflashbrew.com

Country of origin United States
First brewed 2006
Alcohol content 9.2% abv
Serving temperature 55°F, 13°C

The "green" in Green Flash does not refer to the abundant use of hops that occurs with most of the beers coming out of this San Diego–located brewery. Green flash describes the natural phenomenon occurring at sunrise or sunset in coastal areas when part of the sun flashes a different color, usually green.

Not only will Green Flash brewmaster Chuck Silva pack hops into beers where they are expected, but also some where they may surprise, such as Le Freak. This is one of a growing number of crossbred beers. Le Freak begins with the same malt base as in Green Flash Imperial IPA, rather than the Tripel, and is jammed with hops from the American northwest, to the tune of 101 IBUs. For fermentation, Silva's house yeast, an American strain, combines with a Belgian strain to bring Le Freak forward, creating the fruit-and-spice character common in Belgian tripels. **SH**

Tasting notes
Pours a rather cloudy orange. Nose grassy with citrus notes, underlying sweetness as it warms. More hops in the flavor, orange marmalade and subtle spiciness. Ends on bitter notes.

Liberty Ale

Anchor Brewing Company
www.anchorbrewing.com

Country of origin United States
First brewed 1975
Alcohol content 6% abv
Serving temperature 46°F, 8°C

In 1975, Anchor started the annual tradition of brewing a Christmas ale. Each batch was different, giving Anchor's president Fritz Maytag and his brewers a chance to experiment with new things. In 1983, Anchor brewed its Christmas Ale with pale malts and Cascade hops; it was also dry hopped with Cascade. The beer was an absolute hit and Maytag decided to add it to their permanent repertoire under the name Liberty Ale.

It was a groundbreaking beer for the United States. Liberty was one of the first beers to feature Cascade hops, then virtually unknown to most brewers. Today they are regarded as the quintessential American hop, valued for their exuberant citrus, piney, and resinous qualities, and have opened the door to other varieties. Liberty Ale was the first in a new generation of beers that would highlight more unique American hop varieties and help spark the craft beer revolution. **MO**

Tasting notes
The crisp aroma is dominated by citrus and a resiny hop character with honey and light bready notes. On the palate, a gentle sweetness opens into a distinct hop bitterness.

Lindeboom Pilsener

Lindeboom Bierbrouwerij
www.lindeboom.nl

Country of origin Netherlands
First brewed 1912
Alcohol content 5% abv
Serving temperature 39°–43°F, 4°–6°C

In the Dutch village of Neer in the province of Limburg, a young farmer, in 1867, decided to brew beer. He traveled to Germany to study the craft, and on returning in 1870, he began brewing Geenen's Bier (his name was Willem Geenen). He renamed the brewery he built next to his house in honor of an eighty-year-old Linden tree nearby (*boom* is Dutch for "tree").

By 1912, the popularity of pilsner beers was rising. Lindeboom opened a new brewhouse equipped with a steam machine and refrigeration and jumped aboard the good ship pilsner. The hoppy taste of the brewery's refreshing new beer caught on and nearly drowned out the top-fermenting beers in the region.

In 1996, in honor of its 125th year of existence, Lindeboom was declared a supplier to the Dutch royal family. Other beers produced by Lindeboom include Oud Bruin, Herfstbok, and Venloosch Wit. **RP**

Tasting notes
Clear and gold colored with a slight and shy fragrant nose. On the palate, clean and refreshing, malt and hop flavors kept in perfect balance. A quick and slightly bitter finish.

Lipan Světlý Ležák

Pivovarský dvůr Dražič
www.pivovarlipan.cz

Country of origin Czech Republic
First brewed 1998
Alcohol content 5% abv
Serving temperature 44°F, 7°C

Central Europe is home to an unknown number of beer styles that have been pushed aside in the wake of industrial lager production. One of the least well-known is the *kvasnicové pivo*, or "yeast beer," of today's Czech Republic.

After lagering, fresh yeast is added to the finished brew, creating a pronounced cloudiness as well as doughy, yeasty aromas and a vibrancy rarely seen in industrial lagers. It is most often found in pale beers, though dark lagers can be similarly yeasted. Two of the best are produced at the Pivovarský dvůr Dražič brewpub. Brewer Jan Papula makes a pale and a dark *kvasnicové pivo*, both of which are only available on draft. As yeast beers are "live," alcohol measurements can be imprecise, though Pivovarský dvůr Dražič keeps a remarkable alcoholic balance, with its strength hard to notice beneath the flavors of malt and hops. **ER**

Tasting notes
One of the country's most distinctive remaining yeast beers, this extremely cloudy pale lager has rich fruitcake and stewed fruit flavors in the nose with a full, malty mouthfeel.

Łomża Export

Browar Łomża | www.browarlomza.pl

Country of origin Poland
First brewed 1968
Alcohol content 5.7% abv
Serving temperature 46°F, 8°C

Łomża Export is one of the most popular beers in the northeast of Poland. It comes from a beautiful land of more than 1,000 lakes and extensive forests, which are full of bison, lynx, wolves, and wild ponies. Given all this, it is not surprising that the beer comes in a green bottle with a green label. The couple—or the dolls as they are affectionately known—who appear on the label wear the folk dress of the Kurpie people, a group of independent foresters who have uniquely survived to this day. Łomża Export aims to share this green atmosphere with the rest of the world, and it seems to be working. The beer is adept at winning international recognition: it won an award from the International Taste and Quality Institute in 2008, while 2009 saw a bronze medal at the Australian International Beer Awards and a gold medal at the Monde Selection in Belgium.

Browar Łomża is unique among regional Polish breweries. Unlike most breweries of its size, it does not have a long history stretching back to the industrial revolution and to a time when monks jealously guarded their beer recipes. Rather unromantically, Łomża was founded in 1968 as a government-run enterprise, after an excellent underground water source was discovered in the area. It was the first purpose-built brewery to be established in Poland after World War II. The brewery was privatized after the fall of communism, and in 2007 it became a wholly owned subsidiary of Royal Unibrew Polska. The brewery is a strong supporter of local festivals, particularly the Łomża beer festival, which features some of the most popular Polish rock acts of yesteryear. **RZ**

Tasting notes

Łomża Export has a bright yellow color, a notable grainy fragrance, and a sweet malty palate, which is followed by gentle hop notes and a deliciously smooth finish. As refreshing as forest air, this is a beer to enjoy outdoors on a balmy summer evening.

Löwen Bräu Bartholomäus Festbier

Löwen Bräu Buttenheim | www.loewenbraeu-buttenheim.de

Country of origin Germany
First brewed 2006
Alcohol content 5% abv
Serving temperature 46°F, 8°C

Johann Modschiedler, owner of Löwen Bräu Buttenheim, is a very committed man. By day, he is involved in community politics and holds office as a judge; by night, he pours beer for the guests in his brewpub. And, when he brews, he does it right. For example, he develops new beers by himself at his own site instead of using the services of a research institute, as is common among his colleagues. Taking this path, he has created a new light lager that contains less alcohol and, more recently, a new Festbier.

With two seasonal festival beers in his portfolio, he decided to offer a third as a year-round regular. Löwen Bräu Bartholomäus Festbier is a deep golden delight seducing with fruity-sweet and flowery aromas, a creamy body with hints of vanilla, and an elegant bitterness. It is made of Münchner and pilsner malts, which work in tandem with the aroma hops of the German variety Hallertauer Perle and Tettnanger—with the last addition added at just the right moment to retain the delicate bouquet. Bartholomäus has immediately become the second most popular of the Löwenbräu product range, number one being the classic Kellerbier.

The Löwen Bräu brewpub dates back to 1880, and Modschiedler is the fourth generation to run the family business. When he took control, he modernized the facilities, replacing an ancient open cool ship with a closed cooling device. Luckily, the cool ship can still be seen at brewery tours. It is so vast that it is easy to imagine how children used to ice skate on it in winter, as Modschiedler recounts. **SK**

Tasting notes

Deep golden, brilliant color with a fine, moist foam. Expect a sweet fruity-floral hop aroma reminiscent of tropical fruits. The palate has a soft and creamy body, hints of vanilla, and an elegant bitterness with enchanting floral head notes. Dry finish.

+Lupulus

Companyia Cervesera del Montseny | www.ccm.cat

Country of origin Spain
First brewed 2007
Alcohol content 5.4% abv
Serving temperature 46°–54°F, 8°–12°C

On leaving college after studying chemistry, Pablo Vijande traveled to eastern England and worked for almost four years at the Wolf brewery in Norfolk, a county that was once described as a beer desert but in the last two decades has seen many operations like Wolf thrive. Vijande learned the tricks and trades of brewing, such as how to select the best ingredients; he was also able to put his chemistry knowledge into practice. When he returned to Catalonia, he started up his microbrewery in a village north of Barcelona, using second-hand machinery that he bought from Wolf.

Employing English production methods such as the infusion mash, he and brewing parent Jordi Llebaria produce traditional hand-crafted beers. This is artisanal brewing at its most basic, and the beer really is made using mostly manual processes. The brewers call it an Iber Ale. The reason for the name is to be found in ancient history, when the Iberians populated what became the Iberian peninsula. Remains found in Catalonia prove that this population already brewed its own beer so, as a tribute to this heritage, Vijande decided to call this style Iber Ale.

It is brewed as an ale with top-fermentating yeast, but made with ingredients some of which would be at home in a lager: pils malt, caramalt, and wheat malt in the mash tun, although the hopping regime is more eclectic with Cascade, Fuggle, Nugget, Target, and Styrian Golding in the boil. All this gives the beer a very fresh and perfectly balanced sense of bitterness. Served in bottle, this is unpasteurized and unfiltered, so expect some sediment or turbidity. **SS**

Tasting notes

Gold orange in the glass beneath a snow-white, foamy head; boasts a pleasant hop nose with floral notes. On the palate, any tendency to overbitterness is perfectly balanced by the crisp, rich maltiness. Full-bodied and satisfying mouthfeel that leads to a lasting finish.

Maingold Landbier

Kulmbacher Brauerei | www.kulmbacher.de

Country of origin Germany
First brewed 1846
Alcohol content 5.4% abv
Serving temperature 46°F, 8°C

Literally translated, Landbier means "a beer of the countryside," or "a beer with rustic origins." Given that the brewers of this beer can be found in the confines of the Bavarian city of Kulmbach, it would be stretching the truth to call it a rural beer; on the other hand, it is one of the oldest brands still brewed. It first saw the light of day at the Mönchshof brewery, which was also located in the city before being bought up by Kulmbacher in the 1990s.

Not quite a style of beer in the way Weissbier or Märzen are, you could argue that Landbier is the name given to a particular brand. In general, Landbiers tend to have low levels of carbonation and are seen as beers for everyday drinking, although the 5.4 percent alcohol content of Maingold Landbier is a bit high to class it as a session beer. Sometimes these beers are filtered, other times they're not.

Mönchshof's Maingold Landbier is popular and reassuringly old fashioned, thanks to the fact that it is one of those rare bottles with a swing top—this in itself is another sign of yesteryear and a comfortable link to a past that acts as a bulwark to fast and frenetic modern life. As for the ingredients, summer barley, a special yeast, and water from the clear springs of the nearby Fichtelgebirge help to shape this Landbier. Noble hops, yes, but it is not an especially hoppy brew. A great way to drink this beer, a way that makes a statement, is to order it in a restaurant or beer hall and receive it fresh from the cellar and out of a jug—the same way Landbier was drunk when the Mönchshof brewmaster first brewed it. **WO**

Tasting notes

Maingold Landbier pours a golden yellow color in the glass. Quiet and shy nose with hints of sweetish grain and a deep note of caramel in the background. Clean and crisp on the palate with dry grainy notes, followed by a fine, dry, and bittersweet finish.

Malheur 10

Brouwerij Malheur | www.malheur.be

Malheur Bière Brut

Brouwerij Malheur | www.malheur.be

Country of origin Belgium
First brewed 1999
Alcohol content 10% abv
Serving temperature 50°F, 10°C

Country of origin Belgium
First brewed 2000
Alcohol content 11% abv
Serving temperature 44°F, 7°C

Emmanuel (Manu) De Landtsheer opened Brouwerij De Landtsheer, now called Malheur, in 1997, near the site of his grandfather's old brewery in the Flemish Brabant village of Buggenhout. The original brewery closed in the 1960s, the victim of the growing popularity of lager in Belgium. The 18th-century building that housed it still exists and can be seen from the roof of the current brewery.

De Landtsheer is a big fan of hoppy brews. Malheur 10 was created as a strong ale that also had the bitterness to balance the sweetness of such a malty beer. The result is a complex ale with a fine hoppy character, thanks to the fact that whole hop flowers are used, both for aroma and flavor. The name Malheur translates as "misfortune" in French, but it is certainly no misfortune that the Malheur beers exist for beer lovers to enjoy! **CC**

Malheur's Emmanuel De Landtsheer wanted to create a new style of beer, one that would wow consumers with both its taste and presentation. Bière Brut was also created to help give Malheur a higher profile in the world of brewing. Without question, the beer succeeded on all fronts, and not long after, another brewery in Buggenhout came up with the same idea.

Bière Brut begins life in the same way as Malheur 10. After a four-week period of cold fermentation, things change a lot. The beer is put in a new champagne bottle, with a plastic stopper, called a *bidule*, inserted into the bottle's neck. When the beer is ready to be bottled, the bottle's neck is frozen for five minutes. The crown cork is removed, and the bidule and frozen yeast pop out. The bottles are then cleaned, dried, and corked. Malheur Bière Brut is a hugely complex ale, with impressive presentation to boot. **CC**

Tasting notes

Aroma is powerful: yeasty, citrusy, with some peppery character. There are notes of honey, citrus, and a pleasant bitterness. A very easy-drinking, medium-bodied brew.

Tasting notes

Notes of apricot, lemon, and orange on the nose. On the palate, an incredibly rich character, with a hint of sweet malt that hides its alcohol beautifully. Dry aftertaste, bitter finish.

Mata Artesian

Aotearoa Breweries | www.mata.net.nz

Matilda

Goose Island Beer Company | www.gooseisland.com

Country of origin New Zealand
First brewed 2005
Alcohol content 5% abv
Serving temperature 39°–43°F, 4°–6°C

Country of origin United States
First brewed 2005
Alcohol content 7% abv
Serving temperature 41°F, 5°C

When Tammy Viitakangas and Jaysen Magan returned to New Zealand in late 2003, they wanted to go into business together and to create something that was a celebration of New Zealand, but they had no idea what. Tammy began trial brews in her kitchen, and the couple soon found their friends were choosing her beers over commercial brands. Encouraged by this support, they made the brave decision to buy a brewery.

Warm fermented like an ale, but given an extended cold maturation in the manner of a lager, Mata Artesian is loosely modeled on a German Kölsch. The brewery's range includes a sweetish brew flavored with Manuka honey and another much drier one that is made with perfumey Feijoa fruit. Mata beers are made without preservatives, additives, finings, animal products, or added sugars and are the only beers currently certified by the New Zealand Vegetarian Society. **GG**

"This beer started in my head in 1993," says Goose Island's brewmaster Greg Hall, and it was inspired by a trip to Orval, the Belgian monastery that brews a similarly pale and earthy beer. "We didn't want to copy Orval," says Hall. "We were looking for a different beer, something a little richer, with more caramel malt, one that would be a really good food beer."

In 2004, the team started taking Belgian beers seriously. "It took us a while to figure it out at the production brewery. We use two fermentations with Belgian yeast, one started a few weeks earlier and inoculated with *Brettanomyces*," a slow-growing wild yeast that gives the beer its characteristic "barn full of pineapples" aroma. The beer is centrifuged to get the chunks out, but this gentle method allows some of the yeast to remain in the package, so the beer evolves nicely with age. It holds up well for two years or more. **RM**

Tasting notes

A bright, golden brew with a delicate, biscuity malt sweetness, gentle carbonation, and subtle hopping. Exceptionally easy to drink, yet robust enough to stand up to smoky and spicy dishes.

Tasting notes

On the nose, musky honeyish tones of pineapple and ripe tropical fruit plus hints of earthiness. Fairly sweet, thick-textured middle on the palate. Spicy finish.

Meta Beer

Meta Abo Brewery | No website

Country of origin Ethiopia
First brewed 1963
Alcohol content 5% abv
Serving temperature 44°–50°F, 7°–10°C

This lager is conjured from the holy waters of St. Abo, which flow through the scenic hills of Sebata, a town about fifteen miles outside the Ethiopian capital of Addis Ababa. Although usually consumed from one of the "steinie" bottles, the best way to sample Meta is at the brewery or at the main distribution depot in Addis Ababa. Only in these two locales can beer drinkers find the much-coveted, unfiltered version of this beer.

At the brewery, nestled in the Managesha foothills of Mount Wuchacha, you can enjoy an unfiltered draft on the veranda, or stroll through the Meta Abo grounds for spectacular mountain and waterfall views—the brewery runs trails to educate visitors about protecting the habitat from which they draw the pure mountain spring water used in brewing. It is also possible to find the bottled export lager version of Meta at Ethiopian restaurants across Europe and North America. **CO**

Tasting notes
Pours straw blond into the glass and is crowned with a brief, full, white head. On the nose, a noble hop bouquet leads to a sweet malt kiss on the palate backed with hop bitterness.

Meteor Pils

Brasserie Meteor | www.brasserie-meteor.fr

Country of origin France
First brewed 1927
Alcohol content 5% abv
Serving temperature 43°F, 6°C

Meteor has an abbey beer, a wheat beer, and various seasonal beers, but is best known for its Pils. This is an all-malt beer, with Alsatian-grown Strisselpalt and Czech Saaz hops and the beer is filtered but not pasteurized before going out into the wider world in bottle. This means that it has a shorter shelf life than a lot of its rivals, but it makes for a fresher beer.

Brewing has been carried out on the company's site in the village of Hochfelden since the 1640s. The brewery finally became known as Meteor in 1925. Two years later, the then-chairman Louis Haag helped to bring Meteor Pils on the scene (the Haag family are still in charge). This was a beer influenced by Bohemian pilsners and it also used Czech hops to give it an aromatic presence that was missing from a lot of its competitors' beers. Since then it has been a constant in the brewery's beer portfolio. **ATJ**

Tasting notes
Pale blond in color with a thin white collar of foam.
The nose has hints of grassy, sweetish malt and spicy hop notes, while the mouthfeel is soft and gently carbonated.

The Czech hops that make Meteor such a distinctive pilsner. →

Mexicali

Cerveceria Mexicana | www.mexicalibeer.com.au

Country of origin Mexico
First brewed 1923
Alcohol content 5% abv
Serving temperature 32°–39°F, 0°–4°C

The original recipe for Mexicali was formulated by Adolfo Bindher, a German brewery chemist working at the behest of Don Miguel Gonzalez and Don Heraclio Ochoa to make a beer to put the Mexican border town of Mexicali firmly on the map. Once satisfied with their product, the two gentlemen opened the doors of La Cerveceria de Mexicali on July 4, 1923—the first industrial brewery in the state of Baja California.

The Mexican drinking public took the pilsner-style beer to its collective heart instantly, and for five decades Mexicali enjoyed the status of best-selling beer in Baja California. Production grew from 600 barrels per month in its first year to 6,000 per month by 1960. However, the sadness that greeted the death of Don Miguel in 1973 was further compounded by the decision of his family to close the plant.

It appeared as though Mexicali had become little more than a footnote in the history of Mexican beer, usurped by the emergence of less inspiring Mexican drinks that export prodigiously throughout the world. Thankfully it was merely the end of another chapter, and Mexicali climbed back into the brewing ring in 1996. Production reconvened under the supervision of the Tecate brewery in the town of the same name, and the deep golden yellow brew remains a pilsner-style beer with a perfect balance of two-row barley malt and Chinook, Mount Hood, and Peerless hops. Although unlikely to again top the sale charts considering the depth of competition within the country, Mexicali has found many new converts in the United States among pale lager aficionados. **SG**

Tasting notes

A bright, golden yellow color with a subtle nose of sweetened malts and herbal hoppiness. The palate tingles with lightly spiced hops and sweet grain malt, leaving a semidry finish. Mexicali makes a perfect partner to a serving of ceviche.

Moa Original

Moa Brewing Company | www.moabeer.co.nz

Country of origin New Zealand
First brewed 2003
Alcohol content 5.5% abv
Serving temperature 43°F, 6°C

Named after one of the giant flightless birds that used to roam New Zealand, Moa was the brainchild of Josh Scott. The son of a pioneering winemaker, Scott wanted to make super premium boutique beers that would appeal equally to beer aficionados and wine lovers. His plan was to make a range of bottle-refermented beers employing the winemaking techniques used to produce champagne-style sparkling wines.

The brewery's first beer, Moa Original, a dry, hoppy, golden, pilsner-style lager, was launched in December 2003. This was followed by Moa Noir, a dark lager; Moa Blanc, a wheat beer; Moa Harvest, a cherry beer; and 5 Hop Winter Ale, an extravagantly hopped, strong pale ale. More recently, a Belgian-style tripel called St. Joseph's has appeared, and there are plans for a new, strong, wood-aged dark beer.

The Moa range is packaged in 25-ounce (750-ml) and 13-ounce (375-ml) champagne bottles. Although the smaller bottles are filled directly from secondary fermentation tanks and the beer is designed to condition in the bottle, the larger variants undergo the classic riddling, disgorging, and topping-up techniques used in "methode traditionelle" wine production.

Extended yeast contact rewards the Moa beers with distinctive toasty flavors, as well as a delightfully soft natural carbonation with very fine bubbles. The persistent bead also creates a lingering, fluffy white head and excellent lacework. The two palest beers (Moa Original and Moa Blanc) have a racy, white-winelike crispness that makes them terrific either as aperitifs or paired with shellfish or oily dishes. **GG**

Tasting notes

Bright yellow gold hue beneath a pillowy white head. The aroma combines biscuity malt sweetness with grassy, lemony notes from the New Zealand hops. The palate is spritzy, tart, and quenching, often exhibiting hints of vanilla and white pepper. Hoppy pilsner meets spicy saison!

Moinette Blonde

Brasserie Dupont | www.brasserie-dupont.com

Country of origin Belgium
First brewed 1955
Alcohol content 8.5% abv
Serving temperature 50°F, 10°C

In 1950, Dupont started to specialize in producing strong, bottle-conditioned ales. Moinette was one of these. As it passes through the upper reaches of its serene middle age, Moinette is now seen as the quintessential strong golden ale of Wallonia. Further proof of its maturity is its position as the benchmark by which others of its genre are often judged. As many as half a dozen yeasts may contribute to its complex profile, while fine hops add much to the beer's character. Moinette was created in response to the rising popularity of strong ales in Belgium in the 1950s, and since then has become Dupont's biggest seller at home.

Dupont is one of the classic breweries of Belgium. It has the oldest operating brewhouse in the country, which dates back to 1844. The squat copper brewing kettles are survivors of World War I, during which the German army requisitioned most of them for their armaments industry. The open mash tun is another survivor—it dates back to before 1890. The Rimaux-Deridder family opened the original brewery, but in 1920 Alfred Dupont bought it. It was no mere commercial venture: he used it to convince his son to stay in Belgium rather than immigrate to Canada, and the brewery has remained with the family ever since.

This farmhouse brewery oozes with a sense of heritage, but it does not neglect new technology. The stainless steel fermenters, as well as the kegging and bottling lines, are modern adaptations. Regular tours can be undertaken, and most of the Dupont beers can be sampled at La Forge, a fine local café in the village square of Tourpes. **CC**

Tasting notes

Pale golden-colored brew that pours with a rocky white foam. Mild fruit, pepper, and coriander in the nose. The taste is similar: pepper, light coriander, and other spices, with a pleasant bitterness in its dry finish. Try this full-bodied beer with asparagus, seafood, and lighter meats.

Montestella

Birrificio Lambrate | www.birrificiolambrate.com

Country of origin Italy
First brewed 1996
Alcohol content 4.9% abv
Serving temperature 46°F, 8°C

Despite its growing reputation and increasing output, Birrificio Lambrate was founded as a community project and it remains one. If there's one thing that a local pub or bar needs, it's a reliable, tasty, session beer that is available at all times. Montestella is it.

Back in 1996, Gianpaolo and Davide Sangiorgi, along with their friend Fabio Brocca, were considering opening a bar that catered for young people in Lambrate. The spark came from Gianpaolo and Davide's father, Franco, who suggested that they also brew their own beer. More than a decade later, there is a strong commitment to the local community—but thirsty travelers who are venturing this far off the beaten track are also most welcome. At Birrificio Lambrate, happy hour isn't just an excuse to flog cheap booze across the counter. Indeed, the beer is slightly cheaper at this time, but there's also a free food buffet of antipasti and other light snacks to make sure that nobody has to drink on an empty stomach.

A community local needs a proper session beer: an easy-drinking, tasty brew acting as a social lubricant for people who meet there after a day's work. And Montestella is just that, being as old as the brewery. Named after Monte Stella, the hill born out of a pile of wartime rubble in San Siro, a suburb west of Milan, Montestella is a slightly unorthodox tackle at a Kölsch that doesn't actually try to be one. Beware, you may start with one glass of Montestella and the intention of moving on to other beers after that, and soon find yourself having a session on Montestella alone, because it fits the spirit of the place so well. **LM**

Tasting notes

Straw-colored with a very slight haze and lasting white head. Fresh flowery hops dominate the nose and palate, a good pale malt backbone with fruity notes gradually giving way to a crisp final bitterness. Easy drinking but tasty and complex.

Moo Brew Pilsner

Moo Brew | www.moobrew.com.au

Country of origin Australia
First brewed 2005
Alcohol content 5% abv
Serving temperature 39°F, 4°C

Moo Brew appears to be almost as driven by art as it is by beer. David Walsh, the owner of the brewery, is reputed to have made a fortune developing gambling systems while still in his twenties—he then bought a winery in 1990 and started Moo Brew in 2005. In 2006 he paid $3.2 million for a 1954 painting depicting a downtrodden barmaid pausing during service in the infamous "6 o'clock swill."

Each of the Moo Brew beers is beautifully presented with its own specially commissioned artwork from Australian artist John Kelly, who, appropriately enough, is famous for his paintings of cows. In the case of the pilsner, the featured painting is intended to pay homage to Australian artist Sidney Nolan. A John Kelly painting exists for each of the beers in the Moo Brew range, the meanings of which will no doubt remain elusive to all but the most sophisticated of drinkers.

It goes without saying that the most expensive beer labels the world has ever seen would mean nothing without the beers to back them up. Head brewer Owen Johnston has made sure that this happens. Drawing on his formal qualifications from the International Centre for Brewing and Distilling in Scotland, he has won acclaim for each of his beers for its own sake, most recently for his Imperial Stout, which is oak- and bottle-conditioned for more than a year before being released.

The Moo Brew brewery is located on the banks of the Derwent River, not far from Hobart. Moo Brew beers can be found on tap in many of the pubs dotted throughout Tasmania. **DD**

Tasting notes

The golden translucence of Moo Brew Pilsner is its true art, along with the passion fruit aromas that are only revealed after you inhale with a flourish. Crisp malt and honey notes will be painted on your tongue before a crisp, refreshing finale.

John Kelly on the Champs-Elysées, where his cow sculpture was displayed in 1999.

Morrissey Fox Blonde

Morrissey Fox Brewery | www.morrisseyfox.co.uk

Country of origin England
First brewed 2008
Alcohol content 4.2% abv
Serving temperature 44°–48°F, 7°–9°C

There aren't many beers that are launched with their own TV series. But then, there aren't many brewers who are household names on TV. British actor Neil Morrissey has always been passionate about good pubs and great beer, and in 2008 he joined up with TV beer chef Richard Fox to buy a pub, Ye Olde Punch Bowl Inn in the Yorkshire village of Marton-cum-Grafton, and create a brewery. Their attempts to launch a beer and revive the pub were the subject of a three-part TV series, *Neil Morrissey's Risky Business*.

The pair felt passionately that cask ale was unfairly maligned with a dowdy, elderly, slightly geeky image, and set themselves the task of attacking this head on. The brief was to create an ale that lager drinkers would find appealing. The answer was clearly to create a blond ale, the style that was already wooing new drinkers to ale, and Morrissey Fox Blonde was born. Brewed with pale ale and lager malt and Hercules, Riwaka, and Challenger hops, Morrissey Fox Blonde has the light, citrus, tangy refreshment expected of the style. But it also has smart, fresh, irreverent branding, which uses photos of the brewers taken by top fashion photographer Rankin. The reaction was immediate: More than 4,000 pubs have stocked the cask version, and the bottle rapidly gained nationwide distribution, too.

Some rivals have complained about the whole thing being a gimmick. But Morrissey has announced his desire to step back from acting and run the brewery full time. And with Brunette, Best Bitter, and a range of other beers now making up an expanding portfolio, it's clear that the actor is very serious about the brand. **PB**

Tasting notes

Morrissey Fox Blonde is pale gold with a delicate fruity hop aroma and a light, sweet malty flavor, finished off by a gentle hop buzz. As intended, the refreshing bite of a lager combines well with the fruity, more complex hoppiness of an ale.

Naturperle

Brauerei Locher | www.appenzellerbier.ch

Country of origin Switzerland
First brewed 1996
Alcohol content 5.2% abv
Serving temperature 46°–50°F, 8°–10°C

How does an established local brewery whose sales volume has been pretty stable for over a century multiply its business fivefold over a period of fifteen years, all while the total volume of beer sold in the country falls by 25 percent? Cousins Karl and Raphael Locher can answer that riddle, because they achieved just that. The fifth generation of the dynasty, which began in 1886 when Johann Christoph Locher bought a brewery in Appenzell, the Locher cousins took over the running of the brewery in 1996.

They aimed their beers at niche markets, thus developing one of the widest beer ranges in Switzerland. The most successful of those markets has been in organic beer, or "Bio-Bier" as it's known in German. When they released Naturperle in 1996, as a companion to their already successful Quöllfrisch unfiltered lager, Locher was the first Swiss brewery to come up with a certified organic beer.

Naturperle is brewed using a base of German organic malt supplemented by a variable amount (5 to 20 percent) of Swiss organic malt from barley grown in the Engadine mountains, which impart an intense grainy flavor to the beer. The hops are organic, too, and 100 percent Swiss, from the Ackermann family farm in Wolfwil, between Solothurn and Olten, in the heart of Switzerland. The beer is unfiltered and unpasteurized for optimal freshness, albeit with a limited shelf life.

Following Naturperle's success, Locher began contract brewing own-label organic pale lagers for the Swiss supermarket chain Coop. These lagers are slightly lower in alcohol (4.8 percent). **LM**

Tasting notes

Naturperle is a malt-accented, straw-colored lager with a slight haze, fine condition, a yeasty touch, and a nice spicy hop edge. The finish is long, malty, and spicy with a moderate hop bitterness at the very end to achieve the right balance. A great session lager.

Neumarkter Lammsbräu Urstoff

Neumarkter Lammsbräu | www.lammsbraeu.de

Country of origin Germany
First brewed 1963
Alcohol content 4.7% abv
Serving temperature 46°F, 8°C

At a time when most people did not even know the word "ecology," let alone the complexity of its meaning, Franz Ehrensperger, the sixth-generation owner of Neumarkter Lammsbräu, set his mind on the organic production of beers. He was in his twenties when he took over the family brewery in 1971. Challenged by a difficult market that was seeing breweries close or combine, he was confident that his would survive if he brewed the best possible beer. He wanted to lead a sustainable enterprise, an attitude mainly inspired by the first report of the newly emerged Club of Rome—*The Limits to Growth*. Ehrensperger set off to convert the brewery bit by bit. He defined environment protection as a business goal while focusing on organic ingredients that he was convinced would make a better beer. However, there was a problem: there were no such ingredients available. He thus had to win over farmers, but in the beginning earned nothing but rejection.

Eventually, a few farmers participated, and after many tests, the first two all-organic styles were released in 1987. Urstoff, conventionally produced since 1963, became "Bio," as "organic" is known in Germany, in 1994; a year later the conversion of all of Neumarkter Lammsbräu's beers was complete. Urstoff is a medium-bodied, malty beer characterized by a delightful harmony. Distributed nationally mostly in health food shops, it has acquired high renown. The formerly derided Ehrensperger is today overwhelmed with honors and awards. Neumarkter Lammsbräu now also has a gluten-free beer in its portfolio. **SK**

Tasting notes

Brilliant golden orange, fine white moist head. The nose offers malty flavors with hints of a citrusy hop aroma. The first taste is all about softness. A medium body of decent light malt flavors evolves, inspired by floral top notes. Supporting bitterness goes through to a mild finish.

Nils Oscar God Lager

Nils Oscar Brewery | www.nilsoscar.se

Country of origin Sweden
First brewed 1997
Alcohol content 5.3% abv
Serving temperature 46°–50°F, 8°–10°C

When Nils Oscar began production in 1996, most beers available in Sweden were the ubiquitous, delicately flavored imitation pilsners. Sweden's nascent craft brewing movement reacted to this by embracing the American love of the hop, creating powerful, aromatic brews that were designed to show the Swedish drinker what beer can do.

When head brewer Patrick Blomqvist arrived at Nils Oscar, the portfolio was full of beers like this, including a powerfully bitter lager that was "a concerto for hops." The brewers felt there was also room for a rounder, maltier, more balanced beer, and God Lager was born. Although the brewery holds its beers in high regard, it is not claiming divine provenance: "God" is simply Swedish for "good." Brewed with pils and Vienna malts and German hops including Hallertau and Tettnang, God Lager is a craft brewer's take on a traditional Vienna-style lager, with malt and hops held in a fine balance in a beer that shines with a golden glow. Nils Oscar is almost unique in its "grain to glass" approach, growing its own barley and managing the whole production chain from crop to finished beer. Only the hops are imported, because Sweden is too far north to grow its own.

Nils Oscar brews all its beers with food in mind, and God Lager complements a wide variety of dishes. It goes particularly well with roast and fried foods, which complement its malty roundness. God Lager accounts for half of Nils Oscar's output and is the twelfth biggest beer in Sweden. It is now also distributed widely throughout the United Kingdom. **PB**

Tasting notes

Nils Oscar God Lager pours a pale, sunset color with a clean, malty aroma and a hint of floral hop. A fresh, clean, malty flavor with hints of sweetness and a clean, crisp finish. A full-bodied lager that loses nothing in terms of refreshment.

Nora

Birrificio Baladin
www.birreria.com

Country of origin Italy
First brewed 2001
Alcohol content 6.8% abv
Serving temperature 50°–54°F, 10°–12°C

It all began in the small hill town of Piozzo in the Piedmont region of Italy when Teo Musso turned his beer pub into a brewpub in 1996 and launched his new ales under the moniker Le Baladin. Without a doubt, Le Baladin is a pioneer of the Italian craft brewery movement, which was just nascent when the top-fermenting beers began appearing.

One of Le Baladin's most famous and intriguing beers is Nora. It is dedicated to Egyptian culture, one of the world's ancient brewing traditions. Kamut, an ancient cereal variety supposedly rediscovered from an Egyptian tomb, makes up 22 percent of the grain bill in the recipe. The very low amount of hops used is just a formality, so that Nora can still be called beer under law. Musso substitutes the hops with a special Ethiopian resin that comes from a plant in the same family as myrrh. The resin gives the beer an aroma similar to incense and a strange bitterness and aftertaste that have a balsamic quality. In fact, people perceive this bitterness differently because it is not a flavor sensation that most are used to experiencing. Ginger is added to the brew to give the beer some light citrus notes. While devising this recipe, the myrrh was very difficult to work with, but Le Baladin certainly found the right equilibrium, and the result is an enticing ale with a Middle Eastern flair. **MO**

Tasting notes

A thick head tops this orange golden ale. Nose is intense with peppery notes, citrus, incense, and light ginger; a fine bubble makes a very elegant mouthfeel. A unique tannic finish.

Nottingham Extra Pale Ale

Nottingham Brewery
www.nottinghambrewery.com

Country of origin England
First brewed 1999
Alcohol content 4.2% abv
Serving temperature 50°F, 10°C

Philip Derby and Niven Balfour first started brewing commercially in 1995 when they set up the Bramcote Brewery in the English city of Nottingham. Entering into partnership with a small but progressive local pub-owning company, they moved to a city-center site and, at the same time, rechristened the brewery "Castle Rock," after the nearby outcrop on which Nottingham Castle stands. Unfortunately things did not work out, so Derby and Balfour decided to start again from scratch.

Derby and Balfour discovered that the name of the defunct Nottingham Brewery Company was no longer registered, and so the Nottingham Brewery was reborn, back in its hometown. Derby and Balfour have modeled their portfolio of beers on the original "Rock Ales" that were brewed by their namesake and so called because the beers were matured in sandstone caves beneath the old brewhouse.

Extra Pale Ale is made using low-color Maris Otter malt and is seasoned in stages with Challenger, Fuggle, and Golding hops, with a late addition of Bobek Styrian Golding for aroma. It is widely distributed locally, but export markets have yet to be tapped. However, Nottingham Extra Pale Ale is a regular tipple at the South Pole, courtesy of the scientific research vessel RSS *Ernest Shackleton*, which delivers a welcome supply each time it makes the trip. **JW**

Tasting notes

Pale gold with an appetizingly fruity hop aroma, the palate is crisp, citrusy, and full bodied, with juicy malt notes adding balance and culminating in a lingeringly dry, refreshing finish.

A sculpture of a brewer (*ca.* 2465–2323 B.C.E.) at the Egyptian Museum, Cairo.

Odell IPA

Odell Brewing Company | www.odellbrewing.com

Country of origin United States
First brewed 2007
Alcohol content 7% abv
Serving temperature 55°F, 13°C

Three years after Odell Brewing built a new and larger fifty-barrel brewery in 1994, the company invested in a smaller five-barrel system on which its brewers can create and refine new recipes. The more successful experiments end up on tap in the tasting room, and the best of those may graduate to regular production. Not surprisingly, that's where 5 Barrel Pale Ale got its start, and, later on, the India Pale Ale. The pale ale receives eight different hop additions using six hop varieties, whereas the IPA has seven additions with six varieties. Both beers feature Northwest American hops, and Odell's brewers fill a specially designed hop-back with whole flowers in the process of making them.

Although Colorado's breweries don't have quite the same reputation for heavily hopped beers as those on the West Coast, many of them have funded research on growing organic hops in their home state. "To grow hops in Colorado would not only be beneficial to the state's craft breweries but to the agricultural economy as well," says founder Doug Odell. His brewery used the first small amounts in its seasonal brew Hand Picked Ale.

Odell's upgraded its five-barrel operation in 2008, making it not only a pilot system for test batches but essentially a small brewery producing beers for its tasting room and limited distribution. The first beer made on the new five-barrel system was called Pre-Nup Pilsner, a wedding beer made for two employees who met at the brewery and became the fifth married couple to do so. Employees from all departments have an opportunity to brew on the five-barrel system. **SH**

Tasting notes

A frothy white head stands in contrast to the orangey body, throwing off aromas of mango and tangerine. The hops dance nicely between adding citrus flavors and balancing dryness. Long finish, blending final herbal impression and hop flavors.

Old Empire

Marston's | www.marstonsbeercompany.co.uk

Country of origin England
First brewed 2003
Alcohol content 5.7% abv
Serving temperature 46°–54°F, 8°–12°C

Marston's has a curious heritage: It is the only brewer in the legendary beer town of Burton-on-Trent that survives today with an unbroken lineage back to the town's mid-19th-century heyday. But in more than 130 years, Marston's has never brewed the beer that made Burton world famous: India Pale Ale. Burton became the home of IPA because the unique composition of mineral salts in the local spring water added an extra dimension to a pale ale from London, creating a clearer, drier, tastier, and above all more durable beer that usually reached Calcutta in perfect condition. Marston's flagship brand, Pedigree, shares some characteristics of these fabled beers, but never went to India and is not quite an IPA.

Old Empire is brewed with Optic malt and packed with traditional English Fuggle and Golding hops. The introduction of American-grown Cascade hops for aroma may raise questions for some about its authenticity. But at the height of the town's success, Burton's brewers were using more hops than British farmers could grow, and the importation of American hops for use in Burton IPA is well documented.

Old Empire is served on draft in pubs throughout the English Midlands. Given the average English male's insistence that beer should only be drunk in pints, the alcohol level was held at 5.7 percent, a little lower than is traditional. But it's still a full-bodied beer that combines weight and depth with drinkability. It lacks the full in-your-face hoppiness of its U.S. counterparts, but in its balance it is more truly representative of what was being quaffed on Indian verandas a century ago. **PB**

Tasting notes

An initial sulfury whiff of the famous Burton Snatch quickly gives way to a spicy, earthy hop nose with just a hint of lemon. On the palate, Old Empire offers a rich, citrus juiciness balanced by a crunchy maltiness, leading to a pronounced dry finish.

Opat Bitter

Pivovar Broumov | www.pivovarbroumov.cz

Country of origin Czech Republic
First brewed 2007
Alcohol content 4.2% abv
Serving temperature 44°F, 7°C

Coriander, chestnut honey, black pepper, laurel—the brewery in the tiny village of Olivětín has a penchant for innovative lagers with unusual flavorings. But perhaps the most impressive new concoction from brewmaster Jaroslav Nosek is flavored with an old favorite: plenty of *žatecký poloraný červeňák* (Saaz semi-early red) hop cones go into the brewery's *extra-chmelené*, or extra-hopped, pale lager. It is called bitter, but the effect is more aromatic than acrid, creating a fragrant showcase for Saaz, albeit with such a moderate alcohol level that the beer qualifies as a session brew.

Founded by Benedictine monks under powers granted by Holy Roman Emperor Charles IV in Prague, the brewery was functioning at least by 1348. The current brewhouse, a stunning brick tower surrounded by linden trees, dates from 1866, and is considered one of the most beautiful in the Czech Republic. Until it was nationalized in 1948, Pivovar Broumov was a monastery brewery, giving rise to the beer's name of Opat, or "abbot." After the Velvet Revolution, it was privatized and has been under the same ownership since 1997.

Unlike many breweries in the Czech lands, Pivovar Broumov maintains its own maltings, buying raw barley and producing malt to its own specifications. It is also known for the Rampuš, Novic, and Převor beers it makes for a major international supermarket chain. **ER**

Tasting notes
A pronounced grassy nose of fresh Saaz hop cones with resinous and peppery overtones. In the mouth it balances a honeylike malt sweetness with a highly aromatic hop finish.

Oppale

32 Via dei Birrai | www.32viadeibirrai.com

Country of origin Italy
First brewed 2006
Alcohol content 5.5% abv
Serving temperature 46°–50°F, 8°–10°C

His studies in food technologies have given 32 Via dei Birrai's head brewer Fabiano Toffoli a very precise, quite scientific approach to ingredients and temperatures, and the high quality of the range of beers that he makes is the perfect mirror of his personality. He opened the microbrewery with two friends in 2006 in Venice, quite close to the Dolomiti Mountains, and success in the Italian market was quick to follow.

Pure water arrives from two different springs in the mountains, hops are selected and bought in the Belgian town of Poperinge, and malts are usually German. Oppale is one of the first beers that Toffoli made, and he describes it as a mixture and meeting of different beer cultures: Belgian, German, and British. Caramel malt is the main base of the beer, a pale-colored variety—chosen because the brewer wanted a pale beer with a great body. Some pilsner malt is also added. Hops are British varieties: Challenger for bitterness and Brewer's Gold for aroma. After forty days, the beer is bottled with fresh yeast and sugar to kick-start refermentation. After ten days of rest, this top fermenting ale is ready to go.

Oppale is a very drinkable beer and has the lowest alcohol content of 32 Via dei Birrai's products. Toffoli wanted to make a beer that was intense and rich in body and aroma, but still easy to drink. **MM**

Tasting notes
A golden pale ale; lightly cloudy. Intense nose, a wave of hoppy notes of citrus and chamomile. In the palate, it starts with a rich sweetness but hops come back for a long, pleasant aftertaste.

Strong graphic branding distinguishes 32 Via dei Birrai beers.

Via del birrai

ADMIRAL

ATRA

OPPALE

AUDACE

NEBRA

CURMI

Original Alt

Brauerei Pinkus Müller | www.pinkus-mueller.de

Country of origin Germany
First brewed 1830
Alcohol content 5% abv
Serving temperature 46°F, 8°C

Even though Düsseldorf is seen as the center of Altbier, there are outposts of the beer style farther afield in Germany (and even in the United States where the beer was a popular choice in pre-Prohibition times). Pinkus Müller in the city of Münster was founded in 1816 by Johannes Müller, who also owned a bakery. It gets its colloquial "Pinkus" name from a time when Müller's great-grandson Carl had been on a drinking spree that involved finishing off a six-liter capacity Bullenkopp (bull's head) jug. Naturally, after so much liquid, Müller had to pay heed to the call of nature. As he was out walking with a couple of friends who had shared his jug of Altbier, the call came—and as it so happens "Pinkus" is German slang for such an act.

Nowadays, Pinkus Müller is best known for its beers' organic status and its full-bodied Pinkus Alt, in particular. With a grist of just malted barley (malted wheat used to go into the lauter tun at one stage as well), this beer is lighter than Düsseldorf's Altbiers, although it still has that trademark amber hue.

Like many other breweries in the region, Pinkus Müller has a brewery restaurant-cum-beer hall. This is a comfortable tavern whose four separate drinking areas are dotted with classic Westphalian furniture. As well as enjoying this popular Altbier, drinkers can sample a wonderful range of meaty dishes that are well matched with this style of beer. And given the tiny cloistered corridors of this ancient building, visitors are amazed at the modern equipment that services Müller, including gleaming stainless steel tanks where the beer ripens and matures. **WO**

Tasting notes

In the glass, Original Alt is an appealing gold amber in color. The nose is as fresh as the feeling on the palate, where a little sweetness is perfectly combined with the light bitterness of the hops. A full-bodied and pleasant Altbier with a good long finish.

Oro de Calabaza

Jolly Pumpkin Artisan Ales | www.jollypumpkin.com

Country of origin United States
First brewed 2004
Alcohol content 8% abv
Serving temperature 50°F, 10°C

Jolly Pumpkin is one of only a small number of breweries in the United States that uses open fermentation for all its beers—a traditional process in which beer is allowed to ferment without being sequestered in completely sealed containers. The practice was once standard procedure but has been outmoded for decades among most U.S. brewers, who opt for sealed stainless steel fermenters that provide fewer changes for organisms such as wild yeast strains to enter the beer during fermentation.

Since opening in 2004, Jolly Pumpkin's ales have been on many fans' must-try beer lists. Among them is the brewery's two-time Great American Beer Festival winner, Oro de Calabaza, (Pumpkin's Gold), a Franco-Belgian–inspired strong golden ale that is in year-round production at the brewery. As is the case with all of Jolly Pumpkin's beers, Oro de Calabaza ages in oak with naturally occurring wild yeast before it is refermented in the bottle.

With extended conditioning, the beer can become quite carbonated. For this reason, owner and brewmaster Ron Jeffries recommends opening it only when well chilled, treating it as you would champagne—open it with care and have a favorite glass handy. He also suggests allowing the beer to warm a bit in the glass before imbibing, but asserts that the ideal serving temperature is up to the enjoyment of the drinker. And for the musically minded, Jeffries cites a long list of music styles, from Latin American to 1980s punk, and musicians such as Billie Holiday as his inspirations for the beer. **LM**

Tasting notes

Aptly named, Oro de Calabaza pours a pale gold in color. Reminiscent of champagne, a tingly effervescence dances in the mouth, emphasizing a pleasant, slightly sour apple and pear tang that is highlighted by generous spicy and peppery aromas and flavors.

Ostravar Premium

Pivovar Ostravar | www.ostravar.cz

Country of origin Czech Republic
First brewed 1898
Alcohol content 5.1% abv
Serving temperature 44°F, 7°C

Many beers in the eastern industrial city of Ostrava were founded as Czech-owned competitors to brands owned by ruling German-speaking minorities in the area. Ostrava already had a successful pale lager from its Dampfbrauerei, or Steam Brewery, which was owned by Markus Strassmann, but the town's Czechs wanted their own beer. In 1897, just as the citizens of Budweis had done two years previously, a group of Czechs in Ostrava put down the money to found the *Český akciový pivovar v Moravské Ostravě*, or Czech Stock Brewery. Their first batches of pale lager rolled off the line the following spring.

Both breweries ran until 1950, at which point the Communist-era planners closed the Strassmann brewery. The other brewery was nationalized and renamed the Moravian Ostrava City Brewery. It called its beer Ondráš until just after the Velvet Revolution in 1990, at which point it was renamed Ostravar.

Ostravar has produced some of the most interesting brews in the Czech Republic, including Kelt (discontinued in 2009), which was a very good stout, and Velvet, an unusual amber beer with a Guinness-like cascade effect. But it is Premium, the original pale lager, that is Ostravar's flagship pint: a rich golden brew with very moderate carbonation and pronounced citrus hop notes over rich malt. It is brewed at 12 degrees Plato and, like most Bohemian-style pilsners, it retains a healthy amount of residual sugar, giving it substantially more heft in the body than most German pale lagers. It is produced using two-row spring barley and is still fermented in traditional open vessels. **ER**

Tasting notes

This malty, orange-blossom-scented brew balances a hefty maltiness with an equal amount of Saaz hop aroma and a bitter finish. Although traditionally served at cooler temperatures, the hop aromas expand greatly at slightly warmer temperatures.

Otley O1

Otley Brewery | www.otleybrewing.co.uk

Country of origin Wales
First brewed 2005
Alcohol content 4% abv
Serving temperature 46°–50°F, 8°–10°C

When the Otley family opened their brewery in 2005, they wanted their first beer to be one that people could drink a couple of pints of without worrying about the effects. And they wanted it to be golden. Golden ale was sweeping the country, regularly winning prizes at beer festivals, but it was not yet widespread in their native South Wales.

The Otleys realized that golden ale was thriving because it challenged stereotypes about cask ale and bottle-conditioned beer. It promised lagerlike refreshment as well as ale-type body, and looked attractive in the glass to people who might be nervous about trying real ale. When it came to packaging and naming, the Otleys felt that too many beers had names and designs that evoked a cozy country pub. By contrast, O1 looks smart and modern in a monochrome design that evokes the album sleeves of alternative rock bands, and the stark, catalog-style naming scheme creates a discordant contrast with the obvious craft values inherent in the beer, suggesting it is a brewery with a new set of ideas.

O1 is brewed with Celeia hops from Slovakia, which give it a powerful aroma that's not quite in the realm of North American beer styles, but suggests that the family are keeping a close eye on what's happening across the Atlantic, looking to balance intensity of flavor with the ability to drink a few pints. The result? O1 was named Champion Golden Ale at the Great British Beer Festival in 2008 and is now selling in those cool bottles in an ever-increasing radius beyond South Wales. **PB**

Tasting notes

Pours a pale straw color, with a crisp floral aroma seasoned with citrus notes. That fruit comes through on the flavor, but is held in a pleasing balance by a caramel maltiness with hints of toffee, before a satisfying dry finish. Bitter, refreshing, and smooth.

Otley O8

Otley Brewery | www.otleybrewing.co.uk

Country of origin Wales
First brewed 2005
Alcohol content 8% abv
Serving temperature 46°–50°F, 8°–10°C

Once they had established their pilot brew, O1, the Otley brewers wanted to see how far a beer style could be stretched, and O8 was the result. O1 is a golden ale that reaped awards as soon as it was released, thus gaining Otley a reputation as a golden ale specialist. As the name suggests, O8 is 8 percent, but the brewers insist that it is still a golden ale.

Such weighty beers need a firm body to balance what would otherwise be a syrupy alcohol hit. O8 is brewed with generous doses of Whitbread Golding Variant (WGV) hops, a little-known variant of the classic Golding that has a more pronounced sweet fruit version than the Kent classic—an English hop with North American aspirations, if you will. This is complemented with Willamette hops to create a mélange of assertive citrus and blackcurrant aromas. It's not easy to create a balanced, pale beer at this strength, but O8 is deceptively smooth and easy to drink, with the alcohol creeping up slowly.

So when does a golden ale stop being a golden ale? The Campaign for Real Ale classifies this beer as a barleywine, despite the protests of the brewers. But this hasn't gotten in the way of success, and O8 has won gold medals every year since it was first brewed. Despite being what some may describe mistakenly as an "extreme" beer, O8 is attracting new drinkers, particularly women, in significant numbers. Many are lured by the fact that it's a brilliant match with food. Golden and pale ales always go well with fish and Asian food, and stronger beers match deeper, richer flavors. O8 finds itself able to do both, and more. **PB**

Tasting notes

Definitely a blond-colored ale, but with a bruised hue. Concentrated hop aromas are floral and citrusy, and the beer fools the tongue into thinking that tart citrus fruit is present. Then, the alcohol asserts itself and leaves you with a long, warming finish.

Ozeno Yukidoke IPA

Ozeno Yukidoke Beer | www.ryujin.jp

Country of origin Japan
First brewed 2005
Alcohol content 5% abv
Serving temperature 54°F, 12°C

This IPA was originally brewed by Ozeno Yukidoke as a special seasonal beer, and made for hard-core beer fans who wanted more hop character and stronger flavors. While recent years have seen the appearance of several brands of American-style double IPAs, this beer seems similar only in terms of hopping level, while a comparatively normal gravity and 5 percent abv keep it distinct from the stronger versions.

In keeping with the American-style approach, hops used for both bittering and aroma are primarily Cascade along with smaller amounts of American hops also selected for their citruslike flavor notes. Since a lot of hops are used in this brew, care is taken to make sure the wort is brighter and more tightly filtered. This is to assure a greater clarity in the hop flavors. It also brightens the orange bronze color, making the beer more attractive.

The parent company, Ryujin Shuzo, is a regional sake brewery that also produces distilled shochu spirits. Their initial beer offerings when the brewery was opened in 1997 were more conventional flavor profiles; however, by 2006 they had produced quite a number of special beers, and so decided to create a line of premium beers.

Ozeno Yukidoke IPA joins this line of premium beers, which includes Heavy Heavy Barleywine and a strong dark ale called 10th, created for the brewery's tenth anniversary. While those beers are priced higher, the IPA sells for the same price as other conventional beers, such as Brown Weizen, White Weizen, and Stout, since it has the same 5 percent alcohol content. **BH**

Tasting notes

Ozeno Yukidoke IPA has a hazy bronze orange color, with an off-white head. It features a powerful citrusy hop aroma, which continues into the flavor. While the body features a strong malt profile, it is quickly overpowered by the bitter hop flavor.

Pabst Blue Ribbon

Pabst Brewing | www.pabst.com

Country of origin United States
First brewed 1844
Alcohol content 4.7% abv
Serving temperature 36°F, 2°C

In the 1986 movie *Blue Velvet*, Dennis Hopper's sinister character, after going into a foul tirade against one of the world's best-selling beers (Heineken), hails the virtues of Pabst Blue Ribbon. Thus was born America's prototypical "retro" beer—an uninteresting, factory-made, corn-based lager now consumed with abandon by counterculture hipsters. Never mind that Pabst has been around for more than a century and a half; Hopper's curse set the tone for this thoroughly modern creation of underground marketing, loathed and adored like no other beer ever brewed.

Retro beer is your father's beer, or more likely your grandfather's, served as a déclassé alternative to trendy craft beer. Retro beer is fashion, yes, but it is also antifashion. It is the repudiation of mainstream advertising and the affirmation of nostalgia.

Pabst Brewing, originally known as the Empire Brewery and later Best and Co., was founded in 1844 in Milwaukee and grew under steamship captain Frederick Pabst into America's biggest beer maker. For more than a century, it battled the giants—Miller, Anheuser-Busch, and Schlitz—for market domination.

Today, it is a brewery in name only. The company is owned by a nonprofit charitable foundation. Its products are made under contract by companies, including MillerCoors. The flagship, known widely as PBR, gets its name from the many blue ribbons it won at late 19th-century beer exhibitions. PBR is not necessarily an award-winner today, but a sip of this yellow lager will give you a visceral appreciation for an important segment of today's beer culture. **DR**

Tasting notes

Brightly carbonated with a sparkling aroma of malt and corn. Crisp and refreshing, the flavor is dominated by malt sweetness with only a slight suggestion of hop bitterness to pave the way for the next quaff straight out of the can.

Fashionably anti-fashion: PBR is nostalgia in a glass.

Pale Rider

Kelham Island | www.kelhambrewery.co.uk

Paulaner Nockherberger

Paulaner Brauerei | www.nockherberg.com

Country of origin England
First brewed 1992
Alcohol content 5.2% abv
Serving temperature 54°F, 12°C

Country of origin Germany
First brewed 2003
Alcohol content 5.2% abv
Serving temperature 46°F, 8°C

When Dave Wickett started Kelham Island brewery in Sheffield in 1990, he opened the doors to the public. During brewery tours he noted that men liked the aroma from rubbing the bittering hops, but women didn't. The same thing happened at the tastings—women didn't like the bitterness and many of them only drank lager. So he decided to make an ale full in flavor but low in bitterness. Using Maris Otter malted barley as a base along with aromatic North American hops, his team brewed up a one-off batch of beer, named after the eponymous film, and sent it out to the pub trade.

Reports came back that the beer was flying out, enjoyed by both men and women, and within three months was the most popular beer the brewery had ever made. Pale Rider was picking up handfuls of awards within a year of its debut, including the Champion Beer of Britain award in 2004. **MC**

This Paulaner Kellerbier is named Nockherberger (meaning "not too high") for the hill in Munich where the great beer hall of the Paulaner brewery is located and where every year the world-famous strong beer festival, Starkbierfest, takes place. The restaurant and beer hall are set on the most important beer mountain (known to Munich residents as Salvator) in Bavaria and it is only here that Nockherberger is brewed and served.

The beer is one of the youngest and, perhaps, most unusual of the traditional beers in the city. Nockherberger is a rather light and aromatic specialty Kellerbier, which is left unfiltered according to the old tradition, giving it a naturally cloudy appearance. This Kellerbier is available throughout the year but visitors enjoy it during the summer in particular, when one of the most beautiful large beer gardens in town, Biergarten am Nockherberg, is open. **WO**

Tasting notes
Visually appealing with its rich, sunset-orange color, the beer has a delicious baked peach and brioche nose that leads into a rich flavor of raspberries and nectarines. Epically drinkable.

Tasting notes
The Nockherberger is yellow and typically cloudy. It is an unfiltered, typical Kellerbier with a very aromatic taste. A light bitter finish showcases the hops in, with a malty touch of barley.

Perła Chmielowa

Perła Browary Lubelskie | www.perla.com.pl

Petrus Aged Pale

Brouwerij Bavik | www.bavik.be

Country of origin Poland
First brewed 1846
Alcohol content 6% abv
Serving temperature 46°F, 8°C

Country of origin Belgium
First brewed *ca.* late 1990s
Alcohol content 7.3% abv
Serving temperature 46°–54°F, 8°–12°C

Karl Vetter founded the Lublin Brewery in 1846 and started by brewing what was then a modern bottom-fermented beer—a lager, in other words. In 1912 Vetter's brewery merged with the Jewish-founded Browar Parowy Jeleń (Steam Deer Brewery), which had specialized in kosher beers. Nationalized by the Communist government in 1948, the brewery returned to private ownership after the fall of communism and is now partly owned by Royal Unibrew and an American-Canadian private equity fund.

Lublin Perła Chmielowa Pils is the brewery's flagship beer and firmly rooted to its origins. A golden bottom-fermented pils, it continues the lager tradition started by Karl Vetter so long ago; it is also the region's most popular beer. Perła means "pearl," no doubt a reference to those enchanting streams of white bubbles in a freshly poured glass. **RZ**

Bavik is not a small brewery. In fact, it really ought to be called De Brabandere, which is the name of the family who still owns it. The origin of Petrus Aged Pale dates back to when beer writer Michael Jackson turned up at Bavik and asked to taste the brewery's old beer, straight from the barrel. The beer Jackson requested happened to be a pale. Later, he contacted them and placed an order for this beer to be bottled just as he had tasted it—he wanted to offer it to his beer club in the United States. The brewery did as he requested for export—so it was first bottled in 2001 after twenty-four to thirty months' maturing—and then all hell broke loose.

Those who drank it in the United States loved it. Then, the beer connoisseurs of Belgium cried blue murder and wanted it, too. Among the whole Petrus range, this is really the jewel in the crown. **JPa**

Tasting notes
Clear gold in color while the nose offers up inviting hoppy notes. The mildly tangy palate leads to a pleasant finish that is dominated by a gentle, slightly spicy hop-driven finish.

Tasting notes
Vinous, woody nose, which is joined by lemony and green apple notes. There is a very discernible wood character in the taste. Long wooden notes and alcohol warmth in the finish.

Phillips Original IPA

Phillips Brewing Company | www.phillipsbeer.com

Country of origin Canada
First brewed 2001
Alcohol content 6.5% abv
Serving temperature 46°F, 8°C

It is a safe bet that more than a few of the many hundred craft breweries that populate North America were built on credit card debt. And likely an equally good number were also the product of a single individual's determination, grit, and self-sacrifice. Even within such a context, however, the story of Phillips Brewing is a rather extraordinary one.

A journeyman of British Columbia craft brewing, Matt Phillips decided at the dawn of the new century that the world in general, and Vancouver Island in particular, needed at least one more craft brewery—his. And so began a journey through the banks, as Phillips collected rejection after rejection, eventually reaching the conclusion that the credit card applications readily available in each bank would likely finance his dream a lot sooner than would the banks.

He was right. It turned out, however, that buying brewing equipment entirely on credit left little extra cash for rent, and so Phillips took up residence in his brewery, setting up halogen lights to imitate the sunrise during the darkest winter months and showering daily at his local gym.

Of the first three brands that Phillips produced in 2001, only the IPA has stood the test of time. Crafted in a style more in keeping with what was being brewed in the Pacific Northwest of the United States than what British Columbia's brewers were offering at the time, it was a bold statement of individuality. It was ultimately a key player in the evolution of the western Canadian beer culture beyond blond ales, pallid pale ales, and hemp beers. **SB**

Tasting notes

Richly fruity on the nose with peach and golden raisin notes, this impressive IPA starts lightly sweet and honeylike before adding assertive hop bitterness to the mix, eventually easing to the finish with full and citrusy bitterness. Perfect with hamburgers and grilled meats.

Pickla Pils

Nynäshamns Ångsbryggeri | www.nyab.se

Country of origin Sweden
First brewed 2000
Alcohol content 4.8% abv
Serving temperature 46°–50°F, 8°–10°C

The story of Nynäshamns Ångsbryggeri, which is based on the rocky coast of Sweden not too far from the capital Stockholm, is a microbrewery classic. Three friends with an interest in beer formed a club to meet and drink beer. Their interest grew from drinking to brewing. They got together once a week in the kitchen to revisit the home-brewing of their youth (not uncommon in a country with restrictive alcohol laws) and discovered that they had a talent. A home-brewing course followed, and almost ten years after they first met to drink beer, they opened a brewery.

Tony Magnusson, Christer Johansson, and Lasse Ericsson started as enthusiasts and continue to brew in the same spirit. The brewery has grown rapidly despite making a virtue of spending next to nothing on marketing and relying on word of mouth to get their beers known. They still get daily phone calls from restaurateurs wanting to stock their beers and also have a listing in the "systembolaget"—the alcohol shops run by the government. Their success has led to steadily increasing volumes and a move away from hand-bottling and labeling to mechanized production in an old electricity substation.

Pickla Pils was created to introduce Swedish drinkers to a traditional pilsner with a profile closer to the Czech originals, with a hoppier taste and drier finish. Pickla Pils uses pilsner and some caramalt, while the hops are Saaz from the Czech Republic. It's fermented with a fairly neutral pilsner yeast for one week before being matured for three to four weeks at near-freezing temperatures. **AA**

Tasting notes

This is a classic blond pilsner with a snow-white head, and it is matched with a similarly recognizable aroma of straw and grass. Pickla has a malty, dry citrus bite on the palate, balanced bitterness, and a slightly sour but refreshing grapefruit aftertaste.

Pike IPA

Pike Brewing Company | www.pikebrewing.com

Country of origin United States
First brewed 1990
Alcohol content 6.3% abv
Serving temperature 43°–48°F, 6°–9°C

"We start with sea water from the 18th century, flown over from England," quips Pike Brewing Company's founder Charles Finkel. "We were one of the first to do an IPA on the West Coast. We wanted, as much as possible, to recreate an 18th-century India Pale Ale, but with a local flavor as well." In 1990, the bitterness, at 65 IBUs, was "shockingly high," but by today's standards it's pretty mellow. "With our brewer at the time, Fal Allen, our goal was balance rather than beating people over the head with hops," says Finkel. "We ended up with a beer that is really good with food."

He should know. Finkel was one of the earliest practitioners of the art of combining beer and food. Merchant du Vin, the American importing company that he and his wife Rose Ann built up, was one of the first to focus on world-class beers, and to do so in the broader context of gastronomy. Along with a few others, such as the famed beer writer Michael Jackson, the Finkels had the notion, outrageous in the late 1970s, that beer was worthy of serious contemplation and deserved a place at the dinner table.

They incorporate local ingredients as much as possible, using pale ale, crystal, and Munich malts from Gambrinus up in British Columbia, and Columbus, Willamette, Chinook, and Golding hops from Yakima. All this gives the beer a solid malty base to balance the bright juiciness of the Northwest hops. If you're looking for old school, Pike IPA delivers flavor that captures the exuberance of the era and still manages to remain timelessly tasty liquid evidence of just how great the classics can be. **RM**

Tasting notes

On the nose, earthy and piney notes come to the fore with some caramelly maltiness and hints of apricot fruitiness. The palate is massaged by very balanced flavors of crisp and slightly nutty pale malt. There is a modestly bitter mid-taste, with a long, clean, bitter, and fruity aftertaste.

Pike Monk's Uncle Tripel Ale

Pike Brewing Company | www.pikebrewing.com

Country of origin United States
First brewed 2006
Alcohol content 9% abv
Serving temperature 48°F, 9°C

Seattle's Pike Place Public Market is best known for its fish market, where staff hurl the day's fresh catch to one another, and the location where Starbucks served its first cup of coffee. It is also the place where Charles and Rose Ann Finkel decided to establish a brewery in 1989. Finkel had been in the wine business, then entered the beer industry with Merchant du Vin, a company that imported brands such as Orval, Ayinger, Lindemans, and Samuel Smith's at a time when the U.S. craft brewing movement was just taking hold.

Pike Monk's Uncle Tripel was originally brewed in 2006 to celebrate the fact that the Finkels had re-acquired the Pike Brewing Company after an eight-year absence. A total of 500 limited-edition bottles were given to key accounts and friends of the brewery to say thank you for their support. The brewery decided to create the Belgian-style tripel because it was different from the English ales for which Pike was known, such as Pike IPA, Pike Extra Stout, and Pike Old Bawdy Barley Wine Style Ale. A limited amount of Monk's Uncle was served on draft at the Pike Brewery pub, then it was released as a spring seasonal in both 2007 and 2008. After winning a reader's choice award from *Northwest Brewing News* as the best Belgian-style ale, Pike decided to launch Monk's Uncle as a year-round offering in 2009.

The beer is brewed with organic pale and pilsner malts, 7 percent organic sugar, and Nugget and Saaz hops. The addition of the much-prized Westmalle Trappist yeast adds to its Belgian lineage and gives the ale a crisp, dry, and fruity flavor. **RL**

Tasting notes

This Belgian-style ale pours the traditional golden straw color of a tripel together with a solid lacy head that remains throughout. There is an overall fruity background flavor to this brew, with just a hint of honey and a touch of spice.

Pikeland Pils

Sly Fox Brewing | www.slyfoxbeer.com

Country of origin United States
First brewed 2002
Alcohol content 4.9% abv
Serving temperature 39°F, 4°C

Each year in summer, brewers across the United States scan their inventory for their finest crafted ales and lagers, sampling them for flaws, selecting the very best, in order to ship them to Denver to be judged at the Great American Beer Festival. The awards are cherished bragging rights for everyone from the tiniest brewpub to the largest industrial brewery.

In 2007, Sly Fox brewer Brian O'Reilly was hustling to meet the shipping deadline when he realized that it was too late to bottle his brewery's flagship, Pikeland Pils. "So I just grabbed a six-pack of cans from a pallet and sent them out," he says. Brewery reps believe the gold medal awarded to Pikeland Pils that year was the first ever for a canned craft beer. Local fans of this suburban Philadelphia brewery just shrugged; to them, the brightly colored cans are a favorite, perfect for stashing in portable coolers for softball games or picnics.

O'Reilly's Pils has been piling up medals since he first made it. His inspiration was Jever, the classic pilsner from northern Germany. "When I studied in Austria," he says, "I'd remember waking up in the middle of the night after sessions with Jever, and my mouth would be so dry I had to run for a drink of water."

The hop choices are vital to this pils. Noble hops—Hallertau from Bavaria, Saaz from Bohemia—provide the dryness; Tettnanger gives it a slight brassy aftertaste. One might be tempted to pour this wondrous golden lager into the proper glassware to enjoy its beauty and aroma. Go ahead, but this beer seems even more special after a long, hot day of work or play, guzzled straight from the can. **DR**

Tasting notes

Light straw color, and a pinelike or floral aroma rises from a thin, quickly dissipating collar of foam. Light body, somewhat grainy and earthy with distinctive German hop bitterness. Crisply refreshing with a dry finish that encourages one sip after the next.

← Pikeland Pils takes its logo from the female flower cone of the hop.

P.I.L.S.

Pausa Café | www.pausacafe.org

Country of origin Italy
First brewed 2007
Alcohol content 4.2% abv
Serving temperature 43°F, 6°C

Pausa Café is a cooperative involving two prisons—the Lorusso e Cotugno in Turin and the Rodolfo Morandi in Saluzzo. It also involves three communities of coffee and cocoa producers in Guatemala, Mexico, and Costa Rica. In Turin, coffee and cocoa are roasted and packed; in Saluzzo, since 2009, beer is produced.

Pausa Café's brewer is Andrea Bertola, a former Troll brewery worker who decided to produce his own beer. He started in a factory in Venice before moving his new brewery to the prison where it has a strong social value—primarily, to teach prisoners a job that they can continue once they are released. The link with the Latin American farmers means that many of the beers are also produced using products that come from their communities. Coffee and cocoa are prime ingredients, but even quinoa and amaranto get used.

P.I.L.S. is produced in the style of a Czech pilsner in its most traditional way. It is brewed with bottom- (or cold-) fermenting yeast and lagered; it is also gold in color, while Saaz whole-flower hops are added to give the all-important aromatic and grassy nose. They also help to give it an appetizingly bitter character on the palate. The production process follows venerable Czech traditions: the beer is matured in wooden barrels, while more hops are added in a triple infusion, giving different characteristics at different stages. **ES**

Tasting notes

Pale yellow, with gold flashes, and a persistent foam head. On the nose, there are clear notes of Saaz hops, which are grassy with a little honeylike sweetness. In the mouth, it is bittersweet.

Pilsner Urquell

Pilsner Urquell | www.pilsner-urquell.com

Country of origin Czech Republic
First brewed 1842
Alcohol content 4.4% abv
Serving temperature 44°F, 7°C

At one point in the 1830s, the beer from the Bohemian town of Pilsen was considered undrinkable, with many locals preferring the new lagers arriving from Bavaria. Unfortunately, the main brewery in Pilsen didn't have room to switch to the new style of production, and the quality of its own top-fermented beer fell. One day in 1838, locals protested by dumping thirty-six barrels of spoiled beer in front of the town hall. The citizens with brewing rights agreed to build a new brewery.

Hiring Josef Groll as brewmaster might have been their real stroke of luck. Hailing from the Bavarian town of Vilshofen, Groll had experience working with bottom fermentation, as well as the knowledge he had received from his brewmaster father. Still, the first batch brewed in 1842 came as a shock. With the combination of bottom fermentation, triple-decocted pale barley malt, and the city's extremely soft water, Groll had created the world's first clear, pale, bottom-fermented beer. It tasted different as well, in part due to the delicate floral aroma and light bitterness from a healthy dose of Bohemia's long-treasured Saaz hops.

The beer was selling in Vienna by 1856, in Paris by 1869, and in the United States as early as 1873. Meaning "original source," the Urquell name was trademarked in 1898. Now part of the SABMiller group, Pilsner Urquell is considered one of the best large-volume brews. **ER**

Tasting notes

A fine balance between its own sweet pilsner malt and delicately bitter and aromatic Saaz hops, this is one pale lager that is remarkably rich in the body.

A vintage advertisement for Pilsner Urquell. ➡

Pinkus Special

Brauerei Pinkus Müller | www.pinkus-mueller.de

Country of origin Germany
First brewed 1979
Alcohol content 5.1% abv
Serving temperature 46°F, 8°C

Pinkus Special is a global pioneer. It was the first beer to be brewed with all-organic malts, an act that marked the beginning of a decisive change in the production at the family brewery of Pinkus Müller in Münster, Westphalia. It all started back in 1979, when Hans Müller was offered a batch of organic malts; having been unhappy with the declining quality of malts, he was eager to try out the new ingredient. The outcome was delightful. In 1982, with the help of fellow organic pioneers Neumarkter Lammsbräu, Pinkus Müller got hold of organic hops, and all of the brewery's production became organic in 1991.

The brewery, which dates back to the year 1816, is the last of more than 150 alt beer breweries in Münster, while its pub Altbierküche (Alt Beer Kitchen) is a landmark in the town. Today, with Hans's daughter Barbara and her husband Friedhelm Langfeld both at the brewing helm, the new generation has joined in with the management.

Pinkus Special is unfiltered. After approximately three months' storage at around 32 degrees Fahrenheit (0° C), it develops a natural clarity. It is a smooth, mild blond lager with moderate bitterness and decent flowery notes. As Langfeld emphasizes, the beer's flavor might alter depending on the state of the natural hops. Their aroma composition changes through storage. That, however, does not turn off beer lovers all over the world. The beer was a success from the beginning and is still the most popular within the Pinkus Müller product range. It is available in the region, at organic food shops nationally, and is exported worldwide. **SK**

Tasting notes

A golden, slightly opalescent lager beer with fine white foam atop. The nose offers rather sweet, decent flowery and citrusy aromas. On the palate, there's a smooth mouthfeel, mild flavors of floral and vanillalike notes, and a moderate bitterness with a semidry finish.

Poperings Hommel Bier

Brouwerij Van Eecke | www.brouwerijvaneecke.tk

Country of origin Belgium
First brewed 1981
Alcohol content 7.5% abv
Serving temperature 46°F, 8°C

It doesn't take much sampling of Belgian ales to realize that, so far as they can be characterized in general terms, they tend more toward the malty than the hoppy. An early and notable exception to this imperfect rule is Poperings Hommel Bier. The beer is named after the town of Poperinge, which is located near the famous World War I battle site of Ypres. Today the area is also well known as the capital of hop production in the country. The word for hop in the local dialect is *hommel*.

As the heart of hop country and home to a tri-annual hop festival, it was only natural that Poperinge should have a beer of its own, and what was at one time the hoppiest beer in Belgium at that. Perhaps better known for the Kapittel range of abbey-style ales, the family-owned Van Eecke brewery have been brewing since 1862, when they purchased a castle brewery that was reconstructed after being destroyed during the French Revolution (the castle itself was left in ruins). Renaming it the Gouden Leeuw—or Golden Lion—the family operated it as a mostly local concern until the post–World War II reconstruction era, during which the Kapittel line was introduced.

Although the Kapittel beers have no direct connection with an abbey—the name refers to the hierarchy of monks within a monastery—the Hommel Bier has over the years developed a very strong, if unofficial, tie to the region in general and the town in particular. Indeed, even if it is no longer the hoppiest of Belgium's many brews, it no doubt remains the most famous of her hoppy creations. **SB**

Tasting notes

Those expecting IPA-style hoppiness will be disappointed, as its bitterness is not assertive, but rather studiously integrated within a maltiness of light caramel, orange, and honey. Off-dry throughout, it is a curiously refreshing quaff for an ale of its significant strength.

Potsdamer Stange

Braumanufaktur Forsthaus Templin | www.braumanufaktur.de

Country of origin Germany
First brewed 2005
Alcohol content 4.8% abv
Serving temperature 44°–50°F, 7°–10°C

Potsdam is the Prussian version of Versailles: a town just outside the walls of the capital, with a spacious castle for the king to reign untroubled by the big city. The king who made Potsdam his residence in place of Berlin was Frederick II ("the Great"). He might be the only king in history who was a skilled brewer: his father, who considered young Fritz too much of an effeminate bookworm, sent him as an apprentice to a brewery. It is most likely that Fritz brewed something similar to Potsdamer Stange, a style named after the glasses the brew is served in. The stangen (poles) are tall, slender, and straight—as were the goose-stepping Prussian soldiers. What a relief that the content of these glasses is anything but stiff.

Potsdamer Stange is a krausened beer and especially effervescent. The style was brewed sporadically in the old German Democratic Republic and West Berlin in the 1970s. Since 2005, its renaissance has been celebrated in this organic beer made at Braumanufaktur Forsthaus Templin, a brewery, tavern, and beer garden on the banks of Lake Templin in Potsdam.

Thomas Köhler and Jörg Kirchhoff—two brewers who learned their craft at the nationally owned VEB-Getränkekombinat Potsdam—bought the complex in 2002, remodeled the tavern, installed a brewhouse, and reopened in 2003. Their Potsdamer Stange is a bottom-fermented beer made with pilsner, Munich, and wheat malts and Hallertau hops. At second fermentation, they add krausen (fermenting wort) to revive the yeast. The result is a brisk and harmonious beer fit for a king. **SK**

Tasting notes

Orange to amber with a honey haze and a fine head. The nose has a sweet honey aroma. The first pass on the palate is all about the effervescent carbonation. Then comes the sweet flavors supported by bitterness and balanced by a hint of quenching sourness. A dry and mild finish.

Prime Max

Hite | www.hite.com

Country of origin South Korea
First brewed 2002
Alcohol content 4.5% abv
Serving temperature 39°F, 4°C

It was the Europeans who brought beer to Korea. There was no tradition of drinking beer, with locals preferring to use the grain from rice to make soju, a wine similar to Japanese sake. With Korea's hot, humid subtropical climate, however, the refreshing qualities of light American- or German-style lagers were quickly recognized. Modern brewing techniques also mean that beer can be brewed anywhere in the world—there is no need for the Hite brewery's chimney to be within sight of a barley field.

Prime Max is an all-malt beer, which means that unlike other beers from the same brewery, it is not brewed with the addition of adjuncts, such as corn or rice. It shares the yellow color typical of this type of lager, along with an energetic, carbon dioxide effervescence that helps form a white-collar head on top. Its flavor has some depth to it, and as it warms in the glass, wafts of malt flavors, with sweet hints of bubble gum, can be detected. American Cascade hops are used, which add a light floral, citrus quality to the nose.

Given the similarity of most of the beers sold in Korea, food matching is not a particularly sophisticated art. However, most beers are served in bars to accompany local foods, such as *samgyeopsal-gui* (grilled strips of pork belly). Prime Max's unobtrusive taste profile makes it an ideal snacking and sipping beer. Its lack of challenge to the palate and its thirst-quenching qualities mean that it allows the taste of spicy food to come through. Prime Max is aimed at the premium end of the beer market—a beer for tourists and successful local business people. **TH**

Tasting notes

Pale orange yellow to the eye, while light floral notes courtesy of the hop can be detected on the nose. Its mouthfeel is light and the taste is dominated by a syrupy sweetness, which while refreshing quickly disappears in the finish.

Prinz

Bayern Meister Bier | www.bmbier.com

Country of origin Japan
First brewed 2007
Alcohol content 5.5% abv
Serving temperature 46°–50°F, 8°–10°C

Stephan Rager came from Germany to Japan in 1996 to set up a small Japanese brewery. He worked at the brewery until the end of 2001, then remained to do consulting work for breweries in conjunction with German and Danish companies. Then, in the summer of 2004, he started his own brewery on the eastern side of Mount Fuji. At present, he brews an array of German-style beers, centering on two popular types. The Prinz is a conventional German-style pilsner, while his Edelweiss is a wheat beer. While the Edelweiss is quite popular with young Japanese people, Prinz is a favorite with the German community in Japan, where it is in regular demand with the German embassy, German restaurants, and German expatriates.

Rager explains that Prinz was created with Japan in mind. He says he needed a comparatively light-bodied beer to match much of the fish-based dishes in Japanese cuisine. The beer would not only create a good appetite for the food, but it would also need to support its flavors. He explains that the most difficult aspect of brewing Prinz, as well as his other beers, is keeping oxygen out of the beer so it stays fresher for a longer period of time.

All ingredients in all his beers are from Germany, with the exception of the local water, which is from Mount Fuji and of very high quality. Prinz is fermented at normal lager temperatures, from 41 to 46 degrees Fahrenheit (5 to 8°C), then lagered as low as 30 degrees Fahrenheit (-1°C). The result is a well-crafted beer that suits Japanese food perfectly, while also pleasing the many German customers who want to be reminded of home. **BH**

Tasting notes

The beer pours pale gold, with an off-white head. In the aroma, there is perfect balance between malt and hops, while in the taste, the malt flavor has a remarkably high definition, with a very soft mouthfeel leading to a dry, quenching finish.

Proper Job

St. Austell Brewery | www.staustellbrewery.co.uk

Country of origin England
First brewed 2004
Alcohol content 5.5% abv
Serving temperature 52°–55°F, 11°–13°C

When Roger Ryman left Maclays in Scotland to join the Cornish brewery St. Austell, he joined a company whose reputation was suffering, with "St. Awful" being just one of its nicknames. In the years since his arrival as head brewer in 1999, St. Austell's reputation has gone from strength to strength. New beers have emerged, all of which were first tried out at the small, two-barrel microbrewery that Ryman set up, and then debuted at the brewery's annual one-day beer festival in December. Proper Job is one of the most successful of these, a British cask-beer take on an American IPA.

The origins of the beer go back to 2004, when Ryman returned home after a month's sabbatical at BridgePort Brewery in the United States. He was a big fan of BridgePort IPA, and this beer was very much in his mind when he designed Proper Job. At first it was 5.5 percent alcohol content, although after a request from the marketing department, it was then reduced to 4.5 percent, so that it would be more manageable at the handpumps in British pubs and bars (the bottle-conditioned version, however, remains 5.5 percent).

The beer is made with Maris Otter pale ale malt, with barley grown in Cornwall and malted by Tuckers Maltings in Newton Abbot (one of the last traditional floor maltings left in the United Kingdom). The hops are all American: Willamette and Chinook for bitterness and a mix of Willamette, Chinook, and Cascade for aroma. The beer is dedicated to a Cornish regiment who fought during the Indian Mutiny in 1857 and whom Queen Victoria made a Light Infantry regiment in recognition of the "proper job" they had done. **ATJ**

Tasting notes

Pale gold in color. On the nose, resiny hop plus a well-filled fruit bowl of pineapple, melon, and guava. The same tropical fruits turn up on the palate, but the stern malt base keeps any inclination to over-fruitiness in line before a striking bitter finish. Great with strong, creamy blue cheese.

Punk IPA

BrewDog | www.brewdog.com

Country of origin Scotland
First brewed 2007
Alcohol content 6% abv
Serving temperature 44°–59°F, 7°–15°C

Taking much of their marketing inspiration from the microbrewing revolution in the United States, BrewDog have kicked British beer squarely between the legs and encouraged a new audience to sample craft beer. Set up in 2007, BrewDog has a ten-barrel brewhouse in place at the company's home in Fraserburgh on the northeast coast of Scotland, and from the start they've used it, along with their branding, to send an assertive and postmodern message to beer fans.

The aim at BrewDog was to challenge the palate of the British and test the boundaries of ale, having become tired of the cask ale dominance in the craft beer market. "James (Watt) and I . . . were both on the same wavelength with our disenchantment of the British brewing scene and knew that it was about time there was some excitement and intrigue and cool put back into the British industry," says the brewery's cofounder Martin Dickie.

Punk IPA is the flagship brand and has enjoyed phenomenal success, largely due to the poke from the hops. There's a mix of three in the beer—Chinook, Crystal, and Motoeka—and combined, they knock your socks off. The brewers are keen to point out, though, that it has been recognized for its balance, and the Maris Otter extra pale malt is very evident. Also, due to the complexity, don't be surprised to find plenty of tropical range to the fruits in there. However, with 65 IBUs washing around your mouth, you'll still know you're in for a sharp ride, and it pays plenty of homage to the American interpretation of this British style. **TS**

Tasting notes

Light gold in color. The first thing to hit you will be the pine notes on the nose. As you'd hope on tasting, it's bitter at the back of the palate, but before you get there, there's a lovely balance with the sweet malt. It's a perfect match for spicy food, and it cuts beautifully through a nice blue cheese.

Racer 5

Bear Republic Brewing | www.bearrepublic.com

Country of origin United States
First brewed 1996
Alcohol content 7% abv
Serving temperature 50°F, 10°C

Already popular with wine tourists, the town of Healdsburg, California, became a top beer destination in 1996 when the Norgrove family opened Bear Republic Brewing. Its beers have proved so popular that the family have since built a production brewery in nearby Cloverdale. On its tenth anniversary, Bear Republic won Small Brewing Company of the Year at the Great American Beer Festival.

Although famous wine appellations and wineries are a short drive away, Sonoma County was once a hop-growing region. In fact, one winery is located in former hop kilns. Members of the Norgrove family have lived in Sonoma County for four generations, part of an underlying community that wine tourists often overlook. The brewpub is truly a family venture, with father Richard R. Norgrove tending to much of the business side and son Richard G. Norgrove (known as Ricardo) taking charge of the brewing, with both their wives also pitching in.

Racer 5 quickly became Ricardo's top-selling beer, although Rocket Red Ale was the original flagship. The former is an IPA that packs a punch at 84 IBUs, but is as noteworthy for its aromatic blend of Northwest American hops—Cascade, Columbus, and Chinook. While Bear Republic has gained fame for its hoppy ales, the brewpub serves a wide variety of choices. For instance, at the Great American Beer Festival in 2008, its Double Aught, designed as a throwback to the 19th century when American breweries made pilsners without adjuncts, and another lager, El Oso (Spanish for "The Bear"), both earned medals. **SH**

Tasting notes

Orange at the pour and plenty of orange (citrus) in the nose, cleverly blended with floral and piney aromas. Flavors of cotton candy and continued citrus notes on the palate balanced by hints of biscuit and persistent bitterness. A beer that leaves you burping hops.

Red Stripe Strong Lager

Separates you from the herd.

Red Stripe

Desnoes & Geddes | www.redstripebeer.com

Country of origin Jamaica
First brewed 1928
Alcohol content 4.7% abv
Serving temperature 44°F, 7°C

Red Stripe is the beer forever associated with the laid-back, easy vibe of Jamaica. The international brand with its distinctive bold horizontal red stripe logo spent its formative years modeled on English ale, a heavy taste that found few friends among the locals. In 1938, Paul H. Geddes, son of the founder, and his colleague Bill Martindale transformed the beer into the now-familiar pale, golden lager. The light texture and crisp, refreshing nature of the beer corresponded perfectly with the scorching Caribbean climate.

World War II witnessed an influx of American and Canadian troops to Jamaica, dramatically increasing sales and taking Red Stripe to an overseas audience for the first time. In the 1970s, it entered the U.K. market and parts of Europe. The beer's enduring popularity in the hip rock world has guaranteed Red Stripe's youthfulness and vibrancy as a brand. **SG**

Tasting notes
Pale, clear golden color with a rapidly receding white head. A soft grainy and hoppy aroma is detectable, and the palate picks up sweet, caramel traces with a hop bitterness finish.

Reissdorf Kölsch

Privat-Brauerei Heinrich Reissdorf | www.reissdorf.de

Country of origin Germany
First brewed 1894
Alcohol content 4.8% abv
Serving temperature 50°F, 10°C

The brewery was founded in 1894 by a uniform tailor and brewed only top-fermenting beers, though it dabbled with bottom-fermenting ones starting in 1923. Just over a decade later, it became the first brewery in Cologne to bottle its Kölsch. After World War II, as a protest against the ban on higher-gravity beers, the surviving Cologne brewers began a campaign with the slogan "Echt Kölsch" (Real Kölsch). It was a success, and Cologne once again became a Kölsch town.

In 1986, Reissdorf and twenty-three other Cologne brewers created the Kölsch-Konvention. This defines that Kölsch must be: a Vollbier (with original gravity of 11 to 15.9 percent), top-fermented, light-colored, filtered, dry (that is, not malty), hoppy, and produced in Cologne (with some exceptions). Today, Reissdorf only makes Kölsch, though they do produce a bottled schnapps, Bierbrand, which is distilled from beer. **RP**

Tasting notes
Served at the brewpub, the beer is clear golden with a small white head. The aroma is softly malty and hoppy. In the bottle, it is highly carbonated; mildly malty with a very dry finish.

Red Stripe—crisp Caribbean cool.

Reserva 1925

Cervezas Alhambra | www.cervezasalhambra.es

Ripper

Green Jack Brewery | www.green-jack.com

Country of origin Spain
First brewed 1998
Alcohol content 6.4% abv
Serving temperature 43°–46°F, 6°–8°C

Country of origin England
First brewed 1994
Alcohol content 8.5% abv
Serving temperature 46°–54°F, 8°–12°C

In 1925, Cervezas Alhambra was founded in Granada by Carlos Bouvard, then-owner of La Moravia brewery, and Antonia Knorr, who came from a long line of brewers. At the time, the brewery lay on the edge of the city, close to the foot of the snowcapped Sierra Nevada Mountains—the source of Spain's finest water. Today, it is snugly part of the downtown area.

Owners have come and gone down the years—SA Damm took it over from the original founders in 1954. It is currently owned by the brewing behemoth, the San Miguel-Mahou group, but it still manages to operate with a fair amount of independence.

Reserva 1925 was made to celebrate the brewery's founding. It has a slow-controlled fermentation of thirty-five days, which is rare for a corporately owned lager. This classy artisanal brew comes in a subtle but incredibly stylish embossed, green glass bottle. **MC**

Ripper is brewed with pale malt, caramalt, wheat, maize, and candy sugar, and seasoned with Challenger and Celia hops. If it had been brewed in Belgium, it would be termed a tripel, but because it is brewed in the United Kingdom, it is a barleywine.

Cultural differences came into play when Ripper was launched. A Belgian tripel would be sipped slowly from a branded glass at a sidewalk café. An English barleywine is drunk in a pub, though, served in pint or half pint glasses—amid a cultural belief that real men drink only pints.

Ripper finds great favor at beer festivals, where it routinely sells out early and wins big. In 2007 it was named Champion Winter Beer of Britain and has since then attracted attention on a much wider basis, leading to the construction of a new brewhouse and the launch of a bottled version of the beer. **PB**

Tasting notes
Dark blond when poured into the glass. On the nose, rich caramelized orange notes are followed with just a hint of fresh blossom. The palate is grainy and slightly fiery.

Tasting notes
A straw-colored ale with gentle hop aromas and hints of sweetness on the nose. Remarkably smooth for a barleywine, and dangerously drinkable.

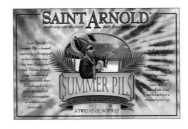

Rychtář Premium 12°

Pivovar Hlinsko | www.rychtar.cz

Saint Arnold Summer Pils

Saint Arnold Brewing | www.saintarnold.com

Country of origin Czech Republic
First brewed 1913
Alcohol content 5% abv
Serving temperature 44°F, 7°C

Country of origin United States
First brewed 1997
Alcohol content 4.9% abv
Serving temperature 48°F, 9°C

Many of the beers in the Czech Republic's Vysočina, or Highlands, emphasize maltiness and a full body, rather than hop presence and bitterness. That is certainly the case for the Rychtář brewery in "Hlinsko in Bohemia," a ski resort that lies about halfway between the Saaz hopyards and the barley fields in Moravia's Haná valley. There is a pronounced sugary note to the brewery's 12-degree pale lager, Premium.

The modern brewery in Hlinsko originally brewed pale lagers of 10 and 12 degrees Plato. During the Nazi occupation of Czechoslovakia, however, the brewery was only allowed to make one at 7 degrees, in limited amounts, until the end of the war. It was nationalized in 1948, after which it reintroduced a 12-degree lager called Blesk. In the late 1970s, that was discontinued and a 12-degree lager returned only in the early 1980s. The brewery is now privately owned. **ER**

There's a good reason that America's largest breweries spend even more on advertising their pale yellow lagers in Texas than other parts of the country. "In Texas, it's cool to be a cowboy with a longneck in your hand" says Brock Wagner, cofounder of Saint Arnold Brewing. Saint Arnold brews a full line of traditional styles. After years of tinkering with what looks like a simple recipe—one malt, two hops—Saint Arnold Summer Pils (originally known as Summerfest) won three medals in five years at the Great American Beer Festival, albeit as a Münchner-style Helles.

Founded in 1994, Saint Arnold is the oldest and largest craft brewery in Texas, taking its name from the patron saint of beer. It did well with seasonal beers from the beginning, including its Summer Pils, the distinctive label of which features Saint Arnold himself sporting sunglasses. **SH**

Tasting notes
Clear, brassy gold with a loose white head. A grainy, malty nose hints at a rich sugariness in the mouth. Hops are less evident in the aroma, more so in the lasting bitter finish.

Tasting notes
Pours bright yellow below a billowing white foam. Fresh floral and grainy aromas on the nose, followed by mild biscuit flavor, while hops leave spicy and grassy impressions. Crisp, dry finish.

Saison Athene

Saint Somewhere Brewing
www.saintsomewherebrewing.com

Country of origin United States
First brewed 2007
Alcohol content 7.5% abv
Serving temperature 46°F, 8°C

Beer is a recent pursuit for Bob Sylvester. He only started brewing in 2001, after he received an all-in-one home-brew kit as a gift. Five years and a handful of blue ribbons later, he opened Saint Somewhere on Florida's Gulf Coast. The tiny brewery produces a mere 250 barrels a year, but Sylvester is earning a steadily growing cult following for his Belgian styles.

This saison, named for Athena, the Greek goddess of wisdom and peace, was the first he bottled as a pro. It starts with standard Belgian and pilsner malts with a touch of wheat and fragrant East Kent Golding hops. In what turned out to be a fluke, Sylvester added rosemary from his backyard. Added to beer, rosemary tends to produce a piney, resiny flavor, not unlike the Centennial hop; the chamomile notches back that influence just a bit. The result is a wonderfully complex saison with a delightful finish. **DR**

Tasting notes
A fluffy cloud of foam floats above a golden body with the aroma of a spring garden of honeysuckle and lemon zest. A peppery bite and soft apple notes give the malt complexity.

Saison de Pipaix

La Brasserie à Vapeur
www.vapeur.com

Country of origin Belgium
First brewed 1785
Alcohol content 6% abv
Serving temperature 46°–50°F, 8°–10°C

In the early 19th century, this was a typical small industrial brewery of the period, but it finally fell victim to changes in the industry that saw the big brewing groups rise on a tide of fizzy lager, drowning many smaller concerns. By 1983 it was derelict.

Enter local teacher and beer fanatic Jean-Louis Dits, who'd nurtured a dream of brewing since a visit to the nearby brewery of Dupont. He bought the brewery and set about restoring it, renaming it "Steam Brewery" after the vintage machine that provided the motive power. Dits dug into the archives for heritage recipes, interpreting them with his own imaginative flair and redeploying long-forgotten spices and flavorings. This, his signature brew, is typical, rejecting the contemporary hoppy saison model for a complex and exotic mélange infused with pepper, ginger, sweet and bitter orange peels, and star anise. **DdM**

Tasting notes
Fluffy, bubbly white head and a toffeeish malt aroma dosed with herbal notes and invitingly dark aniseed-like spicing. Gently bittering orange fruit and brown sugar on the finish.

Saison d'Erpe-Mere

Brouwerij De Glazen Toren
www.glazentoren.be

Country of origin Belgium
First brewed 2004
Alcohol content 6.9% abv
Serving temperature 44°F, 7°C

When Brouwerij De Glazen Toren opened in 2004, the trio behind the brewery—Jef Van den Steen, Dirk De Pauw, Mark De Neef—decided that brewing the first Flemish saison would be a great way to put their new brewery on the map. It was a gamble that paid off.

Pilsner and wheat malt go into the mash, while the hopping regime includes Hallertauer hops grown locally, plus English Target and Czech Saaz. A sense of theater is added by presenting the beer wrapped in multicolored tissue paper.

Such has been the success of the brewery that it once more expanded in 2009, on its fifth anniversary. Over its five years, several beers have been added to the lineup, but Saison d'Erpe-Mere remains the crown jewel. De Glazen Toren exports to France, Italy, the Netherlands, the United Kingdom, Canada, the United States, and Japan. **CC**

Tasting notes

Hazy yellow orange that pours with a big head. Yeasty, citrusy, and earthy aroma, with a hint of mild pepper. Palate is earthy and floral, with fruity notes. Pleasantly bitter in the finish.

Saison Dupont

Brasserie Dupont
www.brasserie-dupont.com

Country of origin Belgium
First brewed *ca*. 1930
Alcohol content 6.5% abv
Serving temperature 46°–54°F, 8°–12°C

In Belgium, the most sought-after beer from Dupont is the Moinette Blonde, but in some of the export markets the Saison is more in demand. The Saison is, perhaps, the beer that is most emblematic for this brewery. After all, Dupont is, historically speaking, a saison brewery, and theirs is probably the only one to remain most faithful to the traditional Hainaut saisons.

Not that Saison Dupont hasn't changed over the years. The strength of 6.5 percent might have been constant since the 1950s, but prior to that, it was really a drink for summer labor at the farm; even fermented out, it probably never exceeded 4.5 percent. Strangely enough, Saison Dupont used to be seen as a bit of an oddball compared to the other saisons still available thirty to forty years ago. The reason was the brewery's deep, special well that yielded very soft liquor and gave a slightly sourish-metallic flavor to the beer. **JPa**

Tasting notes

Hazy, yellow orange beer. Lively nose, lemony, then soft cheese aromas such as Brie, plus tart orange zest. On the palate, spicy, yeasty. Dry, yet at the same time refreshing.

Saison-Brett

Boulevard Brewing | www.blvdbeer.com

Country of origin United States
First brewed 2008
Alcohol content 8.5% abv
Serving temperature 55°F, 13°C

Boulevard Brewing in Kansas City, Missouri, went a decade without introducing a new full-time beer—this was not because its brewers lacked a creative streak, but because they were busy making an already established lineup of beers twenty-four hours a day, seven days a week. Not until a new brewhouse went online in 2007 did they have the facilities to produce a special Smokestack Series that includes four year-round beers and four seasonals sold in 750-ml bottles. The additions include the seasonal Saison-Brett, which has the wild yeast *Brettanomyces* added upon bottling.

"The inspiration came from some of the great Belgian saisons and also from my childhood when I grew up on a farm in Belgium," said brewmaster Steven Pauwels. "We would help out farmers during the harvest. The dusty smell of hay when we were loading it on the field and the barn smell when we were unloading it are completely different but very unique. . . . I tried to get the fresh hay smell through dry hopping and the barn smell with the *Brett*."

Pauwels began working on a saison in 2004, soon realizing *Brettanomyces* would be a necessary addition for the seasonal version. "Our main business is non-Brett beers and we did not want to spoil this fun. So we installed a bottling line in a warehouse away from the brewery to keep the Brett away from the brewery," he said. In 2006, he sent a batch to a festival in Cooperstown, New York, home of the Baseball Hall of Fame, calling the beer "George Brett," a play on the name of Kansas City's most famous baseball player and the unique yeast strain. **SH**

Tasting notes

Pours hazy and orange after being released with a large pop from the corked bottle. Earthy and complex, a myriad of spicy and grassy aromas. Bready, funky in the mouth, very lively on the tongue, then dry, leaving an impression of champagne.

Sakara Gold

Al Ahram Beverages Company | www.alahrambeverages.com

Country of origin Egypt
First brewed 1999
Alcohol content 4% abv
Serving temperature 37°–43°F, 3°–6°C

Egypt is low in the world rankings for beer consumption despite a 5,000-year history of brewing, almost as ancient as that of the Sumerians of Mesopotamia, the supposed discoverers of beer. Texts indicate that pyramid laborers drank beer three times a day. Five different styles are described, and the god Osiris is credited with teaching man how to brew.

In the modern era, Al Ahram Beverages Company (known as the Pyramids Brewing Company until 1953) has been brewing its dominant beer brand Stella (unrelated to Stella Artois) since 1897. For decades, there was a thriving bar and club scene in downtown Cairo, and during World War II thousands of Allied troops slaked their desert thirsts on the local beer. Increased Muslim conservatism since the 1970s has brought about a decline in the local bar and club trade and a growing focus on exports. Today, tourists consume 40 percent of Al Ahram's annual beer output, while exports go to ten countries as far apart as Senegal, Madagascar, and Indonesia.

In 1997, wine specialists El Gouna Beverages decided to challenge Al Ahram's beer-market monopoly. Based at the resort town of Hurghada on the Red Sea, El Gouna came out with Sakara Gold, a higher-priced, higher-quality rival to Al Ahram's Stella, in 1999. Sakara Gold addressed Stella's downmarket reputation and poor consistency and rapidly bit a chunk out of Al Ahram's market dominance; but in February 2001, El Gouna was taken over by Al Ahram. The label depicts the stepped pyramid located at Saqqara, after which the beer is named. **JP**

Tasting notes

A straw-colored thirst-quencher offering a subtle aroma of sweet malt. A balanced flavor: medium bitterness, a hint of lemon sweetness from the malt, and a good hop character at the back of the palate. Finely effervescent without being overcarbonated.

Since 1795

Samson ®

Budweiser Bier

Samson Budweiser Bier Premium

Budějovický Měšt'anský Pivovar
www.budweiser1795.com

Country of origin Czech Republic
First brewed *ca.* 1950s
Alcohol content 4.7% abv
Serving temperature 46°F, 8°C

Brewing originated in the South Bohemian town of České Budějovice (Budweis in German) in 1265, when citizens residing within its walls were granted the right to brew beer. Established in 1795, Budějovický Měšt'anský is České Budějovice's oldest brewery, senior to its neighbor Budweiser Budvar by 110 years. Beer is still brewed to the Bavarian Reinheitsgebot law of 1516, with much of its reputation resting on the extreme softness of its water, drawn from the artesian wells below the town. Only prized floral Saaz hops are used and sweet Moravian malted barley, while its current yeast strain has been cultivated for 150 years. Open-vat fermenters are still in use and long lagering (storing) conditions are strictly observed.

BB Budweiser Bier is the best-known brand, but much of the range is marketed under the Samson label, conforming to the accepted concept—which Samson Budweiser Bier Premium illustrates perfectly—that moderate bitterness and high hop aromas are balanced by a malty, slightly sweet, bready body.

The company began exporting to the United States in 1871, though Anheuser-Busch registered the Budweiser brand seven years later, starting a long series of trademark disputes that continue to this day. **AG**

Tasting notes
Golden in color with vanilla and citrus on the nose, followed by a honeyed, sweet malty palate. The soft mouthfeel is one of the defining characteristics due to its celebrated water.

Sankt Gallen Yokohama XPA

Sankt Gallen Brewery
www.sanktgallenbrewery.com

Country of origin Japan
First brewed 2008
Alcohol content 6% abv
Serving temperature 50°–54°F, 10°–12°C

Sankt Gallen has the distinction of being the first unofficial microbrewery in Japan. Before regulations were changed to allow small breweries, its parent company operated a small bar in Tokyo's Roppongi district, where a small brewing setup was installed to make beer of less than 1 percent alcohol, effectively eliminating the need for a brewing license.

The Sankt Gallen Brewery opened in 1997 in a small suburb near Yokohama. Initially, the company brewed Golden Ale, Pale Ale, Amber Ale, and Black Porter. But in recent years they have released unusual beers with sweetish flavor profiles, such as Imperial Chocolate Stout, aimed at female customers. This XPA is another example of their pioneering spirit, though the flavor profile is rather conventional. Since the malt character and hop bitterness are quite pronounced, it was hard at first for the general public to drink it, so initial acceptance was slow. Yet once this hurdle had been passed, Yokohama XPA attracted a dedicated following among Japanese beer fans.

Even more remarkable is the purity of the water used for brewing: it's sourced from the City of Yokohama's Water Works, and is certified to be pure to 0.0000 percent. **BH**

Tasting notes
Pours a very bright gold, with an off-white head. Brisk hoppiness in the aroma, backed by pale malt. The rich malt flavor is balanced nicely by herbal hops. A brisk, hoppy finish.

Samson: another fine beer from the famous brewing city Budweis.

Sarajevsko Pivo

Sarajevska Pivara | www.pivara.ba

Country of origin Bosnia and Herzegovina
First brewed 1864
Alcohol content 4.9% abv
Serving temperature 46°F, 8°C

During the war in the Balkans between 1992 and 1995, the city of Sarajevo endured the longest military siege in modern European history. Astonishingly, Sarajevska Pivara never ceased production—raw materials for brewing (along with other much-needed supplies for the inhabitants) came via a concealed, hand-dug tunnel stretching beneath the airport. Understandably, quality suffered to some extent and output was greatly reduced, but the continuing presence of the city's beer was an important emblem of the embattled inhabitants' spirit of resistance and determination to carry on as best they could. More importantly, the brewery's three deep artesian wells provided the only source of fresh drinking water for the entire city throughout most of the ordeal. It is not difficult, therefore, to see why Sarajevska Pivara and the beers it produces continue to be held in such high esteem by the locals to this day.

In 2004, the impressive, barrel-vaulted Pivnica HS beer hall opened right next door to the brewery, creating a superb drinking environment in which fresh, albeit slightly hazy, unfiltered, and unpasteurized Sarajevsko Pivo can also be enjoyed, dispensed straight from the conditioning tanks. Today the brewery has over five hundred employees, but although it is seeking to develop export markets, including the United States and the United Kingdom, distribution is still mainly concentrated in Bosnia and Herzegovina, and the Sarajevo region in particular. Hopefully this will change, as there can be little doubt this is a beer that deserves a much wider audience. **JW**

Tasting notes

Pale gold with a tight white head; a heady aroma of resiny hops greets the nose, whilst tangy, citrus hop flavors again dominate the palate. Developing biscuity malt notes then combine to create a full-bodied beer with a hugely, refreshingly long and dry, hop-infused finish.

Since 1996, Sarajevska Pivara has made significant investments in its brewing equipment.

Schell Pilsner

August Schell Brewing Company | www.schellsbrewery.com

Country of origin United States
First brewed 1985
Alcohol content 5.6% abv
Serving temperature 40°–42°F, 4°–6°C

August Schell immigrated to the United States in search of a better life, alongside waves of enterprising Germans and other Europeans. In southern Minnesota, Schell found the local water well suited for brewing and demand for German-style beer strong, and there he established what is now the second-oldest family-owned brewery in the United States. Over the decades, the brewery adapted to setbacks such as Prohibition and persevered through most of the 20th century with the classic adjunct-based mainstream lagers.

By the mid 1980s, the brewery had a new family member in charge: current president Ted Marti. It became clear to him that mainstream beer was being increasingly dominated by big players, and, in order to survive, the brewery would need to change direction. Spurred on by Charles Finkel of Merchant Du Vin, who sold the beers across the country, Schell introduced this all-malt pilsner and a Weissbier. They sold well and bolstered the formidable little brewery's reputation.

The company still brews its mainstream beers, but it is known today for its high-quality craft-oriented beers. It's a testament to an authentic pilsner that there's not much to say about it: 100 percent pilsner malt and Hallertau hops for that classic herbal German hop aroma, carefully brewed to avoid anything interfering with the delicate flavors and aromas. Looking back at the slow unraveling of the mass-market beers that claim to be pilsners, it's hard to understand how the noble style could have been so completely subverted. One sip of this beer makes you glad that there are still some real traditionalists around. **RM**

Tasting notes

On the nose, soft, herbaceous aromas backed by bready, slightly yeasty notes. Malty on the tongue, with just a hint of sweetness, then building to a fine, crisp balance from the noble hops. Schell Pilsner finishes softly malty, with a clean bitterness.

Schiehallion

Harviestoun Brewery | www.harviestoun.com

Country of origin Scotland
First brewed 1994
Alcohol content 4.8% abv
Serving temperature 46°F, 8°C

Beer names come from all corners of the imagination. Schiehallion (pronounced she-ha-lee-on) is a much-loved Perthshire mountain that comes second only to Ben Nevis in Scottish affections. It was this mountain that sprung to mind when Harviestoun first produced Schiehallion—the cask-conditioned lager—in 1994, at a time when most of the brewery's beers were more "traditional" Scottish ales. They were based on the old 70/-, 80/-, and 85/- styles, bearing names such as Original, Waverley, Montrose, Old Manor, and Ptarmigan (only Ptarmigan is still produced).

According to head brewer Stuart Cail, who had joined from Sunderland's Vaux Brewery, "during the mid-1990s, the market started to move from darker malty beers towards lighter hoppier ones. So as the sales of the darker beers declined, the lighter beers increased. From the first batch, Schiehallion grew in popularity and soon became our best seller at the time."

Schiehallion has been festooned with all manner of awards, including being several times a gold winner at the Great British Beer Festival, though, as Cail points out, "It was in the speciality section, which is interesting as it is brewed solely with water, malt, hops, and yeast!"

Lager malt, wheat malt, and a blend of Challenger, Hersbrücker, and Styrian hops go into the brew. It is fermented at a low temperature with a lager yeast. The use of the German Hersbrücker hop is a delightful play on Harviestoun founder Ken Brooker's name (which would be Herr Brooker in Germany). He established the brewery in a 200-year-old former cowshed on the Harviestoun estate at Dollar, Clackmannanshire. **AG**

Tasting notes

A beautifully crafted pale straw-colored lager beer with a grapefruit-laced aroma and a crisp freshness in the flavor. This also has some floral sweetness but is dominated by a full malted biscuit palate. The hop influence reappears in the pleasingly bitter aftertaste.

Schimmele

Ruppaner Brauerei | www.ruppaner.de

Country of origin Germany
First brewed 1992
Alcohol content 5% abv
Serving temperature 46°F, 8°C

Given its position on both the river Rhine and the shores of Lake Constance, the south German city of Konstanz is in a bit of a strange position. Set on the southern shore (the "Swiss shore") of the Rhine, it was brutally cut off from its natural hinterland when the surrounding countryside was invaded by Swiss troops in 1460. Konstanz tried to join the Swiss Confederacy, but the request was rejected and Konstanz soldiered on, a German city on the "wrong" shore of the Rhine.

In terms of beer, Konstanz's remaining German has had positive effects, in that local brewers have easy access to the hop crop from nearby Tettnang, along the northern shore of Lake Constance. They tend to take full advantage of it, whereas local breweries in nearby Switzerland tend to be shy about hops, though hops are grown on the southern shore, too. The area is also famous for its apples, pears, and cider, so maybe the locals are simply more into apples than hops.

Ruppaner was founded in 1795 and has been in the hands of the Ruppaner family for seven generations, since 1872. Their Schimmele (literally "moldy," but better understood as "cloudy") is typical of the pale lagers brewed in the area: crisp and dryish, with liberal amounts of Tettnanger hopping. The major difference is that it is an unfiltered version, which vouches for added crispness and subtle complexity. **LM**

Tasting notes

This is a pale straw-colored, cloudy beer with a fine white head. The pale malt base is present enough for good balance, as the flowery, peppery hops are quite powerful overall.

Schlappeseppel Export

Eder & Heylands Brauerei | www.schlappeseppel.de

Country of origin Germany
First brewed *ca.* 1631
Alcohol content 5.5% abv
Serving temperature 46°F, 8°C

As a beer style, export is a common beer in a brewery's portfolio, and they are often named after an auspicious event in the company's history—Schlappeseppel Export is no different. The story of this beer reputedly goes back to 1631, when Germany was in the throes of the destructive Thirty Years War. The Swedish army marched into the city of Aschaffenburg, and there was a great demand for beer. However, the local brewery was dry, so the Swedes looked for a soldier who was able to brew. They came upon Joseph Lögler, who was lame and called "the lame Seppel" ("Seppel" being a nickname for Joseph), thus the name "schlappe Seppel." This is the officially recognized date of the beer's birthday, even though it has immeasurably changed down through the centuries (for instance, it would have been dark when first brewed).

As the war ground on, Schlappeseppel beer was produced in a small brewery connected to a beer hall. Nowadays, the Schlappeseppel brand of beers (which also includes a pils, dunkel, and kellerbier) is owned by the brewing combination of Eder and Heylands, a family-owned operation that joined forces in 2001 and that does all the brewing in Großostheim. However, the beer hall that bears the same name still exists in the ancient city of Aschaffenburg and is popular with both residents of the town and visitors. **WO**

Tasting notes

Golden colored and clear with a light aroma of hops on the nose; this reoccurs in the long finish. The nose is very fresh, with light aromas of fine yeast and a crisp malty taste.

King Gustav Adolph of Sweden leads his army into Aschaffenburg in 1631.

Schwechater Zwickl

Brauerei Schwechat | www.schwechater.at

Country of origin Austria
First brewed 1995
Alcohol content 5.4% abv
Serving temperature 44°F, 7°C

Unfiltered "Zwickl" beers became popular in Austria during the late 1980s and early 1990s. Schwechater's brewmaster Johann Bruck picked up on the trend and developed his own interpretation. While most Zwickl beers of the time only had a slight haze from the yeast, Bruck decided to go for a massive turbidity. He put more than 60 percent malted wheat on the grain bill, which not only made the beer hazy but also gave it a full-bodied character unparalleled in other Zwickl beers.

The packaging in nostalgic green bottles is part of Schwechater's success story, drawing on the brewery's status as the largest and oldest existing brewery in Vienna's metropolitan area. Peter Descrolier founded it in 1632, and it was acquired by Franz Anton Dreher in 1796. His son Anton developed modern lager-brewing methods—the result was the reddish Vienna-style lager that was first released in 1841. Austrian brewers claim that this was the invention of lager beer as such—although there had been lager beers before in Bavaria. Dreher's real innovation was the temperature control in the cellars and massive cooling efforts. His Vienna lager beer proved to be an instant success.

With a capacity of 26.4 million gallons (1 million hl), Schwechater remains the largest brewery in the region. It became part of Brau A. G. in the 1970s and is now part of Heineken's brewing empire. **CS**

Tasting notes
Arguably the haziest Zwickl one can imagine. The aroma is dominated by an herbal hop character. Soft, creamy mouthfeel and an intense hop finish. Refreshing.

Session Lager

Full Sail Brewing | www.fullsailbrewing.com

Country of origin United States
First brewed 2005
Alcohol content 5.1% abv
Serving temperature 39°F, 4°C

A long time ago, the United States was home to a vast number of breweries that made beer mostly for local consumption. Then came Prohibition, which made it illegal to make and sell all alcohol. By the time Prohibition was repealed, the tasty lager that many breweries had made before Prohibition had become a lost tradition, giving way to increasingly lighter-flavored beers brewed using adjuncts such as corn and rice.

Full Sail Brewing set out to revive pre-Prohibition lager when it released Session. It is an all-malt lager that is available only in squat 11-ounce (330-ml) bottles known as stubbies. "A bunch of us in the brewery always talked about how much we liked the look of the stubbies, and how you just didn't see them anymore," says brewmaster John Harris. "We kept talking about how fun and different it would be to make a beer and put it in stubbies. Harris says there was no discussion over what kind of beer would go into these retro-looking bottles. "It had to be a pre-Pro lager," he says. "You couldn't put an ale in a bottle like that. It just wouldn't be right."

In the past, stubbies often featured a quote or an image under the cap. On the underside of each Session cap, Full Sail has placed a symbol for "rock," "paper," or "scissors," so you can play a round of the game while having a "session" with friends. **LMo**

Tasting notes
Hints of sweet malt and a touch of citrus waft slightly to the nose. Smooth, crisp, and refreshing to drink, Session Lager pairs well with shellfish and salads as well as spicy food.

Full Sail set out to revive the kind of beer that disappeared after Prohibition.

Shiga Kogen IPA

Shiga Kogen Beer | www.tamamura-honten.co.jp

Country of origin Japan
First brewed 2004
Alcohol content 6% abv
Serving temperature 43°–46°F, 6°–8°C

Founded in the fall of 2004, Shiga Kogen Beer is one of the newest Japanese breweries, though the parent company, sake brewer Tamamura Honten, has been in business since 1805. The brewery is located in a mountainous corner of rural Nagano Prefecture, and thanks to their two centuries of doing business there, they have quite a strong presence in the market. Shiga Kogen is a popular ski area, and its beers can be found on tap in a number of ski resort bars.

The lineup of beers is impressive, ranging from the 7 percent Miyama Blonde and 5.5 percent Pale Ale to the 5.5 percent Porter, all of which are masterfully brewed. In all its beers, Shiga Kogen takes a serious approach, going as far as planting its own hops; recently, the company has been "wet-hopping" certain seasonal brews using fresh-picked hops. Of particular note, however, is this strongly flavored India Pale Ale, a variation of their massive 8 percent House IPA, which is a limited-edition brew available on draft.

Brewmaster Eigo Sato sums this beer up by saying that it has taken the brewery about five years to get the flavor profile finished. At first, he explains, due to the higher quantity of malt used to make such a high-gravity beer, it really didn't have the aroma and flavor he was after. With each batch, adjustments were made in both the malt and hops used. At present, the beer primarily makes use of hops from the United States, including Warrior and Chinook for bittering, followed by Centennial, Cascade, and Amarillo for aroma. Sato admits that he will likely continue to tweak this beer to achieve further improvements. **BH**

Tasting notes

The beer is a hazy orange bronze, with an ivory-colored head. There is a citruslike hop aroma, followed by a crisply bitter initial taste. The citrus-infused malt flavors then unfold, with clearly defined American hop flavors, leading to a brisk and refreshing finish.

Sierra Nevada Pale Ale

Sierra Nevada Brewing Company | www.sierranevada.com

Country of origin United States
First brewed 1980
Alcohol content 5.6% abv
Serving temperature 44°–48°F, 7°–9°C

Take the corner of this page and dog-ear it. This is one of the most important beers in this book. Sure, there are much bigger and more outrageous beers nowadays, but it took a lot of nerve and spirit at the time to put Sierra Nevada Pale Ale on the market.

Sierra Nevada's founder Ken Grossman wanted to make a beer that didn't reference English pale ales, and that had a pronounced hop aroma—there weren't that many in those days. He looked at some of the newer hop varieties becoming available. Up to that time, it had just been Cluster, a good-yielding hop with a coarse aroma that was the bitter foundation of almost all American beer at one time.

After countless home-brews and a dozen batches on the home-built ten-barrel system, Sierra Nevada Pale Ale was born. The brewery has always used whole-cone hops. After extensive trials, Grossman remains convinced that they offer "cleaner flavors . . . and are less vegetative" than the finely ground cones that form the basis of hop pellets. They chose Cascade, a racy new variety at the time, aromatically the best of the new breeds that appeared in the 1970s.

So, at 5.6 percent it's not very extreme. It doesn't use the latest boutique hops or wild yeast. And in its original packaging, it's so ubiquitous that it's easy to take for granted. But you know what? This beer quite simply tastes good, and offers the kind of simple pleasure craft brewing can give when it's done right. If it weren't for the vision, persistence, and technological skill of Ken Grossman and the rest of his crew in Chico, craft beer might taste very different today. **RM**

Tasting notes

Fresh grassy, resiny hop nose with orangy undercurrents; also fruity with maybe just a hint of peachiness. In the mouth, it is crisp and dry up front, with a slightly toasty malt character that then blends into a clean, assertive hop bitterness and a long, perfumed bitter finish.

Singha

Boon Rawd Brewery | www.singhabeer.com

Country of origin Thailand
First brewed 1933
Alcohol content 5% abv
Serving temperature 39°–43°F, 4°–6°C

In the context of Southeast Asian beer, Singha is imbued with provenance. It was the first beer to be brewed in Thailand, by royal appointment. Founded by Boonrawd Srethabutra, today it remains in family hands.

An international premium brand, Singha has an all–malt barley base. It was previously 6 percent alcohol, but the change helped distinguish it from its stronger domestic rival, Chang. The beer that you drink at home tastes the same as the beer in Thailand—Singha isn't brewed outside of the country. Yet while holding its own at home, Singha lags behind Chang internationally. This is being addressed: Boon Rawd have signed a distribution deal for the United Kingdom with Molson Coors, a company that has had success in developing niches for exotic imports. That said, Singha is clearly best enjoyed on a beach overlooking Thailand's invitingly clear waters. **LN**

Tasting notes
Color is of runny honey. The nose offers sweet graininess, citrus lemony hop, and a hint of herbal spice. Mouthfeel provides biscuity malt balanced with floral hop bitterness.

Small Craft Warning

Clipper City Brewery | www.ccbeer.com

Country of origin United States
First brewed 2004
Alcohol content 7.25% abv
Serving temperature 46°F, 8°C

Clipper City Brewery's strong regional identity was one of its key assets after it began production in Baltimore in the mid 1990s. As Clipper City grew, though, it needed to establish an identity outside of Baltimore. Thus, the Heavy Seas line was created.

Labeled with cartoon pirates facing various calamities, Heavy Seas beers seem like a gimmick that would be more at home on a box of cereal. But a full taste of each reveals a serious, well-crafted, robust version of a classic style that, in the words of the brewery, is "extrAARGHdinary." All are bottle-conditioned and strong, ranging from 7 percent up to 10 percent. Small Craft Warning is a self-described "uber pils." Initially, the style seems a contradiction of terms; a classic pilsner, after all, is delicate—the opposite of "uber." But this unique hybrid somehow goes both light and heavy at once, with considerable complexity. **DR**

Tasting notes
Classic golden pilsner body radiates the sweet aroma of malt and spicy hops. Bready malt on the first sip evolves into a huge candylike flavor that is surprisingly well balanced.

Snowdonia Ale

Purple Moose Brewery | www.purplemoose.co.uk

Country of origin Wales
First brewed 2006
Alcohol content 3.6% abv
Serving temperature 54°F, 12°C

Purple Moose Brewery is a thriving microbrewery in Porthmadog, North Wales. Its founder, Lawrence Washington, a keen home-brewer, joined forces with Arthur Frampton, formerly of Moor Beer in Somerset, using Frampton's equipment to produce trial runs of recipes. When these proved to be a hit, Lawrence knew he could turn professional.

All Purple Moose beers are sold under dual Welsh and English names. In 2009, the brewery received a major boost when its pale session ale, appropriately named Cwrw Eryri, or Snowdonia Ale, was judged Champion Beer of Wales. It is brewed from pale malt, with a little crystal malt and torrified wheat thrown in for good measure, and laced with Pioneer, Savinjski Golding, and Lubelski hops. The last two add a Central European slant to proceedings, coming from Slovenia and Poland, respectively, and a fresh, piney, citrus note to the beer. **JE**

Tasting notes

A bright golden ale with a clean aroma of pine and citrus, along with some hints of tea. The taste is crisp and bittersweet with a citrus freshness and piney hop notes, before a dry finish.

St.-Ambroise Pale Ale

Brasserie McAuslan Brewing | www.mcauslan.com

Country of origin Canada
First brewed 1989
Alcohol content 5% abv
Serving temperature 41°F, 5°C

After two years of planning and development with the help of brewing consultant Alan Pugsley, Peter McAuslan opened Brasserie McAuslan Brewing in February 1989. The first beer delivered was a pale ale named for the street on which the brewery was situated.

In developing St.-Ambroise Pale Ale with brewer and partner Ellen Bounsall, along with Pugsley, McAuslan wished to build a beer that emulated those of his youth; it would be unabashedly Québécois in character, with a firmly fruity malt backbone and ample hoppiness. His theory was that a taste of the past would resonate well with Quebeckers, given their notoriously long memories and borderline reverence for their collective history—the years since his beer's launch have proven him correct. St.-Ambroise remains an icon of modern Québécois brewing and a fixture in stores and bars across the province and beyond. **SB**

Tasting notes

Deep gold in color, this pale ale combines a robustly fruity aroma (apricot, peach) with a balanced and moderately hopped, off-dry maltiness. Ideal with well-aged cheddar.

St. Bernardus Tripel

Brouwerij St. Bernardus | www.sintbernardus.be

Country of origin Belgium
First brewed 1994
Alcohol content 8% abv
Serving temperature 48°F, 9°C

Even though a smiling monk proffers a foaming chalice of beer on the labels of most of the beers from Brouwerij St. Bernardus, you're no more likely to find maize, rice, or other brewing shortcuts in their beers than you would find a man of the cloth striding through the secular surroundings of this brewery in Watou. It wasn't always so. Up until 1992, the brewery produced beers under license for the Trappist monks at St. Sixtus in Westvleteren. This came to an end when Westvleteren's beers went in-house and what became known as Brouwerij St. Bernardus began to stand on its own two feet. A sign of the brewery's confidence was the debut, in 1994, of this tripel. Hopped with both Target and Styrian Golding, and as golden as a sunny day, this beer was an instant success and showed that even an increasingly commonplace beer could be a real winner (which is what the Tripel was at the World Beer Championships in 2003).

Since its debut, other beers have joined the regular range of Brouwerij St. Bernardus, which now exports to more than twenty countries. A new visitor's center has also been built, which houses a bar that is filled with old brewery memorabilia. Brouwerij St. Bernardus only uses locally grown hops from nearby Poperinge, although it plans to start growing its own hops next to the brewery in the near future. Malt comes from northern France. Although many Belgian breweries have switched to stainless steel brew kettles in the last twenty years, St. Bernardus sticks to its 1960s copper kettles. Many beer lovers and brewers feel that copper produces a more complex beer. **CC**

Tasting notes

The Tripel is dark gold in color with a flowery, fruity, slightly yeasty taste. It pours with a big white head, and also has a mild sweetness and hint of bitterness on the palate. This well-balanced brew pairs well with lighter meats such as chicken or fish.

St. Bernardus features on a Belgian postage stamp. ➡

St.Bernard – St.Bernardus
Belgique-België

25

1990 (16)
PH

St.-Feuillien Tripel

Brasserie St.-Feuillien | www.st-feuillien.com

Štěpán Pale Lager

Pivovarský Dům | www.gastroinfo.cz/pivodum

Country of origin Belgium
First brewed 1998
Alcohol content 8.5% abv
Serving temperature 44°F, 7°C

Country of origin Czech Republic
First brewed 1998
Alcohol content 4% abv
Serving temperature 44°F, 7°C

Brasserie Friart opened in 1873 and closed in 1977. Eleven years later, it reopened as Brasserie St.-Feuillien under the same family. Prior to closing the original brewery, the Friart family had brewed blond and brown beers, and St.-Feuillien Tripel was created when the brewery reopened. Many Belgian brewers have a tripel (or triple, if you want): light-colored, sweetish, possibly looking to Westmalle's classic for inspiration. The trick is to make one that stands out in a crowded beer market. This one does. Many of St.-Feuillien's beers have been contract brewed at Brasserie Du Bocq in Purnode, but all of their Tripel has been brewed at the home site in Le Roeulx. Is this the secret of its success?

In 2008, the brewery completed a major upgrade program, including the construction of a new building and the installation of up-to-date equipment. All the old buildings were also meticulously restored. **CC**

The leader of a wave of innovative new Czech microbreweries, Pivovarský Dům has raised eyebrows with its unusual lagers, brightened with doses of cherry, banana, coffee, lime, almond, and even nettles and potatoes. But beyond the quirks is a line of classic Bohemian beer styles, the flagship of which is a remarkable pale lager known as Štěpán, or Stephen.

Owners Václav Potěšil and Jan Šuráň consult with breweries around the Czech Republic and as far away as Vietnam and Mongolia, sending recipes originally developed as the brewpub's specialty beers off to be produced elsewhere. However, there is only one Štěpán Pale Lager, a charismatic, cloudy "yeast beer" made under the supervision of young brewmaster Martin Vávra. It is not available in bottles, and is generally only available at Pivovarský Dům and its sister beer bar, Pivovarský Klub, also in Prague. **ER**

Tasting notes

Golden orange color that pours with a hefty white foam. Very aromatic on the nose, with notes of mild citrus, malt sweetness, even pepper. A very complex tripel.

Citrus blossom, orange peel, and honeyed fruit dominate the nose. To the eye, it is often quite cloudy, due to the addition of fresh wort and yeast and lack of filtration.

Stiegl Goldbräu

Stieglbrauerei zu Salzburg | www.stiegl.at

Country of origin Austria
First brewed 1912
Alcohol content 4.9% abv
Serving temperature 44°F, 7°C

When Stiegl registered the Goldbräu brand in 1912, the brewery had already been active for 420 years. It started in 1492 in Salzburg and moved to its present location outside the former city walls in 1863. The Stiegl Brewery buildings have been well preserved by the Kiener family, which own Austria's largest independent brewery.

The Goldbräu is Austria's single best-selling beer and could be considered style-defining for what Austrians call "Märzenbier." While "Märzen" refers to the stronger Festbier (festival beers) in Bavaria, and pretty much the rest of the world, Austria's Märzen typically has only between 11.5 and 12.5 degrees Plato and is a bit lighter both in color as well as in alcohol.

Stiegl insists the Goldbräu will always be brewed with a strength of 12 degrees Plato, as it was introduced at that strength in 1912. Only in wartime—and when legally required—has the strength been lowered. **CS**

Tasting notes
Grassy and hoppy notes in the nose go along with a sweet maltiness that dominates the aroma and the palate. It finishes with a hint of almondlike bitterness.

Stille Nacht

De Dolle Brouwers | www.dedollebrouwers.be

Country of origin Belgium
First brewed 1980
Alcohol content 12% abv
Serving temperature 50°F, 10°C

The Stille Nacht ("Silent Night") is De Dolle's winter seasonal. Originally it was a dark beer, but after people began to refer to it as "the good Oerbier," brewer Kris Herteleer grew frustrated and decided to change the beer entirely. Since 1982, it has been golden in color.

In the 1990s, De Dolle fermented Stille Nacht with a yeast strain from the Rodenbach Brewery, until they ceased offering it to brewers in 2000. Up to then, the yeast was weaker and complex. In an attempt to keep the beer's character, Herteleer cultured what he had left of the yeast. Its complexity led the strain to mutate and grow stronger while losing much of the lactic acid and bacterial characteristics. He changed his brewing methods to regain some of its complexity; now 20 percent of the wort is fermented with lactic acid bacteria, and then blended back with the rest of the beer, adding a sour sharpness and improving its drinkability. **MO**

Tasting notes
Thick aroma suggests stone fruits, candy sugar, and a slight earthiness. The mouth starts sweet with a velvety body, a sour backbone, and notes of spices and yeasty esters; dry finish.

Stone & Wood Pale Lager

Stone & Wood | www.stoneandwood.com.au

Country of origin Australia
First brewed 2009
Alcohol content 4.7% abv
Serving temperature 39°F, 4°C

Matilda Bay Brewery was established by Phil Sexton in 1984 and was acquired by Carlton and United Breweries in 1990. Although this acquisition increased the profile of Matilda Bay Brewery's craft beer offerings, to many it was the beginning of the end when it came to the very features of the beers that had attracted drinkers to them in the first place. The man credited with breathing new life into these old brands, as well as offering a few worthy new ones, is brewer Brad Rogers.

Having largely achieved his goals at Matilda Bay Brewery, Brad decided to set up a craft brewery with Ross Jurisich and Jamie Cook in the beachside town of Byron Bay in northern New South Wales. Byron Bay is the home of a diverse and accepting community of surfers, tourists, hippies, and other eclectics. Along with its beautiful beaches, abundant sunshine, and tanned locals, it is surely one of the most desirable places in the world to set up a brewery.

It was with the local environment in mind that Brad Rogers designed Stone and Wood's first beers: the Draught Ale and Pale Lager. Throwing away the style guide, his decision was simply to brew beer that people who lived in Byron Bay would want to drink when they wandered up to a sunny beer garden after a morning in the surf. This meant that refreshment and drinkability were paramount considerations, and although these qualities are of themselves given little credence by many beer commentators, one suspects their opinion might differ after a day of sun, sand, and frolic at Byron Bay! **DD**

Tasting notes

This highly sessionable beer draws on five different kinds of malt to offer a smooth mouthfeel while the hops play second fiddle. Designed for refreshment, the Pale Lager is best consumed with mates in the hot Australian sun after a morning at the beach.

Stone IPA

Stone Brewing | www.stonebrew.com

Country of origin United States
First brewed 1997
Alcohol content 6.9% abv
Serving temperature 55°F, 13°C

The Stone Brewing World Bistro, north of San Diego, California, artfully combines bare industrial elements with a lush beer garden, and is every bit as bold as the beer that financed its construction, graphically illustrating how quickly American beer drinkers embrace the type of beers Stone makes. Only ten years before they threw open the doors of the World Bistro in 2006, cofounders Greg Koch and Steve Wagner started Stone Brewing in a warehouse not far away.

They released Stone IPA as their first-anniversary beer, knowing it would then take a place in the regular lineup—and also establish the fact that each anniversary release would be an event itself. Like other Stone beers, the IPA sets itself apart because the recipe doesn't include any of the Cascade hops common in most West Coast hop-centric beers—instead, Chinook, Columbus, and Centennial provide the spice and bitterness.

Similar to many other relatively small breweries in the United States, Stone is environmentally friendly. In 2009, it was honored with a local sustainability award after initiating two major green projects. A solar system provides about 40 percent of the facility's total electrical power. With this amount of clean energy, the system could offset more than 583,000 pounds (22,070 hl) of carbon emissions over its lifetime, comparable to planting 200 acres (80 ha) of trees. An on-site wastewater treatment facility eliminated the need to truck 40,000 (1,514 hl) gallons of wastewater to San Diego each month, a step that sets a good example for a potential future eco-generation of business. **SH**

Tasting notes

Pale golden in the glass, topped by a white head that turns into thick lacing that tracks your sipping history. Bold from the start, with citrus and pine dominating the aroma; balanced by a measure of sweet malt on the palate. Long, bitter, finally dry finish.

Stone Ruination IPA

Stone Brewing | www.stonebrew.com

Country of origin United States
First brewed 2002
Alcohol content 7.7% abv
Serving temperature 55°F, 13°C

Stone Brewing celebrated its first anniversary in 1997 by releasing its first India Pale Ale and its second with a Double IPA. It stuck to a Double IPA for its third, fourth, and fifth anniversaries, each one a little hoppier than the last. For the sixth anniversary, Stone went in another direction, releasing a cranked-up version of its Smoked Porter. "We decided we couldn't put any more hops into that (the Double IPA) beer," says brewmaster Steve Wagner. So they made Stone Ruination, brewed basically to the recipe of the fifth-anniversary Double IPA beer, a member of the regular lineup, and took the anniversary beers in a variety of directions in each subsequent year.

"We'd got to know Vinnie (Cilurzo) at Blind Pig," Wagner says, talking about a growing interest in hoppy beers in the 1990s. Cilurzo brewed what is considered the first commercial Double IPA in America at a brewery just north of San Diego, and made one each year for the anniversary of the now-defunct brewery. Cilurzo had a tasting room at the brewery where customers would bring their Blind Pig growlers back for refills. Greg Koch, Stone Brewing Co.'s founder, had his growler filled with the last drop of Second Anniversary Ale, out of the brewery's final keg.

From the start, Wagner gave Stone's beers a different taste by forgoing the use of Cascade hops. "When I brewed at Pyramid Brewery (in Washington) we made a Cascade Pale Ale, and I was a little sensitive about redoing what we'd done at Pyramid," he says. So Stone declared itself completely Cascade free and charted its own happy hoppy way. **SH**

Tasting notes

Pours a slightly hazy orange, with bright citrusy and floral hops literally jumping out of the glass. Layers of fruit on the palate, from both the hops and fermentation. Pungent, piney, and spicy, but the bitterness never overwhelms the solid malt backbone.

Stoner

Birrificio Brùton | www.bruton.it

Country of origin Italy
First brewed 2006
Alcohol content 7.5% abv
Serving temperature 50°–54°F, 10°–12°C

The city of Lucca in Tuscany is one of the most famous areas for vineyards and wine in the whole of Italy, and everyone is used to drinking and enjoying wine that is produced here. But now things are changing, and a generation of brewers is emerging and persuading traditional consumers that beer can be just as good as wine. One of these brewers is twentysomething Jacopo Lenci, who in 2006 opened the Brùton microbrewery with the aid of a friend. His passion for tasty beers, beers that are different from the usual lagers that dominate the Italian market, was his first motivation, and the immediate success of Birrificio Brùton is a striking validation of his initial instincts.

Lenci started off with four beers, but now the brewery produces eight different ones, including three seasonal specialties. They are all top-fermenting beers, and include a strong ale and one inspired by the Belgian abbey style. Stoner is the strong ale, and it is a deceptive ale: its strength is not apparent and it is easy to drink. Dangerous but drinkable.

The beer is a blend of pale German malts, such as pilsner malt and carapils, with a good addition of malted wheat and malted rye and just a pinch of rolled oats. Saaz is added to give it a floral aroma, but Lenci also puts in some cane sugar during the boil and, at the end, some bitter orange peel and a nip of coriander. It's a compelling beer, but well rounded and smooth thanks to the presence of rye and oats. On the dining table, it's good company for white meat, such as chicken cooked with spices, or a risotto with pumpkin or asparagus. **MM**

Tasting notes

Brilliant golden color with a thick creamy foam. Very fruity nose with hints of apricots and caramelized fruit. When in the palate, it's well balanced and shows a round body with crisp maltiness and still fruit flavors. In the finish, there is a long and pleasant aftertaste.

Stoudt's Pils

Stoudt's Brewing Company | www.stoudtsbeer.com

Country of origin United States
First brewed 1988
Alcohol content 5.4% abv
Serving temperature 44°F, 7°C

When Carol and Ed Stoudt decided to add a brewery to their famous restaurant, Stoudt's Black Angus Steakhouse in Adamstown, Pennsylvania, they discovered a quirk in the state's law that required them to keep the brewery and the steakhouse as separate businesses. So Ed remained owner of the restaurant while Carol became one of the first female brewers in America when she opened Pennsylvania's first microbrewery in 1988.

Being of German ancestry, the pair traveled throughout Bavaria gathering ideas for exactly how they wanted to brew their beer. Initially, their pilsner was "a less dry Bavarian-style pils," according to Carol Stoudt. It evolved by trying different pilsner malt varieties, brew techniques, and experimentation. Their first pilsner won a silver medal in the European Pilsner category the first time they entered it at the Great American Beer Festival. However, by 1993, they felt all their tinkering with the recipe had really paid off and they had perfected it to the point where it was exactly what they wanted. The Pils then went on to win gold medals at the Great American Beer Festival in 1993, 1994, and 1997, along with a silver medal in 1999.

The beer was first available only in draft, then in 26-ounce (750-ml) bottles, and by 2002 in 11-ounce (335-ml) six-packs and cases. The beer is brewed all year-round and the sales are growing each year. Stoudt's Pils is a traditional German-style pils, brewed with Saaz hops. It is brewed to have an aggressive bitterness, at 42 IBUs on the International Bitterness Units scale, as well as those characteristic Saaz hop aromas. **JB**

Tasting notes

Stoudt's Pils is a bright clear pale golden color with a generous, pillowy white head. The nose has a beautiful signature noble hop aroma that's very traditional. The flavors are rich, clean, and well balanced, with great hop character and a long dry finish.

Strzelec Jasne Pełne

Browar Jędrzejów | www.piwostrzelec.pl

Country of origin Poland
First brewed 1995
Alcohol content 5.2% abv
Serving temperature 46°F, 8°C

Jędrzejów is a small town in central Poland that is famous for three things: its medieval Cistercian monastery, its astronomical museum, and its beer. The monastery was founded in 1142, and with it Jędrzejów's rich brewing tradition started. For many centuries, the white-robed Cistercian monks—also later known as Trappist monks—enjoyed a monopoly on the production and sale of beer in the busy market town. This ended in 1817 when the monastery was dissolved by the Austrians who had occupied this part of the country following the first partition of Poland.

In 1823, Karol and Ludwika Bilewicz founded a large private brewery near a bubbling stream. Ponds were established for the production of ice in winter, which was then stored in cellars and used in summer to cool beer. In the first decade of the 20th century, the site was remodeled into one of the largest modern pils breweries in the region. The brewery then changed hands a number of times until it was nationalized at the end of World War II. As a government enterprise, it became a subsidiary of the large Okocim brewery. After the fall of Communism, it was separated from the parent company in 1995, sold as an independent operation, and renamed the Strzelec Brewery. In 2005, it was acquired by Royal Unibrew.

Strzelec Jasne Pełne is the brewery's best seller. It is a pils-style beer made according to a traditional local recipe. In 2009, Strzelec Jasne Pełne attained its first truly international success and was awarded a silver Monde Selection medal by the International Institute for Quality Selections in Brussels. **RZ**

Tasting notes

In the glass Strzelec, Jasne Pełne is a light golden color with a solid head and a pleasant bouquet. The malty mouthfeel is well balanced by the crisp bitter aftertaste. Perfect with a few kabanosy, a very long and thin smoked pork sausage.

P.G. WODEHOUSE

SUMMER
LIGHTNING

Summer Lightning

Hop Back Brewery | www.hopback.co.uk

Country of origin England
First brewed 1988
Alcohol content 5% abv
Serving temperature 54°F, 12°C

The quintessential English summer ale, Summer Lightning was one of the first beers of the golden ale style to be produced in Britain. At a time when most real ales were dark, rich, and heavy, Summer Lightning was at the forefront of a revolution—ale that was light, cool, and refreshing, and ideal for quenching your thirst on long summer evenings.

The Hop Back Brewery that produces Summer Lightning had inauspicious beginnings in the cellar and back garden of a public house in Salisbury, England—the Wyndham Arms. Here, John Gilbert, who had a history of making beers, started making his own home-produced ales.

The high quality of these local brews was soon recognized by aficionados, particularly members of CAMRA. By 1992, demand had outstripped what Gilbert could produce in his pub, and he established the Hop Back Brewery (named after the vessel that strains the hop cones from the finished beer).

Gilbert designed Summer Lightning when he was asked to come up with something a little different for a local beer festival. He used traditional English ingredients but he didn't have his malt kilned as heavily as normal. This resulted in a fresher flavor and a lighter color. He also added an extra dose of hops at a late stage during the boil, which gave it a fresh citrus taste. It differed from other real ales at the time in that, rather than a blend, it was brewed using only one variety of hop—East Kent Golding. The beer's name came from the title of a P. G. Wodehouse novel, which Gilbert was reading when he created the beer. **JM**

Tasting notes

The nose sings with light, fragrant, fresh hoppy and grassy aromas; while on the palate, this refreshing clean straw-colored beer is bittersweet and citrusy at first, but then leads to a long dry bitter finish. Dangerously drinkable for its strength.

The P. G. Wodehouse novel after which Summer Lightning is named.

Svijanský Rytíř

Pivovar Svijany | www.pivovarsvijany.cz

Country of origin Czech Republic
First brewed 2000
Alcohol content 5% abv
Serving temperature 44°F, 7°C

Though the pale lager known as Svijanský Rytíř (meaning "Svijany Knight") was first produced as such in the year 2000, one could conceivably assign almost any date to the beers from the Bohemian town of Svijany. Historical records for the area go as far back as 1345, and the brewery itself claims a founding date of 1564. Certainly by the early 17th century the Svijany Brewery was very well known, as it is listed among the properties of the anti-Habsburg nobleman Jáchym Ondřej Šlik in 1602.

Of course, the beers made at Svijany during the brewery's early days were probably quite different than the one named in Šlik's honor. Rather than clear and pale, they were probably dark and cloudy, and while there is now some academic speculation that Bohemians might have been producing lager beers at this time, it seems likely that their beers were probably top-fermenting wheat beers or hearty, rustic ales.

By contrast, Svijanský Rytíř is a paragon of the refined pale lager style, a perfect pairing for spicy Asian dishes or excellent as a well-chilled aperitif. While the brewery remains one of the Czech Republic's most traditional, the flagship Svijanský Rytíř beer is slightly more bitter and more aromatically hoppy than the average Czech *světlý ležák* (or light lager), due to its unusual dry-hopping technique. Although, it does have a Bohemian pilsner's typical malt fullness from a traditional decoction mash. As with all the beers from this brewery, Svijanský Rytíř is unpasteurized, leaving the Saaz hop aromas full, spicy, and well pronounced. **ER**

Tasting notes

A flagship pilsner-style beer from the homeland of the style: look for clear deep gold in the glass with a thick white foam on top, a nose of grassy Saaz hops over a honey-malt body followed by a noticeably dry and bitter finish.

Švyturys Ekstra

Švyturio Alaus Darykla | www.svyturys.lt/en

Country of origin Lithuania
First brewed 1995
Alcohol content 5.2% abv
Serving temperature 39°–44°F, 4°–7°C

The functional, postwar, concrete building that houses Švyturys brewery in Klaipeda is not a pretty sight. Penetrate the facade, however, and you'll find a state-of-the-art brewhouse lurking behind it.

In charge of operations is brewmaster Dzuljeta Armoniene. The range of beers has changed dramatically in her twenty years there, and now includes the wheat beer, Baltas, plus a pils, a bock, and a Vienna-style lager. The most significant new beer is Ekstra, a smooth, satisfying beer created in 1995 that has now become the country's biggest seller.

The concept behind the new beer was simple: to provide a very drinkable beer for Lithuania's pubs. Armoniene has certainly succeeded. It's a beer broadly in the Dortmunder Export style—which implies a milder hop presence than a pilsner, with a full, sweet, malty backbone. But Armoniene confesses that she didn't have any particular style in mind when she set about brewing it for the first time. In the home market, the beer is not pasteurized when sold on draft, ensuring a clean, fresh flavor. For export, the bottles are pasteurized, which brings a touch more of a malty-toffee note to the palate, but you can also buy an unpasteurized version in bottle called Ekstra Draught, which is closer to the Lithuanian pub version.

The grist, mainly of lager malt, also contains 10 percent rice—"to soften the taste and add drinkability," reveals Armoniene—and there are two German hops involved in the copper, Magnum for bitterness and Spalt for aroma. The beer has been a winner in the World Beer Cup and keeps on impressing. **JE**

Tasting notes

A golden beer with herbal hops and gentle pale malt in the aroma, along with a little squeeze of lemon. Lemon features in the full, bittersweet taste, too, with more hops and a mild alcoholic warmth, before a dry, hoppy, lemony, bitter finish.

Tannenzäpfle

Badische Staatsbrauerei Rothaus | www.rothaus.de

Country of origin Germany
First brewed 1956
Alcohol content 5.1% abv
Serving temperature 46°–50°F, 8°–10°C

The anachronistic label design shows a woman in traditional Black Forest dress smiling and holding two glasses of beer. Inside the small bottle, an astonishingly smooth, aromatic, and harmonious pils awaits.

Tannenzäpfle needed neither advertising nor communication. It was different and just waiting to be discovered, which was enough for it to become a favorite in urban avant-garde environments such as could be found in Hamburg or Berlin. As legend has it, certain resourceful retailers introduced the beer to bars and clubs and thus kicked off its rise in the 1990s. But how its rise really began is hard to say, since the demand literally increased by word of mouth and made the beer a national cult brand.

Brewed since 1956, this pils was named after the cones on its label: Tannenzäpfle means "fir cone." Due to its popularity, it was the first of a series of small-bottle editions named Zäpfle; others include Rothaus Hefeweizen and Rothaus Eiszäpfle. The Black Forest woman has smiled on Rothaus's labels since the 1930s. Beer lovers named her Birgit, to be pronounced like the vernacular for "beer gives."

The beer owes its overall smooth and harmonious quality to the extremely soft water from seven natural sources. Furthermore, the careful selection of malts and Hallertauer and Tettnanger aroma hops contributes to its sophistication. However, every cult needs a site. Therefore, the state-owned brewery has established a kind of amusement park on its grounds with self-guided tours, events, and a shop. Rothaus expects up to 40,000 pilgrims to visit the site every year. **SK**

Tasting notes

Tannenzäpfle is light blond and brilliant in the glass with a volatile head. On the nose, an aromatic hop character with a hint of citrus. The first taste is soft and fluffy, revealing a medium body with an herbal bitterness. The finish is citrusy and bitter.

Taras Boulba

Brasserie de la Senne | www.brasseriedelasenne.be

Country of origin Belgium
First brewed 2006
Alcohol content 4.5% abv
Serving temperature 44°F, 7°C

The beer's label shows one man preparing to smash a barrel over another man's head. It is inspired by the Russian novel *Taras Boulba,* about an old Cossack who kills his own son after the lad falls for a Polish girl. Swap "Cossack" with "Flemish" and "Polish" with "Wallonian" and you have a tale fit for Belgium's own divisions.

The brewers see Belgium's linguistic squabbles as pointless, and made the label to take a swipe at them. Meanwhile, Taras Boulba the beer makes a statement of its own. It began literally as a brewers' beer. Bernard Leboucq and Yvan De Baets first made a batch in 2004 to quench their own thirsts after long workdays. They liked it so much that they kept making it, tweaking it here and there, and these days Taras Boulba's popularity outstrips their ability to make the stuff.

The beer stands out from the pack of Belgian specialty ales for at least a couple of reasons. The first is its assertive hop character, which is grassy and classy, much like the brewery's other ales. The second is its utterly reasonable alcohol content. While there is plenty of complexity for those who want to stop, sip, and savor, this is a true session beer—a drinking beer—made for gulping all afternoon and then walking home on your own two feet. Taras Boulba achieves a subtle spiciness and citrus zing without any actual spices in it. That's just yeast, hops, and malt doing the talking. One can taste the ingredients in this beer, which despite its Brussels identity could pass for a traditional Hainaut saison—the rustic, low-alcohol ales that kept seasonal farm workers happy and healthy. It may do the same for you. **JS**

Tasting notes

A bright golden beer with a fluffy and persistent white foam, enticing on a summer's day. Fine, floral, grassy hop nose with citric notes like grapefruit. Quite bitter and dry with a faintly tart, quenching acidic edge. Flavorful yet quaffable.

Taybeh Beer Golden

Taybeh Brewing Company
www.taybehbeer.com

Country of origin Palestinian Territories
First brewed 1995
Alcohol content 5.2% abv
Serving temperature 46°F, 8°C

This is the story of a craft brewer in Boston, who started his love affair with beer as a home-brewer and then moved on to an MA in brewing engineering at University California Davis with the intent of starting his own brewery. The man in question is Nadim Khoury, who returned to his native Palestine following the Oslo Accords in 1993 to found Taybeh Brewing, in a Christian town on the occupied West Bank.

Taybeh Beer Golden is an all-malt beer, brewed to the exacting standards of Germany's Reinheitsgebot. No adjuncts or preservatives are added to the beers. The hops are from Bavaria along with aromatic Saaz varietals from the Czech Republic. The fruits of Khoury's persistence are difficult to find outside the Palestinian Territories. The brands were contract brewed in Belgium for a spell to expand the brewery's markets, but this arrangement seems to have ended. **LN**

Tasting notes

Light gold in appearance with attractive carbonation. The nose gives a dry maltiness with floral hop notes. The mouthfeel is chewy with biscuit maltiness balanced by generous bittering.

Tegernseer Spezial

Herzoglich Bayerisches Brauhaus Tegernsee
www.braustuberl.de

Country of origin Germany
First brewed *ca.* 1817
Alcohol content 5.6% abv
Serving temperature 43°–46°F, 6–8°C

Picturesquely situated on the east banks of Tegernsee, a lake south of Munich, the pub and beer garden of Herzoglich Bayerisches Brauhaus Tegernsee is one of Upper Bavaria's best-known taverns and certainly the ideal place to drink their wonderful Spezial. The impressively large vaulted hall attracts not only tourists but also many locals. Young and old, families and couples, and clubs and associations go to the Bräustüberl to enjoy Bavarian beer culture at its best.

Helles might be the best seller of the Herzoglich Bayerisches Brauhaus, but the better beer, according to general manager Christian Wagner and many beer enthusiasts, is the Spezial. It is an outstanding example of a Bavarian-style light lager. Wagner will not tell the secrets of the company's brewing art, but he will reveal that the beer has a "gentle" lagering in lying tanks—room cooled, which is especially costly. **SK**

Tasting notes

Light blond and brilliant, with a finely poured white head. A sweet nose with a biscuit lightness. On the palate, expect a pronounced maltiness. Semidry, mild finish.

A beer advertisement that promotes peace as well as beer.

Terrapin Rye Pale Ale

Terrapin Beer Company | www.terrapinbeer.com

Country of origin United States
First brewed 2002
Alcohol content 5.5% abv
Serving temperature 41°F, 5°C

Terrapin Beer Company brewers Brian Buckowski and John Cochran first got together at the Atlanta Brewing Company. The pair looked at the pale ales, brown ales, and stouts typically being produced in the Southeast and felt that they could do something different. When Buckowski told people that he planned to brew a hoppy pale ale, they warned him that it would be an uphill battle convincing consumers in the Southeast to buy it. Buckowski did not listen and instead created a pale ale recipe with a twist: Terrapin Rye Pale Ale. Less than six months after the launch of the new beer, it won a gold medal at the Great American Beer Festival.

At the core of the ale is malted rye that is blended with Munich, Victory, and honey malts to add complexity and softness. Five different types of hops go into the ale: Magnum, Fuggle, East Kent Golding, and Cascade, and then it is dry hopped with Amarillo. Terrapin Rye Pale Ale's use of rye as a raw ingredient helped the marketing of the beer. In a sea of pale ales, it is a point of difference that helps the brand secure tap handles and shelf space at retail. Rye whiskey's recent resurgence among U.S. consumers has added to Terrapin's crossover attractiveness.

After starting out contract brewing, Terrapin now has its own large brewing facility and has launched several seasonal and limited-edition offerings, including Rye Squared, All American Imperial Pilsner, Big Hoppy Monster, and Wake-n-Bake Coffee Oatmeal Imperial Stout. The brewery's core lineup includes the Rye Pale Ale, Golden Ale, and India Style Brown, which was first brewed to celebrate the company's fifth anniversary. **RL**

Tasting notes

This ale opens with an inviting golden golden color, floral aromatics on the nose, and a firm rocky head that laces the glass. There is a spicy hop up front, with an adequate amount of malt in the finish to balance the beer. Very smooth finish.

Thornbridge Jaipur

Thornbridge Brewery | www.thornbridgebrewery.co.uk

Country of origin England
First brewed 2005
Alcohol content 5.9% abv
Serving temperature 50°–54°F, 10°–12°C

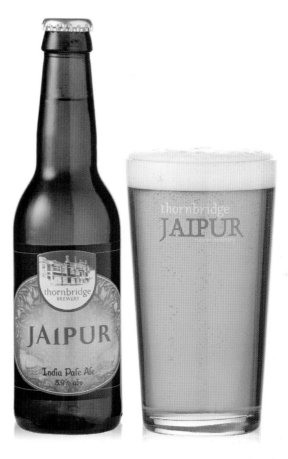

A visit to Thornbridge Hall is a visit to another world. Visitors approach the Hall through green and wooded parkland; occasional weathered statues are dotted about, as if playing hide-and-seek. The Hall stands ahead, imposing and imperious, but welcoming, too. Until September 2009, Thornbridge Brewery was also at home in the stable block, but then it moved to a new site a couple of miles away in the picturesque town of Bakewell. "Although our brewery is only just over four years old, we have been at full capacity for most of that time," said Thornbridge's Managing Director Jim Harrison at the time. "We began planning the new brewery with a determination to use the best technology available but also to ensure our brewing team maintain hands-on control of the process so that we have a brewery that allows creativity."

A major part of the brewery's success has rested on Jaipur, a marvelously hoppy take on the IPA style that looks to the U.S. rather than Burton-on-Trent for its inspiration. It was named after the Indian city famous for its "pink" walls (hence the label's colors). Hops utilized are the U.S.-grown Ahtanum, Centennial, and Chinook, all varieties that produce both good aromatic and fruity notes, while pale ale malt goes into the mash tun. Despite its strength of 5.9 percent, this is a beer that the brewery recommends to be drunk young—so that its succulent hoppy notes can be savored. It's clearly found favor with the British drinking public, as at the time of writing it has won sixty awards at various beer festivals, including the prestigious garland of Best Strong Bitter in the U.K. in 2008. **ATJ**

Tasting notes

Straw yellow with golden tints; on the nose, immediate wafts of tropical fruit such as lychee and grapefruit plus hints of softly toasted barley. Tropical-fruit-flavor bombs on the palate are kept in balance by a slight honeyed sweetness before its long, dry, bittersweet finish.

Thornbridge Kipling

Thornbridge Brewery | www.thornbridgebrewery.co.uk

Country of origin England
First brewed 2006
Alcohol content 5.2% abv
Serving temperature 46°–50°F, 8°–10°C

"Never ordinary" is just one of Thornbridge Brewery's mottos, and also one of the most fitting. Since opening in 2004, this small independent has carved out a reputation as one of the most innovative craft breweries in the United Kingdom. Based in the grounds of a beautiful stately home in Derbyshire, Thornbridge Hall, it is constantly looking to the rest of the world for inspiration for its new brews.

So it was that in 2005, in the middle of a cold British winter, Thornbridge's Italian head brewer, Stefano Cossi, received some hop samples from the sunnier parts of the world. One of them was an entirely new variety from New Zealand called Nelson Sauvin. He and Martin Dickie (Thornbridge's other brewer at the time) did some trials with this new hop and were amazed at the intense passion fruit, mango, and grapefruit aromas. They knew they had to use it.

First they tried to use this new wonder-hop in a wheat beer but, without a cereal cooker, found the grain difficult to convert. They then tried using a torrified wheat, but that was no better. Lastly, they tried an addition of Munich malt to balance the hops, and Kipling was born. They call it a "South Pacific Pale Ale" because the tropical aromas are similar to those found in New Zealand Sauvignon Blanc. Kiwi brewer Kelly Ryan joined Thornbridge in 2007 after Dickie left to set up his own brewery, BrewDog, and this, Cossi laughs, officially gives them the right to use this "made up" style category. The Kipling part comes from when Thornbridge once had an outbuilding containing a small bay window from Rudyard Kipling's caravan. **ST**

Tasting notes

A classic pale ale with plenty of full, fruity aromas. Flavors of passion fruit and kiwi, with a touch of citrusy grapefruit and biscuity malt lies underneath. Deliciously refreshing, and a great aperitif when served chilled. Try pairing it with fish and chips.

Stained glass panel at Thornbridge Hall by Edward Burne-Jones and William Morris.

Tiger Beer

Asia Pacific Breweries | www.tigerbeer.com

Country of origin Singapore
First brewed 1932
Alcohol content 4.8% abv
Serving temperature 39°–43°F, 4°–6°C

In many ways Tiger Beer is the first fruit of the internationalization of the brewing industry. Heineken and a Singapore-based conglomerate, Fraser and Neave, formed a brewing joint venture in 1931, which was called Malayan Breweries. Today it is known as Asia Pacific Breweries. A year later, Tiger Beer was first brewed in Singapore. It is the centerpiece of Asia Pacific's strategy of creating a pan-Asian lager brand. The beer is brewed in eleven countries, with India the most recent entrant, and in unlikely brewing centers such as Vientiane in Laos and Ulan Bator in Mongolia.

Asia Pacific speaks proudly of the many medals that Tiger has won over the years, but is vague regarding its ingredients. In 1998, Tiger came out ahead of 118 other packaged lagers in the Brewing Industry International Awards (BIIA), winning gold. The little-known BIIA carries great weight in the industry because its judging panel is composed entirely of professional brewers. Mongolian-produced Tiger got silver in the Australian International Beer Awards in 2009, in a competition that awarded no gold medals.

As to its ingredients, Asia Pacific notes that Tiger is brewed from yeast that is especially cultured in the Netherlands, working its alcohol-producing magic from malted barley from Australia and Europe, supplemented by rice to ensure a dry finish. The beer is varietal hopped for its bitter notes, relying on high alpha acid Zeus hops from the United States. Today the brewery is rolling out brand extensions, including Tiger Crystal, Tiger Super Cold, and Ice Freeze Tiger, which blends Tiger Beer with ice-crystallized beer. **LN**

Tasting notes

The aroma is generous, with biscuit maltiness supplemented by light citrus and melon notes and—surprise—a hint of clove. The mouthfeel offers sweet, soft malt and a touch of citrus hops, although no bitterness. The finish is short and sweet.

Tipopils

Birrificio Italiano | www.birrificio.it

Country of origin Italy
First brewed 1996
Alcohol content 5.2% abv
Serving temperature 46°–50° F, 8°–10° C

Agostino Arioli is considered to be a real pioneer of the Italian craft beer renaissance. He started as a home-brewer when he was still studying at school. He is passionate about all beer, but has a specific love for the bottom-fermenting variety and, in particular, the pils style. Every year, Arioli goes to Bavaria to personally choose and buy the hops that he uses in his brewery. In all aspects of brewing, he has a scientific, quite obstinate approach, but this is what probably guarantees the consistently high quality of his beers. Tipopils was brewed just before the official opening of Birrificio. It was the brewery's first beer, and, after more than ten years, Arioli's "Tipo" is still the favorite choice for beer lovers visiting the brewpub.

Tipopils is considered to be a sort of Italian-style pils: hoppy, but not too much, well balanced, easy to drink, but with a fine body. No doubt a real parameter for all the Italian craft pils that came after it. It is well characterized by three kinds of hops, all of which are grown in Germany: Northern Brewer, to give the bitterness to the beer; and Hallertauer Perle and Hallertauer Spalter Select for their aromatic qualities. Two different malts (pilsner and caramel) and yeast from Weihenstephan complete the recipe. After a long primary fermentation, the beer needs to mature for three weeks; but during this time, a dry hopping with Spalter Select is done to give an additional kick to the beautiful floral and hoppy bouquet. Between November and February, Arioli also produces an Extra Hop, which is served with a Mittelfrau hop cone on the top of its foam. **MM**

Tasting notes

Brilliant golden color with a thick white foam. Well-balanced aroma that is immediately reminiscent of fresh hops but with a malty undertow. When on the palate, it initially reveals hints of acacia honey, but finishes with a pleasantly sharp touch of bitterness.

Tirana

Birra Malto | www.birratirana.com

Titan IPA

Great Divide Brewing | www.greatdivide.com

Country of origin Albania
First brewed 1961
Alcohol content 4% abv
Serving temperature 37°–43°F, 3°–6°C

Country of origin United States
First brewed 2004
Alcohol content 6.8% abv
Serving temperature 55°F, 13°C

For centuries, wine and the fiery, throat-burning brandy raki were the Albanian drinks of choice. It wasn't until the 1930s that Albania's first brewery was set up. Under Communist rule, in 1960 Enver Hoxha's regime received funding and expertise to set up a state-owned brewery. The brewing company Birra Malto was a subsidiary of the state agriculture department Kombinati Ushqimor. Using barley from the Korça region and hops from Pogradec, a pilsner and a dark beer were made. The pilsner, named after the capital city Tirana, proved popular. In 1983, the aging Russian brewery was expanded and equipped with modern technology. In 1993 investment and increased marketing know-how resulted in new international trade. The brewery was denationalized in 2001. Tirana is now exported to other Balkan states, the United States, and, sometimes, the United Kingdom. **JP**

Not long before Great Divide Brewing in Denver celebrated its tenth anniversary in 2004, the brewery added two strong, hop-laden beers, distinguishing them from the rest of the brewery's range by giving them their own brand name: "Maverick." In short order, Maverick Imperial Stout came second in the Alpha King Challenge, a competition for hoppy beers, while Maverick IPA (boasting a substantial but not outlandish 65 IBU, in contrast with some of the Californian hop-head favorites) found a growing audience. Great Divide sales surged in the next five years, fueling further expansion—the brewery added a taproom in 2007 and underwent major expansion in 2008.

Titan IPA exhibits the balance characteristic of all Great Divide beers but also packs plenty of hops. It quickly became the best-selling beer outside the brewery's home region. **SH**

Tasting notes
A pale gold pilsner with a rapidly diminishing head and good lacing. Aroma of sweet, bready malt. Light mouthfeel with champagne-like carbonation. Dry and thirst quenching.

Tasting notes
Bright-orange-colored body topped by a tall, firm white head. Fruity nose of grapefruit and oranges, with peppery notes of pine. Malt backbone on the palate with some sweetness on the tongue.

A pair of old Tirana beer labels from a private Australian collection.

Tricerahops Double IPA

Ninkasi Brewing | www.ninkasibrewing.com

Country of origin United States
First brewed 2007
Alcohol content 8.8% abv
Serving temperature 44°–54° F, 7°–12°C

When Eugene, Oregon, brewer Jamie Floyd left Steelhead Brewing to start Ninkasi Brewing, one of the beers he knew he wanted to brew was a double India Pale Ale. He had already worked on some double IPAs previously—in fact, Steelhead's Hopasaurus Rex was the first Double IPA to win a medal at the Great American Beer Festival.

Originally, when he wanted to brew a new double IPA for Ninkasi, he wanted to call it Hoptimus Prime after the Transformers hero, but another brewery had already used it. Instead, Floyd decided to continue the trend he had started with Hopasaurus Rex at Steelhead, and named the new beer Tricerahops, after the three-horned dinosaur, triceratops.

"I decided on Tricerahops for a few different reasons," says Floyd. "One of them was because Hopasaurus Rex stayed behind at Steelhead. So it was kind of fun because Steelhead couldn't be mad at me for the similarity in dinosaur names because I named both of the beers. Secondly, the guy who makes Ninkasi's tap handles is one of my best friends, and he worked on an art vehicle called Triceratops—a panel truck that has been turned into a giant steel Triceratops and travels to different things like art events and music festivals. The name is a result of both influences."

Floyd says his other, unofficial name for the massive Tricerahops beer is Sleepytime: "This beer has had a common effect of letting people become extremely familiar with the shape of any chair that they are sitting in while drinking it," he says. "Two pints, and it's often nap time." **LMo**

Tasting notes

Floral notes predominate and play well with citrus and pine hop flavors before a malty sweetness makes an appearance. Despite its heavy dosing of hops and its higher alcohol content, this is a well-balanced beer that is surprisingly smooth and light on its feet.

Tripel de Ripple

Brugge Brasserie | www.bruggebrasserie.com

Country of origin United States
First brewed 1995
Alcohol content 9.8% abv
Serving temperature 43°F, 6°C

Brugge Brasserie is a gastro-pub that is the inspiration of brewer Ted Miller. Indianapolis might not feel much like the ancient Belgian city of Brugge, but your taste buds will tell a different story. Brugge Brasserie combines Belgian-style ales and Continental lagers, with a sophisticated menu that goes well beyond typical pub grub. Menu items like waterzooi, carbonnade flamande, and moules frittes transport dinners across the Atlantic.

Brugge Brasserie came when Ted Miller and his wife Shannon joined forces with their childhood friends to bring the gastro-pub concept to the Broad Ripple section of Indianapolis. The Brugge LLC restaurant group is owned by Abraham Benrubi, Ted and Shannon Miller, Charlie Midgley, Eli Schloss, and Renee Stoltz. Actor Benrubi is best known for his roles on television series *ER* and *Parker Lewis Can't Lose*.

Tripel de Ripple was the first beer brewed by the company. As they were preparing for opening day, Miller and the restaurant's night manager had started the brewing process and had mashed in, betting that the critical sugar for the recipe would arrive in time. After missing the driver, however, the night manager took off in search of a UPS truck and found one just three blocks from the brewery. It was the wrong truck. A frantic search yielded a second UPS truck, which contained the brewer's sugar, just in the nick of time.

Brugge's lineup also includes other brews: Keller Bier, Saison D'etre, Imperial Wit, and Old Dog Belgian Strong Pale Ale. But it was the Tripel de Ripple that won a silver medal at the Great American Beer Festival. **RL**

Tasting notes

Tripel de Ripple pours a cloudy golden color with a thin white head. It gives off a slightly floral and citrus nose that leads to a tart flavor base; hints of ripe fruit with some fleeting sweetness around the edges. The ale finishes with lime zest.

Tripel Karmeliet

Brouwerij Bosteels | www.bestbelgianspecialbeers.be

Country of origin Belgium
First brewed 1996
Alcohol content 8% abv
Serving temperature 43°–44°F, 6°–7°C

Tripel Karmeliet made a revival in the 1990s, having allegedly been originally formulated as long ago as 1679 in a Belgian Carmelite cloister. Whether historical fact or marketing hyperbole, the fact that three types of grain (barley, wheat, and oats) are used in this beer would fit well into the historic picture. One source on this beer even claims that all three grains are used in both malted and unmalted form, and that Styrian Golding is the hop used.

The Bosteels brewery itself dates from the late 18th century, and is still in the hands of the original family, who are now in their seventh generation of descendants. The elegant brewers' house, in the center of the brewery, also hints at a grand past. Following in this noble tradition, more and more of Bosteels' beers are conceived of as specialty treats, usually with an interesting historical background.

Apart from the highly successful and renowned Tripel Karmeliet, Pauwel Kwak has also become world-famous, while the DeuS beer has sparked interest by supposedly being brewed fully by the sparkling wine Méthode Champenoise. Until a few years ago, it was rumored that Tripel Karmeliet was actually brewed at Van Steenberge, a larger regional brewer in the north of the same province. However, recent reports all converge on the evidence that the Tripel really is brewed at Buggenhout. For discerning tasters, it is also of some importance that this beer has a disconcerting habit of doing very well in blind tastings, often coming out better than very famous competitors that might have hoped to fare better. **JPa**

Tasting notes

A clear yellow-golden beer beneath a fluffy white head. Nose of grain, wheat, a little smoked, and becoming roasted-spicy. Sweet, malty taste, but with a sharp, nearly astringent mouthfeel, like partly roasted malt. Perhaps it's the oats that lend it a spicy, roasted streak throughout.

Trois Dames IPA

Brasserie Trois Dames | www.brasserietroisdames.ch

Country of origin Switzerland
First brewed 2005
Alcohol content 6.5% abv
Serving temperature 54°F, 12°C

Set in the Jura Mountains, Brasserie Trois Dames is one of the up-and-coming Swiss breweries. Precision brewing is one way to describe its appeal: clear-cut, clean beers with an assertive, balanced character, complex beers that will satisfy seasoned beer enthusiasts, yet remain fathomable enough for beginners to understand and appreciate.

Raphaël Mettler used to be one of millions of Swiss people who do not like beer. Then some North American pale ale crossed his path and changed his life. First a home-brewer, then a part-time brewer before finally going full-time in the spring of 2008, Raphaël's trajectory may have been meteoric, but his first beer love remains: hops. And what else would you brew to celebrate hops but an IPA at a strength that does justice to the style?

Brewed from German malts and a hopping based on the North American varieties Centennial, Cascade, and Simcoe (a serious hopping that produces an assertive but not over-the-top 60 IBUs), Trois Dames's IPA falls in between the stronger British IPAs and modern U.S. IPAs. Its hop character is unmistakably North American, yet its not-too-thick body clearly hints at the British tradition. Swiss brewers often are a bit on the shy side when it comes to assertively hoppy beers, and this IPA, along with its Ale/ESB, Pacific Northwest Pale Ale, and Saison Houblon stable mates, is clearly challenging Swiss drinkers' palates to explore the delights of bitterness. Judging by sales figures, with the IPA now surprisingly outselling the tamer Ale/ESB, that challenge is clearly being taken. **LM**

Tasting notes

Literally oozing with resiny, citrusy hops, the crystal malt backbone is just sturdy enough to pad out the powerful, slightly earthy final bitterness, so that a complex palate of citrus, pine, red and exotic fruit with a hint of blackcurrant can comfortably unfold in a thoroughly enjoyable balance.

Trumer Pils

Trumer Privatbrauerei | www.trumer.at

Country of origin Austria
First brewed 1977
Alcohol content 4.9% abv
Serving temperature 44°F, 7°C

Trumer Pils is the most prestigious (and hence the most expensive) pilsner beer brand in Austria. The success of this particular beer is not only built on its quality but also on the consistent quality of the marketing strategy that positioned the brand as a gem among Austrian beers.

When the brewery introduced their pils, they introduced the right glassware to drink it in at the same time—an unusual move in the 1970s that strengthened the awareness for this unusual product. Unlike many other beers of its category, Trumer Pils is distinctively hopped—and the brewery is proud to tell consumers about it.

For more than twenty-five years, Trumer's "Bier Akademie" has taught consumers about brewing and beer and its rich history. Brewing began in 1601 in Obertrum, about fifteen minutes north of Salzburg. In 1775, Josef Sigl, a hop merchant from Perlesreuth in Bavaria, acquired the brewery for the sum of 12,000 guilder. The brewery has been a family business ever since, with the current owner being Josef Sigl VII.

Along with branded glassware, the Sigl family also introduced several innovations to the Austrian beer market. In the early 1970s, they were the first to brew a filtered wheat beer called "Champagnerweizen." It was then branded "Weizengold" and distributed nationally. The Weizengold brand was later sold to Stiegl, while the Sigl family decided to focus on the production of Trumer Pils. This single-minded focus has been successful: the beer has won several awards, including the European Beer Star and the World Beer Cup. **CS**

Tasting notes

This straw-colored pils has a firm white head that produces a lot of lace in the glass. There are plenty of resiny and floral hop aromas, which are emphasized by the intense carbonation—thus hop aromas and bitterness are very present in the mouth.

Tsingtao

Tsingtao Brewery | www.tsingtaobeer.com

Country of origin China
First brewed 1903
Alcohol content 4.8% abv
Serving temperature 46°F, 8°C

This fresh and crisp tipple claims the title of the first Chinese beer, although, despite the brewery's location in a busy Chinese seaport, it owes its origin more to German colonists than the indigenous population. Pronounced "ching-dow," Tsingtao is a corruption of the name of the Chinese province in which it is produced, Qingdao. It was here, in 1903, that German colonists set up what is now the oldest brewery in China.

The colonists used the pure spring water from the Laoshan mountain region and locally grown rice, barley, and hops, and applied German brewing techniques to create a Chinese version of a German beer. This fusion of East and West must have gotten something right because the beer was awarded a gold medal at the Munich International Exhibition in 1906. Today, this sparkling lager is one of the most exported Chinese beers, and Tsingtao can be found in fifty countries throughout the world.

Barley, originally grown on-site, is now sourced from high-quality varieties grown in Canada and Australia. This is combined with natural spring water, rice, and hops, and the brew is fermented for at least twenty-eight days using a special yeast strain cultivated at the brewery. The result is quite a sweet beer, and it provides a refreshing complement to any Chinese meal. The brewery is proud of its German roots, even holding an annual international beer festival similar to the Oktoberfest. It also boasts a museum where visitors can see the brewery's history and even visit the "tipsy room," where the effects of being drunk are created by strange perspectives. **JM**

Tasting notes

This crisp and refreshing clear and pale lager has a bubbly but fine head on the initial pour. Its mild yet pleasant aroma is in stark contrast to its slightly sweet and malty highly hopped flavor. With hints of nuttiness, citrus, and fruit, it lingers on the palate with a lasting honey sweetness.

Tusker Lager

East African Breweries | www.eabl.com

Country of origin Kenya
First brewed 1922
Alcohol content 4.2% abv
Serving temperature 39°F, 4°C

Kenya Breweries was founded by two British immigrants, George and Charles Hurst. Brewing equipment was brought over from the United Kingdom, as was a brewer from the northwest of England. Hops were shipped from Kent, wood burning stoves heated the mash tun and brewing kettle, and the brewery began with a stout and an ale. A year later, Tusker beer came onto the scene; however, it is uncertain if it was a lager as, according to some sources, the brewery didn't start producing bottom-fermenting beers until 1930.

With its image of an elephant on the label, Tusker is one of the best-known beers in Africa and is also brewed under contract in Tanzania and Uganda. Low on bitterness, it is a thirst-quenching beer that is perfect for the region's hot climate; it is brewed with barley malt that comes from the tropical, equatorial Kenyan Rift Valley, while water comes from springs in the Aberdare Mountain ranges.

It is best drunk for refreshment—rather than taste—so it is not easy to pair with strong-tasting foods. However, Tusker goes well with simple foods if it is well chilled—grilled or barbecued fish, a salad, or even pasta. The writer Ernest Hemingway visited the region to hunt for game and to find himself as he went through one of his mid-life crises. Tusker is said to have become his favorite beer while in the area. **TH**

Tasting notes
Pale, almost straw-colored yellow in the glass. The beer has a crisp palate, soft malty nose, and even a hint of malted biscuits or sweet corn before it disappears into a light finish.

Tusker Malt Lager

East African Breweries | www.eabl.com

Country of origin Kenya
First brewed 1996
Alcohol content 5% abv
Serving temperature 39°F, 4°C

Tusker dominates Kenya's beer market and is a national institution. In the *hepis* (bars) of Nairobi, it's not unknown for the entire clientele to stand to attention with arms clamped across their chests when the patriotic advertisements for the beer appear on TV.

Perhaps mindful of the fact that almost every Western visitor buys a Tusker T-shirt to take home, East African Breweries recognized the potential to build an export business. Although the beer is unbeatable in the equatorial heat of the Masai Mara, the brewer realized that beers enjoyed on holiday may not taste quite as good when cracked open under gloomier, more temperate skies. And so he developed Tusker Malt.

Most African beers are served in identical recycled brown bottles, Tusker Malt is packaged in green bottles that say "premium" the world over. Unlike other African beers, it's 100 percent malt, derived from fine equatorial barley grown at the base of Mount Kenya, and it is brewed with Aberdare spring water. The result is a beer with a bolder lager character than many imitation pilsners from around the world.

Kenyans soon demanded this high-quality beer for themselves, and in just over ten years Tusker Malt gained 4 percent of the domestic market. Kenya increasingly sees itself as a global player. Tusker Malt is not just a lager: it's a statement of intent. **PB**

Tasting notes
Pours a deeper gold than most lagers, with a thick white head. A malty aroma with a faint grassiness leads into a light sweetness on the palate, with a gentle hoppiness and dry finish.

A freshly painted bar in Malindi, Kenya, advertises the Tusker brand. ➡

TŪ

FINES

TUSKER
FINEST QUALITY LAGER

TUSKER
FINEST QUALITY LAGER

Two Hearted Ale

Bell's Brewery, Inc. | www.bellsbeer.com

Country of origin United States
First brewed 1992
Alcohol content 7% abv
Serving temperature 39°–43°F, 4°–6°C

When owner Larry Bell pulled Kalamazoo Brewing out of the Illinois market—temporarily—he set off a near riot among beer lovers in the Chicago area, and this beer is a good part of the reason. Two Hearted is a true enthusiast's beer, dripping with the pine and citrus punch of Centennial hops.

Today it's a flagship beer brewed by the renamed Bell's Brewery, but the beer's prospects were not always so bright. The original Two Hearted was a failed project combining English malt and Wisconsin-grown hops, according to Larry Bell, who had enjoyed drinking his own hoppy home-brews while fishing in Michigan's Upper Peninsula. Eventually, a more successful formula was found and the beer became a regular product—and the fish stayed on the label.

Bell is a pioneer in many ways. Early on the scene, he fearlessly pushed ahead, following his passions in a fashion that could even be called "eccentrovation." His brewery has five regular stouts and has brewed as many as a dozen in a single year. Emptying the kettle after brewing his Eccentric Ale revealed an assortment of hops, sticks, licorice roots, and who knows what else. After a bad distribution deal, Bell pulled out of Illinois to gasps, then cheers—and he made that risky move work for him. He's a legend.

Two Hearted was one of the first really hoppy beers to catch fire in the Midwest. With its simple but plentiful charms, it's as fine an IPA as you can find anywhere. If you're ever fortunate enough to taste it in its rare cask-conditioned form, you will have something very special in your glass. **RM**

Tasting notes

Perfumed hoppy nose with plenty of grapefruit, plus apricot and honey notes, and a whiff of alcohol. Taste is sweetly malty for a heartbeat, then you have a mess of hops in your face. Malt hangs in, barely, as the beer winds down to a dry, hoppy finish.

Union Jack IPA

Firestone Walker Brewing | www.firestonewalker.com

Country of origin United States
First brewed 2007
Alcohol content 7.5% abv
Serving temperature 50°F, 10°C

During the first year after Firestone Walker released Union Jack, the beer won a gold medal in the World Beer Cup in San Diego, a gold medal at the European Beer Star Awards in Germany, and a gold medal in the Great American Beer Festival in Denver. Not only do judges like Union Jack, but when Firestone Walker opened new markets in the United States's Northwest in 2009—where there are plenty of hop-accented beers to choose from—the IPA was the brewery's best seller.

Brewmaster Matt Brynildson and his crew spent the best part of a year developing the beer. They brewed test batches every other month, blending some into other beers and selling some in the tasting room in order to get customer feedback. Union Jack evolved into something different from the beer that Brynildson had envisioned after a trip to Great Britain to learn about English malts. He expected UK malts would be part of the recipe and that a portion of Union Jack, the name obviously pointing across the Atlantic, would ferment in wood, as do the other Firestone pale ales, Double Barrel and Pale Ale 31.

"We were trying to integrate the oak, but we gave up. It just didn't work with hops," Brynildson says. Likewise, leaner North American two-row pale malt also better served the emerging beer. Union Jack screams of Northwest American hops, with large doses added for flavor and aroma. Firestone's brewers have since made an imperial version of the beer, basically employing the recipe they use in Union Jack but producing a little less beer, taking extra steps to coax all the flavor they can out of each ingredient. **SH**

Tasting notes

Bright golden in the glass, topped by an off-white head, followed by generous lacing. Pine and citrus perfume on the nose; a touch of cotton candy sneaking around underneath. Solid but lean malt backbone stands up to persistent hop flavor and bitterness.

Urbock 23°

Castle Brewery Eggenberg | www.schloss-eggenberg.at

Country of origin Austria
First brewed 1976
Alcohol content 9.6% abv
Serving temperature 50°F, 10°C

The Eggenberg brewery in central Austria is a family business dating back to the 14th century, idyllically surrounded by mountains and lakes. The family home and original center for the business is an attractive, pale yellow–colored country chateau, but the success of its beers led to the construction of a new state-of-the-art brewing complex alongside in spring 2000.

Eggenberg is widely known for the formidable but rather special Samichlaus, a 14 percent lager brewed for Christmas. The brewery acquired the beer from the Swiss company Hürlimann, after it was taken over by rival Feldschlössen, but Eggenberg already had a fine reputation for producing strong beer, most notably with the excellent Urbock 23°. The name of this beer, with its 23° suffix, sounds threatening, but don't be alarmed. The figure of 23 only relates to the amount of sugars in the beer prior to fermentation: the strength is a mere 9.6 percent. Like all great beers, however, somehow the alcohol level is not really an issue when you begin to sip it. It certainly means that you treat the beer with respect, but the whole malt-and-hop package is so seductive that strength seems almost secondary.

Plenty of pilsner malt in the mash provides a sweet, syrupy bedrock for the beer, then four strains of hop—Magnum, Muehlviertler, Spalter Select, and Hallertauer Mittelfrüh—chime in with balancing bitterness. The smoothness is due to the fact that Urbock is cold conditioned in the chateau's cellars for nine months, to round off any rough edges. The beer also ages rather well in the bottle, with hop character slowly declining as sherry notes gradually push through. **JE**

Tasting notes

A golden lager with a heady aroma of creamy malt, sherry, sultanas, and spice. Sweet oranges and dried fruits lead in the smooth taste, nicely balanced by bitterness and a gentle caramel note. Oranges then linger into the long, dry, tangy finish.

Urthel Hop-It

Brouwerij de Leyerth | www.urthel.com

Country of origin Netherlands
First brewed 2005
Alcohol content 9.5% abv
Serving temperature 46°F, 8°C

Music aficionados of a certain age will recall the way in which U.S. rock 'n' roll once cast its spell across the Atlantic onto the shores of Britain, where artists from Keith Richards to Jimmy Page felt the inspiration of the music of Chuck Berry and Little Richard, among many others. Shortly thereafter, the Brits returned the favor by way of the now-legendary British invasion. And so it goes, too, with beer. After years of finding stylistic inspiration among the artisanal breweries of Belgium, the Yanks finally reversed the course in the early days of the new millennium, as visiting Belgian brewers like Hildegard van Ostaden returned home inspired by what they had found stateside.

One of only a handful of female brewers in Belgium, van Ostaden recalls at the tender age of thirteen being fascinated by the "little torches of foam" arising from the open fermenters at the Het Anker brewery. Scant years later, she was in brewing school learning how to raise her own little torches.

The Urthel brand was created after Hildegard and husband Bas van Ostaden decided to book space at the Van Steenberge brewery to create their own line of ales, rather than build a separate facility. The first few Urthel brands were decidedly Belgian in character, with ample strength and body and a malty flavor profile. But Hildegard was inspired by the IPAs that she found in the United States and soon created a more hop-driven brand, Hop-It. The beer was so well received that the couple made the decision to move production to the larger Koningshoeven brewery in the Netherlands. **SB**

Tasting notes

Pouring light gold, Hop-It offers a pear and green-grape aroma that belies the robust bitterness found in the body, along with notes of muddled fruit and an almost floral maltiness. Potent indeed, hoppy and spicy, but at the same time almost refreshing.

Utenos Alus

Švyturys-Utenos Alus | www.utenosalus.lt/en

Vapeur en Folie

La Brasserie à Vapeur | www.vapeur.com

Country of origin Lithuania
First brewed 1979
Alcohol content 5% abv
Serving temperature 39°–44°F, 4°–7°C

Country of origin Belgium
First brewed 1986
Alcohol content 8% abv
Serving temperature 55°–59°F, 13°–15°C

The common perception of beer in the former U.S.S.R. is that it had something of a rough deal. While the state showered vodka distilleries with money to modernize equipment, the breweries were largely ignored. Utenos Alus was established in the small Lithuanian city of Utena in 1977, and its flagship brand Utenos Alus followed a couple of years later.

A team of experts from some of the finest breweries in Czechoslovakia was brought in to advise on how the brewery should be organized. They began with the installation of Czech brewing equipment and an insistence on using higher-quality malt, yeast, and hops than was normal practice within the USSR. This formula elevated Utenos Alus above the inferior competition, but it took privatization and foreign investment to improve the quality levels to a standard enjoyed in the rest of Europe. **SG**

Brasserie à Vapeur can be found in the old center of Pipaix, close to the Hainaut town of Leuze, which boasts no fewer than three active breweries. Until 1983, it was known as Brasserie Biset-Cuvelier, but old brewer Gaston Biset sold it to a young schoolteacher, Jean-Louis Dits, who gave the brewery its current name.

Vapeur is a saison brewery, and Saison de Pipaix is exemplary of the style. Back in 1986, Jean-Louis was dismayed to learn that contemporary beer drinkers were starting to prefer strong beers, and Vapeur en Folie was his first capitulation to this trend (which culminated in a third beer baptized "Cochonne" or "Pigsty"). The labels, by a cartoonist friend, clearly display his sentiments; they are also collectors' items and vary from year to year. En Folie is less sour and also less spiced than the brewery's saison, although it contains orange peel and cumin, among other spices. **JPa**

Tasting notes
Pale, golden-yellow color with a gently receding white head. The nose hints at sweet malts, corn, and lemon, whereas the palate picks up spicy hops with a somewhat bitter lemon taste.

Tasting notes
Fine garden herbs in the nose such as lemongrass, apples, and earthy farmyard notes. Malty, grainy on the palate. Spicy, with sweet alcohol, resulting in a heavy-handed finish.

This jovial sculpture invites potential drinkers into a Lithuanian beer hall.

Velkopopovický Kozel

Plzensky Prazdroj | www.beer-kozel.cz

Veltins

Brauerei C. & A. Veltins | www.veltins.com

Country of origin Czech Republic
First brewed 1874
Alcohol content 4.8% abv
Serving temperature 46°F, 8°C

Country of origin Germany
First brewed 1926
Alcohol content 4.8% abv
Serving temperature 46°F, 8°C

The Velké Popovice brewery, located in the eponymous town near Prague, can trace its roots back to the 15th century. Ownership eventually passed into the ecclesiastical hands of the Benedictine Monastery of St. Nicholas in the 17th century, but real progress wasn't felt until the business came into the possession of the Ringhoffers, a family of industrialists who built a complete new facility on the original site in 1874. By 1934, Kozel was the third-largest beer producer in the country, and Velkopopovický Kozel Premium is currently the best-selling Czech beer abroad.

Kozel's famous emblem (the name means "goat") was created by a traveling French artist in return for the hospitality he received. It is a symbol of potency and strength. The company has two goats as mascots, which live on the brewery site. Tradition insists that both must be called Olda. **AG**

Germany is a land of more than 1,000 breweries. Many of these are small and family run, and reserve their products only for lucky customers who live locally. Very few German breweries have a national presence, and even fewer an international one.

The Veltins brewery is located in the peaceful, hilly region known as the Sauerland. Much of this area is preserved as a natural park, and Veltins—via investment in modern technology—prides itself on doing its bit for the environment. The company's green and white branding is an illustration of this, it claims. The emphasis is solely on the pilsner style, and, although there are light and alcohol-free versions, most of the effort is channeled into the beer called Veltins. Brewed from soft, local spring water and spring barley malt, and generously seasoned with hops from the Hallertau region, Veltins is a crisp, clean, highly quaffable beer. **JE**

Tasting notes
This straw-colored Bohemian pilsner is intensely florally hoppy and lively with an evenly composed crisp malt palate and engaging bitterness. Finishes grassy, dry, and bitter.

Tasting notes
A golden pilsner-style lager with a welcomingly clean, herbal-hoppy aroma. Tangy herbal hop notes fill the palate, with a delicate, soft malty sweetness behind for balance.

Vendelín Světlý Ležák

Rodinný Pivovar Vendelín | No website

Via Emilia

Birrificio del Ducato | www.birrificiodelducato.it

Country of origin Czech Republic
First brewed 1999
Alcohol content 4.8% abv
Serving temperature 44°F, 7°C

Country of origin Italy
First brewed 2006
Alcohol content 5% abv
Serving temperature 43°–46°F, 6°–8°C

The tiny Vendelín brewery and pub is a very small enterprise without even so much as a website, and to call it a brewpub almost seems like an exaggeration: the logo on the brewery's delivery truck says *"rodinný pivovar,"* meaning "family brewery," and the setting seems to be the Krkoška family home.

Produced in a shed in the garden, the beer is brewed in small batches on a daily basis. The kettles are direct-fired with wood, a practice that long ago disappeared from most breweries in Bohemia, which might account for some of the rich caramel flavors in the beer. It is unfiltered, unpasteurized, and dosed with an addition of fresh yeast, resulting in a slightly cloudy and very flavorful brew. Krkoška uses ingredients from some of the most famous suppliers in the country: hops from Žatec, malt from Sladovna Jablonec, and yeast from Budweiser Budvar, as well as water from a well in his garden. **ER**

For this pils, Giovanni Campari took inspiration from Germany rather than from the traditional home of pilsner in Bohemia. His purpose was to brew a very drinkable pilsner, rich in floral and hoppy aromas, refreshing, and thirst quenching. The malt profile is very simple: pilsner malt with just a pinch or two of carapils to help with the body. All the hops come from Germany: Magnum and Perle are first in the boil for bitterness. Tettnang Tettnanger is then used for three weeks of dry hopping. The Tettnang variety is chosen for the terroir that gives a particular floral aroma, which characterizes Campari's personal interpretation of the pils style. After ten days of primary fermentation and at least one month of lagering, the beer is made.

The result rarely, if ever, fails to please beer lovers. It can be drunk easily on its own, or match it with fresh goat's cheese or some good Parma ham. **MM**

Tasting notes

Slightly breadlike in aroma due to its addition of fresh yeast. In the mouth is a filling sweetness and very moderate carbonation, followed by a long and crisp Saaz-hop finish.

Tasting notes

Initially hoppy and balsamic notes on the nose, then an elegant floral aroma. On the palate, a light crisp hoppy body, while the finish has delicate notes of honey and almonds.

Victory Golden Monkey

Victory Brewing | www.victorybeer.com

Country of origin United States
First brewed 1998
Alcohol content 9.5% abv
Serving temperature 37°F, 3°C

Victory Brewing Company may very well have been conceived on a school bus. As fifth graders in 1973, Bill Covaleski and Ron Barchet met on the way to a new school, just 20 miles (32 km) from where Victory is now located. After college, the two discovered home-brewing and took a trip of beer discovery to Europe in 1987. The next year, they traveled to the Great American Beer Festival and were impressed by what was taking place among early craft brewers.

Barchet spent a year as an apprentice brewer at Baltimore Brewing and then moved on to the Technical University of Munich at Weihenstephan in 1990. Covaleski took over his slot at Baltimore Brewing to learn the basics of the brewhouse, then he went to Doemens Institute in Munich. In 1994, the pair agreed it was time to start working on their own brewery. They turned a disused bakery in Downington, Pennsylvania, into a brewery restaurant and served the first beer in February 1996. Victory has been a major part of the East Coast beer scene ever since.

Golden Monkey was originally created to be a one-off limited-edition bottling. The reaction to the Belgian-style tripel was so positive that Victory decided to keep on brewing the ale, adding it to the brewery's year-round lineup. Imported two-row malt, European hops, and crushed coriander seed are the ingredients used to make the beer. The yeast that sparks the ale's fermentation was obtained by Victory from a small brewery in Wallonia, Belgium. The beer is sold on draft, in six-packs, and—like classic Belgian tripels—in corked 25-ounce (750-ml) bottles. **RL**

Tasting notes

Golden Monkey is a straw-colored ale with a white puffy head that laces the glass. There is a spicy aroma leading to a summery flavor profile that has hints of tart fruit, earthiness, and exotic spices. This beer is deceptively smooth and drinkable.

Victory Prima Pils

Victory Brewing | www.victorybeer.com

Country of origin United States
First brewed 1997
Alcohol content 5.3% abv
Serving temperature 39°F, 4°C

"Not another pilsner!" It was the last thing the distributors wanted from Victory Brewing, as partners Bill Covaleski and Ron Barchet began to expand their portfolio in the late 1990s. The two friends had plotted to brew a crisp, hoppy pilsner ever since they had worked together at the now-closed Baltimore Brewing.

"DeGroen's Pils was an important beer for the brewery, and we knew it was only a matter of time till we introduced one at Victory," Covaleski says. "But when we went to our distributors, they said 'no thanks.'" At the time, most small brewers were specializing in ales and other dark, heavy varieties; the time of the hop-heavy IPA was also about to dawn. Pilsner—at least the variety available in the United States—was generally seen as characterless, a fizzy yellow liquid with lots of money for promotion but little taste. Miller, for example, was advertising its Lite as "a true pilsner," and the salesmen worried that craft beer drinkers— even those savvy enough to appreciate the delicate flavors produced by a small-batch brewery—would turn their backs on yet another pils.

"But being stubborn," Covaleski says, "we persevered." With their training in Germany, the partners' Prima Pils would bear no resemblance to Lite. Hops—lots of hops—are this beer's signature. Whole-flower Hallertau, Tettnanger, and Saaz provide a solid bitterness and aroma that are entirely absent from the big-name pilsners. For many Americans weaned on insipid mass-market light beer, Victory's pilsner would be a revelation. Here, for the first time, was a U.S.-made pils that exhibited a solid hop character. **DR**

Tasting notes

Prima Pils is a clear and golden beer with a sweet, grassy, floral hop aroma. Its big bitterness is balanced perfectly with a blend of smooth, biscuity German malts. Hints of its alcohol are evident, whereas it finishes dry and amply thirst quenching.

Vollmond Bier

Brauerei Locher | www.appenzellerbier.ch

Country of origin Switzerland
First brewed 1991
Alcohol content 5.2% abv
Serving temperature 46°–50°F, 8°–10°C

Although Switzerland is often associated with chocolate and cuckoo clocks, it has a proud brewing heritage: in 1885, there were 530 breweries. That number has declined to around thirty, and the majority of beers are sharp and clean-tasting lager styles, but the last few years has seen an upsurge in innovation.

One of the more forward-thinking breweries is Brauerei Locher, a family-run business since 1886. It has developed a name for high-quality and innovative beers, and it is one of very few Swiss breweries to produce a lager matured for a full year in wooden barrels, while open fermenters and classic horizontal lagering (storing) vessels also remain in use.

The Locher family believe that lunar influences give Vollmond (full moon) beer its special characteristics, so it is brewed only on the night of a full moon. This tradition was revived in 1991 when two innkeepers, fed up with the influx of mass-produced foreign beer, approached the Lochers to come up with a beer that reflected Swiss brewing heritage. They had studied customers in their pubs and noticed that whenever there was a full moon, people would act differently, such as friendly regulars becoming agitated and introverted women being more generous. So, at 9 P.M. precisely on the evening of a full moon, Brauerei Locher's head brewer opens a valve to allow soft spring water to surge into the copper. Malt and hops are added to the boil and, at 6 A.M., the yeast is pitched in. The bottle label reads: "Blessed by the mythical powers of the celestial body in all is glory, within Vollmond Bier lies the magical force of nature." **AG**

Tasting notes

Totally organic with a superb malty aroma that continues through the flavor and on to a dry finish. It's beautifully golden and rather innocent looking, which disguises a fairly strong and significant beer. Helpfully, the label lists all full moons until the best-by date.

Wadadli

Antigua Brewery | www.antiguabrewery.com

Country of origin Antigua
First brewed 1993
Alcohol content 4.8% abv
Serving temperature 43°F, 6°C

When Christopher Columbus first sighted this speck of land in 1493, he named it Santa Maria la Antigua in honor of a Spanish patron saint. But he never set foot on the island, leaving colonization to the British, who shortened the name and, in 1632, established the first settlement at Parham. After more than three centuries of British rule, Antigua gained its independence in 1981, but it was another twelve years before the islanders could lay claim to having their own brewery. Although the main structure of the German-designed brewery was erected in 1993, its two impressive copper brewing kettles are of much older origin. They were manufactured in Germany in the mid-1950s.

Antigua itself presents any prospective brewer with a major problem: there is precious little fresh water to be found anywhere on the island. As a result, Antigua Brewery operates its own reverse osmosis desalination plant in order to supply its needs by purifying seawater, which is one very good reason for its coastal location.

Wadadli Lager recalls the name originally given to the island by the Arawaks, who settled here some 2,000 years ago. It is brewed using pilsner malt imported from Britain, while Cascade, Millennium, and Columbus hops from the United States give the beer its distinctive bittersweet character, helped along by the addition of a small amount of brewing sugars to satisfy the local preference for a slightly sweeter palate. It is claimed that Antigua has 365 beaches, one for every day of the year, and surely there can be no better place to relax and enjoy a really well-crafted, local beer. **JW**

Tasting notes
Pale gold in the glass with a delightfully floral, citrusy aroma, Wadadli Lager is crisp, refreshing, and full bodied, with zesty hops and hints of grapefruit on the palate, balanced by a gentle maltiness and concluding in a satisfyingly long, bittersweet finish.

Waldhaus Diplom Pils

Privatbrauerei Waldhaus Johannes Schmid | www.waldhaus-bier.de

Country of origin Germany
First brewed 1956
Alcohol content 4.9% abv
Serving temperature 44°–48°F, 7°–9°C

This beer has won so many awards that the brewery owners, the Schmids, changed the name to Diplom Pils in 1978, thus referring to the many certificates hanging on the brewhouse walls. In fact, the Black Forest brewers from Waldhaus not only pride themselves on a decades-long sequence of German quality awards, but also on receiving international decorations from the likes of the World Beer Cup and European Beer Star Awards for their main product.

Even though its style category is a plain one in its motherland—60 percent of beers poured in Germany are pilsners, some of which are sufficiently described as "blond and bitter"—Waldhaus Diplom Pils is anything but plain. It has become a favorite with many beer connoisseurs due to its well-toned body, lighthearted malt character, and complex aromatic hop character. As Dieter Schmid, the fourth-generation owner of the brewery, claims: "The hops are a carefully guarded family secret." Thus they only put in hops stemming from the three German growing areas of Spalt, Hallertau, and Tettnang. Another important feature of a good pilsner is the soft water. Waldhaus take theirs from five sources directly out of Black Forest rocks; this helps to produce an extremely soft quality. Moreover, the beer is neither pasteurized nor short-term heated and is filtered with a cold membrane device.

Waldhaus Diplom Pils is mainly sold in Germany's southwest region of Baden, but is also known by beer enthusiasts in Hamburg, Berlin, and Cologne. It is also increasingly found in other European countries and even as far as Russia and China. **SK**

Tasting notes

This beer captures the senses with an aromatic bouquet of spicy, floral hops. It enchants the palate with an elegant fizz and a soft mouthfeel, presenting a slim and straight crisp malt body balanced with a complex bitterness and floral, citrus notes. The finish is dry, bitter, and crisp.

Wartmann's No. 2 Bitter Ale

Brauhaus Sternen | www.wartmanns.com

Country of origin Switzerland
First brewed 2006
Alcohol content 9% abv
Serving temperature 54°F, 12°C

When Actienbrauerei Frauenfeld contracted its production out to Heineken in 1997, Martin Wartmann stayed at the brewery and launched Weizentrumpf, the first Swiss Hefeweizen, and Ittinger Klosterbier, a clean, crisp, and hoppy amber lager. He was also instrumental in launching BeerCulture, the first Swiss online beer shop, which introduced many a Swiss drinker to specialty beers until Heineken pulled the plug on it. However, the itch to brew his own beer became too much, and Wartmann took the plunge. In 2003, he opened Brauhaus Sternen, a brewpub, in the disused Actienbrauerei Frauenfeld brewery premises.

Brauhaus Sternen's original offerings were pretty good, if somewhat pedestrian, Germanic-style beers, which were basically what local drinkers were expecting. Once the brewery was up and running, Martin Wartmann came up with a bold range of four high-gravity specialty beers in 25-ounce (75-cl) bottles called "Wartmanns Bier für Freunde" (Wartmann's beer for friends), soberly numbered from one to four. The series includes a Belgian-style barleywine, a cocoa stout, and a grand cru wit. Yet the one that challenges Swiss brewers' and drinkers' palates the most is the No. 2, dubbed simply a "bitter," although it stands somewhere between an American double IPA and a British barleywine. Brewed with malt, malt extract, and some invert sugar, No. 2 is hopped with Saaz for bitterness, followed by a generous dosage of Cascade for aroma. It is available in both the original glass bottles or in shiny aluminum bottles. And yes, it can be shipped abroad if you ask! **LM**

Tasting notes

A pale bronze beer with fine condition, No. 2 boasts a spicy, hoppy, citrusy nose. The palate is quite full bodied, not overly sweet, with a spicy yeast edge and a massive hop presence, leading to a complex, long, throat-warming, and hoppy finish that's not as bitter as you'd expect at first.

Weihenstephaner Pilsner

Bayerische Staatsbrauerei Weihenstephan
www.brauerei-weihenstephan.de

Country of origin Germany
First brewed 1908
Alcohol content 5.1% abv
Serving temperature 43°–46°F, 6°–8°C

Bayerische Staatsbrauerei Weihenstephan declares itself to be the oldest brewery in the world. Originally, the brewery was part of the Weihenstephan monastery, which was founded in 725; more than three centuries later, the monks established a brewery in 1040. Between 1085 and 1463, the monastery burned to the ground no fewer than four times. Disease, famine, and an earthquake also made their marks. The monks, however, did not give up easily. After every disaster, they rebuilt and sometimes even expanded. In 1921, the brewery received the name it still uses today, and, two years later, the emblem of the state of Bavaria became the brewery's official logo.

Brewing equipment has been updated, but the basic method of production remains virtually unchanged since 1040. However, with a current lagering time of thirty days for the Pilsner, it is likely that this part of the process was longer during the Middle Ages. Introduced in 1908, when the brewery was noted more for its wheat beers, the Pilsner is brewed with lightly kilned pilsner malt and Hallertauer Perle, Hallertauer Taurus, and Hallertauer Tradition hops. It is a worthy brew with which to toast the longevity of Weihenstephan. **RP**

Tasting notes

Clear golden color in the glass. The taste is a slight combination of the fruitiness that one might find in a Hefeweizen with the bitterness one expects from a pilsner.

Weihenstephaner Vitus

Bayerische Staatsbrauerei Weihenstephan
www.brauerei-weihenstephan.de

Country of origin Germany
First brewed 2007
Alcohol content 7.7% abv
Serving temperature 46°F, 8°C

The Bavarian brewery of Weihenstephan in Freising is noted for its Weissbiers. Weihenstephaner Vitus is the brewery's newest beer, and it is a Weizenbock—a hardy wheat beer that is approached with caution. It is also a beer that those who fast through Lent can drink for sustenance. One question: given that Schneider's Aventinus has been wowing drinkers for the best part of a century, what took Weihenstephan so long?

After all, it's not as if the saint after whom the beer is named, St. Vitus, or Veit, is a recent arrival. Martyred in the 4th century, he was one of the fourteen protecting patrons of the Catholic church and had his sainthood bestowed on him around the start of the 7th century. There is also a connection between him and brewing. There's an old German rural saying: "If it is raining on St. Veit's day, the barley does not like it."

Vitus is a special beer, produced by a brewery that brews class instead of mass, quality instead of quantities of beer. Vitus undergoes a longer than usual cold storage in the brewery's cellars, which helps to smooth out the flavors. Much to the relief of its followers, this beer is available throughout the whole year, even though it was initially launched during the Lenten time of March. **WO**

Tasting notes

Golden in color and cloudy from the yeast that remains in the bottle. On the nose, malt sweetness; on the palate, a cluster of spicy, clovelike notes before a bittersweet, spicy finish.

Part of the evocative mural that adorns the wall of the Weihenstephaner brewery.

Weltenburger Barock Hell

Klosterbrauerei Weltenburger
www.weltenburger.de

Country of origin Germany
First brewed *ca.* 19th century
Alcohol content 5.6% abv
Serving temperature 46°F, 8°C

The beers crafted in the little brewhouse in the Weltenburg Abbey courtyard veer toward the darker end of the spectrum, but there are also lighter beers in the range. These are brewed at the Bischofshof brewery in nearby Regensburg.

The brewers at Bischofshof also run the monastery brewery, which is owned by the bishop of Regensburg. Just in case anyone doubts the authenticity of the Regensburg offerings, they all bear the name "Marke Weltenburger" as opposed to "Weltenburger Kloster," which indicates beer from the monastery. The quality is equally high, which makes Barock Hell a real treat. It's a wonderfully smooth blond lager, benefiting from eight weeks of lagering and the inclusion of first-rate lager malt and local Hallertauer hops. **JE**

Tasting notes
The aroma is fresh and hoppy with lemon notes from the plentiful hops that continue into the full, smooth, bittersweet taste. Hops then dominate the dry, full, satisfying finish.

West Coast India Pale Ale

Green Flash Brewing
www.greenflashbrew.com

Country of origin United States
First brewed 2005
Alcohol content 7.5% abv
Serving temperature 55°F, 13°C

Given the reputation for hop-focused beers in the San Diego area, Green Flash Brewing set the bar high for itself when it gave West Coast IPA its name.

Brewmaster Chuck Silva packs 95 IBUs into the beer. That's more than in many double or imperial IPAs. Southern California IPAs don't differ simply because they contain more hops. Since Vinnie Cilurzo brewed Blind Pig Double IPA in 1994, the San Diego style has signaled paler-colored and less-sweet beers, but beers that still have the malt character to stand up to plenty of hops. These are generally hop varieties developed in the Northwest: pungent, with flavors of many different citrus fruits and pine. Many brewers use Simcoe, a hop described as "catty" by those with sensitive noses. **SH**

Tasting notes
Pours a hazy orange with hints of green glimmering in the light. The aroma includes pine, tropical fruit, and zesty citrus, especially grapefruit. Long, dry, bitter finish.

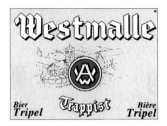

Westmalle Trappist Tripel

Brouwerij van de Abdij der Trappisten van Westmalle | www.trappistwestmalle.be

Country of origin Belgium
First brewed 1934
Alcohol content 9.5% abv
Serving temperature 46°–54°F, 8°–12°C

In 1934, the Antwerp Trappist monks at Westmalle Abbey celebrated a brand-new brewhouse by launching an extra-strong, sparkling golden ale; their strongest (dark) beer was dubbed "dubbel," and thus a name imposed itself. It was only in 1956 that the tripel, as we know it, was perfected by famed father-brewer Brother Thomas. The new beer gained esteem, and, by the 1980s, there were few pubs in Flanders where one couldn't obtain a Westmalle Tripel.

Both beers gained international recognition, and now the world equates tripel with a pale, strong beer. Demand remains high. An indirect result of this insatiable appetite for Westmalle's Tripel is that the brewery's third beer (named Extra) is brewed only ever so often—and for the monks only. **JPa**

Tasting notes
Golden beer with orange shine. Grain and white candy sugar make themselves present on the nose. Hops come out in the taste, while the palate remains fruity, estery, and sweet.

Wild Hare

Bath Ales
www.bathales.com

Country of origin England
First brewed 2005
Alcohol content 5% abv
Serving temperature 46°–54°F, 8°–12°C

Bath Ales was founded in 1995 by long-term friends Roger Jones and Richard Dempster. The pair had previously worked together in a Bristol-based brewery called Smiles, one of the pioneers of the British microbrewing revolution in the 1970s.

First brewed in 2005 as an organic cask ale, but now found solely in bottles, Wild Hare is Bath Ales's answer to light-colored ales such as Summer Lightning. Organic Maris Otter pale ale malt is supplied from a traditional floor-maltings, and the use of the organically farmed First Gold hop helps to give the beer a luscious grapefruit aroma. According to Jones, the reason the brewery produces an organic ale is that "few brewers have the appetite to brew a certified organic beer—so it's a basic point of difference." **JM**

Tasting notes
A crisp, full-flavored pale ale that tantalizes with a fresh citrus and hoppy aroma. On the palate, this organic summer beer is malty and hoppy with light fruit notes. Dry, bitter finish.

Windhoek Lager

Namibia Breweries | www.nambrew.com

Country of origin Namibia
First brewed 1920
Alcohol content 4% abv
Serving temperature 39°–44°F, 4°–7°C

The last-minute scramble for African colonies between the major European powers in the late 19th century saw Namibia fall under the control of Germany. The colony was ruled by a brutal and repressive regime, whose actions still have the power to leave unhealed scars. From such an inglorious time, it may appear somewhat insensitive to describe the introduction of brewing techniques as one positive remnant, yet today Namibians are intensely proud of their beer, with none inducing national pride more than Windhoek Lager.

German settlers were drawn by the economic possibilities in farming and diamond mining. During the early days of colonization, all commercial alcoholic beverages were imported from Europe, but this arduous journey drastically affected taste, and thus opportunities arose for brewmasters to open breweries in the region. In 1920, two businessmen, Carl List and Hermann Ohlthaver, acquired four breweries to form South West Breweries—a move that would radically alter the face of beer production in Namibia.

The fledgling company's aim was to produce a beer modeled on those from the owners' homeland by brewing according to the Reinheitsgebot of 1516. This method has been followed verbatim, and the Windhoek Lager brewed today contains no genetically modified organisms, only the finest barley malt from Germany, hops from the Hallertau region in Bavaria, and pure water sourced from the S. von Bach storage dam near Okahandja. Windhoek has won the gold medal for three consecutive years (2007–2009) at the International DLG Awards in Berlin. **SG**

Tasting notes

Poured correctly, a pale yellow brew is crowned with a foamy head that dissipates quickly. Grainy aromas compete with traces of grass, while the palate combines sweet grainy malts and spicy hops to deliver a dry, crisp, clean finish.

Witkap-Pater Stimulo

Brouwerij Slaghmuylder | www.witkap.be

Country of origin Belgium
First brewed 1932 Verlinden; 1979 Slaghmuylder
Alcohol content 6% abv
Serving temperature 44°–52°F, 7°–11°C

The Slaghmuylder brewery is located in Ninove, in the province of East Flanders. Strangely enough, its Witkap abbey ales are very much in the tradition of beers from the province of Antwerp. Indeed, they once were the brainchildren of the famed prewar brewmaster Hendrik Verlinden, whose role in the development of the famous Westmalle beers is far from negligible.

He started his own brewery in Brasschaat, northeast of Antwerp, in the early 1930s. However, in the mid-1970s, Verlinden's brewery had to be closed, and a new place was found in Ninove. Interestingly enough, Brouwerij Slaghmuylder specialized in bottom-fermenting beers (which it still produces), so the jump to these top-fermenting styles was pretty impressive.

Originally, there were three Witkap beers: the blond-colored Stimulo, the equally hued Tripel, and the dark Dubbel Pater. Since 2009, a Special has joined these; it is a seasonal beer that was originally known as the unpronounceable Greut Lawauitj. The Witkap beers are unpasteurized and refermented on the bottle, and Stimulo boasts both Czech and Belgian hops.

Slaghmuylder is still very much a family-owned brewery. Head brewer Karel Goddeau is very driven to perfect the whole Slaghmuylder range, which has already resulted in some of the beers being recognized as regional specialties. The brewery also has a working steam engine as its living heart, and the annual open brewing day is an excellent occasion to view a working museum piece in action. In the United States, the Stimulo is sold under the meaningless "Abbey Singel ale" (sic) name. Don't let that spoil your fun. **JPa**

Tasting notes

Witkap-Pater Stimulo is a pale yellow beer with a thick white head. Fresh, herbal, grassy nose, and a hint of hop. The taste comes out spicy—hints of mustard seed? Fruity flavors to finish: papaya and prickly pear. Well bodied for a beer that is not that strong.

Woodforde's Headcracker

Woodforde's | www.woodfordes.co.uk

Country of origin England
First brewed 1985
Alcohol content 7% abv
Serving temperature 55°F, 13°C

Woodforde's Brewery sits in the heart of the Norfolk Broads, a network of waterways that, come summer, are packed with tourists cruising at a leisurely pace through drowsy days before mooring for the evening at one of the many pubs that line the riverbank. It's at places like these that Headcracker on draft does good business. "People grab a few pints and head back to their boats with it," says head brewer Bruce Ash. "They don't have to get up for work in the morning, and I think that's when it comes into its own."

Headcracker is an appropriately named traditional barleywine that combines the complexity of a fine red wine with a dangerously smooth and easy drinkability. It doesn't taste like a 7 percent beer, and where it's sold on draft, people approach it with caution after having succumbed to one too many the first time. Headcracker does great business at beer festivals, where people are more adventurous in their drinking, and it does very well in bottles—the brewer himself usually has one with an Indian meal. The bottles carry a "best before" date of about a year from bottling, but this is a beer that will improve and mellow long after that.

Headcracker is brewed only with Maris Otter pale malt, hence its surprisingly pale color for a barleywine, and uses Golding hops for bittering and Slavinsky Syrian hops also for bittering. It's remarkable how ingredients that are commonly associated with light, easy-drinking beers have been used here to create a beer that's perfectly balanced at 7 percent. You can definitely taste the alcohol, but it's held in check and complements beautifully the rest of the flavor. **PB**

Tasting notes

A dark gold beer with enormous complexity on the nose: orange fruitiness, piney hoppiness, and a faint undertone of whiskeylike spiciness. In the mouth, there's rich damson and plum, balanced by a dry hoppiness, with a warming alcohol finish.

XX Bitter

Brouwerij de Ranke | www.deranke.be

Country of origin Belgium
First brewed 1997
Alcohol content 6.2% abv
Serving temperature 46°–50°F, 8°–10°C

The financial address of the De Ranke brewery is in Wevelgem, in the province of West Flanders. However, the state-of-the-art brewing plant is in Dottignies, a town in the neighboring province of Hainaut, in Wallonia. Given the proud sense of identity that Flemish and Wallonian brewers possess, this division of loyalties requires some explanation. De Ranke's founders Nino Bacelle and Guido Devos are both West Flemish, and back in the 1990s, the duo began brewing using the equipment at the Deca brewery, also in the same province. Being passionate brewers, though, they never left the idea of having their own brewery, and in 2005 finally set up shop in Dottignies.

Both Guido and Nino are big champions of outspoken flavors—as long as this doesn't mean sweet. It's no wonder then that many of their brews are inspired by sour beers, such as lambic, and hoppy ones of a kind not usually found in Belgium. Indeed, XX Bitter might be a very unoriginal name, especially in the English-speaking beer nations, but in Belgium it was a statement of intent: a robust rebuttal to the average Belgian drinker who, alas, thought of bitterness as a sign of poor brewing. This attitude has led to some Belgian ales retreating toward more easily accessible flavors—for that, read "sweeter"—and today, 60 percent of De Ranke beers are exported.

XX Bitter has never compromised. It boldly sports Brewer's Gold and Hallertau in its hop mix, based upon a palate of pale malts. Taste the beer, and the hops are there! Today, XX Bitter can be seen as a trendsetter for the new style of would-be-IPA Belgian beers. **JPa**

Tasting notes

Light golden color with a slight, white head. The nose is totally dominated by the hops. The palate undergoes an immediate bitter attack of hops and roasted malt notes. Medium bodied, with the hoppiness going on and on in the finish.

Yankee

Rooster's | www.roosters.co.uk

Country of origin England
First brewed 1994
Alcohol content 4.3% abv
Serving temperature 54°F, 12°C

Created by Sean Franklin when he set up Rooster's five-barrel plant in Knaresborough, Yorkshire, Yankee beer came about after he saw an article in a brewing research paper about a selection of new hop varieties that were touted as the most floral in the world. Franklin decided to start experimenting with the then-rare Cascade hops, choosing to use only a pale malt base to ensure that these incredible hops were showcased and that none of the heady aroma was lost.

"The Cascade variety was a revelation in terms of showcasing that hops can have the same aromas as grapes," says Franklin. "If you have to liken it to any wine, it's close to a Gewürztraminer, and I used to be in the wine trade, so it seemed like an interesting parallel. Since then, we rarely use darker malts in our beers, preferring to let the hops do the talking."

The name Yankee was chosen because, at the time, Franklin was going through a little bit of a James Dean phase. Given that the beer is brewed using a U.S. hop, the name Yankee just seemed to be the ideal fit. Yankee was truly a groundbreaking beer and can be credited alongside brands such as Summer Lightning as breaking the golden ale style that has gone on to be so very popular across the United Kingdom. The drinkability and cross-gender appeal of the beer mean that it's still widely sought after to this day. **MC**

Tasting notes
On the nose, there are masses of tropical fruit notes; on the palate, the fresh, almost grasslike, barley taste combines with the soft Yorkshire water to provide a sensuously creamy drink.

Yona Yona Ale

Yoho Brewing | www.yohobrewing.com

Country of origin Japan
First brewed 1997
Alcohol content 5.5% abv
Serving temperature 55°F, 13°C

Yona Yona Ale is one of the most widely available craft beers in Japan, and one of the best known. The beer was envisioned to be much like a U.S.-style pale ale, and was intended to be unique in Japan. According to Yoho Brewing's president Naoyuki Ide, Yona Yona was the first canned craft beer product in Japan.

Maintaining a consistent flavor for Yona Yona has been a continual effort. The flavor profile of this beer is based on the Cascade hop, and owing to variations from shipment to shipment, it became necessary early on to check and analyze each batch of beer. When it was released to the market, it was radically different from mass-produced beers, and consumers gave a continual stream of comments to the brewery. People said the flavor was too strong, the aroma was too pronounced, and the beer was entirely too bitter. In the long run, the fact that the beer was unusual led an increasing number of people to try it.

While current economic difficulties have adversely impacted the industry, the brewery is still experiencing sales increases every year. It hopes to strengthen nationwide sales and become the most popular craft brewery in Japan. One means to achieve this is via the brewery's website; it has been created purely for image and entertainment and is virtually meaningless to those who cannot understand Japanese. **BH**

Tasting notes
Initial aroma of citruslike hops, backed by dried fruit and malt. The flavor of Yona Yona is briskly hoppy at first, followed by dry malt flavors, leading to a clean and tangy quick finish.

The name and pump art for Yankee are inspired by the U.S. hop used in making it.

Young's Special London Ale

Wells & Young's | www.wellsandyoungs.co.uk

Country of origin England
First brewed 1998
Alcohol content 6.4% abv
Serving temperature 50°–54°F, 10°–12°C

Young's Brewery in Wandsworth, London, is sadly no more. It closed in 2006, after more than 400 years of producing beers for the capital's drinkers. The valuable site was sold for redevelopment, and Young's merged its brewing interests with Charles Wells in Bedford.

A number of Young's beers survived the transfer to the Bedford brewery, one being this exceptional strong ale. Special London Ale caught the wave of the bottle-conditioned beer revival at the end of the 1990s. A pet project of brewer Derek Prentice, it was not a new brew as such. A version had been sold under the name of "Young's Export," and this had even been brewed under license in Belgium. Getting the new product ready for launch took a while, as they mastered the art and science of including live yeast in the bottle for a secondary fermentation there. But the effort proved worthwhile. Not only has Special London Ale become a firm favorite, it's also notched up numerous awards, not least for the Campaign for Real Ale's Champion Bottle-Conditioned Beer in 1999.

The full, smooth body is a product of the generous loading of the mash tun with Maris Otter pale malt and crystal malt. Fuggle and Golding hops in the copper provide the firm, fruity bitterness that is the hallmark of this beer, but the hops' work is not done at the end of the boil. After primary fermentation, and prior to bottling, the beer enjoys three weeks' warm conditioning over a bed of whole Target and Golding hops. This really emphasizes the hop character, which is beautifully illustrated on the palate by tangy, bitter orange marmalade notes. **JE**

Tasting notes

An orange golden beer, with the zest of oranges and grapefruit in the aroma. Full and smooth, the bittersweet taste has marmalade orange notes, plus other citrus fruit, but delicate malt flavors are also present, before a long, dry, bitter, enjoyably hoppy finish.

Žatec

Žatecký Pivovar | www.zateckypivovar.cz

Country of origin Czech Republic
First brewed 1964
Alcohol content 4.6% abv
Serving temperature 44°F, 7°C

The ancient Bohemian town of Žatec, in the northeast of the Czech Republic, has long been hailed for the quality of its hops, which are documented as having been grown since the 11th century. Unfortunately, Žatec misses out on a bit of the credit, as much of the world knows the hops by their German name, Saaz, rather than the Czech name, Žatec. They remain among the world's most expensive hops, and were the first to receive a Protected Designation of Origin from the European Union in 2007.

The town's long brewing tradition, which dates at least to 1261, also seems to run slightly under the radar. At various times, there were as many as seven breweries in town, including a very famous factory owned by Anton Dreher the Younger. Today, just two breweries remain: the noncommercial *pivovar* of the Žatec Hop Institute, used for research purposes, and this commercial brewery on the town's main square, built in 1801. It is believed to be the Czech brewery with the longest continuous tradition of making beer in the same location. As such, it is perhaps unsurprising that modern conveniences are few and far between. The brewery still uses traditional open fermentation vessels. Only Moravian two-row spring barley is used, along with three varieties of the town's great hops: Žatecký poloraný červeňák—or Saaz semi-early red—as well as the two Saaz subvarietals Sládek and Premiant. Žatec Bright Lager is filtered before undergoing cold conditioning for a lengthy period of forty-five days. The result is a beer of remarkable balance, with an understated—yet noble—Saaz hop presence. **ER**

Tasting notes

Despite its hop-centric origins, this harmoniously composed pilsner is far from a 100-IBU imperial IPA. Look for a rich, malty heart counterbalanced by a headful of Saaz hop dreams: slightly peppery and aromatic florid notes with a crisp, bitter buzz in the finish.

Zhujiang Beer

Guangzhou Zhujiang Brewery
www.zhujiangbeer.ca

Country of origin China
First brewed 1985
Alcohol content 5.3% abv
Serving temperature 46°F, 8°C

Zhujiang Brewery was set up in 1985 with the help of Interbrew (as Anheuser-Busch InBev was then called), just as China was opening up to the world. It is based in the city of Guangzhou and is owned in partnership with A-B InBev. This has allowed plenty of investment and—presumably—a cross-cultural exchange on all things brewing, which is possibly why its light and crisp pilsner, named after the brewery, has become South China's top-selling beer.

Imported hops and malt, plus rice, make up the building blocks of the beer, and it is fermented with the help of German yeast. Given the excellent tradition of Cantonese cuisine, this is a beer that marries well with a lot of the province's dishes, such as wonton soup and steamed scallops with ginger and garlic. Zhujiang also produces several other variations on the pale lager theme. **ATJ**

Tasting notes
Pale yellow gold in color sitting beneath a slight collar of snow-white foam. Slender sweetish malt notes on the nose joined by a whisper of sweet lemon; crisp, light, and refreshing on the palate.

Zinnebir

Brasserie de la Senne
www.brasseriedelasenne.be

Country of origin Belgium
First brewed 2002
Alcohol content 6% abv
Serving temperature 44°F, 7°C

Brewer Bernard Leboucq first launched Zinnebir as a beer that he wanted to make distinctive enough to represent the citizens of Brussels. Sweet, overspiced, or otherwise boring blond and pale ales tend to still permeate the Belgian scene, although a growing cadre of more characterful beers have appeared in recent years. Zinnebir is one such beer, with its generous hopping and only a light sweetness coming from the malt. Its subtle spicy character and zesty aroma comes mainly from the yeast—the brewery adds no spices to its beers.

Leboucq's small Sint-Pieters brewery became the Brasserie de la Senne in 2005, after brewer and beer activist Yvan De Baets joined the team. Zinnebir is no longer confined to beer-specialist haunts in the capital, and has gained popularity in the city's younger and hipper cafés. **JS**

Tasting notes
Floral, grassy hop aromas with estery notes of grapefruit zest. Crisply bitter with lightly sweet center. Lively in the mouth and refreshingly dry on the finish.

Zlatý Bažant 12%

Heineken Slovensko
www.zlatybazant.sk

Country of origin Slovakia
First brewed 1969
Alcohol content 5% abv
Serving temperature 46°F, 8°C

Poor old Slovakia. When we think of beer in this part of the world, the mind immediately crosses the border to the pilsner styles of the neighboring Czech Republic, but Zlatý Bažant 12%, or "Golden Pheasant," flies the flag for Slovakian beer throughout the world.

The brewery is based in Hurbanovo, where in 1967 a new maltings was established. A couple of years later, the brewery opened up, and along with it came Zlatý Bažant 12%. The beer, a pale, golden-colored pilsner, was a success from its very inception, and it was also exported abroad—although like a lot of breweries behind the Iron Curtain, the majority of countries it went to were fellow Soviet satellites, such as Poland. The brewery was noted for being the first in the country to introduce a canning line for its beers, in 1971. As well as the 12-degree-Plato version, the brewery also produces a weaker 10-degree beer and a dark beer. **ATJ**

Tasting notes
Pours the color of sunlight. The nose is slight with gently toasted grain and a hint of lemon; soft and refreshing mouthfeel with sweetish malt character. The finish has a crisp bitterness.

Żywiec

Grupa Żywiec
www.zywiec.com.pl

Country of origin Poland
First brewed 1856
Alcohol content 5.6% abv
Serving temperature 43°F, 6°C

One of the fastest-growing beer brands of the early 21st century comes from a quiet little town in the far south of Poland. Żywiec is not easy to spell and it's even harder to ask for, but despite these handicaps, this bright and golden strong lager soon gained a substantial following.

The crown in the beer's logo hints at its royal past, so it's no surprise to learn that a member of the Habsburg family founded the business in the 1850s. After World War II, Żywiec came under state control, but with the collapse of Communism, it returned to private hands in 1991. Heineken acquired a majority holding three years later. The 1913 brewhouse was decommissioned in 1996 to make way for a state-of-the-art symphony in stainless steel. Here, Żywiec is produced, using river water that cascades down from the local hills. **JE**

Tasting notes
A pale golden, smooth, strong lager with creamy pale malt and herbal hops in both the aroma and the bittersweet taste. The finish starts off bittersweet but becomes more bitter.

WHITE BEERS

3 Ravens White

3 Ravens Brewery | www.3ravens.com.au

Country of origin Australia
First brewed 2006
Alcohol content 5.2% abv
Serving temperature 36°–37°F, 2°–3°C

Engineers in Australia are primarily known for solving problems and drinking beer. It is little surprise then that the engineers at the Zektin Group, in Melbourne, Australia, started to brew their own beer when faced with the problem of their local pub no longer serving real ale. Of course, being engineers, they engaged in a process of continuous improvement with each batch until the staff bar became one of the more attractive reasons for people to work at the company. Eventually, production levels got so high they had little choice but to consider sharing the beer with the locals.

Marcus Cox was hired by then-brewer Ben Pattison to take the operation to the next level. Although he had a home-brewing background, Cox had never brewed commercially and was under pressure to learn how to satisfy the growing expectations of a large quality-assurance team of engineers and a burgeoning fan base. The team's technical ability increased further when Matt Inchley arrived from Red Hill Brewery. Together they produce a diverse range of traditional ales, including the popular American Pale Ale.

Being a Belgian-style wheat beer, 3 Ravens White's flavor profile is assisted by the addition of buckets—literally—of organic coriander seeds, handfuls of orange peel, and differing amounts of various other spices, such as cardamom and the West African grain of paradise or Melegueta pepper. As the beer is made without any preservatives, and these spices go to the heart of things, the brewery prefers to keep distribution at a local level to ensure that their essence is not lost in transport. **DD**

Tasting notes

Citrus and spice are the prominent features in this cloudy, yellow beer. Orange and coriander should tease you in the pour and follow you all the way to the slightly tart finish. 3 Ravens White is an excellent companion to poached salmon.

Andechser Weissbier Hefetrüb

Klosterbrauerei Andechs | www.andechs.de/brauerei

Country of origin Germany
First brewed 1764
Alcohol content 5.5% abv
Serving temperature 41˚–54˚F, 5˚–12˚C

Since the mid-15th century, beer of one sort or another has been brewed in this Bavarian Benedictine abbey on the Holy Mountain above the eastern shore of Lake Ammersee. A century later, Weissbier was first brewed in Bavaria, but the right to brew it was later withdrawn by the royal family and it wasn't until 1602 that it was made in Bavaria again. During the Napoleonic era, the abbey was shut, but returned to its otherworldly preoccupations in 1850. Throughout the upheavals, the monks have gotten on with brewing beers in the traditional way, and little changed until the 20th century, when the brewing facilities were renovated and replaced, in some cases, more than once: the maltings, for example, was replaced in 1906, while in 1972 a new brewery was installed. Around 2.5 million gallons (100,000 hl) of beer are produced annually, of which about 5 percent is set aside to serve visitors to the abbey and its public houses. The abbey brewhouse includes a lagering cellar, and beers are typically lagered for four to six weeks before distribution.

The abbey was founded in the 10th century and is now the only monastery (and one of only two breweries) in Germany that brews and distributes a bock beer all year long. Andechs was, of course, not founded solely to produce beer, its purpose being to look after the pilgrims visiting the abbey and the Holy Mountain. In the Middle Ages, as today, the demands of climbing the Holy Mountain are met by stopping at the abbey's beer garden or beer hall, where this refreshing Weissbier is a big favorite and naturally encourages contemplation of the more secular nature. **RP**

Tasting notes

In the glass, Andechser Weissbier Hefetrüb is cloudy orange with a lively, firm, large white head. The aroma is somewhat spicy, but otherwise fairly standard for a Weissbier. On the palate, it has a pleasant fruity, malty taste and finishes on a slightly bitter note.

Ayinger Ur-Weisse

Brauerei Aying | www.ayinger.de

Country of origin Germany
First brewed 1979
Alcohol content 5.8% abv
Serving temperature 44°–46°F, 7°–8°C

Aying is a small village to the southeast of Munich, a rural hideaway surrounded by great swathes of forest, and a picture in itself; however, this beautiful-looking community is also the home of Brauerei Aying. The presence of this much-acclaimed brewery (plus its adjoining restaurant and beer hall) makes it a place of pilgrimage for beer lovers from all over the world. As can be expected with such a solid and venerable establishment, the brewery is family owned, by the Inselkammer family, who have run it since 1878. Given all this, you would expect to be able to find their beer during the Oktoberfest activities in nearby Munich; but you will search in vain, as those big tents with their oompah music and massive steins are solely devoted to breweries within the city limits of Munich. Those who travel to the festival and go no further than a few Paulaners do not know what they are missing.

Ur-Weisse is a dark amber wheat beer, a survival from the 1950s when drinks of this sort were popular with older citizens—soothing and contemplative beers to sip as the world rushed by. They also had a relatively restorative reputation compared to what the younger generation was drinking. It was a time when gleaming golden lagers shone a light on the revitalization and rebuilding of postwar West Germany; a time when Weissbier, both dark and blond, was seen as very much a minority drink. However, Ayinger brought out their own version at the end of the 1970s, as drinkers were ready to be beguiled by an old-fashioned kind of beer, especially over in New York, where Ur-Weisse still fetches a premium price in specialist beer bars. **WO**

Tasting notes

Ur-Weisse is a very successful double act between the freshness of wheat and the heft of dark malt. Amber-colored and cloudy; initial aromatic impressions are of clear aromas of malt; the palate is fruity then dry, while the bitterness is very smooth in the finish.

Berliner Kindl Weisse

Berliner-Kindl-Schultheiss-Brauerei | www.berliner-kindl.de

Country of origin Germany
First brewed 1870
Alcohol content 3% abv
Serving temperature 46°–50°F, 8°–10°C

The roots of the famed Berliner Weisse beer most likely go back to 1526, when Cord Broihan, a brewer from Halberstadt, attempted to re-create the then-popular Hamburger Bier. He produced a beer that came to be called Halberstädter Broihan and was soon known of throughout north Germany. In the mid-17th century, brewers in Berlin modified the recipe and produced a Weissbier. This had become a favorite of Berliners by 1700, and within a hundred years, there were no fewer than 700 pubs in Berlin serving it. When Napoleon's soldiers sampled it in the 19th century, they dubbed the Weissbier the "champagne of the north."

In the early years, Berliner Weisse was often drunk with an herbal liqueur. At the start of the 19th century, a local brewer tried adding herbs directly to the beer, and eventually this led to the use of herbal syrups (usually raspberry or woodruff), which were mixed in the glass or in the bottle; the practice continues today.

Unlike many of the beers for which Germany is famous, Berliner Weisse is top-fermented. It is also a protected name—it may only be brewed in Berlin (just as Kölsch may only be brewed in Cologne). By 1900, there were more than seventy breweries in Berlin making Berliner Weisse. Until 2006, there were three left. Today, there are only two: Berliner-Kindl-Schultheiss-Brauerei and Berliner Bürgerbräu. The latter produces pre-mixed Berliner Weisse. In 2006, Berliner Kindl and Schultheiss joined forces and the Schultheiss brand was dropped, thus forcing the total output of Berliner Weisse to fall again, making it perhaps one of the rarest beer styles in Europe. **RP**

Tasting notes

Perhaps unsurprisingly, this beer is similar in appearance to a Belgian Wit. However, the resemblance ends on tasting: the Berliner Weisse is quite sour, though in a rather pleasant way. In fact, it is not hard to understand how this beer might be wonderfully refreshing on a warm summer's day.

Bio-Dinkel Weisse

Weissbräu Unertl | www.brauerei-unertl.de

Country of origin Germany
First brewed 2000
Alcohol content 5.2% abv
Serving temperature 46°–50°F, 8°–10°C

Television viewers best know brewer Wolfgang Unertl as the world's fastest beer-bottle opener; he has broken his own world record repeatedly on camera since 1999, yet there is more to him than popping bottle tops. At night, Unertl likes to fill his malt room, brew-house, and fermentation and lager cellars in the Bavarian town of Mühldorf with the sound of Mozart, Bach, or Mendelssohn. Just like Italian brewer Teo Musso of Le Baladin, he believes the music creates beneficial vibrations for his beers.

In 2000, Unertl created his award-winning spelt wheat beer. He had become fascinated with spelt because of its incorruptible, primordial character. As he points out, the primeval wheat plant grows solely on simple soils, is very resistant, and defies genetic manipulation. The beer is made only from organic ingredients and is neither filtered nor pasteurized. Instead, Unertl uses water from an artesian source that is additionally swirled in an energetic procedure.

Originally, Unertl wanted to become a healer; it was his sense of responsibility that brought him back to his family's brewery. Producing Bio-Dinkel Weisse is costly—spelt malt is four to five times more expensive than barley or wheat malt—and the brewery does not make money with it. But Unertl sticks to it, knowing that life is not always a matter of breaking speed records. **SK**

Tasting notes
Copper-colored with orange tints, creamy off-white head. A sweet aroma reminiscent of banana. Notes of grain and oranges imbue the palate, balanced by a lively sourness.

Blanche de Chambly

Unibroue | www.unibroue.com

Country of origin Canada
First brewed 1992
Alcohol content 5% abv
Serving temperature 41°F, 5°C

For most North Americans, their first exposure to the Belgian style of wheat beer came when the now-legendary reviver of Hoegaarden White, Pierre Celis, decamped from his homeland to Austin, Texas. Here, he began producing a beer known as Celis White. However, en route to establishing his Texas operations, Celis stopped off in Québec to help a novice brewery owner develop what eventually emerged as the first true North American–brewed white: Blanche de Chambly.

Retired Québec businessman André Dion was approached by a consortium of domestic craft brewers who had the idea of setting up a common distribution front for all their brands. Although this project never got off the ground, Dion became interested in importing beer and followed this course to Belgium, where he discovered the Riva Brewery and its typical Riva Blanche, spiced with coriander and orange peel. Trading a 10 percent stake in his business for a copy of the Riva recipe, Dion returned to Québec to set up operations and, with the help of Celis, began brewing Blanche de Chambly.

The taste was unique to Québec. Eye-catching label graphics, supported by aggressive advertising in the local arts and alternative media, helped to make the beer a hit, and it went on to win many awards. **SB**

Tasting notes
A shining example of balance between coriander spice and citrusy fruit, with a body perhaps a bit fuller than most in its class, but nevertheless a lively, refreshing disposition.

← All of Wolfgang Unertl's beers are brewed with love—and marked accordingly.

Blanche de Saisis

Brasserie Ellezelloise
www.brasserie-ellezelloise.be

Country of origin Belgium
First brewed *ca.* 1993
Alcohol content 6.2% abv
Serving temperature 46°F, 8°C

The tale of how Pierre Celis almost single-handedly revived witbier in the small town of Hoegaarden has become part of Belgian beer lore. Since the 1960s, several breweries have concocted fond imitations of the original—orange peel, coriander, and all—often under the supervision of Celis himself. Meanwhile, flying under the radar are a handful of Belgian wheat beers that excel without the addition of spices. Blanche de Saisis might be the best of them.

The brewery is in a former farmstead perched on a hilltop overlooking the village of Ellezelles. This is northern Hainaut, saison country, and the brewery's beers all have certain farmhouse leanings. They are full-flavored but simple enough that you can taste the ingredients. For the Blanche, that means 60 percent barley malt and 40 percent unmalted wheat. Hopping is generous for bitterness and flavor, as it is with all Ellezelloise beers, while the subtle impression of spices comes mainly from the yeast.

Despite a full body, the beer is highly refreshing. It can liven up a wide variety of lighter meals, from salads to omelets to seafood. The bitterness of Blanche de Saisis means it can stand up to meatier, spicier dishes, too. For those who make the pilgrimage, Ellezelloise is one of Belgium's most visitor-friendly breweries. Its tasting café is open to the public nearly every day. **JS**

Tasting notes
Cereals and notes of lemon, orange, and pepper on the nose. Flavor is nearly devoid of sweetness; just a full and welcome bitterness, dry and grassy, with a lingering orange-peel note.

Blanche des Honnelles

Brasserie de l'Abbaye des Rocs
www.abbaye-des-rocs.com

Country of origin Belgium
First brewed 1991
Alcohol content 6% abv
Serving temperature 43°–46°F, 6°–8°C

Former excise officer Jean-Pierre Eloir started brewing in 1979 in the small Wallonian village of Montignies-sur-Roc, situated on the French border in the province of Hainaut. This made him one of the pioneers of the new wave of microbreweries in Belgium. Once brewing began, matters evolved naturally with the output as well as the range of beer expanding rapidly.

In 1991, this wheat beer was produced alongside the regular offerings, which up until then had been broadly based upon abbey ale styles. Immediately, Blanche des Honnelles set itself apart from the ever expanding range of witbiers, all of them preying upon the success of Pierre Celis's ubiquitous Hoegaarden. This was not only because Honnelles was marginally stronger, as well as darker than most, but also because it showed remarkable constraint in the matter of spicing, which is often a curse in this style.

The beer takes its name from the neighboring rivulets, Grande and Petite Honnelle, and is made from three malted cereals—wheat, barley, and oats. As with all of Abbaye des Rocs' beers, the brewing liquor springs from its own well, and hops are Hallertau and Brewer's Gold. The beer is bottled in various sizes, but it is also kegged, unfiltered, in tall but small kegs. It is quite a restrained beer and can be enjoyed on a hot day without too much reservation. **JPa**

Tasting notes
An orange gold beer beneath a white head. Citrusy nose, like tangerines, with a sweetish background. The palate is dry, with oranges and herbal hints, while keeping a sweet base.

H.G. Jossot satirizes beer drinkers in this 1902 magazine illustration.

Blue Moon

Blue Moon Brewing Company | www.bluemoonbrewingcompany.com

Country of origin United States
First brewed 1995
Alcohol content 5.4% abv
Serving temperature 48°F, 9°C

The tiny SandLot Brewery at Coors Field baseball stadium in Denver, Colorado, could not possibly make enough beer to satisfy a game-day crowd. So if you order a Blue Moon from a vendor in the stands, the chances are that it will have been brewed elsewhere within the brewing family of Molson Coors. Only by venturing into the pub will you find a glass of Blue Moon made on the small system within the park, where it was first developed by Keith Villa not long after he earned a Ph.D. in brewing at the University of Brussels.

Blue Moon was hardly an overnight success. Coors Brewing, before its merger with Molson and partnership with Miller, recognized in the mid-1990s that beer drinkers were attracted to what they called "craft beer," in part because the beers come from small breweries. Rather than put the Coors name on the beer and support it with a large advertising budget, the company created the Blue Moon Brewing Company, which some drinkers thought was based in Belgium. In 1999, the Confederation des Brasseries de Belgique filed a lawsuit against the Colorado brewing company, accusing it of misleading the U.S. public with its labeling.

Not until Blue Moon had been on the market nearly ten years did its sales begin to soar, and it outsold the imported Hoegaarden several times over. Large and small breweries alike took notice. The smaller craft brewers looked toward the Belgian tradition, taking their inspiration from Pierre Celis and including oats and unmalted wheat in their recipes. **SH**

Tasting notes

Blue Moon pours a hazy gold; it possesses a very aromatic nose, dominated by citrus and "green" coriander that hints at celery. Light on the tongue, with more orange flavors and a moderate sweetness balanced by tartness from the wheat.

Bohemian Wheat Lager

Pivovar Herold | www.pivovar-herold.cz

Country of origin Czech Republic
First brewed 1993
Alcohol content 5% abv
Serving temperature 46°F, 8°C

As detailed in Ludvík Fürst's 1941 monograph *How We Used To Brew Beer*, the Bohemian town of Březnice was once well known for its wheat beers. Records show that as early as 1580, the Březnice castle brewery had been making *bilé pivo* (white beer), the name for wheat beers at the time, in addition to its *staré pivo* (old beer), the common term for beers made from barley.

Unfortunately, the majority of Czech wheat beers were killed off after the spread of industrial pale lager production around the end of the 19th century. The style received a deathblow from the Communist planning committees that deliberately streamlined beer production in the 1950s, and it disappeared almost entirely from the Czech lands. The first to reappear after the Velvet Revolution had brought freedom of choice to both citizens and brewers was the so-called Wheat Lager from Březnice's Herald brewery, which arrived in its current form in 1993, when the castle brewery was under U.S. ownership. Unfortunately, the beer was discontinued in 2007.

One year later, the brewery went through a change of ownership, passing back into Czech hands. In addition to new management and a surge of capital, the brewery got another chance to brew its wheat beer, which reappeared to some fanfare in early 2009. Although the label calls this "wheat lager," it is not bottom-fermenting. Instead, the term on the label is an English-language approximation of the Czech brewing term *"ležák,"* referring to the relative strength of the beer, covering those beers produced with an original gravity of 11 degrees and 12 degrees Plato. **ER**

Tasting notes

Look for a very pretty, slightly cloudy gold in the glass topped by a fluffy white head. In Bohemian Wheat Lager, there's just a touch of clove in the nose, with tobacco and whole grains in the mouth, finishing with a lagerlike note of pilsner malt.

Boréale Blanche

Les Brasseurs du Nord
www.boreale.com

Country of origin Canada
First brewed 2004
Alcohol content 4.2% abv
Serving temperature 41°F, 5°C

One of the curiosities of the Québec beer market is a borderline obsession with color—perhaps it's because the words "ale" and "lager" have no direct French translation. Beer is referred to principally by hue. So, rather than being offered, say, a pale lager, brown ale, or stout, you'll more likely be met with a list of blonde (blond), rousse (russet), and noire (black) beers.

Boréale Blanche doesn't quite fit into the Belgian white beer style. Brewed with oats in addition to wheat and malted barley, for a slightly creamier mouthfeel, and seasoned with the traditional coriander and orange peel and other, unidentified spices, it is also fermented to a lighter strength than is typical, thus affording the beer a refreshing character and fascinating flavor profile. **SB**

Tasting notes

White beers tend to be mostly about aroma, and this one especially so, with a fragrant citrus nose that hints at florals, pepper, and ginger. Light, refreshing body and dry finish.

Brooklyner-Schneider Hopfen-Weisse

Brooklyn Brewery
www.brooklynbrewery.com

Country of origin United States
First brewed 2007
Alcohol content 8.5% abv
Serving temperature 46°F, 8°C

Brooklyn head brewer Garrett Oliver first met Schneider brewmaster Hans-Peter Drexler in New York: "He'd never had a stout or IPA before, and first tasted these styles here at Brooklyn Brewery. It turned out that Hans-Peter is really a hophead."

Ten years later they decided to brew a beer together: a strong, hoppy wheat beer. Essentially, they would both make the same beer, but with different hops. In Germany, the beer (Schneider-Brooklyner Hopfen-Weisse) is dry hopped with Hallertau Saphir; in Brooklyn, they use Amarillo and Palisades. Both beers are fermented with the proprietary Schneider yeast. However, the true measure of this wheat beer is not solely on the palate; it is in the collaboration of two professionals, two friends. **DR**

Tasting notes

Carries the expected banana and clove aroma of a standard wheat beer, but with the outstanding addition of earthy fresh hops. Bready malts, citrus, and bitterness blend in a light body.

Celis
White

Michigan Brewing
www.michiganbrewing.com

Country of origin United States
First brewed 1992
Alcohol content 5% abv
Serving temperature 46°F, 8°C

Dancing Camel
Trog Wit

Dancing Camel
www.dancingcamel.com

Country of origin Israel
First brewed 2006
Alcohol content 6.5% abv
Serving temperature 44°F, 7°C

Having revived the spiced Belgian wheat beer style and sold his business, Pierre Celis headed west to set up a new brewery in Austin, Texas, where the Belgian wit style was again his primary focus. The attraction of limestone-filtered water (high in calcium and ideal for wheat beer production) and wheat from the state's Hill Country drew him to this part of the world.

Celis White is made from a mix of unmalted wheat and barley malt, and laced with coriander and curaçao orange peel. The beer was a success, and, just like Hoegaarden in Belgium, it kick-started an interest in wheat beer brewing in the United States. Today the beer is produced in the United States by Michigan Brewing, and in Belgium, on Pierre's behalf, by the Van Steenberge Brewery in Ertvelde, East Flanders. **JE**

Israel isn't particularly well known as a beer country, primarily because its arid landscape and hot, dry climate do not lend themselves to the cultivation of barley and hops. Although only a small minority of the population adheres to cultural or religious prohibitions on alcohol, the average Israeli's annual consumption of beer is only about 0.5 gallon (2 l)—compared to 21 gallons (81 l) in the United States.

Brooklyn-born David Cohen uprooted his family in 2003 to pursue his dream: to create a brewery in Israel. Dancing Camel's Trog Wit is ostensibly a wheat beer in the Belgian style, but the bitter orange peel is replaced by "etrog," the yellow citron, *Citrus medica*. Etrog is referred to in the Bible and is traditionally used by Jews during the Sukkot holiday. **JP**

Tasting notes
(Belgian version) Suggestions of iced tea, lemon, and orange feature in the aroma. Earthy bitterness from coriander seeds lingers in the dry, chewy finish that turns fairly sweet at the end.

Tasting notes
Wheaty malt flavor is sweet with some hints of fruit sourness, coriander, and rose petal. Flavor develops some caramel and yeastiness. Bitter and citrus to finish.

Distelhäuser Kristall-Weizen

Distelhäuser Brauerei Ernst Bauer
www.distelhaeuser.de

Country of origin Germany
First brewed 1960
Alcohol content 5.4% abv
Serving temperature 46°–54°F, 8°–12°C

Duchmaus Weissbier

Rodinný pivovar U Rybiček
www.urybicek.eu

Country of origin Czech Republic
First brewed 2007
Alcohol content 5.6% abv
Serving temperature 46°F, 8°C

This fruity, effervescent, and remarkably dry beer is one of the best examples of the German wheat beer style. As brewmaster Peter Köhler notes, the Kristall-Weizen is very well fermented with a final attenuation of less than 2 percent. Kristall is the filtered version of the brewery's Hefeweizen. Since all of the yeast has been removed, this beer has a straighter and more clear-cut temperament than its unfiltered sisters.

Distelhäuser brews its wheat beer in a classical one-step decoction mash that provides for a high yield of sugar-rich wort. Uniquely, the grain husks are sifted out during milling, a process that helps to achieve the beer's characteristic smoothness. In 2008, Kristall-Weizen won gold at both the World Beer Cup and the European Beer Star. **SK**

In addition to its classic Czech pale and dark lagers and fruit-flavored beers, the Rodinný pivovar U Rybiček brewpub also chose to make the older Bohemian style of wheat beer called *bilé pivo* (white beer).

U Rybiček's version was named after the town's legendary elf, the Duchmaus. Although the Duchmaus has rarely revealed himself directly to humans, he was known for playing tricks from his underground lair. Such a famous name could only go with a very special beer, and U Rybiček's version has become one of its most popular. It is brewed at an original gravity of 14 degrees Plato, far stronger than most wheat beers, and the flavors strike a delicate balance between the crispness of the wheat and a lagerlike malt body, finishing more sweet than many Bavarian Weizen. **ER**

Tasting notes
A pronounced bananalike aroma enchants the nose with hints of citrus. Elegantly sparkling, this beer is fruity with a pinch of spice balanced by a sourish note. Spicy yet mild finish.

Tasting notes
Very cloudy, golden amber beer. Look out for a hint of toffee and spice in the nose, a rich maltiness in the mouth, and an unexpectedly semisweet yet long-lasting finish.

Estrella Damm Inedit

S. A. Damm
www.damm.es

Country of origin Spain
First brewed 2008
Alcohol content 4.8% abv
Serving temperature 39°–46°F, 4°–8°C

Estrella Inedit was developed in association with one of the best chefs in the world—Spain's Farran Adria. Adria and the team of sommeliers from his iconic El Bulli restaurant were challenged to create a beer that would sit comfortably on a dinner table, partly to provide a high-class alternative to wine.

It took nearly a year to develop the beer, the team finally settling on a wheat-beer style that closely followed the Belgian approach, with coriander seeds and orange peel. For an added twist, there is also some licorice thrown in. The company has packaged the beer in a chic, black, champagne-style bottle that sports a single gold star on the front and a neck label that simply reads "Estrella Inedit." Spanish beer has come a long way from being just a *caña*. **MC**

Tasting notes
Citrus and spice on the nose, with a hint of licorice. On the palate, a pleasantly rich delivery of spice and wheat—and a stronger licorice note—then the citrus comes back to finish.

Flying Fish Exit 11

Flying Fish Brewing Company
www.flyingfish.com

Country of origin United States
First brewed 2009
Alcohol content 6.2% abv
Serving temperature 46°F, 8°C

Flying Fish's Exit Series began in 2009 as a plan to design a different beer for each of the New Jersey Turnpike's eighteen exits. Its first, Exit 4, is a hoppy Belgian tripel, labeled with a generic white-and-green highway sign and a local road map. The authority that oversees the Turnpike complained about copyright infringement. One official said that the Exit Series sent out the "wrong message" to consumers: that it was okay to drink and drive.

Blasted by both drivers and beer drinkers for its bureaucratic meddling, the authority backed down. Good thing, too, because Flying Fish immediately followed with Exit 11, which is a confluence of styles: a U.S.-style wheat beer brewed with Belgian pale malt, English ale yeast, and Pacific Northwest hops. **DR**

Tasting notes
A light, fruity tartness up front is followed by the bitter snap of hops. Rich and complex, the body is layered with malty sweetness, yeast spiciness, and refreshing fruit.

Franziskaner Hefe-Weisse

Spaten-Franziskaner-Bräu | www.franziskaner.com

Country of origin Germany
First brewed 1974
Alcohol content 5% abv
Serving temperature 48°–54°F, 9°–12°C

The roots of this brewery go back to 1363, when a small brewing enterprise was started near the Franciscan (Franziskaner) monastery in Munich. Its founder, Seidel Vaterstetter, first sold it in 1377, with the purchaser selling it on again within a year. By 1381, things had turned full circle, with the founder of the brewery renting it back from the third owner! In fact, for almost 500 years the brewery was very successful, attracting new owners with clockwork-like regularity.

In 1815, due to a lack of space, a second brewery was opened in Au, which lay just outside the city at the time. In 1841, Augustin Deiglmayr, who was married to Caecilia Sedlmayr, the eldest daughter of the owner of Spaten Brauerei, purchased the brewery. Their son Augustin took over its management from his father in 1858. In that same year, Augustin joined his cousin Josef Sedlmayr, owner of the Leist Brauerei and son of the famous blond lager pioneer Gabriel Sedlmayr of Spaten, in a joint venture. By 1861, Augustin had thrown in the towel and given his shares to his cousin Josef. Thus was born Franziskaner-Leist Brauerei. In 1922, it joined the Spaten Brauerei (owned by relatives) and became Spaten-Franziskaner Bräu.

During the early 1960s, Spaten-Franziskaner produced a Weissbier under the name "Champagner Weissbier." Unlike traditional Weissbiers, this variation has the clarity of a pilsner. It sold well enough to encourage, in 1974, the introduction of Franziskaner Hefe-Weiss, a fresh and fruity example of the style, which is relatively unique in that 75 percent of the mash is taken up by malted wheat. **RP**

Tasting notes

In the glass, pours hazy blond, with a large and firm white head. The aroma features primarily banana and clove notes. On the palate, it is very refreshing, with notes of cloves, fruit, and vanilla coming to the fore. Spicy and fruity finish.

Fujizakura Heights Weizen

Fujizakura Heights Beer | www.fuji-net.co.jp/beer

Country of origin Japan
First brewed 1997
Alcohol content 5.5% abv
Serving temperature 43°–46° F, 6°–8°C

Weizen is a style of beer that Japanese drinkers particularly enjoy, and the one brewed by Fujizakura is considered one of the country's best. It has recently taken over the top-selling spot from the brewery's pilsner, which is also a fine beer in its own right.

In keeping with German brewing practices, the ratio of pilsner malt to wheat malt is forty/sixty, with bittering provided by a single addition of Perle hops. The beer is known for its creamy texture, as well as for its rather pronounced Weizen aroma, which is often described as bananas and cloves, but sometimes simply as bubble gum by Japanese enthusiasts. It is perhaps the fruity character of this beer that has made it popular, particularly among women drinkers. In the greater Tokyo area, there is even a well-organized fan club for Weizen-style beers, which always attends Oktoberfest events and other German beer parties. They can be spotted by their various items of German clothing and hats. It turns out that Fujizakura Weizen is one of their favorite beers.

Compared with Fujizakura Rauch, the Weizen has grown in popularity more rapidly, and is clearly the favorite brew among the customers of the Sylvan's Restaurant at the brewery. The beer goes well with such favorites as pizza and sausages, as well as fried potatoes. The restaurant itself features a large outdoor area in the back and provides stunning views of Mount Fuji. On weekends, it is visited by numerous large groups that arrive in tour buses to take advantage of the all-you-can-drink plans that can be selected from the menu. **BH**

Tasting notes

The beer is a hazy whitish yellow, with a thick, white head. It has a powerful aroma of Weizen esters (bubble gum included), with a solidly quenching combination of acidity and hop bitterness. The texture is very creamy, particularly toward the finish.

Grolsch Premium Weizen

Koninklijke Grolsch | www.grolsch.nl

Country of origin Netherlands
First brewed 2005
Alcohol content 5.5% abv
Serving temperature 44°F, 7°C

Oktoberfest may or may not be the largest beer festival in the world, but it is almost certainly the best known (although it is not actually a beer festival, but rather a festival at which much beer is served and consumed). Unsurprisingly, its fame has led to many other countries holding autumnal celebrations of beer consumption. In 2005, an Oktoberfest in Varsseveld, a small Dutch town near the German border, was more than just a jolly beery party, being also the occasion for the introduction of Grolsch Premium Weizen (Grolsch, incidentally, is located in a small Dutch town, north of Varsseveld). The first version of the beer was actually brewed in 2004 by brewmaster Guy Evers to celebrate the opening of a new brewery in its hometown of Enschede—by naming it after the German word for "wheat" rather than the Dutch equivalent ("*weit*" or "*tarwe*"), Grolsch put its wheat beer in the German beer camp. It is said that several hundred German brewmasters visiting the brewery were surprised by the appearance of this Weizen (whether pleasantly or otherwise is not recorded).

The beer is produced following the German Reinheitsgebot, and in keeping with that statute, it contains water, hops, malted barley, and wheat; it is also brewed and sold all year round. While a beer must be made of 50 percent wheat to be called a Weizen, Grolsch uses 60 percent.

One of the more interesting notes about this beer is that it is a masterful companion to steamed asparagus, due to a sweetness in the asparagus that chimes with the understated sweetness of the beer. **RP**

Tasting notes

Pale gold and cloudy with a frisky carbonation. Banana custard on the nose, banana and vanilla on the palate; there's an understated sweetness and childlike simplicity about these flavors, while the mouthfeel is a light dance of bubbles. Quick finish.

Gulpener Korenwolf

Gulpener Bierbrouwerij | www.gulpener.nl

Country of origin Netherlands
First brewed 1994
Alcohol content 5% abv
Serving temperature 39°–46°F, 4°–8°C

In 1825, Laurens Smeets founded this brewery in the southern Dutch town of Gulpen in the province of Limburg. It is still there and still owned by the same family (though Grolsch bought a minority interest in 1995). The brewery focuses on local connections—not only as an employer but also as a consumer of locally-produced goods, and as a means by which local traditions may be maintained, primarily through the beers it produces.

The products offered by the brewery are a determined mixture of traditional local beers and beers typically found on the other side of the Dutch border—Limburg is squeezed between two major beer nations, Germany and Belgium, which could be why the beers of the province can seem such a mixed bag of styles. The company sees the pilsner-dominated uniformity of the market as a barrier that must fall. Toward that end, they offer one of the broadest assortments of beers of any small Dutch brewery.

Gulpener Korenwolf—the beer is named for a local sort of wild hamster—is a mixed-grain wheat beer (witbier) that is also top-fermented. The grains used include wheat, oats, rye, and barley; other ingredients include herbs and the blossoms of elderberries. The brewery is keen on sustainability: hops, for example, are sourced from local farmers, while labels are recycled, and the brewing facilities make use of green technologies (such as solar panels) to minimize energy consumption.

Summer in Limburg is considered to be the optimal time (and place) to drink this beer. **RP**

Tasting notes

A smoky-golden color, this beer has a rich white head and the aroma of a German Hefeweizen. The taste sits somewhere between a German Hefeweizen and a Belgian witbier. No lemon necessary, as there is a citrusy tang in the taste.

Gumballhead

Three Floyds | www.3Floyds.com

Country of origin United States
First brewed 2003
Alcohol content 4.8% abv
Serving temperature 46°F, 8°C

For years, U.S. brewers have struggled to create an American version of Bavaria's famous Hefeweizen with uneven success. Some come close, but many lack the complex citrus-and-spice character of this distinctive style. Or, as Lincoln Anderson, the sales manager at Indiana's offbeat Three Floyds Brewing, bluntly put it: "Nick Floyd (the founder) felt most American wheat beers basically sucked."

Rather than mimic the original German style, Floyd started from scratch to create an entirely new hybrid that would reflect America's growing fondness for hops. His creation, the oddly named Gumballhead, might be described as a cross between a classic wheat beer and a pale ale. The familiar banana and clove esters of Bavarian wheat beer are decidedly muted. Possibly because of its name, some tasters are convinced it carries the subtle aroma of bubble gum. Its dominant character, though, is grapefruit, orange, and lemon. The aroma is a product not solely of yeast fermentation, but of Floyd's ample use of Amarillo hops in the final dry hopping stage. Tart and acidic, the hops mimic citrus fruit and newly mown grass.

A fresh glassful is thirst-quenching with a lively, smooth, dry finish. With a relatively low alcohol content, Gumballhead is intended for a long, hot summer afternoon on a shaded backyard patio. Moody and iconic, the yellow, cigarette-smoking cat on the beer's label is so popular among the brewery's fans, some have tattooed him as a keepsake. His creator, artist Rob Syers, describes the character as "a wandering rogue." The same goes for the beer itself. **DR**

Tasting notes

A citrusy billow of aroma rising from a hazy golden body suggests a classic German wheat beer, but one sip of its grapefruitlike hops reveals its American roots. Smooth and medium bodied, it finishes with a light, tart kiss of lemon.

Gutmann Hefeweizen

Brauerei Friedrich Gutmann | www.brauerei-gutmann.de

Country of origin Germany
First brewed 1913
Alcohol content 5.2% abv
Serving temperature 41°–46°F, 5°–8°C

Gutmann Hefeweizen shines like a ripe wheat field, as if directly picked from the sunny golden slopes of the Franconian Alb north of Eichstätt. And given that Gutmann is not only a brewery but also a farm, this analogy is not too far from the truth. Until the 1970s, they cultivated their own hops, while it was only in 1996 that they ceased animal husbandry. They remain linked to the soil, however, by growing their own barley and wheat (though some cereals for their wheat beers are bought from farmers in the area).

The family has owned the brewery since 1855, with brewhouse, farm, and malthouse situated in a beautiful medieval complex that had once been a moated castle—a prince-bishop in 1707 first installed a brewery here. Today the brewery is led by the fifth and sixth generations of the Gutmann family.

The brewery used to offer a much larger portfolio of Franconian beer styles before they specialized in wheat in the 1990s, a decision that has obviously paid dividends. While industrial production of wheat beer increases and more and more pasteurized versions enter the market, Gutmann focuses on the Bavarian wheat beer tradition. After the first fermentation in open vessels, fresh yeast is added for a second fermentation exclusively in bottles. The beer is not pasteurized, so only the fine haze of the living yeast shines through and brings in delicious fresh flavors. This attention to detail and quality has been successful: Gutmann Hefeweizen has acquired a top reputation and is demanded in bars and restaurants in places such as Nuremberg, Erlangen, and Munich. **SK**

Tasting notes

Light golden with a shiny haze and fine white head. This beer offers a decent banana-like aroma with some citrusy moments. The first taste is mild, soft, and fluffy, before a decent fruitiness evolves into pronounced phenolic flavors. The finish reverberates with a distant mild bitterness.

Hacker-Pschorr Hefe Weisse

Hacker-Pschorr Bräu | www.hacker-pschorr.de

Country of origin Germany
First brewed 1972
Alcohol content 5.5% abv
Serving temperature 41°–54°F, 5°–12°C

The first mention of this brewery, in 1417, places it at 14 Sendlinger Strasse—these days the address for "Altes Hackerhaus," a pub where Hacker-Pschorr beers are served. However, the hyphenated name didn't arrive until 1793, when Joseph Pschorr married Maria Theresia Hacker, whose father owned a brewery. Pschorr, the son of a brewer, did the natural thing and took over the Hacker-Brauerei. In 1820, he was busy again, buying Zum Bauernhansl and renaming the enterprise Hacker-Pschorr Brauerei. Under Pschorr's leadership, his new brewery became as popular as the one he had inherited from his father-in-law.

The brewery achieved early fame during Joseph Pschorr's tenure. In 1821, for example, the combined enterprise was producing nearly 8 million gallons (300,000 hl) per annum, which was, at the time, considered an unbelievable amount. This was no fluke: between 1813 and 1823, the lager cellar was so huge that it set a record for industrial beer production. The size of the cellar was also no accident: its dimensions enabled the beer to stay fresh even in the summer, and so, for the first time, it became possible to lager beer for the entire year.

It was not until 1972 that the two breweries became one; that year, Hacker-Pschorr Hefe Weisse was born, at a time when this beer style was becoming popular once more. Today, Hacker-Pschorr is one of the largest Munich breweries and, as it is brewed within the city limits, this traditionally unfiltered and top-fermented Weissbier is one of the beers visitors to the Oktoberfest will quaff in vast quantities. **RP**

Tasting notes

Poured into the glass, the beer is golden orange and the head is creamy but firm. The aroma is bready and includes notes of banana and spices as well. The taste is quite full, yet refreshing, with a hint of fruit in addition to cloves.

A poster from the 1950s advertising another of Hacker-Pschorr's famous beers.

Hef

Burleigh Brewing | www.burleighbrewing.com.au

Country of origin Australia
First brewed 2008
Alcohol content 5% abv
Serving temperature 43°F, 6°C

Burleigh Heads is a stunning strip of beach on the Gold Coast in Queensland, Australia. The sun shines brightly at Burleigh Heads most of the time, and the area is famous for its surf, sand, and beautiful women. You do not have to spend long there to work out why Australians have a profound and almost unassailable love of icy cold lager; a few pots of a local drop in the sun at a surf club overlooking the beach is surely one of the best beer experiences available.

In short, it is not the place that you would expect to find a beer that needs to warm a little after it comes out of the fridge. And certainly not a beer that can be coaxed into releasing one of the most profound banana aromas you will ever encounter in a brew. The Hef, or "Banana Beer" to some, does exactly that and is the creation of Brennan Fielding, the brewer and co-founder of Burleigh Brewing. Like another famous Australian brewer, Chuck Hahn, Brennan is American by birth but has chosen to settle down in Australia.

Rather than distributing their ales as widely as possible, Fielding and his wife Peta adhere to the old German logic that beer should only be drunk within a day's horse-and-cart ride from the brewery. This equates to about four hours' drive in modern parlance, and Burleigh Brewing's core range of beers is not distributed outside of this area. While the Hef has reluctantly been given an Australia-wide distribution, the Fieldings have only allowed this in the knowledge that the beer will be much more aromatic and fresh than a Hefeweizen that has been shipped all the way from the style's traditional homeland. **DD**

Tasting notes

Even beer skeptics will be able to smell the banana that works its way through the bright white head on this beer. A mouthful should reveal hints of cloves along with a malt sweetness that nicely complements roasted snapper fish with fennel.

Hell or High Watermelon Wheat

21st Amendment Brewery | www.21st-amendment.com

Country of origin United States
First brewed 2002
Alcohol content 5.5% abv
Serving temperature 44°F, 7°C

The 21st Amendment Brewery took its name from the much-welcomed amendment that ended Prohibition in 1933. Many of its initial offerings paid homage to San Francisco's rich pre-Prohibition brewing heritage, such as South Park Blonde, Amendment Pale Ale, Potrero ESB, and General Pippo's Porter.

A year after opening, brewmaster and co-founder Shaun O'Sullivan hit upon what has become the brewery's most popular beer: Hell or High Watermelon Wheat Beer. Originally a summer seasonal, it's now canned all year round. O'Sullivan took a U.S.-style wheat beer as his base and added 400 pounds (181 kg) of fresh watermelon for each twelve-barrel batch. The fruit gives the wheat beer just a touch of tartness that's proved ideal for beating the heat, and at 4.9 percent, it's a beer you can enjoy for hours on end. At the brewpub, they serve it in a tall wheat beer glass with a wedge of watermelon.

In order to meet demand, the brewery originally had to buy watermelon from all over the world, wherever it was in season. Initially, that was enough to keep the beer flowing throughout the year, but once it began packaging the beer, the brewery was unable to keep the beer consistent because watermelon grown in different places can vary a great deal. It turned to a company that takes fresh watermelon and makes puree concentrate. Now the brewers can make their watermelon wheat beer taste the same no matter when they brew it. It is brewed with two-row pale malt and wheat, plus Magnum hops, and the watermelon is added during a secondary fermentation. **JB**

Tasting notes

The color is pale straw with subtle, tart, fruity aromas. The fruit flavors are likewise subtle, giving just a hint of their presence, so the overall effect is simply refreshing and the beer is very easy to drink. The finish is clean, too, with just a pleasant lingering tartness.

Hitachino Nest Beer White Ale

Kiuchi Brewery | www.kodawari.cc

Country of origin Japan
First brewed 1998
Alcohol content 5.5% abv
Serving temperature 54°–56°F, 12°–13°C

It was certain that the popularity of Hoegaarden White in Japan inspired Hitachino Nest to create this popular beer. Since White Ale also contains fruit and spices, it is considered different from beer and is taxed at a lower rate, provided it contains only 50 percent malt. Accordingly, reducing the malt level in this beer proved to be quite a challenge.

The parent company of Hitachino Nest is a long-established sake brewery, dating back to 1823. It offers a wide product lineup that even extends to wines and spirits. With a huge store of expertise and experience, creating a low-malt beer was well within its capabilities. To maintain a 50 percent malt content, the brewery used flaked barley and flaked wheat, along with the pilsner malt on which the brew is based. The beer is bittered with Perle, with Styrian Golding used for aroma. It is further spiced with coriander, nutmeg, and orange peel, while a small amount of orange juice concentrate is added to contribute to a brisk flavor profile. Naturally, it is this ingredient that most greatly distinguishes the beer from Hoegaarden White.

White Ale is now the most popular beer among Hitachino Nest offerings, displacing Weizen some years back. The brisk flavor and light body make it pair well with many Japanese foods, particularly the seasonal foods of spring and summer. It has become very popular in the United States, which imports some 300,000 bottles each year. In fact, nearly half of Hitachino Nest beer production is now sold in the United States. The company built a new brewery a few years back to help it cope with increasing demand. **BH**

Tasting notes

The beer pours a hazy light golden yellow with a short-lived white head. There are faintly citrus and sweet spice aromas. The flavor is largely wheat beer joined by coriander and nutmeg, with tangy citrus notes. The finish exhibits both creaminess and tangy flavors.

Hoegaarden

Brouwerij van Hoegaarden | www.hoegaarden.com

Country of origin Belgium
First brewed 1966
Alcohol content 4.9% abv
Serving temperature 36°–37°F, 2°–3°C

Take a look at a bottle of Hoegaarden. There's a date printed on the collar that reads 1445. It implies that this beer was first produced in that year. The truth is rather different, although the beer does hold an important place in brewing history.

Hoegaarden is the savior of the Belgian witbier— the light, spritzy wheat beer style flavored with herbs and spices. It's a style of beer that was being produced in the eastern part of Belgium back in the 15th century, as the bottle label suggests, when monks took advantage of the local wheat harvest to brew a beer that was pale and turbid in appearance. The brewers also included some of the exotic spices that Dutch seafarers were bringing back from their far-flung travels, and this may have been a way of disguising beer that turned sour very quickly in the days when the wonders of fermentation were not fully understood. The precise history of the Hoegaarden brand, however, is very different. The beer owes its existence to a former dairyman, Pierre Celis. By the 1960s, witbier had mostly disappeared; Celis decided to do something about it by opening a brewery in the town of Hoegaarden. His beer became a roaring success, and hundreds of copycat beers are now sold worldwide.

Hoegaarden is produced from a sixty/forty mix of barley malt and unmalted wheat. The hops are unspecified, with the major flavoring coming from the mix of coriander and bitter orange peel that is added to the copper. Some critics say that the beer is not the classic it once was. Its place in beer history, however, cannot be denied. **JE**

Tasting notes

Pear, lemon, and mandarin orange, with a peppery coriander accent, feature in the aroma of this easy-drinking, pale yellow beer, with a soft balance of citrus fruit, coriander, and clove in the taste. Expect a dry and chewy finish with more coriander and cloves.

Huber Weisses Original

Hofbräuhaus Freising | www.hofbraeuhaus-freising.de

Country of origin Germany
First brewed *ca.* 1890s
Alcohol content 5.4% abv
Serving temperature 44°–46°F, 7°–8°C

Freising is a small and beautiful town to the north of Munich. As well as having the dubious distinction of living with Munich airport on its doorstep, it is famous for being the home of Weihenstephan, the ancient and venerable brewery that claims to be the oldest in the world. Just down the road, however, you will find Hofbräuhaus Freising, which has a history of beer making going back to the 12th century. It's not as old as Weihenstephan, perhaps, but is certainly antique and hallowed compared to the mere striplings who came along several centuries later.

The brewery's Huber beers use what looks like a polar bear for their logo. Although it would be tempting to see this as a comment on global warming, it is in fact a celebration of the role a bear played in the life of the town's first bishop, who is said to have tamed one after it killed his packhorse. Freising's coat of arms now includes a saddled-up bear.

Frank Xaver Huber first brewed Huber Weisses Original at the end of the 19th century, which makes it one of the longest-established Weissbiers currently in production. The brewpub for which the beer was first produced has long gone, but Hofbräuhaus Freising take pride in brewing their Weissbiers in a traditional way, and it is a beer noted for being much lower in carbonation and much fruitier than many of its rivals.

The current brewery was built before World War I. At the time, it was seen as the most modern brewery in Germany and an example for other breweries across the brewing world, a reputation that—several renovations later—it still maintains. **WO**

Tasting notes

Golden in color with a light haze from the yeast. Traditional trademark Weiss aromas of bananas and cloves. It is mild on the palate because of its low carbonation, but there is an appetizing bitterness and refreshing fruitiness before its malty finish.

In-Heat Wheat

Flying Dog Brewery | www.flyingdogales.com

Country of origin United States
First brewed 2001
Alcohol content 4.7% abv
Serving temperature 48°F, 9°C

Eric Warner, who created Flying Dog's In-Heat Wheat, literally wrote the book on wheat beers. *German Wheat Beer*, published in 1992, became a road map for U.S. craft brewers who wanted to create beers similar to the Hefe Weissbier, or Hefe Weizen, style found in southern Germany. Sales of such beers were booming in Germany but, other than imports, the style was almost unknown in the United States.

Warner, who studied at the Technical University of Munich at Weihenstephan and then interned in the south of Germany, helped start Tabernash Brewing in Denver. Tabernash Weiss quickly won gold at the 1994 Great American Beer Festival and further ignited interest in the style among small-batch brewers. Tabernash eventually merged with Left Hand Brewing, and Warner went on to become "lead dog" at Flying Dog. Although beers brewed in the manner of German Hefe Weizen didn't become as popular as some predicted in the mid-1990s, wheat beer sales continue to surge across a variety of styles.

The United States had little wheat beer tradition when Anchor Brewing introduced Anchor Wheat in 1984. Furthermore, Anchor's version of a wheat beer featured none of the traditional fruit-and-clove character associated with the beers of Bavaria. "Wheat has been very regionalized," says Warner. "You've got the Widmer style in the Northwest, wheat totally rocks in the Midwest, and with Blue Moon spending on advertising, people are learning more about Belgian wit." In fact, Woody Creek White Belgian Wit has turned into a popular summer release for Flying Dog. **SH**

Tasting notes

Billowing white head tops a properly hazy, orange body in the glass. Fruit dominates the nose, mostly bananas but also apples, just a bit spicy. More fruit flavors in the mouth, but it's also here that the spices and cloves emerge. Nicely balanced.

Jacobsen Sommer Wit

Husbryggeriet Jacobsen | www.jacobsenbryg.dk

Country of origin Denmark
First brewed 2008
Alcohol content 5.1% abv
Serving temperature 37°–44°F, 3°–7°C

Sommer Wit is a seasonal variation of the witbier brewed by Jacobsen, one of the beers that the brewer tries to take in a slightly different path from most craft and microbrewers by infusing the flavors of the Nordic region with well-established styles. Instead of massive hops and malts, Jacobsen has, guided by Jens Eiken and latterly Morten Ibsen, experimented with ingredients such as chamomile, pinecones, sweet woodruff, and, in this case, elderberries.

The idea came from the "Nordic Beer Manifesto" prepared by Jens Eiken and noted Danish hand brewer Per Kølster from Fuglebjerggaard, after the 2007 Nordic Brewers Symposium. The manifesto encourages local brewers to take inspiration from the region, its heritage, and raw materials, and complements the "Nordic Food Manifesto" that has catapulted some Scandinavian restaurants into the gastronomic premier division.

Like many of the Jacobsen beers, Sommer Wit has a subtle taste that achieves a harmonious balance lacking in some craft beers. In the place of risky high-wire acts with hops and malt is a down-to-earth precision-juggling of ingredients that doesn't shock but does entertain; this makes Sommer Wit a good accompaniment to food, as the tight flavor profiles don't detract from the overall experience. Sommer Wit uses the same traditional Belgian wit yeast and Belle de Boskoop apples as the Jacobsen Bramley Wit. In place of the Bramleys, however, is an extract of elderberries to give a slightly sour taste. It also uses pilsner malt, raw wheat, malted wheat, and oats, with fresh orange peel and coriander seeds. **AA**

Tasting notes

A slightly red color with a creamy head. The aroma is of wheat beer clove with an added fruity character backed by a citrus note. In the mouth, the beer has a refreshing carbonation with fruit and a slightly sour bitterness of elderberries.

Jan de Lichte

Brouwerij De Glazen Toren | www.glazentoren.be

Country of origin Belgium
First brewed 2005
Alcohol content 7% abv
Serving temperature 44°F, 7°C

Jef Van den Steen is a retired professor of math. He is also one of Belgium's premier beer writers, who is now spending his retirement as one of Belgium's top brewers. Along with partners Dirk de Pauw and Marc de Neef, he began planning the construction of a brewery in 2002, and De Glazen Toren eventually opened in 2004 on the outskirts of Erpe-Mere, an ancient East Flanders village close to Aalst, which itself has a reputable brewing and hop-growing history.

Both Van den Steen and de Pauw are graduates of the brewing school at the Catholic University of Ghent. They completed a three-year course that equipped them with the technical expertise and knowledge that has, in a very short time, taken a new brewery to a respected position among beer lovers. The brewery is nicknamed the "Glass Tower," a name that has survived from the 19th century. In those days, the area around the brewery was open farmland, except for one very large structure with big glass windows, in which ladies in various states of undress could be seen.

This idea of local tradition and history also extends to the beers. Most of the names of De Glazen Toren's brews come from local history, and this luscious four-grain "double" witbier is no different. While researching a name for their new beer, Van den Steen came across the name of Jan de Lichte. He was an infamous brigand in the area during the late 18th century, but the law finally caught up with him and he suffered an inglorious end on a medieval torture device in Aalst, at the age of twenty-three. Needless to say, he would have led a longer life if he had taken up brewing. **CC**

Tasting notes

Straw yellow in color, it pours with a generous head of foam and leaves noticeable traces of gorgeous-looking lacework as it descends in the glass. The mouthfeel is light to medium, with lemony and grapefruit notes on the palate, joined by a lightness of touch in the spicing.

Kapuziner Weissbier

Kulmbacher Brauerei | www.kulmbacher.de

Country of origin Germany
First brewed 1987
Alcohol content 5.4% abv
Serving temperature 46°F, 8°C

Brewed in the Bavarian city of Kulmbach, which is famous for its beery know-how, Kapuziner Weissbier gets its name from the old order of the Kapuziner monks. You could argue, however, that its branding is very much a secular tongue-in-cheek slice of modern branding, as it was only launched in the late 1980s, when the resurrection of Weissbier was in full swing. Since then, this top-fermented beer with its seventy/thirty wheat/barley grain bill, and which is packaged in bottles with traditional bottle tops, has become one of the top-ten German best sellers of its style, a remarkable success for such a short brewing history. It has also won many awards: it was honored with gold at the German Agricultural Society brewing contests in 2004 and 2005—a welcome reward, as the event is known for being the "hardest beer test in the world."

Beer is central to the life of Kulmbach, even though its main brewery—Kulmbacher AG—is a massive enterprise. The last Saturday of July sees the start of a nine-day-long beer festival, which attracts up to 120,000 guests annually. For nine days, the beer flows and generous portions of the local food are sold, while traditional music plays in the beer gardens and beer halls. A special "festival" beer is brewed for the week, with every Kulmbacher Brewery brand having its own. Kapuziner is an independent brand within the group, alongside brands from EKU and Mönchshof. Its beers are available in six different qualities: the unfiltered Weissbier here, the clear Kristal, a dark version called "Schwarz" rather than "Dunkel," a seasonal Winter-Weissbier, plus "light" and alcohol-free variants. **WO**

Tasting notes

Orange yellow in color, featuring a soft aroma of vanilla and cloves, with hints of barley sugar in the background. Quenching orangy palate, with cloves, grainy maltiness, and a slightly prickly fruitiness following in its trail before its light, spicy finish. Very refreshing.

König Ludwig Weissbier Hell

König Ludwig Schlossbrauerei Kaltenberg | www.koenig-ludwig-brauerei.com

Country of origin Germany
First brewed 1979
Alcohol content 5.5% abv
Serving temperature 43°–46°F, 6°–8°C

Wheat beer was once, officially, the drink of royalty. Back in the late 16th century, the dukes that ran Bavaria introduced a law that forbade ordinary folk from brewing beer that contained wheat. Some historians reckon this was because the more refined character of pale, quenching wheat beers was deigned by royalty to be "above" the tastes of a populace used to dark, smoky beers. Others insist that the move was a money-making venture, with the rulers able to sell licenses to others to brew wheat beer. Whatever the reason, this odd monopoly held for some 200 years.

With history in mind, there seems no more fitting brewery to produce wheat beer today than König Ludwig Schlossbrauerei Kaltenberg. This once-royal brewery is still run by the great-grandson of Bavaria's last ruler and makes full use of its connections, naming its beers after the dethroned family.

The brewery produces a range of wheat beers, both dark and light, and all are brewed not at Kaltenberg's fairy-tale castle brewery just outside Munich, but at a modern brewery 12 miles (19 km) away at Fürstenfeldbruck that has been set up for Weissbier production. The most commonly found beer in the selection is the pale wheat beer, König Ludwig Weissbier Hell. It is a genuine, nonpasteurized, living Weissbier, crafted from malted barley, malted wheat, water, and yeast. In true Weissbier fashion, it is the yeast that provides the magic, laying complex fruit and spice notes on top of a crisp, chewy sweetness provided by the mix of cereals. **JE**

Tasting notes

Fresh banana, apple, and soft clove lead in the aroma of this hazy yellow beer, before a pleasant blend of creamy banana, lemon, and subtle spice comes through in the taste. The finish is dry, chewy, and softly bitter with more banana and gentle spices.

La Grande Blanche

De Proefbrouwerij | www.proefbrouwerij.com

Country of origin Belgium
First brewed 2007
Alcohol content 7.5% abv
Serving temperature 44°F, 7°C

De Proefbrouwerij is possibly the cleanest brewery in Belgium, and is certainly one of the most versatile and high-tech. There is little room for error when you brew *Brettanomyces*-infused beers beside Czech-style pils, German-style Dunkelweizens, and imperial stouts.

Dirk Naudts founded the brewery, and, given his background as a brewing engineer, it is no surprise to discover that the technical accuracy of De Proefbrouwerij is extremely impressive. The laboratory is a sight to behold. Naudts keeps a plethora of different yeast strains in cryogenic storage. It is not unknown for visitors to be shown a rack of these strains, all kept in test tubes.

La Grande Blanche could be called a double witbier and it is part of the Brewmaster's Collection, a range of five beers produced for export to the United States. It was created after a request by the brewery's U.S. importer, SBS, who, on noticing how successful "imperial" beers were in the United States, wanted to see how enthusiastically an authentic Belgian double white would be received. Needless to say, the reception has been very positive.

De Proefbrouwerij brews beers under commission for private customers. It has also collaborated on occasion with several U.S. breweries to create some very eclectic brews, known as the Brewmaster's Collaboration series. **CC**

Tasting notes
Floral aromas and citrus fruit flavors are followed by a soft wheaty taste. Finishes with a hint of hoppiness and coriander. More body and more alcohol than most Belgian witbiers.

Maisel's Weisse

Brauerei Gebrüder Maisel | www.maisel.com

Country of origin Germany
First brewed 1955
Alcohol content 5.2% abv
Serving temperature 44°F, 7°C

Brothers Hans and Eberhardt Maisel founded this Bayreuth-based brewery in 1887, just as the town was becoming a magnet for lovers of Richard Wagner's opera cycle *The Ring*. Maisel's Weisse, which was introduced in 1955, was first known as "Champagner-Weizen." This marketing gambit apparently paid off handsomely: over the next few decades, the firm came to be one of the largest Weissbier producers in Germany. Jeff Maisel, the fourth generation of the family, now runs the company. Maisel's Weisse, brewed to the Bavarian Purity Law of 1516, is a well-regarded example of this style.

Maisel's Weisse is considered to have contributed significantly to the current market for Weissbier. While this sort of beer had largely been restricted to Bavaria, Maisel engaged in national advertising for its brand, and suddenly its beers could be found everywhere, from Munster to Münich. Aside from its successful campaign to make all of Germany into potential customers for its beer, the company's brewing activities are creative in other fields. Maisel's Dampfbier is a steam beer that is rarely made anymore. The brewery has also developed Edelhopfen Diät-pilsner, a low-calorie beer, as well as Kritzenthaler Alkoholfreies pilsner (alcohol-free), which surprised some beer writers by actually tasting of beer. **RP**

Tasting notes
A hazy orange copper color and a firm, very large white head. The aroma is malty, with cloves and some fruit notes. The taste is superbly refreshing, very full bodied, and well balanced.

Traditional sign inviting customers to enjoy a Weissbier in the beer garden.

Mothership Wit

New Belgium Brewing | www.newbelgium.com

Country of origin United States
First brewed 2007
Alcohol content 4.8% abv
Serving temperature 55°F, 13°C

It didn't come as much of a surprise to brewing observers in 2007 when New Belgium produced Mothership Wit as an organic beer. More surprising was the fact that the brewery hadn't gotten around to releasing an organic beer earlier. This is a brewery that has had the carbon footprint of its beers analyzed and that compiles an annual sustainability report. New Belgium became the first wind-powered brewery after employees voted unanimously for the program, even though it reduced their profit-sharing pool.

Hearteningly, New Belgium is not unique among U.S. breweries, many of which have been at the forefront of promoting good environmental practices. In 2008, *Outside* magazine also rated New Belgium as the best place to work in the United States. For example, the company gives employees a fat tire bike after one year on the job, while after five years, they receive a trip to Belgium complete with brewery tours.

In 1991, New Belgium—a tiny 125-gallon (5-hl) system that was first set up in the basement of its founders Jeff Lebesch and Kim Jordan—was not the first Belgian-inspired brewery that Americans took note of. That year, Pierre Celis, the man credited with resurrecting the Belgian White beer style, founded the Celis Brewery in Texas. Although that brewery did not survive, Michigan Brewing now owns the Celis brand. Meanwhile, the little environmentally obsessed brewery in Colorado thrived. With a neat sense of historical symmetry, Mothership Wit won a gold medal at the Great American Beer Festival in 2008, sixteen years after Celis White did the same. **SH**

Tasting notes

Pours more yellow than white, with a fluffy white head and lingering lacing. Aromas of both fleshy and citrus fruits on the nose, but also slightly pungent and spicy with hints of pepper. Sweet with orange notes more apparent on the tongue, lively and mildly tart. A refreshing beer.

Napa Smith Wheat Beer

Napa Smith Brewing | www.napasmithbrewery.com

Country of origin United States
First brewed 2008
Alcohol content 4.8% abv
Serving temperature 48°F, 9°C

While Napa Smith Brewery is a relatively new enterprise, its pedigree runs all the way back to the beginning of the craft beer movement. Napa Smith's brewmaster is Don Barkley, who was the assistant brewer at New Albion Brewery, the first modern microbrewery in America, which opened in 1977. After New Albion closed in 1983, Barkley bought the equipment and co-founded the Mendocino Brewing Company in nearby Hopland, where a century before hops had been grown in California.

In 2008, Barkley was persuaded to see if lightning could again strike and joined the Smith Family in creating the Napa Smith Brewery in the heart of the Napa Valley wine country. He appreciated the Smith's philosophy in wanting to make beer that paired well with all food types. The first version of the wheat beer was originally formulated as a pale ale around 1985, but Barkley resurrected it as a wheat beer, but with his own unique stamp on it. Unlike most wheat beers, he uses lager yeast at a cool temperature, but without lagering it. They also run the mash temperaure hot to impart sweetness, a touch of diacetyl, and a dry finish. The malt build is half wheat, half two-row barley with just a small amount of Franco-Belges kiln amber malt, which imparts a toasty flavor, like a tortilla.

With low bittering, using Cluster and Perle hops, two additional herbs give the Napa Smith Wheat beer its unique character. The first is raw ginger root and the second—the secret ingredient—is a traditional herb that pre-dates the use of hops and grows locally. It gives the beer a high flowery, herbal character. **JB**

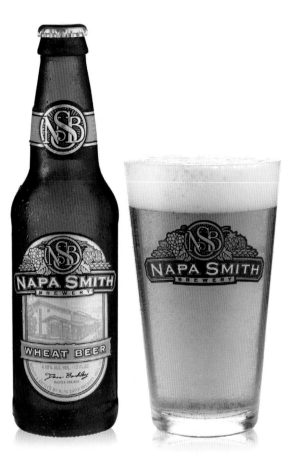

Tasting notes

Napa Smith's wheat beer is straw colored with a very thick white head. It boasts an herbal nose with fruity, spruce, and pine aromas. The mouthfeel is very creamy with lemon zesty flavors and a wild herbal character. The balance is pitch perfect.

Okell's Mac Lir

Okells | www.okells.co.uk

Country of origin Isle of Man
First brewed 2002
Alcohol content 4.4% abv
Serving temperature 48°–54°F, 9°–12°C

Head brewer Mike Cowbourne is a soft-spoken Yorkshireman who learned his craft at Watney Mann in the East End of London before moving on to Wilson's of Manchester. Toward the end of the 1980s he turned up at Okells, where he inherited the beer recipes and was told to keep them the same. When the brewery moved to its current site in Kewaigue, just outside the island's capital, Douglas, in 1994, Cowbourne felt secure enough to start bringing in American and Czech hops. Other changes followed: although the brewery's two main ales are a mild and a bitter, the growth of the specialty beer market and the fact that more people were drinking bottled beer at home gave the brewery and Cowbourne food for thought.

As well as regular monthly specials, they began producing special beers, one of which was this bottled wheat beer. However, the Manx Beer Purity Law—the Reinheitsgebot of the Isle of Man—only allows beer brewed there to contain malt, hops, sugar, and water. Ingredients not permitted included raw cereal, corn syrup, and opium, so the brewery had to approach the Tynwald, the island's parliament, to get a special dispensation. It took six months to get approval, but then Mac Lir (named for the mythological figure Manannán Mac Lir, who, according to Manx legend, was the island's first ruler) was on its way.

Malted wheat makes up to 50 percent of the mash, while the hops are Target and First Gold for bitterness and Hallertau and Saaz for aroma. According to Cowbourne, "It's not a typical German wheat beer, nor is it meant to be." **MC**

Tasting notes

After you've finished admiring the beautiful label, you will find a light lemon and slight herbal presence on the nose, which leads into a pleasantly resinous and citrus flavor on the palate, finishing off with what a lot of wheat beers lack: a lingering—but refreshing—bitter finish.

Olivaria Beloe Zoloto

Olivaria Brewery | www.olivaria.by/en

Country of origin Belarus
First brewed *ca.* 2008
Alcohol content 5% abv
Serving temperature 46°–50°F, 8°–10°C

Even though it seemed like a dying beer style in the 1960s, Bavarian Weissbier has rejuvenated itself in the years since. One of the more telling signs of its Lazarus-like revival is its spread eastward to Poland, the Baltic states, and even farther. Many breweries in the East now have a Weissbier (for instance, Svyturys's Baltas White and Ukraine's Etalon) and Belarus's Olivaria is no different, as their unfiltered Beloe Zoloto (meaning "White Gold") demonstrates. With a good proportion of malted wheat in the mash and the use of traditional Bavarian yeast, this has all the trademarks of a Weissbier—bananas, vanilla, and spicy clove-like notes. For a brewery like this to produce such a beer suggests a degree of confidence in the growing Belarus beer market and high hopes for its marketing potential.

Based in the city of Minsk, the brewery has a history and heritage going back to 1864, when it was first set up. Given the turmoil and tragedies that have afflicted Minsk since then, it's amazing to note that the brewery is still located on the same site, in an old part of the city that managed to avoid major wartime damage. In fact, recent work on the outside of the building uncovered an old sign—Brauerie Minsk—a remainder of the Nazi occupation during World War II. This is just one of several names the brewery has been known as until its designation as Olivaria in 1994. At one stage in the 1970s, the brewery was merged with the newly built Krinitsa Brewery (now one of its competitors) and, because of its age, was expected to fall by the wayside. It didn't and currently is leading its home market with a variety of brands, including a strong Baltic porter. **ATJ**

Tasting notes

Hazy golden orange beneath a whipped egg-white head; nose is spice, sultanas, and hints of lemon curd. Palate is sweetish, spicy, lemon, banana custard, vanilla, and a hint of white pepper; quick, dry finish. Refreshing and well-made approximation of a Weiss.

Orchard White

The Bruery | www.thebruery.com

Country of origin United States
First brewed 2008
Alcohol content 5.7% abv
Serving temperature 48°F, 9°C

Patrick Rue's "Bruery" began, just like so many brewing ventures, as a hobby. When Rue was a first-year law student at Chapman Law School in Orange, California, he took up home-brewing as a way to relax and do something physical after hours reading about law. Gradually, his skill as a brewer improved and his passion ignited. By the time his studies were over, he had decided on a different path to law.

Rue and his wife Rachel opened the Bruery in 2008. It is located in Orange County, not far from Disneyland. In the beginning, the couple were only joined by head brewer Tyler King. The trio planned and built the brewery, and Rue blogged about the experience, which helped him get his name out there and win support even before the first keg was tapped.

In only one year, they went from three to a dozen employees, with Bruery beer sold in ten states, an unheard-of feat for a start-up craft brewery. They specialize in unique Belgian-style and Belgian-inspired ales. Their stated goal is "to create beers with character and depth using the simplest and purest of means." They don't filter or pasteurize their beers, and all of their bottled beers are bottle conditioned.

Orchard White is a Belgian-style witbier that is traditionally spiced with coriander and orange peel. Less traditional is the addition of lavender to the boil and whirlpool. A spicy, fruity yeast strain is used to give complexity, and rolled oats find their way into the mix, which Rue believes gives the beer a silky texture. At the beginning of 2009, *DRAFT* magazine chose Orchard White as one of the Top 25 Beers of 2008. **JB**

Tasting notes

Orchard White is slightly cloudy amber with a billowy white head. The nose is rich and complex, with floral, citrus, and peppery aromas. The flavors are equally complex, with refreshing wheat character, a fresh, effervescent mouthfeel, and spicy, lavender, and zesty citrus notes.

Primátor Weizenbier

Pivovar Náchod | www.primator.cz

Country of origin Czech Republic
First brewed 2003
Alcohol content 5% abv
Serving temperature 44°F, 7°C

The Pivovar Náchod brewery in Náchod, East Bohemia, has developed so many unusual beers that it now markets itself as "a specialist in specialties," complementing the standard pilsner and dark lager styles of its homeland with a dry stout, a Baltic porter, several strong lagers, and even a British-style pale ale made with imported hops. However, its line of unusual brews really took off with this Bavarian-style wheat beer, which, in deference to the brewery's neighbor to the west, was called by a German name—Weizenbier.

In fact, wheat beers have been brewed in the Czech lands for hundreds of years, and there is some speculation that wheat beers may have gone to Bavaria from Bohemia, rather than the other way around. Writing in his seminal text *The Art of Beer Brewing* in 1794, the Czech brewing scientist František Ondřej Poupě said that at least twenty years earlier wheat was the main grist of many brews in Moravia, the eastern half of today's Czech Republic. It was clearly not the grain he preferred. "Wheat is for cakes, oats are for horses, and just barley goes in beer," Poupě wrote, a view that could account for the widespread disappearance of wheat brewing from Bohemia and Moravia in the wake of his book's publication.

Thus, the arrival of a bottled wheat beer from a respected regional producer such as Pivovar Náchod was thought of in Bavarian terms, and this popular beer has much of a Bavarian wheat beer's clove notes in the nose. Like a true Hefeweizen, it is bottled unfiltered, with a substantial yeast sediment. However, it is hopped, quite gently, with Czech Saaz hops. **ER**

Tasting notes

Pouring a very cloudy pale gold, this wheat beer is topped with a chalky white head. Look for plenty of clove in the nose, as well as some banana notes, with a semi-malty body followed by a crisp, slightly bitter finish. Excellent with fish, seafood, and similar light summer fare.

Riegele's Weisse

Brauhaus Sebastian Riegele | www.riegele.de

Country of origin Germany
First brewed *ca.* 1911
Alcohol content 5% abv
Serving temperature 44°–46°F, 7°–8°C

For a brewery to stand out in Bavaria, it has to be good. This part of southern Germany is home to around six hundred breweries, so it's not easy to get noticed. Riegele, however, has been popular locally for more than a century and is now gaining international recognition. The brewery is based in the city of Augsburg and its origins date back to 1386, when the Golden Horse brewery was established. The business was acquired by Sebastian Riegele in 1884 and, under his guidance, rapidly expanded. Riegele's son, also called Sebastian, took the brewery to another level when he built a new brewhouse on the edge of town in 1911. The largest brewery in the city today, it is still family run, with the fifth generation in charge.

The beer selection is extensive, running to pils, export, and dunkel styles, as well as seasonal beers and the ever-popular Riegele's Weisse. This Weissbier is named in honor of the second Sebastian, who not only built the new brewery but also endowed Augsburg with one of its most striking landmarks, the art nouveau Riegelehaus. Three types of malt—pilsner, wheat, and Munich—are used to create this refreshing beer. Hops don't play a major role in the flavor of a Weissbier, but they are important for the balance they bring to the sweetness of the cereals and for their natural preservative qualities. The hops here are Opal and Hersbrucker and they add an important bitterness. What especially appeals to the connoisseur is that Riegele's Weisse is not an overly commercial or sweet Weissbier. The tart fruitiness and higher bitterness make it challenging, and hence more rewarding. **JE**

Tasting notes

A pale yellow beer with a wonderful aroma of bananas, apples, and bubble gum, tinged with a hint of sourness. The fairly bitter taste is dry and not too full, and also has sour apple, banana, and vanilla flavors that linger in the dry finish.

Rothaus Hefe Weizen

Badische Staatsbrauerei Rothaus | www.rothaus.de

Country of origin Germany
First brewed 1995
Alcohol content 5.4% abv
Serving temperature 46°–50°F, 8°–10°C

Rothaus is one of three state-owned breweries in Germany, along with the Staatsbrauerei Weihenstephan in Freising and Hofbräu in Munich, both Bavarian. It was founded in 1791 in Rothaus-Grafenhausen at the brewhouse of the monastery St. Blasius. Since 1922, the brewery has operated as a stock corporation, and today Baden-Württemberg is its only shareholder. The federal state knows just how to do it right: whereas the German beer market is losing volume, Rothaus's business is growing.

Situated in the middle of the Black Forest, Rothaus brews with water from seven sources in a protected area deep in the woods. This soft and clean water—together with locally grown and carefully selected malts, as well as aroma hops from the German growing areas Tettnang and Hallertau—gives a remarkable smoothness to their beers. Furthermore, Rothaus are known to add a bit more malt and make their beers a touch stronger. Their Hefeweizen has an abv of 5.4 percent, whereas the average alcohol content of many German Weissbiers is around 4.9 percent. Thus, Rothaus Hefe Weizen leaves a quite tasteful impression.

Due to the "Zäpfle"-mania—the popularity of the smaller editions of Rothaus beers called "Tannenzäpfle" (Fir Cone) and "Eiszäpfle" (Icicle)—Black Forest brewers were the first in Germany to release their Hefeweizen not only in the usual 17-ounce (0.5-l) bottles but also in 10-ounce (0.3-l) bottles that they called "Hefeweizen Zäpfle." Interestingly, these small bottles were especially popular with women drinkers. **SK**

Tasting notes

Golden orange, hazy; mountainous white head. The nose has a fruity aroma reminiscent of green banana with hints of clove and caramel. On the palate, expect a soft, lean taste and banana flavors with an effervescent green kick. Mild and dry finish.

Schneider Weisse

Weisses Bräuhaus G. Schneider & Sohn | www.schneider-weisse.de

Country of origin Germany
First brewed 1872
Alcohol content 5.4% abv
Serving temperature 46°F, 8°C

It was in Munich, in 1850, when Georg Schneider I—the first member of the family to head this illustrious Bavarian brewery—was given permission by King Ludwig I (whose statue stands proudly outside the current home) to make wheat beer. The recipe for the sumptuously fruity and spicy Schneider Weisse dates back to 1872 and remains a closely guarded secret.

Prior to 1850, the brewing of wheat beer was a privilege only allowed to the royal family, while the rest of society had to make do with murky brown-colored ales. The capital of Bavaria was the Schneider home through revolution, coups, and two world wars, the second of which saw it destroyed in a bombing raid. In the late 1940s, the Schneider family moved north of Munich to the medieval town of Kelheim, which stands on the Danube and is in the center of the Hallertau hop-growing area. With a mixture of luck and foresight, Georg Schneider IV had brought the brewhouse back in the 1920s. It was built in 1607, which makes it one of the oldest establishments making beer in the world. Nowadays, tradition and a modern approach to marketing mark out Schneider as one of the top Weissbier producers in the world.

Georg VI is a tireless promoter of the brewery's products; while more recently, brewmaster Hans-Peter Drexler has embarked on a creative collaboration with Brooklyn Brewery. Visitors to Kelheim are directed to the Weissen Brauhaus, a few minutes from the brewery, where Schneider Weisse (as well as other Schneider beers) can be sampled and celebrated close to the original source. **WO**

Tasting notes

Gold amber in color, Schneider Weisse has an aroma of cloves, bananas, and a hint of vanilla; on the palate, there are more bananas, cloves, a custard-like sweetness, and a hint of bubble gum, before its descent into a tingling, fruity finish.

Sierra Nevada Kellerweis Hefeweizen

Sierra Nevada Brewing Company | www.sierranevada.com

Country of origin United States
First brewed 2009
Alcohol content 4.8% abv
Serving temperature 46°–52°F, 8°–11°C

Although a relative newcomer, Kellerweis os a beer that was years in the making. The idea began when Sierra Nevada wanted to make a lighter, easy-drinking beer to act as a counterpoint to the brewery's more robust ales. "There was intense debate as to what beer, or even what style of beer, to make," says Sierra Nevada Communications Coordinator Bill Manley, adding that they eventually decided to brew a Hefeweizen, the first of which was released around 2006. "The beer was good, and relatively popular, but something was unfortunately missing," Manley says.

Happily, while the brewers were redeveloping the Hefeweizen, a German friend visited the brewery bearing the gift of a rare sample of authentic Bavarian Hefeweizen yeast. This new yeast was legendary for its profound banana and clove notes and its clean, tart, lemony finish. Manley says they used this new yeast and brewed test batch after test batch, but something still wasn't quite right. After six months of trials and thousands of gallons of beer, brewmaster Ken Grossman and some of the other brewers headed to Germany on a whirlwind tour of the legendary wheat beer breweries of Bavaria. There, they noticed that the smaller breweries making the most traditional Hefeweizen used open-vessel fermentation.

On their return, the brewers got working and Kellerweis was born. "Breweries in general have been investing in the newest equipment, the latest technology, to make the science of brewing more efficient—occasionally at the expense of the art," says Manley. He pauses, "old is the new 'new.'" **LMo**

Tasting notes

Wafts of ripe banana, clove, bubble gum, and spices rise from the glass, with a light floral-citrus finish to keep things crisp. Like a great jazz combo, all the elements are so tightly woven, it almost seems like the entire combination of flavors is one.

Southampton Double White

Southampton Ales & Lagers | www.southamptonbrewery.com

Country of origin United States
First brewed 1998
Alcohol content 6.7% abv
Serving temperature 41°F, 5°C

Sometime during the early 1990s, before everybody including Coors was making a white beer, an American home-brewer named Phil Markowski set off on his obligatory pilgrimage to Mecca, also known as Belgium, to taste the cloudy, near-mythical brew called Hoegaarden. The former milk deliveryman Pierre Celis had famously raised the tart, aromatic witbier style from the dead some thirty years earlier. It was a success story that any brewer on either side of the Atlantic might look to for inspiration.

"You could hardly find it in the United States," Markowski remembers. "I just loved it and decided I had to make my own… I guess I went after it like a typical American." Which is to say: B-I-G. Markowski added more unmalted wheat, more extra pale barley malt, and more flaked oats to his recipe. Instead of a relatively light drink with just 5 percent alcohol, his invention tipped the scale at close to 7 percent. More body, more aroma, more buzz. Where Hoegaarden is made for quaffing, Double White is a full-flavored sipper, especially when paired with grilled dishes.

While it's true that a "double white" is rather a contradiction of terms, its appearance on shelves in the late 1990s was a bit of a watershed for American beer. It not only anticipated the 21st-century trend of "imperialized" beer styles, it essentially erased any boundaries: after Southampton Double White, any style no matter how light—a pilsner, a helles, a Kölsch—might be doubled into a stronger beer. Markowski is reluctant to take credit for the trend. "It's a tribute to American tastes. We've come a long way." **DR**

Tasting notes

Hazy and yellow as the New York City sky in August, this aromatic (citrus and spice) witbier looks like a summer cooler. One gulp of its big, malty body tells you to slow down. Begins tart, like unsweetened orange juice, finishes sweet and fizzy with a warming alcohol knock.

Sprecher Hefe Weiss

Sprecher | www.sprecherbrewery.com

Country of origin United States
First brewed 1986
Alcohol content 4.2% abv
Serving temperature 44°F, 7°C

Bavarian Hefeweizen is tricky to brew. Wheat is huskless, so draining the mash can be slow, and for complicated reasons a simple single-temperature infusion mash won't do. The yeast—a different species than regular ale yeast—is especially finicky about temperature. Just a few degrees up or down and you've got a bananarama of a beer or one that's all clove or bubble gum. The idea is to have all these crazy flavors in balance. "I discovered as soon as I started experimenting with brewing Weissbier that the big banana isn't my thing," says Randy Sprecher, founder of this Milwaukee-area brewery.

"We were brewing with the Weihenstephan yeast cultures, just trying to figure this beer out," says Sprecher, "then we accidentally stumbled onto the fact that the Weiss in one fermenting tank seemed to come out better." That led to a quest to learn how to coax the yeast into making the best possible beer. It turned out to be all about good reproduction and better "viability" of the yeast cells, which change malt sugars into alcohol and carbonation, but are also responsible for the fruit salad of flavors.

This approach is typical of Sprecher: diving right in and dealing with things in a practical way. Before he moved to a newer facility in suburban Glendale, the original Milwaukee-located brewery was cobbled together from old dairy tanks, which used to litter the front yard of the brewery. Even with much more up-to-date equipment, the tinkering spirit lives on these days at Sprecher. As he says, "We're having fun perfecting our beers." **RM**

Tasting notes

A spicy and fruity nose with no single thing jumping out. A tad sweet, with a creamy weightiness from the wheat. Gentle hop bitterness provides ample balance. Finish is barely dry and nicely fruity, just quenching enough to make you want another sip.

St. Bernardus Wit

Brouwerij St. Bernardus | www.sintbernardus.be

Country of origin Belgium
First brewed 2001
Alcohol content 5.5% abv
Serving temperature 43°F, 6°C

If one asks people—Belgian or otherwise—about what they think is the definitive witbier, chances are that the answer will be Hoegaarden. However, wheat beer has been common currency in almost every rich farming area in Belgium, even before Hoegaarden's beers were well known outside their region of origin. Yet, by the 1960s, the last brewery in Hoegaarden had closed, and no real Hoegaardse was brewed anymore. Then Pierre Celis, who as a child had helped out in the last active brewery, came along and resuscitated the style in 1966, making it into a massive success story.

These days, the whole world imitates Hoegaardse; and in the town of Hoegaarden, it is still produced by a large beer factory as a soulless global brand. It's safe to say that it is no longer Celis's brainchild. However, he never really left the business, and his activities brought him into contact with the St. Bernard brewery, in the west Flemish town of Watou. The brewery was then in the throes of a revolution—for years it had been producing the St. Sixtus range, a semi-Trappist brand of beers for Westvleteren. That arrangement having ended they were establishing a whole new range under the St. Bernardus name. One beer was sorely missing—witbier.

What could have been more natural than asking Pierre Celis, the godfather of the style, for advice? Which he gave, with good grace. Brewers Hans Depypere and Tom Vanoverbeke worked out the final package, but if you are on the hunt for the real taste of Oud Hoegaarden, then you are advised to try their bottle-conditioned offering. **JPa**

Tasting notes

Hazy orange-colored beer beneath a slight, white head. The nose comes in with citrus, orange peel, pepper, and coriander. Curaçao orange is repeated in the palate, which is also spicy on a slightly sour-sweet base. A clinging, wheaty mouthfeel, just a bit dry, completes the picture.

Švyturys Baltas

Švyturio Alaus Darykla | www.svyturys.lt/en

Country of origin Lithuania
First brewed 2004
Alcohol content 5% abv
Serving temperature 39°–44°F, 4°–7°C

A lot of things have changed in Eastern Europe since the collapse of the Soviet Union. Happily, for the beer lover, many of these changes have taken place in breweries. With the withdrawal of the Iron Curtain, and the expansion of the European Union, both the migration of people and the movement of trade have increased dramatically, meaning that citizens of countries such as Poland and Lithuania have taken up residence in the West, where they are supplied with products they know and love from home. Beer, of course, is high on the list.

The beer exported from the former Soviet countries is a vastly improved product to what was on sale there before. International investment has seen big money spent on refurbishing tired breweries. That's certainly been the case in the Lithuanian port city of Klaipeda, home of the country's biggest brewery, Švyturys, which is part of the Carlsberg-owned Baltic Beverages Holding. Now drinkers in other countries are enjoying the wide range of beers it produces, including the refreshing wheat beer Baltas.

The name Baltas translates as "white," echoing the name of the beer style from which it takes its lead—the Bavarian Weissbier. Baltas is made with 60 percent malted wheat and 40 percent malted barley and is seasoned with German Magnum hops. Weissbier depends heavily on the action of the yeast for its character, with complex fruit and spice notes created during fermentation. Baltas is true to type, packed with vanilla, clove, and banana, all on top of the refreshing lightness that wheat brings to the mash tun. **JE**

Tasting notes

A cloudy yellow beer with the classic Weissbier nose of bubble gum, clove, and banana. This is followed in the mouth by tart apple and lemon, vanilla, banana, clove, and pink bubble gum flavors, before a dry, bready finish with more clovelike bitterness. Refreshing.

Three Boys Wheat

Three Boys Brewery | www.threeboysbrewery.co.nz

Country of origin New Zealand
First brewed 2005
Alcohol content 5% abv
Serving temperature 43°–46°F, 6°–8°C

With a qualification in wine science and ten years' experience as a biochemist and physiologist, Dr. Ralph Bungard had always hoped he would some day get into winemaking or brewing. Five years working in Sheffield, U.K., and gaining an appreciation of England's cask-conditioned real ales finally tipped the balance.

Having returned to New Zealand to take up a lecturing role at Canterbury University, Bungard made the decision to open a brewery in 2005. Four years on, and after a recent increase in batch size from 160 gallons to 530 gallons (600 l to 2,000 l), the biochemist-turned-brewer produces an award-winning range of craft beers in the Christchurch suburb of Woolston.

A genuine family business, Three Boys Brewery is named after Bungard and his two young sons, Marek and Quinn. But there's a "girl" involved, too; Bungard's wife Brigid is responsible for much of the non-brewing work. That includes painstakingly hand-applying neck labels containing the beer's batch number and best-before date to each bottle. Bungard explains, "It allows our drinkers to appreciate and celebrate the subtle differences that occur from batch to batch in a microbrewery—just as wine vintages are celebrated for their differences."

Whenever possible, Three Boys uses locally grown ingredients. Hops are from the Nelson region, while the bulk of the malts are sourced from a local maltster, Gladfield of Dunsandel, just south of Christchurch. Bungard is keen to maintain stylistic integrity with his beers, but points out that he sets out to make modern, New World beers, not simply to mimic the classics. **GG**

Tasting notes

Pours a hazy yellow gold, beneath a pillowy white head. Aroma and palate suggest lemon peel, with hints of ginger and coriander. Soft, champagne-like spritziness precedes a tart, spicy finish, with a hint of grassy hops. Great with Thai food and shellfish.

Trade Winds

Cairngorm Brewery | www.cairngormbrewery.com

Country of origin Scotland
First brewed 2003
Alcohol content 4.3% abv
Serving temperature 46°F, 8°C

The Cairngorm Brewery was established in 2001 in Aviemore, Scotland's premier ski resort. The Highland village also sits within the Cairngorms National Park, amid some of the country's most stunning scenery that varies from wild moorlands and soaring mountain peaks to spectacular rivers and tranquil lochs. Its watercourses are among the cleanest in Scotland, a feature that the Cairngorm Brewery maintains is the key to quality beer.

The mission from the beginning was to brew traditional ales with a fresh new edge and, with multiple industry awards to its name, that dream seems to have been realized. Once it had established a base range of products, such as Wildcat and Stag, the brewery introduced the seasonal beers Trade Winds and White Lady. Trade Winds in particular was an immediate success and quickly gained a permanent spot in the portfolio. "We brought Trade Winds in to complement our range," said Cairngorm's then-Managing Director Robbie Walker. "The beer was originally brewed for the Tall Ships race prior to 2003, so our head brewer Sean Tomlinson brewed a completely new beer but kept the name. It really is a specialty beer, being a cross between a traditional ale and almost a continental wheat beer." The addition of dried elderflower works well with the whole-flower hops to accentuate its floral aroma and flavor.

Trade Winds has been named Champion Speciality Beer of Britain on three occasions. It has also picked up Champion Beer of Scotland awards and was Britain's Champion Best Bitter in 2006. **AG**

Tasting notes

A light golden-colored beer with a nose of apricot and grapefruit. A high proportion of wheat in the mash leaves a stark freshness to the flavor before a massive buildup of floral hops and citrus fruit is overlaid with an elderflower sweetness.

Two Jokers Double Wit

Boulevard Brewing | www.blvdbeer.com

Country of origin United States
First brewed 2009
Alcohol content 8% abv
Serving temperature 55°F, 13°C

It makes complete sense that Boulevard Brewing, located in the heart of America's Midwest, would include wheat as a major ingredient in 70 percent of the beers it brews. Boulevard Unfiltered Wheat is perfect for humid nights in the brewery's home of Kansas City and accounts for most of the wheat bill. However, the brewery also makes a full spectrum of wheat-based beers, including Two Jokers Double Wit.

"The beer and the name is based on duality," says Boulevard brewmaster Steven Pauwels. "On one side, you have the old-school way of making a tart white beer, while on the other side you have the U.S. craft beer movement straining to make everything bigger and more complex. This beer is an approach to overcome these differences." He uses what brewers call a "sour mash" to create much of the tartness in this beer, a method employed in Belgium at the beginning of the 20th century instead of using "wild" yeast beloved of lambic brewers. "I like the idea of tartness in white beers," says Pauwels, who is Belgian-born and trained. "Nowadays we tend to over spice these beers to reach that goal, while they were pretty simple beers at the start of the 1900s."

The recipe for Two Jokers includes both malted and unmalted wheat and some oats. It is spiced with coriander, orange peel, cardamom, and grains of paradise, but not in quantities that make them easy to spot. "I think beer aficionados in the Midwest are on par with Belgian beer drinkers," says Pauwels. "There is a lot of tradition in Belgium, while there is a lot more experimentation going on over here in the U.S." **SH**

Tasting notes

Pours hazy orange into the glass with an off-white head. Citrus and spices jump from the glass, followed by sweet notes of cotton candy. Tart on the tongue, pleasantly grainy, with refreshing orange and lemon zest flavors. Complex and lively.

Unertl Weissbier

Unertl Weissbier | www.unertl.de

Country of origin Germany
First brewed 1895
Alcohol content 4.8% abv
Serving temperature 44°–48°F, 7–9 °C

There is no dark one, there is no pale one, there is just Unertl Weissbier and it pours amber with a copper hue and a yeasty haze, wearing its creamy head up high. The top-fermented beer has presented itself like this since the foundation of Unertl in 1895 in the southern Bavarian village of Haag (not to be confused with Weissbräu Unertl in Mühldorf). When other Weissbier brewers began offering variations of the style, the family brewery stuck to its unique Ur-Weiss. The beer is now an icon, offering unusual maltiness complemented by outrageous fruitiness. All in all, however, its body is well toned and the character harmonious.

As third-generation owner Alois Unertl stresses, his brewery is quality driven. He brews with 70 percent instead of the customary 50 percent of wheat malt that many other breweries use. This higher share of wheat helps to give the beer its freshness. Another quality-control feature is the labor-intensive decoction mash: part of the mash is taken out, boiled in a separate vessel, then reintroduced into the mashing tun to heat the remainder. The mode of boiling enhances the color and provides caramel notes. Furthermore, open fermenting vessels allow the brewers both to take off unpleasant by-products and to "harvest" their own fresh yeast for future fermentations. Gentle bottle fermentation completes the rounded flavor.

Alois Unertl points out that they neither advertise their beer nor do they engage sales representatives to push it into the market. "Our Weissbier is made for people who can make up their own mind and trust their taste buds," he says. **SK**

Tasting notes

Amber to copper, with a fine, firm, cream-colored head. The nose offers caramel and fruity aromas. On the palate, expect distinct malty flavors with hints of coffee and roasted malts balanced by a citrus fruitiness and a certain tartish bite. Mild finish.

Weihenstephaner Hefe Weissbier

Bayerische Staatsbrauerei Weihenstephan
www.brauerei-weihenstephan.de

Country of origin Germany
First brewed 1933
Alcohol content 5.4% abv
Serving temperature 43°–46°F, 6–8°C

Like many other breweries in southern Germany, Weihenstephan continues to pay allegiance to the Reinheitsgebot of 1516, listing the four ingredients in their beer: water, hops, yeast, and grains.

Weihenstephan gets its grains from local farmers, then sends them to a malting house where they are transformed into a brewing malt. The Hefe Weissbier is brewed with Hallertauer Perle and Magnum hops and dark and light barley malt, as well as wheat malt. After the ingredients have been mixed and a "young beer" has been created, the liquid is brought to the storage cellar. Located under the abbey garden, the beer sits in large tanks for some thirty days, by which time it is mature and ready to drink. It is filtered and poured into bottles or kegs. **RP**

Tasting notes
On the palate, somewhat fruity with a bit of a bubblegum flavor. The beer is well balanced between bitter and malty, but does possess a strong undercurrent of bitterness.

Weissbier Etalon

Ridna Marka Corporation
www.ridnamarka.com.ua

Country of origin Ukraine
First brewed 2003
Alcohol content 5% abv
Serving temperature 39°–44°F, 4°–7°C

Ukraine has achieved international recognition for its Weissbier Etalon, which has won countless accolades since its first batch was brewed in 2003.

This unfiltered wheat beer is brewed by the Ridna Marka Corporation. Based on old recipes that had been brought eastward by a Bavarian brewmaster, and apparently modeled on a wheat beer made by the now-defunct Hopf brewery, this is unsurprisingly the first Ukrainian foray into the style; indeed, the company claims it's a national first for brewing with a top-fermenting yeast. The production process is rigid, and the beer's blend of wheat and barley malt and the fermentation temperature of around 68 degrees Fahrenheit (20°C) help to deliver its characteristic warm bronze color. **TS**

Tasting notes
There's a sour, but not overwhelming, bite here, and it is complemented by the hop bitterness. The warm color is as appealing as the vanilla, banana, clove, and apple on the nose.

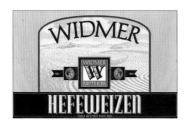

Widmer Hefeweizen

Widmer Brothers Brewing
www.widmer.com

Country of origin United States
First brewed 1986
Alcohol content 4.9% abv
Serving temperature 48°F, 9°C

In 1984, brothers Kurt and Rob Widmer opened either the first or second microbrewery in the state of Oregon (accounts differ). Widmer Hefeweizen came about after a local pub owner asked them for an exclusive beer. It is brewed with U.S. hop varieties Cascade, Alchemy, and Willamette, and four types of barley and wheat malt. With a Hefeweizen that has crisp, clean flavors, but does not have the signature character of its German cousins, the Widmers created the new U.S.-style Hefeweizen. It has won gold medals at the Great American Beer Festival twice, in 1998 and 2006, and has been awarded a gold medal at the World Beer Cup in both 2004 and 2008.

Widmer Hefeweizen is the best-selling Hefeweizen in the United States and is popular year-round. **JB**

Tasting notes
Light, effervescent flavors dance on the tongue and refresh both the body and soul. The clean finish leaves a tingly fruit sensation. Lovely paired with salads, seafood, and spicy dishes.

Zvíkovský Rarášek

Pivovarský dvůr Zvíkov
www.pivovar-zvikov.cz

Country of origin Czech Republic
First brewed 2007
Alcohol content 4.5% abv
Serving temperature 44°F, 7°C

For good reason, central Europe is generally not thought of as a land of spice. Ginger, however, has been part of the culinary landscape for centuries, and has occasionally been used to flavor beers. One of the most remarkable ginger beers to return to the Czech lands is the top-fermented Rarášek beer of the Pivovarský dvůr Zvíkov brewpub in the south Bohemian town of Zvíkovské Podhradí. It is located just below Zvíkov castle, a major tourist destination.

Zvíkovský Rarášek (or Zvíkov Imp) takes its name from a 19th-century theatrical comedy. It is an excellent thirst quencher on warm summer days. Combined with Czech hops, the beer's ginger creates delicious citrus overtones not unlike the crisp fruitiness of a Bavarian Hefeweizen. **ER**

Tasting notes
Complex nose of gingery spice and lambiclike barnyard notes. In the mouth, more spice, sweet whole grains, and citrus fruit, with a finish of fresh pink grapefruit and Meyer lemons.

DARK BEERS

10 Commandments

The Lost Abbey | www.lostabbey.com

Country of origin United States
First brewed 2007
Alcohol content 9% abv
Serving temperature 55°F, 13°C

When Tomme Arthur, director of brewing operations at Port Brewing and The Lost Abbey, took up home-brewing in 1995 during his senior year at Northern Arizona University, he and his brewing partner "left everything behind" when they began thinking about the third batch they'd make. They wanted to make a watermelon beer, so they bought a bunch of Jolly Rancher candies and boiled them down to add watermelon flavor to their beer. To this day, Arthur continues to consider nontraditional sources when he wants to add a particular flavor to a beer.

Ten Commandments descended from a beer Arthur first brewed in 2001 at Pizza Port–Solano Beach; he called it SPF 8. The name was a play on how sunscreens are classified; one with a low number offers less protection and allows a deeper tan, and SPF 8 was a dark beer. Already immersed in brewing beers inspired by the farmhouse ales of Belgium, Arthur was taken aback while drinking Fantome's Black Ghost with friends. He knew he wanted to brew a dark saison-style beer, but one that was dark in color without the taste components of traditional dark beers, such as the roast and chocolate notes found in stouts and porters.

He came up with the idea of blackening raisins and adding them at the end of the boil. Caramelized raisins remain a key ingredient in 10 Commandments, along with honey and rosemary (picked fresh on the first day he brewed SPF 8). Arthur has since decided to add the wild yeast *Brettanomyces* at the bottling stage, thus boosting the complexity and making the beer even more refreshing. **SH**

Tasting notes

Pours dark brown with mahogany highlights, topped by a thick tan head. Rich dark fruits, dark chocolate, and caramelized candy on both the nose and palate, brightened by a dusting of earthy spices and a solid dose of barnyard funk, keeping it light on the tongue.

A. Le Coq Porter

A. Le Coq | www.alecoq.ee/eng

Country of origin Estonia
First brewed 1999
Alcohol content 6.5% abv
Serving temperature 46°F, 8°C

Porter is a dark, bold beer and a sip of history in a glass. It was described by brewery historian Peter Mathias as "the first beer technically suited for mass production at contemporary standards of control." The drinking of dark beers in the Baltic region also has a long history. From the 1780s, during the reign of the British king George III, beers of this style took the long and often dangerous sea journey to Russia. One of the most successful exporting companies was founded by a Belgian named A. Le Coq in 1807. For more than a century, the beers brewed on A. Le Coq's behalf plied their way by sea from London. In 1912, however, the Le Coq company bought the Tivoli brewery in Tartu and began brewing its stout in the Russian Empire. Production of the beer ended in the early 1920s, though, as the beer's imperial links proved too much for the new Communist regime.

The brewery survived, however, and the Soviets changed its name to the Tartu Brewery, which started brewing nondescript, lager-style beers. It did continue to brew a porter until 1969. In 1997, it reverted once again to its A. Le Coq name when it was privatized by Finnish brewery Olvi in the wake of the fall of the U.S.S.R. and Estonia becoming independent.

The porter was brewed for the first time two years later, but its current alcohol strength of 6.5 percent is relatively low compared with the original, which would have been around 9 to 10 percent. However, for those seeking historical accuracy, Harvey's Brewery in England has produced a version of A. Le Coq's renowned Imperial Russian Stout. **TH**

Tasting notes

A strong dark beer, A. Le Coq Porter has poise and great balance. Its nose is a warming bouquet of roasted chocolate malts and mouthwatering molasses, with overlays of spicy hops and rich, dark soft fruits. Extra-dark caramel malts give the beer its color.

ABC Extra Stout

Asia Pacific Breweries
www.apb.com.sg

Country of origin Singapore
First brewed 1931
Alcohol content 8% abv
Serving temperature 46°F, 8°C

ABC Extra Stout is a great favorite with Singaporean beer drinkers. Asia Pacific Breweries was the first commercial brewery in Singapore and was established in 1931 under German ownership. Tiger was launched a year later and it has become the flagship brand of Asia Pacific Breweries.

The portfolio also includes Anchor, a typical, easy-drinking pilsner introduced by German brewmasters, the full-bodied Baron's Strong Brew, and the rich and tasty ABC Extra Stout (as well as being a blue-collar favorite in Singapore, it is very popular with young professionals in Cambodia). The brewery has also made a different version of the beer flavored with ginseng. "We felt that adding ginseng, a traditional Chinese herbal root known for its medicinal properties, would give a refreshing twist to the original version of the stout," said a spokesperson. **ATJ**

Tasting notes

As dark as midnight, it sits beneath an espresso foam–colored head. Mild, milky coffee and chocolate notes on the nose; on the palate, roast barley and chocolate. Sweetish, malty finish.

The Abyss

Deschutes Brewery
www.deschutesbrewery.com

Country of origin United States
First brewed 2006
Alcohol content 11% abv
Serving temperature 55°F, 13°C

The Abyss was first released in 2006 with little fanfare, but interest was sparked almost immediately when beer fans started buzzing about the intensity and complexity of this imperial stout. By the time the next batch was ready, about a year later, The Abyss had created such a cult following that enthusiastic demand for the brew far exceeded availability.

The Abyss is the result of a "brew-off" competition between brewers at Deschutes. Two imperial stouts were initially made, one that featured strong flavors from blackstrap molasses and one that benefited from a dose of brewers' licorice. The brewers took individual kegs of each of these beers and experimented with a variety of spices, procedures, and blends. The resulting Abyss is made with molasses, licorice root, and cherry bark, and aged in oak wine and whiskey barrels then blended near the end of the fermentation process. **LMo**

Tasting notes

Should be served in a tulip glass and allowed to warm up as you consume it, taking you on a fantastic journey as it releases layers of chocolate, coffee, licorice, fruits, nuts, and molasses.

Adam

Hair of the Dog Brewing
www.hairofthedog.com

Country of origin United States
First brewed 1994
Alcohol content 10% abv
Serving temperature 55°F, 13°C

When Alan Sprints set up Hair of the Dog Brewing, the first beer he released wasn't a popular pale ale or porter. It was a style that had been enjoyed as far back as 200 years before, but had since become extinct. "Adambier was the original name of our beer, and also the name of the style we brewed," Sprints says.

The style is based on a Dortmunder made in the 1700s and 1800s and documented by beer writers and historians such as Michael Jackson and Fred Eckhardt. Due to their work, Sprints knew how strong the beer should be; he made assumptions on what ingredients should go into the beer based on knowledge about what had been available in the area at the time. "I determined that Adambier would probably be brewed with some of the smoked malt used in many of the beers in the Bamberg region. It was the way that the malt was dried in the region at that time," he says. **LMo**

Tasting notes

Aromas of chocolate and smoke predominate. Dried fruit, spice, and wood flavors follow the initial cocoa and smoke. Creamy and rich in flavor; great as a drink with dessert.

Alaskan Smoked Porter

Alaskan Brewing
www.alaskanbeer.com

Country of origin United States
First brewed 1988
Alcohol content 6.5% abv
Serving temperature 55°F, 13°C

When U.S. brewers began to experiment with smoked beers in the 1980s, they didn't look to Germany's Rauchbiers for inspiration, but instead to the American past. The most famous result is Alaskan Smoked Porter. Brewery founders Geoff and Marcy Larson discovered that Alaskan breweries at the end of the 19th century brewed porter using colored malts that they kilned themselves over wood fires. The wood would surely have been alder, the only true hardwood in southeast Alaska and used for centuries by Native Americans to smoke fish. Alaskan decided to smoke its own malt, too, for its once-a-year release, each one vintage dated, and the beer became an instant classic.

In 1993, Alaskan made Smoked Porter a little stronger and stopped filtering the beer. Geoff Larson told his customers to keep some bottles back in order to experience different flavors. **SH**

Tasting notes

Pungent smoke arrives with the first whiff and remains through the flavor and finish. Oily texture adds to chocolate richness on the tongue, playing against char flavors of dark burned fruits.

Aldaris Porteris

Aldaris | www.aldaris.lv

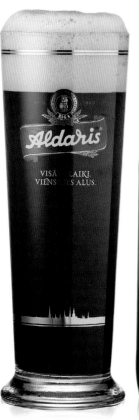

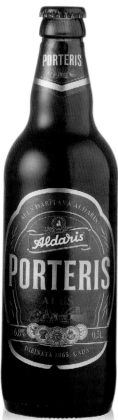

Country of origin Latvia
First brewed 1937
Alcohol content 6.8% abv
Serving temperature 50°–55°F, 10°–13°C

The Baltic porter beer style seems to be on the ropes. In countries such as Lithuania and Latvia, it was a beer that once took up at least a third of the market, and no Eastern European or Baltic brewery worth its salt would have been without one. Times have changed, and the beer that so enthralled Catherine II of Russia is becoming harder to find: ask for a dark beer in some Baltic state bars and you will most likely be served a Guinness. No one knows the reason for the decline.

Aldaris, which is situated on the outskirts of Riga, is one of only two breweries remaining in Latvia that still supplies a porter brew. Its gates were first opened in 1865 by the Bavarian Joachim Dauder, who named the brewery Waldschlosschen (Forest Gate) and set about creating one of Europe's most modern breweries of its time. Despite the popularity of its beer, Waldschlosschen ceased production at the outbreak of World War I, and the copper kettles remained empty until Aldaris took over the building in 1937.

The name may have changed but adherence to the traditional recipes of yesteryear remains steadfast. Slight concessions have been made with the use of hop pellets over hop cones and a shorter maturation process. Yet, as is typical with Baltic porters, Aldaris's version is brewed with bottom-fermenting rather than top-fermenting yeasts, creating a soft roundness in the beer. Seemingly a beer out of time—it accounts for only 2 to 3 percent of Aldaris's overall production—Porteris is still a perfect winter warmer that continues to find new converts, most notably among the Latvian female populace. **SG**

Tasting notes

A dark ruby color topped with an inviting, chunky, creamy head with admirable retention and lacing. The nose works overtime with an aroma flickering from malt, raisins, vanilla, and molasses, while licorice, dark berry fruits, and smoky malt tiptoe across the palate into a syrupy finish.

Alhambra Negra

Cervezas Alhambra | www.cervezasalhambra.es

Country of origin Spain
First brewed 1925
Alcohol content 5.4% abv
Serving temperature 46°–50°F, 8°–10°C

Like Italy, its neighbor across the Mediterranean, Spain is a country where wine has always had the edge on beer, yet it can deliver a selection of beery surprises. There are a handful of brewpubs in cities such as Barcelona, Madrid, and Seville, but it is Alhambra that rules the roost.

Carlos Bouvard and Antonio Knorr founded the brewery in 1925 in the southern Spanish city of Granada. The name of the brewery is a tribute to the medieval Moorish palace of Alhambra that dominates the center of the city, an ironic tribute given the prohibition that Islam places on all things alcoholic. Both men already had experience in the brewing industry, but to make sure that they got their own brewery completely right, they also made use of the technical and management expertise of La Moravia, an older and very famous brewery with which they had links. In 1954, S. A. Damm acquired the company; but twenty-five years later, it passed into the hands of private investors who began expanding production, increasing capacity, and modernizing the equipment. This investment also saw the start of Alhambra exporting to other European countries, as well as to the United States, Australia, and Japan. In 2007, the merry-go-round of ownership continued when Grupo Mahou-San Miguel acquired the brewery.

Alhambra Negra is the company's dark beer, but forget all ideas of Spanish stouts: in Spain, dark beers are seen as an alternative to the golden lagers that dominate the mass market. They are closer to Munich dunkel beers, with roast malt featuring in the mix. **SS**

Tasting notes

Dark reddish–hued lager. On the nose, caramel and roasted malt notes, which are strongly confirmed in the palate, where the mild roasted malt is intensified by a fine carbonization and accompanied by a hint of anise. Perfect with meat dishes.

Altenburger Schwarze

Brauerei Altenburg
www.brauerei-altenburg.de

Country of origin Germany
First brewed 1873
Alcohol content 4.9% abv
Serving temperature 46°F, 8°C

Originally from eastern Germany, this is a deep, dark beer whose popularity has grown since the reunification of Germany in 1990, effectively saving a unique beer style from extinction. Altenburger's version, brewed in the city of the same name, is one of the most popular.

In an age of fickle fashions, especially in the world of beer, it is heartening to report that Altenburger Schwarze is very much an old-fashioned beer, harking back to an era before the tide of blond lagered beers that swept through late 19th-century Germany. Before this time, brown beer was the mainstay of many German brewers—and from this the Schwarzbier developed, both beers sharing a common use of dark roasted malt. Even though it is dark, Schwarzbier is not strong, usually veering between 4 and 5 percent.

The brewery was founded in 1871, and a quarter of a century later it was producing significant quantities of beer of all kinds. Before the Berlin Wall came down, when Schwarzbier was still a novelty to beer drinkers in the West, the city of Altenburg was better known for its manufacture of playing cards. Nowadays it is famous for its beer, too, and the Altenburger Schwarze, which is sold in a swing-top bottle, is a firm favorite. **WO**

Tasting notes
A deep black color and an intense malt aroma, topped with a fine note of hops. The sweetness on the palate combines with light bitter aromas in the finish.

Anchor Porter

Anchor Brewing Company
www.anchorbrewing.com

Country of origin United States
First brewed 1972
Alcohol content 5.6% abv
Serving temperature 46°–57°F, 8°–14°C

Fritz Maytag, owner of Anchor Brewing, has become the godfather of the U.S. microbrewing scene during the renaissance of the past thirty years. In the mid-1960s, when Maytag bought the ailing Steam Brewery, he set about revolutionizing U.S. beer. The global respect and celebration that Anchor beer gained could have ensured Maytag mass-market success, but he was keen to keep the operation true to its craft roots.

Since that time, the San Francisco brewery has used traditional brewing methods, with sugar banished from the brew kettles and whole hops introduced next to a two-row imported barley. With no additives and high standards of cleanliness, it was no surprise that the first brew—Anchor Steam—was well received. Anchor Porter followed the same pattern of pushing U.S. beer boundaries and then went on to do the same globally. Indeed, the dark brew revived a style oft neglected.

The beer raises eyebrows thanks to the high hopping rate during brewing. The addition of whole fresh hops next to the 100-percent malted barley gives it a standout flavor. A top-fermenting yeast and the two-row barley malt ensure that this naturally carbonated porter has a lush creamy foam and an incredibly rich flavor. **TS**

Tasting notes
Pours rich and black, and the burned cereal and heavy hops give it a bitter bite. There's a sweetness, too, and plenty of rich chocolate and toffee, making it great with chocolate cake.

Andechser
Doppelbock Dunkel

Klosterbrauerei Andechs
www.andechs.de

Country of origin Germany
First brewed *ca.* 1800s
Alcohol content 7.5% abv
Serving temperature 46°F, 8°C

Progress has a long tradition at the Benedictine abbey of Andechs, south of Munich. The brewing tradition dates back to 1455, and the facilities have been consistently renewed over the past 150 years. Investment in 2006 saw the modernization of the brewhouse and the expansion of the fermentation and lagering cellars.

Its most famous brew is Andechser Doppelbock Dunkel. This dark beauty, with its fiery hue, voluptuous aroma, and velvety flavor, has delighted many monks and pilgrims, as well as other beer lovers around the world. It is widely available throughout most of Europe, Russia, and Japan. No matter how far away this beer is exported and despite the modernity of the facilities, its brewing methods remain traditional. The doppelbock is brewed with the three-step decoction method, whereby on three separate occasions part of the mash is taken out and boiled, then returned to heat the remainder. Even though this procedure takes more time and energy than modern mashing methods, the monastery holds onto it for the sake of quality and taste. As a result the doppelbock gets the full malt body that is so highly esteemed by beer connoisseurs. Cold fermentation and long cold lagering give the beer enough time to mature and reach its full complexity. **SK**

Tasting notes
A grainy aroma with notes of dried fruit and cocoa. On the palate, expect a rich malty body with flavors of coffee, cocoa, and fruity sherry notes. A warming alcoholic finish.

Antares
Stout Imperial

Cerveza Artisanal Antares
www.cervezaantares.com

Country of origin Argentina
First brewed *ca.* 1998
Alcohol content 8.5% abv
Serving temperature 50°F, 10°C

The most popular beer in Argentina is the Anheuser-Busch InBev–owned Quilmes, which has a hold on about 80 percent of the market. It's a blond lager from a brewery that first opened its doors in 1888, and it is nothing spectacular. It is a straightforward thirst quencher to wash away the dust of the day or to enjoy in the company of grilled steak or ribs from the *asado*.

There's not much wrong with a beer like this, but much lower down the Argentinian pecking order you will find Antares, a young and lively brewery that looks to North American craft brewing for its inspiration. Based at the New Patagonia Brewery in the seaside resort of Mar del Plata, it has its roots in a small brewery set up by Leo Ferrari and Mariana Rodriguez. In 1998, they were joined by Pablo Rodriguez, and Antares started production in Mar del Plata. Now they also have a brewpub in Buenos Aires, which is popular with both young drinkers and passing tourists.

Just like its North American cousins, Antares brews a range of beers, including a Scotch ale, a Kölsch-style beer, a pale and viscous barleywine, and this strong, smooth Stout Imperial. In the brew go pils and chocolate malt, plus caramalt, while Fuggle and Cascade hops join in the fun. **ATJ**

Tasting notes
Pours dark chestnut brown. Savor the rich and fruity chocolate and smoky notes on the nose. On the palate, it has roast coffee beans, dark chocolate, dark fruit, and an appealing dryness.

Arctic Global Warmer

North Cotswold Brewery | www.northcotswoldbrewery.co.uk

Country of origin England
First brewed 2007
Alcohol content 15% abv
Serving temperature 54°F, 12°C

Arctic Ale is a long-forgotten style of strong ale that first made its appearance in 1852, when Burton-on-Trent brewery Allsopp was commissioned to provide a special beer for an Arctic expedition in search of the missing explorer Sir John Franklin. The ale was such a success that it was taken on other expeditions to the polar regions. A century later, Ind Coope's Arctic Ale traveled with the British North Greenland expedition, an event that formed part of an advertising campaign. The Arctic Ale style was described as being less sweet than a barleywine and "as mellow as old Burgundy and nourishing as beefsteak." The beer vanished in the 1960s, but was briefly brought back to life by West Country brewery Teignworthy at the end of the 1990s.

This was an ideal beer to be given a makeover by Jon Pilling, who runs the North Cotswold Brewery near Moreton in the Marsh in Gloucestershire. "I've been around the world in search of beer," he says. "I am passionate about beer flavors and styles. I grew up near Henley, and the aroma of Brakspear's got to me young." As well as this extra-strong beer, Pilling produces the 10 percent Monarch IPA and the luscious Smoked Maple Porter among his special beers. Getting a beer up to and beyond 12 percent abv always requires a lot of care and attention at the fermentation stage, as ale yeasts tend to give up the ghost. Pilling doesn't disclose the type of yeast he uses to continue the fermentation, but does say that in order to keep the yeast working, he has to rouse it a couple of times. He's definitely a dedicated brewer: for Monarch IPA, he mashes in on Christmas Day, and the beer is not released until the summer. **ATJ**

Tasting notes

A shy nose of dark vinous fruit, chocolate, and mocha coffee; the mouthfeel is smooth, with layers of treacle, toffee, and Demerara sugar, all tempered with an assertive hop bitterness. Gorgeous, elegant, sooty, and smoky—a beer to cherish and chew, to contemplate.

Asahi Black

Asahi Breweries | www.asahibeer.co.uk

Country of origin Japan
First brewed 1995
Alcohol content 5% abv
Serving temperature 37°–43°F, 3°–6°C

Dark beers have enjoyed a healthy resurgence in recent times, with milds, stouts, and porters all coming back into popularity. These are all top-fermented, ale-type beers, but there's also been a revival of dark, bottom-fermented lagers—notably in Germany, the Czech Republic, and, surprisingly, Japan.

The Osaka Brewing Company began production in 1889 and, three years later, launched a beer called Asahi, which—translating as "Rising Sun"—is today the name given to the whole business. Its most widespread beer is the golden Asahi Super Dry, but in 1995 the company took the plunge and invested in a new dark lager. Asahi Kuronama, more commonly known as Asahi Black, is an interesting development because it comes from a brewery that has a big following among young drinkers. It also has strong marketing and has been able to go where many dark beers have feared to tread—into the trendy bars.

The beer is only brewed at Osaka from a mix of barley, maize, and rice, but with three dark malts—crystal, black, and Munich. The hops are Czech and American, but low key, as you'd expect from a beer that relies mainly on grain for its flavor. The other major influence on the taste comes from the lagering process. As Asahi Black enjoys a month's cold conditioning after primary fermentation, it presents a crisp, smooth texture to offset the roasted malts. In essence, it is a beer with the roasted character of a stout, but the lightness of touch of a clean pilsner. The beer has echoes of the German Schwarzbier in flavor and appearance, but it is genuinely Japanese. **JE**

Tasting notes

A black beer with coffee, chocolate, and licorice in the aroma. There are gentle caramel and licorice flavors in the crisp, bittersweet taste, along with dry, dark malt notes that run on into the finish, bringing suggestions of roasted coffee beans.

Aventinus

Weisses Bräuhaus G. Schneider & Sohn | www.schneider-weisse.de

Country of origin Germany
First brewed 1907
Alcohol content 8.2% abv
Serving temperature 46°–54°F, 8°–12°C

Aventinus is the Bavarian wheat Doppelbock with the longest pedigree and, it comes as a surprise when you consider the male environment of the Bavarian brewing industry in the first years of the 20th century, to learn that it was created by a woman. In 1905 Georg Schneider III, the owner of the then Munich-based brewery, died at the tender age of thirty-five. His successor was only six years old and in the place of her young son, his widow Mathilde Schneider took over the family business. Not only did she help to create this fabulous beer (named after a medieval Bavarian chronicler), but under her direction the company expanded to become the largest wheat beer brewery of southern Germany in the years before World War I.

Based on the recipe of the Schneider Weisse Original, Aventinus is made of wheat and barley malts with additional roasted malts that create its dark ruby color. The traditional brewing process, alongside its open fermenting vessels and a costly bottle fermentation, makes this beer a gem: intense and subtle at the same time, complex but nicely balanced. Today Aventinus is a world classic and is the pride of the family brewery now run by Georg Schneider VI.

Every year the beer is celebrated at the start of spring with a festival at the brewery's Weisses Bräuhaus in Kelheim. Schneider also produces a vintage edition by lagering bottles for three years in a cave, then packaging each bottle separately to sell abroad. As long as Germans don't develop a taste for this delicacy, international fans are lucky; all of what is in the cave is theirs. **SK**

Tasting notes

Ruby-dark in color with a compact and persistent head. The nose is fruity, tart, with hints of chocolate. A slightly sour palate combines with a full, fluffy mouthfeel, balanced by flavors of banana, pear, caramel, dark chocolate, before sliding into a dry, spicy clove finish.

Aventinus Weizen-Eisbock

Weisses Bräuhaus G. Schneider & Sohn | www.schneider-weisse.de

Country of origin Germany
First brewed 2002
Alcohol content 12% abv
Serving temperature 50°–55°F, 10°–13°C

If you think Aventinus, the first Bavarian wheat doppelbock, is the most intense wheat beer, try Aventinus Eisbock. It is literally a concentrate of the world beer classic, but when you look to its flavor profile it has a character of its own. The nose offers fruity and alcoholic aromas reminiscent of the plum brandy slivovitz. The flavor develops from an intense fruitiness of dried plums and figs to a full-blown maltiness of dark chocolate aromas. Perhaps surprisingly, it is a good digestive.

Legend has it that current brewmaster Hans-Peter Drexler heard tales about an extra-special Aventinus resulting from partial freezing during a cold winter in the late 1930s. What had happened was that, through freezing, water was extracted from the beer in the form of ice, leaving a liquid with an intensified flavor and alcohol content. His memory of hearing this story was jogged by a request from an American importer for an extra-strong beer.

Drexler decided to recreate this classic "mistake," and G. Schneider created a modern controlled facility for which it now owns a patent. From this frozen distillation, only half of the original quantity of beer comes out as what is usually called "Eisbock." Interestingly enough, along with the water, yeast gets extracted, making bottle conditioning—an otherwise traditional Schneider Weisse feature—impossible.

Eisbock has many fans, but not enough to make nationwide distribution worthwhile. Therefore, at the time of writing, it can only be purchased at the brewery's Weisse Brauhaus brewpubs or online. **SK**

Tasting notes

Deep mahogany in color. The nose offers ripe plums and bananas alongside pronounced alcoholic notes. On the palate, the drinker will experience a creamy sweetness, the taste of dried plums, and Viennese coffee before its rhubarblike, brut finish—very complex and warming.

Baden Baden Stout

Cervejaria Baden Baden | www.cervejariabadenbaden.com.br

Country of origin Brazil
First brewed 2001
Alcohol content 7.5% abv
Serving temperature 46°–54°F, 8°–12°C

Mention Brazil and the first images that come to mind for many people are stunning beaches, tropical rain forest, carnival celebrations, and exotic cocktails. An award-winning and internationally acclaimed stout will be the last thing on their minds. When Baden Baden's Stout was awarded the gold medal in the dry stout category at the 2008 European Beer Star Awards in Germany, it became the first-ever South American beer to achieve this honor. It did it in style as well, overcoming strong competition from countries more usually associated with this style of beer. Baden Baden Stout remains true to traditional stout recipes and achieves its glorious black color from carefully selected roasted malts, rather than from the caramelization of sugar like many imitators from the subcontinent.

The brewery is located in Campos do Jordão, a mountainous region of São Paulo state where the climate and topography resemble northern Europe. Many immigrants from Germany and Switzerland were attracted to the region in centuries past for this reason. The location offers the brewery an excellent source of water essential to production. Ingredients that cannot be sourced locally are imported to the brewery, where the stout is made. The result is a truly outstanding beer that is ideal for the chilly wintry weather the region experiences.

Baden Baden is now owned by Schincariol, the largest Brazilian-owned brewery, prompting fears that quality may be compromised in a drive for increased production. Thankfully, this has not yet been the case, and the beer continues to grow in popularity. **AH**

Tasting notes

A very pleasant woody aroma is present in the palate, where roasted malt and some chocolate and coffee notes are also present. Smooth with a pleasingly bitter finish. An ideal accompaniment to oysters or a rich chocolate dessert such as a mousse.

Baltika 6

Baltika Brewery | www.baltika.ru

Country of origin Russia
First brewed 1994
Alcohol content 7% abv
Serving temperature 46°–50°F, 8°–10°C

Baltika has come a long way since the Baltika Brewery opened in 1990 as part of the Leningrad Association of the Beer Brewing and Nonalcoholic Beverages Industry. Today, it is part of the Carlsberg empire and is Russia's biggest brewer, commanding more than 40 percent of the country's domestic beer market. In 1990, the Baltika brands did not exist. Then, its main beers were Zhigulevskoye, Rizhskoye, Admiralteiskoye, and Prazdnichnoye. However, the collapse of Communism and the privatization of the company in 1992 saw the adoption of European-style marketing methods and the development of the Baltika beers. There are nine numbered beers in the range, which spans several beer styles, from a low alcohol to a wheat beer.

Baltika 6 is a porter that draws on the heritage of porter drinking in the St. Petersburg area. According to Baltika's chief brewer, Irina Tlekhuray, the beer is brewed using an old English recipe. She explains that being able to make a good porter indicates the skill of the brewer. As with most porters, dark, burned malts are added to the grist. The blackened, crunchy grains impart little in the way of fermentable sugars, but they bring a lot of flavor and color to the brew.

Baltika 6 porter was launched in 1994 as part of a move by the company to improve the image of beer in Russia. Traditionally, most beer in the country has been sold relatively cheaply and is packaged in plastic PET (polyethylene terephthalate) bottles. Baltika 6 is sold in a smart, glass bottle and has cemented the company's reputation as a quality brewery. It was judged best porter at the World Beer Awards in 2009. **TH**

Tasting notes

A smooth, well-balanced beer with a smoothness that tantalizingly masks its strength. Dark, roasted, chocolate malt and dark, almost-burned, sugar flavor the mouth, which is overlain by a subtle hop finish. There is a suggestion of fruit and complex alcohol on the nose.

Bamberg Rauchbier

Cervejaria Bamberg
www.cervejariabamberg.com.br

Country of origin Brazil
First brewed 2008
Alcohol content 5% abv
Serving temperature 46°F, 8°C

Alexandre Bazzo, founder of Cervejaria Bamberg, is a focused young man who brews traditional German-style beers. This might seem odd in a country like Brazil, but there is a strong German-tinged brewing tradition that goes back more than a century. Bazzo's beers are characterful, tasty, and true to their origins.

Bamberg is Germany's most vibrant brewing center, a town perhaps most famous for its smoked, or *rauch*, beer. A few hundred years ago, beer with a smoky aroma was common, because malt was frequently dried with wood. As technology improved, brewers were quick to abandon what they saw as an inferior and rustic flavor, and by 1800, smoked beer was merely a quaint specialty. Bamberg Rauch uses 50 percent smoked malt from Weyermann in Bamberg, plus pils, Munich, and an aromatic caramel malt, for a classic smoked Märzen in the Bamberg tradition. **RM**

Tasting notes

A smoky campfire nose, with hints of rich malt. On the palate, a modest body, with just a hint of caramel sweetness, met nicely by the dry, smoky beer and building into a firm hoppiness.

Bärni Dunkel

Brauerei Felsenau
www.felsenau.ch

Country of origin Switzerland
First brewed 1998
Alcohol content 5.2% abv
Serving temperature 46°F, 8°C

Felsenau was started in 1881 by Johann Gustav Hemmann, who swapped his restaurant for the then-basic brewery site. The brewery is still independent and caters mostly for customers within a 30-mile (48-km) radius of Bern.

Felsenau was among the first to introduce unfiltered lagers—Zwickelbier—and is pretty much the only brewery in Switzerland to come up with a dark Zwickelbier, which is called Bärni. Basically, it is a back-to-basics version of the traditional Swiss dark lager. Unfiltered and unpasteurized, Bärni is available in flagons that are filled straight from the lagering tanks on the brewery ramp, every Friday afternoon. The bottles are filtered, but are unpasteurized, which gives them a nice, fresh, crisp taste, but a relatively limited shelf life of five months. The label on the bottle features Bern's emblematic brown bear. **LM**

Tasting notes

A smooth, crisp, malty yet dry, dark reddish-brown lager with a very slight buttery edge, gentle bitterness, and moderate carbonation. It's a great beer for drinking after work.

BB10

Birrificio Barley
www.barley.it

Country of origin Italy
First brewed 2006
Alcohol content 10% abv
Serving temperature 59°–61°F, 15°–16°C

BB10 simply stands for Birrificio Barley 10, with the number referring to the alcohol content. Not satisfied with brewing a strong beer, brewer Nicola Perra wanted to personalize it, which he did by adding the "sapa" (concentrated grape must) of Cannonau grapes. Five different kinds of malts, both British and Belgian, and two hop varieties, Cascade and WGV, are also used. BB10 is produced once a year after the Cannonau harvest and in a very limited quantity. The brewing process is very long, with the final maturation in bottle lasting around six months. However, this is definitely a beer to hunt out and treasure.

The result of the complex production process is extraordinary: BB10 cannot be bracketed into any one style (although Perra suggests an imperial stout). Rich and complex, it is an ideal nightcap but it's also a good choice with game meat or chocolate dessert. **MM**

Tasting notes
Dark with hazelnut tints. Rich and complicated aroma; toasted notes come to the fore, followed by red fruits, licorice, and soy sauce. Full-bodied mouthfeel; very long aftertaste.

Beerlao Dark Lager

Lao Brewery
www.beerlao.la

Country of origin Laos
First brewed 2005
Alcohol content 6.5% abv
Serving temperature 44°–50°F, 7°–10°C

When Sivilay Lasachack was appointed brewmaster for the Lao Brewery, she set about revising the beer portfolio, not least by increasing the proportion of home-grown rice used in the mash. This imparted a smoother, mellower character to the beer, which was found to be more in tune with local tastes.

By 1993, foreign investment saw several Thai companies involved in the brewery, but they sold their stake in the business back to the Lao government in 2002. Soon Carlsberg Asia and its regional partners took over, and they have set about promoting the brand to a wider international audience.

Beerlao Dark is a distinctive lager brewed in the pilsner style, and it has quickly gained a loyal local following, as well as finding favor with the growing number of tourists now visiting this landlocked but scenically stunning part of Southeast Asia. **JW**

Tasting notes
Chestnut brown with a whisper of toffee and freshly ground coffee on the nose; the palate is smooth, with more toffee, dried fruit, and caramel notes. Hoppy, bittersweet finish.

Bercloux Bière Stout

Brasserie de Bercloux | www.bercloise.com

Bernard Dark

Rodinný Pivovar Bernard | www.bernard.cz

Country of origin France
First brewed 2000
Alcohol content 5% abv
Serving temperature 50°–57°F, 10°–14°C

Country of origin Czech Republic
First brewed 1995
Alcohol content 5.1% abv
Serving temperature 46°F, 8°C

Head brewer Philippe Laclie started learning his craft at the Irish Brewing Company in County Kildare, Ireland, in 1999. The roasted, nutty, and toasted bread–influenced stouts he experienced inspired him to create something similar—with even more flavor extractions. Laclie borrows the family cognac-distilling equipment to boil the wort, and water is fed directly from one of two wells on the farm.

The brewery's barley is grown in northern France and malted in Belgium, which Laclie maintains is essential for its aroma, color, and consistency. All Bercloise beers are top-fermented and conditioned for between fifteen and twenty-one days. Spicy hops sourced from Alsace deliver an aromatic burst. Nottingham ale yeast was selected for its tolerance to low fermentation temperatures and for its ability to allow the full natural flavor of malt to develop. **AG**

Stanislav Bernard's greatest claim to fame is his brewery, Rodinný Pivovar Bernard. Co-owner Josef Vávra is the brewmaster and has created lagers that have brought a small regional producer a relatively large share of the country's premium beer market.

In the Czech Republic, the brewery has made much of the fact that its beers are unpasteurized. Even moderate amounts of pasteurization can diminish the dynamics of the aromas and flavors in lagers, and Bernard's beers particularly seem to benefit from the lack of flash heating. Certainly Bernard Dark has few competitors that come close to its levels of richness, depth, and complexity. Brewed from five different malts at an original gravity of 13 degrees, the beer fits in with the premium category of Czech "speciál" beers. It is lagered at cold temperatures for a minimum of forty days, which results in a rich, malty body. **ER**

Tasting notes
As black as its Irish counterparts with an effervescent head. Chocolate joins licorice maltiness to gather rich fruitcake flavors for a dry finish and smoky afterglow.

Tasting notes
Pours a clear, very dark amber. The aroma is of freshly baked rye bread and grainy malt. In the mouth, molasses and coffee flavors give way to a dry, long-lasting, bitter finish.

◄ Brasserie de Bercloux's barley hails from northern France.

Big Swede

Viking Brewing Company | www.vikingbrewing.com

Country of origin United States
First brewed 1997
Alcohol content 8% abv
Serving temperature 59°F, 15°C

The small Wisconsin town of Dallas, which is the home of Viking Brewing, is tucked away in the northwest corner of the state. When Viking opened in 1994, it was the first microbrewery in the region, and it brought back the time-honored tradition of a local, family-run brewery. What Viking may lack in size it more than makes up for in its variety of beer. The brewery regularly turns out twenty-two different beer styles, working out of the former Dallas Creamery building, which is sited beside a picturesque millpond. The range goes from basics such as a bock, wheat, and IPA to more esoteric brews, such as Hot Chocolate, which boasts cocoa and cayenne pepper in the mix, and Whole Stein, a coffee, oatmeal, and milk porter. If you find yourself in Dallas on a Saturday, the brewery tour includes samples of at least a half-dozen brews.

Viking takes purity seriously. No fining agents, chemicals, or preservatives are used in any of their beers. They are natural, unpasteurized, and not sterile filtered, and they contain active brewer's yeast, which means that they continue to age and develop over time. Clearly, the Big Swede Swedish Style Imperial Stout could be kept in a quiet corner of your fridge for a couple of years and produce wonderful results.

The name "Viking" reflects the Scandinavian heritage of owners Randy and Ann Lee; he's Norwegian and she's a Swede. Randy gained notoriety in 2002 when he launched a low-budget and ultimately unsuccessful bid to become Wisconsin's governor, as a candidate for the BEER (Balance Education Environment Reform) Party. **RL**

Tasting notes

This brew pours thick black, producing a tan head. There is a roasted-grain and oaky aroma. On the palate, deep dark chocolate notes with hints of dark berries, molasses, coffee, and even a little Irish cream. A big beer that evolves over the course of a glass.

Black

Brasserie de Bellevaux | www.brasseriedebellevaux.be

Country of origin Belgium
First brewed 2007
Alcohol content 6.3% abv
Serving temperature 46°–50°F, 8°–10°C

This beer might be a Scotch and it might be brewed in the Wallonian province of Liège, but brewer Wil Schuwer is a true . . . Dutchman. A former pharmacist, in 2004 he took his wife and children to live in the small tourist town of Malmedy, not far from the Dutch border. He brews on the site of a beautiful old farmhouse (although the brewery is a Japanese-made state-of-the-art plant), and the surrounding countryside is popular with walkers and skiers.

All Wil's beers have some features in common—they're 100 percent malt beers, with oats added; they also include carefully thought-out blends of special malts from various sources. All are unfiltered, but eschew secondary forced refermentation. The water is local, from a common village well. External hints suggest their common origin, with all four beers starting with the letter "B": the French language allows for the Blonde, Brune, and Blanche; but, for the Scotch, Wil borrowed from the language of Shakespeare. Apart from this linguistic distinction, the Black also proudly sports the addition of Fuggle hops. Meanwhile, the striking logo on the rhomboid label hints at local nobility—Bellevaux being their family name.

All Bellevaux beers have been carefully planned, tested, and executed, yet many connoisseurs agree that the Black is really the one that stands out. The beer is available in bottles here and there across Belgium, but the draft version is as rare as hen's teeth and is really kept for the locals. Should you find yourself in the Belgian Ardennes, it is well worthwhile searching for this hidden black. **JPa**

Tasting notes

Small yellow beige head looms over a red-shot black beer. If the nose excels in fruits, such as blackcurrant and blueberries, as well as a pinch of nutmeg and pepper, the taste is more that of dried berries, chalky even. Generally, very dry indeed.

Black Adder

Mauldons | www.mauldons.co.uk

Black Albert

De Struise Brouwers | www.struisebrouwers.be

Country of origin England
First brewed 1987
Alcohol content 5.3% abv
Serving temperature 54°–57°F, 12°–14°C

Country of origin Belgium
First brewed 2007
Alcohol content 13% abv
Serving temperature 50°–57°F, 10°–14°C

Brewer Peter Mauldon was either being foolhardy or forward thinking when he launched a dark, bitter stout in 1987. At the time, dark beers were out of fashion, and golden beers were the future.

Mauldon was among a new wave of brewers who were convinced that there was a market for new, interesting, and tasty beers—so, he created Black Adder. This potent, bittersweet stout, with its dangerous drinkability, quickly proved to be a firm favorite, and in 1991, it was crowned Champion Beer of Britain. In 2000, Mauldon retired, and Steve and Alison Sims bought the brewery and relocated to a glass-fronted building situated high on a hill overlooking Sudbury. Behind the glass is a gleaming collection of brewing vessels. The investment in this new kit is an obvious sign of the Sims's commitment to brewing in an area whose history is so linked to beer production. **TH**

Three brewing friends, under the patronage of brewmaster Urbain Coutteau, decided to rent Deca brewery, which had a lot of spare capacity that they could use to brew. Aardmonnik (Flemish Oud Bruin) and Struiselensis (sour *Brettanomyces* ale) were among the first beers to emerge, but then, in 2007, their foreign contacts incited them to brew an imperial stout. As Belgium is a kingdom, they dubbed it "Royal Stout" and then borrowed the name of the reigning Belgian monarch for its final name. Weighing in at 13 percent in alcohol strength, Black Albert is certainly potent enough, if maybe less over-the-top than some U.S. or Scandinavian attempts at the style.

Black Albert has already spawned impressive offspring, such as Cuvée Delphine (lagered in bourbon vats). The bottles sport artwork reminiscent of the glass partitions in Belgian pubs of a century ago. **JPa**

Tasting notes

A strong, bittersweet stout with treacle, licorice, and roast malt on the nose, plus a burned, estery fruitiness. The palate is rich, smoky, and slightly sweet, with espresso and a hint of vanilla.

Tasting notes

Dark beige, dense, creamy head over black beer. A concentrated hop nose suggesting U.S. hopping and drying grapes on straw. Velvety, viscous, nearly chewy in the mouth.

Inside the mash tun at De Struise Brouwers' Deca site. →

Black Bavarian

Sprecher | www.sprecherbrewery.com

Country of origin United States
First brewed 1985
Alcohol content 5.9% abv
Serving temperature 61°F, 16°C

"I was stationed in Augsburg, Germany, in 1968 to 1969," recalls Randy Sprecher, founder of the eponymous brewery, "and I used to love that Paulaner Salvator. Of course I was underage, but the inn I used to go to had a little room for me where I'd have my schnitzel and those great dark beers. Sometimes I could barely get my ass upstairs." Like so many others, Sprecher was dogged by the memory of those great beer experiences in Europe. He re-created those flavorful beers first as home-brews in the early 1970s, and eventually as Sprecher Black Bavarian.

Bavaria has a long history of schwarz, or "black," beers, especially in Kulmbach, Köstritz, and Augsburg. Stylistically, Sprecher Black Bavarian fits the style, which may have been influenced by the popularity of porter in the late 18th century. Like all Schwarzbier, Black Bavarian balances a moderately sweet body with the slight bitter edge of black malt, which adds up to a luxurious chocolate flavor. The real magic is that all this happens in a session beer of 5.9 percent alcohol. Black Bavarian is satisfying and drinkable, a great combination.

The recipe has remained the same all these years, but recent tinkering with the fermentation has made it "leaner in the middle," according to Sprecher, "while keeping that really rounded mouthfeel." It ranks at or near the top of session beers on the beer-rating sites, and lately has been winning converts even in places such as hop-mad California. As a flagship for a U.S. craft brewery, it is absolutely unique. Black Bavarian is proof that there are unexpected treasures to be found if you just look a little closer. **RM**

Tasting notes

Big roasty nose with some cakelike malt as well, plus something that smells a bit like roasted pecans. Sweetish on the palate at first, but balancing nicely as the black malt kicks in. Creamy texture and a smooth roasty finish with an almost smoky character.

Black Butte Porter

Deschutes Brewery | www.deschutesbrewery.com

Country of origin United States
First brewed 1988
Alcohol content 5.2% abv
Serving temperature 39°–55°F, 4°–13°C

Deschutes's beers are only sold in fourteen western states, including Alaska and Hawaii and the West Coast east to Wyoming and south to parts of Texas. But despite the brewery's limited distribution, Black Butte Porter continues to be the best-selling porter in the United States.

Black Butte Porter is named after a geographic feature that looms over the picturesque town of Bend, Oregon, where Deschutes has been brewing for more than twenty-one years. At the base of the tall butte runs River Metolius, starting at a mysterious source hidden deep within the ancient, ebony-colored lava flows that form the base of Black Butte. The namesake beer is just as dark.

The beer was originally formulated by Frank Appleton, a British-born Canadian brewer who designed Deschutes's original pub brewing system. The roasty porter was one of the brewery's trio of original beers, along with Cascade Golden Ale and Bachelor Bitter, both of which are also still enjoyed today, but are not nearly as popular as the porter.

Deschutes's founder and president Gary Fish credits Black Butte Porter's success, in part, to Jim Kennedy, one of the first distributors of craft beer in Oregon and the United States. Kennedy had advised Fish to focus on promoting the inky-black beer when Deschutes opened for business in 1988, a time when almost all beers in the country were pale yellow and fizzy. Crafted from chocolate and crystal malts, Black Butte Porter remains its flagship beer to this day, enjoying a loyal and passionate following. **LMo**

Tasting notes

Pours a deep mahogany with a khaki-colored head; aromas of milk chocolate and roasted coffee dance from the glass. Expect flavors of chocolate and espresso with a creamy finish that would pair well with many foods—from cheeses to grilled meats to desserts.

Black Chocolate Stout

Brooklyn Brewery | www.brooklynbrewery.com

Country of origin United States
First brewed 1994
Alcohol content 10.0% abv
Serving temperature 55°F, 13°C

In the early 1990s when Garrett Oliver was toiling at a small brewpub in downtown Manhattan, he took up the challenge to invent a winter beer for the growing Brooklyn Brewery on the other side of the East River. It had to be strong, dark, warming, and taste like chocolate. Oliver designed possibly the most chocolaty beer in the United States, but, astonishingly, it doesn't contain an ounce of chocolate.

Brewed in the style of a classic Russian imperial stout, it takes three separate mashes to produce enough wort for this monster. The grain bill includes roasted barley, black barley, black malt, and chocolate malt, but nothing remotely related to cacao. A substantial amount of Willamette and American-grown Fuggle hops provides the needed balance. "Each one has a particular role in creating the flavor profile," Oliver says. "The interesting thing is that the beer becomes much more chocolatelike over its first year in the bottle." Though the stout can stand on its own as a cold-weather sipper, it's a flexible partner at dinnertime. It complements strong cheese and plays well with fudge.

Significantly, the beer is not actually brewed at Brooklyn's own facility. It's contracted to a larger upstate New York brewery, where there is ample tank space for it to be properly conditioned for two months before bottling. The stout's superb flavor and excellent reputation for consistency helped put to rest a growing debate in the 1990s that such U.S. contract brews were somehow inferior products. Needless to say, it also earned Oliver a job across the river. **DR**

Tasting notes

Black as ink with a tight brown head. Sweet chocolate and dark-roasted malt in the nose. While cocoa does not dominate, other chocolatelike characters of bitterness, espresso, dark fruits, and burned toast are recognizable. Hugely satisfying with a strong, challenging alcohol kick.

Black Forest

Matt Brewing Company | www.saranac.com

Country of origin United States
First brewed 1997
Alcohol content 5.3% abv
Serving temperature 46°F, 8°C

With this dark, malty Schwarzbier, The Matt Brewing Company, established in 1888, has reached back to the very roots of its pioneering founder. Francis Xavier Matt was already on the road to success as a trainee at the famous Duke of Baden Brewery in the Black Forest region of Germany when, in 1885, he decided to move to the United States. His dream, like so many other immigrants from the Old World, was to open his own business. His new start came at the Bierbaur Brewery in Utica, New York. This quaint but burgeoning town, tucked into the leafy foothills of the Adirondack Mountains, surely must have reminded him of home. Facing competition from no fewer than eleven other local breweries, Bierbaur nearly collapsed. Then, serving as both its star salesman and brewmaster, Matt reorganized it as one of the town's largest and most successful.

Over the years, the brewery—later renamed after Matt—grew, suffered through Prohibition, and grew again under the leadership of his sons Walter and Frank. It created Utica Club, one of the Northeast's prototypical regionally distributed lagers. As other regional brewers succumbed to the dominance of mass-marketed mega-brands, Matt continued to grow, thanks largely to the tenacity of its owners. Part of Matt's success is due to the unique "contract" brewing arrangements it has built with other brands. Some would say that Matt brews the best for itself, under its own Saranac label. Among its more than thirty ales and lagers is this superbly malty, engagingly refreshing black beer, named for its founder's home. **DR**

Tasting notes

Toasty malt aroma with a light touch of hops rises from an inviting dark brown body. Its medium body is well carbonated, filling the mouth with a pleasing balance of bready malt and earthy hops, finishing with sweet molasses and chocolate.

Black Gold Bourbon Imperial Stout

Full Sail Brewing | www.fullsailbrewing.com

Country of origin United States
First brewed 2006
Alcohol content 10.5% abv
Serving temperature 48°F, 9°C

Black Gold Imperial Stout is released every year, but the barrel-aged version is only available every other year, after it has spent about ten months in bourbon barrels. Full Sail's brewers began experimenting with aging beer in barrels when they put two beers in bourbon ones back in 1997. "That's when we started playing with bourbon barrels; those first ones were Jim Beams from Kentucky," says Full Sail brewmaster John Harris. "We threw our imperial porter and our barleywine in those. They spent a year in them."

Harris says he and the other brewers learned a lot from that first foray into bourbon barrels and beer. "At first, the beer picks up just the bourbon, and it's pretty hot," he says. "You don't get the wood right away. All you get is a lot of fire and the spirit. A lot of folks freak out because the alcohol is so strong, and they will pull the beer out then. But we learned from those experiments that the wood's influences arrive later." Continuing their experiments, in 2005, the brewers chose to age some of the imperial stout in bourbon barrels. The next year, the brewery released two versions of the imperial stout, with half of it aged in the bourbon barrels and half aged in stainless steel. The idea was for people to taste the difference of each one.

Full Sail releases the bourbon-barrel-aged versions of Top Sail Imperial Porter and Black Gold Imperial Stout on alternate years, so one bourbon-barrel beer is released each year. On the years when the beers don't appear as barrel aged, they are produced simply as Top Sail and Black Gold, the brewery's imperial porter and imperial stout. **LMo**

Tasting notes

Bourbon and vanilla hit the nose with a touch of toasted coconut and almond. This beer does not hide the fact that it has spent some time in bourbon barrels, but the influence is nicely rounded. A hearty beer intended for slow sipping.

Black Hawk Stout

Mendocino Brewing Company | www.mendobrew.com

Country of origin United States
First brewed 1983
Alcohol content 5.2% abv
Serving temperature 48°F, 9°C

Mendocino Brewing Company began life as the Hopland Brewery. The California town of Hopland, a couple of hours north of San Francisco, was one of the early hop-growing regions in the western United States. When Hopland Brewery opened on August 14, 1983, it was one of the first brewpubs in America. In less than a year, the company had to expand because its 400-barrel brewhouse could not keep pace with demand. Today things are a little different. Mendocino still runs the original Hopland brewpub, but most of the company's beer flows from breweries in Ukiah, California, and Saratoga Springs in New York State. The company now distributes to forty-one states.

Hopland went public in 1994 by selling stock to fans through flyers that were stuffed in six-packs. But the brewery hit a tough business patch in 1997, and Vijay Mallya, the Indian billionaire who is chairman of United Breweries Group, Kingfisher Airlines, and Scotland's Whyte and Mackay Distillery, acquired a majority interest in Mendocino. Red Tail Ale is the company's flagship brew, and they also make Blue Heron Pale Ale, Red Tail Lager, Eye of the Hawk Select Ale, and White Hawk Select IPA. The company actively contract brews for other brands and makes India's Kingfisher Premium Lager for sale in the United States.

Black Hawk Stout is one of the company's original brews and was served at Hopland's grand opening in 1983. It was designed to be a traditional, dry, Irish-style stout, using two-row pale ale malt and roasted black caramel malts in the mash with whole-leaf Warrior and Cascade hops in the wort. **RL**

Tasting notes

A thick, creamy, tan head and a rich, roasted aroma open this dark-as-night stout. There are also plenty of coffee and dark chocolate notes. A big, filling brew with a rich mouthfeel and some burned grain notes in the finish. Crisp and refreshing, it goes well with shellfish and roasted meats.

Black Sand Porter

Kona Brewing Company | www.konabrewingco.com

Country of origin United States
First brewed 2002
Alcohol content 6.8% abv
Serving temperature 44°–50°F, 7°–10°C

In action since 1995, this once modest operation was started by father-and-son team Cameron Healy and Spoon Khalsa, and has since grown by an incredible 585 percent, producing 310,000 gallons (12,400 hl) each year. Thanks to an alliance with Widmer Brothers Brewing Company in 2003, the beer is now distributed nationwide through Anheuser-Busch Sales.

As well as Black Sand Porter, there are a host of brews coming out of Kona, and the range is fantastic, with color traveling from blond to black and flavor from tangy through hoppy to roasty. Others worth a quaff include the Longboard Island, a crisp and not-too-hoppy lager, and Fire Rock Pale Ale, which is a medium-to-full-bodied beer.

Black Sand Porter stands out, however, as evidence that climate should not impede innovation or experimentation when it comes to brewing. The beer won a gold medal at the Great American Beer Festival back in 2005. There's a healthy dose of bittering in this brew—the blend of Centennial and Northern Brewer hops delivering a 40 IBU dose to the mix. As with all good porters, though, the balance comes through the malts. While not as easy to track down as some beers, this one is available at Kona Brewing's Kailua-Kona Pub on Hawaii's Big Island and, frankly, is best enjoyed while sitting in the Hawaiian sun. **TS**

Tasting notes
The malt selection is complex with chocolate, Munich, caramel, carapils, and black delivering a rich, sweet flavor. Hops add bitterness and round it off.

Bock Damm

S. A. Damm | www.bockdamm.com

Country of origin Spain
First brewed 1888
Alcohol content 5.4% abv
Serving temperature 43°–46°F, 6°–8°C

After the foundation of its brewery in Barcelona in 1876, Bock Damm was the second beer that S. A. Damm produced. Nearly a century and a half on, having survived civil war, fascist dictatorship, and the complete domination of the Spanish brewing scene by blond lagers, Bock Damm remains one of the most popular dark lagers in Spain. Look at the label and you will see a woodcut-style image of a rearing billy goat, based on the original icon that appeared on the bottle when it was first introduced to the public. This image is a pun on the beer's name (*bock* is German for "billy goat"), although the beer has more in common with a Munich dunkel in its flavor profile and strength.

With Munich malts and German hops going into the mix, this is not a very bitter beer, which has made it a favorite with female drinkers. Once the company realized this in the 1960s, the company dedicated a whole advertising campaign to women.

However, if you fancy another dark beer in this part of the world, then make for Barcelona's brewpub, Cervesera Artesana. This is a comfortable bar, hidden down a side street. There are Belgian beers on tap, but there is also a choice of beers that have been brewed at the back. The star of the show is the Iberian Stout: a gorgeous, roasty, full-bodied creature that is eminently refreshing and complex. **SS**

Tasting notes
On the nose, sweet malt aromas that continue on the palate, where the beer demonstrates a range of toasted malt notes. A gentle bitterness tempers the sweetness of the finish.

Bock Damm's distinctive icon plays on "bock," the German word for "billy goat."

Bock 1888 Damm

Premium Quality Dark Beer

NEGRA MUNICH

Bock-Damm es una Cerveza sing...
...tuado sabor tostado, final suave y...

Bock 1888 Damm

Premium Quality Dark Beer

NEGRA MUNICH

La Negra Bock-Damm es una Cerveza singular que se caracte...
por su acentuado sabor tostado, final suave y discretamente am...

Borefts Stout

Brouwerij De Molen | www.brouwerijdemolen.nl

Country of origin Netherlands
First brewed 2006
Alcohol content 7.2% abv
Serving temperature 50°F, 10°C

When De Molen started in 2004, most of its beers were variations on the standard types found in the Netherlands and Belgium: a few bokbiers, witbiers, abbey beers, and so on. However, since 2008 the brewery has started to move more toward British and U.S.-influenced beers: twenty-two of the current line of approximately forty beers are described as belonging to either the English or U.S. school. Porter and stout alone account for nine.

Perhaps the change of direction in the brewery happened during the spring of 2008, when it brewed De Molen 1914 Triple Stout and De Molen 1914 Porter. These beers were re-created from British stout and porter brewing recipes from 1914. This experience inspired brewmaster Menno Olivier to look at his beers from a completely different angle. One of the first results of this new look at ingredients was Cuvée 1, a cask-conditioned beer that was a hit at the European Beer Festival in the autumn of 2009. The beer was not only served from a cask, but was gravity-poured as well.

Borefts Stout is one of the brewer's first attempts at a stout. As it came before the historic brewing reenactment of the 1914 records, Olivier concentrated more on an attempt to duplicate a modern stout based on currently available ingredients. However, the brewery's newer stouts and porters (Rasputin Russian Imperial Stout, Tsarina Esra Imperial Porter, and Hemel and Aarde), rather than being based on currently fashionable varieties, seem to harken back to what was perhaps a golden age for this type of beer in the United Kingdom. **RP**

Tasting notes

As the name says: a stout. The beer explodes from the bottle in a froth of cappuccino foam. The beer is dark to the point of being completely opaque. The nose is quite bitter, while the palate is intensely bitter—think burned coffee—with some balancing sweetness.

Bourbon County Stout

Goose Island Beer Company | www.gooseisland.com

Country of origin United States
First brewed 1992
Alcohol content 13% abv
Serving temperature 50°–55°F, 10°–13°C

"It was 1992 and we were coming up on our 1,000th batch at the pub," says Goose Island brewmaster Greg Hall. "I had been invited to bring some growlers to a tasting that also included the whiskey legend Booker Noe, and I sat next to him all night. Somehow, I got the idea during our conversation that aging some beer in bourbon barrels might be a fun thing to do." Noe shipped Hall a few recently emptied barrels from his Jim Beam distillery. The resulting beer was almost 29 degrees Plato, a massive wort that fermented "like a freight train," outstripping the glycol system's ability to keep the fermenting beer cool.

After one hundred days in the barrels, the big stout finally emerged, spiked with the lovely vanilla perfume only an old bourbon cask can provide. Despite its appeal, it remained a once-a-year winter specialty for the pub, but was expanded into a packaged product in 2004. Bourbon County Stout became a defining beer for Goose Island and helped spawn a whole new category of bourbon-barrel-aged beers. "Right now, we've got 950 Heaven Hill barrels full of stout, just waiting," says Hall, "and we're sitting on fifty barrels that once held twenty-three-year-old bourbon for something really special."

Bourbon County Stout is a fine dessert beer, either as a pair for something rich and sinful or as a kind of liquid pudding in itself. One writer has rhapsodized about eating dark chocolate–malted milk balls with the beer, and has gone on to write that he could not tell where one left off and the other began. Not many beers can do that. **RM**

Tasting notes

A load of vanilla, caramel, and chocolate on the nose.
Tastes a lot like chocolate ice cream with whiskey sauce.
Substantial middle, but balanced and not overly sweet.
Smooth, bittersweet finish, long and very dessertlike.
Notes based on a three-year-old sample.

Brains Dark

SA Brain & Company | www.sabrain.com

Country of origin Wales
First brewed *ca.* 1920
Alcohol content 4.1% abv
Serving temperature 52°F, 11°C

The decline of mild has been much lamented in British beer circles. This malty style of beer, less bitter than pale ale and generally lower in alcohol, once oiled the wheels of industry. Miners, foundry workers, farmers, and the like made a point of calling into a pub on the way home from work, not just to slake their thirsts but also to enjoy the replenishing nourishment that mild, with its abundant malty sugars, provided.

Mild remained the biggest-selling style of beer in the United Kingdom right up to the late 1950s, but, as heavy industry declined, so did mild. In certain heartlands, it lingered longer and remains popular still. That is certainly the case in south Wales, where a mild brewed in the capital city, Cardiff, continued to be its brewer's most popular beer right up to the 1980s, and is still an important part of the portfolio today.

Brains was founded in 1882 and, although we don't know the exact year it was first brewed, a mild was certainly prominent among the company's earliest offerings. In later years, the mild became known as Red Dragon, mirroring the proud, fiery emblem of Wales, with this abbreviated at one point to RD Dark, and finally, just Dark. With its moody, mahogany appearance and creamy texture, it has become an icon of its home city.

Brewed from pale and chocolate malts, Dark is smooth and rich, belying its modest alcohol level, yet not overly sweet for a mild, thanks to the generous addition of Challenger, Fuggle, and Golding hops. The result is a drink with widespread appeal that goes beyond mild's traditional audience. **JE**

Tasting notes

A deep garnet beer with biscuity malt, chocolate, and a hint of licorice in the aroma. The taste is mostly bitter and dry, but with some welcome sweetness and dark chocolate and roasted grain flavors. Nutty, dry, bitter finish with coffee notes.

Brodie's Prime

Hawkshead Brewery | www.hawksheadbrewery.co.uk

Country of origin England
First brewed 2004
Alcohol content 4.9% abv
Serving temperature 54°F, 12°C

Hawkshead is a village in the Lake District National Park in the county of Cumbria in northwest England. It is just north of Esthwaite Water, which itself is between the larger lakes of Windermere and Coniston Water. Its jumble of car-free alleyways is a living reminder of the village's medieval origins. For three centuries, until 1909, Hawkshead had a grammar school, and the poet William Wordsworth was its most famous former pupil. He described the village in his autobiographical poem "The Prelude."

In 2002, Hawkshead lent its name to a new brewery being built in an old farm building outside the village. Alex Brodie was a journalist, foreign correspondent, and broadcaster familiar to listeners of BBC's Radio 4 and World Service, who reported extensively on Pakistan, Iran, and Israel. Yearning to put political and military strife behind him, he craved the tranquillity of the Lake District—and beer. He bought a house there, enabling him to juggle broadcasting commitments with creating a brewery.

The first beers he brewed, Hawkshead Bitter and Hawkshead Best, rapidly gained a foothold in the pubs of the Lake District, and new beers were developed. The flavors provided by their combination of British and American hops came as a pleasant surprise to the generally conservative drinkers of a region accustomed to more prosaic cask ales. Brodie's Prime isn't an easy brew to categorize: it seems to sit between being a stout, a porter, and a winter ale, while possessing a modern American influence provided by a generous helping of Cascade hops. **JP**

Tasting notes

A generous and inviting aroma of toffee and forest fruits. The palate has roasted malt with abundant fruit and herbal flavors such as red and black currant and sarsaparilla. Malt sweetness is disguised by hop bitterness and dryness. Herby, fruity finish.

Brokát Dark

Pivovar Kaltenecker | www.kaltenecker.sk

Country of origin Slovakia
First brewed 1997
Alcohol content 5% abv
Serving temperature 43°–46°F, 6°–8°C

Despite its past relationship with the Czech Republic, Slovakia's beer culture lags far behind its former partner. However, there has been a perceptible growth in brewpubs and microbreweries in the past few years, although many have also come and gone. At the time of writing, there are eight small breweries and brewpubs trying to compete with nearly a dozen larger outfits, many of which are foreign owned.

Set up by Peter Legnár and Ladislav Kováč in 1997, Kaltenecker is one of the better known survivors and is celebrated for the sense of diversity it brings to its beers. It is a thriving outfit situated on the outskirts of the town of Rožňava, and its beers are popular with tourists from nearby Hungary and farther afield, and with those who want more than just another golden beer. There's also a restaurant, and the idea of food and beer is keenly promoted. Naturally, the brewery produces several variations on the color scheme, but it has also branched out and produced beers flavored with honey, vanilla, ginger, and chili (not at the same time!), as well as an IPA and a Rauchbier. A bit less ambitious but still deviating from the golden norm is Brokát Dark, a dark, rich, bittersweet lager that has more than a touch of dunkel about it.

The small town of Rožňava is popular with tourists who visit for its historic center, and, like most European towns, it is twinned with several others elsewhere on the Continent. Was it deliberate or just coincidence that its Polish twin is Cieszyn, which is home to Bracki Browar Zamkowy? Beer town greets beer town. **ATJ**

Tasting notes

Dark in color, though with tints of chestnut when held up to the light; mocha coffee and malt sweetness on the nose. The palate is rich and roasty (although not overbearing), with chocolate notes coming through. Brokát Dark has a dry finish.

Brother Thelonious

North Coast Brewing | www.northcoastbrewing.com

Country of origin United States
First brewed 2006
Alcohol content 9.3% abv
Serving temperature 55°F, 13°C

Brother Thelonious was not the first Belgian-inspired beer from North Coast Brewing in Fort Bragg, California, but because of its fine label and connection to jazz it has gained international fame. The brewery first released the beer in conjunction with the Thelonious Monk Institute of Jazz, and for every case sold makes a contribution to support jazz education. As a result, it has landed on the menu in many jazz clubs and festivals.

North Coast was looking for a monastic reference when it named the strong dark beer, and tried the sound of Latin-sounding names that monks might have taken, such as Brother Octavius and then Brother Thelonious. The "Monk" connection was obviously too inviting to resist. Sales manager Doug Moody is a serious jazz fan, with his own local radio show, and he quickly put the link with the Monk Institute in place.

When North Coast brewmaster Mark Ruedrich first came up with the recipe for a golden ale called PranQster in the mid-1990s, few other U.S. craft breweries used yeast of Belgian origin. "One of the things that's appealing about the Belgian styles is the freedom. . . . It's expected to be idiosyncratic," he said. That required shedding the fear, shared by many American breweries, of bringing another yeast strain into the brewery. "You've got to be willing to take a long time to get to know its ins and outs," Ruedrich says, talking about what he was seeking. "Flavor and fermentation characteristics. Fruit, pepper, clove. Personality. Independent and interesting, but able to work well as part of a team." **SH**

Tasting notes

Pours a rich, reddish brown with a tall tan head that doesn't linger. A quick blast of alcohol tickles the nose, opening it for aromas of caramelly dark bread. Slightly boozy dark fruits—plums and raisins—dominate on the palate. Contemplative, pairing well with Monk's music.

Broughton Scottish Oatmeal Stout

Broughton Brewery | www.broughtonales.co.uk

Country of origin Scotland
First brewed 1981
Alcohol content 4.2% abv
Serving temperature 57°F, 14°C

Broughton is a small independent brewery situated in the beautiful countryside of the Scottish Borders, south of Edinburgh, between the towns of Biggar and Peebles. It was founded in 1980 and was an early pioneer in the microbrewing revolution that was convulsing the British brewing scene. Three decades later, the company has an array of brands, including eleven bottled beers and half-a-dozen cask ales.

The brewery draws on local history, literature, and legend for the names of its beers: Greenmantle Ale, The Ghillie, Black Douglas, and Exciseman's 80/- celebrate Scotland's heritage and present a cultural backdrop to one of the nation's most historic regions. However, enticing branding is one thing, but it also helps that Broughton's beers have an excellent reputation both at home and in the United States.

The label of Scottish Oatmeal Stout portrays Robert Younger, founder of the renowned Younger's Brewery in Edinburgh, a pioneer in every aspect of brewing and the licensed trade, and great-grandfather of David Younger, one of the two creators of Broughton Brewery. Oatmeal has a long history in Scottish culinary traditions. Being better suited to a short, wet growing season than wheat, it therefore became the staple grain of the country.

Pinhead oats are used in the brewing of Scottish Oatmeal Stout to enhance the flavor and to create a softness in the mouthfeel. Oatmeal Stout's other main ingredients are optic pale ale malt, black malt, and roasted barley, along with English-grown Fuggle, First Gold, and Challenger hops. **AG**

Tasting notes

Black malt and roasted barley give this traditional beer its rich dark color, strong, complex toasted aroma, and distinct flavor through great waves of coffee and dark chocolate. These flavors are offset by a good level of hop bitterness and a silky palate.

Budweiser Budvar Tmavý Ležák

Budweiser Budvar | www.budweiser-budvar.cz

Country of origin Czech Republic
First brewed 2004
Alcohol content 4.7% abv
Serving temperature 46°F, 8°C

In April 2004, the renowned Czech brewer Budweiser Budvar announced that it would add a dark lager to its lineup. At that point, beers from the brewery in České Budějovice only included pale lagers of the pilsner and pale Schankbier styles, as well as Bud Super Strong, a pale bock. The brewery's production is in line with the highly conservative tastes of Czech consumers, who famously consume the largest annual amounts of beer in the world: about 280 imperial pints (160 l) for every Czech man, woman, and child. Of that, more than 98 percent is composed of pale lager, with the average Czech drinker consuming less than five glasses of dark beer in a year.

All of this made the arrival of a new dark lager from the brewery something of a surprise. In fact, Budweiser Budvar made dark lagers at earlier points in its hundred-year history, some of which went by the name "granát," or garnet, a common name for amber and dark beers in Bohemia. As if to hedge its bets, its *tmavý ležák*, or dark lager, was only offered on draft until 2006, when it first appeared in bottles.

Like the brewery's classic pale lager, the dark lager is brewed with water drawn from deep artesian springs and 100 percent Czech hops of the Saaz semi-early red varietal, added in whole cones. In addition to Moravian pale malt, Munich, caramel, and roasted malts are used. Since it was reintroduced, it has become an international favorite, winning awards and picking up a gold medal for best dark beer from the Sdružení přátel piva, the Czech Republic's beer consumers' organization, in 2006. **ER**

Tasting notes

Look for a clear deep amber, almost black, in the glass with a fluffy head of camel-colored foam. The aroma evokes cold coffee, cola, ginger, and spice, with a sugary malt rush in the mouth followed by a semisweet, slightly herbal finish.

Cascade Stout

Cascade Brewery | www.cascadebrewery.com.au

Country of origin Australia
First brewed 1832
Alcohol content 5.6% abv
Serving temperature 41°–50°F, 5°–10°C

Max Burslem started brewing for Cascade in 1969. Now head brewer, he has tasted Cascade Stout almost every day for forty years as part of his quality assurance testing, and swears that the flavor profile has remained the same during this time. Burslem is rightly proud of the fact that Cascade still malts its barley at the brewery, using its own maltster and local Tasmanian produce. The only change to the brewing process has been the introduction of a double mash: the first of pale malt and the second of a mixture of pale malt and roasted barley. Both mashes are combined and local Tasmanian Pride of Ringwood hops are added to bring a bitter finish to proceedings after an extra long boil.

Cascade brewer Tully Hadley considers that the real secret to Cascade Stout is the special Cascade yeast. It gives the beer its smooth, clean flavor rather than the harsher burned notes often seen in lesser stouts. **DD**

Tasting notes
Best consumed in the middle of winter. Presents with a thick brown head over a midnight black body before following through with bold, roasted, chocolate and coffee flavors.

Castle Milk Stout

SABMiller | www.sabmiller.com

Country of origin South Africa
First brewed 1895
Alcohol content 6% abv
Serving temperature 39°–46°F, 4°–8°C

Fans of Castle Milk Stout are unequivocal about its status in the world of beer: they claim that it is one of the best. Brewed for more than one hundred years, it has cult status, and drinkers say the brand is rooted in the traditions of Africa. The use of lactose milk sugars gives it the status of a traditional milk stout, and therefore it has more in common with the light sweetish stouts developed in England at the start of the 20th century.

In South Africa, stout is popular in low-income areas, and Castle Milk Stout has a solid consumer base. Its iconoclastic positioning is reinforced by its tag line, "True Greatness Comes From Within." The tenor of the marketing encourages drinkers to be great men by upholding their African values and to take pride in who they are and where they come from. Castle Milk Stout is the fifth most popular beer in the country. **TH**

Tasting notes
The beer's body is ebony and topped with a sun-bleached color of white foam. The strong malty flavor is tempered by its satisfying sweetness and warming finish.

Celebrator

Brauerei Aying | www.ayinger.de

Černá Hora Granát

Černá Hora | www.pivovarch.cz

Country of origin Germany
First brewed 1982
Alcohol content 6.7% abv
Serving temperature 46°F, 8°C

Country of origin Czech Republic
First brewed 1896
Alcohol content 4.5% abv
Serving temperature 48°F, 9°C

This award-winning doppelbock was first designed for the U.S. market, where it became a favorite of beer enthusiasts before it was discovered and celebrated in its motherland. Celebrator owes its existence to Charles Finkel, a pioneer in the marketing of craft beer. In the 1980s, when the U.S. craft beer revolution was in its early stages, Finkel looked to the Old World for handcrafted specialties to bring to his thirsty compatriots.

Celebrator is characterized by its dark color, roasted, malty flavor, and its relatively high final attenuation, which means that only a little residual sugar is left. Brewmaster Hans-Jürgen Iwan uses caramel, dark, and coffee malts in a three-step decoction, which enhances color and caramelization. He also adds the German Hallertauer Perle hops that provide an aromatic and rounded bitterness. The long maturation contributes to the harmonious complexity of the beer. **SK**

Černá Hora's first written brewing record is dated 1530, but beer production in the town is believed to have begun much earlier. Documents exist that relate how a religious law ceremony was celebrated in July 1298 "with Černá Hora beer." This would have been the product of one of many cottage brewers, but Černá Hora nevertheless uses this date as part of its logo.

Consumers refer to Černá Hora Granát as a "black beer," and, because of its sweeter nature, it is also known as "women's beer." The name is derived from the mysterious red color—resembling the garnet group of minerals—that glows out of its deep dark hue when the beer is held up to the light. No nation makes dark lagers quite like the Czech Republic, and most breweries feature at least one in their portfolios. Black lagers actually predate the more familiar golden ones, which didn't come into existence until the mid-19th century. **AG**

Tasting notes
This beer enchants the nose with dark chocolate and coffee aromas, hints of dried fruit and nuts. Grainy notes, marzipan moments, and velvet roasted flavors flatter the palate.

Tasting notes
Reddish-brown in color with a vigorous head and plummy aroma. A distinct caramel sweetness emerges from its dark maltiness, which also reveals contrasting bitter traces.

Chimay Bleue

Bières de Chimay | www.chimay.com

Country of origin Belgium
First brewed 1948
Alcohol content 9% abv
Serving temperature 55°F, 13°C

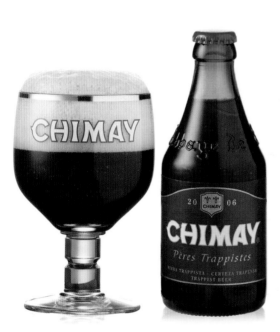

Undoubtedly, some of the best known of Belgium's beers are the products of the country's six Trappist abbey breweries. And unquestionably the most famous of these is Chimay. Officially known as the Abbaye de Notre-Dame de Scourmont, the monastery situated just outside the town of Chimay is, like all the Trappist breweries in Belgium, a picture of bucolic wonder. As per the guidelines laid out for Trappist accreditation, the brewing takes place on the abbey grounds and is officially overseen by the monks, although lay workers operate the brewery and off-site bottling facility.

For those who find it odd that monks produce beer, a little history lesson is in order. Since the Middle Ages and possibly earlier, monasteries have been centers of brewing, providing citizens with nutritious ales that were often far safer than the local drinking water because any contaminants would have been removed during the boiling process. The Trappist edict dictates that the monks are prohibited from accepting charity and must therefore participate in commerce in order to both survive and fund any charitable works.

Blue is the strongest and maltiest of Chimay's four different ales, all of which, apart from one (the Dorée, a lower strength beer, mainly found at the brewery tap down the road from the abbey), are widely sold around the world. As well as coming in a blue-capped bottle, the Blue is also available in cork-finished form, as Grande Réserve. This is the prince of the Chimay range, a beer that improves with age—in fact, some argue that it is best left for five years before drinking. **SB**

Tasting notes

Although some have argued that this beer has lost body through recent years, it still offers fine, spicy aromatics, ample chocolaty and faintly peppery malt, and suitable richness of character. A generously warming finish completes the picture. As it ages, it gets drier and stronger.

Chocarrubica

Birrificio Grado Plato | www.gradoplato.it

Country of origin Italy
First brewed 2007
Alcohol content 7% abv
Serving temperature 54°–57°F, 12°–14°C

The founder of Birrificio Grado Plato, Sergio Ormea, only started home-brewing in 1994, but such was his enthusiasm and the high quality of his beers that he made the next step in 2003 and opened his brewpub in the town of Chieri, not far from Turin. If Chieri has a good gastronomic reputation for its snails, then Grado Plato's beers are famous for their variety, as well as the skill and spirit of discovery of the brewer and his penchant for working with local ingredients. Among his beers, Ormea has some made with the addition of local honey or chestnuts.

His most unique beer, however, is Chocarrubica. Ormea was often tempted to make a chocolate stout, but he had his moment of inspiration one night while watching a documentary about the Allied landings in Sicily during World War II. The sight of American soldiers throwing chocolate bars to the Sicilian children, whose only sweets until then had been carobs, stuck in his mind. This image gave birth to Chocarrubica, a meeting between the "new" chocolate and the "old" carobs.

The beer also has a large proportion of oats (30 percent) in the mash, which Ormea hopes to locally source in the near future, plus Maris Otter barley and black and chocolate malts. English East Kent Golding hops go into the kettle for aroma, while Slovenian Premiant is used for bitterness. During the boil, cacao beans are added first, followed by the carobs. The beer gets a secondary fermentation in the bottle for ten days, with a final fortnight for maturation before going out into the world. **MM**

Tasting notes

A beautiful mahogany color, topped by a creamy, abundant, and persistent foam. On the nose, the carob is distinctive, sweet, and intense, with notes of toffee and cacao. Surprisingly fresh at the start on the palate, lightly astringent, with a return of the fruity and toffee notes.

Clotworthy Dobbin

Whitewater Brewery | www.whitewaterbrewery.co.uk

Country of origin Northern Ireland
First brewed 1996
Alcohol content 5% abv
Serving temperature 50°F, 10°C

Had you been strolling down Royal Avenue, Belfast, in 1820, you would doubtless have been captivated by the malty aromas coming from the premises of Mr. Clotworthy Dobbin, master brewer. Dobbin later his brewery to Smithfield Square and there he took on his most famous apprentice, Thomas Caffrey, who later became heir to the brewery. While Caffrey's legend lives on in the name of a different beer, Dobbin sank into the mists of history.

Until 1996, that is, when the Whitewater Brewery in County Down was looking for a name to lend gravitas to its finest ale. Who better than Belfast's original brewing maestro to conjure up the sense of time-honored brewing quality? Ironically, when Thomas Caffrey's ultimate successor (InBev) closed its Belfast brewery in 2005, Whitewater became Northern Ireland's largest beer maker, with Clotworthy Dobbin at the forefront of Ulster's native ales once more.

Although we know little of what was produced at the brewery, it is almost certain that porter would have been a major part of it. Clotworthy Dobbin is a ruby red version of this classic 19th-century style. It's made from a cocktail of malts, including crystal, for that typical Irish sweetness; chocolate, for a lush and warming character; plus a pinch of black, for a dryness that keeps the drinker coming back for more. The hops are mostly traditional U.K. varieties, and a dose of U.S. Cascade is added at the end to give a citrusy punch. Unsurprisingly, the awards for Clotworthy Dobbin have been pouring in, including a place in the world's top fifty beers in the International Beer Challenge 2007. **JD**

Tasting notes

The unique combination of malt and hops creates a chocolate-coated raisin character. Heavy and filling, yet light enough to demand a second bottle, Clotworthy Dobbin works as a session beer, but also pairs well with strong cheeses and tart fruit pies.

Coopers Best Extra Stout

Coopers Brewery | www.coopers.com.au

Country of origin Australia
First brewed 1862
Alcohol content 6.3% abv
Serving temperature 39°F, 4°C

Stout has been popular in Australia since the 19th century, and, notwithstanding the early adoption of lager in the colonies, most of the Australian breweries from that period have continued to offer at least one credible stout. Coopers Best Extra Stout is among the richest and darkest of the stouts that have survived since those colonial days. The beer has continued to be developed over the subsequent five generations of Coopers and it is now a world-class example of the style. Extra stout it is, weighing in at an impressive 6.3 percent, and ideal slow drinking in cold Adelaide winters.

Although the popularity of stouts in Australia has been generally on the decline since the 1960s, Coopers Best Extra Stout has grown in stature over the past twenty years, as awareness of the Coopers brand has increased throughout Australia and abroad. In a move comparable to selling lager to the residents of Pilsen, Coopers commenced exporting Best Extra Stout directly to Dublin for distribution in Ireland in 2007. By contrast, the introduction of Guinness into the South Australian market forty years earlier resulted in an increase in the sales of Best Extra Stout, because the locals went out of their way to let their preferences be known.

Coopers Best Extra Stout is bottle fermented, which means that, in accordance with Coopers's tradition, you should consider whether you wish to roll or tip the bottle to distribute the yeast evenly before pouring. South Australian residents are known to serve this beer with oxtails or beef shin braised with Best Extra Stout and thyme. **DD**

Tasting notes

Expect roasted-malt darkness of this beer, which pours with a thick light brown head. Careful consideration of aromas may reward with coffee, smoked wood, and licorice. A velvety mouthfeel is followed by hints of chocolate and a bitter finish.

Cusqueña Malta

Backus and Johnston | www.cusquena.com.pe

Country of origin Peru
First brewed 1911
Alcohol content 5.6% abv
Serving temperature 36°F, 2°C

In the Peruvian Andes, the production of beer has been in evidence for more than 1,000 years. Recently, archaeologists discovered an ancient brewery dating from the Wari Empire, where large vats held a fermented corn drink, known as "chicha." As with much of Latin America, Peru's modern brewing methods can be traced back to the arrival of German nationals in the mid-19th century. The Cervesur brewery opened a factory in the city of Cuzco in 1911, the site where Cusqueña Malta was first produced.

Cusqueña is brewed with natural ingredients, including 100 percent malt, Saaz hops, and glacial melt water from the Andes. The dark version, Cusqueña Malta, has the same brewing process as a lager, undergoing bottom fermentation, but then imported ingredients such as coffee and candy malts are added to give a richer and more complex flavor than the pils version. **SG**

Tasting notes
Expect a dark brown body with thin beige head and a nose of malt sweetness. The rich flavor of bitter chocolate and coffee culminates in a sweet finish. Excellent with oysters.

Cutthroat Porter

Odell Brewing Company | www.odellbrewing.com

Country of origin United States
First brewed 1993
Alcohol content 4.8% abv
Serving temperature 50°F, 10°C

In 1993, U.S. beer writer Jim Parker approached Doug Odell, of the Fort Collins brewery, and asked him to create an exclusive beer for his Mountain Tap Tavern in Fort Collins, Colorado. Parker came up with "Cutthroat Porter," named after Colorado's official state fish. Parker explained what he wanted the beer to taste like, but he left the actual recipe to the brewers at Odell.

They started with basic two-row pale malt and added some crystal and chocolate malts along with a touch of roasted barley. Inspired by the classic London porters, they looked to the United Kingdom for hops, too, using Fuggle and East Kent Golding. Despite the English hops, the beer is 43 IBUs, pushing the upper limit for bittering in a British-style porter. It's also drier than the average porter. When Odell Brewing added a bottling line in 1997, Cutthroat Porter was among the first beers it packaged. **JB**

Tasting notes
Inky black with a rich tan head. Malty sweet on the nose, with rich coffee and dark chocolate aromas. Velvety smooth mouthfeel, and the finish is dry and smoky.

CUTTHROAT®

PORTER

ODELL BREWING CO.

D. Carnegie & Co. Porter

Carlsberg Sverige | www.carlsberg.se

Country of origin Sweden
First brewed 1836
Alcohol content 5.5% abv
Serving temperature 50°–55°F, 10°–13°C

When it comes to Baltic porters, this sucker takes some beating; indeed, it is a perfect example of type. With its firm heritage, Carnegie Porter has been making its way out from Scandinavia for more than 150 years. Given the complex relationship the Swedish state has had with alcoholic drinks over that time, though, this porter has seen a reduction in its typically high alcohol content.

The Baltic porter stylebook dictates that this beer should have a roasty flavor and complementary color, and it doesn't disappoint, with the color being near opaque black and the taste well hopped and heavily malted. The nose is equally complex, as the brewer achieves an almost licorice quality to the scent, not to mention plenty of almost chocolate richness. The color and style will naturally urge some beer fans to compare this beer with Guinness and there *are* Celtic links with the beer. Indeed, the brewery's original founder David Carnegie Jr. came to Gothenburg from Montrose in Scotland, and at age twenty-three he purchased a porter brewery and sugar mill. By 1836, he had Carnegie Porter up and running, and it is now listed as one of Sweden's oldest registered trademarks, currently under the guardianship of Carlsberg.

This drink is a very different proposition from Guinness. It's true that the long roasting process and the slightly burned edge to it ensure that there are similar qualities, but porter as a style is much sweeter, and Carnegie's subtle caramel and chocolate elements add depth. Don't rush this one though; the beer will only get better with age, and the brewing team here recommend anything up to ten years of maturing. **TS**

Tasting notes

The color of Carnegie Porter is a glorious pitch black, and the complexity of flavor sees roast and sweet malt up front, backed by a stunning acidic bitterness; this all provides a beer that matches perfectly with a smoked meat or earthy cheese.

Dark Force

HaandBryggeriet | www.haandbryggeriet.net

Country of origin Norway
First brewed 2006
Alcohol content 9% abv
Serving temperature 50°–59°F, 10°–15°C

The Norwegian market is a hostile environment for craft breweries because the sale of beer is controlled by a government monopoly, taxation of drink is punitive, and any kind of marketing activity is, at best, frowned upon. Therefore, if you're in the business of handcrafting quality ale, then you may as well do it properly and give the drinker lots of bangs for the wallet-load of bucks he will have to shell out.

On the surface, Dark Force is a stout: the black, roasty, malt-driven beer familiar to drinkers the world over. HaandBryggeriet has taken this basic model, walked around it, kicked the tires, and then set about embellishing it royally. First of all, the alcohol content is ramped up to 9 percent, enhancing the flavors and making it a beer to stop and take time over. No suspect fermentables were added to make the beer stronger—no sugar or syrups—it's all malt, but instead of the usual barley, the brewery has opted for wheat. In combination with a specially chosen wheat beer yeast, this imparts a soft fruitiness to the flavor and a distinct spiciness of the kind you get with Germany's dark Weissbiers; a solid dose of roasted grains adds that dry coffeelike taste that makes stout so popular.

And then there's the hops. Pounds and pounds of bittering, flavoring, and aroma hops are thrown in and really make their presence felt, adding yet a further dimension to an already complex beer. A green bitterness hits the nose right before the fruity wheat, and a tasty citrusy kick remains on the lips long after the beer is swallowed. When opening a Dark Force, forget everything you thought you knew about stout. **JD**

Tasting notes

A real flavor roller coaster, Dark Force runs the gamut from bitter hops through mellow roasted coffee, licorice, and dark sweet fruits. Working best as a fireside sipper, it also pairs with hot chocolate puddings and strong blue cheese. Anything port can do, this can do better.

Dark Horizon

Nøgne Ø A/S | www.nogne-o.com

Country of origin Norway
First brewed 2007
Alcohol content 16% abv
Serving temperature 61°–64°F, 16°–18°C

Inspired by a Mephistopheles Stout by Avery Brewing, brewer Kjetil Jikiun sat down with the idea to produce a dessert beer that could be enjoyed like a fine port or Madeira, with a long and lingering aftertaste. As the Nogne Ø brewery was moving into new, larger premises, Jikiun had more room to brew and extra fermenters that weren't earmarked for anything.

Dark Horizon is produced using a double fermentation process. First an extra-strong and dark stout is brewed with ordinary ale yeast. Then several tons of brown sugar are added with homemade coffee extract and wine yeast to take the alcohol content higher. In Norway, most beer is pale, pasteurized, and filtered, so Dark Horizon certainly wasn't the most commercial choice with regard to the domestic market. However, with more than 70 percent of Nogne Ø's production going for export, the less sophisticated Norwegian market wasn't such a concern. And Dark Horizon found a ready market in the United States where strong, hopped beers have their spiritual home.

It can be argued that Dark Horizon is a global brew: it has inspiration from the American Midwest, malt from England, bottles from Germany, its name from Japan, sugars from Mauritius, hops from the Pacific rim, yeast from Canada, and coffee from Colombia, and it is brewed in Grimstad, Norway. Dark Horizon bottles come individually wrapped in tissue paper inside a metal sleeve, showcasing the contemporary style that has won Nøgne Ø acclaim for its use of design in its home country. **AA**

Tasting notes

Dark Horizon pours gloriously black with a slight purple tinge. A notable coffee and raisin aroma rises from the dark brown head, but on tasting, it turns into a velvety chocolate dessert, with lingering coffee and licorice and balanced bitterness.

Dark Island

Orkney Brewery | www.orkneybrewery.co.uk

Country of origin Scotland
First brewed 1988
Alcohol content 4.6% abv
Serving temperature 50°F, 10°C

Former pub landlord Roger White set up Orkney Brewery in 1988 with equipment sourced from England, Wales, and France, and Dark Island soon emerged as its flagship brew. Orkney merged with Atlas Brewery in 2004 and took the name Highland and Islands Breweries; two years later, it was taken over by Sinclair Breweries.

Dark Island has twice been awarded Champion Beer of Scotland. According to head brewer Andrew Fulton, "Dark Island is a very tricky beer to categorize. Some regard it as a dark mild; however, I have never really been comfortable with that label. In essence it is a traditional Scottish heavy with a larger dose of chocolate malt than is normal for that style. The heavy style of beers were always reddish colored and malt-led in character, traditionally using crystal malt and black malt, which gave a slight sweet caramel hint to the beers. Dark Island's malt profile has always been led by chocolate malt, which gives it a depth and complexity of character not found in other traditional heavy beers. I think it is the combination of being different to, but also reminiscent of, traditional Scottish beers that has given the beer its enduring appeal."

The brewery started life in the old schoolhouse in Quoyloo, near the fabled Skara Brae, the incredibly well-preserved stone village with its intricate maze of dwellings whose stone beds, lintels, and cupboards remain intact from Neolithic times. The Dark Island label depicts the mysterious Ring of Brodgar that is generally assumed to have been erected between 2500 and 2000 B.C.E. **AG**

Tasting notes

Dark Island is a very dark beer with a deep ruby tint and a tight, off-white head. The aroma weaves around bitter chocolate and dried fruits with hints of roasted malt, coffee, and toffee, before a medley of roast malt flavors and more fruit on the palate.

Dark Lord

Three Floyds | www.3Floyds.com

Country of origin United States
First brewed 2002
Alcohol content 13% abv
Serving temperature 55°F, 13°C

The Dark Lord exists mainly by reputation. His power is rumored, his character praised with cultlike obsession, yet he is rarely seen. Until, that is, Dark Lord Day, a holiday ritual for the devoted who flock from around the world to Three Floyds Brewing in Munster, Indiana, for his annual appearance. Held on the last Saturday of April, it is a day of raucous celebration, with music and a tasting of other rare beers. Lucky attendees clutch onto golden tickets allowing them to purchase a maximum of four precious bottles. And then, by the end of the day, Dark Lord is gone, reverently cellared by his minions to be savored in coming months and years. Or, perhaps, dispatched to eBay, where a single 22-ounce (650-ml) bottle will sell for a hundred dollars.

Dark Lord is brewed with a senseless amount of malt and barley, with Indian sugar, molasses, vanilla beans, and hundreds of pounds of espresso beans from a local coffee roaster. Some is aged in oak casks to enhance its character. It ferments and conditions for months, slowly building its power. At an average of 13 percent alcohol content, this is a Russian imperial stout from the Cold War days, when the world shook as the premier pounded his shoe.

Each annual vintage, coded with a different colored wax seal, is charted and compared in copious notes. It is among the perennial top two or three beers at ratebeer.com, ranking with the likes of the less rare Trappist ale from Belgium's Westvleteren abbey. Beer drinkers bow in its presence. Yet, the iconoclastic brewers at Three Floyds regard it without awe: "We make it; we drink it. That's all." **DR**

Tasting notes

Dark and foreboding with the aroma of sweet, boozy dried fruits. A tentative sip fills the mouth with an explosion of roasted malt flavors: coffee, burned toast, raisin, and chocolate. Its strong alcohol is somewhat tempered by vanilla, light honey, and a surprisingly tart finish.

Deep Water Dopplebock Lager

Thomas Creek Brewery | www.thomascreekbeer.com

Country of origin United States
First brewed 1999
Alcohol content 7% abv
Serving temperature 44°F, 7°C

Tom Davis created Deep Water Dopplebock in 1984 as a home-brewer and worked on perfecting the recipe before he brewed the dark lager commercially in 1999. However, it was not until the summer of 2007, when South Carolina legalized higher gravity beers—popping the cap on the 6.25 percent limit that had been in place—that the Thomas Creek Brewery could adjust the recipe and brew a true dopplebock.

Six different malts, including Bonlander Munich malt, are used in Deep Water Dopplebock. On the days when the beer is made, the brewery is filled with delectable chocolate and roasted malt aromas. The beer has quickly gained acclaim as one of the best examples of its style and won a silver medal at the 2008 Great American Beer Festival.

Thomas Creek Brewery is part of an emerging contingent of craft brewers in Palmetto State. Until very recently, the beer market in South Carolina was dominated by pale lagers and light beer. Tom Davis and his father Bill joined the microbrewery movement when they took over a disused brewpub in downtown Greenville. After using Bill's architectural skills to add a second brewhouse, the first batch of Thomas Creek beer was released to the public in July 1998. They also operate a full-service home-brew shop at the location.

Thomas Creek makes six year-round brews, including amber ale, IPA, pilsner, porter, red ale, and the dopplebock, plus four seasonals. The Davis team turns out specialty brews and test batches from a ten-barrel system and uses a sixty-barrel system as the company's production brewery. **RL**

Tasting notes

This beer pours with a creamy tan head that laces the glass. It is a traditional dopplebock mahogany color that glows around the edges. A sweet malt aroma leads to a rich roasty flavor with hints of cocoa and coffee and a substantial malty background.

Devonshire 10'der'

Country Life Brewery | www.countrylifebrewery.com

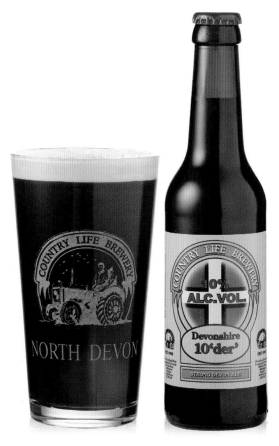

Country of origin England
First brewed 2006
Alcohol content 10% abv
Serving temperature 46°–54°F, 8°–12°C

When Simon Lacey left the army in 1997 he went straight to the pub—the Pig on the Hill, owned by his in-laws in a small village close to the north Devon port of Bideford, England. As well as serving behind the bar, he set up Country Life Brewery, which in the beginning was based at the back of the pub. "In the early days," Lacey recalls, "the pub was ideal to test the beers out on people, and it was great to see their reactions."

By the summer of 2002, Lacey moved the brewery to the nearby Big Sheep, a theme park devoted to all things ovine; he also bought a new brewing plant. Even though Lacey's bread-and-butter beers include Old Appledore, an amber session ale, and a golden ale called "Pot Wallop" (named after an annual event in the village of Appledore), the sense of experimentation that existed in the early days of the brewery still runs like a river through Devonshire 10'Der,' a barleywine/old ale hybrid that is brewed once or twice a year. "We made it because we wanted an 'extreme' beer," says Lacey, who is himself noted for his own enthusiasm for extreme sports, "and we also wanted it to be 10 percent in alcohol content. We had tried to do this before but only managed to hit 8.5 percent, so after some research we put everything in place and got to 10 percent." Challenger and the U.S.-grown Willamette are used as hops, and the beer is mainly bottled, where it continues to condition; however, a few casks are also filled. This is a beer that certainly wears its Devon heritage with pride "because we come from Devon and are proud of it, the name reflects the county and its strength." **ATJ**

Tasting notes

Chestnut brown in color. Sweet, alcoholic, fruitcake nose. Well-rounded, voluptuous hybrid of barleywine and old ale, with fruitcake and fiery alcoholic notes on the palate, tempered with a malty smoothness. Finish has an alcoholic warmth and hop tingle.

Dogbolter Dark Lager

Matilda Bay Brewing Company | www.matildabay.com.au

Country of origin Australia
First brewed 1987
Alcohol content 5.2% abv
Serving temperature 39°–46°F, 4°–8°C

Matilda Bay Brewing is recognized as Australia's first microbrewery of the modern era. Australia had been through almost a century of bland, cold lager when Phil Sexton and others challenged its sense of what beer can be with a range of tasty brews in 1984. The original owners sold their interests to Carlton and United Breweries in 1990, and to its credit, Australia's largest brewer has continued to treat Matilda Bay as a craft branch with as much creative independence as can be expected in the circumstances.

However, every beer whose brewer moves on faces the risk that its nature will drift over time as the scale of production changes, costs are reduced, and focus is shifted. To many of the older fans of Dogbolter, this seemed to be exactly what happened to their beloved dark lager. It was just not as rich and rewarding as it once was. No doubt in many cases complaints like this are just the lament of those who consider a craft beer lost as soon as it is acquired by a serious brewery. But in the case of Dogbolter, there seemed to be some substance to the concerns.

Brad Rogers, then head brewer of Matilda Bay, was having none of it. He tracked down the original brewers and spoke to them about Dogbolter's initial flavor profile and their approach to brewing. He then tweaked his own ingredients and processes, including making use of no less than six barley and wheat malts, in an attempt to restore Dogbolter's reputation. The current version is one of the more seductive and rewarding dark lagers available. It is hard to imagine the original being any better. **DD**

Tasting notes

Although Dogbolter should be stored in the refrigerator, those in the know suggest letting this beer warm up for a while after admiring its thick head and dark ruby tinge. This will let the sweet roasted malt flavors come through along with hints of chocolate and a long, gentle finish.

Dogfish Head World Wide Stout

Dogfish Head | www.dogfish.com

Country of origin United States
First brewed 1999
Alcohol content 18% abv
Serving temperature 55°F, 13°C

Some day we'll tell our grandchildren about the high-octane beer wars of the early 21st century, about the combat between extreme beers that used high-tech yeast strains to convert fermentable sugar into ever-increasing levels of synapse-loosening alcohol. Some day we'll tell them—assuming our capacity for long-term memory was not among the casualties.

Herewith is one of the weapons of mass destruction: a black beer with five times the alcohol content of the world's most popular stout. Sounding not unlike Edward Teller before the first hydrogen bomb, Dogfish Head founder Sam Calagione says, "Our goal was to brew the world's strongest beer. And we succeeded . . . for one month." World Wide Stout was quickly surpassed by Sam Adams Millennium. Even when Dogfish Head managed briefly to notch its alcohol to 23 percent in 2002, Boston Beer roared back with Utopias, which is now at 27 percent .

WWS's distinction from these powerhouses, however, is that it actually resembles beer, with the body, aroma, and basic flavor of an imperial stout. As the brewery brags, the base of this stout is "a ridiculous amount of barley." But it is Dogfish Head's proprietary yeast strain that does the heavy lifting. Typical ale yeast peters out as it reaches double-digit strength, literally poisoned by the very alcohol it creates. How does the brewery do it? "All I can say is we have a quality-control team that is constantly analyzing under a microscope to maintain the best environment for alcohol-tolerant yeast," says Calagione. Mad scientists at work. Teller would be proud. **DR**

Tasting notes

World Wide Stout pours black with a hint of ruby and little foam. Dried fruit and a waft of warming alcohol bursts from the glass. Roasted malt, some licorice, and booze-soaked raisins in the palate. Portlike with a tart, warming, porterlike finish.

Dorothy Goodbody's Wholesome Stout

Wye Valley Brewery | www.wyevalleybrewery.co.uk

Country of origin England
First brewed 1989
Alcohol content 4.6% abv
Serving temperature 54°F, 12°C

When former Guinness brewer Peter Amor set up his own brewery in 1985, there was only one beer that he really wanted to brew. He'd loved the traditionally brewed Guinness of the 1960s, and took it as his inspiration. Dorothy Goodbody's Stout is brewed with pale malt and roasted barley for a rich, dark hue, and flaked barley for a full and creamy head, finished off with a generous dose of Northdown hops to add a resiny dryness to the taste. It has been widely hailed as a classic example of a simple stout.

So why not Amor's Stout or Wye Valley Stout? Peter felt these names might be a little boring, so he did what any self-respecting brewer would do: grabbed a few friends, went out for a few beers, and thought about it. Later that evening, Dorothy Goodbody was born. No one can really remember who it was that conceived her. On bottle labels, Dorothy evokes a wholesome, timeless glamor. She looks like the kind of woman who could work in the Herefordshire fields harvesting barley, have a couple of beers afterward, then shower and change to become the belle of the ball.

No mere illustration either, she comes with a backstory of being a hop grower's daughter who developed an interest in brewing when she began courting a head brewer. The range of bottled beers that bears her name was intended to include only seasonal beers inspired by a range of "quintessentially English ales" brewed by Dorothy herself. Her Wholesome Stout was always the most famous of these, and, after it was named Champion Winter Beer of Britain in 2002, it has been brewed all year around. **PB**

Tasting notes

Wholesome Stout pours almost black with a feisty, boisterous beige head. Mocha and toffee with a hint of licorice on the nose followed by a dry-roast, burned chocolate maltiness and a surprising clean, dry finish that leaves a hint of hoppy buzz.

Dragon Stout

Desnoes & Geddes | www.jamaicadrinks.com

Country of origin Jamaica
First brewed 1961
Alcohol content 7.5% abv
Serving temperature 55°F, 13°C

Eugene Peter Desnoes and Thomas Hargreaves Geddes first shook hands while working at the West Indies Mineral and Table Water Company in Kingston, Jamaica. The friends became partners in 1918 when they set up a soft drink plant, rapidly establishing Desnoes and Geddes as a producer of quality sodas and distributor of imported liquor.

Within a decade, the pair had opened the Surrey Brewery with a vision to produce a Jamaican beer that would make a mark on the world stage—a feat they accomplished with Red Stripe. Peter S. Desnoes, son of the company founder, became chairman in 1952, overseeing the building of a modern facility in Hunts Bay and a period of intense expansion. It was during these boom years that Dragon Stout emerged, a beer with links to the island's colonial past just as Jamaica freed itself from British rule. Brewed using a mixture of black malt, corn syrup, caramel malt, and hop extract, the beer is primed with sugar before bottling to satisfy those with a palate predisposed for all things sweet—a sweetness that can often disguise the strength of the drink.

In 1970, D and G offered 8 percent of its shares to the public to fund further growth and ventures with other brewers, including an agreement to produce the U.K. stout brand Mackeson on the island. By 1993, it had sold a 51 percent holding stake in the company to Guinness (now Diageo). With the backing of the Guinness Group—no stranger to marketing stouts internationally—Dragon Stout has gained a wider audience, as drinkers are seduced by its dark, creamy, and sweet charms. **SG**

Tasting notes

In the glass, this beer appears a very dark brown with a slight red tinge and thin beige head. The aroma of molasses instantly hits the nose, and the palate is overwhelmed with a sweet, dark chocolate and caramel flavor. It goes surprisingly well with a good chocolate ice cream.

Dragonstooth Stout

Elysian Brewing | www.elysianbrewing.com

Country of origin United States
First brewed 1996
Alcohol content 7.2% abv
Serving temperature 44°–55°F, 7°–13°C

With a name like Elysian, one might anticipate that the brewery's wares would carry Greek mythological names. Indeed, this Seattle-based brewery's lineup of beers includes names such as Zephyrus Pilsner and Perseus Porter. Dragonstooth Stout is also named from Greek mythology, but in a less obvious way, perhaps. This imperial stout is named for the founders of the Greek city Thebes. The myth says that the Phoenician prince Cadmus destroyed a dragon and sowed its teeth in the ground. From the teeth sprang a race of fierce, armed men, five of whom assisted Cadmus in building Thebes, and thus became the founding fathers of the city.

"Dragonstooth was a carryover from a strong oatmeal stout I used to brew at a previous job," says head brewer of Elysian Brewing Dick Cantwell. "As soon as it ran out, people wanted it back. So, when we started Elysian, our newer version became part of the permanent lineup." This version of Dragonstooth was Elysian's second brew, after the Wise ESB, but it wasn't as fierce as the one that stands today. "About two years after Dragonstooth Stout was first released, our lead brewer took it as a personal challenge to make an imperial-weight version of the beer," Cantwell says. "The only real change to create the current imperial stout was to add more pale malt and a commensurate amount of bittering hops to maintain the balance in the beer while creating a richer version at the same time."

Organic rolled oats make up 10 percent of the grain bill, along with roasted barley and chocolate malt. Dragonstooth is bittered with Magnum hops and finished with Cascade and Centennial. **LMo**

Tasting notes

The balance between the malts and the rolled oats makes Dragonstooth a strong stout of rare richness, but the beer also exhibits a surprising amount of hop character. Allowing it to warm up after refrigeration gives this dragon an even more beguiling personality.

Drayman's Porter

Berkshire Brewing Company
www.berkshirebrewingcompany.com

Country of origin United States
First brewed 1995
Alcohol content 6.2% abv
Serving temperature 50°F, 10°C

The label for Drayman's Porter features an old-fashioned, horse-drawn beer delivery wagon, and, as is the case for all the labels of Berkshire Brewing's beers, vows that what is inside the bottle is fresh and local. Since founding their brewery in 1994, Gary Bogoff and Chris Lall have put that promise first, delivering unfiltered, unpasteurized beer to a growing market centered on their Western Massachusetts base.

The partners built much of the brewery themselves, and they started brewing with secondhand equipment. They were still bottling by hand until they got to the stage of producing 10,000 barrels annually. Unlike most breweries, Berkshire handles the distribution of almost all of its beers from its own warehouses, selling most within 100 miles (160 km) of its brewery. **SH**

Tasting notes
Rich aromas, flavors, and mouthfeel—sweet chocolate and caramel malt throughout, offset early by roasty/toasty coffeelike character and later on by an earthy hop bitterness.

Dreher Bak

Dreher
www.dreher.hu

Country of origin Hungary
First brewed 1997
Alcohol content 7.3% abv
Serving temperature 50°–54°F, 10°–12°C

Anton Dreher was renowned as one of the great forward thinkers of the modern brewing industry. In 1840, while working in Vienna, he pioneered the use of large cold maturation cellars for his new malty, amber-colored, clear beer—Vienna Lager. Dreher's achievement was the competitive spur for the people in the town of Pilsen to hire his protégé Josef Groll, who produced a style of beer that is now drunk all over the world, carrying the town's name.

Much later, South African Breweries acquired the rights to use the historic Dreher name, and, in 1997, Dreher Classic and Bak were born. *Bak* is the Hungarian word for "bock," although the beer has hints of a strong dunkel about it. Given its strength, it is especially welcome on a cold day in Budapest. **TH**

Tasting notes
Rich and full-bodied dark beer poured beneath a large creamy head. On the nose, sweetish aromatic notes of malt and caramel with a delicate scent of hops in the background.

The Duck-Rabbit
Baltic Porter

Duck-Rabbit Craft Brewery
www.duckrabbitbrewery.com

Country of origin United States
First brewed 2006
Alcohol content 9% abv
Serving temperature 50°F, 10°C

There's nothing like a dark, high-alcohol porter to take the chill off a bleak, wintry night. Yet Farmville, North Carolina, is home to this classic Baltic porter.

Swimming against the mainstream is how this three-man brewery has quickly earned a reputation as a southern gem. The brewery unapologetically makes only dark beer. "I aim all for delicious," says brewery owner Paul Philippon. "I'm not saying I always hit it on the mark, but I don't brew anything I don't love." Despite his individualistic approach, Philippon is a fairly conventional brewer, focusing only on traditional styles. Velvety smooth with no acrid bitterness, Duck-Rabbit Baltic Porter is clean, well-rounded and complex. It is a rich, contemplative ale that seems fit for a chilly night beside a roaring fireplace. **DR**

Tasting notes
Tantalizing traces of berries and cocoa mingle with the warmth of alcohol. Despite its forbidding roasted-malt heft, the body is exceptionally smooth and easy on the palate.

The Duck-Rabbit
Milk Stout

Duck-Rabbit Craft Brewery
www.duckrabbitbrewery.com

Country of origin United States
First brewed 2004
Alcohol content 5.7% abv
Serving temperature 44°F, 7°C

The Duck-Rabbit Craft Brewery released its first beer in 2004. The brewery bills itself as "dark beer specialists," and its beer lineup pays off that claim. When founder Paul Philippon launched the company, he felt darker brews were underrepresented in the southeast part of the United States, and he set out to produce a range that now includes a brown ale, Baltic porter, wee heavy scotch ale, and other styles.

Duck-Rabbit Milk Stout is brewed with lactose, which helps to balance the weight of the roasted grains. Philippon did not know what to expect when the product was launched, but consumer acceptance of the new beer was fairly rapid, and the dark brew has been Duck-Rabbit's top-selling beer every month since it was introduced. **RL**

Tasting notes
Pours a deep, dark brown with a tan head. The aroma is roasted malt with a hint of cocoa. Silky mouthfeel with semisweet milk chocolate elements and a roasted coffee base.

Dunkler Weizenbock

Brauerei Michael Plank | www.brauerei-plank.de

Country of origin Germany
First brewed 2001
Alcohol content 7.8% abv
Serving temperature 46°–50°F, 8°–10°C

When Maria Plank, brewpub landlady and head of the Plank brewing family, celebrated her fiftieth year, a big party took place in the small village of Laaber near Regensburg. Brauerei Plank invited many guests to their tavern and it was for this occasion in 2001 that Maria's son, Michael Plank, created the Dunkler Weizenbock. Or to be more precise he re-created and improved a recipe from a beer that his brewery had offered until the 1980s, before it was abandoned owing to a lack of demand.

The new creation not only won over the party guests but it is also adored by beer enthusiasts worldwide. It was awarded a gold medal at the World Beer Cup in 2004. This balanced beer is refreshing and complex at the same time. To achieve this balance of flavors, Plank works with open fermentation vessels and then stores the beer for about four days in unbunged tanks before bottling. The subsequent bottle fermentation at warm temperatures lasts another week followed by storage in a cooling house for another two to three weeks, all of which contributes to the complexity of the beer.

The Dunkler Weizenbock is exported mainly to the United States, but it can also be found in Austria, China, and Australia. For his home market, Plank only brews two batches a year to ensure that it remains rare and precious. As a strong beer, the Weizenbock can lay in the cellar for years and develop an even more complex character. According to Michael Plank, such vintage editions are available in gourmet restaurants in the United States. **SK**

Tasting notes

Light brown with orange tints and slightly hazy; beige head. This beer offers a citrus aroma with roasted notes and hints of spicy clove. The palate is spicy-sweet with a sour bite evolving into roasted, coffeelike flavors. A mild finish with an alcoholic kick.

Echigo 90 Days Stout

Echigo Beer | www.echigo-beer.jp

Country of origin Japan
First brewed 2005
Alcohol content 7% abv
Serving temperature 54°F, 12°C

Echigo Stout was one of the original beers brewed at Echigo's brewpub, which opened in early 1995. The first beers were craft beer classics, generally in the U.S. style, and often of high gravity. Fortunately, Echigo continues to brew these original beers, such as Amber Ale, Pale Ale, Weizen, and Stout, at this same location.

Founder Seiichiro Uehara relates that his original image for the brewpub was that of an abbey brewery. Nestled on the side of a hill, the white building gives the impression of a cathedral, but inside the feeling is bright and spacious, owing to the great number of windows, white walls, and the extensive use of light-colored wood. After opening, the Echigo brewpub was a popular destination for beer enthusiasts, primarily for its unique nature, but also because there weren't any other brewpubs in operation at the time. Recently the Echigo brewpub has become a bit quieter, opening only on weekends and for personal parties.

Echigo Stout has gradually grown in popularity. Earlier in this decade, a decision was made to produce the stout in Echigo's larger brewery. Since the batch size is some twenty times greater than that at the brewpub, the recipe had to be altered to produce it efficiently on the larger equipment. The original recipe calls for some wheat malt, which Echigo has found does not ferment in a particularly stable manner, so quantities had to be adjusted. This process took time, but in 2005 the new version of stout, named 90 Days Stout after its nominal aging period, was finally offered for sale. The stout is bittered with Northern Brewer hops, and Hersbrucker hops are used for aroma. **BH**

Tasting notes

Very deep reddish brown, it sports a loose tan head. There is a faint dark-toffee aroma, with a tangy nutty flavor and dark caramel notes that linger long into the finish. There are practically no deep-roasted flavors, so it is more like a porter in style.

Eclipse Imperial Stout

FiftyFifty Brewing | www.fiftyfiftybrewing.com

Country of origin United States
First brewed 2008
Alcohol content 9.5% abv
Serving temperature 55°F, 13°C

Todd Ashman wasn't the first brewer to put beer in bourbon barrels, but he was a driving force in establishing barrel-aged beers as a separate category in the world of beer. When he was at Flossmoor Station Brewing in Illinois, his beers that had been aged in bourbon barrels won Great American Beer Festival medals in 1998 and 1999 as "experimental" beers, before they were considered a style of their own. His Eclipse Imperial Stout at FiftyFifty Brewing is a direct descendant of those creations.

"It's amazing how many people have begun using barrels. It's a minute percentage of your business, but you garner a lot of attention with those barrels," he says. Ashman was looking for a style that would stand up to the intense flavors left in a bourbon barrel, and he began experimenting with barrels in Flossmoor, a suburban Chicago brewpub. He'd heard about Goose Island's Bourbon County Stout but hadn't been able to taste the beer. "Stout provides a backdrop. It's very intense, very resilient. You can add all these things, flavor and character, and that resiliency remains," he says. Of course, he didn't stop there. Old Conundrum Barley Wine, also aged in bourbon barrels, was his 1999 experimental medal-winning beer.

The recipe for the Eclipse Imperial is as complex as the beer that ends up in the glass. Ashman used fourteen malts in brewing the 2009 batch, as well as mesquite honey, Indian palm sugar, and brown rice syrup solids. Some of the first batch he brewed in 2008 was kept out of the barrel-aging process—this also won a medal at the Great American Beer Festival. **SH**

Tasting notes

Eclipse Imperial Stout pours black with a tan head. Bourbon and oaky vanilla notes are apparent on the nose, balanced by a rush of aromas and flavors: dark chocolate and dark fruits, coffee and toffee, molasses and licorice ... the list is long.

A Bonda tribesman harvests the kind of sugar palm sap used in Eclipse Imperial Stout. ➡

Eel River Organic Porter

Eel River Brewing | www.eelriverbrewing.com

Country of origin United States
First brewed 1995
Alcohol content 5.8% abv
Serving temperature 50°F, 10°C

Eel River Organic Porter started its life as Ravensbrau Porter and wasn't originally an organic beer. But the year after it was first brewed, in 1996, it was certified organic after changes to the ingredients were made. Four years later, Eel River also stopped using the Ravensbrau brand.

Ted Vivatson, the founder of Eel River Brewing, now brews only organic beers in a 100 percent bio-mass-powered brewing facility that he opened in 2008. And that's only the half of it. The new building itself, where the brewery is located, is also recycled, having formerly been a Redwood lumber mill in Scotia, a town in northern California. In fact, Eel River was the first brewery in the United States to be certified organic. They use no animal by-products either, making their beers not just organic, but also vegan. Their tagline says it all: "Be natural, drink naked!"

The porter uses five varieties of organic malted barley, including caramel and chocolate malt. Vivatson believes that these "compliment and highlight one another in a harmonious mixture." Two hop varieties are then added to the boil. The first is Hallertau, a German variety. The other is Pacific Gem, an organic hop developed in New Zealand at the Oldham family farm, which grows only organic hops.

Eel River Organic Porter has won twenty awards during the last decade, including ten gold medals at competitions both large and small, from the California State Fair to the Great American Beer Festival. *DRAFT Magazine* also recently included it in its list of the "Top Twenty-Five Beers in the World." **JB**

Tasting notes

Deepest mahogany in color, with a solid buff head, Eel River Organic Porter has a milk chocolate nose with a touch of caramel and espresso. The mouthfeel is very creamy with flavors of cocoa and roasted coffee with underlying nutty notes. The finish is smooth and velvety.

Eisenbahn Dunkel

Sudbrack Brewery | www.eisenbahn.com.br

Country of origin Brazil
First brewed 2002
Alcohol content 4.8% abv
Serving temperature 37°–41°F, 3°–5°C

Nuremberg 2007. The European Beer Star Awards. Fifty-four expert judges sample 575 beers from twenty-eight different countries. Prestigious breweries with long traditions enter their "star beers." The competition is fierce, and there is simply no room for anything other than outstanding quality. In the dunkel category, Eisenbahn Dunkel wins the bronze medal, the first South American beer to earn such a prestigious award —an honor it shared with Eisenbahn Weizenbock, which won bronze in the category of the same name. This recognition has placed Eisenbahn on the map in the world of brewing, and considering the brewery only started brewing in 2002, this really is a remarkable feat.

Dunkel (meaning "dark" in German) is a beer style that originated in the Munich area. The traditional practice used a complex method of triple decoction, and Munich malts gave dunkels their distinctive dark color. Eisenbahn Dunkel uses a blend of five malts and is a superb version of this style. Like all Eisenbahn beer, Dunkel follows the traditional 1516 Bavarian Purity laws, which forbid any other ingredients in beer other than water, grains, hops, and yeast.

The Eisenbahn brewery is in the southern interior city of Blumenau, Brazil's most German city. The many German immigrants in the region have left their mark on the architecture, food, music, and, most importantly, beer. Blumenau now boasts the largest Oktoberfest outside Germany, attracting huge crowds to enjoy everything that you would expect to find at the German event, including truly excellent beers such as Eisenbahn Dunkel. **AH**

Tasting notes

Rich and complex, the beer is dark and the aroma is toasted malt. The roasted and chocolate malts come through more strongly on the palate and give a coffee flavor. Goes well with sausages, cheese, mushrooms, and ham, as well as chocolate desserts.

El Toro Negro Oatmeal Stout

El Toro Brewing Company | www.eltorobrewing.com

Country of origin United States
First brewed 1996
Alcohol content 5.5% abv
Serving temperature 55°F, 13°C

In the spring of 1994, Geno and Cindy Acevedo built the El Toro Brewing Company, a small seventeen-barrel system, on their land in the rural residential area of Morgan Hill, California, in Santa Clara County. The county is better known as Silicon Valley, and Morgan Hill is south of San Jose, the nearest major city. The brewery takes its name from El Toro, a small mountain that casts its shadow over the entire town, and its silhouette is used on the city's official logo. Due to El Toro's unique combination of volcanic and seismic activity, it's also the only place in the world one can find the semiprecious stone Poppy Jasper. In fact, El Toro's first beer was Poppy Jasper Amber.

In 2006, the Acevedos opened a brewpub in downtown Morgan Hill. In a former bank, complete with a private room inside the vault, it's a two-story building with the Poppy Jasper bar. It also features a three-barrel brewery where they brew more than twenty-five different beers. Their Negro Oatmeal Stout was the 181st batch of beer. Brewmaster Geno Acevedo's inspiration was the oatmeal stout being made at the time by other local brewers, such as Anderson Valley and Seabright breweries. With oats making up nearly a third of the mash, they provide a unique smoothness and a touch of sweetness.

The use of oats in beer originated during medieval times but died out by the 1700s. It was reintroduced at the end of the 19th century in restorative beers, inspired by the popularity of porridge, before retreating again until the late 1970s. Samuel Smith brewed the first modern oatmeal stout in 1979. **JB**

Tasting notes

As black as night with a very thick, dense tan head. The nose is milk chocolate with espresso aromas. The flavors are oats, strong roasted coffee, and a touch of tobacco, with a creamy mouthfeel and a very long, bitter finish. Try it with roast poultry, smoked meats, veal, and chocolate desserts.

Enigma

The Twisted Hop | www.thetwistedhop.co.nz

Country of origin New Zealand
First brewed 2007
Alcohol content 10.5% abv
Serving temperature 54°–59°F, 12°–15°C

The Twisted Hop brewpub was the brainchild of two expatriate Englishmen, Martin Bennett and Stephen Hardman. Having arrived with their families on separate flights in February 2003, the two were blissfully unaware that they shared the same dream of bringing English-style ales to New Zealand. After combining forces, the pair decided to build a real ale brewpub and seawrched for a suitable building. Their timing was impeccable; Christchurch city council was developing an old part of the city and transforming it into a retail and hospitality hub. The area, known as the Lichfield Lanes, reminded Martin and Stephen of parts of London, and they bought one of the old warehouses. They then set about installing the brewery and bar, while carefully preserving the beams, columns, and bare bricks of the original structure.

Despite the building's history, The Twisted Hop is the antithesis of a typical English pub. Although set in a quiet back street and with a pleasant curbside drinking area, The Hop is bright, airy, and modern, with large glass windows to the rear of the bar looking into the brewery beyond. Since opening for business in August 2004, it has made a name for itself as one of New Zealand's leading beer destinations.

Enigma is an English-style barleywine that is aged in wine casks. The oak casks contribute hints of vanilla and a tannic dryness to what is a deeply complex and satisfying sipping beer. Initially christened "Epiphany," the beer's name was later changed when it was found that another New Zealand brewpub, Galbraith's of Auckland, already had a beer of the same name. **GG**

Tasting notes

Copper colored beneath a tan head. The aroma has notes of toffee, banana, and coffee. Smooth and warming, the palate combines resiny hops with chewy malt, sappy oak, vanilla, and a hint of smoke. Finishes with a deep, lingering bitterness. Perilously drinkable!

Erdinger Dunkel

Privatbrauerei Erdinger Weissbräu | www.erdinger.de

Country of origin Germany
First brewed *ca.* 1890s
Alcohol content 5.6% abv
Serving temperature 41°–54°F, 5°–12°C

Erdinger Weissbräu, as it is less formally known, was established in the town of Erding, to the northeast of Munich, in 1886. With its current annual output of 40 million gallons (1.5 million hl), it is considered the largest Weissbier brewery in the world. However, it did not start brewing Weissbier until the 1890s, and it was not until 1935 that it came into the hands of the Brombach family who currently own it. In fact, the brewery did not even receive its current name until 1949. In 1965, when the son of Franz Brombach (who purchased the brewery in 1935) took over operations, the brewery was delivering 1 million gallons (40,000 hl) of beer per year. In only thirteen years, he managed to increase production by a factor of more than five.

In the early 1960s, Weissbier had only a very small share of the Bavarian beer market. It was still made in a traditional style, but, by the late 1960s, the "new" Champagnelike Kristall style was taking hold. It only took a few more years before the style changed yet again—this time back to the cloudy form that had been the mainstay of the small Weissbier market in the early 1960s. Today, the traditional style holds sway, and its market share in Bavaria has climbed to 25 percent.

Erdinger Dunkel is one of the long-term survivors of the brewery: a light, appetizing beer that undergoes a secondary fermentation in bottle (as do most of the brewery's range). Even though the brewery only makes Weissbier, there are ten variations on a theme, including a festival beer and several seasonals. Aficionados of the beer make for the center of town to enjoy the full range at the brewery's tap. **RP**

Tasting notes

Dark tan/chestnut brown in color. The nose has soft notes of darkish, lightly roasted malt plus an undercurrent of fruitiness. On the palate, it is mild tasting, with the light chocolate/coffee flavors of the roasted malts acting in concert with the soft, fruit, wheat notes. Refreshing.

Erdinger Pikantus

Privatbrauerei Erdinger Weissbräu | www.erdinger.de

Country of origin Germany
First brewed 1968
Alcohol content 7.3% abv
Serving temperature 46°F, 8°C

If we speak about Weissbier, Erdinger is the global leader of this brewing specialty. Founded in 1886, the production was just 66,043 gallons (250,000 l) when the current owners, the Brombach family, acquired it during the 1930s. By 2007, the production had more than tripled. The best seller is Erdinger Weissbier.

However, beyond the Weissbier, perhaps the most exceptional beer of the brewery is Pikantus, a 7 percent weizenbock that enthralls beer lovers throughout the whole year, even though it is a style that is normally associated with the beers originally produced by monks for the springtime Lenten period. It is believed that the first commercially produced weizenbock was brewed in 1907, at Kelheim near Regensburg. It took another sixty years or so before Erdinger decided it was time to add one to its portfolio. It is intriguing that it chose this time to bring out this beer, because Weissbiers of all sorts were considered to be in decline then; they were wrongly or rightly associated with the older generation, and pale pilsners were the cooler and more fashionable choice. However, Weissbier made a remarkably strong comeback (mirroring the rediscovery of Belgian witbier), especially with the young, so Erdinger showed great foresight to produce this beer (or was just lucky).

Pikantus is a pleasure throughout the year, but for a truly historic drinking experience, the best time to contemplate a glass is during and after Lent. Thanks to its strength, Pikantus matures well in the bottle, becoming mellower and even more delectable. Those monks were on to something good! **WO**

Tasting notes

Dark amber in color. The use of high-quality wheat and barley in the grist produces a full-bodied and spicy beer; it has a pleasant and enjoyable finish with a light bitterness of hop coming through. Erdinger Pikantus is a smooth and delicious weizenbock.

Espresso

Dark Star | www.darkstarbrewing.co.uk

Country of origin England
First brewed 2000
Alcohol content 4.2% abv
Serving temperature 44°F, 7°C

Brighton, which is about 50 miles (80 km) south of London, has long been seen as the city's seaside suburb: convenient for day trips or long weekends but not too far from the metropolis. It is an energetic, buzzy town for people who enjoy the finer things in life, beer included. Four hundred pubs cater for a permanent population of 156,000 and countless thousands more visitors every year. Rail passengers from London to Brighton embark at Victoria Station, many ready for a beer. Once in Brighton, a beer temple is conveniently located just around the corner on Surrey Street—the Evening Star, the spiritual home of Dark Star beers. There are two sister pubs elsewhere in Sussex: the Stand Up Inn at Lindfield and the Duke of Wellington at Shoreham.

Rob Jones created the original Dark Star beer (named for a song by the Grateful Dead) for Pitfield Brewery, and it went on to win Champion Beer of Britain in 1987. Jones later joined forces with pub owners Peter Halliday and Peter Skinner, and in 1994, the beer name became a brewery name.

Espresso was originally a regular stout driven by nitrogen, occupying the role normally reserved for Guinness; but in 2000, this stout became a coffee beer. The coffee is provided by Brighton's Red Roaster Coffee House, and 15 pounds (7 kg) are added late in the brew. The beer's dryness and abundant coffee flavor lend it to pairing with almost any food combining chocolate and sweetness. In fact, Dark Star Espresso allows after-dinner coffee to be served alongside pudding to great effect. **JP**

Tasting notes

A big coffee aroma accompanies a fast-diminishing, pale brown head with lacing. The flavor is dry, bitter, and roasted—like munching on coffee beans with a hint of chocolate. There is little evidence of hop character and no concession to sweetness.

Exmoor Beast

Exmoor Ales | www.exmoorales.co.uk

Country of origin England
First brewed 1992
Alcohol content 6.6% abv
Serving temperature 54°F, 12°C

Exmoor National Park is one of the most glorious places in southwest England. It's a landscape of deep wooded valleys and high windswept moors where the heather blazes imperial purple in the autumn. It is also a place where, in the 1970s, tales were swapped in isolated pubs about the Exmoor beast, a wild cat that supposedly roamed the moors and dined out on the local sheep. The authorities were so sure that there was something out there that a detachment of Royal Marine snipers were sent out to try and catch it.

Nothing was found, but in 1992, Exmoor Ales, a small brewery in Wiveliscombe, on the edge of the national park, produced this popular rich porter that was mischievously named after the mysterious big cat. "The idea of a strong porter was conceived by our then–marketing manager Jim Laker," says Peter Turner, the brewery's managing director at the time. "We joked about having the abv of 6.66 percent on the pump clip, but, being god-fearing and curiously superstitious, decided against it."

At first, the beer was only produced from October to April, until demand made it into a year-round brand. Brewed with pale ale, chocolate, and crystal malts, and hopped with Golding, Challenger, and Brewers Gold, this is a beer to be sipped slowly on a winter's night while the weather does its worst (and maybe the beast is abroad). It can be served slightly chilled in warmer weather or as a beer drinker's version of an Irish coffee (try it with Stilton cheese). It is also used as an ingredient in Exmoor Beast fruitcake with whiskey icing, which is made by a local baker. **ATJ**

Tasting notes

On the nose, espresso coffee beans, currants, raisins, cocoa, and a fiery hint of brandy or rum. More fruitcake, alcohol, coffee beans, and chocolate follow through on the palate. All are nicely kept in line with a spicy hoppiness, before the complex, long aftertaste.

Farsons Lacto

Simonds Farsons Cisk
www.farsons.com

Country of origin Malta
First brewed 1946
Alcohol content 3.8% abv
Serving temperature 55°F, 13°C

Today it is hard to imagine a beer being advertised as "perfect for invalids," but things were different in the late 1940s, when Lacto was launched in Malta. Simonds Farsons drew heavily on its English heritage, and it is no surprise that it decided to brew a style of beer that was popular in Britain. Beer is often described as liquid bread, and milk stouts, which have added unfermentable sugars known as lactose or milk sugar, acquired a reputation for being a nutritional food supplement and a source of calories.

The style had been brewed in Britain from the start of the 20th century, and many people drank milk stouts as an addition to their meager diets. Beers can no longer be sold as nutritional pick-me-ups—but Farsons still produces Lacto in very small quantities. It can be found in bars in Malta, although the health claims have long since been dropped from the label. **TH**

Tasting notes
Deep black brew, topped by an espresso-colored head. Smooth and full of blackcurrant and dark chocolate notes. Caramel sweetness gives way to a slight tartness. The finish is dry.

Fat Dog Stout

Stoudt's Brewing Company
www.stoudtsbeer.com

Country of origin United States
First brewed 1998
Alcohol content 9% abv
Serving temperature 50°F, 10°C

With a name like Stoudt, you'd guess this family-owned brewery would specialize in, well, stout. Guess again. "We always wanted to do just German beers," says Carol Stoudt, who is one of very few female brewers. The thriving business—which also includes a restaurant, antique market, bakery, and innovative Bavarian-style "village"—is deep in the heart of Pennsylvania Dutch country. And when the Stoudts welcome visitors, it's with liters of helles lager, amber-hued bock, and copper-colored Festbier.

Pennsylvania is primarily a draft beer market, and the Stoudts soon faced pressure to brew an ale. Eventually they gave in and bottled a Belgian-style abbey ale, a very English-like extra-special bitter, and, at last, a stout. Rich and luscious with its sizable addition of oatmeal, Fat Dog Stout numbs the noggin with a massive load of alcohol. **DR**

Tasting notes
Rich malt aroma with solid chocolate notes. Some light-roasted bitterness with a touch of fruit is evident. Finishes smoothly, its potent alcohol well hidden in its creamy body.

Feast Of Fools

Magic Hat Brewing Company
www.magichat.net

Country of origin United States
First brewed 2002
Alcohol content 5.3% abv
Serving temperature 50°F, 10°C

Magic Hat Brewery is an oddball U.S. original, whose self-titled founder is the "Conductor of Cosmic Symphonies." The brewers hide nonsensical sayings beneath bottle caps ("Make your move to improve your groove"), and the marketing department takes their outstanding beers and gives them psychedelic names.

Feast of Fools is the name of Magic Hat's annual winter variety pack, an enjoyable way to sample the madness. But savvy fans of the brewery know that Feast of Fools is also the name of its exceptionally rare annual holiday stout. The dark, sensuous ale is made with two pounds of raspberries for every gallon of beer. It is packaged in jet-black, corked, and foil-wrapped champagne bottles, which the brewery makes available only to a limited number of friends and family. But anyone can enjoy a growler to go. All it takes is a trip to the brewery's tasting room. **DR**

Tasting notes
As black and forbidding as the elixir in a witch's cauldron. Surprisingly light bodied, a full sip is tart with a mild, lingering sweetness followed by a bitter bite of chocolate.

Flekovský Tmavý Ležák 13°

Pivovar U Fleků
www.ufleku.cz

Country of origin Czech Republic
First brewed 1499
Alcohol content 4.6% abv
Serving temperature 44°F, 7°C

Grand, gothic, dark, and intimate—there is no pub in the Czech capital quite like U Fleků. Its records date back only as far as the purchase of the building, in 1499, although archaeological evidence suggests that beers might have been produced here as early as 1360. In 1762, the tavern was acquired by Jakub Flekovské and his family, who later named it U Fleků, or "At the Fleks."

Its lengthy history has made the pub a favorite with beer lovers, especially after it converted from the earlier top-fermented yeast to bottom-fermented lager brewing, starting in the late 19th century. With an original gravity of 13 degrees Plato, this beer ranks as a "speciál" in Czech brewing terms. Brewed from four types of malt using a traditional decoction mash, the beer is very rich and creamy. In its heyday, the pub was frequented by Jaroslav Hašek, the author of *The Good Soldier Švejk*. **ER**

Tasting notes
Pitch black with glinting amber notes, topped by a whipped-cream crown of thick foam. Chocolate and sugary malt in the mouth that is followed by a lightly bitter Saaz-hop finish.

Forst Sixtus

Forst | www.forst.it

Country of origin Italy
First brewed 1901
Alcohol content 6.5% abv
Serving temperature 46°F, 8°C

Forst was founded in 1857 and still remains one of the few Italian independent brewing companies. The founding Fuchs family remains in charge, which means that a high standard is maintained across the entire production process. Forst is located in the Alto Adige region, quite close to the Austrian border, and the style of its beers definitely looks to the German brewing tradition of bottom-fermenting beers. Seven regular brands, including a very attractive pils, plus two seasonals, complete the brewery's portfolio.

Sixtus was brewed for the first time more than a century ago to celebrate the birth of Hans Fuchs. It was originally dedicated to Saint Sixtus, to whom Fuchs's mother was particularly devoted. After many years, the name of the beer was shortened to just Sixtus, but the recipe is still the same, with only the alcohol percentage being lowered from 8 to 6.5 percent.

Sixtus is a bock-style beer, made with different malts. The main malt in the grist is Munich, and the hop variety is Northern Brewer, which is grown in the Hallertau region; the water comes from a spring hidden high in the mountains. Fermentation lasts about seven days and is then followed by a maturation period of two weeks to refine the flavors and aromas. The ultimate maturation is very long: three months at a low temperature. Then the beer is filtered.

Sixtus is the strongest beer produced by Forst, and it marries well with matured cheese, some pasta dishes, and even chocolate dessert. It is also a kind of winter warmer, best sampled in one of the beautiful pubs owned by the brewery in the Alto Adige region. **MM**

Tasting notes

Brilliant mahogany color with amber reflections. Thick and persistent foam. The aroma is rich in notes of caramel, toasted malt, red fruits, and hints of chestnut honey. On the palate, this beer has a rounded body full of malty notes, but there is also a spicy and toasted undercurrent.

Founders Breakfast Stout

Founders Brewing Co. | www.foundersbrewing.com

Country of origin United States
First brewed 2001
Alcohol content 8.3% abv
Serving temperature 44°F, 7°C

Most college students dream of what it would be like to run their own brewery. Mike Stevens and Dave Engbers actually did it, and Founders Brewing was born in 1997. It took a year of hard work to renovate the vacant and rundown Wolverine Brass Works building in Grand Rapids, Michigan. As with any project of this size, it was hit with delays and unexpected turns. Once Founders Brewing started churning out beer, the pair soon discovered that, although the beer they were making was good, it was fairly unremarkable. Sales were sluggish. The venture floundered in near-bankruptcy before Stevens and Engbers decided to follow their instincts and brew beer they were passionate about.

Bigger and fuller bodied beers started to flow from Founders, and beer fans began to discover the small brewery. Experimentation with spices, coffee, chocolate, fruits, vegetables, honey, and other ingredients followed, and Founders Breakfast Stout was born out of this wanderlust in 2001. The beer is brewed with flaked oats, bitter and imported chocolates, plus Sumatra and Kona coffee. At 8.3% alcohol content, this is not a beer to start off your morning with! Instead, it is the perfect drink for the end of an evening or even to go along with a rich piece of chocolate cake at the climax of a meal.

Thanks to this fortuitous change in the kind of beers it brews, the future of Founders is fairly secure. A new brewery was built in 2007 about a mile from the original location to fuel a growing expansion of the brand across the Midwest. **RL**

Tasting notes

If you like coffee, you can skip Starbucks and go straight to this beer. Dark black color with a tan head and plenty of roasted aromas. Wonderful stout flavor notes surrounded by espresso and cocoa with a finish that lingers for quite some time.

Fuller's London Porter

Fuller Smith & Turner | www.fullers.co.uk

Country of origin England
First brewed 1996
Alcohol content 5.4% abv
Serving temperature 50°–55°F, 10°–13°C

"When a man is tired of London, he is tired of life." In the past few decades, the much-repeated maxim of the 18th-century wit Doctor Johnson has applied to a variety of London brewers, such as Truman, Watney, Worthington, and, more recently, Young's, who have all shut up shop. However, Fuller's still occupies a pristine position by the River Thames, and is owned and managed by the same families who have been in place for more than 150 years. There is continuity in the site as well. The Griffin brewery has been around in one shape or another for well over 300 years. London Pride is the brewery's flagship beer and its best seller, but under both its previous head brewer, Reg Drury, and current incumbent, the irrepressible John Keeling (who took over in 1999), a variety of stunning beers has emerged.

London Porter was first brewed on Drury's watch, a revised recipe that looked back to the early part of the 20th century when the brewery produced a similar beer. According to Keeling, who worked with Drury, "We had released 1845 to coincide with the 150th anniversary of the Fuller Smith and Turner partnership, and it had been a real success. We needed another beer to follow on from this, and so we looked back again into our past. London is the spiritual home of porters, and we are a London brewery." The judicious use of brown malt and crystal helps to give the beer its roasted coffee notes, whereas the Fuggle hop helps to balance any over-tendency to malty sweetness. The result is an elegant and luxuriant beer that is wonderful in bottle and on draft. **ATJ**

Tasting notes

Dark as midnight, although crimson tints appear if held to the light. A soft and smooth nose of creamy toffee. The palate sees the luxuriant toffee character joined by roasty notes, before yielding to a smooth, dry, and long finish, which also has a hint of vanilla.

Fuller's: a brewery with more than 150 years of family history. ➡

FULLER, SMITH & TURNER'S

NOURISHING STOUT

IN SMALL BOTTLES

Griffin Brewery, 4½ᴰ Chiswick.

General Washington's Tavern Porter

Yards Brewing | www.yardsbrewing.com

Country of origin United States
First brewed 2003
Alcohol content 7% abv
Serving temperature 46°F, 8°C

One of the most popular tourist destinations in Philadelphia is the City Tavern, a modern re-creation of the colonial tavern where the Founding Fathers raised their tankards and plotted revolution. Just a short stroll from Independence Hall, the tavern's walls seemingly echo the toasts that surely accompanied the signing of the Declaration of Independence.

However, what did the gentlemen drink on such a heady occasion? Almost certainly, the porter of Robert Hare, America's first professionally educated brewer. Trained at Burton-on-Trent, his dark ale would eventually rival even the original porters of England. The British troops who occupied Philadelphia, and, later, Hare's brewery itself, were said to have favored it over the porters of London. There are reports of shipments leaving Philadelphia and making it to Calcutta without spoilage.

Today, the City Tavern serves this authentic, colonial-style porter, brewed by Philadelphia's Yards Brewing. Located just steps away from the site of Hare's long-gone shop, Yards makes an entire line of so-called "Ales of the Revolution." Thomas Jefferson's Tavern Ale is based on an old Mount Vernon recipe. Poor Richard's Tavern Spruce Ale follows Benjamin Franklin's directions for making beer with spruce instead of hops. This porter is based on an old recipe found in George Washington's letters. Not surprisingly, many raw goods were hard to come by in the years after the Revolution. So, like those early porters, this one contains molasses to sweeten the beer. It's the product of good old American ingenuity. **DR**

Tasting notes

Garnet hued with the aroma of roasted malt and chocolate. Its light body carries sweet molasses and malt flavors with a touch of dried fruit. Though a bit strong for a porter, a tankard empties quickly thanks to its mild, palate-cleansing bitterness.

Ghisa

Birrificio Lambrate | www.birrificiolambrate.com

Country of origin Italy
First brewed 1998
Alcohol content 5% abv
Serving temperature 50°F, 10°C

Birrificio Lambrate is one of the pioneers of the Italian brewpubs and microbrewery scene, but it is hard to pin down as it is both a community local as well as a brewery distributing its beer all over Italy and beyond. Despite this, it remains very much Italian despite the obvious, but rather superficial German influences.

Tucked away on a side street in Lambrate, a working-class suburb east of Milan's city center and once the cradle of the mythical Lambretta scooters, the pub itself is a rather cramped affair with dark wood panels, very much Bavarian in style. It has just the right amount of Italian chic, however; the brewery's logo is more akin to a sports car badge than to a beer brand. No big shiny coppers are prominently displayed in the middle of the room either. The brewery itself is in another part of the building, along a passage leading to a courtyard. The beer range reflects the feel of the place, as the obvious German influence on most of the range, where one can spot a Weizen, a Kölsch, and an Altbier, quickly subsides as one notices beers showing Belgian, British, and American influences, too.

The name Ghisa comes from the early 20th century nickname for Milan's traffic wardens. What looks at first glance like a Rauchbier turns out to be a top-fermented stout brewed with birch-smoked Bavarian malt. When it first appeared in 1998 it was a little bit stronger and a lot smokier than it is today, but it remains all the same a rather unexpected thing to find in Italy, and more than enough of an excuse to leave trendy downtown Milan behind and seek out Birrificio Lambrate on a journey of beer discovery. **LM**

Tasting notes

A smooth, roasty, chocolaty, jet black stout with a pale beige head and a clearcut birch smoke edge. Some meaty, almost salty, soy saucelike notes lurk in the malty depths and make Ghisa a winner with both oily fish and scamorza affumicata (a smoked Italian cow's milk cheese).

Gonzo Imperial Porter

Flying Dog Brewery | www.flyingdogales.com

Country of origin United States
First brewed 2005
Alcohol content 7.8% abv
Serving temperature 55°F, 13°C

After author Hunter S. Thompson committed suicide in 2005, the Flying Dog Brewery chose to honor his memory the best way they knew how—by making a limited edition beer. The first batch of Gonzo Imperial Porter, named with a nod to Thompson's "gonzo" style of journalism, was 9 percent abv. It proved popular enough for Flying Dog to make it a regular release (although they did drop its strength to 7.8 percent). Ralph Steadman, who illustrated much of Thompson's work and began creating Flying Dog artwork in 1995, drew the label with a skeletal portrait of Thompson and a voice bubble saying, "OK, let's party!"

Flying Dog's relationship with Thompson went back to the days when the brewery was founded in Aspen, Colorado, the same town in which Thompson lived. The brewery's "gonzo" link was further cemented in 1995, when Steadman drew his first label for them, for Road Dog Porter. The Colorado Liquor Enforcement Division rejected the label because it included the words "Good Beer, No Shit." The American Civil Liberties Union challenged the rejection as an unconstitutional restriction of Flying Dog's right to free speech, and after years of legal battles, the brewery was finally allowed to use the wording in 2001.

Flying Dog moved from Aspen to Denver in 2004, then closed its Denver brewery in 2008 after buying another one in Frederick, Maryland. Its corporate headquarters remain in Denver and its links to Thompson and Steadman stay strong. That wouldn't matter if the beer were just a gimmick, but in 2008, it earned a gold medal in the World Beer Cup. **SH**

Tasting notes

Pours black with a thick tan head, leaving abundant lacing. Smells of roasted coffee beans, dark fruits, and piney hops. Complex on the tongue, with smooth, chocolate, and caramel notes added to the mix. Lingering coffee and hops leave a final bittersweet impression.

Gouden Carolus Christmas

Brouwerij Het Anker | www.hetanker.be

Country of origin Belgium
First brewed 2002
Alcohol content 10.5% abv
Serving temperature 50°–57°F, 10°–14°C

Few long-established family breweries have such an eventful history as Het Anker, the oldest brewer still left in the town of Mechelen. Until 1990, it was firmly in the hands of the Van Breedam family, but hard times struck, and first the ill-fated RIVA emporium and then the John Martin business became involved. Fortunately, Charles Leclef, the last owner and heir of the Van Breedam family, decided to go solo again and steered the old family brewery toward a better future.

History might be a heavy burden, but it has also been a salvation, especially with the name "Gouden Carolus," which has proved very commercially viable. The brewery decided to back this successful horse, rebaptizing the essential Gouden Carolus beer a classic, and broadening or renaming the rest of the portfolio to variations upon a theme.

In 2002, after a thirty-eight-year break, it brewed a Christmas special, which started life as "Gouden Carolus Noël," and was soon anglicized to "Christmas." Brewed in August, this beer is lagered for several months and is ready for sale toward the turn of the year. With a hefty alcohol content of 10.5 percent and flavored with six different spices, this beer lends itself perfectly to aging (just like the brewery's equally weighty Cuvée van de Keizer beers). A further sense of the preciousness of this beer comes from the use of three different kinds of Belgian-grown hops.

Lovers of this beer—and there are many—find themselves in good company: Gouden Carolus Christmas has managed to win several distinctions, including in the prestigious World Beer Cup. **JPa**

Tasting notes

Dark, deep color with an obvious red shine. It has a nose of Madeira, raisins, roasted malts, and molasses. The taste shows fruity, estery, and spicy hints, ending in a long aftertaste with fruity and spritzy acids balancing the heavy malt load and alcohol warmth.

Gouden Carolus Classic

Brouwerij Het Anker | www.hetanker.be

Country of origin Belgium
First brewed *ca.* 1930s
Alcohol content 8.5% abv
Serving temperature 44°–50°F, 7°–10°C

The Anker brewery in the Belgian city of Mechelen has origins dating back more than 600 years. The Van Breedam family took over back in 1873 and is still in charge today (with Charles Leclef at the helm); this was despite flirtations with bigger breweries that took interest in the business at the end of the 20th century. Recent developments include a refurbishment of the 19th-century brewhouse and the addition of a hotel to the site. One of the long-standing features of the brewery is a beer called Gouden Carolus Classic.

This strong, satisfying ale was first brewed from an older recipe in the years leading up to World War II. It was known as "Keizersbier" at the time, but was renamed "Gouden Carolus" in 1961. "Carolus" refers to the 16th-century Holy Roman Emperor Charles V, who was brought up in Mechelen; a Gouden Carolus was a gold coin minted during his reign.

The brewery maintains that this is the sort of beer that was once drunk by foxhunters prior to the chase, to raise their spirits and enliven the atmosphere. At 8.5 percent, it is easy to see why. Such has been its success that a range of beers has developed in its wake—there's now a Gouden Carolus Ambrio, Gouden Carolus Tripel, and Gouden Carolus Hopsinjoor, as well as seasonal beers sharing the name.

Pilsner malt, caramel malt, and roasted malt are joined by wheat malt in the mash, with Belgian Challenger hops added to the copper. The result, according to the brewery, is a drink "that combines the warmness of wine and the freshness of beer." This satisfying Belgian brown has won many awards. **JE**

Tasting notes

A full-bodied, attractive, ruby-colored beer that opens up with a mellow aroma of toffeelike malt. The rich taste is equally mellow and smooth, with toffee and raisin notes balanced by a crisp bitterness. A light bitterness then continues into the malty finish.

Grand Baltic Porter

Garrison Brewing Company | www.garrisonbrewing.com

Country of origin Canada
First brewed 2008
Alcohol content 9% abv
Serving temperature 50°F, 10°C

Introducing an "out there" style of beer into a conservatively minded market is always a challenge, and especially for a brewery without a recognized reputation for such mischief. Doing so with a beer style often misunderstood by even those who profess to follow beer closely can be the brewing equivalent of ascending Mount Everest without oxygen! Garrison Brewing therefore deserves ample credit for even attempting the sometimes-confounding beer style of Baltic porter in the Canadian Maritime province of Nova Scotia. That they did so with character, panache, and stylistic integrity makes the accomplishment all that much more impressive.

The Baltic porter style is an off-shoot of imperial stout, the high-strength black beer whose creation, or at least naming, is often attributed to a Belgian named Le Coq. A 19th-century exporter of beer from England to Russia, Le Coq built his business on the region's mighty thirst for robust stouts, even donating beer to the hospitals where Russian troops were treated during the Crimean War. This earned Le Coq an imperial warrant from the tsar, and the style was born.

While imperial stout is now widely brewed in the West, in the Baltic regions it morphed into a sweet, lager-fermented beer that became known as "Baltic porter." As such, a beer true to the style should have a thinner body than one would expect, with less complexity, restrained fruitiness, and notable alcohol. Like Grand Baltic Porter. As well as undergoing a stylistically correct lager fermentation, it receives an untraditional dose of molasses and dates in the boil. **SB**

Tasting notes

The molasses that is added to this black beer shows prominently on the nose, along with sweet coffee and dark chocolate. In the body, too, the molasses figures, supported by notes of coffee, burned toffee, and black licorice, all leading to a soothing and warming finish.

Great Lakes Edmund Fitzgerald Porter

Great Lakes Brewing Co. | www.greatlakesbrewing.com

Country of origin United States
First brewed 1991
Alcohol content 5.8% abv
Serving temperature 50°F, 10°C

The *Edmund Fitzgerald* was one tough freighter. It took three swings of a champagne bottle to properly launch her in 1958. She plied the waters for the next seventeen years, carrying ore and raw materials from mines to foundries through the region—Detroit, Gary, Toledo, and, of course, Cleveland. And then came disaster. The wreck of the *Edmund Fitzgerald* in 1975 is a searing memory for those who live on the shores of Huron, Ontario, Michigan, Erie, and Superior, and not just because the tale became a popular song.

It might seem strange to name a beer after a shipwreck, but for Great Lakes Brewing it's a strong, identifying link to the history of this region. The brewery's portfolio nods toward a local hero (Commodore Perry IPA) and a Cleveland financier (Rockefeller Bock). One ale smirks at a city laughing stock (Burning River Pale Ale); another (Elliot Ness Amber Lager) is a tribute to the lawman who left his mark at the taproom's bullet-riddled, grand Tiger Mahogany bar.

The brewery has earned a reputation as a strong supporter of local urban-renewal projects and is a leader in environmental sustainability and energy-efficient practices. Its beer garden, for example, is an eco-friendly, indoor/outdoor dining area with a retractable canvas roof, straw-bale wall, and radiant-heat floor and fireplace. It is a perfect place to snuggle up with a glass of this superbly rich, dark porter. A sip of its outstanding roasted malt body puts one in the mood to listen to the song of that fateful night, when, in the words of songwriter Gordon Lightfoot, "the gales of November came slashing." **DR**

Tasting notes

A massive roasted malt aroma rises from an ink-black pint glass. Despite its forbidding appearance, the body is light and quite easy to swallow, offering an outstanding complexity of rich malt flavors, especially burned toast and bitter chocolate. The finish is rich, satisfying, and clean.

Green Man Stout

Green Man | www.greenmanbrewery.co.nz

Country of origin New Zealand
First brewed 2007
Alcohol content 7% abv
Serving temperature 46°–50°F, 8°–10°C

Tom Jones began his association with craft brewing in 2004 while working for Emerson's, one of New Zealand's leading craft brewers. At the time, the pioneering Dunedin brewery was expanding fast and selling ever-increasing volumes of beer, much of it packaged in 17-ounce (500-ml) bottles that were imported by the container-load from Germany.

A self-confessed "greenie," Jones was concerned that the expensive recyclable glass bottles weren't being washed and reused, and he decided to survey craft beer drinkers on the issue. Encouraged by the results, he figured the time was right to instigate a bottle-reusage scheme in the local area and start his own fully organic brewery. The timing was perfect; by 2005, Emerson's was relocating to a larger facility, and Jones secured the lease for his new microbrewery. In September 2006, just six months after brewing started in its own premises, Green Man was recognized with a major brewing industry award for its recycling work.

Brewmaster Enrico Gritzner crafts a range of eight full-time beers and occasional seasonal specialties. The Green Man range, which comprises mostly German and British styles, includes New Zealand's—and possibly the world's—strongest organic beer, Enrico's Cure (14.5 percent abv). Green Man Stout is fermented with a traditional English ale yeast, but the recipe also includes German cara-aroma, Munich, and carafa malts and New Zealand hops. Given Enrico's nationality and expertise, the beer could be deemed a Teutonic/Kiwi interpretation of the classic foreign export style. **GG**

Tasting notes

Pours inky black beneath a tan-colored head. There's a rich, malty aroma with caramel and mocha most prominent. Medium bodied with an edge of tartness, the palate shows an early sweetness with roasted, dark fruit, and charred notes before an emphatic, dry finish.

Guinness

St. James's Gate Brewery | www.guinness.com

Country of origin Ireland
First brewed 1779
Alcohol content 4.3% abv
Serving temperature 41°–46°F, 5°–8°C

Some beers need no introduction and, with 10 million pints drunk every day all around the world, Guinness slots neatly into this category. No longer just the drink of Ireland, this famous stout is produced in more than fifty breweries across the globe.

The drink is named after its creator, Arthur Guinness, who started brewing ale in a small town called Liexlip in Ireland. In 1759, he signed the lease on a dormant Dublin brewery called St. James's Gate Brewery; he clearly had his eye on the future even then because he signed a 9,000-year lease for the plot. Some thirty years later, it claimed the title of Ireland's largest brewery. Initially, Guinness brewed ales, but the popularity of porter drew him to stop producing ales in 1799 and focus on porter, which in the 19th century became the ubiquitous stout (Guinness stopped brewing their porter in the 1970s). After this fortuitous switch, six generations of the Guinness family were involved in the drink's production—turning it from a small concern to a worldwide phenomenon.

For more than 250 years, Guinness has been produced using the same four ingredients—barley, water, hops, and yeast. Although it is often described as "the black stuff," Guinness is in fact a ruby stout, getting its dark red color (and distinctive taste) from the addition of a small quantity of roasted barley that cannot be fermented. For a long time, the drink's much-trumpeted slogan was "Guinness is good for you," but nowadays the company makes no such claim, despite recent reports suggesting that Guinness may work as well as aspirin to prevent heart clots. **JM**

Tasting notes
Pours dark amber with a deep creamy head. Its aroma gives away the fact that it contains roasted barley and provides light coffee and chocolate notes. On the palate, it has a rich burned malt taste, with undertones of caramel and roasted barley, ending with a deeply satisfying bitter aftertaste.

The legendary Guinness toucan first appeared in 1935.

Guinness Foreign Extra

St. James's Gate Brewery | www.guinness.com

Country of origin Ireland
First brewed *ca.* 1900s
Alcohol content 7.5% abv
Serving temperature 52°F, 11°C

Guinness has to be one of the most well-known beer names in the world, and one that is synonymous with Ireland. However, most British and Irish lovers of a pint of "the black stuff" are perhaps unaware that Guinness's best seller worldwide is this potent 7.5 percent brew. Guinness Foreign Extra Stout has a dark ruby brown color and a rich, powerful taste, and is one of the strongest beers in the Guinness family. Like all of Guinness's variants, it gets its intensity of color and flavor from the use of barley that has been roasted in a giant drum within the St. James's Gate Brewery.

When Foreign Extra Stout is made in Dublin, some beer is stored in vats for 100 days, which produces an intense lactic flavor; this is then blended with a freshly matured stout. The blend has a hint of sourness that reputedly comes from the use of a *Brettonamyces* yeast. The beer is produced in many countries across Africa, Asia, and the Caribbean. The basis for all of them is an unfermented and concentrated hopped wort that is produced in the Dublin brewery and then shipped worldwide, before being fermented and conditioned locally.

The company's reputation has been built on the quality and success of its advertising. Over the years, memorable lines have been used, such as "Guinness is good for you." In 1929, a campaign for Extra Stout targeted the medical profession, saying Guinness was good for the nerves, digestion, insomnia, and fatigue. Some of the best-known advertising images by artist John Gilroy can be seen at the Storehouse visitor center in Guinness's former Dublin brewhouse. **TH**

Tasting notes

The beer is dark, but not black, and topped by a wispy brown head. The nose is dominated by hops, which give way to notes of burned breakfast toast and rich malty flavors, including coffee, licorice, blackcurrant, and a hint of banana.

Guinness Foreign Extra (Nigeria)

Arthur Guinness & Son | www.guinness-nigeria.com

Country of origin Nigeria
First brewed 1962
Alcohol content 7.5% abv
Serving temperature 34°F, 1°C

Nigerians first started to drink imported Guinness in the 1940s, when their country was a British colony. Guinness made the decision to build a local brewery rather than import the beer when Nigeria gained its independence in 1960. A modern, purpose-built brewery was completed in Ikeja to meet the growing local demand. It was Guinness's first brewery outside the British Isles. Today, Nigeria is the second-largest market for Guinness in the world: locals drink more than the Irish, and some experts predict consumption will overtake the United Kingdom's in the next few years. Perhaps that isn't so surprising considering Nigeria's population is thirty times larger than Ireland's. However, despite Guinness's success, lager is by far the most popular type of beer in Nigeria, and Star, which is brewed by Nigerian Breweries, leads brand sales.

Irish images are not used to sell Nigerian Guinness, and few local drinkers have heard of the significance of St. Patrick's Day to Irish culture. Guinness in Nigeria is sold as an aspirational African drink, using slogans such as "Are you the Warrior?" and "Millions of Nigerians Choose Greatness," and featuring the Guinness harp logo transformed into a map of Africa. Typically, advertisements show successful business people or allude to physical prowess.

It is not sold on draft, and, although the beer looks similar to other bottled Guinness, the taste is different. A dark stout wort concentrate is imported from Dublin, and this is blended with a Nigerian-brewed pale beer made from locally grown sorghum and maize, resulting in a sweeter beer. **TH**

Tasting notes

The color of Nigerian Guinness is ruby black, and it is topped by a wispy brown head. Initially, there is a sweet, almost-syrupy intensity of flavor, which comes from the use of sorghum and maize. There are underlying hints of coffee, licorice, and berries.

Gulden Draak

Brouwerij Van Steenberge
www.vansteenberge.com

Country of origin Belgium
First brewed *ca.* 1980
Alcohol content 10.5% abv
Serving temperature 43°–50°F, 6°–10°C

In 1111, the Norwegian King Sigrid Magnusson gave the Emperor of Constantinople a sculpture of a golden dragon. Almost a century later, Baldwin IX, count of Flanders, took a liking to the statue and removed it to his home in Flanders. For a while, the dragon was in Bruges, but neighboring Ghent claimed it, sparking a minor war between the two cities. So the story goes.

Historically a brown ale brewer, Van Steenberge majors on strong specialties, and it focused on Gulden Draak (Golden Dragon) when it entered the export market in the mid-1990s. This farsighted venture was well rewarded in 1998 when the American Culinary Institute named it best beer in the world. This dark, strong, spicy ale, conditioned in distinctive white bottles, is hard to classify—the brewery suggests it's a barleywine, whereas some writers have described it as what seems like a contradiction, a dark tripel. **DdM**

Tasting notes

Dark ruby with a foamy, pinkish head and a sharpish but malty, gooseberry-tinged aroma. Rich, tart, fruity prune palate, a fluffy, herbal swallow, and gooseberry and custard to finish.

Hakim Stout

Harar Brewery Factory
No website

Country of origin Ethiopia
First brewed Unknown
Alcohol content 5.5% abv
Serving temperature 46°F, 8°C

The ancient city of Harar is the fourth holiest place in Islam. An unlikely place for a brewery? Perhaps. But then, Ethiopia is a diverse country, composed of roughly equal parts Christian and Muslim, and even a small population of Jews. Such heterogeneity may explain why Harar's mainly Muslim population tolerates a brewery—or maybe it is due to the flavor of the brewery's nonalcoholic malt beverage, Harar Sofi.

Outside the city's eastern Sanga Gate, sipping a Hakim Stout can calm the nerves while observing the gatesmen feeding scraps to the town's population of spotted hyenas. The "hyena men" know each animal by name and conduct this daily ritual at dusk. No visit to Harar is complete without a rest stop at the Cottage Bar, just inside the westernmost Harar Gate, where one may ponder the day's activities while sipping from a glass of Hakim Stout. **CO**

Tasting notes

Garnet with a faint layer of froth, deep caramel sweetness, and nary a hint of roastiness, which is why some people prefer to enjoy this stout with a drop of Harar's other famous brew: coffee.

Harpoon Munich Dark

Harpoon Brewery
www.harpoonbrewery.com

Country of origin United States
First brewed 1998
Alcohol content 5.5% abv
Serving temperature 46°F, 8°C

Harpoon Brewery was founded in 1987 by three Harvard classmates in an old shipbuilding warehouse. The brewery began small but grew quickly into one of New England's largest producers of beer.

Most of the brewery's brands are English-style ales, presumably not much different than what would have been enjoyed by early colonists. But its most remarkable full-time label is a dark, malty dunkel that would seem more at home in a Bavarian beer garden. Munich Dark is made with a blend of roasted malts that produce a deep brown hue, a mellow, breadlike flavor, and a medium body. Its appearance suggests a heavy, potent glass, such as a bock, yet it goes down with the easy-sipping enjoyment of a light, refreshing lager. Curiously, this lager is fermented with ale yeast.

Widely available in bottles, it's even richer and more complex when served on draft. **DR**

Tasting notes
The warm malty nose is complemented by subtle hops. A medium body fills the palate with balanced flavors of bitter chocolate and toasted, buttered muffins.

Harvestmoon Schwarz

Harvestmoon Brewery
www.ikspiari.co.jp/harvestmoon

Country of origin Japan
First brewed 2000
Alcohol content 4.5% abv
Serving temperature 50°–54°F, 10°–12°C

Brewmaster Tomoko Sonoda first thought of brewing a Schwarzbier in 1997, because she found most of the dark beers in Japan to be too bitter and strongly flavored. Her first version was brewed with Tettnanger hops for bittering and Saaz for aroma. After several batches, it was decided that the flavors were too sharp. The current version has been changed, with Northern Brewer hops for bittering and Tettnanger for aroma, over a grain bill of German (and some Canadian) pilsner, caramel, and black malt. She believes that keeping the alcohol level at a comparatively low 4.5 percent contributes to the beer's drinkability.

This well-crafted Schwarzbier is just one among a variety of beers Sonoda has created for Harvestmoon. Others in the year-round lineup include a U.S.-style brown ale, a European-style pilsner, a Belgian-style wheat beer, and an English-style pale ale. **BH**

Tasting notes
Dark chocolate brown with a light brown head, with the aroma of toffee, dark rye bread, and coffee. The rich flavor and hint of licorice lead to a brisk refreshing finish.

Harveys Imperial Extra Double Stout

Harveys Brewery | www.harveys.org.uk

Country of origin England
First brewed 1999
Alcohol content 9% abv
Serving temperature 57°–61°F, 14°–16°C

In 1998, Harveys Brewery was asked by a U.S. importer to re-create a beer last brewed in 1921 in the province of Livonia, now Estonia. The beer was Albert Le Coq's legendary Imperial Extra Double Stout. Since the early 19th century, Belgian entrepreneur Albert Le Coq had been buying Extra Stout from London brewer Barclay Perkins, bottling it under his own label, and exporting it to the Baltic regions. A gift of five thousand bottles to the Russian military hospitals founded by Catherine the Great was rewarded with an Imperial Warrant of Appointment, and Imperial Extra Double Stout was born. Later on, Le Coq was invited by the tsarist government to brew this beer within the Russian empire, and in 1912, production commenced in Tartu.

Harveys's head brewer Miles Jenner says, as far as the recipe was concerned, the Tartu Brewery was as helpful as it could be, but it was not exactly precise. "I relied heavily on the recollections of the generation of brewers who had produced Barclay Perkins Russian Stout in the 1950s," he says. A recipe was eventually compiled, and the beer brewed and stored for nine months before its export to the United States. Disaster nearly struck when the beer underwent a rigorous secondary fermentation, shooting the corks out of some of the bottles. "Upon reflection, we should have heeded the fact that Georgian brewers and, indeed, Barclay Perkins, had apparently held their stouts for twelve months rather than the nine we had afforded," says Miles. Today, the beer is still being brewed, but a crown replaces the cork, and it is conditioned for twelve months before bottling to avoid explosions. **TH**

Tasting notes

Pitch black in color, its aroma is warming and vinous. Roast, alcoholic, and spicy notes combine to produce a sweet and sour beer with hints of blue cheese. It has a cascade of flavors, including espresso, prunes, licorice, chocolate, burned sugar, orange, and figs.

Hemel & Aarde

Brouwerij De Molen | www.brouwerijdemolen.nl

Country of origin Netherlands
First brewed 2008
Alcohol content 9.5% abv
Serving temperature 61°F, 16°C

De Molen ("the Mill" in English) was founded in 2004 by brewmaster Menno Olivier. Starting as a home-brewer in his own kitchen, Menno eventually found work at several small Dutch breweries. After twelve years' experience working for others, he started de Molen in an old windmill in the town of Bodegraven. He bought much of the equipment secondhand, with his kettles having previously seen service on a dairy farm. Although the brewery has met with considerable success, it is still run largely as a one-man operation.

Currently, de Molen produces more than forty different beers. The product line is described by the country of origin of the beer type: American, British, German, and Belgian. Most beers are British, with nine different porters and a stout, plus an Irish ale and a cask-conditioned ale. There are also ten in the American style. Virtually all of de Molen's beers are top-fermenting beers. Although bottom-fermenting pils-type beers have a stranglehold on the beer market in his native country, Menno has had no problem swimming upstream: His beers have found an international audience. With the help of U.S. beer-fan websites, de Molen is recognized by a substantial number of foreign beer lovers as one of the best, if not *the* best, brewery in the Netherlands.

In 2008, de Molen, Picobrouwerij Alvinne, and de Struise (the latter two are in Belgium) formed an informal arrangement whereby they hold events at each other's breweries and feature beers from all three. This has been a big attraction for beer fans from abroad and has brought considerable commercial success. **RP**

Tasting notes

Is it a porter or a stout? It pours as dark as the darkest moonless night. The nose has notes of smoke, tar, and roast coffee beans. The taste is a complex combination of dried fruit, coffee, and a touch of smokiness—thanks, no doubt, to the use of peated malt from a Scottish distillery.

Hercule Stout

Brasserie Ellezelloise | www.brasseriedeslegendes.be

Country of origin Belgium
First brewed 1993
Alcohol content 9% abv
Serving temperature 55°F, 13°C

The wry Belgian sense of humor is hard at work with "Les Bières des Collines," as the products from Ellezelloise are known. Although the brewery sits on a hillside, it is very much a singular bump in what is otherwise a generally flat countryside. The offspring of brewer Philippe Gerard, who had logged more than two decades in breweries prior to realizing his dream of going it alone, Ellezelloise is named after the town it overlooks from its hilltop perch, Ellezelles, birthplace of Agatha Christie's fictional detective, Hercule Poirot.

Distinctive in their stopper-topped, heavy glass bottles, the beers of Ellezelloise found favor both locally and among the growing ranks of the Belgian beer cognoscenti. Subsequently, almost inevitably for Belgian beers, it seems, they made their way into export channels. In addition to the Hercule Stout, a "Belgian stout," which was first produced in the debut year of the brewery, Gerard also garnered praise for the assertive Quintine Blonde and the more gentle, malty Quintine Ambrée, both named for a witch of local legend, as depicted on the brewery's labels.

In 2006, Gerard sold his brewery to the nearby Brasserie des Géants, creating in the process Brasserie des Légendes. The sale caused some observers to scratch their heads in bewilderment and others to assert that the quality of the Ellezelloise beers suffered for the takeover; but at least what has been called Belgium's most distinctive stout emerged relatively unscathed. Good news for all those who appreciate fine ale, no doubt, but especially so for the "hill people" of Ellezelles. **SB**

Tasting notes

As dark as coal, this stout does not hold back with its roastiness or its licorice character, offering both in an otherwise coffeelike aroma and creamy and spicy body. A formidable beer built for accompanying dark chocolate or late-night contemplative sipping.

Herold Bohemian Black Lager

Pivovar Herold | www.pivovar-herold.cz

Country of origin Czech Republic
First brewed 2001
Alcohol content 5.3% abv
Serving temperature 44°F, 7°C

The castle brewery at Březnice boasts a written history dating back to at least 1506, when state archives note that it was sold, along with the chateau and surrounding property, to the nobleman Zdeněk Malovec z Chejnova. It is believed to have been producing beer for many years before that. Despite the long history, the brewery's remarkable Bohemian Black Lager is a relatively new development. Unlike most Czech darks, this beer finishes on the dry side, rather than sweet, and has less of a typical Czech dark lager's sugary cola notes. As such, it can be thought of as more in line with the Schwarzbier tradition of Saxony and Thuringia than with the sweeter dunkel beers of Bavaria.

Now known as Herold, the Březnice brewery has maintained many traditions that have been abandoned by other producers under the guise of modernization. Conditioning is still extremely time consuming, taking up to seventy days in this case. Herold is one of the few Czech beer makers to continue to use its own maltings, and in addition to classic Czech-style pale, amber, and black lagers, it also brews a celebrated wheat beer.

After several changes of hands following the Velvet Revolution of 1989, Herold once again finds itself under competent local ownership, and it is continuing to make a name for itself among beer enthusiasts, in part due to its varied, high-quality beer lineup. However, beers from Herold remain relatively difficult to find in the Czech capital, despite being brewed less than an hour from Prague. When the Bohemian Black Lager is spotted on draft, it is considered a rare treat. **ER**

Tasting notes

Pouring very dark amber with a sandy head, this dark and mysterious lager has a solid malt body with complex layers of licorice, chocolate, and dry cocoa. Expect a slightly astringent finish that practically begs for another sip. A perfect match for rich Czech goulash.

Hertog Jan Grand Prestige

Hertog Jan Brouwerij | www.hertogjan.nl

Country of origin Netherlands
First brewed 1982
Alcohol content 10% abv
Serving temperature 50°–54°F, 10°–12°C

Today, Hertog Jan is one of the most familiar and easily obtainable brands of domestic specialty beer in the Netherlands. It is therefore unlikely to be the first choice of beer geeks, especially since one of the reasons for this ubiquity is the backing it receives from the world's biggest mega-brewer, AB-InBev. Yet, if there was a single turning point in the modern resurgence of Dutch craft brewing, it is arguably the management buyout of what was then De Drie Hoefijzers (The Three Horseshoes) brewery at Arcen, Limburg, in 1981.

Ironically, the new owners had specialty ales thrust upon them. Founded in 1915, the brewery had been in the hands of British-based Allied Breweries (now part of Carlsberg) since 1968, and the owners only agreed to sell rather than close the brewery with the anti-competitive provision that no lager be made there. It was relaunched as the Arcense Stoombierbrouwerij (Arcen Steam Beer Brewery), and shortly afterward, unveiled the Belgian-sounding Hertog Jan range, in recognition that Dutch drinkers were discovering new tastes through visits to their southern neighbors.

The French-monikered Grand Prestige was the apex of a range that also included a dubbel and a tripel, and at one point, this barleywine-cum-abbey-ale was the strongest beer brewed in the Netherlands and the flagship of Dutch craft brewing. AB-InBev has so far kept the brewery open, although in 2002 it stopped bottle conditioning. It is still a distinctive strong dark ale and a reliable mainstay in places where smaller brewers have little presence. **DdM**

Tasting notes

Dark ruby with a low yellow head and an estery raisin and cola aroma. Grand Prestige has a caramel and gravy malt palate with a powerful charge of drying hops, and Vermouth, fruitcake, dark marmalade, and chewy hops on the finish.

Highgate Old Ale

Highgate Brewery | www.highgatebrewery.com

Country of origin England
First brewed 1898
Alcohol content 5.3% abv
Serving temperature 54°–57°F, 12°–14°C

The story of this beer is one of remarkable survival. The Highgate Brewery still stands in Walsall, near Birmingham in the English Midlands, with much of its original equipment, such as the wooden mash tuns and copper kettles, still intact from when it was built in 1898. Highgate Old Ale was one of the first beers brewed; it was a winter warmer full of rich Christmas pudding flavors that was brewed in October and November. It was a popular beer, but not as popular as Highgate Mild, a weaker version of the same beer that was for many years the staple drink of working men.

Both beer and brewery survived the intense bombing of the region in World War II. Yet, ten years after hostilities ended, Highgate was taken over by nearby rivals Mitchell and Butler's, who subsequently merged with Bass. Production of Old Ale was halted to focus on Highgate Mild and the new owners' Butler's Old Ale. Highgate Old Ale was revived in the late 1980s, only to be threatened with extinction a few years later when Bass decided to close the brewery. A management buyout secured the future, and since then, Old Ale has gone from strength to strength. Still only available on draft in winter, a bottle-conditioned version is now sold year-round.

Despite its temporary demise and otherwise extraordinary longevity, Highgate Old Ale is still brewed to its original Victorian recipe, with pale, crystal, and black malts, molasses syrup and caramel, and Fuggle and Progress hops. In 2008, it was awarded a silver medal in the Champion Beer of Britain competition; its first international brewing award was won in 1913. **PB**

Tasting notes

Highgate Old Ale pours a rich ruby color. The malt dominates the nose with significant chocolate and coffee aromas. These are joined on the palate by dollops of dark red fruit and a faint vein of sherry warmth. An ideal pairing for rich desserts.

Highland Oatmeal Porter

Highland Brewing Company | www.highlandbrewing.com

Country of origin United States
First brewed 1995
Alcohol content 5.8% abv
Serving temperature 43°F, 6°C

Highland Oatmeal Porter was born out of the failed attempts by the Asheville-based brewery in North Carolina to create a lager as a companion for its flagship Gaelic Ale. Founder Oscar Wong and brewmaster John Lyda had already dumped three consecutive batches of lager that did not live up to their standards. The pair agreed that Highland Brewing, which released its first beer at the end of 1994 from a brewhouse that was using reconfigured dairy equipment, just could not afford to dump a fourth batch of lager. Instead, the base lager was blended with roasted grains and oatmeal. A new beer was born, and it quickly became a favorite. Over time Highland tweaked the brew, weaning the Oatmeal Porter off the use of its base lager to a more traditional ale recipe, but the beer retains pleasing soft notes.

Highland Brewing's backbone is a family of British-style ales, and the brewery itself is named to honor the Scots-Irish who first settled the Blue Ridge Mountains around Asheville. The brewery makes five year-round beers, including an IPA, stout, and pale ale, to go along with the Oatmeal Porter and Gaelic Ale. Three seasonal brews include the extremely popular Cold Mountain Winter Ale that features a different combination of spices each year. The company has also released a pair of certified organic brews: Black Mountain Bitter and Cattail Peak Wheat Beer.

Highland's popularity grew rapidly and forced the brewery to contract brew some of its bottled product for a time in Maryland, before a larger brewery was opened just to the east of Asheville in 2006. **RL**

Tasting notes

This porter delivers a robust tan head with small bubbles that produce a gorgeous lace. The nose has a hint of roasted grains, and the flavor opens with satisfying maltiness. Extremely smooth with dark chocolate notes and a balancing hop bite in the finish.

Hoepfner Porter

Privatbrauerei Hoepfner | www.hoepfner.de

Country of origin Germany
First brewed *ca.* 1900
Alcohol content 5.8% abv
Serving temperature 44°–50°F, 7°–10°C

Hoepfner Porter is a wonderful example of the rare species of German porters. The first one is said to have been brewed in the mid-19th century in the wake of the style's growing popularity, which had spread from the United Kingdom. During the Cold War, East German brewers kept brewing the style in small quantities, though in West Germany, Hoepfner became the last representative after Dressler, a former Bremer brewery, had ceased the production of their porter in the 1970s. In 1980, even Hoepfner removed theirs from the market, due to a lack of demand. Thankfully, they revived it in 1998 on the occasion of their 200th anniversary. Today, the porter is Hoepfner's signature brew, marking out the Karlsruhe-based business as specialty brewer. This is even more the case since the long-established family brewery was sold to the Heineken joint venture BHI in 2004. Thankfully, Hoepfner still acts independently, and their porter is still made with care and insight.

Brewmaster Peter Bucher uses Munich and caramel malts (from Hoepfner's own malthouse) in a two-step decoction mash. However, when asked about the brewing techniques, he is careful not to reveal all of his tricks. Only so much: For the beer to acquire a low final attenuation, they meticulously regulate the mashing to extract both fermentable and non-fermentable sugars. To balance the sweetness, hops are added; Bucher uses the German aroma hop breed Tettnanger. Compared to English porters, the German varieties are mostly bottom-fermented beers. Open fermentation vessels, their proper yeast strain, and a prolonged lagering of six weeks result in a distinguished, complex savor. **SK**

Tasting notes

Clear mahogany brown, creamy beige head. This beer offers dark cacao aromas with floral, citrusy top notes. The first taste is creamy. Dark chocolate flavors evolve with hints of bread, balanced by roasted tastes and bitterness. Finish is bitter with herbal, citrusy hop notes.

Hook Norton Double Stout

Hook Norton Brewery | www.hooky.co.uk

Country of origin England
First brewed *ca.* 1900
Alcohol content 4.8% abv
Serving temperature 52°F, 11°C

In the village of Hook Norton in north Oxfordshire, the streets still echo to the sound of horses' hooves as they pull the brewery's dray to deliver beer to local pubs. The brewery dates from 1849, but its famous and distinctive six-story Victorian tower was built in the late 1890s and is still powered by a steam engine installed in 1899. Believed to be the last steam engine of its age still in regular use for its original purpose in the United Kingdom, the building shakes and vibrates as the belts, cogs, and wheels whirl into life. It is not hard to imagine sweating brewery workers in the 1900s using what was then state-of-the-art technology to haul the heavy sacks of dark malts to the top floor of the brewery. There, they would be poured into a grist mill to be crushed, before being mixed with water from the brewery's own well to release the sugars in the mashing process. The grist mill was also installed in 1899 and is another example of original machinery that is still in use; it may be the last one of its kind.

Double Stout was brewed up until 1916, but its production ceased during World War I when supplies of darker malt were harder to find. It returned to full production in 2005, when brewer James Clarke wanted to re-create a beer that was full of taste and character that could persuade a generation of lager drinkers to try something different—Double Stout was reborn. It is sold on draft as a seasonal beer but is available in bottle all year round—whereas a bottle-conditioned version can be bought from the brewery's visitor center. **TH**

Tasting notes

Hook Norton Double Stout has a long satisfying dryness, which is induced by the use of brown malt. Black malt enriches the color and teases the palate with an unmistakable fresh toast flavor. The beer has a refreshing hoppy aftertaste.

Huon Dark Ale

Two Metre Tall Company | www.2mt.com.au

Country of origin Australia
First brewed 2006
Alcohol content 5.5% abv
Serving temperature 55°F, 13°C

Ashley and Jane Huntington made wine in the south of France for eight years before returning to establish a winery in Tasmania, Australia. Unfortunately, it would be three years before their first crop of grapes could be harvested, and so they turned to beer as a way of filling in the time. This filler gradually turned into a passion, and the vines for that first harvest have been displaced indefinitely with crops of hops and grains.

But that is not to say that the time spent making wine has not been of use. It has brought a perspective to beer making that Ashley and Jane would not have had otherwise. The main consequence is that they treat their beer as a product of the land, rather than something that is assembled using raw material grown by someone else (often overseas). However, sourcing suitable seeds for their crops has proved to be a more difficult exercise than they expected, due to a lack of demand for varied hops and grain in Australia. Their most recent grain seeds have had to be obtained from a cereal museum that has been propagating them since the 1950s. The hop plants that are harvested on their farm annually have not seen Australian sun for more than one hundred years.

A background in wine also makes Ashley more willing to take risks with his beer. The Huon Dark Ale, for example, contains unfiltered, unpasteurized apple juice. Ashley's thinking was that the fruit sweetness would soften some of the bitter charred notes of the darkened grains, and also provide some acidity. Either way, the combination can come as a surprise to those looking for a traditional taste. **DD**

Tasting notes

Check the brew date on your bottle because your experience will change with the seasons. Your beer may pour with a coffee darkness and pillowy head, and follow with roasted and chocolate flavors balanced by some acidity from the apple juice.

Ichtegem's Oud Bruin

Brouwerij Strubbe | www.brouwerij-strubbe.be

Iwate Kura Oyster Stout

Iwate Kura Beer | www.sekinoichi.co.jp/beer

Country of origin Belgium
First brewed 1982
Alcohol content 5.5% abv
Serving temperature 43°–46°F, 6°–8°C

Country of origin Japan
First brewed 2004
Alcohol content 7% abv
Serving temperature 41°–46°F, 5°–8°C

Strubbe is an old-style family brewer in West Flanders. Its strength is brewing top-fermenting ales, especially of the regional kind affectionately known as "Oud Bruin" (Old Brown). This is the typically sweet-sour, lactic, blended beer of the area.

Ichtegem's Oud Bruin started off at 4.9 percent abv and was later brought by head brewer Marc Strubbe to its current strength. It is made in the traditional way. The malt grist is three-quarters lightly cured pilsner malt and 20 percent amber malt, with the balance being dark caramel malt; local hops go into the boil. After the first fermentation, the batch is split, with 80 percent undergoing a slow conventional fermentation, while the rest gets a spontaneous lactic fermentation; this can last as long as eighteen months. The soured beer is then blended with the younger, sweeter beer before bottling. **JPa**

Japanese brewmaster Wataru Satoh had read once that oysters go well with Guinness and other dark beers, and so he became interested in oyster stout. His brewery is located in Iwate prefecture, which is famous for oysters, so he decided to give it a try since he wanted to brew a beer with a strong Iwate identity. Best of all, the famous Hirota Bay oyster beds nearby made it easy for the brewery to procure a very fresh supply of suitable oysters during the season, which lasts from October to February.

In making this beer, the oysters are shucked and added to the wort after the addition of the shells. His first discovery was that oyster shells promote strong fermentation of the wort; his second discovery was that oysters themselves complement the flavors of dark beer. The beer itself is made from pale malt, chocolate malt, caramel malt, and wheat malt. **BH**

Tasting notes

Lactic acid, vinous, and oak notes, and fruity impressions carry the nose. The taste has similar flavors, but they are masked by an extra, rather outspoken sweetness; the body is medium heavy.

Tasting notes

A deep opaque brown with a dark tan head. The brisk hoppy aroma carries hints of the sea. The rich bittersweet chocolate flavor has a strong, almost-meaty foundation.

Jämtlands Heaven

Jämtlands Bryggeri | www.jamtlandsbryggeri.se

Country of origin Sweden
First brewed 2000
Alcohol content 5% abv
Serving temperature 41°F, 5°C

If you brew a beer called "Hell," it sort of stands to reason that one day it should be complemented by another beer named "Heaven." And if the former is a blond lager—the name is an allusion to the German word for "pale"—then, then logically Heaven should be dark and mysterious.

During a brainstorming period between two world-class beer bars, Oliver Twist and Akkurat, in Stockholm, the idea was born to create a golden pilsner-style lager. The beer they produced was Hell, and it was one of the hoppiest lagers that Sweden had ever seen. It was an immediate hit, and its success prompted its creators to produce a follow-up beer called "Heaven," which edges strongly toward black in color. Also a lager, Heaven emerged and was neither close to a Baltic porter nor in the style of a schwarzbier: in other words, it was a second singular brew. **SB**

Tasting notes
A coffeelike aroma, holding notes of roast, smoke, and burned
spice. On the body, roasty malt supports licorice root,
overroasted coffee beans, and earthy, moderately bitter dryness.

Kapittel Prior

Brouwerij Van Eecke | www.brouwerijvaneecke.tk

Country of origin Belgium
First brewed *ca.* 1948/1962
Alcohol content 9% abv
Serving temperature 54°–55°F, 12°–13°C

One source says that the Kapittel Abbey range was first brewed in 1948, whereas another pinpoints 1962 as year zero. Whatever the truth, this very successful range has had an eventful history. There is also no denying the role of brewer Jan van Gysegem; this is the man responsible for gems such as Eylenbosch Druivenbier and Hoegaarden Grand Cru.

In 1962, the dark Prior topped the brewery's range, although later the blond Abt took the peak spot. Prior was dark and lively and—due to the intricacies of its fermentation—often rather explosive on opening; in some bars this led to patrons ordering the Prior as "beer champagne." But fans didn't mind losing a bit on the pouring, as the beer was phenomenal—sour-sweet, with unbelievable depth. These days Prior, which has caramel and spices in the mix, is better behaved, with a predictably pronounced sweet-roasted character. **JPa**

Tasting notes
Brown beer, with red orange reflections and a creamy head.
A nose of raisins, port, and a hint of rich fruitcake. The palate
has smoked wood, bittering hops, licorice, and roasted malts.

Ke To Re Porter

Birra del Borgo | www.birradelborgo.it

Kneitinger Bock

Brauerei Kneitinger | www.kneitinger.de

Country of origin Italy
First brewed 2006
Alcohol content 4.6% abv
Serving temperature 54°–57°F, 12°–14°C

Country of origin Germany
First brewed 1862
Alcohol content 6.8% abv
Serving temperature 46°–54°F, 8°–12°C

Why smoke tobacco when you can drink it? Leonardo Di Vincenzo, a talented young brewer of the Italian craft beer movement, had this original idea after a cigar tasting in 2003 at a club called Maledetto Toscano. At the beginning, it was a sort of challenge. Di Vincenzo enjoyed the rich and sweet aromas of the tobacco and decided to use it in a beer.

The recipe is a classic porter, with a minimum percentage of tobacco. The tobacco is lightly fermented and then dried and poured in the infusion for just a few minutes. British malts are the backbone of this beer: mainly pils, crystal, and some chocolate. Hops are Northern Brewer for bitterness and East Kent Golding and Willamette for aroma. The brewing process lasts about two months: a long fermentation; then, after a week of rest, one month in the bottle for the secondary fermentation and maturation. **MM**

When Pope Benedict XIV was a resident of Regensburg, apparently he loved Kneitinger beers. This may or may not be true, but in the German beer world Kneitinger's beers are as famous as the Vatican—especially the bock. This strong and dark beer is available between October and April, which means that it is an excellent winter warmer.

During this time, a visit to Kneitinger's beer hall in the center of Regensburg will prove how popular the beer is, because most of the drinkers will be nursing this near-black beer in their huge glasses. It is often said that bock beer lovers are used to a very sweet drink where the pleasure can often pale after the first glass. But that is not the case with this beer: Kneitinger Bock is not too sweet and even a little bit dry, so one can drink more of it than a sweet doppelbock (but not too much, because 6.8 percent abv is still a bit hefty). **WO**

Tasting notes

Dark, ebony-colored beer, with a hazelnut foam that is thick and persistent. The aroma is complex with lots of different notes: coffee, chocolate, hazelnut, and a hint of sweet tobacco.

Tasting notes

Nearly black-colored beer with light hop floral notes on the nose. The palate is fruity, harmonious, and smooth in the mouthfeel. The finish is a mixture of hop and light dry notes from the malt.

A cautionary tale in a window of a Regensburg restaurant. ➡

Polizeiſtunde

Kodiak Brown Ale

Midnight Sun Brewing Co. | www.midnightsunbrewing.com

Country of origin United States
First brewed 1995
Alcohol content 5% abv
Serving temperature 44°F, 7°C

A midnight sun, a natural phenomenon, occurs in the summer months near both the Arctic and Antarctic circles. When it happens, the sun can still be seen in the sky at midnight and, if the weather is good, can even remain visible for twenty-four hours. The closer to the pole you go, the better the odds of an increase in the number of days a midnight sun might appear.

Midnight Sun Brewing is located in Anchorage, Alaska's largest city. The company was founded by Mark Staples and Barb Miller in 1995, with a focus on "an art-marries-science approach, mixing tradition with innovation, to design and craft bold, distinctive beers for Alaska . . . and beyond." It has been named a top brewery in Alaska and several times a top brewery in the United States and the world.

The Kodiak Brown Ale was its very first beer and has been the best-selling Midnight Sun beer ever since. It's brewed with the traditional malts of a Northern English brown: pale and chocolate malt. The hopping rate is also along lines typical for the style, at 24 IBUs, but with rather more unusual hop varieties: German Perle and American Willamette. These hop varieties give the brown ale a decidedly nontraditional taste profile, which adds to its very unique character. Another curious mix is the music that head brewer Gabe Fletcher plays while brewing Kodiak: usually the American thrash/punk metal band Darkest Hour and the English acid jazz/funk/soul/disco band Jamiroquai.

The brown ale is named after the Kodiak brown bear, which can be found on the Kodiak Archipelago, a group of islands in southern Alaska. **JB**

Tasting notes

With an apt, deep brown color, Kodiak Brown Ale also boasts a thick tan head. The nose is malty with nutty, toffee aromas. It's smooth, with a clean mouthfeel. The flavors are complex with a predominately malty sweet character, nutty notes, and a lingering hoppy finish.

König Ludwig Dunkel

König Ludwig Schlossbrauerei Kaltenberg | www.koenig-ludwig-brauerei.com

Country of origin Germany
First brewed 1976
Alcohol content 5.1% abv
Serving temperature 43°–46°F, 6°–8°C

Pinch yourself; you could be in Disneyland. This is the feeling that strikes you when you stand in front of the gates at Kaltenberg Brewery. Set out before you is a stunning fantasy castle, complete with its own medieval jousting ground. Tap on the walls, though, and reality hits home. There's no plastic here. This astonishing structure is solid stone and wood. It is home to a royal family, and, even though it operates as a commercial brewery, there's a real live prince in charge.

Kaltenberg was built in the 17th century and remodeled in neo-gothic fashion in the 1800s. The royal owners lost their throne after World War I, but, even though they are private citizens today, they still wear their titles with pride. Running the family brewery (now known as König Ludwig International) is Prinz Luitpold, great-grandson of the last Bavarian king, Ludwig III. He took over the business in the mid-1970s, at a time when its fortunes were in decline. His solution was simple yet bold: go back to the past. Luitpold remembered how dark lager was the most popular drink locally in the 1920s and, rather than try and compete with hundreds of brewers of pils, he decided that Kaltenberg would revive the style.

The strategy has been successful. Kaltenberg has cornered the local market in dark beer through its König Ludwig Dunkel, which is responsible for nearly half of all dark lager sales in Bavaria. The beer is brewed using local malt (pale and roasted) and Hallertau hops to make a satisfying, full-flavored beer that has an intriguing slight sourness, courtesy of the addition of a second yeast culture during fermentation. **JE**

Tasting notes

A ruby brown beer with a creamy aroma of dark malt. This leads to herbal and sweet malty flavors in the taste, which is also a little smoky and sour with suggestions of chocolate and dried fruit. Roasted grains and hoppy dryness characterize the bitter finish.

Köstritzer Schwarzbier

Köstritzer Schwarzbierbrauerei | www.koestritzer.de

Koutský Tmavý Speciál 18°

Pivovar Kout na Šumavě | www.pivovarkout.cz

Country of origin Germany
First brewed 1543
Alcohol content 4.8% abv
Serving temperature 46°F, 8°C

Country of origin Czech Republic
First brewed 2006
Alcohol content 9% abv
Serving temperature 48°F, 9°C

State control of breweries in Eastern and Central Europe following World War II proved to be a mixed blessing. While many companies suffered from a lack of investment, others prospered and were guaranteed a market for their products through a strict regional control of distribution. This meant that some beers that survived easily could have perished if left to their own devices in a more competitive environment.

This seems to have been the case with Köstritzer Schwarzbier. The Köstritzer brewery has its origins in the 15th century, in the spa town of Bad Köstritz, near Weimar. A new brewhouse was added early in the 1900s, but, with the postwar division of Germany, it found itself confined in the Soviet Bloc. When Germany was reunified, the business was in urgent need of a cash injection. This came courtesy of the Simon family, owners of Bitburger, who acquired the business in 1991. They took a particular interest in the Schwarzbier. The Bitburger brewers saw the potential in this unusual beer, but they felt it needed a little life support. They took a long, hard look at the recipe and decided to make some changes, the most substantial of which was to raise the strength from a flimsy 3.5 to 4.8 percent. Today, the beer is produced from pilsner malt, Munich malt, and what the brewery describes as "special malt." Hops come from the Hallertau region. **JE**

The strong dark beers known as Baltic porters are associated with the cold-climate countries of northeast Europe. During the late 19th and early 20th centuries, these dark lagers were also brewed throughout Eastern and Central Europe, with beers called "porters" appearing from Slovakia's Martinský Pivovar as well as from breweries in today's Czech Republic. However, after the spread of industrial pilsner production, many such beers were discontinued, and by 2006 only Pardubický Porter remained in the former Czechoslovakia.

Originally founded in 1736, the brewery at Kout na Šumavě added a strong dark lager to its lineup when it started brewing again. According to current Czech brewing law, "porter" is a term that is reserved for dark, bottom-fermented beer of 18 degrees or higher, brewed from malted barley. Although Pivovar Kout na Šumavě does not call its beer a porter, preferring instead the term "*tmavý speciál*," or "dark special," the brew does meet the requirements for the term. It was originally launched as a festive beer, but is now produced on a more constant basis.

The beer has virtually no alcoholic heat in the mouth. As a thick, viscous, and semisweet beer, it is not anything close to a session beer, but rather appears most often as a nightcap or winter warmer. **ER**

Tasting notes
Slightly sour aroma, with hints of coffee and dark chocolate. The gentle sourness runs on into the bittersweet taste, along with creamy dark malt, coffee, and plain chocolate.

Tasting notes
Pours a clear black-brown with a loose tan head of limited lifespan. Look for complex aromas of plum compote and holiday spice, with rich chocolate and gingerbread notes.

Maintaining the pressure at the Kout na Šumavě brewery. ➡

Krušovice Černé

Pivovar Krušovice | www.krusovice.cz

Country of origin Czech Republic
First brewed *ca*. 1900
Alcohol content 3.8% abv
Serving temperature 44°F, 7°C

New owners can make an impact on a brewery, and nowhere is that more clear than in Krušovice, a small town west of Prague. In 1583, the Holy Roman Emperor Rudolph II bought the local brewery for 11,500 Meissner kopa, instantly raising this modest regional property to the status of an aristocrat.

Later owners were less kind. Stripped, in 1945, from the noble Fürstenberk family of Bohemia who had owned it for two centuries, the brewery was nationalized in 1948. It became one of the workhorses of Communist Czechoslovakia, bringing in much-needed foreign currency by producing a pale lager said to be good enough to occasionally pass for Pilsner Urquell in the export market. After the Velvet Revolution, the brewery went through several transfers of ownership, with the quality of the lagers seeming to suffer at every turn. Its purchase in 2007 by the Heineken group may just have been its salvation.

Although the brewery's pilsner-style beers sell in large volumes, it is Krušovice's dark that stands out. It appears in the pot almost as often as on the table—promoted by several high-profile chefs as a marinade for roasts and often listed as the base ingredient in a hearty goulash. It is one of the few Czech lagers to use the term *černé*, or "black," and it seems a couple of steps stronger in flavor than your average Czech *tmavé*, or "dark beer." It first appeared around 1900 as "Grand," a burly 14 degrees Plato lager of nearly 6 percent alcohol, before being modified to a more manageable 10 degrees Plato and 3.8 percent. In 2009, this beer was named World's Best Dark Lager at the World Beer Awards in London. **ER**

Tasting notes

A remarkable beer of moderate strength but powerful flavors, Krušovice Černé pours nearly black with deep amber glintings and a long-lasting, sandy-colored head. It is complex for a lager, featuring cola, coffee, and spice notes, with a licoricelike, slightly herbal finish.

Lancaster Milk Stout

Lancaster Brewing Company | www.lancasterbrewing.com

Country of origin United States
First brewed 1996
Alcohol content 5.3% abv
Serving temperature 50°F, 10°C

With nearly 100,000 cows grazing on the green fields of its Amish and Mennonite farmers, Lancaster County, Pennsylvania, is known more for milk than beer. In this verdant land, there are more than 1,800 family-owned dairy farms and only four breweries. Lancaster Brewing brews one of the United States's rare milk stouts.

Milk stout, of course, does not contain milk. This dark, exceptionally rich ale is made with an addition of lactose—milk sugar—that cannot be fermented by beer yeast. This gives the beer a lightly sweet flavor to complement the deeply roasted malt's compelling bitterness. U.K. authorities long ago banned the word "milk" on beer labels, mainly because the style was frequently marketed as a health benefit. It was often claimed, for example, that milk stout was good for nursing mothers. U.S. regulators don't object to "milk stout," however, because it's a recognized historic beer style.

Brewery owner John Frantz says that Lancaster Milk Stout is one of his oldest brands, originally designed as a sweet alternative for stout fans who wanted something less bitter than an Irish stout. It quickly became one of the brewery's staples because "it's smoother than Guinness, and around these parts it's definitely fresher." Made with two-row barley and exceptionally dark malts, it's bursting with roasted barley dryness, with hints of chocolate and coffee. Cascade and Styrian Golding hops are present, but only enough to balance the sweetness. The dark beer is extremely popular in the region; another of the brewery's favorite brands is Strawberry Wheat. **DR**

Tasting notes

An aggressively poured glass fills with the color of dark espresso coffee topped by tight froth. Bitter chocolate crosses the palate first, quickly followed by mellow coffee and sweet cream. A smooth creaminess in the finish is countered by a slight roasted malt bitterness.

Laurentina Preta

Cervejas de Moçambique | www.sabmiller.com

Country of origin Mozambique
First brewed 1932
Alcohol content 5% abv
Serving temperature 44°F, 7°C

Europeans first came to Mozambique in 1498 when the navigator Vasco da Gama briefly dropped anchor on his way to India; so began almost 500 years of Portuguese rule in the area. Independence was finally gained in 1974 when a bloody and destructive civil war took place, at the end of which Mozambique was rated officially the poorest nation on Earth.

Today, Mozambique is moving away from its troubled past, as a visit to the seafront capital, Maputo, will testify. A walk along the palm-lined avenidas reveals bustling cafés and restaurants where locals and tourists are almost inevitably relaxing with a bottle of Laurentina. The Preta version is a premium dark lager, brewed using a combination of four malts including a distinctive toasted black malt and caramel. It is a firm favorite with beer connoisseurs and found fame in Europe after winning a gold medal at the 2008 Monde International Institute for Quality Selection in Belgium.

Mozambique's best-loved brewery began life in 1912 as the Victoria Ice and Soft Drink Plant and became known as the Laurentina Brewery twenty years later. Precious little is known of the company prior to independence, but the domestic market was dominated by Laurentina and 2M (brewed by Mac Mahon Brewery) for several years until civil war incapacitated production. Remarkably, the Laurentina Brewery survived this dark time and is today one of the few successful African breweries exporting outside the continent. Laurentina somewhat inevitably found itself swallowed up by the South African brewing giant SABMiller and operates under the subsidiary Cervejas de Moçambique. **SG**

Tasting notes

Expect to discover a black beer with a long-lasting, creamy, tan head with ample lacing. The nose is dominated by dark malts and a trace of chocolate that comes through on the palate with notes of coffee and molasses to leave a roasted malt finish.

Left Hand Milk Stout

Left Hand Brewing | www.lefthandbrewing.com

Country of origin United States
First brewed 2001
Alcohol content 5.3% abv
Serving temperature 55°F, 13°C

From the time that Anchor Brewing in San Francisco began introducing American beer drinkers to English beer styles, U.S. craft brewers have taken inspiration from traditional brewing nations. At times, they've tried to faithfully replicate the originals, but at others they've chosen styles no longer or seldom brewed. Left Hand wasn't the first small U.S. brewery to make milk stout, but its version has been a particularly popular and critical success.

Popularized by Mackeson at the beginning of the 20th century, milk stouts evolved into sweet, low-alcohol beers that breweries hoped women would buy. Left Hand's version is a throwback to Mackeson's 1907 recipe—in fact, it's a little stronger—containing the same key ingredient of lactose, or milk sugar. When the brewery introduced the beer, brewmaster Dick Doore had to carefully explain that it included no dairy products and that the addition of unfermentable sugar "gives it great mouthfeel and a sweet finish." That first year, Left Hand brewed just ten beer barrels of Milk Stout, and the next year doubled that to twenty. Today, it sells that amount many times over.

It makes an interesting contrast to Left Hand Imperial Stout, a seasonal brew that graduated into a regular beer. "I will get asked all year long when the Imperial Stout will be on," co-founder Eric Wallace noted when it was available only once a year. Then Doore made it clear that the beer, now a 10.4 percent monster, drew its inspiration from their home-brewing roots. "Basically, we fill up the mash tun and we get whatever we get. We keep pouring in two-row until we stop." **SH**

Tasting notes

Nearly pitch black in the glass, showing a few ruby highlights under a tan head. Chocolate and burned toast in the aroma and flavor are constantly balanced by creamy sweetness. The beer turns dry at the finish, leaving a final impression of coffee and cream.

Limfjords Porter

A/S Thisted Bryghus | www.thisted-bryghus.dk

Country of origin Denmark
First brewed 1989
Alcohol content 7.9% abv
Serving temperature 54°–59°F, 12°–15°C

Thisted Bryghus is perched at the northern tip of Jutland and is one of only a handful of independent Danish brewers that have stayed out of the hands of its bigger competitors. Formed in 1899, it began production with a dark Bavarian-style lager, instead of the local top-fermented ale. It went bust, only to be reborn in 1902 and grow to become the second-largest employer in the area and a local institution.

Thisted was the birthplace of the cooperative movement in Denmark and that is reflected in the brewery's history. Fierce local pride in the company has helped it survive, and many of the shares are still in the hands of the community. The company's annual general meeting is a close second to Christmas as a social occasion in Thisted, with around 1,300 of the brewery's 1,900 shareholders taking part. Its growth from a local company with only two beers to an acknowledged brewer of specialist beers is thanks to brewmaster and managing director Peter Klemensen, who retired in June 2009. He strengthened the company's reputation beyond Denmark with special beers such as the well-loved Limfjords Porter.

Limfjords Porter was first sold by the Urban Brewery in Ålborg, but the name was bought in 1986 when the brewery closed. Klemensen continued to experiment with the recipe until 1997, when he decided that the beer had the right blend of caramel, smoked, and colored malts, and licorice. It lives up to the seafaring heritage of other Baltic porters with a tarry, smoky taste that has been described as "maritime" by some and "like licking an ashtray" by others. **AA**

Tasting notes

A dark brown beer with a mocha head, from beneath which emerges a toasted malt, slightly smoky aroma alongside a hint of licorice. Stronger smoke flavors, with dried fruit and licorice, lead into an intense charred taste and a slightly bitter, antiseptic finish.

Lion Stout

Ceylon Brewery | www.lionbeer.com

Country of origin Sri Lanka
First brewed 1881
Alcohol content 8% abv
Serving temperature 54°F, 12°C

The former British colony of Sri Lanka is not well known for its beery heritage, and in the past a coconut-based spirit was a local favorite with those who drank alcohol. However, Nuwara Eliya, a former colonial retreat high up in the mountains, has had a pivotal part to play in the history of brewing in the area.

Tea was (and still is) grown here, but the Victorian tea planters who settled in the place and nicknamed it "Little England" also brought something else that was close to their hearts: beer. In 1881, a Sir Samuel Baker set up a brewery in the area. Nearly one hundred years later, the intrepid beer hunter Michael Jackson made the precarious journey here and found the brewery's Lion Stout being dispensed by hand pump in a couple of bars in the area. Not only that, but the beer was also bottle conditioned, and it was a revelation. Since Jackson's discovery of Lion Stout, it has remained a beer to be enjoyed and treasured (although, sadly, the two bars that dispensed what seemed like cask-conditioned stout have long since vanished).

There has been one other important change, too. The brewery has now come down from its mountain heights and is located near the capital city of Columbo; but the stout still remains a great beer, full of creamy and soothing flavors. Lion Lager is the Ceylon Brewery's best-selling beer. It also brews Carlsberg's lager and Special Brew under contract, but it is to the company's credit that it continues to produce this niche dark beer, an historic relic that, through the endeavors of Jackson, went out across the world and found new fans. **ATJ**

Tasting notes

Very dark. On the nose, bitter chocolate; soft, rounded mouthfeel with coffee bean and fruity hints that lead to a bitter chocolate finish. An expansive and rich-tasting stout with a slight sweetness replacing the usual roasted and dry flavors of stout.

Longfellow Winter Ale

Shipyard Brewing
www.shipyard.com

Country of origin United States
First brewed 1995
Alcohol content 5.8% abv
Serving temperature 46°F, 8°C

Shipyard Brewing is located on the waterfront site of the birthplace of poet Henry Wadsworth Longfellow. In 1995, the company marked its first birthday, and the bard's 188th, with this dark, wintertime warmer.

Available between November and January, the ale is not generally sold outside of New England, but it is hugely popular among the literary buffs who trek to Portland every year to mark Longfellow's birthday. The bars and restaurants toast the occasion by tapping the season's last kegs of this full-bodied ale. The beer itself is the masterwork of Shipyard's chief, Alan Pugsley, the British-trained disciple of famed Ringwood brewer Peter Austin. Longfellow Winter Ale has distinctive British roots. Pugsley says, "It might be called a hybrid between an English porter and a Scottish ale." Full bodied with complex malt notes, it's sweeter than the classic porter, while finishing far drier than a Scottish. **DR**

Tasting notes
Dark brown with a pleasing aroma of toast and almonds. Slightly sweet up front, then smoothing out to a roasted malt bitterness. Its body is light, smooth, and refreshing.

Mackeson Stout

Anheuser-Busch
www.ab-inbev.com

Country of origin England
First brewed 1907
Alcohol content 3% abv
Serving temperature 55°F, 13°C

This one tugs hard on the nostalgic heartstrings. Mackeson is a remnant of a style long since lost for many. Uttering the words "milk stout" might make some beer drinkers rush for their coats, but this historic style deserves a chance. The way it's made means the residual dextrins and unfermented sugars provide more than the usual when it comes to sweetness, so there is a fine depth to this beer.

This particular example has plenty of depth when it comes to its ingredients. The color immediately reveals that, as with stouts, the beer has a burned malty quality to it, something easily picked up on the nose with an almost woody scent. The taste also delivers a rich chocolate front with enough bitterness at the end to ensure that it's a balanced quaff. What will surprise, however, is that this beer can be chilled and provides a refreshing change from a pale ale or lager. **TS**

Tasting notes
Make sure you drink it alongside a good piece of dark chocolate. Pours dark brown with a nice foamy head and gives off those chocolate sweet aromas before a nice balanced mouthfeel.

MacKroken Flower

Le Bilboquet
www.lebilboquet.qc.ca

Country of origin Canada
First brewed 2008
Alcohol content 10.8% abv
Serving temperature 50°F, 10°C

Brasserie Bilboquet became the fourth brewpub in the province of Québec when it first opened in 1990 in St.-Hyacinthe. A decade later, the MacKroken Flower was first brewed, but not at Bilboquet.

As is the case with a number of other commercial brewers, Mac, as the beer is known around the brewery, began life as a home-brew—the creation of former Bilboquet employee and brewing enthusiast Jean-Philippe Barbeau. In 2004, this dark beer won its category in the prestigious Canadian Amateur Brewers Association contest; it then went on to do the same in a similar competition in Québec. The latter, however, came with the prize of having the beer commercially brewed, but still not by Le Bilboquet. The honey-influenced Scotch ale finally found a permanent home at Le Bilboquet when the brewery received its bottling license in 2008. **SB**

Tasting notes
Richly malty and floral nose, as if from fresh flower honey and malt. On the palate, notes of candied plum, molasses, and caramel leading to an almost port wine–like finish.

Mahou Negra

Grupo Mahou San Miguel
www.mahou-sanmiguel.com

Country of origin Spain
First brewed 1908
Alcohol content 5.5% abv
Serving temperature 43°–44°F, 6°–7°C

Grupo Mahou San Miguel has its origins back in 1890, when the sons of Casimiro Mahou founded a company in Madrid to produce beer and ice. The company developed a reputation for keeping up with industry developments: in 1922, it substituted the cork with the aluminum cap, and in the 1960s, it swapped its aluminum barrels for traditional wood ones.

Its bread-and-butter beer is the unremarkable blond lager Mahou Clásica, along with the ubiquitous San Miguel, which can be found throughout Spain. However, Mahou Negra has a lot more going for it. It was created in 1908, together with Clásica, with the aim of introducing some German-style beers to the Iberian public. As the name "Negra" suggests, this is a dark, Munich-style beer with a luscious toasted malt character. It is perfect to serve with shellfish tapas or just to sip on its own. **SS**

Tasting notes
Clear, dark reddish brown color, with a thick, cream-colored head. On the nose, a bittersweet malty aroma; the palate has an appetizing mix of bitter and toasted coffee notes.

Mahr's Der Weisse Bock

Mahr's Bräu | www.mahrs-braeu.de

Country of origin Germany
First brewed 1994
Alcohol content 7.5% abv
Serving temperature 46°–50°F, 8°–10°C

Every year on Ash Wednesday, a select group of people congregate at the brewpub of Mahr's Bräu, in Bamberg's borough of Wunderburg. The gathering includes brewers from the Netherlands, some from Belgium, a few Danes, the mayor of Bamberg, and some officers from the nearby U.S. base. In all, about twenty people celebrate the release of Mahr's Der Weisse Bock, a strong wheat ale only available during Lent.

Since its launch in 1994, this beer has won many loyal fans, purely by word-of-mouth recommendation. For the six weeks before Easter, beer enthusiasts from Austria, Italy, Switzerland, Scandinavia, and other European countries rally to the small Bamberg brewhouse to get as many cases of the wheat bock as their vehicles can carry.

Junior brewmaster and fourth-generation owner Stephan Michel uses dark wheat malts, Munich, and pilsner malts in a classic two-step decoction mash to make the beer as full-flavored as possible. Before Michel accepted responsibilities in the brewery in 1997, he traveled to the United States. Not just for the beer, he emphasizes, but to get a sense of what makes the U.S. beer market tick. With regard to Der Weisse Bock, Michel developed a slightly stronger beer to satisfy transatlantic demands: the U.S. version is 8.5 percent abv. The beer also goes to other countries, but once was rejected by some Japanese customers, who found it too strong. Whatever the strength and country it appears in, Der Weisse Bock is strictly seasonal, which should give more people around the world a reason to celebrate Ash Wednesday. **SK**

Tasting notes

Intense brown, orange tints, hazy; giant light-brown head. This beer seduces with fruity aromas, a touch of dark chocolate as well as toast. Smooth, fruity flavors imbue the palate and are balanced by roasted notes and a touch of smoke. Full-flavored yet dry finish.

Malheur 12

Brouwerij Malheur | www.malheur.be

Country of origin Belgium
First brewed 2001
Alcohol content 12% abv
Serving temperature 50°F, 10°C

Some would call Malheur 12 a barleywine, but not many people in Belgium use that phrase; others might call it a strong ale, but that is stating the obvious. You wouldn't call it a blond, given that it is dark and ruddy in complexion. It's dark, then, so why not call it a stout? No roast character, I'm afraid. What to call Malheur 12? That is the question.

Being a Malheur beer means that the brew is going to be thoroughly well crafted: a beer that has character, taste, and virtue. Yes, it's strong, but, if you know how to brew, it's relatively easy to produce very strong beers in Belgium. The real trick is bringing ones forth into the world that manage to hide their alcohol well, and have a deep complexity to boot. Malheur does that trick with style, as evidenced by the 12. Only whole hop flowers of the Hallertauer and Styrian varieties are used. Malheur's president, the cheerful and welcoming Manu de Landtsheer (a man who works hard, plays hard, and is a serious businessman, too), feels it's best to use whole hops in his beers, even though they are more expensive and more difficult to work with than pellets or extracts. That's good. Like all of Malheur's beers, 12 is filtered but it's unpasteurized and refermented in the bottle, and available in crown-capped 11-ounce (330-ml) bottles, as well as in the 26-ounce (750-ml) size with cork.

Malheur 12 has another function: it is the base beer for the Brut Noir. Both are fine beers for savoring beside a roaring fire. Or, one might choose either beer to accompany a meal of beef, deer, or even bison. You'll almost certainly be glad if you do. **CC**

Tasting notes

A dark brown beer with a thick, creamy head. Very malty and yeasty in the nose. Notes of dark candi sugar, fruitlike esters, chocolate, and a deep malty complexity. Alcohol is subdued for such a strong brew. Pair this one with dark Belgian chocolate!

Malheur Dark Brut

Brouwerij Malheur
www.malheur.be

Country of origin Belgium
First brewed 2002
Alcohol content 12% abv
Serving temperature 43°F, 6°C

Creating beers using the Méthode Champenoise had its genesis at the turn of the last millennium, when several Belgian brewers had the idea of greeting the 21st century with luxurious beer instead of champagne. The first beers that they produced were blond, but Malheur then came up with the idea of making a dark version, initially dubbed "Chocolat Noir."

Brouwerij Malheur is based in Bouggenhout, a small town in East Flanders that has two active family-owned breweries. It stopped brewing in 1939 but kept bottling and selling beer, until Emmanuel "Manu" De Landtsheer decided to start a microbrewery in 1997. The brewery offers a whole range of beers of varying strengths, from a very modest 4 percent to the super-powerful Brut beers, such as this one. The Brut range has opened doors to sales across the world, including the United States and Italy.

This dark version is light-years ahead of the blonds in its distinctiveness. It offers the advantages of a dark, malted beer, aged perfectly on kilned American oak barrels, together with a champagne-like spritziness. The result is something truly amazing. Malheur Dark Brut, as well as its blond equivalent, is an ideal beer for food pairing. Even though the chocolate character has been slightly in retreat since it was first brewed, it is an excellent partner to many desserts. **JPa**

Tasting notes
A woody, vinous, fruity nose with a hint of walnuts. The taste is of a very tannin-rich bitterness with truckloads of malt. Full bodied, near syrupy with a long, sweet aftertaste.

Manns Brown Ale

Marston's
www.marstonsbeercompany.co.uk

Country of origin England
First brewed 1902
Alcohol content 2.8% abv
Serving temperature 46°–50°F, 8°–10°C

Although Manns is a brown ale, don't expect it to share a tasting profile with the brown ales that are popular in the northeast of England. It is sweetish, lightly hopped, and very low in alcohol. In its heyday, because of its low strength, it was a beer that could be drunk purely for refreshment and sugar content. Some regarded it as almost a soft drink.

It's a survivor of a time when most English brewers had a beer of this style. Low in bitterness, the ales typically shared a dark, burned caramel coloration. Manns is regarded as the oldest British beer brand and has been continuously brewed since 1902, when it was developed and bottled (a revolution in itself) by Thomas Wells Thorpe, the head brewer at Mann, Crossman, and Paulin in East London.

This beer has a tradition as a mixer. Drinkers in London and the south of England would order a "brown and bitter" or a "brown and mild." They would also mix a half pint of draft beer with a bottle of brown ale. The carbonation in the bottled beer would often help to add new vitality to the draft beer, which all too often was poorly kept and rough on the palate. These days, it's very much a specialist beer and is recommended as an ingredient in cooking. It adds fullness to rich fruit puddings, light caramel flavors to creamy stews, and a deliciously mellow body to walnut bread. **TH**

Tasting notes
Light and refreshing, it has hints of raisins and chocolate. Dark ruby black in color, the beer is topped with a light caramel-colored head. It has a malty sweet aroma.

Manns—more soft drink than working man's beverage?

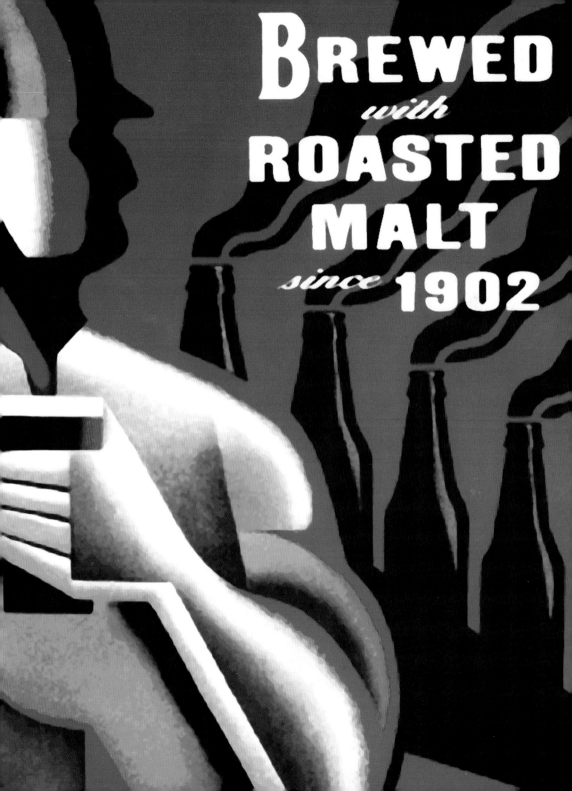

Maredsous 8

Duvel Moortgat | www.duvel.be

Country of origin Belgium
First brewed 1963
Alcohol content 8% abv
Serving temperature 46°–54°F, 8°–12°C

Belgian abbey ales are a mixed bunch. Some of the outstanding ones from smaller brewers have no genuine monastic links at all. Meanwhile, a good few bearing the official "Certified Belgian Abbey Beer" logo (indicating they are brewed under license from a monastic institution and contribute royalties to it) turn out to be industrial beers from big brewers.

The trio of bottle-conditioned beers marketed under the Maredsous name by the Duvel Moortgat Group in the small Flemish town of Breendonk are one honorable exception. Although often overlooked beside a certain celebrated world classic from the same brewery, these beers do consistently well in blind tastings and are arguably the best of the readily available "certified" abbey beers.

The Benedictine abbey at Maredsous is in a picturesque area that is part of the commune of Denée, in the French-speaking Namur province. It's a neo-Gothic structure dating from the 1870s, founded by Bavarian monks when Belgian monasticism was re-establishing itself after suppression by Napoleon. The monastery brewed its own beer until 1963, when it struck the deal with Duvel Moortgat. Back then, most abbey beers were brown; the golden ones only began to proliferate following the popularity of Leffe Blonde in the 1970s. Today, Maredsous 8 is the only brown in a range that includes a Blond 6 and a Triple 10, and, discounting the divine, is undoubtedly the closest to the monks' original inspiration. Some have speculated that its luscious caramel and raisin flavors indicate the Trappist ales of Rochefort as its original model. **DdM**

Tasting notes

Very dark ruby with a rocky white head. Hints of pine and licorice in a caramel and fruit aroma. There's caramel and raisin alongside sweet black coffee in a lightly drying palate, with slight roasted notes, coal tar, and salty gravy on the finish. Recommended with rich meaty dishes.

Martha's Mild

Teignworthy Brewery | www.teignworthybrewery.com

Country of origin England
First brewed 2002
Alcohol content 5.3% abv
Serving temperature 59°F, 15°C

Symbiosis is a scientific term for cases when two entities live and work together, to mutual advantage. That fairly sums up the arrangement between Teignworthy Brewery and Tucker's Maltings in Devon, England. The maltings is one of the few surviving floor maltings left in the United Kingdom, and to aid its preservation it has bolted tourism onto its business.

The century-old malthouse now attracts many visitors each year. Part of the attraction is Teignworthy Brewery; it is a separate business but rents a corner of the historic building. The steam from the copper adds a hoppy accent to the maltings air, which is already filled with the aromatics of toasted grain. At the end of the maltings tour, a glass of Teignworthy beer slakes the thirst you have worked up climbing the many stairs.

John Lawton is Teignworthy's founder and brewer. He produces a wide range of ales, including beers that celebrate the gradual extension of his own family. The first of these arrived in 1997, shortly after John's wife Rachel gave birth to daughter Amy. There are now four "baby beers" in the Teignworthy collection. As well as Amy's Ale, you can try Harvey's Special Brew, Pippa's Pint, and the particularly interesting Martha's Mild, named for Martha, born in 2002.

This deep-ruby-colored beer is a rare beast in British brewing circles: a strong mild, such as would have been popular a hundred or more years ago. The rich, malty character is the result of a clever blending of pale, crystal, amber, and chocolate malts, with a little wheat malt to lighten the tone. Fuggle and Golding hops keep things firmly traditional. **JE**

Tasting notes

A ruby beer with coffee, chocolate, and nuttiness in the inviting aroma. Similar dark malt flavors also appear in the sweetish taste, joined by hints of licorice and pear drop candy, while the finish is dry and bitter, with yet more coffee and nut.

Maxlrainer Jubilator

Schlossbrauerei Maxlrain | www.maxlrain.de

Country of origin Germany
First brewed *ca.* 1938
Alcohol content 7% abv
Serving temperature 46°F, 8°C

There are at least five Jubilators in Germany: late-winter bocks with which to toast the imminence of spring, celebrate the chaos of carnival, and maintain a sense of Lenten probity. However, Maxlrainer Jubilator is probably the most prominent one of all, and it comes from Schlossbrauerei Maxlrain, which is situated within the grounds of the castle of the same name.

The brewery prides itself on being "small but fine," as its motto goes. Jubilator has built up a formidable reputation for itself (and won many awards), not only in its home valley of Mangfall in Upper Bavaria, but also in other regions. The beer first emerged toward the end of the 1930s, when it was brewed for a special Christmas party at the brewery. After that, no doubt the brewmaster realized he had a winner on his hands, and it became an annual treat.

As is the case with many other breweries that produce beers of this sort, the arrival of Jubilator is usually greeted with some ceremony as it is tapped: a Bavarian brass band playing their hearts out, local dignitaries testing the first stein, and a general sense of goodwill. Even though Lent was traditionally a time when beers like Jubilator were supposed to sustain those who were fasting, the brew also goes well with typical Bavarian dishes such as roast pork and beef and, of course, sausage.

Schlossbrauerei Maxlrain was founded in 1636 and is one of only five castle breweries in Germany. Thirteen different brands are brewed during the year, including an impressive Weissbier and an amber-colored Christmas beer. **WO**

Tasting notes

Maxlrainer Jubilator is dark amber in color; on the nose, fresh and spicy notes with crisp malt in the background; the palate is restrained in its sweetness, with spicy notes coming through in the middle; finish is well balanced with light hop notes hovering about.

Mc Chouffe

Brasserie d'Achouffe | www.achouffe.be/en

Country of origin Belgium
First brewed *ca.* 1986
Alcohol content 8% abv
Serving temperature 46°–54°F, 8°–12°C

In most Anglo-Saxon countries, Scotch has always been understood to be a whisky from Caledonia. However, until the 1970s, in Belgium and especially in Wallonia, asking for a Scotch would get you a glass of dark, nearly black ale, reeking of burned malts and sugars. For some reason, people were convinced that this was the kind of beer that Highlanders must be drinking to keep warm in their damp castles—you get the picture. In reality, Belgian brewers had developed a wholly national style of beer (yet another one).

In the early years of their brewery, when the ubiquitous La Chouffe wowed beer lovers, Achouffe's founders Pierre Gobron and Chris Bauweraerts had also been trying out other brews. During a tour, Chris offered trial samples of a very dark beer and asked for opinions. "It's quite like a Walloon Scotch . . . " was my response. This was actually the case, and in true Chouffe style (should you have missed the semantics of this, a Chouffe is a kind of hobbit, native to the Ardennes hills. Unlike the Tolkien kind, he is unkempt, mischievous to the point of being nasty, and—impervious to the effects of alcohol—he makes desperate attempts at Chouffe-powered flight), they invited the Mc Chouffes into the fold.

Mc Chouffe has since become the other beer of the brewery and is available all year around. It has also won a number of international awards. The beer is spiced, but there is no heather involved—it is not brewed in Scotland after all. Make no mistake, this is a Chouffe-interpretation of an ancient style—and it is unfiltered, of course. **JPa**

Tasting notes

Dark amber beer under a creamy head, sporting a nose of roasted and caramel malts and spices. Has a thick malt base, but the sweetness is reminiscent of licorice. Full bodied, with a subtle but always present hint of alcohol, while the spices last until the end.

Meantime London Porter

Meantime Brewing | www.meantimebrewing.com

Country of origin England
First brewed 2005
Alcohol content 6.5% abv
Serving temperature 52°F, 11°C

Under the auspices of its founder Alastair Hook, Meantime Brewing has been producing great beers since 1999. Based in Greenwich—hence the name—where Hook and co-founder Ben Joseph grew up, the brewery started slow and then took off when it began brewing own-label beers for major U.K. supermarket Sainsbury's. However, it is for his dedication to research and re-creating historic beer styles, such as India Pale Ale, that Hook has become rightly famous—and the Meantime London Porter is seen as being at the very pinnacle of its class.

Hook says that this porter is a re-creation of a 1750s recipe, with seven malts and an awful lot of Fuggle hops. Although it can't be a direct representation of that beer—because of modern malting and gristing methods, not to mention single-strain yeast cultivation methods—we know it was an incredibly popular drink, as a French visitor to London observed.

"Another kind of beer is called 'porter,' meaning 'carrier,' because the greater quantity of this beer is consumed by the working classes. It is a thick and a strong beverage, and the effect it produces, if drunk in excess, is the same as that of wine; this porter costs threepence the pot. In London, there are a number of alehouses where nothing but this beer is sold. It is said that more grain is consumed in England for making beer than for making bread."

Whatever its popularity then, there is no doubt that porter and its cousin, stout, are making a comeback in the U.K., and Meantime's own version certainly has a lot to do with that. **MC**

Tasting notes

From its statuesque 25-ounce (750ml) champagne cork–enclosed bottle pours a rich, dark, and complex beer. With caramelized currants, coffee, and charred-oak notes on the nose, it has burned-rum caramel and chocolate on the palate, which gives way to a pleasing, but astringent, finish.

The Greenwich Union—flagship pub of Meantime Brewing.

Meantime London Stout

Meantime Brewing | www.meantimebrewing.com

Country of origin England
First brewed 2008
Alcohol content 4.5% abv
Serving temperature 46°–50°F, 8°–10°C

Having created authentic versions of the two beers they felt defined modern brewing—porter and India Pale Ale—Meantime Brewing wanted to take its historical interest in beer styles in a slightly different direction. Both beer styles were originally developed in London, but they actually evolved elsewhere, to such a degree that they became synonymous with other towns. Porter fueled London's industrial revolution before being imitated by a certain Irish brewery, who developed an extra-stout porter with the addition of unmalted roast barley. This became known as "stout," and the brewer, Guinness, became so famous that it eclipsed the style's London origins.

In London, porter brewing disappeared, only returning with the recent craft beer revival. Brewer Alastair Hook pondered how porter would have evolved if it had remained popular. How would it be different from Irish stout? The result is Meantime London Stout—a beer that draws a straight line from 18th-century porter to modern-day stout, and which does not deviate via Dublin. It has a lower alcohol content than porter once had, in line with the late-19th and 20th century trend to lighter drinks. The key difference from Guinness is that it contains 100 percent malt grist with no roast barley. The brown and black malts combine with London water to give less astringency and a softer, more velvety mouthfeel and mellower taste than stout drinkers may be accustomed to. Meantime London Stout is the descendant of a beer style that was all about London, and is best thought of as a cousin to Irish stout. **PB**

Tasting notes

Pours black with a satisfying beige head. Aromas of coffee, vanilla, and dark chocolate are followed by a velvety smooth beer on the palate with flavors of coffee, caramel, molasses, and vanilla. A fine balance of bitter and sweet. Excellent with oysters but also good with duck and cold meats.

Midtfyns Imperial Stout

Midtfyns Bryghus | www.midtfyns-bryghus.dk

Country of origin Denmark
First brewed 2007
Alcohol content 9.5% abv
Serving temperature 50°–57°F, 10°–14°C

An American moved to Denmark and took over a failing microbrewery that was producing bad Scottish ales; he turned it around to win New Beer of the Year, as voted for by Danish beer consumers. This description of Eddie Szweda's Midtfyns Bryghus reads like a fairy tale by Hans Christian Andersen, but at the time Szweda felt that the company he invested in was more like the ugly duckling.

Midtfyns Bryghus was set up in 2005 by two local businessmen hoping to capitalize on the growing demand for microbrewed beer. They chose to brew Scottish ales under license, but failed to win over the locals' palates with the flat, unpasteurized beer. They sold the brewery in 2006 to Eddie and a partner. It was time for a change, and Eddie, who previously had worked in Denmark selling jam and wine, put his irrepressible energy to work. Eddie has become well known on the island of Funen, right in the middle of Denmark, where the brewery is based, and has taken every opportunity to speak and promote the brewery to the local population. His commercial savvy and tireless efforts have gone hand in hand with a completely new range of beers that has attracted the attention of Danish beer drinkers farther afield, too.

Within a year, Eddie and brewmaster Jan Thaagaard Jensen had two beers in the Danish Beer Enthusiasts' Beer of the Year competition, and Imperial Stout won the New Beer of the Year award. Imperial Stout is a Danish beer that underlines the nation's love of dark, roasted malty beers. It is brewed with several roasted malt types and matured in oak casks. **AA**

Tasting notes

Dark with a coffee head, Imperial Stout has an initial aroma of roasted malt with caramel and milk chocolate that makes way for a balanced chocolate sweetness in the mouth, ahead of the beer's moderate bitterness and a finish of dried fruit, smoke, and oakiness.

Mikkeller Beer Geek Breakfast

Mikkeller | www.mikkeller.dk

Country of origin Denmark
First brewed 2005
Alcohol content 7.5% abv
Serving temperature 52°–55°F, 11°–13°C

Beer Geek Breakfast started life when the brewery's co-founder Mikkel Borg Bjergsø and his old brewing partner Kristian Klarup Keller set out to make an oatmeal stout with a great deal of body. From the outset, this was a brewer's indulgent experiment, as the pair sought out every single malted grain they thought highly of, which translated into seven varieties—pilsner, oat, smoked, CaraMunich, brown, pale chocolate, and chocolate malts plus roasted barley and flaked oats.

As Bjergsø himself says: "We wanted to combine all the best flavors of all the different grains that we'd been experimenting with, even to the point where it's 25 percent oats, because we wanted to add great body and creaminess." But, despite throwing the metaphorical kitchen sink at the brew, they were sadly disappointed when they tried the initial final product, finding it lacking in that oomph factor they were after. So, Mikkel came up with the idea of adding coffee and, after contacting Alesmith Brewery in California to see how its coffee beer was created, they set the percolator running, and the rest, as they say, is brewing history.

Bjergsø says, "Some brewers might think we are crazy spending five or six hours a day brewing coffee, but we always want our beers to stay the same. After all, this is probably still our most famous beer despite it being one of the first." That said, the brewery does sometimes produce special variations for beer festivals including chocolate and chili in place of the coffee, using yeast from De Dolle in Belgium, or upgrading to the startlingly expensive Civet coffee. **MC**

Tasting notes

The genius of this beer is in the use of Centennial and Cascade hops, which means that the malts and coffee don't overwhelm completely. There's a balance of bitter chocolate-covered raisins and coffee beans with a lighter, tingly freshness that makes it refreshing enough for brunch.

Mikkeller Black

Mikkeller | www.mikkeller.dk

Country of origin Denmark
First brewed 2007
Alcohol content 17.5% abv
Serving temperature 59°F, 15°C

Brewer Mikkel Borg Bjergsø describes this imperial stout as "one of my experiments." It is one of many that have succeeded as the Danish brewer has quickly proved himself as a craftsman of challenging beers since the first brew in 2006. He started (originally with colleague Kristian Klarup Keller) with the aim of competing not only with the established Danish brewers, but also the growing number of microbreweries. The idea, he says, was to test the limits of what could be done with beer—in taste and alcohol strength—rather than copy American microbreweries. His beers live up to the original aim, especially with the amount of hops used, leading to surprised looks from classically trained brewers. The big, bold flavors Bjergsø produces have won many fans both in Denmark and in the United States. The tendency to go big has led to accusations of going over the top on occasion, but whether this is true or not, Bjergsø's beers are always interesting.

Unlike other microbrewers, Bjergsø is a nomad, brewing at various breweries around Europe. He has brewed in Denmark, Belgium, Norway, England, and Scotland. Black is no exception and was brewed at De Proef Brouwerij, which can be found in Lochristi-Hijfte, Belgium, with the help of Dirk Naudts. Naudts, known as "the Prof," is a specialist in beers with a heavy alcohol content and has created many recipes for Belgian breweries. Mikkeller Black follows the pattern of many of Bjergsø's other brews, with plenty of hops and roasted malts. It is brewed first with ale yeast, before dark cassonade sugar is added and a secondary fermentation started with champagne yeast. **AA**

Tasting notes

Black with a coffee-colored head, it packs an immediate punch with a strong alcohol nose with hints of dark fruits. The taste starts chocolaty and then develops into a dark roasted maltiness bordering on tarry, with strong sweetness and sharp, lingering bitterness.

Mikkeller From To

Mikkeller | www.mikkeller.dk

Country of origin Denmark
First brewed 2007
Alcohol content 8% abv
Serving temperature 50°–54°F, 10°–12°C

In 2006, the Danish brewing scene underwent a minor revolution, with microbreweries opening at the rate of one every two weeks. This was the frenetic environment in which Mikkeller appeared, brought to life by young home-brewers Mikkel Borg Bjergsø and Kristian Klarup Keller (the latter left and currently edits a rock music magazine). Bjergsø is now the sole brewer, but this hasn't stopped his creative brewing juices from flowing, and he has produced an array of different beers, alongside various collaborations with breweries such as Scotland's BrewDog and Belgium's De Struise.

Of the many small breweries in Denmark, Mikkeller is perhaps among the most lionized and loved. Their beers are exported across Europe and to the United States, where they have become particularly popular with devotees of the Internet beer sites Ratebeer and Beer Advocate.

This is a porter brewed annually for the Christmas season. Given that this is a time for giving, the bottle's label is printed as a gift card so that drinkers can fill in the "from" and "to" names. An aspect of Mikkeller's creative anarchy is that the beer does not follow a fixed recipe, but changes slightly annually. The last vintage saw several malts, roasted barley, a trio of hops, and all manner of spices going into the mix. Somewhat oddly, so does the name of the beer. "From To" in Danish is "Fra Til," but the beer has also been called "Til Fra" and "Fra via Til." It is not only Americans who recognize Mikkeller's beer passion. They have twice been voted Danish Brewery of the Year. **RP**

Tasting notes

This porter pours black with a chocolate brown head. There is a very deep aroma of chocolate and coffee with a fruity background. The taste is what one expects of a stout/porter—chocolate and coffee—but in this case, lightened by a slight fruitiness.

Moonraker

J. W. Lees | www.jwlees.co.uk

Country of origin England
First brewed *ca.* late 1970s
Alcohol content 7.5% abv
Serving temperature 52°F, 11°C

Manchester-based brewery J. W. Lees started brewing in 1828 and, like most breweries of the time, produced strong ale. However, its award-winning barleywine Moonraker only appeared in the late 1970s. It is a potent ale of high strength that was often packaged in small bottles called "nips." These were either used as mixers with bitter or drunk at the end of an evening in the same way that some drinkers savor a brandy or single-malt whisky. The name "Moonraker" pays tribute to the tale told of local farm workers, who, late one evening after a few beers, saw the reflection of a full moon in a stream. They thought it was a cheese in the water and tried to rake it out. Could they have been drinking an earlier version of Moonraker?

English barleywines are a memory of the time when country brewers tried to give at least one of their beers the cachet and strength of wine. However, another story of the origins of "barleywine" relates that the term came into use in the 18th and 19th centuries when England was often at war with France—some say that it was the duty of patriots, usually from the upper classes, to drink ale rather than claret.

Moonraker is made with Maris Otter malted barley and East Kent Golding hops, and it is still brewed in the brewhouse built in 1876 by John Willie Lees. Today, production is overseen by a sixth-generation member of the family, Michael Lees-Jones. With its rich fruit flavors, preponderance of alcohol, and dark port-style characteristics, Moonraker has proved to be an ideal partner with red meat and cheeses—especially dry, crumbly cheeses such as Lancashire. **TH**

Tasting notes

The powerful nose is sweet, rich, and warming; on the palate, dark chocolate and alcohol notes overlay a marvelous roasted toasty base. Dark amber to the eye and still in the glass; the fruit and licorice sweetness gives way to a dry, lingering finish.

Moonshine

Grand Ridge Brewery | www.grand-ridge.com.au

Country of origin Australia
First brewed 1989
Alcohol content 8.5% abv
Serving temperature 43°–46°F, 6°–8°C

Microbreweries have sprung up all over Australia since the early 1980s, for all sorts of reasons. First and foremost, it has been due to a frustration with the range of icy cold lagers that have dominated the Australian drinking scene for more than a hundred years. Rarely has it been about the money (if only because it is so hard to make). In the case of Eric Walters, it was part frustration and part opportunity that prompted him and a group of mates to take over a failed brewery in rural Victoria in 1988.

About two hours' drive east of Melbourne, the brewery is set in an old butter factory, which opened in 1891, and it has an excellent water supply. Although the previous brewery's owner had only survived in the business for twelve months, Eric claims to have made up his mind about the purchase as he drove between the picturesque mountain ridges after which the brewery is named. It's very much a local affair, and Walters's co-owners include a mechanic, baker, lawyer, accountant, and full-time mother. Despite this modest beginning, Grand Ridge has gone out of its way to produce ales that challenge the perception of what it means for a beer to be Australian. Moonshine is one of its triumphs and was designed to be a classic barleywine able to stand side by side with world-class beers.

Appropriately enough, the locals refer to Grand Ridge brewery as "the monastery on the mountain." It would appear that they prefer the old butter factory providing a steady stream of Moonshine (or its venerable grandfather, the 11 percent Supershine) to slabs of butter for their Vegemite on toast. **DD**

Tasting notes

The dark ruby colors in your glass should be covered with a fleeting head that entices beer drinkers with soft, caramel aromas. Carefully sipped at a warm temperature, Moonshine ale rewards with a rich malt flavor that hints of your favorite pudding.

Moorhouse's Black Cat

Moorhouse's Brewery | www.moorhouses.co.uk

Country of origin England
First brewed 1979
Alcohol content 3.4% abv
Serving temperature 50°F, 10°C

Black Cat was a beer born of desperation to bring luck to an ailing brewery and, in this case, superstition paid off. At the time, Moorhouse's Brewery (based in the northwest English town of Burnley) was only making one beer—the 3.7 percent session ale Premier. Its main focus was on non-alcoholic hop bitters for export and for use in shandy concentrates for soft drink companies.

Black Cat came about through the need to use up some of the concentrate licorice that had been lying around. The brewery started to experiment with more traditional ingredients, and when chocolate malt was added to provide flavor, Black Cat Mild sprang to life. When it was launched, it seemed like a rather mad move because mild was declining against lager sales in the United Kingdom. But the northwest of England has always been a staunch mild heartland, and passionate customers in the local pubs kept the brand alive, because they wanted a cask mild to replace those that the major breweries had stopped brewing.

In 2000, the word "mild" was dropped from the name, with the aim of broadening its appeal. The same year also saw it win the Campaign for Real Ale's Champion Beer of Britain. This was the first time a mild had won the acclaimed prize in twenty-seven years. Moorhouse's itself came very close to closing its doors in 1985, before locally born businessman Bill Parkinson stepped in to save the company. He was enjoying a pint of Premier and was told that the brewery was about to shut within days. As the story has it, he liked the beer so much that he bought the brewery and remains owner to this day. **MC**

Tasting notes

Black Cat's mocha latte nose gives way to chocolate, coffee, and licorice tones, tempered by a dry fruit note and a slight creaminess that—when served at a slightly more chilled temperature than most ales—can be both satisfying and refreshing.

Motor Oil

Birrificio Beba | www.birrabeba.it

Murphy's Irish Stout

Murphy Brewery | www.murphys.com

Country of origin Italy
First brewed 1999
Alcohol content 6.8% abv
Serving temperature 46°–50°F, 8°–10°C

Country of origin Ireland
First brewed 1856
Alcohol content 4% abv
Serving temperature 46°–50°F, 8°–10°C

Villar Perosa is a small village not too far from Turin, where brothers Enrico and Alessandro Borio produce their wide range of artisanal beers. The two brothers had no previous experience; they weren't even home-brewers or even real beer lovers. However, Enrico spent a few months in the United Kingdom as a student and enjoyed a few decent pints of cask ale. The beer compared so favorably to mass-market Italian lagers that he decided to brew his own.

Beba started off with bottom-fermenting beers, until the brothers decided that lager would be a better option. Motor Oil is one of the "family": a strong dark lager. Lots of pils, some Munich, and a pinch of chocolate malts make up the grist, while Hallertau Tradition hops are added during the boil just to give a clean bitterness to the beer. Try Motor Oil with a well-matured cheese or well-flavored pasta dishes. **MM**

Murphy's is an Irish dry stout, which means it is a touch lighter than a full-bodied stout. Its low carbonation makes it an extremely quaffable beer, often enjoyed in the traditional pubs of its Munster heartland.

The Murphy's family has a rich Irish heritage, having set themselves up in the Cork area in the early 1700s. But it was not until 1825 that beer production really picked up pace, when James J. Murphy invested heavily to take it to new heights. Since then, the beer has gone from strength to strength, picking up awards such as the gold medal at the Brewing Industry International Awards in 2005. The reason? Well, it stands up as a true example of the style: roast and bitterness in the taste, but a balance with the sweetness and low carbonation that lends itself to a sessionable stout. It also has a wonderful creaminess, so can be enjoyed in summer or winter in equal measure. **TS**

Tasting notes
On the nose, the aroma is quite complex, rich in roasted grainy notes, coffee beans, and licorice. Well balanced on the palate, a medium body, with a pleasant return of the roasted notes.

Tasting notes
It pours as black as peat and has all the roast flavor a good stout should have. There's a slight hop profile, not as easily detected, but sure enough, it's bitter. Pair it with red meat.

Time for a Murphy's? A stout clock face in Cork, Ireland. ➡

Murray's Best Extra Porter

Murray's Craft Brewing Co. | www.murraysbrewingco.com.au

Country of origin Australia
First brewed 2008
Alcohol content 8% abv
Serving temperature 46°F, 8°C

A successful property developer, Murray Howe was traveling through America in 2004 when he had a beer epiphany after being exposed to some of the local craft offerings. Determined to reproduce the experience back home, Murray bought the historic pub in Taylors Arm—the original pub with no beer—and used it to set up a brewery that brewed the type of beer he wanted to drink.

The fifty inhabitants of this small New South Wales village gave Murray's beers a mixed response. Some of the older drinkers in particular were rusted onto their old loves, and either refused to taste the interloper or quickly returned to the icy comfort of their favorite drop. Other skeptics became converts. Thirsty travelers spread the word, and before too long, Murray's beers were being distributed nationally. Increased production eventually meant that the brewery had to be moved to the picturesque Port Stephen's Winery, where Murray now delights in changing visiting wine drinkers' perception of beer.

Renowned New Zealand brewer Graeme Mahy designed Murray's Best Extra Porter to be a complex winter warmer suited to careful sipping, like a port or brandy. The beer is now maintained by former home-brewer Shawn Sherlock, who surprised no one outside of the University of Newcastle when he put his Australian history PhD studies on hold to follow his passion as Graeme's assistant. Now head brewer, Shawn tweaks Graeme's original recipe each year as the temperature drops, to keep things interesting both for himself and for followers of this seasonal delight. **DD**

Tasting notes

The unusually high level of alcohol adds warmth and sweetness to this ruby dark beer, while light carbonation allows the malt-driven complexity to linger on the palate. Murray's Best Extra Porter is best enjoyed slowly with a nibble of the finest dark chocolate.

+Negra

Companyia Cervesera del Montseny | www.ccm.cat

Country of origin Spain
First brewed 2007
Alcohol content 5.2% abv
Serving temperature 48°F, 9°C

Together with +Malta and +Lupulus, the recipe for this stout style was created while brewmaster Pablo Vijande was still a home-brewer. This one, he believes, was the hardest to get to the stage where he was happy with it. This was because it always came out too sweet. His final recipe was more complicated and refined. As well as crystal, caramalt, chocolate, and black malts, he selected four cereals—flaked wheat, roasted barley, flaked oats, and flaked rye—while the perfectly proportionate bitterness was obtained with Hallertau Hersbrücker, Northern Brewer, and Styrian Golding hops. At the end of all this work, he must have felt it was worth all his efforts: Cervesera del Montseny's +Negra was elected Beer of 2008 at Jafre Fair, a Spanish craft beer festival.

Founded in 2007 in Sant Miguel de Balenyà (Seva), in the heart of Catalonia, Companyia Cervesera del Montseny produces five different beers, brewed using traditional methods and ingredients. One of its first aims was to re-create what was seen as the lost beer culture of Spain, which is a big beer consumer but whose drinkers do not have much knowledge about what goes into the glass. The largest segment of the Spanish beer market is dominated by light and easy beers that Spanish drinkers are used to consuming at any time of day. It is hard to introduce the concept of craft beer, not to mention feature a stout that is so very different from the popular *caña*—Iberian pint—people are used to. Yet with enthusiasm, passion, and good beer, Cervesera del Montseny are meeting with some measure of success in achieving their aims. **SS**

Tasting notes

An intense darkness in color, beneath a brawny persistent head. On the nose, aromatic notes combine with sweetness from the cereals and a roastiness from the dark malts; this balance and combination continue on the palate accompanied by a measured bitterness from the hops.

Nightmare

Nick Stafford's Hambleton Ales | www.hambletonales.co.uk

Country of origin England
First brewed 1994
Alcohol content 5% abv
Serving temperature 54°F, 12°C

In the Hambleton Hills in north Yorkshire, a white horse is etched into the hillside. Its distinctive image also appears on the labels of Nick Stafford's Hambleton Ales, a brewery based 12 miles (19 km) away, close to the village of Melmerby.

In 1989, Stafford resigned as the headmaster of a preparatory school. He worked briefly in banking and even considered buying a pub, before his brother Martin, the founder of Dent Brewery in Cumbria, suggested that he start his own brewery. Stafford created his brewery in his mother-in-law's barn, while using a garden shed as an office. He began brewing with a capacity of ten barrels in 1991, but within six months he was producing thirty barrels a week.

Stafford decided to brew beers to satisfy local Yorkshire tastes. The "new brand but familiar flavors" approach worked. By 1997, the brewery had outgrown the barn and moved elsewhere locally. Stafford also embarked on bottling, for himself and other small breweries, and, to this day, contract bottling forms a large part of the Hambleton business. Stafford is influential in the Society of Independent Brewers (SIBA), for whom he created a scheme whereby members could sell to Britain's big pub chains, otherwise commercially out-of-bounds to small brewers.

Stafford describes Nightmare as a "stout porter." The beer won the brewery's first major prize, Champion Winter Beer of Britain, in 1997, and it has since been a brewery favorite. Beer historians often bicker over the definitions of stout and porter, but whatever it is, Nightmare is a beer of distinction. **JP**

Tasting notes

Creamy off-white head and dark red brown body. A soft aroma of cold black coffee with an undercurrent of treacle toffee and chocolate. Smooth, luxurious mouthfeel. Flavors of dark fruits, such as plums and blueberries, accompany the roasted malt. More roast and bitter flavors linger.

Nikšićko Tamno

Trebjesa Brewery | www.ab-inbev.com

Country of origin Montenegro
First brewed *ca.* 1890s
Alcohol content 6.2% abv
Serving temperature 41°F, 5°C

Long before Inspector Morse and his love of English ale, there was Nero Wolfe, another fictional detective with a liking for beer, a man of Falstaffian girth who often drank five quarts a day and kept his bottle tops in a drawer so that he could keep an eye on his drinking. Wolfe was from Montenegro, although the books never recorded if he ever enjoyed a pint from Trebjesa Brewery, which, since the country's independence in 2006, has been its sole brewery. The brewery brewed its first batch of beer in 1896, and Interbrew (as Anheuser-Busch InBev was then called) bought the place in 1997.

As is usual for this part of the world, where beer has always co-existed with fiery spirits as well as locally produced wine, pale lagers dominate the market, and Nikšićko Pivo is the best seller. It is a fairly standard pils, designed to be served cold—refreshing and thirst quenching and ideal with a plate of *prsuta*, a smoked ham that is similar in style to prosciutto.

Montenegrins are fiercely proud of Nikšićko Pivo, and woe betide travelers who wish to buy a bottle of beer from, say, neighboring Croatia or Serbia: it has been known for patriotic cashiers to refuse to serve them anything other than Nikšićko. As well as producing a couple of other beers on a pils theme, and bottling Beck's, Trebjesa also brews Nikšićko Tamno, the brewery's take on the Munich dunkel style. Even though dark beers only make up a small sector of the market, it is heartening to see the continued survival of this beer, which is surprisingly refreshing and light on the palate despite its strength. **ATJ**

Tasting notes

Dark with chestnut tints, Nikšićko Tamno sits beneath a rocky espresso-colored head. On the nose, sweetish caramel malt, with a tingle of fruit in the background. Palate is chocolaty, with hints of coffee bean and condensed milk, before it descends into a quick finish.

Nils Oscar Imperial Stout

Nils Oscar Brewery | www.nilsoscar.se

Country of origin Sweden
First brewed 1999
Alcohol content 7% abv
Serving temperature 54°–59°F, 12°–15°C

We may call it "Russian imperial stout," but the drink perfected in England for consumption in the courts of the czars was enjoyed all around the Baltic. The trip to St. Petersburg may not have been as arduous as the voyage of India Pale Ale, but it was still long and difficult. The key difference was there were many other potential markets along the way. The chances of a profitable voyage could be greatly increased by building business en route in Holland, Prussia, Denmark, Poland—and Sweden.

Throughout the 18th and 19th centuries, imperial stout was enormously popular in Sweden. However, it had disappeared by the 20th century, as those who continued to drink in a largely anti-alcohol climate followed the rest of Scandinavia into its love affair with pilsner lager. As in most of the world, stout meant only Guinness by the time Nils Oscar made a millennial Christmas present to the nation, reintroducing Sweden to its lost love in 1999.

Nils Oscar Imperial Stout was so popular that what had been intended as a seasonal beer has been brewed regularly ever since. Brewed with generous amounts of roasted barley, various malts, and malted oats, as well as Magnum and East Kent Golding hops, it's a rounded, smooth stout, definitely English rather than Irish in style. It soon proved popular at home and abroad, winning several golds at the Stockholm Beer Festival and also thriving at the World Beer Cup. Less challenging than hard-core fans of the style are used to, at 7 percent, Nils Oscar Imperial Stout is still a weighty beer, and can be cellar aged for up to ten years. **PB**

Tasting notes
Pours near-black with a deep reddish hue. A deep, sweet roasted aroma of chocolate, coffee, and dark fruit, followed by additional hints of raisins, treacle, earthiness, and licorice on the palate. A nice balance of dark roast and sweet fruit.

Nils Oscar Rökporter

Nils Oscar Brewery | www.nilsoscar.se

Country of origin Sweden
First brewed 2007
Alcohol content 6% abv
Serving temperature 54°–59°F, 12°–15°C

When first asked, Nils Oscar head brewer Patrick Holmqvist says cryptically of Rökporter that it was simply "a beer he wanted to brew." Then he reveals that it's a beer that contains 75 percent beechwood smoked malt, as well as caramel, chocolate and crystal malts, and is seasoned with English Fuggle and American Amarillo hops.

There's a brutally simple logic behind what might seem—from the recipe—an enormously complex beer. Alcohol sales in Sweden are controlled by a state-owned monopoly, the Systembolaget. When a product is submitted to them, they ask what category it belongs to. If the supplier replies with a category they recognize, there is a tasting competition for products within that category, and the winner instantly gains nationwide distribution. In beer, one category is "complex porter or stout." Nils Oscar created Rökporter specifically to win the tasting in that category, duly did so, and now has a fine, complex beer that sells very well throughout Sweden.

Rökporter simply translates as "smoked porter," and smoked beers have a reputation for dividing the beer world. While aficionados adore them, many feel strongly that their beer shouldn't resemble bacon or smoked cheese. What makes Rökporter an incredible beer is that, even with 75 percent smoked malt, it retains a wonderful balance. The beechwood aroma is present, but doesn't dominate. The complex malts give a delicate roundness of flavor, and the complexity serves to marry the smoke character into the whole, making it fit, rather than leaving it to intimidate. **PB**

Tasting notes

Pours dark with a beige head, and a complex aroma blends smoke with creamy coffee and chocolate. On the palate, these flavors are joined by licorice, bitter chocolate, and sweet malt, before a dry finish with hints of charcoal. Matches well with fried, grilled, and barbecued foods.

Nøgne Ø Imperial Stout

Nøgne Ø A/S | www.nogne-o.com

Country of origin Norway
First brewed 2005
Alcohol content 9% abv
Serving temperature 57°F, 14°C

Nøgne Ø—or "Naked Isle" in English—takes its name from the bare, rocky islands that dot the Norwegian coastline. There's nothing bare or naked about the beers brewed by Kjetil Jikiun and his company, but the scenery is certainly reflected in the uncompromising attitude Nøgne Ø takes toward its beer.

Jikiun, a former airline pilot and home-brewer, nursed his dream of a brewery for years, bringing back bags of malt and hops from his flights to the United States. Also among his luggage were bottles of U.S. beer that served as the inspiration for a long line of impressive brews that have since won great acclaim. Apart from impressing the brewing world in general, Jikiun and Nøgne Ø have also made an impact in Norway, introducing terms such as "IPA" and "imperial stout" to the highly regulated Nordic market. It hasn't all been easy going, and the company had endured several changes of shareholders before the brewing and commercial sides of the business came together.

Nøgne Ø Imperial Stout is Jikiun's interpretation of a style that should be sweet, dark, and bitter, but without losing balance. He has brewed it to be easily drinkable—so that it is possible to finish a bottle with your taste buds still in one piece. Jikiun believes balance is important and that it is possible to get away with extreme ingredients as long as they are in harmony. Imperial Stout doesn't hold back on ingredients and contains roasted barley, Maris Otter pale ale, Munich, black, and chocolate malts combined with Columbus and Crystal hops, English ale yeast, and local Grimstad water. **AA**

Tasting notes

In the glass, a wonderfully dark body topped by a dark head. The aroma has coffee and chocolate notes that dovetail perfectly into a complex roasted malt taste with hints of fruit and vanilla, followed by a long, warming, balanced bitter finish.

Norwegian Wood

HaandBryggeriet | www.haandbryggeriet.net

Country of origin Norway
First brewed 2006
Alcohol content 6.5% abv
Serving temperature 50°–54°F, 10°–12°C

"Most of the brewing traditions of Norway were lost when the lager brewers conquered the country, but we are trying to re-create the beers." These words, from Jens Maudal, one of four friends who run the HaandBryggeriet brewery, sum up the company's philosophy in the same way as its name—translating as "hand brewery"—conveys the attention to detail they put into their beers.

The brewery is housed in a 200-year-old wooden building just south of Oslo. Here the old style of brewing is dusted off and put to good use in harness with modern techniques to ensure first-rate beers for today's drinker. A great example of the range comes in the beer they call "Norwegian Wood." The mash for this brew incorporates various malts, including smoked (from Bamberg), crystal, amber, and Munich. Old Norway then plays a hand when juniper branches, loaded with berries, are placed in the mash tun. These are not bought in, but harvested from local woods. They echo Norwegian farmhouse brewing, when a beer like this would have been produced for special events such as christenings, weddings, and funerals.

To balance the spiciness of the wood and berries, and the sweetness and aromatics of the malt, American Cluster and Centennial hops are added to the copper. These contribute a New World twist, but then the past comes calling again with fermentation provided by an old-style yeast. This clever mix of ingredients and the blending of past and present result in a fascinating, complex dark beer that drinks very well with cured hams and smoked meats. **JE**

Tasting notes

A biscuity, lightly smoky aroma of nut and coffee, followed by a light-textured, crisp, and nutty taste with sweet coffee notes. Burned grain lingers pleasantly in the dry, increasingly bitter, coffeelike finish. Both smoke and scented juniper flavors are well restrained in this red brown beer.

Oak Aged Yeti Imperial Stout

Great Divide Brewing
www.greatdivide.com

Country of origin United States
First brewed 2003
Alcohol content 9.5% abv
Serving temperature 50°F, 10°C

Oak Aged Yeti Imperial Stout is an imposing beer that makes its presence known right from the start. "When we first made (the original) Yeti Imperial Stout, we just wanted to make a big, chewy stout," says brewery founder Brian Dunn. They experimented with oak and eventually settled on a combination of French and American oak. Dunn says that only oak chips are used in this beer because he didn't want the flavor to be affected by any properties that come from previously used wood vessels, such as bourbon barrels.

The effect is a smoother, drier version of the original Yeti. Great Divide continues to push the limits with different versions of its original Yeti Imperial Stout, including a Chocolate Oak Aged Yeti, made with cocoa nibs and a hint of cayenne pepper. **LMo**

Tasting notes
Creamy, soft, moderately carbonated body accompanies sweet whispers of vanilla, chocolate milk, roasted coffee, toasted oak, and almonds.

Oatis Oatmeal Stout

Ninkasi Brewing
www.ninkasibrewing.com

Country of origin United States
First brewed 2007
Alcohol content 7.2% abv
Serving temperature 44°–55°F, 7°–13°C

Oatis is a beer with a massive dose of oatmeal added to each batch. "I love oatmeal stout. It is my favorite of the stout styles. And there are not a lot of commercial examples of the style in the marketplace," says brewer Jamie Floyd. The brewery decided to make an oatmeal stout its flagship beer. It debuted as a seasonal but became so popular that it is brewed year-round.

Ninkasi Brewing was named to honor the ancient Sumerian goddess of beer. The Sumerians gave up their nomadic way of life when they began to grow barley, making them among the first known brewers. Their beer is documented in a hymn to Ninkasi that is considered the first beer recipe. "It is our goal at Ninkasi Brewing to promote beer's historic and continued role in the cultivation of civilization," Floyd says. **LMo**

Tasting notes
A tall, dark beer that, thanks to a generous hand with the oatmeal, is a smooth operator, too. Black coffee and chocolate caress the gentle, roasted bitterness and subtle sweetness.

Ripe oats growing in the Willamette Valley, Oregon, near the Ninkasi brewery. →

O'Hanlon's Port Stout

O'Hanlon's Brewing Company | www.ohanlonsbeer.com

Country of origin England
First brewed 1999
Alcohol content 4.8% abv
Serving temperature 54°F, 12°C

Kerry-born John O'Hanlon was a keen rugby player in the town of Dublin. After the match, battered and bruised as was the norm for rugby players, a few pints of stout was the clarion call. Next morning, equally battered and bruised, some would make their way to the bar for a lunchtime libation. It is said that one canny barman used to mix in a glass of port with the stout; the name of this drink was "corpse-reviver." Years later, living in London and running his own brewery, John O'Hanlon remembered this drink, and it became the foundation of O'Hanlon's magnificent Port Stout.

Optic pale ale malt, caramalt, crystal, and roast barley go into the mash, and the British "hedgerow" hop Pilot and Styrian Golding are added during the boil (the latter for aroma). The port is added when the beer is being racked, in order to give it a slightly sweetish vinous edge that balances superbly with the roasted notes of the stout. According to O'Hanlon's head brewer Alex Bell, "This was born before my time with O'Hanlon's, but I think the original recipe was dreamed up by John and Rob Jones, later of Dark Star Brewery fame. The Dry Stout recipe from which it is drawn had a lower original gravity than now, as it used a lower attenuating strain of yeast. I changed the yeast to allow more of the malt character to come through."

O'Hanlon's is located on an old farm near Exeter. It is owned by John and wife Liz, who upped sticks from their former brewing site (and pub) in London in 2000. Along with their Port Stout, they have also won plaudits for a sprightly golden ale, Yellowhammer, and their re-creation of Thomas Hardy's Ale. **ATJ**

Tasting notes

Dark chestnut brown with ruby highlights. On the nose, mocha coffee, milk chocolate, and a hint of roasted malt. The mouth is filled with mocha coffee, bitter chocolate, and roasted malt, and in the background the sweetness of the port. Dry, grainy, malty finish.

O'Hara's Irish Stout

Carlow Brewing Company | www.carlowbrewing.com

Country of origin Ireland
First brewed 1998
Alcohol content 4.3% abv
Serving temperature 50°F, 10°C

Carlow Brewing Company has been one of the success stories of Ireland's craft beer industry. Since 1996, they have been turning out beers from their six-person microbrewery into a hostile market where heavily advertised international brands rule supreme. It is not even possible to buy a pint of Carlow beer in Carlow town: craft beer seekers are better served by traveling the 50 miles (80 km) to Dublin to try the beer specialists there. Rather than local emphasis, Carlow has built its success on export, and its stout is available in parts of Europe and as far away as the United States and Australia. Bottling has been the key to this, and yet even here there are challenges. The brewery has to tanker the fresh beer across the Irish Sea to England to be bottled, and then re-import it to Ireland for sale.

Having a mostly bottled product is a distinct advantage when it comes to stout. Since the 1960s, draft Irish stout has been almost exclusively served with nitrogen gas, the chemistry of which traps the aromas and flavors of the beer inside the liquid to preserve that distinctive creamy head. However, with an ordinarily carbonated bottle, as with cask, all of the taste and smell is free to roam unimpeded.

While clearly a member of the dry Irish stout family, O'Hara's is boosted by a generous dose of sweet chocolate malt to complement its dry roasted coffee bitterness. Like almost all Irish craft beer, it's a simple, no-nonsense product in a traditional style. It won't get any awards for exotic flavors or ingredients. However, when only a simple pint of session plain will do, Irish stout doesn't get any better. **JD**

Tasting notes

A brief chocolate overture on the nose is followed swiftly by a stunningly dry, almost sulfurous flavor. After a second, the bitter, roasted coffee notes rise to take the edge off, and then the chocolate makes a reappearance for a smooth, sweet finish.

Okells Aile Smoked Celtic Porter

Okells | www.okells.co.uk

Country of origin Isle of Man
First brewed 2005
Alcohol content 4.8% abv
Serving temperature 50°–55°F, 10°–13°C

With a strong presence in Scandinavia, where they love dark strong beers, Okells was always going to be onto a winner with that market when it produced Aile. The beer was born after a conversation that head brewer Dr. Mike Cowbourne had with one of the brewery's distributors, Steve Holt of Vertical Drinks. Holt suggested that Cowbourne should look into brewing a "quirkier beer."

Cowbourne went away and looked to his malt supplier, Simpsons, for some peated malt. He started to play around with it a bit, looking initially to the German Rauchbier style for inspiration. Producing this beer proved to be somewhat of a nightmare though, as its initial incarnation of the brewery's standard bitter, brewed to a higher strength with the addition of the peated malt, was utterly undrinkable because it reeked and tasted rather like antiseptic. Cowbourne persisted, however, and nine months later, the smoked porter was born.

It's quite likely that traditional London porters had a certain element of smoke to them, as they were brewed over direct heat from coal or wood. When attempting to come up with a name for this unusual brew, Cowbourne initially hit a dead end. He then had the inspiration to search in the Manx dictionary for the words "smoked," "peat," and various others, before finding the word "fire"—or "Aile"—and understandably settling on that. The label on the bottle is probably the most striking of the brewery's range, with its fiery nymph on the back of a dragon, and the Aile beer itself is no less stunning. **MC**

Tasting notes

On the nose, there are rich smoky, malted milk, coffee, and licorice notes. These lead into a sumptuously rich and satisfying smoky and chicory flavor, with hints of chocolate and licorice on the palate that give way to a surprisingly astringent finish.

Old Engine Oil

Harviestoun Brewery | www.harviestoun.com

Country of origin Scotland
First brewed 1999
Alcohol content 6% abv
Serving temperature 55°F, 13°C

Harviestoun began life in a 200-year-old cow byre in Clackmannanshire, later relocating to a purpose-built plant at Alva, a neighboring village that delights in the dramatic backdrop of the Ochil Hills. Ken Brooker, who founded the brewery in 1985, spent much of his early life crafting wooden design prototypes for the Ford Motor Company in Dagenham, Essex, so it's no real surprise that he named this strong and dark ale in honor of another of his great passions: the internal combustion engine.

The wickedly smooth and mysteriously opaque Old Engine Oil is in the style of an imperial Russian stout, exhibiting strong malt flavors and dessertlike rich dark fruits. It is constructed—unusually for a dark beer—with pale malt, roasted barley, and oats. Two U.S. hop varieties, Willamette and Galene, combine with the classic English varieties Fuggle and Golding to produce aromas of aniseed and dry earth with hints of chocolate, coffee, and licorice. It was originally conceived for a winter beer competition that invited only bespoke beers. It won in a convincing manner and gained a nationwide profile as part of the prize.

First experimentations used chocolate powder and smoked malt to produce the desired effect. But the flavor profiles were eventually achieved through the careful selection of malted barley and a clever hop regime that combines aggressive characteristics with more temperate, earthy flavors. It has been described as "the perfect postprandial beer" for its port wine–like attributes of encouraging quiet contemplation and self-satisfaction. **AG**

Tasting notes

A deeply dark beer to savor and mull over. On the palate, it is enormously complex, with flavors of nut, spice, and smoke enhancing and alternating with rich chocolate, coffee, and licorice, before moving on to roasted grain and vinous fruits.

Old Freddy Walker

Moor Beer Company | www.moorbeer.co.uk

Country of origin England
First brewed 1997
Alcohol content 7.3% abv
Serving temperature 54°F, 12°C

Moor Beer started on a farm outside the Somerset town of Glastonbury back in the 1990s. The brewery is still in Somerset, although at a different location, and it is run by Californian Justin Hawke. "My dad educated me in world beer styles when I was growing up," he says, "then I visited England as a teenager and fell in love with cask ale." After graduating from West Point in 1993, he gained practical experience with European beers by traveling through the United Kingdom, Belgium, and the Czech Republic. After leaving the army, he returned to the United States and learned to brew. In 1997, he returned to England "with plans to open our own brewery, fusing cask ale with our global beer inspiration and Californian innovation."

Originally brewed in the late 1990s and named after a retired Royal Navy submariner who lived in the brewery's then–home village, Old Freddy Walker is a block-busting dark ale that is one of the brewery's oldest and most successful beers. (It was once the Campaign for Real Ale's Winter Beer of the Year.) Pale ale, lager, black, crystal, and wheat malts go into the grist, whereas the hops are Liberty and Bramling Cross. Hawke won't release the beer for sale with less than a month of conditioning. "It is drinkable at that point," he says, "but my personal preference is to give it at least three months, and it continues to improve with age." He has also done port and brandied versions of OFW, as well as aging it in wooden barrels that once held cider brandy made from local cider. In 2007, Hawke further demonstrated his U.S. craft brewing credentials with JJJ, a 9 percent double IPA. **ATJ**

Tasting notes

As dark as a moonless night. A soothing nose of licorice, mocha coffee, cocoa powder, and milk chocolate. The palate features a smooth and creamy milk chocolate start that is balanced by an appetizing smokiness; the finish is creamy and smooth hand in hand with a drying graininess.

Old No. 38 Stout

North Coast Brewing | www.northcoastbrewing.com

Country of origin United States
First brewed 1988
Alcohol content 5.5% abv
Serving temperature 44°–50°F, 7°–10°C

"This was the first beer we ever brewed for our 'giant' seven-barrel fermenter," says North Coast founder Mark Ruedrich. Like so many craft brewers, he had returned from a stint in England and found American beer culture "lacking anything fit to drink." Tired of the whining, a friend gave him a home-brewing book and urged him to "shut up and do something about it." The recipe for Old No. 38 was taken from that book by Dave Line, one of the few home-brewing texts available in the late 1970s, and filled with recipes that used treacle and glucose chips, among other exotica.

Old No. 38 was first produced as a home-brew, and the recipe has changed only a little since then. As is traditional for Irish-style stouts, roasted unmalted barley gives a crisp, bittersweet, roasted edge to the beer without tasting charred. At 5.5 percent, it's light enough to qualify as a session beer, but it has great depth of flavor and an overall creaminess that really ties it all together. Bitterness is high at 53 IBUs, but not lip-peelingly so. It's easy enough to brew a stout, but very difficult to create one with this much personality and finesse. The late beer writer Michael Jackson was particularly fond of Old No. 38, calling it "possibly the best stout made in America."

North Coast is located in Fort Bragg in northern California. The name of this beer plays on the area's heritage and comes from a California Western Railroad steam engine that ran through the redwood forests nearby. The beer began life as Old No. 45, but fears of a collision with a similarly numbered malt liquor led to the choice of a less provocative number. **RM**

Tasting notes

Bright roastiness in the nose, with hints of herby, almost-minty hops and a little estery fruitiness. Very soft and smooth on the palate; highly drinkable. Nicely integrated flavors and a really velvety texture. The finish is long, clean, and chocolaty.

Old Peculier

Theakston | www.theakstons.co.uk

Country of origin England
First brewed 1890
Alcohol content 5.6% abv
Serving temperature 55°F, 13°C

Old Peculier is a rich, full-bodied, smooth-tasting ale that made the town of Masham in North Yorkshire famous, especially in the 1970s when the consumer organization Campaign for Real Ale was formed, rekindling an interest in cask-conditioned beer. It is a beer that stands out from the crowd and not just because of its strange name, which refers to the Peculier of Masham, the town's 12th-century ecclesiastical court. This allowed the church to levy fines for a range of crimes, including drunkenness!

Old Peculier is a deep, ruby-colored, strong old ale that is luxurious and full bodied. It is a comfort beer that is best sipped slowly, allowing the complexity of its exuberant and rounded character to dance over the tongue. Pale and crystal malt, cane sugar, and caramel all contribute to the sweetness and color of the beer. The aroma and bitterness, which are so characteristic of an English ale, come from Fuggle hops, which are boiled in the sweet wort and then dry hopped into every cask. An old ale has probably been brewed by the Theakston family since 1827, when they bought a brewpub in the town called the Black Bull. They moved to their present site fifty years later, when a maltings and a small tower brewery were built.

In 2003, in a reversal of more than two decades of ownership, first by Matthew Brown and then Scottish and Newcastle, four Theakston brothers, whose great-great-grandfather had started the firm 176 years before, returned the company to family ownership. Located in the aptly named Paradise Fields, Theakstons has a visitor center and offers brewery tours. **TH**

Tasting notes

A harmonious burst of burned sugar and dark fruit flavors envelops the tongue. A warming sweetness caresses the mouth. There is a long, smooth, dry, satisfying finish. There are hints of licorice, chocolate, and a bold fruitiness that includes ripe plums.

Old Rasputin Russian Imperial Stout

North Coast Brewing | www.northcoastbrewing.com

Country of origin United States
First brewed 1995
Alcohol content 9% abv
Serving temperature 55˚F, 13˚C

North Coast brewmaster Mark Ruedrich was still a home-brewer in the mid-1980s when he first sampled an imperial stout made by the late and lamented craft brewing pioneer, Bert Grant. This was well before Ruedrich and his partners opened their brewpub in Fort Bragg, California. "I thought it was the best beer I had ever tasted," he recalls. Nearly ten years after drinking that beer, Ruedrich had what he calls a "taste" dream. "The residue remained" the next day, when it came time to check the progress of his first imperial stout, which became Old Rasputin. By then, he was making beer at both the brewpub and the microbrewery they'd opened across the street. "We were tasting it from the tank," he says, "and it was the beer I had tasted in my dream."

First released on draft in 1995 and then bottled shortly afterward, Old Rasputin soon earned attention in 1996 for what was in the bottle as well as on the label—a striking portrait of Grigori Rasputin, the famed Russian mystic said to have been a lover of imperial stouts—and started winning multiple awards. To celebrate Old Rasputin turning ten years old in bottle, Ruedrich brewed a special batch in 2006, aging it in bourbon barrels until it was ready to drink a year later. Called "Old Rasputin X," it was followed by Old Rasputin XI in 2008, then Old Rasputin XII. Bourbon and time change the beer considerably, rounding any rough edges with vanilla notes and overtaking chocolate flavors with bourbon. Although the alcohol content climbs from 9 to 11.6 percent, the "X" version leaves an almost silky-smooth impression. **SH**

Tasting notes

Black in the glass, with mahogany highlights at the edges. Roasted coffee beans and toffee-chocolate sweetness on the nose, with more of the same in the mouth. Complex and creamy; dark fruits as well as nutty chocolate. Long, dry finish with lingering bitterness.

Old Slug Porter

RCH Brewery | www.rchbrewery.com

Country of origin England
First brewed 1992
Alcohol content 4.5% abv
Serving temperature 55°F, 13°C

The letters "RCH" stand for Royal Clarence Hotel. That's the establishment on the promenade in Burnham-on-Sea, Somerset, where the brewery began life in 1982. It wasn't the ideal location. As the brewery began to build up trade with other pubs and awards started to roll in, it was soon clear that larger premises would be required, preferably in a location where the demands of the brewhouse wouldn't divert water away from the hotel's guest rooms. The result was a move in 1993 to an old cider farm close to Weston-super-Mare.

Another reason for relocating was a problem with slugs, which just loved Burnham's sandy soil and regularly invaded the brewhouse. They've now been consigned to the past, but they're not forgotten thanks to this first-rate porter, which was jokingly named because, as you drink the beer, it leaves a trail like a slug's down the side of the glass.

Back in the early 1990s, porter as a beer style was almost forgotten. Its near-neighbor, stout, was still kicking around thanks to the huge advertising budget of Guinness; but porter, with its slightly sweeter, lighter-bodied profile, had largely disappeared. RCH was among the earliest microbreweries to revive the style, which today enjoys a much healthier presence in British licensed premises.

The ingredients of Old Slug are simple but effective. Crystal malt and black malt add color and roasted grain character to the sweetness provided by pale malt. Fuggle and Golding hops contribute to the balancing bitterness. It's an enjoyable combination that has won the beer many prizes. **JE**

Tasting notes

A dark, garnet-colored porter with a light, airy body and an aroma of smooth coffee and creamy chocolate. The mostly bitter taste features roasted grain and coffee flavors, as well as a gentle hop tang, rounded off by a dry, bitter, coffee finish.

Old Tom Strong Ale

Frederic Robinson | www.frederic-robinson.co.uk

Country of origin England
First brewed 1899
Alcohol content 8.5% abv
Serving temperature 52°F, 11°C

One of the most precious items kept safely at the Unicorn Brewery in the northern English town of Stockport is a notebook from 1899 belonging to Frederic Robinson's then–head brewer, Alfred Munton. On a page dated Wednesday, November 1, he records his first brew of Old Tom—complete with a sketch of the brewery's cat. More than a century later, this strong, dark, luxurious ale is still being brewed: an elegant barleywine with a full-throated chorus of glorious sensory sensations.

Available on draft and from a bottle, it is a beer that changes over time. When freshly poured, it smells of burned molasses and vinous fruit. It is a winter warmer that does precisely what you expect it to: the alcohol caresses the tongue in a cordial embrace, leading on to peppery rich overtones. It is bittersweet, but not too sweet; the yeast has taken most of the fermentable sugars and turned them into alcohol.

The beer's complexity comes from Halcyon and Pipkin pale malts, crystal malt, a little flaked maize, and torrified wheat, plus some caramel for color. Whole flowers of Golding hops are added to a rolling, boiling, sweet wort before the fermentation begins, and after that more hops—Golding again and Northdown—are added to the cask.

The brewery was founded in 1859 by Frederic Robinson, and Oliver Robinson is the sixth generation of the family to have worked at the brewery. He prefers Old Tom to be served with a slight chill, rather than at cellar temperature. That said, it is a beer that looks its best when served in a brandy glass. **TH**

Tasting notes

Almost-black black currant in color with chestnut tints, it has a stupendous nose of toffee and malt followed by hints of caramel and fruit. A superbly balanced, mouth-filling, fruity, vinous, and warming ale that also contains hints of the smokiness of whiskey.

Olivaria Porter

Olivaria Brewery | www.alivaria.by

Country of origin Belarus
First brewed 2009
Alcohol content 6.8% abv
Serving temperature 54°F, 12°C

Given that Belarus has only existed as an independent country since the early 1990s, it's no surprise that the world of beer has taken little notice of what is going on in its brewing industry. However, Belarus has a native brewing industry, and Olivaria (or "Alivaria," as it is spelled in Belarusian) is one of the oldest, having been established in Minsk in 1864 with financial help from the provincial government of the time. In the years prior to the 1917 revolution, the brewery went through a series of owners, including one from Austria, who exported its beers to the likes of Vilnius—now capital of Lithuania—and Brest, where the treaty that ended the war between Germany and Russia was signed in 1918. History has not been kind to this part of the world: revolution and wars have rolled back and forth over its lands. But Olivaria is unique in that it still produces its beers on the same site as it did in 1864.

Olivaria Porter is a dark and strong variation on the Baltic porter style, and it was first brewed in 2009 for the 145th anniversary of the brewery's founding. When the beer was launched, the brewery held beer tastings at various hypermarkets in Minsk, which was a novel experience for people of the city. This proved to be popular. The brewery has also recommended that the porter be warmed in a saucepan with an added spoonful of honey and lemon juice. According to those in the know, this gives a result that is similar to a German Glühwein and warming enough to help cope with a Belarusian winter's day, which can sometimes see the mercury drop to -22 degrees Fahrenheit (-30°C). **ATJ**

Tasting notes

In the glass, very dark chestnut in color beneath a demerara sugar–colored head; butter toffee on the mellow nose. Butter toffee and demerara sugar sweetness on the palate, which is almost suggestive of sugared mocha coffee. Dangerously drinkable given its strength.

Ommegang Abbey Ale

Brewery Ommegang | www.ommegang.com

Country of origin United States
First brewed 1997
Alcohol content 8.5% abv
Serving temperature 50°F, 10°C

Sitting amid the gently rolling hills outside the upstate New York village of Cooperstown, the picturesque Brewery Ommegang can easily be confused with a traditional farmhouse brewery of Wallonia. The brewery, founded in 1997 by Wendy Littlefield and her husband Don Feinberg, was inspired by the farms and breweries they visited as importers of Belgian ales. Built on a 19th-century hop farm, it is white and rustic, and it greets visitors who enter through a gated archway with the aroma of freshly milled grain and steaming malt. One mouthful from a chalice of the brewery's flagship dubbel will have you convinced it was poured at one of those charming inns that invariably stand near Belgium's Trappist monasteries.

The beer was formulated by Bert DeWit of Belgium's Affligem, then perfected by American Randy Thiel. Phil Leinart, who now oversees the brewery (it's owned by Duvel Moortgat), says its recipe is fairly typical of the style, relying on aromatic malts and dextrose. The secret may be in the spices, he says: coriander, sweet orange peel, star anise, licorice root, and cumin. The flavor is sublime and well rounded.

When Belgian beer expert Tim Webb conducted a blind tasting at the Great British Beer Festival a few years ago, he and the majority of participants favored Ommegang when matched against Chimay's highly honored Grande Reserve. "I did not believe it at first," Webb later said. "I thought there must have been a misunderstanding." Each summer, Ommegang hosts a Belgian-style ale gala called "Belgium Comes to Cooperstown." The truth is, it's already there. **DR**

Tasting notes

Deep burgundy with a pillowy layer of foam that holds its form throughout. Rich and aromatic with hints of anise, fresh apricot, and honey. On the tongue it offers caramel, fig, and currant flavors with a luscious mouthfeel. Finishes with pleasant warmness.

Optimator

Spaten-Franziskaner Bräu | www.spatenbraeu.de

Country of origin Germany
First brewed *ca.* 1890s
Alcohol content 7.2% abv
Serving temperature 50°F, 10°C

This may be a Bavarian doppelbock, a strong and virile beer with which to ride out the virtuous period of Lent, but for some reason most of what the brewery produces of Optimator is exported to the United States. There, it is available throughout the year, a constant reminder of the traditional beers that have their roots in the period when monks and monasteries ruled the roost when it came to brewing.

Optimator started off its life in the late 19th century as just one of a series of Lent beers with which the good folk of Munich celebrated the imminent coming of spring. Most of these beers' names ended with the suffix "ator," a tradition started by the Paulaner Brauerei in 1773: Salvator means "savior." Various breweries started producing generically named "Salvators," but after a trademark case in 1896 gave the rights to the name to Paulaner, they had to change the names, but often kept the suffix "ator."

The first mention of a brewery on the site where Spaten-Franziskaner Bräu has its home was in 1397, and the next 300 years saw several changes of ownership. This included the Spatt family, who gave the company the actual name. But the most famous name in the brewery's history is that of Sedlmayr: from 1807 to 1922, they were at the helm in a period of fast and furious technical and economical innovations (today's name "Spaten-Franziskaner" dates from 1922, when the union between Spaten and Franziskaner-Leist-Bräu began). The ready embrace of changes such as steam power and refrigeration helped lay the foundation for the brewery's lasting success. **WO**

Tasting notes

Optimator is a deeply dark amber in color; the taste is full bodied and sweet, a little bit sticky but also very malty. It lacks the bittersweet finish that is normally so typical for a strong beer of this style, though this is perhaps a concession to U.S. palates.

A waitress hefts a stein in a Spaten poster from the 1930s. ➜

Palliser Porter

Bushwakker Brewing Company | www.bushwakker.com

Country of origin Canada
First brewed 1991
Alcohol content 5.8% abv
Serving temperature 50°F, 10°C

Saskatchewan has not been lucky when it comes to beer. Despite several efforts, commercial craft brewing has been less than successful in Canada's central prairie province. When the government made the decision to link brewpub licenses with permission to operate lucrative cold beer stores, they pretty much guaranteed that a large number of operators would get involved in the brewing business—not for the love of beer, but for the revenue potential.

Fortunately, Saskatchewan's capital city of Regina was fortunate in at least one brewing aspect: it had Bev Robertson teaching at its university. Returning from a year's sabbatical in Germany, Robertson had developed a taste for north German pilsners and found he could not slake his thirst any longer in Canada. He decided to start his own brewpub, and after a false start or two, Bushwakker Brewing Company opened its doors on Robbie Burns Day, January 25, in 1991. It was, by all reports, a success from almost day one, pouring what was then the province's only all-grain brewpub beers—the other brewpubs, including those licensed during the first round of permits, used malt extract to make their beers. He supplemented it with a pub food menu that is now what one might consider the equal of some of the best gastropub fare.

It is still necessary to visit the brewery directly to purchase bottles of Palliser Porter or any of its other beers, but the trip is well worth it. The anchor of a historic strip in the heart of the capital, the Bushwakker is as atmospheric as its beers are flavorful. **SB**

Tasting notes

A wonderfully versatile food accompaniment, this porter offers a nicely balanced mix of roasted malt and coffee notes in the aroma and an off-dry character carrying drying rather than bittering hop notes alongside chocolate and cocoa flavors.

Pannepot

De Struise Brouwers | www.struisebrouwers.be

Country of origin Belgium
First brewed 2004
Alcohol content 10% abv
Serving temperature 54°F, 12°C

Pannepot is not so well known in Belgium, but American beer geeks in particular—many of whom tend to fall for strong, brash beers of uncompromising character—have nurtured a love affair with this spicy dark ale. Once they started making and exporting the sort of intense brews they themselves liked best, the Struise brewers of West Flanders quickly developed a cult following across the Atlantic.

Struise is technically a beer firm, and the arrangement whereby they rent equipment at Deca, which is just a few minutes' drive from Westvleteren and the famous Sint-Sixtus abbey, seems to work well for them. Fans of the beer complain only about its scarcity, wishing that the "Sturdy Brewers" had the capacity to make more of the stuff.

Pannepot is sweet but far from simple. Its medley of spices—cinnamon, coriander, thyme, and orange peel, among others—adds complexity rather than dominates any aspect of the flavor. There is a big, sugary, dark-malt core that gives the yeast something to chew on for several years. In fact that yeast may be the real star here, adding a definite aspect that increases somewhat over time. No mistake: this one does get better with age.

The boat on the label is a P50 Pannepot, a fishing boat from the Belgian coastal village of De Panne. The painting is of the P50 boat that was owned by one of the brewers' grandparents. The story goes that the grandparents made a strong, spiced brew for keeping warm in inclement weather, and it became the inspiration for Pannepot, the "old fisherman's ale." **JS**

Tasting notes

Pours very dark brown, nearly black, with a tall and enduring chestnut brown head. The contemplative nose includes dark candy sugar and notes of chocolate, dried figs, and red grapes. Tastes quite sweet, with restrained alcohol warmth and spice coming through the aftertaste.

Pardubický Porter

Pivovar Pernštejn | www.pernstejn.cz

Country of origin Czech Republic
First brewed 1890
Alcohol content 8% abv
Serving temperature 57°F, 14°C

On October 1, 1889, Antonín Šimonek began his tenure as the brewmaster at Pivovar Pernštejn in Pardubice, Bohemia. Although the brewery was primarily producing Bohemia's traditional pale and dark lagers, within a few months he had begun work on a special new beer intended for an upcoming exposition in Prague. In March 1890, Šimonek brewed his very first batch of Pardubický Porter. By the time the General Global Exhibition took place in 1891, Šimonek had perfected the recipe, and his beer—a thick, malty black lager named after the porter style of the Baltics—earned a gold medal. In 1904, it earned another gold at Vienna's International Exhibition of the Culinary Arts.

Today, it is one of the few such porters remaining in the former Czechoslovakia. It is currently developing a cult following among chefs due to its versatility as a culinary ingredient that creates soylike complexity and coffeelike flavors when cooked. Pardubice is famous for a kind of spiced cake called *perník*. Although there is no ginger in the cake, *perník* is often translated as "gingerbread," and similar notes of aniseed and gingery spice come through in the beer.

As with all of the beers from the Pernštejn brewery, Pardubický Porter is bottom-fermented with traditional lager yeast. Following Šimonek's original recipe from 1890, it is produced at an original gravity of 19 degrees Plato, using four types of malt from the brewery's own maltings. It is very good slightly chilled, but excels when served closer to room temperature, which allows the full malt body and aromatic bouquet to expand with rich layers of flavor. **ER**

Tasting notes

Despite the tan head, this rich black lager looks like a cola, and there are notes of cola, ginger, aniseed, and coffee among its many flavors. It pairs exceptionally well with roast meats and Bohemian-style goulash, and may be successfully aged for several years.

Petrus Oud Bruin

Brouwerij Bavik | www.bavik.be

Country of origin Belgium
First brewed 1993
Alcohol content 5.5% abv
Serving temperature 48°F, 9°C

Twenty years before the historic region of West Flanders became part of one of the most devastating battlefields of World War I, the Brabandere family switched from making beer for their own consumption to brewing it for the public at large. The German army confiscated the brewery, although the pioneering brewmaster Joseph de Brabandere got it going again once the guns fell silent. Prior to the war, the popularity of golden-colored pilsners had not gone unnoticed and, ironically enough given the brewery's fate in 1914, Bavik pils was very successful. It remains so to this day, being popular in France and the Netherlands as well as locally. However, Bavik, a medium-sized brewery located in Bavikhoeve, near Kortrijk, also produces a variety of other beers, the most artisanal of which are marketed under the Petrus brand (representatives of the famous Bordeaux chateau once paid a courtesy visit and left close friends).

Oud Bruin, which is sometimes called "Old Dark" for export purposes, is a classic Flemish old brown ale that is part young and part wood-aged ale. The base beer, an aged pale, is matured in oak barrels for two years and blended with young brown ale to produce the Oud Bruin. This method of maturing beers has been a tradition in Flanders for centuries. The style of beer is typically moderate in alcohol and refreshing. Tradition and technology are respected at Bavik, as both an older copper brewhouse and a new stainless steel brewery come into play for the various beers. In the barrel room, there are fifteen huge oak casks where the base beer for Oud Bruin is matured. **CC**

Tasting notes

Petrus Oud Bruin pours with a dark, ruby red color and sits in the glass beneath rocky, tannish foam. Aroma is dark fruits, oak, and sweet and sour notes. The taste is mildly sour with some sweetness, a medium mouthfeel, and good malt character. Notes of oak and sour cherries are present.

Plevna Imperial Stout Siperia

Plevna Brewery
www.plevna.fi

Country of origin Finland
First brewed 2006
Alcohol content 8% abv
Serving temperature 50°–54°F, 10°–12°C

Plevna Brewery is an integrated brewpub and restaurant that was set up in the city of Tampere in 1995. A variety of beers are produced here, including an American-style IPA, a pils (both blond and dark), and even a smoked beer. Then there is Siperia, the brewery's take on the old imperial Russian stout style that would have been a familiar beer in these parts during the 19th century.

For a dark strong stout, this has a very hoppy character thanks to the use of U.S. varieties Tomahawk, Mount Hood, Simcoe, and Vanguard, a hopping regime that will come as a bit of a shock to those used to less bitter beers of this sort. Thankfully, it works, although the beer is not bottled and only sold on draft at Plevna's brewpub. A trip to Finland beckons. **ATJ**

Tasting notes
Dark and delectable in the glass. Nose hints at coffee beans, earthy hops, dark chocolate, and some roasted barley. The mouthfeel is rich and luxurious before the bitterness sets in.

The Poet

New Holland Brewing Company
www.newhollandbrew.com

Country of origin United States
First brewed 1998
Alcohol content 5.2% abv
Serving temperature 39°–43°F, 4°–6°C

The trick with brewing stouts is to find a way to temper the sharp bitterness that comes from the highly roasted grain. That's where the oats come in. "The concept was to make a dark, rich, and creamy beer," says New Holland's Fred Bueltman. "It was discovered that there were many options for oats, and the brewers settled on steel-cut oats for their superior mouthfeel and creaminess." You can certainly taste them in this beer, as a kind of round richness that plays off the roasted malt.

"The Poet has brought many people to the world of dark beers," says Bueltman. "It's a brewery favorite." Despite a love of good coffee and chocolate, many Americans balk at the thought of a dark, roasty beer. Using something familiar, like oatmeal, helps make the beer more approachable. **RM**

Tasting notes
Big roasty nose with hints of a campfire and a bit of fruitiness evident. Sweet on the palate at first, then very creamy and roasty. Long, clean finish of black malt and hoppy bitterness.

Point Reyes Porter

Marin Brewing Co.
www.marinbrewing.com

Country of origin United States
First brewed 1989
Alcohol content 6% abv
Serving temperature 50°F, 10°C

Marin Brewing's Point Reyes Porter was the third batch of beer brewed at the California brewpub and was on tap the day it first flung open the doors on April Fools' Day, 1989. In its various incarnations, it has won five medals at the Great American Beer Festival.

Today's version of the porter is made with a blend of English and North American pale ale malt, along with specialty malts such as Munich, chocolate, and black. Its English pedigree is further enhanced by using a strain of yeast very similar to Fuller's. It's a robust porter and, as befits its West Coast origins, is hoppier than most, thanks to a good dose of East Kent Golding hops in the whirlpool. It is rich, velvety, and luscious, and is divine drunk alongside Mexican *mole poblano*, hearty meat dishes, and chocolate desserts. **JB**

Tasting notes
Inky black with a tight tan head and great lace. The nose is filled with chocolate and coffee aromas. With a creamy mouthfeel, the flavor profile is dry with rich espresso and chewy chocolate.

Porterhouse Oyster Stout

Porterhouse Brewing Company
www.porterhouse.ie

Country of origin Ireland
First brewed 1996
Alcohol content 4.8% abv
Serving temperature 44°F, 7°C

Porterhouse Oyster Stout is on the sweeter side of the flavor spectrum, but, unlike other sweet stouts, this flavor derives not from sugary malts but succulent Carlingford oysters, shucked into the kettle in the late stages of brewing. This sits on top of a classically dry and slightly bitter traditional Irish stout, just a fraction stronger than the usual. There is a definite blast of sea air to the beer, an invigorating mix of salt and iodine. The fine balance between sweet and salt is the key to this gourmet beer, and the silky-smooth texture and enticing aroma add to its elegance.

Brimming with class, the interplay of flavor sensations rewards considered sipping. The Porterhouse in Dublin's Temple Bar will happily serve you up a half-dozen oysters with your pint if you wish. **JD**

Tasting notes
Deep ruby red in color, topped with an off-white head. Sweet at first then distinctly salty, with a dry finish. As well as oysters, it matches well with any seafood and will add zing to salads.

Primátor Double 24%

Pivovar Náchod | www.primator.cz

Country of origin Czech Republic
First brewed 1999
Alcohol content 10.5% abv
Serving temperature 55°F, 13°C

Often mistaken for a doppelbock because of its name, the Double 24% beer from Pivovar Náchod is actually a high-octane take on the Baltic porter style. In the category of strong lagers, such differences are subtle but noticeable, especially with regard to the darkness of this beer and its stark bitterness, both of which greatly surpass those of a typical doppelbock.

Primátor Double 24% is brewed from four types of barley malt and a small addition of wheat malt to a remarkable original gravity of 24 degrees Plato, thus "double" the standard 12 degrees Plato that marks the high end for many breweries in the Czech Republic. Two varieties of the noble Saaz hops are used, both in pellet form as well as hop extract. The beer is cold conditioned for two months, resulting in a very powerful 10.5 percent abv, which makes it one of the strongest bottom-fermented year-round brews in Europe.

Although the brew is bitter, the beer's hoppy notes are balanced with an addition of brewing sugar, which renders Primátor Double very sweet in the finish. At its best, the beer has a full and sticky mouthfeel, lush notes of coffee and maple syrup, toasty malt tones, and a bright, peppermintlike, hoppy spike in the finish. When Primátor Double is used as a culinary ingredient, most often as a marinade or in a soup or sauce, the complexity of the flavors can increase dramatically, creating rich layers of taste and aroma.

Primátor Double will never be a best seller in the pale lager–loving Czech Republic: it is too strong, too dark, and too richly bittersweet. But for those who know where to find it, it remains a beloved secret. **ER**

Tasting notes

Lager beers are known for clarity, not complexity, but this strong lager presents complex flavors including maple, stone fruits, vanilla, cocoa, and coffee, as well as vinous portlike tones. Look for a beautiful blackish brown color in the glass topped by a loose tan head.

Pullman Brown Ale

Flossmoor Station Brewing Company | www.flossmoorstation.com

Country of origin United States
First brewed 1996
Alcohol content 6% abv
Serving temperature 50°F, 10°C

This luscious brown ale tells a complex tale of beers, brewers, and breweries. Although the Pullman name predated his arrival, brewmaster Todd Ashman takes the credit for reinventing this beer when he arrived at Flossmoor in late 1996. It's barely a brown ale in any sense but brownness; this chestnut-colored ale resembles a historic porter as much as anything else. Whatever it is, this in-your-face ale still finds a way to be deliciously drinkable.

Perhaps it is the sheer variety of ingredients, which means there's always something on which to focus one's attention. The recipe includes seven different malts plus toasted oats for "that cookie thing," as Ashman says. Several gallons of blackstrap molasses lighten the palate while adding layers of deep, nutty flavors. When Todd Ashman left the brewery, the recipe came under the care of Matt Van Wyk, who tweaked it, but with the original spirit very much in mind. Now that Van Wyk has left, the new brewer will be in charge, adding his own touches.

Flossmoor Station is a smart brewpub on Chicago's Far South Side. Located in a renovated train station, it was founded in 1996. The brewery was named Best Small Brewpub in the United States at the Great American Beer Festival in 2006.

Despite its bravado, this is a beer that harmonizes with many foods. The huge range of malty flavors makes it go well with many grilled, roasted, or baked foods. It also has a particular affinity with cheese: try it with a runny, washed-rind Camembert for a sort of "liquid grilled cheese sandwich" effect. **RM**

Tasting notes

Very complex nose of deeply caramelized malt, burned sugar, dried fruit, and a deep, almost smoky chocolate character. The palate is sweet up front and then dries a bit to a luxurious, toasty fruit finish. The hop bitterness is modest, just there for balance.

Raven Stout

Mitchell's Knysna Brewery
www.mitchellsknysnabrewery.com

Country of origin South Africa
First brewed *ca.* late 1980s
Alcohol content 5% abv
Serving temperature 55°F, 13°C

It must have been with some trepidation that Lex Mitchell set up his microbrewery in the West Cape more than twenty-five years ago. For years, the South African brewing scene has been dominated by the mighty South African Breweries.

Mitchell first produced Raven Stout as a seasonal brew, but its popularity grew so quickly that it became a regular and is now available all year-round. The beer is top-fermented and undergoes a lengthy secondary fermentation at a lowish temperature, which rounds off the flavors perfectly. In South Africa, they have a saying "local is lekker," which means "local is delicious." There can hardly be a more sublime combination than a glass of Raven Stout paired with oysters harvested from the clear waters of the River Knysna estuary. It is a classic match that proves that a good white wine need not be the only drink to partner oysters. **TH**

Tasting notes
Ebony black, it is topped by a head that looks like a tempting sugar honeycomb. It is full bodied and bursting with burned sugar and ecpresso flavors. Well balanced in the mouth.

Red Duck Porter

Red Duck
www.redduckbeer.com.au

Country of origin Australia
First brewed 2005
Alcohol content 6.4% abv
Serving temperature 46°–50°F, 8°–10°C

It is extremely difficult to set up a microbrewery in Australia in the modern era and make money out of it. But some brewers are not driven by fiscal goals. Scott Wilson-Browne of the Red Duck brewery just wants Australians to start drinking real beers, and ales in particular. To this end, he has designed his Red Duck Porter to be rich and dark, yet balanced and approachable. Strongly malt driven, Red Duck Porter is brewed using Australian malts because Scott believes that the cleaner air of the southern hemisphere results in a cleaner-tasting malt and a cleaner beer.

Essentially self-taught, Scott brews using a specially designed kettle and rain that falls on the property. His first batches were sold to locals at the markets. Distribution is difficult, but sales are increasing as people discover his beer, and, if you know where to look, you can buy it in many Australian cities. **DD**

Tasting notes
Red Duck delivers with dark, roasted warmness that takes you back to your favorite chocolate indulgence. This beer is best enjoyed in winter with a plate of beef stew and butter mash.

Redoak Baltic Porter

Redoak Brewery
www.redoak.com.au

Country of origin Australia
First brewed 1996
Alcohol content 9% abv
Serving temperature 50°–54°F, 10°–12°C

David Hollyoak of the Sydney-based Redoak Brewery often travels abroad to gain inspiration and knowledge about traditional beer styles and modern trends. Way back in 1994, he ventured into Eastern Europe. One of his stops was in a café in Krakow, Poland. It had a magnificent old cellar, full of wine and beer that had been acquired over a long history. Hollyoak selected a murky porterlike beer and marveled at its complexity and depth of flavor. Part of his interest was because he could not pinpoint the style, and nobody at the café could give him any information about who brewed it.

Research at the local university revealed that the brewery that made the beers had gone out of business in 1952. Drinking forty-two-year-old beers of such quality had Hollyoak hooked, and within two years he had produced his own version of a style of beer that was just becoming known as Baltic porter. **DD**

Tasting notes

The chocolate and fruit aromas intensify as you let a glass of this dark, ruby-edged beer warm up in your hands. Balanced malt complexity, warming smoothness, and a lingering finish.

Redoak Special Reserve

Redoak Brewery
www.redoak.com.au

Country of origin Australia
First brewed 1996
Alcohol content 12% abv
Serving temperature 46°F, 8°C

Special Reserve is a difficult beer to track down, and little wonder when you consider what is involved in brewing it. To start with, the fermentation takes twelve months. This extended period is required to get the alcohol to a level suitable for the barleywine style. The reason it takes so long is that the yeast suffers from alcohol fatigue as it wallows in its own by-product. Apparently an alcohol-resistant yeast has been developed in the United States, but, because it is more traditional, Hollyoak prefers to put an English old ale yeast to work while he tends to other brews.

After twelve months of waiting, the process isn't over yet. The beer is matured in three different oak barrels for at least two years. Each of the oaks contributes to the complexity of the beer. The greater the anticipation, the richer the reward when this most luscious of beers passes across the lips. **DD**

Tasting notes

The beer has a sublimely complex oak, malt, and alcohol-driven aroma of dried fruits, vanilla, and brandy. Small sips reveal a balanced malt sweetness and a warming finish.

Richter Černý Speciál 14°

Richter Brewery
www.pivovarubulovky.cz

Country of origin Czech Republic
First brewed 2004
Alcohol content 5.5% abv
Serving temperature 48°F, 9°C

When František Richter opened his Prague brewpub in 2004, he brought a lifetime of work experience from breweries in Germany. The brewpub makes both Bavarian and Prague-style wheat beers, as well as versions of some of Germany's few remaining top-fermented styles. The Černý Speciál, or "black special," however, was designed in the tradition of a Czech classic.

First appearing as a medium-strong dark beer, this brew evolved into a traditional and slightly stronger beer. It is brewed in a single decoction mash, which is composed of pilsner, Munich, caramel, and carahell malts; some earlier experiments included small amounts of oats and wheat malt. It is hopped three times with pellets, using the classic Saaz semiearly red varietal with another Saaz version, the higher alpha-acid Premiant, added for bitterness. After a week of primary fermentation, it lagers for at least six weeks at very cold temperatures, finishing with 5.5 percent abv.

All Richter's special beers are brewed on a rotating basis, and the only constantly available beer is Richter Ležák, a classic Bohemian pilsner. However, beer fans in the Czech capital welcome the Černý Speciál's few yearly appearances, when it is an extremely welcome accompaniment to the brewpub's excellent cuisine. **ER**

Tasting notes
Near black with a thick crown of cappuccino foam. In the mouth, it starts out sweet and rich before revealing ginger, coffee, and spice notes, finishing with a remarkable hop bitterness.

Ridgeway Foreign Export Stout

Ridgeway Brewing
www.quaffale.org.uk/php/brewery/830

Country of origin England
First brewed 2006
Alcohol content 8% abv
Serving temperature 50°F, 10°C

Peter Scholey was the last head brewer at Brakspear's in Henley-on-Thames, England. When that much-loved, historic brewhouse was closed in 2002, he decided to branch out on his own. Wisely avoiding the major cost of leasing a site to launch a brewery, he started a business by brewing beer himself using spare capacity at other breweries.

Scholey offers a wide range of high-quality beers, many for export, and Foreign Export Stout is typical of this quality. Initially, the beer was a rebranding of a stout for Christmas that Scholey called "Lump of Coal." With a slightly different recipe, it is now a brew in its own right. Scholey generally brews it either at Hepworth and Co. in Horsham, Sussex, or closer to home at Cotswold Brewing in Oxfordshire. The cereal grist includes pale, pilsner, crystal, amber, and black malts, as well as roasted barley and malted oats, while the hops are whole-leaf English Challenger and Styrian Golding. Fruitiness is restrained a little by carefully controlling the speed of fermentation.

Scholey thinks the Foreign Export, being conditioned in the bottle, will keep for at least two years after release and may change subtly during that time. Young or older, it's an impressive, satisfying drink. **JE**

Tasting notes
A near-black stout with chocolate, coffee, and tangy hops in the aroma. Sweet to start, the taste features creamy chocolate, nut, soft caramel, and raisins, as well as a suggestion of tea.

← Harvesting the Saaz hops that go into Richter's "black special."

Rip Tide

BrewDog | www.brewdog.com

Country of origin Scotland
First brewed 2008
Alcohol content 8% abv
Serving temperature 50°–57°F, 10°–14°C

The strength of the contemporary Anglo-American craft beer scene is its passion for looking both ways: digging deep into history to revisit classic, sometimes extinct, beer styles, and reviving them not entirely faithfully, but with a modern twist. BrewDog position themselves as the punks of the beer scene, but like much of their often controversial label copy, this is best read with a healthy dose of irony. Punks wanted to destroy the past and start at Year Zero. With a beer such as Rip Tide, BrewDog have taken an old aristocrat and, instead of destroying it, they have treated it with respect—renovating it, dusting it down, and giving it a modern set of clothes.

Rip Tide is a "contemporary Scottish take" on imperial Russian stout, the beer brewed in the United Kingdom and exported to the court of the czars. According to contemporary accounts, it was thick, almost meaty, spirituous, and sensual. BrewDog's version is brewed with dark muscovado sugar and four types of malt, to provide a muscular, challenging body for First Gold and Galena hops to season.

BrewDog's serving suggestion for Rip Tide is to "enjoy with an air of aristocratic nonchalance." While this is a beer that would be at home in blue-blooded company, it would be extremely difficult to approach it with anything resembling indifference. Instead, enjoy the tongue-in-cheek packaging in the spirit in which it's intended, before getting down to some very serious contemplation of an ageless classic, and marvel at the unique way in which beer can combine irreverence and beauty. **PB**

Tasting notes

BrewDog say: "conceited, lurking, tormenting, under the cursed shadows and flow." This writer says: "inky black with aromas of coffee, port, and sweet toffee, followed by rich dark chocolate, treacle, and coffee grounds slowly revealing myriad other taste allusions."

Ritterbock

König Ludwig Schlossbrauerei Kaltenberg | www.koenig-ludwig-brauerei.com

Country of origin Germany
First brewed *ca.* 1980s
Alcohol content 9% abv
Serving temperature 43°–46°F, 6°–8°C

Munich's annual beer jamboree is the Oktoberfest. The event sprang to life in 1810, when the marriage of Crown Prince Ludwig of Bavaria and Princess Theresa of Saxony was the catalyst for lively celebrations in the city. These days, however, the Oktoberfest is rivaled by the Ritterturnier, an event staged 30 miles (48 km) away on the first three weekends in July. This colorful, atmospheric jousting tournament has the perfect setting of Kaltenberg Castle, the striking Wagnerian home of König Ludwig Schlossbrauerei Kaltenberg.

Kaltenberg is run by Prinz Luitpold, great-great-grandson of Crown Prince Ludwig, whose marriage kick-started the Oktoberfest. Strangely, the Prinz's own brewery has been excluded from supplying beer to the Oktoberfest, which is restricted to brewers from Munich itself. The Prinz's response has been to make the Ritterturnier an even more spectacular event, attracting 120,000 visitors annually with its mixture of jousting, stunt shows, and "medieval" market stalls.

Kaltenberg beers are naturally well in evidence at the tournament, from which the splendid Ritterbock (Knight's Bock), a rich and fruity strong lager, derives its name. This triple bock, one of the strongest beers in Bavaria, is made from local barley malt and Hallertau hops and is then lagered for five months. It is complex and full bodied, impressive enough to claim the title of World's Best Strong Lager in the World Beer Awards, run by the now-defunct *Beers of the World* magazine, in 2008. The brewery recommends it with roast meats and other hearty dishes, the sort of substantial fare that is readily available during the tournament itself. **JE**

Tasting notes

A ruby brown beer with chocolate and caramel notes, plus dried figs in the malty aroma. The taste is malty, figgy, and sweet with chocolate and raisin flavors, rounding off dry, bittersweet, and malty with more raisins. A satisfying, gently warming, strong brew.

Robert the Bruce

Three Floyds | www.threefloyds.com

Country of origin United States
First brewed 1997
Alcohol content 6.5% abv
Serving temperature 39°F, 4°C

The Three Floyds style is hard to peg at first, a little like the tale of the blind men encountering an elephant, where trunk, tail, and leg give vastly different impressions. Take a sip of Alpha King or Dreadnaught and it's all about the hops; the appeal and pull of Dark Lord Imperial Stout is its pulverizing strength; the Gorch Fock Helles is orthodoxy itself. However, taste a Robert the Bruce and you will swear that the men at Three Floyds are totally obsessed by malt. All of this is true, which is the beauty of Three Floyds.

From the Chicago suburb of Munster, Indiana, Three Floyds is turning out a bewildering array of characterful beers. Robert the Bruce is a bit of a nod to the Scottish origin of the Floyd name, but more importantly it was to fill a niche in the Chicago market, according to founder Nick Floyd. "Everybody was doing ambers, Irish reds, and pale ales. Bruce was meant to be the opposite of the brewery's flagship Alpha King," and was named after the 14th-century Scottish king and freedom fighter.

Scotland has an ancient brewing tradition that mirrors English brewing but with some differences. Due to the colder climate, Scottish ales were fermented a little cooler than their English cousins, which can give them a sort of lager smoothness (one of lager's first footholds in the British Isles was Scotland). Also, because of the distance from the hop yards of southern England, the beers tended to be on the malty side. Hopping is therefore light at 35 IBUs, just barely enough bitterness to balance what Floyd calls "the best dark malts money can buy." **RM**

Tasting notes

Appetizing nose of chocolate brownies, with hints of dried fruit: raisins and prunes. Deeply caramelized, maybe even a bit smoky. Sweet and full on the palate, but with this smooth, soft roastiness it's not cloying. Long cocoa finish. Ah, the joys of malt!

Rogue Mocha Porter

Rogue Ales | www.rogue.com

Country of origin United States
First brewed 1995
Alcohol content 5.1% abv
Serving temperature 44°–54°F, 7°–12°C

"If you're going to be irreverent and do some crazy stuff then you better make dammed sure you're making great beer." So says Jack Joyce, former lawyer and director of the Nike clothing company and current co-owner of the Rogue Brewery. The brewery and indeed Jack are the kings of difference when it comes to beers, and for more than twenty years this Oregon-based operation has been rustling brewing feathers. Irreverent the beer certainly is, but as the man says, it's also great stuff and, as a result, has been recognized by peers and in awards throughout the United States. Most of the palate range is covered by the amazing sixty beers brewed at Rogue—from floral in the Juniper Pale Ale to smoky in the aptly named take on a Bamberg Rauchbier, Smoke Ale. There's something for everyone in Jack's portfolio.

The Mocha, meanwhile, is a prime example of the U.S. porter style, a beer that was inspired by its English cousin but has burst out of the blocks with plenty of Yankee twist. Rogue's take on it is to make sure you know all about that coffee; but, as is their way, the brewing team has managed to go a step further by making sure the hop profile is distinct. As a malty offering, the porter features a complex mix of Northwest Harrington and Klages, 80 crystal, Beeston chocolate, black, Munich, and carastan malts. While the bittering only adds 54 IBUs, there's no mistaking the wonderful Perle and Centennial hop character. Coffee isn't listed in the ingredients, but there's no mistaking its presence, making this not only incredibly tasty but an interesting addition to the dinner table. **TS**

Tasting notes
A strong hint of coffee on the nose and the dark ruddy color aids the comparison, but this is a complex beer, smooth in the mouth, with a lovely light chocolate flavor. Great simply out of the fridge but try it with a barbecue to get the most from it.

Royal Extra Stout

Carib Brewery | www.caribbeer.com

Country of origin Trinidad and Tobago
First brewed *ca.* 1930s
Alcohol content 6.6% abv
Serving temperature 50°–54°F, 10°–12°C

In Trinidad, there are a couple of beery echoes of British Empire days in the range produced by the main local brewery, Carib. Carib's leading product is the light, quenching Carib Lager, but the portfolio also features a strong version of Mackeson Stout, as well as the intriguing Carib Royal Extra Stout. This latter beer was inherited by Carib from an earlier brewery named Walter's, which it took over in the 1950s. Pilsner and black malts form the basis of the mash, with caramel added for color. Hops are not a major feature, as this is a predominantly sweet drink primed with cane sugar and lactose, which adds to the body.

Royal Extra Stout is a wonderful dessert beer, such is its sugary nature, but, at 6.6 percent, it's not a beer to take lightly under the relentless West Indian sun. **JE**

Tasting notes
A deep ruby-colored beer with bitter chocolate, caramel, buttery malt, licorice, and dried fruit in the aroma. The taste is full and sweet, with chocolate, coffee, and hints of licorice.

Ryan O'Sullivan's Imperial Stout

Moylan's Brewing Co. | www.moylans.com

Country of origin United States
First brewed 1996
Alcohol content 10% abv
Serving temperature 52°F, 11°C

Ryan O'Sullivan's Imperial Stout was created in 1996 to honor the bagpipe player who appears at Moylan's Brewery and Restaurant every St. Patrick's Day to play tunes to mark the holiday. Owner Brendan Moylan promised the musician that if he played at every St. Patrick's Day celebration, the brewery would name a beer for him. O'Sullivan wasn't sure if Moylan was being serious, but he agreed to the deal, and sure enough Ryan O'Sullivan's Imperial Stout was born.

The imperial stout, which is now distributed in more than twenty-one states, plus British Columbia and Guam, gets its rich, complex flavor from a total of nine different malts. Like the original imperial stouts that were built to withstand the voyage from England to Russia, this brew packs a considerable punch. **RL**

Tasting notes
This brew is as black as a moonless night. It has a rich mocha head that stays thick and an inviting malty aroma. Roasted, sweet malt base, with a touch of vanilla and a hint of cocoa.

Sacramento Russian Imperial Stout

Sacramento Brewing | www.sacbrew.com

Country of origin United States
First brewed 1997
Alcohol content 8.1% abv
Serving temperature 55°F, 13°C

The original inspiration for Sacramento Brewing's Russian Imperial Stout was another local California version—North Coast's Old Rasputin. In 1997, brewery owners Jeri and Sam Petersen wanted to create their own interpretation of the originally English style of beer created for the Russian imperial court.

The beer is brewed with a blend of six different malts: two-row, Munich, roasted barley, pale chocolate, Special B, and de-husked black malt from Castle Malting in Belgium, along with a large portion of oats, utilizing a multi-batch fermentation process. By filling their fermenter over several days and manipulating the aeration that the unfermented wort receives, they create a strong ale that is smooth and approachable when released but can be cellared for many years. **JB**

Tasting notes
Pours jet black with a dark tan head and great Brussels lace. The nose is rich dark chocolate with aromas of vanilla, roasted coffee, and figs. The mouthfeel is velvety smooth.

Sagres Preta

Sagres | www.sagresbeer.com

Country of origin Portugal
First brewed 1940
Alcohol content 4.3% abv
Serving temperature 48°F, 9°C

Sagres Preta was born the same year as Sagres Branca—the omnipresent flagship lager that sponsors premier Portuguese soccer. Over time, Sagres went from being the product of a tightly controlled economy to a modern-day marketing machine subject to the global economy—now owned by Heineken.

Mega-corporations are not often known for making decent beer, so the fact that this beer has survived is a real mystery. It's entirely possible that Sagres Preta's resilience owes something to its compatibility with food. Its roasty and mildly sweet caramel flavor makes it friendly with grilled meat and fish, whether in Portugal or in your own backyard. It has refreshment value and character, a useful combination that shouldn't be so hard to find. **JS**

Tasting notes
Tan head sits atop a near-black beer. Some caramel and sweetened coffee with cream in the nose, and a lightly sweet flavor checked only by roast, faint bitterness. Very quaffable.

Saku Porter

Saku Brewery
www.saku.ee

Country of origin Estonia
First brewed *ca*. 1990s
Alcohol content 7.5% abv
Serving temperature 54°–57°F, 12°–14°C

Even though brewing in Estonia has a long and venerable history, the country still only has a handful of breweries. Saku is one of the oldest, with a history going back to 1820. As is the case with brewing traditions in all the Baltic countries, it comes as no surprise to discover that bottom-fermenting lagered beers rule the Estonian roost (Saku's best seller is a strong pale lager, Originaal), although many of the bigger breweries are also going in for gimmicky mixes.

There doesn't seem to be much room now for Baltic porters on their home turf, even though these rich, dark, bittersweet beers are very popular in foreign markets, especially the United States. There are various reasons for the decline in the popularity of Baltic porters: it may be that the Balts are keen to show their desire to be part of the West by following the drinking preferences of their new European partners. Or it could be that the big brewing companies that have moved into the region have brought with them marketing folk who scratch their heads over the relatively long maturation times Baltic porters need (Saku are owned by Carlsberg). Saku Porter is a rare survivor. Full of chocolate and coffeelike character, it is brewed once a year for enjoyment in the winter. **ATJ**

Tasting notes
A subtle nose of coffee and roast malt. The palate is soothing with a restrained malty sweetness opening up the proceedings followed by coffee, toffee, and more roast notes.

Samuel Smith's Imperial Stout

Samuel Smith | www.tadcaster.uk.com/breweriesSamuelSmith.htm

Country of origin England
First brewed 1986
Alcohol content 7% abv
Serving temperature 59°F, 15°C

Aside from India Pale Ale, there is no beer more evocative of a period in history than Russian imperial stout. Although Smith's doesn't use the "Russian" prefix, that's what this beer is—an intense stout, in the style that used to be exported from London to the court of Catherine the Great in the late 18th century.

Smith's played a major part in reviving the style in the mid 1980s, when imperial stout was something of a rarity. Somewhat incongruously, the style has been given an enthusiastic reception by the new wave of U.S. craft breweries. What has this to do with Samuel Smith's brewery, you may ask? Garrett Oliver, brewmaster of the Brooklyn Brewery, takes up the story: "I apprenticed to head brewer Mark Witty, who had been a senior brewer at Samuel Smith's. There can be little doubt that our beers were much influenced by the Sam Smith's beers. Similarly, when I first brewed Brooklyn Black Chocolate Stout in 1994, Samuel Smith's Imperial Stout was the touchstone for the style."

Despite being revived in 1986, everything about the beer harks back to a much earlier time, from the style of the beer itself to the hand-drawn Victorian feel of the label. An era of luxury is alluded to in Smith's serving suggestions: caviar, champagne, and cigars. **ZA**

Tasting notes
Huge, intense aroma of espresso, dark chocolate, and slightly burned fruitcake. Slightly viscous on the tongue, initially sweet, but with an enjoyable bitterness emerging.

Samuel Smith's: a Russian stout in all but name.

Samuel Smith's Taddy Porter

Samuel Smith | www.tadcaster.uk.com/breweriesSamuelSmith.htm

Country of origin England
First brewed 1979
Alcohol content 5% abv
Serving temperature 55°F, 13°C

Tadcaster in north Yorkshire is one of England's historic brewing towns. The quality of its natural water supply has encouraged the development of a number of breweries, three of which have survived for a century or more. The name of the town is honored in a beer produced by one of those breweries, the popular but somewhat camera-shy Samuel Smith, which was founded in 1884 when Samuel took over the site formerly run by John Smith's brewery, which had moved next door. Sam was John's nephew.

There's a strange, unconventional silence that surrounds Sam's today. It remains in the hands of the founder's descendants but is a deeply private company that shuns all media inspection, instead allowing its beers to do the talking. In this publicity-conscious world, it's a refreshingly different approach to marketing, and with the beers saying plenty of good things, Sam's doesn't seem to be losing out.

While the company makes a number of fine draft beers, its fame around the world has been built on the quality of its bottled-beer offering—beers such as Nut Brown Ale, Oatmeal Stout, Winter Welcome, and the robust Taddy Porter. The latter was introduced in 1979, against the trend of the time, when porters were seldom found in the United Kingdom. The rave reviews it received no doubt prompted other breweries to reassess their dark beer provision. It's too much to expect Sam's to let us in on the brewing secrets behind this beer, but there's clearly an ample helping of dark grain in the mash tun to bring out that deep ruby color and rich roasted barley flavors. **JE**

Tasting notes

A deep ruby beer with chocolate, caramel, and sweet tobacco in the aroma. The taste is tangy and gently bitter, with bitter chocolate, licorice, and coffee notes, followed by a dry, bitter, and nutty finish, with roasted grain coming to the fore.

Sara

Brasserie Silenrieux | users.belgacom.net/gc195540/#

Country of origin Belgium
First brewed 1992
Alcohol content 6% abv
Serving temperature 50°F, 10°C

This brewery was created for the purpose of producing beers using interesting and ancient grains. Its first two beers, Sara and Joseph, use buckwheat and spelt, respectively, in addition to barley. Both beers are certified 100 percent organic by Ecocert, the organization that is the controlling authority over biological certification in the European Union.

The use of buckwheat gives Sara a brownish color, a refreshing taste, and a medium-to-full body; it also gives its name to the beer, with "Sara" being derived from the French word for "buckwheat," *sarrasin*. Buckwheat is commonly grown and used in places such as Russia, southern Europe, and much of the Far East, especially China and Japan. It is believed that the Greeks brought it from the Middle East and introduced it to Europe. Buckwheat, sometimes called the "black" grain, is a hearty plant that grows quickly and can prosper in poor soil. It became more popular in areas that were occupied by the Germans during World War II, when barley, oats, and wheat had to be sold to the invading army. The recipe for Sara is based on an old brewing recipe from the region.

Brasserie Silenrieux is a two-man operation, with Benoit in charge of brewing and Edouard Descendre looking after business matters. With these two literally doing everything in the brewery, it is a small-scale operation that produces approximately 26,400 gallons (1,000 hl) of beer per year. Despite the Lilliputian scale of brewing, however, Silenrieux still manage to export its beers to France, Spain, Italy, Switzerland, the USA, and Japan. **CC**

Tasting notes

Reddish-brown colored beer that pours with a big tan foam; notes of wheat, dark fruits like prunes, yeast, and spices in the aroma. Flavor is malty, yeasty, mildly hoppy and somewhat earthy, with a bittersweet aftertaste. Try pairing with flounder or trout dishes.

Sarah Hughes Dark Ruby

Sarah Hughes Brewery
www.sarahhughesbrewery.co.uk

Country of origin England
First brewed 1921
Alcohol content 6% abv
Serving temperature 54°F, 12°C

The Beacon Hotel in the town of Sedgeley, England, is a little Victorian gem. Two cozy front bars, a longer, wood-paneled back room, and an endearing little servery are happy survivors of days when many pubs looked like this. At the rear of the pub stands a classic brewhouse of the same 19th-century vintage, ergonomically designed so that the brewing process could proceed by gravity, with malt fed in on the top floor and the finished beer rolling out at the bottom.

The pub and brewery were acquired by a local widow named Sarah Hughes in 1920. She had lost her husband in a mining incident and used the insurance money to fund her new enterprise. She took to brewing herself and, a year later, came up with the recipe for one of the most acclaimed beers to emerge from the Midlands. Sarah's grandson, John Hughes, reopened the brewery in the 1980s. In a bid to work out the recipe for Sarah's renowned ale, John pored over record books and old invoices. Then, the chance discovery of the original recipe in a local bank vault ensured that he could make his beer totally authentic.

Sarah Hughes Dark Ruby is a rare survivor, one of the few existing strong milds. Pale and crystal malts fill the mash tun, with caramel added to deepen the color. Fuggle and Golding hops do their modest but vital work in the copper. **JE**

Tasting notes

Soft pear-drop candy notes, a little chocolate, and smooth malt feature in the winey aroma. The taste is mellow and malty with a slightly vinous bite to offset the sweetness.

Schmaltz's Alt

August Schell Brewing Company
www.schellsbrewery.com

Country of origin United States
First brewed 1989
Alcohol content 5.1% abv
Serving temperature 43°–44°F, 6°–7°C

A big chunk of Schell's production is an old-school mainstream lager called "Grain Belt," which it acquired in 2002, but August Schell brews quite a few bona fide craft beers as well. Founded in 1860, it is the United States's second-oldest family-owned brewery, and one of the most beautiful. Situated in parklike grounds in southwest Minnesota, the forested property is also a deer park. Fourth-generation owner Ted Marti now runs the brewery and was responsible for its shift in focus from mainstream to craft beer in the 1990s.

Schmaltz's is an Altbier (meaning "old" in German) and a style of beer that is top-fermented, a process that is common in parts of Germany. Today the center of the style is in Düsseldorf. "We had been producing a series of seasonal Blizzard Ales," says Marti, "and had been pretty successful with darker, malty beers. We had wanted to try an ale and thought an Altbier would be appropriate for a brewery like ours with a German heritage. It was also a bit of a tribute to my dad." According to the story on the neck label, as a youth, Marti's father was fond of shooting rats at the city dump under the tutelage of a man named Schmaltz. The elder Marti was nicknamed Schmaltz, and it stuck.

Compared with most modern German Altbiers, Schmaltz's is a tad over the top in flavor, body, and color. But heck, if the beer tastes good, why not? **RM**

Tasting notes

On the nose, this has deep, raisiny, caramel notes with soft hints of roastiness. The rich aroma belies a modest body, with a smooth, mocha roastiness. Aftertaste is long, smooth, and bittersweet.

The bottling line at the August Schell brewery in New Ulm, Minnesota. ➡

Schwarzer Kristall

Brauerei Locher | www.appenzellerbier.ch

Country of origin Switzerland
First brewed 2007
Alcohol content 6.3% abv
Serving temperature 46°–50°F, 8°–10°C

As the fifth generation at the head of the brewery in Appenzell since their ancestor Johann Christoph Locher bought it in 1886, Karl and Raphael Locher have established a niche-market development policy that has proved relatively successful in the rather conservative Swiss-German brewing context. This policy has seen the gradual development of a wide range of specialty beers.

After their initial success with the organic beer Locher Naturperle in 1996, Brauerei Locher already had more new beers in the pipeline. First to follow was Appenzeller Hanfblüte, a hemp-flavored lager, joined over the years by the chestnut beer Castégna; an oak-aged amber lager Holzfassbier; the low-alcohol Appenzeller Légère; the alcohol-free beers Leermond and Sonnwendling; and then Birra da Ris, brewed with rice from the northernmost European rice fields in Tessin, to name but a few. This was an impressive beer range indeed, well mastered all the way.

Yet the most impressive of them all was yet to come, and it took many a Swiss beer buff by surprise on its 2007 release. Schwarzer Kristall (Black Crystal) is bottom-fermented, but underneath the lyrical, almost gothic label blurb hinting at founder Johann Locher, Schwarzer Kristall is based on a late 19th-century recipe, albeit with a touch of modern-day artistic license. It boasts a bold, clear-cut, slightly smoky character that's both unexpected and very welcome as a wake-up call in the Swiss beer landscape. Schwarzer Kristall is unfiltered and, just like all the other Locher beers, unpasteurized. **LM**

Tasting notes

Pours an oily jet black, with a fine beige head. Massive roasty, malty, meaty, slightly smoky nose, all reflected in the smooth, silky mouthfeel, yet not really heavy on the palate. A black delight that screams for a proper aged Swiss Gruyère on the side, not to mention the obvious sushi.

Sexual Chocolate

Foothills Brewing | www.foothillsbrewing.com

Country of origin United States
First brewed 2006
Alcohol content 9.7% abv
Serving temperature 44°F, 7°C

Foothills Brewing opened in 2005 in Winston-Salem, North Carolina. It makes seven year-round brews, including Hoppyum IPA, Total Eclipse Stout, Torch Pilsner, and Salem Gold. On the seasonal side, the brewery churns out ten limited-release beers, with Gruffmeister Maibock, People's Porter, and Hurricane Hefeweizen part of the lineup. Foothills Festive, the company's holiday beer, varies its spice recipe from year to year. Foothills also pushes the envelope with side projects like Seeing Double IPA, which is aged in Pappy Van Winkle bourbon barrels. Even with this impressive collection of brews, for many the discussion of Foothills comes down to two words: Sexual Chocolate.

Sexual Chocolate was originally conceived in 1996 as a home-brewed beer to celebrate St. Valentine's Day. A decade later, the beer was produced commercially for the first time at Foothills, and word spread quickly. Brewmaster and co-owner Jamie Bartholomaus uses cocoa nibs that are cold infused in the stout after fermentation and during conditioning. The beer's name is a semiobscure reference to the 1988 comedy movie *Coming to America,* which starred Eddie Murphy and Arsenio Hall. In the movie, a fictional band named Sexual Chocolate perform the song "Greatest Love of All" at a church-sponsored event.

Sexual Chocolate has become Foothills's most sought-after beer. The company does a limited bottling of the beer and releases it once a year at the Foothills brewpub. The day has turned into a semiofficial beer holiday, and beer lovers head to Winston-Salem to line up and get a few of the precious bottles. **RL**

Tasting notes

This beer pours a thick black color that does not allow light to pass through. The tan head is thin, but stays throughout. There is an immediate baker's chocolate aroma. Rich roasted flavors blend throughout a big beer delivery, with cocoa, coffee, toffee, and roasted grains combining.

Shakespeare Stout

Rogue Ales | www.rogue.com

Country of origin United States
First brewed 1988
Alcohol content 5.8% abv
Serving temperature 50°F, 10°C

Shakespeare Stout is an imperial stout that is one of Rogue's original beers. It is named to recognize the Oregon Shakespeare Festival, which takes place annually over several months in the small, arty community of Ashland, where Rogue was originally located.

Fate played a hand in Rogue's current location, though. In early 1989, in the middle of a nasty blizzard, one of the brewery's main partners, Jack Joyce, was persuaded by Mohave Neimi, the owner of Mo's Clam Chowder, a chain of famous Oregon coast restaurants, to open a new brewpub in a building that her family owned on Newport's lively waterfront. The property negotiations included a promise that Rogue would always display a picture of Neimi, naked in a bathtub, in the pub. Neimi died several years ago, but the picture is still there today; you can find it just to the left of the bar. Her image, clothed this time, also graces the label of a Rogue beer.

Eventually, Rogue left Ashland entirely and expanded its brewing operations in Newport. The city is now the location of Rogue's world headquarters, also known as Rogue Nation, where a museum, tasting room, and distillery share space with the brewery. Rogue's original brewer, Greg Kebkey, created Shakespeare Stout, adding oats to the brew to create a smooth, luscious mouthfeel. When current brewmaster John Maier got on board in the late 1980s, he Americanized the Hallertau-based hop profile by switching to Cascade hops, but otherwise left the recipe alone. "It's a beer for all seasons," Maier says. "Warm or cold, it's always rich." **LMo**

Tasting notes

Shakespeare Stout is deep ebony in color with a rich creamy head. It has a bright, yet earthy flavor, and a mellow, chocolate and coffee finish. This beer goes well with beef and cheese, or try pouring it over vanilla ice cream for a tasty dessert.

Shonan Liebe

Shonan Beer | www.kumazawa.jp

Country of origin Japan
First brewed *ca*. 1997
Alcohol content 5% abv
Serving temperature 41°–44°F, 5°–7°C

Kumazawa Shuzo started off as a sake maker in 1872. More than a century later, in 1996, it moved across into brewing and started Shonan Beer. Mokichi Kumazawa (who is currently the sixth-generation president of Kumazawa Shuzo) was inspired by his visits to a number of microbreweries in the United States. Back in Japan, the hardest part was getting information on brewing beer. Microbrewing was a new thing in Japan at the time, and everyone was scrambling to find out how to do it. Mokichi believed that microbrewing was a worthy endeavor for his company; it only made sake during the winter months, so there was enough time to brew beer at other times.

Although its first beer, a pilsner, is still its most popular, Liebe was its third effort and is now just behind the pilsner in sales. It is a Schwarzbier and was conceived as a special for St. Valentine's Day. A great deal of effort went into enhancing its smoothness. As a result, the beer received a very good response at the brewery's restaurant. After it won a few awards, too, it was retained as a regular product.

Shonan Beer brews several rather intriguing styles, such as IPA and imperial stouts. However, its main beers are more conventional and are sold primarily to restaurants. Liebe, along with Ruby (an Altbier) and Bitter (a pilsner), defines this category. Water for these beers, as well as the sake products, comes from an old well on the property that is fed by an aquifer from the Tanzawa mountains. Said to take seventy-five years to travel underground from the mountains to the well, the water is of extremely high quality. **BH**

Tasting notes

The beer is deep reddish brown with a tan head. The aroma is of coffee and dark caramel. The rich flavor exhibits minimal sweetness with good tanginess. There is just enough hop bitterness to keep everything in balance. The finish is long with roasty flavors.

Sinebrychoff Porter

Oy Sinebrychoff | www.sinebrychoff.fi

Country of origin Finland
First brewed 1957
Alcohol content 7.2% abv
Serving temperature 50°–64°F, 10°–18°C

At the end of the 18th century, the Russian nobleman Pyotr Sinebrychoff packed his family into wagons and set off toward the Grand Duchy of Finland to make his fortune. There he founded "a beer fermentation room" for the soldiers of the garrison town of Ruotsinalmi. When the garrison moved on, he stayed put, but his son Nicolai followed the troops, prospering in the wars between Sweden and Russia by supplying the Russian army. With a keen eye for new business, he noticed the growth in beer consumption, and in 1819, he won a ten-year license for the brewing and selling of beer in Helsinki, marking the founding of the company.

Porter brewing has a long history in the company—going back to the 1860s—but production has been sporadic. To begin with, only small amounts were brewed during the winter months, and then production ended in the 1930s. It wasn't until 1957 that Sinebrychoff Porter was introduced. Unlike many Baltic porters, Sinebrychoff's version is brewed with top-fermenting yeast—from Guinness no less. The beer is unfiltered, although excess yeast is removed by separation. It is brewed with four different malts—pilsner, Munich, brown, and caramel—and hopped with Saaz and Nugget hops.

Beer writer Michael Jackson was a great supporter of Baltic porter and one of the first beer writers from outside the region to promote the style. Sinebrychoff Porter was reputedly a favorite of his. The Beverage Testing Institute in Chicago ranked it among the United States's best import beers, and it has twice won silver in the Brewing Industry International Awards. **AA**

Tasting notes

Dark with a dark tan head. It has a fairly plain, roasted malt aroma without too many notes, but on tasting, it develops into a stronger, slightly burned coffee flavor, with hints of toast, licorice, and dried fruit. Bitterness is balanced and hangs on just long enough to finish off the experience.

S'muttonator

Smuttynose Brewing | www.smuttynose.com

Country of origin United States
First brewed 2005
Alcohol content 8.8% abv
Serving temperature 46°F, 8°C

Tasting notes

Near black with a ghostly ruby shade, topped by an ample collar of foam. A waft of alcohol warns of a solid alcohol content, but the flavor is all malt, with an appetizing mix of raisin, molasses, and chocolate. Chewy with a creamy, smooth finish.

If it weren't for a lousy, broken-down pump on David Yarrington's brew kettle at the Smuttynose Brewery in Portsmouth, New Hampshire, the world might never have experienced the joys of this massively malty double bock. Smuttynose's system does double duty, pumping the mash from the kettle into the lauter tun, then filtering the wort back into the kettle. One day in the middle of a brew a few years ago, however, the aforementioned pump broke down and, unexpectedly, the mash began feeding back into the kettle.

Yarrington cursed, then thought about what had happened. He had witnessed the age-old process of decoction, a method of removing a portion of the mash, boiling it, then returning it to the full brew. Lager brewers have done it for centuries to reduce cloudiness and produce a richer malt profile. It's a long process and largely unneeded today because of the improved consistency of highly modified malts and temperature controls on equipment. Few brewers bother with the step, but Yarrington says, "It gave us the idea to try a double decoction on a double bock."

It was a curious decision because Smuttynose was known mainly for English-style ales that didn't require the added brewing step. Double decoction turned a typical eight-hour brewing shift into a fifteen-hour day. The additional work is well worth the effort. Yarrington credits the slow process with pulling added malt character from the mash without adding extra sweetness. Instead of a cloying finish, this beer leaves the palate with a roasted malt bite and just enough hops to encourage another gulp. **DR**

Southwark Old Stout

South Australian Brewing | www.lion-nathan.com

Country of origin Australia
First brewed 1984
Alcohol content 7.4% abv
Serving temperature 44°F, 7°C

Southwark Old Stout is a beer of some intrigue. There are few who recall its beginnings, and it perhaps has not been a beer of sufficient fame for its origin to have been publicly recorded. John Harvey was head brewer of South Australian Brewing (or SAB) at the time Southwark Old Stout was released in the early 1980s. Harvey recalls that Southwark had not produced a stout since it ceased brewing Guinness under license in 1975. That is not to say that Southwark did not have a tradition of brewing stout, as most of the older Australian breweries do, but rather, SAB had agreed to cease brewing its stouts in 1964 as part of its agreement to brew Guinness.

It was to these earlier stouts that SAB turned when it revitalized the tradition in 1984. In particular, it drew from the work of its head brewer from 1946, Lance Walters, who had developed West End Export Stout, which was stronger, thicker, and more bitter than its predecessors. Harvey also drew from learnings gained from the twelve years SAB spent brewing Guinness. Southwark Old Stout was released to much fanfare, and by all accounts, the journalists present at the launch enjoyed themselves a little more than they expected due to its high alcohol content.

One of the young lads working at SAB at the time of the release was Tony Jones, who was following in the footsteps of his father and uncle. Within ten years, he was head brewer. Although he now works at another brewery in Sydney, when pressed, Tony will confess to sneaking in the odd Southwark Old Stout when winter is upon him. **DD**

Tasting notes

Expect a generous creamy head that hints of roasted coffee and dark fruits as it weaves light brown laces down your glass. Each sip releases a comforting warmth and gentle malt sweetness before a lingering bitter finish that perfectly matches your mother's chocolate brownies.

Speedway Stout

AleSmith Brewing | www.alesmith.com

St.-Ambroise Oatmeal Stout

Brasserie McAuslan Brewing | www.mcauslan.com

Country of origin United States
First brewed 2002
Alcohol content 12% abv
Serving temperature 55°F, 13°C

Country of origin Canada
First brewed 1991
Alcohol content 5% abv
Serving temperature 50°F, 10°C

Many of today's craft brewers got their start at home, but few breweries strut their home-brew pedigree with more enthusiasm than AleSmith Brewing. Its advertising plays on the fact that all its employees are home-brewers. Peter Zien, who bought the brewery from home-brewer turned pro Skip Virgilio in 2002, is himself a "grand master" home-brew judge.

Virgilio first brewed Speedway Stout in 1998 as a more modest 8 percent abv offering flavored with coffee. The entrepreneur who'd come up with the idea and the Speedway Stout name soon lost interest, and AleSmith brewed only two batches of the beer. In 2001, Virgilio took inspiration from Rogue Ales Imperial Stout: "I wrote a fresh recipe and revived the Speedway Stout name. This time, the beer was 12 percent." A portion of the batch also became AleSmith's first barrel-aged beer. **SH**

A year after the launch of their Montréal craft brewery, Peter McAuslan and his partner brewer Ellen Bounsall decided that the time had come to add a seasonal brand to their portfolio. Oatmeal Stout, or Bière Noire à l'Avoine, as it is called in French, was not a style well known in Québec. It's unclear precisely when and how the oatmeal stout style originated, but it was almost certainly in Britain and most likely during the late 19th and early 20th centuries, when brewers sought to promote the healthiness and vitality of the products.

Oats in the mash give the beer a creaminess, some might even say a silkiness, that an un-oated stout simply does not possess. It is a difficult process for a brewer to handle, because even minor additions of oats can gelatinize during the boil and gum up the works quite badly. But when done correctly, as it is in the McAuslan version, the results are spectacular. **SB**

Tasting notes

Dark color with a creamy off-white head. Roasted coffee beans dominate the nose, followed by chocolate and nuts. Tastes of coffee, joined by creamy chocolate, dark fruit, and caramel.

Tasting notes

Hints of coffee, raisin, date, and plum on the nose, and a creamy, mouth-coating body offers the palate flavors of dark chocolate, espresso, roasted malt, and a touch of anise.

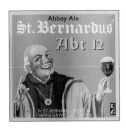

St. Bernardus Abt 12

Brouwerij St. Bernardus | www.sintbernardus.be

St. Nikolaus Bock Bier

Penn Brewery | www.pennbrew.com

Country of origin Belgium
First brewed 1946
Alcohol content 10.5% abv
Serving temperature 54°F, 12°C

Country of origin United States
First brewed 1989
Alcohol content 7.5% abv
Serving temperature 50°F, 10°C

First brewed in 1946, as Belgium was recovering from the ravages of World War II, St. Bernardus Abt 12 was part of the arrangement to brew beers for the monks at the nearby St. Sixtus abbey (now known as Westvleteren). The commercial arrangement with the abbey ended in 1992, and the brewery entered the marketplace on its own.

Brouwerij St. Bernardus doesn't cut corners in the production of its beers—making very complex, flavorful strong ales takes time. This beer has an overall production period of more than three months, from primary fermentation to maturity, which includes two months of cold conditioning and a further two weeks of warm conditioning. The recipe includes both the Alexis and Prisma varieties of pale malt, plus a pinch of roasted malt that gives the beer its muscular body, while Target and Styrian Golding hops add spice. **CC**

It's a little-known fact that St. Nicholas is the patron saint of brewers, and how he earned that distinction is unknown. There's no record that Nicholas, a 4th-century bishop of Myra (now Turkey), ever brewed or even drank beer. He's known more for miraculously visiting every child on a certain night of the year.

St. Nikolaus Bock is released during the Christmas season by Pittsburgh's Penn Brewery. It is a strong, dark, Munich-style bock made with five different roasted malts. It's no surprise that Penn chose a classic German style as its Christmas beer. Its founder's family goes back to the very beginnings of German immigration in the United States, and its brewhouse and restaurant are located in the former Eberhardt and Ober Brewery, a historically certified, 19th-century building in the city's Deutschtown, where German-style lager was first brewed in 1848. **DR**

Tasting notes
A very dark brown beer that leaves a noticeable lacing in the glass. It has notes of banana, chocolate, candi sugar, and dark fruits. The mouthfeel is very full and creamy.

Tasting notes
Very dark brown with a hint of Santa Claus red. Caramel and dark fruit flavors swirl with just a touch of spice, then finish with a tight, roasted malt bitterness. Toffee malt aroma.

St. Peter's Cream Stout

St. Peter's Brewery | www.stpetersbrewery.co.uk

Country of origin England
First brewed 2001
Alcohol content 6.5% abv
Serving temperature 50°–54°F, 10°–12°C

All the beers at St. Peter's Brewery in Suffolk are made using locally grown barley and water drawn from the brewery's own well. The water is unusually soft for the area and absolutely ideal for brewing. St. Peter's Cream Stout is one of twelve year-round bottled beers, plus a few seasonals—a staggering range for a brewery that is still relatively small.

A cream stout is one that has a smoother palate and a less bitter character than a "dry" stout. This cream stout was created by head brewer Mark Slater, who based it on a traditional, pre-Guinness stout recipe. The brief was to create a beer with lots of character and flavor. Fuggle and Challenger hops from Kent, plus a blend of four locally grown, floor-malted barleys, create an aromatic, strong, dark chocolate cream stout with a satisfying bittersweet aftertaste. Sounds appetizing? It is. **ST**

Tasting notes
Think burned toast and espresso with hints of dark chocolate. An undeniably bitter palate but with a surprisingly light mouthfeel, hints of dark fruits, and a bittersweet finish.

Stolichno Bock

Zagorka Brewery | www.zagorka.bg

Country of origin Bulgaria
First brewed 2000
Alcohol content 6.5% abv
Serving temperature 41°F, 5°C

These days, Bulgaria has a surprisingly large offering of home-grown beers, given that brewing doesn't have a long tradition and heritage in the country. Bulgaria's reputation as a wine producer has meant that the fermented juice of the grain and the grape have often vied with each other for drinkers' attentions.

In a sea of Continental lagers, travelers searching for something more satisfying should head toward Stolichno Bock Beer. This beer was originally created at the Ariana Brewery in Sofia, but the plant closed in 2004 and production was shifted to Zagorka Brewery. Although Stolichno's recipe is a closely guarded secret, it is known that three types of malt are used to maintain that all-essential balance on the palate: a caramel malt for its strong flavor, a coffee malt to produce its saturated color, and a light malt to give the beer a thicker taste. **JM**

Tasting notes
Beneath the foamy head of this dark chestnut-colored beer, expect a deep and thick malty flavor, with strong hints of coffee and caramel. Slightly fiery finish reminiscent of cognac.

Cream Stout's flask-shaped bottle is a replica of a 1770 antique.

Stone Smoked Porter

Stone Brewing | www.stonebrew.com

Country of origin United States
First brewed 1996
Alcohol content 5.9% abv
Serving temperature 55°F, 13°C

Stone Smoked Porter was released not long after Stone Brewing opened, and it was meant to be a one-off; it was also meant to be sold solely on draft and only in the San Diego area. Today it's the most widely available smoked beer in the United States, and it's distinctively different from many of the other popular smoked, or rauch, beers. This popularity could have something to do with the fact that Stone uses Hugh Baird peat-smoked malt in its porter, as opposed to the beechwood-smoked malt common in German Rauchbier and its U.S. cousins, or the alder-smoked malt in Alaskan Smoked Porter. The latter two conjure images of smoked meat or fish because those woods are commonly used in curing. Peat-smoked malt, on the other hand, has the same pungent aroma found in intense single-malt whiskeys from Islay.

Stone uses the smoked malt with restraint. Although the brewery is known first for its hop-centric beers, its range continues to grow. In 2002, Stone began a series of eleven annual releases of Vertical Epic Ale. Each is brewed to a different recipe and meant to be aged. The first was released on February 2, 2002, the second on March 3, 2003, and so on until the final release on December 12, 2012.

The brewery has also collaborated with other breweries to release special beers, a practice becoming more common as U.S. brewers work together or with brewers from other countries. Stone, in fact, has often teamed up with others on the same beer; for example, it created a triple with Mikkeller from Denmark and AleSmith, who are just down the road in San Diego. **SH**

Tasting notes

Pours reddish brown in the glass, leaving a trail of white foam. On the nose, there is smokiness at the outset, which complements rich, coffeelike notes. There is more smoke on the palate, intermingling with chocolate flavors, a harmony and bond that ultimately ties the beer together.

Störtebeker Schwarzbier

Stralsunder Brauerei | www.stralsunder.de

Country of origin Germany
First brewed 1991
Alcohol content 5% abv
Serving temperature 46°F, 8°C

The Stralsunder Brauerei named their black lager after Germany's medieval buccaneer Klaus Störtebeker, who fought the merchants of the Hanseatic League in the North and Baltic seas around 1400. There is another reason: the last name of this mysterious figure is said to derive from the Low German idiom for gulping down a jar of alcohol. With such a name, no wonder the beer has become Stralsunder Brauerei's best seller.

In a sense it is a foundation beer, even though the brewery's origin dates back to 1827. In the 19th century, Stralsunder Brauerei became main purveyor to the Baltic seaside resorts. After World War II, East Germany nationalized the company, and their beers acquired quite a reputation during the 1970s. After reunification, the large western German wholesaler Nordmann bought the site and also established his headquarters there. They modernized the brewery and released three beers at first—two styles of the regional brand Stralsunder and the premium Schwarzbier.

This velvety-black specialty is malty but not sweet, offers roasted but no burned notes, and is bitter but not harsh. All in all, this beer is wonderfully balanced and yet full of character. Markus Berberich, brewmaster and managing director, brews it with five barley malts in the traditional time-consuming decoction mash. He also uses organically grown aroma hops to bring in a spicy but smooth bitterness. The beer is unfiltered, which contributes to the rounded taste.

Störtebeker Schwarzbier is mainly available in the northern regions. As becomes an untamed buccaneer, it often emerges here and there in other Baltic states. **SK**

Tasting notes
Coffee brown, slightly hazy, with a cream-colored head. On the nose, caramel and roasted aromas with hints of cocoa. On the palate, a smooth first taste builds up to a rich body of coffee, chocolate, and roasted flavors, supported by a modest bitterness. Velvety finish with roasted notes.

Stouterik

Brasserie de la Senne | www.brasseriedelasenne.be

Country of origin Belgium
First brewed 2005
Alcohol content 4.2% abv
Serving temperature 55°F, 13°C

Brewers have influenced each other across borders for centuries. Even the idiosyncratic Belgians are known to steal good ideas now and then. Stout, for example. That was a good idea.

The Belgians made stouts for most of the 20th century, originally inspired by English and Irish beers. But the brewers gradually ripped them free of their roots, and they became fruitier, stronger, and sweeter over time. Perhaps not coincidentally, Belgian stouts also lost popularity and were virtually extinct. A few have appeared in recent years, but these often commit the sins that condemned them in the first place.

Stouterik is the kind of authentically dry Irish stout that is rarely made anymore—even in Ireland. It retains a certain Belgian sparkle, comparatively thin and lively on the tongue, but its signature trait is a bone-dry, thirst-provoking roast flavor. Only a touch of malt sweetness remains, contending with a fair dose of hop bitterness. This one's not for those with a sweet tooth.

Incidentally, *stouterik* in the Flemish and Brussels dialects means "strongman," like the kind you might see at a circus. Mothers use the word more commonly to admonish headstrong children—something like "you little brute." From the muscle-bound workers on the label, one can guess that the brewers conceived this as a stout for quaffing at the end of a long day. The low alcohol content also might encourage that sort of behavior. Like their Taras Boulba, the Stouterik springs from the brewers' belief that beer need not be strong in alcohol to be strong in flavor—an idea that is perhaps more rare in Belgium than it ought to be. **JS**

Tasting notes

Black beer with a tan head, smelling of roast walnut and espresso. Raspy, chocolate-malty taste offers a fleeting impression of sweetness before going crisply bitter and as dry as cobwebs in a dark desert cave. Pleasant aftertaste, like chewing on roasted malt.

Strong Suffolk Vintage Ale

Greene King | www.greeneking.co.uk

Country of origin England
First brewed *ca.* 1980s
Alcohol content 6% abv
Serving temperature 52°F, 11°C

Strong Suffolk Vintage Ale is an unusual beer that uses a technique of blending two ales prior to bottling: Old 5X, which is brewed to around 12 percent and aged for at least two years in a hundred-barrel oak tun whose lid is lined with a fine-grain clay called Suffolk Marl, and BPA, a dark, malty sweet, 5 percent freshly brewed beer. The result is a dark and fruity beer of great depth. Neither Old 5X nor BPA are sold as beers in their own right, but brewer John Bexon sometimes allows visitors to taste them in the brewery's cellars. (Those who have been lucky to experience Old 5X speak of a nose reminiscent of a very dry Fino—musty, yeasty, almost tangy—and the body is thin but with plenty of woodiness, raisins, and a sour-sweetness.)

Both beers are brewed with pale and crystal malts and hopped with Challenger and First Gold, while Old 5X has the addition of the bittering hop Target. The technique of aging beers and blending them was commonly used in Britain in the late 1700s and 1800s as a way of balancing sweetness and acidity while adding vitality to a brew that had stood maturing for at least two years. Beers from the Rodenbach brewery in Belgium are still blended in a similar way. It is said that in 1878 Eugene Rodenbach traveled to England, where he learned how to blend beers the English way. Some speculate that he visited Greene King.

Suffolk Vintage Ale (sold as Olde Suffolk in the United States) has never been a big seller, but Greene King has shown their commitment to it by installing a second tun to store the Old 5X, as the beer is now highly regarded as a specialty brew. **TH**

Tasting notes

A dark, full-bodied, fruity beer that is full of oaky flavors and some chocolate sweetness. The bittering hops add great depth and complexity to the taste. Its strength makes it warming in the mouth. It pairs excellently with fruitcake or Christmas pudding.

Super Bock Stout

União Cervejeira | www.superbock.pt

Country of origin Portugal
First brewed 2003
Alcohol content 5% abv
Serving temperature 50°F, 10°C

It's tricky to find beers with this much character in the pale lager paradise of Portugal. More like a German-style Schwarzbier or dunkel, Super Bock Stout is a relatively new entry in the Portuguese tradition of dark lagers called "preta." The Portuguese beer scene has long been dominated by two giant companies, Unicer and Centralcer. They flood the market with light lagers, and then fight for the scraps by contriving ways to attract those drinkers who want something different. In Portugal, dark beer still qualifies as different.

Super Bock Stout is an attractive beer that offers some malt backbone. The proper setting for one may well be an old-fashioned *cervejaria*—a Portuguese beer hall. Imagine a glass of nearly black beer casting its shadow on a plate of salt cod (*bacalhau*) or grilled meat. Its reasonable alcohol content means that the beer need not end with the meal. **JS**

Tasting notes
Pours black with a tall tan head. Aroma of weak, sugared black coffee and currants on the nose. Prevailing flavor is a mild sweetness, accented by a light, roasted malt bitterness.

Super Vintage

Hakusekikan Beer | www.hakusekikan-beer.jp

Country of origin Japan
First brewed 1999
Alcohol content 14.3% abv
Serving temperature 54°F, 12°C

Super Vintage is one of the most notable beers on the Japanese craft beer scene. Its popularity can be attributed to its long and deep flavor profile, which is created during its extended fermentation and aging times. It was designed by brewmaster Satoshi Niwa. He initially fermented the beer with wine yeast to achieve a high alcohol content, but several attempts were not successful because the yeast did not ferment maltose well. He then started off the fermentation with beer yeast, then continued with wine yeast and achieved better results.

Using pale malt as a base, Niwa also adds crystal malt, chocolate malt, and wheat malt to achieve the complex flavors. Challenger hops from England are used for both bittering and aroma. Super Vintage is now brewed once a year, then laid down for two years before being released for sale. **BH**

Tasting notes
Striking aroma of dark malt and alcohol. Flavor is refreshingly tart, with a layered malt profile very like a strong Belgian ale. Strong bitterness lingers on a background of dried stone fruit.

← A vintage beer tap and Azulejos tiles in Bairro Alto, Lisbon.

Terrible

Unibroue | www.unibroue.com

Country of origin Canada
First brewed 2002
Alcohol content 10.5% abv
Serving temperature 50°F, 10°C

An iconic line from the early days of rap music explains that something or someone bad could be "not bad meaning bad, but bad meaning good!" And so it is with Terrible, a pitch-black and intimidating strong ale first unleashed on the public at the 2002 edition of the Montréal beer festival, La Mondial de la Bière.

It was released alongside a similarly packaged golden strong ale called Fringante, and neither beer was originally intended for sale beyond the provincial borders. Greatly positive reviews of both beers, in particular the Terrible, forged reputations that quickly spread, feeding demand as they did so. It was not long before Terrible was spotted at better beer destinations over the border in the United States.

While all of this was occurring, though, a behind-the-scenes battle for control of Unibroue was well underway, with the Ontario-based Sleeman Breweries demonstrating ever-increasing degrees of interest in its Québec contemporary. A strong regional brewery operating in all other parts of the country, Sleeman was anxious to have a firm foothold in Québec and saw Unibroue as the means with which to get it.

The deal finally came through in the spring of 2004; but only a few years after that, Sleeman and its holdings, including Unibroue, were acquired in turn by Sapporo of Japan. Thereafter structural changes in the company occurred, including the withdrawal of several brands from certain markets. Part of this retrenchment was the return of Terrible to its original purpose as primarily a Québec-only brand, although small amounts are still exported from time to time. **SB**

Tasting notes

Most striking in the aroma of this jet-black ale is the appearance of something resembling Asian spice, alongside black licorice and molasses. The complex body continues spicy, adding dark chocolate, espresso beans, and blackstrap molasses to the enticing mix.

Thornbridge Bracia

Thornbridge Brewery | www.thornbridgebrewery.co.uk

Country of origin England
First brewed 2008
Alcohol content 9% abv
Serving temperature 54°F, 12°C

When it comes to brewing innovation, there are few breweries doing it better than Thornbridge in the English county of Derbyshire. Bracia is absolute proof of this theory, although you could argue that the beer is hardly a new idea.

"Bracia" is likely to have been the Celtic name for an Iron Age beverage, to which a Roman reference has been found not far from Thornbridge at Haddon Hall. Although little is known about the historic brew, head brewer Stefano Cossi uncovered that it was definitely high in alcohol, and made with different grains and, almost certainly, honey. So, being Italian, he set out to follow in his Roman forefathers' footsteps and uncover how this brew may have tasted. He started by making a stout in the same way that they would have done in the old days, taking the first runnings off two mashes.

To do this, he took seven malts, the key one being brown malt, and used large quantities for a smooth chocolate note; he also used a smoked malt, which helped to partially re-create some of the flavors that historic open kilning of the grains would have added. He then added four different types of hops, including the very unusual Sorachi Ace, and as a final flourish added bittersweet Italian chestnut honey. Then, as if all the dedication to ingredients wasn't enough, after ordinary fermentation, the beer undergoes a second three-month cold maturation before being put into bottles with champagne yeast for a third fermentation. This is most definitely a sipping beer, and Cossi recommends that it be served in a wide-based stemmed glass and savored. **MC**

Tasting notes

Upon pouring, there are waves of chestnut honey, white chocolate, mocha, prunes in syrup, and a hint of sandalwood; this then develops on the palate as velvety chocolate, hazelnuts, coffee, and molasses, ending in a little licorice, peat, and a lot of slightly astringent cocoa.

Thornbridge Saint Petersburg

Thornbridge Brewery | www.thornbridgebrewery.co.uk

Country of origin England
First brewed 2005
Alcohol content 7.7% abv
Serving temperature 54°F, 12°C

In 2009, Thornbridge Brewery moved from their original stately home to an ultramodern brewery in the nearby town of Bakewell, a cathedral of gleaming stainless steel where the brewery's ever-inquisitive brewing team could continue their devotion to good beer. This all makes for a contemporary cutting-edge attitude to brewing and promotion, but Thornbridge has also always tried to make something of its history.

In 1790, a local merchant named John Morewood bought Thornbridge Hall. He had made his fortune selling linen to St. Petersburg, then the Russian capital, a fact that helped to name the imperial Russian stout. "With this beer we are looking back to the sort of beer that might have been drunk in the house's early days," says the brewery's director Simon Webster about a style of beer that was imported regularly to the Baltic.

Maris Otter, torrified wheat, chocolate, roasted barley, dark crystal, and peated malts go into the mash tun, while the hops include Vanguard, Sorachi Ace, and a variety that always changes (Galena and Bramling Cross have been used before). Dark muscovado sugar is added toward the end of the boil.

In 2007, the brewery wood-aged a consignment of Saint Petersburg. "We got hold of three former whisky hogsheads," says head brewer Stefan Cossi, "Macallan, Mortlach, and Caol Ila. The beer and wood were infused for three months and then bottled with sugar and yeast. Caol Ila is the one that aged better." The experiment has not been repeated, but given the brewery's sense of adventure, chances are something similar will happen again. **ATJ**

Tasting notes

Dark color with an espresso head. On the nose, fiery alcohol, soot, mocha, condensed milk, and cigar box. It's a beguiling palate with more mocha and condensed milk, bitter fruit, hops, and malty softness coming in, before a long, lasting bitter finish with roasted graininess returning.

Tokyo Black

Yoho Brewing | www.yohobrewing.com

Country of origin Japan
First brewed 2005
Alcohol content 5% abv
Serving temperature 55°F, 13°C

Tokyo Black is a superbly crafted session porter introduced by former brewmaster Toshi Ishii. It was intended as a second brand to the ever-popular Yona Yona Ale. Brewery president Naoyuki Ide relates that the company recognized the popularity of Guinness in Japan, and wanted to offer a beer that could eventually exceed it. He explains that because his beers are brewed in Japan, they are perceived as being fresher. Furthermore, in recent years, Japan's major brewers have been introducing more dark beers in order to capitalize on the nascent popularity of stout, often going as far as selling a dark lager as a stout. In reality, it seems that Japanese drinkers prefer a porter.

According to Ide, creating Tokyo Black was not difficult. The beer is based on an existing recipe from a U.S. brewery and only required tweaking to make it appeal to Japanese palates. Moreover, the brewery spent a great deal of effort giving the beer a distinctly Japanese image for greater local appeal. While Yona Yona Ale is the main beer featured on the company's website, Tokyo Black and another newer product, an IPA named Ao-oni, are featured peripherally. In fact, the website is a full celebration of Japanese imagery. The three beers, however, have individually distinct flavor profiles, and seem to be aimed at different segments of the market.

The parent company, Hoshino Resort, is located in a mountainous area of Nagano Prefecture. Although the area is more famous for the whiskey being produced there, the link to very good quality water is obvious, and this has been a great asset for Yoho Brewing. **BH**

Tasting notes

It is dark opaque brown with a medium tan head. There is a faintly sweet dark caramel aroma, with a touch of vanilla. It has a tangy flavor, quite like chocolate. The deep roast flavors are minimal, with a taste more like brownies, making it closer to a porter than a stout.

Tomislav Pivo

Zagrebacka Pivovara | www.ozujsko.com

Country of origin Croatia
First brewed 1925
Alcohol content 7.3% abv
Serving temperature 44°F, 7°C

As well as being the king of Croatian beers, the deep, dark malty brew Tomislav Pivo is named after the country's first king. It was created to commemorate the 1,000-year anniversary of the crowning of the first king of Croatia, Tomislav I. Although very little is known about him, Tomislav I is still remembered as a hero in Croatia today. He may have only reigned for three years, but before claiming the throne, he used his vast military force to unite the country's two warring factions, and, for the first time, Croatia came under independent rule. Such a powerful ruler needs an equally potent drink to honor him, and Tomislav Pivo certainly delivers on this level. It remains one of the strongest beers produced in Croatia and is a drink that Croatians save for special occasions.

Although it has the appearance of a stout, Tomislav is a dark lager, a close cousin of the beer styles that are greatly enjoyed in the Czech Republic and Bavaria, with a slight nod toward the taste profiles of the porters of the Baltic. Meanwhile, the addition of a fair amount of roasted malt in the mix gives it a luscious, caramelized flavor. As with most Croatian beers, it is traditionally served very cold. When you consider that this beer has remained popular for more than eighty years, you realize that it has something genuinely special about it. Just don't have more than three. **JM**

Tasting notes
Old-fashioned, chocolate-tinged dark lager with a thick creamy head and a strong malty aroma. This deep malt flavor remains on the tongue with sweet notes of caramel and wine.

Tosta

Pausa Café | www.pausacafe.org

Country of origin Italy
First brewed 2007
Alcohol content 14% abv
Serving temperature 46°–50°F, 8°–10°C

Along with Chicca—a dark beer produced with coffee beans—Tosta is the beer that most represents what the far-sighted and innovative Pausa Café is trying to achieve with its brews: unusual beers that are also eminently drinkable. Pausa Café classes Tosta as a fairly traditional barleywine, although at 14 percent abv, it is much stronger than most British examples. Unlike some beers of this strength, however, it is not bottle conditioned and remains still in the glass when poured. Another difference is that cocoa beans are added to the mix, which contribute to the beer's aroma in two ways: on one hand, the beans add the traditional roast notes that can be found in barleywine, although these are usually the by-product of roasted malts; on the other hand, they also give the sort of smooth acidity that can be found in strong chocolate.

The use of cocoa beans like this is possible because the brewing equipment has a separate system of filters that allows the brewmaster, Andrea Bertola, to work with a denser wort than usual. Moreover, the coppers are not heated with direct fire, but with steam, which helps to provide a more measured and slower heat for the wort, avoiding burned or caramelized notes in the final product. The result is a very rich beer, with strong roast notes and sensations that are more common in wine than in beer. **ES**

Tasting notes
Tosta has a dark chocolate color with a slight foam on the head. On the nose, there are clear roasted notes. On the palate is a smooth acidity that is common in cocoa.

← A monument to King Tomislav I in Zagreb, Croatia.

T'Owd Tup

Dent Brewery | www.dentbrewery.co.uk

Country of origin England
First brewed 1991
Alcohol content 6% abv
Serving temperature 55°F, 13°C

Dent Brewery is in the Yorkshire Dales. From that, you might assume that it is also in Yorkshire, which is the largest county in England (and Britain). You would be wrong. It is in Cumbria, England's most northwesterly county, famed for the rural beauty of the Lake District National Park. This anomaly occurred in 1974, when counties were rearranged. Cumbria was created out of Cumberland, Westmoreland, a chunk of North Lancashire and a slice of the former West Riding of Yorkshire. The ancient name "Cumbria" (from the same Celtic root as *Cymru*) was revived for the new county.

The Dent Brewery was created in 1990 by Martin Stafford. A year later, Martin's brother founded Nick Stafford's Hambleton Ales 40 miles (65 km) to the east in North Yorkshire. In 2005, Martin Stafford sold the brewery to Paul and Judith Beeley of Keighley, who have improved the marketing of the beers by having pump clips and bottle labels professionally designed.

The one constant in the Dent history is head brewer Paul Goodyear, who joined the company following a work experience placement when leaving school in 1990. He has played a key role in developing all the beers—regular and seasonal—the brewery has ever produced. Sheep are an unavoidable feature of the hilly landscapes of Cumbria and they have inspired most of Dent's beer names and associated imagery.

Dent's most acclaimed beer is T'Owd Tup, which is dialect for "the old ram." This strong winter ale won CAMRA's Champion Winter Beer of Britain in 1999. Its complex malt profile makes it suitable to sup with hearty winter stews of beef or, even better, mutton. **JP**

Tasting notes

Dark red/walnut ale with a big aroma of dark chocolate, treacle, and licorice. The dry and roasted flavor of the malt hints at molasses, sarsaparilla, and pipe tobacco with a hint of spicy vinous acidity. Hop character is minimal and bitterness moderate.

Trappistes Rochefort 10

Brasserie de l'Abbaye Notre-Dame de St. Remy | www.trappistes-rochefort.com

Country of origin Belgium
First brewed 1953
Alcohol content 11.3% abv
Serving temperature 54°–59°F, 12°–15°C

After World War II, the Trappist brewery near Rochefort in the province of Namur had suffered serious damage. New equipment had to be bought in, including some from its brother Trappist brewery at Chimay. In the same breath, two new beers were conceived—the 6 degrees and the 10 degrees—named for their density in Belgian degrees. (The 6 has an original gravity of 1060 and the 10 a gravity of 1100. "Original gravity" refers to the amount of the dissolved sugar present in the wort before fermentation—the higher the figure, the stronger the beer). Rochefort's current brewer is Gumer Santos. Although his parents were Spanish, he is a Rochefortois, born and bred.

All three Rochefort beers (there is also an 8 degrees) share the same basic recipe. They are not, however, the same beer—every batch is specifically aimed at one of the three versions with just the amount of liters per batch differing. All the beers are made with barley malt, wheat starch, brown and white candi sugar, Hallertau and Styrian hop pellets, and, it's rumored, a tad of coriander. However, the strangest thing in the Rochefort recipe is the yeast. It consists of three different strains, each rekindled and mixed a couple of times a year: it is first used on the 6 degrees, then transferred to the 8, and finally to the 10.

When Rochefort 10 was launched in 1953, it was nicknamed "la Merveilleuse" ("the Magnificent"), although today that moniker has virtually vanished. In Belgium, there's a legend about an even stronger Christmas version, but the truth is that pubs in the area used to blend it with port wine during the season. **JPa**

Tasting notes

Dark brown beer with a reddish shine and creamy head. The nose has banana, toffee, ripe pear, and chocolate liqueur, which on the palate turns into Mexican mole (spicy chili and bitter chocolate sauce), enriched with port, raisins, and spices. Ends as a rich Armenian brandy on wood.

Traquair Jacobite Ale

Traquair House Brewery | www.traquair.co.uk

Country of origin Scotland
First brewed 1995
Alcohol content 8% abv
Serving temperature 54°–59°F, 12°–15°C

Records show that a brewery was working at full tilt in Traquair House, near Peebles in the Scottish Borders, when Mary Queen of Scots visited in 1566. A large copper was installed in 1739 in the brewhouse beneath the chapel, and today the beers are made to traditional recipes sourced from the house's archives. Traquair Jacobite Ale is based on an18th-century formula and has proved so popular that it earned a permanent position in the brewery's range. It was named Champion Winter Beer at the World Beer Championship in 1997 and won a gold medal at the Stockholm Beer Festival in 1998. The 20th Laird of Traquair, the late Peter Maxwell Stuart, started brewing in 1965 after he discovered the old mash tun, open coolers, and wooden stirring paddles—all in perfect condition—that had lain silent since the early 1880s.

Jacobite Ale was brewed to mark the Jacobite Rebellion of 1745, an attempt to restore the Stuart kings to the thrones of Scotland and England. The earls of Traquair had had a long tradition of Catholicism and supported the Jacobite cause. In 1745, when the fifth earl bade farewell to Prince Charles Edward Stuart— Bonnie Prince Charlie—the Bear Gates, then the main entrance to the house, were shut with a promise that they would not be opened until the Stuarts were restored to the throne. They have remained closed. **AG**

Tasting notes
Rich and almost winelike in raisin-fruit intensity, this beer develops a chocolate and spice (coriander) palate on the way to a bittersweet finish. Remarkably easy to drink.

Trois Pistoles

Unibroue | www.unibroue.com

Country of origin Canada
First brewed 1997
Alcohol content 9% abv
Serving temperature 50°F, 10°C

The name of this beer does not refer to a trio of pistols, although overconsumption of this potent yet almost quaffable ale could lead to feeling like one has been knocked in the head by at least one or two heavy metallic objects. Instead, the ale is named after a small village in the Québec region of Les Basques, the name of which refers to three coins rather than any firearms.

Like many of Unibroue's beers, the label of Trois Pistoles makes a reference to a Québécois legend—in this case, one that naturally enough emerged from the town's 300-year history. It relates to a local bishop who evoked the assistance of a good devil in order to complete the construction of the new church. Since the devil took the form of a muscular black steed, work progressed quickly, until someone removed the bridle from the horse and it vanished with one last stone still to be set. This legend explains both the presence of the black horse on the ale's label and the absence of a single stone from the village church at Trois Pistoles.

Like many of its stablemates, Trois Pistoles is of a lineage most easily traced to Belgium. It is spiced, strong, and bottle fermented, as are many Belgian beers, yet its character differs from anything commonly seen out of Europe. The brewery promotes it as an ideal companion for food, specifically chocolate desserts, and maintains that it will age well for up to a decade. **SB**

Tasting notes
Almost black in color, Trois Pistoles is spicy enough on the nose, but in the body presents more dark, stewed fruit and chocolate notes. Of moderate sweetness for its strength.

A label inspired by legend; a beer to be quaffed with care. ➡

trois pistoles

The Troobacz

Pivovar Štramberk
www.relaxvpodhuri.cz/en

Country of origin Czech Republic
First brewed 2005
Alcohol content 4.3% abv
Serving temperature 46°F, 8°C

When brewmaster Marek Pietoň made his first batch of lager in the north Moravian hill town of Štramberk in 2005, he was renewing a 650-year-old tradition that had ended in 1854, when the town's brewing kettles had been fired for the last time.

For his brewery, Pietoň chose a historic building on the town's central square, in house No. 5, one of the twenty-two original houses with brewing rights in town. Štramberk had received its so-called "one-mile right" from Jan, Margrave of Moravia, on December 4, 1359. This privilege granted a town the monopoly on brewing and dispensing beer within a radius of one Bohemian mile, equal to almost 7 miles (11 km).

While earlier beers in Štramberk are thought to have been top-fermenting ales, the new beers from Pivovar Štramberk are bottom-fermenting lagers, produced over longer periods of time at very cold temperatures. As well as an excellent pilsner, the brewery produces lagers flavored with cherries and plums. The Troobacz is in the style of Prague's legendary Flekovské Pivo, pouring a very dark amber, almost black, with deep coffee and spice flavors. Like the town's *štramberské uši*, or Štramberk ears, a type of pastry, the Troobacz has an understated sweetness, making it a fine dessert beer. It is almost always only seen on tap, very rarely outside of its hometown. **ER**

Tasting notes
This black beer is topped with a tan head. Expect remarkable complexity for a lager, with coffee, cola, and ginger flavors brightened by bakery spice and an addictive semibitter finish.

Turbodog

Abita Brewing
www.abita.com

Country of origin United States
First brewed 1989
Alcohol content 6.1% abv
Serving temperature 55°F, 13°C

The village of Abita Springs in Louisiana was famous for its "healing waters" long before Abita Brewing began shipping 2.5 million gallons of this water, in the form of beer, to most parts of the United States. The springs closed long ago but the town remains popular with tourists who come for the local beer and nearby hiking trails. Founded in 1986 and currently the biggest craft brewery in the United States south of the Mason-Dixon Line, Abita moved to a larger facility outside the town in 1994. Its beers are found in the original brewpub, which serves a full lineup of Abita beers to accompany spicy Louisiana fare.

Most Americans associate Abita beers with nearby New Orleans. Fortunately, the brewery was mostly untouched by Hurricane Katrina when the city was devastated in 2005, and it began brewing Fleur-de-Lis Restoration Ale almost immediately, donating part of each sale to a disaster recovery fund. Although Abita Amber can be found on tap in hundreds of bars, one of the joys of drinking in New Orleans is that adults are allowed to wander about with an alcoholic drink in hand. Bars sell beer in "to go" cups, and almost any convenience store will open a bottle and put it in a paper sack for you. The malt-forward Turbodog, named the best beer in the United States in 2005 by *Stuff* magazine, does particularly well in this setting. **SH**

Tasting notes
Pours a deep brown with ruby highlights; hints of roasted nuts and chocolate on the nose. Sweet chocolate and toffee on the palate. Coffee rather than hop bitterness at the end.

Launched as a specialty, Turbodog has a faithful following. ➡

Uerige DoppelSticke

Uerige Obergärige Hausbrauerei | www.uerige.de

Country of origin Germany
First brewed 2005
Alcohol content 8.5% abv
Serving temperature 46°F, 8°C

This luscious beauty of a beer is the result of a creative conspiracy in the kitchen of Uerige's brewpub. It is a beer so rich and complex that it must have had a special moment of creation, which indeed it did, although Michael Schnitzler, owner and brewmaster of Uerige Obergärige Hausbrauerei in Düsseldorf, tells the story in a more down-to-earth way.

At 8.5 percent, DoppelSticke is even stronger than that other famous Uerige alt variant, Sticke, which is a more modest 6.5 percent. DoppelSticke is made of so much more malt that it takes two mashes to get the usual quantity of wort. Pilsner and caramel malts are used alongside hops such as Spalter and Hallertauer Perle. As the name *alt* (old) can indicate, Uerige actually brews using the old (top-fermenting) way, a process that can be observed at its beautiful brewhouse where the brewing team still operates a cool-ship and a drip cooler.

Like Sticke, the DoppelSticke is dry hopped and lagered for a long time. It pours almost like oil, bringing along a fruity-sweet, herbal-bitter complexity that is reminiscent of Italian bitters. Therefore, it is ideal as an aperitif. Likewise, it is a delightful companion to dessert and a cheese board. While Uerige Sticke comes out twice a year, the DoppelSticke is brewed on demand, and it is usual to find individual bottles available at the pub. So, what motivated brewmaster Schnitzler to create such a fine beer? As he tells it, it was a transatlantic call from U.S. importer Matthias Neidhart, who wanted an extra-strong Uerige to please U.S. palates. Down-to-earth indeed, but still magical. **SK**

Tasting notes

Dark brown with ruby tints, the beer offers a sweet nose with a floral hop aroma. It has a pronounced bitterness balanced by a firm caramel body. Malty sweetness and complex herbal notes are imbedded in an almost oily mouthfeel. Yet it has a dry and astringent finish.

Uff-da

New Glarus Brewing Co. | www.newglarusbrewing.com

Country of origin United States
First brewed 1993
Alcohol content 7.3% abv
Serving temperature 48°F, 9°C

After having lived—and brewed—in Germany, Montana, Colorado, and Oregon, Dan Carey settled in the tidy tourist town of New Glarus in southern Wisconsin with his wife and partner Deb, to found the eponymous brewery in 1993. Carey is one of those rare lager brewers adept with both halves of his brain. This shows in the clean, flawless presentation as well as the enduring personality of beers such as this one. Uff-da is a classic dark bock, a full-bodied, nourishing brown brew, that is rare now even in its own Bavarian homeland. Bocks were once popular in North America, celebrated as springtime tonics and harbingers of the approaching summer.

Carey first brewed this recipe at Montana's Kessler Brewery in 1983, on equipment he "had cobbled together from scrap," according to his wife. At the time, beer writer Michael Jackson called it "the best bock in North America." It was the second beer to be brewed at New Glarus and is a favorite of the Careys. "I named it because my Norwegian grandfather had a habit of saying 'Uf da' whenever he lifted something heavy," which certainly describes this beer. Deb Carey describes it as "big and balanced. Nice coffee and chocolate things happening." Those dark roasted flavors are crucial. Beers in this style are not heavily hopped, so they rely on the bitter, roasted character to balance the caramelly sweetness that otherwise would dominate. The resulting beer has a fine sense of balance despite its weight. This is not an everyday beer, but does suit any occasion where you can wrap your head around its malty charms. **RM**

Tasting notes

A mocha-with-caramel-syrup kind of nose. Slightly chocolaty, but with serious toffeelike notes as well. Flavor is a tad sweet at first, but balances out as the bitterness of the hops and roasted malt start to show. Aftertaste is very long, smooth, and bittersweet.

Union Temno Pivo

Pivovarna Union | www.pivo-union.si

Ursus Black

Ursus Brewery | www.sabmiller.com

Country of origin Slovenia
First brewed 1989
Alcohol content 5.2% abv
Serving temperature 46°F, 8°C

Country of origin Romania
First brewed 1878
Alcohol content 6% abv
Serving temperature 44°–50°F, 7°–10°C

If you ask for a beer in Slovenia, chances are that you will be given a light-colored lager style. If you want something a little bit different, it will require a bit more patience and a devotion to beer hunting.

Two breweries dominate the beer market in Slovenia: Lasko, from the town of the same name, and Union, which is based in the capital Ljubljana. In 1989, the Union brewery (founded in 1864) bucked the light lager trend and released Union Temno Pivo (also known as Crni Baron or Black Baron): a dark and strong beer that was pitched at a more discerning market than was usual. As is the case with many dark beers throughout Central Europe and the Balkans, this beer looks to the dunkel style for its inspiration, offering a sweetish, toasty character. The brewery markets it as a beer for dessert, but its relatively low alcohol content suggests it would work just as well as a social beer. **ATJ**

This tasty beer, one of the leading lights in Romania, is brewed in Cluj-Napoca, a town in the western region of Transylvania. It is a Schwarzbier and, although this style is about burned and roasty characteristics, it also has a tendency to prove deceptively light.

The brewery call Ursus "the king of beers," and once you've got your taste buds around it, you'll agree that it stands up as a very fine expression of the Schwarzbier style. There's an obvious undertone of roasted flavors and coffee here, the brewer observing the traditional brewing methods to ensure that it stays faithful to the style; but it is carefully put together and well balanced as a result. There is a caramel quality to the sweetness and a rich molasses edge. Although lighter than other beers that appear the same—a porter or stout, for example—this remains a decent medium-bodied brew. **TS**

Tasting notes
Dark chestnut in color, with a slight head of foam; on the nose, roast coffee bean and sweetish malt notes. On the palate, a caramel maltiness plus a sweetness that doesn't turn too syrupy.

Tasting notes
Pours deathly black, and you would swear there is a tinge of blood red in the brown head. Lots of coffee on the nose, and it delivers a sweet up front and bitter finish. Refreshing.

The "U" on the last building of Dortmund's former Union Brewery.

Utenos Porteris

Švyturys-Utenos Alus | www.utenosalus.lt

Country of origin Lithuania
First brewed 1979
Alcohol content 6.8% abv
Serving temperature 50°–55°F, 10°–13°C

Baltic porter was long admired by kings and queens, but it was an emperor who inadvertently became its savior. Revered in France, reviled in much of Europe, and afforded a place on the marble frieze of the U.S. Supreme Court in recognition of his Civil Code, Napoleon Bonaparte divides opinion like few other historic figures. However, beer lovers may like to know that without Napoleon, the Baltic porter could have been obsolete today, rather than merely in its current heightened state of potential extinction.

Russian imperial stout arrived in Eastern Europe in the late 18th century from suppliers in London, such as Thrale's Anchor Brewery. The beer transported in British trading ships was characterized by a stronger, more robust flavor than those traditionally brewed in London, to ensure it survived the long journey. Devoured by czars and noblemen alike, the shipments of imperial stout were placed under threat at the start of the 19th century by the blockading of Baltic ports by Napoleon's forces. The solution to this trade restriction was resolved when local breweries created an heir to imperial stout in the form of Baltic porter.

Utenos Porteris is bottom-fermented and brewed according to a traditional Baltic porter recipe, with caramel malt to give that familiar sweet flavor and rich color. It has a shorter history than its counterparts, having only arrived during the dog days of the Communist era, when it was first brewed by Utenos Alus. Despite the domination of golden lagers in Eastern Europe, Utenos Porteris is still fighting fit, as you would expect from the drink that not even Napoleon could stop. **SG**

Tasting notes

Pours a deep, brownish red color with a foamy, beige head that displays a full malty nose with toffee and faint traces of chocolate. A strong, smooth caramel taste fills the mouth, followed by a hint of licorice and banana to leave a sweet finish.

Verdi Imperial Stout

Birrificio del Ducato | www.birrificiodelducato.it

Country of origin Italy
First brewed 2007
Alcohol content 8.2% abv
Serving temperature 57°–64°F, 14°–18°C

This microbrewery is located in Roncole Verdi, a little village that is famous as the birthplace of Giuseppe Verdi, Italy's most important composer. Here, close to the house where Verdi may well have played his first notes, Giovanni Campari and his partners started their brewing adventure. Campari learned a lot as a pupil of Agostino Arioli from Birrificio Italiano, but soon developed a personal approach toward his beers.

Campari got the idea to produce an imperial stout after a short holiday in New York, where he tasted different variants of the style from U.S. craft brewers. He enjoyed them all, but wanted to make his own imperial stout: strong in alcohol and rich in flavor, yet very drinkable. He found his "secret weapon" in chili peppers, which he adds very carefully to the recipe. Other ingredients are several different malts, above all Maris Otter, but also specials such as chocolate malt, rolled oats, and a small amount of smoked malted barley. British hops such as Fuggle give the bitter flavor and aroma to the beer, but the chili is what, in Campari's words, "cools down the palate" and makes you want another sip. He claims that the chili makes this imperial stout "slimmer" compared to more traditional ones.

Primary fermentation lasts one week. After a rest of five days, the beer has a second fermentation in bottle, where it matures for at least three weeks. Campari believes that the beer is at its best after two months and will age well. With this beer, he also marked the coming of age of the Italian craft beer movement. It won the gold medal at the European Beer Star in 2008—a first for an Italian beer. **MM**

Tasting notes

Beautiful ebony color with a thick, quite persistent hazelnut foam. Immediate notes of cacao, coffee, and hints of tobacco. Very intriguing indeed. In the palate, it is surprisingly easy to drink with flavors of licorice and again roast coffee. Very smooth and silky, with a long aftertaste.

Victory Storm King Imperial Stout

Victory Brewing | www.victorybeer.com

Country of origin United States
First brewed 1998
Alcohol content 9.2% abv
Serving temperature 50°F, 10°C

Victory's brewmaster Bill Covaleski says that his German training as a brewer makes him appreciate even more the artistic freedom that brewers have in the United States. Victory's beer collection clearly shows strong traditional elements mixing well with creativity.

Victory Prima Pils is a classic European pilsner. Victory Lager is a German helles. Victory Donneybrook Stout is a solid Irish dry stout. St. Victorious is a rich doppelbock. Old Horizontal is a powerful barleywine-style ale. Victory Whirlwind is a seasonal witbier perfect for the summer. All offer up stylistic lessons in what the U.S. craft brewing movement is capable of achieving.

Storm King Imperial Stout started life as a fall seasonal, but fans kept asking for it year-round. Heavily roasted two-row malt and a blend of Pacific Northwest hops give the beer its intense flavor. It's a big, imposing brew that caused the brewery's expensive German-manufactured malt mill to grind to a halt, literally, when the equipment was first installed in 2004. Victory had to revise its process so that the hard-kilned malt did not render the milling equipment useless. The end result is that Victory has an award-winning ale that makes a bold, classic imperial stout statement and is perfect for supping during a cold winter. **RL**

Tasting notes

Pours an opaque black with a cappuccino-colored, thick, rocky head. The flavor is a bustling combination of baker's chocolate and roasted malt that is well balanced by a firm hop finish.

Villa Pola Soci's Schwartz

Birrificio Barchessa di Villa Pola | www.villapola.com

Country of origin Italy
First brewed 1993
Alcohol content 4% abv
Serving temperature 46°F, 8°C

Cavaso del Tomba is a village close to the mountains around Venice, where the first Italian home-brewers club was founded in 1993. Soci dea Bira immediately started brewing all-malt beers and began with a chestnut ale, Monfenera, and Soci's Schwartz. The brewers travel every year to Bavaria to buy malts and hops, not only for their own production, but also for Barchessa di Villa Pola, a brewpub where Paolo De Martin, one of the founders of the home-brewers club, has worked as a brewer since 2006.

De Martin is probably one of the best Italian brewers and technicians around. His skills are good enough to make him one of the most appreciated consultants for the emerging boom of microbreweries in Italy. For Soci's Schwartz, he chose a special Bavarian roasted malt, toasted for a very long time and at a lower temperature than usual. It gives something special to the beer, even though it makes up only 10 percent of the grist—the rest is pilsner malt. Two German hops are used, both from the Hallertau region: the first is Magnum, which provides a sturdy bitterness, and then some Tradition. A couple of weeks for fermentation and around three months of lagering help the beer to reach a perfect harmony and balance. **MM**

Tasting notes

Complex but delicate aroma with hints of toasted notes, cacao, and a fruity underlining of plum. Easy to drink, with toasted and fruity notes again in the palate and a long, dry aftertaste.

Victory takes its name from the victory over Prohibition and the Temperance League.

Weltenburger Kloster Asam Bock

Klosterbrauerei Weltenburger | www.weltenburger.de

Country of origin Germany
First brewed 1997
Alcohol content 6.9% abv
Serving temperature 46°F, 8°C

Although less famous than the Trappist monastery breweries of Belgium and Holland, Weltenburger has a longer history of brewing than them all. The monks arrived here on the banks of the Danube in the 7th century and probably began making beer immediately. No records exist, but it is known that the abbey was brewing in 1050, which makes Weltenburger second only to Weihenstephan, just north of Munich, in the list of the world's oldest breweries (the year of 1050 is also claimed for the genesis of this beer, but it changed considerably over the centuries).

The monks have not brewed continuously on this site, however. Markers painted on the abbey walls reveal just how high the Danube floodwaters have reached over the years, causing the brotherhood to abandon their holy ship at various times. In 1974, the abbey brewhouse was in urgent need of investment. The monks sought an outside party to refurbish the equipment and found the perfect partner in the Bischofshof brewery in Regensburg. Today, Bischofshof brews some beers and others are produced at the monks' own brewhouse at Weltenburg.

Asam Bock is brewed at the abbey. It is named for the Asam brothers who built the abbey's splendid church, and, in true bock fashion, it is a substantial beer, loaded with sweet malts, balanced by local Hallertauer hops, and lagered for twelve weeks. The nourishing quality leads you to imagine the monks contentedly sipping this heady brew on fasting days when solid food is prohibited. Indeed, the term "liquid bread" could have been coined for this beer. **JE**

Tasting notes

Aromas of biscuity dark malt, chocolate, coffee, and raisin lead onto a full, bittersweet taste loaded with nutty dark malt, chocolate, and prunelike fruit. Malt and chocolate linger in the thick, bittersweet finish, with bitterness building. Smooth and ruby colored.

Weltenburger Kloster Barock Dunkel

Klosterbrauerei Weltenburger | www.weltenburger.de

Country of origin Germany
First brewed *ca.* 1860s
Alcohol content 4.7% abv
Serving temperature 46°F, 8°C

There's a neat divide among the beers brewed under the Weltenburger name. The paler beers are produced by Bischofshof brewery in Regensburg, while, at the abbey's own brewhouse, the Bischofshof brewers, on behalf of the monks, focus on dark beers. This is, they say, in keeping with the monastic tradition. It certainly seems that the darker beers, with their full complement of malts, do lend themselves better to a monastic lifestyle, when days of fasting mean that a meal in a glass provides welcome nourishment.

These beers are not just popular with the monks. The 750,000 visitors who make the journey by pleasure boat up the Danube from Kelheim, or along the twisting roads on the river bank, enjoy the diverse delights of Weltenburg Abbey—notably, a stein of the local brew, served along with hearty Bavarian cooking in the monastery courtyard beer garden. Barock Dunkel, which takes its name from the ornate baroque church on the site, is the most popular draft beer here.

It's crafted from a mix of lager malt, dark malt, and caramel malt, but that's as much as the brewers will reveal in their almost Trappistlike silence on the subject of ingredients. Hops come from the Hallertau region, just to the south, and the water from a well below the abbey. Behind the tiny brewhouse, carved into the hillside, lie the lagering cellars, and it's here that Barock Dunkel spends eight lazy, chilly weeks while the yeast nibbles away at the sugars and rounds off the rougher edges of the green beer. The result is a smooth, full-flavored, yet not too chunky, brew that really hits the spot. **JE**

Tasting notes

A malty, nutty aroma with suggestions of biscuit preludes a bittersweet, nutty taste with roasted malt notes, raisin, a hint of toffee, and some soft chocolate. Nutty, roasted grain features prominently in the dry, pleasantly bitter finish. Not too heavy and very quaffable.

Wild Rose Cherry Porter

Wild Rose Brewery
www.wildrosebrewery.com

Country of origin Canada
First brewed 2002
Alcohol content 6.5% abv
Serving temperature 50°F, 10°C

Wild Rose first opened its doors in a Calgary industrial park in 1996. Sensing perhaps that the going could be tough in retail stores, founders Michael Tymchuk and Alan Yule spent their first six years brewing only draft ales for bar and restaurant sales. The first bottling run at Wild Rose took place in 2002, around the time that Yule departed the company. A spurt of growth came after the company moved the beers into smaller bottles and six-packs.

In a province that does not have too many indigenous breweries and has even fewer noteworthy seasonal beers, Cherry Porter has become a much-anticipated release, usually launching at the start of November and selling out around Christmas. Each batch consumes an impressive 176 pounds (80 kg) of cherries and is made with nine barley malts, thus creating a beer of no small amount of complexity and character. **SB**

Tasting notes

This ebony ale combines ample fruitiness with dark chocolate in the nose and a tasty mix of cherry fruit, mocha, sweet spice, toasted malt, and concentrated plum in the body.

Winter Humbug'r

MacTarnahan's Brewing
www.macsbeer.com

Country of origin United States
First brewed 1996
Alcohol content 5.3% abv
Serving temperature 50°F, 10°C

MacTarnahan's brewers Alan Kornhauser and Brett Porter wanted to create "a porter that was as creamy as possible, but without the bite of many dark beers." They added oats to the malt build to give the beer its distinctive smoothness. To this, they added a "ton of very lightly roasted caramel malt." Northern Brewer hops were used in the first two hop additions, and East Kent Golding for the third and for dry hopping. To get softer flavors, a lager yeast was employed. Fermenting the beer at a cooler temperature provided subtle fruit esters. The new beer was named Blackwatch Cream Porter and it won gold medals at the Great American Beer Festival in 2001 and 2008.

This holiday seasonal is still brewed with caramel malt, black roasted malt, unmalted wheat and, most importantly, oats, but the name has been changed to "Winter HumBug'r." **JB**

Tasting notes

The nose is filled with chocolate aromas and a hint of fruitiness. With a very smooth mouthfeel, the effervescent flavors are chocolaty with coffee and nutty notes.

Wrasslers XXXX Stout

Porterhouse Brewing Company
www.theporterhouse.ie

Country of origin Ireland
First brewed 1996
Alcohol content 5% abv
Serving temperature 44°F, 7°C

Complaining that stout isn't what it used to be is something of a national pastime in Ireland. The big breweries' accountants have made sure that the modern pint of plain is as cold and bland as possible to appeal to the widest segment of the population, thereby ensuring that no one is upset by the more alarming aspects of stout, such as flavor. Powerful and uncompromising, Wrasslers XXXX hits the palate like a blackthorn stick to the side of the head.

Porterhouse traces the recipe back to Deasy's Brewery, founded in 1800 in Clonakilty, County Cork. "The Wrestler" was its most famous porter, later becoming known in the local dialect as "Wrastler's" or "Wrasslers." Deasy's closed in 1942, but Wrasslers XXXX lives on at the Porterhouse, where its strong, old-fashioned taste has been a regular favorite with those who appreciate a good traditional Irish stout. **JD**

Tasting notes
Black with a tan-colored head, it is bitter at first, almost metallic. As the palate adjusts to the bitterness, more complexities come out: luxurious dark chocolate and fine aromatic cigars.

Xingu Black Lager

Cervejarias Kaiser SA
www.cervejaxingu.com.br

Country of origin Brazil
First brewed 1988
Alcohol content 4.6% abv
Serving temperature 37°–43°F, 3°–6°C

This beer pays homage to an age before the Portuguese colonists arrived in 1500, when women in Brazil did most of the brewing while the men hunted. The earliest account of black beer brewed by the indigenous people of the Amazon region dates back to 1557. These beers were originally brewed with roasted corn or manioc roots. They were fermented with wild yeast and were very important in traditional ceremonies.

Xingu premiered in Boston in 1998 at the Culinary Institute of America and then became more widely available across the country. In 2002, Kaiser brewery in Brazil took ownership of the Xingu brand and made some minor modifications. Although it looks like a stout, Xingu is actually a dark lager. One of its common traits is that, like other Brazilian dark beers, it has a tingle of sweetness, which might make it too much for those who like a scorching hop bitterness in their beer. **AH**

Tasting notes
Opaque black in appearance with a very creamy tan head. A rich malt and nutty aroma is followed up by roasted malt and coffee on the palate. Slight touch of bitter hops and citrus.

XS: Imperial Stout

Rogue Ales | www.rogue.com

Country of origin United States
First brewed 1994
Alcohol content 11% abv
Serving temperature 50°–55°F, 10°–12°C

Tackling a massive beer such as an imperial stout is not something that phases Rogue Ales's brewmaster John Maier, who brews around sixty beers from the humongous Rogue portfolio. True to the U.S. spirit, he has applied his own sense of innovation to the style. He joined Rogue from Alaska Brewing in 1989, having previously tried his hand as a technician at Hughes Aircraft Company in El Segundo. He had bumped into the brewery's founder Jack Joyce during a business trip, and the chance to come back to his native Oregon was too good an opportunity to miss. After twenty years with Rogue, he has won hundreds of awards.

The imperial stout has had a demanding audience since its inception back in the late 1700s. It was initially brewed for the Russian czar, so it had to be large. With the massive, roasted, burned malt mixed with spicy fruit, it remains exactly that; at 11 percent abv, it is certainly not one for the faint hearted. Maier created a quaff with an incredible twelve ingredients. For malts see Great Western, Harrington and Klages, Hugh Baird XLT-80, black, Munich, chocolate, and rolled; yeast and water are made up of Rogue's Pacman yeast and free-range coastal water. As ever, though, Rogue makes its mark with a hop profile to die for; in this mix, you'll find Willamette, Cascade, and Chinook hitting the chops with 88 IBUs. Rogue doesn't disappoint, and if you're looking for an example of this style with an extra bite, then you have to give this beer a whirl. This is the sort of behemoth of a beer that can be either sipped on its own or matched with chocolate cake or dark meat. **TS**

Tasting notes

This imperial stout pours like an oil leak, black and slick, and the color alone will leave you drooling. The hop profile is daunting, but the balance is perfect and the most prominent flavor is chocolate. Match it with chocolate cake or dark meat.

The Rogue Nation World Headquarters in Newport, Oregon.

Yuengling Dark Brewed Porter

D. G. Yuengling & Son | www.yuengling.com

Country of origin United States
First brewed 1829
Alcohol content 4.7% abv
Serving temperature 41°F, 5°C

Yuengling is the oldest brewery in the United States, and historians cite the Yuengling Dark Brewed Porter as the world's oldest surviving example of the style, produced without interruption since the brewery was founded in 1829. Yuengling's variety is made with bottom-fermenting lager yeast, not the ale yeast that traditionalists say helped to produce the sour, fruitlike character of the original porters. The Yuengling porter's yeast and corn tend to lighten the body and flavor, making it a less filling porter than the variety once quaffed in London. However, this doesn't make it any less authentic.

Porter has been a favorite in the United States since the Revolution, when George Washington made it a focal point in his "Buy American" campaign. **DR**

Tasting notes
Offers only a faint malty aroma and little hops. The mouthfeel is surprisingly light for such a dark, robust brew, while its roasted malt flavor finishes with a slightly sour, chocolate bite.

Žamberecký Kanec Imperial Stout

Pivovar Žamberk | www.pivovarzamberk.wz.cz

Country of origin Czech Republic
First brewed 2006
Alcohol content 5.5% abv
Serving temperature 50°F, 10°C

The Czech Republic's craft beer scene is fueled in part by an active network of home-brewers, of whom one of the most mysterious is known as Anteňák, or "Antenna Man." His recipes have shown up in several Czech breweries and brewpubs, most notably in the form of the unusual imperial stout at Pivovar Žamberk.

It is brewed from pilsner and wheat malts as well as roasted barley, which give the beer its murkiness and dark coloring. It is top-fermented using ale yeast and is hopped roughly twice as much as one of the brewery's Czech pilsners, using whole hop cones as well as hop extract and hop pellets for both bittering and aroma. It is listed as slightly weak for the style, although it makes up for any lack of alcohol with a rich, bitter corpulence. **ER**

Tasting notes
A thick dark body topped with camel-colored foam, this creamy stout plays heavily on its bitter notes, with coffee and rye bread coming through in the nose and a chewy thickness in the mouth.

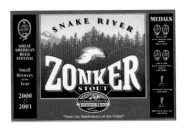

Zonker
Stout

Snake River Brewing | www.snakeriverbrewing.com

Country of origin United States
First brewed 1994
Alcohol content 5.4% abv
Serving temperature 55°F, 13°C

A sign on the crowded walls, decorated with scores of brewing awards, at Snake River Brewing in Jackson, Wyoming, reads, "We don't aim to make the most beer; just the best."

Like most brewpubs, Snake River offers quite a wide range of beers, most of them inspired by classic styles, but often with a twist. Zonker Stout—a "zonker" is a large, underwater fishing fly—contains seven different malts in the recipe and is hopped with American, British, and German hops. The beer won a silver medal at the Great American Beer Festival the year Snake River opened, and has won six more medals at the United States's premier craft brewing events. Snake River Brewing itself also won Small Brewery of the Year at both the 2000 and 2001 festivals. **SH**

Tasting notes

Aromas include sweet malts and roasted coffee beans. The complex palate has dry chocolate, robust coffee, and nutty flavors. Earthy mouthfeel with a long, dry, bitter finish.

Żywiec
Porter

Grupa Żywiec | www.zywiec.com.pl

Country of origin Poland
First brewed 1881
Alcohol content 9.5% abv
Serving temperature 46°–54°F, 8°–12°C

In the past few years, Polish beer has become incredibly popular in Western Europe, but among the plethora of pale pilsners, there hasn't been too much room for the classic Baltic porter.

In these days of rapid fermentation and maturation, the ninety-day production process of Żywiec Porter bucks the short-order trend. After fermentation, the Porter travels to the lagering cellars, cold and musty spaces built into the side of a hill. Here, the Porter undergoes a long slumber, and its flavors are smoothed out. Tasted directly from the tank, the nose is nutty and similar to cough medicine, whereas the palate has more of the cough medicine note, joined by roast cereals, dark fruit, and a bitter finish. The survival of this beer in an age of brand portfolios is a cause for celebration. **ATJ**

Tasting notes

As dark as a moonless night. Chocolate, mocha coffee, roast barley, and vinous fruits all jostle for attention on the palate. Creamy mouthfeel with a bitter, dry, roasty finish.

SPECIALTY BEERS

3 Fonteinen Oude Geuze Vintage

Brouwerij 3 Fonteinen | www.3fonteinen.be

Country of origin Belgium
First brewed 2002
Alcohol content 6% abv
Serving temperature 48°–57°F, 9°–14°C

Back in the 1950s, the famed Flemish writer Herman Teirlinck urged his friend Gaston Debelder to blend geuze and kriek beer. Teirlinck wanted to preserve geuze for posterity, and the blends became a regular feature in Gaston's new restaurant, De 3 Fonteinen.

All 3 Fonteinen beers qualify under European Union specifications as oude geuze or kriek. This means that they have been made in the traditional way by spontaneous fermentation. As is often the case with artisanal products, some batches are better than others. The first of the blendings was the 1998, a kind of tryout for the Millennium Geuze. This was such a success that, from 2002 onward, the best batches were kept for this geuze, which was dubbed "Oude Geuze Vintage"—the best blending. **JPa**

Tasting notes

A citrusy nose over leather soap, horse-blanket, and distinctive wheat aromas. Mild, smoked taste, and a whisper of malty sweetness. More well bodied than is usual for a geuze.

3 Fonteinen Oude Kriek

Brouwerij 3 Fonteinen | www.3fonteinen.be

Country of origin Belgium
First brewed 1953
Alcohol content 6% abv
Serving temperature 55°F, 13°C

The mark of a great brewery is one that only produces superb beers, and 3 Fonteinen (Three Fountains) is such a brewery. The current owner, Armand Debelder, is an important figure in the Belgian beer world. He is noted for being the driving force of HORAL, a group of ten lambic breweries and blenderies, which seeks to promote and preserve traditional lambic beers.

Nowadays, Debelder is much more optimistic about the survival of his brewery and traditional lambic beers than in years past. The 3 Fonteinen complex is a pilgrimage spot for beer lovers and has put the town of Beersel on the international beer map. All the beers are complex masterpieces, and the Oude Kriek is no exception. It uses whole cherries from Eastern Europe that are steeped in the brewery's Oude Geuze. **CC**

Tasting notes

Deep reddish color with an incredibly rich, prominent cherry flavor. Very dry, with a light bitterness. Very tart and refreshing, it bombards the palate with lambic and fruit character.

Owner and brewer Armand Debelder pours a glass of his marvelous lambic. →

1488 Whisky Beer

Tullibardine Distillery | www.traditionalscottishales.co.uk

Country of origin Scotland
First brewed 2005
Alcohol content 7% abv
Serving temperature 41°F, 5°C

Distillers of fine whisky are rarely known for their beer making, preferring to reserve their malted barley for the production of stronger concoctions than ale. However, there are always exceptions, and one of these resulted in 1488 Whisky Beer.

Located in the heart of Perthshire in Scotland is the Tullibardine Distillery. Here, they noticed that there were a lot of empty whisky barrels lying around doing nothing, and as this distillery is located on the site of Scotland's oldest public brewery (which switched over to distilling in the 1940s), what better product to fill those barrels with than fine ale?

To make it, the wash (fresh mountain spring water and malted barley), quantities of local water, and yeast are taken from the distillery to the Bridge of Allan Brewery in Sterling. The beer is lightly hopped and fermented for a bit longer than would be usual for a normal beer, with the addition of some sugar—hence the strong alcohol content. The beer is then aged in recently emptied whisky barrels for up to twelve weeks. Previously, the barrels had been filled with bourbon for a decade and then single malt for a further ten years, and the American oak passes a deep whisky flavor to the ale. It is then sterile filtered, bottled, and sealed to keep its unique taste as fresh as possible.

The name is inspired by the year King James IV of Scotland had his coronation, and also when records show that he bought beer from the brewery on the site where the Tullibardine Distillery now stands. And there seems no better way to commemorate his memory than by downing a wee dram of whisky beer. **JM**

Tasting notes

The deep golden color is reminiscent of a single malt, as is its fruity yet smoky aroma. Very mildly hopped, it imparts warmth in the throat as it is drunk. Despite its strength, it's deceptively light and refreshing, with sweet vanilla and tart notes, and a strong whisky finish.

Angel's Share Ale

The Lost Abbey | www.lostabbey.com

Country of origin United States
First brewed 2006
Alcohol content 11.5% abv (vintages vary)
Serving temperature 55°F, 13°C

The Lost Abbey might have seemed somewhat precocious when they won the champion's trophy for Small Brewing Company at both the 2007 Great American Beer Festival (GABF) and World Beer Cup before even reaching their second anniversary. However, the brewery's pedigree was already in place. Lost Abbey is an extension of the Pizza Port family, and in both 2003 and 2004, Pizza Port–Solana Beach won champion Small Brewpub at the GABF. In 2006, the new brewery opened in San Marcos, taking over the space that Stone Brewing had outgrown.

Tomme Arthur, director of brewing operations, also brought a few recipes with him. The beer at the center of Angel's Share is very much like the strong ale at the heart of the Late Harvest 15th Anniversary Ale that Arthur and Jeff Bagby created in 2002. After aging in American oak barrels, some of that beer was blended with grape juice (Carignan grapes) and fermented a second time with a Cabernet wine yeast. Angel's Share doesn't get any of the wine treatment, but different versions are aged in brandy and bourbon barrels respectively. The term "angel's share" refers to the portion of a wine or distilled spirit that is lost to evaporation while aging in barrels. The alcohol content varies according to different vintages.

"When we secured the brandy barrels, I had a feeling these flavors were more in line with what I was expecting back in 2002," Arthur said, after watching Angel's Share climb to the top of the charts on Internet beer-rating sites. "In this way, the beer soars in a way the other could not." An angelic upstart, indeed. **SH**

Tasting notes

Pours dark brown with a tan head. A laundry list of aromas and flavors, with new ones emerging each time you revisit the glass: dark dried fruit, vanilla, coconut, wood tannins, bourbon, maple syrup, brandy, caramel, toffee, molasses. Amazingly unified.

Anniversary Ale

Firestone Walker Brewing
www.firestonewalker.com

Country of origin United States
First brewed 2006
Alcohol content Variable
Serving temperature 55°F, 13°C

To celebrate Firestone Walker's tenth anniversary in 2006, the brewers created four strong special beers (a barleywine, an imperial stout, an imperial brown, and a double IPA) and aged them in six varieties of oak barrels, including retired whiskey and brandy barrels. The brewers held a tasting to set the blend, which resulted in a beer that is a wonderful example of collaboration between the grape and the grain.

Firestone X weighed in at 10 percent abv. The brewery repeated the process in 2007 with Firestone XI growing to 11 percent, and following that with Firestone XII at 12 percent. Each year the brewers create new parts of the blend, but brewmaster Matt Brynildson now has the luxury of using a variety of barrels that have been aging for several years. **SH**

Tasting notes
Each batch has grown more complex as it ages: an ebb and flow of dark fruits, sweet notes of molasses, flavors of the spirits the barrels held before, and other notes associated with wood.

Bam Bière

Jolly Pumpkin Artisan Ales
www.jollypumpkin.com

Country of origin United States
First brewed 2005
Alcohol content 4.5% abv
Serving temperature 39°–43°F, 4°–6°C

Bam is proof that session beers needn't be insipid, mild mannered, or boring. It has no modern counterpart in Belgium, but it does reflect a tradition of oak-fermented small beers that largely died out there in the early 20th century. Bam is fermented in large oak *foudres*, or vertical oak tanks. Wood is a very hospitable medium for the kind of wild yeast and other microbes that give Bam its earthy charm. First among them is *Brettanomyces*, a type of wild yeast known mostly for a barnyard aroma.

Like the Belgian witbiers that it superficially resembles, Bam is ghostly pale and luminously hazy. As with all Jolly Pumpkin beers, Bam is bottle conditioned for an additional layer of flavor and a fine-textured carbonation. Dry hopping adds a herby perfume. **RM**

Tasting notes
Very complex aroma of wood, earth, and pineapple fruit. Taste is bright, tart, backed up by a little sweetness. Builds to woody middle, modest hop bitterness, and a touch of bready maltiness.

Bard's The Original Sorghum Malt Beer

Bard's Tale Beer
www.bardsbeer.com

Country of origin United States
First brewed 2005
Alcohol content 4.6% abv
Serving temperature 44°F, 7°C

Barley is the most common grain used to make beer. However, along with other grains, it poses a hidden danger to roughly 1 percent of the population who cannot tolerate gluten, which is found in many grains.

Bard's was created by Craig Belser and Kevin Seplowitz, both of whom are gluten intolerant. They refer to their beer as the "first gluten-free craft beer made with sorghum." Bard's has no syrups, extracts, or sugars. Making a gluten-free beer is much more difficult than ordinary beer. Using naturally gluten-free ingredients is the safest option at present, and for that reason, sorghum is the most popular choice. However, more than 10,000 kinds of sorghum exist and little study has been done to determine the best ones for brewing. As a result, they are unpredictable. **JB**

Tasting notes
The nose is sweet with sharp, pleasant aromas that include hints of coffee and butterscotch. The flavors are smooth and sweet with a nice hop presence, hints of butterscotch, and a long finish.

Bastarda Doppia

Birrificio Amiata
www.birra-amiata.it

Country of origin Italy
First brewed 2007
Alcohol content 8.5% abv
Serving temperature 54°–57°F, 12°–14°C

Birrificio Amiata is located near Mount Amiata in Tuscany, an area that is surrounded by chestnut woods. Naturally, when Claudio Cerullo started the brewery, everybody asked him to brew a chestnut ale. The first attempt was Bastarda Rossa, an easy-drinking ale with the light flavor of chestnuts. This was not enough for the locals, so Cerullo had to do something stronger and more chestnutlike: Bastarda Doppia.

This top-fermenting beer needs about 88 pounds (40 kg) of chestnuts for every 242 pounds (110 kg) of malt. This is a huge quantity, but it is necessary in order to have a chestnut aroma, chestnut flavor, and chestnut aftertaste. Strong in alcohol, but elegant and charming, this beer is surely the best alternative way to taste the special chestnuts of Mount Amiata. **MM**

Tasting notes
The chestnut aroma is joined by an undercurrent of fruity notes and some smokiness. On the palate, the beer has a warming and pleasant mouthfeel, followed by a long aftertaste.

Bee's Organic Ale

Arkell's Brewery | www.arkells.com

Country of origin England
First brewed 2001
Alcohol content 4.5% abv
Serving temperature 55°F, 13°C

Brewing honey beers can be tricky. Choose the wrong honey and you end up with a beer that smells sickly and floral. Put too much honey in and the taste can be unbearably sweet and cloying. Get the combination of honey and quantity right, however, and beer takes off into another dimension. It can even draw in drinkers who do not normally even like honey.

Arkell's Brewery is responsible for one of the most successful honey beers. It has been part of the railway town of Swindon in Wiltshire since 1843. It's still family run and operates a 150-year-old brewhouse that is an historic treasure. Today, alongside long-standing favorites such as the malty best bitter 3B, the even maltier, chunky but smooth Kingsdown Ale, and the highly quaffable light bitter 2B, it now turns out a selection of seasonal and occasional ales.

Bee's Organic is available on draft roughly four times a year and in bottle at all times. It was added to the range in 2001 and required serious consideration on the part of head brewer Don Bracher to achieve that subtle sweetness and delicate smoothness that make it one of the best honey beers around. The brew begins with pale and crystal malts, plus a little wheat malt, in the mash tun. The honey—organic, like the other ingredients, and sourced from places like India and Brazil—is added during the copper boil, where it joins First Gold hops. As the beer is being strained through the hop back, more hops are added, this time Hallertauer from New Zealand. The clever combination of fruit from the hops and soft, floral notes from the honey ensures widespread appeal. **JE**

Tasting notes

A golden beer with a malty, spicy, and honey-floral aroma that has hints of pineapple. The taste is silky-smooth and gently bitter, without overbearing sweetness or floral notes from the honey, but with a little pineapple. Hops are only mild, until the soft finish.

Bell's Cherry Stout

Bell's Brewery, Inc. | www.bellsbeer.com

Country of origin United States
First brewed 1988
Alcohol content 8.5% abv
Serving temperature 44°–50°F, 7°–10°C

This is a "love it or leave it" beer according to Bell's Brewery's founder, Larry Bell. However, for many drinkers, this "chocolate-covered cherry in a bottle," which is available through the winter, is irresistible. Bell makes a comparison to wine: "It's like Pinot Noir. That first sip can be kind of awkward, but soon you are asking for more."

The beer began as a "tip of the cap" to a local home-brew club, which had developed a bit of a specialty with cherry stout. Bell brewed his early versions with cherry juice that leaked through a cloth conveyor belt at a local fruit cannery. It was one of the earliest fruit beers in the United States. "The government took a long time to approve that one, because they just weren't sure what to make of a beer with fruit in it."

Fruit beers have a long history, but have been typically produced only in fruit-growing areas for local consumption, and only in the last few decades have they been made more commercially. Dark ones are still very rare. Bell brews his from Traverse City cherry concentrate these days. With its 8.5 percent strength, it's a sipper, not a quaffer. Between the cherries and the sharpness of the black malts, this beer has a fair amount of acidity. While it takes some getting used to, that's a good thing, because the acidity brightens and defines the fruit flavors considerably.

While most beers are best when fresh, this is a beer that stands up to a little aging. Over time, the acidity softens, and the dark fruit and malt flavors knit together for a more elegant, winelike experience. **RM**

Tasting notes

Chocolaty nose with cherry top notes and a dab of alcohol and fruity esters. On the palate, it is mouthwateringly tangy, the sweet-and-sour balance augmented by the deep roasted malt flavors. Finishes bright and fruity with roastiness at the very end.

Bière Cognac

Brasserie de Bercloux | www.bercloise.com

Country of origin France
First brewed 2000
Alcohol content 7% abv
Serving temperature 46°–50°F, 8°–10°C

France is associated with the great wines of the world, but its beer is rarely mentioned in elevated terms. Brasserie de Bercloux head brewer Philippe Laclie was introduced to his craft in 1999 at the Irish Brewing Company in County Kildare, Ireland. The family business has been in wine and cognac production since 1889 and it is one of a dwindling band of independent cognac distillers in the area around Cognac, where light, chalky soil adds to the mystical *terroir*. This background meant that when Laclie started brewing, demand for his new beers among friends and family grew to such a pitch that he had to choose between the grape and the grain. The grain settled on top and brewing got off to a start in 2000.

Laclie borrows the family cognac still to boil the wort (the only brewery in the world to do so). This is the *alembic charentais*, an exotic-looking, onion-shaped boiler with a long thin neck. Bière au Cognac is matured for three weeks with the addition of six-year-old Laclie Cognac, which highlights its light floral and fruit nature. Brasserie de Bercloux has carved a niche out of an impressive market for its portfolio. All the beers are top-fermented, and Blanche and Stout are unfiltered. **AG**

Tasting notes
This copper-colored beer's wood-tinged aroma, biscuity maltiness, sweet palate, and definite alcohol kick make it one to savor at leisure. "Une belle harmonie."

Bière des Naufrageurs Miel

Brasserie des Naufrageurs | www.oleron-plages.fr

Country of origin France
First brewed 1995
Alcohol content 7.5% abv
Serving temperature 46°F, 8°C

Naufrageur is the French word for "shipwrecker," and the brewery's label features a donkey with a lamp hanging from its neck, luring a sailing ship onto the rocks, its crew and passengers to be overwhelmed by unscrupulous brigands. Presumably, this refers to the history of the location of this tiny microbrewery: the Isle d'Oleron, off France's west coast. Vast quantities of the world-renowned Marennes oysters are harvested here, and the landscape varies from pine forest to marshland, cliffs to creeks, and salt-beds to sand dunes.

Brewery owner Jean Luc Metayer runs a honey farm producing all manner of merchandise, such as beeswax, royal jelly, and spiced honey cake. He set up the brewery in 1995 and also produces a honey beer, Naufrageurs Miel, which is complex, full, and well balanced, with a lingering, honeyed, bittersweet character and a gentle warmth. Metayer's other beers include Naufrageurs à la Bergamot, Blonde, and Mure (blackberry). All are top-fermented, unfiltered, and unpasteurized. The barley for the beers is grown on Isle d'Oleron, but is sent to the mainland to be malted. Summer brewing can cause problems because of the high temperatures. This means that Naufrageurs' beers are produced mainly in cooler months. **AG**

Tasting notes
Rich, red brown in appearance with an inviting, honeyed malt nose. More honey on the palate with some bitter hop evident to balance all that sweetness and hefty warmth. Gently complex.

Naufrageurs' label: the donkey lures another ship to its doom. ➡

Bière des Naufrageurs

Brassée sur l'Ile d'Oléron

Blandford Fly

Hall & Woodhouse | www.hall-woodhouse.co.uk

Country of origin England
First brewed 2000
Alcohol content 5.2% abv
Serving temperature 52°F, 11°C

It's always nice to find a beer that has a good local story behind it, and Hall and Woodhouse's ginger-flavored beer Blandford Fly has exactly that. It is named after a particularly snappy local insect, residing around and about the nearby River Stour. Local folklore has it that only zingibain, an active component of ginger that is widely used in alternative medicine circles, has the ability to reduce the fever and swelling inflicted by the creature's bite.

The beer was developed in 2000 by Dr. Tim Morris, head brewer of the Dorset-based brewery, following the successful launch of one of the brewery's other popular beers, Champion, which is flavored with elderflower and was seen as a bold move at the time it was released. The idea behind Blandford Fly was to create a ginger beer for adults designed to take both the spice and sweet aspects of the soft drink ginger beer and add in some brewing heritage to ensure its adult appeal.

The traditional beer aspect comes from the use of Tipple pale malt (an increasingly popular replacement for Optic) and three different types of hops: Magnum and Hallertau Tradition for bittering and Select as the subtle aroma hop. All those selected are fairly light, so as not to overpower the delicate ginger scents and flavors. The beer is primed back with some sucrose and a little caramel, to assist with the sweetness, which the brewery believes provides a much cleaner flavor profile than using malts. It is a very versatile food beer that goes extremely well with everything from Thai curries to ribs. **MC**

Tasting notes

A sparkling, light-colored ale, it offers ginger, apricots, and vanilla on the nose. On the palate, it is tingly, with the ginger and carbonation combining to great effect and offset by the residual sweetness, ensuring that there isn't too much of a "bite."

Boon Oude Geuze

Brouwerij Boon | www.boon.be

Country of origin Belgium
First brewed 1975
Alcohol content 6.5% abv
Serving temperature 55°F, 13°C

Oude geuze has been described as the champagne of beers, due to its effervescent carbonation as well as the extreme dryness of most examples. It is a fine choice as an introduction to the style, as the level of its sourness and tartness is not too extreme, with the funkiness of its wild *Brettanomyces* yeast being more pronounced. Boon uses the same blending ingredients as most lambic breweries to produce an oude geuze; 90 percent of the blend has, on average, been aged for two years in oak barrels. Into the blend, 5 percent each of one- and three-year-old lambics are also added.

Frank Boon is one of a handful of individuals who had stepped up to help save traditional lambic and oude geuze beers from extinction in the 1970s. These brews—tart, sour, and with a noticeable horse-blanketlike character—were the antithesis of the sweet drinks that were becoming so popular in Belgium and all over the world at that time. Lambic breweries, faced with a fast-disappearing market, either sweetened their beers or vanished, except for a sterling few such as Boon and Cantillon.

Boon bought the old De Vits blending house in 1977, and soon set about producing lambic beers there. In 1990, Boon entered a partnership with Palm, and with extra investment, an authentic lambic brewhouse was installed. Such is the high quality of the unfermented wort of Boon that it is commonly used by the three remaining lambic blending houses—De Cam, Hanssens, and Oud Beersel. In the small world of lambic brewing, where not everyone sees eye to eye, Frank Boon is well respected among his colleagues. **CC**

Tasting notes

Hazy, golden orange color with a big rocky head. Aroma is earthy and musty, with notes of fruits, such as lemons and apples. Taste is sour grapefruit, apples, pears, and a light oakiness, with a moderate, pleasant sourness. Try with a Roquefort cheese!

Boon Oude Geuze Mariage Parfait

Brouwerij Boon | www.boon.be

Country of origin Belgium
First brewed 1978
Alcohol content 8% abv
Serving temperature 55°F, 13°C

This is the top of the Boon range—the crown jewel of the brewery. Mariage Parfait has the best lambics from Boon in its blend, chosen by owner Frank Boon himself. This beer has a higher percentage of three-year-old lambics than would be normal; this adds complexity, tartness, and dryness to the blend. Boon created this beer to be the pinnacle of his brewery. It is first blended then usually bottled every March.

All the lambics at Boon are spontaneously fermented on site, and then aged in oak barrels for between one to three years. The Boon complex, which was formerly an iron foundry, is quite large, and one of the cavernous rooms contains dozens of huge oak barrels, or *foeders*. The foundry complex offered much more space than the De Vits site where Boon originally began to blend lambics.

Samples taken right from several of the *foeders* showed how much lambic changes over time: from a soft, somewhat sweet, two-week-old version, to the tart, sour, beautifully refreshing three-year-old one. Six-month and two-year-old versions are evidence of the lambics' progression.

Brouwerij Palm owns 50 percent of Boon, which uses the Palm beer distribution network. This helps the beers get much more exposure and distribution in Belgium than they might otherwise. However, Palm has a very hands-off approach to the brewery, and Frank Boon retains a firm control over the goings-on in Lembeek. At a number of Palm-owned or affiliated cafés in Belgium, unblended, unfiltered Boon Lambiek is served on draft from hand pumps. **CC**

Tasting notes

Hazy, golden straw color with a tannish-white foam. Aroma is very earthy and barnyardlike, with a prominent Brettanomyces *horse-blanket character. The taste is similar to the aroma, with tartness and acidity added, along with funky citrus notes. Good with steamed mussels.*

The huge oak barrels where Brouwerij Boon's beers age. ➡

Cantillon Grand Cru Bruocsella

Brasserie Cantillon | www.cantillon.be

Country of origin Belgium
First brewed 1986
Alcohol content 5% abv
Serving temperature 54°–59°F, 12°–15°C

What kind of a beer is Grand Cru Bruocsella? First off, it isn't a geuze. Cantillon brews lambic, and that is what Bruocsella (the Latin name for Brussels) is—a pure, three-year-old, hence "Grand Cru," lambic, bottled straight from the big wooden vats (*foeders*) that slumber in this museum of a brewery. As a result, it is bone-dry and the real thing for connoisseurs.

Brasserie Cantillon dates from the very start of the 20th century, and began as a geuze blender, blending lambic into Brussels's famous champagne, geuze. Later, the Cantillon family started brewing lambic themselves. Today's brewer, Jean Van Roy, is the grandson of the last Cantillon.

Lambic, which is regulated by both Belgian and European laws, contains 30 percent raw wheat, malted barley, and aged hops (for preserving purposes only, not for bittering). It also has a formula-determined minimum content of organic acids. It is spontaneously fermented. This means that exclusively wild yeasts start and finish the fermentation, with *Brettanomyces* yeasts carrying out the end fermentation, no doubt the most important one of the whole cycle.

If the main bulk of lambic production goes into the blending of geuze, or the fruit-laden derivatives such as kriek and framboise, Cantillon gives you the opportunity to sample the basic but special lambic at home (usually served by gravity pull from the cask), in the form of the Grand Cru Bruocsella. The brewery itself describes its flavor as toasted bread, with a discreet acidity. It compares it to Chardonnay and recommends serving it in wine glasses. **JPa**

Tasting notes

Golden-colored beer with no head. Aromas of aged oak wood, old leather-bound books, and wild mushrooms leap out of the glass, while tasting yields more wood, tannins, an unlikely hint of sweetness, and aged sherry casks. Perfect with delicate fish or crustaceans, and sauerkraut.

Cantillon Gueuze 100% Lambic Bio

Brasserie Cantillon | www.cantillon.be

Country of origin Belgium
First brewed 2001
Alcohol content 5% abv
Serving temperature 55°F, 13°C

This extraordinary brewery opened in Brussels in 1900, and it is the last remaining lambic brewery in the city. Cantillon is at once a living museum and an operating brewery that crafts some of the most highly respected and most sought-after lambic beers in the world. Its central location and its openness to the public make it a must-visit destination. The brewery is open six days a week, and no reservations are required—you can merely show up, pay the entry fee (which includes a beer), and wander about. Beers can be purchased and tasted right in the heart of the brewery.

At Cantillon, as is the case for most of the other lambic breweries, hot wort (unfermented beer) is pumped into a rectangular-shaped copper vessel located on the top floor of the brewery. As the wort cools overnight, wild yeasts begin the process of fermentation. This wort is then transferred to wooden barrels, where it will be aged.

The Gueuze 100% Lambic is a blend of one- two- and three-year-old lambics, which are carefully chosen by brewmaster Jean Van Roy and his father Jean-Pierre. The older lambic gives most of the intense, sour, and complex flavors to the beer, and the one-year-old lambic, which is still fermenting, provides the sugar necessary for refermentation in the bottle.

This beer is certified as "bio" in Belgium, meaning its ingredients—barley, grain, hops, and wheat—are organically produced. The beer was organically certifed in 2003 and is part of the brewery's declared intention to support farmers who do not use chemical fertilizers or pesticides in the production of crops. **CC**

Tasting notes

Pours a hazy golden color, with an effervescent head. Aroma is citrus fruits, lambic "funkiness," and tartness. Flavor is mouth-puckeringly sour, with notes of lemon, sour grapes, even melons. Very complex. A bone-dry beer with a medium mouthfeel that finishes with a hint of bitterness.

Cantillon Iris

Brasserie Cantillon | www.cantillon.be

Country of origin Belgium
First brewed 1996
Alcohol content 5.5% abv
Serving temperature 50°–54°F, 10°–12°C

You would be wrong if you called Cantillon Iris a lambic or a geuze. It is an ale, albeit one made by spontaneous fermentation, but lambic needs at least 30 percent unmalted wheat. Iris, however, is a full-malt (barley, that is) beer, and, therefore, legally not a lambic. There are more differences: the beer is hopped partly with fresh hops, although 50 percent of the hops used are also aged, as is common with lambics.

Fresh Styrian Golding hops were used the first time it was brewed, but variations on the hopping theme are a characteristic of this beer. Iris matures for two years in the wood, is dry hopped (another geuze antithesis), and then ferments in the bottle, thanks to a little glucose addition. Despite all this deviation from the lambic theme, Iris carries the Cantillon stamp all over, but with a variation. Although first brewed by former brewer Jean-Pierre Van Roy, it owes more to the sensibilities of his son Jean, the current brewmaster. He is much less of a hardliner than his father and likes to experiment, for example, with unusual fruit or fresh, powerful American hops, such as Cascade or Amarillo.

The first Iris batch was brewed in 1996 and bottled two years later in readiness for the brewery museum's twentieth anniversary. Since then, several more batches have been made and each has presented a more outspoken hop character. Iris also has a historic connection. Cantillon's forefathers brewed a similar beer as a typical Brussels ale; while the iris, the wetland lilylike flower, stands as a symbol for Brussels's development over the centuries from its original marshy surroundings around the River Senne. **JPa**

Tasting notes

Light amber color. Lambic character very present in the nose, with fresh and cheesy old hops, plus fruity notes and hard exotic wood. Fruity taste with subdued bitterness, ending in a very outspoken dry finish. This has a complexity not found in other Cantillon lambics.

Cantillon Lou Pepe

Brasserie Cantillon | www.cantillon.be

Country of origin Belgium
First brewed 2001
Alcohol content 5% abv
Serving temperature 54°–59°F, 12°–15°C

For better or worse, Cantillon is seen as the archetypal lambic traditionalist. Therefore, it's somewhat ironic to discover that the Lou Pepe range of beers doesn't actually meet the European Union's requirements for classification as "old" lambic, geuze, or kriek.

Let's dissect the name first. Lou Pepe is neither Dutch, French, nor even Broessels (as they call the dialect of Brussels). Its etymology is in the language of the southwest of France, the Languedoc. There, "Lou Pepe" is the affectionate term used to address a grandfather. Former brewer Jean-Pierre Van Roy and his wife, Claude Cantillon, often took their family on vacation to this part of the world. Also, Jean-Pierre often collaborated with renowned French vintners for some of his products, and used Bergeron apricots for Fou'Foune, another idiosyncratic creation. Lou Pepe was created as part of a "super" range of products to honor Jean-Pierre when he was planning to step down (whether his presence will ever leave the brewery is yet another matter).

The idea behind Lou Pepe was, as with so many Cantillon brews, to preserve the most authentic taste of the best old lambic and that of the finest fruits available. The best barrels of old lambic are initially selected, and a good glucose solution is added as primer. This is a very neutral and qualitative sugar source, which is completely fermented out by the time the lagering within the bottle is completed. For the Framboise Lou Pepe, the addition of raspberries is one and a half times the usual amount used for the Rosé de Gambrinus, Brasserie Cantillon's main Framboise. **JPa**

Tasting notes

Unbelievable deep cherry red color with a large pink head. On the nose, a bucket of fresh raspberries, wet wood at the back, plus a waft of wet chalk on blackboard. The taste is of wild raspberries, with woody overtones. Deeply refreshing, with raspberries lingering and tart fruit adding liveliness.

Cantillon Rosé de Gambrinus

Brasserie Cantillon | www.cantillon.be

Country of origin Belgium
First brewed 1986
Alcohol content 5% abv
Serving temperature 41°F, 5°C

Brewery tours, it is said, lack the romance of winery tours because the latter tend to mix nature with history and artistry. Cantillon may lack the beauty of row after row of carefully tended vines, but the air of history and almost palpable sense of artistry make its tour equal to any winery visit. Moreover, there is a taste of history in every Cantillon brand, providing you have taken care to school yourself in the ways of spontaneously fermented and aged lambic beers.

The educated palate might by now be scoffing, imagining that raspberry lambics (framboises) are but modernist interpretations of age-old lambic traditions, but this is not so. The patriarch of Cantillon, Jean-Pierre Van Roy, has effected considerable research into the subject and found that although it is difficult to determine the exact time raspberry lambics began to be served in the Payottenland, they have most certainly been around for at least a century.

To craft this beer, pounds of whole raspberries are added to barrels of semimature lambic, promoting further fermentation and adding a significant, though not sweet or overwhelming, fruit character to the beer. The fruitiness will fade with age, and so Van Roy recommends drinking his rosé as one would enjoy its wine equivalent—that is to say, young. This beer is not actually called "framboise." The reason, given on the brewery website, is that by 1986, the very word was associated with only "sweet, artificially flavored beer," and so a separate declaration was required. A rosé dedicated to Gambrinus (the god of beer) rather than Bacchus (the god of wine) seemed apt. **SB**

Tasting notes

This soft pink beer offers tart, dry, and barnyardy aromatics, mixed with fresh raspberry and citrus peel notes. In the body, the fruit is all skin and seeds, the berry's residual sugar long since fermented, with a dry and almost puckering tartness and floral lemon notes behind.

Cascade Cuvée du Jongleur

Cascade Brewing | www.raclodge.com

Country of origin United States
First brewed 2005
Alcohol content 8.4% abv
Serving temperature 48°F, 9°C

Cascade Brewing's Cuvée du Jongleur is a beer that is hard to pin down. For a start, there's the issue of the name. "'Cuvée' is a French term used on wine labels to denote wine of a specific blend or batch. The word originates from the French word *cuve,* meaning 'vat,'" explains Cascade's brewmaster Ron Gansberg. "'Jongleur' refers to an entertainer or juggler in medieval England and France," he adds, revealing that the name "Cuvée du Jongleur" made perfect sense to him as he juggled barrels from nine different lots of beer to create the finished product. The beer is the result of a careful blending of select barrels of sour red ales, aged in excess of a year; soured Belgian tripels aged in oak for up to eighteen months; and fresh blond quadrupels. After bottling, the beer is laid on its side in racks, like champagne, for eight months of further conditioning.

Cascade Brewing was one of dozens of craft breweries in the metro area of Portland, Oregon, but it skyrocketed out of anonymity shortly after Gansberg and his crew began experimenting with sour beers, a move that came partially out of necessity as well as creativity. "Our sour beer program got started in order to lay down beers of quality for the long term, so they were out of the main product flow of tanks and cooler storage," says Gansberg. "In addition to being in one of the biggest craft beer regions in the world, we live in a vibrant wine-producing region. That generates a lot of affordable, used French oak wine barrels from pinot noir aging. My background in wine has served me well in creating our sour beers." **LMo**

Tasting notes

Cuvée du Jongleur presents a fine balancing act that manages to keep many flavors going at the same time while making it all seem effortless. Enjoy oak, sweet-and-sour fruit, along with lemon peel tartness all tied up in a dramatic finish.

Cascade Kriek Ale

Cascade Brewing | www.raclodge.com

Country of origin United States
First brewed 2006
Alcohol content 8.1% abv
Serving temperature 50°F, 10°C

Art Larrance is one of the fathers of the craft beer movement in the Pacific Northwest. He co-founded Portland Brewing in 1985 and started the Oregon Brewers Festival, which takes place each year at the end of July and is recognized as one of America's best beer events. In 1998, Larrance started the Racoon Lodge and Brewpub in Portland's Raleigh Hills neighborhood. Working with former winemaker Ron Gansberg, who spent time learning the brewing craft at BridgePort Brewing, the pair use a ten-barrel system to make Cascade's unique ales.

Cascade Brewing Company turns out eight draft beers on a yearly basis, but it is the collection of oak barrels at the brewery that generates much of the buzz. Here, fruit is married with ale to undergo lactic fermentation for months at a time until the beer is hand transferred into champagne-style bottles. In addition to the Kriek, Cascade makes an Apricot Ale and The Vine, which is made with white wine grapes from the region, plus some Belgian-style sour ales.

Cascade is committed to utilizing the region's agricultural bounty. The Pacific Northwest is noted for producing outstanding cherries, and Cascade blends blood-red Bing cherries and sour pie cherries to get the right taste profile for the beer. The goal is to make a kriek unique to Cascade and not attempt to simply copy Belgian krieks. The base of Cascade Kriek is the company's Northwest Sour Red Ale, which is similar to a Flanders red ale. The brewery blends a fresh mixture of whole cherries with ale, which then spends more than six months aging in French oak wine barrels. **RL**

Tasting notes

This beer pours a rich reddish brown color with a thick, healthy head. An inviting fruit and spice aroma is instantly present. Vibrant, tart sourness dominates the flavor, punctuated by fruit from the whole cherries that have been soaked in the beer.

Coconut Porter

Maui Brewing Co. | www.mauibrewingco.com

Country of origin United States
First brewed 2005
Alcohol content 5.7% abv
Serving temperature 44°–50°F, 7°–10°C

A lot of people love Coconut Porter and it's easy to see why: this robust porter contains natural toasted coconut to further enhance North America's affection for innovation. If you like coconut, this is a beer for you.

With two sites for brewing, the company is always keen to support the local community and proud to say that production is based on the island, as opposed to using the mainland for support. Brewing takes place in Kahana, where handcrafted beer comes through small seven-barrel batches, with another site in Lahainatown, where there is a larger brewhouse and automatic canning line.

At its heart, Maui Brewing remains artisan in outlook, and, as with all U.S. craft brewers, there's plenty of variety here: the Big Swell IPA and Penguin XX Imperial Stout are both well worth a try. The Coconut Porter, meanwhile, fits into the U.S. porter style and takes on attributes of its English ancestor, yet incorporates plenty of innovation through the addition of coconut. Those fearing a sickly sweet drink should prepare for a shock because this is a wonderfully balanced concoction with incredible depth. The bitterness truly contrasts with the sweet to provide a lingering, thought-provoking drinking experience. The 32 IBUs do not dominate, but the subtle presence means the smooth mouthfeel is countered by a final zing on the tongue.

Big on the eco-friendly tip, the chaps at Maui also put the beers in cans, one of the most recycled materials on the planet, and refute the claim that this makes the beer taste tinny. **TS**

Tasting notes

Pours rich black with a tan foamy head, and the coconut is prominent up front from the first taste. The beer has a sound coffee backbone that helps with bitterness and balance. An excellent addition to the dinner table and particularly good with calamari and Cajun crab cake.

Consecration

Russian River Brewing | www.russianriverbrewing.com

Country of origin United States
First brewed 2009
Alcohol content 10.5% abv
Serving temperature 55°F, 13°C

Russian River brewmaster and co-owner Vinnie Cilurzo grew up as the son of a winemaker in southern California, and as a youth he could often be found helping out in the cellars. Nowadays, he appreciates the irony that he turned to home-brewing because he discovered he could make beer in twenty-one days, but now some of his beers need a much longer time to prepare. Among his barrel-aged beers, Consecration goes to market after about six months or so in wood, aging in barrels from one of the country's premier cabernet sauvignon wine producers.

"I'm more of a pinot (noir) guy, but I love our cab (cabernet) barrels," Cilurzo says, while filling recently acquired pinot barrels with what would go on to become Supplication. His challenge was finding the right fruit to stand up to rich flavors still in the cabernet barrels. He decided to use currants after brewing an anniversary beer for the Toronado, a legendary bar in San Francisco. That one was a blend of five beers, and although there was no fruit in any of them, drinkers often commented on the dried cherry and currant flavors.

He brews a strong, dark Belgian-inspired beer as the base for Consecration, marrying it with currants and a strain of *Brettanomyces* (a wild yeast known for its earthy or barnyard character), which then rests with a family of cabernet barrels. After a few months, he tops the barrels with the same blend of additional wild yeast strains that he uses in other beers, such as Temptation and Supplication; this all helps to boost the levels of sourness and acidity. **SH**

Tasting notes

Pours reddish brown, purple around the edges. Intoxicating vinous aromas, black fruit, then funk that would make a winemaker crazy. Those aromas blend into similar flavors, herbal and spicy, most notably green peppercorns, as well as vanilla and oak. Long, earthy finish.

Cottonwood Pumpkin Spiced Ale

Carolina Beer Company | www.carolinabeer.com

Country of origin United States
First brewed 1997
Alcohol content 6% abv
Serving temperature 37°F, 3°C

Carolina Beer Company operates from a modern brewery in Mooresville, North Carolina. The company's beer lineup is just one part of the operation, which includes a contract packaging business for a leading energy drink, malt beverage, and distilled spirit brands. J. Michael Smith and John Stritch founded the brewery in 1997, the same year Cottonwood Pumpkin Spiced Ale was first brewed at a microbrewery in Boone, North Carolina. A brewer who relied heavily on his grandmother's pumpkin pie recipe created the original recipe, which included real pumpkin, ginger, allspice, cinnamon, and cloves, as it still does today.

Pumpkin beers are said to have been used in place of malt at harvest time in colonial America. The modern version of these ales originated in 1985 when Bill Owens at Buffalo Bill's Brewpub in Hayward, California, used Atlantic giant pumpkins to brew. Carolina Beer purchased the Cottonwood Ales brand from the original Boone brewery in 1999. The Pumpkin Spiced Ale is Carolina Beer's most popular seasonal brew. To this day, whenever Pumpkin Spiced Ale is being brewed, the aroma of pumpkin pie is overwhelming throughout the brewery. Each year when the first batch of the ale is made, the brewery celebrates by hosting a pumpkin-carving contest for employees and the community. The reputation of the pumpkin ale is such that the 700-plus barrels of the beer brewed each year is sold out in advance.

The brewery's other seasonal beers include Almond Stout, American Wheat, Irish Style Red, Scottish Ale, and Frostbite, a strong winter warmer. **RL**

Tasting notes

This brew has a rich amber color, an ample white head, and the full body of a pumpkin pie. Generous amounts of cinnamon, ginger, allspice, and cloves appear on the palate, with a hint of brown sugar and maple syrup in the finish.

Cuvée de Tomme

The Lost Abbey | www.lostabbey.com

Country of origin United States
First brewed 1999
Alcohol content 11.5% abv
Serving temperature 55°F, 13°C

Tomme Arthur, who is director of brewing operations for both Port Brewing and The Lost Abbey, brews many "beers that don't have homes" when it comes to classifying them by style. This seemed to be a big deal in 1999 when he first took Cuvée de Tomme to the Great American Beer Festival, entering it as an experimental beer and seeing it win medals in consecutive years.

Cuvée started from a dark, strong ale that was fermented with yeast from Belgium. Arthur added the ale to a used bourbon barrel dosed with cherries and three different strains of *Brettanomyces* wild yeast. He intended to age Cuvée in wine barrels, but didn't have time to track down a wine barrel when he was ready to brew the first batch. Instead, a gently used bourbon barrel was available. "It was never designed to be a bourbon barrel–based beer, although in retrospect it made a perfect fit," he said. **SH**

Tasting notes
New flavors emerge as quickly as you can identify them: cherries, smoky chocolate, dark fruits, dried fruit (figs), bourbon caramel, and woody vanilla. Balanced by an acidic finish.

De Cam Oude Kriek

Geuzestekerij De Cam | www.decam.be

Country of origin Belgium
First brewed *ca.* 2002
Alcohol content 6.5% abv
Serving temperature 50°F, 10°

First, let's get the definitions right. A *geuzesteker* is a blender of lambic beer, whereas a lambic brewer brews lambics, which can then be blended into geuze. *Geuzestekers* were once plentiful, but now De Cam is one of two *geuzestekerijen* still plying its ancient trade.

De Cam covers more than just the blending of lambics. Karel Goddeau is the man in charge, and he is an ideal blender, although for him it's more of a hobby: he is also the head brewer at Slaghmuylder brewery in Ninove. Goddeau is a perfectionist and doesn't like to do things by half. That is why the cherries for Oude Kriek De Cam (*kriek* is the Flemish name for sour cherry varieties) usually hail from his family's orchards in the village of Gooik. Such is his devotion to the cause of blending that if the harvest isn't enough, he will join fellow lambic brewer and enthusiast Frank Boon and buy in Polish cherries. **JPa**

Tasting notes
A vinous nose, fruity, but not expressly cherrylike. Sour cherries arrive in the taste, fresh fruit–like; the beer is not overly lambic, yet it is pretty acidic and well carbonated.

Decadence

AleSmith Brewing | www.alesmith.com

Country of origin United States
First brewed 2005
Alcohol content 9.9%–11% abv (variable)
Serving temperature 50°F, 10°C

Peter Zien, an accomplished home-brewer, bought the AleSmith Brewery from the original founders in 2002. Since taking over the brewery, Zien has won more than 400 medals and honors. Decadence was first brewed in 2005 to commemorate the tenth anniversary of AleSmith Brewing. As befits the small, iconoclastic brewery, each year a completely new and different beer is created. The only running thread is that each is a big beer and ideal to be laid down and aged.

The first Decadence Anniversary Ale was a classic English-style old ale combining abundant malt flavors balanced by fresh English hops. The 2008 brew is a traditional English-style barleywine weighing in at 11 percent. AleSmith used floor-malted barley and English hops, in addition to a true top-cropping English yeast, giving it an intensely malty character overflowing with caramel and toffee flavors. **JB**

Tasting notes
The nose is dark chocolate and coffee, with hints of nutty and earthy aromas. It's liquid cake, initially sweet, rich, and chewy, with cocoa, coffee, and dark fruit flavors. The finish is bitter.

Demoiselle

Cervejaria Colorado | www.cervejariacolorado.com.br

Country of origin Brazil
First brewed 2008
Alcohol content 6% abv
Serving temperature 43°F, 6°C

Cervejaria Colorado's founder, Marcelo Carneiro da Rocha, admits that it was pretty hard to sell people on flavorful beers when he started fourteen years ago in Ribeirão Preto, in southern Brazil. But with enthusiasm and perseverance, Colorado has grown with the Brazilian beer scene. With the vibe of a U.S. craft brewery, its beers feature uniquely Brazilian flavors like manioc, local honey, and rapadura cane sugar.

In addition to German specialty malts, this coffee porter uses estate-grown, organic "blue" coffee beans. The brewery roasts the beans, then cold-extracts the coffee and adds it toward the end of fermentation for a clean, smooth coffee aroma. The result is a subtle mix of roasted aromas, with the coffee picking up right where the malt leaves off. At 6 percent, it's not a powerhouse, but something more elegant. Demoiselle is rich and creamy without being overly sweet. **RM**

Tasting notes
A soft cocoa nose with sharp espresso notes and fruity hints of dried cherries on top. Very creamy on the palate, with chocolate drying out to brighter espresso flavors. A luxurious finish.

The Dissident

Deschutes Brewery | www.deschutesbrewery.com

Country of origin United States
First brewed 2006
Alcohol content 9% abv
Serving temperature 50°F, 10°C

The Dissident is aptly named, as it is truly a departure on several levels for the award-winning Deschutes Brewery. It was first brewed in 2006 as part of Deschutes's Reserve Series of specialty brews. The Dissident marked a duo of firsts for the brewery, which is based in Bend, Oregon: it was the first time it had ever crafted a fruit beer—Washington State cherries were added about six months into the fermentation—and the first time the brewery had used the wild yeast strain *Brettanomyces* (affectionately known by many U.S. craft brewers as "Brett") during fermentation.

In some European wines, Brett is known for creating earthy undertones, but in the beer fermentation process, it can be used to create strong flavors typically associated with Belgian beers. Compared with traditional yeasts, Brett takes longer to ferment and requires additional barrel finishing time to balance the sour flavors. In the Dissident's case, this meant aging a portion of the beer in pinot and cabernet wine barrels for more than three months to help mellow it out and give it the properties of a Flanders-style oud bruin.

Although Brett is desired in some beer styles, it can also create what could be considered "off" flavors in others. Deschutes's brewers did not therefore want to take a chance at the wild yeast contaminating the brewery. The Dissident was kept in isolation under lock and key away from the rest of the brewing operations. The brewery chose the name because it can also mean "to sit apart." The Dissident won a gold medal at the 2008 Great American Beer Festival. **LMo**

Tasting notes

Magically tart and sweet at the same time, the fruit and acidity make this beer very food friendly, cutting the heaviness of creamy dishes or cooling spicy ones. Thanks to the cherry notes, the beer also pairs well with chocolate.

Draco

Birrificio Montegioco | www.birrificiomontegioco.com

Country of origin Italy
First brewed 2006
Alcohol content 11% abv
Serving temperature 46°–50°F, 8°–10°C

Thanks to the enormous ability and imagination of brewer Riccardo Franzosi, Montegioco's beers are always of a high standard, while a huge variety of styles is also produced. Many of the beers are aged in wooden barrels that have previously been used for wine, while others have fruit added to them. This gives the beers an incredibly diverse aromatic profile. At Montegioco, it is possible to find beers that are closer to wine than they are to the ale family, for example, T-Beer, which is produced with Timorasso—a white regional variety of grape. There are also delicate and perfumed beers, such as the Quarta Runa, to which Volpedo peaches have been added.

The fruit is always added after it is cooked. The aim is not to add acidity to the beers, but to contribute to their flavor and aroma, which the fruit-cooking process emphasizes. Draco (or dragon) is a version of Demon Hunter that has cooked and mashed blueberries added during a second fermentation. This beer has three fermentations—two in steel tanks and one in bottle.

There are two versions of this beer: the basic one and the Draco Metodo Cadrega (*cadrega* means "chair" in the Piedmont dialect). The latter is an oxidized version of the beer that has been matured for a longer period. When Franzosi is asked about the origins of the name "Cadrega," he explains that, with this method, all he can do is sit down and see what happens.

Draco is a warm and strong beer, with the fruit playing a central part, rather like a Christmas ale. This makes it an obvious choice for winter, but it is also great with a piece of Piedmontese blue cheese. **ES**

Tasting notes

Strong amber color, with a persistent foamy head. The nose is rich and spiced, with strong notes of dried fruits that can be linked to panettone or Christmas pudding. In the mouth, the beginning is sweet, followed by fresh fruit notes, which then turn warm and rich again.

Marie
de
Bourgogne
1457 1482

Duchesse de Bourgogne

Brouwerij Verhaeghe Vichte
www.brouwerijverhaeghe.be

Country of origin Belgium
First brewed *ca.* 1900s
Alcohol content 6.2% abv
Serving temperature 50°F, 10°C

Breweries have been aging beer in wooden barrels for as long as there has been commercial brewing, but the practice has fallen off dramatically with the advent of more durable and less flavor-imparting stainless steel. In parts of Flanders, however, wood aging endures through the persistence of several beer styles, including the red ales sometimes known as the burgundies of Belgium.

Brewed with a minority portion of darker malts, these beers are generally fermented with yeast that contains some souring bacteria and conditioned in wooden barrels that have been allowed to serve as host to a variety of microflora. The resulting brews are, to differing degrees, tart and dry, full of fruity notes, and marvelous as aperitif drinks.

A stylistically similar beer, known as oud bruin, is produced over the border in East Flanders. **SB**

Tasting notes
The aroma combines enticing red berry with pomegranate, light spice, and notes of good balsamic vinegar. The body is sweet and tart, with considerable fruitiness and a dry finish.

Eliščino Královské 13°

Pivovar Rambousek
www.rambousek.wz.cz

Country of origin Czech Republic
First brewed 2006
Alcohol content 6.2% abv
Serving temperature 48°F, 9°C

Originally founded as little more than a hobby brewery in 2002, Pivovar Rambousek expanded to a new location in 2007. The brewery is believed to be the smallest commercial producer in the country with an annual output of around 1,275 gallons (51 hl).

The tradition of brewing with chestnuts is well known in Corsica and Italy. More than a millennium ago, Slavic tribes in Eastern Europe sweetened their beers with honey. The two traditions meet in Eliščino Královské 13°, an unusual lager brewed with chestnut honey. Czech pilsner malt composes the bulk of the grist, with an addition of chestnut blossom honey from Slovenia, also the source of the wort's four additions of hops. It is bottom-fermented, then lagered for six to seven weeks. The result is a finely bitter, lightly sweet amber lager of unusual aromatic complexity. All the beers are brewed to order, and most are sold out months in advance. **ER**

Tasting notes
This cloudy, deep amber brew has little foam, making it easier to detect the complex aroma of chestnut blossom and bakery spice. In the mouth, it is semisweet with rich layers of flavor.

← The duchess herself, Mary of Burgundy, in a 15th-century portrait.

Elixir

Birrificio Le Baladin | www.birreria.com

Country of origin Italy
First brewed 2004
Alcohol content 10% abv
Serving temperature 39°F, 4°C

The Langhe wine region is considered to be one of the top areas in Italy for unique wines and, above all, is best known for its Barolo and Barbaresco varieties, both being made from Nebbiolo grapes. A journey through the hills of this part of Piedmont is a journey through the rich tapestry of wine country, a land where beer seemingly has no place. However, reach the little village of Piozzo and a surprise is in store. Piozzo was once noted for its pumpkins, but now it's beer: It is the home of Matterino (better known as Teo) Musso, the brewmaster of Le Baladin. Here beer is taking on wine—and winning.

Musso is known for his desire and passion for breaking through the borders of what constitutes normal brewing. To some he is more than a brewer, an artist that loves to play with malts, hops, spices, and yeast. He learned to brew at the Brasserie à Vapeur at Pipaix, Belgium, but since then he has simply followed his dreams; this journey has included some fairly unorthodox methods (for example, headphones are attached to fermentation tanks to see what kind of music the yeast enjoys). Elixir is an example of his desire to challenge people's expectations of beer.

Elixir undergoes fermentation with the sort of yeast strain that is normally used in the whiskies of Islay in Scotland. It could be called a "demi sec" beer, having the sort of gentle sweetness that you would find in champagne. Given its strength, this beer is best as a nightcap, although considering Musso's love of matching beer and food, it's also welcome on the table: try it with game or a mature cheese. **MM**

Tasting notes

Copper color with brilliant orange tints and a thick, persistent foam. Charming nose with plenty of fruitiness and a distinctive note of fudge. Complex and warming in the mouth, with hints of dessert fruit such as dates; a very long, but dry, finish.

Éphémère (Apple)

Unibroue | www.unibroue.com

Country of origin Canada
First brewed 2002
Alcohol content 5.5% abv
Serving temperature 41°F, 5°C

In the early part of the new century, the minds behind Unibroue made the decision to release a line of seasonal fruit beers under the moniker of Éphémère: apple for the summer, cassis for the fall, cranberry for the winter, and peach for the spring. Thanks in part to the popularity of Belgian beers, some of which had fruit in the mix, drinkers were starting to look beyond what traditionally constituted a beer. Unibroue, no doubt, wanted to reach out to them. As it turned out, the apple, or Éphémère Pomme, as it was known in Québec, was the only one to survive long-term.

Built on a white beer base (presumably something roughly similar to Blanche de Chambly), each beer was crafted using fruit, sometimes combined with juices or essences. The problem the range faced was addressing the market outside Québec; as each beer had a very similar label, there was some confusion. Meanwhile, making certain that the seasons did not overlap when the distributors and stores were, in some cases, hundreds of miles from the brewery could also be problematic. Eventually, the Éphémère line was pared down until only the apple remained (although a raspberry beer, Éphémère Framboise, has since been added for the Québec audience).

Unlike many other fruit beers, which make generous use of juice and post-fermentation flavorings, Éphémère is still made with macerated Granny Smith apples, along with nutmeg, ginger, and cinnamon. This fact is no doubt responsible for the genuine apple aromas and flavors commented on by so many tasters and advocates of the beer. **SB**

Tasting notes

Fresh and lively in the glass, there's no mistaking the green apple aroma or the accompanying spiciness. On the palate, it's light and crisp, with more apple and a more-or-less harmonious spicy, grainy taste that suits it well to serving with salads.

Erika

Birrificio Baladin | www.birreria.com

Country of origin Italy
First brewed 2007
Alcohol content 9% abv
Serving temperature 54°–57°F, 12°–14°C

Erika is a gold-colored beer that, as is the case with all of this innovative brewery's beers, is far from an ordinary ale. It includes heather honey and fir honeydew honey in its list of ingredients. Both these honeys are added during different phases of the brewing process and they contribute in their diverse ways to the aromatic profile of the beer.

Heather is a spring honey that is produced from bees in Tuscany. It has aromas of caramel, licorice, and tamarind and is added to the wort during the boil. As well as contributing to the aroma, it gives a fine sweetness to the beer. Fir honeydew honey is a summer product that comes from the Trentino Mountains. It is added in the bottle as a sugar for the second fermentation; it also helps to give a strong balsamic and quite bitter flavor that can be found in the beer. Together with the English hops, this helps balance the sweetness. With judicious use of the ingredients, the result is a balanced and rich beer that is excellent when paired with soft cheeses.

Along with Birrifico Italiano, Le Baladin was one of the first microbreweries to open in Italy in the 1990s. With the restlessly experimental Teo Musso at the helm, the brewery is noted for its eclectic and unusual range of beers. In the spring of 2009, Musso started a pub called Open in the village of Cinzano near Cuneo. The pub is named after one of his beers and serves only Italian beers, both bottled and draft. Open beer is unusual in that its recipe can be downloaded from the Internet, with Musso keen to allow home-brewers to try and re-create it at home. **ES**

Tasting notes

Pale golden yellow, with a good and persistent foam. The nose is very sweet and rich, with balsamic and spicy notes of tamarind. In the mouth it is warm, thanks to the alcohol with a good final bitterness produced by the work of the honeydew and English hops.

Fantôme Chocolat

Brasserie Fantôme | www.fantome.be

Country of origin Belgium
First brewed 2004
Alcohol content 8% abv
Serving temperature 43°F, 6°C

Belgian beer leads the world in eccentricity and Dany Prignon's creations at Fantôme are widely regarded as the strangest of the lot. Those lucky enough to encounter his beers either love or hate them. While some critics have detected a spicy, infected mess of inconsistency, fans enjoy the unusual flavors and playful creativity. Fantôme beers are never boring.

They are saisons in that they are farmhouse ales following seasonal whims, but they do not adhere to the more modern tradition typified by Saison Dupont. Nor are Fantôme beers like the quenching, low-alcohol saisons traditionally served to Wallonian farmhands. In their ingredients they more closely resemble the much older tradition of gruit—medieval beers made with a medley of spices, before hops really caught on. Prignon generally hops his beers, but is just as likely to reach for the spice cabinet.

It would have been a surpise if Prignon had made a chocolate beer that actually looks and tastes like chocolate. First, the color is not dark but amber, looking more like a pale ale than anything else. Real cacao powder takes on most of the bittering work but its flavor is quite subtle—although pairing the beer with a bite of dark, bitter chocolate helps it come out of hiding. Chili might be what adds some zing, or there may be other spices at work. Prignon's recipes typically change from year to year. Intentional or not, the telltale tartness of infection adds a certain refreshing quality and helps hide the beer's alcoholic strength—although the barnyard notes might be too much for those who prefer a finer drink. **JS**

Tasting notes

Cloudy amber ale with some off-white froth. The nose has some fruity yeast esters and cereals competing with serious barnyard notes. On the palate it's tart and spicy, with some caramel sweetness managing to show through. Very subtle cocoa in the backdrop.

Fraoch Heather Ale

Williams Brothers Brewing Company | www.williamsbrosbrew.com

Country of origin Scotland
First brewed 1992
Alcohol content 5% abv
Serving temperature 50˚F, 10˚C

A lot of beers claim to have a long ancestry, but few claim a lineage as far back as heather ale. Brewed with heather flowers, Fraoch is a type of beer whose origins go as far back as 2000 B.C.E. It's a distinctive brew—hops wouldn't have been available in those far-off times, so heather flowers were used; their preserving properties helped to keep the ale from spoiling.

Bruce Williams, the owner of a home-brew beer shop in Glasgow, took a gamble on reviving this ancient brewing technique in 1986. He obtained an old Gaelic family recipe for Leann fraoch (heather ale). After testing various concoctions brewed from different types and quantities of heather flowers, Bruce finally perfected the recipe. By 1992, he had reintroduced heather ale to Scotland. It was instantly popular, despite only being stocked in six pubs, and the following year Scotland's oldest family brewers, Maclay, agreed to let Bruce brew larger quantities in its Alloa-based brewery during the heather season.

Fraoch is made by adding bog myrtle and the purple flowers of wild heather to the boil (hops are used in small amounts for their preservative properties). Once cooled slightly, the hot mixture is poured into vats of fresh heather flowers and left to infuse for an hour before being fermented. The ale that results from this has a floral peaty aroma and a dry finish and is a perfect accompaniment to rich and spicy foods. To date, this historic ale, made only from naturally occurring ingredients, has won more than thirty prestigious awards from international food and drink associations. **JM**

Tasting notes

A light floral scent accompanies this honey amber beer, which boasts a dry winelike finish. It has a full malt character and is slightly sweet, with earthy, haylike undertones and a spicy, herbal flavor. There's no finer choice to wash down your haggis on Burns Night.

Gale's Prize Old Ale

Fuller, Smith & Turner | www.fullers.co.uk

Country of origin England
First brewed *ca.* 1920s
Alcohol content 9% abv
Serving temperature 50°–55°F, 10°–13°C

Before the closure of Gale's in 2005, its Prize Old Ale was one of the diamonds in the brewing crown of England, a strong, dark barleywine that improved with age. It was a beer that had a three-hour boil (most beers get ninety minutes), was matured for six months at the brewery, and bottle conditioned. Gale's closed after being bought by London brewery Fuller's, and many aficionados thought that this was the last they would see of the beer. However, John Keeling, Fuller's head brewer, had other ideas and brought the beer back to life in 2007. He has overseen new versions of the brew every year from then on.

Keeling admits that he wasn't a fan of the original beer. As he recalls, "I felt it was too flat. I said to the former head brewer of Gale's that he shouldn't be putting it in a corked bottle, as it loses its fizz through the cork—it is never going to be true to its potential if it doesn't have fizz. The company wasn't very keen on doing it either, but I am glad I have done it; it is an unusual beer, it is a beer that grows on you."

The 2007 vintage of Prize Old Ale was brewed at Gale's and matured at Fuller's; but from then onward, Keeling has used the old recipe to brew the ale, mixing it with a batch of the last brew to be produced at Gale's in 2005. "We have forty barrels of this sitting in tanks," says Keeling, "and when we brew one and mix it in with the barrels, every bottling will have some of the original Gale's Prize Old Ale in it." The survival (and some would say, improvement) of this magnificent ale is testimony to the seriousness with which Keeling treats his craft. **ATJ**

Tasting notes

Dark reddish brown. Nose hints at cherry brandy with subtle traces of a geuzelike softness in the background. On the palate, a sherrylike richness before a sharp and sweet grapefruitlike character emerges. Lambic, geuze, and aged barleywine in one glass.

Genziana

Birra del Borgo | www.birradelborgo.it

Country of origin Italy
First brewed 2006
Alcohol content 6.2% abv
Serving temperature 54°–57°F, 12°–14°C

Leonardo Di Vincenzo began his career in brewing as a home-brewer while he was finishing his degree in biochemistry. After traveling through Europe to study historic beer styles and do some practical training, Di Vincenzo opened Birra del Borgo in 2005 in the small mountain community of Borgorose, just forty-five minutes from Rome, in the Lazio region of Italy.

Many from the Italian craft beer renaissance, including Di Vincenzo, brought a new twist into the brewhouse, using original and exciting ingredients. The inspiration for Genziana came from the alpine plant that is the beer's namesake, gentian (*genziana* in Italian), which is commonplace in Borgorose. Its root is used almost exclusively in bitters produced in the region. It is a medicinal herb that can be toxic if consumed in excess.

With the Genziana, the brewer wanted to create a beer that captured the aroma of the gentian, but not its extreme bitterness. The plant is quite potent, so a very small quantity in the kettle goes a long way—just enough to impart that smell of roots and forest floor. The brewer also adds coriander to deepen the nose with some balsamic notes. The beer is fermented with a Belgian yeast strain to harmonize the aroma profile. The gentian root is added during the last few minutes of the boil and is removed before the whirlpool. As the plant is endangered, it is prohibited to harvest it, and del Borgo get the root from a licensed grower nearby. The best compliment Di Vincenzo ever received for this beer was from another Italian brewer who said: "It has the scent of a woman." **MO**

Tasting notes

A light amber-colored ale with a white head. The complex nose offers floral and medicinal herbal smells, with wildflower honey, and a subtle citrus. On the palate, a fluffy mouthfeel with peppery notes. The finish leaves balsamic aromas and a firm clean bitterness.

Girardin Gueuze 1882

Brouwerij Girardin | horal.be/girardin.php

Country of origin Belgium
First brewed 1882
Alcohol content 5.5% abv
Serving temperature 50°–57°F, 10°–14°C

If any lambic brewer in the Payottenland heartland can claim the title of first among equals, there's no doubt it is the long-established Brouwerij Girardin, hidden away in the remote Flemish Brabant village of St.-Ulriks-Kapelle. Its picturesque location on top of a hill heightens this sense of the venerable: Armand Debelder, who is chairman of HORAL (a professional organization for the preservation of the art of spontaneous fermentation), has dubbed this brewery "the Château d'Yquem of the lambic brewers."

Girardin was very much shaped and styled by its former brewer Louis Girardin, who died in 2000. He made it into a very closed-off enterprise, a brewery going its own way, ignoring the rest of the world. His sons Jan and Paul, who run the brewery today, have retained a little bit of this attitude, but they have opened up toward their lambic-brewing brethren by joining HORAL. The public has also benefited from this slight change of heart. Girardin now participates in the annual Toer de Geuze, an organized visit of several lambic brewers and geuze blenders.

Louis Girardin might have had his reasons to keep his premises firmly closed. Rare pictures from inside the brewhouse show an immaculate environment, in sharp contrast to the often shabby premises seen elsewhere. While all the Girardin geuze are labeled "Girardin 1882," they have two other labels—black and white. The white label is used for the filtered and pasteurized product, while the black label stands for the real unfiltered thing. Most beer aficionados plump for the latter—the splendid Oude Gueuze. **JPa**

Tasting notes

Golden color with slight orangey shine. Nose of horse blanket, fresh flowers, sulfur, green apples, and drying hay. Very dry, rich in tannins, with flavors of citrus, pineapple, green apples, drying hay, lime, and lactic acid. There is also a hint of sweetness.

Goedecke's Döllnitzer Ritterguts Gose

Brauhaus Hartmannsdorf | www.leipziger-gose.com

Country of origin Germany
First brewed 1824
Alcohol content 3.9% abv
Serving temperature 46°F, 8°C

Having survived the turbulences of German history, the sour beer style of gose is these days establishing itself as one of the country's most exquisite regional specialties. First mentioned in around 980, the style originated in the Harz Mountains, where people used the water of the Gose creek for brewing. In medieval times, it reached Saxony, and in 1738, production began in Leipzig, which later became known as "the gose town." Goedecke's Döllnitzer Ritterguts Gose dates to 1824, when a merchant named Goedecke founded a gose brewery between Halle and Leipzig.

After World War II, the owners were dispossessed, the brewhouse dismantled, and the owner's son Adolf Goedecke fled to West Germany. With the last of the Saxony gose brewers closing down in 1966, the sour beer style would have been gone forever if it were not for Hartmut Hennebach and Lothar Goldhahn. They found the old Döllnitzer recipe in the 1980s and began brewing the beer. After reunification, Adolf Goedecke returned and reestablished the family brand in 1999.

Today, Döllnitzer Ritterguts Gose is produced on Goedecke's behalf at the Brauhaus Hartmannsdorf. It is said to be the most true to the Leipzig gose style of the three brands still existing. Top-fermented, using wheat and barley malts, and spiced with coriander and salt, Döllnitzer Ritterguts Gose undergoes an alcoholic and lactobacterial fermentation, the latter giving it its sour character. Goedecke recently found a sixty-year-old case of gose bottles from which he plans to cultivate the yeast, so that beer lovers can drink a Döllnitzer fermented by the original strain. **SK**

Tasting notes

Intense golden orange in color, with a meringue-like foam. Phenolic coriander aroma with sour moments. The palate offers a velvet sourness reminiscent of the fruitiness of ripe lemons. Smooth, not pungent, it is balanced by a decent saltiness with hints of resiny hop aroma.

Green Peppercorn Tripel

The Brewer's Art | www.thebrewersart.com

Country of origin United States
First brewed 2003
Alcohol content 9.2% abv
Serving temperature 46°F, 8°C

"It was just one of those creative moments," says Volker Stewart, the founder of Baltimore's popular Brewer's Art brewpub. "Someone just wondered, 'What would be fun to throw into this firkin of tripel?'" Poll a hundred brewers and the vast majority of them would say fruit, maybe candy sugar. However, a bright spark at Brewer's Art came up with the idea of peppercorns. Instead of coming off like a bowl of over-spiced broth, this rich golden ale has a snappy, palate-awakening bite. It's loud but never overheated. "I can't think of a single person who tasted it and didn't like it," Stewart says.

With the cask pouring freely, patrons regularly fill the brewery's restaurant, a Victorian-era mansion just a couple blocks from the city's symphony house. The bar, with its ornately decorated lounge and clubby downstairs pub, is an essential stop for beer (and music) lovers in Baltimore. In 2009, *Esquire* magazine—chronicler of all things trendy—rated it the number-one bar in the United States.

It soon became clear that Brewer's Art had a hit in their quirky peppered ale. This off-the-cuff experiment became the brewery's first bottled product. Packaging it in the cramped brewpub is impossible, however. Several times a year, the brewers troop north to the Sly Fox Brewery outside Philadelphia, where they churn out a few hundred cases of corked bottles. When they show up on regional shelves, word spreads, and they're gone in an instant. "It's really a beer for the beer geeks," Stewart says. And for readers. A portion of the proceeds from sales of Green Peppercorn Tripel supports a local literacy program. **DR**

Tasting notes

A tulip glass is brightened by a golden orange sunset beneath lusciously billowing clouds of foam. Its tropical aroma hints at refreshing fruitiness (banana, pineapple, mango), with a bubblegum sweetness. Never cloying, it cleans the palate with a sharp, finishing pepper snap.

Hanssens Artisanaal Oude Gueuze

Hanssens Artisanaal | www.proximedia.com/web/hanssens.html

Country of origin Belgium
First brewed 1896
Alcohol content 6% abv
Serving temperature 55°F, 13°C

Members of the Hanssens family have been blending lambic beers to produce their Oude Gueuze since just after World War I. In 1914, the invading German army ended more than forty years of lambic brewing by Hanssens when they took away their copper brew kettles for the war effort. With no money to buy new ones, Bartholomeus Hanssens decided that he would rather continue as a blender than give up entirely on the beer business.

This *geuzestekerij* is now run by Sidy Hanssens (daughter of the late Jean Hanssens) and her husband, John Matthys, and they still blend geuze as it was done in the old days. Wort is purchased from lambic brewers such as Boon, Girardin, and Lindemans, and is then put into barrels at Hanssens for aging. Typically, their lambic is aged from a few months right up to three years. Usually, one-, two-, and three-year-old lambics are blended to create Oude Gueuze.

Hanssens has an interesting collection of old barrels from many of the different lambic breweries. However, these barrels, some of which are one hundred years old, are not museum pieces. They are the living, breathing heart that still creates lambic today. The fact that beer lovers in many countries can still purchase a brew that has been matured in century-old barrels is remarkable in itself, even without considering the high quality of the beer.

Sidy Hanssens and John Matthys sell beer directly from the blendery on Friday afternoons and Saturdays. Both have full-time jobs and don't rely on the blendery as a primary source of income. **CC**

Tasting notes

Hazy, golden-colored brew that pours with very light carbonation. Very full bodied and dry, with notes of tart citruslike fruits, oak, and a distinct barnyard, horse-blanket aroma and flavor. Tart, sour, and acidic, but pleasantly so. Ever so slight sweetness in the finish.

Hemp Ale

Nectar Ales | www.nectarales.com

Country of origin United States
First brewed 1998
Alcohol content 5.7% abv
Serving temperature 48°F, 9°C

Considering the laid-back atmosphere and quirky character of Northern California's Humboldt County, this brewery's origin came from a decidedly mainstream source. Brewery founder Mario Celotto was a member of the 1980 Super Bowl–winning American football team, the Oakland Raiders. After researching how to build a brewery, he took the bonus money from the Super Bowl win and used it to start the Humboldt Brewing Company in 1987.

With Humboldt County's reputation as one of the biggest marijuana-growing areas in California, it's surprising that the first hemp beer wasn't brewed there. That distinction went to Hempen Ale from Maryland's Fredericksburg Brewing Company, but this was later discontinued. A hemp ale from Humboldt seemed a natural, though, and they first toked up the brew kettle in 1998.

In 2003, Firestone Walker bought Humboldt and rebranded their beers under the name "Nectar Ales." Shortly after taking over the brand, head brewer Matt Brynildson was named Mid-Size Brewing Company Brewmaster of the Year at the 2003 Great American Beer Festival, and then Champion Brewmaster for Mid-Size Brewing Company at the 2004 World Beer Cup.

The ale is spiced with hemp seeds, which are mixed into the mash and add a sweet spiciness to the flavor. Of course, the seeds are sterilized and there's no tetrahydrocannabinol (THC). Since the seeds are not water soluble, any remaining traces of THC would not make it through the initial boil. Hemp Ale will not get you high, only drunk, if you enjoy enough bottles of it. **JB**

Tasting notes

Hemp ale pours deep amber, nearly brown, but is streaked with reddish tints. The nose is subtly spicy with chocolate notes. The flavor profile is primarily sweet malt, but with spicy undertones and good hop character. The finish is clean and quick.

Honey Dew

Fuller, Smith & Turner | www.fullers.co.uk

Country of origin England
First brewed 1999
Alcohol content 5% abv
Serving temperature 43°–46°F, 6°–8°C

Despite the fact that 1999 is down as the year when this beer was first brewed, Fuller's had actually been making a honey beer since 1996. However, it was as a seasonal and was not an organic beer. In the late 1990s, the eco-revolution had started to take hold in the United Kingdom. Some canny marketing folk at the Griffin Brewery in Chiswick, London, saw the organic wave begin to build, and Honey Dew was positioned to ride it all the way in. It is now the country's best-selling organic beer.

Not only was Honey Dew one of the United Kingdom's first organic beers, it was also one of the first honey beers. Yet, you would be mistaken if you categorized it as a beer for women. At sampling shows, it's amusing to see just as many tough-looking men quaffing back this delicately sweet, golden beer as women.

Organic beer is not easy to brew, purely because the number of those producing organic malt and hops is small. Despite this, John Keeling, Fuller's masterbrewer, manages to find just enough organic raw materials. Farmers have had to relearn a variety of techniques from the 18th century, such as planting crops to attract predators away from the hops or barley, without the need for pesticides. Organic honey is another issue. With so much intensive farming in the United Kingdom, honey farmers can't control where the bees roam. The only place to get organic honey in enough quantities for brewing is from South America, where there are huge tracts of uncultivated land for bees to collect their pollen. **ST**

Tasting notes

Light and golden with a spicy, citrus edge and a delicate sweetness from the honey. Gently bitter and drying as the hops build. Easy to drink and surprisingly versatile with food. Try it with creamy pasta dishes, fish starters, or mushroom dishes.

Honey Spice Triple

Sharp's Brewery | www.sharpsbrewery.co.uk

Country of origin England
First brewed 2009
Alcohol content 9% abv
Serving temperature 46°F, 8°C

Honey beer tends to be a bit of a hit-and-miss option for many people—often it can be overwhelmingly sweet and thin—but this is not the case with Sharp's Honey Spice Triple. Head brewer Stuart Howe had always been a bit skeptical about using honey in beer, until someone gave him some citrus flower honey to brew with, which smells like it has been dry hopped with Styrian Golding. He used it to make the original 2007 version of this beer, which went on to win a number of prizes and critical acclaim.

The project was stopped in its tracks when Howe returned to his producer to get some more honey and discovered that the bees were dead. After that, he tried a few different honeys in the same recipe, but it never came out as well. He went back to the drawing board to design a similar beer around a different honey.

In the 2009 Triple version, Howe used an ivy honey, which is about as big in taste as honey gets. This is because ivy honey is so hard that even the bees can't use it, which means brewing with it is a sustainable and eco-friendly thing to do. As with the original Honey Spice beer, Howe used wheat to add a tartness to counter the sweetness of the barley and the honey; but this time, he used a more extensive mixture of herbs and spices that had been grown by Cornwall's Eden Project. This includes ginger, cinnamon, and coriander as well as yarrow, bay, and alecost. Five hops were used: English-grown Northdown, Slovenian Bobek, Hallertauer Brewer's Gold from Germany, and Cascade and Chinook from the United States. The result is an outstanding example of the brewer's craft. **MC**

Tasting notes

A truly complex and outstanding beer, its plethora of spice and herbs is present in an almost bewildering, yet enticing, array on the nose. On the palate, there is wonderful balance of all those complex aromas, balanced out with a sweet, resinous tinge from the honey.

Hop-15

Port Brewing Company
www.portbrewing.com

Country of origin United States
First brewed 2002
Alcohol content 10.5% abv
Serving temperature 54°F, 12°C

Hop-15 was originally produced as a draft beer in 2002 to celebrate the fifteenth anniversary of the Pizza Port restaurant in Solana Beach, California. It is now brewed all year-round. Hop-15 is made using fifteen different hop varieties. In the original brew, the name of each hop variety was written on a piece of paper and placed into a hat. Each brewer pulled out a piece of paper with a hop name on it, and added 15 ounces (425 g) of that particular hop variety to the brew kettle.

The hops were added to the brew in the order pulled, which, along with the actual variety of hops used, is a closely kept secret among the brewers. The order of the hops as they were first drawn is still followed precisely every time Hop-15 is brewed, with each hop variety going into the brew kettle at intervals of fifteen minutes. The timing makes for an unusually lengthy boiling period of more than three hours. **LMo**

Tasting notes
A huge hop aroma spills out as soon as Hop-15 is uncapped. The flavors follow through on the hoppy promise, with a backbone of malty sweetness and a pleasant measure of alcohol.

Ichtegem's Grand Cru

Brouwerij Strubbe
www.brouwerij-strubbe.be

Country of origin Belgium
First brewed 2006
Alcohol content 6.5% abv
Serving temperature 54°F, 12°C

Carolus Strubbe founded this brewery in 1830, and since then the brewery has stayed in the family, with the sixth generation recently taking its place over the mash tun. The release of Ichtegem's Grand Cru marked the brewery's 175th birthday, as well as the arrival of Marc Strubbe as head brewer.

The Grand Cru is based on Ichtegem's Oud Bruin. It is a fairly traditional Flemish red ale, brewed partly with amber and dark caramel malts and getting very light bitterness from aged hops. The Oud Bruin is a blend of young sweet ale and older stuff that has spent up to eighteen months souring and fermenting in metal tanks, ending up fairly sweet with an odd, dusty-sour backtaste. The Grand Cru, on the other hand, not only skips the young beer but also the metal, getting to spend its maturation period in oak tuns. The result is a tart, vinous beer that is nonetheless easy to drink. **JS**

Tasting notes
A thin, beige head sits atop a reddish brown beer, releasing a nose of tart cherries, berries, and balsamic vinegar. Tastes quite tart and fruity with a lightly sweet, malt center.

iJuba Special

United National Breweries
www.kzn.org.za/index.php?view_page+59192

Country of origin South Africa
First brewed Unknown
Alcohol content 3%–4% abv
Serving temperature 54°F, 12°C

Sorghum beer is brewed at home and commercially throughout southern Africa, especially among the Zulus; it is often brewed with a mix of sorghum and corn. United National Breweries markets sorghum beers under several labels, including iJuba, which means "dove" in the Zulu language. iJuba is consumed while fermentation is still occurring, so it is packaged in paper cartons and plastic jugs with holes punched in the lids to prevent the containers from bursting. Foam gently gurgling from the vents indicates freshness.

Sorghum beer is struggling to maintain popularity in prosperous, modern South Africa. The beer isn't set to disappear overnight, but a marketing makeover may be required for this half-traditional, half-global hybrid brew to thrive. To attract younger drinkers, the brewery has created Nini-Nanini, a sorghum beer flavored with banana or pineapple. **CO**

Tasting notes
Pinkish in color; on the palate, it is sour and a little sweet. The mouthfeel is thick and could be compared to a beer porridge. It is traditionally served in a hollowed-out gourd.

Imperial Pumking

Southern Tier Brewing
www.southerntierbrewing.com

Country of origin United States
First brewed *ca.* 2006
Alcohol content 9% abv
Serving temperature 41°F, 5°C

Southern Tier Brewing's first two flagship brands were a pilsner and a mild ale. They were, the brewery openly admits, flops. Its third beer, however, a highly hopped India Pale Ale, was a huge success. Founders Phineas DeMink and Allen Yahn realized that beer drinkers in New York and Pennsylvania like big flavors.

Southern Tier began focusing on distinctive ales with an edge: an imperial pale ale, a heavy-duty hefeweizen, a crème brûlée–flavored stout, and this one, a knee-buckling imperial pumpkin ale. Pumpkin ale is an increasingly popular seasonal that is threatening to replace Oktoberfestbier as the favorite among U.S. microbreweries. Its recipe goes back to colonial days when the American brewers, unable to obtain malt, used pumpkins as a substitute. Flip off the cap, and big spicy aromas—cinnamon, clove, nutmeg, baked pie crust—rise and suggest it's time for dessert. **DR**

Tasting notes
This orange brew greets the nose with a plume of freshly baked spices. Cinnamon, clove, nutmeg, brown sugar, and toast are dominant in a silky body that is never sweet.

Innis & Gunn Oak Aged Beer

Innis & Gunn Brewing Company | www.innisandgunn.com

Country of origin Scotland
First brewed 2003
Alcohol content 6.6% abv
Serving temperature 52°F, 11°C

Serendipity is said to have played its part in the development of this beer. In 2002, whisky producer William Grant wanted to make an ale-flavored whisky so he approached brewer Dougal Sharpe, who fashioned a strong ale for putting into a used bourbon cask, as was traditionally used by whisky makers for storing the spirit. The idea was that the beer would impart some of its flavors into the white American oak barrels that would then be transferred to the whisky. Originally, the beer was going to be discarded, but the story goes that the distillery workers supped the brew, rather than wasted it, after it had been in the barrel for thirty days prior to the whisky going in. It proved a great hit, as the white oak imparted a smoky malt flavor together with massive orange fruit and vanilla and honey notes. And a new beer was born.

The use of oak to store beer is nothing new, but traditionally its effect is benign and not intended to impart flavor. Dougal and his brother Neil decided that there would be a commercial market for the beer and established a company to market it, and Innis and Gunn was born. The beer is contract brewed for the brothers and, like many beers, it ferments for seven days. It is then poured into oak barrels where it is matured, slowly gathering flavors from the wood for thirty days. The beer is then blended and stored in a large steel marrying tun for at least forty-seven days, where some of the harsher flavors mellow and soften. The brothers have also experimented with beer aged in rum casks and a triple-matured beer, which is aged for 147 days before being bottled. **TH**

Tasting notes

Honey colored. The nose has wistful, woody, spiritlike aromas, whereas the palate starts off with burned butterscotch flavors, followed by a toffee sweetness accentuated by a strong vanilla note and hints of apple and spice. The finish is warm, long, and sweetly satisfying.

Kinshachi Nagoya Red Miso Lager

Kinshachi Beer | www.kinshachi.jp

Country of origin Japan
First brewed 2005
Alcohol content 6% abv
Serving temperature 55°F, 13°C

Kinshachi Beer first brewed this beer for the 2005 World Expo in the Japanese prefecture of Aichi. The brewery is a subsidiary of Morita Shuzo, a venerable sake brewer that also makes soy sauce and miso, a fermented soybean paste that is used as a seasoning in Japanese cooking. Morita's miso is used for this beer, but it is said that the idea to use the paste in the beer was not readily accepted throughout the company. Many were afraid that the beer would taste too salty, or too much like seasoning; others thought that the idea was too radical even for a specialty beer.

In the actual brewing process, the biggest difficulty is determining the quantity of miso paste to be used. What works best is an amount that contributes to a subtle background flavor, yet is enough to give the beer an interesting body. However, the lager characteristics of this darker beer provide a good foundation for the miso. Less fruity than ale, the beer is quite smooth and easy to drink.

Red Miso Lager is a popular product in the Kinshachi line. Initially, many people buy it as a one-off gift purchase, but, after hearing how well it is received, they end up buying it for themselves. It is popular among Nagoya-based chain restaurants because it suits the strong flavors in Nagoya's highly seasoned foods. It is also a good match for Chinese food. In recent years, Red Miso Lager has surpassed Kinshachi Pilsner in sales and become the brewery's best seller. Kinshachi also produces a lager with black Hatcho miso, along with an Altbier, an IPA, and a beer made with premium Japanese green tea. **BH**

Tasting notes

The beer pours a deep reddish brown, with a light tan head. The aroma is of dark caramel and dried fruit. There is some initial bitterness in the rich malty flavor, with sweetened miso in the background. The taste of light fruitcake and some bitterness leads to a long finish.

Kriek De Ranke

Brouwerij de Ranke
www.deranke.be

Country of origin Belgium
First brewed 2000
Alcohol content 7% abv
Serving temperature 50°F, 10°C

This is a beer with a history. De Ranke's brewers, Guido Devos and Nino Bacelle, started out as avid home-brewers who both loved lambic beers. The pair had about half a batch of an amber ale that they had brewed in 1998, which was not as hoppy as their usual beers. Also, this batch was a little on the "funky" (i.e. lambiclike) side, which did not go down very well with customers. Guido and Nino saved this batch and added fresh, whole sour cherries from Poland and allowed them to macerate in the beer for six months. However, they were not completely happy with the result. In a flash of inspiration, the pair decided to add young lambic to the blend—in this case, from the esteemed Brouwerij Girardin. As soon as they tasted the brew, they knew they had hit the mark.

The result? A quasi-lambic, quasi–oud bruin, quasi-kriek beer with lots of wild, farmhouse character. **CC**

Tasting notes
Aroma has tart cherries, citrus, and horse-blanket funk. Taste is acidic, tart, fruity, dry, and earthy. Medium-bodied beer that finishes with fruit and mild alcohol. Pair with a Belgian waffle.

La Choulette Framboise

Brasserie La Choulette
www.lachoulette.com

Country of origin France
First brewed 1983
Alcohol content 6% abv
Serving temperature 46°F, 8°C

Brasserie La Choulette brews La Choulette Framboise using its Ambrée as a base, to which pure raspberry juice is added, combined with Hallertau hops from Germany and pale malted barley. It is unusual in that this sort of fruit beer is more common in Belgium, either made by adding fresh fruit to lambic or with the addition of various syrups and juices to the base beer.

La Choulette's beers remain part of the traditional mode of bière de garde style of presentation. They have a champagne-style cork and a twist-off wire cage that adds a sense of theater to their opening and pouring. La Choulette Framboise throws a fine head with attractive pink traces ready to reveal several waves of flavors flowing from sharp to sour. The beer scored a gold at the Concours International de Bières de Montréal in 1998 and was a gold medal winner at the World Beer Championships in 2003. **AG**

Tasting notes
Some fruity malt appears in the flavor with hints of almonds, then it passes through astringency on to sourness. The malt base reappears in the finish with more red fruit developing.

La Folie

New Belgium Brewing
www.newbelgium.com

Country of origin United States
First brewed 2000
Alcohol content 6% abv
Serving temperature 55°F, 13°C

New Belgium releases a variety of beers that draw their flavor and character from wooden barrels, but La Folie was the star the moment it was first released.

Not long after he began at New Belgium in 1996, brewmaster Peter Bouckaert bought twelve used wine barrels. He purchased a variety of *Brettanomyces* and other wild yeasts, then found others along the way—harvesting what returned in old kegs of other New Belgium beers, for instance. Bouckaert tasted the beer every fourteen days, and the tastings became among the best attended at the brewery. When the time came to bottle the first batch in 2000, employees from the brewery enthusiastically pitched in.

The first batches of La Folie were sold only at the brewery, before being released to a broader market. When it comes to bottling this sour ale, employees from throughout the brewery still show up to help. **SH**

Tasting notes
Some vintages pour redder than others, just as the degree of sourness may vary. Complex fruity aromas, including everything from orange to cherries, then oak and vanilla.

La Meule

Brasserie des Franches-Montagnes
www.brasseriebfm.ch

Country of origin Switzerland
First brewed 1998
Alcohol content 6% abv
Serving temperature 54°F, 12°C

This is one of the original beers that La Brasserie des Franches-Montagnes brewed in 1998, along with La Salamandre ("the Salamander"), a complex, sharp blanche of Belgian inspiration, and La Torpille ("the Torpedo"), a strong spiced dark ale with prunes.

The inspiration for La Meule is probably found in Saison Dupont—dryish, hoppy blond ale with a spicy edge and not-too-high alcohol content. Yet, as the brewery's founder Jérôme Rebetez stated from the start, merely copying beers does not interest a self-respecting brewer. Thus, there's a little twist in La Meule, in the form of sage leaves, which bring an herbal note and an almost gingerlike citrusy spiciness to this classic brew. Crisper, hoppier, and drier than when it first appeared more than a decade ago, La Meule has come into its own over time and is a testimony to Rebetez's idiosyncratic genius. **LM**

Tasting notes
The initial fruity softness quickly gives way to a spicy, citrus kick, where notes of fresh ginger, lemon peel, thyme, and sage meet an almost minty herbal edge. Crisp, dry finish.

La Mummia

Birrificio Montegioco | www.birrificiomontegioco.com

Country of origin Italy
First brewed 2006
Alcohol content 5% abv
Serving temperature 43°–46°F, 6°–8°C

Undoubtedly, the most important characteristic of Montegioco is its continual research into linking its beers with the surrounding terroir. For an Italian beer, produced with imported malt and hops, this can be a difficult task. To achieve the strongest connection possible, brewer Riccardo Franzosi only uses fruit that grows in the valleys of south Piedmont (Volpedo's peaches, Timorasso grapes) and wine-producing elements such as barrique or champagne yeasts.

La Mummia (or "the Mummy") is one of the best examples of a terroir beer in Italy. It is so called because it is left for a long period in a sort of wooden sarcophagus. It has been made since the brewery opened in 2006, but because of the long maturation period, it only went on the market in 2008. Its tortuous path of production means that it is only available in very small quantities.

There is no precise style into which Mummia falls. It starts off as Runa, the basic beer of Montegioco, a blond beer refermented in the bottle. This beer is then left in barrels that were originally used for aging Barbera dei Colli Tortonesi, a local red wine with a strong fruitiness. The maturation gives the beer a clear aromatic profile that covers both the wood notes and the acidity. These come as a consequence of bacterial infections, which are quite typical of beers aged in wooden barrels. After twelve months, Mummia is bottled and refermented with a wine yeast used for another local wine, the white sparkling wine Cortese. This yeast gives it a closeness to a *spumante* wine, with notes of baked bread and a nice acidity. **ES**

Tasting notes

In the glass, it is turbid with an evanescent foam. On the nose, there are notes of wood, vanilla, peach, with a general sensation of freshness. In the mouth, it has a good, soft acidity with notes of white fruits such as pear and peach. A perfect aperitif; good with fish and vegetables.

La Petrognola

Birrificio La Petrognola | www.lapetrognola.com

Country of origin Italy
First brewed 2005
Alcohol content 5.5% abv
Serving temperature 46°–50°F, 8°–10°C

Garfagnana is one of the few corners of Tuscany that has not been invaded by tourists, even though it is full of small villages, free-flowing rivers, crystal-clear lakes, and forests. Here, you will find the village of Piazza al Serchio, where La Petrognola officially started brewing in 2005. "Officially," because founder Roberto Giannarelli had already been cultivating his passion for beer for many years by home-brewing on weekends.

In Garfagnana, a lot of farming land is dominated by the cultivation of spelt. Grown in the areas free from the forest, spelt was for centuries a traditional remedy for the local population, but it is now used in the preparation of fresh pasta, soups, and many other kinds of foods. When Giannarelli decided to brew, spelt was his first and immediate choice as an ingredient for his beers. Now every beer that emerges from La Petrognola has spelt in the mix.

For La Petrognola, the recipe involves 70 percent malted barley and 30 percent raw spelt, while Saaz is added for bitterness and aroma. After a primary fermentation of four days, the beer is bottled for its final fermentation and maturation (the entire production of La Petrognola is in bottle). This is a brewing process that usually lasts a little less than two months. The beer is ready to drink when it is sold, but the best choice is to leave it for a further three or four months in the cellar, where it can become even more harmonious. La Petrognola is an interesting and original beer, and on the dining table it's a graceful companion to chicken dishes, as well as vegetable soups, possibly made with barley or spelt. **MM**

Tasting notes

Pale amber, cloudy, topped by a white, abundant foam. Aroma is intriguing, rich in citrus and floral notes. Hints of spices, too. In the palate, starts quite sweet with notes of cereals, but it ends with a fresh hoppy underlining. Well-balanced brew.

La Roja

Jolly Pumpkin Artisan Ales | www.jollypumpkin.com

Country of origin United States
First brewed 2004
Alcohol content 7.2% abv
Serving temperature 39°–43°F, 4°–6°C

This is a beer that looks forward and backward at the same time. Forward, because Jolly Pumpkin is among a handful of truly cutting-edge small breweries in the United States. However, La Roja's roots stretch back to the dim shadows of the Middle Ages. It is in the style of a Flemish red ale, a type of beer that has been brewed for centuries in what is now Belgium. Its main distinguishing feature is not its color, though, but the fact that it is a blend of beers that have been aged in oak for between two and twelve months.

Located in Dexter, Michigan, just outside of Ann Arbor, Jolly Pumpkin Artisan Ales was founded by brewer Ron Jeffries in 2004 with the intention that every single one of its beers would spend time in contact with oak. Brewing, as he says, "just plain wicked awesome beers from wild, natural cultures" is a pretty radical business plan, but he's stuck to it. These are the beers he loves, and in these heady days, what inflames one fanatical devotee is sure to gather a following of like-minded enthusiasts. In keeping with their generally whimsical theme, La Roja means "the Red One."

Jeffries says, "It's all about doing things the hard way," and given the uncertainties of fermenting in barrels and producing a consistent product, that's an understatement. La Roja is uncompromisingly rooted in something deep and profound. If you're a jaded Pinot lover, searching for a beer with the depth and charm of a great red wine, this could be your beer. If you're a beer adventurer, then this ruddy-amber-colored beer is well worth trying. **RM**

Tasting notes

La Roja presents a tangy acidic nose, with hints of estery fruit and a tiny dab of vanilla. It's brightly acidic but layered with soft caramel, a dry bitterness, and the smack of American oak. Dry, nearly vinous, it still manages to be fun and refreshing.

La Semeuse Espresso Stout

Brasserie Trois Dames | www.brasserietroisdames.ch

Country of origin Switzerland
First brewed 2008
Alcohol content 7.5% abv
Serving temperature 54°F, 12°C

When he's not challenging Swiss beer drinkers' palates by flinging crisp, hoppy beers at them, Brasserie Trois Dames' founder, Raphaël Mettler, loves to experiment with new brews, some of which later appear as limited-release beers. His unspiced, crisp, complex Belgian saisons, namely La Récolte (plain), Saison Houblon (dry hopped with Cascade), and Saison Framboise (with raspberry juice), for example, are opening up new perspectives on what Swiss beer can be. Newer releases, such as Fraîcheur du Soir (a grand cru wit) and Oud Bruin (unexpectedly, a matured blend of strong stout and apricot wine), hint at mouthwatering things to come. The clear winner among these experiments, though, is La Semeuse Espresso Stout.

The idea of adding coffee to a stout to bring out the roasted, torrified notes in the beer is nothing new. Yet La Semeuse has two trump cards tucked up its sleeve. First, the base beer is a rich, rounded 7.5 percent abv stout, not a standard-strength one, which gives a lot of depth and padding to it. Then there's the way the espresso coffee is added, to ensure that only the aromatic part ends up in the beer, warding off any harsh notes reminiscent of over-stewed coffee beans.

The blend yields a Jekyll-and-Hyde of a brew: warming, cordial, almost soothing, with a stimulating, reviving, and fresh-coffee edge kicking in. It works fine as an aperitif or a beer after work, but it truly comes into its own as an after-dinner treat or with sturdy desserts. It effortlessly cuts through the creaminess of a tiramisù and stands up even to the richest and darkest of chocolate cakes. **LM**

Tasting notes

A rich, deep, and luxurious stout with dark chocolate and cocoa as the main character, mellowed by a touch of vanilla. The crisp, razor-sharp espresso coffee edge is seamlessly merged in, gradually taking over the long, luxurious, and bitter finish.

L'Abbaye de Saint Bon-Chien

Brasserie des Franches-Montagnes
www.brasseriebfm.ch

Country of origin Switzerland
First brewed 2004
Alcohol content 11% abv (variable)
Serving temperature 59°F, 15°C

The brewery was founded in 1997 by Jérôme Rebetez, a young oenologist who turned to beer. In a world where more and more brewers are dabbling with wood aging, Jérôme is very much one step ahead of the pack, as his oenologist's training gives him the skill necessary to blend oak-aged beer to perfection.

Abbaye de Saint Bon-Chien is a sour mash beer that's fermented with a traditional ale yeast, and then transferred into a collection of oak casks that have contained all kinds of wines or spirits. Since some of the casks bring more to the nose and some more to the palate, the trick to blending is to combine them to reach a balanced beer without faults or blurry bits. The few casks that stand well enough without blending are sold as Abbaye de Saint Bon-Chien Grand Cru. **LM**

Tasting notes
Every vintage is different, but expect an almost flat, oily, sour ale, reminiscent of oud bruins and fortified wines. Spices, dark fruit, wood, and leather merge into a rich, smooth beer.

Liefmans Cuvée-Brut

Liefmans Brouwerij
www.liefmans.be

Country of origin Belgium
First brewed *ca.* 1937
Alcohol content 6% abv
Serving temperature 44°F, 7°C

Brewing is in the very air of the East Flemish town of Oudenaarde. The town was once a center of production for Flemish old brown ales, but now just a brace of breweries remains in the area.

The base beer for this kriek is Liefmans Oud Bruin. The wort is put into open copper fermenters, yeast is added, and it does its work for seven days. There is also likely to be some fermentation by wild yeasts during this period, which may explain the tartness of the beer. The wort is moved to closed stainless steel vessels for further maturation. For the kriek, whole cherries from Belgium and Denmark are used. The cherries sit on the base of Oud Bruin and ferment for about twelve months. This brew is blended with Oud Bruin and Goudenband of different ages, resulting in a very complex beer. **CC**

Tasting notes
The aroma is of sour cherries, with some sweet malt. Taste is tart cherries with a mild sweetness, perfectly in balance. Great with chocolate cake, fruit pie, ice cream, and other rich desserts.

A year of fermentation awaits these cherries at Liefmans. ➡

Mamma Mia! Pizza Beer

Pizza Beer Company | www.pizzabeer.net

Country of origin United States
First brewed 2006
Alcohol content 4.6% abv
Serving temperature 44°F, 7°C

Pizza and beer may be the ultimate pairing of food and brew, but pizza-flavored beer? For all but those with iron stomachs, the mere suggestion of this unique beverage produces raised eyebrows and instant gastric distress. That is, until you actually taste it. Somehow, Illinois home-brewer Tom Seefurth has discovered the secret of combining the spicy tang of oregano, garlic, and tomatoes with the refreshing flavor of a golden ale. Surprisingly well balanced, Mamma Mia! Pizza Beer will appeal to anyone who enjoys the bite of a hoppy IPA.

The first batch was just a lark. Tom and his wife Athena were sitting around on a holiday weekend trying to figure out what to do with a bunch of leftover ingredients. Tom says, "We had some tomatoes, and I thought about using those. And I had a neighbor who was always talking about doing a garlic beer, so we added that. I had some fresh oregano, some basil, an old packet of yeast, and I said, 'it probably won't work. If it doesn't, we can just cook with it.'"

Fermentation did its trick; the couple bottled the home-brew, waited for it to carbonate, and then gave it a try. They were surprised at how good it was. A couple weeks passed. One night they ordered a pizza—one of those stuffed Chicago pies—and popped open the beer. They realized it was a perfect partner to pizza and renamed their unique product.

Tom gave up his job as a mortgage broker to work full time on his quirky beer. Bottled under contract by a commercial brewery, it's a cult beer with an unusual flavor that's much more enjoyable than it sounds. **DR**

Tasting notes

The underlying tomato character brings to mind a tart-tasting rye ale, with the spice tingling away like a peppery Belgian saison. Flavorful, full bodied, and fun—it's certainly no mere gimmick and naturally goes well with a pizza.

Meantime Coffee Porter

Meantime Brewing | www.meantimebrewing.com

Country of origin England
First brewed 2005
Alcohol content 6% abv
Serving temperature 44°–50°F, 7°–10°C

There was a time when drinkers would have spluttered at the suggestion of coffee-flavored beer. Surely, you have one in the morning after plenty of the other? Meantime Brewing has successfully challenged such a notion, however, and produced in its Coffee Porter something that beautifully combines the two.

Meantime is a company that has always been happy to test the boundaries. As well as paying tribute to some wonderful native British beers through their portfolio, here is a team that is always ready to push innovation. Founded by Alastair Hook, the brewery is now the second largest in London, a position Meantime earned after ten short years. In even less time, the beers produced have established a strong pedigree, particularly in competitions, where they often pick up gold medals.

With a tremendous passion for brewing heritage, Meantime has breathed new life into classic styles such as London porter and India Pale Ale. Nor is the brewing team daunted by the prospect of less familiar projects, such as bringing a helles, old smoked bock, raspberry, and even chocolate beer to the attention of British palates.

Meantime Coffee Porter is a fantastic example of this love of innovation. It is a superbly executed beer, essentially in the English porter style. The Arabica coffee beans used in the brew are grown by the Maraba Cooperative in Butare Province, Rwanda, and hand-roasted by Union Coffee Roasters. The beans work in unison with a roasted barley backbone, and the beer packs a definite caffeine punch. **TS**

Tasting notes

You can't hide from the chocolate, and there's a nice sweet vanilla edge, too, so it works well with truffles. As you'd expect, it pours dark, almost black, and the "espresso-cum-mocha" profile is subtler than expected, with just the right amount of bitterness.

Midas Touch

Dogfish Head | www.dogfish.com

Country of origin United States
First brewed 1999
Alcohol content 9% abv
Serving temperature 44°F, 7°C

According to legend, King Midas turned everything he touched into gold. There was a real Midas, however, who ruled Phrygia (now Turkey) 2,700 years ago. His tomb, discovered in the 1950s, contained a stunning collection of Iron Age drinking vessels. Forty years after the excavation, a University of Pennsylvania molecular archaeologist, Patrick McGovern, determined that the residue left behind in the vessels was probably alcohol. McGovern found traces of barley, grapes, and honey—a mix of beer, wine, and mead. A beer aficionado himself, McGovern searched for a brewery that would be willing to re-create the mixture for a special feast in honor of Midas. Delaware-based Dogfish Head, known for its "extreme beers," was a natural choice for this task.

"When we opened," says brewery founder Sam Calagione, "we were looked on as freaks and heretics, creating unusual styles with weird ingredients." The brewery had already produced other styles with raisins, chicory, juniper berries, vanilla, and maple syrup. When a beer with grapes and honey was suggested, Calagione thought, why not? His intuition was right, and the beer was an instant hit, though initially among wine enthusiasts who compared it to champagne.

Today, Midas Touch is brewed year-round and is the brewery's most heavily awarded beer. It has spawned other historic styles, including unusual varieties based on analyses of archaeological sites in Honduras and China. Says Calagione: "Pat McGovern's analysis validated our creative approach to brewing in a way that we could never do ourselves." **DR**

Tasting notes

Just as advertised, it pours royally gold with a firm collar of foam and some yeast cloudiness. The fruity aroma of grapes, honey, and spices is fit for a king. The sweet flavor of honey mead and fruity wine up front overshadows light malt and saffron. The finish is dry and smooth.

Midnight Sun

Williams Brothers Brewing Company | www.williamsbrosbrew.com

Country of origin Scotland
First brewed 2008
Alcohol content 5.6% abv
Serving temperature 55°F, 13°C

At one time, eight breweries operated in the small Scottish town of Alloa. Today, there is only one, the Williams Brothers Brewing Company (formerly New Alloa Brewery) owned by Bruce and Scott Williams, who have reinvigorated the craft sector while building a reputation for innovation. Based on the banks of the River Forth, the brewery has a forty-barrel brew length with in-house bottling and packaging lines.

Midnight Sun is an English porter–style ale, a virtually black beer made from roasted barley, oats, and chocolate malt, balanced with a generous hop content and slivers of fresh root ginger. According to Bruce Williams, "We reviewed many old recipes from the Scottish Brewing Archives at Glasgow University and noticed that many old porter styles, including some from the old Maclay's Brewery and George Younger's of Alloa, had used licorice, linseed, and ginger to give the beer a 'warming' feel. We use whole fresh ginger in other recipes and tried adding small amounts to our standard porter. . . . The ginger and a late addition of Fuggle hops is the only special treatment, except the generous addition of porridge oats in the mash tun."

This beer has a more international aspect than the brothers' more "Scottish" beers, though Williams counters, "I guess the porter style is a London thing, but this has the additional Scottish flare!" Midnight Sun is part of the brothers' color-coded range of beers (Black, Gold, Red), a series of beers that the brewery says is based on the "golden ratio," an irrational mathematical constant found in nature. **AG**

Tasting notes

Almost pure black in density with a cream-colored head and a chocolate-and-coffee aroma with some hints of fresh tropical fruit. Dark chocolate continues through the flavor with oats, bitter hop, and a surprise helping of ginger notes on the finish.

Mill Street Coffee Porter

Mill Street Brewery | www.millstreetbrewery.com

Country of origin Canada
First brewed 2002
Alcohol content 5.5% abv
Serving temperature 50°F, 10°C

For many years, in the heart of downtown Toronto, there lay the empty and useless shell of the long-disused Gooderham and Worts Distillery, which was once the second-largest distillery in the British Empire. Since the new millennium, the old site has been converted into a commercial and cultural center known as the Distillery District. This housed Mill Street Brewery when it opened in late 2002 with a trio of flagship brands, including its Coffee Porter.

Since the 1990s, when the landmark downtown beer bar, C'est What, commissioned its own coffee porter, the city of Toronto has had an ambivalent relationship with coffee-flavored brews, welcoming the arrival of new variations on the theme and, occasionally, scarcely bemoaning their departure. Of them, just the draft-only C'est What version and Mill Street's bottled brew have endured.

Making the Mill Street Porter just that much more unusual is the fact that the brewer who created it, Michael Duggan, doesn't even drink coffee. He had to rely on other palates at the brewery and the coffee bean–roasting skills of his Distillery District neighbors, Balzac's Coffee, to ensure proper balance in the beer. Amazingly, it worked well.

In 2008, Mill Street decamped to an industrial part of the city's east end and turned the original brewery into a brewpub. Duggan, meanwhile, left the company and veteran Toronto brewer Joel Manning took the helm of the new operation. New brands were added and the Coffee Porter survived the transition, taking on what the brewery refers to as "cult status." **SB**

Tasting notes

One sniff of this mahogany brew is enough to tell you they are serious about their coffee at Mill Street, as the aroma of freshly roasted beans mixes with dark chocolate and malt. The body stays true to the nose, with the addition of a soft hoppy bitterness, ending in an off-dry finish.

Monk's Café Flemish Sour Ale

Brouwerij Van Steenberge | www.vansteenberge.com

Country of origin Belgium
First brewed 1923
Alcohol content 5.5% abv
Serving temperature 46°–50°F, 8°–10°C

The sour red ales of Dutch-speaking Belgium are sometimes known as "the Burgundies of Flanders" thanks to their reddish color and vinous flavor; but there is a deeper historic connection. In 1384, Flanders passed to the neighboring state of Burgundy, which was renowned at the time for its art, music, luxurious living, and partying. Some Belgians still identify their appreciation of fine living as a Burgundian legacy, so it's not surprising to find the region name-checked on more than one Flemish beer.

The Van Steenberge brewery is in the village of Ertvelde in the Meetjesland, a flat but pretty stretch of countryside between Bruges and Ghent. Although Van Steenberge was founded in 1874 as a farm brewery, the beer remained a sideline until 1922, when the brewery was taken over by Paul Van Steenberge. He launched a new brown ale called "Bios" (Greek for "life") that blended "stale" beer, which had been matured for two years, with a fresh brew.

Today, the brewery is a modern operation with a computerized brewhouse and bottling line. The brown ale has become something of an infrequently brewed footnote to a range that majors on stronger specialties and contracts—a shame given the rarity of the style. It received a boost in 2002 when the Monk's Café beer bar in Philadelphia asked the brewery to supply the ale and relabeled it as their own brand, "Flemish Sour." Unlike the better-known examples, it's matured in metal rather than wooden casks, which some say makes it harsher. However, it's still refreshing enough to count as an indulgent Burgundian pleasure. **DdM**

Tasting notes

A deep ruby brown beer with an off-white lacy head and a sour, ironlike cherry aroma. Salty minerals and sweet-and-sour fruit on the palate, with a maltier note than some. There is a fruity, sour, and salty finish with late hints of grainy malt.

Ola Dubh

Harviestoun Brewery | www.harviestoun.com

Country of origin Scotland
First brewed 2006
Alcohol content 8% abv
Serving temperature 59°F, 15°C

Ola Dubh is Gaelic for "black oil," which instantly forms a close and neat connection with Harviestoun's rich, dark ale, Old Engine Oil. A version of the latter forms the basis for this collaboration between the brewery and Highland Park Distillery. Located on the Orkney Islands, off the country's north coast, the distillery's roots can be traced back to 1798. Although the barley it uses now comes from the mainland, it is malted and dried over locally cut peat, which hugely influences the smoky, dry, and elegant whisky. Highland Park's eighteen-year-old topped a list of the world's best 110 spirits, with judges citing its excellent balance of floral sweetness and restrained peat notes. So this is the class act that Old Engine Oil has to match up to, because, after being brewed, it is matured in casks previously used to mature single-malt whisky.

The initial concept for the project came from Harviestoun's North American distributor, B. United International. Harviestoun's Matthias Neidhart says: "There is a thirst for highly individual products with unique flavor profiles like Ola Dubh." It cannot have escaped Neidhart and the brewery's attention that barrel-aged beers were also finding fans both in the United States and in the United Kingdom. However, what made this idea so unique was that the beer became available in three "expressions," from casks that once held Highland Park twelve-year-old, sixteen-year-old, and thirty-year-old single malt. Each has its own characteristics, ranging through a nose of truffle oil, cocoa, and faint smoke to a palate that slips easily between heathery peat, orange, and dried fruit. **AG**

Tasting notes

Ola Dubh Special 30 Reserve is deep brown with a burgundy flush and an oily appearance, with an oatmeal-tinged head. It laps between flavors of honey, toasted malts, vanilla, red fruits, and espresso beans before a long, oaky finish. Great with Stilton cheese and oatcakes or fruitcake.

Oud Beersel Oude Geuze

Brouwerij Oud Beersel | www.oudbeersel.com

Country of origin Belgium
First brewed 1882
Alcohol content 6% abv
Serving temperature 50°F, 10°C

This lambic brewery opened in 1882, just a couple of hundred meters from its current site, which dates to 1930. Old copper hopbacks, an open copper fermenter, paintings of old lambic café scenes, lambic brewing tools, and lots of brewery ephemera make Oud Beersel a very interesting and historic brewery to visit. On-site brewing stopped in 2002, when European Union health inspectors forced the brewery to close under new food-production safety rules. Such overzealous regulations threaten Belgium's artisanal brewing heritage.

Gert Christiaens and his father Jos purchased the brewery from Henri Vandervelden in 2005. Oud Beersel was Gert's favorite lambic brewery during his university years, and he did not want it disappear forever. Gert and Jos have Brouwerij Boon brew their wort for them, using the original recipe of Oud Beersel. The wort is brought by tanker truck to Beersel and put in the original Oud Beersel barrels. Some of these 124 oak barrels, which can hold up to 158 gallons (600 l) of beer each, are more than 100 years old.

Oud Beersel blends one-, two-, and three-year-old lambics to produce their Oude Geuze. The older lambics contribute to the tartness, complexity, and fruitiness of the beer. The young lambic is still fermenting, so with the help of a little sugar at bottling, the Oude Geuze has a third fermentation in the bottle. A group of beer enthusiasts called "De Geuzen van Oud Beersel," which has 160 members, leads tours of the brewery on the first Saturday of each month. The blendery sells beer on Saturdays. **CC**

Tasting notes

Golden orange-colored brew that pours with a moderate head. Notes of citrus fruits, oak, and sour apple on the nose. The taste is dry, yeasty, earthy, and fruity, with lemon and orange notes. This beer is tart, but not overly so. Very refreshing, it has a mild bitterness in the finish.

Our Special Ale

Anchor Brewing Company | www.anchorbrewing.com

Country of origin United States
First brewed 1975
Alcohol content 5.5%–6% abv
Serving temperature 55°F, 13°C

Anchor's winter seasonal has an official name—Our Special Ale—but most people, including Anchor's employees, call it simply "Christmas Ale." First brewed in 1975, it was the first new U.S. holiday beer made in modern times, and remains one of the few that changes its recipe each year. Anchor's owner Fritz Maytag got the idea from the tradition of medieval villages brewing special beers for festivals.

The first recipe was an all-malt brown ale that was dry hopped with Cascade. For the first few years, it remained the same; but then each year, the brewers began tinkering with the recipe and, by the late 1980s, experimenting with different mixes of spices (although what they use remains a closely guarded secret). Trying to figure out what spices are in each year's version has become great sport for beer lovers, although the brewery steadfastly refuses to reveal any details. Some of the flavorings people believe they have identified over the years include allspice, chestnut, cinnamon, cloves, coriander, evergreen, ginger, juniper, lemon zest, licorice, and nutmeg. The only detail that the brewery has so far disclosed is that they've never used cloves.

The label on Anchor's Christmas Ale changes each year also. It features a different hand-drawn tree and, since 1982, has included the scientific name of the tree. Until recently, the beer was released on the Monday before Thanksgiving each year, but now Anchor Christmas Ale is available beginning in early November through January. It comes in magnums as well as regular bottles, perfect for holiday parties. **JB**

Tasting notes

While varying from year to year, the 2008 version, like most years, is a dark mahogany color with a rich, tan head. The nose is a complex mélange of spices with a tinge of bitterness. Flavors are likewise complex and spicy, with a chewy, rich malt backbone and a lusciously long finish.

The original Anchor brewery on Pacific Street was destroyed in the great earthquake of 1906.

Panil Barriquée Sour

Birrificio Panil
www.panilbeer.com

Country of origin Italy
First brewed 2002
Alcohol content 8% abv
Serving temperature 57°F, 14°C

Wine is in Renzo Losi's blood. His father was a wine producer, and the family still has a vineyard at Torrechiara near Parma. Losi himself was a wine producer for many years, but the love for beer finally won, and Birrificio Panil is now one of the most interesting microbreweries in Italy. Some of his beers really seem to have a connection to the world of wine.

Barriquée Sour is definitively one of these. It starts off as a normal dark ale but then is refined for months in old barrels. Losi starts with a wort obtained with different German malts, such as pils, caramel, and some chocolate. Hops are German Perle, for bitterness, and British East Kent Golding, added at the end for aroma. After the primary fermentation, the beer goes into the barrel, which is about fifty years old, and rests from five to eight months. During this time, the bacterial flora gives the sour flavor to the beer. **MM**

Tasting notes

Beautiful mahogany color. Fascinating nose, rich with wood, leather, and a hint of green lemon. On the palate, it is very complex, fresh but lightly astringent, with notes of sweet citrus.

Panil Enhanced

Birrificio Panil
www.panilbeer.com

Country of origin Italy
First brewed 2005
Alcohol content 9% abv
Serving temperature 50°F, 10°C

If a brewer deals with both wine and beer, as is the case with Renzo Losi, it's not easy to keep the two things separate. On the other hand, when interesting beers are produced as a direct result of a cultural contamination, why worry about keeping them separate?

Panil Enhanced does not go into wooden barrels or barriques. At the beginning of the process, and with regard to most of the ingredients, it is a straightforward beer that is easy to understand. The beer's backbone is pils and a small quantity of Munich malts, and two different hops are used: German Perle for bitterness and some Willamette added at the end of the boil and also used in dry hopping. The secret of this beer is the yeast that is used: Bajanus, which is normally used in wine production. It gives elegant aromas of muscat grapes, and, in Enhanced, is the touch that gives the aromatic profile to the beer. **MM**

Tasting notes

Golden and cloudy, with abundant white foam. Intriguing aroma, with notes of grape and apple. On the palate, it is very elegant, with a hint of pleasant acidity and a long, dry aftertaste.

Paradox

BrewDog
www.brewdog.com

Country of origin Scotland
First brewed 2007
Alcohol content 10% abv
Serving temperature 46°F, 8°C

When BrewDog emerged in 2007, it was very much like the appearance of a new rock band. However, behind the hype and the noise, co-founders Martin Dickie and James Watt possess serious beer brains.

According to Dickie, "The thinking behind the Paradox series was to utilize the enormous variance in flavor profile in Scotch whisky distilleries to create a wonderfully unique, flavorful beer series. These were the first beers in the U.K. to utilize a strong stout that was big enough to complement the powerful whisky flavors that leach from the oak during maturation." There are three "editions" in the Paradox series: Smokehead, whose Isle of Islay location produces smoky, seaweedy, and iodine notes; Isle of Arran, where the beer was matured in former sherry casks; and Springbank Distillery in Campbeltown. With the base beer a ravishingly strong imperial stout, these are seriously big beers. **ATJ**

Tasting notes
Springbank is black brown, with vanilla, buttery toffee, earthy hops, ripe strawberry, and alcohol on the nose. Mocha coffee and marzipan flavors before a lingering, wood-sweet finish.

Pliny the Elder

Russian River Brewing
www.russianriverbrewing.com

Country of origin United States
First brewed 1999
Alcohol content 8% abv
Serving temperature 55°F, 13°C

When Vinnie Cilurzo started Blind Pig Brewing in Temecula, California, in 1994, he conjured up a monstrously bitter beer. This was the start of the double IPA revolution. "Our equipment was pretty antique and crude, so I wanted to start out with something that was big and, frankly, could cover up any off flavors," Cilurzo says. He aged the beer on oak for nine months and served it on the brewery's first anniversary as Inaugural Ale. When he took it to the Great American Beer Festival, he described it as a double IPA.

Cilurzo continued to make the beer annually to celebrate Blind Pig's anniversary until he left to brew at Russian River Brewing. When he made Pliny the Elder for the first time in 1999, he used a totally new recipe, basically scaling up the one he used for Russian River IPA. He named the beer after the Roman scholar who created the botanical name for hops. **SH**

Tasting notes
Bright golden, with beautiful lacing. Aroma of hop cones, pine, and citrus. Hops hang on a clean malt backbone, providing abundant flavors, peppery notes, and pure bitterness.

Quarta Runa

Birrificio Montegioco | www.birrificiomontegioco.com

Country of origin Italy
First brewed 2005
Alcohol content 7% abv
Serving temperature 44°F, 7°C

Birrificio Montegioco's Riccardo Franzosi chooses fruits and spices to flavor his beer because those fruits and spices are found all around him in the Piedmont region of Italy. His beers reflect the territory, and there's always a logical path that he follows from the original idea to the final recipe. Quarta Runa is no exception to this rule. The name, like many of his beers, comes from his passion for local history. "Runa" is an ancient Celtic word and, indeed, Celts once inhabited the area.

Franzosi first produced Quarta Runa in 2005, after recognizing the excellent quality of Volpedo's peaches, a local historic variety of peach that is highly appreciated on the Italian market. The peaches are first washed and then de-stoned; Franzosi then makes a sort of jam from them to concentrate all the flavors and aromas. When this jam is cooled, it is added to the fermentation tank and, after a short while, the yeast is pitched in. The yeast—*Saccharomyces bajanus*—is mainly used for white and sparkling wines and, together with the peaches, adds to the distinctive value of the beer. Quarta Runa is a pleasant and delicate beer, with an intriguing aroma. Only pils malt is used, and just a small quantity of Hallertau Hersbrucker hops for bitterness and aroma. The beer ferments in tanks for around eight days, then rests elsewhere for two weeks at a low temperature.

At the end of this process, the beer finally reaches the bottle, where it develops the final fermentation and maturation, which usually takes about two months. It can also further develop in the cellar for another two to three years. **MM**

Tasting notes

Golden, cloudy color with a white foam that is not too persistent. Lots of immediate peach notes at the nose and then a light almond undercurrent. On the palate, a pleasant acidity is noticeable, and the aftertaste returns to the memory of the first aromatic impression.

Raison D'Être

Dogfish Head | www.dogfish.com

Country of origin United States
First brewed 1995
Alcohol content 8% abv
Serving temperature 46°F, 8°C

It's tempting to shrug off "extreme beer" as the unsubtle product of hop-and-alcohol crazed brewers seeking to push toward the uncharted edge of palatability. Double-digit alcohol content, triple-digit IBUs—it's territory colonized mainly by iron livers and leather tongues. There is another definition of "extreme," however, that has nothing to do with strength, and that is beer made with nontraditional ingredients. This is where adventuresome brewers leave behind the Reinheitsgebot and ransack the pantry. We're talking herbs, fruit, spices, coffee, honey, or, in the case of Raison D'Être, beet sugar and green raisins.

"That's the one we took a lot of flak for back when we started," says Sam Calagione, whose Dogfish Head Brewery's very slogan defines the extreme beer niche: off-centered ales for off-centered people. "People were saying, 'Putting grapes in beer? What the hell are you doing?'" In fact, Raison D'Être has its roots in wine. One of the earliest recipes at Dogfish Head's first brewpub in Rehoboth Beach, Delaware, it was designed as a substitute for the bottle of full-bodied red that one might otherwise pair with a grilled steak. The mahogany-hued ale's fruitlike flavor is a product of not only those raisins and sugar, but also its select roasted malts and Belgian yeast.

Initially attracting a cultlike following of beer geeks, Raison D'Être soon won praise from food writers and gourmet magazines, who compared it to a Burgundy that could take its place at the finest tables. This dark ale signaled the dawn of the new trend of beer as a legitimate substitute for wine. **DR**

Tasting notes

Poured into a tulip glass, it's dark reddish brown with a tight head, producing an aroma of raisins, caramel, and dark rum. Toffee notes on the first sip, followed by complex flavors of coffee, toffee, raisins, Burgundy, and lightly smoked malt.

Red Poppy Ale

The Lost Abbey | www.lostabbey.com

Country of origin United States
First brewed 2008
Alcohol content 5.5% abv
Serving temperature 55°F, 13°C

Consider these two statements from Tomme Arthur, the director of brewing at the Lost Abbey in California: "Perhaps the single most defining beer moment for me came when I experienced my first Rodenbach Grand Cru. It was a seminal moment, as I only then began to understand that beer could possess a range of flavors outside of bland and watery. The beer was ruby with brown highlights. It was at once sweet and sour, woody and dry. This beer was an epiphany for me." Then there is this: "For a while, people were trying to replicate the world styles, but I don't know that I ever set out to copy another beer."

Arthur could apply many of the same words he once used when talking about Rodenbach Grand Cru to describe his own Red Poppy Ale, but you wouldn't mistake one of those beers for the other. He also wouldn't have much reason to brew Red Poppy if you did. It is one of a dizzying number of sour beers the Lost Abbey has produced in its first three years of operation. Such was the pace of innovation that barrels quickly overflowed the original barrel room, filling up any available space in the rest of the brewery as well as spilling over into a storage facility nearby.

Red Poppy starts innocently enough with a blend of two beers, one of which is the award-winning dark mild called Dawn Patrol. It ages a year in French oak barrels, which are old enough that the oak character is muted. Then it is dosed with sour cherries—different sour cherries from those in Cuvee de Tomme—and then with what's become the proprietary Red Poppy yeast culture. The effect is magical. **SH**

Tasting notes

Lovely ruby and brown in the glass, with aromas of sour dark fruits apparent from the start. Sweet caramel and red fruit flavors are quickly met with tart sour cherries and pleasant notes of balsamic vinegar. With hints of wine, the oak and vanilla are subdued and delightfully complex.

Redoak Framboise Froment

Redoak Brewery | www.redoak.com.au

Country of origin Australia
First brewed 1994
Alcohol content 5% abv
Serving temperature 41°F, 5°C

It is quite possible that Australia has never known a brewer as prolific and relentless as David Hollyoak of the Redoak Brewery. At its peak, his small brewery was producing almost forty beers, almost all of them world-class examples of their style regardless of the country of origin or historic context. After being brewed in a secret, undisclosed location, they appear as though by magic in his Sydney beer bar and offer a perspective-changing experience that hints of genius.

Hollyoak did not waste any time learning his trade. He started brewing ginger beer in his home at the tender age of fourteen. His little brewery followed him into adulthood and was the cause of much tension among those who lived with him and did not fully appreciate his interest. His girlfriend was one such person. Despite being from Belgium, she did not enjoy beer and could not see the value of Hollyoak's equipment taking up so much of their kitchen. He responded by brewing her a raspberry wheat beer that not only won her affection but would also one day challenge the brewers of her homeland as a quintessential version of their own fruit beer.

The raspberries are sourced from a farm in the Yarra Valley, Victoria, that belongs to Hollyoak's cousin. About a handful per beer is used in the brewing, and stains can often be seen on Hollyoak's hands after he's been making the beer (and even more especially so after making a batch of Framboise Froment's cousin, the Blackberry Hefeweizen). The best place to have a glass is in the Redoak Boutique Beer Cafe, which is not far from the Sydney Opera House. **DD**

Tasting notes

Expect a striking pink color best highlighted in a champagne flute, and hints of bananas, cloves, and raspberries. A delicate sip should reveal fruit-infused wheat flavors followed by a considered, tart finish. Enjoy served with eggs Benedict at a Framboise Froment breakfast.

Riedenburger Historisches Emmer Bier

Riedenburger Brauhaus | www.riedenburger.de

Country of origin Germany
First brewed 2004
Alcohol content 5.5% abv
Serving temperature 46°–50°F, 8°–10°C

In the 1980s, Martha and Michael Krieger were part of the protest against the construction of the Rhine-Main-Danube Canal; they felt it would upset the ecological balance of the Altmühl Valley Nature Park. Although the protest did not prevent the canal, the movement helped to fire up the environmental awareness of people like the Kriegers. As a result, they decided to organize their Riedenburger brewery on more ecological lines and, in 1994, completed the conversion to an all-organic brewery. They also began to research older and more environmentally friendly cereals and discovered einkorn and emmer wheat, both of which bring low yields but many benefits for the environment. Emmer contains more proteins, magnesium, and iron than usual wheat and brings about a wonderfully mild, fruity flavor.

On the occasion of the first historic city festival of Riedenburg, the Kriegers brewed their first emmer ale, which went down well with the locals. The Kriegers included the beer in their portfolio, even though in the beginning there were not enough ingredients available. Together with the nearby monastery of Plankstetten, which provides the Kriegers with all their ingredients, they have overcome their supply problems and have been officially honored as substantial contributors to the revival of ancient crops.

Emmer Bier is remarkably creamy at first taste, offering a full fruity body and a surprisingly dry finish. It is made with natural hops whose tannins contribute to the prolonged stability. The beer is appreciated in many European countries and can be found in most parts of Germany, especially in whole food shops. **SK**

Tasting notes

Emmer Bier is hazy copper to brown, with a creamy beige head. A grainy, nutty aroma with hints of plums. On the palate, expect a creamy first taste evolving into a fruity body inspired by spicy yet decent aroma hop bitterness. Mild, surprisingly dry finish.

Rodenbach

Brouwerij Rodenbach | www.rodenbach.be

Country of origin Belgium
First brewed 1821
Alcohol content 5.2% abv
Serving temperature 43°–46°F, 6°–8°C

There are few beers capable of sharpening the palate as much as Rodenbach. What makes this Belgian classic so refreshing is its natural acidity, acquired from a long aging process in ancient oak tuns. Rodenbach is today part of Palm Breweries, but its origins lie in the 1820s, when a member of the influential Rodenbach family became a partner in a brewery in the West Flanders town of Roeselare.

The business has long been known as the world leader in the production of oak-aged, sour beer, and these days Rodenbach's red ale is brewed from a blend of three different malts and an addition of maize in a state-of-the-art brewhouse. The hops added to the copper are local, from Poperinge, but they are not fresh: the brewers are not looking for the flavor of hops but rather their preservative qualities. After primary fermentation, the beer is lagered for four weeks before being pumped into the Rodenbach cellars. A visitor to these vaults is met with an extraordinary sight: row after row of giant, wooden vessels, some dating back to 1830. The temperature here is set at a relatively balmy 59 degrees Fahrenheit (15°C), and the beer stays here for two years, during which time wild yeasts and microorganisms that live in the old tuns do their work, feeding off the oxygen that permeates the oak and turning the beer sour and acidic.

When you taste beer straight from the wood, it is shockingly tart, fruity, and earthy. It is also flat, so it needs to be blended with lively, young beer for bottling. Rodenbach is the "everyday" beer; for a more intense experience, there's Rodenbach Grand Cru. **JE**

Tasting notes

A ruby-colored beer with a distinctly tart, oaky, and acetic aroma of winey fruit. The taste cleverly combines sweetness and tartness, with winey fruit sharpening up smooth malt and an oaky dryness. The finish is also acidic, tart, and sweet, leaving more woody dryness.

Rodenbach Grand Cru

Brouwerij Rodenbach | www.rodenbach.be

Country of origin Belgium
First brewed *ca.* 1885
Alcohol content 6% abv
Serving temperature 43˚–46˚F, 6˚–8˚C

The Rodenbach family was once very famous in the world of Belgian and Flemish politics and literature. The family bought into a brewery in their hometown of Roeselare in 1821, and in 1836 the brewery became Brouwerij Pierre Rodenbach Wauters. Eugène Rodenbach studied brewing in England, and fate brought him to the English east coast, where in those days, the process of blending matured, cask-ripened beer with young, fermenting beer was still very much the rule. He brought this concept home, and a couple of years before his untimely death in 1889, Rodenbach was producing essentially blended beers.

Subsequent directors of the firm encountered difficulties with the cost of running such a venture and were forced to sell to a bigger Belgian regional, Palm, in 1998. Indeed, the Rodenbach beers are very costly to produce. A visit to the brewery will tell you why: row upon row of toweringly huge oak vats, which are indispensable for the complex mixed fermentation, fill large cellars and halls. They have to be maintained by skilled carpenters and other craftsmen—there's more to Rodenbach than just brewing.

The "ordinary" Rodenbach is a blended beer, and this is well known. What is less well-known is that the Grand Cru is also blended: one-third young and two-thirds matured beer. Like the classic Rodenbach, Grand Cru is filtered and pasteurized, and very discreetly chaptalized (sugar is added to unfermented wort in order to increase the alcohol content after fermentation). Remarkably, given the color of the beer, all malts are pale, rather than colored. **JPa**

Tasting notes

Brown with a burgundy shine under a dense, lacy head. Woody nose with lactic acid, black cherries, and Black Forest cake. Vinous taste, sharp notes of lactic and acetic acid, with some sweetness. Yet tart, even astringently dry. Fruity esters, but clean metallic in the palate.

Róisin

Williams Brothers Brewing Company | www.williamsbrosbrew.com

Country of origin Scotland
First brewed 2007
Alcohol content 4.2% abv
Serving temperature 46°F, 8°C

Alloa in Scotland was often referred to as the "Burton-on-Trent of the North" because of the preeminence of brewing in the town. It also had a heritage of producing varied and distinctive ales from some of the country's most notable brewing families, such as the Youngers, Calders, and Arrolls. At one time, eight breweries bubbled and boiled in the central Scotland town of barely 15,000 inhabitants, and much of its reputation rested on the output of the original 1810 Alloa Brewery. Nowadays, there is only one brewing establishment, the New Alloa Brewery owned by Bruce and Scott Williams, who have reinvigorated the sector while building a huge reputation for enterprise and innovation topped off with fine ale. The brothers' beers have secured an enviable position in their homeland's culinary heart.

Róisin (pronounced *row-sheen*) is a tayberry-flavored beer made from the distinctive fruit that grows in abundance in the fertile soil along the course of the River Tay in Perthshire, one of Scotland's premier salmon rivers. It is a hybrid of a blackberry and a raspberry, but it is much larger, sweeter, and more aromatic than its half siblings.

Belgian brewers in particular are masters at concocting fruit beers with flavors of raspberry, strawberry, and cherry, and the Williams brothers have come close to emulating them with Róisin (Gaelic for "red"). Each season, the berries are harvested by hand and frozen until required. Other wild Scottish ingredients used in the brothers' range include myrtle, meadowsweet, pine, and spruce. **AG**

Tasting notes

An interesting, full, fruit beer with red berry notes and a faint malt flavor anchoring the bittersweet tayberry. It is dusky pink in appearance, pouring brownish red. The dominant tayberry flavor is joined by traces of blackberry then followed by a malty sweetness.

Rosée d'Hibiscus

Brasserie Artisanale Dieu du Ciel!
www.dieuduciel.com

Country of origin Canada
First brewed 2006
Alcohol content 5% abv
Serving temperature 41°F, 5°C

Looking at the exclamation mark that the founders of the Dieu du Ciel! brewpub in Montréal elected to place at the end of the company's name, one might guess that they knew their brewery was destined for greatness. In fact, it was more for emphatic effect, and it is meant to be taken in the sense of how one might exclaim "God in Heaven" upon receiving a surprise—such as a beer flavored with hibiscus flowers. Indeed, the brewpub has delighted in surprising its patrons with unusual, interesting, and occasionally outrageous brews.

Brewer Jean-François Gravel has shown a deft hand with almost all the styles he touches, but particularly so with unusual ingredients. Rosée d'Hibiscus is a delicate ale flavored with the petals of hibiscus flowers. The flower petals provide not only a pinkish color, but also a slight acidity that dries the wheat beer and gives it an added element of refreshment. **SB**

Tasting notes
Floral nose, but the citrusy notes from the wheat add extra dimensions. The acidity, soft fruitiness (melon, lychee), and whispers of grain give the body a multifaceted character.

Route des Épices

Brasserie Artisanale Dieu du Ciel!
www.dieuduciel.com

Country of origin Canada
First brewed 2002
Alcohol content 5% abv
Serving temperature 46°F, 8°C

The casual observer could be forgiven for thinking the Dieu du Ciel! brewpub to be little more than a neighborhood local, such is its modest size, street corner location in the residential Plateau de Montréal, and general lack of airs. Brewer Jean-François Gravel is quiet and unassuming, and might go entirely unnoticed as he sits at the bar, watching the crowds as they enjoy, appreciate, and, at times, marvel at his latest twist of the brewing arts.

Gravel crafts classics out of ingredients that arguably have no place in beer, such as the black peppercorns that add to the remarkable aroma and trademark spiciness of Route des Épices. He says that he managed to hit the right proportions of both rye grain and peppercorns in his very first test brew of the ale, something any brewer will tell you should not logically have occurred. **SB**

Tasting notes
The aroma offers fragrant black pepper mixed with notes of cocoa and light, dried fruit. In the body, the pepperiness initially subsides, replaced by a mocha and caramel maltiness.

Sam Adams Utopias

Boston Beer
www.samueladams.com

Country of origin United States
First brewed 2001
Alcohol content 27% abv
Serving temperature 59°F, 15°C

There are many people who will insist that Utopias is not a beer: 27 percent alcohol content, the strong, liquorlike flavor and body of a fine cognac, not even a single bubble of carbonation. Jim Koch, chief executive of Samuel Adams, smiles at the doubters and replies, "I know it's beer because I have to pay a nickel deposit on the bottle in Massachusetts."

Utopias is essentially made like any other beer, albeit with an insane amount of barley plus maple syrup that produces a wort whose gravity is an unheard-of 48 degrees Plato. The alcohol is produced completely by yeast fermentation, the company says—no distillation or added spirits. It's then aged in a variety of barrels, including bourbon, Madeira, and brandy, and blended with previous batches dating to 1994. Each vintage differs, but it is generally sweet and malty with vanilla and caramel notes. **DR**

Tasting notes

Strong, aromatic notes of caramel, hazelnut candy, and maple syrup. Intended for measured sipping, it crosses the tongue with a thin, oily coat of complex sweetness and languid alcohol.

Schäazer Rogg'n

Brauerei Drei Kronen
www.kronabier.de

Country of origin Germany
First brewed 2009
Alcohol content 5.5% abv
Serving temperature 46°F, 8°C

Rye ales are rare in Germany, and Josef Lindner, brewmaster of Drei Kronen brewery, had no experience with the ingredient. He consulted his maltster and a rye-experienced brewer and developed a recipe based on a minimum of 50 percent rye malt and some wheat and barley malts. He mashed them with the two-step decoction method that had proved to be successful with his wheat beer. Furthermore, he used the same efficient yeast that he adds to his award-winning weizenbock. When Lindner tasted the beer during the second fermentation, he became skeptical. The extra "something" was missing.

Luckily, he figured out what that something was. By increasing the compression of the tanks, he improved the carbonation. After bottling, the yeast made an unforeseen extra effort, and the result was remarkable. The first batch sold out within three weeks. **SK**

Tasting notes

The nose is sweet, reminiscent of honey and tropical fruits, with a touch of grain. The palate experiences a fluffy carbonation. Spicy flavors like clove or nutmeg lift the fruity body.

Shangrila

Birrificio Troll | www.birratroll.it

Country of origin Italy
First brewed 2003
Alcohol content 8.5% abv
Serving temperature 46°–50°F, 8°–10°C

Troll first opened as a restaurant in 1983, situated in a beautiful location up in the mountains near the French border. It was owned and run by a couple of brothers, one of whom worked as a cook and was said to resemble a troll, hence the name of the establishment.

In 2003, Troll became a brewpub after being bought by Alberto Canavese, who brought in brewers Daniele Meinero and Andrea Bertola to help him complete the transformation. There was a sense of adventure in the brewing, which would eventually lead them to experiment with aging beers. They started with a couple of beers: the Belgian-style witbier Panada, and Shangrila, a beer that again looked to Belgium for inspiration, although with a twist, as Himalayan spices play a central role. The use of these spices led to the name of the beer, as it was inspired by the mountain utopia described in *Lost Horizon* by James Hilton, a place full of peace and happiness.

The spices in this beer are three different kinds that are used commonly in Indian cuisine—pepper, cinnamon, and star anise—which might make the recipe seem a little bit crazy. However, the skill of the brewers has produced a perfectly balanced beer. Six different malts and English hops are also used in this complex and rich brew. Another version of this beer is the Shangrila Fumé—brewed with peated malt, typical of Scottish distilleries, and with fewer spices and hops than normal. The beers served at Troll are always matched with food, and this is why Shangrila Fumé was created: there was a need for a beer that was good enough to be matched with barbecued meat. **ES**

Tasting notes

Amber in color with a persistent and creamy foam. The nose is rich with clear notes of spices. In the mouth, Shangrila is warm, spicy, and velvety, with a pleasant sweetness. Not to be served too cold, it is perfect with stewed meat or with salami.

Siamese Twin Ale

Uncommon Brewers | www.uncommonbrewers.com

Country of origin United States
First brewed 2008
Alcohol content 8.5% abv
Serving temperature 50°F, 10°C

The aptly named Uncommon Brewers are fast making a name for themselves by taking traditional styles and turning them on their heads, utilizing all-organic ingredients and unconventional flavorings. Inspired originally by Belgian-style dubbels, in 2002, they began playing with a number of different spices; for example, Indian coriander, which is a variety that has more prominent citrus notes than hot spices.

One nontraditional ingredient used in Siamese Twin Ale is lemongrass, which is grown on a neighboring organic establishment. Its official name is *Cymbopogon*, and it consists of about fifty-five species of grasses native to India and the Far East. Another unique ingredient is Kaffir lime leaves, an aromatic flavoring often used in Thai cuisine. This type of lime is a rough, bumpy fruit with distinctively shaped leaves. It is not currently grown in Northern California, so the brewery is trying to find a farmer who is willing to start growing it, as the climate there is similar to its native Thailand.

Like all the beers produced by the Uncommon Brewers, Siamese Twin Ale is 100 percent organic. The owners felt that by starting a new brewery in the green-conscious San Francisco Bay Area, they had to make a commitment to working with organic ingredients, despite the limitations that this brings with regard hop varieties and malts. In spite of these hurdles, the brewery is obviously on to a winner with Siamese Twin Ale: the beer won big in the first competition that it entered, taking first place at the National Organic Brewing Challenge in 2008. **JB**

Tasting notes

Hazy orange in color with a massive ivory head. The nose is fresh fruit, spicy, and sweet. With a creamy mouthfeel, it's as unusual as it is delicious; the lemongrass and Kaffir lime leaves are an excellent foil for the sweetness of this classy Belgian-style dubbel.

Smokin' Bishop

Invercargill Brewery | www.invercargillbrewery.co.nz

Country of origin New Zealand
First brewed 2007
Alcohol content 7% abv
Serving temperature 46°–50°F, 8°–10°C

Outside of Ireland, there can be few breweries whose best-selling beer is a stout, but this is the case with Invercargill Brewery. Mind you, the brewery is in New Zealand's southernmost city, and the beer, a robust, chocolaty stout called Pitch Black, is ideal fortification against the southerly winds that regularly blast their way up from the Antarctic. The brewery's owner, Steve Nally, began brewing twenty-five years ago when he responded to a magazine advertisement for home-brewing supplies. "I asked Dad if we could give it a crack, which we did, and it tasted like rubbish," he recalls candidly. "This didn't deter me . . . While in a supermarket, I discovered a box of hops and found recipes for beer on the back; I bought a large tin of Maltexo (malt extract), went home, brewed up some beer, and this time it tasted great!"

Since first firing its kettle in 1999, the brewery has gone from strength to strength, and today, Nally is regarded as one of the rising stars of New Zealand's craft brewing scene. Nally's diverse beer range includes a hoppy English-style pale ale, a so-called "honey pilsner," and an intriguing seasonally brewed wheat beer flavored with boysenberries. But the brewery's most celebrated brew is Smokin' Bishop, New Zealand's first smoked beer.

Designed by Nally's apprentice Pru Bishop, the inspiration for Smokin' Bishop came from the malty bock beers of Bamberg in Bavaria, where local brewers still malt over fire. However, while the German brewers cure their malts over beech wood from local forests, Nally uses wood from native Manuka trees. **GG**

Tasting notes

Pours a lustrous, reddish amber hue beneath a tan-colored head. The aroma is reminiscent of bacon cooking on a bonfire. The palate begins sweet with hints of caramel and licorice, then there's a piquant, lingering, spicy smokiness that suggests Lapsang souchong tea.

St. Peter's Fruit Beer (Grapefruit)

St. Peter's Brewery | www.stpetersbrewery.co.uk

Country of origin England
First brewed 1997
Alcohol content 4.7% abv
Serving temperature 43°–46°F, 6°–8°C

The phrase "never judge a book by its cover" certainly applies to St. Peter's. What at first appears to be an old farm conceals a modern, custom-built brewery. The distinctive bottle shape might seem like nothing more than a cool piece of contemporary design, but it is in fact a replica of an 18th-century bottle. And what might at first appear to be a gimmicky, fruit-flavored beer is also much more historic.

Ever since beer first touched the lips of our Mesopotamian ancestors, humankind has been chucking all kinds of fruits, herbs, and spices into beer to make it taste nice—and St. Peter's is not shy when it comes to experimenting with nature's bounty. Grapefruit beer is one of the earliest St. Peter's beers, created by the first brewer Richard Eyton-Jones, who brewed a trilogy of fruit beers, including Lemon and Ginger, and Elderberry. The brewery has also experimented with an Apple and Cinnamon Ale, but these have all since fallen by the wayside. Only the Grapefruit beer remains, and it is a hugely successful example of the style.

St. Peter's own Bavarian-style wheat beer is used as a base for the fruit, which is added as an infusion toward the end of fermentation. The bitterness provided by the addition of the zesty, pithy grapefruit is remarkably hoplike, which doesn't make it an odd combination at all and actually extenuates the citrus character of the hops. The delicate balance between bitter fruit and bitter hops makes this a very grown-up fruit beer, lacking any of the sickly sweetness found in some other examples of the style. **ST**

Tasting notes

Fresh and floral with a citrus, undeniably grapefruit character. Combined with the tropical fruit flavors from the wheat beer, this makes for an enormously refreshing drink. Ideal with curries and spicy foods, yet also suitable for drinking with hot puddings and citrus desserts.

Supplication

Russian River Brewing | www.russianriverbrewing.com

Country of origin United States
First brewed 2005
Alcohol content 7% abv
Serving temperature 55˚F, 13˚C

Seats at the bar in the Russian River brewpub in Santa Rosa, California, look into a room where beers age in wine barrels, aided and abetted by both fruit and wild yeast strains. A sign that once belonged to the New Albion Brewery (the United States's first post-Prohibition microbrewery) hangs above the glass window. Nothing seems out of place. Co-owners Natalie and Vinnie Cilurzo—who operate both the brewpub and a nearby production brewery—love Pinot Noir wine, but Vinnie brews beers that are cherished for their hop flavor and bitterness.

Cilurzo had already aged a beer that he called "Temptation" in chardonnay barrels with a single strain of *Brettanomyces* wild yeast before he created Supplication. He picked Pinot Noir barrels for the next experiment because of his passion for this wine. He decided to add more varieties of wild yeast, plus 25 pounds (11 kg) of cherries in each barrel because "we were trying to take the next step, and still just exploring." Supplication spends twelve to fifteen months in barrels. "It probably has the cherry and barrel flavor after about nine months but will be lacking acidity," Cilurzo says.

Some drinkers compare the resulting beer with a Belgian-brewed lambic, although it does not ferment spontaneously like lambics. However, Cilurzo and his friend Tomme Arthur (brewmaster at Lost Abbey Brewing) hit on a way to spontaneously ferment beer in California. At Russian River, this beer is called "Beatification" and it is yet another one aging in barrels behind the big glass window. **SH**

Tasting notes

Pours the color of a not-quite-ripe cherry, with an off-white head. Sour cherries and ripe grapes on the nose, supplemented by raspberry and strawberry notes, and smokiness; an incredibly complex nose. On the palate, fruit flavors are balanced by tart acidity and oak tannins.

Surly Coffee Bender

Surly Brewing | www.surlybrewing.com

Country of origin United States
First brewed 2006
Alcohol content 5.2% abv
Serving temperature 55°F, 13°C

You'd think that uplifting caffeine and somnambulistic alcohol would be incompatible rivals, but that is not the case with Surly Brewing's Coffee Bender. To create the coffee-infused beer, Surly brewers start with Bender, their flagship oatmeal brown ale. Using Belgian and British malts, they give Bender cocoa, coffee, caramel, and hints of vanilla and cream. Oatmeal adds a velvety smoothness and rounds out the beer.

They then take the base Bender beer, 20 gallons (75 l) at a time, and cold-press it for twenty-four hours in ground coffee beans from the Vinca Vista Hermosa plantation in Guatemala. This process removes a portion of the acidity, giving it less bite and smoother flavors. Surly's brewers developed this unique cold-extraction process to give Coffee Bender "intense coffee aromatics." The beer is meant to be similar to an iced coffee and is designed to be as aromatic as a bag of whole beans.

The brewery name comes from a trip that founder Omar Ansari and his wife Becca took to the beer haven of Portland, Oregon, in 2005. While discussing the issue of bars with poor beer selections, the question was posed: "How do you feel when you go into a bar and there is no good beer?" Becca came up with the reply: "You get surly, and say, 'Let's go to another bar that cares about decent beer.'" And that's how the brewery became surly, too. Surly Brewing was founded on that idea, defining it as "the anger fueled by the inability to find good beer." Since 2006, they've been doing their level best to make sure that doesn't happen in any place where their beer is served. **JB**

Tasting notes

Coffee Bender is deep amber brown in color with a fluffy tan head. The nose is redolent of fresh roasted coffee and sweet malt. Thick with coffee flavor, it's surprisingly drinkable and well balanced, with sweet toffee, caramel, and vanilla notes, and just a touch of hops in the finish.

Survival "7-Grain" Stout

Hopworks Urban Brewery | www.hopworksbeer.com

Country of origin United States
First brewed 2008
Alcohol content 5.3% abv
Serving temperature 50°F, 10°C

Survival "7-Grain" Stout is like a Swiss Army knife; it could be all you need to endure just about any situation. "The concept for Survival Stout is that it's everything you need to survive in one bottle," says Hopworks Urban Brewery's Ben Love. "We took the idea that beer is 'liquid bread' one step further."

In addition to common beer ingredients such as barley, wheat, and oats, Hopworks Urban Brewery uses the ancient grains amaranth, quinoa, spelt, and kamut in Survival Stout. Love remarks that brewers usually try to avoid adding high amounts of protein to their beers because it can make the beer too foamy. But because Survival Stout also includes a healthy shot of strong coffee in each bottle, the proteins are a plus. "Most coffee beers have little or no head, because of the oils from the coffee," he says. "I think the complex proteins from the grains actually help this beer have incredible foam stability, even with the coffee."

The coffee addition is a labor of love for the brewers. They start by adding pounds of coffee to filtered water in each of three buckets. The coffee is left in a cooler for four days to cold brew, and then strained through a fine mesh bag to remove the grounds. The resulting very strong coffee is then bubbled with CO_2 to remove any oxygen before being added to the stout during filtration. The seven ancient grains provide needed nutrients. The alcohol level in the beer makes you happy and mellow, but is low enough to keep you quick on your feet. And a shot of strong coffee helps you stay focused. Survival Stout might just be your Armageddon beer. **LMo**

Tasting notes

Roasted grains and coffee aromas give way to a semisweet chocolate creaminess that enters the dance with additional layers of strong java. It ends with a clean, smooth finish and a slight suggestion of pleasant bitterness that leaves you wanting more.

Temptation

Russian River Brewing | www.russianriverbrewing.com

Country of origin United States
First brewed 2000
Alcohol content 7.2% abv
Serving temperature 55°F, 13°C

Temptation was the first Russian River beer that Vinnie Cilurzo aged in wood and also fermented with a wild yeast strain, but this pioneer has been followed by many others. "It started with the idea [that] I wanted to make a blond barrel-aged beer," Cilurzo says. "I love Belgian lambics, so I decided to take one component of lambic (the wild yeast) and do that in this beer. The idea of extracting some of the wine flavor (from the barrels) happened on its own." He had only recently settled on the idea of making an entire series of "-ation" beers, taking their inspiration from those brewed in Belgium. At the time, Korbel Champagne Cellars in Guerneville, California, owned Russian River Brewing. Cilurzo and his wife Natalie have since bought the brand and started their own brewpub and brewery.

The first batch of Temptation filled two wine barrels and aged for more than a year. Cilurzo added a single wild strain of *Brettanomyces* to the barrels along with the beer. Today, he defines a batch as sixty wine barrels, and long ago started adding other varieties of wild yeast, enhancing the acidity and complexity of his barrel-aged beers.

The number of "-ation" beers in the series has increased. The first was Damnation, a golden beer often compared with Duvel. Previously, Cilurzo had brewed the beer at home, but needed a name for it. He was driving back from work one evening when a song titled "Hell" by the band Squirrel Nut Zippers came on the radio. In the song, the Zippers spell out "damnation." "I instantly knew we could do a whole line of '-ation' beers," he said. **SH**

Tasting notes

Golden in the glass, with an abundance of tight bubbles. Initial white grape and citrus (particularly pineapple) aromas are followed by earthy, musty, wild notes. More of the same on the palate: orchard fruits blending with grapes, oak, and vanilla to the fore. Crisp, acidic finish.

Thornbridge Alliance

Thornbridge Brewery | www.thornbridgebrewery.co.uk

Country of origin England
First brewed 2007
Alcohol content 11% abv
Serving temperature 50°–52°F, 10°–11°C

The name of this remarkable beer refers to the coming together of the brewers from Thornbridge with Brooklyn Brewery's Garrett Oliver, although it may also be a nod toward the alliance between the barleywine and the sherry and Madeira casks in which the brew is aged.

Since it started brewing in 2005, Thornbridge's young brewing team has been heavily influenced by the fresh ideas coming from U.S. craft brews. Thornbridge was one of the pioneers of wood aging, whereas Oliver had always been interested in brewing an old British ale. He brought the recipe (and the Brooklyn yeast); Thornbridge's Stef Cossi provided the brewery, Thornbridge yeast, and Maris Otter barley, as well as Hallertau Magnum, East Kent Golding, and Marynka hops, and the wooden barrels.

The team will never forget brewing day—and not just because Cossi keeps meticulous records. Brewing required a second mash to get the strength and volume that the brewers wanted. The next day, fermentation was so vigorous that the yeast was spouting like a geyser from the fermenters. It was then conditioned for eighteen months before being finished in Pedro Ximénez casks or Madeira casks for a further three months. Each of the variants was bottled with champagne yeast and added sugar.

Early reviews proclaimed it to be one of the best beers in the world. Within months, the brewery had sold out, but it's likely that bottles will be changing hands for years to come. This is a beer that will continue to improve with age—and the asking price is bound to reflect this. **PB**

Tasting notes

For the 2008 vintage, the base beer sees strong orange fruitiness vying with butterscotch and caramel maltiness and a thick, warming, alcohol thread. The casks add oak, vanilla, and wine, with dried fruit in the sherry and nutty fruitiness in the Madeira.

Three Philosophers

Brewery Ommegang | www.ommegang.com

Country of origin United States
First brewed 2003
Alcohol content 9.8% abv
Serving temperature 50˚F, 10˚C

What is your ideal beer? A hoppy British ale? An aromatic German hefeweizen? An Oregon home-brewer named Noel Blake sat down a number of years ago and pondered this question for a "Create a Great Beer" contest. For him, the matter of one's ideal beer is not simply about style or even ingredients; it's really a philosophical question whose answer can be debated endlessly. It's a question, Blake imagined, that might have stymied the three philosophers of the poet William Blake's 18th-century dramatic satire *An Island in the Moon*. The home-brewer's essay won the contest and ultimately led to the creation of a dream beer.

Three Philosophers is a strong ale, a Belgian-style quadruppel. According to brewer Phil Leinart, it is the only one of Ommegang's highly regarded, Belgian-inspired ales that is brewed without the addition of spices. Instead, it is flavored with a small amount of kriek, the cherry-flavored lambic from Belgium. Leinart won't disclose who makes the kriek, but he does say that it's an authentic, commercially available lambic. The brand is of little consequence, because the flavor of cherry is just one of the multitude of players in this masterpiece. It's largely spirited by very dark caramel malt and Ommegang's house yeast, which produces contemplative aromas of chocolate, raisins, and coffee.

Is this the ideal beer? It's a question that William Blake's three philosophers might have tackled. The Epicurean, the Cynic, and the Pythagorean, the English poet wrote, sat together "thinking of nothing." At nearly 10 percent abv, this ale would have the same happy effect on anyone. **DR**

Tasting notes

Pours a deep, winelike ruby with a nose of roasted malt, dark fruits, vanilla, sweet and sour cherries, coffee, currants, brandied raisins, and chocolate. Exceedingly smooth on the palate, never cloying. Finishes warm with an assertive but comfortable alcohol blast.

Timmermans Framboise Lambic

Brouwerij Timmermans-John Martin | www.anthonymartin.be

Country of origin Belgium
First brewed *ca.* 1980
Alcohol content 4% abv
Serving temperature 43°–46°F, 6°–8°C

The distinctive sour taste and horse-blankety aroma of lambic divides the beer-drinking community and often provides a shock to those who first taste it. However, lambic also makes an undeniably good base for Belgian fruit beers such as this.

Based in Itterbeek in the Senne Valley, where all true lambic beers are made, Timmermans Brewery has been successfully making lambic since 1781. Today, under the watchful eye of brewmaster Jacques Van Cutsem, Timmermans produces a range of fruit beers with a distinctive lambic character. As well as Framboise, there is a traditional Kriek and a not-so-traditional Pêche, made using peach juice.

Timmermans's lambic base is made from an old wheat beer recipe. Hops are added, but only after they have been aged for two to three years; they impart a very gentle bitterness but are mostly to protect the beer from undesirable infections. The all-important airborne yeasts penetrate the wort during the cooling and start the spontaneous fermentation. Next, the beer is transferred to oak casks in the maturing room. After maturing for six months, the beer is known as "young lambic" ("old lambic" has to be matured for two to three years). Whole ripened raspberries are added, and the sugars and natural yeasts kick-start another period of fermentation, and the beer is left to mature for a further six to ten months. Then, and only then, the transformation is complete. The sour beer with an acquired taste has been transformed into a pink, sparkling, raspberry aperitif. It's a classic Cinderella story (only with beer). **ST**

Tasting notes

An elegant beer with the dryness of pink champagne. Smooth, crisp, and intensely raspberrylike. Any excess sweetness is tempered by the lambic tartness, with a pleasantly dry, almondy finish. Serve in a champagne tulip. Ideal as an aperitif or with dessert.

Tokyo*

BrewDog | www.brewdog.com

Country of origin Scotland
First brewed 2009
Alcohol content 18.2% abv
Serving temperature 54°–57°F, 12°–14°C

It's illustrative of the difference between British and U.S. beer cultures that a craft beer that wouldn't have raised too many eyebrows in the United States had a motion proposed against it in the Scottish Parliament. The most talked-about British beer of 2009 alarmed many with its 18.2 percent strength. Those who believe that beer can only be drunk in pints seemed to genuinely believe that this limited run of 3,000 bottles, retailing at $15.99 (£9.99) for 11 ounces (330 ml), posed a significant threat to the nation's health.

As is usual in any moral panic, the protesters made their case without having tried this complex imperial stout. BrewDog, the leading British exponents of wood-aging beer, raised their game with Tokyo*. Brewed with Maris Otter, dark crystal, caramalt, and chocolate malts, and roast barley, and flavored with Galena hops, jasmine, and cranberries, the beer is then heavily dry hopped and aged on French toasted oak chips.

Appropriately enough for a brewery in Scotland, tasting the beer is closer to drinking a fine malt whisky than anything else. It's impossible to do anything with this beer other than savor a small amount, slowly. It's sad, though inevitable, that strength became the main talking point, because there are very few beers in the world that have this depth of character and push the edges of what beer can be to such an extent. Tokyo* is a beer that begs to be drunk with the ripest, smelliest cheese you can find—few other foods have a hope of standing up to it. But the beer will mature and improve for at least a decade, offering future flavor sensations that even the brewers can only guess at. **PB**

Tasting notes

A dark ruby stout with powerful aromas of whisky, alcohol, treacle, and hints of resiny hops and fresh woodiness. A strong initial hit of vanilla gives way to cherries, cream, and chocolate with a satisfying, drying earthiness toward the finish.

Upstream Gueuze-Lambic

Upstream Brewing Company | www.upstreambrewing.com

Country of origin United States
First brewed 2005
Alcohol content 6.5% abv
Serving temperature 44°F, 7°C

"Omaha" is a Native American word that translates as "upstream" or "against the current." At first, the idea of a brewery in Nebraska making barrel-aged Belgian-style ales sounds a little like swimming against the flow, but on tasting Upstream's unique ales, beer lovers are realizing that Flanders might not be that far away.

Founded in 1996, Upstream operates two popular brewpubs in Omaha. Its draft offerings feature the brewpub standards you would expect, such as pale ale, blond ale, and wheat beer. They also make the interestingly named Bugeater Root Beer. However, it is the special bottlings of Belgian-style and barrel-aged beers that set them apart from the pack.

Oud bruin, Flanders red ale, lambic, geuze, gose, and Berliner weisse are all styles that fit into the sour beer category. These ales have an acidic sourness that would in most beers be considered a major defect. For the makers of sour ales, the presence of *Lactobacillus*, *Brettanomyces*, or *Pediococcus* yeasts in a brewhouse is not the cause for concern it would be elsewhere—they are positively welcomed.

Upstream first brewed its Geuze-Lambic in 2005 to launch a barrel-aging program after the arrival of twenty former Cabernet Sauvignon French oak barrels at the brewery. To create the Geuze-Lambic, a Belgian wheat beer is fermented with a variety of wild Belgian microflora, the actions of which impart a sour character in this beer. Each year, fresh wheat beer is added to the ale to tone down the sourness a touch. Typically, eighteen months to two years may go by between the brewing and bottling of this ale. **RL**

Tasting notes

Pours a cloudy orange amber in the glass, producing a robust head that persists throughout. An immediate citrus and woody aroma emerges. The assertive mouthfeel surrounds taste buds with tart, sour flavor notes. Hints of oak, citrus, honey, and slight earthy qualities.

The Vine

Cascade Brewing | www.raclodge.com

Country of origin United States
First brewed 2006
Alcohol content 9.2% abv
Serving temperature 46°F, 8°C

Despite what some might think, The Vine is not a Belgian-style sour ale. Cascade Brewing's brewmaster Ron Gansberg prefers to call it—and all of its popular sour beers—"Northwest-style sour ale." The name references the Pacific Northwest region of the United States. "Starting out, our beers were inspired by the beers of Belgium," Gansberg says. "As our first sour beers came to market, we were calling them 'Belgian Style Red' and such, but over time our beers have taken on their own flavor and style. . . . Our beers are made in the Pacific Northwest and reflect our conception of sour ales—individual and distinct from other beers and other regions."

The area where Cascade Brewing is located is also a well-known and highly respected wine-making region. The Vine is the result of Gansberg's interest in the concept of marrying a beer with the juice of an American white wine grape varietal through the process of fermentation. It took the brewery two years to develop a spiced Belgian blond ale that became the base for The Vine. For the grape juice, nearly 500 pounds (227 kg) of white wine grapes are picked by hand and then pressed on-site at the brewery. The fresh juice is added to the barrel-aged beer and fermented in stainless steel for three months.

Gansberg, who worked in wine cellars before becoming a brewer, blends soured tripels, blonde quadrupels, and golden ales with the base beer to create The Vine. It then spends more than six months of lactic fermentation and aging in small oak barrels before it is ready to be released. **LMo**

Tasting notes

Surprisingly crisp and effervescent for a higher alcohol beer, The Vine offers a pleasantly tart, vinous quality that gives way to a slight vanilla sweetness. This beer is a marriage of both wine and beer that would please fans from either camp.

Wells Banana Bread Beer

Wells & Young's | www.wellsandyoungs.co.uk

Country of origin England
First brewed 2002
Alcohol content 5.2% abv
Serving temperature 50°–54°F, 10°–12°C

Banana isn't the first ingredient that springs to mind when you think about beer, but many an inquisitive ale drinker has been pleasantly surprised when they've taken a chance on Wells Banana Bread Beer. This fruity ale, launched in 2002 by Charles Wells Brewery (as it was then known) and created by brewmaster Jim Robertson, was added to their range of beers in an attempt to attract younger customers. This is no alcopop, however. It is a genuine thoroughbred bitter, the sort of thing you would expect from a 130-year-old company steeped in tradition. Today, Wells and Young's is the largest independently owned, family-run brewery in the United Kingdom.

When tasting Banana Bread Beer, the sweet smell is the first thing to hit you: fresh, clean, and very reminiscent of natural bananas. However, when it comes to drinking it, the nutty banoffee aroma takes a back seat to the lightly sparkling hoppy bitter. It's a taste combination that has to be experienced to discover just how well these flavors work together.

The inclusion of "bread" in the title comes from the Saxon phrase for beer—"liquid bread"—from a time when beer was safer to drink than water. It is made using high-quality ingredients—peppery Golding and Challenger hops, crystal malt, and water drawn from the brewery's own well sunk through a limestone and chalk hill in the middle of the English countryside. The bananas that are pulped and added to the mash are all Fair Trade Certified. The brew is then left to ferment for seven days to allow the banana flavor to completely infuse through the beer. **JM**

Tasting notes

A silky, crisp, and rich amber-colored ale with a fluffy head and strong banana note on the nose. Its strongly hoppy bitterness has underlying notes of toffee and sweet banana and a dry tangy finish. It is crisp and refreshing on the palate as well.

Wheat Wine Ale

Smuttynose Brewing | www.smuttynose.com

Country of origin United States
First brewed 2005
Alcohol content 11.4% abv
Serving temperature 46°F, 8°C

If barleywine is strong ale made with an ample helping of barley, what is wheat wine? Where the typical American barleywine presents a challenging mouthful of roasted malt and bitter hops, this wheat wine, created by Smuttynose brewer David Yarrington, is seductive, luring the palate with soft notes of vanilla and fruit.

Phil Moeller of California's Rubicon Brewing generally gets the credit for inventing the wheat wine–style in the late 1980s. A few other West Coast breweries—Marin, Lagunitas, and Steelhead—toyed with it over the years. But it was Yarrington of New England's Smuttynose Brewing who brought the style east and bottled what may be the defining version. "Defining" though, was problematic from the start.

Federal authorities rejected Smuttynose's first attempts to label its novel ale as wheat wine because it's not actually wine: "wheat wine," the feds said, would "confuse and mislead the consumer." The first batch sat around for a year, conditioning and mellowing in naked bottles till Yarrington finally convinced the authorities that his brew was legitimate. The result was a singularly smooth, delicately balanced strong ale that likely will never be repeated.

Nonetheless, each year's edition is remarkable for its complex array of gentle aromas that seem to carry an otherwise heavy, high-alcohol beer on their shoulders. There are few commercial examples of the style, but Smuttynose's excellence helped convince the Great American Beer Festival to recognize wheat wine as an official judged category. **DR**

Tasting notes

Lacking the familiar hoppy aromatics of an American barleywine, it's the malt of this hazy pink and burned-orange hybrid that shines on the nose. After the first sip, which is silky and sensual on the palate, a complex swirl of vanilla and apricot emerges.

Wisconsin Belgian Red

New Glarus Brewing Co. | www.newglarusbrewing.com

Country of origin United States
First brewed 1995
Alcohol content 5.1% abv
Serving temperature 37°–43°F, 3°–6°C

In 1985, New Glarus brewer and co-owner Dan Carey was serving as an apprentice in the well-respected Ayinger Brewery, south of Munich in Germany. According to his wife and business partner Deb, they took a road trip to Belgium. Although he was pursuing the strict discipline of lager brewing at the time, "Dan was totally enamored with spontaneous fermentation and fruit in beer." This began a quest that spanned several states and many trial batches, "sometimes with messy results," until the right approach was found. The beer became a real motivation. "His cherry beer was a lot of the reason I believed we should start our own brewery," says Deb. New Glarus has turned into a sizeable craft brewery, so successful in its home state that there's none left for anyone else. You'll have to go to Wisconsin to get your hands on it.

There are plenty of fruit beers about, but the cost and difficulty of using good fresh fruit keep most of them pretty timid. This one makes no compromises: with a pound of fruit in every bottle, it screams "cherries" from its ruby depths to the top of its pink foam. The brew begins with a spontaneously fermented brown ale. Luxurious amounts of Door County Montmorency sour cherries are added, and the resulting creation is aged in wooden tanks before being packaged in bottles that have been hand-dipped in cheesemakers' wax. The wild fermentation is not just a novelty; the acidity of the sour ale is needed to bring the fruit to life and give the beer a pleasant sweet-sour balance. Wisconsin Belgian Red is the most awarded fruit beer in the United States. **RM**

Tasting notes

On the nose, spicy Montmorency cherry pie aromas blend with slight cinnamon and earthy tinges. It is sharp and puckery on the palate, brightening the fruit. Underneath is a serious Belgian-style sour brown ale, bringing winelike depth. Finishes dry, fruity, and clean.

Xyauyù

Birrificio Baladin | www.birreria.com

Country of origin Italy
First brewed 2003
Alcohol content 13.5% abv
Serving temperature 57°–61°F, 14°–16°C

Xyauyù is the name given by Italian craft brewer Teo Musso's daughter to her imaginary friend, and it's no surprise that he adopted this word to name what is probably his most imaginative beer. It is also very difficult to define, bridging as it does the worlds of wine and beer—Musso has described it as an "Italian-style barleywine." Definitions, in this case, are not so important. Xyauyù is the perfect demonstration of how wide the borders of beer can be. Many, on first tasting it, are ready to swear that the drink is not a beer. Yet, malted barley, yeast, hops, water, and a few teaspoons of sugar are its only ingredients. The secret is in the brewing process.

It was in 1996 that Musso first thought of trying to create an oxidized beer that was similar to Madeira, although it wasn't baptized until 2003. The wort is initially boiled for a longer time than is normal in order to obtain a very dense liquid; then a particular yeast from an Islay distillery—the same as in Elixir—is added. The primary fermentation is difficult, slow, and very long, usually thirty or forty days; then the temperature is lowered to 32 degrees Fahrenheit (0°C) and kept at that point for another three months. The filtration is carried out, and, finally, the beer rests in an open tank and in a sterilized room for between fourteen and eighteen months. Finally, it is kept in bottle for a further five to six months.

The next batch of Xyauyù will be ready in 2010 and will only consist of around 7,000 bottles, but its unique aromas and flavors make it a genuine "must have" for every beer hunter in the world. **MM**

Tasting notes

No foam at all, but the color is reminiscent of a dark amber. Very complex, fascinating aroma rich with dates, figs, tropical fruits, and a hint of salty soy sauce. On the palate, it is smooth, silky, and very close in character to a Madeira or a Vino Santo.

YSPRID Y DDRAIG

6.5% ABV

6.5% ABV

THE BRECONSHIRE BREWERY

Ysprid y Ddraig

Breconshire Brewery
www.breconshirebrewery.com

Country of origin Wales
First brewed 2003
Alcohol content 6.5% abv
Serving temperature 54°–57°F, 12°–14°C

Breconshire Brewery was born in 2002 when Welsh drinks distributor Howard Marlow bought a brew kit and began looking for a brewer. Justin "Buster" Grant heard about the opening and decided to stop by after attending a friend's wedding in the area. The minute he stepped through the door, he was greeted with the phrase, "Nice to meet you, when can you start?" Buster left his job at Brakspear Brewery on the Friday and started at Breconshire the following Monday.

Buster has developed a core range of award-winning beers for Breconshire Brewery, but inspiration for Ysprid y Ddraig struck while enjoying a glass or two of a whisky that had been matured in an ale cask. Buster acquired a whisky cask from a local whisky company and filled it with the brewery's Golden Valley Extra Ale, then left it to mature for St. David's Day. The five firkins of Ysprid y Ddraig disappeared remarkably quickly—so swiftly, in fact, that Grant only had a small taste himself—and he felt it a good idea to brew the beer again. He bought and filled more whisky casks, and now each batch is aged in a different oak, including Bowmore. Ysprid y Ddraig is a seasonal beer, only brewed in very limited quantities for occasions such as St. David's Day on March 1. The name means "Spirit of the Dragon" in Welsh—and a spirited beer it is indeed. **MC**

Tasting notes

On the palate, there are slight medicinal notes up-front, which develop into kirsch-soaked cherry flavors with a burned-toast edge. It finishes cleanly with a flinty, mineral edge.

Žatec Xantho

Žatecký Pivovar
www.zateckypivovar.cz

Country of origin Czech Republic
First brewed 2007
Alcohol content 5.7% abv
Serving temperature 48°F, 9°C

Hops are not only addictively aromatic and delicious in beer, they have also been used in folk medicine for millennia. In 2006, the Czech Research Institute of Malting and Brewing experimented with Lady Beer, a brew that capitalized on the phytoestrogens that are present in hops. The target audience was women going through menopause who suffer health problems due to reduced estrogen levels.

Although Lady Beer never made it to market, the next year saw the arrival of a similar idea, Xantho from Žatecký Pivovar. Xantho, however, is not your typical, extremely bitter hop bomb. Developed in conjunction with the Žatec Hop Institute, the beer includes higher amounts of xanthohumol and isoxanthohumol, two antioxidant flavonoids from hops that are believed to offer significant health benefits, including a reduction in oxidative stress, the stabilization of cholesterol levels, and possibly reversing the effects of osteoporosis in menopausal women.

The possible health benefits in Xantho seem to arrive without making any difference to its flavor or aroma. Brewed to an original gravity of 14 degrees Plato, it is a strong dark beer with a typical Czech dark lager's rich molasses and burned-bread notes in the mouth, followed by a touch of licorice in the finish. Its hop presence is surprisingly refined. **ER**

Tasting notes

Very moderate carbonation and a long-lasting sandy head of densely packed foam. Despite its chemistry, the bitterness levels are moderate, with a primary aroma of licoricelike malt.

← A Welsh dragon for a Welsh beer: Ysprid y Ddraig.

Glossary

Abbey Ale
Beers with a monastic brewing heritage, although now often produced under license by secular brewers.

ABV
Alcohol by volume—the percentage of alcohol in a finished beer.

Adjuncts
Additions to the mash, such as wheat flour, rice, corn, maize, or sorghum; these are usually employed for reasons of cost or to make a beer lighter in body.

Ale
The name derives from the Anglo-Saxon *ealu*, which was originally a malted alcoholic drink with added herbs and spices to clarify, season, or preserve it. Up until the introduction of hops to Britain, the words "beer" and "ale" were interchangeable. Afterward, "beer" came to mean just the hopped variant.

Alpha Acid
The component in the hop that produces bitterness. The higher the alpha acid, the more bitter the hop.

Alt
The top-fermented, cold-conditioned beer of Düsseldorf, which is amber or copper in color.

Aroma Hops
Hops that are low in alpha acids and added to the boil in the latter stages to impart flavor.

Attenuation
The degree to which fermentable sugars are changed into alcohol and carbon dioxide by yeast during fermentation. The more attenuation, the drier and stronger the beer.

Barley
A cereal crop whose grain is part germinated and kilned. This produces malted barley, which is used in the first step in brewing.

Barleywine
Strong, warming ale that appeared in the United Kingdom at the end of the 19th century.

Beer
Derived from the Anglo-Saxon word *beor*, the term "beer" was interchangeable with "ale" until the appearance of hops. "Beer" denotes a beverage produced by fermented grain, chiefly malt, which has been hopped.

Bière de Garde
The beer of northern France, once brewed on farms and packaged in champagne-style bottles, usually amber in color and over 6 percent abv.

Bitter
Top-fermenting beer that emerged at the end of the 19th century in the United Kingdom and was mainly sold on draft in pubs, where it is still best enjoyed.

Bittering Hops
Hops high in alpha acids that give bitterness to the beer. They are added at the start of the boil. Also called "copper hops" and "kettle hops."

Bock
Strong, bottom-fermented, lagered beer that supposedly has its origins in the northern German brewing town of Einbeck. Doppelbock is a stronger version, which is occasionally superseded by the even more powerful Eisbock.

Bottom Fermentation
Fermentation that takes place at a low temperature, with yeast sinking to the bottom of the vessel. Generally used for lagers and also known (perhaps more accurately) as "cold fermentation."

Brown Ale
As the name suggests, dark amber or chestnut in color; those of northern England tend to be stronger than their sweeter counterparts in the south.

Burtonization
A brewing process that began in the 19th century in which mineral salts similar to those found naturally in Burton-on-Trent's local water are added to the brewing liquor by other brewers eager to replicate Burton's beers.

Cooper
The person who makes and repairs the wooden casks in which beer has traditionally been kept. A rarity today.

Copper
Brewing vessel in which the wort is boiled and hops and other flavorings are added. Also called the kettle.

Decoction Mashing
The method of mashing used for lager brewing where some of the wort is taken out, heated up, and added back to the mash. Supposed to help with converting starch into malt sugar.

Dortmunder Export
Bottom-fermented lagered beer that is drier, slightly stronger, and less bitter than the average pilsner or Helles; was once popular with the industrial workers of Dortmund but is a style that is harder to find and define these days.

Double IPA
Stronger, hoppier version of India Pale Ale.

Dry Hopping
The practice of adding a handful of hops (or hop pellets) to beer in the cask.

Dubbel
Darker version of an abbey ale, usually 6 to 7 percent abv.

Dunkel
Dark wheat or lagered beer.

Esters
Volatile flavor compounds produced by the work of the yeast on fermenting beer. They often produce a fruity complexity in both aroma and taste.

Extreme Beer
American craft brewing phenomenon that is represented by brewers experimenting with techniques as diverse as wood-aging beer, using triple amounts of hops, or adding various combinations of fruit, vegetables, and spices in the mash tun. The brewing equivalent of BASE jumping.

Framboise/Frambozen
Raspberry-flavored lambics or oud bruin beers; a mainstay of Belgian beer.

Geuze
A blend of young and older lambic, which produces a sprightly champagne-like freshness; different spellings refer to the French (geuze) and Flemish (gueuze) variations.

Gose
Top-fermenting wheat beer with spices and salt in the mix, a speciality of Leipzig.

Grist
Crushed or milled barley malt ready to be mashed.

Helles
The Bavarian answer to pilsner, a fresh-tasting golden beer with a soft maltiness.

IBU
International Bittering Units, a scale that measures the bitterness of beer.

Imperial Stout/Porter
Extra strong versions of stout and porter, with the latter famously being exported from the United Kingdom to imperial Russia at the end of the 18th century.

India Pale Ale
Beer that is heavily hopped and high in alcohol to withstand the journey from Britain to India by sea. First brewed in the 19th century, it found fame in the Indian Raj and has been expertly revived in recent years.

Kellerbier
German beer that is served unfiltered straight from the cellar.

Kilning
The process where the partially germinated malt is dried in massive malting kilns.

Kölsch
Gold-colored beer that is produced with top-fermenting yeast in and around the city of Köln.

Kräusen
The process that takes place during lager maturation (or lagering) where partially fermented wort is added to the brew to boost the secondary fermentation.

Kriek
Lambic that has had cherries added.

Lager
General term for a whole family of bottom-fermenting beers that have been matured (lagered).

Lagering
Period of maturation for lager (in German, *lager* means "to store"). Supposed to have originated in 15th-century Bavaria when beers were stored in cool caves where the lower temperature encouraged a slower fermentation.

Lambic
Spontaneously fermented beer whose traditional home is in the Pajottenland area around Brussels.

Märzen
Beer originally brewed at the end of the brewing season in March and tapped in September; darker in color than Oktoberfest beers.

Mash
Process where milled malt is steeped in hot liquor in a mash tun for the purpose of extracting fermentable sugars. This is aided by sparging (or spraying) the mash with hot water to get out all of the fermentable sugars. Mainly used in British brewing.

Mild
Lightly or mildly hopped ales that are mainly dark in color.

Old Ale
Beers brewed for the winter months, which were matured for some time and developed vinous traits; more modern interpretations are called "winter warmers," which are sweeter.

Original Gravity
Unit of measurement of the strength of a beer, based on the amount of dissolved fermentable malt sugars present in the wort after the mash has taken place. Water is defined as having an original gravity of 1,000, so a beer with an original gravity of 1,040 (the usual amount for ordinary bitter) is approximately 4 percent denser than water.

Oud Bruin
Flemish beers that receive long periods of aging, usually in oak casks, also known as "Old Brown."

Pale Ale
Originating in the late 19th century, the name comes from the practice of using pale malts in the grist. In the United Kingdom it usually refers to bottled beers, though it has been revived by U.S. craft brewers to mean amply hopped (though not as much as IPAs) beers.

Pasteurization
Treating filtered beer with heat for the purpose of killing off any remaining yeast cells. Once beer is brewed, it can be left to continue its secondary fermentation or it can be filtered and pasteurized before being bottled, canned, or kegged.

Pilsner
Pale, bottom-fermenting beer with subtle, spicy hop notes.

Session Beer
Beer that is not too strong in alcohol (usually between 3.6 and 4 percent abv), which enables drinkers to have several pints without getting drunk.

Steam Beer
Traditionally a bottom-fermenting beer that was matured at ale temperatures.

Stock Ale
Strong beer that was traditionally brewed to be aged and used for blending with younger and weaker beers.

Stout
After porter, stronger versions were called "stout porters," and the dark beer style has since taken on a life of its own; various permutations include Irish dry stout, milk stout, and oatmeal stout.

Top Fermentation
Fermentation that takes place at 59–68 degrees Fahrenheit (15–20°C). Not all sugars are fermented, which results in a fruitier, sweeter beer than those that undergo bottom fermentation. Also known as "warm fermentation."

Trappist
Beers produced at seven Trappist monasteries, six of them in Belgium and one in Holland.

Tripel
Blond and high in alcohol, with Westmalle's Tripel often seen as the model.

Contributors

Andrew Arnold (AA) is based in Copenhagen. He has fifteen years' experience writing for food and drink publications and worked at Carlsberg as a PR consultant for six years. He writes about the history of lager in the United Kingdom at www.lager-frenzy.com.

Zak Avery (ZA) was the British Guild of Beer Writers Writer of the Year for 2008. He runs one of the best beer shops in the United Kingdom and shares his passion via his blog, Are You Tasting the Pith?, at www.thebeerboy.co.uk.

Stephen Beaumont (SB) has been writing about beer and other liquid pleasures for longer than he cares to admit. A frequent contributor to any number of North American magazines, he is also the author of six books and overseer of www.worldofbeer.com.

Jay R. Brooks (JB) has been writing about beer for nearly twenty years. He's the former general manager of the *Celebrator Beer News* and currently writes a syndicated column, "Brooks On Beer," which appears in newspapers throughout the United States.

Pete Brown (PB) is the author of several best-selling books including *Hops and Glory: One Man's Search for the Beer that Built the British Empire*. He travels the world in search of great beer and blogs at www.petebrown.blogspot.com.

Melissa Cole (MC) is one of the United Kingdom's leading beer experts, with ten years' experience of writing about brewing, pubs, and the hospitality industry. She has also judged at some of the world's leading beer contests.

Charles D. "Chuck" Cook (CC) is a freelance writer who lives in the United States. He has visited nearly 100 Belgian breweries and over 200 beery cafés during nineteen trips to "The Beer Country." He is currently working on his own book about Belgium's beer culture.

Des de Moor (DdM) is one of the United Kingdom's leading experts on bottled beer. Since 2002, he has written the regular bottled beer review column and occasional features for the Campaign for Real Ale's magazine, *BEER*.

David Downie (DD) is one of Australia's leading beer commentators and has written about beer and beer culture since the late 1990s. He is a founder of AustralianBeers.com and a partner in a major law firm.

John Duffy (JD) lives in Dublin and blogs about the beer scene in Ireland and abroad at thebeernut.blogspot.com. He is an administrator of Ireland's main online resource for beer and brewing: www.irishcraftbrewer.com.

Jeff Evans (JE) has edited eight editions of the Campaign for Real Ale's *Good Beer Guide* and has written seven editions of the *Good Bottled Beer Guide*. He has been judged Beer Writer of the Year by his colleagues in the British Guild of Beer Writers. More of Jeff's work can be found at www.insidebeer.com.

Alastair Gilmour (AG) is one of the United Kingdom's sharpest beer writers. A multi-award winner, he writes regularly in newspapers and specialist publications. He has contributed to two best-selling books and judged beer events in cities across the world.

Simon Gray (SG) is a freelance writer and music playlist designer for restaurants and bars. Based in Hertfordshire, his specialist fields are travel, music, and food and drink.

Geoff Griggs (GG) Beer Hunter Michael Jackson wrote, "I first met Geoff Griggs over pints of Fuller's, in our neighborhood local in west London. Now he is a tireless and fastidious reporter of the New Zealand brewing scene."

Tim Hampson (TH) has one of the best jobs in the world—he is paid to drink beer for a living. A regular writer and broadcaster on beer, he travels the world in pursuit of the perfect drink.

Bryan Harrell (BH) is a Tokyo-based beer writer with a wide knowledge of the Japanese craft beer scene. He publishes a newsletter on beer in Japan at www.bento.com/brews.html.

Stan Hieronymus (SH) has traveled the United States many times over while writing about beer. He is the author of seven books, including *Brew Like a Monk* and *Brewing With Wheat*. He comments regularly at his website, www.appellationbeer.com.

Andrew Howitt (AH) is a well-traveled freelance journalist, translator, and beer writer specializing in South American beers. Andrew spends much of his time in Brazil exploring the emerging craft beer scene there.

Sylvia Kopp (SK) is a freelance beer writer. She holds a Diploma as beer-sommelier from Doemens Academy, a brewing school near Munich, gives sensory trainings and tastings, and judges beers in international contests such as the World Beer Cup (United States) and European Beer Star (Germany).

Rick Lyke (RL) has written for numerous publications, including *All About Beer*, *DRAFT*, *Cigar Aficionado*, and the *Brewing News* regional brewspapers. His blog, Lyke2Drink, covers beer, wine, and spirits. Lyke founded the Pints for Prostates (www.lyke2drink.com/pints) campaign.

Maurizio Maestrelli (MM) is an Italian food, wine, and beer journalist. He is a regular contributor to many magazines, including *Gambero Rosso*, *Il Mondo della Birra*, and *De Vinis*. In 2006, he was elected

Best Beer Journalist by Unionbirrai, the Italian Association of Craft Beer Producers.

Jamie Middleton (JM) is a freelance writer who lives in Bath, England, with his wife and one-year-old son. With over a decade's experience in critiquing bars and restaurants, he particularly enjoys reviewing alcoholic beverages.

Lisa Morrison (LMo) loves to "talk beer" and has done so in person, in print, on the radio, and on TV for over a dozen years. Known as "The Beer Goddess," she reminds us that "every beer has a story."

Randy Mosher (RM) has been writing about beer since 1989 and is the author of *The Brewers Companion* (1991), *Radical Brewing* (2004), and *Tasting Beer* (2009). Randy is a member of the faculty of Chicago's Siebel Institute.

Laurent Mousson (LM) is a French-speaking Swiss with a long-lasting love of British ales. He has been involved in the European Beer Consumers' Union for over a decade.

Larry Nelson (LN) is editor and publisher of *Brewers' Guardian*, the international brewing industry magazine; and, from late 2005, editor and publisher of *The Brewery Manual and Who's Who*, the authoritative annual guide to the United Kingdom's alcoholic drinks trade.

Werner Obalski (WO) is a freelance journalist and writer who covers spirits, beer and wine. In 2008, he published books about sherry and tequila and contributed to *The Beer Book*.

Chris O'Brien (CO) is the author of *Fermenting Revolution: How To Drink Beer and Save the World*. He is Director of Sustainability at a U.S. university by day and blogs at BeerActivist.com by night.

Michael Opalenski (MO) has liked beer ever since happening upon a home-brewing kit in Pollenzo, Italy, while attending the University of

Gastronomic Sciences. His passion fermented and matured, leading to his graduate thesis. Today he works in the industry with a U.S. beer importer.

Ron Pattinson (RP), bon vivant and archive junkie, haunts the Internet with his pub guides and blog. Lager, AK, gose, mild, Barclay Perkins, and dragging his kids around pubs are his main obsessions. He lives in Amsterdam.

Joris Pattyn (JPa) is a renowned commentator on fine beers and has judged brewing contests worldwide. Flemish born, he has also contributed to various publications on beer.

Jeff Pickthall (JP) founded the legendary beer bar Microbar in London in 2001. He later worked for Utobeer at London's Borough Market and helped to set up their bar, The Rake.

Evan Rail (ER) is based in Prague. He is the author of the *Good Beer Guide: Prague and the Czech Republic* and a writer on beer and travel throughout Europe. He has a nearly unquenchable thirst for lambic and geuze.

Don Russell (DR) is better known as Joe Sixpack, beer reporter for the *Philadelphia Daily News*, where his weekly column appears. He is an author, speaker, elbow-bender, ink-stained newsman, and two-time American Beer Writer of the Year.

Tom Sandham (TS) is an award-winning writer who has contributed to and edited leading drink industry magazines. He has also written for national newspapers and magazines and is co-author of the *Good Beer Guide: West Coast USA*.

Conrad Seidl (CS) is a Vienna-based writer. He has regular columns on beer in *Getränkefachgroßhandel* and *Falstaff* and is regularly published in German and American magazines, including *All About Beer* and *Brewer's Guardian*. He is the founder of Kampagne für Gutes Bier and the editor of *Conrad Seidl's Bierguide*.

Eugenio Signoroni (ES) graduated with a degree in Gastronomic Sciences in 2008 and worked on the *Italian Beer Guide 2009*. He has also worked with *The World of Fine Wine* magazine and assisted guidebooks and restaurants as a consultant and cook.

Stefania Siragusa (SS) was born in Torino, Italy, and is a graduate of the University of Gastronomic Sciences. She writes about gastronomy for Italian magazines and collaborates with the international journal of *Haute Cuisine Apicius*, published by Montagud Editores (Spain).

Joe Stange (JS) is a freelance journalist living in Brussels. Along with brewer Yvan De Baets, he is co-author of *Around Brussels in 80 Beers*, published by Cogan & Mater (www.booksaboutbeer.com). Joe is a former Associated Press reporter and hails from Springfield, Missouri.

Adrian Tierney-Jones (ATJ) is an award-winning freelance journalist. He started off working for the rock music press, but these days it's beer, brewing, and pubs that gets him up in the morning. Author of several books, and contributor to many magazines and newspapers, he scours the United Kingdom and Europe in search of beer.

Sally Toms (ST) was editor of *Beers of the World* magazine from 2006 to 2009. She is a regular judge in the World Beer Awards and enjoys writing about beer almost as much as drinking it.

John Westlake (JW) is an award-winning member of the British Guild of Beer Writers. He has visited every continent where beer is brewed and over 150 individual countries in search of interesting and unusual beer styles.

Rafal Zakrzewski (RZ) is one of the founders of AustralianBeers.com. He holds a doctorate in law from Oxford University and works as a solicitor with Clifford Chance.

Index of Beers by Brewery

Brasserie Pietra
Pietra 227

Brasserie Silenrieux
Sara 797

Brasserie Silly
Scotch Silly 256

Brasserie St.-Feuillien
St.-Feuillien Triple 496

Brasserie Theillier
La Bavaisienne 168

Brasserie Thiriez
Etoile du Nord 372

Brasserie Trois Dames
La Semeuse Espresso Stout
901
Trois Dames IPA 523

Brasseries Fischer
& Adelshoffen
Adelscott 30

Brasseries Kronenbourg
Premier Cru 228

Braucommune Freistadt
Freistädter Rotschopf 126

Brauerei Altenburger
Altenburger Schwarze 620

Brauerei Aying
Ayinger Ur-Weisse 560
Celebrator 653

Brauerei Bischofshof
Bischofshof Zoigl 61

Brauerei C. & A. Veltins
Veltins 534

Brauerei Clemens Härle
Clemens Ohne Filter 88

Brauerei Drei Kronen
Schäazer Kronabier 253
Schäazer Rogg'n 925

Brauerei Drummer
Dunkles Vollbier 108

Brauerei Felsenau
Bärni Dunkel 628

Brauerei Friedrich Gutmann
Gutmann Hefeweizen 577

Brauerei Ganter
Wodan 295

Brauerei Gebrüder
Maisel
Maisel's Weisse 590

Brauerei Göller
Göller Kellerbier 381

Brauerei im Füchschen
Füchschen Alt 127

Brauerei Kneitinger
Kneitinger Bock 718

Brauerei Locher
Hanfblüte 145
Naturperle 437
Schwarzer Kristall 800
Vollmond Bier 538

Brauerei Michael Plank
Dunkler Weizenbock 674

Brauerei Pinkus Müller
Original Alt 446
Pinkus Special 464

Brauerei Rosengarten
Einsiedler Lager Hell 370

Brauerei Schlenkerla
Aecht Schlenkerla Rauchbier
33

Brauerei Schleswig
Asgaard Das Göttliche
46

Brauerei Schönram
Altbayrisch Dunkel 39

Brauerei Schumacher
Schumacher Alt 254

Brauerei Schwechat
Schwechater Zwickl 488

Brauerei Spezial
Spezial Rauchbier 266

Brauhaus Faust
Faust Kräusen 376

Brauhaus Hartmannsdorf
Goedecke's Döllnitzer
Ritterguts Gose 886

Brauhaus Schweinfurt
Advents-Bier 311

Brauhaus Sebastian Riegele
Commerzienrat Riegele Privat
351
Riegele's Weisse 598

Brauhaus Sternen
Wartmann's No. 2 Bitter Ale
541

Braumanufaktur Forsthaus
Tenplin
Potsdamer Stange 466

Breconshire Brewery
Ysprid y Ddraig 945

BrewDog
Paradox 915
Punk IPA 470
Rip Tide 788
Tokyo* 937

Brewer's Art, The
Green Peppercorn Tripel 887

Brewery Ommegang
Ommegang Abbey Ale 773
Three Philosophers 935

BridgePort Brewing
Company
BridgePort India Pale Ale 72
BridgePort Old Knucklehead
73

Brooklyn Brewery
Black Chocolate Stout 638
Brooklyn Lager 75
Brooklyn Local 1 335
Brooklyner-Schneider Hopfen-
Weisse 568

Broughton Brewery
Broughton Old Jock Ale 77
Broughton Scottish Oatmeal
Stout 650

Brouwerij 3 Fonteinen
3 Fonteinen Oude Gueuze
Vintage 848
3 Fonteinen Oude Kriek
848

Brouwerij Bavik
Petrus Aged Pale 455
Petrus Oud Bruin 779

Brouwerij Boon
Boon Oude Geuze 859
Boon Oude Geuze Mariage
Parfait 860

Brouwerij Bosteels
Deus 360
Pauwel Kwak 223
Tripel Karmeliet 522

Brouwerij Contreras
Tonneke 280

Brouwerij Corsendonk
Corsendonk Agnus Tripel 353

Brouwerij De Glazen Toren
Jan de Lichte 587
Saison D'Erpe-Mere 477

Brouwerij De Koninck
De Koninck Amber 96

Brouwerij de Leyerth
Urthel Hop-It 531
Urthel Samaranth 287

Brouwerij De Molen
Borefts Stout 644
Hemel & Aarde 707

Brouwerij de Ranke
Guldenberg 386
Kriek De Ranke 896
XX Bitter 549

Brouwerij De Ryck
Special De Ryck 265

Brouwerij der Abdij van
St. Sixtus
Westvleteren Abt 12° 294

Brouwerij der Trappistenabdij
De Achelse Kluis
Achel Blond 8° 310
Achel Bruin Bier Extra 29

Brouwerij Girardin
Girardin Gueuze 1882 885

Brouwerij Het Anker
Gouden Carolus Christmas
695
Gouden Carolus Classic 696
Gouden Carolus Hopsinjoor
383

Brouwerij Huyghe
Delirium Tremens 358

Brouwerij Malheur
Malheur 10 426
Malheur 12 733
Malheur Bière Brut 426
Malheur Dark Brut 734

Odell Brewing Company
5 Barrel Pale Ale 22
90 Shilling 25
Cutthroat Porter 658
Odell IPA 442

O'Hanlon's Brewery
O'Hanlon's Port Stout 762
Thomas Hardy's Ale 275

Okells
Doctor Okell's IPA 363
Okells Aile Smoked Celtic
Porter 764
Okell's Mac Lir 594

Olde Mecklenburg Brewery
OMB Copper 217

Olivaria Brewery
Olivaria Beloe Zoloto
595
Olivaria Porter 772

Orkney Brewery
Dark Island 663
Red MacGregor 237
Skull Splitter 262

Oskar Blues Brewery
Dale's Pale Ale 94

Ostfriesen Bräu
Ostfriesenbräu Landbier
Dunkel 219

Otley Brewery
Otley O1 449
Otley O8 450

Otter Brewery
Otter Head 220

Oy Sinebrychoff
Sinebrychoff Porter 805

Ozeno Yukidoke Beer
Ozeno Yukidoke IPA 451

Pabst Brewing
Pabst Blue Ribbon 452

Paulaner Brauerei
Paulaner Nockherberger
454
Paulaner Salvator 222

Pausa Café
P.I.L.S. 462
Tosta 823

Pelican Pub & Brewery
India Pelican Ale 158
Kiwanda Cream Ale 408

Penn Brewery
St. Nikolaus Bock Bier 809

Perła Browary Lubelskie
Perła Chmielowa 455

Phillips Brewing Company
Amnesiac Double IPA 314
Phillips Original IPA 456

Pike Brewing Company
Pike IPA 458
Pike Monk's Uncle Tripel Ale 459

Pilsner Urquell
Pilsner Urquell 462

Pink Elephant
Mammoth 185

Pivovar Broumov
Opat Bitter 444

Pivovar Chodovar
Chodovar Zámecký Ležák
Speciál 348

Pivovar Eggenberg
Eggenberg Dark Lager 111
Eggenberg Pale Lager 369

Pivovar Herold
Bohemian Wheat Lager 567
Herold Bohemian Black
Lager 709
Herold Bohemian Blond 388

Pivovar Hlinsko
Rychtář Premium 475

Pivovar Jihlava
Jihlavský Grand 402

Pivovar Kaltenecker
Brokát Dark 648

Pivovar Kocour Varndsorf
IPA Samuraj 158

Pivovar Kout na Šumavě
Koutská Desítka 410
Koutská Nefiltrovaná
Dvanáctka 410
Koutský Tmavý Speciál 18° 722

Pivovar Krušovice
Krušovice Černé 724

Pivovar Náchod
Primátor Double 24% 782
Primátor Exklusiv 16% 230
Primátor Polotmavý 13%
231
Primátor Weizenbier 597

Pivovar Ostravar
Ostravar Premium 448

Pivovar Pernštejn
Pardubický Porter 778

Pivovar Rambousek
Eliščino Královské 13° 877

Pivovar Regent Bohemia
Regent Prezident 331

Pivovar Štramberk
Troobacz, The 828

Pivovar Svijany
Svijanský Rytíř 506

Pivovar U Fleku
Flekovský Tmavý Ležák 13°
687

Pivovar Vyskov
Jubiler 402

Pivovar Žamberk
Žamberecký Kanec Imperial
Stout 844

Pivovarna Union
Union Temno Pivo 833

Pivovarský Dum
Štěpán Pale Lager 496

Pivovarský dvůr Chýně
Chýně Rauchbier 87

Pivovarský dvůr Dražlč
Lipan Světlý Ležák 421

Pivovarský dvůr Zvikov
Zvíkovský Rarášek 611

Pivovary Staropramen
Staropramen Granát 266

Pizza Beer Company
Mamma Mia! Pizza Beer
904

Plevna Brewery
Plevna Imperial Stout Siperia
780

Plzeňský Prazdroj
Master Polotmavý 191
Velkopopovický Kozel 534

Port Brewing Company
Hop-15 892

Porterhouse Brewing Company
Porterhouse Oyster Stout 781
Wrasslers XXXX Stout 841

Privatbrauerei Bolten
Boltens Ur-Alt 67

Privatbrauerei Erdinger Weissbräu
Erdinger Dunkel 682
Erdinger Pikantus 683

Privatbrauerei Ernst Barre
Barre Alt 51

Privat-Brauerei Heinrich Reissdorf
Reissdorf Kölsch 473

Privatbrauerei Hoepfner
Hoepfner Maibock 152
Hoepfner Porter 713

Privatbrauerei Vitzthum
Einhundert 100 Bitterpils 369

Privatbrauerei Waldhaus Johannes Schmid
Waldhaus Diplom Pils 540

Proefbrouwerij
Beersel Lager 318

Propeller Brewing Company
Propeller Extra Special Bitter
232
Propeller IPA 233

Purple Moose Brewery
Snowdonia Ale 493

Pyramid Breweries
Snow Cap 264

Pyraser Landbrauerei
6-Korn Bier 24

RCH Brewery
East Street Cream 109
Old Slug Porter 770

Red Duck
Red Duck Porter 784

Stone Brewing
Arrogant Bastard Ale 45
Stone IPA 499
Stone Ruination IPA 500
Stone Smoked Porter 812

Stoudt's Brewing Company
Fat Dog Stout 686
Stoudt's Pils 502

Stralsunder Brauerei
Störtebeker Schwarzbier
    813

Sudbrack Brewery
Eisenbahn Dunkel 679
Eisenbahn Kölsch 370
Eisenbahn Pale Ale 112

Surly Brewing
Surly Coffee Bender 931
Surly Furious 271

Švyturio Alaus Darykla
Švyturys Baltas 605
Švyturys Ekstra 507

Švyturys-Utenos Alus
Utenos Alus 533
Utenos Porteris 834

Taybeh Brewing Company
Taybeh Beer Golden 511

Teignworthy Brewery
Martha's Mild 737

Terrapin Beer Company
Big Hoppy Monster 59
Terrapin Rye Pale Ale 512

Thai Beverage Plc
Chang 346

Theakstons
Old Peculier 768

Theresianer
Theresianer Strong Ale 274

Thomas Creek Brewery
Deep Water Doppelbock
    Lager 665

Thornbridge Brewery
Thornbridge Alliance 934
Thornbridge Bracia 819
Thornbridge Jaipur 513
Thornbridge Kipling 515
Thornbridge Saint Petersburg
    820

Three Boys Brewery
Three Boys Wheat 606

Three Floyds
Alpha King 38
Dark Lord 664
Gumballhead 576
Robert the Bruce 790

Timothy Taylor
Timothy Taylor's Landlord 278

Tommyknocker Brewery
Tommyknocker Butthead
    279

Traquair House Brewery
Traquair House Ale 282
Traquair Jacobite Ale 826

Trebjesa Brewery
Nikšićko Tamno 755

Tröegs Brewing
Mad Elf Ale 181
Troegenator Double Bock 283

Trumer Privatbrauerei
Trumer Pils 524

Tsingtao Brewery
Tsingtao 525

Tuatara Brewing
Tuatara Indian Pale Ale 284

Tullibardine Distillery
1488 Whisky Beer 850

Twisted Hop, The
Enigma 681

**Two Brothers Brewing
    Company**
Cane and Ebel 81
Domaine DuPage 99

Two Metre Tall Company
Forester Pale Ale 123
Huon Dark Ale 715

U Medvídku
X-Beer 33° 299

**Uerige Obergarige
    Hausbrauerei**
Uerige Alt 284
Uerige DoppelSticke 830

Uncommon Brewers
Siamese Twin Ale 927

Unertl Weissbier
Unertl Weissbier 609

União Cervejeira
Super Bock Stout 817

Unibroue
Blanche de Chambly 563
Éphémère (Apple) 879
Maudite 191
Terrible 818
Trois Pistoles 826

United National Breweries
iJuba Special 893

Upstream Brewing Company
Upstream Gueuze-Lambic 938

Ursus Brewery
Ursus Black 833

Victory Brewing
Victory Golden Monkey 536
Victory HopDevil 288
Victory Prima Pils 537
Victory Storm King Imperial
    Stout 837

Viking Brewing Company
Big Swede 632

Wadworth
Wadworth 6X 290

Weissbrau Unertl
Bio-Dinkel Weisse 563

**Weisses Bräuhaus
    G. Schneider & Sohn**
Aventinus 624
Aventinus Weizen-Eisbock 625
Schneider Weisse 600

Weitra Bräu Bierwerkstatt
Hadmar 143

Wellington County Brewery
Iron Duke 159

Wells & Young's
Wells Banana Bread Beer 940
Wells Bombardier 293
Young's Special London Ale 552

Weltenburg Kloster Brauerei
Weltenburger Barock Hell 544
Weltenburger Kloster Asam
    Bock 838
Weltenburger Kloster Barock
    Dunkel 839

Westerham Brewery Co.
British Bulldog 74
Little Scotney Pale Ale
    180

Weyerbacher Brewing
Double Simcoe IPA 103

White Shield Brewery
Worthington's White Shield
    297

Whitewater Brewery
Clotworthy Dobbin 656

**Widmer Brothers
    Brewing**
Drop Top Amber Ale 106
Widmer Hefeweizen 611

Wild Rose Brewery
Wild Rose Cherry Porter
    840

**Williams Brothers Brewing
    Company**
Fraoch Heather Ale 882
Midnight Sun 907
Róisin 923

Woodforde's
Woodforde's Headcracker
    548
Woodforde's Wherry 296

Wychwood Brewery
Hobgoblin 150

Wye Valley Brewery
Dorothy Goodbody's
    Wholesome Stout 669
Hereford Pale Ale 387

Yards Brewing
General Washington's
    Tavern Porter 690

Yoho Brewing
Tokyo Black 821
Yona Yona Ale 551

Zagorka Brewery
Stolichno Bock 811

**Zagrebacka
    Pivovara**
Tomislav Pivo 823

Žatecký Pivovar
Žatec 553
Žatec Xantho 945

Every effort has been made to credit the copyright holders of the images used in this book. We apologize for any unintentional omissions or errors and will insert the appropriate acknowledgment to any companies or individuals in subsequent editions of the work.

37 Steve Terrill/Corbis **44** Stone Brewing **55** Travelpixs/Alamy **76** Broughton Brewery **85** Brasserie D'Achouffe **100** Peter M. Wilson/Alamy **107** Widmer Brothers Brewing **110** Alberto Paredes/Alamy **115** Carlsberg **125** Hair of the Dog Brewing **131** Fuller, Smith & Turner **134** Furthermore Beer **142** Getty Images/Hulton Archive/Imagno **144** Brauerei Locher **153** Lebrecht Music & Arts/Corbis **171** David Sanger Photography/Alamy **177** Duvel Moortgat **187** Duvel Moortgat **190** Plzensky Prazdroj **196** Jason Row/Alamy **203** Nils Oscar Brewery **209** Browar Okocim **224** Iain Cooper/Alamy **251** Mark Sunderland/Alamy **252** Interfoto/Alamy **267** Chris Fredriksson/Alamy **273** Silverport Pictures/Alamy **277** Consorcio Cervecero De Baja California **291** Aa World Travel Library/Alamy **298** Travelpixs/Alamy **300** Guildhall Library & Art Gallery/Imagestate Rm/Photolibrary **308** Dogfish Head **321** Angelo Hornak/Corbis **324** Thomas Cockrem/Alamy **332** Charles D. Cook **337** Jan Holm/FotoLibra **342** Advertising Archive **345** SABmiller **352** Brouwerij Corsendonk **354** Private Collection/Giraudon/The Bridgeman Art Library **384** Koninklijke Grolsch **429** Andia/Alamy **435** Orban Thierry/Corbis Sygma **440** The Print Collector/Imagestate Rm/Photolibrary **445** 32 Via Dei Birrai **453** Lebrecht Music And Arts Photo Library/Alamy **460** Envision/Corbis **463** Upperhall Ltd/Robert Harding Travel/Photolibrary **472** Advertising Archive **480** Budějovický Měšťanský Pivovar **483** Sue Cunningham Photographic/Alamy **487** Interfoto/Alamy **489** Getty Images/Hulton Archive/Imagno **495** Hipix/Alamy **504** Everyman/Illustration: Andrzej Klimowski/Design: Peter B. Willberg **510** Taybeh Brewery Company **514** Martin Jenkinson/Alamy **518** Birra Malto/Michael Doulton **527** Imagestate Media Partners Limited – Impact Photos/Alamy **532** Norman Price/Alamy **543** Janet Czekirda/FotoLibra **550** Rooster's **562** Imagebroker/Alamy **564** The Art Archive/Kharbine-Tapabor **578** AKG-Images **591** Mauritius Images Gmbh/Alamy **630** Ian Shaw/Alamy **635** Charles D. Cook **677** Christophe Boisvieux/Corbis **691** Fuller, Smith & Turner **701** Advertising Archive **719** Pat Behnke/Alamy **723** Pivovar Kout Na Sumave **735** Marston's **740** Jack Carey/Alamy **751** Neil Setchfield/Alamy **761** David R. Frazier Photolibrary, Inc./Alamy **775** Mary Evans Picture Library/Alamy **786** Getty Images/Sean Gallup **795** Samuel Smith **799** August Schell Brewing Company **802** Rogue Ales **810** St. Peter's Brewery **816** Travelpixs/Alamy **822** Simon Belcher/Alamy **827** Unibroue **829** Innovative Advertising/Abita Brewing **832** Friedrich Stark/Alamy **836** Corbis **842** Rogue Ales **849** Owen Franken/Corbis **857** Brasserie Des Naufrageurs **861** Brouwerij Boon **876** White Images/Scala, Florence **903** Duvel Moortgat **913** Anchor Brewing Company

Commissioned photography

Simon Pask 23 28 29 30 31 32 40 49 50 52 53 58 60 62 69 70 71 72 74 75 78 79 80 84 90 91 96 102 109 112 114 117 118 119 129 130 132 133 137 138 150 151 162 163 165 167 172 184 185 186 193 194 199 200 201 202 205 213 218 220 221 222 223 225 226 227 230 231 232 233 237 239 242 244 245 246 249 250 256 258 262 263 265 269 272 275 278 286 287 289 290 293 296 297 301 304 305 307 310 315 320 327 328 331 336 338 339 340 346 347 349 353 357 360 363 364 365 367 372 373 381 391 392 393 398 400 401 404 405 407 412 413 414 415 416 417 419 422 424 430 431 432 433 436 439 443 449 450 457 465 467 469 470 479 482 485 494 503 505 507 509 512 513 515 516 522 525 529 530 531 538 539 546 547 548 549 552 553 559 561 566 572 574 575 579 583 586 589 594 595 597 598 600 604 605 606 607 615 618 619 622 623 625 626 627 633 639 643 644 646 647 648 650 651 654 656 657 660 661 662 663 666 669 670 679 681 682 683 684 685 690 695 696 699 700 702 703 706 707 708 709 710 711 714 721 724 725 726 728 729 736 737 739 741 742 743 744 745 746 747 747 749 752 753 754 755 756 757 758 759 762 763 764 765 766 768 770 771 772 777 779 782 788 789 796 797 800 805 815 819 820 821 824 825 834 838 839 850 854 858 859 860 862 863 864 865 866 882 883 888 890 891 894 902 905 907 909 910 921 922 923 926 928 929 934 936 940 941 942

Creative Publishing International (Anna DePagter, Audrey Johnson, Nick Lindemann, Keith Long, Katie Taylor) 22 25 34 35 38 42 47 59 63 64 65 68 73 81 82 83 89 94 97 99 103 104 105 106 116 122 136 139 146 147 157 164 166 170 173 174 175 182 183 192 198 210 211 212 214 215 216 217 234 238 243 247 248 260 261 264 279 281 288 292 306 312 314 322 323 324 325 326 334 335 343 356 362 374 380 382 390 406 408 418 442 447 447 452 456 458 459 461 471 478 484 491 499 500 502 512 520 521 528 536 537 576 581 585 592 593 596 601 602 603 608 614 632 636 637 638 640 641 645 649 659 664 665 668 671 676 678 680 689 692 694 697 698 712 720 727 767 770 773 776 783 790 791 801 803 806 812 818 831 843 851 855 867 868 869 870 871 874 879 887 889 900 904 906 908 912 915 917 918 927 930 931 932 933 935 938 939

Marc Veit Schwär 24 33 39 46 51 57 61 88 108 113 127 156 188 189 219 254 268 311 376 377 378 395 437 446 464 466 508 523 540 541 560 577 584 588 599 609 624 674 713 732 738 774 800 830 901 920

Angelo Rosa 41 48 56 95 98 178 204 235 236 257 274 326 375 394 399 501 521 655 688 693 835 875 878 880 884 898 899 914 916 926 943

John Hollingshead 123 148 160 161 179 241 255 313 330 396 397 409 434 498 558 580 667 715 807 919

Brent Bossom Photography 43 128 149 195 240 366 451 468 490 573 582 675 804 895

Karel Kita 341 348 379 448 506 567 778

Frank Croes 383 587 888 911

Adrian Tierney-Jones would like to give special thanks to:

Sam Houston at the Impact Agency, Pierhead Purchasing, and Rupert Ponsonby and all at R'n'R for their help in supplying bottles and glasses.

Also a big thanks to all the brewers, wherever they are in the world, who sent in beers and glasses, as well as the writers and editors who helped organize this sterling logistical feat. Thanks also go to Richard Cabburn for his help with Wadadli bottles and to renowned beer smuggler Jeff Pickthall for doing the same with Sakara Gold.

Plus a special thanks to Jane and James for their forbearance.

Dedicated to the memory of "The Beer Hunter," Michael Jackson (1942–2007)

Quintessence would like to thank all of the breweries who sent bottles, glasses, and images—this book would not have been possible without their help. In addition, thanks go to the following organizations and individuals for their assistance in the creation of this book:

Simon Pask; Michele Lanci-Altomare (Creative Director at Creative Publishing International); Rich Milligan ("Beer Glass Collector" at myweb.tiscali.co.uk/beerglasscollector); Corey Gray and Nathan Wiger at www.beerlabels.com; Beers of Europe, Ltd. www.beersofeurope.co.uk; Utobeer in Borough Market, London www.utobeer.co.uk; Chris Taylor; Meghan Bulmer at Alamy; The Advertising Archive; Natascha Wintersinger at AKG-images; John Moelwyn-Hughes at Corbis; Gwyn Headley and Yvonne Seeley at FotoLibra; Hayley Newman at Getty Images; Tim Kantoch at Photolibrary; Danny Browne at Scala Archives; Belgo Centraal in Covent Garden, London, U.K.; Belgo Clapham on Clapham High Road, London, U.K.; The Eagle on Old Street, London, U.K.; The White Horse on Parson's Green, London, U.K.; The Bread and Roses on Clapham Manor Street, London, U.K., and The Old Fountain on Baldwin Street, London, U.K.